Lecture Notes in Computer Science 16543

Founding Editors

Gerhard Goos
Juris Hartmanis

The series Lecture Notes in Computer Science (LNCS), including its subseries Lecture Notes in Artificial Intelligence (LNAI) and Lecture Notes in Bioinformatics (LNBI), has established itself as a medium for the publication of new developments in computer science and information technology research, teaching, and education.

LNCS enjoys close cooperation with the computer science R & D community, the series counts many renowned academics among its volume editors and paper authors, and collaborates with prestigious societies. Its mission is to serve this international community by providing an invaluable service, mainly focused on the publication of conference and workshop proceedings and postproceedings. LNCS commenced publication in 1973.

Joan Daemen · Emmanuel Thomé
Editors

Advances in Cryptology – EUROCRYPT 2026

45th Annual International Conference on the Theory
and Applications of Cryptographic Techniques
Rome, Italy, May 10–14, 2026
Proceedings, Part III

Editors
Joan Daemen (ORCID)
Radboud University
Nijmegen, The Netherlands

Emmanuel Thomé (ORCID)
Inria
Nancy, France

ISSN 0302-9743   ISSN 1611-3349 (electronic)
Lecture Notes in Computer Science
ISBN 978-3-032-25323-1   ISBN 978-3-032-25324-8 (eBook)
https://doi.org/10.1007/978-3-032-25324-8

This Springer imprint is published by the registered company Springer Nature Switzerland AG
The registered company address is: Gewerbestrasse 11, 6330 Cham, Switzerland

If disposing of this product, please recycle the paper.

Preface

These are the proceedings of the 45th Annual International Conference on the Theory and Applications of Cryptographic Techniques (EUROCRYPT 2026), held in Rome, Italy, from May 10 to May 14, 2026. The conference series is organized by the International Association for Cryptologic Research (IACR).

EUROCRYPT 2026 received a new record number of 701 submissions. Out of these, 6 were withdrawn, 20 were desk-rejected due to violation of anonymity or formatting rules and the remaining 675 formally went to the review process. We assigned every submission in a double blind way to three program committee members and for papers by PC members we assigned four reviewers. During the process we assigned for some submissions additional reviewers, in particular for papers with only low-confidence reviews, or cases with clashing reviewer opinions or where PC members were not able to deliver their reviews in time nor find subreviewers. In the end we had 7 papers where we were unable to get more than 2 reviewers. For 3 of these papers the area chairs and reviewers had an in-depth discussion and finally 1 of them was accepted and 2 rejected. For the remaining 4 papers the two reviews that did come in were so negative that it was extremely unlikely that a third review could turn things around so they were rejected.

After the individual reviewing phase and a quick discussion round, we selected 382 papers to enter the second round. These remaining papers were offered a rebuttal stage to answer questions and react to concerns raised by the reviewers. After several weeks of subsequent discussions, we ultimately selected 142 papers for acceptance. This comes down to an acceptance rate of roughly 20%. For four of these, acceptance was conditional and we had PC members as shepherds overseeing whether the final paper satisfied the conditions. The entire process was managed using the IACR version of the HotCRP software.

In order to handle such a large number of submissions, we appointed 10 area chairs:

- Lejla Batina: efficient implementations, security models, side-channel attacks, masking;
- Geoffroy Couteau: public-key cryptography with advanced functionalities, (fully) homomorphic encryption;
- Helena Handschuh: cryptographic protocols, real-world cryptography, SSE, secure messaging;
- Dakshita Khurana: quantum and information-theoretic cryptography;
- Sarah Meiklejohn: proof systems, zero-knowledge proofs, succinctness;
- Claudio Orlandi: multi-party computation, secret-sharing, consensus, broadcast;
- Giuseppe Persiano: foundations, obfuscation, correlated pseudorandomness, oblivious transfer and RAM, private information retrieval;

- Ron Steinfeld: public-key encryption, signatures, key exchange, threshold cryptography;
- Gilles Van Assche: symmetric cryptographic primitives, constructions, modes and cryptanalysis;
- Benjamin Wesolowski: isogenies, elliptic curve, mathematical cryptanalysis.

They each led the discussions and the paper selection in their respective area, and they advised us in certain strategic decisions.

Similarly important was the great work of the program committee; it consisted of 104 top cryptography researchers from all the relevant areas and from all over the world. In total, PC members did more than 1156 reviews, the area chairs did 2, and there were 997 by 705 different external subreviewers. Clearly some subreviewers did multiple reviews and we have indicated these in the list below. During the reviewing and decision-making process more than 6500 comments were posted. The continuously increasing number of submissions, but also the fact that nowadays submissions often come with a large appendix that cannot be reviewed given the tight schedule, poses a serious challenge to the reviewing process. In this context we wish to mention the following PC members for doing truly outstanding work, as recognized by the area chairs: Anamaria Costache, Dario Fiore, Felix Günther, Simon Holmgaard Kamp, Gabriel Kaptchuk, Tomoyuki Morimae, Morten Øygarden, Alice Pellet-Mary, Willy Quach and Marloes Venema.

We continued the recently introduced initiative to offer an artifact evaluation process, in order to support open and reproducible research. This process offers authors of accepted papers the possibility to submit artifacts associated with their papers (such as software or datasets) for review, in a collaborative process between authors and the artifact review committee, with the aim to make them publicly archived by the IACR at https://artifacts.iacr.org. The authors of 17 papers made use of this possibility. We thank the chair Francisco Rodríguez Henríquez and the entire artifact review committee for handling this process.

Out of the accepted papers, two were decorated with an award after we consulted the PC and area chairs. The Best Paper Awards went to Shan Chen, Kaige Pan and Olga Sanina for their paper "Provable Security and Privacy Analysis of WPA3's SAE and SAE-PK Protocols" and to Lars Ran for his paper "Wedges, Oil, and Vinegar – An Analysis of UOV in the Exterior Algebra", where the latter happened to be an early-career paper. Congratulations to the recipients!

In addition to the contributed papers, EUROCRYPT 2026 featured invited talks by Anna Lysyanskaya and Luca De Feo and the traditional Rump Session with numerous short talks. Furthermore, several cryptography workshops were co-located with the conference, held in the preceding weekend. We would like to thank the IACR Board of Directors for their trust in us, and for all the valuable work they are doing for the good of the field. A special thank you goes to Kevin McCurley and Kay McKelly, for their always prompt help on technical matters with the HotCRP system and IACR hosted websites. We are also grateful to our predecessors Serge Fehr and Pierre-Alain Fouque, who allowed us to profit from their experience and were always quick in answering our questions. A big round of applause goes to the general chairs, Edoardo Persichetti and Daniele Venturi, who did a fantastic job with the local organization of the conference. It was a pleasure to work together with them towards this event and to enjoy the result of our work during the conference.

May 2026

Emmanuel Thomé
Joan Daemen

Organization

General Co-chairs

Edoardo Persichetti   Florida Atlantic University, USA
Daniele Venturi   Università di Roma Sapienza, Italy

Program Co-chairs

Joan Daemen   Radboud University, the Netherlands
Emmanuel Thomé   Inria, France

Area Chairs

Lejla Batina   Radboud University, the Netherlands
Geoffroy Couteau   CNRS, Université Paris Cité, France
Helena Handschuh   QuSecure and SCI Semiconductors, USA
Dakshita Khurana   University of Illinois Urbana-Champaign and NTT Research, USA
Sarah Meiklejohn   University College London and Google, UK
Claudio Orlandi   Aarhus University, Denmark
Giuseppe Persiano   Università di Salerno, Italy
Ron Steinfeld   Monash University, Australia
Gilles Van Assche   STMicroelectronics, Belgium
Benjamin Wesolowski   CNRS and ENS Lyon, France

Program Committee

Masayuki Abe   NTT Social Informatics Laboratories, Japan
Navid Alamati   VISA Research, USA
Diego F. Aranha   Aarhus University, Denmark
Carsten Baum   Technical University of Denmark, Denmark
Gabrielle Beck   CNRS, University of Montpellier, France
Alexander Bienstock   J.P. Morgan, USA
Olivier Blazy   Ecole polytechnique, France
Xavier Bonnetain   Inria Nancy, France

Joppe Bos	NXP Semiconductors, Belgium
Cecilia Boschini	ETH Zurich, Switzerland
Katharina Boudgoust	CNRS, University of Montpellier, France
Matteo Campanelli	Offchain Labs, Denmark
Sébastien Canard	Télécom Paris, IMT, IPP, France
Wouter Castryck	KU Leuven, Belgium
Dario Catalano	Università di Catania, Italy
Binyi Chen	Stanford University, USA
Céline Chevalier	Université Paris-Panthéon-Assas and DI/ENS, France
Sherman S. M. Chow	Chinese University of Hong Kong, China
Kai-Min Chung	Academia Sinica, Taiwan
Andrea Coladangelo	University of Washington, USA
Deirdre Connolly	Oracle, Selkie Cryptography, USA
Anamaria Costache	École polytechnique, France
Dana Dachman-Soled	University of Maryland, USA
Maria Eichlseder	Graz University of Technology, Austria
Reo Eriguchi	AIST, Japan
Antonio Faonio	EURECOM, France
Dario Fiore	IMDEA Software Institute, Spain
Lorenzo Grassi	Eindhoven University of Technology, the Netherlands
Felix Günther	IBM Research Europe – Zurich, Switzerland
Qian Guo	Lund University, Sweden
Mohammad Hajiabadi	University of Waterloo, Canada
Rachelle Heim Boissier	UCLouvain, Belgium
Julia Hesse	IBM Research Europe – Zurich, Switzerland
Minki Hhan	UT Austin, USA
Alexander Hoover	Stevens Institute of Technology, USA
Michael Hutter	UniBw M and PQShield, Germany
Charlie Jacomme	Inria Nancy, France
Tibor Jager	University of Wuppertal, Germany
Stanislaw Jarecki	University of California, Irvine, USA
Simon Holmgaard Kamp	Ruhr University Bochum, Germany
Gabriel Kaptchuk	University of Maryland, College Park, USA
Julia Kastner	CWI, the Netherlands
Mustafa Khairallah	Nanyang Technological University, Singapore
Michael Klooß	Karlsruhe Institute of Technology, Germany
Chelsea Komlo	University of Waterloo and NEAR One, Canada
Juliane Krämer	University of Regensburg, Germany
Péter Kutas	Eötvös Loránd University, Hungary and University of Birmingham, UK

Yi-Fu Lai	Ruhr-University Bochum, Germany and KU Leuven, Belgium
Eysa Lee	Barnard College, USA
Gaëtan Leurent	Inria Paris, France
Bart Mennink	Maastricht University and Radboud University the Netherlands
Simon-Philipp Merz	ETH Zurich, Switzerland
Daniel Moghimi	Google, USA
Tomoyuki Morimae	Kyoto University, Japan
María Naya-Plasencia	Inria Paris, France
Ruben Niederhagen	Academia Sinica, Taiwan and University of Southern Denmark
Maciej Obremski	National University of Singapore
Sabine Oechsner	Vrije Universiteit Amsterdam, the Netherlands
Emmanuela Orsini	Bocconi University, Italy
Morten Øygarden	Simula UiB, Norway
Elena Pagnin	Chalmers and University of Gothenburg, Sweden
Lorenz Panny	Technische Universität München, Germany
Alice Pellet-Mary	CNRS and Université de Bordeaux, France
Léo Perrin	Inria, France
Duong Hieu Phan	Télécom Paris, IPP, France
Federico Pintore	University of Trento, Italy
Thomas Pornin	NCC Group, Canada
Eamonn W. Postlethwaite	King's College London, UK
Sihang Pu	CNRS, IRIF, France
Willy Quach	CISPA Helmholtz Center for Information Security, Germany
Håvard Raddum	Simula UiB, Norway
Shahram Rasoolzadeh	Ruhr University Bochum, Germany
Divya Ravi	University of Amsterdam, the Netherlands
Michael Reichle	ETH Zurich, Switzerland
Nicolas Resch	University of Amsterdam, the Netherlands
Damien Robert	Centre Inria de l'Université de Bordeaux, France
Francisco Rodríguez-Henríquez	Technology Innovation Institute (TII), UAE
Lior Rotem	The Hebrew University, Israel
Adeline Roux-Langlois	CNRS Caen, France
Sujoy Sinha Roy	Graz University of Technology, Austria
Markku-Juhani Saarinen	Tampere University, Finland
Olivier Sanders	Orange, France
Yu Sasaki	NTT Social Informatics Laboratories, Japan and NIST Associate, USA

Or Sattath	Ben-Gurion University, Israel
Christian Schaffner	University of Amsterdam and QuSoft, the Netherlands
Sven Schäge	Eindhoven University of Technology, the Netherlands
Patrick Schaumont	Worcester Polytechnic Institute, USA
Gregor Seiler	IBM Research Europe, Switzerland
Daniel Slamanig	Universität der Bundeswehr München, Germany
Benjamin Smith	Inria and École polytechnique, Institut Polytechnique de Paris, France
Ling Song	Jinan University, China
Katerina Sotiraki	Yale University, USA
Katherine E. Stange	University of Colorado Boulder, USA
Mehdi Tibouchi	NTT Social Informatics Laboratories, Japan
Monika Trimoska	Eindhoven University of Technology, the Netherlands
Serge Vaudenay	EPFL, Switzerland
Marloes Venema	University of Wuppertal, Germany
Xiao Wang	Northwestern University, USA
Bas Westerbaan	Cloudflare, the Netherlands
Ke Wu	University of Michigan, USA
Sophia Yakoubov	Aarhus University, Denmark
Kevin Yeo	Google, USA
Yupeng Zhang	University of Illinois Urbana Champaign, USA
Vassilis Zikas	Georgia Tech, USA

Additional Reviewers

Marius A. Aardal	Nouri Alnahawi (2)
Behzad Abdolmaleki (2)	Bar Alon
Simon Abelard	Orestis Alpos
Damiano Abram (4)	Miguel Ambrona
Hamza Abusalah	Ghous Amjad
Gora Adj (2)	Ignacio Amores (2)
Amit Agarwal	Gaspard Anthoine
Siddharth Agarwal	Ananya Appan (2)
Adya Agrawal	Sven Argo
Aikata Aikata (2)	Frederik Armknecht
Gorjan Alagic (2)	Gal Arnon (2)
Martin Albrecht	Rotem Arnon-Friedman
Andreea Alexandru	Sarah Arpin
Jens Alich	Kyoichi Asano

Haetham Al Aswad
Shahla Atapoor
Noor Athamnah
Thomas Attema
Daniel Augot
Thomas Aulbach
Noam Avidan
Melissa Azouaoui
Aron van Baarsen (3)
Kaniuar Bacho
Renas Bacho (4)
Matilda Backendal
Ruben Baecker
Karim Baghery
David Balbás (2)
Marshall Ball (3)
Brieuc Balon
Henry Bambury (2)
Harrison Banda (2)
Gustavo Banegas
Shalini Banerjee
Razvan Barbulescu
Mohammed Barhoush (2)
Augustin Bariant (2)
Matilde Baroni
James Bartusek (3)
Andrea Basso
Michele Battagliola
Jules Baudrin
Balthazar Bauer (2)
Agathe Beaugrand (2)
Amit Behera (2)
Christof Beierle (2)
Amos Beimel
Yanis Belkheyar (2)
Mario Marhuenda Beltrán (4)
Emad Heydari Beni
Benjamin Benčina (2)
Robin Berger
Loris Bergerat (2)
Sebastian Berndt
Slim Bettaieb
Ward Beullens
Ritam Bhaumik (4)
Nidhish Bhimrajka

Beatrice Biasioli
Jean-Francois Biasse (3)
Bruno Blanchet
Erica Blum
Jan Bobolz
Aurélien Boeuf
Andrej Bogdanov (2)
Madalina Bolboceanu
Maxime Bombar (2)
Joseph Bonneau
Jonathan Bootle
Giacomo Borin
Sebastiano Boscardin
Samuel Bouaziz-Ermann
Alexandre Bouez (2)
Christina Boura (2)
Clémence Bouvier (2)
Zvika Brakerski
Pedro Branco (3)
Nicholas Brandt
Lennart Braun (2)
Pierre Briaud (2)
Jan Brinkmann
Carlo Brunetta (2)
Alessandro Budroni
Dung Bui (2)
Jakob Burkhardt
Julien Béguinot
Benedikt Bünz
Alper Cakan (2)
Alessio Caminata
Luca Campa (2)
Isaac Canales-Martínez (2)
Ran Canetti
Anne Canteaut
Pedro Capitão
Davide Carnemolla
Kévin Carrier
Ignacio Cascudo (2)
David Cash (2)
Gaëtan Cassiers (2)
André Chailloux
Rutchathon Chairattana-Apirom (2)
Avik Chakraborti
Debasmita Chakraborty (2)

Alexander Frolov
Honghao Fu
Yuuki Fujita (2)
Phillip Gajland
Pierre Galissant (2)
Antonio Merino Gallardo
Mariana Gama
Chaya Ganesh
Antoine Gansel (2)
Rachit Garg
Albert Garreta
Pierrick Gaudry
Robin Geelen (2)
Rosario Gennaro (2)
Simon Gerhalter (2)
Baptiste Germon
Wissam Ghantous
Surendra Ghentiyala
Diana Ghinea (3)
Riddhi Ghosal
Satrajit Ghosh
Shibam Ghosh (2)
Lukas Giner
Emanuele Giunta (5)
Kristian Gjøsteen (2)
Lewis Glabush (4)
Noemi Glaeser (2)
Eli Goldin
Guillaume Goy
Vipul Goyal
Matthew Gray
Scott Griffy
Alex B. Grilo
Koen Groenland
Jiaxin Guan (2)
Ziyi Guan
Zichen Gui (3)
Antonio Guimarães (4)
Aditya Gulati
Sam Gunn (2)
Chun Guo
Kanav Gupta
Rishav Gupta
Aparna Gupte (2)
Kamil Doruk Gur

Julia Guskind
Jincheol Ha
Calvin Abou Haidar (3)
Mathias Hall-Andersen (2)
Miro Haller (2)
Ariel Hamlin
Lucjan Hanzlik
Keisuke Hara
Keitaro Hashimoto
Valerian Hatey
Ryuya Hayashi
David Heath
Aditya Hegde (4)
Lena Heimberger (5)
Raphael Heitjohann (4)
Paul Hermouet
Laura Hetz
Hans Heum (2)
Jonas von der Heyden (2)
Taiga Hiroka
Taiga Hirooka
Martin Hirt
Keitaro Hiwatashi
Clément Hoffmann (2)
Thomas den Hollander (2)
Blake Holman
Jan Horning
Máté Horváth (3)
Akinori Hosoyamada
Marc Houben
Patrick Hough
Martha Norberg Hovd (2)
Yao-Ching Hsieh (3)
Kai Hu (4)
Shengyuan Hu
William Hu
Miryam Huang
Yizhi Huang
Yu-Hsuan Huang
Vincent Hwang
Sorina Ionica
Nadiia Ichanska
Atsunori Ichikawa
Riccardo Invernizzi
Tetsu Iwata

Samuel Jacques
Joseph Jaeger
Vahid Jahandideh (3)
Jonas Janneck
Ruta Jawale
Sönke Jendral
Corentin Jeudy (2)
Ashwin Jha (2)
Yanxue Jia (2)
Haoxiang Jin (2)
Thomas Johansson
Daniel Jost
Hiroto Kaihara
Giannis Kaklamanis
Saqib Kakvi
Fatih Kaleoglu
Nikolay Kaleyski
Anna Kaplan
Harish Karthikeyan
Andes Y. L. Kei
Adrian Perez Keilty
Hannah Josephine Keller
John Kelsey
Oleksandr Kholosha
Hamidreza Khoshakhlagh
Jean Kieffer
Jaehyung Kim
Jaeseon Kim
Jiseung Kim
Seongkwang Kim
Taechan Kim
Elena Kirshanova (2)
Fuyuki Kitagawa (2)
Ivana Klasovitá
Alexander Koch
Lisa Kohl
Sebastian Kolby (2)
Dimitris Kolonelos
Niels Kornerup
Katharina Koschatko (3)
Liliya Kraleva (2)
Rucha Kulkarni
Naman Kumar
Noboru Kunihiro
Ashley Kurian (2)

Shuto Kuriyama
Russell W. F. Lai
Virginie Lallemand
Eran Lambooij (3)
Roman Langrehr
Oleksandra Lapiha (2)
Jun Bo Lau (2)
Lucia Lavagnino
Abel Laval
Jonas Lazard
Arthur Lazzaretti (2)
Jason LeGrow (2)
Byeonghak Lee (2)
Changmin Lee
Keewoo Lee
Yeongmin Lee (2)
Barry van Leeuwen
Charlotte Lefevre (3)
Antonin Leroux
Afonso Li
Baiyu Li
Douglas Li
Hanjun Li (2)
Jianwei Li
Kang Li
Yunqi Li
Zhe Li
Zihao Liao
Wei-Kai Lin
Yao-Ting Lin (2)
Eik List
Fukang Liu
Hanlin Liu (2)
Haolin Liu
Huimin Liu
Jiahui Liu (2)
Linsheng Liu
Qipeng Liu (2)
Tianren Liu
Tianyi Liu
Xiangyu Liu
Yong Liu
Zeyu Liu
Chen-Da Liu-Zhang (4)
Simon Ljungbeck

Riccardo Lolato
Phuoc Pham Van Long
Riccardo Longo
Gioella Lorenzon
Paul Lou
Georgu Lu (3)
Yun Lu
Yin Lv
Dounia M'foukh
Jack P. K. Ma
Rasoul Akhavan Mahdavi
Luciano Maino
Jules Maire (2)
Monosij Maitra
Christian Majenz (2)
Eleftheria Makri
Giulio Malavolta
Bence Mali
Lola-Baie Mallordy
Shuping Mao
Siva Maradana
Varun Maram
Christian Martin
Lisa Masserova (2)
Loïc Masure
Surya Mathialagan
Takahiro Matsuda
Florent Mazelet
Ian McQuoid
Jeremias Mechler (2)
Liam Medley
Jonas Meers
Willi Meier
Fredrik Meisingseth
Kelsey Melissaris (2)
Nikolas Melissaris (2)
Nicolas Meloni
Alessio Meneghetti
Ben Merbaum
Michael Meyer
Charles Meyer-Hilfiger
Peihan Miao
Bastien Michel
Francesco Migliaro (2)
Brice Minaud (2)

Kazuhiko Minematsu (2)
Omid Mir
Chalres Momin
Mickael Montessinos
Ethan Mook (2)
Thorben Moos (2)
Aditya Morolia
Travis Morrison
Jonathan Mosheiff
Nicky Mouha
Tamer Mour
Changrui Mu
Ananta Mukherjee
Anisha Mukherjee (2)
Saswata Mukherjee
Marzio Mula (2)
Marta Mularczyk
Takao Murakami
Guilhem Mureau
Saachi Mutreja
Mari Muurman
Erik Mårtensson (2)
Denis Nabokov (2)
Marcel Nageler (3)
Phillip Nazarian
Barak Nehoran
Rohit Nema
Patrick Neumann (4)
Lucien K. L. Ng
Duy Nguyen
Hai Nguyen
Jérôme Nguyen
Khoa Nguyen
Thi Thu Quyen Nguyen
Ky Nguyen (3)
Alexander Nilsson
Guilhem Niot (2)
Ryo Nishimaki (2)
Anca Nitulescu
Zhongfeng Niu
Ariel Nof
Miguel Cueto Noval
Julian Nowakowski (2)
Arne Tobias Ødegaard
Adam O'Neill

Miyako Ohkubo
Chrysa Oikonomou
Yasuaki Okinaka
Eli Orvis
Michał Osadnik (2)
Massimo Ostuzzi
Johannes Ottenhues (2)
Lucas Ottow
Cavit Özbay
Yupeng Ouyang
Aurel Page (2)
Thales Paiva
Tapas Pal
Ying-Yu Pan
Laz Panard
Mahak Pancholi (3)
Yanxin Pang
Roberto Parisella (2)
Jai Hyun Park
Aditi Partap (2)
Sikhar Patranabis
Yevhen Perehuda (2)
Hilder V. L. Pereira (2)
Octavio Perez-Kempner (2)
Paola de Perthuis
Thomas Peyrin (2)
Atharva Phanse
Stjepan Picek
Krzysztof Pietrzak
Lucas Piske
Daan Planken
Bertram Poettering (2)
Erik Pohle (2)
Simon Pohmann
David Pointcheval
Guru Vamsi Policharla
Antigoni Polychroniadou
Alexander Poremba (2)
Tejas Balasaheb Pujari
Kirthivaasan Puniamurthy
Pierre Pébereau
Luowen Qian
Kexin Qiao
Apurva Rai
Markus Raiber

Justin Raizes
Simon Rastikian
Fabian Regen
Krijn Reijnders (2)
Farzin Renan
Emeline Repel (2)
Mahshid Riahinia
Artur Riazanov
Berenika Richterová
Doreen Riepel (2)
Peter Rindal
Thomas Ristenpart
Silvia Ritsch
Bhaskar Roberts
Ricardo Rodriguez-Reveco
Felix Rohrbach
Francesco Romeo
Michael Rosenberg
Yann Rotella
Ron Rothblum
Lawrence Roy (5)
Alexander Russell
Luigi Russo (3)
Éric Sageloli (2)
Abishanka Saha
Yusuke Sakai
Olga Sanina
Antonio Sanso
Maria Corte-Real Santos
Sidhant Saraogi
Rahul Satish (3)
Federico Savasta
Matteo Scarlata
Sina Schaeffler (2)
Markus Schiffermüller
Fabian Schmid
Phil Schmieder (3)
Tobias Schneider (2)
Gabe Schoenbach
Markus Schofnegger
Peter Scholl (2)
André Schrottenloher
Jacob Schuldt
Gabrielle Scullard
Massaer Seck

Michel Seck (2)
Okan Seker
Ben Sela
Joon Young Seo
István András Seres
Karn Seth
Yannick Seurin (2)
Alessandro Sferlazza (2)
Akash Shah
Aria Shahverdi (2)
Zehua Shang
abhi shelat
Yaobin Shen
Yixin Shen
Danping Shi
Kecheng Shi (2)
Maurice Shih
Kazumasa Shinagawa
Manasi Shingane
Yuki Shirakawa
Edoardo Signorini
Janno Siim (3)
Mark Simkin (2)
Jaspal Singh (2)
Satvinder Singh
Luisa Siniscalchi (2)
Boris Skoric
Luiza Soezima
Yongha Son
Fang Song
Gary Song
Yongsoo Song (3)
Yuanming Song
Chiara Spadafora
Pierre-Jean Spaenlehauer
Florian Speelman
Sebastian A. Spindler (2)
Nicholas Spooner (2)
François-Xavier Standaert
Gilad Stern (2)
Jure Sternad (2)
Silvan Streit
Marco Streng
Patrick Struck
Bing Sun

Yao Sun
Elias Suvanto (3)
Moeto Suzuki
Erkan Tairi (3)
Kaoru Takemure
Kel Zin Tan
Quan Quan Tan
Er-Cheng Tang
Gang Tang
Rui Tang
Samuel Tap
Ertem Nusret Tas
Athina Terzoglou
Brady Testa
Lea Thiemt
Rachel Thomas
Yosuke Todo
Kabir Tomer
Jacques Traoré
Filip Trenkic (2)
Ni Trieu
Kien Tuong Truong
Giorgos Tsimos
Ida Tucker
Nirvan Tyagi
LaKyah Tyner
Aleksei Udovenko
Akin Ünal (2)
Jorge Urroz
Lalitha Vadlamani
Shannon Veitch (2)
Michiel Verbauwhede
Javier Verbel
Damien Vergnaud
Nikita Veshchikov
Irene Villa (2)
Quoc Huy Vu (4)
Weiqiang Wen (4)
Benedikt Wagner (3)
Alexandre Wallet
Bow-Yaw Wang
Dachao Wang
Gaoli Wang
Hongxiao Wang
Mingyuan Wang

Qingju Wang
Ruihan Wang
Shichang Wang
Wenhao Wang
Xiaoyun Wang
Yunhao Wang (2)
Zhiheng Wang
Yohei Watanabe
Robin Webbers
Yu Wei (3)
Maximiliane Weishäupl
Mor Weiss
Chenkai Weng
Wessel Van Woerden
Ronald de Wolf
Harry W. H. Wong (2)
Keita Xagawa
Wenwen Xia (2)
Binwu Xiang
Hua Xu
Jiayu Xu
Shogo Yamada
Shota Yamada (2)
Takashi Yamakawa (2)

Kazuki Yamamura
Kang Yang (3)
Qianqian Yang
Yibin Yang (2)
Yizhou Yao (2)
Arkady Yerukhimovich
William Youmans
Zihan Yu
Aaram Yun
Thomas Zacharias
Oliver Zajonc (2)
Riccardo Zanotto
Arantxa Zapico (2)
Hadas Zeilberger (5)
Runzhi Zeng
Jiaheng Zhang (2)
Jiayu Zhang
Tianyu Zhang (2)
Wenhao Zhang
Zhiyu Zhang
Mingxun Zhou
Chenzhi Zhu (3)
Chiara Marie Zok

Contents

Multi-Party Computation

Traceable Secret Sharing Schemes
for General Access Structures

Oriol Farràs[iD] and Miquel Guiot[(✉)][iD]

Universitat Rovira i Virgili, Tarragona, Spain
{oriol.farras,miquel.guiot}@urv.cat

Abstract. Traceable secret sharing complements traditional schemes by enabling the identification of parties who sell their shares. In the model introduced by Boneh, Partap, and Rotem [CRYPTO'24], a group of corrupted parties generates a reconstruction box R that, given enough valid shares as input, reconstructs the secret. The goal is to trace R back to at least one of the corrupted parties using only black-box access to it.

While their work provides efficient constructions for threshold access structures, it does not apply to the general case. In this work, we extend their framework to general access structures and present an information-theoretic traceable scheme supporting them.

In the course of our construction, we also contribute to the study of anonymous secret sharing, a notion recently introduced by Bishop et al. [CRYPTO'25], which strengthens classical secret sharing by requiring that shares do not reveal the identities of the parties holding them. We further advance this area by proposing new and stronger definitions, and presenting an anonymous scheme for general access structures that satisfies them.

Keywords: Secret sharing scheme · anonymity · traceability

1 Introduction

A secret sharing scheme is a cryptographic primitive in which a dealer shares a secret among a set of parties, ensuring that only certain subsets of them, called authorized, can recover the secret. The collection of these authorized subsets is known as the access structure of the scheme. The primary measure of efficiency for such schemes is the size of the shares.

Secret sharing schemes were introduced independently by Shamir [Sha79] and Blakley [Bla79] in 1979. They presented schemes for threshold access structures, where any subset of parties can recover the secret as long as their size exceeds a given threshold. Since then, secret sharing schemes have been used as a building block in many cryptographic protocols, including secure multiparty computation and threshold cryptography [Bei25]. Although threshold schemes are suitable for many of these applications, some scenarios call for more general access structures, such as in weighted cryptography or attribute-based encryption.

© International Association for Cryptologic Research 2026
J. Daemen and E. Thomé (Eds.): EUROCRYPT 2026, LNCS 16543, pp. 3–32, 2026.
https://doi.org/10.1007/978-3-032-25324-8_1

In this context, secret sharing schemes for general access structures were first presented by Ito, Saito and Nishizeki [ISN87]. Following that, several works presented more efficient schemes [BL88, LV18, ABF+19, ABNP20, AN21], but the best known information-theoretic construction still has shares of exponential size.

While these schemes focus on ensuring that unauthorized subsets cannot recover the secret, they do not address other dishonest behaviors. In particular, most constructions do not prevent parties from copying or selling their shares. This lack of accountability can be problematic in certain scenarios, as it gives parties an opportunity to leak or sell their shares without facing consequences.

Recently, to address this issue, Goyal, Song, and Srinivasan [GSS21], and Boneh, Partap, and Rotem [BPR24] introduced the notion of traceable secret sharing schemes. In the model presented in the latter work [BPR24], the adversary uses the shares of an unauthorized subset of parties to construct a reconstruction box, which can then reconstruct the secret once it receives enough valid shares. It is assumed that this reconstruction box is eventually obtained by the authorities, who can interact with it in a black-box manner in order to trace it back to its original constructors. Within this framework, a traceable secret sharing scheme must satisfy two key properties: *traceability*, the ability to identify at least one party whose share was used in building the reconstruction box; and *non-imputability*, which ensures that no honest party is falsely blamed. In addition, the scheme must guarantee that the secret remains hidden throughout the tracing procedure.

Although the aforementioned tracing proposals are efficient in terms of share size, they are limited to threshold access structures. This work builds on the framework of [BPR24], with the aim to provide a traceable secret sharing scheme for general access structures.

1.1 Our Results

In this work, we present an information-theoretic traceable secret sharing scheme for general access structures. This constitutes an initial step towards efficient traceable secret sharing beyond threshold access structures. As part of our contribution, we extend and generalize the definitions of traceable secret sharing introduced by Boneh, Partap, and Rotem to handle arbitrary access structures.

In the course of our construction, we also contribute to the emerging line of research on *anonymous secret sharing* [PCO20, EBG+24, BGI+25], which strengthens standard secret sharing by requiring that shares do not reveal the identity of the parties they belong to. We enrich this framework by providing further definitions and constructing a new anonymous scheme for general access structures. This notion plays a central role in our traceable scheme and is of independent interest. Our main result is stated below.

Theorem 1.1 (Informal). *For any access structure over n parties, there exists a traceable secret sharing scheme with perfect privacy and statistical correctness, traceability, and non-imputability. Moreover, the tracing procedure only requires $O(\text{poly}(n))$ queries to the reconstruction box.*

As in the work of Boneh, Partap, and Rotem [BPR24], the guarantees of statistical correctness and traceability rely on the fact that the shares and the secret come from a domain of super-polynomial size, which ensures that both tasks succeed with overwhelming probability. Similarly, our statistical guarantee for non-imputability also stems from this domain size. However, in contrast to their approach, we do not rely on one-way functions, as we deliberately design our construction to be fully information-theoretic. In terms of efficiency, although the share size is exponential (as inherent in all known information-theoretic constructions for general access structures), the number of queries required by our tracing algorithm is polynomial.

To construct such a scheme, a necessary first step is to expand and generalize the definitions of traceable secret sharing to the setting of general access structures. This generalization is technically involved, as it must account for the more complex configuration of authorized and unauthorized subsets. More in detail, the threshold case is simpler because all parties are treated uniformly, and authorized subsets are determined solely by their size. Therefore, the reconstruction box only needs to handle queries containing a fixed number of shares, which corresponds to the number of additional parties required to meet the threshold when combined with the corrupted subset. In contrast, for general access structures, authorized subsets may have an intricate description and do not depend only on their size. As a result, the definition of reconstruction box must be generalized to handle input queries consisting of any unauthorized subset that, when combined with the corrupted parties, forms an authorized set.

Additionally, we also extend the notion of reconstruction boxes to handle a more challenging and realistic setting in which they may leak only partial information about the secret, rather than the full value. In particular, we focus on the minimal case where the reconstruction box outputs just a single bit, representing the smallest unit of useful information that can still be exploited by the tracer. These aspects are discussed in more detail in Sect. 4.

Furthermore, we show that we can get efficient traceable schemes with polynomial share size for the family of *low slices*. These are access structures over n parties with a threshold $t \ll n$, where the authorized subsets include all subsets of size greater than t, along with an arbitrary collection of subsets of size exactly t. The statement is given below.

Corollary 1.2 (Informal). *For any t-slice access structure over n parties with $t = O(1)$, there exists a traceable secret sharing scheme with perfect privacy and statistical reconstruction, traceability and non-imputability. Moreover, its share size is $\tilde{O}(\mathrm{poly}(n))$ and the tracing procedure only requires $\tilde{O}(\mathrm{poly}(n))$ queries to the reconstruction box.*

As pointed out in [BPR24], to trace efficiently, i.e., with a polynomial number of queries, shares cannot be linked to the parties to which they belong. Although this requirement may seem counterintuitive, given that the goal of traceability is to identify corrupted parties based on a reconstruction box that operates on their shares, it is in fact essential (see Sect. 5.1).

To formalize this requirement, we build upon the notion of anonymous secret sharing schemes [PCO20, EBG+24, BGI+25], where the identity of any unauthorized subset of parties remains hidden from their shares. We extend the definitions introduced by Bishop et al. [BGI+25] by additionally requiring that the reconstruction process itself does not leak any information about the identities of the participating parties, and we provide a scheme satisfying this strengthened notion of anonymity. Furthermore, we show that slight modifications to classical ideal schemes for threshold access structures also satisfy our anonymity requirements. These results are formalized in the following theorem.

Theorem 1.3 (Informal). *For any access structure over n parties, there exists an anonymous secret sharing scheme with perfect privacy and statistical correctness. In the special case of threshold access structures, perfect correctness can also be achieved.*

Finally, we take a step further and define the notion of *hiding anonymous secret sharing*, which strengthens anonymity by adding two requirements: the reconstruction algorithm must operate independently of the access structure, and the shares must not leak any information about it. We construct such a scheme for general access structures by building on top of our anonymous scheme, and it serves as a key component in the design of our traceable secret sharing scheme.

Theorem 1.4 (Informal). *For any access structure over n parties, there exists a hiding anonymous secret sharing scheme with perfect privacy and statistical correctness.*

Indeed, we show that hiding the access structure is a necessary step if one wants to trace back all corrupted parties, rather than identifying only one of them.

Theorem 1.5 (Informal). *There does not exist any traceable secret sharing scheme for general access structures that traces back all the corrupted parties and keeps the access structure public.*

1.2   Our Techniques

Our construction of a traceable secret sharing scheme for general access structures proceeds in three main steps. First, we build an anonymous scheme by extending the classical DNF construction. Next, we enhance this scheme to satisfy the stronger notion of hiding anonymity, ensuring that neither the shares nor the reconstruction algorithm reveal any information about the access structure. Finally, we build on this hiding anonymous scheme to design our traceable construction. This approach is motivated by an observation from [BPR24], who noted that for certain threshold access structures, efficient tracing (i.e. a polynomial number of queries) requires anonymity.

Anonymous Schemes for General Access Structures. To construct an anonymous secret sharing scheme, where neither the shares nor the reconstruction procedure reveal the identity of the parties, we adopt a combinatorial approach. Specifically, we eliminate any reliance on the configuration of the access structure, as this could potentially leak information about which parties hold which shares. Instead, we additively share the secret independently for each authorized subset.

However, this strategy results in each party receiving one share for every authorized subset it belongs to, and thus the size of a party's share leaks the number of such subsets, breaking anonymity. To address this, we assign dummy random shares to each party for every authorized subset it does not belong to, thereby equalizing the share size of each party.

To enable reconstruction, each authorized subset of parties must identify the portion of their shares corresponding to their subset. However, they cannot do so directly because their shares reveal no information about their role in the access structure. To overcome this challenge, we employ an indicator technique: in addition to the actual secret, we also share a fixed indicator value (namely, 0) using the same anonymous scheme. This allows the parties to test different combinations of their shares and identify the correct subset (i.e., the one that reconstructs the indicator). Moreover, if the domain of shares is sufficiently large, the probability that an incorrect reconstruction involving dummy shares yields the indicator is negligible.

When a subset of parties want to reconstruct the secret, we need to ensure that the process does not reveal their identities. For that, each party only provides the portion of its shares that is labeled by the size of the subset. This approach aligns with a common feature in many secret sharing schemes, where only a specific part of each share is needed during reconstruction. We formalize this idea through a deterministic algorithm called Projection, which models a local computation that each party performs on its share based solely on the size of the reconstructing subset. This step is crucial for preserving anonymity, as revealing the entire share during reconstruction could inadvertently expose party identities. For example, if the reconstructing subset is not minimal, exposing full shares might reveal which of its proper subsets are minimal, thereby leaking structural information of the parties.

Finally, we note that our anonymous scheme differs from the one proposed by Bishop et al. [BGI+25], and we discuss these differences in detail in Sect. 3.1.

Example 1.6. We illustrate these ideas with a toy access structure Γ over three parties p_1, p_2, p_3 given by $\Gamma = \{\{p_1, p_2\}, \{p_2, p_3\}, \{p_1, p_2, p_3\}\}$.

Let $\mathbb{Z}_m$ be the ring of integers modulo m for a sufficiently large m, and let $s \in \mathbb{Z}_m$ be the secret. First, we show how to share the secret s among Γ:

1. For each $A \in \Gamma$, share s independently among A with the additive scheme[1]:

$$\mathsf{sh}_1 = \{r^s_{1,1}, r^s_{3,1}\}, \ \mathsf{sh}_2 = \{s - r^s_{1,1}, r^s_{2,2}, r^s_{3,2}\}, \ \mathsf{sh}_3 = \{s - r^s_{2,2}, s - r^s_{3,1} - r^s_{3,2}\}.$$

---

[1] At this point, the size of the share of p_2 is different from the size of the shares of p_1 and p_3, which reveals its identity.

8   O. Farràs and M. Guiot

2. For each $A \in \Gamma$, send dummy random values to the parties not in A[2]:

$$\mathsf{sh}_1 = \{r^s_{1,1}, r^s_{2,1}, r^s_{3,1}\}, \qquad\qquad \mathsf{sh}_2 = \{s - r^s_{1,1}, r^s_{2,2}, r^s_{3,2}\},$$
$$\mathsf{sh}_3 = \{r^s_{3,1}, s - r^s_{2,2}, s - r^s_{3,1} - r^s_{3,2}\},$$

    where the blue color indicates that these shares are not the result of any sharing process, but are instead sampled uniformly at random from $\mathbb{Z}_m$.

3. Repeat the steps (1) and (2) with the indicator 0 and group the parts of the shares in pairs of the form (indicator, secret):

$$\mathsf{sh}_1 = \{(r^0_{1,1}, r^s_{1,1}), (r^0_{2,1}, r^s_{2,1}), (r^0_{3,1}, r^s_{3,1})\},$$
$$\mathsf{sh}_2 = \{(-r^0_{1,1}, s - r^s_{1,1}), (r^0_{2,2}, r^s_{2,2}), (r^0_{3,2} r^s_{3,2})\},$$
$$\mathsf{sh}_3 = \{(r^0_{3,1}, r^s_{3,1}), (-r^0_{2,2}, s - r^s_{2,2}), (-r^0_{3,1} - r^0_{3,2}, s - r^s_{3,1} - r^s_{3,2})\}.$$

    Next, we show how the authorized subset $\{p_2, p_3\}$ recovers the secret s from their shares $\mathsf{sh}_2, \mathsf{sh}_3$:

1. Since p_2, p_3 is an authorized subset of size two, each party computes its projected share of level two. These projected shares correspond to the portions of their shares associated with all authorized subsets of size two:

$$\mathsf{psh}_2 = \{(-r^0_{1,1}, s - r^s_{1,1}), (r^0_{2,2}, r^s_{2,2})\}, \ \ \mathsf{psh}_3 = \{(r^0_{3,1}, r^s_{3,1}), (-r^0_{2,2}, s - r^s_{2,2})\}.$$

2. Reconstruct for all the indicator shares to check which indicator corresponds to the value 0:

$$-r^0_{1,1} + r^0_{3,1} \neq 0, \quad r^0_{2,2} + (-r^0_{2,2}) = 0.$$

3. For the corresponding component, reconstruct the secret using its shares:

$$r^s_{2,2} + (s - r^s_{2,2}) = s.$$

Hiding Anonymous Schemes for General Access Structures. To enhance our anonymous scheme to satisfy the hiding property, we first observe that its reconstruction algorithm already operates independently of the access structure: authorized subsets can locally test combinations of their shares using the indicator technique, without requiring any knowledge of the access structure itself. Then, what remains is to ensure that the shares do not leak information about the access structure. In our anonymous scheme, the size of any share reflects the

---

[2] Now, the size of the share of p_2 is equal from the size of the shares of p_1 and p_3, hiding its identity.

number of authorized subsets in the access structure, which leaks information about it.

To prevent this, we increase the shares of each party with a dummy share for each unauthorized subset of the access structure. As a result, every party receives a share of uniform size, determined solely by the total number of parties. This modification suffices to transform our anonymous scheme into a hiding anonymous one.

Traceable Schemes for General Access Structures. The core idea behind our traceable secret sharing scheme is to make the reconstruction box itself reveal the identities of the corrupted parties who built it. To keep the exposition clear, in this discussion we assume that the reconstruction box outputs the full secret rather than a single bit. The technically more challenging and general case, in which the reconstruction box outputs only one bit, is handled and explained in detail in Sect. 5.

At a high level, omitting some technical subtleties discussed later in Sect. 4, this is achieved by exploiting two key properties of our hiding anonymous scheme. First, sets of shares generated from the same scheme but corresponding to different secrets are indistinguishable to unauthorized subsets.[3] Second, due to anonymity, these shares cannot be linked to any specific parties.

Using these facts, we proceed as follows. For each unauthorized subset, we select one party and assign it a unique secret identifier. We then additively share this identifier for an authorized subset that contains the unauthorized subset. The parties in the unauthorized subset receive their corresponding additive shares, while all other parties in the access structure receive dummy shares[4]. The remaining real additive shares are kept by the tracer and later used as queries to the reconstruction box.

More specifically, in order to trace the corrupted parties, the tracer iteratively tests all such retained shares by querying the reconstruction box with them and checking whether the output matches the identifier of a party. Since the reconstruction box cannot distinguish these shares from the valid ones associated with the actual secret, it accepts them as legitimate input. In particular, when the query includes the retained shares corresponding to the unauthorized subset that built the reconstruction box, it reconstructs the associated identifier, thereby revealing the identity of one of the corrupted parties.[5] The hiding property of our scheme, which ensures that no information about the access structure is leaked, plays a subtle but essential role in this step: it prevents the reconstruction box from detecting inconsistencies in the reconstruction process, a technical detail further discussed in Sect. 5.

---

[3] This property is referred to as *multi-dealer anonymity* in the work of Bishop et al. [BGI+25], and is discussed in more detail in Sect. 3.

[4] These dummy shares ensure anonymity by keeping share sizes uniform.

[5] See the full version of this work [FG25] for an optimization that enables tracing multiple corrupted parties.

Example 1.7. We illustrate these ideas again with the access structure Γ in Example 1.6. Let $\mathbb{Z}_m$ be the ring of integers modulo m for a sufficiently large m, let $s \in \mathbb{Z}_m$ be the secret, and assume that we have already shared s among $\{p_1, p_2, p_3\}$ with a hiding anonymous scheme Σ for Γ.

First, we show how we add traceability for the unauthorized subset $\{p_1\}$:

1. Select an identifier $\mathsf{id}_1 \in \mathbb{Z}_m$.
2. Select an authorized subset A of Γ containing $\{p_1\}$: $A = \{p_1, p_2\}$.
3. Generate the shares of id_1 according to Σ for the authorized subset A:

$$(\mathsf{sh}_1^{\mathsf{id}_1}, \mathsf{sh}_2^{\mathsf{id}_1}, \mathsf{sh}_3^{\mathsf{id}_1}) \leftarrow \Sigma(\mathsf{id}_1, A),$$

   where the blue color indicates that these shares are not the result of any sharing process, but are instead sampled uniformly at random from $\mathbb{Z}_m$.
4. Generate a dummy random share sh_2^r for the party p_2.[6]
5. Send $\mathsf{sh}_1^{\mathsf{id}_1}$, sh_2^r, and $\mathsf{sh}_3^{\mathsf{id}_1}$ to p_1, p_2, and p_3 respectively.
6. Retain $\mathsf{sh}_2^{\mathsf{id}_1}$ for the tracer.

The procedure to add traceability for the remaining unauthorized subsets is analogous. Next, we show how to trace back the corrupted subset $\{p_1\}$:

1. Query the reconstruction box R with each of the shares sh given to the tracer during the sharing phase, gathering the corresponding outputs:

$$\mathsf{output} \leftarrow R(\mathsf{sh}).$$

2. For each query, check if the output of the reconstruction box R is the indicator id of any of the parties. If the check passes, accuse the corresponding party:

$$\mathsf{output} \overset{?}{=} \mathsf{id}.$$

3. Since the corrupted set $\{p_1\}$ constructed the reconstruction box R, with high probability it will only output the indicator id_1 when queried with $\mathsf{sh}_2^{\mathsf{id}_1}$:

$$\mathsf{id}_1 \leftarrow R(\mathsf{sh}_2^{\mathsf{id}_1}).$$

Therefore, party p_1 is accused.

1.3   Related Work and Open Questions

In this section, we review prior work on traceable secret sharing schemes and the main open questions. We refer to the full version of this work [FG25] for related work on secret sharing schemes for general access structures, anonymous secret sharing schemes, and other open problems.

The notion of traceable secret sharing was first explored by Goyal, Song, and Srinivasan [GSS21], who proposed a construction for threshold access structures based on the Goldreich-Levin decoding algorithm [GL89]. Subsequently, Boneh,

---

[6] Since $p_3 \notin A = \{p_1, p_2\}$, $\mathsf{sh}_3^{\mathsf{id}_1}$ is already a dummy random share.

Partap, and Rotem [BPR24] revisited this concept and introduced an alternative traceability model, presenting two new constructions for threshold access structures based on the classical schemes of Shamir [Sha79] and Blakley [Bla79].

Following these foundational contributions, recent works have extended traceable secret sharing to broader settings. Hoffmann [Hof24] proposed a construction for weighted threshold access structures, while Baghery et al. [BEMS25] designed a traceable verifiable secret sharing scheme for threshold access structures. Moreover, some new lines of research have introduced notions closely related to traceable secret sharing, such as secret sharing with snitching [DFLM24], traceable verifiable random functions [BPR25], and deniable secret sharing [CDK+25].

After making public this work, Goyal, Jain, and Partap [GJP25] proposed an alternative construction of traceable secret sharing schemes for general access structures. Their approach, however, differs substantially from ours. First, they adopt a modified and incomparable setting in which the reconstruction box also includes a label specifying an unauthorized subset I, and correctness is only required when the box is queried with the shares of all parties in I. This modeling choice eliminates the need for anonymous secret sharing. Moreover, although their construction is efficient in terms of share size, it is computational in nature and relies on indistinguishability obfuscation, whereas our scheme is information-theoretic and linear.

Our results raise two main open questions about traceable secret sharing schemes. A clear direction for future research is to construct information-theoretic traceable schemes for general access structures using more efficient underlying schemes than the DNF-based one. In particular, it is natural to ask whether any of the recent general constructions, which achieve significantly smaller share size, can be extended to support traceability. Another related question is to develop efficient traceable secret sharing schemes for useful families of access structures, such as graphs or slices. As in the case of threshold access structures, their structural constraints might allow for more efficient solutions.

An alternative line for future work is understanding the lower bounds for traceable schemes. Unlike common secret sharing schemes, which are mainly focused on privacy, traceable schemes must also guarantee that leaked shares can be traced back to their parties. This extra requirement may impose additional constraints on the constructions of such schemes, potentially leading to higher lower bounds on the share size.

1.4 Organization

In Sect. 2, we present the notation used in this work. In Sect. 3, we introduce the notions of anonymous and hiding anonymous secret sharing schemes, highlight their similarities and differences with the definitions proposed by Bishop et al. [BGI+25], and construct the schemes for general access structures of Theorem 1.3 and Theorem 1.4. In Sect. 4, we extend the definition of traceable secret sharing from [BPR24] to support arbitrary access structures. Later, in Sect. 5, we present the traceable secret sharing scheme for general access structures of Theorem 1.1.

We defer to the full version of this work [FG25] an extended discussion on the related work and open questions, the preliminaries on secret sharing schemes,the second statement of Theorem 1.3, all the proofs, the introduction of a weaker traceability model, and a scheme for general access structures in that model.

2 Preliminaries

The definitions and basics of secret sharing schemes are standard, and they are deferred to the full version of this work [FG25]. Next, we introduce the notation used in the paper.

We notate $\mathbb{N}$, $\mathbb{Z}$, and $\mathbb{R}$ for the sets of natural, integer, and real numbers, respectively. For $m \in \mathbb{N}$, we denote the ring of integers modulo m by $\mathbb{Z}_m$, and for any prime power $q \in \mathbb{N}$, we notate $\mathbb{F}_q$ for the finite field of q elements.

For $n \in \mathbb{N}$, we denote the set $\{1, \ldots, n\}$ as $[n]$. For a set S, we denote its cardinal by $|S|$, its power set by 2^S, and we denote by $s \leftarrow_\$ S$ the process of sampling a value s from the uniform distribution over S.

We denote vectors $\boldsymbol{x}$ using bold symbols, and their i-th coordinates as x_i. The unary vector is denoted by $\mathbf{1}^n \in \{0,1\}^n$, and the zero vector is denoted by $\mathbf{0}^n \in \{0,1\}^n$.

We say that a function $\mathrm{negl} : \mathbb{N} \to \mathbb{R}$ is negligible if for every positive polynomial $p(\lambda)$ there exists $\lambda_0 \in \mathbb{N}$ such that $\mathrm{negl}(\lambda) \leq \frac{1}{p(\lambda)}$ for every $\lambda \geq \lambda_0$.

3 Anonymous Secret Sharing

In this section, we study anonymous secret sharing schemes. We begin by introducing new definitions that extend the existing framework and compare them with the notions proposed by Bishop et al. [BGI+25]. Next, we present a general construction that realizes any access structure under our anonymity definitions. Finally, we introduce the notion of *hiding anonymous schemes* and construct such a scheme for general access structures. All proofs are deferred to the full version of this work [FG25], where we also describe simple and efficient anonymous schemes for specific families of access structures, compare our general construction with those of [PCO20,BGI+25], and present further optimizations.

3.1 Definition

Anonymous secret sharing schemes, as defined by Bishop et al. [BGI+25], extend classical secret sharing by adding two properties beyond correctness and privacy. The first, *share anonymity*, requires that the shares of any unauthorized subset do not reveal any information about the identities of the parties holding them. The second, *anonymous reconstruction*, ensures that the reconstruction procedure can be performed without knowing the identities of the parties involved.

To formalize share anonymity, Bishop et al. [BGI+25] introduce a hierarchy of three definitions: *single-dealer anonymity*, *multi-dealer anonymity*, and *uniform anonymity*. The weakest, single-dealer anonymity, requires the shares of any unauthorized subset to be indistinguishable from those of any other unauthorized subset of the same size. Multi-dealer anonymity strengthens this by requiring indistinguishability between shares derived from the same secret and shares derived from two independently chosen secrets. Finally, uniform anonymity is the strongest notion, requiring the shares of any unauthorized subset to be indistinguishable from uniformly random values. These definitions are related, with uniform anonymity implying multi-dealer anonymity, which in turn implies single-dealer anonymity. In their work [BGI+25], schemes satisfying both uniform anonymity and anonymous reconstruction are called *fully anonymous schemes*. We refer the reader to [BGI+25] for the precise definitions and a detailed comparison.

Our definition of anonymous secret sharing extends this framework by strengthening the notion of anonymous reconstruction. Specifically, we require not only that the reconstruction algorithm does not rely on the identities of the parties, but also that the inputs provided to it do not leak any information about those identities. That is, the inputs given by any two authorized subsets of the same size must be indistinguishable. We refer to this stronger requirement as *projected anonymous reconstruction*.

To support this, we introduce an additional algorithm, Projection, which models a local transformation applied by each party to their share. This deterministic algorithm takes as input a share and an integer indicating the size of the subset attempting reconstruction, and returns the portion of the share relevant for authorized subsets of that size. This approach reflects a natural principle: in many secret sharing schemes, only a portion of each share is needed for reconstruction.

Intuitively, since the goal is to prevent the reconstruction process from leaking any information about the parties, it must avoid relying on the internal structure of the access structure. Therefore, the only information that parties are allowed to use is the size of the subset they belong to, as this is inherently revealed during reconstruction. The Projection algorithm captures this constraint, ensuring that each party only exposes the minimal part of their share needed for reconstructing the secret.

In this context, our anonymous secret sharing schemes must satisfy the share anonymity condition (in the sense of [BGI+25]) and projected anonymous reconstruction. We now formalize the definition.

Definition 3.1 (Anonymous Secret Sharing Scheme). *Let $\mathcal{S}$ be a finite set of secrets with $|\mathcal{S}| \geq 2$, and let Γ be an access structure over n parties. An anonymous secret sharing scheme for Γ it is a triple of the following algorithms:*

- $\mathsf{Share}(s) \mapsto \{\mathsf{sh}_i\}_{i \in [n]}$ *is the randomized share algorithm. It takes as input a secret $s \in \mathcal{S}$. It outputs a set of shares $\{\mathsf{sh}_i\}_{i \in [n]}$.*

- $\mathsf{Proj}(\mathsf{sh}_i, k) \mapsto \mathsf{psh}_{i,k}$ *is the deterministic projection algorithm. It takes as input a share sh_i and a size $k \in [n]$. It outputs the projected share $\mathsf{psh}_{i,k}$ of level k.*
- $\mathsf{Rec}(\{\mathsf{psh}_{i,k}\}_{i \in A}, k) \mapsto s$ *is the deterministic reconstruction algorithm. It takes as input a set of projected shares of level k for an authorized subset A and the level k. It outputs the secret s.*

Apart from the perfect correctness and privacy requirements, these algorithms must satisfy the following requirements:

- ***Perfect projected correctness.*** *For any secret $s \in \mathcal{S}$ and any authorized set A with $|A| = k$, it holds that*

$$\mathbf{P}[s = \mathsf{Rec}(\{\mathsf{Proj}(\mathsf{Share}(s)_i, k)\}_{i \in A}, k)] = 1.$$

- ***Perfect share anonymity.*** *For any secret $s \in \mathcal{S}$, any unauthorized sets A, B with $|A| = |B| = k$, and any possible set of k shares $\{\mathsf{sh}_i\}_{i \in [k]}$, it holds that*

$$\mathbf{P}[\mathsf{Share}(s)_A = \{\mathsf{sh}_i\}_{i \in [k]}] = \mathbf{P}[\mathsf{Share}(s)_B = \{\mathsf{sh}_i\}_{i \in [k]}].$$

- ***Perfect projected anonymous reconstruction.*** *For any secret $s \in \mathcal{S}$, any authorized sets A, B with $|A| = |B| = k$, and any possible set of k projected shares $\{\mathsf{psh}_{i,k}\}_{i \in [k]}$ of level k, it holds that*

$$\mathbf{P}[\{\mathsf{Proj}(\mathsf{Share}(s)_i, k)\}_{i \in A} = \{\mathsf{psh}_{i,k}\}_{i \in [k]}]$$
$$= \mathbf{P}[\{\mathsf{Proj}(\mathsf{Share}(s)_i, k)\}_{i \in B} = \{\mathsf{psh}_{i,k}\}_{i \in [k]}].$$

Remark 3.2. In the above definition, we adopt the weakest notion of share anonymity, namely *single-dealer anonymity*. This choice is motivated by the fact that, for constructing traceable secret sharing schemes, this weaker notion is sufficient.

Remark 3.3. As in the standard definition of secret sharing, the requirements of anonymous secret sharing can also be relaxed. In particular, instead of demanding perfect guarantees, one can define *statistical share anonymity* and *statistical projected anonymous reconstruction*. These relaxed variants lead to the definition of statistical anonymous secret sharing schemes.

In the full version of this work [FG25], we discuss an additional extra property that may be desirable for some applications of anonymous secret sharing schemes.

3.2   Anonymous Scheme for General Access Structures

We now describe an anonymous secret sharing scheme for general access structures, based on the classical DNF construction. Our goal is to ensure that neither the shares nor the reconstruction procedure reveals the identities of the participating parties. To this end, we adopt a combinatorial approach that eliminates any reliance on the internal structure of the access structure, as such dependencies could leak information about which parties hold which shares.

As in the DNF construction, the secret is shared independently for each authorized subset. To do so, we employ the DNF additive scheme, which is also anonymous, as a building block. However, a direct application of this idea results in parties receiving shares only for the subsets they belong to. Since the number of such subsets varies across parties, this causes their share size to differ, which can leak information about their position in the access structure. To prevent this, we ensure that each party receives one share for every authorized subset (filling in with dummy random shares when necessary), which leads to a uniform share size across all the parties.

To further prevent parties from inferring the identity of other parties during reconstruction, we carefully define the **Projection** algorithm. In our construction, it simply selects the parts of the shares corresponding to authorized subsets of the same size as the subset currently attempting to reconstruct the secret. This restriction is essential to preserve anonymity: if a party were to reveal its full share, it could leak information about him. For example, if the reconstructing subset is not minimal, exposing the full shares could reveal which proper subset of it is minimal, thereby leaking information of the parties.

For the reconstruction process, we would like it to be as in the DNF scheme. However, the parties cannot directly identify which portion of their shares corresponds to their authorized subset, since the secret is unknown and the inclusion of dummy shares obscures the access structure. To address this, we incorporate an indicator technique. Alongside the actual secret, the dealer also distributes a known public indicator (specifically, the value 0) using the same sharing process. Parties can then test subsets of their projected indicator shares to identify the one that reconstructs the indicator 0, revealing the correct portion of their projected shares from which they must recover the secret. If the underlying field is large enough, the probability that an incorrect combination of projected indicator shares reconstructs the indicator is negligible, ensuring statistical correctness.

Finally, another potential source of leakage arises from the ordering of the authorized subsets during the sharing process. If the dealer selects subsets of a given size in a fixed order, parties might infer their position in the access structure by identifying the index of the share component they use to recover the secret. To prevent this, the dealer samples a fresh random permutation over the authorized subsets of each given size and distributes the shares according to this randomized order. This guarantees that the ordering of share components does not reveal any structural information.

The complete description of this anonymous scheme for general access structures is given in Fig. 1, and its formal statement follows below. The full version of this work [FG25] contains the proof, a comparison with the constructions of [PCO20, BGI+25], and additional optimizations of the scheme.

Notation:

1. Let Γ_k be the family of authorized subsets in Γ of size k.
2. Let P_k denote the set of permutations of $|\Gamma_k|$ elements.

Share(s):

1. For $k \in [n]$
   (a) Select a permutation $\sigma_k \in P_k$ uniformly at random, i.e. $\sigma_k \leftarrow_\$ P_k$.
   (b) For $A \in \Gamma_k$
       i. Set $B \leftarrow \sigma_k(A)$.
       ii. Share $0, s \in \mathbb{Z}_m$ with the DNF additive scheme Σ among the parties in A, i.e.

$$\{(\mathsf{sh}^0_{i,k,B}, \mathsf{sh}^s_{i,k,B})\}_{i \in A} \leftarrow (\Sigma(0, A), \Sigma(s, A)).$$

       iii. Set $\mathsf{sh}_{i,k,B} \leftarrow (\mathsf{sh}^0_{i,k,B}, \mathsf{sh}^s_{i,k,B})$ for $i \in A$.
       iv. Send two random elements $r_0, r_s \in \mathbb{Z}_m$ to each of the parties not in A, i.e.

$$\mathsf{sh}_{i,k,B} \leftarrow_\$ (\mathbb{Z}_m, \mathbb{Z}_m) \text{ for } i \in [n] \setminus A.$$

   (c) Set $\mathsf{sh}_{i,k} \leftarrow \{\mathsf{sh}_{i,k,B}\}_{B \in \mathcal{J}}$ for $i \in [n]$, where $\mathcal{J} = \{\sigma_k(A) : A \in \Gamma_k\}$.
2. Set $\mathsf{sh}_i \leftarrow \{\mathsf{sh}_{i,k}\}_{k \in [n]}$ for $i \in [n]$.
3. Output $\{\mathsf{sh}_i\}_{i \in [n]}$.

Proj(sh_i, k):

1. Parse sh_i as $\{\mathsf{sh}_{i,k}\}_{k \in [n]}$.
2. Set $\mathsf{psh}_{i,k} \leftarrow \mathsf{sh}_{i,k}$, i.e. the projection algorithm is the projection function.
3. Output $\mathsf{psh}_{i,k}$.

Rec($\{\mathsf{psh}_{i,k}\}_{i \in A}, k$):

1. Parse $\mathsf{psh}_{i,k}$ as $\{\mathsf{sh}_{i,k,B}\}_{B \in \Gamma_k}$ for $i \in A$.
2. Set $s' \leftarrow_\$ \mathbb{Z}_m$.
3. For $B \in \Gamma_k$
   (a) Parse $\mathsf{sh}_{i,k,B}$ as $(\mathsf{sh}^0_i, \mathsf{sh}^s_i)$ for $i \in A$.
   (b) Set $u \leftarrow \sum_{i \in A} \mathsf{sh}^0_i$.
   (c) If $u = 0$, set $s' \leftarrow \sum_{i \in A} \mathsf{sh}^s_i$ and **break**.
4. Output s'.

Fig. 1. Anonymous secret sharing scheme for any access structure Γ.

Theorem 3.4. (Theorem 1.3 restated). *Let Γ be any access structure over n parties, let $\lambda \in \mathbb{N}$ be the security parameter with $\lambda = \Omega(n)$, and let $m = 2^{\Theta(\lambda)}$. For any $s \in \mathbb{Z}_m$ the protocol of Fig. 1 is an anonymous secret sharing scheme with statistical reconstruction realizing Γ with a share size of $O(2^n \log m)$.*

3.3 Hiding Anonymous Secret Sharing

In this subsection, we first introduce the notion of hiding anonymous secret sharing schemes, which strengthens the notion of anonymity already presented. Then, we present such a construction for general access structures.

Definition. The definition of hiding anonymous schemes builds upon the notion anonymous schemes. In particular, apart from requiring that shares and reconstruction do not reveal the identities of the participating parties, we now consider a setting where the access structure itself is unknown to the parties. Instead, they are only aware that the access structure belongs to some known family of candidate access structures. In this context, the goal is to ensure that any set of parties learn no additional information about the specific access structure being used beyond what is inherently unavoidable.

More in detail, due to the correctness of scheme, a subset of parties will naturally learn which of their subsets are authorized and which are not, simply by testing whether reconstruction is possible. However, beyond this, a hiding anonymous scheme requires that the parties cannot distinguish which access structure, among all those compatible with their observed authorized and unauthorized subsets, was actually used to generate their shares.

To formalize this, we generalize the standard secret sharing model to consider schemes defined over a family of access structures, rather than a single one. In this framework, the Share algorithm receives as input the specific access structure from the family under which it must share the secret. In contrast, the Projection and Reconstruction are independent of the access structure, ensuring that reconstruction works uniformly across the entire family.

Finally, we require that, for every access structure in the family, the restriction of the scheme to that structure, that is, the Share algorithm instantiated with that specific access structure together with the common Projection and Reconstruction algorithms, must satisfy all the properties of an anonymous secret sharing scheme. The precise definition follows.

Definition 3.5. (Hiding Anonymous Secret Sharing Scheme). *Let $\mathcal{S}$ be a finite set of secrets with $|\mathcal{S}| \geq 2$, and let $\mathcal{F}$ be a family of access structures over n parties. A hiding anonymous secret sharing scheme for $\mathcal{F}$ is a triple of the following algorithms:*

- $\mathsf{Share}(s, \Gamma) \mapsto \{\mathsf{sh}_i\}_{i \in [n]}$ *is the randomized share algorithm. It takes as input a secret $s \in \mathcal{S}$ and an access structure $\Gamma \in \mathcal{F}$. It outputs a set of shares $\{\mathsf{sh}_i\}_{i \in [n]}$.*
- $\mathsf{Proj}(\mathsf{sh}_i, k) \mapsto \mathsf{psh}_{i,k}$ *is the deterministic projection algorithm. It takes as input a share sh_i and a size $k \in [n]$. It outputs the projected share $\mathsf{psh}_{i,k}$ of level k.*
- $\mathsf{Rec}(\{\mathsf{psh}_{i,k}\}_{i \in A}, k) \mapsto s$ *is the deterministic reconstruction algorithm. It takes as input a set of projected shares of level k for an authorized subset A of some $\Gamma \in \mathcal{F}$ with $|A| = k$ and the level k. It outputs the secret s.*

These algorithms must satisfy the following requirements:

- **Restricted Anonymous Schemes.** *For any $\Gamma \in \mathcal{F}$, the restriction of the* Share *algorithm to Γ together with the* Projection *and* Reconstruction *algorithms form an anonymous secret sharing scheme for Γ.*
- **Perfect Hideout.** *For any $s \in \mathcal{S}$, $k \in [n]$, any subset $A \subseteq [n]$ such that $|A| = k$, any two access structures $\Gamma, \Gamma' \in \mathcal{F}$ such that Γ and Γ' agree in all subsets of A, and any possible set of k shares $\{\mathsf{sh}_i\}_{i \in [k]}$, it holds that*

$$\mathbf{P}[\mathsf{Share}(s, \Gamma)_A = \{\mathsf{sh}_i\}_{i \in [k]}] = \mathbf{P}[\mathsf{Share}(s, \Gamma')_A = \{\mathsf{sh}_i\}_{i \in [k]}].$$

Remark 3.6. As in Remark 3.3, the requirements of hiding anonymous schemes can also be relaxed. In particular, instead of demanding perfect guarantees, one can define *statistical restricted anonymous schemes* and *statistical hideout.* These relaxed variants lead to the definition of statistical hiding anonymous secret sharing schemes.

The Scheme. We now explain the idea behind the construction of hiding anonymous secret sharing schemes for a family of access structures. The main challenge in this setting is to prevent the parties from learning any information about the specific access structure used, beyond what is inherently revealed by the ability (or inability) to reconstruct the secret.

The anonymous scheme from Fig. 1 is already close to satisfying this notion. In particular, its Projection and Reconstruction algorithms are independent of the access structure, and thus already compatible with the hiding requirement. The only obstacle preventing the scheme from being hiding is that the total share size of each party depends on the number of authorized subsets in the selected access structure. Therefore, if the family contains access structures with varying numbers of authorized subsets, the share size itself would leak information about which access structure was used.

To address this issue, we modify the scheme as follows. Instead of generating shares only for the authorized subsets of the selected access structure, we consider the set of all authorized subsets that appear in any access structure in the family. For those subsets that belong to the selected access structure, we apply the same procedure as in Fig. 1, using the anonymous additive scheme to share both the secret and the indicator. For all other subsets, we simply assign dummy shares to the parties. This padding ensures that the share size is uniform across all access structures in the family and thus does not leak any structural information. The rest of the scheme remains unchanged, and the correctness, privacy, and anonymity guarantees follow from the ones in the previous construction.

A full specification of the hiding anonymous scheme for a family of access structures is presented in Fig. 2, its statement follows. The full version of this work [FG25] contains the proof and further optimizations of the scheme.

Theorem 3.7. (Theorem 1.4 restated). *Let $\mathcal{F}$ be a family of access structures over n parties, let $\lambda \in \mathbb{N}$ be the security parameter with $\lambda = \Omega(n)$, and let $m = 2^{\Theta(\lambda)}$. For any $s \in \mathbb{Z}_m$, the protocol of Fig. 2 is a hiding anonymous secret sharing scheme for $\mathcal{F}$ with statistical reconstruction and share size $O(2^n \log m)$.*

Notation:

1. Let $\Delta = \bigcup_{\Gamma' \in \mathcal{F}} \Gamma'$ be the family of authorized subsets of access structures in $\mathcal{F}$.
2. Let Δ_k be the family of subsets in Δ of size k.
3. Let P_k denote the set of permutations of $|\Delta_k|$ elements.

$\mathsf{Share}(s, \Gamma)$:

1. For $k \in [n]$
   (a) Select a permutation $\sigma_k \in P_k$ uniformly at random, i.e. $\sigma_k \leftarrow_\$ P_k$.
   (b) For $A \in \Delta_k$
      i. Set $B \leftarrow \sigma_k(A)$.
      ii. If $A \in \Gamma$
         A. Share $0, s \in \mathbb{Z}_m$ with the DNF additive scheme Σ among the parties in A, i.e.
         $$\{(\mathsf{sh}^0_{i,k,B}, \mathsf{sh}^s_{i,k,B})\}_{i \in A} \leftarrow (\Sigma(0, A), \Sigma(s, A)).$$
         B. Set $\mathsf{sh}_{i,k,B} \leftarrow (\mathsf{sh}^0_{i,k,B}, \mathsf{sh}^s_{i,k,B})$ for $i \in A$.
         C. Send two random elements $r_0, r_s \in \mathbb{Z}_m$ to each of the parties not in A, i.e.
         $$\mathsf{sh}_{i,k,B} \leftarrow_\$ (\mathbb{Z}_m, \mathbb{Z}_m) \text{ for } i \in [n] \setminus A.$$
      iii. If $A \notin \Gamma$
         A. Send two random elements $r_0, r_s \in \mathbb{Z}_m$ to each of the n parties, i.e.
         $$\mathsf{sh}_{i,k,B} \leftarrow_\$ (\mathbb{Z}_m, \mathbb{Z}_m) \text{ for } i \in [n].$$
   (c) Set $\mathsf{sh}_{i,k} \leftarrow \{\mathsf{sh}_{i,k,B}\}_{B \in \mathcal{J}}$ for $i \in [n]$, where $\mathcal{J} = \{\sigma_k(A) : A \in \Delta_k\}$.
2. Set $\mathsf{sh}_i = \{\mathsf{sh}^k_i\}_{k \in [n]}$ for $i \in [n]$.
3. Output $\{\mathsf{sh}_i\}_{i \in [n]}$.

$\mathsf{Proj}(\mathsf{sh}_i, k)$: The same as in the general anonymous scheme of Fig. 1.

$\mathsf{Rec}(\{\mathsf{psh}_{i,k}\}_{i \in A}, k)$:

1. Set $t \leftarrow \binom{n}{k}$.
2. Parse $\mathsf{psh}_{i,k}$ as $\{\mathsf{sh}_{i,k,B}\}_{B \in \Delta_k}$ for $i \in A$.
3. Set $s' \leftarrow_\$ \mathbb{Z}_m$.
4. For $B \in \Delta_k$
   (a) Parse $\mathsf{sh}^k_{i,j}$ as $(\mathsf{sh}^0_i, \mathsf{sh}^s_i)$ for $i \in A$.
   (b) Set $u \leftarrow \sum_{i \in A} \mathsf{sh}^0_i$.
   (c) If $u = 0$, set $s' \leftarrow \sum_{i \in A} \mathsf{sh}^s_i$ and **break**.
5. Output s'.

Fig. 2. Hiding anonymous secret sharing scheme for any access structure Γ of a family of access structures $\mathcal{F}$.

4   Traceable Secret Sharing for General Access Structures

In this section, we focus on generalizing the definitions of traceable secret sharing from [BPR24] to accommodate arbitrary access structures. First, we outline how we extend their tracing model to the general case. Later, we define traceability for general access structures. The full version of this work [FG25] introduces a restricted yet simpler notion of traceability, which we refer to as *projection traceability*, which serves as a useful stepping stone towards towards building the general notion of traceability.

4.1   The Tracing Model

Our tracing framework builds on the model of [BPR24], which formalizes traceability in the context of threshold secret sharing, and extends it to support arbitrary monotone access structures. In their setting, the adversary uses the shares of an unauthorized subset of parties to construct a reconstruction box, which can later reconstruct the secret when provided with a sufficient number of valid shares. It is assumed that this reconstruction box is eventually obtained by the authorities, who are able to interact with it in a black-box manner in order to trace it back to the corrupted parties who built it from their shares.

Within this framework, a traceable secret sharing scheme must satisfy two main requirements: *traceability*, which ensures that the tracer can correctly identify at least one corrupted party whose share was used to build the reconstruction box; and *non-imputability*, which guarantees that no honest party is falsely blamed. To support the tracing procedure, the Share algorithm outputs not only the individual shares, but also a tracing key and a verification key. The tracing key is given to the tracer and is used to generate a proof that links the reconstruction box to one or more corrupted parties. The verification key is given to a verifier and enables to check the correctness of the proof presented by the tracer.

We generalize this model in two important directions. First, we incorporate the Projection algorithm already defined for anonymous schemes and introduce an additional randomized algorithm, denoted ShareGeneration. This algorithm models a local computation based on the tracing key that allows the tracer to generate projected *pseudoshares*, that is, artificial projected shares that simulate valid projected shares. These projected pseudoshares are used to interact with the reconstruction box during the tracing procedure while maintaining anonymity. This process is described in more detail later.

Second, we extend the notion of reconstruction boxes beyond the threshold setting. Rather than assuming that the reconstruction box operates on a fixed number of shares, as is the threshold case, we allow it to accept any subset of shares that satisfies a general access structure. As a result, the tracing procedure must be designed to accommodate this more flexible and expressive behavior.

In this context, together with the extended notion of traceability, we also introduce a restricted variant that we call *projection traceability* (see the full version of this work [FG25]). At a high level, the two notions differ in the amount of information that parties must provide to the reconstruction box built by the adversary. Specifically, in the projected traceability setting, it is assumed that the reconstruction box only requires the projected shares of the parties to recover the secret. In contrast, in the traceability setting, the reconstruction box is allowed to reconstruct the secret only when it receives the full shares. As we will discuss in Sect. 5, assuming that the reconstruction box receives only projected shares simplifies the tracing procedure.

4.2   Traceable Secret Sharing

We next introduce the notion of traceability for general access structures. However, as we will discuss in Sect. 5, enabling tracing in this setting requires more than anonymity; the scheme must also hide the access structure itself. Consequently, since we will work with hiding anonymous schemes, it is convenient to define traceable schemes with respect to a family of access structures rather than a single one. The definition follows.

Definition 4.1. (Traceable Secret Sharing Scheme). *Let S be a finite set of secrets with $|S| \geq 2$, and let $\mathcal{F}$ be a family of access structures over n parties. A traceable secret sharing scheme for $\mathcal{F}$ is a sextuple of the following algorithms:*

- *$\mathsf{Share}(s, \Gamma) \mapsto (\{\mathsf{sh}_i\}_{i\in[n]}, \mathsf{tk}, \mathsf{vk})$ is the sharing algorithm. It takes as input parameter the secret and the access structure. It outputs a set of shares $\{\mathsf{sh}_i\}_{i\in[n]}$, a tracing key tk and a verification key vk.*
- *$\mathsf{Proj}(\mathsf{sh}_i, k) \mapsto \mathsf{psh}_{i,k}$ is the deterministic projection algorithm. It takes as input a share sh_i and a size $k \in [n]$. It outputs the projected share $\mathsf{psh}_{i,k}$ of level k.*
- *$\mathsf{Rec}(\{\mathsf{psh}_{i,k}\}_{i\in A}, k) \mapsto s$ is the deterministic reconstruction algorithm. It takes as input a set of projected shares $\mathsf{psh}_{i,k}$ of level k for an authorized set A with $|A| = k$ and the level k. It outputs the secret s.*
- *$\mathsf{ShGen}(\mathsf{tk}, k, k', p) \mapsto \{\mathsf{sh}'_i\}_{i\in[k']}$ is the randomized share generation algorithm. It takes as input a traceable key $\mathsf{tk} = (\mathsf{vk}_1, ..., \mathsf{vk}_n)$, two sizes $k, k' \in [n]$ such that $k + k' \leq n$, and an index p of one of the identifier's bits. It outputs a set of k' pseudoshares $\{\mathsf{sh}'_i\}_{i\in[k']}$.[7]*
- *$\mathsf{Trace}^R(\mathsf{tk}) \mapsto (\mathcal{I}, \pi)$ is the randomized tracing algorithm. It takes as input a tracing key $\mathsf{tk} = (\mathsf{tk}_1, ..., \mathsf{tk}_n)$ and it gets oracle (black-box) access to a reconstruction box R. It outputs a subset $\mathcal{I} \subset [n]$ of identities of corrupted parties and an associated proof π.*
- *$\mathsf{Verify}(\mathsf{vk}, \mathcal{I}, \pi) \mapsto \{0, 1\}$ is the deterministic verification algorithm. It takes as input a verification key $\mathsf{vk} = (\mathsf{vk}_1, ..., \mathsf{vk}_n)$, an alleged traitor subset $\mathcal{I}$, and an associated proof π. It outputs 1 (resp. 0) when accepting (resp. rejecting) the proof π that the parties $\mathcal{I}$ are guilty.*

Apart from the standard notions of correctness and privacy, these algorithms must also satisfy the following requirements:

---

[7] In this setting, the $\mathsf{ShareGeneration}$ algorithm outputs full pseudoshares instead of projected pseudoshares because the reconstruction box takes as input the whole shares.

- **Perfect Tracer Privacy.** *For any secrets* $s, s' \in \mathcal{S}$, *any unauthorized set* A, *and any possible set of shares* $\{\mathsf{sh}_i\}_{i \in A}$ *and any possible tracing key* tk, *it holds that*

$$\mathbf{P}[(\{\mathsf{sh}_i\}_{i \in A}, \mathsf{tk}) = \mathsf{Share}(s, \Gamma)_{A, \mathsf{tk}}] = \mathbf{P}[(\{\mathsf{sh}_i\}_{i \in A}, \mathsf{tk}) = \mathsf{Share}(s', \Gamma)_{A, \mathsf{tk}}],$$

  where $\mathsf{Share}(s, \Gamma)_{A, \mathsf{tk}}$ *corresponds to the restriction of the* Share *algorithm to the shares of* A *and the whole tracing key.*
- **Perfect Traceability.** *See Definition 4.3.*
- **Perfect Non-imputability.** *See Definition 4.4.*

To define the notions of traceability and non-imputability, we first introduce the notion of good reconstruction boxes. Intuitively, a reconstruction box is considered good if, when provided with a sufficient number of valid shares, it reconstructs the secret with high probability. As discussed earlier, we generalize the definition of Boneh, Partap, and Rotem [BPR24] to handle general access structures and allow the reconstruction box to output only the minimal useful information, namely a single bit, rather than the full secret.

In addition, since our traceable schemes are defined over a family of access structures, the definition of good reconstruction boxes must reflect this generality. In particular, we require the reconstruction box to be correct for all access structures in the family that are compatible with the corrupted subset, that is, for all access structures in which the corrupted parties form an unauthorized set. For each of these access structures, the reconstruction box must successfully reconstruct the secret when it is given full shares generated under that access structure, as long as the shares corresponding to the corrupted parties coincide with those from the original sharing. This condition is justified by the fact that the reconstruction algorithm is independent of the access structure, which remains hidden from the parties.

Another key difference from the model of [BPR24] lies in how the correlation between the shares of corrupted parties and those used as input to the reconstruction box is modeled. In [BPR24], this correlation is made explicit through a correlation string, which is used by the sharing algorithm to ensure consistency between the two sets of shares. In contrast, we require that the shares assigned to the corrupted parties coincide with the ones produced by the sharing procedure that generates the shares used as input to the reconstruction box. This choice is motivated by our setting, where the secret is shared under two potentially different access structures (though they agree on the behavior of the corrupted set), making it infeasible to use the same correlation string for both cases. Instead, requiring that the shares of the corrupted parties match in both sharing procedures provides a natural way to ensure consistency among the shares.

Definition 4.2. (Good Reconstruction Box). *Let* $\mathcal{S}$ *be a finite set of secrets with* $|\mathcal{S}| \geq 2$, *let* $\mathcal{F}$ *be a family of access structures over* n *parties, let* Γ *be an access structure in* $\mathcal{F}$, *and let* Σ *be a traceable secret sharing for* $\mathcal{F}$. *For* $\epsilon \in [0, \frac{1}{2}]$, *secrets* $s_0, s_1 \in \mathcal{S}$, *a bit* $b \in \{0, 1\}$, *an unauthorized subset* $A \notin \Gamma$, *and a corresponding set of shares* $\mathbf{sh} = \{\mathsf{sh}_i\}_{i\in A}$, *a reconstruction box* R *is* $(\mathcal{F}, A, \mathbf{sh}, s_0, s_1, b, \epsilon)$*-good if for any access structure* $\Gamma' \in \mathcal{F}$ *that is consistent with* A, *any unauthorized subset* $B \notin \Gamma'$ *such that* $A \cap B = \emptyset$ *and* $A \cup B \in \Gamma'$, *it holds that*

$$\mathbf{P}[R(\{\mathsf{sh}'_i\}_{i\in B}) = b] \geq \frac{1}{2} + \epsilon,$$

where the probability is taken over $(\{\mathsf{sh}'_i\}_{i\in[n]}, \mathsf{tk}, \mathsf{vk}) \leftarrow \mathsf{Share}(s_b, \Gamma')$ *conditioned on* $\{\mathsf{sh}'_i\}_{i\in A} = \mathbf{sh}$, *and the random coins of* R.

Once the notion of good reconstruction boxes is established, we proceed to formalize the definitions of traceability and non-imputability. We start by presenting the traceable experiment in Fig. 3, followed by the formal definition of the traceability requirement in Definition 4.3.

Experiment $\mathbf{ExpTrace}_{\mathcal{A},\Sigma,\epsilon}$

1. $(J, s_0, s_1, \mathsf{state}) \leftarrow \mathcal{A}(\mathcal{F})$.
2. $\Gamma \leftarrow_\$ \mathcal{F} \setminus \bigcup_{\substack{\Gamma' \in \mathcal{F} \\ J \in \Gamma'}} \Gamma'$.   ▷ The subset J must be unauthorized in Γ.
3. $b \leftarrow_\$ \{0, 1\}$.
4. $(\{\mathsf{sh}_i\}_{i\in[n]}, \mathsf{tk}, \mathsf{vk}) \leftarrow \mathsf{Share}(s_b, \Gamma)$.
5. $\mathbf{sh} = \{\mathsf{sh}_i\}_{i\in J}$.
6. $R \leftarrow \mathcal{A}(\mathsf{state}, \mathbf{sh})$.
7. $(J^*, \pi) \leftarrow \mathsf{Trace}^R(\mathsf{tk})$.
8. $\mathsf{GoodBox} := (J \notin \Gamma) \wedge (R \text{ is } (\mathcal{F}, J, \mathbf{sh}, s_0, s_1, b, \epsilon)\text{-good})$.
9. If $(J^* \nsubseteq J) \wedge (\mathsf{Verify}(\mathsf{vk}, J^*, \pi) = 1)$ then return 1.
10. If $\neg\mathsf{GoodBox}$, then return 0.
11. If $(J^* \neq \emptyset) \wedge (J^* \subseteq J) \wedge (\mathsf{Verify}(\mathsf{vk}, J^*, \pi) = 1)$ then return 0, else return 1.

Fig. 3. The tracing experiment for a traceable secret sharing scheme Σ for a family of access structures $\mathcal{F}$.

Definition 4.3. (Perfect Traceability). *Let* $\mathcal{S}$ *be a finite set of secrets with* $|\mathcal{S}| \geq 2$, *let* $\mathcal{F}$ *be a family of access structures over* n *parties, and let* Σ *be a traceable scheme for* $\mathcal{F}$. *For any* $\epsilon \in [0, \frac{1}{2}]$, Σ *is perfect traceable if for every adversary* $\mathcal{A}$, *it holds that*

$$\mathsf{Adv}^{\mathrm{trac}}_{\mathcal{A},\Sigma,\epsilon} := \mathbf{P}[\mathbf{ExpTrace}_{\mathcal{A},\Sigma,\epsilon} = 1] = \frac{1}{2}.$$

We now describe the non-imputability experiment in Fig. 4, and then formally define the non-imputability requirement in Definition 4.4.

Experiment $\mathbf{ExpNI}_{\mathcal{A}, \Sigma}$

---

1. $(\Gamma, i^*, s, \mathsf{state}) \leftarrow \mathcal{A}(\mathcal{F})$.
2. $(\{\mathsf{sh}_i\}_{i \in [n]}, \mathsf{tk}, \mathsf{vk}) \leftarrow \mathsf{Share}(s, \Gamma)$.
3. $(J^*, \pi) \leftarrow \mathcal{A}(\mathsf{state}, \{\mathsf{sh}_i\}_{i \in [n] \setminus \{i^*\}}, \mathsf{tk})$.
4. If $(i^* \in J^*) \wedge (\mathsf{Verify}(\mathsf{vk}, J^*, \pi) = 1)$ then return 1, else return 0.

Fig. 4. The non-imputability experiment for a traceable secret sharing scheme Σ for a family of access structures $\mathcal{F}$.

Definition 4.4. (Perfect Non-imputability). *Let $\mathcal{S}$ be a finite set of secrets with $|\mathcal{S}| \geq 2$, let $\mathcal{F}$ be a family of access structures over n parties, and let Σ be a traceable scheme for $\mathcal{F}$. Then, Σ is non-imputable if for every adversary $\mathcal{A}$, it holds that*

$$\mathsf{Adv}^{\mathrm{ni}}_{\mathcal{A}, \Sigma} := \mathbf{P}[\mathbf{ExpNI}_{\mathcal{A}, \Sigma} = 1] = 0.$$

Remark 4.5. In contrast to the non-imputability definition of [BPR24], our definition does not grant the adversary access to the verification key, as doing so would allow it to falsely accuse an honest party in our construction. This restriction is inherent to the information-theoretic setting. In the full version of this work [FG25], we show that by relying on computational assumptions, this limitation can be overcome, and we explain how to modify our scheme to support a fully public verification key, thereby achieving public verifiability.

Furthermore, as in Remark 3.3, the requirements of traceable schemes can also be relaxed: instead of demanding perfect guarantees, one can define *statistical tracer privacy*, *statistical traceability* and *statistical non-imputability*. These relaxed variants lead to the definition of statistical traceable schemes.

We conclude this subsection by introducing an additional requirement for traceable schemes: *minimal set indistinguishability*. This notion strengthens the security guarantees of the scheme by ensuring that the pseudoshares generated during the tracing procedure are indistinguishable from real shares held by honest parties, where the union of these parties and the corrupted subset forms a minimal authorized subset in some access structure within the same family.

More precisely, consider two disjoint subsets $A, B \subseteq [n]$ such that $A, B \notin \Gamma \cup \Gamma'$ for some $\Gamma, \Gamma' \in \mathcal{F}$, and $A \cup B$ is minimal in Γ. Minimal set indistinguishability requires that, when the secret is sampled uniformly at random, the distribution of the shares of the parties in $A \cup B$ generated according to Γ is equal to the joint distribution of the shares of the parties in A generated according to Γ', and $|B|$ pseudoshares generated using the tracing key associated with Γ'.

Intuitively, this captures the idea that a reconstruction box built from the shares of an unauthorized subset cannot distinguish whether it is being queried with real shares generated under an access structure in which the parties from the query together with the corrupted subset form a minimal authorized subset, or with simulated pseudoshares generated according to a different access structure.

This requirement is crucial for our tracing experiment because it guarantees that the reconstruction box behaves consistently for both real and simulated inputs, which allows the tracer to extract meaningful identifying information from it. However, as explained later in Sect. 5.1, to support effective tracing in this setting, the indistinguishability must hold specifically with respect to a minimal authorized subset. The formal definition follows.

Definition 4.6. (Perfect Minimal Set Indistinguishability). *Let $m > 1$ be a power of two, let $\mathcal{S}$ be a finite set of secrets with $|\mathcal{S}| = m^2$, let $\mathcal{F}$ be a family of access structures over n parties, and let Σ be a traceable scheme for $\mathcal{F}$. Then, Σ is minimal set indistinguishable if for any secret $s \in \mathcal{S}$, any $p \in [2 \log m]$, any pair of access structures $\Gamma, \Gamma' \in \mathcal{F}$, and any pair of disjoint subsets $A, B \subseteq [n]$ such that $A, B \notin \Gamma \cup \Gamma'$, and $A \cup B$ is a minimal authorized subset in Γ, it holds that the distributions*

$$(\{\mathsf{sh}_i\}_{i \in A \cup B}) \text{ and } (\{\mathsf{sh}_i'\}_{i \in A}, \{\mathsf{sh}_i''\}_{i \in [k']})$$

are equal, where $k = |A|$, $k' = |B|$, $s \leftarrow_\$ \mathcal{S}$, $(\{\mathsf{sh}_i\}_{i \in [n]}, \mathsf{tk}, \mathsf{vk}) \leftarrow \mathsf{Share}(s, \Gamma)$, $(\{\mathsf{sh}_i'\}_{i \in [n]}, \mathsf{tk}', \mathsf{vk}') \leftarrow \mathsf{Share}(s, \Gamma')$, and $\{\mathsf{sh}_i''\}_{i \in [k']} \leftarrow \mathsf{ShGen}(\mathsf{tk}', k, k', p)$.

5   A Traceable Scheme for General Access Structures

In this section, we construct a traceable scheme for general access structures in the information-theoretic setting. We start by explaining why anonymity and hiding the access structure are essential for achieving traceability. After that, we provide an outline of the scheme. All proofs, details, and optimizations are deferred to the full version of this work [FG25].

5.1   The Need for Anonymity and Hiding the Access Structure

Anonymity. At first glance, anonymity and traceability may seem at odds: while anonymity hides the identities of the parties holding shares, traceability aims to reveal which corrupted parties contributed to constructing a malicious reconstruction box. However, as observed by [BPR24], anonymity is in fact a fundamental ingredient for achieving efficient traceability. Specifically, it is necessary to ensure that the tracing procedure can be carried out with a polynomial number of queries.

The core reason is that if shares were linked to party identities, then a malicious reconstruction box could recognize whether a given query comes from the tracer. In particular, a reconstruction box built by a set of corrupted parties A could inspect the identifiers associated with the shares in a query and check whether any of them belong to A. If so, since none of these parties would query their own reconstruction box, it could deduce that the query contains non-valid or simulated shares and refuse to respond meaningfully by returning $\perp$.

This forces the tracer to avoid querying the reconstruction box with any shares from the corrupted parties. However, since the tracer does not know which parties built the reconstruction box, ensuring that a query avoids all corrupted parties is non-trivial. In some cases, for access structures with a large number of unauthorized subsets, this can lead to an expected exponential number of queries before obtaining a useful response. This issue is illustrated in [BPR24] for the case of threshold access structures in which both the threshold and the number of corrupted parties are a constant fraction of the total number of parties.

Hiding the Access Structure. In order to achieve traceability for general access structures in the setting introduced by [BPR24], it is essential to hide the access structure from the participating parties. To understand why, we first observe that all known tracing strategies in this model, including those from [BPR24] for threshold structures and our own generalization to arbitrary access structures, rely on a common approach.

These strategies exploit the assumption that the reconstruction box is *good*, meaning that it reconstructs the secret with high probability when given a valid set of shares as input. Then, the general tracing procedure involves querying the reconstruction box with carefully crafted shares. When these shares, combined with those internally held by the box, form a valid authorized subset, the box is expected to output the secret or, in the case of our construction, an identifier that can be used to trace one of the corrupted parties.

However, a subtle but crucial assumption underlies this strategy: the reconstruction box always uses all available shares when computing the output. This assumption is justified only if the union of the corrupted subset and the query corresponds to a *minimal* authorized subset. If the union is non-minimal, the box may use only a subset of the available shares, those sufficient to form a minimal authorized subset, making it difficult for the tracer to know which shares actually influenced the output. This uncertainty can break the tracing mechanism.

More specifically, in the case of our hiding anonymous scheme, when the combined set of shares includes more than one minimal authorized subset, the reconstruction box has several valid reconstruction paths. Therefore, if these different paths produce inconsistent outputs (a situation that may occur when the input query includes simulated shares used for tracing) the box can detect this inconsistency, realize that it is being queried by a tracer, and simply return $\perp$.

This issue is especially problematic for general access structures, as there are cases where an unauthorized subset is not contained in any minimal authorized subset. For example, in a graph access structure, a corrupted subset made up of two nodes with no edge between them cannot be extended to form a minimal authorized set. In such situations, existing tracing techniques break down. To address this issue, our approach hides the access structure from the parties, revealing only a family of access structures to which the actual one belongs. This allows the tracer to trick the reconstruction box into believing that the query shares, together with those of the corrupted parties, form a minimal authorized set in some structure of the family, enabling the tracing procedure to work.

Furthermore, if the goal is to trace all corrupted parties that contributed to the construction of the reconstruction box, rather than just a single one, hiding the access structure becomes essential. In particular, for access structures in which two or more parties play equivalent roles, corrupted parties can exploit this symmetry when building a reconstruction box to ensure that at least one of them cannot be traced. By hiding the access structure, such strategies are no longer available. The formal statement follows and its proof is deferred to the full version of this work [FG25].

Theorem 5.1. (Theorem 1.5 **restated).** *There does not exist any traceable secret sharing scheme for general access structures that traces back all the corrupted parties and keeps the access structure public.*

In the full version of this work [FG25] we discuss scenarios where it is reasonable to assume that parties do not know the access structure and we show how to modify our traceable scheme to enable tracing all corrupted parties.

Covering Families of Access Structures. Unfortunately, the strategy described above only works under a specific condition: for every unauthorized subset in any access structure from the family, there must exist another access structure in the same family in which that subset is strictly included in a minimal authorized subset. This property is necessary to ensure that the tracer can always simulate a minimal authorized set during the tracing procedure.

To formalize the class of families where our tracing approach is applicable, we introduce the notion of a *covering family of access structures*: a family in which every unauthorized subset of every access structure within the family is strictly contained in a minimal authorized subset of some access structure in the same family. Its definition and a lemma stating that the family of all access structures satisfies it are presented next. The proof of the lemma is deferred to the full version of this work [FG25].

Definition 5.2. *A family of access structures over n parties $\mathcal{F}$ is a* covering family *if for every $\Gamma \in \mathcal{F}$ and every subset $A \notin \Gamma$, there exists $B \subseteq [n]$ and $\Gamma' \in \mathcal{F}$ such that $A \subsetneq B$ and B is minimal in Γ'.*

Lemma 5.3. *For every $n \in \mathbb{N}$, the family of all access structures over n parties is a covering family.*

5.2   The Scheme

For simplicity, we assume in this subsection that the tracer knows in advance the exact number of corrupted parties c. In the full version of this work [FG25], we explain how to relax this assumption. Our construction combines the hiding anonymous secret sharing scheme of Fig. 2 with a key observation: any two shares generated by the same scheme for the same party, even if they correspond to different secrets, are indistinguishable to that party.[8] The core ideas underlying each of the algorithms in our construction are as follows.

---

[8] This holds due to the scheme's satisfaction of the stronger anonymity notion known as *multi-dealer anonymity* [BGI+25], as discussed in Sect. 3.

Share. We begin by sharing the secret s among the parties according to the access structure Γ using the hiding anonymous scheme of Fig 2, but now defined over the domain $\mathbb{Z}_m^2$. In addition, each party i is assigned a secret identifier $\mathsf{id}_i = (\mathsf{id}_i^1, \mathsf{id}_i^2)$, sampled uniformly from the same domain. The first component, id_i^1, forms part of the tracing key and will be used by the tracer to identify corrupted parties, while the second component, id_i^2, forms part of the verification key and allows the verifier to validate the accusation issued by the tracer.

Next, for each unauthorized subset $A \notin \Gamma$, we find the smallest disjoint subset $B \subseteq [n]$ such that $A \cup B$ forms a minimal authorized subset in some access structure of the covering family $\mathcal{F}$ of Γ. This ensures that the corrupted parties can always be embedded into a minimal authorized subset of some access structure in the family, which is essential for the tracing procedure to succeed. After selecting B, we create $|B|$ dummy parties $d_1, \ldots, d_{|B|}$ and uniformly at random select one party $i \in A$. Then, for each bit $b \in \{0, 1\}$ of the identifier id_i, we independently share the corresponding value s_b among the set $A \cup d_1, \ldots, d_{|B|}$ using the DNF additive scheme. The shares assigned to the dummy parties are included in the tracing key and will later allow the tracer to reconstruct bitwise the identifier id_i, thereby identifying the corrupted part i.

Finally, note that access structures in the covering family $\mathcal{F}$ may have different numbers of unauthorized subsets. Since we share a tracing identifier for every unauthorized subset of the selected access structure Γ, the total number of components in the share could vary depending on which access structure was chosen. To prevent this, we pad each party's share with dummy random values until its size matches the maximum number of unauthorized subsets in $\mathcal{F}$, ensuring uniform share sizes that do not leak information about Γ.

Intuitively, this procedure makes the unauthorized set A perceive the shares of the bitwise encoding of id_i as actual shares of the secret s for the minimal authorized set $A \cup B$. Since these shares are indistinguishable, the reconstruction box cannot tell whether they correspond to s or to the encoding of id_i. Hence, when for each bit b of id_i the tracer queries the box with the dummy parties' shares $\{d_1, \ldots, d_{|B|}\}$, it treats them as valid shares of s for $A \cup B$ and outputs the corresponding value s_b. By repeating this process for all bits, the tracer reconstructs the identifier id_i, exposing a corrupted party.

Projection & Reconstruction. These algorithms are identical to those of Fig. 2 because the secret is shared using that hiding anonymous scheme.

Share Generation. At a high level, in this step we use the tracing key to construct projected pseudoshares of level $k + k'$ for the p-th bit of the identifier that are indistinguishable from genuine projected shares of the same level. We then extend them with enough dummy random values to match the size of a full share. These pseudoshares are later used to fool the reconstruction box during the tracing procedure. In addition, this method enables us to trace simultaneously all unauthorized subsets of size k that require k' extra shares to become authorized.

More in detail, for given sizes k and k', and an index p of a bit of the identifier, the algorithm ShareGeneration is executed by the tracer during the tracing procedure to construct k' full pseudoshares, each containing meaningful projected pseudoshares of level $k+k'$ for the p-th bit of the identifier. Specifically, each projected pseudoshare is built from the dummy shares in the tracing key, which were generated by secret sharing the identifiers across all subsets of the form $A \cup \{d_1, \ldots, d_{k'}\}$, where $A \subseteq [n]$ is an unauthorized subset of size k and $d_1, \ldots, d_{k'}$ are dummy parties. To obtain a full pseudoshare, we then pad each projected pseudoshare with uniformly random values so that its size matches that of a real full share.

Trace. The tracing procedure is run by the tracer and proceeds iteratively for each bit of id_i. Since the reconstruction box only accepts full shares, for each level $\ell \in [n-c]$ and for each identifier's bit b, we generate ℓ full pseudoshares that contain projected pseudoshares of level $c+\ell$ using the ShareGeneration algorithm, and we query the box with them. As previously explained, the reconstruction box cannot distinguish these projected pseudoshares from genuine shares of the secret. Therefore, when queried with them, a *good* reconstruction box will run the Reconstruction algorithm on the pseudoshares and output s_b, which reveals the bit b of the identifier id_i.[9]

After completing the $2 \log m$ queries needed to recover all bits of id_i, the tracer reconstructs the full identifier. It then compares the first component id_i^1 with the corresponding part of the identifiers present in the tracing key. This step ensures that the output is a valid identifier and determines the corresponding party i. Once this check is satisfied, the second recovered component id_i^2 is used as a proof π, which is then provided to the verifier.

Since the reconstruction box is not perfect, for each bit of the identifier the tracing procedure is repeated $\mathrm{poly}(\lambda)$ times, and the tracer outputs the majority value among the responses. By the Chernoff bound, this majority-vote rule ensures that, at the correct level[10], the reconstruction box returns all the correct bits of the identifier id_i with overwhelming probability.

Verify. The verification procedure is executed by the verifier and consists of a simple check: it verifies whether any of the values provided in the proof π matches the second component of the identifier from the verification key corresponding to the accused party. If so, it outputs 1; otherwise, it returns 0. Intuitively, for a malicious tracer to falsely accuse an honest party i, it would need to correctly guess the second component id_i^2 of that party's identifier. Thus, if this value is sampled uniformly from a large domain, the probability of such a guess succeeding is negligible.

We provide in Fig. 5 an outline of the scheme's construction, while its the full description is given in the full version of this work [FG25]. The formal statement is presented in Theorem 5.4, and its proof is deferred to the full version.

---

[9] See the full version of this work [FG25] for an optimization that enables tracing multiple corrupted parties.

[10] That is, the level corresponding to the actual number of additional parties required for the corrupted parties to form an authorized set.

Share(s, Γ):

1. Share the secret $s \in \mathbb{Z}_m^2$ among Γ with the general hiding anonymous scheme of Fig. 2.
2. Assign a uniformly random identifier $\mathsf{id}_i = (\mathsf{id}_i^1, \mathsf{id}_i^2) \in \mathbb{Z}_m^2$ to each party $i \in [n]$.
3. Append all the first parts of the identifiers id_i^1 in the tracing key.
4. Append all the second parts of the identifiers id_i^2 in the verification key.
5. For each $A \notin \Gamma$
   (a) Find a subset $B \notin \Gamma$ such that $A \cup B$ is a minimal authorized subset for some $\Gamma' \in \mathcal{F}$.
   (b) Consider $|B|$ dummy parties $d_1, ..., d_{|B|}$.
   (c) Select randomly a party $i \in A$.
   (d) For each bit $b \in \{0, 1\}$ of id_i
      i. Share s_b among $A \cup \{d_1, ..., d_{|B|}\}$ with the DNF additive scheme.
   (e) Ensure a uniform share size among all parties sending dummy random values to them.
   (f) Append the shares of the dummy parties $d_1, ..., d_{|B|}$ in the tracing key.
6. For each $A \in \Gamma$ such that there exists $\Gamma' \in \mathcal{F}$ for which $A \notin \Gamma'$
   (a) Ensure a uniform share size among all access structures sending dummy random values to the all the n parties.

Proj(sh_i): The same as in the general anonymous scheme of Fig. 1.

Rec($\{\mathsf{psh}_{i,k}\}_{i \in A}, |A|$): The same as in the general anonymous scheme of Fig. 1.

ShGen(tk, k, k', p):

1. Use as the k' pseudoshares the portions of the shares corresponding to the dummy parties $d_1, \ldots, d_{k'}$ that are obtained by secret sharing the p-th bit of the identifier with all unauthorized subsets of size k.
2. Ensure that all k' pseudoshares match the size of actual shares by padding dummy random values to them.

Trace$^R(\mathsf{tk}, c, \lambda)$:

1. For each size $\ell \in [n - c]$.
   (a) For each bit $b \in \{0, 1\}$ of id_i
      i. Repeat poly(λ) times
         A. Compute ℓ pseudoshares using the ShGen algorithm.
         B. Query the reconstruction box R with these pseudoshares.
         C. Store the output bit b^*.
      ii. Take as the bit b the majority value among all the poly(λ) outputs b^*.
   (b) If the first part of the reconstructed identifier matches any first part of the identifiers in the tracing key, terminate and output the second part of the reconstructed identifier as the proof π.

Verify($\mathsf{vk}, \mathcal{I}, \pi$):

1. If the proof π matches the second part of the identifier included in the verification key vk corresponding to the party specified by I, output 1.
2. Otherwise, output 0.

Fig. 5. Outline of a traceable secret sharing scheme for any access structure Γ of a covering family of access structures $\mathcal{F}$.

Theorem 5.4. *Let $\mathcal{F}$ be a covering family of access structures over n parties, let $\lambda \in \mathbb{N}$ be the security parameter with $\lambda = \Omega(\mathrm{poly}(n))$, let $m = 2^{\Theta(\lambda)}$, and let $\epsilon(\lambda) \in [0, \frac{1}{2}]$ be a non-negligible function. For any $s \in \mathbb{Z}_m^2$, the protocol Σ of Fig. 5 is a traceable secret sharing scheme with statistical reconstruction, traceability, and non-imputability realizing $\mathcal{F}$ with a share size of $O(2^n\mathrm{poly}(\log m))$ and $O(\mathrm{poly}(\lambda, n)\log m)$ queries.*

As a simple corollary of Theorem 5.4, we get our traceable scheme for general access structures. Its proof is deferred to the full version of this work [FG25].

Corollary 5.5. (Theorem 1.1 restated). *Let $\mathcal{F}$ be the family of all access structures over n parties, let $\lambda \in \mathbb{N}$ be the security parameter with $\lambda = \Omega(\mathrm{poly}(n))$, and let $m = 2^{\Theta(\lambda)}$. For any $s \in \mathbb{Z}_m^2$ there exists a traceable secret sharing scheme with statistical reconstruction, traceability, and non-imputability realizing $\mathcal{F}$ with a share size of $O(2^n\mathrm{poly}(\log m))$ and $O(\mathrm{poly}(\lambda, n)\log m)$ queries.*

Acknowledgments. We thank Yuval Ishai for providing us with early access to [BGI+25] and for valuable discussions, and Eurocrypt reviewers for their suggestions. The authors are supported by the projects ACITHEC PID2021-124928NB-I00 and MATSE PID2024-156636NB-C22 funded by MCIN/AEI/10.13039/501100011033, and by the project HERMES, funded by the European Union NextGenerationEU/PRTR via INCIBE.

References

ABF+19. Applebaum, B., Beimel, A., Farràs, O., Nir, O., Peter, N.: Secret-Sharing Schemes for General and Uniform Access Structures. In: Ishai, Y., Rijmen, V. (eds.) EUROCRYPT 2019. LNCS, vol. 11478, pp. 441–471. Springer, Cham (2019). https://doi.org/10.1007/978-3-030-17659-4_15

ABNP20. Applebaum, B., Beimel, A., Nir, O., Peter, N.: Better secret sharing via robust conditional disclosure of secrets. In STOC **2020**, 280–293 (2020)

AN21. Applebaum, B., Nir, O.: Upslices, Downslices, and Secret-Sharing with Complexity of 1.5^n. In: Malkin, T., Peikert, C. (eds.) CRYPTO 2021. LNCS, vol. 12827, pp. 627–655. Springer, Cham (2021). https://doi.org/10.1007/978-3-030-84252-9_21

Bei25. Beimel, A.: Secret-sharing schemes for general access structures: an introduction. Cryptology ePrint Archive, Paper 2025/518 (2025)

BEMS25. Baghery, K., Ebrahimi, E., Mirzamohammadi, O., Sedaghat, M.: Traceable verifiable secret sharing and applications. Cryptology ePrint Archive, Paper 2025/318 (2025)

BGI+25. Bishop, A., Green, M., Ishai, Y., Jain, A., Lou, P.: Fully anonymous secret sharing. In: Tauman Kalai, Y., Kamara, S.F. (eds.) CRYPTO 2025. Springer, Cham (2025). https://doi.org/10.1007/978-3-032-01884-7_12

BL88. Cohen Benaloh, J., Leichter, J.: Generalized secret sharing and monotone functions. In: Goldwasser, S. (eds.) CRYPTO '88, vol. 403, LNCS, pp. 27–35. Springer, Cham (1988)

Bla79. Robert Blakley., G.: Safeguarding cryptographic keys. In: Proceedings of the 1979 AFIPS National Computer Conference, vol. 48, pp. 313–317 (1979)

BPR24. Boneh, D., Partap, A., Rotem, L.: Traceable secret sharing: strong security and efficient constructions. In: Reyzin, L., Stebila, D., (eds.) CRYPTO 2024, pp. 221–256. Springer, Cham (2024)

BPR25. Boneh, D., Partap, A., Rotem, L.: Traceable verifiable random functions. Springer International Publishing, In EUROCRYPT (2025)

CDK+25. Canetti, R., Damgård, I., Kolby, S., Ravi, D., Yakoubov, S.: Deniable secret sharing. Cryptology ePrint Archive, Paper 2025/525 (2025)

DFLM24. Dziembowski, S., Faust, S., Lizurej, T., Mielniczuk, M.: Secret sharing with snitching. In: Proceedings of the 2024 on ACM SIGSAC Conference on Computer and Communications Security, CCS '24, pp. 840–853. New York, NY, USA (2024). Association for Computing Machinery

EBG+24. Eldridge, H., Beck, G., Green, M., Heninger, N., Jain, A.: Abuse-resistant location tracking: balancing privacy and safety in the offline finding ecosystem. In: Proceedings of the 33rd USENIX Conference on Security Symposium, SEC '24, USA, 2024. USENIX Association

FG25. Farràs, O., Guiot, M.: Traceable secret sharing schemes for general access structures. Cryptology ePrint Archive, Paper 2025/1120 (2025)

GJP25. Goyal, V., Jain, A., Partap, A.: Traceable secret sharing revisited. Cryptology ePrint Archive, Paper 2025/1980 (2025)

GL89. Goldreich, O., Levin, L.A.: A hard-core predicate for all one-way functions. STOC '89, pp. 25–32, New York, NY, USA (1989). Association for Computing Machinery

GSS21. Goyal, V., Song, Y., Srinivasan, A.: Traceable Secret Sharing and Applications. In: Malkin, T., Peikert, C. (eds.) CRYPTO 2021. LNCS, vol. 12827, pp. 718–747. Springer, Cham (2021). https://doi.org/10.1007/978-3-030-84252-9_24

Hof24. Hoffmann,C.: Traceable secret sharing based on the Chinese remainder theorem. Cryptology ePrint Archive, Paper 2024/811 (2024)

ISN87. Ito, M., Saito, A., Nishizeki, T.: Secret sharing schemes realizing general access structure. In: Globecom 87, pp. 99–102 (1987). Journal version: Multiple assignment scheme for sharing secret. J. Cryptol. 6(1), 15–20 (1993)

LV18. Liu, T., Vaikuntanathan, V.: Breaking the circuit-size barrier in secret sharing. In: 50th STOC, pp. 699–708 (2018)

PCO20. Paskin-Cherniavsky, A., Olimid, R.F.: On cryptographic anonymity and unpredictability in secret sharing. Inf. Process. Lett. 161, 105965 (2020)

Sha79. Shamir, A.: How to share a secret. Commun. ACM 22, 612–613 (1979)

Traceable Secret Sharing Revisited

Vipul Goyal[1], Abhishek Jain[1,2], and Aditi Partap[3(✉)]

[1] NTT Research, Sunnyvale, USA
vipul@vipulgoyal.org
[2] Johns Hopkins University, Baltimore, USA
abhishek.jain@ntt-research.com
[3] Stanford University, Stanford, USA
aditi712@cs.stanford.edu

Abstract. In a secret sharing scheme for a monotone access structure $\mathcal{A}$, one can share a secret among a set of parties such that all subsets of parties authorized by $\mathcal{A}$ can reconstruct the secret while all other subsets learn nothing. However, what if an unauthorized subset of parties collude and offer their shares for sale? Specifically, suppose that the parties pool their shares to create a reconstruction box that reveals the secret upon receiving enough additional shares as input. To deter this behavior, Goyal et al. (CRYPTO'21) introduced the notion of *traceable secret sharing* (TSS), where it is possible to provably trace reconstruction boxes containing leaked secret shares back to their respective parties. Goyal et al. and subsequent work presented definitions and constructions of TSS for the threshold access structure.

In this work, we revisit the notion of TSS.

- We identify shortcomings in previous formulations of TSS and present new, strengthened definitions that are not achieved by known constructions. We show that it is easy to build reconstruction boxes for which the tracing guarantees of *all* previous works fail.
- We extend the study of TSS beyond threshold to *general* access structures. Our new definitions are, in fact, necessary for this setting as natural adaptations of existing definitions become vacuous for general access structures.
- We present new constructions of TSS that satisfy our definitions for all access structures captured by monotone circuits. One of our constructions relies solely on one-way functions while the other additionally relies on indistinguishability obfuscation.

1 Introduction

In a secret sharing scheme [8,51] for a monotone access structure $\mathcal{A}$, a dealer can share a secret s among a set of parties such that all authorized subsets of parties $A \in \mathcal{A}$ can recover s while all other subsets learn nothing about s. Secret sharing is a fundamental cryptographic primitive with many applications, most notably to secure multiparty computation [4,16,29] and threshold cryptography [18,19].

J. Daemen and E. Thomé (Eds.): EUROCRYPT 2026, LNCS 16543, pp. 33–63, 2026.
https://doi.org/10.1007/978-3-032-25324-8_2

Traceable Secret Sharing. Suppose that a subset of parties collude and sell the shares in their possession to whoever is willing to meet their price. In most secret sharing constructions, there is no way to hold such parties accountable, meaning that they have a risk-free incentive to sell the secret information.

To address this issue, Goyal et al. [35] introduced the notion of *traceable secret sharing* (TSS). Subsequently, new definitions were introduced by Boneh et al. [11], and investigated by several follow-up works. The basic idea is as follows. Suppose that an unauthorized subset of parties collude and pool their shares to create a *reconstruction box*. This box takes as input additional secret shares, and outputs the secret if it receives "enough" shares.[1] One may think of the reconstruction box as either an obfuscated program or a tamper-proof hardware device. The main requirement in a TSS scheme is *traceability*: There exists an efficient tracer algorithm that can provably identify the parties responsible for constructing the reconstruction box given only black-box access to the box. To protect against malicious tracers, a TSS scheme must also satisfy *tracer non-imputability*, namely, even a malicious tracer should not be able to generate a false proof implicating an honest party, and *tracer secrecy*, namely, the secret remains hidden from the tracer even if it colludes with any unauthorized subset of parties.

Prior works [11,35] formalized TSS for the threshold access structure and presented various constructions. Recently, [24] investigated TSS for general access structures in a *non-standard* model where the access structure is assumed to be hidden from the adversary (see Sect. 1.2 for details).

This Work. In this work, we revisit the notion of traceable secret sharing. First, we identify shortcomings in prior formulations of TSS and propose new and strengthened definitions that address these gaps. In particular, our definitions capture stronger traceability guarantees that are not achieved by known constructions. Second, we generalize the notion of TSS beyond threshold to general access structures. Finally, we give new constructions of TSS for all monotone access structures described by monotone circuits.

Before describing our results, we first provide an overview of the main themes of our work.

I. How to Model Traceability?. The notion of traceability is centered on the idea of a reconstruction box constructed by a subset of parties. Like any program or device, a reconstruction box must come with a user manual. For brevity, we refer to such a manual as the box *label*. In prior work, this label simply corresponds to a number $f < t$, where t is the reconstruction threshold. The box is guaranteed to work correctly if it receives a *good* set of shares where a set $I \subset [n]$ is said to be good if it satisfies the following:

- **No overlap:** It contains no overlapping shares with the reconstruction box. That is, $I \cap J = \emptyset$, where $J \subset [n]$ is the set of shares used to create the reconstruction box.

---

[1] What constitutes 'enough' shares is specified by the instruction manual accompanying the box; we discuss this later.

– **Minimal:** I is *minimal* in the sense that it contains exactly f shares and $f + |J| = t$. That is, the total number of input and corrupted shares is equal to the reconstruction threshold t.

Traceability is defined for reconstruction boxes that work correctly for *all* good sets.

We now highlight the key shortcomings of the above definition. The first issue concerns with the usability of the box: It is not clear how someone can ever get such a reconstruction box to work. Indeed, someone who buys the box needs to source sufficient shares from parties outside the set J, without knowing J, to satisfy the no-overlap requirement. This may require a super-polynomial number of queries to the reconstruction box if J is large, limiting the usability of such boxes.

The second and more pressing issue concerns the guarantees provided by the traceability definition: It only captures a rather limited class of reconstruction boxes. In particular, it does not capture boxes that work correctly only for:

– *Non-minimal* input sets, i.e., sets I s.t. $|I| + |J| > t$.
– A few good sets as opposed to *all* good sets.

Let us focus on the minimal set requirement. Intuitively, this only captures "well-behaving" adversaries that ask for minimal shares that suffice for reconstruction and no more. But why would an adversary not require non-minimal input sets, especially if it could help evade tracing? In fact, as it turns out, existing tracing strategies completely *fail* if the reconstruction box requires even one "extra" share, that is, $f = t - |J| + 1$. Note that such a box is easy to build, yet, as we explain in Sect. 2.1, it evades the tracing guarantees of *all* previous works[2]. Furthermore, as we explain below, if we extend the above requirements to the setting of general access structures, the notion of traceability becomes vacuous as minimal sets may simply *not* exist.

In this work, we present new definitions of traceability that overcome these limitations and, in particular, are meaningful for general access structures.

II. General Access Structures. Prior work on TSS has focused on the threshold access structure, leaving open the problem of TSS for other structures. In this work, we fill this gap and extend the study of TSS to general access structures.

As we alluded to earlier, existing definitions do not extend in a meaningful way to general access structures. First, for access structures where authorized sets are not symmetric, share count is clearly not an appropriate way to label a box. Second, and more importantly, for general access structures, we must necessarily allow for reconstruction boxes that might require *non-minimal* input sets: For any monotone access structure $\mathcal{A}$ and any set J that is unauthorized with respect to $\mathcal{A}$, let I be any set such that $I \cup J$ is authorized. We say that I is minimal if no subsets of $I \cup J$ are authorized; otherwise, I is non-minimal. Now consider an access structure over four parties: $(1 \vee 2) \wedge (3 \vee 4)$. For $J = \{3, 4\}$,

---

[2] Concurrent and independent of our work, Goyal and Waters also made this observation [33].

it is easy to see that for any choice of I, $I \cup J$ is "over-authorized"; i.e., *all* sets I are non-minimal. In fact, this is true for many access structures.

On a technical level, TSS for general access structures poses fundamentally new challenges. For one, we must necessarily trace in the over-authorized setting, which for reasons that we discuss later, is challenging and requires new techniques. Furthermore, known efficient secret sharing schemes for general access structures (see, e.g., [5,6,37,52]) allow unauthorized sets of parties to perform a "partial reconstruction" on their shares such that the resulting value holds no information about the identities of the parties involved in the reconstruction, but can still be used towards full reconstruction given additional shares. This is fundamentally at odds with traceability since an adversary could simply create a reconstruction box with a partially reconstructed secret; there is no way to trace corrupt parties using such a box. We elaborate on these challenges in Sect. 2.1.

III. Boxes that do not Output Full Secret. So far, we have only discussed traceability for boxes that output the entire secret. However, in scenarios where even partial information about the secret is valuable, the corrupt parties may construct a box that does not output the full secret; instead, it may only output partial information, say, a *single bit*. Is it possible to trace in this setting?

The work of [35] considers such boxes, but allows for *non-black-box* tracing where the tracer algorithm has knowledge of how the reconstruction box was constructed. In this work, we remove this restriction and define black-box tracing for such boxes. A key benefit of our new notion is that it can be used to generically compile other cryptographic primitives, such as secret-key encryption schemes, to their traceable counterparts in the one-time use setting.[3]

1.1   Our Results

In this work, we give new definitions and constructions of TSS for general access structures. All our results are in the computational setting where the secrecy property of secret sharing holds against computationally bounded adversaries. We summarize our contributions in the following.

New Definitions. We start by modeling "minimally-useful" reconstruction boxes, namely, boxes that are accompanied with a label specifying a set of party identities I, such that they work correctly upon receiving shares of parties in the set I. Roughly speaking, upon receiving correct inputs, the box outputs one bit of information about the secret with some non-negligible probability. We formulate this via a semantic-security-style game (following [35]), where the box can distinguish between shares of two secrets s_0, s_1.

This models all useful boxes since any reconstruction box must work correctly on at least *one* share set; otherwise it is not useful. This is in contrast to prior work that only considers boxes that are guaranteed to work correctly on *all* good input sets (as per the definition of good sets described earlier). We formalize two notions of black-box traceability for minimally-useful boxes:

---

[3] Achieving multi-use security would require a form of *reusable* secret sharing [20]. We leave exploration of this direction to future work.

- **$\emptyset$-Strong Traceability:** In this notion, we consider reconstruction boxes where I and J have no overlapping parties, i.e., $I \cap J = \emptyset$, where J is the set of corrupt parties whose shares were used to construct the box. We place no other restrictions on the box label; in particular, I can be non-minimal w.r.t. J.
- **Strong Traceability:** This notion is the same as above, except that we remove the no-overlap requirement. That is, we allow $I \cap J \neq \emptyset$.

We emphasize that *both* of these notions are stronger than existing notions of traceability. Following prior work, we also model security against malicious tracers by defining tracer non-imputability and tracer secrecy.

We are now ready to state our results.

I. TSS with $\emptyset$-Strong Traceability. Our first result is a TSS scheme for all access structures described by monotone circuits that achieves $\emptyset$-Strong Traceability as well as tracer non-imputability and tracer secrecy. Our scheme relies on the sub-exponential security of indistinguishability obfuscation (iO) [3,26,39,40] and one-way functions. To minimize the share size, our scheme is described in the public information model [1], where a public share is available to each party in addition to its private share.

Theorem 1.1 (Informal). *Under the sub-exponential hardness of iO and one-way functions, there exists a TSS scheme for access structures described by monotone circuits, that achieves $\emptyset$-Strong traceability, tracer secrecy and tracer non-imputability in the public information model. For an access structure with monotone circuit C and n parties, public information is of size $\mathsf{poly}(\lambda, n, |C|)$ and private share size is $\mathsf{poly}(\lambda, \log n)$, where λ is the security parameter.*

We also show that in the case of a single dealer sharing multiple secrets, the public information can be re-used. Whenever the dealer wants to share a new secret (with the same access structure), it only needs to publish a short public share whose size is independent of n and the circuit size (see the full version [34, Sec. 5] for details).

II. TSS with Strong Traceability. Next, we investigate the stronger notion of strong traceability. We first show that it is *impossible* to simultaneously achieve strong traceability and security against malicious tracers.

Theorem 1.2 (Informal). *There does not exist TSS for threshold access structures and large secrets with strong traceability that also satisfies either tracer non-imputability or tracer secrecy.*

While strong traceability, in isolation, is a stronger property than $\emptyset$-strong traceability, the above result shows that TSS with $\emptyset$-strong traceability, tracer secrecy and tracer non-imputability is *incomparable* to TSS with strong traceability without tracer secrecy and tracer non-imputability (we will use TSS with strong traceability to refer to this notion from now on). In fact, we are able to construct TSS with strong traceability for monotone circuits relying solely on one-way functions. We obtain our result by devising a general compiler based on one-way functions from any secret sharing scheme for a monotone access structure $\mathcal{A}$ to a strongly-traceable TSS scheme for the same access structure. Our compiler preserves the share size of the underlying scheme up to a multiplicative factor in the number of parties n.

Theorem 1.3 (Informal). *Assuming one-way functions, if there exists an efficient secret sharing scheme* SS *for a monotone access structure $\mathcal{A}$, then there exists a strongly-traceable TSS scheme for the same access structure $\mathcal{A}$ with share size n times the share size of* SS.

By applying our compiler to Yao's secret sharing scheme for monotone circuits [52], we obtain TSS with strong traceability for monotone circuits based on one-way functions. Finally, we show that we can also extend our scheme in Theorem 1.1 to achieve strong traceability at the cost of tracer secrecy and tracer non-imputability, while retaining the same share size (see the full version [34, App. B]).

Application to One-time Traceable Secret-key Cryptography. Our constructions of traceable secret sharing (TSS) can be used to generically obtain one-time traceable secret-key encryption for general access structures.

We introduce the notion of $\emptyset$-strong traceability in the encryption setting, defined with respect to a minimally-useful decryption box labeled by a set I and a ciphertext. This box takes as input decryption shares of parties in I, and outputs decryption of the ciphertext. We then show how to compile any one-time secret-key encryption scheme to a traceable scheme for general access structures, by simply secret-sharing the decryption key using our TSS. Crucially, since our TSS schemes achieve black-box tracing for boxes that only output partial information about the secret, we can trace boxes that only output the decryption of a ciphertext (and not the reconstructed decryption key). Indeed, this compiler cannot be realized using prior TSS constructions (even for the threshold access structure), since [11] only support tracing boxes that output the full secret and [35] do not achieve black-box tracing. We present the compiler in the full version [34, App. C].

Open Problems. Our work leaves open several interesting questions for future research. First, determining minimal assumptions for achieving our new, strengthened notions of TSS remains open. While the use of obfuscation seems crucial to the design of our first TSS scheme (see Sect. 2), it is not clear whether obfuscation or even public-key cryptography is necessary. This question remains open even for the case of threshold access structures.

The second question concerns with share-size efficiency of TSS. Our first scheme has succinct private shares, but requires a large public share whose size grows with the size of the access structure. Minimizing the size of the public share will likely require building upon recent advances in succinct secret sharing [38,45]; we leave exploration of this direction to future work.

1.2   Related Work

Traceable Secret Sharing. The notion of traceable secret sharing was introduced by Goyal et al. [35], who proposed a construction for threshold access structures based on the Goldreich-Levin decoding algorithm [28]. Subsequently, Boneh et al. [11] revisited this concept and introduced an alternative traceability model, presenting two new constructions for threshold access structures based on the schemes of Shamir [51] and Blakley [8]. Hoffmann [36] proposed a construction for threshold access structures using Mignotte's scheme [46] albeit only achieving weak (inverse polynomial) secrecy. Baghery et al. [2] designed a traceable verifiable secret sharing scheme for threshold access structures.

Recently, Farràs et al. [24] investigated TSS for general monotone access structures in a non-standard model where the access structure is assumed to be hidden from the adversary. If this assumption is violated, their tracing guarantee does not hold. In this work, we consider the standard model and do not make such assumptions on the adversary. Beyond this distinction, there are additional differences between their work and ours. Similarly to prior work, their traceability definition suffers from the limitations discussed in Sect. 1. Their scheme is linear and achieves information-theoretic security, but requires share size and reconstruction time exponential in the number of parties. Our constructions, in contrast, are efficient but only achieve computational security.

In a concurrent work, [44] construct a TSS scheme for threshold access structures based on Asmuth-Blum secret sharing. Their definitions suffer from the same limitations as described in Sect. 1.

Anonymous Secret Sharing. Anonymous secret sharing requires that shares from an unauthorized subset of parties do not reveal any information about party identities or even that the shares were generated together. We refer the reader to [7] for a survey of this line of work. We note that the partial reconstruction challenge that arises in the design of TSS (see Sect. 2) is also a barrier to achieving anonymity. In particular, to achieve anonymity, one must ensure that any attempt at partial reconstruction does not reveal that the shares were generated together. We note, however, that hiding such correlations is *not* necessary for TSS. Indeed, unlike [7], we are able to address the partial reconstruction problem using only one-way functions in the setting of strong traceability.

Secret Sharing with Snitching. The goal of holding secret-share holders accountable has inspired another line of work called secret sharing with snitching [14,23]. These works consider a different adversarial model wherein if an authorized set of parties collude to reconstruct the secret, then one of the colluding parties learns a "snitching proof" indicating that some party participated in illegal secret reconstruction.

Traitor Tracing. In the traitor tracing setting, a central authority issues a single encryption key, and n decryption keys, one per receiver. If any coalition of receivers comes together and produces a pirate decoder box D that can decrypt well-formed ciphertexts, then this box can be traced back to at least one of the receivers who contributed to it. Many traitor tracing schemes have been proposed over the years (see, e.g., [9, 13, 15, 17, 21, 22, 25, 27, 30, 31, 41, 43, 47, 48, 50, 53, 54]). As we explain in Sect. 2, traitor tracing techniques can be used to build TSS for the star graph access structures, but do not suffice for general access structures.

2   Technical Overview

In this section, we describe the main ideas that underlie our results. We start by providing an overview of the main challenges towards achieving our notions of traceability. We describe our construction that achieves $\emptyset$-strong traceability in Sect. 2.2. Finally, we discuss the case of strong traceability in Sect. 2.3.

2.1   Main Challenges

In the following, we discuss two key challenges that we must overcome to realize our notions of TSS.

Challenge I: Over-authorization. Recall that in our traceability definitions, a reconstruction box built using shares of parties in J may require input shares of sets I s.t. $I \cup J$ is over-authorized, i.e., there are multiple ways to reconstruct the secret using shares of $I \cup J$. For example, let us consider the t-out-of-n threshold access structure. Suppose that J consists of f parties and the box requires input sets I consisting of $t - f + 1$ shares different from J. In this case, the box has $t + 1$ different ways to reconstruct the secret.

Known tracing algorithms [11,35] run the reconstruction box with "fake" shares that despite not being "real", are consistent with adversarial shares. For example, in the TSS scheme of [11] based on Shamir secret sharing, each share consists of an evaluation of a random degree $(t-1)$ polynomial (with the constant term set to the secret) on a random point. The tracer algorithm in this scheme prepares the shares of an input set I by sampling random field elements. When $|I| = t - f$, fake shares are indistinguishable from real shares to the reconstruction box since a randomly sampled set of $t - f$ points forms a unique degree $t - 1$ polynomial when combined with the f shares in the box.

However, this strategy *fails* when $|I| > t - f$. Note that in this over-authorized setting, the box may run the reconstruction algorithm using different authorized subsets of $I \cup J$ and abort if the answers do not match. Unfortunately, in this setting, there is no way to sample shares consistent with adversarial shares without knowledge of real shares. For example, let $f = t - 1$ and $|I| = t - f + 1 = 2$. Then, each of the two different shares sampled by the tracer will form a different degree $t - 1$ polynomial with the adversarial shares. Indeed, for this reason, existing tracing strategies cannot work in the over-authorization setting. This necessitates new tracing techniques.

Challenge II: Partial Reconstruction. The standard methodology for constructing efficient secret sharing for general access structures (see, e.g., [5,6,37,52]) involves a recursive design: To share a secret s for an access structure, say $\mathcal{A} = \mathcal{B} \wedge \mathcal{C}$, we first share s into $s_\mathcal{B}$ and $s_\mathcal{C}$ for the $\wedge$ gate and then recursively share $s_\mathcal{B}$ (resp., $s_\mathcal{C}$) w.r.t. $\mathcal{B}$ (resp., $\mathcal{C}$). For example, consider the access structure $(1 \vee 2) \wedge (3 \vee 4)$. Here, secret s is first additively shared into s_ℓ and s_r, and parties 1 and 2 are assigned s_ℓ as their share. Similarly, parties 3 and 4 are assigned s_r.

Now suppose that party 1 is corrupt and uses its share s_ℓ to construct a reconstruction box. Since this box could also have been constructed by the party 2 (since they are both authorized for the left gate $\vee$), there is no way to definitively trace the box to party 1. More generally, for any sub-access structure G within an access structure $\mathcal{A}$, a set of parties that are authorized w.r.t. G could use their shares to reconstruct the value s_G associated with the output wire of G. If there are multiple subsets of parties that are authorized w.r.t. G, then s_G contains no information about the reconstructing set of parties. Thus, if the corrupt parties create a reconstruction box using s_G, there is no way to trace their identities.

Note that this issue does not arise in the case of Shamir secret sharing for threshold access structure (for threshold greater than one). To see why, consider a reconstruction box built by a set of parties J, that takes as input shares of a set I. Although some partial reconstruction is possible by combining the shares of J using Lagrange coefficients for the set $J \cup I$, the box will still have to store some information about the set J so that it can compute Lagrange coefficients for the input shares of I. Indeed, this is why prior work that focused on the threshold access structure does not need to separately tackle this issue. For the case of general access structures, however, new ideas are required to address this.

We now proceed to describe the main ideas underlying our constructions, starting with our construction of TSS with $\emptyset$-Strong Traceability.

2.2   TSS with $\emptyset$-Strong Traceability

Our Strategy in a Nutshell. We start by giving a bird's eye view of how we address the challenges discussed above, and then provide more details.

Recall that in order to achieve our traceability definitions, we must address the over-authorization challenge: The tracer must seemingly provide shares for parties in the set I as input to the reconstruction box, while ensuring consistency with the shares of corrupt parties J—even when $I \cup J$ forms an over-authorized set. At first, this seems impossible; indeed, as discussed earlier, existing tracing techniques [11,35] fundamentally break down in this setting.

To address this challenge, we eliminate the tracer's burden of preparing consistent shares. Instead, we design a scheme where any inconsistencies in the shares are *invisible* to the adversary. We design our scheme in the public information model, where an additional public share is essential for reconstruction. This share will enable two *indistinguishable* modes of reconstruction:

– Normal mode, where reconstruction succeeds only with consistent shares.
– *Tracer* mode, where it is possible to *program* the output of reconstruction using shares generated by the tracer.

Since the two modes are indistinguishable, the adversary cannot tell whether the output comes from honest reconstruction or from the tracer's programmed shares. Thus, even if the box attempts reconstruction using different authorized subsets of $I \cup J$, it will always see the same output programmed by the tracer-generated shares of I (even if these shares are inconsistent with adversarial shares). We implement this blueprint using indistinguishability obfuscation (iO). Roughly speaking, the public share will be an obfuscation of a modified reconstruction algorithm with two indistinguishable modes of operation.

To address the partial reconstruction challenge, we implement an *all-or-nothing* design: The reconstruction algorithm reveals *nothing* unless the input shares form an authorized set. In other words, partial reconstruction is not possible. Technically, we achieve this by programming the obfuscated reconstruction algorithm to abort whenever invoked on shares corresponding to an unauthorized subset. Later, in Sect. 2.3, we design a different mechanism to implement an all-or-nothing strategy using only one-way functions in the setting where we do not require tracer secrecy.

Warm-Up: Tracing by Observing "Jumps". Before describing our scheme, we describe a tracing technique that we will use in our constructions. This tracing technique underlies many works on traceable encryption for the 1-out-of-n access structure (commonly referred to as traitor tracing) [12,17,27,30,31,53–55].

To explain this technique, we consider a warm-up task of constructing TSS for the star graph access structure on $n+1$ parties, where an authorized set consists of the "star" party $n+1$ together with any one of the "leaf" parties $1,\ldots,n$. A simple secret sharing scheme for this access structure can be constructed as follows: We additively share the secret s as $s = s_{n+1} + s_{[n]}$, giving s_{n+1} to the star party $n+1$ and $s_{[n]}$ to each of the leaf parties. Now consider an adversary who corrupts a subset $J \subseteq [n]$ and constructs a reconstruction box labeled with $I = \{n+1\}$. In this case, since the box has no information about which party out of $\{1,\ldots,n\}$ contributed to the box, tracing is impossible.

Fortunately, we can address this by building a different secret sharing scheme using a special encryption scheme called Private Linear Broadcast Encryption (PLBE) [12]. An n-party PLBE scheme achieves the following properties:

- Any normal (i.e., honestly generated) ciphertext can be decrypted by any of the n parties, where each party holds a *distinct* decryption key.
- It is possible to create "special" ciphertexts that can only be decrypted by a subset of the parties, where the subset is specified by a contiguous range (i, n) for $i \in [n]$. For convenience, we refer to this range as the ciphertext *tag*. It follows that a special ciphertext with tag $(1, n)$ is the same as a normal ciphertext.
- The special ciphertexts satisfy *index-hiding*, which means that two special ciphertexts with tags (i, n) and $(i+1, n)$ are indistinguishable to an adversary holding keys for all parties $\ell \neq i$.

Intuitively, special ciphertexts allow for *selective disabling* of the keys of some parties. Crucially, the ciphertext reveals minimal information about which parties have been disabled: A party that is allowed to decrypt will learn that it is indeed not disabled, but nothing more.

Given a PLBE scheme, we can construct a TSS for the star graph as follows. To share a secret s, we create a normal encryption of s and set it as the share of the star party. Each leaf party in $\{1, \ldots, n\}$ receives a distinct decryption key. For tracing, recall that we are considering a reconstruction box that requires as input the share of party $n + 1$, which is a ciphertext. The tracer is given as input an encryption key that allows it to create special ciphertexts. Using this key, the tracer runs the box many times with different ciphertexts, wherein it disables each party one by one. Specifically, it creates the share of party $n + 1$ with a special ciphertext for set $\{1, \ldots, n\}$, then $\{2, \ldots, n\}$, and so on until $\emptyset$.

When the box is run with a ciphertext for $\{1, \ldots, n\}$ that can be decrypted by any party (like a normal ciphertext), a useful box must be able to decrypt. On the other hand, given a ciphertext such that all the parties are disabled, i.e., for the set $\emptyset$, the box cannot decrypt. This means that there must be a *jump* in the behavior of the box. Concretely, there must exist a party $j^* \in [n]$ such that when the tracer disables this party by encrypting to set $\{j^* + 1, \ldots, n\}$, the box will suddenly stop working, or at the very least, the probability with which the box can reconstruct the secret (relative to a ciphertext where this party is not disabled) will noticeably reduce. The tracer blames this party j^*. Correctness of this strategy hinges on the index-hiding property: without the key of j^*, the adversary cannot tell whether j^* was disabled or not. Thus, the jump in behavior correctly implicates j^*.

Our First Attempt. Armed with this jump-based tracing technique, we now proceed to implement our blueprint for constructing TSS with $\emptyset$-strong traceability. Initially, we will only focus on achieving traceability. Later, we will extend our solution to also achieve security against malicious tracers.

Our construction relies on a symmetric-key encryption scheme $\mathsf{SKE} := (\mathsf{KeyGen}, \mathsf{Enc}, \mathsf{Dec})$ and a signature scheme $\mathsf{Sig} := (\mathsf{KeyGen}, \mathsf{Sign}, \mathsf{Verify})$. Looking ahead, we will, in fact, require stronger tools even for achieving standard secrecy: Specifically, a *puncturable* encryption scheme and a *constrained* signature scheme. However, for now, we ignore these details. We share a secret s as follows:

- We sample keys for the encryption and signature schemes: $\mathsf{sk}_{\mathsf{SKE}} \leftarrow\!\!\$\, \mathsf{SKE}.\mathsf{KeyGen}(1^\lambda)$ and $\mathsf{sk}, \mathsf{vk} \leftarrow\!\!\$\, \mathsf{Sig}.\mathsf{KeyGen}(1^\lambda)$.
- For each party $i \in [n]$, the share contains an encryption to zero, i.e., $\mathsf{ct}_i \leftarrow\!\!\$\, \mathsf{SKE}.\mathsf{Enc}(\mathsf{sk}_{\mathsf{SKE}}, 0)$. Roughly speaking, this is an encryption with respect to the set $\{1, \ldots, n\}$, i.e., no party is disabled (note that there is no message being encrypted here). In general, we will encrypt to a set $\{j + 1, \ldots, n\}$ by simply encrypting j using SKE.
- The share of each party additionally contains a signature on the party's index and ciphertext, i.e., $\sigma_i \leftarrow\!\!\$\, \mathsf{Sig}.\mathsf{Sign}(\mathsf{sk}, (i, \mathsf{ct}_i))$. We set $\mathsf{sh}_i := (\mathsf{ct}_i, \sigma_i)$ for all parties. Looking ahead, the signature will act as an authentication key.
- We compute the obfuscation of a program P. For now, let us assume that we have virtual black-box (VBB) obfuscation [3]. This program P has the secret s, the circuit C representing the access structure, the symmetric key $\mathsf{sk}_{\mathsf{SKE}}$ and the signature verification key vk hard-coded. It takes as input the shares of a

subset of parties. Figure 1 gives an overview of this program – at a high level, it outputs the secret if and only if, the subset of input parties that remain enabled with respect to the ciphertexts in their shares is still authorized under C. Otherwise, it simply outputs $\perp$. This obfuscated program serves as the public share of our scheme.

Hard-coded inputs: Secret s, Access structure C, Signature verification key vk, Decryption key $\mathsf{sk}_{\mathsf{SKE}}$.

1. For each input share $\mathsf{sh}_i = (\mathsf{ct}_i, \sigma_i)$:
   (a) Verify the signature, i.e., ignore this share if $\mathsf{Sig.Verify}(\mathsf{vk}, \sigma_i, (i, \mathsf{ct}_i)) = 0$.
   (b) Decrypt the ciphertext to get an index, i.e., $j_i \leftarrow \mathsf{SKE.Dec}(\mathsf{sk}_{\mathsf{SKE}}, \mathsf{ct}_i)$.
   (c) Ignore shares of all disabled parties, i.e., all parties $\leq j_i$.
2. Output the secret s if the remaining set of parties is still authorized. Otherwise, output $\perp$.

Fig. 1. An overview of the reconstruction algorithm for our first attempt to achieve $\emptyset$-Strong traceability. An obfuscation of this algorithm forms the public information.

To reconstruct the secret, an authorized set of parties simply runs the obfuscated program in the public share, with their shares as input. Correctness follows because the share of each party contains an encryption of 0, which corresponds to the set $\{1, \ldots, n\}$. Hence, when run with the shares of any authorized set, the program will not ignore any party, meaning that it will always output the secret. In contrast, when invoked on any unauthorized set, the program returns $\perp$, thereby preventing partial reconstruction.

We now turn to traceability, postponing the discussion of secrecy until later in this section. Our goal is to incorporate the jump-based tracing approach described earlier. Recall that the tracer gets as input the label I such that the reconstruction box only works when given shares of parties in I. At a high level, tracing proceeds by repeatedly running the box on different tracer-generated shares of I, where the ciphertexts in those shares progressively disable parties one by one. Concretely, the tracer prepares shares of I with ciphertexts corresponding to sets $\{1, \ldots, n\}$, $\{2, \ldots, n\}$, and so on till $\emptyset$. To enable the tracer to prepare such ciphertexts as well as signatures on these ciphertexts, the encryption and signing keys, i.e., $\mathsf{sk}_{\mathsf{SKE}}$ and sk are included in the tracing key.

By the same reasoning as in the standard jump-based approach, when the box is run with shares containing ciphertexts that enable all parties (like real shares), a useful box must output information about the secret. On the other hand, when run with shares containing ciphertexts that disable all parties, i.e., for the set $\emptyset$, the box cannot work. Intuitively, this is because, all the box can do is run the obfuscated program on shares of authorized subsets of $I \cup J$, since the box does not have a valid authentication key, i.e., signature for any party outside of this set. Next, since J is unauthorized by definition, any authorized subset of $I \cup J$ must contain at least one party in I. This means that, if the box runs the obfuscated program for any authorized subset of $I \cup J$, the program will never output the secret because the ciphertexts in the tracer-generated shares of I disable all parties. Hence, there must exist an index j^* such that the output behavior of the box changes by a noticeable amount when the tracer disables this index. It remains to show that this jump in behavior cannot occur at an honest party.

Intuitively, since no party has access to the decryption key $\mathsf{sk}_{\mathsf{SKE}}$, the only way for the adversary to distinguish whether a party j is enabled by the share of a party i is to compare the outputs of the obfuscated program on $i \cup S$ versus $i \cup S \cup j$ for some set $S \subseteq [n] \setminus \{i, j\}$. However, producing the latter input requires a valid share for party j, which in turn requires forging a signature. Hence, an adversary without the real share of party j^* cannot tell whether this party is allowed by the ciphertexts in shares of I. The tracer therefore safely accuses j^* as corrupt. This first attempt can be viewed as an adaptation of the iO-based PLBE framework of [13].

Insufficiency of PLBE. Unfortunately, there is a flaw in the above argument. While the adversary only has the authentication keys, i.e., signatures for the corrupt parties J, the reconstruction box receives as input the tracer-generated shares of I. These shares contain ciphertexts as well as valid authentication keys for all parties in I. Consequently, the adversary effectively has access to authentication keys for I, and may be able to distinguish whether a party $j^* \in I$ has been disabled. In this case, the box could cause a jump just at index $j^* \in I$ and nowhere else, meaning that the tracer will fail to identify any corrupt party! Therefore, to achieve $\emptyset$-strong traceability, we need to strengthen the jump-based tracing technique.

Private *Set* Broadcast Encryption. At a high level, our solution is to never disable the parties in I during the tracing process. To achieve this, we generalize the PLBE primitive so that we can encrypt to sets of the form $\{1, \ldots, n\} \cup I$, $\{2, \ldots, n\} \cup I$ and so on till $\emptyset \cup I$ for an arbitrary set $I \subseteq [n]$. We refer to this as *private set broadcast encryption* – a generalization of private linear broadcast encryption. Given such a scheme, we can now modify the jump-based tracing strategy as follows: the tracer prepares shares of label I with ciphertexts for $\{1, \ldots, n\} \cup I$, $\{2, \ldots, n\} \cup I$ and so on till $\emptyset \cup I$. It then identifies the index j^* at which the box's behavior exhibits a jump, and blames this party.

Let us now see why this private set broadcast encryption based approach solves the problem. As in our first attempt, a useful box must output information about the secret when provided shares with ciphertexts for $\{1, \ldots, n\} \cup I$. On the other hand, the box cannot work when given shares containing encryptions for I, which disable all parties outside I. Indeed, note first that the label I must not be an authorized set – a box that asks for shares of an authorized set as input is not useful, since one could simply reconstruct the secret using shares of I. Then, by a similar argument as above, the obfuscated program will never output the secret when run with any authorized subset of $I \cup J$ (which must contain some party in I), because the only set of parties allowed by the ciphertexts in shares of I, is the set I, which is unauthorized to begin with. Thus, there must be an index j^* such that the behavior of the box changes when the tracer disables this index. This index cannot be in $[n] \setminus (I \cup J)$, as argued for our first attempt. But crucially, this jump cannot be in I either, since parties in I are never disabled. Hence, the tracer is guaranteed to always find a corrupt party.

To implement this private set broadcast encryption based strategy, we need to modify the ciphertexts contained in each share so that the tracer can encrypt to sets of the form $\{j, \ldots, n\} \cup I$, when preparing shares of the label set I. A natural first attempt is to simply use symmetric key encryption to encrypt both the set I and the index j, and modify the obfuscated program to only allow parties in $\{j + 1, \ldots, n\} \cup I$, when it is given such a ciphertext. While correct, this approach leads to ciphertexts of size $|I|$, which can grow with $\Theta(n)$.

To avoid this blow-up in the share size, we exploit the fact that the tracer does not need to embed the set I in the ciphertext for *every* party's share in I. Instead, we modify the encryption in each ciphertext to encrypt a one-bit flag f denoting whether this share is tracer-generated, together with an index j (as before). Specifically, each party's share will now include an encryption of $f = 0, j = 0$ (along with a signature, as before). During tracing, the tracer will set the flag to 1 for all the shares that it prepares, and varies the index j from 0 to n, as before. The obfuscated program is modified so that it never ignores shares marked with $f = 1$. Figure 2 depicts the modified obfuscated program. As discussed above, the tracer will find at least one jump, and this jump must be corrupt. Crucially, the share size now grows only poly-logarithmically in the number of parties.

Hard-coded inputs: Secret s, Access structure C, Signature verification key vk, Decryption key $\mathsf{sk}_{\mathsf{SKE}}$.

1. For each input share $\mathsf{sh}_i = (\mathsf{ct}_i, \sigma_i)$:
   (a) Verify the signature, i.e., ignore this share if $\mathsf{Sig.Verify}(\mathsf{vk}, \sigma_i, (i, \mathsf{ct}_i)) = 0$.
   (b) Decrypt the ciphertext to get a flag and an index, i.e., $f_i, j_i \leftarrow \mathsf{SKE.Dec}(\mathsf{sk}_{\mathsf{SKE}}, \mathsf{ct}_i)$.
   (c) Ignore shares of all disabled parties $\leq j_i$ without the flag, i.e., ignore all j such that $f_j = 0$ and $j \leq j_i$.
2. Output the secret only if the remaining set is still authorized. Otherwise, output $\perp$.

Fig. 2. An overview of the reconstruction algorithm for our TSS scheme that achieves $\emptyset$-Strong traceability. The public information contains an obfuscation of this algorithm.

Achieving Secrecy. So far, we assumed VBB obfuscation, under which secrecy is straight-forward. Since VBB obfuscation is impossible in general, we instead use iO to obfuscate the program in our public share. To argue secrecy with iO, we proceed via a sequence of hybrid experiments in which the secret is gradually removed from the obfuscated program. We then need to argue that an adversary with the shares of an unauthorized set $J \subset [n]$ cannot tell that the secret has been removed. This requires that the obfuscated program's functionality remains unchanged for such an adversary. In particular, we must ensure that no valid signatures exist for parties outside the corrupt set J. With this property, the program ignores all shares outside J, and since J is unauthorized, it never outputs the secret—allowing us to argue that removing the secret does not alter observable behavior. To achieve this, we need to use a *constrained signature scheme*, which allows generating a *constrained verification key* vk^* under which *no valid signatures exist* for messages satisfying a given constraint. Similarly, to argue traceability in the iO setting, we need to instantiate the symmetric-key encryption using a puncturable PRF.

Achieving Tracer Secrecy via *Doubly* Constrained Signatures. A careful reader might observe that the scheme does not achieve tracer secrecy. Recall that the tracing key contains both the decryption key $\mathsf{sk}_{\mathsf{SKE}}$ and the signing key sk, to allow the tracer to prepare shares for tracing. This means that the tracer can simply generate fresh, valid shares for all parties by generating encryptions to flag 0 and index 0, along with valid signatures, and run the obfuscated program with these shares to learn the secret.

To prevent this, we need to restrict the tracer's power so that it cannot generate real shares of any party; at the same time, it must still be able to trace. We observe that for tracing, it suffices that the tracer can sign ciphertexts encrypting flag $f = 1$ and arbitrary indices j—it does not need to sign ciphertexts with $f = 0$. Hence, we define a new type of signature scheme that we call *doubly-constrained signature*, wherein we can generate a *constrained* signing key, which can only be used to sign messages that satisfy a certain constraint. We call this doubly-constrained since it also allows generating a constrained verification key (as defined above), such that valid signatures only exist on messages that satisfy a certain constraint. We now use this scheme to sign the ciphertext in each share. The tracer is given a constrained signing key as part of the tracing key, which can only sign ciphertexts that encrypt the flag set, i.e., $f = 1$, ensuring that the tracer cannot generate valid, real shares with the flag $f = 0$.

However, the obfuscated program in Fig. 2 would still output the real secret even if the inputs contain tracer-generated shares with flag $f = 1$. To ensure tracer secrecy, we also need to modify the obfuscated program to never output the real secret if it sees any such tracer-generated share. But, what should it output instead? Clearly, the program must output a value that is identically distributed as the secret (or at least be computationally indistinguishable from the secret's distribution), as otherwise the reconstruction box can trivially distinguish between real shares and tracer-generated shares. To solve this, we observe that the tracer does indeed know the distribution of the secret. Recall that the reconstruction box can distinguish between shares of two secrets s_0, s_1, which are also known to the tracer. This means that the real secret is distributed uniformly at random between these two values. Hence, if we could *program* the output of the obfuscated program, then we can force it to output something that comes from the same distribution as the secret, when given tracer-generated shares.

We achieve this by modifying the ciphertext in each share to now encrypt three values, a flag f used to indicate tracer-generated shares, an index j used for tracing, and a value m. This value is set to 0 for real shares of all parties. But during tracing, the tracer samples a value s^* from the same distribution as the secret – it simply picks one of s_0, s_1 uniformly at random. Then, when preparing shares for all parties in I, it generates ciphertexts encrypting s^* as the value (along with flag $f = 1$ and index j ranging from 0 to n). We modify the obfuscated program to simply output this value when it sees any share with the flag set, i.e., $f = 1$[4]. This allows us to achieve tracer secrecy; roughly speaking, the tracer can only generate shares encrypting the flag set, and the obfuscated program when run with such shares, never outputs the real secret. Combining this with the tracing technique described above, we have constructed a TSS with both $\emptyset$-Strong traceability and tracer secrecy.

In the full version [34, App. D], we present a construction of doubly constrained signatures from sub-exponential hardness of iO. In Sect. 4, we give a formal description and security analysis of our TSS construction.

Achieving Tracer Non-imputability. Recall that to achieve security against a malicious tracer, we also need tracer non-imputability, meaning that a malicious tracer must not be able to blame an honest party. In the scheme described so far, there is nothing stopping a malicious tracer from just blaming any honest party i, by simply outputting the index i. To achieve tracer non-imputability, informally, there must be some secret value in the share of each party, which is only known to this party; and if the tracer can extract this secret value for some party from the reconstruction box, then it can be used as proof for blaming that party. Concretely, we assign a random identifier $x_i \in \{0, 1\}^\lambda$ from a large space to each party $i \in [n]$. We also include a one-way function of this identifier $\mathsf{OWF}(x_i)$ in the tracing and verification key. Now, the tracer must recover this identifier to blame a party i. Intuitively, falsely accusing an honest party i would amount to inverting $\mathsf{OWF}(x_i)$ for a randomly chosen x_i.

But it is unclear how to trace now; the tracer not only needs to identify a corrupt party j, it must also extract the corresponding identifier x_j from the box. To do so, we observe that this problem is similar to a notion called embedded-identity traitor tracing [32,49], wherein each party also has an *identity* (which may be a string) along with an index, and the tracer must extract the identity of a corrupt party along with its index. The identifier x_j in our scheme can be interpreted as the identity of that party.

Based on this connection, we adapt techniques from [32] to extract the identifier from a reconstruction box. At a high level, we generalize the encryption scheme so that we can disable parties based on not only their index and flag (as done above), but also on a single bit of their identifier. This will allow the tracer to extract the corrupt identifier one bit at a time. In more detail, the tracer

---

[4] This can be seen as the *tracer* mode of the obfuscated program, that we alluded to in the beginning of this section.

does the following: First, it extracts the index j^* of a corrupt party by using the jumps approach as described above. Then, for each position of the identifier, it will prepare shares of parties in I with ciphertexts that disable party j^* if its identifier is 0 at that position (in addition to disabling parties $< j^*$ based on their flags). Roughly speaking, if the box can distinguish between these ciphertexts and the ciphertexts that only disable parties $< j^*$ based on their flags, then x_{j^*} must be 0 at that position (and 1 otherwise).

To implement this technique, we again use symmetric-key encryption to encrypt a position $u \in \{0, \ldots, \lambda\}$ and a bit $b \in \{0, 1\}$ (along with a flag f, an index j, a value m as above). The share of party i will contain an encryption ct_i to position 0, bit 0 (and flag 0, index 0 and value $m = 0$ as above), and a signature, which now also signs the identifier x_i, along with the index i and ciphertext ct_i. We also modify the obfuscated program to take as input shares of the form $(i, x_i, \mathsf{ct}_i, \sigma_i)$ and interpret them as follows:

- Verify the signature and if valid, decrypt the ciphertext to get (u, b, f, j, m).
- If $u = 0$, the program disables all shares for parties $\leq j$, but keeps all shares with flag $f = 1$. This is essentially equivalent to an encryption to (f, j, m) as described above.
- If $u > 0$, then the program also disables $j+1$ if the uth bit of the corresponding identifier x_{j+1} is b.

The rest of the program remains the same as before: it outputs $\bot$ if the remaining set of parties is not authorized; otherwise, it outputs the programmed value or the real secret, based on the flags in the shares. We give a formal description of our scheme with tracer non-imputability in the full version of the paper [34, Sec. 5.3].

2.3   TSS with Strong Traceability

Impossibility Result. We start by providing brief intuition on our impossibility result. Recall that in the definition of Strong traceability, we consider reconstruction boxes with very little restriction on the label I. In particular, the label may even contain corrupt parties, i.e., $I \cap J \neq \emptyset$. We present a negative result in the full version [34, App. A], which states that it is in fact impossible to achieve this notion of traceability simultaneously with tracer secrecy or tracer non-imputability, if the secret comes from a large space.

To understand why, consider a particular reconstruction box with a label I such that $I \cap J$ is indeed a non-empty set. This box simply aborts if the shares given as input do not match the real shares for parties in $I \cap J$; it can do this because the box already has the real shares of all corrupt parties in J. Hence, to get such a box to output something meaningful, the tracer will need to prepare shares of I such that the shares of all parties in $I \cap J$ are exactly the same as their real shares. On the other hand, if the tracer has the ability to prepare real shares for $I \cap J$, then it can also break tracer secrecy! It can simply corrupt an unauthorized set of parties S such that $S \cup (I \cap J)$ is authorized, then run the reconstruction algorithm on shares of S and the shares of $I \cap J$ that it prepared. Since all of the prepared shares for $I \cap J$ are the real shares, the reconstruction algorithm will indeed output the secret by correctness.

Similarly, if the tracer has the ability to prepare real shares for $I \cap J$, then it can also break tracer non-imputability. It can simply prepare a reconstruction box with the shares of $I \cap J$, and run the Trace on this box. By strong traceability, we know that the Trace algorithm must find at least one party in $I \cap J$ along with a valid proof; hence allowing the tracer to blame this party without ever querying for their real share.

We now describe our construction of TSS with Strong traceability from one-way functions.

Starting Observations Towards Positive Result. To achieve Strong traceability, we leverage the impossibility result to our benefit. Given that there is no hope of achieving tracer secrecy, we can make the task of tracing easier by simply providing the real shares of all parties as part of the tracing key. The tracer can then use the real shares when preparing shares of the label I. This allows us to completely bypass the first challenge – the real shares are consistent with the adversarial shares by definition! Hence, we now only have to deal with the second challenge, i.e., partial reconstruction when designing a traceable scheme. While we used obfuscation to achieve this in the last section, we will only rely on one-way functions here. We start with describing our approach for tracing reconstruction boxes with label I that does not overlap with the corrupt set J, i.e., $I \cap J = \emptyset$; we will discuss how to remove this restriction later in the section.

Dealing with Partial Reconstruction. To get around this challenge, we need to take the *all-or-nothing* approach mentioned in Sect. 2.2 to design the reconstruction algorithm such that an unauthorized subset of parties cannot learn anything meaningful. Moreover, for our tracing via jumps approach to work, we still need the ability to create shares of parties such that we can disable shares of certain parties.

As a naive first attempt, let us encrypt the secret using any encryption scheme, and publish the resulting ciphertext as the public share. Then, we secret share the decryption key using any secret sharing scheme SS for monotone circuits [1,45,52], and give the shares of the key as secret shares to all parties. While this avoids partial reconstruction of the secret, a subset of parties can still partially reconstruct the key! We conclude that any one-level secret sharing approach (where we share the secret or a key hiding the secret) will not be enough to avoid partial reconstruction.

Our Approach. Instead, we devise a *two-level* sharing procedure to address the partial reconstruction challenge. At a high level, our approach is to first share the secret using any secret sharing scheme SS for monotone circuits [1,45,52], and then compute a *special* encryption of each share. This special encryption scheme is a generalization of private set broadcast encryption (which in turn, generalizes PLBE) to general access structures. It has three key properties:

- A normal ciphertext can only be decrypted if an authorized subset of parties comes together (as opposed to any single party being able to decrypt).
- It is possible to create "special" ciphertexts with respect to any set S as the tag, such that only authorized subsets of S are allowed to decrypt, essentially disabling all parties outside S.
- The special ciphertexts leak limited information about the tag S – parties in S can learn that they are not disabled, but nothing more. This generalizes the notion of index-hiding for PLBE.

Roughly speaking, each party will only get the special encryption of its share (along with the special decryption key corresponding to its index). The first property will ensure that, if an unauthorized subset of parties collude, they will not be able to decrypt any of the shares, hence no partial reconstruction would be possible. The second and third properties will allow us to use the tracing via jumps approach described in Sect. 2.2.

We now describe our TSS scheme, including how we implement the special encryption with these properties. We will use a secret-key encryption scheme $\mathsf{SKE} := (\mathsf{KeyGen}, \mathsf{Enc}, \mathsf{Dec})$ and a secret sharing scheme $\mathsf{SS} := (\mathsf{Share}, \mathsf{Rec})$ for monotone circuits as building blocks. To share a secret s with respect to a monotone circuit C as the access structure, we do the following:

- Share s using SS, i.e., $(\mathsf{sh}'_1, \ldots, \mathsf{sh}'_n) \leftarrow_\$ \mathsf{SS.Share}(1^\lambda, s, C)$.
- For each $i \in [n]$, sample a fresh secret-key encryption key, i.e., $\mathsf{sk}_i \leftarrow_\$ \mathsf{SKE.KeyGen}(1^\lambda)$.
- For each $i \in [n]$, we compute a special encryption of sh'_i as follows:
    - Compute *sub-shares* of sh'_i using SS for the same access structure, i.e.,$(\mathsf{sh}'_{i,1}, \ldots, \mathsf{sh}'_{i,n}) \leftarrow_\$ \mathsf{SS.Share}(1^\lambda, \mathsf{sh}'_i, C)$.
    - Encrypt the jth sub-share using the jth key, i.e., $\mathsf{ct}_{i,j} \leftarrow_\$ \mathsf{SKE.Enc}(\mathsf{sk}_j, \mathsf{sh}'_{i,j})$.
    - Set $\mathsf{ct}_i \leftarrow (\mathsf{ct}_{i,1}, \ldots, \mathsf{ct}_{i,n})$. This is an encryption of sh'_i with respect to the set $S = \{1, \ldots, n\}$.
- For each $i \in [n]$, assign the ith encryption key along with the special encryption of sh'_i as the share of this party. Formally, $\mathsf{sh}_i := (\mathsf{sk}_i, \mathsf{ct}_i)$.

For reconstruction, an authorized subset of parties $S \subseteq [n]$ can decrypt an authorized set of sub-shares of sh'_i for all $i \in S$, which can be used to reconstruct sh'_i. The secret can then be reconstructed using the sh'_i values for all $i \in S$.

Let us now see why our special encryption scheme indeed achieves all three properties. First, observe that to decrypt any single share, we need to decrypt an authorized subset of its sub-shares, which requires knowing the secret keys sk_i of an authorized subset of parties. Hence, an unauthorized subset of parties cannot decrypt the ciphertext of even a single share, as desired.

For the remaining properties, we first show how we can modify our encryption scheme to encrypt to arbitrary sets. To encrypt a share sh'_i with respect to a set $S \subseteq [n]$, we encrypt the jth sub-share using the jth key as above, for all parties in S. Formally, for all $j \in S$, $\mathsf{ct}_{i,j} \leftarrow_\$ \mathsf{SKE.Enc}(\mathsf{sk}_j, \mathsf{sh}'_{i,j})$. But, for all other parties, i.e., $j \in [n] \setminus S$, we encrypt some garbage value (say, 0) instead of the real sub-share $\mathsf{sh}'_{i,j}$, i.e., $\mathsf{ct}_{i,j}$ would be $\mathsf{SKE.Enc}(\mathsf{sk}_j, 0)$ for all $j \in [n] \setminus S$. This means that, the sub-shares for all parties $\in [n] \setminus S$ are essentially useless for reconstruction, hence, a share sh'_i encrypted in this manner can only be decrypted by an authorized subset of S, as desired. Lastly, to see why the third property holds, observe that an adversary that does not have the key for a party ℓ, cannot learn whether the ciphertext $c_{i,\ell}$ encrypts a real sub-share or zero, by semantic security. Hence, this adversary cannot learn whether party ℓ has been disabled or not. Our special encryption scheme can be seen as a generalization of the trivial PLBE scheme [10].

For tracing, we can simply use the tracing via jumps approach described in the previous section. Recall that the tracer is given the real shares of all n parties (since we cannot achieve tracer secrecy anyway). Hence, the tracer can use the keys $(\mathsf{sk}_1, \ldots, \mathsf{sk}_n)$ and shares $(\mathsf{sh}'_1, \ldots, \mathsf{sh}'_n)$ to prepare shares of all $i \in I$, wherein it encrypts sh'_i with respect to sets $\{j, \ldots, n\} \cup I$ for different values of j. By similar arguments as in the last section, the second and third properties of our special encryption imply that the tracer must find a jump at some index j^*, and this index cannot be honest. Hence, the tracer simply blames party j^{*5}.

Handling Overlapping Sets. Recall that in the definition of strong traceability, the label I may contain corrupt parties. But then, the above tracing algorithm will completely break down – the tracer samples fresh ciphertexts for parties in I whenever it runs the box. But the box will immediately observe that the input shares do not match real shares of parties in $I \cap J$ and simply abort.

To solve this problem, we will exploit the fact that the tracer has access to the real shares of all n parties. At a high level, the tracer will run the reconstruction box with the real shares of I, and then replace the share of each party in I with a freshly sampled share (encrypted to set $\{1, \ldots, n\}$ like a real share), one-by-one. We consider two cases:

1. There is a jump in behavior of the box when switching the share of a party $j^* \in \mathcal{I}$ from real to freshly-sampled: Observe that, for any honest party, the freshly-sampled share, i.e., a fresh encryption of the share to $[n]$ is distributed identically as the real share. Hence, the box cannot distinguish between the two for an honest party. Consequently, the only scenario where the box can distinguish between real and freshly-sampled shares is if it already has the real share for party j^*. This implies that j^* must be corrupt. Hence, the tracer simply blames this party.
2. There is no jump in the box's behavior: This means that the box outputs information about the correct secret with non-negligible probability, even when given freshly sampled shares of all parties in I as input. We can now rely on the same tracing procedure described above – we prepare shares of I to disable parties one-by-one and blame the party where we find a jump.

---

[5] Concurrent and independent of our work, Goyal and Waters [33] also proposed a TSS scheme for the threshold access structure, based on similar ideas, that achieves our notion of strong traceability.

Reducing Share Size. The share of each party contains a symmetric decryption key sk_i, along with an encryption of sh'_i. If the share size for the scheme SS is w, then the encryption of sh'_i is of size $(w)^2 \cdot n$. To avoid this quadratic overhead in w, we use a hybrid encryption approach. Specifically, to encrypt sh'_i with respect to a set S, we first sample a fresh symmetric encryption key k and encrypt sh'_i with this key to get $\hat{c}_i$. Next, we encrypt the key k (which is of size $\Theta(1)$ as opposed to w) with respect to the set S, exactly as described above. This allows us to reduce share size to $w + w \cdot n$. We describe the full compiler in Sect. 5.

2.4   Organization

In Sect. 3, we introduce our new TSS definitions. Section 4 presents our TSS scheme achieving $\emptyset$-strong traceability and security against malicious tracers. Section 5 describes our generic compiler for constructing TSS with strong traceability. The impossibility result can be found in the full version [34, App. A].

3   New Definitions of TSS

In this section, we formally define traceable secret sharing for access structures captured by monotone circuits. We start with some preliminaries.

Preliminaries. Our constructions rely on standard primitives such as indistinguishability Obfuscation (iO) and puncturable Pseudorandom functions (pPRF). We defer the reader to the full version [34, Sec. 3] for their formal definitions.

We use $[n]$ to denote the set $\{1, \dots, n\}$. For any set $J \subseteq [n]$, we use $x_J \in \{0,1\}^n$ to denote a bit string such that $\forall\, i \in J,\, x_i = 1$, and $\forall\, i \in [n] \setminus J,\, x_i = 0$.

Syntax. A traceable secret sharing for a circuit ensemble $\{\mathcal{C}_\lambda\}_\lambda$ is a tuple of four PPT algorithms, $\mathsf{GTSS} = (\mathsf{Share}, \mathsf{Rec}, \mathsf{Trace}, \mathsf{Verify})$.

- $\mathsf{Share}(1^\lambda, s, C) \to (\{\mathsf{sh}_i\}_{i \in [n]}, \mathsf{pp}, \mathsf{tk}, \mathsf{vk})$ is the randomized secret sharing algorithm. It takes as input the security parameter 1^λ, the access structure in the form of a poly-sized monotone circuit $C : \{0,1\}^n \to \{0,1\}$ such that $C \in \mathcal{C}_\lambda$ and the secret $s \in \mathcal{S}_\lambda$, where $\mathcal{S} = \{\mathcal{S}_\lambda\}_{\lambda \in \mathbb{N}}$ is the space of secrets. It outputs the secret shares of all parties $\{\mathsf{sh}_i\}$, public information pp, the tracing key tk and the verification key vk.
- $\mathsf{Rec}(\mathsf{pp}, \{\mathsf{sh}_i\}_{i \in J}) \to s$ is the deterministic secret reconstruction algorithm. It takes as input secret shares of a set $J \subseteq [n]$ and outputs a secret s or $\bot$.
- $\mathsf{Trace}^R(\mathsf{pp}, \mathsf{tk}, 1^{1/\delta}, s_0, s_1, \mathcal{I}) \to (\mathcal{J}, \pi)$ is the randomized tracing algorithm. It takes as input a tracing key tk, an error parameter δ and two secrets s_0 and s_1 in $\mathcal{S}_\lambda$. It also gets oracle (black-box) access to a reconstruction box R along with a 'label' $\mathcal{I}$. It outputs a subset $\mathcal{J} \subseteq [n]$ of identities of leaking parties and an associated proof π.
- $\mathsf{Verify}(\mathsf{vk}, \mathcal{J}, \pi) \to \{0,1\}$ is the deterministic verification algorithm. It takes as input the verification key vk, an alleged traitor subset $\mathcal{J}$, and an associated proof π, and outputs a bit denoting whether the proof is valid.

Correctness and Secrecy. A traceable secret-sharing scheme must satisfy the standard notions of correctness and secrecy for any secret sharing scheme. We defer the formal definitions to the full version of the paper [34, Sec. 4].

Additionally, a traceable secret-sharing scheme should satisfy tracer secrecy, $\emptyset$-strong traceability, and tracer non-imputability.

Tracer Secrecy. Tracer secrecy requires that secrecy is maintained even against the tracer. That is, that the tracing key tk does not help in breaking secrecy. This is made formal in the following definition.

Definition 3.1 (Tracer Secrecy). *Let* GTSS = (Share, Rec, Trace, Verify) *be a traceable secret-sharing scheme for secrets in* $\mathcal{S} = \{\mathcal{S}_\lambda\}_{\lambda \in \mathbb{N}}$. *We say that* GTSS *satisfies* **tracer secrecy** *if for every* $\lambda \in \mathbb{N}$, *any two secrets* $s_0, s_1 \in \mathcal{S}_\lambda$, *every monotone circuit* $C : \{0,1\}^n \to \{0,1\}$ *such that* $C \in \mathcal{C}_\lambda$, *and every subset* $\mathcal{J} \subseteq [n]$ *such that* $C(x_{\mathcal{J}}) = 0$, *every* PPT *algorithm* D, *the following advantage is negligible in* λ:

$$\mathsf{Adv}^{t-sec}_{D,\mathsf{GTSS}}(\lambda) := \left| \Pr\left[b^* = b : \begin{array}{c} b \xleftarrow{\$} \{0,1\} \\ (\{\mathsf{sh}_i\}_{i \in [n]}, \mathsf{pp}, \mathsf{tk}, \mathsf{vk}) \xleftarrow{\$} \mathsf{Share}(1^\lambda, s_b, C) \\ b^* \xleftarrow{\$} \mathcal{A}(\mathsf{state}, \mathsf{pp}, \{\mathsf{sh}_i\}_{i \in \mathcal{J}}, \mathsf{tk}, \mathsf{vk}) \end{array} \right] - \frac{1}{2} \right|$$

$\emptyset$-Strong Traceability. Suppose an unauthorized set of parties $\mathcal{J} \subseteq [n]$ of parties i.e., $C(x_{\mathcal{J}}) = 0$, constructs a reconstruction box R using their shares. This R is an algorithm that takes in secret shares of all parties in the label set $\mathcal{I}$ and can distinguish whether the shares correspond to secret s_0 or s_1. Intuitively, if this R is a "minimally-useful" reconstruction box, then it should be possible to trace it back to at least one of the parties who "contributed" its share to it. We require that tracing should be done given only black-box access to R.

In more detail, say that the secret shared among the parties is s_b. Then, R is a minimally-useful reconstruction box with respect to a label $\mathcal{I}$ if it guesses b with non-negligible probability, when given shares of s_b for the set $\mathcal{I}$ as input. Definition 3.2 below formally defines such reconstruction boxes.

Definition 3.2 (Minimally-useful Reconstruction Box). *Let* GTSS *be a traceable secret-sharing scheme. Let* $\lambda \in \mathbb{N}$, *let* $C : \{0,1\}^n \to \{0,1\}$ *be a monotone circuit. For* $\epsilon \in [0,1]$, *secrets* $s_0, s_1 \in \mathcal{S}_\lambda$, *a bit* $b \in \{0,1\}$, *a set* $\mathcal{J} \subseteq [n]$ *such that* $C(x_{\mathcal{J}}) = 0$, *and corresponding shares* $\{\mathsf{sh}_i\}_{i \in \mathcal{J}}$, *and a label* $\mathcal{I} = \{i_1, \ldots, i_f\}$, *a reconstruction box* R *is* $(C, \mathcal{I}, \{\mathsf{sh}_i\}_{i \in \mathcal{J}}, \mathsf{pp}, s_0, s_1, b, \epsilon)$-*minimally-useful if,*

$$\Pr\left[R(\mathsf{sh}_{i_1}, \ldots, \mathsf{sh}_{i_f}) = b \right] \geq \frac{1}{2} + \epsilon,$$

where $(\{\mathsf{sh}_i\}_{i \in [n]}, \mathsf{pp}, \mathsf{tk}, \mathsf{vk}) \xleftarrow{\$} \mathsf{Share}(1^\lambda, s_b, C)$ *and the probability is taken over the random coins of* R.

Equipped with this notion, the $\emptyset$-Strong traceability experiment is presented in Fig. 3 and the definition is given in Definition 3.3.

Definition 3.3 ($\emptyset$-Strong Traceability). *Let* GTSS $=$ (Share, Rec, Trace, Verify) *be a traceable secret-sharing scheme, and let* $\epsilon = \epsilon(\lambda)$ *be a function of the security parameter. We say that* GTSS *is **traceable**, if for every probabilistic polynomial time adversary* $\mathcal{A}$, *the following function is negligible in* λ:

$$\mathsf{Adv}^{\emptyset-\mathrm{str}-\mathrm{trac}}_{\mathcal{A},\mathsf{GTSS},\epsilon}(\lambda) := \Pr\left[\mathbf{Exp\emptyset StrongTrace}_{\mathcal{A},\mathsf{GTSS},\epsilon}(\lambda) = 1\right].$$

Remark 3.4 (On the $\emptyset$-Strong traceability definition). Some remarks are in order:

- **Requiring $\mathcal{I} \cap \mathcal{J} = \emptyset$.** We do not require $\mathcal{I} \cup \mathcal{J}$ to be minimal in $\emptyset$-strong traceability. In the full version [34, Sec. 4.1], we give an even stronger definition of tracing where we lift this restriction.
- **Private tracing:** In the tracing experiment, the adversary is not given access to the tracing key tk and the verification key vk. This is because, for our constructions, knowledge of these keys can allow an adversary to evade tracing. We leave the problem of constructing secret sharing schemes with public tracing as an avenue for future work.

Experiment $\mathbf{Exp\emptyset StrongTrace}_{\mathcal{A},\mathsf{GTSS},\epsilon}(\lambda)$

1:   $(C, \mathcal{J}, s_0, s_1, \mathsf{state}) \leftarrow \mathcal{A}(1^\lambda)$ // $\mathcal{A}$ chooses the parties to corrupt

2:   $b \leftarrow\!\!\$ \{0,1\}$; $(\{\mathsf{sh}_i\}_{i\in[n]}, \mathsf{pp}, \mathsf{tk}, \mathsf{vk}) \leftarrow\!\!\$ \mathsf{Share}(1^\lambda, s_b, C)$

3:   $(R, \mathcal{I}) \leftarrow\!\!\$ \mathcal{A}(\mathsf{state}, \mathsf{pp}, \{\mathsf{sh}_i\}_{i\in\mathcal{J}})$

4:   $(\mathcal{J}^*, \pi) \leftarrow\!\!\$ \mathsf{Trace}^R(\mathsf{pp}, \mathsf{tk}, 1^{1/\epsilon}, s_0, s_1, \mathcal{I})$

5:   $\mathsf{GoodBox} := (\mathcal{I} \cap \mathcal{J} = \emptyset) \wedge C(x_\mathcal{J}) = 0 \wedge C(x_\mathcal{I}) = 0 \wedge$

6:               (R is $(C, \mathcal{I}, \{\mathsf{sh}_i\}_{i\in\mathcal{J}}, \mathsf{pp}, , s_0, s_1, b, \epsilon)$-minimally-useful)

7:   **if** $\mathcal{J}^* \not\subseteq \mathcal{J} \wedge \mathsf{Verify}(\mathsf{vk}, \mathcal{J}^*, \pi) = 1$ **then return** 1

8:   **if** $\neg\mathsf{GoodBox}$ **then return** 0

9:   **if** $\mathcal{J}^* \neq \emptyset \wedge \mathcal{J}^* \subseteq \mathcal{J} \wedge \mathsf{Verify}(\mathsf{vk}, \mathcal{J}^*, \pi) = 1$ **then return** 0 **else return** 1

Fig. 3. The $\emptyset$-strong tracing experiment for a traceable secret-sharing scheme GTSS and an adversary $\mathcal{A}$.

Tracer Non-imputability. Lastly, we require that a traceable secret-sharing scheme satisfy the notion of tracer non-imputability, stating that honest parties cannot be wrongly blamed by a cheating tracer. In more detail, this means that even a malicious tracer cannot produce an accepting proof for the culpability of an honest party. This is formally captured by the security experiment in Fig. 4. There, the adversary gets the tracing and verification keys tk and vk, and may obtain the secret shares of any party of its choosing, as long as it is not the honest party it tries to blame.

Experiment $\mathbf{ExpNI}_{\mathcal{A},\mathsf{GTSS}}$

1 : $(C, i^*, s, \mathsf{state}) \leftarrow\!\!\$\ \mathcal{A}(1^\lambda)$

2 : $(\{\mathsf{sh}_i\}_{i\in[n]}, \mathsf{pp}, \mathsf{tk}, \mathsf{vk}) \leftarrow\!\!\$\ \mathsf{Share}(1^\lambda, s, C)$

3 : $(\mathcal{J}^*, \pi) \leftarrow\!\!\$\ \mathcal{A}(\mathsf{state}, \mathsf{pp}, \{\mathsf{sh}_i\}_{i\in[n]\setminus\{i^*\}}, \mathsf{tk}, \mathsf{vk})$

4 : **if** $i^* \in \mathcal{J}^* \wedge \mathsf{Verify}(\mathsf{vk}, \mathcal{J}^*, \pi) = 1$ **then return** 1 **else return** 0

Fig. 4. The tracer non-imputability experiment for GTSS and an adversary $\mathcal{A}$.

Definition 3.5. *Let* $\mathsf{GTSS} = (\mathsf{Share}, \mathsf{Rec}, \mathsf{Trace}, \mathsf{Verify})$ *be a TSS scheme. We say that* GTSS *achieves* **tracer non-imputability**, *if for every probabilistic polynomial time adversary* $\mathcal{A}$, *the following function is negligible in* λ:

$$\mathsf{Adv}^{\mathrm{ni}}_{\mathcal{A},\mathsf{GTSS}}(\lambda) := \Pr\left[\mathbf{ExpNI}_{\mathcal{A},\mathsf{GTSS}}(\lambda) = 1\right],$$

where the experiment $\mathbf{ExpNI}_{\mathcal{A},\mathsf{GTSS}}$ *is as defined in Fig. 4.*

4   **GTSS** with ∅-Strong Traceability from iO

We now present our traceable secret sharing scheme for monotone circuits which achieves ∅-strong traceability, tracer secrecy and tracer non-imputability.

4.1   Building Block: Doubly-Constrained Signatures

In this section, we define a new primitive that we call doubly-constrained signatures. While this primitive is related to constrained signatures [13] and splittable signatures [42], the notion we define and achieve has not been considered before.

Informally, a doubly constrained signature scheme allows the computation, given circuits C_1 and C_2, of (i) a constrained public key pk_{C_1} and a corresponding signing key sk_{C_1} and (ii) a constrained signing key sk_{C_2}. The public key pk_{C_1} has the property that for any message x such that $C_1(x) = 0$, there are no valid signatures on x relative to pk_{C_1}. For security, we require that pk_{C_1} is indistinguishable from a valid, honestly generated public key for any adversary that can query signatures on any x such that $C_1(x) = 1$. The constrained signing key sk_{C_2} can only be used to sign messages x such that $C_2(x) = 1$. Moreover, signatures generated using sk_{C_2} should be indistinguishable from those generated using sk_{C_1}. Note that we do allow the public key and secret key to be constrained by different circuits, i.e., C_1 may not be equal to C_2.

More formally, a doubly-constrained signature scheme for a circuit ensemble $\{\mathcal{C}_\lambda\}_\lambda$ is a tuple of four PPT algorithms $\mathsf{DCS} = (\mathsf{KeyGen}, \mathsf{Sign}, \mathsf{SignVerify}, \mathsf{ConstPK})$:

– $\mathsf{KeyGen}(1^\lambda, \ell, z, C_1) \to (\mathsf{pk}, \mathsf{sk}, \mathsf{sk}_{C_1})$ takes as input the security parameter λ, an upper bound on the message length ℓ, a circuit $C_1 : \{0,1\}^\ell \to \{0,1\}$ in $\mathcal{C}_\lambda$

and an upper bound $z = \max_{C \in \mathcal{C}_\lambda} |C|$ on the size of the circuits handled by the scheme. It outputs a valid (unconstrained) secret/public key pair $(\mathsf{pk}, \mathsf{sk})$ along with a constrained secret key sk_{C_1}. We will use $\mathsf{len}_\sigma = \mathsf{len}_\sigma(\lambda, \ell, z)$ to denote the length of a signature for the scheme.

- $\mathsf{Sign}(\mathsf{sk}, m) \to \{0,1\}^{\mathsf{len}_\sigma}$ is the randomized algorithm that takes as input the secret signing key and a message m, and outputs a signature σ_m.
- $\mathsf{SignVerify}(\mathsf{pk}, m, \sigma_m) \to \{0,1\}$ is the deterministic algorithm that takes as input the public key, the message and a signature, and outputs whether the signature is valid.
- $\mathsf{ConstPK}(1^\lambda, \ell, z, C_1, C_2) \to (\mathsf{pk}_{C_2}, \mathsf{sk}_{C_2}, \mathsf{sk}_{C_1})$ takes as input the security parameter, message length ℓ, an upper bound z on the size of the circuits, and two circuits $C_1, C_2 \in \mathcal{C}_\lambda$. It outputs a constrained public key-secret key pair $(\mathsf{pk}_{C_2}, \mathsf{sk}_{C_2})$ along with a constrained secret key sk_{C_1}.

Correctness. We require two notions of correctness. First, an honestly generated signature should verify successfully with the corresponding public key. This should hold for the key pairs generated by KeyGen as well as $\mathsf{ConstPK}$. Second, we require that for any m that does not satisfy C_2, there should be no valid signature with respect to pk_{C_2}. We give formal definitions in the full version [34, Sec. 5.1].

Security. We require two key properties. First, the distribution of signatures generated by a constrained signing key sk_{C_1} should be indistinguishable from that generated by an unconstrained key sk, for all messages such that $C_1(m) = 1$. Definition 4.1 formalizes this notion.

Definition 4.1. *A doubly-constrained signature scheme* DCS *is said to have identically-distributed signatures if the following advantage is negligible for all PPT adversaries:*

$$\mathsf{Adv}_{\mathcal{A},\mathsf{DCS}}^{\mathsf{id-dist}}(\lambda) := \left| \Pr[\mathbf{ExpIdDist}_{\mathcal{A},\mathsf{DCS}}(\lambda) = 1] - \frac{1}{2} \right|,$$

where the experiment $\mathbf{ExpIdDist}_{\mathcal{A},\mathsf{DCS}}$ *is as defined in Fig. 5.*

Experiment $\mathbf{ExpIdDist}_{\mathcal{A},\mathsf{DCS}}$	Oracle $\mathsf{SignO}(m)$
1 : $(\ell, z, C_1, \mathsf{state}) \leftarrow\!\!\$\ \mathcal{A}(1^\lambda)$	1 : **if** $C_1(m) = 0$ **then**
2 : $(\mathsf{pk}, \mathsf{sk}, \mathsf{sk}_{C_1}) \leftarrow\!\!\$\ \mathsf{KeyGen}(1^\lambda, \ell, z, C_1)$	2 : **return** $\mathsf{Sign}(\mathsf{sk}, m)$
3 : $b \leftarrow\!\!\$\ \{0,1\}$; $\mathsf{sk}^* := \mathsf{sk}$ **if** $b = 0$ **else** sk_{C_1}	3 : **else return** $\mathsf{Sign}(\mathsf{sk}^*, m)$
4 : $b^* \leftarrow\!\!\$\ \mathcal{A}^{\mathsf{SignO}(\cdot)}(\mathsf{state}, \mathsf{pk})$	
5 : **return** 1 **if** $b = b^*$ **else** 0	

Fig. 5. The Identical-Distribution property for normal keys, of a doubly-constrained signature scheme DCS.

The second property requires that an adversary cannot distinguish between the constrained public key pk_{C_2} and a normal public key pk, even if the adversary is allowed to query signatures on arbitrary messages m that satisfy $C_2(m) = 1$. Moreover, if C_1 is more restrictive than C_2, then the adversary additionally gets access to the constrained signing key sk_{C_1}, but it should still not be able to distinguish between the two public keys. Formally, a circuit C_1 is more restrictive

---

$\underline{\mathsf{Share}(1^\lambda, s, C)}$:

1. Sample PRF key $k \leftarrow\!\!\$ \ \{0,1\}^\lambda$ and doubly-constrained signature keys $(\mathsf{pk}, \mathsf{sk}, \mathsf{sk}_1) \leftarrow\!\!\$ \ \mathsf{DCS.KeyGen}(1^\lambda, \ell, z, C_1)$ where $C_1 : [n] \times \mathsf{CT} \rightarrow \{0,1\}$ is defined as, $C_1(i, \mathsf{ct}) = 1$ if and only if, $\mathsf{Dec}(k, \mathsf{ct}) = (1, \cdot, \cdot)$. // $\mathsf{CT} := \{0,1\}^\lambda \times \{0,1\}^{1+\log(n+1)+\log(|\mathcal{S}_\lambda|)}$ and $\ell = \ell(n, \lambda)$, $z = z(\lambda, n)$ will be specified later.
2. $\forall \ i \in [n]$, let $\mathsf{ct}_i \leftarrow\!\!\$ \ \mathsf{Enc}(k, (0,0,0))$, $\sigma_i := \mathsf{DCS.Sign}(\mathsf{sk}, (i, \mathsf{ct}_i))$.
3. Obfuscate the program P described below, i.e., $\hat{\mathsf{P}} \leftarrow \mathsf{Obf}(\mathsf{P})$.
4. Output $\{\mathsf{sh}_i = (i, \mathsf{ct}_i, \sigma_i)\}_{i \in [n]}, \mathsf{pp} \leftarrow \hat{\mathsf{P}}, \mathsf{tk} \leftarrow (k, \mathsf{sk}_1), \mathsf{vk} \leftarrow \perp$.

$\underline{\mathsf{Enc}(k, (f, j, m))}$:

1. Sample $r \leftarrow\!\!\$ \ \{0,1\}^\lambda$. Output $\mathsf{ct} \leftarrow (r, \mathsf{ct}' \leftarrow \mathsf{PRF.F}(k, r) + (f||j||m)) \in \mathsf{CT}$.

$\underline{\mathsf{Dec}(k, \mathsf{ct})}$:

1. Parse ct as (r, ct') and output $\mathsf{ct}' - \mathsf{PRF.F}(k, r)$.

$\underline{\mathsf{P}(\{i, \mathsf{ct}_i, \sigma_i\}_{i \in J})}$:

1. **Constants**: C, k, pk, s.
2. Let $\hat{J} = J$. For all $i \in J$, if $\mathsf{DCS.SignVerify}(\mathsf{pk}, (i, \mathsf{ct}_i), \sigma_i) = 0$, set $\hat{J} \leftarrow \hat{J} \setminus \{i\}$.
3. $\forall \ i \in \hat{J}$, let $(f_i, j_i, m_i) \leftarrow \mathsf{Dec}(k, \mathsf{ct}_i)$, $S_i := \{j_i + 1, \ldots, n\}$ and $S := \bigcap_{i \in \hat{J}} S_i$.
4. $\forall \ i \in \hat{J}$ s.t. $f_i = 1$, set $S \leftarrow S \cup \{i\}$. Set $\hat{J} = \hat{J} \cap S$. Abort if $C(x_{\hat{J}}) = 0$.
5. If $\forall \ i \in \hat{J}$, $f_i = 0$, then output s.
6. Otherwise, output m_{i^*} where $i^* = \min_{i \in \hat{J}, f_i \neq 0}(i)$.

$\underline{\mathsf{Rec}(\mathsf{pp}, \{\mathsf{sh}_i\}_{i \in J})}$:

1. Parse pp as $\hat{\mathsf{P}}$. Output $\hat{\mathsf{P}}(\{\mathsf{sh}_i\}_{i \in J})$.

$\underline{\mathsf{Trace}^R(\mathsf{pp}, \mathsf{tk}, 1^{1/\epsilon}, s_0, s_1, \mathcal{I})}$:

1. Parse tk as (k, sk_1). Sample $b^* \leftarrow\!\!\$ \ \{0,1\}$, and set $s^* := s_{b^*}$.
2. Let $\mathcal{J}^* := \perp$. For $j \in \{0, \ldots, n\}$:
   (a) Let $p_j \leftarrow 0$. For $q \in \{1, \ldots, N\}$: // $N = \frac{8\lambda \cdot n^2}{\epsilon^2}$
     i. $\forall \ i \in \mathcal{I}$, let $\mathsf{ct}'_i \leftarrow\!\!\$ \ \mathsf{Enc}(k, (1, j, s^*))$ and $\sigma'_i \leftarrow \mathsf{DCS.Sign}(\mathsf{sk}_1, (i, \mathsf{ct}'_i))$.
     ii. Query R on $\{\mathsf{sh}^*_{i,j} \leftarrow (i, \mathsf{ct}'_i, \sigma'_i)\}_{i \in \mathcal{I}}$. Let b denote R's response.
     iii. If $s_b = s^*$, then set $p_j \leftarrow p_j + 1$.
   (b) Compute $p'_j \leftarrow p_j / N$. If $j > 0$ and $p_{j-1} - p_j > \epsilon/4n$, then set $\mathcal{J}^* \leftarrow \mathcal{J}^* \cup \{j\}$.

Fig. 6. Our iO-based scheme iOGTSS with $\emptyset$-strong traceability and tracer secrecy. In the full version [34, Sec. 5.3], we show how to modify this scheme to also achieve tracer non-imputability.

than C_2 if $C_1(m) = 1 \implies C_2(m) = 1$. We will use $C_1 \implies C_2$ as a short-hand for this. This definition is a generalization of security for constrained signatures. We defer the formal definition to the full version [34, Sec. 5.1].

4.2 Our Construction

We start with describing a simpler construction that does not achieve tracer non-imputability. In the full version [34, Sec. 5.3], we describe how to modify this scheme to achieve tracer non-imputability.

We use a puncturable PRF : $\{0,1\}^\lambda \times \{0,1\}^\lambda \to \{0,1\} \times \{0,1,\ldots,n\}$, a doubly constrained signature scheme DCS and indistinguishability obfuscation Obf as building blocks. Figure 6 gives a formal description. We do not describe a Verify algorithm since this scheme does not provide tracer non-imputability.

We prove correctness, tracer secrecy and $\emptyset$-strong traceability of our scheme in the full version [34, Sec. 5.2], by relying on security of PRF, DCS and Obf. We focus on a semi-adaptive notion of $\emptyset$-Strong traceability, wherein the adversary sends the label $\mathcal{I}$ along with the corrupt set $\mathcal{J}$ in the first step of the game.

5 A Generic Compiler for **GTSS** with Strong Traceability

Figures 7 and 8 present our generic compiler to construct traceable secret sharing schemes with strong traceability, from any secret sharing scheme for monotone

---

$\mathsf{Share}(1^\lambda, s, C):$ $\!\!/\!\!/$ $C : \{0,1\}^n \to \{0,1\}$

1. $\forall\ i\ \in\ [n]$, sample $k_i\ \leftarrow\!\!\$\ \mathsf{SKE.KeyGen}(1^\lambda)$. Run $(s_1,\ldots,s_n,\mathsf{pp})\ \leftarrow\!\!\$$
   $\mathsf{SS.Share}(1^\lambda, s, C)$.
2. $\forall\ i \in [n]$, set $\mathsf{sh}_i \leftarrow (k_i, (\hat{c}_i, c_i) \leftarrow\!\!\$ \mathsf{ShareEnc}(\{k_i\}_{i\in[n]}, s_i, [n], C)\ )$.
3. Output $\{\mathsf{sh}_i\}_{i\in[n]}$, $\mathsf{pp} \leftarrow \mathsf{pp}$, $\mathsf{tk} \leftarrow \{\mathsf{sh}_i\}_{i\in[n]}$, $\mathsf{vk} \leftarrow \perp$.

$\mathsf{ShareEnc}(\{k_i\}_{i\in[n]}, m, S \subseteq [n], C):$

1. Sample $\hat{k} \leftarrow\!\!\$ \mathsf{SKE.KeyGen}(1^\lambda)$ and $(u_1,\ldots,u_n) \leftarrow\!\!\$ \mathsf{SS.Share}(1^\lambda, \hat{k}, C)$.
2. Compute $\hat{c} \leftarrow\!\!\$ \mathsf{SKE.Enc}(\hat{k}, m)$ and $\forall\ j \in S$, compute $c_j := \mathsf{SKE.Enc}(k_j, u_j)$.
3. $\forall\ j \in [n] \setminus S$, sample $\hat{u}_j \leftarrow\!\!\$ \mathcal{SH}_{\mathsf{SS},j,\lambda}$ and let $c_j := \mathsf{SKE.Enc}(k_j, \hat{u}_j)$. Output
   $(\hat{c}, c = (c_1, \ldots, c_n))$.

$\mathsf{ShareDec}(\{k_i\}_{i\in J}, \hat{c}, c):$

1. Parse c as $(c_1, \ldots, c_n)$. For all $j \in J$, compute $u'_j \leftarrow \mathsf{SKE.Dec}(k_j, c_j)$.
2. Run $\hat{k}' \leftarrow \mathsf{SS.Rec}(\{u_j\}_{j\in J})$. If $\hat{k}' = \perp$, output $\perp$ else output $\mathsf{SKE.Dec}(\hat{k}', \hat{c})$.

$\mathsf{Rec}(\mathsf{pp}, \{\mathsf{sh}_i\}_{i\in J}):$

1. Output $\mathsf{SS.Rec}(\{s'_i\}_{i\in J})$ where $s'_i \leftarrow \mathsf{ShareDec}(\{k_i\}_{i\in J}, \hat{c}_i, c_i)\ \forall\ i \in J$.

Fig. 7. The $\mathsf{Share}, \mathsf{Rec}$ algorithms for our generic compiler Π_{GTSS} to construct TSS with strong traceability. Here, $\mathcal{SH}_{\mathsf{SS},j,\lambda}$ denotes the space of secret shares of party $j \in [n]$ for SS. The Trace algorithm can be found in Fig. 8.

$\mathsf{Trace}^R(\mathsf{pp}, \mathsf{tk}, 1^{1/\epsilon}, s_0, s_1, \mathcal{I})$:

1. Parse tk as $\{\mathsf{sh}_i\}_{i \in [n]}$, and for all $i \in [n]$, parse sh_i as $(k_i, \hat{c}_i, c_i)$.
2. Let $J \subseteq [n]$ be any subset such that $C(x_J) = 1$. Let $s \leftarrow \mathsf{Rec}(\{\mathsf{sh}_i\}_{i \in J})$.
3. For $i \in [n]$, compute $\hat{s}_i \leftarrow \mathsf{ShareDec}(\{k_i\}_{i \in J}, \hat{c}_i, c_i)$. Let $\mathcal{J}^* := \perp$.
4. Let $\mathcal{I} = \{i_1, \dots, i_f\}$. For $j \in \{0, \dots, f\}$:
   (a) Let $q_j := 0$. For $q \in \{1, \dots, N\}$: $/\!/\ N = \frac{8\lambda n^2}{\epsilon^2}$
       i. $\forall\, \nu \in [j]$: $c''_{i_\nu} \leftarrow\!\!\$ \mathsf{ShareEnc}(\{k_i\}_{i \in [n]}, \hat{s}_{i_\nu}, [n], C)$. Let $\mathsf{sh}''_{i_\nu, j} := (k_{i_\nu}, c''_{i_\nu})$.
       ii. For $i \in \{i_{j+1}, \dots, i_f\}$, set $\mathsf{sh}''_{i,j} := \mathsf{sh}_i$.
       iii. Run $b \leftarrow\!\!\$ R(\{\mathsf{sh}''_{i,j}\}_{i \in \mathcal{I}})$. If $s_b = s$, set $q_j \leftarrow q_j + 1$.
   (b) Compute $q'_j := q_j/N$. If $j > 0$ and $q'_{j-1} - q'_j > \epsilon/4n$, set $\mathcal{J}^* \leftarrow \mathcal{J}^* \cup \{i_j\}$.
5. If $\mathcal{J}^* \neq \perp$, output $\mathcal{J}^*$. Else, compute $\hat{\epsilon} := \epsilon/2$. For $j \in \{0, \dots, n\}$:
   (a) Let $p_j := 0$. For $q \in \{1, \dots, \hat{N}\}$: $/\!/\ \hat{N} = \frac{8\lambda n^2}{\hat{\epsilon}^2}$
       i. For $i \in \mathcal{I}$, $(\hat{c}'_i, c'_i) \leftarrow\!\!\$ \mathsf{ShareEnc}(\{k_i\}_{i \in [n]}, \hat{s}_i, \mathcal{I} \cup \{j+1, \dots, n\}, C)$.
       ii. Run $b \leftarrow\!\!\$ R(\{\mathsf{sh}^*_{i,j} := (k_i, \hat{c}'_i, c'_i)\}_{i \in \mathcal{I}})$. If $s_b = s$, set $p_j \leftarrow p_j + 1$.
   (b) Let $p'_j := p_j/\hat{N}$. If $j > 0$ and $p_{j-1} - p_j > \hat{\epsilon}/4n$, then set $\mathcal{J}^* \leftarrow \mathcal{J}^* \cup \{j\}$.
6. Output $\mathcal{J}^*$.

Fig. 8. The Trace algorithm for our generic compiler Π_{GTSS}.

circuit access structures SS (without traceability) and a CPA-secure secret-key encryption scheme SKE, which can be instantiated using one-way functions. We prove that it achieves correctness, secrecy and strong traceability by relying on secrecy of SS and LR-CPA security of SKE, in the full version [34, Sec. 6].

Acknowledgements. Part of this work was done while the authors were visiting the Simons Institute for the Theory of Computing.

References

1. Applebaum, B., Beimel, A., Ishai, Y., Kushilevitz, E., Liu, T., Vaikuntanathan, V.: Succinct computational secret sharing. In: Saha, B., Servedio, R.A. (eds.) 55th ACM STOC, Orlando, FL, USA, pp. 1553–1566. ACM Press (2023)
2. Baghery, K., Ebrahimi, E., Mirzamohammadi, O., Sedaghat, M.: Traceable verifiable secret sharing and applications. Cryptology ePrint Archive, Report 2025/318 (2025)
3. Barak, B., et al.: On the (im)possibility of obfuscating programs. In: Kilian, J. (ed.) CRYPTO 2001. LNCS, vol. 2139, pp. 1–18. Springer, Heidelberg (2001). https://doi.org/10.1007/3-540-44647-8_1
4. Ben-Or, M., Goldwasser, S., Wigderson, A.: Completeness theorems for non-cryptographic fault-tolerant distributed computation (extended abstract). In: 20th ACM STOC, Chicago, IL, USA, pp. 1–10. ACM Press (1988)
5. Benaloh, J., Leichter, J.: Generalized secret sharing and monotone functions. In: Goldwasser, S. (ed.) CRYPTO 1988. LNCS, vol. 403, pp. 27–35. Springer, New York (1990). https://doi.org/10.1007/0-387-34799-2_3

6. Bertilsson, M., Ingemarsson, I.: A construction of practical secret sharing schemes using linear block codes. In: Seberry, J., Zheng, Y. (eds.) AUSCRYPT 1992. LNCS, vol. 718, pp. 67–79. Springer, Heidelberg (1993). https://doi.org/10.1007/3-540-57220-1_53

7. Bishop, A., Green, M., Ishai, Y., Jain, A., Lou, P.: Fully anonymous secret sharing. In: Advances in Cryptology – CRYPTO 2025: 45th Annual International Cryptology Conference, Santa Barbara, CA, USA, 17–21 August 2025, Proceedings, Part IV, pp. 356–389. Springer, Heidelberg (2025)

8. Blakley, G.R.: Safeguarding cryptographic keys. In: Proceedings of AFIPS 1979 National Computer Conference, vol. 48, pp. 313–317 (1979)

9. Boneh, D., Franklin, M.: An efficient public key traitor tracing scheme. In: Wiener, M. (ed.) CRYPTO 1999. LNCS, vol. 1666, pp. 338–353. Springer, Heidelberg (1999). https://doi.org/10.1007/3-540-48405-1_22

10. Boneh, D., Partap, A., Rotem, L.: Accountability for misbehavior in threshold decryption via threshold traitor tracing. In: Reyzin, L., Stebila, D. (eds.) CRYPTO 2024, Part VII. LNCS, vol. 14926, pp. 317–351. Springer, Cham (2024a)

11. Boneh, D., Partap, A., Rotem, L.: Traceable secret sharing: strong security and efficient constructions. In: Reyzin, L., Stebila, D. (eds.) CRYPTO 2024, Part V. LNCS, vol. 14924, pp. 221–256. Springer, Cham (2024b)

12. Boneh, D., Sahai, A., Waters, B.: Fully collusion resistant traitor tracing with short ciphertexts and private keys. In: Vaudenay, S. (ed.) EUROCRYPT 2006. LNCS, vol. 4004, pp. 573–592. Springer, Heidelberg (2006). https://doi.org/10.1007/11761679_34

13. Boneh, D., Zhandry, M.: Multiparty key exchange, efficient traitor tracing, and more from indistinguishability obfuscation. In: Garay, J.A., Gennaro, R. (eds.) CRYPTO 2014. LNCS, vol. 8616, pp. 480–499. Springer, Heidelberg (2014). https://doi.org/10.1007/978-3-662-44371-2_27

14. Bormet, J., Dziembowski, S., Faust, S., Lizurej, T., Mielniczuk, M.: Strong secret sharing with snitching. Cryptology ePrint Archive, Paper 2025/1119 (2025)

15. Chabanne, H., Phan, D.H., Pointcheval, D.: Public traceability in traitor tracing schemes. In: Cramer, R. (ed.) EUROCRYPT 2005. LNCS, vol. 3494, pp. 542–558. Springer, Heidelberg (2005). https://doi.org/10.1007/11426639_32

16. Chaum, D., Crépeau, C., Damgård, I.: Multiparty unconditionally secure protocols (extended abstract). In: 20th ACM STOC, Chicago, IL, USA, pp. 11–19. ACM Press (1988)

17. Chen, Y., Vaikuntanathan, V., Waters, B., Wee, H., Wichs, D.: Traitor-tracing from LWE made simple and attribute-based. In: Beimel, A., Dziembowski, S. (eds.) TCC 2018. LNCS, vol. 11240, pp. 341–369. Springer, Cham (2018). https://doi.org/10.1007/978-3-030-03810-6_13

18. Desmedt, Y.: Society and group oriented cryptography: a new concept. In: Pomerance, C. (ed.) CRYPTO 1987. LNCS, vol. 293, pp. 120–127. Springer, Heidelberg (1988). https://doi.org/10.1007/3-540-48184-2_8

19. Desmedt, Y., Frankel, Y.: Threshold cryptosystems. In: Brassard, G. (ed.) CRYPTO 1989. LNCS, vol. 435, pp. 307–315. Springer, New York (1990). https://doi.org/10.1007/0-387-34805-0_28

20. Devadas, L., Jain, A., Waters, B., Wu, D.J.: Succinct witness encryption for batch languages and applications. In: ASIACRYPT (2025)

21. Do, X.T., Phan, D.H., Pointcheval, D.: Traceable inner product functional encryption. In: Jarecki, S. (ed.) CT-RSA 2020. LNCS, vol. 12006, pp. 564–585. Springer, Cham (2020). https://doi.org/10.1007/978-3-030-40186-3_24

22. Dodis, Y., Fazio, N.: Public key trace and revoke scheme secure against adaptive chosen ciphertext attack. In: Desmedt, Y.G. (ed.) PKC 2003. LNCS, vol. 2567, pp. 100–115. Springer, Heidelberg (2003). https://doi.org/10.1007/3-540-36288-6_8

23. Dziembowski, S., Faust, S., Lizurej, T., Mielniczuk, M.: Secret sharing with snitching. In: Luo, B., Liao, X., Xu, J., Kirda, E., Lie, D. (eds.) ACM CCS 2024, Salt Lake City, UT, USA, pp. 840–853. ACM Press (2024)

24. Farràs, O., Guiot, M.: Traceable secret sharing schemes for general access structures. Cryptology ePrint Archive, Paper 2025/1120 (2025)

25. Fiat, A., Tassa, T.: Dynamic traitor tracing. In: Wiener, M. (ed.) CRYPTO 1999. LNCS, vol. 1666, pp. 354–371. Springer, Heidelberg (1999). https://doi.org/10.1007/3-540-48405-1_23

26. Garg, S., Gentry, C., Halevi, S., Raykova, M., Sahai, A., Waters, B.: Candidate indistinguishability obfuscation and functional encryption for all circuits. In: 54th FOCS, Berkeley, CA, USA, pp. 40–49. IEEE Computer Society Press (2013)

27. Garg, S., Kumarasubramanian, A., Sahai, A., Waters, B.: Building efficient fully collusion-resilient traitor tracing and revocation schemes. In: Al-Shaer, E., Keromytis, A.D., Shmatikov, V. (eds.) ACM CCS 2010, Chicago, Illinois, USA, pp. 121–130. ACM Press (2010)

28. Goldreich, O., Levin, L.A.: A hard-core predicate for all one-way functions. In: 21st ACM STOC, Seattle, WA, USA, pp. 25–32. ACM Press (1989)

29. Goldreich, O., Micali, S., Wigderson, A.: How to play any mental game or A completeness theorem for protocols with honest majority. In: Aho, A. (eds.) 19th ACM STOC, New York City, NY, USA, pp. 218–229. ACM Press (1987)

30. Gong, J., Luo, J., Wee, H.: Traitor tracing with $N^{1/3}$-size ciphertexts and $O(1)$-size keys from k-Lin. In: Hazay, C., Stam, M. (eds.) EUROCRYPT 2023, Part III. LNCS, vol. 14006, pp. 637–668. Springer, Cham (2023)

31. Goyal, R., Koppula, V., Waters, B.: Collusion resistant traitor tracing from learning with errors. In: Diakonikolas, I., Kempe, D., Henzinger, M. (eds.) 50th ACM STOC, Los Angeles, CA, USA, pp. 660–670. ACM Press (2018)

32. Goyal, R., Koppula, V., Waters, B.: New approaches to traitor tracing with embedded identities. In: Hofheinz, D., Rosen, A. (eds.) TCC 2019. LNCS, vol. 11892, pp. 149–179. Springer, Cham (2019). https://doi.org/10.1007/978-3-030-36033-7_6

33. Goyal, R., Waters, B.: Personal communication (2025)

34. Goyal, V., Jain, A., Partap, A.: Traceable secret sharing revisited. Cryptology ePrint Archive, Paper 2025/1980 (2025)

35. Goyal, V., Song, Y., Srinivasan, A.: Traceable secret sharing and applications. In: Malkin, T., Peikert, C. (eds.) CRYPTO 2021. LNCS, vol. 12827, pp. 718–747. Springer, Cham (2021). https://doi.org/10.1007/978-3-030-84252-9_24

36. Hoffmann, C.: Traceable secret sharing based on the Chinese remainder theorem. Cryptology ePrint Archive, Report 2024/811 (2024)

37. Ito, M., Saito, A., Nishizeki, T.: Secret sharing schemes realizing general access structure. In: Proceedings of the IEEE Global Telecommunication Conference (Globecom 1987), pp. 99–102 (1987)

38. Jain, A., Jin, Z., Mathialagan, S., Paneth, O.: On succinct obfuscation via propositional proofs (or: how to use PV-IO). In: STOC 2025 (2025, to appear)

39. Jain, A., Lin, H., Sahai, A.: Indistinguishability obfuscation from well-founded assumptions. In: Khuller, S., Williams, V.V. (eds.) 53rd ACM STOC, Virtual Event, Italy, pp. 60–73. ACM Press (2021)

40. Jain, A., Lin, H., Sahai, A.: Indistinguishability obfuscation from LPN over $\mathbb{F}_p$, DLIN, and PRGs in NC^0. In: Dunkelman, O., Dziembowski, S. (eds.) EUROCRYPT 2022, Part I. LNCS, vol. 13275, pp. 670–699. Springer, Cham (2022)

41. Kiayias, A., Yung, M.: Self protecting pirates and black-box traitor tracing. In: Kilian, J. (ed.) CRYPTO 2001. LNCS, vol. 2139, pp. 63–79. Springer, Heidelberg (2001). https://doi.org/10.1007/3-540-44647-8_4

42. Koppula, V., Lewko, A.B., Waters, B.: Indistinguishability obfuscation for Turing machines with unbounded memory. In: Servedio, R.A., Rubinfeld, R. (eds.) 47th ACM STOC, Portland, OR, USA, pp. 419–428. ACM Press (2015)

43. Kurosawa, K., Desmedt, Y.: Optimum traitor tracing and asymmetric schemes. In: Nyberg, K. (ed.) EUROCRYPT 1998. LNCS, vol. 1403, pp. 145–157. Springer, Heidelberg (1998). https://doi.org/10.1007/BFb0054123

44. Leslie, M., Dutta, R.: A Traceable Threshold Asmuth–Bloom Secret Sharing Scheme. Cryptology ePrint Archive, Paper 2025/1561 (2025)

45. Lu, G., Nassar, S., Waters, B.: Succinct computational secret sharing for monotone circuits (2025)

46. Mignotte, M.: How to share a secret. In: Beth, T. (ed.) EUROCRYPT 1982. LNCS, vol. 149, pp. 371–375. Springer, Heidelberg (1983). https://doi.org/10.1007/3-540-39466-4_27

47. Naor, D., Naor, M., Lotspiech, J.: Revocation and tracing schemes for stateless receivers. In: Kilian, J. (ed.) CRYPTO 2001. LNCS, vol. 2139, pp. 41–62. Springer, Heidelberg (2001). https://doi.org/10.1007/3-540-44647-8_3

48. Naor, M., Pinkas, B.: Threshold traitor tracing. In: Krawczyk, H. (ed.) CRYPTO 1998. LNCS, vol. 1462, pp. 502–517. Springer, Heidelberg (1998). https://doi.org/10.1007/BFb0055750

49. Nishimaki, R., Wichs, D., Zhandry, M.: Anonymous traitor tracing: how to embed arbitrary information in a key. In: Fischlin, M., Coron, J.-S. (eds.) EUROCRYPT 2016. LNCS, vol. 9666, pp. 388–419. Springer, Heidelberg (2016). https://doi.org/10.1007/978-3-662-49896-5_14

50. Safavi-Naini, R., Wang, Y.: Sequential traitor tracing. In: Bellare, M. (ed.) CRYPTO 2000. LNCS, vol. 1880, pp. 316–332. Springer, Heidelberg (2000). https://doi.org/10.1007/3-540-44598-6_20

51. Shamir, A.: How to share a secret. Commun. Assoc. Comput. Mach. **22**(11), 612–613 (1979)

52. Vinod, V., Narayanan, A., Srinathan, K., Rangan, C.P., Kim, K.: On the power of computational secret sharing. In: Johansson, T., Maitra, S. (eds.) INDOCRYPT 2003. LNCS, vol. 2904, pp. 162–176. Springer, Heidelberg (2003). https://doi.org/10.1007/978-3-540-24582-7_12

53. Wee, H.: Functional encryption for quadratic functions from k-lin, revisited. In: Pass, R., Pietrzak, K. (eds.) TCC 2020. LNCS, vol. 12550, pp. 210–228. Springer, Cham (2020). https://doi.org/10.1007/978-3-030-64375-1_8

54. Zhandry, M.: New techniques for traitor tracing: size $N^{1/3}$ and more from pairings. In: Micciancio, D., Ristenpart, T. (eds.) CRYPTO 2020. LNCS, vol. 12170, pp. 652–682. Springer, Cham (2020). https://doi.org/10.1007/978-3-030-56784-2_22

55. Zhandry, M.: Optimal traitor tracing from pairings. In: Fehr, S., Fouque, P.-A. (eds.) EUROCRYPT 2025, Part III. LNCS, vol. 15603, pp. 305–335. Springer, Cham (2025)

Client-Server Homomorphic Secret Sharing in the CRS Model

Damiano Abram[1], Geoffroy Couteau[2], Lalita Devadas[3],
Aditya Hegde[4(✉)], Abhishek Jain[4,5], Lawrence Roy[6],
and Sacha Servan-Schreiber[7]

[1] University of Edinburgh, Edinburgh, UK
`abram.damiano@protonmail.com`
[2] CNRS, Université Paris Cité, Paris, France
`couteau@irif.fr`
[3] Massachusetts Institute of Technology, Cambridge, USA
`lali@mit.edu`
[4] Johns Hopkins University, Baltimore, USA
`{ahegde3,abhishek}@jhu.edu`
[5] NTT Research, Sunnyvale, USA
[6] Aarhus University, Aarhus, Denmark
[7] Tinfoil, San Francisco, USA
`sacha@tinfoil.sh`

Abstract. Homomorphic secret sharing (HSS) is a distributed analogue
of fully homomorphic encryption (FHE) where clients secret-share their
inputs among two (or more) servers, who then non-interactively compute additive shares of the function output. Unlike FHE, HSS enables
a distributed form of homomorphic computation from a broader set of
cryptographic assumptions.

All known multi-client HSS schemes require a correlated setup that is
used by the clients to share their inputs. In contrast, multi-client delegation of computation using *only* a CRS has been known from assumptions
that imply FHE since the introduction of multi-key FHE (Lopez-Alt et
al., STOC 2012).

We close this gap by providing the first construction of client-server
HSS in the CRS only model from DDH, DCR, and more. Our constructions subsume all existing variants of group-based HSS schemes, including public-key HSS (Boyle et al., Crypto 2016), succinct HSS (Abram
et al., Eurocrypt 2024), and multi-key HSS (Couteau et al., Eurocrypt
2025), and their applications.

1 Introduction

In a homomorphic secret sharing (HSS) [10] scheme for a function family $\mathcal{F}$,
a dealer can secret share its private input x among a set of servers such that
the servers can locally evaluate any function $f \in \mathcal{F}$ over their respective shares
to obtain additive shares of the function output $f(x)$. The key requirement is
succinctness, namely, the size of input and output shares is independent of the

© International Association for Cryptologic Research 2026
J. Daemen and E. Thomé (Eds.): EUROCRYPT 2026, LNCS 16543, pp. 64–93, 2026.
https://doi.org/10.1007/978-3-032-25324-8_3

description size of the function. HSS guarantees input privacy as long as at least one of the servers is honest.

HSS can be viewed as a distributed analogue of fully-homomorphic encryption [26], where the inputs are secret-shared rather than encrypted. In contrast to FHE that is known only from lattice-based assumptions [14,15,26,27] or indistinguishability obfuscation [3,16,30], HSS can be constructed from a broad set of standard assumptions [1,7,8,10,12,13,20,21,23,24,34,35]. This has enabled powerful applications such as private information retrieval [10,20,28], sublinear secure computation [10,17,19–21,23] and pseudorandom correlation generators [6,7] from assumptions not known to imply FHE.

Client-Server HSS. The basic version of HSS only supports computations over one private input. To enable computations over *multiple* inputs, Boyle et al. [12] initiated the study of *client-server* HSS where multiple clients can simultaneously secret-share their inputs to a set of servers. They investigated client-server HSS in a correlated setup model, where a trusted party samples a public key for the clients and evaluation keys for the servers. Using the common public key of the servers, all clients can share their inputs to the servers by encrypting them under the common public key. Subsequently, Abram et al. [1] proposed a *one-round* instantiation of the trusted setup in the common reference string (CRS) model. More recently, Couteau et al. [18] proposed an alternative construction where the servers first publish their public keys (that are sampled using a CRS), and then the clients use the server keys to compute their input shares.[1]

However, to date, all known constructions of client-server HSS either require a correlated setup with a trusted party, or an additional round of interaction. These limitations carry over to the many applications of client-server HSS.

This Work: Client-Server HSS with Just a CRS. In this work, we study client-server HSS in the CRS (*only*) model. Specifically, we eliminate the requirement of a correlated setup or extra interaction required in other schemes to generate a common public key. Instead, computation in our model proceeds similarly to basic (single-input) HSS while supporting many clients:

- **CRS Generation:** First, a CRS is sampled and published.
- **Input sharing:** Given only the CRS, each client shares its input with the servers.
- **Evaluation:** Upon receiving its shares from all clients, each server can locally (i.e., non-interactively) computes an additive share of the function output.

It is easy to see that this notion readily implies a *two-round* client-server secure computation protocol with succinct communication. Such a protocol is currently only known from multi-key fully homomorphic encryption [31,33] or spooky encryption [24]. The primary goal of this work is to broaden the set of assumptions that suffice for obtaining such protocols.

---

[1] Couteau et al. [18] also presented a *two*-party scheme in the CRS only model, where the evaluation must be performed by the input-providing parties i.e., clients and servers are the *same* entities. Unlike standard HSS, this scheme does not support delegation of computation.

1.1 Our Results

We now summarize our results.

Client-Server HSS. Our main result is a construction of multi-client, two-server HSS based on either of the following assumptions: DDH over prime order groups, DCR, or the extended hidden subgroup assumption over class groups. The latter assumption is a DDH-like assumption introduced in [2] and follows other standard variants of DDH. All our constructions support computing restricted multiplication straight-line (RMS) programs—which are sufficiently powerful to compute any function in the class NC^1—over the inputs of an unbounded, polynomial number of clients. The constructions from DCR and class groups have negligible correctness error while the one from DDH has an inverse-polynomial correctness error.

Theorem 1 (Informal). *Let λ be the security parameter. There exist the following instantiations of a client-server HSS scheme for evaluating polynomial size RMS programs over plaintext space of size $B := B(\lambda)$:*

1. *Under the DCR assumption, with a trusted setup, and negligible correctness error, for super-polynomial B.*
2. *Under the small exponent and the extended hidden subgroup assumption over class groups, with a transparent setup, and negligible correctness error, for super-polynomial B.*
3. *Under the DDH assumption over prime order cyclic groups, with a transparent setup, and inverse-polynomial correctness error, for polynomial B.*

Previously, client-server HSS in the CRS model for all polynomial-size circuits could be obtained from spooky encryption [24], which is currently only known from lattice-based assumptions or from obfuscation. Theorem 1 provides the first construction of such a primitive from an assumption not known to imply FHE, thus further extending the line of work initiated by Boyle et al. [10] of studying HSS as an alternative to FHE.

Client-Server *Succinct* HSS. In standard HSS, each share size grows with the input size. Recently, Abram et al. [2] introduced a new notion of *succinct* HSS, where clients can share large inputs $\mathbf{y}$ such that the size of one of the shares is *sublinear* in the size of $\mathbf{y}$. They constructed succinct HSS schemes in a correlated setup model that enable inner-product computations of the form $\langle P_{\mathsf{rms}}(\mathbf{x}), \mathbf{y}\rangle$, for "short" inputs $\mathbf{x} = (x_1, \ldots, x_m)$, long inputs $\mathbf{y} = (\mathbf{y}_1, \ldots, \mathbf{y}_m)$, and RMS programs P_{rms}.

Our second contribution is a construction of succinct client-server HSS, which removes the correlated setup from succinct HSS, and allows clients to share both short and large inputs only using the CRS. We instantiate succinct client-server HSS from the same set of assumptions as client-server HSS. Similar to client-server HSS, it supports evaluating over the inputs of an unbounded, polynomial number of clients.

Theorem 2 (Informal). *Let λ be the security parameter and $N := N(\lambda)$ be a polynomially-bounded length parameter. Under each of the three instantiations* *of client-server HSS from Theorem 1, there exists a succinct client-server HSS scheme that supports evaluating*

$$\langle P_{\mathsf{rms}}(x_1, \ldots, x_m), \ (\mathbf{y_1}, \ldots, \mathbf{y_m}) \rangle,$$

for polynomial size RMS programs P_{rms}, where each $x_i \in \mathbb{Z}$ and $\mathbf{y}_i \in \mathbb{Z}^N$ are shared by clients. In all instantiations, the size of the CRS as well as all input shares sent to one of the servers is $\mathcal{O}(\sqrt{N}) \cdot \mathsf{poly}(\lambda)$ bits.

In fact, we construct a more general variant of succinct client-server HSS where servers compute on clients' short private inputs and long *public* inputs. Specifically, all input shares sent to one server continue to remain sublinear in the length of the long inputs, but privacy of these inputs is not ensured against either server. The non-trivial property here is that only *one* of the servers receives the full description of the long inputs from the clients, yet both servers are able to compute secret shares of a function involving all client inputs. By relaxing the definition to compute over public inputs, we can support evaluation of a larger class of functions of the form $P_{\mathsf{rms}}(\mathbf{x}) \cdot C(\mathbf{y})$, where $\mathbf{x} = (x_1, \ldots, x_m)$ are private inputs, $\mathbf{y} = (\mathbf{y}_1, \ldots, \mathbf{y}_m)$ are public inputs, P_{rms} is an RMS program, and C is an arithmetic circuit over the integers.

Our instantiations of succinct client-server HSS for long public inputs have the same communication efficiency as the ones from Theorem 2 and additionally require the circular power-DDH assumption over the underlying group. In fact, the constructions from Theorem 2 follow as a special case of this variant.[2]

Application to Circuit-Succinct MPC. Theorem 1 immediately implies a two-round, multi-client, two-server MPC protocol for RMS programs with circuit-succinct communication (i..e, communication sublinear in the circuit size) from DCR and class groups. We can also obtain a similar protocol from DDH for NC^1, using known techniques [12] to handle the correctness error in our HSS scheme. These protocols support an arbitrary number of clients and two servers and achieves semi-honest security. Previously, such an MPC protocol was only known from spooky encryption [24].[3]

Application to Input-Succinct MPC. Theorem 2 implies a two-round, client-server MPC protocol with *input succinct* communication from the DCR and class group. More specifically, we obtain a multi-client, two-server MPC protocol for computing the same class of programs as in Theorem 2 where the communication to one of the servers is sublinear in the length of the clients' long inputs.

In particular, this yields a natural notion of *multi-client* Private Information Retrieval (PIR), where clients can perform *joint* queries on a private database shared across two servers (where one of the servers only holds a short digest).

---

[2] In the sequel, we refer to the public input variant as succinct client-server HSS.

[3] While the MPC protocol in [24] is not described in the client-server model, it can be easily adapted to this setting. The notion is also closely related to multi-key FHE, which is implied by spooky encryption.

Specifically, in this model, each client i generates a *local* query q_i, and the joint query q to the database is determined by evaluating a function f over the local queries, i.e., $q = f(q_1, \ldots, n)$, where n is the number of clients. Since our scheme supports an arbitrary NC^1 computation over the client inputs, we can also implement non-trivial access policies on the clients: each local query is now a tuple (a_i, q_i) and $q = f(q_1, \ldots, q_n)$ iff $P(a_1, \ldots, a_n)$ (and $\perp$ otherwise) where P is an access policy. Finally, in the non-private-database setting, it is easy to see that we can also support computations on the database (instead of simply fetching a particular record).

1.2 Organization

We provide a detailed technical overview of our results in Sect. 2. We present our client-server HSS scheme in Sect. 3 and our succinct client-server HSS scheme in Sect. 4. The remaining details are deferred to the full version.

2 Technical Overview

In this section, we provide a technical overview of our constructions. We begin in Sect. 2.1 by explaining the challenges involved in extending existing HSS constructions to the client-server setting. We then review relevant background in Sect. 2.2, and in Sect. 2.3 we present the main ideas underlying our construction of client-server HSS. Finally, in Sect. 2.4, we discuss how our techniques can be extended to obtain succinct client-server HSS.

2.1 Challenges in Building Client-Server HSS

We start by reviewing existing variants of HSS and identifying the key challenges in constructing client-server HSS. In particular, this will serve to highlight why only heavy building blocks like multi-key FHE are known to be sufficient for realizing client-server HSS in the CRS model.

Public-Key HSS. Public-key HSS, first introduced by Boyle et al. [10], allows two servers $\mathsf{S_A}$ and $\mathsf{S_B}$, to non-interactively compute on the inputs of multiple clients to obtain shares of the output. The scheme requires a correlated setup, where a trusted party generates a public pk and evaluation keys $\mathsf{ek_A}$ and $\mathsf{ek_B}$, one for each server. A client can use the public key pk to compute shares $\langle x \rangle_\mathsf{A}$ and $\langle x \rangle_\mathsf{B}$ of its input x, which it then sends to the respective servers. Each server then uses its evaluation key to locally compute on their input shares and obtain shares of the output.

The HSS scheme of Boyle et al. [11] fits a general template—that has subsequently been adopted by a number of works [1,8,12,34,35]—that is built around a public-key encryption scheme. In this template, the public key pk of the HSS scheme is simply the public key h of the underlying encryption scheme, and the evaluation keys are subtractive shares of the corresponding secret key s i.e.,

$ek_A - ek_B = s$. To share an input x, the client encrypts both x and $x \cdot s$ and sends the ciphertexts to the servers. Boyle et al. show that, given such input shares, the servers can then use their evaluation keys to jointly compute on the clients' inputs.

Our goal in this work is to allow clients to share their inputs with the two servers using only the CRS. The main challenge in removing the correlated setup is that the public-key HSS template fundamentally relies on all clients encrypting their inputs under a *single* key s. This common key is what allows the servers to perform non-interactive computation using their evaluation keys, which are shares of s. In the absence of a common public key, however, it is not clear how clients can share their inputs in a way that supports computation across all inputs. A recent work by Couteau et al. [18] addressed this exact problem in the *two-party* setting, which we describe next.

Two-key HSS. Couteau et al. [18] present a two-key HSS scheme[4] that allows any two parties to use the CRS to share their inputs with each other and compute shares of a function evaluated on their joint inputs. However, their scheme does not allow parties to delegate computation to servers. This is because, unlike public-key HSS, where both servers' input shares only contained ciphertexts, a party's own share of its input in two-key HSS includes private state that does not preserve privacy if revealed to the other party. This private state is nevertheless essential to realize *synchronization* of input shares, a mechanism that lies at the heart of the two-key HSS construction of Couteau et al. [18].

In more detail, the primary observation behind the two-key HSS construction is that it suffices for all input shares to be under the same key in order to apply the public-key HSS evaluation template. Motivated by this, the two-key HSS scheme takes the natural approach of having each party—denoted P_A and P_B— independently generate their own key pair (h_A, s_A) and (h_B, s_B) using the CRS, and then share their inputs under their locally generated key. The main technical contribution in [18] is a procedure that allows parties to non-interactively *synchronize* these input shares to obtain encryptions of x and $x \cdot s_{AB}$ under a shared secret key s_{AB}. After synchronization, the situation is identical to the public-key HSS template: for every input x, the parties hold ciphertexts of x and $x \cdot s_{AB}$, together with evaluation keys that are shares of s_{AB}. This allows the parties to directly apply the public-key HSS evaluation template to compute shares of the output.

However, synchronizing an input x shared by P_A requires P_B to use its secret key s_B, and P_A to use the randomness r sampled for sharing x. This poses a challenge to use this approach for client-server HSS even in the simpler two-client setting: revealing s_B to the servers would compromise the privacy of P_B's inputs, while revealing r would compromise the privacy of x, since r is the randomness used in its sharing. Thus, applying the synchronization procedure as is in the client-server setting does not appear viable.

---

[4] [18] refer to it as multi-key HSS; we use two-key HSS to distinguish it from the client-server setting.

Barriers to Delegating Synchronization. A natural question, however, is if we can "delegate" the synchronization step in two-key HSS while preserving privacy; this would allow servers to synchronize the input shares sent by all clients and then use the public-key HSS template for evaluation. To investigate this, we start by sketching a simplified version of the synchronization step in the two-key HSS construction, which remains equivalent to the one described in [18].

Consider a cyclic abelian group $\mathbb{G}$ with generator g. Let B be a positive integer so that g^r for $r \leftarrow \mathbb{Z}_B$ is statistically close to a uniformly random group element. Let f denote the generator of a subgroup $F \subseteq \mathbb{G}$ over which computing discrete logarithms is computationally easy.[5] Recall that in the two-key HSS construction, each party P_σ first locally generates a key pair (h_σ, s_σ), where the public-key $h_\sigma = g^{-s_\sigma}$. To share its input x, P_A sends an ElGamal encryption of x under its public key h_A, namely

$$\left(g^r, h_\mathsf{A}^r \cdot f^x\right) = \left(g^r, g^{-s_\mathsf{A} \cdot r} \cdot f^x\right),$$

where $r \leftarrow \mathbb{Z}_B$. Similarly, it also sends an encryption of $x \cdot s_\mathsf{A}$. The synchronization step in the two-key HSS construction yields ElGamal-style encryptions of $x \cdot s_\mathsf{A}$, $x \cdot s_\mathsf{B}$, and x under the joint key $s_\mathsf{AB} = (s_\mathsf{A}, s_\mathsf{B})$. This means that each synchronized ciphertext consists of three group elements (g_1, g_2, g_3), such that $g_1^{s_\mathsf{A}} \cdot g_2^{s_\mathsf{B}} \cdot g_3 = f^z$, where z is the underlying plaintext. The encryptions of x and $x \cdot s_\mathsf{A}$ sent by P_A can be decrypted using s_A, and therefore trivially constitute an encryption under the joint key s_AB.

Unsurprisingly, the main technical challenge is synchronizing to an encryption of $x \cdot s_\mathsf{B}$ since neither party knows both x and s_B. To do this, parties use the above encryption of x sent by P_A, and compute the following:

$$\mathsf{P}_\mathsf{A} \text{ computes:} \quad \left((h_\mathsf{B})^{-r}, g^{-s_\mathsf{A} \cdot r} \cdot f^x, g^0\right) = \left(g^{s_\mathsf{B} \cdot r}, g^{-s_\mathsf{A} \cdot r} \cdot f^x, g^0\right)$$

$$\mathsf{P}_\mathsf{B} \text{ computes:} \quad \left((g^r)^{s_\mathsf{B}}, g^{-s_\mathsf{A} \cdot r} \cdot f^x, g^0\right) = \left(g^{s_\mathsf{B} \cdot r}, g^{-s_\mathsf{A} \cdot r} \cdot f^x, g^0\right),$$

where P_A obtains P_B's public key h_B as part of its input share. The terms highlighted in red indicate the private values used by each party for synchronization. It is easy to see that the synchronized ciphertext yields $f^{x \cdot s_\mathsf{B}}$ when decrypted using the joint key $s_\mathsf{AB} = (s_\mathsf{A}, s_\mathsf{B})$.

Thus, synchronization ultimately reduces to computing $g^{s_\mathsf{B} \cdot r}$. It is this step in the two-key HSS scheme that crucially relies on parties using private state and is the main barrier in extending this approach to the client-server setting. Intuitively, the computation of $g^{s_\mathsf{B} \cdot r}$ can be viewed as a non-interactive key exchange (NIKE) between P_A holding r, and P_B holding s_B. Privately delegating this computation to the servers seems to amount to a three-party NIKE. Indeed,

---

[5] Concretely, $\mathbb{G}$ can be viewed as the Paillier group, corresponding to the subgroup of quadratic residues of $\mathbb{Z}_{N^2}^*$, for a sufficiently large modulus N that is a product of safe-primes.

we conjecture synchronization can be delegated using tools such as pairings, which are known to imply three-party NIKE. However, this would fall short of our goal of realizing client-server HSS from a broad class of group-based assumptions. For this reason, we depart from synchronization entirely and pursue a different approach for HSS evaluation.

Our Approach. In our client-server HSS construction, each client uses the CRS to locally generate a key pair, which it then uses to share its input—similar to two-key HSS. However, in light of the challenges to extending synchronization to the client-server setting, we move away from the approach of two-key HSS and do not attempt to apply the public-key HSS evaluation template. Instead, we take a step back and ask the following question:

Can we design an alternative approach to HSS evaluation
that does not require all inputs to be encrypted under the same key?

Such an approach would eliminate the need to synchronize input shares. In fact, since client-server HSS subsumes both public-key HSS and two-key HSS, this would yield a more general approach to evaluation compared to the public-key HSS template. Our main technical contribution is providing a positive answer to this question.

We next review relevant background in Sect. 2.2—which readers familiar with prior works may safely skip—and then proceed to the key ideas underlying our construction in Sect. 2.3.

2.2 Background

In this section, we briefly recall the template for public-key HSS evaluation and the primitives it relies on.

Instantiating the Group. As mentioned earlier, we consider a cyclic abelian group $\mathbb{G}$ with generator g. Let B be a positive integer so that g^r for $r \leftarrow \mathbb{Z}_B$ is statistically close to a uniformly random group element. Let f denote the generator of a subgroup $F \subseteq \mathbb{G}$ over which computing discrete logarithms is computationally easy. Concretely, this abstraction captures the Paillier group, where $\mathbb{G}$ is the subgroup of quadratic residues of $\mathbb{Z}^*_{N^{(\nu+1)}}$, for a positive integer ν and a sufficiently large modulus N that is a product of safe-primes. This abstraction also extends to class groups and prime-order cyclic groups, modulo some technical refinements. We assume that a suitable subgroup indistinguishability assumption holds over $\mathbb{G}$ (e.g., DDH in prime order cyclic groups or DCR over the Pailler group, or similar assumptions in class groups).

Distributed Discrete Logarithm. A central tool in building HSS is the distributed discrete logarithm (DDLog) procedure which ensures that for divisive shares $g_1, g_2 \in \mathbb{G}$ of a value x, such that $g_1/g_2 = f^x$,

$$\mathsf{DDLog}(g_1) - \mathsf{DDLog}(g_2) = x.$$

That is, DDLog transforms divisive shares over the group to subtractive shares over the integers. Known DDLog procedures require the value x to lie within a bounded range to guarantee that the outputs are subtractive shares over the integers. This bound is super-polynomial for Paillier and class groups, and polynomial for prime-order cyclic groups. In the latter case, DDLog additionally incurs a (tunable) inverse-polynomial correctness error. For the purpose of this overview, we set these technical details aside and return to them later.

Distributed Decryption. The core of public-key HSS evaluation centers around using DDLog together with a public-key encryption scheme with "exponent-linear" decryption to enable distributed decryption of ciphertexts. Specifically, let (h, s) be a key pair such that $h = g^{-s}$. An ElGamal encryption of x under h is of the form $(g^r, h^r \cdot f^x) = (g^r, g^{-s \cdot r} \cdot f^x)$. Observe that decryption is linear in the secret key since $(g^r)^s \cdot h^r \cdot f^x = f^x$, at which point we can obtain x by computing discrete log with respect to f.

Now, consider two servers $\mathsf{S_A}$ and $\mathsf{S_B}$, such that they hold subtractive shares of $y \cdot \mathsf{sk}$, where $\mathsf{sk} = (s, 1)$. Specifically, each server S_σ holds a tuple $[y \cdot \mathsf{sk}]_\sigma$ such that $[y \cdot \mathsf{sk}]_\mathsf{A} - [y \cdot \mathsf{sk}]_\mathsf{B} = y \cdot \mathsf{sk} = (y \cdot s, y)$. Given the above ElGamal ciphertext, each server S_σ can locally carry out decryption using its share to obtain

$$(g^r)^{[y \cdot s]_\sigma} \cdot (h^r \cdot f^x)^{[y]_\sigma} = g^{[0]_\sigma} \cdot f^{[xy]_\sigma},$$

which constitutes a divisive share of xy since $[y \cdot \mathsf{sk}]_\sigma$ are subtractive shares of $y \cdot \mathsf{sk}$. Consequently, each server can compute

$$[xy]_\sigma := \mathsf{DDLog}(g^{[0]_\sigma} \cdot f^{[xy]_\sigma})$$

to obtain subtractive shares of the product xy. Thus, given an encryption of x, the servers can exploit linearity of decryption and use shares of the secret key "pre-multiplied" by a value y to non-interactively compute subtractive shares of the product xy.

Distributed Evaluation of RMS Programs. In group-based public-key HSS schemes, following the template introduced by Boyle et al., the public key of the HSS scheme is a public key h of the underlying encryption scheme and the evaluation keys correspond to subtractive shares of the corresponding secret key s i.e., $\mathsf{ek_A} - \mathsf{ek_B} = s$. During evaluation, each server S_σ computes over two types of shares: (1) *Input shares* $\langle x \rangle_\sigma$ provided by clients that consist of an encryption of $x \cdot s$ and x, and (2) *Memory shares* $[y \cdot \mathsf{sk}]_\sigma$, where $\mathsf{sk} = (s, 1)$, that form subtractive shares of $y \cdot \mathsf{sk}$. They perform two types of operations on these shares:

– **Addition:** Locally add two memory shares

$$[x \cdot \mathsf{sk}]_\sigma + [y \cdot \mathsf{sk}]_\sigma = [(x + y) \cdot \mathsf{sk}]_\sigma = \left([(x + y) \cdot s]_\sigma, [x + y]_\sigma \right),$$

where the equality follows from linearity of the subtractive sharing.

– **Restricted Multiplication:** Multiply an input share $\langle x \rangle_\sigma$ with a memory share $[y \cdot \mathsf{sk}]_\sigma$ to obtain a memory share of the product $[xy \cdot \mathsf{sk}]_\sigma$. To achieve this, the servers apply the distributed decryption procedure: using $[y \cdot \mathsf{sk}]_\sigma$, they decrypt the ciphertexts of x and $x \cdot s$ to obtain $[xy]_\sigma$ and $[xy \cdot \mathsf{sk}]_\sigma$, respectively. These values together constitute the desired memory shares $[xy \cdot \mathsf{sk}]_\sigma$.

Since the evaluation keys correspond to shares of the secret key s, the servers hold a memory share of 1. They can thus compute memory shares of each input by multiplying the input share with the memory share of 1. This allows the servers to carry out an arbitrary sequence of the above operations on the inputs to eventually obtain memory shares of the output $[z \cdot \mathsf{sk}]_\sigma$, which by definition contains subtractive shares of the output $[z]_\sigma$. A sequence of the above instructions is called a restricted multiplication straight-line (RMS) program and is precisely the class of computation supported by existing group-based HSS schemes. It is known that the RMS programs contain branching programs and thus NC^1 circuits.

2.3   Building Client-Server HSS

We now turn to the key ideas underlying our client-server HSS construction. Recall that a client-server HSS scheme allows a set of clients $\{\mathsf{P}_1, \ldots, \mathsf{P}_m\}$, each holding an input x_i, to share their inputs with two servers S_A and S_B using only the CRS, so that the servers can non-interactively compute shares of a function evaluated on the joint inputs.

We start by having each client P_i use the CRS to locally generate a key pair (h_i, s_i), which it then uses to share its input x_i. As a first step towards supporting distributed evaluation of RMS programs, we define memory shares of y held by server S_σ as $[y \cdot \mathsf{sk}]_\sigma$, where $\mathsf{sk} = (s_1, \ldots, s_m, 1)$. The main challenge towards realizing client-server HSS is enabling servers to non-interactively multiply their input shares of x with memory shares of y to obtain memory shares of the product xy. If this can be achieved, obtaining memory shares of 1 is straightforward: each client P_i simply sends a subtractive share of its secret key $[s_i]_\sigma$ to server S_σ. With this in place, RMS programs can be evaluated on the inputs by first converting input shares into memory shares through multiplication with 1, as described in Sect. 2.2.

Thus, for the remainder of this discussion, we focus on how clients can share their inputs so that servers can multiply input shares with memory shares. For clarity, we first consider the case of two clients P_1 and P_2, and focus on how S_σ can multiply the input share $\langle x \rangle_\sigma$ sent by P_1 with a memory share of y in order to obtain the memory share of the product $[xy \cdot \mathsf{sk}]_\sigma = ([xy \cdot s_1]_\sigma, [xy \cdot s_2]_\sigma, [xy]_\sigma)$. In particular, the challenge lies in computing $[xy \cdot s_2]_\sigma$: the remaining components of the memory share are straightforward to compute by having P_1 include encryptions of $x \cdot s_1$ and x under its public key h_1 in its input share. As we will see later, the solution naturally extends to more than two clients.

Non-interactive Multiplication. The key component of our solution for computing shares of $xy \cdot s_2$ is a technique for non-interactive multiplication (NIM), first introduced in [25], and later applied in the HSS setting in [2].[6] NIM allows two parties, P_1 and P_2, holding private inputs v_1 and v_2 respectively, to compute shares of the product $v_1 v_2$ with a single simultaneous message to each other. Specifically, given a random group element $g_1 \in \mathbb{G}$ as part of the CRS, the parties proceed as follows:

1. **Input Encoding:** P_1 samples $r \leftarrow \mathbb{Z}_B$ and sends $(g_1^r,\ g^r \cdot f^{v_1})$ to P_2. P_2 samples $u \leftarrow \mathbb{Z}_B$ and sends $g_1^u \cdot g^{v_2}$ to P_1.
2. **Decoding:** Upon receiving the other party's message, each party computes

$$
\begin{aligned}
P_1: \quad & \gamma_1 := \left(g_1^u \cdot g^{v_2}\right)^r, & [v_1 v_2]_1 := \mathsf{DDLog}(\gamma_1) \\
P_2: \quad & \gamma_2 := \left(g_1^r\right)^u \cdot \left(g^r \cdot f^{v_1}\right)^{v_2} & [v_1 v_2]_2 := \mathsf{DDLog}(\gamma_2).
\end{aligned}
$$

It is easy to see that γ_2 and γ_1 constitute divisive shares of $v_1 v_2$ since

$$
\frac{\gamma_2}{\gamma_1} = \frac{g_1^{ru} \cdot g^{r v_2} \cdot f^{v_1 v_2}}{g_1^{ur} \cdot g^{v_2 r}} = f^{v_1 v_2},
$$

which in turn implies that $[v_1 v_2]_2 - [v_1 v_2]_1 = v_1 v_2$ constitute subtractive shares of $v_1 v_2$. Privacy of v_2 follows from the fact that g_1^u is (statistically close to) a random group element. Privacy of v_1 intuitively follows from the fact that the discrete log of g_1 with respect to g is hard to compute, and can formally be reduced to the hardness of a suitable subgroup indistinguishability assumption over $\mathbb{G}$.

This construction naturally generalizes to support computing inner-products of vectors held by the parties, with the advantage that the communication from P_2 to P_1 continues to remain a single group element, independent of the length of the vector. It is precisely this succinctness property of NIM that motivated its use in prior works [2,25]. However, for the purpose of constructing client-server HSS, succinctness is not the property we rely on. Instead, the key observation we make is that the decoding procedure of NIM—specifically computation of γ_1 and γ_2—is *linear* in the messages received (highlighted in red above). This linearity allows us to *delegate decoding* to the servers while preserving the privacy of the clients' inputs: given encodings of P_1's input v_1 and P_2's input v_2, each server S_σ can use shares of r, u, and v_2 to compute divisive shares of $v_1 v_2$, which can then be converted to subtractive shares using DDLog.

Leveraging NIM Delegation. We show that the ability to delegate NIM enables the servers to compute shares of $xy \cdot s_2$. At a high level, the servers compute a NIM between P_1's input x and P_2's secret key s_2. Because the decoding procedure is linear, if the shares used for decoding are "pre-multiplied" by y, the servers directly obtain shares of $xy \cdot s_2$.

---

[6] [2] refer to this primitive as half-chosen VOLE. We adopt the term NIM from [9] as it better reflects its role in our construction.

Before proceeding, we note that since P_2 encodes its secret key, the NIM encoding can be simplified. In particular, P_2 no longer needs to sample u to mask its input and can instead simply send g^{s_2}; this is secure because g^{s_2} is just the inverse of its public key $h_2 = g^{-s_2}$. This simplification also carries over to P_1's encoding: it now suffices for P_1 to send $g^r \cdot f^x$.

The servers having obtained the above NIM encodings from the clients, will require shares of $y \cdot s_2$ and $y \cdot r$ to perform the decoding. While each server holds $[y \cdot s_2]_\sigma$ as part of its memory share of y, they do not have shares of $y \cdot r$. Indeed, if the servers had such a sharing, then each server S_σ could locally compute

$$\frac{(g^r \cdot f^x)^{[y \cdot s_2]_\sigma}}{(g^{s_2})^{[y \cdot r]_\sigma}} = g^{[0]_\sigma} \cdot f^{[xy \cdot s_2]_\sigma},$$

which can then be converted into subtractive shares $[xy \cdot s_2]_\sigma$ using the DDLog procedure.

At first glance, it's unclear if we have made any progress; we seem to have merely shifted the problem from computing shares of $xy \cdot s_2$ to computing shares of $y \cdot r$. However, this shift is crucial. The term $xy \cdot s_2$ requires combining y with inputs originating from two different clients—namely, x from P_1 and s_2 from P_2. In contrast, $y \cdot r$ involves only the product of y with r, where r is known to P_1. Indeed, it suffices for P_1 to encrypt r under its public key h_1: since each server holds $[y \cdot s_1]_\sigma$ as part of its memory share of y, it can then perform a distributed decryption of this ciphertext, as described in Sect. 2.2, to obtain $[y \cdot r]_\sigma$. Using this share, the servers can compute $[xy \cdot s_2]_\sigma$, as described above. With this, the servers can non-interactively multiply their input shares with their memory shares, which in turn allows computing RMS programs on the clients' inputs.

Client-Server HSS. To summarize, our approach for HSS evaluation is centered around the linear decoding of NIM. As we show below, this solution immediately extends to multiple clients. Specifically, we reduce multiplying an input share of x with a memory share of y, to computing a NIM between x and the secret key s_i of every client P_i. The linear decoding property of NIM allows clients to delegate the NIM to the servers, while preserving the privacy of their inputs. To allow the servers to carry out the NIM decoding, the client P_j that shares the input x, additionally provides an encryption of the randomness r it used to encode its input. Each server first uses its memory share to perform a distributed decryption of this ciphertext and obtain $[y \cdot r]_\sigma$. This then allows the server to decode the NIM between x and s_i, to obtain the share $[xy \cdot s_i]_\sigma$, where linearity of the decoding ensures that the output is pre-multiplied with y. We next provide a full sketch of the construction in the multi-client setting.

- **Input Encoding:** To share its input x_i, each client P_i locally generates a key pair (h_i, s_i), where $h_i = g^{-s_i}$. It then computes

$$\mathsf{enc} := g^r \cdot f^{x_i}, \qquad \mathsf{rct} := \left(g^u, h_i^u \cdot f^r\right),$$

and subtractive shares $[s_i] = ([s_i]_\mathsf{A}, [s_i]_\mathsf{B})$. It sends $\langle x_i \rangle_\mathsf{A} = ([s_i]_\mathsf{A}, h_i, \mathsf{enc}, \mathsf{rct})$ to S_A and $\langle x_i \rangle_\mathsf{B} = ([s_i]_\mathsf{B}, h_i, \mathsf{enc}, \mathsf{rct})$ to S_B.

- **Evaluation:** S_A and S_B set their memory share of 1 to $[\![1]\!]_A := (1, [s_1]_A, \ldots, [s_m]_A)$ and $[\![1]\!]_B := (0, [s_1]_B, \ldots, [s_m]_B)$, respectively. They evaluate each instruction as follows.
  - **Addition:** Each S_σ adds two memory shares by computing $[\![x + y]\!]_\sigma := [\![x]\!]_\sigma + [\![y]\!]_\sigma$.
  - **Multiplication:** To multiply the input share $\langle x_i \rangle_\sigma$ with $[\![y]\!]_\sigma = ([y]_\sigma, [y \cdot s_1]_\sigma, \ldots, [y \cdot s_m]_\sigma)$, each S_σ does the following.

1: It decrypts rct to obtain $[y \cdot r]_\sigma$, by computing

$$g^{[0]_\sigma} \cdot f^{[y \cdot r]_\sigma} := (g^u)^{[y \cdot s_i]_\sigma} \cdot (h_i^u \cdot f^r)^{[y]_\sigma}, \quad \text{and}$$

$$[y \cdot r]_\sigma := \mathsf{DDLog}\left(g^{[0]_\sigma} \cdot f^{[y \cdot r]_\sigma}\right).$$

2: For each client P_j, it uses enc_i and h_j to decode the NIM between x_i and s_j as

$$g^{[0]_\sigma} \cdot f^{[x_i y \cdot s_j]_\sigma} := (g^r \cdot f^{x_i})^{[y \cdot s_j]_\sigma} \cdot h_j^{[y \cdot r]_\sigma}, \quad \text{and}$$

$$[x_i y \cdot s_j]_\sigma := \mathsf{DDLog}\left(g^{[0]_\sigma} \cdot f^{[x_i y \cdot s_j]_\sigma}\right),$$

to obtain the share $[x_i y \cdot s_j]_\sigma$.

3: It obtains $[x_i y]_\sigma$ by decoding a NIM between x_i and 1, by computing

$$g^{[0]_\sigma} \cdot f^{[x_i y]_\sigma} := (g^r \cdot f^{x_i})^{[y]_\sigma} \cdot g^{-[y \cdot r]_\sigma}, \quad \text{and}$$

$$[x_i y]_\sigma := \mathsf{DDLog}\left(g^{[0]_\sigma} \cdot f^{[x_i y]_\sigma}\right).$$

4: It sets the memory share of the product

$$[\![x_i y]\!]_\sigma := ([x_i y]_\sigma, [x_i y \cdot s_1]_\sigma, \ldots, [x_i y \cdot s_m]_\sigma).$$

Tying Up Loose Ends. Our discussion so far has ignored the fact that the DDLog procedure requires its input to lie within a bounded range in order to guarantee that the outputs are valid subtractive shares over the integers. In our construction, this condition translates to requiring that, for each memory value y, both $y \cdot r$ and $y \cdot s$ fall within the bound, where r is the randomness used for NIM and s is a secret key. When instantiated over the Paillier group, the DDLog bound can be made exponentially larger in the security parameter than the bounds on r and s, which in turn allows evaluating RMS programs on any input whose memory value does not exceed an exponentially large bound. For our class-group instantiation, we additionally rely on the small-exponent assumption to guarantee that r and s remain exponentially smaller than the DDLog bound, thereby once again supporting the evaluation of RMS programs with exponentially large bounds. In case of prime order cyclic groups, where DDLog only supports polynomially bounded values, we use the BHHO [5] encryption scheme. This increases the length of the secret key but ensures that each component is a single bit, and our construction naturally extends to handle longer keys. The randomness r, however, remains large; to address this, we encrypt each bit of r individually. Finally, the inverse-polynomial error of DDLog in this setting translates to a noticeable error for the client-server HSS. We present the full construction in Sect. 3.2.

2.4 Succinct Client-Server HSS

We conclude by providing an overview of our succinct client-server HSS construction.

Client-Server HSS allows clients to share their private inputs among two servers such that the servers can non-interactively compute on the joint inputs. If a client has multiple inputs $\mathbf{x} = (x_1, \ldots, x_m)$, it can share each input x_i separately, but the size of the resulting input share grows linearly with the number of inputs $|\mathbf{x}|$. Succinct client-server HSS extends client-server HSS to additionally support evaluation on long *public* inputs of the clients such that the communication to one of the servers $\mathsf{S_B}$ is sublinear in the length of the input.[7] In particular, we construct succinct client-server HSS for computing $P_{\mathsf{rms}}(x_1, \ldots, x_{m_1}) \cdot \mathsf{C}(\mathbf{y}_1, \ldots, \mathbf{y}_{m_2})$, where P_{rms} is an RMS program, C is an arithmetic circuit over the integers, and the inputs are defined and shared as follows.

- **Private Inputs:** The client holding $x_i \in \mathbb{Z}$ computes the input shares $\langle x_i \rangle_\mathsf{A}$ and $\langle x_i \rangle_\mathsf{B}$ using the CRS and sends it to the respective servers, as in the scheme of Sect. 2.3. Each share $\langle x_i \rangle_\sigma$ ensures that the input x_i remains private to S_σ.
- **Public Inputs:** The client holding $\mathbf{y}_i \in \mathbb{Z}^N$ computes a hash of its input d using the CRS and sends $(\mathbf{y}_i, \mathsf{d})$ to $\mathsf{S_A}$ and only d to $\mathsf{S_B}$. Note, however, that the input remains public: $\mathsf{S_A}$ receives $\mathbf{y}_i$ in the clear, and d is not required to preserve the privacy of $\mathbf{y}_i$.

The size of each d as well as each input share $\langle x_i \rangle_\sigma$ is sublinear in N, which in turn ensures that communication to $\mathsf{S_B}$ is succinct.

Computing on Long Private Inputs. Succinct client-server HSS already provides a non-trivial property by allowing computation on even public inputs of clients while ensuring succinct communication. Nevertheless, we note that it can also be used to compute a smaller class of functions on long private inputs of clients. Specifically, to compute $\sum_{i=1}^{N} P_{\mathsf{rms}}^{(i)}(x_1, \ldots, x_m) \cdot \mathbf{y}^{(i)}$, where $\mathbf{y}^{(i)}$ denotes the i-th component of $\mathbf{y}$, the client holding $\mathbf{y}$ samples a PRG seed k and uses it to mask its input as $\mathbf{c} := \mathbf{y} - \mathbf{u}$, where $\mathbf{u} = \mathsf{PRG}(k)$. It then uses $\mathbf{c}$ as its long input and shares the PRG seed k as its short private input. Now, observe that to compute shares of $P_{\mathsf{rms}}^{(i)}(x_1, \ldots, x_m) \cdot \mathbf{y}^{(i)}$, it suffices for servers to compute shares of $P_{\mathsf{rms}}^{(i)}(x_1, \ldots, x_m) \cdot \mathbf{c}^{(i)}$ and $P_{\mathsf{rms}}^{(i)}(x_1, \ldots, x_m) \cdot \mathbf{u}^{(i)}$, since

---

[7] Note that it is information theoretically impossible to have communication to both servers be sublinear in the length of the input.

$$P_{\mathsf{rms}}^{(i)}(x_1, \ldots, x_m) \cdot \mathbf{c}^{(i)} + P_{\mathsf{rms}}^{(i)}(x_1, \ldots, x_m) \cdot \mathbf{u}^{(i)}$$
$$= P_{\mathsf{rms}}^{(i)}(x_1, \ldots, x_m) \cdot (\mathbf{y}^{(i)} - \mathbf{u}^{(i)} + \mathbf{u}^{(i)})$$
$$= P_{\mathsf{rms}}^{(i)}(x_1, \ldots, x_m) \cdot \mathbf{y}^{(i)}.$$

Succinct client-server HSS supports computing shares of both these values since servers receive input shares of the PRG seed k—specifically, servers can compute shares of $P_{\mathsf{rms}}^{(i)}(x_1, \ldots, x_m) \cdot \mathbf{c}^{(i)}$ directly using the primitive and they can compute shares of $P_{\mathsf{rms}}^{(i)}(x_1, \ldots, x_m) \cdot \mathbf{u}^{(i)}$ by evaluating a modified function on the private inputs that first expands the PRG seed k to compute $\mathbf{u}^{(i)}$ and then computes $P_{\mathsf{rms}}^{(i)}(x_1, \ldots, x_m) \cdot \mathbf{u}^{(i)}$. As long as the PRG can be evaluated by an RMS program, it is not too difficult to show that the modified function can be computed by an RMS program too. Because the servers obtain subtractive shares of the output, which are linear, it is straightforward to extend this hybrid encryption technique to compute an inner-product between the long private inputs of clients and RMS programs evaluated on the short inputs. Finally, using techniques introduced by Behera et al. [4], this idea can be extended to support computing polynomially bounded Waring rank functions on the long private inputs of clients.

Building Succinct Client-Server HSS. The starting point of our succinct construction is the client-server HSS scheme described in Sect. 2.3. The client-server HSS construction allows clients to share their private inputs with servers, who can then evaluate RMS programs on the joint inputs and obtain shares of $P_{\mathsf{rms}}(x_1, \ldots, x_{m_1})$. To do so, the servers first convert input shares into memory shares by multiplying with a memory share of 1. As observed by Couteau et al. [22], if the servers already hold a memory share of some value z, they can instead use this for the conversion, which amounts to evaluating the RMS program on the inputs pre-multiplied by z. As a result, the servers obtain shares of $P_{\mathsf{rms}}(x_1, \ldots, x_{m_1}) \cdot z$. Thus, to build succinct client-server HSS it suffices for each server S_σ to compute a memory share of the circuit C evaluated on the long public inputs, namely $[\mathsf{C}(\mathbf{y}_1, \ldots, \mathbf{y}_{m_2}) \cdot \mathsf{sk}]_\sigma$, where $\mathsf{sk} = (s_1, \ldots, s_{m_1}, 1)$ are the secret keys used to share the private inputs. Note that our goal is for the servers to compute this while ensuring succinct communication to S_B.

We observe that exploiting the *succinctness* of NIM, as in prior works [2,25], together with its linear decoding property, provides a way for servers to obtain shares of $\mathbf{y} \cdot s$ for every long input $\mathbf{y}$ and each secret key s used to encrypt a private input. In particular, NIM succinctness ensures that the hash d and each input share $\langle x \rangle_\sigma$ is succinct, while the linear decoding property allows servers to carry out the NIM decoding, while preserving privacy of the private inputs. Given shares of $\mathbf{y}_i \cdot s$, where the server S_A knows each long input $\mathbf{y}_i$ in the clear, we can leverage techniques introduced in recent works [29,32] to enable servers to compute $\mathsf{C}(\mathbf{y}_1, \ldots, \mathbf{y}_{m_2}) \cdot s$. Specifically, Ishai et al. [29] introduce a primitive called *algebraic homomorphic MACs* (aHMAC) which allows two parties that holds shares of $\mathbf{y} \cdot s$, where one of the parties also holds $\mathbf{y}$ in the clear, to compute shares of $\mathsf{C}(\mathbf{y}) \cdot s$. While these works [29,32] introduce these techniques in the context of garbling, where one party wishes to compute its output share before learning the inputs, we observe that they can be leveraged in our setting too. Equipped with aHMACs, the servers can compute shares of $C(\mathbf{y}_1, \ldots, \mathbf{y}_{m_2}) \cdot s$ for each secret key s used to encrypt a private input. Since S_A can also compute $C(\mathbf{y}_1, \ldots, \mathbf{y}_{m_2})$ in the clear, each server S_σ obtains the memory share $[C(\mathbf{y}_1, \ldots, \mathbf{y}_{m_2}) \cdot \mathsf{sk}]_\sigma$. This can then be used with client-server HSS to compute $P_{\mathsf{rms}}(x_1, \ldots, x_{m_1}) \cdot C(\mathbf{y}_1, \ldots, \mathbf{y}_{m_2})$, as discussed earlier.

We conclude by sketching how succinctness of NIM allows servers to compute shares of $\mathbf{y} \cdot s$, for a long input $\mathbf{y} \in \mathbb{Z}^N$ held by P_1 and a secret key $s \in \mathbb{Z}$ held by P_2. First, we describe how servers can compute shares of an inner-product between n-length vectors $\mathbf{y}$ and $\mathbf{x}$, held by two clients, P_1 and P_2, respectively. We then extend this to compute shares of $\mathbf{y} \cdot s$, while ensuring messages sent by both clients to S_B are succinct. To compute shares of the inner-product, given n random group elements $g_1, \ldots, g_n \in \mathbb{G}$ in the CRS, P_1 and P_2 compute d and enc as

$$\mathsf{d} := \prod_{i=1}^{n} g_i^{y_i}, \quad \text{and} \quad \mathsf{enc} := \left(g_1^r \cdot f^{x_1}, \ldots, g_n^r \cdot f^{x_n}\right),$$

where y_i and x_i denote the i-th component of $\mathbf{y}$ and $\mathbf{x}$, and P_2 samples $r \leftarrow \mathbb{Z}_B$. P_1 then sends d to both servers and additionally sends $\mathbf{y}$ to S_A. P_2 sends shares of r to both servers and additionally sends enc to S_A. The servers can then use linear decoding of NIM to non-interactively compute divisive shares of the inner-product $\langle \mathbf{x}, \mathbf{y} \rangle$ as

$$S_A: \quad g^{[0]_A} \cdot f^{[\langle \mathbf{x}, \mathbf{y} \rangle]_A} := \prod_{i=1}^{n} \left(g_i^r \cdot f^{x_i}\right)^{y_i} \cdot \mathsf{d}^{[r]_A}$$

$$S_B: \quad g^{[0]_B} \cdot f^{[\langle \mathbf{x}, \mathbf{y} \rangle]_B} := \mathsf{d}^{[r]_B},$$

and then convert it into subtractive shares $[\langle \mathbf{x}, \mathbf{y} \rangle]_\sigma$ using DDLog. This naturally extends to compute shares of $\mathbf{y} \cdot s$: P_1 breaks its input $\mathbf{y}$ into n-length chunks $\mathbf{y}_i$ and sends the hash d_i of each chunk, while P_2 sends an encoding enc_i each row of $I \cdot s$, where I is the $n \times n$ identity matrix. By using d_i and enc_j, for every combination of i and j, to compute inner-products as above, the servers can obtain shares of $\mathbf{y} \cdot s$, as desired. Observe that each hash d_i is a single group element which means that P_1 sends N/n group elements to S_B. On the other hand, P_2 sends n shares to S_B. Thus, by setting $n := \sqrt{N}$, the total client communication to S_B is $O(\sqrt{N})$ bits (ignoring factors polynomial in the security parameter). Finally, we note that the computation of d is deterministic and thus does not ensure privacy of $\mathbf{y}$. However, this is fine for succinct client-server HSS, since $\mathbf{y}$ corresponds to the public input. On the other hand, because P_2 only sends shares of the randomness used in its NIM encoding, privacy of s—and consequently of the private inputs shared by P_2—is preserved. We present the full succinct client-server HSS construction in Sect. 4.1.

3 Client-Server Homomorphic Secret Sharing

In this section, we define and construct client-server HSS.

Definition 1 (Client-Server Homomorphic Secret Sharing). *Let $\mathcal{P} :=$ $\mathcal{P}(\lambda)$ be a program class over the integers. A client-server homomorphic secret sharing scheme for $\mathcal{P}$ is a tuple of algorithms $\mathsf{HSS} = (\mathsf{Setup}, \mathsf{Share}, \mathsf{Eval})$ with the following properties.*

- *Syntax:*
  - $\mathsf{Setup}(1^\lambda) \to (\mathsf{crs}, B_{\mathsf{prog}})$ *is a* PPT *algorithm that takes the security parameter 1^λ as input and outputs a common reference string crs and a positive integer B_{prog}.*
  - $\mathsf{Share}(\mathsf{crs}, x) \to (\langle x \rangle_{\mathsf{A}}, \langle x \rangle_{\mathsf{B}})$ *is a* PPT *algorithm that takes as input the common reference string crs and a message $x \in \mathbb{Z}$ and outputs a sharing $\langle x \rangle = (\langle x \rangle_{\mathsf{A}}, \langle x \rangle_{\mathsf{B}})$ of the input.*
  - $\mathsf{Eval}(\mathsf{crs}, \sigma, \langle x_1 \rangle_\sigma, \ldots, \langle x_m \rangle_\sigma, P) =: [z]_\sigma$ *is a polynomial time algorithm that takes as input the common reference string crs, a server identifier $\sigma \in \{\mathsf{A}, \mathsf{B}\}$, an input share $\langle x_j \rangle_\sigma$ from each client, and a program $P \in \mathcal{P}$. It outputs a subtractive share of the evaluation result z.*
- *Correctness Let $m := m(\lambda)$ be a polynomially-bounded positive integer. HSS is ϵ-correct, for some real-valued function $\epsilon := \epsilon(\lambda, m)$, if there exists a negligible function $\mathsf{negl}(\cdot)$ such that for all $\lambda \in \mathbb{N}$, m-input programs $P \in \mathcal{P}$, and $x_1, \ldots, x_m \in \mathbb{Z}$, we have*

$$\Pr\left[\begin{array}{cc} [z]_{\mathsf{A}} - [z]_{\mathsf{B}} & (\mathsf{crs}, B_{\mathsf{prog}}) \leftarrow \mathsf{Setup}(1^\lambda) \\ \neq & : (\langle x_i \rangle_{\mathsf{A}}, \langle x_i \rangle_{\mathsf{B}}) \leftarrow \mathsf{Share}(\mathsf{crs}, x_i), \forall i \in \{1, \ldots, m\} \\ P(x_1, \ldots, x_m) & [z]_\sigma := \mathsf{Eval}\left(\mathsf{crs}, \sigma, (\langle x_i \rangle_\sigma)_{i=1}^m, P\right), \forall \sigma \in \{\mathsf{A}, \mathsf{B}\} \end{array}\right]$$
$$\leq \epsilon + \mathsf{negl}(\lambda),$$

  where the probability is conditioned on $(x_1, \ldots, x_m)$ being B_{prog}-bounded on P.
- *Security For all polynomial size adversaries $\mathcal{A}$, there exists a negligible function $\mathsf{negl}(\cdot)$ such that for all $\lambda \in \mathbb{N}$, we have*

$$\Pr\left[b' = b : \begin{array}{l} (\mathsf{crs}, B_{\mathsf{prog}}) \leftarrow \mathsf{Setup}(1^\lambda) \\ (x_0, x_1, \sigma, \mathsf{st}) \leftarrow \mathcal{A}(\mathsf{crs}) \\ b \leftarrow \{0, 1\} \\ (\langle x_b \rangle_{\mathsf{A}}, \langle x_b \rangle_{\mathsf{B}}) \leftarrow \mathsf{Share}(\mathsf{crs}, x_b) \\ b' \leftarrow \mathcal{A}\left(\langle x_b \rangle_\sigma, \mathsf{st}\right) \end{array}\right] \leq \frac{1}{2} + \mathsf{negl}(\lambda),$$

  where $x_0, x_1 \in \mathbb{Z}$.

3.1   Building Blocks

Our client-server HSS construction requires the following building blocks.

Definition 2 (Group Generator with Distributed Discrete Logarithm).
A group generator with distributed discrete logarithm (DDLog) is a pair of algorithms $\mathsf{GrpGen} = (\mathsf{Gen}, \mathsf{DDLog})$ *with the following properties.*

- ***Syntax:***
    - $\mathsf{Gen}(1^\lambda) \to (\mathsf{par}, \mathbb{G}, F, t, f, B_{\mathsf{ddlog}})$ *is a* PPT *algorithm that takes the security parameter* 1^λ *as input and outputs a parameter string* par, *the description of an abelian group* $\mathbb{G}$, *a finite cyclic subgroup* $F \subseteq \mathbb{G}$ *of order* t *generated by* f, *and a positive integer* B_{ddlog}. *We assume that* par *implicitly defines* $(\mathbb{G}, F, t, f, B_{\mathsf{ddlog}})$ *and it's length is at least* λ *bits.*
    - $\mathsf{DDLog}(\mathsf{par}, h) \to x$ *is a* PPT *algorithm that takes the parameter string* par *and a group element* $h \in \mathbb{G}$ *as input, and outputs an integer* x.
- ***Distributed Discrete Logarithm:*** DDLog *is said to be an* ϵ-*correct DDLog algorithm, where* $\epsilon := \epsilon(\lambda)$ *is a real valued function such that* $0 \leq \epsilon < 1$, *if there exists a negligible function* $\mathsf{negl}(\cdot)$ *such that for all* $\lambda \in \mathbb{N}$, par *in the support of* $\mathsf{Gen}(1^\lambda)$, $x \in \mathbb{Z}$, *and* $h \in \mathbb{G}$, *we have*

$$\Pr\left[\mathsf{DDLog}(\mathsf{par}, h \cdot f^x; r) - \mathsf{DDLog}(\mathsf{par}, h; r) \not\equiv x \bmod t\right] \leq \epsilon + \mathsf{negl}(\lambda),$$

where the probability is over the choice of $r \leftarrow \{0,1\}^\lambda$ *and is conditioned on* $|x| < B_{\mathsf{ddlog}}$, *where* $(\mathbb{G}, F, t, f, B_{\mathsf{ddlog}})$ *are as defined by* par.

Definition 3 (Encryption with Exponent-Linear Decryption).   *Let* GrpGen *be a group generator with DDLog. An encryption scheme under* GrpGen *with exponent-linear decryption is a tuple of algorithms* $\Pi = (\mathsf{Setup}, \mathsf{KeyGen}, \mathsf{Encrypt})$ *with the following properties.*

- ***Syntax:***
    - $\mathsf{Setup}(\mathsf{par}) \to (\mathsf{crs}, \ell_{\mathsf{sk}}, B_{\mathsf{sk}})$ *is a* PPT *algorithm that takes the group parameters* par *as input and outputs a common reference string* crs *and positive integers* ℓ_{sk} *and* B_{sk}. *We assume that* crs *includes* par *and defines* ℓ_{sk} *and* B_{sk}.
    - $\mathsf{KeyGen}(\mathsf{crs}) \to (\mathsf{pk}, \mathsf{sk})$ *is a* PPT *algorithm that takes the common reference string* crs *as input and outputs a public key* pk *and a private key* $\mathsf{sk} \in \mathbb{Z}^{\ell_{\mathsf{sk}}}$, *such that* $\|\mathsf{sk}\|_\infty \leq B_{\mathsf{sk}}$.
    - $\mathsf{Encrypt}(\mathsf{crs}, \mathsf{pk}, x) \to \mathsf{ct}$ *is a* PPT *algorithm that takes the public key* pk *and a message* $x \in \mathbb{Z}$ *as input and outputs a ciphertext* $\mathsf{ct} \in \mathbb{G}^{\ell_{\mathsf{sk}}+1}$, *where* $\mathbb{G}$ *is the group defined by* par.
- ***Exponent-Linear Decryption:*** *For all* $\lambda \in \mathbb{N}$ *and* $x \in \mathbb{Z}$, *we have*

$$\Pr\left[\langle \mathsf{ct}, (\mathsf{sk}, 1)\rangle = f^x : \begin{array}{l} (\mathsf{par}, \mathbb{G}, F, t, f, B_{\mathsf{ddlog}}) \leftarrow \mathsf{GrpGen.Gen}(1^\lambda) \\ (\mathsf{crs}, \ell_{\mathsf{sk}}, B_{\mathsf{sk}}) \leftarrow \mathsf{Setup}(\mathsf{par}) \\ (\mathsf{pk}, \mathsf{sk}) \leftarrow \mathsf{KeyGen}(\mathsf{crs}) \\ \mathsf{ct} \leftarrow \mathsf{Encrypt}(\mathsf{crs}, \mathsf{pk}, x) \end{array}\right] = 1.$$

– **Security:** *For all polynomial size adversaries $\mathcal{A}$, there exists a negligible function* $\mathsf{negl}(\,\cdot\,)$, *such that for all* $\lambda \in \mathbb{N}$, *we have*

Definition 4 (Non-Interactive Multiplication with Exponent-Linear Decoding). *Let* GrpGen *be a group generator with DDLog. A non-interactive multiplication (NIM) scheme under* GrpGen *with exponent-linear decoding is a tuple of algorithms* $\mathsf{NIM} = (\mathsf{Setup}, \mathsf{Encode}, \mathsf{Hash})$ *with the following properties.*

– **Syntax:**
  - $\mathsf{Setup}(\mathsf{par}, 1^n) \to (\mathsf{crs}, B_{\mathsf{nim}})$ *is a* PPT *algorithm that takes the group parameters* par *and a length parameter* 1^n *as input and outputs a common reference string* crs *and a positive integer* B_{nim}. *We assume that* crs *includes* par, *defines* B_{nim}, *and is at least n bits in length.*
  - $\mathsf{Encode}(\mathsf{crs}, \mathbf{x}) \to (\mathsf{enc}, r)$ *is a* PPT *algorithm that takes as input the common reference string* crs *and a tuple* $\mathbf{x} \in \mathbb{Z}^n$ *to encode. It outputs an encoding* $\mathsf{enc} \in \mathbb{G}^n$ *and an integer* $|r| \leq B_{\mathsf{nim}}$, *where* $\mathbb{G}$ *is the group defined by* par.
  - $\mathsf{Hash}(\mathsf{crs}, \mathbf{y}) =: \mathsf{d}$ *is a polynomial time algorithm that takes the common reference string* crs *and a tuple* $\mathbf{y} \in \mathbb{Z}^n$ *as input and outputs a digest* $\mathsf{d} \in \mathbb{G}$, *where* $\mathbb{G}$ *is the group defined by* par.
– **Exponent-linear Decoding:** *For all polynomially-bounded positive integers* $n := n(\lambda)$, $\lambda \in \mathbb{N}$ *and* $\mathbf{x}, \mathbf{y} \in \mathbb{Z}^n$, *we have*

$$\Pr\left[\langle\mathsf{enc}, \mathbf{y}\rangle \cdot \mathsf{d}^r = f^{\langle\mathbf{x},\mathbf{y}\rangle} : \begin{array}{r} (\mathsf{par}, \mathbb{G}, F, t, f, B_{\mathsf{ddlog}}) \leftarrow \mathsf{GrpGen.Gen}(1^\lambda) \\ (\mathsf{crs}, B_{\mathsf{nim}}) \leftarrow \mathsf{Setup}(\mathsf{par}, 1^n) \\ (\mathsf{enc}, r) \leftarrow \mathsf{Encode}(\mathsf{crs}, \mathbf{x}) \\ \mathsf{d} := \mathsf{Hash}(\mathsf{crs}, \mathbf{y}) \end{array}\right] = 1.$$

– **Security:** *For all polynomial size adversaries $\mathcal{A}$ and polynomially-bounded positive integers* $n := n(\lambda)$, *there exists a negligible function* $\mathsf{negl}(\,\cdot\,)$, *such that for all* $\lambda \in \mathbb{N}$, *we have*

$$\Pr\left[b = b' : \begin{array}{r} (\mathsf{par}, \mathbb{G}, F, t, f, B_{\mathsf{ddlog}}) \leftarrow \mathsf{GrpGen.Gen}(1^\lambda) \\ (\mathsf{crs}, B_{\mathsf{nim}}) \leftarrow \mathsf{Setup}(\mathsf{par}, 1^n) \\ (\mathbf{x}_0, \mathbf{x}_1, \mathsf{st}) \leftarrow \mathcal{A}(\mathsf{crs}) \\ b \leftarrow \{0,1\} \\ (\mathsf{enc}, r) \leftarrow \mathsf{Encode}(\mathsf{crs}, \mathbf{x}_b) \\ b' \leftarrow \mathcal{A}(\mathsf{st}, \mathsf{enc}) \end{array}\right] \leq \frac{1}{2} + \mathsf{negl}(\lambda),$$

where $\mathbf{x}_0$ *and* $\mathbf{x}_1$ *are in* $\mathbb{Z}^n$.

3.2   Template for Client-Server HSS

We present our client-server HSS construction in Fig. 1. We refer the reader to Sect. 2.3 for a detailed overview of our construction. Our construction requires the following property, which we call secure key hashing, that states that the hash of the encryption scheme's secret key under the NIM scheme preserves the privacy of the ciphertexts. Informally, this is a 'circular-security'-style assumption since we encrypt the NIM randomness under the encryption scheme but also hash the secret key under NIM. However, this property comes for free in our instantiations since the hash will correspond to the public-key.

Definition 5 (Secure Key Hash). *Let* GrpGen *be a group generator with* $DDLog$, Π *be an encryption scheme under* GrpGen *with exponent-linear decryption, and* NIM *be a NIM under* GrpGen *with exponent-linear decoding.* Π *is said to have* secure key hash *under* NIM *if there exists a* PPT *algorithm* Sim *such that*

$$\left\{ (\mathsf{par}, \mathsf{crs}_\pi, \mathsf{crs}_{\mathsf{nim}}, \mathsf{pk}, \mathsf{d}) : \begin{array}{c} (\mathsf{crs}_{\mathsf{nim}}, B_{\mathsf{nim}}) \leftarrow \mathsf{NIM.Setup}(\mathsf{par}, 1^{\ell_{\mathsf{sk}}}) \\ \mathsf{d} := \mathsf{NIM.Hash}(\mathsf{crs}_{\mathsf{nim}}, \mathsf{sk}) \end{array} \right\}_\lambda$$

$$\overset{c}{\approx}$$

$$\left\{ (\mathsf{par}, \mathsf{crs}_\pi, \mathsf{crs}_{\mathsf{nim}}, \mathsf{pk}, \mathsf{d}) : (\mathsf{crs}_{\mathsf{nim}}, \mathsf{d}) \leftarrow \mathsf{Sim}(\mathsf{par}, \mathsf{crs}_\pi, \mathsf{pk}) \right\}_\lambda$$

where $(\mathsf{par}, \mathbb{G}, F, t, f, B_{\mathsf{ddlog}}) \leftarrow \mathsf{GrpGen.Gen}(1^\lambda)$, $(\mathsf{crs}_\pi, \ell_{\mathsf{sk}}, B_{\mathsf{sk}}) \leftarrow \Pi.\mathsf{Setup}(\mathsf{par})$, *and* $(\mathsf{pk}, \mathsf{sk}) \leftarrow \Pi.\mathsf{KeyGen}(\mathsf{crs}_\pi)$ *are identically distributed in both ensembles.*

Theorem 3. *Let* λ *be the security parameter and* GrpGen *be a group generator with* ϵ*-correct DDLog (Definition 2). Let* Π *be an encryption scheme with exponent-linear decryption (Definition 3) and* NIM *be a NIM with exponent-linear decoding (Definition 4), both under* GrpGen*. Let* PRF_1 *and* PRF_2 *be PRFs. Then, for all positive integers* $B := B(\lambda)$*, the construction described in Figs. 1 and 2 is a client-server HSS (Definition 1) for evaluating polynomial size RMS programs, such that the correctness error on evaluating an* m*-input program* P *is at most*

$$\epsilon \cdot (\ell_{\mathsf{sk}} \cdot \lceil \log_B B_{\mathsf{nim}} \rceil + \ell_{\mathsf{sk}} \cdot m + 1) \cdot |P|,$$

where ℓ_{sk} *and* B_{nim} *are as defined by the common reference string.*

Corollary 1. *Let* λ *be the security parameter.*

- *Assuming DCR, there exists a client-server HSS scheme for evaluating polynomial size RMS programs with* $\mathcal{O}(2^\lambda)$ *bound.*
- *Assuming the* 2^λ*-small exponent assumption and the extended hidden subgroup assumption over class groups, there exists a client-server HSS scheme for evaluating polynomial size RMS programs with* $\mathcal{O}(2^\lambda)$ *bound.*
- *Assuming DDH, there exists a client-server HSS scheme for evaluating polynomial size RMS programs with* $\mathsf{poly}(\lambda)$ *bound and inverse-polynomial correctness error.*

Client-Server Homomorphic Secret Sharing

Public Parameters. Let $B := B(\lambda)$ be a positive integer. Let $\mathsf{GrpGen} = (\mathsf{Gen}, \mathsf{DDLog})$ be a group generator with DDLog (Definition 2), $\Pi = (\mathsf{Setup}, \mathsf{KeyGen}, \mathsf{Encrypt})$ be an encryption scheme under GrpGen with exponent-linear decryption (Definition 3), and $\mathsf{NIM} = (\mathsf{Setup}, \mathsf{Encode}, \mathsf{Hash})$ be a NIM under GrpGen with exponent-linear decoding (Definition 4). Let PRF_1 be a PRF with output space $\{0,1\}^\lambda$ and let PRF_2 be a PRF with output space $\mathbb{Z}_t$, where t will be defined by par output by Gen.

Notation. We use $[1]_\mathsf{A} := 1$ and $[1]_\mathsf{B} := 0$ to denote a trivial sharing of 1. We use DDLog^* as a shorthand to denote $\mathsf{DDLog}^*(h, \mathsf{id}) := \mathsf{DDLog}(\mathsf{par}, h; \mathsf{PRF}_1(\mathsf{k}_\mathsf{prf}^{(1)}, \mathsf{id})) + \mathsf{PRF}_2(\mathsf{k}_\mathsf{prf}^{(2)}, \mathsf{id}) \bmod t$, where par, $\mathsf{k}_\mathsf{prf}^{(1)}$, $\mathsf{k}_\mathsf{prf}^{(2)}$, and t will be defined by the common reference string crs.

$\mathsf{HSS.Setup}(1^\lambda)$

1 : $(\mathsf{par}, \mathbb{G}, F, t, f, B_\mathsf{ddlog}) \leftarrow \mathsf{Gen}(1^\lambda)$

2 : $(\mathsf{crs}_\pi, \ell_\mathsf{sk}, B_\mathsf{sk}) \leftarrow \Pi.\mathsf{Setup}(\mathsf{par})$

3 : $(\mathsf{crs}_\mathsf{nim}, B_\mathsf{nim}) \leftarrow \mathsf{NIM.Setup}(\mathsf{par}, 1^{\ell_\mathsf{sk}})$

4 : $\ell := \lceil \log_B(B_\mathsf{nim}) \rceil$

5 : $\mathsf{k}_\mathsf{prf}^{(1)}, \mathsf{k}_\mathsf{prf}^{(2)} \leftarrow \{0,1\}^\lambda$

6 : $\mathsf{crs} := \left(\mathsf{par}, \mathsf{crs}_\pi, \mathsf{crs}_\mathsf{nim}, \ell, \mathsf{k}_\mathsf{prf}^{(1)}, \mathsf{k}_\mathsf{prf}^{(2)} \right)$

7 : $B_\mathsf{prog} := \dfrac{\min(B_\mathsf{ddlog}, 2^{-\lambda} \cdot t)}{\max(B, B_\mathsf{sk})}$

8 : **return** $(\mathsf{crs}, B_\mathsf{prog})$

$\mathsf{HSS.Eval}(\mathsf{crs}, \sigma, \langle x_1 \rangle_\sigma, \ldots, \langle x_m \rangle_\sigma, P)$

1 : **parse** $\mathsf{crs}_\mathsf{nim}$ from crs

2 : **for** $i \in \{1, \ldots, m\}$

3 :   **parse** $[\mathsf{sk}_i]_\sigma, \mathsf{d}_i$ from $\langle x_i \rangle_\sigma$

4 : $[\![1]\!]_\sigma := ([1]_\sigma, [\mathsf{sk}_1]_\sigma, \ldots, [\mathsf{sk}_m]_\sigma)$

    $\triangleright \; [\![1]\!]_\sigma \in \mathbb{Z}^{\ell_\mathsf{sk} \cdot m + 1}$

5 : $\mathsf{d}_0 := \mathsf{Hash}(\mathsf{crs}_\mathsf{nim}, \mathbb{1}_1^{\ell_\mathsf{sk}})$

6 : **for** $\mathsf{id} \in \{1, \ldots, |P|\}$ evaluate the id-th instruction as described in Figure 2.

$\mathsf{HSS.Share}(\mathsf{crs}, x)$

1 : **parse** $\mathsf{crs}_\pi, \mathsf{crs}_\mathsf{nim}, \ell$ from crs

2 : $(\mathsf{pk}, \mathsf{sk}) \leftarrow \mathsf{KeyGen}(\mathsf{crs}_\pi)$

3 : $\mathsf{d} := \mathsf{Hash}(\mathsf{crs}_\mathsf{nim}, \mathsf{sk}) \quad \triangleright \; \mathsf{d} \in \mathbb{G}$

4 : **for** $i \in \{1, \ldots, \ell_\mathsf{sk}\}$

5 : (enc_i, r_i)

       $\leftarrow \mathsf{Encode}(\mathsf{crs}_\mathsf{nim}, \mathbb{1}_i^{\ell_\mathsf{sk}} \cdot x)$

    $\triangleright \; \mathsf{enc}_i \in \mathbb{G}^{\ell_\mathsf{sk}}, \; r_i \in \mathbb{Z}$

6 : $\left(r_i^{(1)}, \ldots, r_i^{(\ell)} \right) := \mathsf{digits}_{B,\ell}(r_i)$

7 :   **for** $j \in \{1, \ldots, \ell\}$

8 : $\mathsf{ct}_i^{(j)} \leftarrow$

       $\Pi.\mathsf{Encrypt}\left(\mathsf{crs}_\pi, \mathsf{pk}, r_i^{(j)} \right)$

9 : $\mathsf{rct}_i := \left(\mathsf{ct}_i^{(1)}, \ldots, \mathsf{ct}_i^{(\ell)} \right)$

    $\triangleright \; \mathsf{rct}_i \in \mathbb{G}^{\ell \times (\ell_\mathsf{sk} + 1)}$

10 : $[\mathsf{sk}]_\mathsf{B} \leftarrow \left\{ 0, \ldots, 2^\lambda \cdot B_\mathsf{sk} \right\}^{\ell_\mathsf{sk}}$

11 : $[\mathsf{sk}]_\mathsf{A} := \mathsf{sk} + [\mathsf{sk}]_\mathsf{B}$

12 : $\langle x \rangle_\mathsf{A} := \left([\mathsf{sk}]_\mathsf{A}, \mathsf{d}, (\mathsf{enc}_i, \mathsf{rct}_i)_{i=1}^{\ell_\mathsf{sk}} \right)$

13 : $\langle x \rangle_\mathsf{B} := \left([\mathsf{sk}]_\mathsf{B}, \mathsf{d}, (\mathsf{enc}_i, \mathsf{rct}_i)_{i=1}^{\ell_\mathsf{sk}} \right)$

14 : **return** $\left(\langle x \rangle_\mathsf{A}, \langle x \rangle_\mathsf{B} \right)$

Fig. 1. Client-Server HSS for evaluating RMS programs from an encryption scheme with exponent-linear decryption and NIM with exponent-linear decoding.

Client-Server Homomorphic Secret Sharing (continued)

$\mathsf{Convert}(\mathsf{I}_{x_i}) \to \mathsf{M}_{x_i}$

1 : Execute $\mathsf{Mult}(\mathsf{I}_{x_i}, 1)$

$\mathsf{Add}(\mathsf{M}_{y_1}, \mathsf{M}_{y_2}) \to \mathsf{M}_z$

1 : $[\![z]\!]_\sigma := [\![y_1]\!]_\sigma + [\![y_2]\!]_\sigma$

$\mathsf{Output}(\mathsf{M}_y)$

1 : **parse** $[y]_\sigma$ from $[\![y]\!]_\sigma$
2 : **return** $[y]_\sigma$

$\mathsf{Mult}(\mathsf{I}_{x_i}, \mathsf{M}_y) \to \mathsf{M}_z$

1 : **parse** $(\mathsf{enc}_j, \mathsf{rct}_j)_{j=1}^{\ell_{\mathsf{sk}}}$ from $\langle x_i \rangle_\sigma$
2 : **parse** $[\![y]\!]_\sigma = ([y]_\sigma, [y \cdot \mathsf{sk}_1]_\sigma, \ldots, [y \cdot \mathsf{sk}_m]_\sigma)$
   $\triangleright \ [y]_\sigma \in \mathbb{Z}, \ [y \cdot \mathsf{sk}_i]_\sigma \in \mathbb{Z}^{\ell_{\mathsf{sk}}}$
3 : **for** $j \in \{1, \ldots, \ell_{\mathsf{sk}}\}$
4 :   **parse** $\mathsf{rct}_j = \left(\mathsf{ct}_j^{(1)}, \ldots, \mathsf{ct}_j^{(\ell)}\right)$
5 :   **for** $k \in \{1, \ldots, \ell\}$
6 : $h_\sigma := \left\langle \mathsf{ct}_j^{(k)}, ([y \cdot \mathsf{sk}_i]_\sigma, [y]_\sigma) \right\rangle$
7 : $\left[y \cdot r_j^{(k)}\right]_\sigma := \mathsf{DDLog}^* (h_\sigma, \mathsf{id}\|1\|k)$
8 : $[y \cdot r_j]_\sigma := \sum_{i=1}^{\ell} \left[y \cdot r_j^{(k)}\right]_\sigma \cdot B^{i-1}$
9 :   **for** $k \in \{1, \ldots, m\}$
10 : $h_\sigma := \left\langle \mathsf{enc}_j, [y \cdot \mathsf{sk}_k]_\sigma \right\rangle \cdot \mathsf{d}_k^{[y \cdot r_j]_\sigma}$
11 : $\left[x_i y \cdot \mathsf{sk}_k^{(j)}\right]_\sigma := \mathsf{DDLog}^* (h_\sigma, \mathsf{id}\|2\|k)$
12 : $[x_i y \cdot \mathsf{sk}_k]_\sigma := \left(\left[x_i y \cdot \mathsf{sk}_k^{(1)}\right]_\sigma, \ldots, \left[x_i y \cdot \mathsf{sk}_k^{(\ell_{\mathsf{sk}})}\right]_\sigma\right)$
13 : $h_\sigma := \left\langle \mathsf{enc}_1, ([y]_\sigma, \mathbf{0}^{\ell_{\mathsf{sk}}-1}) \right\rangle \cdot \mathsf{d}_0^{[y \cdot r_1]_\sigma}$
14 : $[x_i y]_\sigma := \mathsf{DDLog}^* (h_\sigma, \mathsf{id}\|3)$
15 : $[\![x_i y]\!]_\sigma := ([x_i y]_\sigma, [x_i y \cdot \mathsf{sk}_1]_\sigma, \ldots, [x_i y \cdot \mathsf{sk}_m]_\sigma)$

Fig. 2. Subroutines for evaluating each instruction of the RMS program in the client-server HSS construction described in Fig. 1.

4 Succinct Client-Server Homomorphic Secret Sharing

In this section, we define and construct succinct client-server HSS.

Definition 6 (Succinct Client-Server Homomorphic Secret Sharing).
Let $\mathcal{P} := \mathcal{P}(\lambda)$ be a class of programs over the integers with private and public inputs. A succinct client-server homomorphic secret sharing scheme for $\mathcal{P}$ is a tuple of algorithms $\mathsf{SHSS} = (\mathsf{Setup}, \mathsf{Share}, \mathsf{Eval}_\mathsf{A}, \mathsf{Eval}_\mathsf{B})$ with the following properties.

- **Syntax:**
  - $\mathsf{Setup}(1^\lambda, 1^N) \to (\mathsf{crs}, B_{\mathsf{prog}})$ *is a* PPT *algorithm that takes the security parameter* 1^λ *and a length parameter* 1^N *as input and outputs a common reference string* crs *and a positive integers* B_{prog}.
  - $\mathsf{Share}(\mathsf{crs}, x) \to (\langle x \rangle_\mathsf{A}, \langle x \rangle_\mathsf{B})$ *is a* PPT *algorithm that takes as input the common reference string* crs *and a message* $x \in \mathbb{Z}$ *and outputs a sharing* $\langle x \rangle = (\langle x \rangle_\mathsf{A}, \langle x \rangle_\mathsf{B})$ *of the input.*
  - $\mathsf{Hash}(\mathsf{crs}, \mathbf{y}) =: \mathsf{d}$ *is a polynomial time algorithm that takes the common reference string* crs *and a message* $\mathbf{y} \in \mathbb{Z}^N$ *as input and outputs a digest* d.
  - $\mathsf{Eval}_\mathsf{A}(\mathsf{crs}, \langle x_1 \rangle_\mathsf{A}, \ldots, \langle x_{m_1} \rangle_\mathsf{A}, \mathbf{y}_1, \ldots, \mathbf{y}_{m_2}, \mathsf{d}_1, \ldots, \mathsf{d}_{m_2}, P) =: [z]_\sigma$ *is a polynomial time algorithm that takes as input the common reference string* crs, *input shares* $\langle x_i \rangle_\mathsf{A}$, *inputs* $\mathbf{y}_i \in \mathbb{Z}^N$ *with its digest* d_i, *and a program* $P \in \mathcal{P}$. *It outputs a subtractive share of the evaluation result* z.
  - $\mathsf{Eval}_\mathsf{B}(\mathsf{crs}, \langle x_1 \rangle_\mathsf{B}, \ldots, \langle x_{m_1} \rangle_\mathsf{B}, \mathsf{d}_1, \ldots, \mathsf{d}_{m_2}, P) =: [z]_\sigma$ *is a polynomial time algorithm that takes as input the common reference string* crs, *input shares* $\langle x_i \rangle_\mathsf{B}$, *digests* d_i, *and a program* $P \in \mathcal{P}$. *It outputs a subtractive share of the evaluation result* z.
- **Correctness:** *Let* $m_1 := m_1(\lambda)$, $m_2 := m_2(\lambda)$, *and* $N := N(\lambda)$ *be polynomially-bounded positive integers.* SHSS *is* ϵ-*correct, for some real-valued function* $\epsilon := \epsilon(\lambda, m_1, m_2, N)$, *if there exists a negligible function* $\mathsf{negl}(\cdot)$ *such that for all* $\lambda \in \mathbb{N}$, *programs* $P \in \mathcal{P}$ *with* m_1 *private inputs and* $m_2 N$ *public inputs, and* $x_1, \ldots, x_{m_1} \in \mathbb{Z}$ *and* $\mathbf{y}_1, \ldots, \mathbf{y}_{m_2} \in \mathbb{Z}^N$, *we have*

$$\mathrm{Pr}\left[\begin{array}{c} [z]_\mathsf{A} - [z]_\mathsf{B} \\ \neq \\ P(\mathbf{x}, \mathbf{y}) \end{array} : \begin{array}{l} (\mathsf{crs}, B_{\mathsf{prog}}) \leftarrow \mathsf{Setup}(1^\lambda) \\ (\langle x_i \rangle_\mathsf{A}, \langle x_i \rangle_\mathsf{B}) \leftarrow \mathsf{Share}(\mathsf{crs}, x_i), \ \forall i \in \{1, \ldots, m_1\} \\ \mathsf{d}_i := \mathsf{Hash}(\mathsf{crs}, \mathbf{y}_i), \ \forall i \in \{1, \ldots, m_2\} \\ [z]_\mathsf{A} := \mathsf{Eval}_\mathsf{A}(\mathsf{crs}, \langle \mathbf{x} \rangle_\mathsf{A}, \mathbf{y}, \mathsf{d}, P) \\ [z]_\mathsf{B} := \mathsf{Eval}_\mathsf{B}(\mathsf{crs}, \langle \mathbf{x} \rangle_\mathsf{B}, \mathsf{d}, P) \end{array}\right] \leq \epsilon + \mathsf{negl}(\lambda),$$

  where the probability is conditioned on $(\mathbf{x}, \mathbf{y})$ *being* B_{prog}-*bounded on* P, $\mathbf{x} = (x_1, \ldots, x_{m_1})$, $\mathbf{y} = (\mathbf{y}_1, \ldots, \mathbf{y}_{m_2})$ *and* $\mathsf{d} = (\mathsf{d}_1, \ldots, \mathsf{d}_{m_2})$, *and* $\mathbf{x}$ *and* $\mathbf{y}$ *correspond to the private and public inputs of* P, *respectively.*
- **Input Privacy:** *For all polynomially bounded positive integers* $N := N(\lambda)$ *and polynomial size adversaries* $\mathcal{A}$, *there exists a negligible function* $\mathsf{negl}(\cdot)$ *such that for all* $\lambda \in \mathbb{N}$, *we have*

$$\mathrm{Pr}\left[b' = b : \begin{array}{r} (\mathsf{crs}, B_{\mathsf{prog}}) \leftarrow \mathsf{Setup}(1^\lambda, 1^N) \\ (x_0, x_1, \sigma, \mathsf{st}) \leftarrow \mathcal{A}(\mathsf{crs}) \\ b \leftarrow \{0, 1\} \\ (\langle x_b \rangle_\mathsf{A}, \langle x_b \rangle_\mathsf{B}) \leftarrow \mathsf{Share}(\mathsf{crs}, x_b) \\ b' \leftarrow \mathcal{A}(\langle x_b \rangle_\sigma, \mathsf{st}) \end{array}\right] \leq \frac{1}{2} + \mathsf{negl}(\lambda),$$

  where $x_0, x_1 \in \mathbb{Z}$.

- ***Efficiency:*** *There exists a polynomial* $\mathsf{poly}(\,\cdot\,)$ *such that for all* $\lambda, N \in \mathbb{N}$, *all* $x \in \mathbb{Z}$ *and* $\mathbf{y} \in \mathbb{Z}^N$, *and all* crs *in the support of* $\mathsf{Setup}(1^\lambda)$, *we have the following.*
    1. *The size of* crs *is at most* $\mathsf{poly}(\lambda) \cdot o(N)$ *bits.*
    2. *For all* $\mathsf{d} := \mathsf{Hash}(\mathsf{crs}, \mathbf{y})$, *the size of* d *is at most* $\mathsf{poly}(\lambda) \cdot o(N)$ *bits.*
    3. *For all* $\langle x \rangle_{\mathsf{B}}$ *in the support of* $\mathsf{Share}(\mathsf{crs}, x)$, *the size of* $\langle x \rangle_{\mathsf{B}}$ *is at most* $\mathsf{poly}(\lambda) \cdot o(N)$ *bits.*

4.1   Template for Succinct Client-Server HSS

Building Blocks. In addition to algebraic homomorphic MACs (aHMACs) [29], our succinct client-server HSS construction employs a non-interactive tensor product (NTP) scheme that enables computing the tensor product of a "short" input $\mathbf{x}$ and a "long" input $\mathbf{y}$ while ensuring that the communication to one of the servers is sublinear in $|\mathbf{y}|$. In the full version, we construct NTP directly from NIM by leveraging the reusability of input encodings. Concretely, for a length parameter n, the algorithm $\mathsf{NTP.Share}(\mathsf{crs}, \mathbf{x})$ processes each coordinate $\mathbf{x}^{(i)}$ by computing a NIM encoding of the rows of $\mathbf{x}^{(i)} \cdot I_n$, where I_n denotes the $n \times n$ identity matrix. The output consists of the corresponding NIM encodings together with additive shares of the associated encoding randomness. On the other hand, $\mathsf{NTP.Hash}(\mathsf{crs}, \mathbf{y})$ partitions $\mathbf{y}$ into blocks of length n and hashes each block. The tensor product is then obtained by invoking the NIM evaluation procedure on each pair consisting of an encoding of $\mathbf{x}$ and a hashed block of $\mathbf{y}$.

We present our succinct client-server HSS construction in Fig. 3.

Theorem 4. *Let* λ *be the security parameter,* N *be the length parameter, and* GrpGen *be a group generator with* ϵ-*correct DDLog. Let* Π *be an encryption scheme with exponent-linear decryption,* NIM *be a NIM with exponent-linear decoding, and* aHMAC *be an* ϵ_{mac}-*correct aHMAC, all under* GrpGen.

Then, for all positive integers $B := B(\lambda)$, *and polynomially-bounded positive integers* $n := n(N)$ *such that* $n \in \omega(1)$ *and* $n \in o(N)$, *the construction described in Fig. 3 is a succinct client-server HSS for polynomial size programs in* $\mathsf{RMS} \times \mathcal{C}$. *For all polynomially-bounded positive integers* $m_1 := m_1(\lambda)$ *and* $m_2 := m_2(\lambda)$, *the correctness error on evaluating a program* $P = (P_{\mathsf{rms}}, \mathsf{C})$ *with* m_1 *private inputs and* $m_2 N$ *public inputs is at most*

$$\epsilon \cdot (\ell_{\mathsf{sk}} \cdot \lceil \log_B B_{\mathsf{nim}} \rceil + \ell_{\mathsf{sk}} \cdot m_1 + 1) \cdot |P_{\mathsf{rms}}| + \epsilon \cdot m_1 m_2 N \ell_{\mathsf{mac}} + \epsilon_{\mathsf{mac}} \cdot m_1,$$

where ℓ_{sk}, B_{nim} *and* ℓ_{mac} *are defined by the common reference string.*

Succinct Client-Server HSS

Public Parameters. Let $n := n(\lambda)$ and $B := B(\lambda)$ be positive integers. Let GrpGen be a group generator with DDLog, Π be an encryption scheme under GrpGen with exponent-linear decryption, NIM be a NIM under GrpGen with exponent linear decoding, and aHMAC be an aHMAC under GrpGen.

Notation. We modify HSS.Share to output $\left(\langle x\rangle^{\mathsf{hss}}, \mathsf{sk}\right)$, where $\langle x\rangle^{\mathsf{hss}}$ denotes the shares output by HSS.Share and sk denotes the secret key sampled in step 2 of the algorithm. Similarly, we modify HSS.Eval to take $[\![z]\!]_\sigma$ as an additional input and evaluate $\mathsf{Convert}(\mathsf{I}_{x_i}) \to \mathsf{M}_{x_i}$ instructions by executing $\mathsf{Mult}(\mathsf{I}_{x_i}, z)$ in step 1 instead.

SHSS.Setup$(1^\lambda, 1^N)$

---

1 : $(\mathsf{crs}_{\mathsf{hss}}, B_{\mathsf{rms}}) \leftarrow \mathsf{HSS.Setup}(1^\lambda)$

2 : **parse** par from $\mathsf{crs}_{\mathsf{hss}}$

3 : $(\mathsf{crs}_{\mathsf{ntp}}, B_{\mathsf{ntp}}) \leftarrow \mathsf{NTP.Setup}(\mathsf{par}, 1^N)$

4 : $(\mathsf{crs}_{\mathsf{mac}}, \ell_{\mathsf{mac}}, B_{\mathsf{mac}}, B_{\mathsf{circ}})$
        $\leftarrow \mathsf{aHMAC.Setup}(\mathsf{par})$

5 : $\mathsf{crs} := (\mathsf{par}, \mathsf{crs}_{\mathsf{hss}}, \mathsf{crs}_{\mathsf{ntp}}, \mathsf{crs}_{\mathsf{mac}})$

6 : $B_{\mathsf{prog}} := \min\left(B_{\mathsf{ntp}}/B_{\mathsf{mac}}, B_{\mathsf{circ}}, B_{\mathsf{rms}}\right)$

7 : **return** $(\mathsf{crs}, B_{\mathsf{prog}})$

SHSS.Hash$(\mathsf{crs}, \mathbf{y})$

---

1 : **parse** $\mathsf{crs}_{\mathsf{ntp}}$ from crs

2 : $\mathsf{d} := \mathsf{NTP.Hash}(\mathsf{crs}_{\mathsf{ntp}}, \mathbf{y})$

3 : **return** d

SHSS.Share(crs, x)

---

1 : **parse** crs =
        $(\mathsf{par}, \mathsf{crs}_{\mathsf{hss}}, \mathsf{crs}_{\mathsf{ntp}}, \mathsf{crs}_{\mathsf{mac}})$

2 : $\left(\langle x\rangle^{\mathsf{hss}}, \mathsf{sk}\right) \leftarrow$
        $\mathsf{HSS.Share}(\mathsf{crs}_{\mathsf{hss}}, x)$

3 : $(\boldsymbol{\Delta}, \mathsf{ek}) \leftarrow$
        $\mathsf{aHMAC.KeyGen}(\mathsf{crs}_{\mathsf{mac}}, \mathsf{sk})$

4 : $\left(\langle\boldsymbol{\Delta}\rangle_{\mathsf{A}}^{\mathsf{ntp}}, \langle\boldsymbol{\Delta}\rangle_{\mathsf{B}}^{\mathsf{ntp}}\right) \leftarrow$
        $\mathsf{NTP.Share}(\mathsf{crs}_{\mathsf{ntp}}, \boldsymbol{\Delta})$

5 : **parse** $\langle x\rangle^{\mathsf{hss}} = \left(\langle x\rangle_{\mathsf{A}}^{\mathsf{hss}}, \langle x\rangle_{\mathsf{B}}^{\mathsf{hss}}\right)$

6 : $\langle x\rangle_{\mathsf{A}} := \left(\langle x\rangle_{\mathsf{A}}^{\mathsf{hss}}, \langle\boldsymbol{\Delta}\rangle_{\mathsf{A}}^{\mathsf{ntp}}, \mathsf{ek}\right)$

7 : $\langle x\rangle_{\mathsf{B}} := \left(\langle x\rangle_{\mathsf{B}}^{\mathsf{hss}}, \langle\boldsymbol{\Delta}\rangle_{\mathsf{B}}^{\mathsf{ntp}}, \mathsf{ek}\right)$

8 : **return** $\left(\langle x\rangle_{\mathsf{A}}, \langle x\rangle_{\mathsf{B}}\right)$

Fig. 3. Extending the client-server HSS construction from Fig. 1 to succinct client-server HSS using delegatable succinct NTP and aHMACs. The evaluations algorithms are described in Fig. 4.

Succinct Client-Server HSS (continued)

$\underline{\mathsf{SHSS.Eval_A}\left(\mathsf{crs}, \left(\langle x_i\rangle_\mathsf{A}\right)_{i=1}^{m_1}, \left(\mathbf{y}_i, \mathsf{d}_i\right)_{i=1}^{m_2}, P\right)}$

1 : **parse** $\mathsf{crs} = (\mathsf{par}, \mathsf{crs_{hss}}, \mathsf{crs_{ntp}}, \mathsf{crs_{mac}})$

2 : **parse** $P = (P_\mathsf{rms}, \mathsf{C})$

3 : $\mathbf{y} := (\mathbf{y}_1, \dots, \mathbf{y}_{m_2})$

4 : **for** $i \in \{1, \dots, m_1\}$

5 :   **parse** $\langle x_i\rangle_\mathsf{A} = \left(\langle x_i\rangle_\mathsf{A}^\mathsf{hss}, \langle \boldsymbol{\Delta}_i\rangle_\mathsf{A}^\mathsf{ntp}, \mathsf{ek}_i\right)$

6 :   **for** $j \in \{1, \dots, m_2\}$

7 : $[\boldsymbol{\Delta}_i \otimes \mathbf{y}_j]_\mathsf{A} :=$
$$\mathsf{NTP.Eval_A}\left(\mathsf{crs_{ntp}}, \langle\boldsymbol{\Delta}_i\rangle_\mathsf{A}^\mathsf{ntp}, \mathbf{y}_j, \mathsf{d}_j\right)$$

8 : $[\boldsymbol{\Delta}_i \otimes \mathbf{y}]_\mathsf{A} := \left([\boldsymbol{\Delta}_i \otimes \mathbf{y}_j]_\mathsf{A}\right)_{j=1}^{m_2}$

9 : $[\mathsf{sk}_i \cdot z]_\mathsf{A} :=$
$$\mathsf{aHMAC.Eval_A}(\mathsf{crs_{mac}}, \mathsf{ek}_i, \mathbf{y}, [\boldsymbol{\Delta}_i \otimes \mathbf{y}]_\mathsf{A})$$

10 : $[\![z]\!]_\mathsf{A} := \left(\mathsf{C}(\mathbf{y}), [\mathsf{sk}_1 \cdot z]_\mathsf{A}, \dots, [\mathsf{sk}_{m_1} \cdot z]_\mathsf{A}\right)$

11 : **return**
$$\mathsf{HSS.Eval_A}\left(\mathsf{crs_{hss}}, \left(\langle x_i\rangle_\mathsf{A}^\mathsf{hss}\right)_{i=1}^{m_1}, P_\mathsf{rms}, [\![z]\!]_\mathsf{A}\right)$$

$\underline{\mathsf{SHSS.Eval_B}\left(\mathsf{crs}, \left(\langle x_i\rangle_\mathsf{B}\right)_{i=1}^{m_1}, \left(\mathsf{d}_i\right)_{i=1}^{m_2}, P\right)}$

1 : **parse** $\mathsf{crs} = (\mathsf{par}, \mathsf{crs_{hss}}, \mathsf{crs_{ntp}}, \mathsf{crs_{mac}})$

2 : **parse** $P = (P_\mathsf{rms}, \mathsf{C})$

3 : **for** $i \in \{1, \dots, m_1\}$

4 :   **parse** $\langle x_i\rangle_\mathsf{B} = \left(\langle x_i\rangle_\mathsf{B}^\mathsf{hss}, \langle \boldsymbol{\Delta}_i\rangle_\mathsf{B}^\mathsf{ntp}, \mathsf{ek}_i\right)$

5 :   **for** $j \in \{1, \dots, m_2\}$

6 : $[\boldsymbol{\Delta}_i \otimes \mathbf{y}_j]_\mathsf{B} :=$
$$\mathsf{NTP.Eval_B}\left(\mathsf{crs_{ntp}}, \langle\boldsymbol{\Delta}_i\rangle_\mathsf{B}^\mathsf{ntp}, \mathsf{d}_j\right)$$

7 : $[\boldsymbol{\Delta}_i \otimes \mathbf{y}]_\mathsf{B} := \left([\boldsymbol{\Delta}_i \otimes \mathbf{y}_j]_\mathsf{B}\right)_{j=1}^{m_2}$

8 : $[\mathsf{sk}_i \cdot z]_\mathsf{B} :=$
$$\mathsf{aHMAC.Eval_B}(\mathsf{crs_{mac}}, \mathsf{ek}_i, [\boldsymbol{\Delta}_i \otimes \mathbf{y}]_\mathsf{B})$$

9 : $[\![z]\!]_\mathsf{B} := \left(0, [\mathsf{sk}_1 \cdot z]_\mathsf{B}, \dots, [\mathsf{sk}_{m_1} \cdot z]_\mathsf{B}\right)$

10 : **return**
$$\mathsf{HSS.Eval_B}\left(\mathsf{crs_{hss}}, \left(\langle x_i\rangle_\mathsf{B}^\mathsf{hss}\right)_{i=1}^{m_1}, P_\mathsf{rms}, [\![z]\!]_\mathsf{B}\right)$$

Fig. 4. Evaluation algorithms for succinct client-server HSS construction. The remaining algorithms are described in Fig. 3.

Acknowledgements. L. Roy was supported by the European Research Council (ERC) under the European Union's Horizon 2020 research and innovation programme under grant agreement number 101124977 (DECRYPSIS). A. Hegde and A. Jain were supported in part by NSF CAREER 1942789 and Johns Hopkins University Catalyst award. A. Jain was additionally supported by JP Morgan Faculty Award and research gifts from Ethereum Foundation, Stellar Development Foundation, and Cisco. Lalita Devadas was supported by the Defense Advanced Research Projects Agency (DARPA) under Contract No. HR0011-25-C-0300. Any opinions, findings and conclusions or recommendations expressed in this material are those of the author(s) and do not necessarily reflect the views of the Defense Advanced Research Projects Agency (DARPA). G. Couteau acknowledges the support of the French Agence Nationale de la Recherche (ANR), under the France 2030 ANR Project ANR-22-PECY003 SecureCompute. This work is supported by ERC grant OBELiSC (101115790). D. Abram was supported by a fellowship with the Simons Institute for the Theory of Computing. This work was supported by Input Output (iog.io) through their funding of the Edinburgh Blockchain Technology Lab. Part of this work was conducted while D. Abram, A. Hegde, A. Jain, and L. Roy were visiting the Simons Institute for the Theory of Computing.

References

1. Abram, D., Damgård, I., Orlandi, C., Scholl, P.: An algebraic framework for silent preprocessing with trustless setup and active security. In: Dodis, Y., Shrimpton, T. (eds.) Advances in Cryptology – CRYPTO 2022, Part IV. LNCS, vol. 13510, pp. 421–452. Springer, Cham (2022). https://doi.org/10.1007/978-3-031-15985-5_15

2. Abram, D., Roy, L., Scholl, P.: Succinct homomorphic secret sharing. In: Joye, M., Leander, G. (eds.) Advances in Cryptology – EUROCRYPT 2024, Part VI. LNCS, vol. 14656, pp. 301–330. Springer, Cham (2024). https://doi.org/10.1007/978-3-031-58751-1_11

3. Agrikola, T., Couteau, G., Hofheinz, D.: The usefulness of sparsifiable inputs: how to avoid subexponential iO. In: Kiayias, A., Kohlweiss, M., Wallden, P., Zikas, V. (eds.) PKC 2020, Part I. LNCS, vol. 12110, pp. 187–219. Springer, Cham (2020). https://doi.org/10.1007/978-3-030-45374-9_7

4. Behera, A.R., Meyer, P., Orlandi, C., Roy, L., Scholl, P.: Privately constrained PRFs from DCR: Puncturing and bounded waring rank. Cryptology ePrint Archive, Paper 2025/230 (2025). https://eprint.iacr.org/2025/230

5. Boneh, D., Halevi, S., Hamburg, M., Ostrovsky, R.: Circular-secure encryption from decision Diffie-Hellman. In: Wagner, D. (ed.) CRYPTO 2008. LNCS, vol. 5157, pp. 108–125. Springer, Heidelberg (2008). https://doi.org/10.1007/978-3-540-85174-5_7

6. Boyle, E., Couteau, G., Gilboa, N., Ishai, Y.: Compressing vector OLE. In: Lie, D., Mannan, M., Backes, M., Wang, X. (eds.) ACM CCS 2018: 25th Conference on Computer and Communications Security, Toronto, ON, Canada, Oct 15–19, 2018, pp. 896–912. ACM Press (2018). https://doi.org/10.1145/3243734.3243868

7. Boyle, E., Couteau, G., Gilboa, N., Ishai, Y., Kohl, L., Scholl, P.: Efficient pseudorandom correlation generators: silent OT extension and more. In: Boldyreva, A., Micciancio, D. (eds.) CRYPTO 2019. LNCS, vol. 11694, pp. 489–518. Springer, Cham (2019). https://doi.org/10.1007/978-3-030-26954-8_16

8. Boyle, E., Couteau, G., Gilboa, N., Ishai, Y., Orrù, M.: Homomorphic secret sharing: optimizations and applications. In: Thuraisingham, B.M., Evans, D., Malkin, T., Xu, D. (eds.) ACM CCS 2017: 24th Conference on Computer and Communications Security, Dallas, TX, USA, Oct 31 – Nov 2, 2017, pp. 2105–2122. ACM Press (2017). https://doi.org/10.1145/3133956.3134107

9. Boyle, E., Devadas, L., Servan-Schreiber, S.: Non-interactive distributed point functions. In: Jager, T., Pan, J. (eds.) PKC 2025, Part I. LNCS, vol. 15674, pp. 3–35. Springer, Cham (2025). https://doi.org/10.1007/978-3-031-91820-9_1

10. Boyle, E., Gilboa, N., Ishai, Y.: Breaking the circuit size barrier for secure computation under DDH. In: Robshaw, M., Katz, J. (eds.) CRYPTO 2016, Part I. LNCS, vol. 9814, pp. 509–539. Springer, Heidelberg (2016). https://doi.org/10.1007/978-3-662-53018-4_19

11. Boyle, E., Gilboa, N., Ishai, Y.: Function secret sharing: improvements and extensions. In: Weippl, E.R., Katzenbeisser, S., Kruegel, C., Myers, A.C., Halevi, S. (eds.) ACM CCS 2016: 23rd Conference on Computer and Communications Security, Vienna, Austria, Oct 24–28, 2016, pp. 1292–1303. ACM Press (2016). https://doi.org/10.1145/2976749.2978429

12. Boyle, E., Gilboa, N., Ishai, Y.: Group-based secure computation: optimizing rounds, communication, and computation. In: Coron, J.-S., Nielsen, J.B. (eds.) EUROCRYPT 2017, Part II. LNCS, vol. 10211, pp. 163–193. Springer, Cham (2017). https://doi.org/10.1007/978-3-319-56614-6_6

13. Boyle, E., Kohl, L., Scholl, P.: Homomorphic secret sharing from lattices without FHE. In: Ishai, Y., Rijmen, V. (eds.) EUROCRYPT 2019, Part II. LNCS, vol. 11477, pp. 3–33. Springer, Cham (2019). https://doi.org/10.1007/978-3-030-17656-3_1

14. Brakerski, Z., Gentry, C., Vaikuntanathan, V.: (Leveled) fully homomorphic encryption without bootstrapping. In: Goldwasser, S. (ed.) ITCS 2012: 3rd Innovations in Theoretical Computer Science, Cambridge, MA, USA, Jan 8–10 2012, pp. 309–325. Association for Computing Machinery (2012). https://doi.org/10.1145/2090236.2090262

15. Brakerski, Z., Vaikuntanathan, V.: Efficient fully homomorphic encryption from (standard) LWE. In: Ostrovsky, R. (ed.) 52nd Annual Symposium on Foundations of Computer Science, Palm Springs, CA, USA, Oct 22–25, 2011, pp. 97–106. IEEE Computer Society Press (2011). https://doi.org/10.1109/FOCS.2011.12

16. Canetti, R., Lin, H., Tessaro, S., Vaikuntanathan, V.: Obfuscation of probabilistic circuits and applications. In: Dodis, Y., Nielsen, J.B. (eds.) TCC 2015, Part II. LNCS, vol. 9015, pp. 468–497. Springer, Heidelberg (2015). https://doi.org/10.1007/978-3-662-46497-7_19

17. Couteau, G.: A note on the communication complexity of multiparty computation in the correlated randomness model. In: Ishai, Y., Rijmen, V. (eds.) EUROCRYPT 2019, Part II. LNCS, vol. 11477, pp. 473–503. Springer, Cham (2019). https://doi.org/10.1007/978-3-030-17656-3_17

18. Couteau, G., Devadas, L., Hegde, A., Jain, A., Servan-Schreiber, S.: Multi-key homomorphic secret sharing. In: Fehr, S., Fouque, P.A. (eds.) EUROCRYPT 2025, Part V. LNCS, vol. 15605, pp. 3–33. Springer, Cham (2025). https://doi.org/10.1007/978-3-031-91092-0_1

19. Couteau, G., Kumar, N.: 10-party sublinear secure computation from standard assumptions. In: Reyzin, L., Stebila, D. (eds.) CRYPTO 2024, Part IX. LNCS, vol. 14928, pp. 39–73. Springer, Cham (2024). https://doi.org/10.1007/978-3-031-68400-5_2

20. Couteau, G., Kumar, N., Ye, X.: Multiparty homomorphic secret sharing and more from LPN and MQ. In: TCC 2025 (2025)
21. Couteau, G., Meyer, P.: Breaking the circuit size barrier for secure computation under quasi-polynomial LPN. In: Canteaut, A., Standaert, F.-X. (eds.) EUROCRYPT 2021, Part II. LNCS, vol. 12697, pp. 842–870. Springer, Cham (2021). https://doi.org/10.1007/978-3-030-77886-6_29
22. Couteau, G., Meyer, P., Passelègue, A., Riahinia, M.: Constrained pseudorandom functions from homomorphic secret sharing. In: Hazay, C., Stam, M. (eds.) EUROCRYPT 2023, Part III. LNCS, vol. 14006, pp. 194–224. Springer, Cham (2023). https://doi.org/10.1007/978-3-031-30620-4_7
23. Dao, Q., Ishai, Y., Jain, A., Lin, H.: Multi-party homomorphic secret sharing and sublinear MPC from sparse LPN. In: Handschuh, H., Lysyanskaya, A. (eds.) CRYPTO 2023, Part II. LNCS, vol. 14082, pp. 315–348. Springer, Cham (2023). https://doi.org/10.1007/978-3-031-38545-2_11
24. Dodis, Y., Halevi, S., Rothblum, R.D., Wichs, D.: Spooky encryption and its applications. In: Robshaw, M., Katz, J. (eds.) CRYPTO 2016, Part III. LNCS, vol. 9816, pp. 93–122. Springer, Heidelberg (2016). https://doi.org/10.1007/978-3-662-53015-3_4
25. Döttling, N., Garg, S., Ishai, Y., Malavolta, G., Mour, T., Ostrovsky, R.: Trapdoor hash functions and their applications. In: Boldyreva, A., Micciancio, D. (eds.) CRYPTO 2019, Part III. LNCS, vol. 11694, pp. 3–32. Springer, Cham (2019). https://doi.org/10.1007/978-3-030-26954-8_1
26. Gentry, C.: Fully homomorphic encryption using ideal lattices. In: Mitzenmacher, M. (ed.) 41st Annual ACM Symposium on Theory of Computing, Bethesda, MD, USA, May 31 – Jun 2, 2009, pp. 169–178. ACM Press (2009). https://doi.org/10.1145/1536414.1536440
27. Gentry, C., Sahai, A., Waters, B.: Homomorphic encryption from learning with errors: conceptually-simpler, asymptotically-faster, attribute-based. In: Canetti, R., Garay, J.A. (eds.) CRYPTO 2013, Part I. LNCS, vol. 8042, pp. 75–92. Springer, Heidelberg (2013). https://doi.org/10.1007/978-3-642-40041-4_5
28. Gilboa, N., Ishai, Y.: Distributed point functions and their applications. In: Nguyen, P.Q., Oswald, E. (eds.) EUROCRYPT 2014. LNCS, vol. 8441, pp. 640–658. Springer, Heidelberg (2014). https://doi.org/10.1007/978-3-642-55220-5_35
29. Ishai, Y., Li, H., Lin, H.: Succinct homomorphic MACs from groups and applications. Cryptology ePrint Archive, Paper 2024/2073 (2024). https://eprint.iacr.org/2024/2073
30. Jain, A., Lin, H., Sahai, A.: Indistinguishability obfuscation from LPN over $\mathbb{F}_p$, DLIN, and PRGs in NC^0. In: Dunkelman, O., Dziembowski, S. (eds.) Advances in Cryptology – EUROCRYPT 2022, Part I. LNCS, vol. 13275, pp. 670–699. Springer, Cham (2022). https://doi.org/10.1007/978-3-031-06944-4_23
31. López-Alt, A., Tromer, E., Vaikuntanathan, V.: On-the-fly multiparty computation on the cloud via multikey fully homomorphic encryption. In: Karloff, H.J., Pitassi, T. (eds.) 44th Annual ACM Symposium on Theory of Computing, New York, NY, USA, May 19–22 2012, pp. 1219–1234. ACM Press (2012). https://doi.org/10.1145/2213977.2214086
32. Meyer, P., Orlandi, C., Roy, L., Scholl, P.: Silent circuit relinearisation: Sublinear-size (boolean and arithmetic) garbled circuits from DCR. Cryptology ePrint Archive, Paper 2025/245 (2025). https://eprint.iacr.org/2025/245
33. Mukherjee, P., Wichs, D.: Two round multiparty computation via multi-key FHE. In: Fischlin, M., Coron, J.-S. (eds.) EUROCRYPT 2016, Part II. LNCS, vol.

9666, pp. 735–763. Springer, Heidelberg (2016). https://doi.org/10.1007/978-3-662-49896-5_26

34. Orlandi, C., Scholl, P., Yakoubov, S.: The rise of paillier: homomorphic secret sharing and public-key silent OT. In: Canteaut, A., Standaert, F.-X. (eds.) EUROCRYPT 2021, Part I. LNCS, vol. 12696, pp. 678–708. Springer, Cham (2021). https://doi.org/10.1007/978-3-030-77870-5_24

35. Roy, L., Singh, J.: Large message homomorphic secret sharing from DCR and applications. In: Malkin, T., Peikert, C. (eds.) CRYPTO 2021, Part III. LNCS, vol. 12827, pp. 687–717. Springer, Cham (2021). https://doi.org/10.1007/978-3-030-84252-9_23

Simultaneous-Message and Succinct Secure Computation: Reusable and Multiparty Protocols

Siddharth Agarwal[1], Abhishek Jain[2,3], Akshayaram Srinivasan[1], and David J. Wu[4(✉)]

[1] University of Toronto, Toronto, ON, Canada
{siddharth,akshayaram}@cs.toronto.edu
[2] Johns Hopkins University, Baltimore, MD, USA
abhishek@cs.jhu.edu
[3] NTT Research, Sunnyvale, CA, USA
[4] UT Austin, Austin, TX, USA
dwu4@cs.utexas.edu

Abstract. Recently, Boyle, Jain, Servan-Schreiber, and Srinivasan (EUROCRYPT'25) introduced the notion of simultaneous-message and succinct (SMS) secure computation. In an SMS protocol, after an initial sampling of a common reference string (CRS), two parties—Alice (with a *large* input) and Bob (with a small input)—can simultaneously exchange encodings of their private inputs and obtain additive shares of the output of a function evaluated over their inputs. The key requirement is *succinctness*: namely, the size of the CRS and each input encoding grows only poly-logarithmically in the size of Alice's input and the function output. Boyle et al., and independently Abram, Malavolta, and Roy (STOC'25), constructed SMS for all bounded-depth Boolean circuits from the plain learning with errors (LWE) assumption.

In this work, we extend the study of SMS along two new dimensions:
- **Reusable SMS:** In this setting, the same input encodings can be reused to compute multiple functions.
- **Multiparty SMS:** In the multiparty setting, we consider computations over one large input and *multiple* small inputs. Succinctness in this case means the size of the CRS and input encodings can grow with the total length of the small inputs (but polylogarithmically with the length of the long input and the size of the function output).

Assuming polynomial hardness of LWE (with a sub-exponential modulus-to-noise ratio), we construct reusable two-party SMS for all bounded-depth Boolean circuits with polylogarithmic communication. By additionally assuming indistinguishability obfuscation, we present a generic compiler from reusable two-party SMS to reusable multiparty SMS.

1 Introduction

Consider the following scenario involving three parties, Alice, Bob, and Charlie: Alice holds a large private input $\mathbf{x}_0$, Bob holds a small private input $\mathbf{x}_1$, and

© International Association for Cryptologic Research 2026
J. Daemen and E. Thomé (Eds.): EUROCRYPT 2026, LNCS 16543, pp. 94–123, 2026.
https://doi.org/10.1007/978-3-032-25324-8_4

Charlie wishes to learn the output $f(\mathbf{x}_0, \mathbf{x}_1)$ of some function f evaluated on the inputs of Alice and Bob. There is a simple and communication-efficient insecure protocol for this task: Bob sends his input to Alice, who computes the function output and sends it to Charlie. Is it possible to design a *secure* protocol that achieves, to the extent possible, the communication efficiency and interaction pattern of this insecure protocol?

Simultaneous-Message and Succinct Secure Computation. To address this question, a recent work of Boyle et al. [11] proposed the notion of *simultaneous-message and succinct* (SMS) secure computation. SMS is defined in the common reference string (CRS) model. To compute a function f, the parties proceed in two stages of simultaneous communication:

- **Encode:** Given f, Alice and Bob encode their private inputs and exchange their encodings with each other.
- **Decode:** Upon receiving the input encodings, Alice and Bob compute *additive* shares of the function output and send them to Charlie. Upon receiving the shares, Charlie sums the shares to obtain the function output.

The key requirement is *succinctness*: The size of the CRS and of the input encodings only grows polylogarithmically in the size of Alice's (large) input and the function output.[1] Furthermore, we require simulation-based security in the semi-honest model against collusion between either of the input parties (Alice or Bob) and the output party (Charlie). Compared to the insecure protocol, SMS necessarily requires two additional messages—one from Alice to Bob, and another from Bob to Charlie.[2] Furthermore, the total communication to Charlie is only twice the function output length. Thus, the communication overhead of SMS relative to the insecure protocol is essentially minimal.

SMS extends the notion of private simultaneous messages [27] to require succinct communication and security against collusions. Furthermore, it subsumes the notion of trapdoor hash functions [26], which has applications to high-rate private information retrieval [22,26,37], correlation-intractable hash functions [16,20,36], and hidden-bits generators [19]. It also bears similarity, but is incomparable to existing notions in succinct cryptography, including fully-homomorphic encryption (FHE) [29], laconic function evaluation (LFE) [21,39], and homomorphic secret sharing (HSS) [10,25]. Finally, SMS can be used as a "rate-booster" for cryptographic primitives: for instance, it can be used to generically compile any FHE scheme into a rate-1 FHE scheme [11,14].

Assuming learning with errors (LWE) [40], Boyle et al. [11] constructed an SMS scheme for all bounded-depth Boolean circuits where the input encoding size is polylogarithmic in the size of Alice's input (i.e., the long input) and slightly sublinear in the size of the function output. In an independent work, Abram et al. [1] achieved polylogarithmic efficiency in both Alice's input and

---

[1] Due to information-theoretic lower bounds, we cannot expect to achieve succinctness in the input size of both parties.

[2] These extra messages are necessary to prevent input resetting attacks [32].

the output size under the same assumption. Assuming circular-secure LWE [33], these results can be extended to circuits of unbounded depth.

This Work: Reusable and Multiparty SMS. In this work, we extend the study of SMS along two new dimensions: (1) reusability of users' input encodings, and (2) computations over inputs involving more than two parties. In the following, we expand on each of these directions:

- **Reusable SMS:** In SMS, the input encodings of the parties depend on f. This means that if the parties wish to later compute a different function f' on the same inputs, they must recompute the encodings. This is in contrast to notions such as FHE and HSS that allow for homomorphic evaluations of different functions on the same ciphertext or shares. We address this shortcoming by proposing the notion of *reusable SMS*, where input encodings can be *reused* for computing multiple functions. More specifically, in reusable SMS, the parties execute the encoding stage given only their private input and the CRS. Later, given the description of any function f, they can compute shares of their output using the (same) input encodings.
- **Multiparty SMS:** SMS only supports computations over inputs of two parties. In this work, we extend SMS to the *multiparty* setting where one party holds a large input $\mathbf{x}_0$ and the other parties hold small inputs (say) $\mathbf{x}_1, \ldots, \mathbf{x}_n$. Given a function f, the goal is to compute the function output $f(\mathbf{x}_0, \mathbf{x}_1, \ldots, \mathbf{x}_n)$. The communication model and the efficiency requirements of multiparty SMS are the same as in two-party SMS: namely, the size of the input encodings should scale polylogarithmically with the length of the long input and the length of the function output, but is allowed to scale with the total length of the short inputs. We require semi-honest security against collusions between any subset of the input parties and the output party.

Reusable SMS subsumes and strengthens the notion of succinct HSS proposed by Abram et al. [2]. The key difference is that while succinct HSS (similar to vanilla HSS) allows for a *correlated* public-key setup, reusable SMS only requires a CRS. Succinct HSS with reusable input shares is currently known for a limited class of two-input functions of the form $\langle f(\mathbf{x}_0), g(\mathbf{x}_1) \rangle$, where $\langle \cdot, \cdot \rangle$ denotes an inner product, f is an arbitrary polynomial-size circuit and g is any logarithmic-depth circuit [23,34]. Reusable and multiparty SMS implies the notion of reusable two-round secure multiparty computation [3,4,6–9] while additionally enjoying the same efficiency benefits as SMS relative to standard secure computation.

1.1   Our Results

In this work, we define and the construct the first reusable and multiparty SMS protocols. Throughout this work, we focus on SMS protocols for evaluating Boolean circuits.

Reusable Two-Party SMS. Our first result is a reusable two-party SMS protocol in the common *random* string model based on the LWE assumption.

Theorem 1.1 (Informal). *Assuming LWE (with a sub-exponential modulus-to-noise ratio), there exists a reusable two-party SMS for all bounded-depth Boolean circuits in the common random string model. Specifically, let λ be the security parameter. To evaluate a Boolean circuit $C\colon \{0,1\}^N \times \{0,1\}^k \to \{0,1\}^m$ of depth d and size $\mathsf{poly}(\lambda) \leq 2^\lambda$, our scheme achieves the following efficiency properties:*

- *The CRS has size $\mathsf{poly}(\lambda, d)$.*
- *The encoding of the large input $\mathbf{x}_0 \in \{0,1\}^N$ has size $\mathsf{poly}(\lambda, d)$ and the encoding of the short input $\mathbf{x}_1 \in \{0,1\}^k$ has size $\mathsf{poly}(\lambda, d, k)$.[3]*

Reusable Multiparty SMS. By additionally assuming the existence of indistinguishability obfuscation $(i\mathcal{O})$ [5,28], we can extend the above result to the *multiparty* setting in the common *reference* string model. In fact, we present a general compiler from two-party reusable SMS to a multiparty reusable SMS, assuming $i\mathcal{O}$ together with a non-reusable (two-party) SMS scheme (where the decoding function of the party with the short input has a small circuit description). By instantiating both of the underlying SMS protocols from LWE, we obtain the following theorem:

Theorem 1.2 (Informal). *Assuming sub-exponentially secure iO for circuits and sub-exponentially secure LWE (with a sub-exponential modulus-to-noise ratio), there exists a reusable multiparty SMS scheme for bounded-depth Boolean circuits. Specifically, let λ be the security parameter. To evaluate a Boolean circuit $C\colon \{0,1\}^N \times (\{0,1\}^k)^n \to \{0,1\}^m$ of depth d and size $\mathsf{poly}(\lambda) \leq 2^\lambda$, our scheme achieves the following efficiency properties:*

- *The CRS has size $\mathsf{poly}(\lambda, d, n, k)$.*
- *The encoding of the large input $\mathbf{x}_0 \in \{0,1\}^N$ has size size $\mathsf{poly}(\lambda, d)$ and the encoding of the short inputs $\mathbf{x}_i \in \{0,1\}^k$ has size $\mathsf{poly}(\lambda, k)$.*
- *The evaluation time of parties $\mathcal{P}_1, \ldots, \mathcal{P}_n$ (with the short inputs $\mathbf{x}_1, \ldots, \mathbf{x}_n \in \{0,1\}^k$) is $\mathsf{poly}(\lambda, d, n, k)$,[7] and in particular, does not depend on the description length of f.*

1.2 Related Work

SMS vs. Succinct Cryptography. Fully homomorphic encryption (FHE) [29] allows one to securely compute a function where the communication complexity of the protocol is independent of the size of the circuit being computed. Moreover, the canonical two-message protocol based on FHE for computing over two private

---

[3] Since we always bound $|C| \leq 2^\lambda$, this means $N, m \leq 2^\lambda$. Thus we can absorb polylogarithmic dependencies in the input length N and the output length m into a $\mathsf{poly}(\lambda)$ term..

inputs[4] also achieves communication independent of the input size of one of the parties. However, compared to SMS, this protocol requires sequential (i.e., non-simultaneous) communication. For similar reasons, the dual notion of laconic function evaluation [39] also does not imply SMS.

SMS is incomparable to homomorphic secret sharing (HSS) [10,25]. While SMS requires succinctness in one of the input sizes, HSS only requires succinctness in circuit size. However, HSS requires reusability of input shares, while plain SMS does not require reusability of input encodings for evaluation of different functions.

Finally, as observed in [11], SMS implies trapdoor hash functions [26].

Reusable SMS vs. Succinct HSS. Reusable SMS is closely related to the notion of succinct HSS [2] and shares the key requirements of simultaneous communication, succinctness in the size of one of the inputs, additive output reconstruction, and importantly, reusability of input encodings. The key difference is that succinct HSS is defined in the correlated setup model where a trusted party samples a common public key which is used by the input holders to encode their inputs. In addition the trusted party also samples *correlated* evaluation keys for the parties that are used to compute output shares. Reusable SMS, in contrast, only requires sampling a CRS without any additional correlated setup. In this sense, reusable SMS can be viewed as a strengthening of succinct HSS. Finally, we note that the best known constructions of succinct HSS only support a limited class of computations of the form $\langle f(\mathbf{x}_0), g(\mathbf{x}_1) \rangle$, where $\langle \cdot, \cdot \rangle$ denotes an inner product, f is an arbitrary polynomial-size circuit, and g is any logarithmic-depth circuit [23,34]. In this work, we support arbitrary joint computations over all inputs.

2   Technical Overview

We start with the formal syntax of a *reusable* simultaneous-message and succinct (SMS) secure computation protocol. We start with the two-party setting considered in [11] where one party (denoted $\mathcal{P}_0$) holds a long input $\mathbf{x}_0 \in \{0,1\}^N$ and the other party (denoted $\mathcal{P}_1$) holds a short input $\mathbf{x}_1 \in \{0,1\}^k$. A reusable SMS protocol then consists of three main algorithms:

- **Setup:** The setup algorithm Setup that takes as input the security parameter λ and outputs a common reference string (CRS).
- **Input encoding:** Using the CRS, each party can use the Encode algorithm to encode their input (either $\mathbf{x}_0$ or $\mathbf{x}_1$) to obtain an input encoding ek_i and a decoding trapdoor td_i.

---

[4] Concretely, in this protocol, Bob would first encrypt his input using FHE and send the encrypted input to Alice. Alice then homomorphically evaluates the function on Bob's encrypted input and her private input and sends back the encrypted result. Bob can decrypt and learn the output. Optionally, if we want the parties to obtain additive shares of the joint output, Alice can homomorphically apply a random shift to the output at the end of the homomorphic evaluation process.

- **Circuit evaluation:** Finally, there is a local evaluation algorithm Eval that takes as input the CRS, the parties' input encodings $\mathsf{ek}_0, \mathsf{ek}_1$, the description of a Boolean circuit $C \colon \{0,1\}^N \times \{0,1\}^k \to \{0,1\}^m$, along with a decoding trapdoor d_i (for $i \in \{0,1\}$). The local evaluation algorithm outputs a share d_i.

Moreover, the scheme should satisfy the following properties:

- **Correctness:** The correctness requirement says that if ek_0 is an encoding of $\mathcal{P}_0$'s input $\mathbf{x}_0 \in \{0,1\}^N$ and ek_1 is an encoding of $\mathcal{P}_1$'s input $\mathbf{x}_1 \in \{0,1\}^k$, then the associated shares d_0, d_1 output by Eval are an additive secret sharing of the output $C(\mathbf{x}_0, \mathbf{x}_1)$. Namely, we have that $d_0 \oplus d_1 = C(\mathbf{x}_0, \mathbf{x}_1)$.
- **Security:** The security requirement asserts that a party's evaluation key ek_i should computationally hide their associated input (i.e., ek_0 computationally hides $\mathbf{x}_0$ and ek_1 computationally hides $\mathbf{x}_1$).
- **Succinctness:** The succinctness requirement is that the length of the encoding ek_0 of the long input $\mathbf{x}_0 \in \{0,1\}^N$ scales polylogarithmically with N and the output length m of the circuit C. The length of the encoding ek_1 of the short input $\mathbf{x}_1 \in \{0,1\}^k$ is allowed to scale polynomially with k, but also polylogarithmically with the output length m. For simplicity, throughout this work, we assume the size of the circuit C is at most 2^λ, so we can bound $\log N$ and $\log m$ by the security parameter λ. In this case, our efficiency requirements are

$$|\mathsf{ek}_0| = \mathsf{poly}(\lambda) \quad \text{and} \quad |\mathsf{ek}_1| = \mathsf{poly}(\lambda, k).$$

When considering bounded-depth computations (i.e., settings where the circuit C has depth at most d), we also allow the size of the encodings $\mathsf{ek}_0, \mathsf{ek}_1$ to scale with the depth bound d.

An important feature of the above definition is that the input encoding algorithm is *circuit-independent*. The circuit is only specified at evaluation time rather than encoding time. This means the same input encodings can be reused to evaluate many different circuits. This is similar to primitives like fully homomorphic encryption [29] or homomorphic secret sharing [10] where the same ciphertext or shares can be reused across multiple computations. Thus, we say the SMS scheme is reusable. In the original notion of SMS from [11], the encoding function depended also on the circuit being computed. To evaluate different circuits over the same input, the parties would have to re-encode their input each time. In this work, we focus on the more versatile notion of *reusable* SMS.

2.1 Reusable Two-Party SMS from LWE

Our first contribution in this work is a construction of a *reusable* two-party SMS scheme from LWE. Our construction relies on a new "dual-use" technique of composing an algebraic homomorphic MAC based on lattices introduced in the recent work of Ishai, Li, and Lin [34,35] together with a lattice-based homomorphic encryption scheme. Namely, we consider a setting where the LWE secret key is *reused* across both an algebraic homomorphic MAC and a (leveled) homomorphic encryption scheme. We believe that this type of algebraic composition is of independent interest. In a very different setting, the work of [17] described a dual-use technique of sharing an LWE secret key across a lattice-based attribute-based encryption scheme and a homomorphic encryption scheme. They showed how this composition enables new approaches for predicate encryption and private constrained PRFs.

Algebraic Homomorphic MACs. In an algebraic homomorphic MAC [34, 35] over $\mathbb{Z}_p^n$, a tag $\boldsymbol{\sigma} \in \mathbb{Z}_p^n$ on an input bit $x \in \{0, 1\}$ satisfies $\boldsymbol{\sigma} = x \cdot \mathbf{s} + \mathbf{k} \in \mathbb{Z}_p^n$, where we refer to $\mathbf{s} \in \mathbb{Z}_p^n$ as a "global offset" and $\mathbf{k} \in \mathbb{Z}_p^n$ is a (pseudorandom) blinding term (which we often refer to as the "encoding key" associated with $\boldsymbol{\sigma}$). An algebraic homomorphic MAC allows one to homomorphically operate over tags encoded with respect to the *same* global offset $\mathbf{s}$ (and arbitrary encoding keys). We consider a setting where there are two global offsets $\mathbf{s}_{\mathsf{in}}, \mathbf{s} \in \mathbb{Z}_p^n$, where $\mathbf{s}_{\mathsf{in}}$ is the global offset associated with input values and $\mathbf{s}$ is the global offset associated with the output of a homomorphic computation. Then, an algebraic homomorphic MAC consists of three main algorithms:

- **Setup:** The setup algorithm Setup takes the output global offset $\mathbf{s} \in \mathbb{Z}_p^n$ as input and outputs a public evaluation key evk, a secret key sk, and a global offset $\mathbf{s}_{\mathsf{in}} \in \mathbb{Z}_p^n$ for input values. Note that we provide the output offset $\mathbf{s}$ as an *explicit* input because we will consider scenarios where the *same* $\mathbf{s}$ is reused across the algebraic homomorphic MAC and a leveled homomorphic encryption scheme. This "dual-use" of the offset $\mathbf{s}$ is a central technique introduced in this work.
- **Tag computation:** Take any Boolean circuit $C\colon \{0, 1\}^\ell \to \{0, 1\}^m$ and input $\mathbf{x} \in \{0, 1\}^\ell$. Suppose we have a collection of tags $\boldsymbol{\sigma}_i = x_i \cdot \mathbf{s}_{\mathsf{in}} + \mathbf{k}_i \in \mathbb{Z}_p^n$ encoded with respect to the input offset $\mathbf{s}_{\mathsf{in}}$ and *arbitrary* encoding keys $\mathbf{k}_1, \ldots, \mathbf{k}_\ell$. We will often write this more compactly as

$$\boldsymbol{\sigma}_\mathbf{x} = (\mathbf{x} \otimes \mathbf{s}_{\mathsf{in}}) + \mathbf{k} \in \mathbb{Z}_p^{n\ell}.$$

Then, the *public* evaluation algorithm EvalTag(evk, $C, \mathbf{x}, \boldsymbol{\sigma}_\mathbf{x}$) outputs a tag $\boldsymbol{\sigma}' \in \mathbb{Z}_p^n$ on the output $\mathbf{y} = C(\mathbf{x})$ with respect to the global offset $\mathbf{s}$. Namely,

$$\boldsymbol{\sigma}_\mathbf{y} = (C(\mathbf{x}) \otimes \mathbf{s}) + \mathbf{k}_C \in \mathbb{Z}_p^{nm}. \tag{2.1}$$

A critical property of algebraic homomorphic MACs is the output encoding key $\mathbf{k}_C \in \mathbb{Z}_p^n$ only depends on the circuit C and does *not* depend on the input $\mathbf{x}$. In fact, there is a separate key-computation algorithm (see below) that computes $\mathbf{k}_C$ from the input encoding key $\mathbf{k}$ and the circuit C.
- **Key computation:** Using the secret key sk, the key-computation algorithm EvalKey(sk, $C, \mathbf{k}$) computes the output encoding key $\mathbf{k}_C$ satisfying Eq. (2.1). Importantly, this only requires knowledge of the key $\mathbf{k}$ associated with the input and the description of the circuit C. Moreover, Eq. (2.1) holds for *every* input encoding key $\mathbf{k}$ and tag $\boldsymbol{\sigma}_\mathbf{x} = (\mathbf{x} \otimes \mathbf{s}_{\mathsf{in}}) + \mathbf{k}$.

We can also view the pair $(\boldsymbol{\sigma}_{\mathbf{y}}, \mathbf{k}_C)$ in Eq. (2.1) as a *secret sharing* of the value $\mathbf{y} \otimes \mathbf{s} = C(\mathbf{x}) \otimes \mathbf{s}$ over $\mathbb{Z}_p^{nm}$. Thus, an algebraic homomorphic MAC allows two parties (one holding tags $\boldsymbol{\sigma}_{\mathbf{x}} \in \mathbb{Z}_p^{n\ell}$ on an input $\mathbf{x}$ and the other holding the associated encoding key $\mathbf{k} \in \mathbb{Z}_p^{n\ell}$ and the secret key sk) to *non-interactively* compute a secret sharing of $C(\mathbf{x}) \otimes \mathbf{s}$. This observation lends itself naturally to the structure of an SMS protocol.

A Template for Building SMS from an Algebraic Homomorphic MAC. We now describe a basic template for constructing a two-party SMS protocol using an algebraic MAC. This first template is completely insecure, but illustrates the conceptual ideas underlying our design. Throughout this section, we will assume Alice holds the long input $\mathbf{x}_0 \in \{0,1\}^N$ and Bob holds the short input $\mathbf{x}_1 \in \{0,1\}^k$. Since the input encodings are *reusable*, we can without loss of generality consider evaluating a circuit with a single output bit. We can handle circuits with m output bits by evaluating circuits $C_1, \ldots, C_m$, where C_i computes the ith output bit.

- **Setup:** First, suppose that Alice has an algebraic homomorphic MAC on her input $\boldsymbol{\sigma}_{\mathbf{x}_0} = (\mathbf{x}_0 \otimes \mathbf{s}_{\mathsf{in}}) + \mathbf{k}_0 \in \mathbb{Z}_p^{Nn}$ and Bob has an algebraic homomorphic MAC on his input $\boldsymbol{\sigma}_{\mathbf{x}_1} = (\mathbf{x}_1 \otimes \mathbf{s}_{\mathsf{in}}) + \mathbf{k}_1 \in \mathbb{Z}_p^{kn}$. Suppose also that Bob knows the secret key sk for the algebraic homomorphic MAC as well as the encoding keys $\mathbf{k}_0$ and $\mathbf{k}_1$.
- **Input encoding:** Bob's public input encoding will simply be the algebraic homomorphic MAC on his input $\boldsymbol{\sigma}_{\mathbf{x}_1}$ together with his input $\mathbf{x}_1$. (This is of course insecure, but can be fixed below by replacing $\mathbf{x}_1$ with an encryption of $\mathbf{x}_1$). For now, Alice does not provide any input encoding. By construction, this approach satisfies our efficiency requirements.
- **Circuit evaluation:** Given a circuit $C: \{0,1\}^N \times \{0,1\}^k \to \{0,1\}$, Alice now applies $\mathsf{EvalTag}$ on the circuit C, the inputs $(\mathbf{x}_0, \mathbf{x}_1)$, and the tags $(\boldsymbol{\sigma}_{\mathbf{x}_0}, \boldsymbol{\sigma}_{\mathbf{x}_1})$ to obtain a tag $\boldsymbol{\sigma}_{\mathbf{y}}$. Similarly, Bob applies $\mathsf{EvalKey}$ on the circuit C and the encoding keys $(\mathbf{k}_0, \mathbf{k}_1)$ to obtain a key $\mathbf{k}_C$. The correctness guarantee of the algebraic homomorphic MAC now ensures that

$$\boldsymbol{\sigma}_C = (C(\mathbf{x}_0, \mathbf{x}_1) \otimes \mathbf{s}) + \mathbf{k}_C = C(\mathbf{x}_0, \mathbf{x}_1) \cdot \mathbf{s} + \mathbf{k}_C \in \mathbb{Z}_p^n$$

In particular, Alice and Bob now have a secret sharing of $C(\mathbf{x}_0, \mathbf{x}_1) \cdot \mathbf{s}$. Suppose that we set the first component of the global offset $\mathbf{s}$ to be 1 (i.e., $s_1 = 1$). Then, the first bit of $\boldsymbol{\sigma}_C$ together with the first bit of $\mathbf{k}_C$ represent a secret sharing of $C(\mathbf{x}_0, \mathbf{x}_1)$.

This basic template satisfies our correctness and efficiency guarantees. Notably, the algebraic homomorphic MAC ensures that the two parties' output is an additive secret sharing of the output. However, there are two major problems with this template:

- **Generating a homomorphic MAC on Alice's input.** First, we are assuming that Alice has an algebraic homomorphic MAC $\boldsymbol{\sigma}_{\mathbf{x}_0}$ on her input. It is not clear how she computes this (without knowledge of the secret key).

On the other hand, Bob knows the secret key for the algebraic homomorphic MAC, so he can compute his tag $\sigma_{\mathbf{x}_1}$ himself.

- **Hiding Bob's input.** The second major problem is the algebraic homomorphic MAC only supports computations on *public* inputs. Namely, the EvalTag operation requires knowledge of the input $\mathbf{x}$ associated with the tag $\sigma_{\mathbf{x}}$. In the above template, this means Bob had to reveal his input to Alice in order for Alice to compute on it. Thus, to satisfy the security requirement of an algebraic MAC, we need a way to hide Bob's input.

Below, we show how to address each of these challenges. We handle the first challenge by using a reusable SMS protocol for quadratic polynomials (which was recently constructed in the work of [1]), and tackle the second challenge by having Bob encrypt his input and then employing a new *dual-use* technique that exploits the algebraic structures of lattice-based homomorphic encryption and algebraic homomorphic MACs.

From Public to Private Computation. To hide Bob's input, the natural approach is to *encrypt* it using a (homomorphic) encryption scheme. Consider the following approach:

- We take the basic SMS template from above, but now, instead of Bob sending his input $\mathbf{x}_1 \in \{0,1\}^k$ in the clear, Bob will first encrypt it using a (homomorphic) encryption scheme. Let $\mathbf{c}_1 \in \{0,1\}^t$ be the encryption of $\mathbf{x}_1$. In the SMS protocol, Bob now publishes the ciphertext $\mathbf{c}_1$ together with the tag $\sigma_{\mathbf{c}_1}$ as part of his public input encoding.
- As before, let $C \colon \{0,1\}^N \times \{0,1\}^k \to \{0,1\}^m$ be the circuit the two parties want to compute. Let f_C be the Boolean circuit that takes as input an input $\mathbf{x}_0 \in \{0,1\}^N$ and a ciphertext $\mathbf{c} \in \{0,1\}^t$, and homomorphically evaluates the circuit $C(\mathbf{x}_0, \cdot)$ on the ciphertext $\mathbf{c}$. Namely, $f_C(\mathbf{x}_0, \mathbf{c}_1)$ outputs the binary representation of a ciphertext that decrypts to $C(\mathbf{x}_0, \mathbf{x}_1)$ under the public key pk. Let $\mathbf{d} = f_C(\mathbf{x}_0, \mathbf{c}_1)$.
- Suppose Alice now evaluates the circuit f_C on the tags $(\sigma_{\mathbf{x}_0}, \sigma_{\mathbf{c}_1})$. Let $\sigma_{\mathbf{d}}$ be the resulting tag. The correctness property of the algebraic homomorphic MAC now says that

$$\sigma_{\mathbf{d}} = (f_C(\mathbf{x}_0, \mathbf{c}_1) \otimes \mathbf{s}) + \mathbf{k}_{f_C} = (\mathbf{d} \otimes \mathbf{s}) + \mathbf{k}_{f_C}. \tag{2.2}$$

Observe that this computation only requires knowledge of the ciphertext $\mathbf{c}$ (and the public key for the homomorphic encryption scheme), and does not *require* knowledge of Bob's input $\mathbf{x}_1$. Similarly, Bob can compute the new encoding key $\mathbf{k}_{f_C}$ given knowledge of the input encoding keys $\mathbf{k}_0, \mathbf{k}_1$ and the description of the circuit computing f_C (which does *not* require knowledge of Alice's input $\mathbf{x}_0$).

While this template addresses the security issue of Bob having to reveal his input $\mathbf{x}_1$, it introduces a new problem. At the end of the protocol, Alice and Bob have a secret sharing of $\mathbf{d} \otimes \mathbf{s}$, where $\mathbf{s}$ is the global offset associated with the algebraic homomorphic MAC, and $\mathbf{d}$ is the binary representation of an encryption of

$C(\mathbf{x}_0, \mathbf{x}_1)$; *not* the actual value of $C(\mathbf{x}_0, \mathbf{x}_1)$, which is what we are actually trying to recover.

The Dual-Use Technique. In order to recover $C(\mathbf{x}_0, \mathbf{x}_1)$ from $\mathbf{d}$, we need to implement *decryption*. The crux of the dual-use technique is that the decryption operation in many lattice-based homomorphic encryption schemes (c.f., [13,15, 18,30]) is nearly linear. Namely, a ciphertext (encrypting a bit $\mu \in \{0,1\}$) can be taken to be a vector $\mathbf{c} \in \mathbb{Z}_p^n$, the secret key is also a vector $\mathbf{s} \in \mathbb{Z}_p^n$, and the decryption algorithm simply computes $\mathbf{s}^\mathsf{T}\mathbf{c} \bmod p$. This yields a noisy "encoding" of the message:

$$\mathbf{s}^\mathsf{T}\mathbf{c} = \mu \cdot \lfloor p/2 \rfloor + e \in \mathbb{Z}_p,$$

where e is a small error term. To recover μ, one scales the result by $2/p$ and then rounds to the nearest integer.

Suppose now that the global offset $\mathbf{s} \in \mathbb{Z}_p^n$ in the algebraic homomorphic MAC was *also* the decryption key for the homomorphic encryption scheme, and the homomorphic encryption scheme had a nearly linear decryption procedure. In this case, we can recover shares of $C(\mathbf{x}_0, \mathbf{x}_1)$ from shares of $\mathbf{d} \otimes \mathbf{s}$. To see this, suppose $\tilde{\mathbf{d}} \in \mathbb{Z}_p^n$ is an encryption of $C(\mathbf{x}_0, \mathbf{x}_1)$ and let $\mathbf{d}$ be its binary representation (as computed by $\mathbf{d} = f_C(\mathbf{x}_0, \mathbf{c}_1)$ from above). This means

$$\mathbf{s}^\mathsf{T}\tilde{\mathbf{d}} = C(\mathbf{x}_0, \mathbf{x}_1) \cdot \lfloor p/2 \rfloor + e \in \mathbb{Z}_p,$$

where e is small error. For ease of notation, let $\ell = \lceil \log p \rceil$. Then, we can write $\mathbf{d}^\mathsf{T} = [d_{1,1}, \ldots, d_{1,\ell}, \ldots, d_{n,1}, \ldots, d_{n,\ell}]$ where $(d_{i,1}, \ldots, d_{i,\ell})$ is the binary representation of $\tilde{d}_i \in \mathbb{Z}_p$. In this case, given $\mathbf{d} \otimes \mathbf{s} \in \mathbb{Z}_p^{n^2\ell}$, we can apply a linear map $L \colon \mathbb{Z}_p^{n^2\ell} \to \mathbb{Z}_p$ such that

$$L(\mathbf{d} \otimes \mathbf{s}) = \sum_{i\in[n]}\sum_{j\in[\ell]} 2^{k-j} s_i d_{i,j} = \sum_{i\in[n]} s_i \tilde{d}_i = \mathbf{s}^\mathsf{T}\tilde{\mathbf{d}} = C(\mathbf{x}_0, \mathbf{x}_1) \cdot \lfloor p/2 \rfloor + e \in \mathbb{Z}_p,$$

$$(2.3)$$

where e is a small error term. Since L is a linear function, we can combine it with the algebraic homomorphic MAC invariant from Eq. (2.2) and conclude that

$$L(\boldsymbol{\sigma}_\mathbf{d}) = L(\mathbf{d} \otimes \mathbf{s} + \mathbf{k}_{f_C}) = C(\mathbf{x}_0, \mathbf{x}_1) \cdot \lfloor p/2 \rfloor + e + L(\mathbf{k}_{f_C}).$$

In particular, the pair $(L(\boldsymbol{\sigma}_\mathbf{d}), L(\mathbf{k}_{f_C}))$ is an additive share of $C(\mathbf{x}_0, \mathbf{x}_1)\cdot\lfloor p/2 \rfloor + e$. At this point, we can use the standard local rounding techniques from [12,25] to have Alice and Bob locally round their respective shares and recover additive shares of $C(\mathbf{x}_0, \mathbf{x}_1)$ over $\mathbb{Z}_2$.[5]

To summarize, by having the homomorphic encryption scheme and the algebraic homomorphic MAC share a common $\mathbf{s}$ (as the decryption key and the

---

[5] Specifically, the parties apply a random shift $u \xleftarrow{\text{R}} \mathbb{Z}_p$ to the output (where u is sampled as part of the CRS), scale the result by $2/p$, and then round to the nearest integer. For appropriate choices of p, q, the works of [12,25] show that with overwhelming probability over the choice of u, the result will be an additive share of $C(\mathbf{x}_0, \mathbf{x}_1)$ over $\mathbb{Z}_2$. We refer to the proof of Theorem 4.3 for the full analysis.

output global offset), the algebraic homomorphic MAC evaluation process is implicitly performing both homomorphic evaluation followed by a homomorphic decryption procedure. This allows Alice and Bob to transform secret shares on their input to secret shares of the *decrypted* output.

Bootstrapping from an SMS Scheme for Degree-Two Functions. The remaining wrinkle in our basic template above is our protocol assumes that Alice already has an algebraic MAC on her input $\mathbf{x}_0$ while Bob holds the secret key for the algebraic homomorphic MAC. Thus, we need a mechanism for Alice to learn the tag $\boldsymbol{\sigma}_{\mathbf{x}_0}$ and Bob to learn the associated encoding key $\mathbf{k}_0$ where

$$\boldsymbol{\sigma}_{\mathbf{x}_0} = (\mathbf{x}_0 \otimes \mathbf{s}_{\mathsf{in}}) + \mathbf{k}_0 \in \mathbb{Z}_p^{Nn}. \tag{2.4}$$

Equivalently, we can view the pair $(\boldsymbol{\sigma}_{\mathbf{x}_0}, \mathbf{k}_0)$ as an additive secret sharing of $\mathbf{x}_0 \otimes \mathbf{s}_{\mathsf{in}}$. Thus, an equivalent way of formulating the problem is we need an efficient mechanism for Alice and Bob to derive secret shares of the value $\mathbf{x}_0 \otimes \mathbf{s}_{\mathsf{in}}$. In this case, Alice holds the long input $\mathbf{x}_0$ while Bob holds the short input $\mathbf{s}_{\mathsf{in}}$. Observe now that this is essentially an SMS problem for a *degree-2* computation and where we want the outputs to be an additive secret sharing over $\mathbb{Z}_p^{Nn}$ (as opposed to a secret sharing over $\mathbb{Z}_2$). The recent work of [1] construct a notion called a "reverse trapdoor hash" from the learning with errors assumption, which can be adapted to obtain a reusable two-party SMS for degree-2 functions where the output shares $(\boldsymbol{\sigma}_{\mathbf{x}_0}, \mathbf{k}_0)$ precisely satisfy Eq. (2.4). Using this scheme, we now have an efficient mechanism for Alice to derive the tag $\boldsymbol{\sigma}_{\mathbf{x}_0}$ on her input.

To summarize, our final reusable SMS protocol can be viewed as a way to bootstrap a reusable SMS protocol for degree-2 polynomials into one that supports arbitrary bounded-depth Boolean circuits. The bootstrapping step relies on a dual-use combination of lattice-based algebraic homomorphic MACs with lattice-based (leveled) homomorphic encryption. Putting all the pieces together, our final protocol operates as follows:

- **Setup:** The CRS in our scheme consists of the CRS for the underlying SMS for quadratic functions as well as the local rounding randomness (used for local decryption).
- **Alice's input encoding:** Alice's input encoding consists of an encoding for the underlying SMS scheme on her (long) input $\mathbf{x}_0$. Note that the resulting input encoding is short by succinctness of the underlying SMS for quadratic functions.
- **Bob's input encoding:** Bob samples a secret key $\mathbf{s}$ for the homomorphic encryption scheme and encrypts his input $\mathbf{x}_1$ with the secret key $\mathbf{s}$. Let $\mathbf{c}_1$ be the resulting ciphertext. Next, Bob samples the public evaluation key evk for the algebraic homomorphic MAC with $\mathbf{s}$ as the global offset (associated with the outputs). Let $\mathbf{s}_{\mathsf{in}}$ be the offset associated with the inputs. Bob's input encoding now consists of the evaluation key evk, the encryption $\mathbf{c}_1$ of his input, the tag $\boldsymbol{\sigma}_{\mathbf{c}_1}$ on the ciphertext $\mathbf{c}_1$, as well as the SMS message on the input $\mathbf{s}_{\mathsf{in}}$.

- **Circuit evaluation:** To evaluate a circuit $C\colon \{0,1\}^N \times \{0,1\}^k \to \{0,1\}$ on the input encodings, Alice and Bob perform the following sequence of *local* operations:
  1. Alice and Bob first *locally* run the SMS protocol for quadratic functions on the function $g(\mathbf{x}_0, \mathbf{s}_{\mathsf{in}}) := \mathbf{x}_0 \otimes \mathbf{s}_{\mathsf{in}}$ Let $\boldsymbol{\sigma}_{\mathbf{x}_0}$ be Alice's share and $\mathbf{k}_0$ be Bob's share. Correctness of the underlying SMS protocol says that the local shares $\boldsymbol{\sigma}_{\mathbf{x}_0}$ and $\mathbf{k}_0$ precisely satisfy Eq. (2.4). Hence, we can view $\boldsymbol{\sigma}_{\mathbf{x}_0}$ as an algebraic homomorphic MAC on $\mathbf{x}_0$ with respect to the encoding key $\mathbf{k}_0$ (and input offset $\mathbf{s}_{\mathsf{in}}$).
  2. At this point, Alice can homomorphically evaluate the circuit f_C on the tags $(\boldsymbol{\sigma}_{\mathbf{x}_0}, \boldsymbol{\sigma}_{\mathbf{c}_1})$, where f_C is the circuit that takes input $(\mathbf{x}_0, \mathbf{c}_1)$ and homomorphically evaluates the circuit $C(\mathbf{x}_0, \cdot)$ on the ciphertext $\mathbf{c}_1$. Similarly, Bob homomorphically evaluates f_C on the encoding keys $(\mathbf{k}_0, \mathbf{k}_1)$.
  3. Next, Alice and Bob locally applies the linear function L from Eq. (2.3) to their respective shares. By the dual use technique, Alice and Bob at this point have derived an additive secret sharing of $C(\mathbf{x}_0, \mathbf{x}_1) \cdot \lfloor p/2 \rfloor + e \in \mathbb{Z}_p$.
  4. Finally, using the local rounding procedure [12,25], Alice and Bob recover additive shares of $C(\mathbf{x}_0, \mathbf{x}_1)$ over $\mathbb{Z}_2$, as desired.

Security of our protocol directly reduces to security of the underlying schemes. In particular, Alice's input encoding hides her input by security of the SMS scheme for quadratic functions. Security for Bob's encoding follows also be SMS security of the underlying SMS scheme (to argue that $\mathbf{s}_{\mathsf{in}}$ is hidden), security of the algebraic homomorphic MAC (to argue that the output mask $\mathbf{s}$ is hidden), and security of the homomorphic encryption scheme (to argue that the ciphertext $\mathbf{c}_1$ hides $\mathbf{x}_1$). We provide the full details of our construction in Sect. 4 and defer the proof to the full version of the paper.

Instantiating the Primitives from LWE. Finally, we note that all of the building blocks from the above construction can be instantiated from the plain LWE assumption. As noted previously, the work of [1] can be leverated to obtain a two-party reusable SMS for quadratic functions from LWE and the homomorphic encryption scheme with nearly linear decryption can be instantiated from most lattice-based homomorphic encryption schemes [13,15,18,30]. For the algebraic homomorphic MAC, the recent work of [34,35] describe a construction based on ring LWE (that supports all bounded-depth Boolean circuits). It is straightforward to adapt their construction to one based on plain LWE. We refer to the full version of this paper for the details of this construction.

2.2 A Generic Approach to Multiparty SMS via Indistinguishability Obfuscation

The construction described in Sect. 2.1 gives a reusable two-party SMS protocol for arbitrary bounded-depth Boolean circuit families from the plain LWE assumption. A natural question is whether we can generalize this to a *multiparty* SMS protocol. In this setting, there are $n + 1$ parties $\mathcal{P}_0, \ldots, \mathcal{P}_n$ where party $\mathcal{P}_0$ holds a long input $\mathbf{x}_0 \in \{0,1\}^N$ and the remaining parties $\mathcal{P}_i$ for $i \in [n]$

hold short inputs $\mathbf{x}_i \in \{0,1\}^k$. As in the two-party case, each party can publish an encoding of their respective input. Later, given an arbitrary Boolean circuit $C\colon \{0,1\}^N \times (\{0,1\}^k)^n \to \{0,1\}$, each party can locally compute an additive share of the output $C(\mathbf{x}_0, \mathbf{x}_1, \ldots, \mathbf{x}_n)$. We require that the size of the CRS and the size of the input encodings be polylogarithmic in the size of the long input $\mathbf{x}_0$ as well as the output length of the family of circuits.

Constructing multiparty SMS is much more challenging. For instance, several of the ideas underlying the two-party SMS protocol from Sect. 2.1 do not appear to extend to more than two parties. These include the dual-use technique of composing the algebraic homomorphic MAC with leveled homomorphic encryption as well as the local rounding procedure needed to transform partial decryptions to shares of the underlying message. In the non-input-succinct regime, the work of [25] showed how to lift a two-party spooky encryption scheme to a multiparty protocol with additive reconstruction via a GMW [31] style gate-by-gate computation procedure. However, this does not work in our input-succinct setting. While the lattice techniques do not directly extend to the multiparty setting, we show that if we rely on indistinguishability obfuscation, then we can *generically* lift any two-party SMS protocol into an multiparty SMS protocol.

From Two-Party SMS to Multiparty SMS. The main idea underlying our construction is to delegate the computation of $\mathcal{P}_0$'s share to an obfuscated program in the CRS. The main challenge is to do so in a way that preserves succinctness of the CRS; this latter step will rely on the underlying two-party reusable SMS protocol. To illustrate this idea, we begin with a straw-man scheme that has a *long* CRS.

- **Setup:** First, the CRS will contain a public key pk_i for each party $\mathcal{P}_i$ for each $i \in [n]$. In addition, it will also contain an obfuscated program that has the associated decryption keys sk_i hard-coded inside. Essentially, the obfuscated program will takes as input the (short) encodings keys from all the parties and output the share for $\mathcal{P}_0$. We provide more details on the precise behavior below.
- **Party $\mathcal{P}_0$'s encoding:** In the straw-man scheme, party $\mathcal{P}_0$'s input encoding ek_0 is a succinct commitment to their input $\mathbf{x}_0 \in \{0,1\}^N$.
- **Party $\mathcal{P}_i$'s encoding:** Party $\mathcal{P}_i$ (for $i \in [n]$) encodes their input $\mathbf{x}_i \in \{0,1\}^k$ by first sampling a key k_i for a pseudorandom function (PRF) and then encrypting the pair $(k_i, \mathbf{x}_i)$ under the public key pk_i in the CRS. Succinctness of party $\mathcal{P}_i$'s encoding ek_i follows by construction.
- **Evaluation for party $\mathcal{P}_i$:** On input a Boolean circuit $C\colon \{0,1\}^N \times (\{0,1\}^k)^n \to \{0,1\}$ and the encodings keys $\mathsf{ek}_0, \mathsf{ek}_1, \ldots, \mathsf{ek}_n$ from the other parties, party $\mathcal{P}_i$ computes its output share as $d_i = \mathsf{PRF}(k_i, (C, \mathsf{ek}_0, \ldots, \mathsf{ek}_n)) \in \{0,1\}$.
- **Evaluation for party $\mathcal{P}_0$:** Party $\mathcal{P}_0$ will derive its share of the output using the obfuscated program in the CRS. To ensure correctness, the obfuscated program must output the share $d_0 = C(\mathbf{x}_0, \mathbf{x}_1, \ldots, \mathbf{x}_n) \oplus d_1 \oplus \cdots \oplus d_n$. One way to do this is have the obfuscated program take as input $(C, \mathbf{x}_0, \mathsf{ek}_0, \mathsf{ek}_1, \ldots, \mathsf{ek}_n)$ and then compute the following:

1. Check that ek_0 is a valid commitment to $\mathbf{x}_0$. If the check fails, then the program outputs $\perp$.
2. Decrypt each ek_i to obtain $(k_i, \mathbf{x}_i)$ and compute

$$d_i = \mathsf{PRF}(k_i, (C, \mathsf{ek}_0, \mathsf{ek}_1, \ldots, \mathsf{ek}_n)) \in \{0, 1\}.$$

3. Output $d_0 = C(\mathbf{x}_0, \mathbf{x}_1, \ldots, \mathbf{x}_n) \oplus d_1 \oplus \cdots \oplus d_n \in \{0, 1\}$.

The basic straw-man approach achieves correctness, but does *not* satisfy succinctness. The size of the obfuscated program in the CRS scales linearly with the length of party $\mathcal{P}_0$'s input $\mathbf{x}_0$ *and* the size of the Boolean circuit C (namely, it takes $\mathbf{x}_0$ and C as input).

As we show below, we solve *both* problems using a two-party SMS scheme. In the following description, we write $(\widetilde{\mathsf{ek}}_0, \widetilde{\mathsf{ek}}_1)$ to denote encoding keys and $(\tilde{d}_0, \tilde{d}_1)$ to denote the output shares associated with $\mathcal{P}_0$ and $\mathcal{P}_1$ in the underlying two-party SMS scheme, respectively. As before, we follow the convention that $\mathcal{P}_0$ holds the long input (i.e., "Alice" in the earlier convention) and $\mathcal{P}_1$ holds the short input (i.e., "Bob" in the earlier convention).

Step 1: Encode the long input $\mathbf{x}_0$ using SMS. First, instead of committing to their input $\mathbf{x}_0$, party $\mathcal{P}_0$ instead uses the reusable two-party SMS protocol to construct an encoding $\widetilde{\mathsf{ek}}_0$ of her input $\mathbf{x}_0$. Party $\mathcal{P}_0$ sets their encoding key $\mathsf{ek}_0 = \widetilde{\mathsf{ek}}_0$. This is *short* by definition. With this modification, the obfuscated program no longer needs to take $\mathbf{x}_0$ as input. Instead, the obfuscated program takes $(C, \mathsf{ek}_0, \mathsf{ek}_1, \ldots, \mathsf{ek}_k)$ as input and proceeds as follows:

1. Decrypt each ek_i to obtain $(k_i, \mathbf{x}_i)$. Then, compute an SMS encoding $\widetilde{\mathsf{ek}}_1$ of the concatenated input $(\mathbf{x}_1, \ldots, \mathbf{x}_n)$ using the underlying two-party SMS scheme (as party $\mathcal{P}_1$).[6] By design, the size of $\widetilde{\mathsf{ek}}_1$ is $\mathsf{poly}(\lambda, n, k)$.
2. Use the underlying two-party SMS protocol (as party $\mathcal{P}_1$) to evaluate the Boolean circuit $C \colon \{0, 1\}^N \times (\{0, 1\}^k)^n \to \{0, 1\}$ on the encodings $(\mathsf{ek}_0, \widetilde{\mathsf{ek}}_1) = (\widetilde{\mathsf{ek}}_0, \widetilde{\mathsf{ek}}_1)$. Let $\tilde{d}_1 \in \{0, 1\}$ be the output share.
3. Finally, compute $d_i = \mathsf{PRF}(k_i, (C, \mathsf{ek}_0, \mathsf{ek}_1, \ldots, \mathsf{ek}_n)) \in \{0, 1\}$ and output the blinded share $d_0' = \tilde{d}_1 \oplus d_1 \oplus \cdots \oplus d_n \in \{0, 1\}$ together with the input encoding $\widetilde{\mathsf{ek}}_1$.

Returning now to the multiparty SMS protocol, the evaluation algorithm for parties $\mathcal{P}_i$ is the same as in the straw-man scheme: they simply output $d_i = \mathsf{PRF}(k_i, (C, \mathsf{ek}_0, \mathsf{ek}_1, \ldots, \mathsf{ek}_n)) \in \{0, 1\}$. To compute their share d_0, party $\mathcal{P}_0$ would proceed as follows:

1. Run the obfuscated program on input $(C, \mathsf{ek}_0, \mathsf{ek}_1, \ldots, \mathsf{ek}_n)$ to obtain a *blinded* share $d_0' = \tilde{d}_1 \oplus d_1 \oplus \cdots \oplus d_n$ and an input encoding $\widetilde{\mathsf{ek}}_1$.

---

[6] Technically, the encoding procedure is a *randomized* algorithm. We derandomize this by having the program derive the randomness using a PRF evaluated on the inputs. We refer to Sect. 5 for the full description.

2. Use the underlying two-party SMS protocol (as party $\mathcal{P}_0$) to evaluate the circuit C on the encodings $(\mathsf{ek}_0, \widetilde{\mathsf{ek}}_1) = (\widetilde{\mathsf{ek}}_0, \widetilde{\mathsf{ek}}_1)$. Let $\tilde{d}_0 \in \{0, 1\}$ be the output share.
3. By correctness of the underlying two-party SMS protocol, it holds that

$$\tilde{d}_0 \oplus \tilde{d}_1 = C(\mathbf{x}_0, \mathbf{x}_1, \ldots, \mathbf{x}_n).$$

Output the share

$$d_0 = \tilde{d}_0 \oplus d'_0 = (\tilde{d}_0 \oplus \tilde{d}_1) \oplus (d_1 \oplus \cdots \oplus d_n)$$
$$= C(\mathbf{x}_0, \mathbf{x}_1, \ldots, \mathbf{x}_n) \oplus d_1 \oplus \cdots \oplus d_n \in \{0, 1\}.$$

Thus, the shares $(d_0, d_1, \ldots, d_n)$ derived in this way constitute an additive secret-secret of $C(\mathbf{x}_0, \mathbf{x}_1, \ldots, \mathbf{x}_n)$. This approach removes the need to provide $\mathbf{x}_0$ as an input to the obfuscated program, but it still needs to take the circuit C as input. As such, it still does *not* satisfy succinctness.

Step 2: Encode the circuit C using SMS. To avoid having to provide the description of C to the obfuscated program, we *again* leverage SMS. Much like how we eliminated the dependence on the long input $\mathbf{x}_0$, the idea is to replace the circuit C with an SMS input encoding of C to the obfuscated program. However, in a reusable SMS protocol, the circuit C is not known at encoding time. To get around this, we will instead compose *two* separate SMS protocols: the first SMS protocol handles the input encoding (as described above), while the second handles the circuit encoding. To integrate them together, the first SMS will generate the input encodings for the second SMS instance. More concretely, we start by defining the Boolean circuit G:

1. The circuit G takes the binary representation of $(C, (\widetilde{\mathsf{ek}}_0, \widetilde{\mathsf{ek}}_1, \widetilde{\mathsf{td}}_1))$ as input, where $C \colon \{0, 1\}^N \times (\{0, 1\}^k)^n$ is a Boolean circuit, $\widetilde{\mathsf{ek}}_0, \widetilde{\mathsf{ek}}_1$ are public SMS encodings for the two-party reusable SMS scheme (associated with $\mathcal{P}_0$ and $\mathcal{P}_1$), and $\widetilde{\mathsf{td}}_1$ is the state of $\mathcal{P}_1$ (which $\mathcal{P}_1$ would use to generate its shares of the output). We take C to be the long input (associated with $\mathcal{P}_0$) and $(\widetilde{\mathsf{ek}}_0, \widetilde{\mathsf{ek}}_1, \widetilde{\mathsf{td}}_1)$ to be the short input (associated with $\mathcal{P}_1$).
2. The circuit G computes $\mathcal{P}_1$'s output share obtained by evaluating C on the encodings $(\widetilde{\mathsf{ek}}_0, \widetilde{\mathsf{ek}}_1)$ (using $\widetilde{\mathsf{td}}_1$ as the state of $\mathcal{P}_1$).

In other words, the Boolean circuit G is precisely the computation described in Step 2 of the above protocol. Directly evaluating G (as done previously) would require a circuit that scales with the size of C. However, if we use a two-party *non-reusable* SMS protocol [1,11] where the circuit is part of $\mathcal{P}_0$'s input, and the encoding and share-computation times of $\mathcal{P}_1$ only scales polynomially with the security parameter and the length of $\mathcal{P}_1$'s input (and polylogarithmically with the length of $\mathcal{P}_0$'s input and the output length of the circuit), then we achieve full succinctness.

Concretely, the obfuscated program in the CRS now takes as input a tuple $(\hat{C}_{\mathsf{SMS}}, \mathsf{ek}_0, \mathsf{ek}_1, \ldots, \mathsf{ek}_n)$ where $\hat{C}_{\mathsf{SMS}}$ is a two-party (non-reusable) SMS encoding of the input C for the circuit G (for $\mathcal{P}_0$). The efficiency requirements for the SMS scheme ensures that $\hat{C}_{\mathsf{SMS}}$ has a short description. The obfuscated program now proceeds as follows:

1. Decrypt each ek_i to obtain $(k_i, \mathbf{x}_i)$. Then, compute an SMS encoding $\widetilde{\mathsf{ek}}_1$ of the concatenated input $(\mathbf{x}_1, \ldots, \mathbf{x}_n)$ using the two-party reusable SMS scheme as party $\mathcal{P}_1$. Let $\widetilde{\mathsf{td}}_1$ be the state $\mathcal{P}_1$ would use to derive the output share.
2. Use the two-party (non-reusable) SMS protocol to compute an encoding $\widehat{\mathsf{ek}}_1$ of the input $(\mathsf{ek}_0, \widetilde{\mathsf{ek}}_1, \widetilde{\mathsf{td}}_1) = (\widetilde{\mathsf{ek}}_0, \widetilde{\mathsf{ek}}_1, \widetilde{\mathsf{td}}_1)$ as party $\mathcal{P}_1$.
3. Use the two-party (non-reusable) SMS protocol to compute $\mathcal{P}_1$'s output share $\hat{d}_1 \in \{0,1\}$ with respect to the input encodings $(\hat{C}_{\mathsf{SMS}}, \widehat{\mathsf{ek}}_1)$.
4. Finally, compute $d_i = \mathsf{PRF}(k_i, (f, \mathsf{ek}_0, \mathsf{ek}_1, \ldots, \mathsf{ek}_n)) \in \{0,1\}$ and output the blinded share $d_0' = \hat{d}_1 \oplus d_1 \oplus \cdots \oplus d_n \in \{0,1\}$ together with the input encodings $\widehat{\mathsf{ek}}_1$ and $\widetilde{\mathsf{ek}}_1$.

By construction, the inputs to the obfuscated program consists of an input encoding (for $\mathcal{P}_0$) under a two-party SMS scheme and encryptions of the small inputs. Moreover, the computation performed by the obfuscated program only consists of algorithms that would be run by party $\mathcal{P}_1$ in one of the underlying two-party SMS protocols. Thus, the size of the obfuscated program scales with $\mathsf{poly}(\lambda, k, n, \log N)$, as required.[7] To compute $\mathcal{P}_0$'s share, they now proceed as follows:

1. Use the two-party (non-reusable) SMS protocol to compute an encoding $\widehat{\mathsf{ek}}_0$ of input C for the circuit G. We view $\hat{C}_{\mathsf{SMS}} = \widehat{\mathsf{ek}}_0$ as the succinct encoding of the circuit C.
2. Run the obfuscated program on input $(\hat{C}_{\mathsf{SMS}}, \mathsf{ek}_0, \mathsf{ek}_1, \ldots, \mathsf{ek}_n)$ to obtain a blinded bit $d_0' = \hat{d}_1 \oplus d_1 \oplus \cdots \oplus d_n$ along with input encodings $\widehat{\mathsf{ek}}_1$ and $\widetilde{\mathsf{ek}}_1$.
3. Run the underlying two-party non-reusable SMS protocol on the encodings $(\widehat{\mathsf{ek}}_0, \widehat{\mathsf{ek}}_1)$. Let $\hat{d}_0$ be the output share. By correctness of the two-party SMS protocol, we have

$$\hat{d}_0 \oplus \hat{d}_1 = G(C, (\widetilde{\mathsf{ek}}_0, \widetilde{\mathsf{ek}}_1, \widetilde{\mathsf{td}}_1)) = \tilde{d}_1,$$

where $\tilde{d}_1$ is $\mathcal{P}_1$'s share obtained by evaluating C on encodings $(\widetilde{\mathsf{ek}}_0, \widetilde{\mathsf{ek}}_1)$ in the underlying two-party reusable SMS protocol.
4. Run the underlying two-party reusable SMS protocol on the encodings $(\mathsf{ek}_0, \widetilde{\mathsf{ek}}_1) = (\widetilde{\mathsf{ek}}_0, \widetilde{\mathsf{ek}}_1)$ with the circuit C to obtain an output share $\tilde{d}_0$. By correctness of the underlying SMS protocol, we have

$$\tilde{d}_0 \oplus \tilde{d}_1 = C(\mathbf{x}_0, \mathbf{x}_1, \ldots, \mathbf{x}_n).$$

---

[7] When considering Boolean circuit with m output bits, we incur an additional dependence on $\log m$. The extra $\log m$ factor comes from the fact that the underlying two-party SMS schemes with single-bit output has negligible correctness error, so extending to multiple output bits requires taking a union bound over the number of output bits. Note that in our setting, we can always bound m (as well as N) by 2^λ, so all $\mathsf{poly}(\log N, \log m)$ terms can be absorbed by a $\mathsf{poly}(\lambda)$ term.

5. Output the share

$$
\begin{aligned}
d_0 &= \tilde{d}_0 \oplus \hat{d}_0 \oplus d'_0 \\
&= \tilde{d}_0 \oplus (\hat{d}_0 \oplus \hat{d}_1) \oplus (d_1 \oplus \cdots \oplus d_n) \\
&= (\tilde{d}_0 \oplus \tilde{d}_1) \oplus (d_1 \oplus \cdots \oplus d_n) \\
&= C(\mathbf{x}_0, \mathbf{x}_1, \ldots, \mathbf{x}_n) \oplus d_1 \oplus \cdots \oplus d_n,
\end{aligned}
$$

and correctness follows.

Proving Security. We now provide a brief overview of the main ideas underlying the security analysis. Recall that our objective is to show that each party's input encoding ek_i hides their input $\mathbf{x}_i$. First, consider $\mathcal{P}_0$. By construction, party $\mathcal{P}_0$'s encoding is an encoding of $\mathbf{x}_0$ using an underlying two-party SMS protocol. Thus, security for $\mathcal{P}_0$ follows immediately by security of the underlying two-party SMS protocol.

Security for $\mathcal{P}_i$ (for $i \in [n]$) is more involved. Recall first that $\mathcal{P}_i$'s encoding is an encryption of $(k_i, \mathbf{x}_i)$ under the public key pk_i in the CRS. Moreover, the corresponding decryption key sk_i is hard-wired inside the obfuscated program in the CRS. Thus, we cannot directly invoke semantic security of the underlying public-key encryption scheme to argue that $\mathcal{P}_i$'s encoding hides their input $\mathbf{x}_i$. Instead, we proceed in a sequence of hybrid experiments where in the final distribution, the CRS as well as party $\mathcal{P}_i$'s input encoding is *independent* of their input $\mathbf{x}_i$:

- In the first sequence of hybrids, we replace party $\mathcal{P}_i$'s encoding ek_i (i.e., the encryption of $(k_i, \mathbf{x}_i)$) with an encryption of $\perp$. Note that to ensure functional equivalence for the program in the CRS, we also need to hard wire the value $(k_i, \mathbf{x}_i)$ into the obfuscated program as the "decryption" of ek_i.
  To argue this, we adopt a Naor-Yung approach [38]. Namely, we modify the scheme to include two independent public keys $\mathsf{pk}_{i,0}, \mathsf{pk}_{i,1}$ for each party $i \in [n]$ in the CRS. Then, we have party $\mathcal{P}_i$ encrypt the pair $(k_i, \mathbf{x}_i)$ with respect to $\mathsf{pk}_{i,0}$ *and* $\mathsf{pk}_{i,1}$. Their public encoding now includes a pair of ciphertexts $\mathsf{ct}_{i,0}$ and $\mathsf{ct}_{i,1}$. In addition, $\mathcal{P}_i$ also includes a (simulation-sound) non-interactive zero-knowledge (NIZK) proof [24,41] that the two ciphertexts $\mathsf{ct}_{i,0}$ and $\mathsf{ct}_{i,1}$ encrypt the *same* value. The key insight underlying the Naor-Yung approach is that we can decrypt $(\mathsf{ct}_{i,0}, \mathsf{ct}_{i,1})$ with knowledge of either the secret key $\mathsf{sk}_{i,0}$ associated with $\mathsf{pk}_{i,0}$ or the secret key $\mathsf{sk}_{i,1}$ associated with $\mathsf{pk}_{i,1}$. Thus, we can consider a reduction where the obfuscated program uses $\mathsf{sk}_{i,0}$ to decrypt $\mathcal{P}_i$'s ciphertext while still being able to invoke semantic security for ciphertexts encrypted with respect to $\mathsf{pk}_{i,1}$. Then, we switch the obfuscated program to use $\mathsf{sk}_{i,1}$ to decrypt, which allows us to invoke semantic security with respect to $\mathsf{pk}_{i,0}$. This allows us to replace the ciphertexts in $\mathcal{P}_i$'s encoding with an encryption of a value that is independent of $(k_i, \mathbf{x}_i)$. A similar Naor-Yung approach also featured in the construction of functional encryption from $i\mathcal{O}$ [28].

- After the previous step, party $\mathcal{P}_i$'s encoding key ek_i no longer depends on $\mathbf{x}_i$, but at the same time, we have also hard-coded $\mathcal{P}_i$'s input $\mathbf{x}_i$ into the obfuscated program itself (i.e., the decryption of ek_i is always fixed to be $(k_i, \mathbf{x}_i)$). In the next sequence of hybrids, our goal is to erase the input $\mathbf{x}_i$ from the description of the obfuscated program. To do so, we consider every possible choice of encoding keys $(\mathsf{ek}_0, \mathsf{ek}_1, \ldots, \mathsf{ek}_n)$, and for each possible tuple, we argue that by security of the underlying two-party SMS protocols (as well as of the PRF), we can replace the decryption of ek_i with $\bot$ in the obfuscated program.
  Since this step requires iterating over all possible inputs $(\mathsf{ek}_0, \mathsf{ek}_1, \ldots, \mathsf{ek}_n)$, it is critical that the encoding keys are short (polylogarithmic in the length of the long input $\mathbf{x}_0$). In this case, as long as the underlying two-party SMS protocols, the indistinguishability obfuscation scheme, and the PRF are sub-exponentially secure, security holds.

We refer to Sect. 5 for the detailed construction and defer the security proofs to the full version of the paper

Organization. We define the standard cryptographic primitives used in this work in the full version. We define reusable multiparty SMS protocol in Sect. 3. In Sect. 4, we give our reusable two-party SMS construction from LWE and in Sect. 5, we give our reusable multiparty SMS construction from indistinguishability obfuscation and two-party reusable SMS. In the full version, we give our construction of algebraic homomorphic MAC from LWE and security proofs of our reusable SMS constructions.

3   Reusable Multiparty SMS

In this section, we introduce our notion of reusable multiparty simultaneous-message and succinct secure computation protocols. Consider a setting with n clients $\mathcal{P}_1, \ldots, \mathcal{P}_n$ along with a server $\mathcal{P}_0$. Each client $\mathcal{P}_i$ has a (private) input $\mathbf{x}_i \in \{0, 1\}^k$ and the server has a (private) input $\mathbf{x}_0 \in \{0, 1\}^N$. We typically think of N and m as being much larger than k. A reusable multiparty SMS scheme is a tuple of algorithms (Setup, Encode, Eval) with the following properties:

- The Setup algorithm takes in the security parameter λ and outputs the common reference string crs.
- Each party $\mathcal{P}_i$ can apply the Encode algorithm on their input $\mathbf{x}_i$ to obtain a public encoding key ek_i associated with their input and a secret decoding trapdoor td_i.
- Finally, each party $\mathcal{P}_i$ can apply the evaluation algorithm Eval on a Boolean circuit C, the encoding keys for all of the parties $(\mathsf{ek}_0, \ldots, \mathsf{ek}_n)$, and their decoding trapdoor td_i to obtain a share of the output d_i.

The correctness requirement is that the parties' shares satisfy $d_0 \oplus d_1 \oplus \ldots \oplus d_n = C(\mathbf{x}_0, \mathbf{x}_1, \ldots, x_n)$. For security, we require that each party's encoding key ek_i computationally hide their input $\mathbf{x}_i$. Finally, the succinctness property requires that the size of the encoding key ek and the size of the crs scale polylogarithmically with the length of the server's input N and the length of the output m. Note that since we only consider correctness in settings where $N, m \leq 2^\lambda$, the polylogarithmic terms can be absorbed into a $\mathsf{poly}(\lambda)$ term without loss of generality.

There are two main differences between SMS and reusable multiparty SMS protocols. First, we extend the SMS notion to multiple parties. Second, in the case of SMS, the encoding key generated by $\mathcal{P}_0$ depends on the circuit being evaluated. In contrast, with reusable SMS, the circuit is provided as input to the Eval algorithm. This means the same set of encoding keys could be used to evaluate different circuits. This key property makes the encoding keys reusable in our setting, whereas the encoding keys in the existing SMS notion are not reusable. On the flip side, in a reusable SMS, the amount of computation each party $\mathcal{P}_i$ has to perform to compute their output share d_i can depend on the size of the Boolean circuit C (since we allow the evaluation algorithm to take C as input). In contrast, in vanilla SMS, only the server $\mathcal{P}_0$ has to perform work proportional to the size of C. The remaining parties $\mathcal{P}_1, \ldots, \mathcal{P}_n$ only need to perform work proportional to the length of their (short) input and the length of the output to compute their output share d_i. Note that our reusable multiparty SMS protocol based on $i\mathcal{O}$ (Sect. 5) has the property that $\mathcal{P}_i$'s work scales only with the output length of f (and *not* the size of f), much like in vanilla multiparty SMS.

Definition 3.1 (Reusable Multiparty SMS). *Let λ be a security parameter and let $\mathcal{C} = \{\mathcal{C}_\kappa\}_{\kappa \in \mathbb{N}}$ be a family of bounded-depth Boolean circuits indexed by a parameter κ. We assume that each circuit $C \in \mathcal{C}_\kappa$ is a Boolean circuit of depth at most $d = d(\kappa)$ and of type $C \colon \{0,1\}^N \times (\{0,1\}^k)^n \to \{0,1\}^m$, where $d = d(\kappa)$, $N = N(\kappa)$, $k = k(\kappa)$, $n = n(\kappa)$, and $m = m(\kappa)$ are polynomially-bounded. A reusable multiparty SMS protocol $\Pi_{\mathsf{RM\text{-}SMS}}$ for $\mathcal{C}$ is a tuple of efficient algorithms $\Pi_{\mathsf{RM\text{-}SMS}} = (\mathsf{Setup}, \mathsf{Encode}, \mathsf{Eval})$ with the following syntax:*

- *$\mathsf{Setup}(1^\lambda, 1^\kappa) \to \mathsf{crs}$: On input the security parameter λ and the circuit-family parameter κ, the setup algorithm outputs a common reference string crs. We assume that crs implicitly contains the circuit-family parameter 1^κ.*
- *$\mathsf{Encode}(\mathsf{crs}, i, \mathbf{x}_i) \to (\mathsf{ek}_i, \mathsf{td}_i)$: On input the common reference string crs, a party index $i \in [0, n]$, and their input $\mathbf{x}_i$ (where $\mathbf{x}_i \in \{0,1\}^N$ if $i = 0$ and $\mathbf{x}_i \in \{0,1\}^k$ where $i \in [n]$), the encoding algorithm outputs an encoding key ek_i and a trapdoor td_i.*
- *$\mathsf{Eval}(\mathsf{crs}, (\mathsf{ek}_0, \ldots, \mathsf{ek}_n), C, i, \mathsf{td}) \to d_i$: On input the common reference string crs, a collection of evaluation keys $(\mathsf{ek}_0, \ldots, \mathsf{ek}_n)$, a circuit $C \in \mathcal{C}_\kappa$, a party index $i \in [0, n]$, and their trapdoor td, the evaluation algorithm outputs an output share d_i.*

We want this scheme to satisfy the following properties:

- ***Correctness:** For all polynomials $s = s(\lambda) \leq 2^\lambda$ and $t = t(\lambda)$, there exists a negligible function $\mathsf{negl}(\cdot)$ such that for all $\lambda \in \mathbb{N}$, all $\kappa \in \mathbb{N}$, all inputs*

$\mathbf{x}_0 \in \{0,1\}^N$, $\mathbf{x}_1, \ldots, \mathbf{x}_n \in \{0,1\}^k$, and all circuits $C_1, \ldots, C_t \in \mathcal{C}_\kappa$ where $|C_i| \le s(\lambda)$, we have the probability that the following happens is $\mathsf{negl}(\lambda)$:

- $\mathsf{crs} \leftarrow \mathsf{Setup}(1^\lambda, 1^\kappa)$.
- $\forall i \in [0, n] : (\mathsf{ek}_i, \mathsf{td}_i) \leftarrow \mathsf{Encode}(\mathsf{crs}, i, \mathbf{x}_i)$.
- $\forall i \in [0, n], j \in [t] : d_{i,j} \leftarrow \mathsf{Eval}(\mathsf{crs}, (\mathsf{ek}_0, \ldots, \mathsf{ek}_n), C_j, i, \mathsf{td}_i)$.
- $\hat{d}_j = d_{0,j} \oplus d_{1,j} \oplus \cdots \oplus d_{n,j}$.
- $\exists j \in [t]$ such that $\hat{d}_j \neq C_j(\mathbf{x}_0, \ldots, x_n)$.

- **Security:** *For a bit $b \in \{0,1\}$ and a party index $i \in [0,n]$, we define the security game between an adversary $\mathcal{A}$ and a challenger as follows:*
  - *On input the security parameter 1^λ and the party index $i \in [0,n]$, the adversary $\mathcal{A}$ outputs the circuit-policy parameter 1^κ.*
  - *The challenger samples $\mathsf{crs} \leftarrow \mathsf{Setup}(1^\lambda, 1^\kappa)$ and gives crs to $\mathcal{A}$.*
  - *Algorithm $\mathcal{A}$ outputs two messages $\mathbf{x}_0, \mathbf{x}_1$ where $\mathbf{x}_0, \mathbf{x}_1 \in \{0,1\}^N$ if $i = 0$ and $\mathbf{x}_0, \mathbf{x}_1 \in \{0,1\}^k$ if $i \in [n]$.*
  - *The challenger computes $(\mathsf{ek}_i, \mathsf{td}_i) \leftarrow \mathsf{Encode}(\mathsf{crs}, i, x_b)$ and responds to $\mathcal{A}$ with ek_i.*
  - *Algorithm $\mathcal{A}$ outputs a bit $b' \in \{0,1\}$, which is the output of the experiment.*

We say that $\Pi_{\mathsf{RM\text{-}SMS}}$ is adaptively secure if for all efficient adversaries $\mathcal{A}$, there exists a negligible function $\mathsf{negl}(\cdot)$ such that for all party indices $i \in [0, n]$

$$|\Pr[b' = 1 : b = 0] - \Pr[b' = 1 : b = 1]| = \mathsf{negl}(\lambda)$$

in the above security game. We say that $\Pi_{\mathsf{RM\text{-}SMS}}$ is selectively secure if the adversary $\mathcal{A}$ in the security game has to commit to the input $(\mathbf{x}_0, \mathbf{x}_1)$ at the beginning of the security game before seeing the CRS.

- **Succinctness:** *We say that the scheme satisfies succinctness if there exists a polynomial $\mathsf{poly}(\cdot)$ such that the size of the crs output by $\mathsf{Setup}(1^\lambda, 1^\kappa)$ satisfies $|\mathsf{crs}| = \mathsf{poly}(\lambda, d, n, k)$, and the size of the evaluation keys ek_i output by $\mathsf{Encode}(\mathsf{crs}, i, \cdot)$ satisfies $|\mathsf{ek}_0| = \mathsf{poly}(\lambda, d)$ and for every $i \in [n]$, we have $|\mathsf{ek}_i| = \mathsf{poly}(\lambda, d, k)$.*

Remark 3.2 (Supporting Multi-Bit Outputs). We note that reusable SMS for circuits with single-bit outputs implies reusable SMS for circuits with multi-bit outputs. This is because we can decompose any circuit C with m-bit outputs into m circuits $C_1, \ldots, C_m$ where C_i computes the ith output bit of C. By applying Eval to each circuit $C_1, \ldots, C_m$, the parties can obtain an additive secret sharing of $C_i(\mathbf{x}_0, \mathbf{x}_1, \ldots, \mathbf{x}_n)$ for all $i \in [m]$ and concatenate the shares together to obtain an additive secret sharing of $C(\mathbf{x}_0, \mathbf{x}_1, \ldots, \mathbf{x}_n)$. Correctness for the multi-bit evaluation case now follows immediately from the correctness definition in Definition 3.1 (by taking $t = m$ and more generally, if we consider evaluating t' circuits with m-bit outputs, then we can set $t = mt'$).

Remark 3.3 (Satisfying a Real-Ideal Simulation Definition). Definition 3.1 considers an indistinguishability-based security notion for reusable multiparty SMS. It was shown in [11] that this security notion implies the standard real-ideal simulation definition when we additionally compose with a 2-party non-interactive key exchange (NIKE) protocol.

Reusable Two-Party SMS for Degree-2 Polynomials. In our construction of reusable two-party SMS, we will need a reusable two-party SMS that supports the class of degree-2 polynomials over a ring $\mathbb{Z}_p$ (where $p > 2$). Thus, we consider a generalization of Definition 3.1 to $\mathbb{Z}_p$. Specifically, let the input to $\mathcal{P}_0$ be $\mathbf{x}_0 \in \mathbb{Z}_p^N$ and the input to $\mathcal{P}_1$ be $\mathbf{x}_1 \in \mathbb{Z}_p^k$. We define the class of functions $\mathcal{C}_{\mathsf{Q}}$ as follows:

$$\mathcal{C}_{\mathsf{Q}} = \{f \colon \mathbb{Z}_p^N \times \mathbb{Z}_p^k \to \mathbb{Z}_p \mid f(\mathbf{x}_0, \mathbf{x}_1) = \mathbf{a}^\mathsf{T}(\mathbf{x}_0 \otimes \mathbf{x}_1) + \mathbf{b}^\mathsf{T}\mathbf{x}_0 + \mathbf{c}^\mathsf{T}\mathbf{x}_1 + e.\} \quad (3.1)$$

We can now consider a reusable SMS protocol for $\mathcal{C}_{\mathsf{Q}}$ where the Encode algorithm takes inputs over $\mathbb{Z}_p^N$ and $\mathbb{Z}_p^k$ and the Eval algorithm outputs shares of the output over $\mathbb{Z}_p$. Specifically, if $\mathsf{ek}_0 \leftarrow \mathsf{Encode}(\mathsf{crs}, 0, \mathbf{x}_0)$ and $\mathsf{ek}_1 \leftarrow \mathsf{Encode}(\mathsf{crs}, 1, \mathbf{x}_1)$ where $\mathbf{x}_0 \in \mathbb{Z}_p^N$ and $\mathbf{x}_1 \in \mathbb{Z}_p^k$, we require the evaluation algorithms $\mathsf{Eval}(\mathsf{crs}, (\mathsf{ek}_0, \mathsf{ek}_1), f, 0, \mathsf{td}_0)$ and $\mathsf{Eval}(\mathsf{crs}, (\mathsf{ek}_0, \mathsf{ek}_1), f, 1, \mathsf{td}_1)$ to output shares $d_0, d_1 \in \mathbb{Z}_p$, respectively such that

$$d_0 - d_1 = f(\mathbf{x}_0, \mathbf{x}_1) \in \mathbb{Z}_p. \quad (3.2)$$

We now argue that the reverse trapdoor hash for Boolean circuits from [1, Construction 6.9] implies a reusable SMS for $\mathcal{C}_{\mathsf{Q}}$ with these properties. Consider a Boolean circuit g_i that takes the binary representation of $\mathbf{x}_0$ and $\mathbf{x}_1$ and outputs the ith bit of $\mathbf{x}_0 \otimes \mathbf{x}_1$. The reverse trapdoor hash from [1] outputs a $\mathbb{Z}_2$-secret sharing of $g_i(\mathbf{x}_0, \mathbf{x}_1)$. To do this, [1] first constructs a noisy secret sharing of $g_i(\mathbf{x}_0, \mathbf{x}_1) \cdot q/2$ over $\mathbb{Z}_q$ (where $q = \lambda^{\omega(1)}$) and then applies the $\mathsf{Round}_{q \to 2}$ operation on the noisy shares. This yields additive shares over $\mathbb{Z}_2$ by Lemma 4.1. In our case, we would like an additive secret sharing over $\mathbb{Z}_p$ (where $p > 2$). To obtain an additive secret sharing over $\mathbb{Z}_p$, we proceed as follows:

- First, we modify [1] to first produce a noisy secret sharing $g_i(\mathbf{x}_0, \mathbf{x}_1) \cdot q/p$ over $\mathbb{Z}_q$. This is done by multiplying the output of LFE.Eval and the matrix $\mathbf{A}$ in [1, Construction 6.9] with $\mathbf{G}^{-1}(q/p \cdot \mathbf{u})$ instead of $\mathbf{G}^{-1}(q/2 \cdot \mathbf{u})$.
- Next, we apply $\mathsf{Round}_{q \to p}$ to the noisy shares to obtain a subtractive secret sharing $d_{0,i}, d_{1,i} \in \mathbb{Z}_p$ of $g_i(\mathbf{x}_0, \mathbf{x}_1)$ over $\mathbb{Z}_p$. As long as $q = p \cdot \lambda^{\omega(1)}$, correctness follows from the local rounding lemma (Lemma 4.1). Namely, $d_{0,i} - d_{1,i} = g_i(\mathbf{x}_0, \mathbf{x}_1) \in \mathbb{Z}_p$.
- Using the subtractive shares over $\mathbb{Z}_p$ of the binary representation of the tensor product $\mathbf{x}_0 \otimes \mathbf{x}_1$, parties $\mathcal{P}_0, \mathcal{P}_1$ can scale them by powers-of-2 to obtain subtractive shares of $\mathbf{x}_0 \otimes \mathbf{x}_1$ over $\mathbb{Z}_p^{Nk}$ (i.e., $\mathbf{d}_0, \mathbf{d}_1 \in \mathbb{Z}_p^{Nk}$ where $\mathbf{d}_0 - \mathbf{d}_1 = \mathbf{x}_0 \otimes \mathbf{x}_1$).

Let $f(\mathbf{x}_0, \mathbf{x}_1) = \mathbf{a}^\mathsf{T}(\mathbf{x}_0 \otimes \mathbf{x}_1) + \mathbf{b}^\mathsf{T}\mathbf{x}_0 + \mathbf{c}^\mathsf{T}\mathbf{x}_1 + e$. Party $\mathcal{P}_0$ can locally compute $\mathbf{a}^\mathsf{T}\mathbf{d}_0 + \mathbf{b}^\mathsf{T}\mathbf{x}_0 + e$ and party $\mathcal{P}_1$ can locally compute $\mathbf{a}^\mathsf{T}\mathbf{d}_1 - \mathbf{c}^\mathsf{T}\mathbf{x}_1$. Observe then that

$$(\mathbf{a}^\mathsf{T}\mathbf{d}_0 + \mathbf{b}^\mathsf{T}\mathbf{x}_0 + e) - (\mathbf{a}^\mathsf{T}\mathbf{d}_1 - \mathbf{c}^\mathsf{T}\mathbf{x}_1) = \mathbf{a}^\mathsf{T}(\mathbf{x}_0 \otimes \mathbf{x}_1) + \mathbf{b}^\mathsf{T}\mathbf{x}_0 - \mathbf{c}^\mathsf{T}\mathbf{x}_1 + e = f(\mathbf{x}_0, \mathbf{x}_1).$$

The parties now have a subtractive sharing of the output of f that satisfies Eq. (3.2). We summarize this instantiation in the following theorem:

Theorem 3.4 (Reusable Two-Party SMS for Quadratic Functions [1]).
Assuming LWE with a sub-exponential modulus-to-noise ratio, there exists an adaptively-secure two-party reusable SMS scheme over $\mathbb{Z}_p$ for the function class $\mathcal{C}_Q$. In particular, the Eval function outputs substractive secret shares over $\mathbb{Z}_p$ (i.e., shares that satisfy Eq. (3.2)).

4   Reusable Two-Party SMS Protocol from LWE

In this section, we give our construction of reusable two-party SMS scheme that supports all bounded-depth Boolean circuits based on the plain LWE assumption (with a sub-exponential modulus-to-noise ratio). Our construction relies on a dual-use technique where we share the same secret key between an algebraic homomorphic MAC and a (leveled) homomorphic encryption scheme. We refer to Sect. 2.1 for an overview of this construction. Our construction makes use of the local rounding lemma which we describe below.

Local Rounding. Take $p, q \in \mathbb{N}$ where $q > p$. Define the $\mathsf{Round}_{q \to p} \colon \mathbb{Z}_q \to \mathbb{Z}_p$ function that takes an input $t \in \mathbb{Z}_q$, lifts it to the integers (over the interval $(-q/2, q/2]$) and outputs $\lfloor (p/q) \cdot t \rceil$. We extend the rounding operation $\mathsf{Round}_{q \to p}$ to operate on vectors and matrices component-wise. We now recall the local rounding lemma from [12,25]:

Lemma 4.1 (Local Rounding [12, adapted]).   *Take any $p, q \in \mathbb{N}$ where $q > p$. Then, for all $e \in \mathbb{Z}$,*

$$\Pr[\mathsf{Round}_{q \to p}(t) = \mathsf{Round}_{q \to p}(t + e) : t \xleftarrow{\text{R}} \mathbb{Z}_q] \geq 1 - O\left(\frac{p|e|}{q}\right).$$

Construction 4.2 (Reusable Two-Party SMS). Let λ be a security parameter and let $\mathcal{C} = \{\mathcal{C}_\kappa\}_{\kappa \in \mathbb{N}}$ be a family of bounded-depth Boolean circuits indexed by a parameter κ. We assume that each circuit $C \in \mathcal{C}_\kappa$ is a Boolean circuit of depth at most $d = d(\kappa)$ and of type $C \colon \{0,1\}^N \times \{0,1\}^k \to \{0,1\}$, where $d = d(\kappa)$, $N = N(\kappa)$, and $k = k(\kappa)$ are polynomially-bounded.[8] Our construction relies on the following building blocks:

- A leveled homomorphic encryption scheme $\Pi_{\mathsf{LHE}} = (\mathsf{LHE.KeyGen}, \mathsf{LHE.Enc}, \mathsf{LHE.Eval})$ with nearly-linear decryption, secret key dimension $n = n(\lambda, d(\kappa))$, and modulus $p = p(\lambda, d(\kappa))$. Let $d' = d'(\lambda, \kappa)$ be a bound on the depth of the Boolean circuit computing $\mathsf{LHE.Eval}$. Let $\ell_{\mathsf{ct}} = \ell_{\mathsf{ct}}(\lambda, \kappa)$ be the length of a ciphertext output by $\mathsf{LHE.Enc}$.
- An algebraic homomorphic MAC scheme $\Pi_{\mathsf{AHMAC}} = (\mathsf{AHMAC.Setup}, \mathsf{AHMAC.EvalKey}, \mathsf{AHMAC.EvalTag})$ over $\mathbb{Z}_p^n$.

---

[8] As discussed in Remark 3.2, we can consider circuits with single-bit outputs without loss of generality.

- A reusable two-party SMS protocol $\Pi_{\mathsf{SMSQ}} = (\mathsf{SMS_Q.Setup}, \mathsf{SMS_Q.Encode}, \mathsf{SMS_Q.Eval})$ for computing the class of degree-2 polynomials $\mathcal{C}_Q$ over $\mathbb{Z}_p$ (see Eq. (3.1) and Theorem 3.4).

We construct our two-party reusable SMS scheme $\Pi_{\mathsf{SMS}} = (\mathsf{Setup}, \mathsf{Encode}, \mathsf{Eval})$ as follows:

- $\mathsf{Setup}(1^\lambda, 1^\kappa)$: On input the security parameter λ and the circuit parameter κ, the setup algorithm samples $\mathsf{crs_{SMSQ}} \leftarrow \mathsf{SMS_Q.Setup}(1^\lambda)$, the local rounding randomness $u \xleftarrow{\text{R}} \mathbb{Z}_p$ and outputs $\mathsf{crs} = (1^d, \mathsf{crs_{SMSQ}}, u)$.
- $\mathsf{Encode}(\mathsf{crs}, i, \mathbf{x})$: On input the common reference string $\mathsf{crs} = (1^d, \mathsf{crs_{SMSQ}}, u)$, an index $i \in \{0, 1\}$, and an input $\mathbf{x}_i$, the encoding algorithm proceeds as follows:
  - If $i = 0$, then lift $\mathbf{x} \in \{0, 1\}^N$ to $\mathbf{x} \in \mathbb{Z}_p^N$ and compute $(\mathsf{ek}_0', \mathsf{td}_0') \leftarrow \mathsf{SMS_Q.Encode}(\mathsf{crs_{SMSQ}}, 0, \mathbf{x})$. Output $\mathsf{ek}_0 = \mathsf{ek}_0'$ and $\mathsf{td}_0 = \mathsf{td}_0'$.
  - If $i = 1$, then sample the following:

$$(\mathsf{pk}, \mathbf{s}) \leftarrow \mathsf{LHE.KeyGen}(1^\lambda, 1^d)$$
$$(\mathbf{s}_{\mathsf{in}}, \mathsf{sk}, \mathsf{evk}) \leftarrow \mathsf{AHMAC.Setup}(1^\lambda, 1^{d'}, \mathbf{s})$$
$$(\mathsf{ek}_1', \mathsf{td}_1') \leftarrow \mathsf{SMS_Q.Encode}(\mathsf{crs_{SMSQ}}, 1, \mathbf{s}_{\mathsf{in}}).$$

  Then, for each $j \in [k]$, compute the following:
  * Compute the ciphertext $\mathsf{ct}_j \leftarrow \mathsf{LHE.Enc}(\mathbf{s}, x_j)$. We interpret $\mathsf{ct}_j \in \{0, 1\}^{\ell_{\mathsf{ct}}}$ as a binary string.
  * Sample an encoding key $\mathbf{k}_j \xleftarrow{\text{R}} \mathbb{Z}_p^{n\ell_{\mathsf{ct}}}$ for the ciphertext.
  * Compute an algebraic homomorphic MAC $\boldsymbol{\sigma}_j = \mathsf{ct}_j \otimes \mathbf{s}_{\mathsf{in}} + \mathbf{k}_j$ on ct_j.
  Output the encoding key $\mathsf{ek}_1 = \left(\mathsf{ek}_1', \mathsf{evk}, \mathsf{pk}, \{\mathsf{ct}_j, \boldsymbol{\sigma}_j\}_{j \in [k]}\right)$ and the trapdoor $\mathsf{td}_1 = \left(\mathsf{td}_1', \mathsf{sk}, \{\mathbf{k}_j\}_{j \in [k]}\right)$.
- $\mathsf{Eval}(\mathsf{crs}, (\mathsf{ek}_0, \mathsf{ek}_1), C, b, \mathsf{td})$: On input the common reference string $\mathsf{crs} = (1^d, \mathsf{crs_{SMSQ}}, u)$, evaluation keys $\mathsf{ek}_0 = \mathsf{ek}_0'$ and $\mathsf{ek}_1 = (\mathsf{ek}_1', \mathsf{evk}, \mathsf{pk}, \{\mathsf{ct}_j, \boldsymbol{\sigma}_j\}_{j \in [k]})$, a circuit $C \colon \{0, 1\}^N \times \{0, 1\}^k \to \{0, 1\}$, a party index $b \in \{0, 1\}$, and a decoding trapdoor td, the evaluation algorithm first defines the following functions:
  - Let $g \colon \mathbb{Z}_p^N \times \mathbb{Z}_p^n \to \mathbb{Z}_p^{Nn}$ be the quadratic function where $g(\mathbf{x}_0, \mathbf{s}_{\mathsf{in}}) := \mathbf{x}_0 \otimes \mathbf{s}_{\mathsf{in}}$.
  - Let $f_C \colon \{0, 1\}^N \times \{0, 1\}^{k\ell_{\mathsf{ct}}} \to \{0, 1\}^{n \log p}$ be the Boolean circuit

$$f_C(\mathbf{x}_0, (\mathsf{ct}_1, \dots, \mathsf{ct}_k)) := \mathsf{LHE.Eval}(\mathsf{pk}, C(\mathbf{x}_0, \cdot), (\mathsf{ct}_1, \dots, \mathsf{ct}_k)).$$

  - Let $L \colon \mathbb{Z}_q^{n^2 \log p} \to \mathbb{Z}_q$ be the linear function where $L(\mathbf{c} \otimes \mathbf{s}) := \mathbf{s}^\top \tilde{\mathbf{c}}$, where $\mathbf{c}$ is the binary representation of $\tilde{\mathbf{c}}$.
  Now depending the value of $b \in \{0, 1\}$, the evaluation algorithm proceeds as follows:
  - If $b = 0$, the evaluation algorithm parses $\mathsf{td} = \mathsf{td}_0'$ and computes the tag

$$\tilde{\boldsymbol{\sigma}} = \mathsf{SMS_Q.Eval}\left((\mathsf{ek}_0', \mathsf{ek}_1'), g, 0, \mathsf{td}_0'\right) \in \mathbb{Z}_p^{Nn}.$$

The algorithm parses $\tilde{\boldsymbol{\sigma}}^{\mathsf{T}} = [\tilde{\boldsymbol{\sigma}}_1^{\mathsf{T}} \mid \cdots \mid \tilde{\boldsymbol{\sigma}}_N^{\mathsf{T}}]$ where $\tilde{\boldsymbol{\sigma}}_j \in \mathbb{Z}_p^n$ for all $j \in [N]$. Then, it computes the tag

$$\boldsymbol{\sigma}_{f_C} = \mathsf{EvalTag}\left(\begin{matrix} \mathsf{evk}, f_C, (\mathbf{x}_0, (\mathsf{ct}_1, \ldots, \mathsf{ct}_k))), \\ (\tilde{\boldsymbol{\sigma}}_1, \ldots, \tilde{\boldsymbol{\sigma}}_N, \boldsymbol{\sigma}_1, \ldots, \boldsymbol{\sigma}_k) \end{matrix} \right) \in \mathbb{Z}_p^{n^2} \qquad (4.1)$$

Output the share $d_0 = \mathsf{Round}_{p \to 2}(L(\boldsymbol{\sigma}') - u) \in \mathbb{Z}_2$.
- If $b = 1$, the evaluation algorithm parses $\mathsf{td} = (\mathsf{td}_1', \mathsf{sk}, \{\mathbf{k}_j\}_{j \in [k]})$. Then, it computes the encoding key

$$\tilde{\mathbf{k}} = \mathsf{SMS}_Q.\mathsf{Eval}((\mathsf{ek}_0', \mathsf{ek}_1'), g, 1, \mathsf{td}_1').$$

The algorithm parses $\tilde{\mathbf{k}}^{\mathsf{T}} = [\tilde{\mathbf{k}}_1^{\mathsf{T}} \mid \cdots \mid \tilde{\mathbf{k}}_N^{\mathsf{T}}]$ where $\tilde{\mathbf{k}}_j \in \mathbb{Z}_p^n$ for all $j \in [N]$. Then, it computes the encoding key

$$\mathbf{k}_{f_C} = \mathsf{EvalKey}(\mathsf{sk}, \mathsf{evk}, f_C, (\tilde{\mathbf{k}}_1, \ldots, \tilde{\mathbf{k}}_N, \mathbf{k}_1, \ldots, \mathbf{k}_k)). \qquad (4.2)$$

Finally, it outputs the share $d_1 = \mathsf{Round}_{p \to 2}(-L(\mathbf{k}_{f_C}) + u)$.

Theorem 4.3 (Correctness). *If Π_{LHE}, Π_{AHMAC}, and Π_{SMSQ} are correct and $p > \lambda^{\omega(1)}$, then Construction 4.2 is correct.*

Proof. Take any size bound $s = s(\lambda) < 2^\lambda$ and instance bound $t = t(\lambda)$. Take any security parameter $\lambda \in \mathbb{N}$, circuit family parameter $\kappa \in \mathbb{N}$, inputs $\mathbf{x}_0 \in \{0,1\}^N$ and $\mathbf{x}_1 \in \{0,1\}^k$ and a collection of circuits $C_1, \ldots, C_t \in \mathcal{C}_\kappa$ where $|C_i| \leq s(\lambda)$. Let $\mathsf{crs} \leftarrow \mathsf{Setup}(1^\lambda, 1^\kappa)$. Write $\mathsf{crs} = (1^d, \mathsf{crs}_{\mathsf{SMSQ}}, u)$ where $\mathsf{crs}_{\mathsf{SMSQ}} \leftarrow \mathsf{SMS}_Q.\mathsf{Setup}(1^\lambda)$ and $u \xleftarrow{\mathsf{R}} \mathbb{Z}_p$. Let

$$(\mathsf{ek}_0, \mathsf{td}_0) \leftarrow \mathsf{Encode}(\mathsf{crs}, 0, \mathbf{x}_0)$$
$$(\mathsf{ek}_1, \mathsf{td}_1) \leftarrow \mathsf{Encode}(\mathsf{crs}, 1, \mathbf{x}_1).$$

Fix a function $C \in \{C_1, \ldots, C_t\}$ and compute $d_0 := \mathsf{Eval}(\mathsf{crs}, (\mathsf{ek}_0, \mathsf{ek}_1), C, 0, \mathsf{td}_0)$ and $d_1 := \mathsf{Eval}(\mathsf{crs}, (\mathsf{ek}_0, \mathsf{ek}_1), C, 1, \mathsf{td}_1)$. Consider the value of $d_0 \oplus d_1$:

- First, we can write

$$\begin{aligned} \mathsf{ek}_0 &= \mathsf{ek}_0' & \mathsf{ek}_1 &= (\mathsf{ek}_1', \mathsf{evk}, \mathsf{pk}, \{\mathsf{ct}_j, \boldsymbol{\sigma}_j\}_{j \in [k]}) \\ \mathsf{td}_0 &= \mathsf{td}_0' & \mathsf{td}_1 &= (\mathsf{td}_1', \mathsf{sk}, \{\mathbf{k}_j\}_{j \in [k]}). \end{aligned}$$

- Consider the values of $\tilde{\boldsymbol{\sigma}}$ and $\tilde{\mathbf{k}}$ from the computations of d_0 and d_1. By construction,

$$\tilde{\boldsymbol{\sigma}} = \mathsf{SMS}_Q.\mathsf{Eval}((\mathsf{ek}_0', \mathsf{ek}_1'), g, 0, \mathsf{td}_0') \in \mathbb{Z}_p^{Nn}$$
$$\tilde{\mathbf{k}} = \mathsf{SMS}_Q.\mathsf{Eval}((\mathsf{ek}_0', \mathsf{ek}_1'), g, 1, \mathsf{td}_1') \in \mathbb{Z}_p^{Nn}.$$

Since $\mathsf{ek}_0', \mathsf{ek}_1'$ are encodings of $\mathbf{x}_0 \in \mathbb{Z}_p^N$ and $\mathbf{s}_{\mathsf{in}} \in \mathbb{Z}_p^n$, respectively, we conclude by correctness of Π_{SMSQ}, with overwhelming probability, it holds that

$$\tilde{\boldsymbol{\sigma}} - \tilde{\mathbf{k}} = g(\mathbf{x}_0, \mathbf{s}_{\mathsf{in}}) = \mathbf{x}_0 \otimes \mathbf{s}_{\mathsf{in}}.$$

In particular, this means that for all $i \in [N]$, $\tilde{\boldsymbol{\sigma}}_i = x_{0,i} \cdot \mathbf{s}_{\mathsf{in}} + \tilde{\mathbf{k}}_i$

- Next, consider the value $\boldsymbol{\sigma}_{f_C}$ and $\mathbf{k}_{f_C}$ from the computation of d_0 and d_1 (see Eqs. (4.1) and (4.2)). Since $\boldsymbol{\sigma}_j = \mathsf{ct}_j \otimes \mathsf{s}_{\mathsf{in}} + \mathbf{k}_j$, by correctness of Π_{AHMAC}, with overwhelming probability,

$$\boldsymbol{\sigma}_{f_C} = f_C(\mathbf{x}_0, (\mathsf{ct}_1, \ldots, \mathsf{ct}_k)) \otimes \mathsf{s} + \mathbf{k}_{f_C} = \mathbf{c} \otimes \mathsf{s} + \mathbf{k}_{f_C},$$

where $\mathbf{c}$ is the binary representation of $\tilde{\mathbf{c}} = \mathsf{LHE.Eval}(\mathsf{pk}, f(\mathbf{x}_0, \cdot), (\mathsf{ct}_1, \ldots, \mathsf{ct}_k))$.
- Next, L is a linear function, so

$$L(\boldsymbol{\sigma}_{f_C}) - L(\mathbf{k}_{f_C}) = L(\mathbf{c} \otimes \mathsf{s}) = \mathsf{s}^{\mathsf{T}}\tilde{\mathbf{c}}.$$

By correctness of Π_{LHE}, with overwhelming probability, $\mathsf{s}^{\mathsf{T}}\tilde{\mathbf{c}} = f(\mathbf{x}_0, \mathbf{x}_1) \cdot \lfloor p/2 \rfloor + e$ where $|e| < \sqrt{p}$.
- Since $u \xleftarrow{\text{R}} \mathbb{Z}_p$, with overwhelming probability over the choice of u, it follows from Lemma 4.1 that $d_0 \oplus d_1 = f(\mathbf{x}_0, \mathbf{x}_1)$ except with probability $O(1/\sqrt{p}) = \mathsf{negl}(\lambda)$.

Thus, with overwhelming probability over the randomness of Setup and Encode, we conclude that for any $C \in \{C_1, \ldots, C_t\}$ correctness holds with overwhelming probability. Since $t = \mathsf{poly}(\lambda)$, the claim now holds by a union bound.

Theorem 4.4 (Security). *If Π_{LHE} is semantically secure, Π_{AHMAC} is selectively secure, and Π_{SMSQ} is adaptively secure, then Construction 4.2 is adaptively secure.*

We give the proof of Theorem 4.4 in the full version.

Theorem 4.5 (Succinctness). *If Π_{AHMAC} and Π_{SMSQ} satisfy succinctness, then Construction 4.2 is also succinct.*

Proof. The size of $|\mathsf{crs}_{\mathsf{SMSQ}}| = \mathsf{poly}(\lambda, |\mathsf{s}_{\mathsf{in}}|)$ where $\mathsf{s}_{\mathsf{in}} \in \mathbb{Z}_p^n$. Since $n \log p = \mathsf{poly}(\lambda, d)$, this means $|\mathsf{crs}| = \mathsf{poly}(\lambda, d)$. Next, succinctness of Π_{SMSQ} implies that $|\mathsf{ek}_0'| = \mathsf{poly}(\lambda)$ and $|\mathsf{ek}_1'| = \mathsf{poly}(\lambda)$. By definition, $|\mathsf{pk}| = \mathsf{poly}(\lambda, d)$ and succinctness of the algebraic MAC implies that $|\mathsf{evk}| = \mathsf{poly}(\lambda, d') = \mathsf{poly}(\lambda, d)$ since $d' = \mathsf{poly}(\lambda, d)$. Each ciphertext ct_i and each tag σ_i has size $\mathsf{poly}(\lambda, d)$. Thus, putting everything together, the size of ek_1 is $\mathsf{poly}(\lambda, d, k)$.

Remark 4.6 (Sub-Exponential Security). We note that if each of the underlying building blocks $(\Pi_{\mathsf{LHE}}, \Pi_{\mathsf{AHMAC}}, \Pi_{\mathsf{SMSQ}})$ in Construction 4.2 are sub-exponentially-secure, then the proof of Theorem 4.4 shows that Construction 4.2 also satisfies sub-exponential security.

5   Reusable Multiparty SMS Protocol from $i\mathcal{O}$

In this section, we show how to bootstrap a reusable two-party SMS protocol to the multiparty setting using $i\mathcal{O}$.

Construction 5.1 (Multiparty Succinct HSS). Let λ denote the security parameter and $\mathcal{C} = \{\mathcal{C}_\kappa\}_{\kappa \in \mathbb{N}}$ be a family of bounded-depth Boolean circuits where each circuit $f \in \mathcal{C}_\kappa$ is a Boolean circuit of depth $d = d(\kappa)$ and of type $f\colon \{0,1\}^N \times (\{0,1\}^\ell)^n \to \{0,1\}$, where $d = d(\kappa)$, $N = N(\kappa)$, $\ell = \ell(\kappa)$, and $n = n(\kappa)$ are polynomially-bounded.[9] We define two more security parameters: $\lambda_1 = \mathsf{poly}(\lambda, n, \ell)$ and $\lambda_2 = \mathsf{poly}(\lambda, d, \log N, n, \ell)$. The construction makes use of the following building blocks:

- Let $\Pi_{\mathsf{rSMS}} = (\mathsf{rSMS.Setup}, \mathsf{rSMS.Encode}, \mathsf{rSMS.Eval})$ be a reusable two-party SMS scheme for $\mathcal{C}$ with sub-exponential security.
- Let $\kappa'(\lambda, \kappa)$ be an injective and efficiently-computable mapping, and let $\mathcal{C}' = \{\mathcal{C}'_{\kappa'}\}_{\kappa' \in \mathbb{N}}$ be a family of Boolean circuits that includes circuits of the form

$$G(f, (\mathsf{ek}_{\mathsf{rSMS},0}, \mathsf{ek}_{\mathsf{rSMS},1}, \mathsf{td}_{\mathsf{rSMS},1})) := \mathsf{rSMS.Eval}\left(\begin{matrix} \mathsf{crs}_{\mathsf{rSMS}}, (\mathsf{ek}_{\mathsf{rSMS},0}, \mathsf{ek}_{\mathsf{rSMS},1}), \\ f, 1, \mathsf{td}_{\mathsf{rSMS},1} \end{matrix}\right),$$

  where $f \in \mathcal{C}_\kappa$ and $\mathsf{crs}_{\mathsf{rSMS}}$ is a CRS in the support of $\mathsf{rSMS.Setup}(1^\lambda, 1^\kappa)$. Let $\Pi_{\mathsf{SMS}} = (\mathsf{SMS.Setup}, \mathsf{SMS.Encode}, \mathsf{SMS.Decode})$ be a two-party SMS scheme for the circuit class $\mathcal{C}'$ with sub-exponential security.
- Let $i\mathcal{O}$ be an indistinguishability obfuscation scheme for Boolean circuits that supports the Boolean circuits appearing in the subsequent description and those in the security proof. We require the $i\mathcal{O}$ scheme to satisfy sub-exponential security.
- Let $\Pi_{\mathsf{PKE}} = (\mathsf{PKE.KeyGen}, \mathsf{PKE.Enc}, \mathsf{PKE.Dec})$ be a semantically-secure public-key encryption scheme.
- Let $\Pi_{\mathsf{NIZK}} = (\mathsf{NIZK.Setup}, \mathsf{NIZK.Prove}, \mathsf{NIZK.Verify})$ be a statistical simulation-sound NIZK proof system.
- Let $\Pi_{\mathsf{PRF}} = (\mathsf{PRF.KeyGen}, \mathsf{PRF.Punc}, \mathsf{PRF.Eval})$ be a puncturable PRF family. We require Π_{PRF} to satisfy sub-exponential security.

We assume without loss of generality that the $\mathsf{PKE.Encode}$, $\mathsf{rSMS.Encode}$, and $\mathsf{SMS.Encode}$ algorithms above take at most λ bits of randomness. This is without loss of generality since we can always take the randomness to an algorithm to be the seed of a pseudorandom generator (PRG) and use the PRG to expand the seed into however many bits of randomness the algorithm requires. By a standard hybrid argument, this preserves the security of the underlying scheme. The multiparty succinct HSS is then defined as follows (Fig. 1):

- $\mathsf{Setup}(1^\lambda, 1^\kappa)$: On input the security parameter λ and the circuit-family parameter κ the setup algorithm proceeds as follows:
  1. Sample $\mathsf{crs}_{\mathsf{rSMS}} \leftarrow \mathsf{rSMS.Setup}(1^{\lambda_1}, 1^\kappa)$ and $\mathsf{crs}_{\mathsf{SMS}} \leftarrow \mathsf{SMS.Setup}(1^{\lambda_1}, 1^{\kappa'})$ where $\kappa' = \kappa'(\lambda_1, \kappa)$.
  2. For each $i \in [n]$,

---

[9] In this construction, we use f to denote the Boolean circuit in order distinguish it from the (obfuscated) circuit $\widetilde{C}$ in the CRS. Additionally, we refer to Remark 3.2 on how to support circuits with multiple output bits.

Inputs: $(f_{\mathrm{SMS}}, \mathsf{ek}_0, \ldots, \mathsf{ek}_n)$.

Hardwired: $K, \{\mathsf{pk}_{i,0}, \mathsf{pk}_{i,1}, \mathsf{sk}_{i,0}, \mathsf{crs}_{\mathrm{NIZK},i}\}_{i \in [n]}, \mathsf{crs}_{\mathrm{rSMS}}, \mathsf{crs}_{\mathrm{SMS}}$.

(a) For every $i \in [n]$,
     i. Check $\mathsf{NIZK.Verify}(\mathsf{crs}_{\mathrm{NIZK},i}, (\mathsf{pk}_{i,0}, \mathsf{pk}_{i,1}, \mathsf{ct}_{i,0}, \mathsf{ct}_{i,1}), \pi_i) = 1$.
     ii. If the check fails, output $\perp$.

(b) For every $i \in [n]$,
     i. Compute $(x_i, k_i) \leftarrow \mathsf{PKE.Dec}(\mathsf{sk}_{i,0}, \mathsf{ct}_{i,0})$.
     ii. Compute $\mathsf{mask}_i \leftarrow \mathsf{PRF.Eval}(k_i, (f_{\mathrm{SMS}}, \mathsf{ek}_0, \ldots, \mathsf{ek}_n))$.

(c) Compute $(r_{\mathrm{rSMS}}, r_{\mathrm{SMS}}) \leftarrow \mathsf{PRF.Eval}(K, (\mathsf{ek}_0, \ldots, \mathsf{ek}_n))$.

(d) Compute $(\mathsf{ek}_{\mathrm{rSMS},1}, \mathsf{td}_{\mathrm{rSMS},1}) = \mathsf{rSMS.Encode}(\mathsf{crs}_{\mathrm{rSMS}}, 1, x_1, \ldots, x_n; r_{\mathrm{rSMS}})$.

(e) Compute

$$(\mathsf{ek}_{\mathrm{SMS},1}, \mathsf{td}_{\mathrm{SMS},1}) \leftarrow \mathsf{SMS.Encode}(\mathsf{crs}_{\mathrm{SMS}}, 1, \mathsf{ek}_0, \mathsf{ek}_{\mathrm{rSMS},1}, \mathsf{td}_{\mathrm{rSMS},1}; r_{\mathrm{SMS}}).$$

(f) Compute $d_{\mathrm{SMS},1} \leftarrow \mathsf{SMS.Decode}(\mathsf{crs}_{\mathrm{SMS}}, 1, f_{\mathrm{SMS}}, \mathsf{td}_{\mathrm{SMS},1})$.

(g) Output $(\mathsf{ek}_{\mathrm{rSMS},1}, \mathsf{ek}_{\mathrm{SMS},1}, d_{\mathrm{SMS},1} \oplus \mathsf{mask}_1 \oplus \ldots \oplus \mathsf{mask}_n)$.

Fig. 1. Description of circuit C

     (a) Sample $(\mathsf{pk}_{i,b}, \mathsf{sk}_{i,b}) \leftarrow \mathsf{PKE.KeyGen}(1^\lambda)$ for each $b \in \{0,1\}$.
     (b) Sample $\mathsf{crs}_{\mathrm{NIZK},i} \leftarrow \mathsf{NIZK.Setup}(1^\lambda)$.
3. Sample $K \leftarrow \mathsf{PRF.KeyGen}(1^{\lambda_1})$.
4. Compute $\widetilde{C} \leftarrow i\mathcal{O}(1^{\lambda_2}, C)$ where C is the following circuit:
5. Sample randomness $r \xleftarrow{\mathrm{R}} \{0,1\}^{\lambda_1}$.
6. Output the common reference string

$$\mathsf{crs} = (\mathsf{crs}_{\mathrm{rSMS}}, \mathsf{crs}_{\mathrm{SMS}}, \{\mathsf{pk}_{i,0}, \mathsf{pk}_{i,1}, \mathsf{crs}_{\mathrm{NIZK},i}\}_{i \in [n]}, \widetilde{C}, r). \tag{5.1}$$

– Encode(crs, i, x_i): On input the common reference string crs (with components parsed according to Eq. (5.1)), the party index $i \in [0, n]$, and the input x_i, the encoding algorithm proceeds as follows:
- If $i = 0$, then compute $(\mathsf{ek}_{\mathrm{rSMS},0}, \mathsf{td}_{\mathrm{rSMS},0}) \leftarrow \mathsf{rSMS.Encode}(\mathsf{crs}_{\mathrm{rSMS}}, 0, x_0)$ and output the evaluation key $\mathsf{ek}_0 = \mathsf{ek}_{\mathrm{rSMS},0}$ and the trapdoor $\mathsf{td}_0 = (\mathsf{td}_{\mathrm{rSMS},0}, r)$.
- If $i \in [n]$, then proceed as follows:
     * Sample $k_i \leftarrow \mathsf{PRF.KeyGen}(1^{\lambda_2})$ and set $m_i = (x_i, k_i)$.
     * Compute $\mathsf{ct}_{i,b} \leftarrow \mathsf{PKE.Enc}(\mathsf{pk}_{i,b}, m_i; r_{i,b})$ for each $b \in \{0,1\}$ where $r_{i,b} \xleftarrow{\mathrm{R}} \{0,1\}^\lambda$.
     * Compute $\pi_i \leftarrow \mathsf{NIZK.Prove}\left(\begin{array}{c} \mathsf{crs}_{\mathrm{NIZK},i}, \mathcal{R}, (\mathsf{pk}_{i,0}, \mathsf{pk}_{i,1}, \mathsf{ct}_{i,0}, \mathsf{ct}_{i,1}), \\ (m_i, r_{i,0}, r_{i,1}) \end{array}\right)$
     where $\mathcal{R}$ is the following NP relation:

$$\mathcal{R}\big((\mathsf{pk}_0, \mathsf{pk}_1, \mathsf{ct}_0, \mathsf{ct}_1), (m, r_0, r_1)\big) = 1$$
$$\iff \forall b \in \{0,1\} : \mathsf{ct}_b = \mathsf{PKE.Enc}(\mathsf{pk}_b, m; r_b)$$

$*$ Output the evaluation key $\mathsf{ek}_i = (\mathsf{ct}_{i,0}, \mathsf{ct}_{i,1}, \pi_i)$ and the trapdoor $\mathsf{td}_i = (k_i, r)$.

- $\mathsf{Eval}(\mathsf{crs}, (\mathsf{ek}_0, \mathsf{ek}_1, \ldots, \mathsf{ek}_n), f, i, \mathsf{td}_i)$: On input the common reference string crs (with components parsed according to Eq. (5.1)), evaluation keys $\mathsf{ek}_0, \ldots, \mathsf{ek}_n$, the circuit $f \colon \{0,1\}^N \times (\{0,1\}^\ell)^n \to \{0,1\}$, an index $i \in [0, n]$, and a trapdoor td_i, the evaluation algorithm proceeds as follows:

1. Compute $(f_{\mathsf{SMS}}, \mathsf{td}_{\mathsf{SMS},0}) = \mathsf{SMS.Encode}(\mathsf{crs}_{\mathsf{SMS}}, 0, (f, G); r)$ where G is the circuit

$$G(f, (\mathsf{ek}_{\mathsf{rSMS},0}, \mathsf{ek}_{\mathsf{rSMS},1}, \mathsf{td}_{\mathsf{rSMS},1})) := \mathsf{rSMS.Eval}\left(\begin{array}{c} \mathsf{crs}_{\mathsf{rSMS}}, \mathsf{ek}_{\mathsf{rSMS},0}, \\ \mathsf{ek}_{\mathsf{rSMS},1}, f, 1, \mathsf{td}_{\mathsf{rSMS},1} \end{array} \right).$$

2. If $i = 0$, parse $\mathsf{ek}_0 = \mathsf{ek}_{\mathsf{rSMS},0}$ and the trapdoor $\mathsf{td}_0 = (\mathsf{td}_{\mathsf{rSMS},0}, r)$ and then proceed as follows:
   (a) Compute $(\mathsf{ek}_{\mathsf{rSMS},1}, \mathsf{ek}_{\mathsf{SMS},1}, d_1') \leftarrow \widetilde{C}(f_{\mathsf{SMS}}, \mathsf{ek}_0, \ldots, \mathsf{ek}_n)$.
   (b) Compute $d_{\mathsf{SMS},0} = \mathsf{SMS.Decode}(\mathsf{crs}_{\mathsf{SMS}}, 0, \mathsf{ek}_{\mathsf{SMS},1}, \mathsf{td}_{\mathsf{SMS},0})$.
   (c) Compute $d_{\mathsf{rSMS},0} = \mathsf{rSMS.Eval}(\mathsf{crs}_{\mathsf{rSMS}}, (\mathsf{ek}_{\mathsf{rSMS},0}, \mathsf{ek}_{\mathsf{rSMS},1}), f, 0, \mathsf{td}_{\mathsf{rSMS},0})$.
   (d) Output $d_0 = d_{\mathsf{rSMS},0} \oplus d_{\mathsf{SMS},0} \oplus d_1'$.
3. If $i \neq 0$, parse $\mathsf{td}_i = k_i$ and output $d_i = \mathsf{PRF.Eval}(k_i, (f_{\mathsf{SMS}}, \mathsf{ek}_0, \ldots, \mathsf{ek}_n))$.

We give the proof of correctness, security and the succinct analysis in the full version.

Acknowledgments. We thank Yuval Ishai for many helpful comments and discussions. Akshayaram Srinivasan and Siddharth Agarwal are supported in part by the NSERC Discovery Grant RGPIN-2024-03928. Akshayaram Srinivasan is additionally supported by a SDF academic research award. David J. Wu is supported by NSF CNS-2140975, CNS-2318701, a Sloan Fellowship, a Microsoft Research Faculty Fellowship, a Google Research Scholar Award, an Amazon Research Award, and a gift from the Stellar Development Foundation. Abhishek Jain is supported in part by NSF CAREER 1942789, Johns Hopkins University Catalyst award, JP Morgan Faculty Award, and research gifts from the Ethereum Foundation, Stellar Development Foundation, and Cisco. Part of this work was conducted while Abhishek Jain and David J. Wu were visiting the Simons Institute for the Theory of Computing and supported in part by a grant from the UC Noyce Initiative.

References

1. Abram, D., Malavolta, G., Roy, L.: Succinct oblivious tensor evaluation and applications: adaptively-secure laconic function evaluation and trapdoor hashing for all circuits. In: STOC (2025)
2. Abram, D., Roy, L., Scholl, P.: Succinct homomorphic secret sharing. In: EUROCRYPT (2024)
3. Ananth, P., Jain, A., Jin, Z., Malavolta, G.: Multi-key fully-homomorphic encryption in the plain model. In: TCC (2020)
4. Ananth, P., Jain, A., Jin, Z., Malavolta, G.: Unbounded multi-party computation from learning with errors. In: EUROCRYPT (2021)

5. Barak, B., et al.: On the (im)possibility of obfuscating programs. In: CRYPTO (2001)
6. Bartusek, J., Garg, S., Masny, D., Mukherjee, P.: Reusable two-round MPC from DDH. In: TCC (2020)
7. Bartusek, J., Garg, S., Srinivasan, A., Zhang, Y.: Reusable two-round MPC from LPN. In: PKC (2022)
8. Benhamouda, F., Jain, A., Komargodski, I., Lin, H.: Multiparty reusable non-interactive secure computation from LWE. In: EUROCRYPT (2021)
9. Benhamouda, F., Lin, H.: Mr NISC: multiparty reusable non-interactive secure computation. In: TCC (2020)
10. Boyle, E., Gilboa, N., Ishai, Y.: Function secret sharing: improvements and extensions. In: ACM CCS (2016)
11. Boyle, E., Jain, A., Servan-Schreiber, S., Srinivasan, A.: Simultaneous-message and succinct secure computation. In: EUROCRYPT (2025)
12. Boyle, E., Kohl, L., Scholl, P.: Homomorphic secret sharing from lattices without FHE. In: EUROCRYPT (2019)
13. Brakerski, Z.: Fully homomorphic encryption without modulus switching from classical GapSVP. In: CRYPTO (2012)
14. Brakerski, Z., Döttling, N., Garg, S., Malavolta, G.: Leveraging linear decryption: rate-1 fully-homomorphic encryption and time-lock puzzles. In: TCC (2019)
15. Brakerski, Z., Gentry, C., Vaikuntanathan, V.: (Leveled) fully homomorphic encryption without bootstrapping. In: ITCS (2012)
16. Brakerski, Z., Koppula, V., Mour, T.: NIZK from LPN and trapdoor hash via correlation intractability for approximable relations. In: CRYPTO (2020)
17. Brakerski, Z., Tsabary, R., Vaikuntanathan, V., Wee, H.: Private constrained PRFs (and more) from LWE. In: TCC (2017)
18. Brakerski, Z., Vaikuntanathan, V.: Efficient fully homomorphic encryption from (standard) LWE. In: FOCS (2011)
19. Branco, P., Choudhuri, A.R., Döttling, N., Jain, A., Malavolta, G., Srinivasan, A.: Black-box non-interactive zero knowledge from vector trapdoor hash. In: EUROCRYPT (2025)
20. Canetti, R., Goldreich, O., Halevi, S.: The random oracle methodology, revisited. J. ACM **51**(4) (2004)
21. Cho, C., Döttling, N., Garg, S., Gupta, D., Miao, P., Polychroniadou, A.: Laconic oblivious transfer and its applications. In: CRYPTO (2017)
22. Chor, B., Goldreich, O., Kushilevitz, E., Sudan, M.: Private information retrieval. In: FOCS (1995)
23. Couteau, G., Hegde, A., Pu, S.: Enhanced trapdoor hashing from DDH and DCR. In: EUROCRYPT (2025)
24. De Santis, A., Di Crescenzo, G., Ostrovsky, R., Persiano, G., Sahai, A.: Robust non-interactive zero knowledge. In: CRYPTO (2001)
25. Dodis, Y., Halevi, S., Rothblum, R.D., Wichs, D.: Spooky encryption and its applications. In: CRYPTO (2016)
26. Döttling, N., Garg, S., Ishai, Y., Malavolta, G., Mour, T., Ostrovsky, R.: Trapdoor hash functions and their applications. In: CRYPTO (2019)
27. Feige, U., Kilian, J., Naor, M.: A minimal model for secure computation (extended abstract). In: STOC (1994)
28. Garg, S., Gentry, C., Halevi, S., Raykova, M., Sahai, A., Waters, B.: Candidate indistinguishability obfuscation and functional encryption for all circuits. In: FOCS (2013)

29. Gentry, C.: Fully homomorphic encryption using ideal lattices. In: STOC (2009)
30. Gentry, C., Sahai, A., Waters, B.: Homomorphic encryption from learning with errors: conceptually-simpler, asymptotically-faster, attribute-based. In: CRYPTO (2013)
31. Goldreich, O., Micali, S., Wigderson, A.: How to play any mental game or A completeness theorem for protocols with honest majority. In: STOC (1987)
32. Halevi, S., Lindell, Y., Pinkas, B.: Secure computation on the web: computing without simultaneous interaction. In: CRYPTO (2011)
33. Hsieh, Y., Lin, H., Luo, J.: Attribute-based encryption for circuits of unbounded depth from lattices. In: FOCS (2023)
34. Ishai, Y., Li, H., Lin, H.: Succinct homomorphic MACs from groups and applications. In: FOCS (2025)
35. Ishai, Y., Li, H., Lin, H.: A unified framework for succinct garbling from homomorphic secret sharing. In: CRYPTO (2025)
36. Jain, A., Jin, Z.: Non-interactive zero knowledge from sub-exponential DDH. In: EUROCRYPT (2021)
37. Kushilevitz, E., Ostrovsky, R.: Replication is NOT needed: SINGLE database, computationally-private information retrieval. In: FOCS (1997)
38. Naor, M., Yung, M.: Public-key cryptosystems provably secure against chosen ciphertext attacks. In: STOC (1990)
39. Quach, W., Wee, H., Wichs, D.: Laconic function evaluation and applications. In: FOCS (2018)
40. Regev, O.: On lattices, learning with errors, random linear codes, and cryptography. In: STOC (2005)
41. Sahai, A.: Non-malleable non-interactive zero knowledge and adaptive chosen-ciphertext security. In: FOCS (1999)

Non-interactive Secure Computation with Constant Communication Overhead

Yuval Ishai[1], Ziyang Jin[2], Naty Peter[1,2], and Akshayaram Srinivasan[2(✉)]

[1] Technion and AWS, New York, USA
naty@post.bgu.ac.il
[2] University of Toronto, Toronto, Canada
ziyang@cs.toronto.edu, akshayaram.srinivasan@utoronto.ca

Abstract. We study the communication complexity of non-interactive secure computation (NISC) protocols with security against malicious adversaries. We give a general NISC protocol for any two-party function computed by a Boolean circuit C using only $O(|C|\lambda)$ bits of communication, where λ is an exact security parameter. This protocol is unconditionally secure in the random oracle model, assuming a standard random OT correlations setup. Compared to Yao's semi-honest protocol, our protocol incurs only a constant communication overhead and achieves security against malicious parties with no additional interaction. Prior works achieved such constant overhead by either using a larger number of rounds or more structured correlations.

1 Introduction

Secure computation [24,52] is a fundamental cryptographic primitive with numerous applications. In the commonly studied scenario involving two parties, one party (the receiver) has a private input x, while the other party (the sender) has a private input y. The receiver aims to obtain the output of a two-party function f applied to (x, y). Secure computation allows the receiver to learn this information without learning anything else about the sender's input, while revealing nothing about the receiver's input to the sender.

In the semi-honest setting, garbled circuits [52] combined with a two-round oblivious transfer (OT) protocol provide a straightforward two-message protocol for this task. In the first round, the receiver encodes its private input x as the receiver's choice bits in the OT protocol. The sender generates the garbled circuit $\widetilde{C}$ along with the set of input labels using the circuit representation of the function. Subsequently, the sender sends $\widetilde{C}$, the labels corresponding to its private input y, and then encodes the labels for the receiver's input wires as the sender's message in the OT protocol. The receiver first decodes the OT message from the sender to obtain the labels corresponding to its input x, and then evaluates the garbled circuit to learn $f(x, y)$. Furthermore, we can replace the

---

N. Peter–Work done while at the University of Toronto
This work is not associated with Amazon.

J. Daemen and E. Thomé (Eds.): EUROCRYPT 2026, LNCS 16543, pp. 124–154, 2026.
https://doi.org/10.1007/978-3-032-25324-8_5

two-round OT protocol with random bit-OT correlations, which can be efficiently generated (with a succinct, reusable setup) using pseudorandom correlation generators [8] or pseudorandom correlation functions [9]. Specifically, after a seed setup phase whose communication cost can be polylogarithmic in the number of OT instances, random OT correlations can be generated on the fly via "silent" local expansion.

The above protocol has a number of appealing features. Firstly, it involves only a single message each from the receiver and the sender. This interaction pattern is minimal: viewing the receiver's message as an encryption of its input, any potential sender only needs to locally compute and send the encrypted output to the receiver. For this reason, the model is sometimes referred to as *non-interactive secure computation* (NISC) [34,37]. Secondly, this simple semi-honest NISC protocol can be based on minimal cryptographic assumptions (two-round oblivious transfer) or relies on a minimal correlated randomness setup of random OT correlations along with a pseudorandom generator (PRG). Thirdly, its communication cost is $O(|C|\lambda)$ bits, where λ is (an exact) computational security parameter and C refers to the number of gates in a Boolean circuit C (excluding XOR gates whenever a random oracle is assumed). Unless one relies on "homomorphic" primitives such as fully homomorphic encryption (FHE) [7,12,22,23] or homomorphic secret sharing (HSS) [11,15,36,42,43], this is the best communication cost that one could hope for barring a major breakthrough.

Malicious Setting. If the parties are allowed to deviate arbitrarily from the protocol specification, then the state of affairs is not as clean as in the semi-honest setting. For simplicity, we cast all of the following results by assuming an OT correlations setup. Ishai et al. [34,37] were the first to consider NISC with security against malicious adversaries making a black-box use of cryptography. They achieved a positive result with a multiplicative communication overhead of $\text{polylog}(|C|,\sigma)$ compared to the semi-honest baseline, only making a black-box use of a PRG. (Here and in the following, σ is a statistical security parameter allowing for $2^{-\sigma}$ simulation error.) A subsequent work of Afsar et al. [1] obtained a concretely efficient version of malicious NISC with multiplicative communication overhead of σ, which is asymptotically worse but concretely better than [34] for realistic values of σ. Hazay et al. [25] obtained the first malicious NISC protocol with a constant communication overhead in the random oracle model. However, this protocol only satisfied a weaker notion of security called security with correlated abort. Specifically, in this security notion, the sender can force the receiver to abort if the receiver's private input satisfies a sender-defined predicate. (This is similar to, but slightly stronger than, the type of security achieved by constant-round protocols following the "dual execution" framework [28].) Recently, Dittmer et al. [19] presented malicious NISC protocols with constant communication overhead, but relied on more structured "OLE-style" correlations that are stronger than OT correlations and are much more expensive to generate [8,10]. See Table 1 for a summary of prior work.

Table 1. Comparison of NISC protocols in prior works, where λ is an exact computational security parameter, and σ is a statistical security parameter.

Work	Assumptions	Communication Cost	Security
[34]	OT correlations + PRG	$O(|C|\lambda) \cdot \mathrm{polylog}(|C|, \sigma)$	Standard
[1]	2-round batch-committing OT	$O(|C| \cdot \lambda\sigma)$	Standard
[25]	OT correlations + RO	$O(|C|\lambda)$	Correlated-Abort
[19]	programmable tensor OLE + RO	$O(|C|\lambda)$	Standard
Ours	OT correlations + RO	$O(|C|\lambda)$	Standard

The above state of the art leaves the following natural question open:

Is there a malicious-secure NISC protocol with communication cost $O(|C|\lambda)$ assuming random OT correlations and black-box use of PRG?

Such a protocol will bridge the asymptotic gap between what is known in a semi-honest setting and what is known in a malicious setting.

Our Result. We show that if we replace a PRG by a random oracle, we can indeed close the above gap.

Theorem 1. *Assume random OT correlations and a random oracle. There is a (malicious-secure, two-party) NISC protocol for any Boolean circuit C with a communication cost of $O(|C|\lambda)$ bits, where λ is an exact computational security parameter.*

1.1   Related Work

Following the pioneering works of Mohassel and Franklin [44] and Lindell and Pinkas [41] on "black-box" malicious-secure variants of Yao's protocol, there has been a long line of work [17, 19, 25, 26, 29, 39, 46, 50] on constructing constant-round, malicious-secure two-party protocols with constant communication overhead when compared to semi-honest Yao. The most recent work along this line is due to Cui et al. [17], who gave a 10-round protocol in the VOLE-hybrid plus random oracle model that has $2\times$ overhead when compared to semi-honest Yao.

An orthogonal line of works, originating from the "row reduction" garbled circuit optimization of Naor et al. [45], focused on improving the concrete size of garbled circuits in the random oracle model [27, 40, 49, 53]. For standard Boolean circuits, the state of the art is a garbled circuit construction whose size is $1.5\lambda \cdot N_{\mathsf{AND}}$ where N_{AND} denotes the number of nonlinear 2-input gates in the circuit (e.g., AND) [49]. This has been shown to be nearly optimal with recent lower bounds that apply to natural restricted classes of "gate-by-gate" garbled circuit constructions [38, 51].

Chase et al. [14] introduced a notion called reusable non-interactive secure computation. In such a protocol, the first-round message sent by the receiver could be reused an unbounded number of times with (potentially) different senders. They constructed a reusable NISC protocol in the OLE-hybrid model. The work of Ishai et al. [33] constructed a reusable NISC assuming a 2-round semi-honest OT plus a random oracle.

Ishai et al. [31–33] extended the standard NISC protocol to a two-sided NISC protocol. In the setting of two-sided NISC, both the sender and the receiver speak in each round of the interaction, and at the end of two rounds, they both receive the output $f(x, y)$. In the malicious setting, simply running two instances of one-sided NISC in opposite directions does not work, as nothing prevents the parties from using inconsistent inputs in the two executions.

2   Technical Overview

In this section, we give a high-level overview of the techniques used in constructing a NISC protocol with constant communication overhead.

Bird's Eye View of Our Techniques. Starting with the early works of Mohassel-Franklin [44] and Lindell-Pinkas [41], there has been a long line of work on minimizing the communication overhead of black-box constant-round secure computation. Here, we focus on NISC protocols with constant overhead, and achieve this using OT correlations (a minimal setup) and a random oracle. Previous works with the same setup [25, 31, 34] employed a similar set of techniques, including the IPS watchlist mechanism, but all faced technical barriers that prevented them from achieving the current goal. The first two could only achieve constant overhead with selective failures (satisfying relaxed security with "correlated abort"), and the latter required super-constant overhead due to the incompatibility of packing techniques with their technical approach. The key innovation in our work lies in a new way of using packed secret sharing along with sublinear proof systems to circumvent these previous barriers. The most novel technical aspect is the development of a black-box method to combine Ligero proofs with the watchlist mechanism. We explain these in detail below.

Starting Point. Our NISC protocol builds on the IPS compiler [37]. The IPS compiler gives a generic way to construct constant-round, two-party protocols with security against malicious adversaries by combining three building blocks: an outer protocol, an inner protocol, and a watchlist.

The outer protocol is a client-server secure computation protocol between two clients (namely, the sender and the receiver) and m servers. The clients send an encoding of their inputs to the servers, the servers then perform local computation, and finally they send an encoding of the output to the receiver client. The receiver client decodes the server messages to learn the output of the function. The outer protocol has security against any malicious adversary that corrupts one of the clients and a constant fraction of the servers.

In the IPS compiler, the servers in the outer protocol are virtually emulated by the clients using a semi-honest secure inner protocol. To be a bit more precise, each server in the outer protocol is emulated using an instance of the inner protocol. The private inputs used by the receiver and the sender in the i-th instance of the inner protocol correspond to the messages they send to the i-th server in the outer protocol. At the end of this emulation, the receiver client learns the messages that the servers intend to send to it in the outer protocol. This guarantees correctness. However, the inner protocol is only guaranteed to be secure against semi-honest adversaries, whereas a malicious sender or receiver could cheat in all the inner protocol executions, thereby violating the security of the outer protocol. This could allow the corrupted client to learn the private input of the honest client. This kind of cheating is prevented by the watchlist.

A watchlist protocol prevents a corrupted client from cheating in a large number of inner protocol instances. Specifically, in the watchlist protocol, each client chooses a secret subset of the inner protocol executions as its "watchlist". The watchlist protocol delivers to a client the input and the randomness of the other client in each execution that is present in its watchlist. This allows this client to check consistency between the messages that it received in the inner protocol with the input and randomness it got via the watchlist protocol. If any inconsistency is detected, the honest client aborts. Since the set of executions in the watchlist is chosen uniformly at random, if no cheating is detected in the watchlist executions, it can be argued that a large fraction of the inner protocol executions are honestly emulated. Thus, we can rely on the security of the outer protocol to argue that a corrupted client learns no information about the inputs of the honest client except the output of the function.

The IPS compiler gives a constant-round protocol when one uses a constant-round outer protocol, a constant-round inner protocol, and a constant-round watchlist protocol. Ishai et al. [30,31] gave a round-optimal approach to instantiate the IPS compiler. Specifically, they used a two-round client-server protocol from the work of [35] as the outer protocol, and the two-round semi-honest secure protocol from garbled circuits [52] as the inner protocol. Their main contribution is to weaken the requirement from the watchlist protocol. Specifically, they showed that the set of watchlist executions need not be secret and they can be revealed to the corrupted client after it sends its messages in the inner protocol. This allowed them to instantiate the watchlist in the random oracle model using the Fiat-Shamir heuristic.

While the above works achieved round optimality, their communication cost was far from being optimal. The communication complexity in these works was $\mathsf{poly}(|C|, \lambda)$, a far cry from that of the semi-honest protocol that achieved $O(|C|\lambda)$ bits. Our goal in this work is to bridge this gap. We achieve this via a novel combination of a specialized outer protocol and an inner protocol that is tailored to emulate the server computations in the outer protocol with minimal overhead. We again use the Fiat-Shamir approach to instantiate the watchlist.

2.1 Our Outer Protocol

The outer protocol in our work computes an authenticated version of the BMR garbled circuits [3]. Specifically, it gets an additive share of the wire mask from the sender and the receiver, a MAC key from the receiver, the wire labels from the sender and the precomputed PRG values on the wire labels from the sender and generates an authenticated version of the BMR garbled gate. We make a couple of observations on the garbled gate computation:

- Given the pre-computed PRG values from the sender, each garbled gate entry can be computed via a constant-degree polynomial with a constant number of monomials.
- The MAC prevents a cheating sender from sending incorrect PRG computations. If the sender cheats, then the MAC check will fail.
- Having the wire mask secret shared between the sender and the receiver prevents the sender from mounting an input-dependent abort attack against the receiver.

From these three observations, we conclude that it is sufficient for the outer protocol to compute a constant-degree polynomial on the sender and receiver inputs.

Semi-honest Protocol. Let's for now assume that this outer protocol needs to only be semi-honest secure. In this case, the sender and the receiver can compute Shamir shares of their private inputs and send these shares to the servers. Let d be the degree of the function to be computed and let t be the corruption threshold for the outer protocol. Assume that the number of servers is $O(dt)$. The servers can locally compute a degree-d function on the Shamir shares to get a dt-sharing of the output. They can then send these shares to the receiver[1] who reconstructs the garbled gate entries from the server messages.

Consider the communication cost of this protocol. Fix the finite field size to be 2^λ. The number of private inputs for the sender and the receiver to compute the BMR garbled gate entries are $O(|C|)$ field elements. The threshold t needs to be fixed as $O(\lambda)$. Thus, the total number of servers needed is $O(\lambda)$ as d is a constant. Therefore, the sender and the receiver communicates $O(|C|\lambda)$ field elements in total to the servers. Since each field element is $O(\lambda)$ bits, the total communication between the clients and the servers is $O(|C|\lambda^2)$ bits. As these messages are going to be the inputs to the inner protocol, this serves as a lower bound on the communication cost of our compiler. Therefore, when compared to semi-honest Yao, the outer protocol already incurs a $O(\lambda)$ multiplicative overhead.

Packing to the Rescue. To reduce the communication cost of the outer protocol, we rely on packing techniques introduced by Franklin and Yung [21]. Recall how packed Shamir secret sharing works. Let $\mathbb{F}$ denote the underlying field. We set $|\mathbb{F}| \geq 2^\lambda$. Fix a set of ℓ distinct elements $\beta_1, \ldots, \beta_\ell \in \mathbb{F}$ and fix another disjoint set of m distinct elements $\alpha_1, \ldots, \alpha_m \in \mathbb{F}$. Let $\overline{s} := (s_1, \ldots, s_\ell) \in \mathbb{F}^\ell$ be a vector of secrets to share. To hide the secrets, we sample a random univariate polynomial

---

[1] For the sake of keeping the exposition simple, we are ignoring the random shares of 0 that need to be added to the dt-sharing to prevent the receiver from gleaning more information about the sender inputs.

$p(\cdot)$ of degree $t + \ell$ conditioned on $p(\beta_i) = s_i$ for all $i \in [\ell]$. To compute the shares, for every $j \in [m]$, party j's share is computed as $x_j := p(\alpha_j)$. The vector consisting of all shares $\overline{x} := (x_1, \ldots, x_m) \in \mathbb{F}^m$ is often called a *sharing* of $\overline{s}$. Sometimes we write $[\overline{s}]$ to denote a sharing of $\overline{s}$. When we add/multiply the shares corresponding to a packed secret sharing scheme, we obtain entry-wise addition/product of the secret vectors under the hood. We now explain how to compute constant-degree polynomials using packed secret sharing.

Case of Degree-2. Suppose the outer protocol was tasked to compute only a degree-2 function on the receiver's and the sender's private inputs. Let vector $\overline{x}$ and vector $\overline{y}$ denote the private inputs of the receiver and the sender, respectively. The outer protocol is constructed as follows:

- *Step 1.* Let $\odot$ denote the entry-wise product operation. Let p be a degree-2 polynomial p, and we represent it by a vector of its monomials. Here we abuse the notation p to also mean a vector. We decompose the monomials in p as $p^x \odot p^y$ where vector p^x (resp. p^y) only contains variables in $\overline{x}$ (resp. $\overline{y}$) and constants. For example, for polynomial $p(\overline{x}, \overline{y}) := 1 + y_1 + x_1 y_3 + x_2^2 + x_3 y_2 + y_3 y_4$, and $\overline{x} := (x_1, x_2, x_3)$ and $\overline{y} := (y_1, y_2, y_3, y_4)$, the decomposition is

$$p = \begin{pmatrix} 1 & y_1 & x_1 y_3 & x_2^2 & x_3 y_2 & y_3 y_4 \end{pmatrix},$$
$$p^x = \begin{pmatrix} 1 & 1 & x_1 & x_2^2 & x_3 & 1 \end{pmatrix},$$
$$p^y = \begin{pmatrix} 1 & y_1 & y_3 & 1 & y_2 & y_3 y_4 \end{pmatrix}.$$

- *Step 2.* The receiver and the sender send a packed sharing of p^x and p^y respectively to the servers. The servers locally multiply the shares to obtain shares of the monomials in the polynomial p. To mask the monomials, the sender additionally sends a sharing of a random size-$|p|$ vector $\overline{z}$ conditioned on the sum of its elements being zero. The servers add the sharing of $\overline{z}$ to the sharing of p and send the result to the receiver. In the end, the receiver reconstructs the monomials of $p + \overline{z}$ and adds them together to obtain evaluation of p.

Reducing Constant Degree to Degree 2. Once we have an outer protocol for degree-2 polynomials, we can reduce the computation of any constant-degree polynomial to a degree-2 polynomial as we only have two clients. Specifically, for any constant degree polynomial, the clients can decompose the terms in each monomial from their respective private inputs. For instance, if a monomial is $x_2 y_1 y_3$, then the client decomposes this to $p^x = x_2$ and $p^y = y_1 y_3$. They construct the vector p^x and p^y as above and send packed secret sharing of p^x and p^y to the servers. The rest of the protocol follows identically to the case of degree 2.

Communication Cost. Suppose we used the protocol based on packed secret sharing to compute BMR garbled gate entries with a packing factor of $\ell = O(\lambda)$. The receiver and the sender in this case need to send $O(|C|/\lambda)$ shares to the servers where each share packs $O(\lambda)$ secrets. The number of servers is $O(\lambda)$, and it takes λ bits to represent a field element. Therefore, the total communication cost is $O(|C|/\lambda) \cdot \lambda \cdot O(\lambda) = O(|C|\lambda)$ bits.

Extending to Malicious Adversaries. Note that the above outer protocol is only semi-honest secure but we need it to be secure against malicious adversaries for the IPS compiler. We observe that a malicious client can cheat in the following two ways in the above protocol:

- **Sending incorrectly generated packed shares.** The malicious client could cheat by sending shares that do not lie on a degree-$(t + \ell)$ polynomial. In the case of [35], this was dealt by using a special secret sharing scheme called pairwise verifiable secret sharing and a conditional disclosure of secrets protocol that prevents the adversary from learning any information about the honest party's inputs if it sent inconsistent shares to the honest servers. Unfortunately, this approach incurs at least a $O(\lambda)$ multiplicative overhead in the individual share size and this is something that we cannot afford.
- **Sending shares of incorrectly decomposed values.** The malicious client could send packed shares of p^x or p^y that are incorrectly decomposed. For instance, in the places where there needs to be a constant 1, it can send an arbitrary value. In places where the term needs to $x_1 x_2$, it can send another value and so on. We need to ensure that clients are sending packed shares of correctly decomposed values.

We explain how to deal with these two issues below.

Issue-1: Incorrectly Generated Packed Shares. Observe that a packed Shamir secret sharing can be viewed as a Reed-Solomon codeword, where each server holds a symbol of the codeword. A server receiving an inconsistent symbol from the malicious client can be viewed as a corrupted position in the received codeword. If we can ensure that the number of corrupted positions is within the error-correction distance, then the correct computation result can still be recovered from the result of honest servers' computation. Thus, it comes down to the problem of testing Reed-Solomon proximity—given a received codeword, accept if the received codeword disagrees with its closest exact Reed-Solomon codeword on at most t positions, and reject otherwise. There has been a lot of research on testing Reed-Solomon proximity [5,48]. We use the Ligero proof system [2] that tests Reed-Solomon proximity of multiple codewords together. However, we cannot use the Ligero proof system directly due to a technical issue that we explain next.

Note that each client shares multiple vectors. Let n be the number of vectors and we view them as a matrix of n rows where each row contains the purported codeword sent by a corrupted client. We need to test Reed-Solomon proximity of n codewords together, which seemingly can be achieved by a direct application of Ligero. However, the notion of distance used in Ligero is the maximum distance between any row of the purported codeword to an actual Reed-Solomon code.

This distance notion turns out to be insufficient for our purpose. To see why this the case, let's denote this distance to be d. Consider a purported codeword sent by the corrupt client such that the first d positions of the first row is inconsistent with a Reed-Solomon codeword, the second d positions of the second row is inconsistent with a Reed-Solomon codeword, and so on. In total, there are dn positions across all the rows that are inconsistent with a Reed-Solomon codeword. In the IPS compiler, the servers that correspond to these inconsistent positions are corrupted. This means that the number of servers need to be larger than dn, which is something we cannot afford.

What we really need is the union over the positions across each row that is different from an actual codeword to have small cardinality. If this was the case, we can then corrupt those servers in the outer protocol in the IPS compiler. Thus, in our paper, we define the *distance* between n received codewords and their closest exact RS codewords to be the cardinality of the union of corrupted positions over all n codewords. Under this new definition of distance, we use the result of [4] to prove the soundness of Ligero with improved parameters. This allows us to argue that all the corruptions caused by the malicious client is concentrated on a small subset of servers and therefore error-correction can still be achieved.

At a high level, the Ligero proof for RS proximity views the sharing of all n vectors as a $n \times m$ matrix U as each RS codeword has length m. Each server $j \in [m]$ obtains a column of U. The matrix U is committed column-wise by a straight-line extractable commitment scheme, which can be constructed in the random oracle model [47]. The Ligero proof essentially sends two things: a random linear combination of the rows of U, and openings for a random subset of columns. The intuition is that a random linear combination of RS codewords is a RS codeword, whereas a random linear combination of non-codewords is unlikely to be a codeword. The openings for a random subset of columns allows the verifier to check if the random linear combination is computed honestly.

For communication cost, the resulting codeword of the random linear combination takes $m \cdot \lambda$ bits given our finite field $\mathbb{F}$ of order 2^λ, and openings of columns takes $O(m) \cdot n \cdot \lambda$ bits. The number of vectors n in the outer protocol is $O(|C|/\ell)$. Therefore, the communication cost is $O(m|C|\lambda/\ell)$. Taking packing size $\ell = O(\lambda)$ and the number of servers $m = O(\lambda)$, we obtain the communication complexity $O(|C|\lambda)$ for the Ligero proof.

Issue-2: Incorrectly Decomposed Values. To compute the BMR garbled gate entries, we need to compute a degree-3 polynomial. This means that decomposed vectors p^x or p^y can have degree at least 2 or higher, which makes it non-trivial to test.

To overcome this, we further decompose p^x into vectors $p_1^x, \ldots, p_d^x$ and decompose p^y into vectors $p_1^y, \ldots, p_d^y$ such that each of p_i^x (resp. p_i^y) is linear. As a result, each element of p_i^x (resp. p_i^y) is either a variable from x (resp. y) or a constant. These vectors should satisfy the decomposition requirement $p^x = p_1^x \odot \cdots \odot p_d^x$ and $p^y = p_1^y \odot \cdots \odot p_d^y$, which can be checked by the watchlist.

Now that p_i^x (resp. p_i^y) is linear, we can enforce a set of linear constraints on these vectors to ensure that the corresponding slots are aligned correctly for entry-wise product. For example, suppose we have the following decomposition for p^x:

$$
\begin{aligned}
p^x &= \begin{pmatrix} 1 & x_1 x_2 x_3 & x_2^2 x_4 & x_2 x_4 \end{pmatrix}, \\
p_1^x &= \begin{pmatrix} 1 & x_1 & x_2 & x_2 \end{pmatrix}, \\
p_2^x &= \begin{pmatrix} 1 & x_2 & x_2 & x_4 \end{pmatrix}, \\
p_3^x &= \begin{pmatrix} 1 & x_3 & x_4 & 1 \end{pmatrix}.
\end{aligned}
$$

For each p_i^x, let $p_i^x[j]$ denote the j-th element of the vector. Then, we need to ensure that $p_1^x[3] = p_1^x[4] = p_2^x[2] = p_2^x[3]$ since all these positions hold the same variable x_2, and $p_2^x[4] = p_3^x[3]$ since both positions hold x_4, and $p_1^x[1] = p_2^x[1] = p_3^x[1] = p_3^x[4] = 1$ since these positions should contain the constant 1. These equalities can be translated to a set of linear equations. After this high-degree to linear reduction, we can directly apply the Ligero proof for linear constraints to ensure that the decomposed values p^x and p^y are generated honestly.

Another issue that arises with the BMR garbling process and our outer protocol is that the inputs and the masking bits are boolean values, but our outer protocol performs arithmetic operations over a finite field $\mathbb{F}$. A malicious client may use vectors whose positions are supposed to contain boolean values to actually contain some arbitrary values in $\mathbb{F}$. To deal with this, consider the equation $x(1 - x) = 0$ over $\mathbb{F}$, which enforces the value of x to be 0 or 1. Following this idea, for a vector v, we compute $v_{\mathsf{bool}} := v \odot (1 - v)$ where 1 denotes the all-one vector.[2] For the positions in v that needs to have value 0 or 1, the corresponding positions in v_{bool} must be 0. Note that other positions in v_{bool} are irrelevant and can be ignored. This again gives us a set of linear equations $v_{\mathsf{bool}}[j] = 0$ for all j where $v[j]$ is supposed to be a boolean value. Again, we use the Ligero proof for linear constraints to ensure the boolean values are converted honestly to 0/1 in $\mathbb{F}$.

The communication cost of Ligero proof for linear constraints is also $O(|C|\lambda)$. The difference from the Ligero proof for RS proximity is that instead of sending a linear combination of codewords, the Ligero proof for linear constraints sends a random linear combination of polynomials by sending the coefficients of the resulting polynomial. The resulting polynomial will have degree asymptotically the same as m (the codeword length). Therefore, the communication cost is still dominated by the size of opening of a random subset of columns. Hence, the communication cost is still $O(|C|\lambda)$.

2.2   Our Inner Protocol

The semi-honest inner protocol performs server computation in the outer protocol. In the outer protocol, the receiver (resp. sender) client sends packed secret

---

[2] Note that we can enforce the correct computation of v_{bool} in a similar way to enforcing the correct computation of p^x and p^y.

shares of p_1^x, p_2^x, p_3^x (resp. p_1^y, p_2^y, p_3^y) to the servers as computing a boolean circuit can be reduced to computing degree-3 polynomials. Denote the sharings of these vectors by $[p_1^x], [p_2^x], [p_3^x]$ (resp. $[p_1^y], [p_2^y], [p_3^y]$). Additionally, the sender sends packed secret shares of $\mathbf{z}$, which is a vector of additive secret sharing of zeros to mask the monomials. Denote the sharing of $\mathbf{z}$ by $[\mathbf{z}]$. The server function does two things:

1. It computes $[p^x] = [p_1^x] \odot [p_2^x] \odot [p_3^x]$ and $[p^y] = [p_1^y] \odot [p_2^y] \odot [p_3^y]$.
2. It computes $[p] = [p^x] \odot [p^y] + [\mathbf{z}]$.

For the first operation, observe that $[p^x]$ (resp. $[p^y]$) can be locally computed by the receiver (resp. sender). Thus, the receiver (resp. sender) client also sends a precomputed $[p^x]$ (resp. $[p^y]$) to the servers. We will use the watchlist to ensure that the pre-computation is performed honestly.

For the second operation, suppose the sharings $[p^x], [p^y], [\mathbf{z}]$ are vectors of k elements, the evaluation $[p^x] \odot [p^y] + [\mathbf{z}]$ can be viewed as k parallel oblivious linear evaluations (OLEs).

We note that if we were given k preprocessed random OLE correlations over $\mathbb{F}$ where $|\mathbb{F}| = 2^\lambda$, this can be done trivially. However, generating random OLE correlations is much more expensive than for instance, generating random bit OT correlations. We would like our inner protocol to build on basic assumptions like standard random bit OT correlations.

To solve this problem, we make use of *multiplication-friendly embeddings* (MFEs) [13,20]. Essentially, a MFE is a pair of linear-maps (ρ, μ) where ρ maps a vector of elements in a small ring to a single element in a big ring, and μ maps an element in a big ring to a vector of elements in a small ring. They satisfy $x \cdot y = \rho(\mu(x) \odot \mu(y))$ where x and y are elements from the big ring. We use the result of [16] which states that there exists an explicit MFE family

$$\left(\rho_\lambda : \mathbb{F}_2^{r(\lambda)} \to \mathbb{F}_{2^\lambda}, \ \mu_\lambda : \mathbb{F}_{2^\lambda} \to \mathbb{F}_2^{r(\lambda)} \right)_{\lambda \in \mathbb{N}}$$

with ratio $r(\lambda)/\lambda \to 5.12$ as $\lambda \to \infty$. This allows us to express an OLE in $\mathbb{F}_{2^\lambda}$ by $O(\lambda)$ number of OTs in $\mathbb{F}_2$. Using the linearity property of MFEs, we construct an inner protocol that computes k OLEs in $\mathbb{F}_{2^\lambda}$ using $O(k\lambda)$ number of preprocessed random bit OT correlations. The communication cost of our protocol is only a constant multiple of the trivial protocol based on OLE correlations. We remark that similar protocols have appeared in [6].

For communication cost, the vector p^x, p^y contains $O(|C|)$ field elements and are shared via a packed Shamir secret sharing of packing size ℓ. Thus, we have $k = O(|C|/\ell)$. Each field element takes λ bits to represent. Therefore, the inner protocol has communication cost $O(|C|\lambda/\ell)$. The outer protocol has m servers, and each server runs an instance of the inner protocol. Hence, the total communication cost of the inner protocols used in the outer protocol is $O(|C|\lambda)$ when we take $m = O(\lambda)$ and $\ell = O(\lambda)$.

3   Preliminaries

Basic Notations. Let λ denote the cryptographic security parameter, and we assume that all cryptographic algorithms implicitly take 1^λ as an input parameter. A function $\mu(\cdot) : \mathbb{N} \to \mathbb{R}^+$ is said to be negligible if for any polynomial poly$(\cdot)$, there exists a λ_0 such that for all $\lambda \geq \lambda_0$, we have $\mu(\lambda) < \frac{1}{\mathsf{poly}(\lambda)}$. We will use negl$(\cdot)$ to denote an unspecified negligible function. We use the abbreviation PPT to mean probabilistic polynomial time. We say that two distribution ensembles $\{X_\lambda\}_{\lambda \in \mathbb{N}}$ and $\{Y_\lambda\}_{\lambda \in \mathbb{N}}$ are computationally indistinguishable if for every non-uniform probabilistic polynomial time (PPT) distinguisher $\mathcal{D}$ there exists a negligible function negl$(\cdot)$ such that $\left| \Pr[\mathcal{D}(1^\lambda, X_\lambda) = 1] - \Pr[\mathcal{D}(1^\lambda, Y_\lambda) = 1] \right| \leq$ negl(λ). We use $\{X_\lambda\}_{\lambda \in \mathbb{N}} \approx_c \{Y_\lambda\}_{\lambda \in \mathbb{N}}$ to denote the two ensembles are computationally indistinguishable. For $n \in \mathbb{N}$, we use $[n]$ to denote the set of elements $\{1, 2, \ldots, n\}$. We use $x \leftarrow S$ to mean that x is drawn uniformly at random from the set S. We use $\odot$ to denote the entry-wise product (also called Hadamard product or Schur product) operation of two vectors. For any matrix U, we use U_i to denote the i-th row of U, and we use $U[j]$ to denote the j-th column of U. For a string x, we use $|x|$ to denote the number of bits in x. For a vector v over a finite field $\mathbb{F}$, we use $|v|$ to denote the number of elements in v. All the logs in this paper are by default base 2. For complete description of all the building blocks, we refer the reader to the full version.

4   Outer Protocol

In this section, we progressively define three client-server protocols [18]. The first protocol computes an array of degree-2 polynomials (i.e. quadratics); the second protocol computes an array of constant-degree polynomials; the third protocol computes any two-party functionality f modeled as a Boolean circuit C. The security of these three protocols are defined against specific adversaries that will be described later, which we call "admissible adversaries". Looking ahead, we will use the watchlist method from the IPS compiler [37] and a set of non-interactive zero-knowledge arguments based on Ligero [2] to lift the security from admissible adversaries to standard malicious adversaries.

Conforming Protocol. Our outer protocol is set in the client-server model with two clients and m servers. A two-client, m-server, two-round protocol Φ for computing f can be described by a tuple of algorithms $((\mathsf{Share}_1, \mathsf{Share}_2), \mathsf{Eval}, \mathsf{Dec})$. Additionally, our protocol is *conforming*, meaning that the first-round messages sent from the clients to the servers are shares of a packed Shamir secret sharing scheme. Formally,

Definition 1 (Conforming Protocol). *A two-round, two-client, m-server protocol Φ is said to be conforming if the output of* Share$_1$ *(resp.* Share$_2$*) is of the form* $\{(x_{i,1}, \ldots, x_{i,m})\}_{i \in [n]}$ *(and resp.* $\{(y_{i,1}, \ldots, y_{i,m})\}_{i \in [n]}$*) where n is the number of vectors of share, and for each $i \in [n]$, $(x_{i,1}, \ldots, x_{i,m})$ (resp. $(y_{i,1}, \ldots, y_{i,m})$) are the shares of a packed Shamir secret sharing scheme.*

4.1 Protocol for Computing Quadratics

Notations. Fix a finite field $\mathbb{F}$ with order 2^λ. Denote the receiver's input by $\overline{x} = (x_1, \ldots, x_n) \in \mathbb{F}^n$ and the sender's input by $\overline{y} = (y_1, \ldots, y_n) \in \mathbb{F}^n$. Let $\overline{p} = (p_1, \ldots, p_N)$ where $N \in \mathbb{N}$ be a vector of degree-2 multivariate polynomials over $\mathbb{F}$ to be computed by the protocol. For $i \in [N]$, each polynomial $p_i(\overline{x}_i, \overline{y}_i)$ takes as input vector $\overline{x}_i \subseteq \overline{x}$ and vector $\overline{y}_i \subseteq \overline{y}$. For each $i \in [N]$, we use $|p_i|$ to denote the number of monomials in p_i. Each polynomial p_i is represented in form of the sum of its monomials, denoted by $p_i = m_{i,1} + \ldots + m_{i,|p_i|}$, where the monomials $m_{i,j}$ for $j \in \{1, \ldots, |p_i|\}$ are ordered from low-degree to high-degree and in lexicographic order. We abuse the notation p_i to also mean a vector of its monomials, i.e., $p_i := (m_{i,1}, \ldots, m_{i,|p_i|})$. Furthermore, we abuse the notation $\overline{p} := (m_{1,1}, \ldots, m_{1,|p_1|}, \ldots, m_{N,1}, \ldots, m_{N,|p_N|})$ to mean a long vector of all the monomials of all polynomials concatenated together and let $N_{\mathrm{mono}} = |p_1| + \ldots + |p_N|$ be the total number of monomials in $\overline{p}$. Let $(\mathsf{Share}_{(t,\ell,m)}, \mathsf{Rec}_{(t,\ell,m)})$ be a $(t, t+\ell+1; \ell, m)$-packed Shamir secret sharing scheme over $\mathbb{F}$, where ℓ is the packing size. This means that any t parties gain no information about the secret, while any $t+\ell+1$ parties can recover the secret. For any positive natural number $a, b \in \mathbb{N}$, let $(\mathsf{Share}_{(at+b\ell,\ell,m)}, \mathsf{Rec}_{(at+b\ell,\ell,m)})$ denote a $(at+b\ell, at+b\ell+\ell+1; \ell, m)$-packed Shamir secret sharing scheme.

Decomposition. We describe a deterministic procedure, denoted by $\mathsf{Decomp}(\overline{p})$, that decomposes the polynomials $\overline{p} = (p_1, \ldots, p_N)$ into entry-wise products of linear polynomials. The decomposition works as follows:

Step 1. Recall that $\odot$ is the entry-wise product operation. For each polynomial p_i where $i \in [N]$, we first decompose it as $p_i = p_i^x \odot p_i^y$ where p_i^x (resp. p_i^y) only contains variables in $\overline{x}_i$ (resp. $\overline{y}_i$) or constants. For example, let $p_i(\overline{x}_i, \overline{y}_i) = 1 + y_1 + x_1 y_3 + x_2^2 + x_5 y_2 + y_3 y_5$ for some i, and $\overline{x}_i = (x_2, x_5)$ and $\overline{y}_i = (y_1, y_2, y_3, y_5)$, then the decomposition is

$$
\begin{aligned}
p_i &= \begin{pmatrix} 1 & y_1 & x_1 y_3 & x_2^2 & x_5 y_2 & y_3 y_5 \end{pmatrix}, \\
p_i^x &= \begin{pmatrix} 1 & 1 & x_1 & x_2^2 & x_5 & 1 \end{pmatrix}, \\
p_i^y &= \begin{pmatrix} 1 & y_1 & y_3 & 1 & y_2 & y_3 y_5 \end{pmatrix}.
\end{aligned}
$$

Step 2. We further decompose each of p_i^x and p_i^y into $p_i^x = p_{i,1}^x \odot p_{i,2}^x$ and $p_i^y = p_{i,1}^y \odot p_{i,2}^y$ respectively. For each $k \in \{1, 2\}$, each $p_{i,k}^x$ (resp. $p_{i,k}^y$) contains elements of either a single variable in $\overline{x}_i$ (resp. $\overline{y}_i$) or a field constant. To continue the example above, the further decomposition will be

$$
\begin{aligned}
p_{i,1}^x &= \begin{pmatrix} 1 & 1 & x_1 & x_2 & x_5 & 1 \end{pmatrix}, & p_{i,1}^y &= \begin{pmatrix} 1 & y_1 & y_3 & 1 & y_2 & y_3 \end{pmatrix}, \\
p_{i,2}^x &= \begin{pmatrix} 1 & 1 & 1 & x_2 & 1 & 1 \end{pmatrix}, & p_{i,2}^y &= \begin{pmatrix} 1 & 1 & 1 & 1 & 1 & y_5 \end{pmatrix}.
\end{aligned}
$$

To make the decomposition unique, one can specify a fixed set of decomposition rules. Therefore, each degree-2 polynomial p_i is eventually decomposed into 6 vectors $p_i^x, p_{i,1}^x, p_{i,2}^x, p_i^y, p_{i,1}^y, p_{i,2}^y$. We concatenate the decomposed vectors of all polynomials p_i^x (resp. p_i^y) for $i \in [N]$ into 6 long vectors $\overline{p}^x, \overline{p}_1^x, \overline{p}_2^x, \overline{p}^y, \overline{p}_1^y, \overline{p}_2^y$ as follows:

$$\overline{p}^x = p_1^x || \cdots || p_N^x, \qquad \overline{p}_1^x = p_{1,1}^x || \cdots || p_{N,1}^x, \qquad \overline{p}_2^x = p_{1,2}^x || \cdots || p_{N,2}^x,$$
$$\overline{p}^y = p_1^y || \cdots || p_N^y, \qquad \overline{p}_1^y = p_{1,1}^y || \cdots || p_{N,1}^y, \qquad \overline{p}_2^y = p_{1,2}^y || \cdots || p_{N,2}^y.$$

Observe that $\overline{p}^x = \overline{p}_1^x \odot \overline{p}_2^x$ and $\overline{p}^y = \overline{p}_1^y \odot \overline{p}_2^y$. Hence, the final decomposition can be expressed as $\overline{p}^x, \overline{p}_1^x, \overline{p}_2^x, \overline{p}^y, \overline{p}_1^y, \overline{p}_2^y \leftarrow \mathsf{Decomp}(\overline{p})$.

Linear Constraints from the Decomposition. To ensure that each client in the MPC protocol honestly executes the decomposition described above, we can enforce a set of linear constraints on $\overline{p}_1^x, \overline{p}_2^x, \overline{p}_1^y, \overline{p}_2^y$. Let us use a minimal example to illustrate. Suppose the protocol computes two degree-2 polynomials $\overline{p} = (p_1, p_2)$ where $p_1 = x_1 y_1$ and $p_2 = x_2^2 + x_1 y_2 + y_1^2$. Then the vector representation $\overline{p} = (x_1 y_1, x_2^2, x_1 y_2, y_1^2)$ and the decomposition is

$$\overline{p}^x = \begin{pmatrix} x_1 & x_2^2 & x_1 & 1 \end{pmatrix}, \qquad \overline{p}^y = \begin{pmatrix} y_1 & 1 & y_2 & y_1^2 \end{pmatrix},$$
$$\overline{p}_1^x = \begin{pmatrix} x_1 & x_2 & x_1 & 1 \end{pmatrix}, \qquad \overline{p}_1^y = \begin{pmatrix} y_1 & 1 & y_2 & y_1 \end{pmatrix},$$
$$\overline{p}_2^x = \begin{pmatrix} 1 & x_2 & 1 & 1 \end{pmatrix}, \qquad \overline{p}_2^y = \begin{pmatrix} 1 & 1 & 1 & y_1 \end{pmatrix}.$$

We describe the linear constraints that the receiver should satisfy below, and the constraints for the sender can be derived similarly. To express the linear constraints, let

$$v := (\overline{p}_1^x || \overline{p}_2^x) = (x_1, x_2, x_1, 1, 1, x_2, 1, 1)$$

be a (column) vector of 8 elements. Let $v[i]$ denote the i-th element of v. Observe a correct decomposition should satisfy the following constraints:

- The variables need to be correctly aligned, which means same variable should take the same value across the decomposed vectors. For the example above, for variable x_1 it should satisfy $v[1] = v[3]$, and for variable x_2 it should satisfy $v[2] = v[6]$.
- The "1" slots should take value 1. For the example above, it should satisfy $v[4] = v[5] = v[7] = v[8] = 1$.

The above constraints can be converted into a set of linear equations. We can also write the constraints in matrix form $Av = b$ where A is a $|v| \times |v|$ matrix and b is a vector of size $|v|$.

For the sender, the linear constraints are similar. Additionally, the sender also needs to use additive secret sharings of zero to mask the resulting monomials such that they will not be exposed to the receiver. Specifically, for each p_i where $i \in [N]$, the sender samples a vector $p_i^0 = (r_{i,1}, \ldots, r_{i,|p_i|})$ of random field elements over $\mathbb{F}$ conditioned on the elements of p_i^0 sum to zero. Let $|p_i|$ denote the number of elements in p_i^0. This introduces an additional linear constraint $\sum_{j=1}^{|p_i|} r_{i,j} = 0$. Let $\overline{p}^0 = p_1^0 || \cdots || p_N^0$ denote the concatenation of all p_i^0's. We formally define *linear constraints* over a set of n vectors $v_1, \ldots, v_n$ as follows:

Definition 2 (Linear Constraints). *Let $\mathbb{F}$ be a finite field and let ℓ, n be natural numbers. Consider n vectors $v_1, \ldots, v_n \in \mathbb{F}^\ell$. The linear constraints $\mathcal{R}$ on the set of vectors $\{v_1, \ldots, v_n\}$ is a system of linear equations $Av = b$, where $v = (v_1 \| \ldots \| v_n) \in \mathbb{F}^{n\ell}$ is all vectors concatenated together, and $A \in \mathbb{F}^{n\ell \times n\ell}$ is a sparse matrix and $b \in \mathbb{F}^{n\ell}$.*

Let $\mathcal{R}_x$ denote the linear constraints on the receiver's vectors $\overline{p}_1^x, \overline{p}_2^x$. Similarly, let $\mathcal{R}_y$ denote the linear constraints on the sender's vectors $\overline{p}_1^y, \overline{p}_2^y, \overline{p}^0$, where $\overline{p}^0$ is a vector of additive secret sharing of zeros. Let $\mathcal{R} := (\mathcal{R}_x, \mathcal{R}_y)$ be the combined linear constraints. Note that the linear constraints ensure that the adversary must use consistent values for its variables. For example, if variable x_1 appears in both p_1 and p_2, then the receiver must plug in the same value for x_1 in these two polynomials. On the other hand, if $\overline{p}_1^x, \overline{p}_2^x$ satisfy the linear constraints $\mathcal{R}_x$, then a unique input vector $\overline{x}$ can be extracted from receiver's decomposed vectors $\overline{p}_1^x, \overline{p}_2^x$. Similarly, if $\mathcal{R}_y$ is satisfied, then a unique input vector $\overline{y}$ can be extracted from the sender's decomposed vectors $\overline{p}_1^y, \overline{p}_2^y$.

Admissible Adversary. Let m be the number of servers in the client-server MPC protocol. Let $\overline{p}^x, \overline{p}_1^x, \overline{p}_2^x$ (resp. $\overline{p}^y, \overline{p}_1^y, \overline{p}_2^y, \overline{p}^0$) be the vectors to be packed secret shared by the receiver (resp. sender) as a result of the decomposition described above. For each $j \in [m]$, let $\{\hat{x}_j, \hat{x}_{j,1}, \hat{x}_{j,2}\}$ (resp. $\{\hat{y}_j, \hat{y}_{j,1}, \hat{y}_{j,2}, \hat{0}_j\}$) be the first-round messages sent by the receiver (resp. sender) to server j, which are the purported shares for $\overline{p}^x, \overline{p}_1^x, \overline{p}_2^x$ (resp. $\overline{p}^y, \overline{p}_1^y, \overline{p}_2^y, \overline{p}^0$).

Definition 3 (Admissible Adversary). *An adversary $\mathcal{A}$ corrupting either client and a set of servers T ($|T| \leq t$) is said to be admissible w.r.t. linear constraints $\mathcal{R} = (\mathcal{R}_x, \mathcal{R}_y)$ if*

1. *(Consistency Constraints) The first-round messages $\hat{x}_j, \hat{x}_{j,1}, \hat{x}_{j,2}$ sent by the receiver (resp. $\hat{y}_j, \hat{y}_{j,1}, \hat{y}_{j,2}, \hat{0}_j$ sent by sender) to the honest servers $j \in [m] \setminus T$ are consistent with packed Shamir secret sharings of vectors $\overline{p}^x, \overline{p}_1^x, \overline{p}_2^x$ (resp. $\overline{p}^y, \overline{p}_1^y, \overline{p}_2^y, \overline{p}^0$).*
2. *(Decomposability Constraints) The first-round messages $\hat{x}_j, \hat{x}_{j,1}, \hat{x}_{j,2}$ sent by the receiver (resp. $\hat{y}_j, \hat{y}_{j,1}, \hat{y}_{j,2}$ sent by sender) satisfy $\hat{x}_j = \hat{x}_{j,1} \odot \hat{x}_{j,2}$ (resp. $\hat{y}_j = \hat{y}_{j,1} \odot \hat{y}_{j,2}$) for all honest servers $j \in [m] \setminus T$.*
3. *(Linear Constraints) Assuming the consistency constraint is satisfied, let $\overline{p}^x, \overline{p}_1^x, \overline{p}_2^x$ (resp. $\overline{p}^y, \overline{p}_1^y, \overline{p}_2^y, \overline{p}^0$) be the secret vectors extracted from the first-round messages sent by the receiver (resp. sender) to the honest servers. Then, the vectors $\overline{p}_1^x, \overline{p}_2^x$ (resp. $\overline{p}_1^y, \overline{p}_2^y, \overline{p}^0$) satisfy the linear constraints $\mathcal{R}_x$ (resp. $\mathcal{R}_y$).*

Description of the Protocol. Consider a two-client, m-server conforming MPC protocol (see Definition 1) where one client and at most t servers can be corrupted. Before entering the protocol, both parties execute the decomposition procedure $\overline{p}^x, \overline{p}_1^x, \overline{p}_2^x, \overline{p}^y, \overline{p}_1^y, \overline{p}_2^y \leftarrow \mathsf{Decomp}(\overline{p})$. Note that $\overline{p}^x, \overline{p}_1^x, \overline{p}_2^x, \overline{p}^y, \overline{p}_1^y, \overline{p}_2^y$ contain entries that consist of variables (symbols) and constants, which are known

Protocol Φ_{quad} for Computing Quadratics:

- **Inputs:** Receiver has input $\overline{x}$ and sender has input $\overline{y}$. The common input $\overline{p} = (p_1, \ldots, p_N)$ is a vector of degree-2 polynomials to evaluate. Let N_{mono} be the total number of monomials in $p_1, \ldots, p_N$.
- **Set-up:** Both parties execute $\overline{p}^x, \overline{p}_1^x, \overline{p}_2^x, \overline{p}^y, \overline{p}_1^y, \overline{p}_2^y \leftarrow \mathsf{Decomp}(\overline{p})$ described above.
- **Round 1:**
  The receiver runs $\mathsf{Share}_1(1^\lambda, \overline{x})$ as follows:
  1. It assigns values of monomials in $\overline{p}^x, \overline{p}_1^x, \overline{p}_2^x$ using $\overline{x}$.
  2. It partitions each of $\overline{p}^x, \overline{p}_1^x, \overline{p}_2^x$ into $N' := N_{\mathsf{mono}}/\ell$ short vectors of size ℓ. Denote these vectors by $\overline{v}_1^x, \ldots, \overline{v}_{N'}^x$ and $\overline{v}_{1,1}^x, \ldots, \overline{v}_{N',1}^x$ and $\overline{v}_{1,2}^x, \ldots, \overline{v}_{N',2}^x$ respectively.
  3. For each $i \in [N']$,
     (a) It computes $[\overline{v}_{i,1}^x] = \mathsf{Share}_{(t,\ell,m)}(\overline{v}_{i,1}^x)$ and $[\overline{v}_{i,2}^x] = \mathsf{Share}_{(t,\ell,m)}(\overline{v}_{i,2}^x)$, where $[\overline{v}_{i,1}^x] := (s_{i,1,1}, \ldots, s_{i,m,1})$ denotes a sharing of $\overline{v}_{i,1}^x$, and $[\overline{v}_{i,2}^x] := (s_{i,1,2}, \ldots, s_{i,m,2})$ denotes a sharing of $\overline{v}_{i,2}^x$.
     (b) It computes $[\overline{v}_i^x] = [\overline{v}_{i,1}^x] \odot [\overline{v}_{i,2}^x]$, where $[\overline{v}_i^x] := (s_{i,1}, \ldots, s_{i,m})$ denotes a sharing of $\overline{v}_i^x$.
     For $j \in [m]$, let $\hat{x}_{j,1} := (s_{1,j,1}, \ldots, s_{N',j,1})$, $\hat{x}_{j,2} := (s_{1,j,2}, \ldots, s_{N',j,2})$, $\hat{x}_j := (s_{1,j}, \ldots, s_{N',j})$.
  4. It outputs $\{\hat{x}_j, \hat{x}_{j,1}, \hat{x}_{j,2}\}_{j \in [m]}$.
  The sender runs $\mathsf{Share}_2(1^\lambda, \overline{y})$ as follows:
  1. It assigns values of monomials in $\overline{p}^y, \overline{p}_1^y, \overline{p}_2^y$ using $\overline{y}$.
  2. It samples N vectors $p_1^0, \ldots, p_N^0$ such that for each $i \in [N]$, vector $p_i^0 := (r_{i,1}, \ldots, r_{i,|p_i|})$ contains $|p_i|$ random field elements under the constraint $\sum_{j=1}^{|p_i|} r_{i,j} = 0$ (i.e. an additive secret sharing of 0). Let $\overline{p}^0 := p_1^0 || \ldots || p_N^0$.
  3. It partitions each of $\overline{p}^0, \overline{p}^y, \overline{p}_1^y, \overline{p}_2^y$ into $N' := N_{\mathsf{mono}}/\ell$ short vectors of size ℓ. Denote these vectors by $\overline{v}_1^0, \ldots, \overline{v}_{N'}^0$ and $\overline{v}_1^y, \ldots, \overline{v}_{N'}^y$ and $\overline{v}_{1,1}^y, \ldots, \overline{v}_{N',1}^y$ and $\overline{v}_{1,2}^y, \ldots, \overline{v}_{N',2}^y$ respectively.
  4. For each $i \in [N']$, it computes the sharings $[\overline{v}_{i,1}^y], [\overline{v}_{i,2}^y], [\overline{v}_i^y]$ similarly as above and $[\overline{v}_i^0] = \mathsf{Share}_{(4t+3\ell,\ell,m)}(\overline{v}_i^0)$ where $[\overline{v}_i^0]$ denotes a sharing of $\overline{v}_i^0$. For $j \in [m]$, define $\hat{y}_j, \hat{y}_{j,1}, \hat{y}_{j,2}, \hat{0}_j$ similarly as above.
  5. It outputs $\{\hat{y}_j, \hat{y}_{j,1}, \hat{y}_{j,2}, \hat{0}_j\}_{j \in [m]}$.
- **Round 2:** Server j runs $\mathsf{Eval}(1^\lambda, j, (\hat{x}_j, \hat{x}_{j,1}, \hat{x}_{j,2}), (\hat{y}_j, \hat{y}_{j,1}, \hat{y}_{j,2}, \hat{0}_j))$ for $j \in [m]$ as follows:
  1. **Verify:** It verifies that $\hat{x}_j = \hat{x}_{j,1} \odot \hat{x}_{j,2}$ and $\hat{y}_j = \hat{y}_{j,1} \odot \hat{y}_{j,2}$. Note that this check will eventually be replaced by the watchlist.
  2. **Eval:** It outputs $\phi_j := \hat{x}_j \odot \hat{y}_j + \hat{0}_j$ via N' parallel OLE operations, where ϕ_j is a vector of N' field elements.
- **Output:** The receiver runs $\mathsf{Dec}(1^\lambda, (\phi_1, \ldots, \phi_m))$ as follows:
  1. It reconstructs $\overline{o} = \mathsf{Rec}_{(4t+3\ell,\ell,m)}(\phi_1, \ldots, \phi_m)$, where $\overline{o} := \overline{o}_1 || \ldots || \overline{o}_{N'}$.
  2. Note that $\overline{o}$ is a vector of $N_{\mathsf{mono}} = N' \cdot \ell$ monomials. It re-partitions the monomials in $\overline{o}$ back into N vectors of size $|p_1|, \ldots, |p_N|$ in order. Denote the re-partitions by $\overline{o} = \overline{f}_1 || \ldots || \overline{f}_N$, where $\overline{f}_i := (f_{i,1}, \ldots, f_{i,|p_i|})$, which corresponds to evaluations of monomials in p_i for $i \in [N]$.
  3. For each $i \in [N]$, it computes $z_i := \sum_{j=1}^{|p_i|} f_{i,j}$.
  4. It outputs $\overline{z} := (z_1, \ldots, z_N)$ as the evaluations of polynomials.

Fig. 1. Protocol for Computing Quadratics

to both parties. However, the vectors $\overline{p}^x, \overline{p}_1^x, \overline{p}_2^x$ (resp. $\overline{p}^y, \overline{p}_1^y, \overline{p}_2^y$) become private once the receiver (resp. sender) assigns the values from its private input $\overline{x}$ (resp. $\overline{y}$) into these vectors.

The conforming protocol $\Phi_{\mathsf{quad}}(\overline{p}, \overline{x}, \overline{y}) := ((\mathsf{Share}_1, \mathsf{Share}_2), \mathsf{Eval}, \mathsf{Dec})$ for computing degree-2 polynomials $\overline{p} = (p_1, \ldots, p_N)$ is described in Fig. 1 below.

Recall that there are m servers, and at most t servers can be corrupted. Since the final resulting vectors are recovered using a $(4t + 3\ell, 4t + 3\ell + \ell + 1; \ell, m)$-packed Shamir secret sharing scheme, we need to use a polynomial of degree $4t + 4\ell$ to share the secrets, which means the number of honest servers need to be at least $4t + 4\ell + 1$. If we view the sharing as a Reed Solomon code, then the distance of the code is $m - (4t + 4\ell)$. In order to correct t errors, we need $t \leq \lfloor (m - (4t + 4\ell))/2 \rfloor \implies m \geq 6t + 4\ell$.

For definition of security against the admissible adversary and the security proof, we refer the reader to the full version.

Lemma 1. *Let ℓ be the packing size of packed secret sharing scheme and let number of servers $m \geq 6t + 4\ell$. The two-client, m-server, two-round conforming protocol Φ_{quad} for computing a vector of degree-2 polynomials, is secure against an admissible adversary $\mathcal{A}$ corrupting either client and up to t servers.*

4.2   Protocol for Computing Constant-Degree Polynomials

In this section, we describe the conforming protocol $\Phi_{\mathsf{cons}}(\overline{p}, \overline{x}, \overline{y})$ that computes a vector of constant-degree polynomials, which is a natural extension to the protocol Φ_{quad} in the previous section. We use the same notation as in the previous section, except that now $\overline{p} = (p_1, \ldots, p_N)$ is a vector of constant-degree polynomials over $\mathbb{F}$. Let d denote the maximum degree of these polynomials. The extension is rather straightforward: the decomposition now becomes $\overline{p}^x = \overline{p}_1^x \odot \cdots \odot \overline{p}_d^x$ and $\overline{p}^y = \overline{p}_1^y \odot \cdots \odot \overline{p}_d^y$ and the protocol is updated correspondingly. For detailed description of Φ_{cons}, we refer the reader to the full version.

4.3   Protocol for Computing Boolean Circuits

In this section, we describe the conforming protocol $\Phi_{\mathsf{circ}}(C, x, y)$ for computing an arbitrary two-party functionality $f(x, y)$ expressed as a Boolean circuit C. First, we follow the garbling process of the BMR protocol, which reduces the problem of computing circuit C to computing a vector of degree-3 polynomials. Once this reduction is complete, we invoke Φ_{cons} with degree $d = 3$ as a black box to obtain the evaluations of polynomials. The receiver then uses these evaluations to carry out the BMR evaluation process and obtain the final output $C(x, y)$. This is the final outer protocol that will be used in our compiler. For detailed description of Φ_{circ}, we refer the reader to the full version.

5   Inner Protocol from OT Correlations

In the outer protocol Φ_{circ}, the server's evaluation function Eval needs to perform N' parallel Oblivious Linear Evaluation (OLE) operations. Our two-round, semi-honest inner protocol instantiates these OLE computations. Let $\mathbb{F}$ denote the finite field used in both the outer and inner protocol, with field order $|\mathbb{F}| = 2^\lambda$. We first describe a trivial inner protocol, Π_{OLE}, which is based on preprocessed random OLE correlations over $\mathbb{F}$. Then, with the help of *multiplication-friendly embeddings* (MFEs) [13], we construct a second inner protocol, Π^*_{OLE}, which is based on preprocessed random bit OT correlations. Both Π_{OLE} and Π^*_{OLE} can be composed with the outer protocol in our compiler. For detailed description of inner protocols Π_{OLE} and Π^*_{OLE}, we refer the reader to the full version.

6   Proofs of Reed-Solomon Proximity and Constraints

The security of the outer protocol holds only against the defined admissible adversary. In this section, we progressively remove the constraints imposed on the admissible adversary by replacing them with non-interactive zero-knowledge arguments in the random oracle model. Specifically, we present three argument systems addressing consistency constraints, linear constraints, and Boolean constraints, respectively.

Note that both clients need to prove to the other client that their secret sharing is honest. The sender proves for the shares of $\overline{p}^0, \overline{p}^y_1, \overline{p}^y_2, \overline{p}^y_3$ to the receiver, and the receiver proves for the shares of $\overline{p}^x_1, \overline{p}^x_2, \overline{p}^x_3$ to the sender. We remark that the shares of vector $\overline{p}^x$ (resp. $\overline{p}^y$) is deterministically computed using shares of $\overline{p}^x_1, \overline{p}^x_2, \overline{p}^x_3$ (resp. $\overline{p}^y_1, \overline{p}^y_2, \overline{p}^y_3$) and will be checked by the compiler later.

Notations. Let $||$ denote the concatenation operation. To simplify the notation, we denote the prover's input (the shares of size-ℓ vectors it sends to the m servers) by an $n \times m$ matrix U where row $U_i := (u_{i,1}, \ldots, u_{i,m})$. For each $j \in [m]$, the column $U[j]$ stacks shares sent to server j vertically together. When the receiver client is the prover, column $U[j] = (\hat{x}_{j,1}||\hat{x}_{j,2}||\hat{x}_{j,3})$ (vertically stacked) and the number of rows $n = 3N'$. When the sender client is the prover, it needs to use two separate matrices. The first matrix is for the shares of the vectors $\overline{p}^y_1, \overline{p}^y_2, \overline{p}^y_3$. In this case, column $U[j] = (\hat{y}_{j,1}||\hat{y}_{j,2}||\hat{y}_{j,3})$ (vertically stacked) and the number of rows $n = 3N'$. The second matrix is for the additive secret shares of zeros $\overline{p}^0$, in which case $U[j] := \hat{0}_j$ and the number of rows $n = N'$. We need two matrices because the degree of the polynomial underlying the packed Shamir secret sharing for $\overline{p}^y_1, \overline{p}^y_2, \overline{p}^y_3$ and $\overline{p}^0$ are different. Let $(\mathsf{Com}, \mathsf{Open})$ be a non-interactive, straight-line extractable commitment scheme in the random oracle model [47], where the commitment is of size $O(\lambda)$. With polynomial number of queries to the random oracle, the commitments are statistically binding, computationally hiding, and straight-line extractable. We commit matrix U as follows. For each $j \in [m]$, we commit column $U[j]$ by computing $\mathsf{com}_j := \mathsf{Com}(U[j], s_j)$ where $s_j \leftarrow \{0,1\}^\lambda$ is a uniform random salt. For simplicity and readability, in this section, we hide the random salt parameter and write $\mathsf{Com}(U[j])$ instead. Furthermore, we define $\overline{\mathsf{com}} := (\mathsf{com}_1, \ldots, \mathsf{com}_m)$ as the commitment for matrix U. The random oracle is modeled by hash functions $\mathcal{H} := (H_{\mathsf{com}}, H_T, H_r)$, where H_{com} is used in the commitment scheme $(\mathsf{Com}, \mathsf{Open})$, $H_T : \{0,1\}^* \to S_{m,|T|}$ outputs a uniform random subset $T \subseteq [m]$ and $|T|$ is a constant fraction of m, and $H_r : \{0,1\}^* \to \{0,1\}^*$ generates a random binary string that can be interpreted as field elements of $\mathbb{F}$.

6.1 The Proof System for Consistency Requirements

Recall packed Shamir secret sharing. Fix m distinct points $\overline{\alpha} = (\alpha_1, \ldots, \alpha_m) \in \mathbb{F}^m$ and ℓ distinct points $\overline{\beta} = (\beta_1, \ldots, \beta_\ell) \in \mathbb{F}^\ell$ and $\overline{\alpha}$ and $\overline{\beta}$ are disjoint. We sample a random polynomial p such that $(p(\beta_1), \ldots, p(\beta_\ell))$ equals the vector of size ℓ. The sharing is then $p(\alpha_1), \ldots, p(\alpha_m)$. Since the shares are evaluations of a polynomial, we can view each sharing (i.e. each row of matrix U) as a Reed-Solomon codeword.

Fix $t + \ell$ distinct points $\overline{k} = (\beta_1, \ldots, \beta_\ell, k_1, \ldots, k_t)$ and $\overline{k}$ and $\overline{\alpha}$ are disjoint. Let $k = t + \ell - 1$. Let $\mathsf{RS}_{\overline{\alpha}, \overline{\beta}}[\mathbb{F}, k, m]$ denote the Reed-Solomon code of dimension $k + 1$ (since we use a degree-k polynomial) and block length m over finite field $\mathbb{F}$, where the actual message is evaluated on $\overline{\beta} \in \mathbb{F}^\ell$. In our case, $\overline{\alpha}, \overline{\beta}, \overline{k}$ are pre-determined before the execution of the outer protocol. Thus, to simplify the notation, we write $\mathsf{RS}[\mathbb{F}, k, m]$ when the context is clear. For any message $v \in \mathbb{F}^\ell$, to compute the RS codeword, we sample a random polynomial p of degree k conditioned on $p(\beta_i) = v_i$ for all $i \in [\ell]$, then the codeword is $(p(\alpha_1), \ldots, p(\alpha_m)) \in \mathsf{RS}[\mathbb{F}, k, m]$. If the secrets are honestly shared, then for each $i \in [n]$, $U_i := (u_{i,1}, \ldots, u_{i,m})$ should be an exact RS codeword. For $i \in [n]$, let p_i be the degree-k polynomial used in the packed Shamir secret sharing.

Description of the Non-Interactive Argument System. In Fig. 2 below, we describe the non-interactive argument system, denoted by $(P, V)_{\mathsf{rs}}^{\mathcal{H}}$, to test Reed-Solomon proximity, which shows the shares are consistent with RS codewords in $\mathsf{RS}[\mathbb{F}, k, m]$. This is essentially a zero-knowledge version of the Ligero test [2] for interleaved Reed-Solomon codes, applied with the Fiat-Shamir transformation using the random oracle.

The input of the prover consists of the matrix U and the commitments of U's columns $\overline{\mathsf{com}} = (\mathsf{com}_1, \ldots, \mathsf{com}_m)$, and as witnesses the polynomials $p_1, \ldots, p_n$ used in the packed secret sharing of the rows $U_1, \ldots, U_n$ respectively. The input of the verifier is the commitments $\overline{\mathsf{com}} = (\mathsf{com}_1, \ldots, \mathsf{com}_m)$. We remark that the prover also obtains the associated random salts used in the commitments implicitly. When the prover opens a commitment to the verifier, it also provides the random salt as part of the opening. Both prover and the verifier have access to the random oracle $\mathcal{H} = (H_{\mathsf{com}}, H_T, H_r)$, where H_{com} is used to create the commitments $\overline{\mathsf{com}}$. The size of the random subset T should be a constant fraction of m, and it can be tweaked as a parameter according to the security it wants to achieve in practice. In our final compiled protocol, we invoke $(P, V)_{\mathsf{rs}}^{\mathcal{H}}$ with $|T| = \lambda$.

$(P,V)_{\mathsf{rs}}^{\mathcal{H}}$:

- **Input**: The purported shares represented by matrix U and the commitments $\overline{\mathsf{com}} = (\mathsf{com}_1, \ldots, \mathsf{com}_m)$. The witnesses $(p_1, \ldots, p_n)$ which are polynomials of degree k. Note that $\overline{\mathsf{com}}$ is the common input of both the prover and the verifier.
- **Prover** $P_{\mathsf{rs}}^{\mathcal{H}}(\overline{\mathsf{com}}, U, (p_1, \ldots, p_n))$:
  1. (Insert random row) It samples a random degree-k polynomial p_0. Then it computes $U_0 := (p_0(\alpha_1), \ldots, p_0(\alpha_m)) = (u_{0,1}, \ldots, u_{0,m})$.
  2. For each $j \in [m]$, it computes $\mathsf{com}'_j := \mathsf{Com}(\mathsf{com}_j \| u_{0,j})$. Let $\overline{\mathsf{com}}' := (\mathsf{com}'_1, \ldots, \mathsf{com}'_m)$.
  3. It samples a random salt $s_r \leftarrow \{0,1\}^{\lambda}$. Then, it uses the random oracle to generate a random column vector $r := H_r(\overline{\mathsf{com}}, \overline{\mathsf{com}}', s_r)$, where $r = (r_1, \ldots, r_n) \in \mathbb{F}^n$.
  4. (Folding) It computes $\overline{u}' := r^{\mathsf{T}} U + U_0$, and denote the elements of $\overline{u}'$ as $(u'_1, \ldots, u'_m) \in \mathbb{F}^m$.
  5. It samples a random salt $s_T \leftarrow \{0,1\}^{\lambda}$. Then it uses the random oracle to obtain a random subset $T := H_T(\overline{\mathsf{com}}, \overline{\mathsf{com}}', \overline{u}', s_T) \subseteq [m]$ and $|T| \leq t$.
  6. For each $j \in T$, it computes the openings $\mathsf{open}'_j := \mathsf{Open}(\mathsf{com}'_j)$ and $\mathsf{open}_j := \mathsf{Open}(\mathsf{com}_j)$. Specifically, open'_j should contain $(\mathsf{com}_j \| u_{0,j})$ and open_j should contain $U[j]$.
  7. It outputs $\pi_{\mathsf{rs}} := (\overline{\mathsf{com}}', s_r, s_T, \overline{u}', T, \{\mathsf{open}_j : j \in T\}, \{\mathsf{open}'_j : j \in T\})$.
- **Verifier** $V_{\mathsf{rs}}^{\mathcal{H}}(\overline{\mathsf{com}}, \pi_{\mathsf{rs}})$:
  1. It calls $H_T(\overline{\mathsf{com}}, \overline{\mathsf{com}}', \overline{u}', s_T)$ and checks if it is equal to T sent by the prover. If so, it checks for each $j \in T$ if the openings are successful, i.e. open'_j should successfully open $(\mathsf{com}_j \| u_{0,j})$ and open_j should successfully open $U[j]$.
  2. It calls the random oracle $H_r(\overline{\mathsf{com}}, \overline{\mathsf{com}}', s_r)$ to obtain $r = (r_1, \ldots, r_n)$.
  3. It does the following:
     (a) For each $j \in T$, it computes $r^{\mathsf{T}} U[j] + u_{0,j}$ and checks if it is equal to u'_j sent by the prover.
     (b) It checks if $\overline{u}' \in \mathsf{RS}[\mathbb{F}, k, m]$ (i.e. is an exact RS codeword).
  4. It accepts if and only if all the checks above pass.

Fig. 2. Description of $(P,V)_{\mathsf{rs}}^{\mathcal{H}}$ for Consistency Requirements

Communication Complexity. Consider the message π_{rs} sent by the prover. The commitment $\overline{\mathsf{com}}'$ takes $m \cdot O(\lambda)$ bits. The random salts s_r, s_T takes λ bits each. The result of linear combination $\overline{u}'$ takes $m \log |\mathbb{F}| = m\lambda$ bits. To represent the subset T, it takes $|T| \log m$ bits. The openings $\{\mathsf{open}'_j : j \in T\}$ take $|T| \cdot O(\lambda)$ bits. The openings $\{\mathsf{open}_j : j \in T\}$ take $|T| \cdot O(n\lambda)$ bits as they need to contain the whole column $U[j]$. Summing them up, the total communication is $O(m\lambda) + 2\lambda + m\lambda + |T| \log m + |T| \cdot O(\lambda) + |T| \cdot O(n\lambda)$, which is dominated by the $|T| \cdot O(n\lambda)$ term. Recall that $n \leq 3N'$ and $N' \cdot \ell = N_{\mathsf{mono}} = O(|C|)$. Therefore, the communication complexity of $(P,V)_{\mathsf{rs}}^{\mathcal{H}}$ is $|T| \cdot O(|C|\lambda/\ell)$. If we take $\ell = O(\lambda)$ and $|T| = \lambda$, then the communication complexity becomes $O(|C|\lambda)$.

Completeness. For completeness, it follows directly from the description. Note that $\overline{u}'$ is a linear combination of RS codewords $U_0, U_1, \ldots, U_n$. By linearity of Reed-Solomon code, $\overline{u}'$ is in $\mathsf{RS}[\mathbb{F}, k, m]$ with probability 1.

Soundness. For soundness, note that we share n vectors, and each sharing U_i can be viewed as a (possibly corrupted) RS codeword. Let t be the number of corrupted servers defined in the outer protocol, which is also the number of corrupted columns in U. If the union of all corrupted positions over all n received codewords has size at most t, which means at most t columns are corrupted, then by the error-correcting property of the underlying secret sharing scheme, the secrets can still be recovered.

Before proving the soundness, we introduce some notations. Let U' be a $(n+1) \times m$ matrix with rows $U_0, U_1, \ldots, U_n$. Let $U_i := (u_{i,1}, \ldots, u_{i,m})$ for $i \in \{0, \ldots, n\}$. Let L^{n+1} be a $(n+1) \times m$ matrix, where each row $L_i \in \mathsf{RS}[\mathbb{F}, k, m]$ is the exact RS codeword that is closest in Hamming distance to U_i. Let $d(U_i, L_i)$ denote the Hamming distance between U_i and L_i. Furthermore, for any string $s \in \mathbb{F}^m$, we use $d(s, \mathsf{RS})$ to denote the Hamming distance between s and its closest codeword in $\mathsf{RS}[\mathbb{F}, k, m]$. Let $\Delta(U_i, L_i) := \{j \in [m] : U_{i,j} \neq C_{i,j}\}$ denote the set of indices where U_i disagrees with L_i. Let $h(U', L^{n+1}) := \left| \cup_{i \in \{0, \ldots, n\}} \Delta(U_i, L_i) \right|$ denote the size of the union of indices where U_i disagrees with L_i, over all $i \in \{0, 1, \ldots, n\}$.

To prove soundness, the intuition is that if the rows of U' are not all exact RS codewords, then a linear combination of the rows of U' is unlikely to be close to a RS codeword. This is formally studied as the proximity gap theorem. We state a proximity gap theorem by Ben-Sasson et al. [4] below. Note that we only take t up to the unique decoding bound and we take $t = \Theta(m)$ and $m = \Theta(\lambda)$ and $|\mathbb{F}| = 2^\lambda$. Applying this theorem, we prove the soundness of $(P, V)_{\mathsf{rs}}^{\mathcal{H}}$, which is negligible in λ. For detailed soundness proof as well as proof of zero-knowledge, we refer the reader to the full version.

Theorem 2 (Rephrase of Theorem 1.6 from [4]). *For any $n + 1$ strings $U_0, U_1, \ldots, U_n \in \mathbb{F}^m$, let $S := U_0 + \mathrm{span}\{U_1, \ldots, U_n\} \subset \mathbb{F}^m$ be an affine subspace. If $t \in (0, (m - k)/2)$, and*

$$\Pr_{s \in S}[d(s, \mathsf{RS}) \leq t] > m/|\mathbb{F}|,$$

then there exists a subset of positions $\mathcal{D}' \subseteq [m]$ and $n + 1$ exact Reed-Solomon codewords $L_0, L_1, \ldots, L_n \in \mathsf{RS}[\mathbb{F}, k, m]$ satisfying $|\mathcal{D}'| \geq m - t$ and for all $i \in \{0, 1, \ldots, n\}$, string U_i and codeword L_i agree on all of $\mathcal{D}'$.

6.2   The Proof System for Linear Constraints

Recall the linear constraints requirement of the admissible adversary, where the receiver (resp. sender) needs to show that the vectors they share satisfy linear constraints $\mathcal{R}_x$ (resp. $\mathcal{R}_y$) defined as a system of linear equations $Av = b$. To remove the linear constraints requirement of the admissible adversary, we describe a non-interactive argument system $(P, V)_{\mathsf{lin}}^{\mathcal{H}}$, which is essentially the zero-knowledge version of Ligero test for linear constraints [2], combined with a Fiat-Shamir transformation in the random oracle model. For detailed description of $(P, V)_{\mathsf{lin}}^{\mathcal{H}}$, we refer the reader to the full version.

6.3   The Proof System for Boolean Constraints

There is another constraint that needs to be addressed. In the BMR-style garbling used in the outer protocol Φ_{circ} for computing Boolean circuits, both the sender and the receiver generate masking bits for every wire in C. However, the protocol performs arithmetic operations over the finite field $\mathbb{F}$. Consequently, each masking bit must be converted to an element of $\mathbb{F}$. Similarly, the circuit input bits must also be converted into field elements of $\mathbb{F}$. Since they are bits, they should be mapped to $0/1$ in $\mathbb{F}$. Following similar ideas as in the proof system for linear constraints, we apply Ligero proofs to construct a proof system $(P, V)_{\mathsf{bool}}^{\mathcal{H}}$ that ensures the Boolean constraints. For detailed description of $(P, V)_{\mathsf{bool}}^{\mathcal{H}}$, we refer the reader to the full version.

7   The Protocol Compiler

In this section, we use the IPS-style watchlist to compile the outer protocol Φ_{circ} in Sect. 4 with the inner protocol in Sect. 5 and the succinct non-interactive arguments in Sect. 6 in the random oracle model.

Theorem 3. *Let λ be the security parameter. Let $\mathbb{F}$ be a finite field of order 2^λ. Let f be an arbitrary two-party, single-output functionality modeled by a Boolean circuit C comprised on XOR and AND gates of fan-in 2. Assume the existence of:*

- *A two-round, 2-client, m-server outer protocol Φ_{circ} for computing f that is secure against an admissible adversary corrupting either client and up to t servers, where t is a small constant fraction of m and $m = \Theta(\lambda)$. The outer protocol uses packed Shamir secret sharing of packing size $\ell = \Theta(\lambda)$.*
- *A two-round, semi-honest inner protocol Π_{OLE} that computes $k = O(|C|/\ell)$ instances of OLE over $\mathbb{F}$ in parallel, assuming $O(k)$ preprocessed random OLE correlations over $\mathbb{F}$. Or, equivalently, a two-round, semi-honest inner protocol Π_{OLE}^* that computes k instances of OLE over $\mathbb{F}$ in parallel, assuming $O(k\lambda)$ preprocessed random bit OT correlations.*

Then, there exists a NISC protocol Γ for computing f that makes black-box use of Π_{OLE} (or Π_{OLE}^*) and is secure against static, malicious adversaries in the random oracle model. The communication complexity of Γ is $O(|C|\lambda)$.

Malicious Two-Party NISC $\Gamma(C, x, y)$:

- **Set-up:**
  - The receiver (resp. sender) obtains vector $\overline{x}$ (resp. $\overline{y}$), and as common input linear constraints $\mathcal{R} = ((A^x, b^x), (A^y, b^y))$ and Boolean constraints $\mathcal{B} = (A^x_{\mathsf{bool}}, A^y_{\mathsf{bool}})$ from the set-up of outer protocol $\Phi_{\mathsf{circ}}(C, x, y)$.
  - The receiver (resp. sender) obtains correlations $r_{\mathsf{rec}} := (r_{\mathsf{rec},1}, \ldots, r_{\mathsf{rec},m})$ (resp. $r_{\mathsf{sen}} := (r_{\mathsf{sen},1}, \ldots, r_{\mathsf{sen},m})$) from the set-up of inner protocol Π_{OLE}.

- **The receiver does:**
  1. It obtains $\{\hat{x}_j, \hat{x}_{j,1}, \hat{x}_{j,2}, \hat{x}_{j,3}\}_{j \in [m]} = \mathsf{Share}_1(1^\lambda, \overline{x})$. Let $U \in \mathbb{F}^{n \times m}$ be a matrix formed by $\{\hat{x}_{j,1}, \hat{x}_{j,2}, \hat{x}_{j,3}\}_{j \in [m]}$.
  2. It commits $\overline{\mathsf{com}}^U := (\mathsf{com}_1^U, \ldots, \mathsf{com}_m^U)$, where $\mathsf{com}_j^U = \mathsf{Com}(U[j])$ for $j \in [m]$. It commits $\overline{\mathsf{com}}^x := (\mathsf{com}_1^x, \ldots, \mathsf{com}_m^x)$, where $\mathsf{com}_j^x = \mathsf{Com}(\hat{x}_j)$ for $j \in [m]$.
  3. It runs $\mathsf{makeProofs}$ (described in Figure 4) to generate the Ligero proofs for U, denoted by π^x_{proofs}.
  4. It commits $\overline{\mathsf{com}}^x_{\mathsf{OLE}} := (\mathsf{com}^x_{\mathsf{OLE},1}, \ldots, \mathsf{com}^x_{\mathsf{OLE},m})$, where $\mathsf{com}^x_{\mathsf{OLE},j} = \mathsf{Com}(r_{\mathsf{rec},j})$ for $j \in [m]$. Then it obtains first-round messages $\pi^x_{\mathsf{OLE}} := (\pi^1_{\mathsf{OLE},1}, \ldots, \pi^m_{\mathsf{OLE},1})$, where $\pi^j_{\mathsf{OLE},1} = \Pi_{\mathsf{OLE},1}(\hat{x}_j, r_{\mathsf{rec},j})$ for $j \in [m]$.
  5. It obtains subset $T_x = H_T(\overline{\mathsf{com}}^x, \overline{\mathsf{com}}^U, \overline{\mathsf{com}}^x_{\mathsf{OLE}}, \pi^x_{\mathsf{proofs}}, \pi^x_{\mathsf{OLE}}, \mathsf{tag}^x) \subseteq [m]$ where $\mathsf{tag}^x \leftarrow \{0,1\}^\lambda$. It then computes the openings $\overline{\mathsf{open}}^x := \{\mathsf{Open}(\mathsf{com}_j^x), \mathsf{Open}(\mathsf{com}_j^U), \mathsf{Open}(\mathsf{com}^x_{\mathsf{OLE},j})\}_{j \in T_x}$.
  6. It outputs $\mathbb{T}_x := (\overline{\mathsf{com}}^x, \overline{\mathsf{com}}^U, \overline{\mathsf{com}}^x_{\mathsf{OLE}}, \pi^x_{\mathsf{proofs}}, \pi^x_{\mathsf{OLE}}, \mathsf{tag}^x, T_x, \overline{\mathsf{open}}^x)$.

- **The sender does:**
  1. It runs $\mathsf{verifyProofs}$ (described in Figure 5) for U and $\mathsf{checkWatchlist}(0, \mathbb{T}_x, r_{\mathsf{sen}})$. If any of them outputs 0, it aborts.
  2. It obtains $\{\hat{y}_j, \hat{y}_{j,1}, \hat{y}_{j,2}, \hat{y}_{j,3}, \hat{0}_j\}_{j \in [m]} = \mathsf{Share}_2(1^\lambda, \overline{y})$. Let $V \in \mathbb{F}^{n \times m}$ be a matrix formed by $\{\hat{y}_{j,1}, \hat{y}_{j,2}, \hat{y}_{j,3}\}_{j \in [m]}$. Let $V^0 \in \mathbb{F}^{n_0 \times m}$ be a matrix formed by $\{\hat{0}_j\}_{j \in [m]}$.
  3. It commits $\overline{\mathsf{com}}^V := (\mathsf{com}_1^V, \ldots, \mathsf{com}_m^V)$, $\overline{\mathsf{com}}^{V^0} := (\mathsf{com}_1^{V^0}, \ldots, \mathsf{com}_m^{V^0})$, and $\overline{\mathsf{com}}^y := (\mathsf{com}_1^y, \ldots, \mathsf{com}_m^y)$ similarly as above.
  4. It runs $\mathsf{makeProofs}$ to generate the Ligero proofs for V and V^0, denoted by π^y_{proofs}.
  5. It commits $\overline{\mathsf{com}}^y_{\mathsf{OLE}} := (\mathsf{com}^y_{\mathsf{OLE},1}, \ldots, \mathsf{com}^y_{\mathsf{OLE},m})$, where $\mathsf{com}^y_{\mathsf{OLE},j} = \mathsf{Com}(r_{\mathsf{sen},j})$ for $j \in [m]$. Then it gets second-round messages $\pi^y_{\mathsf{OLE}} := (\pi^1_{\mathsf{OLE},2}, \ldots, \pi^m_{\mathsf{OLE},2})$ where $\pi^j_{\mathsf{OLE},2} = \Pi_{\mathsf{OLE},2}(\pi^j_{\mathsf{OLE},1}, \hat{y}_j, \hat{0}_j, r_{\mathsf{sen},j})$ for $j \in [m]$.
  6. It gets $T_y = H_T(\overline{\mathsf{com}}^y, \overline{\mathsf{com}}^V, \overline{\mathsf{com}}^{V^0}, \overline{\mathsf{com}}^y_{\mathsf{OLE}}, \pi^y_{\mathsf{proofs}}, \pi^y_{\mathsf{OLE}}, \mathsf{tag}^y) \subseteq [m]$ where $\mathsf{tag}^y \leftarrow \{0,1\}^\lambda$. It then computes the openings $\overline{\mathsf{open}}^y := \{\mathsf{Open}(\mathsf{com}_j^y), \mathsf{Open}(\mathsf{com}_j^V), \mathsf{Open}(\mathsf{com}_j^{V^0}), \mathsf{Open}(\mathsf{com}^y_{\mathsf{OLE},j})\}_{j \in T_y}$.
  7. It outputs $\mathbb{T}_y := (\overline{\mathsf{com}}^y, \overline{\mathsf{com}}^V, \overline{\mathsf{com}}^{V^0}, \overline{\mathsf{com}}^y_{\mathsf{OLE}}, \pi^y_{\mathsf{proofs}}, \pi^y_{\mathsf{OLE}}, \mathsf{tag}^y, T_y, \overline{\mathsf{open}}^y)$.

- **Output:** The receiver does:
  1. It runs $\mathsf{verifyProofs}$ for V, V^0 and $\mathsf{checkWatchlist}(1, \mathbb{T}_y, r_{\mathsf{rec}}, \pi^x_{\mathsf{OLE}})$ (described in Figure 6). If any of them outputs 0, then it aborts and outputs $\perp$.
  2. It obtains $\phi_j = \mathsf{out}_{\mathsf{OLE}}(\pi^j_{\mathsf{OLE},2}, r_{\mathsf{rec},j})$ for $j \in [m]$.
  3. It runs $\mathsf{Dec}(1^\lambda, (\phi_1, \ldots, \phi_m))$ and outputs whatever it outputs.

Fig. 3. Description of Two-Round Malicious 2PC

$\mathsf{makeProofs}(n, U, \overline{\mathsf{com}}, (p_1, \ldots, p_n), A, b, A_{\mathsf{bool}})$:
- **Inputs:**
    1. A parameter n. When we need to prove for $U = \{\hat{x}_{j,1}, \hat{x}_{j,2}, \hat{x}_{j,3}\}_{j \in [m]}$ or $V = \{\hat{y}_{j,1}, \hat{y}_{j,2}, \hat{y}_{j,3}\}_{j \in [m]}$, then $n = 3N'$. When we need to prove for $V^0 = \{\hat{0}_j\}_{j \in [m]}$, then $n = N'$. Note that $N' = O(|C|/\lambda)$.
    2. A matrix $U \in \mathbb{F}^{n \times m}$ and the commitment of its columns $\overline{\mathsf{com}} = (\mathsf{com}_1, \ldots, \mathsf{com}_m)$ where com_j is the commitment of $U[j]$ for $j \in [m]$.
    3. An array of polynomials $(p_1, \ldots, p_n)$ used in the packed secret sharing scheme in $\mathsf{Share}_1, \mathsf{Share}_2$ such that row $U_i = (p_i(\alpha_1), \ldots, p_i(\alpha_m))$ for all $i \in [n]$. These polynomials uniquely define the secret vectors $v_i = (p_i(\beta_1), \ldots, p_i(\beta_\ell))$ for all $i \in [n]$. Let $v := v_1 || \ldots || v_n$.
    4. A matrix $A \in \mathbb{F}^{n\ell \times n\ell}$ and a vector $b \in \mathbb{F}^{n\ell}$ that describe the linear constraints by $Av = b$.
    5. A matrix $A_{\mathsf{bool}} \in \mathbb{F}^{n\ell \times n\ell}$ that describes the Boolean constraints by $A_{\mathsf{bool}} (v \odot (1 - v)) = 0$, where $1 \in \mathbb{F}^{n\ell}$ is the all-one column vector and $0 \in \mathbb{F}^{n\ell}$ is the all-zero column vector. When we need to prove for $\{\hat{0}_j\}_{j \in [m]}$, then A_{bool} is not needed.
- **Execution:**
    1. It runs $\pi_{\mathsf{rs}} := P_{\mathsf{rs}}^{\mathcal{H}}(\overline{\mathsf{com}}, U, (p_1, \ldots, p_n))$ with proximity parameter (number of corrupted columns) $t_{\mathsf{rs}} = \lambda$, and random subset $|T_{\mathsf{rs}}| = \lambda$.
    2. It runs $\pi_{\mathsf{lin}} := P_{\mathsf{lin}}^{\mathcal{H}}(\overline{\mathsf{com}}, U, (p_1, \ldots, p_n), A, b)$ with random subset $|T_{\mathsf{lin}}| = \lambda$.
    3. It runs $\pi_{\mathsf{bool}} := P_{\mathsf{bool}}^{\mathcal{H}}(\overline{\mathsf{com}}, U, (p_1, \ldots, p_n), A_{\mathsf{bool}})$ with random subset $|T_{\mathsf{bool}}| = \lambda$. When we need to prove for $\{\hat{0}_j\}_{j \in [m]}$, this is not needed.
    4. It outputs $\pi_{\mathsf{proofs}} := (\pi_{\mathsf{rs}}, \pi_{\mathsf{lin}}, \pi_{\mathsf{bool}})$.

Fig. 4. Description of $\mathsf{makeProofs}$

$\mathsf{verifyProofs}(n, \overline{\mathsf{com}}, A, b, A_{\mathsf{bool}}, \pi_{\mathsf{proofs}} = (\pi_{\mathsf{rs}}, \pi_{\mathsf{lin}}, \pi_{\mathsf{bool}}))$:
- **Context:** The shares sent by the prover are represented by the matrix $U \in \mathbb{F}^{n \times m}$. Let $v := v_1 || \ldots || v_n$, where U_i encodes v_i for $i \in [n]$.
- **Inputs:**
    1. A parameter n. For U, V, set $n = 3N'$. For V^0, set $n = N'$.
    2. The commitments of matrix U's columns $\overline{\mathsf{com}} = (\mathsf{com}_1, \ldots, \mathsf{com}_m)$.
    3. A matrix $A \in \mathbb{F}^{n\ell \times n\ell}$ and a vector $b \in \mathbb{F}^{n\ell}$ that describe the linear constraints by $Av = b$.
    4. A matrix $A_{\mathsf{bool}} \in \mathbb{F}^{n\ell \times n\ell}$ that describes Boolean constraints by $A_{\mathsf{bool}} (v \odot (1 - v)) = 0$. For V^0, this is not needed.
    5. The Ligero proofs $\pi_{\mathsf{proofs}} = (\pi_{\mathsf{rs}}, \pi_{\mathsf{lin}}, \pi_{\mathsf{bool}})$.
- **Execution:**
    1. It runs verifier's algorithm $V_{\mathsf{rs}}^{\mathcal{H}}(\overline{\mathsf{com}}, \pi_{\mathsf{rs}})$.
    2. It runs verifier's algorithm $V_{\mathsf{lin}}^{\mathcal{H}}(\overline{\mathsf{com}}, A, b, \pi_{\mathsf{lin}})$.
    3. It runs verifier's algorithm $V_{\mathsf{bool}}^{\mathcal{H}}(\overline{\mathsf{com}}, A_{\mathsf{bool}}, \pi_{\mathsf{bool}})$ (not needed For V^0).
    4. If any of the verifiers above rejects, it outputs 0. Else, it outputs 1.

Fig. 5. Description of $\mathsf{verifyProofs}$

$\underline{\textsf{checkWatchlist}(k, \mathbb{T}, r_{\textsf{cor}}, \pi_{\textsf{OLE}})}$:

- **Inputs:**
    1. An index $k \in \{0, 1\}$. If $k = 0$, then $\mathbb{T} = \mathbb{T}_x$ is the receiver's message. If $k = 1$, then $\mathbb{T} = \mathbb{T}_y$ is the sender's message.
    2. Transcript

    $$\mathbb{T} = \begin{cases} \left(\overline{\textsf{com}}^x, \overline{\textsf{com}}^U, \overline{\textsf{com}}^x_{\textsf{OLE}}, \pi^x_{\textsf{proofs}}, \pi^x_{\textsf{OLE}}, \textsf{tag}^x, T_x, \overline{\textsf{open}}^x \right), & k = 0; \\ \left(\overline{\textsf{com}}^y, \overline{\textsf{com}}^V, \overline{\textsf{com}}^{V^0}, \overline{\textsf{com}}^y_{\textsf{OLE}}, \pi^y_{\textsf{proofs}}, \pi^y_{\textsf{OLE}}, \textsf{tag}^y, T_y, \overline{\textsf{open}}^y \right), & k = 1. \end{cases}$$

    3. Correlated randomness

    $$r_{\textsf{cor}} = \begin{cases} r_{\textsf{sen}} = (r_{\textsf{sen},1}, \ldots, r_{\textsf{sen},m}), & k = 0; \\ r_{\textsf{rec}} = (r_{\textsf{rec},1}, \ldots, r_{\textsf{rec},m}), & k = 1. \end{cases}$$

    4. An optional parameter $\pi_{\textsf{OLE}}$, which is the message output by the inner protocol. If $k = 0$, then we do not need this parameter. If $k = 1$, then $\pi_{\textsf{OLE}} = \pi^x_{\textsf{OLE}} = (\pi^1_{\textsf{OLE},1}, \ldots, \pi^m_{\textsf{OLE},1})$.
- **Execution:**
    - If $k = 0$, then the sender does:
        1. It checks if $H_T(\overline{\textsf{com}}^x, \overline{\textsf{com}}^U, \overline{\textsf{com}}^x_{\textsf{OLE}}, \pi^x_{\textsf{proofs}}, \pi^x_{\textsf{OLE}}, \textsf{tag}^x)$ equals received T_x.
        2. For each $j \in T_x$,
            (a) It checks if $\textsf{Open}(\textsf{com}^x_j)$ successfully opens $\hat{x}_j$, $\textsf{Open}(\textsf{com}^U_j)$ successfully opens $U[j]$, and $\textsf{Open}(\textsf{com}^x_{\textsf{OLE},j})$ successfully opens $r_{\textsf{rec},j}$.
            (b) It checks if $(r_{\textsf{sen},j}, r_{\textsf{rec},j})$ is a valid pair of correlated randomness. For random bit OT correlations, it checks if $(S^0, S^1) \in \{0, 1\}^2$ is consistent with $(C, R = S^C)$. For random OLE correlations, it checks if $y_r = a_r x_r + b_r$.
            (c) It simulates the inner protocol $\Pi_{\textsf{OLE},1}(\hat{x}_j, r_{\textsf{rec},j})$ and checks if the output is equal to the $\pi^j_{\textsf{OLE},1}$ received.
            (d) It checks if $\hat{x}_j = \hat{x}_{j,1} \odot \hat{x}_{j,2} \odot \hat{x}_{j,3}$.
        If any of the checks above fails, it outputs 0. Else, it outputs 1.
    - If $k = 1$, then the receiver does:
        1. It checks if $H_T(\overline{\textsf{com}}^y, \overline{\textsf{com}}^V, \overline{\textsf{com}}^{V^0}, \overline{\textsf{com}}^y_{\textsf{OLE}}, \pi^y_{\textsf{proofs}}, \pi^y_{\textsf{OLE}}, \textsf{tag}^y)$ equals received T_y.
        2. For each $j \in T_y$,
            (a) It checks if the openings $\textsf{Open}(\textsf{com}^y_j)$ successfully opens $\hat{y}_j$, $\textsf{Open}(\textsf{com}^V_j)$ successfully opens $V[j]$, $\textsf{Open}(\textsf{com}^{V^0}_j)$ successfully opens $V^0[j]$, and $\textsf{Open}(\textsf{com}^y_{\textsf{OLE},j})$ successfully opens $r_{\textsf{sen},j}$.
            (b) It checks if $(r_{\textsf{sen},j}, r_{\textsf{rec},j})$ is a valid pair of correlated randomness.
            (c) It simulates the inner protocol $\Pi_{\textsf{OLE},2}(\pi^j_{\textsf{OLE},1}, \hat{y}_j, \hat{0}_j, r_{\textsf{sen},j})$ and checks if the output is equal to the $\pi^j_{\textsf{OLE},2}$ received.
            (d) It checks if $\hat{y}_j = \hat{y}_{j,1} \odot \hat{y}_{j,2} \odot \hat{y}_{j,3}$.
        If any of the checks above fails, it outputs 0. Else, it outputs 1.

Fig. 6. Description of checkWatchlist

7.1   Construction

Building Blocks. The construction makes use of the following building blocks.

1. A conforming outer protocol $\Phi_{\mathsf{circ}} = ((\mathsf{Share}_1, \mathsf{Share}_2), \mathsf{Eval}, \mathsf{Dec})$ for computing f that is secure against an admissible adversary corrupting either client and up to t servers. The $\mathsf{Share}_1, \mathsf{Share}_2$ algorithms make use of packed Shamir secret sharing of packing size ℓ.
2. A semi-honest inner protocol $\Pi_{\mathsf{OLE}} = (\Pi_{\mathsf{OLE},1}, \Pi_{\mathsf{OLE},2}, \mathsf{out}_{\mathsf{OLE}})$ that computes $k = N' = O(|C|/\ell)$ instances of OLE in parallel from OLE correlations. Or equivalently, a two-round, semi-honest inner protocol $\Pi^*_{\mathsf{OLE}} = (\Pi_{\mathsf{OLE},1}, \Pi_{\mathsf{OLE},2}, \mathsf{out}_{\mathsf{OLE}})$ from $O(k\lambda)$ random bit OT correlations.
3. A straight-line extractable commitment scheme $(\mathsf{Com}, \mathsf{Open})$ constructed unconditionally from random oracle [47].
4. The random oracle modeled as hash functions $\mathcal{H} = (H_{\mathsf{com}}, H_T, H_r)$.
5. Non-interactive arguments $(P, V)^{\mathcal{H}}_{\mathsf{rs}}, (P, V)^{\mathcal{H}}_{\mathsf{lin}}, (P, V)^{\mathcal{H}}_{\mathsf{bool}}$ based on Ligero.

Description of the Protocol. We describe a two-party, two-round, malicious-secure protocol $\Gamma(C, x, y)$ for computing f in Fig. 3 below. Note that the openings $\mathsf{Open}(\mathsf{com}^x_j)$ contains $\hat{x}_j$, $\mathsf{Open}(\mathsf{com}^U_j)$ contains $U[j]$, and $\mathsf{Open}(\mathsf{com}^x_{\mathsf{OLE},j})$ contains $r_{\mathsf{rec},j}$. Similarly, the openings $\mathsf{Open}(\mathsf{com}^y_j)$ contains $\hat{y}_j$, $\mathsf{Open}(\mathsf{com}^V_j)$ contains $V[j]$, $\mathsf{Open}(\mathsf{com}^{V^0}_j)$ contains $V^0[j]$, and $\mathsf{Open}(\mathsf{com}^y_{\mathsf{OLE},j})$ contains $r_{\mathsf{sen},j}$. For detailed communication complexity and security proof, we refer the reader to the full version (Figs. 4, 5 and 6).

Acknowledgments. The authors thank the anonymous reviewers for their detailed comments and Swastik Kopparty for helpful discussions. Yuval Ishai was supported in part by ISF grants 2774/20 and 3527/24 and BSF grant 2022370. This work is not associated with Amazon. Akshayaram Srinivasan and Ziyang Jin are supported in part by the NSERC Discovery Grant RGPIN-2024-03928. Akshayaram Srinivasan is additionally supported by a SDF academic research award.

References

1. Afshar, A., Mohassel, P., Pinkas, B., Riva, B.: Non-interactive secure computation based on cut-and-choose. In: Nguyen, P.Q., Oswald, E. (eds.) EUROCRYPT 2014. LNCS, vol. 8441, pp. 387–404. Springer Berlin Heidelberg, Germany, Copenhagen, Denmark (2014). https://doi.org/10.1007/978-3-642-55220-5_22
2. Ames, S., Hazay, C., Ishai, Y., Venkitasubramaniam, M.: Ligero: lightweight sublinear arguments without a trusted setup. In: Thuraisingham, B.M., Evans, D., Malkin, T., Xu, D. (eds.) ACM CCS 2017, pp. 2087–2104. ACM Press, Dallas, TX, USA (2017). https://doi.org/10.1145/3133956.3134104
3. Beaver, D., Micali, S., Rogaway, P.: The round complexity of secure protocols (extended abstract). In: 22nd ACM STOC, pp. 503–513. ACM Press, Baltimore, MD, USA (1990). https://doi.org/10.1145/100216.100287

4. Ben-Sasson, E., Carmon, D., Ishai, Y., Kopparty, S., Saraf, S.: Proximity gaps for reed-Solomon codes. In: 61st FOCS, pp. 900–909. IEEE Computer Society Press, Durham, NC, USA (2020). https://doi.org/10.1109/FOCS46700.2020.00088
5. Ben-Sasson, E., Sudan, M.: Simple PCPs with poly-log rate and query complexity. In: Gabow, H.N., Fagin, R. (eds.) 37th ACM STOC, pp. 266–275. ACM Press, Baltimore, MA, USA (2005). https://doi.org/10.1145/1060590.1060631
6. Block, A.R., Gupta, D., Maji, H.K., Nguyen, H.H.: Secure computation using leaky correlations (asymptotically optimal constructions). In: Beimel, A., Dziembowski, S. (eds.) TCC 2018, Part II. LNCS, vol. 11240, pp. 36–65. Springer, Cham, Switzerland, Panaji, India (2018). https://doi.org/10.1007/978-3-030-03810-6_2
7. Boneh, D., et al.: Fully key-homomorphic encryption, arithmetic circuit ABE and compact garbled circuits. In: Nguyen, P.Q., Oswald, E. (eds.) EUROCRYPT 2014. LNCS, vol. 8441, pp. 533–556. Springer Berlin Heidelberg, Germany, Copenhagen, Denmark (2014). https://doi.org/10.1007/978-3-642-55220-5_30
8. Boyle, E., Couteau, G., Gilboa, N., Ishai, Y., Kohl, L., Scholl, P.: Efficient pseudorandom correlation generators: silent OT extension and more. In: Boldyreva, A., Micciancio, D. (eds.) CRYPTO 2019, Part III. LNCS, vol. 11694, pp. 489–518. Springer, Cham, Switzerland, Santa Barbara, CA, USA (2019). https://doi.org/10.1007/978-3-030-26954-8_16
9. Boyle, E., Couteau, G., Gilboa, N., Ishai, Y., Kohl, L., Scholl, P.: Correlated pseudorandom functions from variable-density LPN. In: 61st FOCS, pp. 1069–1080. IEEE Computer Society Press, Durham, NC, USA (2020). https://doi.org/10.1109/FOCS46700.2020.00103
10. Boyle, E., Couteau, G., Gilboa, N., Ishai, Y., Kohl, L., Scholl, P.: Efficient pseudorandom correlation generators from ring-LPN. In: Micciancio, D., Ristenpart, T. (eds.) CRYPTO 2020, Part II. LNCS, vol. 12171, pp. 387–416. Springer, Cham, Switzerland, Santa Barbara, CA, USA (2020). https://doi.org/10.1007/978-3-030-56880-1_14
11. Boyle, E., Gilboa, N., Ishai, Y.: Breaking the circuit size barrier for secure computation under DDH. In: Robshaw, M., Katz, J. (eds.) CRYPTO 2016, Part I. LNCS, vol. 9814, pp. 509–539. Springer Berlin Heidelberg, Germany, Santa Barbara, CA, USA (2016). https://doi.org/10.1007/978-3-662-53018-4_19
12. Brakerski, Z., Vaikuntanathan, V.: Efficient fully homomorphic encryption from (standard) LWE. In: Ostrovsky, R. (ed.) 52nd FOCS, pp. 97–106. IEEE Computer Society Press, Palm Springs, CA, USA (2011). https://doi.org/10.1109/FOCS.2011.12
13. Cascudo, I., Cramer, R., Xing, C., Yuan, C.: Amortized complexity of information-theoretically secure MPC revisited. In: Shacham, H., Boldyreva, A. (eds.) CRYPTO 2018, Part III. LNCS, vol. 10993, pp. 395–426. Springer, Cham, Switzerland, Santa Barbara, CA, USA (2018). https://doi.org/10.1007/978-3-319-96878-0_14
14. Chase, M., Dodis, Y., Ishai, Y., Kraschewski, D., Liu, T., Ostrovsky, R., Vaikuntanathan, V.: Reusable non-interactive secure computation. In: Boldyreva, A., Micciancio, D. (eds.) CRYPTO 2019, Part III. LNCS, vol. 11694, pp. 462–488. Springer, Cham, Switzerland, Santa Barbara, CA, USA (2019). https://doi.org/10.1007/978-3-030-26954-8_15
15. Couteau, G., Hazay, C., Hegde, A., Kumar, N.: $\omega(1/\lambda)$-rate boolean garbling scheme from generic groups. In: Kalai, Y.T., Kamara, S.F. (eds.) CRYPTO 2025, Part IV. LNCS, vol. 16003, pp. 489–521. Springer, Cham, Switzerland, Santa Barbara, CA, USA (2025). https://doi.org/10.1007/978-3-032-01884-7_16

16. Cramer, R., Rambaud, M., Xing, C.: Asymptotically-good arithmetic secret sharing over $\mathbb{Z}/p^\ell\mathbb{Z}$ with strong multiplication and its applications to efficient MPC. In: Malkin, T., Peikert, C. (eds.) CRYPTO 2021, Part III. LNCS, vol. 12827, pp. 656–686. Springer, Cham, Switzerland, Virtual Event (2021). https://doi.org/10.1007/978-3-030-84252-9_22

17. Cui, H., Wang, X., Yang, K., Yu, Y.: Actively secure half-gates with minimum overhead under duplex networks. In: Hazay, C., Stam, M. (eds.) EUROCRYPT 2023, Part II. LNCS, vol. 14005, pp. 35–67. Springer, Cham, Switzerland, Lyon, France (2023). https://doi.org/10.1007/978-3-031-30617-4_2

18. Damgård, I., Ishai, Y.: Constant-round multiparty computation using a black-box pseudorandom generator. In: Shoup, V. (ed.) CRYPTO 2005. LNCS, vol. 3621, pp. 378–394. Springer Berlin Heidelberg, Germany, Santa Barbara, CA, USA (2005). https://doi.org/10.1007/11535218_23

19. Dittmer, S., Ishai, Y., Lu, S., Ostrovsky, R.: Authenticated garbling from simple correlations. In: Dodis, Y., Shrimpton, T. (eds.) CRYPTO 2022, Part IV. LNCS, vol. 13510, pp. 57–87. Springer, Cham, Switzerland, Santa Barbara, CA, USA (2022). https://doi.org/10.1007/978-3-031-15985-5_3

20. Escudero, D., Xing, C., Yuan, C.: More efficient dishonest majority secure computation over $\mathbb{Z}_{2^k}$ via Galois rings. In: Dodis, Y., Shrimpton, T. (eds.) CRYPTO 2022, Part I. LNCS, vol. 13507, pp. 383–412. Springer, Cham, Switzerland, Santa Barbara, CA, USA (2022). https://doi.org/10.1007/978-3-031-15802-5_14

21. Franklin, M.K., Yung, M.: Communication complexity of secure computation (extended abstract). In: 24th ACM STOC, pp. 699–710. ACM Press, Victoria, BC, Canada (1992). https://doi.org/10.1145/129712.129780

22. Gentry, C.: Fully homomorphic encryption using ideal lattices. In: Mitzenmacher, M. (ed.) 41st ACM STOC, pp. 169–178. ACM Press, Bethesda, MD, USA (2009). https://doi.org/10.1145/1536414.1536440

23. Gentry, C., Sahai, A., Waters, B.: Homomorphic encryption from learning with errors: Conceptually-simpler, asymptotically-faster, attribute-based. In: Canetti, R., Garay, J.A. (eds.) CRYPTO 2013, Part I. LNCS, vol. 8042, pp. 75–92. Springer Berlin Heidelberg, Germany, Santa Barbara, CA, USA (2013). https://doi.org/10.1007/978-3-642-40041-4_5

24. Goldreich, O., Micali, S., Wigderson, A.: How to play any mental game or A completeness theorem for protocols with honest majority. In: Aho, A. (ed.) 19th ACM STOC, pp. 218–229. ACM Press, New York City, NY, USA (1987). https://doi.org/10.1145/28395.28420

25. Hazay, C., Ishai, Y., Venkitasubramaniam, M.: Actively secure garbled circuits with constant communication overhead in the plain model. In: Kalai, Y., Reyzin, L. (eds.) TCC 2017, Part II. LNCS, vol. 10678, pp. 3–39. Springer, Cham, Switzerland, Baltimore, MD, USA (2017). https://doi.org/10.1007/978-3-319-70503-3_1

26. Hazay, C., Scholl, P., Soria-Vazquez, E.: Low cost constant round MPC combining BMR and oblivious transfer. In: Takagi, T., Peyrin, T. (eds.) ASIACRYPT 2017, Part I. LNCS, vol. 10624, pp. 598–628. Springer, Cham, Switzerland, Hong Kong, China (2017). https://doi.org/10.1007/978-3-319-70694-8_21

27. Heath, D., Kolesnikov, V.: Stacked garbling - garbled circuit proportional to longest execution path. In: Micciancio, D., Ristenpart, T. (eds.) CRYPTO 2020, Part II. LNCS, vol. 12171, pp. 763–792. Springer, Cham, Switzerland, Santa Barbara, CA, USA (2020). https://doi.org/10.1007/978-3-030-56880-1_27

28. Huang, Y., Katz, J., Evans, D.: Quid-Pro-Quo-tocols: strengthening semi-honest protocols with dual execution. In: 2012 IEEE Symposium on Security and Privacy, pp. 272–284. IEEE Computer Society Press, San Francisco, CA, USA (2012). https://doi.org/10.1109/SP.2012.43

29. Huang, Y., Katz, J., Evans, D.: Quid-Pro-Quo-tocols: strengthening semi-honest protocols with dual execution. In: IEEE Symposium on Security and Privacy, SP 2012, 21-23 May 2012, San Francisco, California, USA, pp. 272–284. IEEE Computer Society (2012). https://doi.org/10.1109/SP.2012.43, https://doi.org/10.1109/SP.2012.43

30. Ishai, Y., Khurana, D., Sahai, A., Srinivasan, A.: On the round complexity of black-box secure MPC. In: Malkin, T., Peikert, C. (eds.) CRYPTO 2021, Part II. LNCS, vol. 12826, pp. 214–243. Springer, Cham, Switzerland, Virtual Event (2021). https://doi.org/10.1007/978-3-030-84245-1_8

31. Ishai, Y., Khurana, D., Sahai, A., Srinivasan, A.: Round-optimal black-box protocol compilers. In: Dunkelman, O., Dziembowski, S. (eds.) EUROCRYPT 2022, Part I. LNCS, vol. 13275, pp. 210–240. Springer, Cham, Switzerland, Trondheim, Norway (2022). https://doi.org/10.1007/978-3-031-06944-4_8

32. Ishai, Y., Khurana, D., Sahai, A., Srinivasan, A.: Round-optimal black-box secure computation from two-round malicious OT. In: Kiltz, E., Vaikuntanathan, V. (eds.) TCC 2022, Part II. LNCS, vol. 13748, pp. 441–469. Springer, Cham, Switzerland, Chicago, IL, USA (2022). https://doi.org/10.1007/978-3-031-22365-5_16

33. Ishai, Y., Khurana, D., Sahai, A., Srinivasan, A.: Black-box reusable NISC with random oracles. In: Hazay, C., Stam, M. (eds.) EUROCRYPT 2023, Part II. LNCS, vol. 14005, pp. 68–97. Springer, Cham, Switzerland, Lyon, France (2023). https://doi.org/10.1007/978-3-031-30617-4_3

34. Ishai, Y., Kushilevitz, E., Ostrovsky, R., Prabhakaran, M., Sahai, A.: Efficient non-interactive secure computation. In: Paterson, K.G. (ed.) EUROCRYPT 2011. LNCS, vol. 6632, pp. 406–425. Springer Berlin Heidelberg, Germany, Tallinn, Estonia (2011). https://doi.org/10.1007/978-3-642-20465-4_23

35. Ishai, Y., Kushilevitz, E., Paskin, A.: Secure multiparty computation with minimal interaction. In: Rabin, T. (ed.) CRYPTO 2010. LNCS, vol. 6223, pp. 577–594. Springer Berlin Heidelberg, Germany, Santa Barbara, CA, USA (2010). https://doi.org/10.1007/978-3-642-14623-7_31

36. Ishai, Y., Li, H., Lin, H.: A unified framework for succinct garbling from homomorphic secret sharing. In: Kalai, Y.T., Kamara, S.F. (eds.) CRYPTO 2025, Part IV. LNCS, vol. 16003, pp. 390–425. Springer, Cham, Switzerland, Santa Barbara, CA, USA (2025). https://doi.org/10.1007/978-3-032-01884-7_13

37. Ishai, Y., Prabhakaran, M., Sahai, A.: Founding cryptography on oblivious transfer - efficiently. In: Wagner, D. (ed.) CRYPTO 2008. LNCS, vol. 5157, pp. 572–591. Springer Berlin Heidelberg, Germany, Santa Barbara, CA, USA (2008). https://doi.org/10.1007/978-3-540-85174-5_32

38. Januzelli, J., Rosulek, M., Roy, L.: Lower bounds for garbled circuits from shannon-type information inequalities. In: Kalai, Y.T., Kamara, S.F. (eds.) Advances in Cryptology - CRYPTO 2025 - 45th Annual International Cryptology Conference, Santa Barbara, CA, USA, August 17-21, 2025, Proceedings, Part IV. Lecture Notes in Computer Science, vol. 16003, pp. 589–618. Springer (2025). https://doi.org/10.1007/978-3-032-01884-7_19, https://doi.org/10.1007/978-3-032-01884-7_19

39. Katz, J., Ranellucci, S., Rosulek, M., Wang, X.: Optimizing authenticated garbling for faster secure two-party computation. In: Shacham, H., Boldyreva, A. (eds.) CRYPTO 2018, Part III. LNCS, vol. 10993, pp. 365–391. Springer, Cham, Switzerland, Santa Barbara, CA, USA (2018). https://doi.org/10.1007/978-3-319-96878-0_13
40. Kolesnikov, V., Schneider, T.: Improved garbled circuit: Free XOR gates and applications. In: Aceto, L., Damgård, I., Goldberg, L.A., Halldórsson, M.M., Ingólfsdóttir, A., Walukiewicz, I. (eds.) ICALP 2008, Part II. LNCS, vol. 5126, pp. 486–498. Springer Berlin Heidelberg, Germany, Reykjavik, Iceland (2008). https://doi.org/10.1007/978-3-540-70583-3_40
41. Lindell, Y., Pinkas, B.: An efficient protocol for secure two-party computation in the presence of malicious adversaries. In: Naor, M. (ed.) EUROCRYPT 2007. LNCS, vol. 4515, pp. 52–78. Springer Berlin Heidelberg, Germany, Barcelona, Spain (2007). https://doi.org/10.1007/978-3-540-72540-4_4
42. Liu, H., Wang, X., Yang, K., Yu, Y.: BitGC: garbled circuits with 1 bit per gate. In: Fehr, S., Fouque, P.A. (eds.) EUROCRYPT 2025, Part VII. LNCS, vol. 15607, pp. 437–466. Springer, Cham, Switzerland, Madrid, Spain (2025). https://doi.org/10.1007/978-3-031-91098-2_16
43. Meyer, P., Orlandi, C., Roy, L., Scholl, P.: Silent circuit relinearisation: sublinear-size (boolean and arithmetic) garbled circuits from DCR. In: Kalai, Y.T., Kamara, S.F. (eds.) CRYPTO 2025, Part IV. LNCS, vol. 16003, pp. 426–458. Springer, Cham, Switzerland, Santa Barbara, CA, USA (2025). https://doi.org/10.1007/978-3-032-01884-7_14
44. Mohassel, P., Franklin, M.: Efficiency tradeoffs for malicious two-party computation. In: Yung, M., Dodis, Y., Kiayias, A., Malkin, T. (eds.) PKC 2006. LNCS, vol. 3958, pp. 458–473. Springer Berlin Heidelberg, Germany, New York, NY, USA (2006). https://doi.org/10.1007/11745853_30
45. Naor, M., Pinkas, B., Sumner, R.: Privacy preserving auctions and mechanism design. In: Feldman, S.I., Wellman, M.P. (eds.) Proceedings of the First ACM Conference on Electronic Commerce (EC-99), Denver, CO, USA, November 3-5, 1999, pp. 129–139. ACM (1999). https://doi.org/10.1145/336992.337028
46. Nielsen, J.B., Orlandi, C.: Cross and clean: amortized garbled circuits with constant overhead. In: Hirt, M., Smith, A.D. (eds.) Theory of Cryptography - 14th International Conference, TCC 2016-B, Beijing, China, October 31 - November 3, 2016, Proceedings, Part I. Lecture Notes in Computer Science, vol. 9985, pp. 582–603 (2016). https://doi.org/10.1007/978-3-662-53641-4_22
47. Pass, R.: On deniability in the common reference string and random oracle model. In: Boneh, D. (ed.) CRYPTO 2003. LNCS, vol. 2729, pp. 316–337. Springer Berlin Heidelberg, Germany, Santa Barbara, CA, USA (2003). https://doi.org/10.1007/978-3-540-45146-4_19
48. Polishchuk, A., Spielman, D.A.: Nearly-linear size holographic proofs. In: 26th ACM STOC, pp. 194–203. ACM Press, Montréal, Québec, Canada (1994). https://doi.org/10.1145/195058.195132
49. Rosulek, M., Roy, L.: Three halves make a whole? Beating the half-gates lower bound for garbled circuits. In: Malkin, T., Peikert, C. (eds.) CRYPTO 2021, Part I. LNCS, vol. 12825, pp. 94–124. Springer, Cham, Switzerland, Virtual Event (2021). https://doi.org/10.1007/978-3-030-84242-0_5
50. Wang, X., Ranellucci, S., Katz, J.: Authenticated garbling and efficient maliciously secure two-party computation. In: Thuraisingham, B.M., Evans, D., Malkin, T., Xu, D. (eds.) ACM CCS 2017, pp. 21–37. ACM Press, Dallas, TX, USA (2017). https://doi.org/10.1145/3133956.3134053

51. Xu, F., Hu, H., Xu, C.: Bitwise garbling schemes - A model with $\frac{3}{2}\kappa$-bit lower bound of ciphertexts. In: Kalai, Y.T., Kamara, S.F. (eds.) Advances in Cryptology - CRYPTO 2025 - 45th Annual International Cryptology Conference, Santa Barbara, CA, USA, August 17-21, 2025, Proceedings, Part IV. Lecture Notes in Computer Science, vol. 16003, pp. 459–488. Springer (2025). https://doi.org/10.1007/978-3-032-01884-7_15
52. Yao, A.C.C.: How to generate and exchange secrets (extended abstract). In: 27th FOCS, pp. 162–167. IEEE Computer Society Press, Toronto, Ontario, Canada (1986). https://doi.org/10.1109/SFCS.1986.25
53. Zahur, S., Rosulek, M., Evans, D.: Two halves make a whole - reducing data transfer in garbled circuits using half gates. In: Oswald, E., Fischlin, M. (eds.) EUROCRYPT 2015, Part II. LNCS, vol. 9057, pp. 220–250. Springer Berlin Heidelberg, Germany, Sofia, Bulgaria (2015). https://doi.org/10.1007/978-3-662-46803-6_8

On the Communication Complexity of PSM and CDS for Symmetric Functions

Reo Eriguchi[✉][iD]

National Institute of Advanced Industrial Science and Technology, Tokyo, Japan
`eriguchi-reo@aist.go.jp`

Abstract. Private Simultaneous Messages (PSM) and Conditional Disclosure of Secrets (CDS) are two fundamental primitives in information-theoretic cryptography. In a PSM protocol, each party sends a single message to a referee, who can then compute a function f of their private inputs but learns nothing else. A CDS protocol follows the same model as PSM, but the goal is to disclose a secret shared among all parties to the referee if and only if the function f evaluates to 1. Minimizing the communication complexity of these primitives is a central question in this area. Since the best known constructions for general functions require high communication complexity, recent studies have attempted to obtain more efficient constructions by focusing on symmetric functions, whose outputs are invariant under permutations of inputs. However, the extent to which exploiting symmetry can improve efficiency has remained unclear. In this work, we show upper and lower bounds that relate the optimal communication complexities of PSM and CDS for symmetric functions to those for general functions. When the number of parties is larger than the input domain size, our upper bound for PSM improves the best known communication complexity for symmetric functions. Furthermore, our upper bound for CDS demonstrates for the first time that symmetry can be exploited to reduce communication in CDS protocols. In contrast, when the number of parties is constant, our lower bounds show that focusing on symmetric functions yields only a constant-factor improvement. We also derive an analogous implication for PSM protocols under a plausible conjecture. In addition, our new constructions for symmetric functions lead to improvements over the state-of-the-art results in related models such as ad hoc PSM and secret sharing.

Keywords: private simultaneous messages · conditional disclosure of secrets · secret sharing

1 Introduction

Private Simultaneous Messages (PSM) [27,30] and *Conditional Disclosure of Secrets (CDS)* [29] are two fundamental primitives in information-theoretic cryptography. In a PSM protocol for a function f, each of n parties has an input x_i

© International Association for Cryptologic Research 2026
J. Daemen and E. Thomé (Eds.): EUROCRYPT 2026, LNCS 16543, pp. 155–184, 2026.
https://doi.org/10.1007/978-3-032-25324-8_6

and shares common private randomness. Each party sends a single message to an external party called a referee, who can then compute $f(x_0, \ldots, x_{n-1})$ but learns nothing else on the parties' inputs. In a CDS protocol, the parties also hold a common secret s. The goal is to disclose the secret s to the referee if and only if the function $f(x_0, \ldots, x_{n-1})$ evaluates to 1. Note that in the CDS setting, the parties' inputs x_i are not private and are known to the referee. Despite their simplicity, PSM and CDS have been used as building blocks for many other cryptographic primitives, including constant-round secure computation [32,33], attribute-based encryption [28], and secret sharing for general access structures [5,35].

The central question in this area is to determine the optimal communication complexity of PSM and CDS protocols for a function f, where communication complexity is defined as the total bit length of parties' messages. This question has been extensively studied both for general functions and for functions with specific representations, e.g., [4,6–8,15–17,30,37]. Let $\mathcal{F}_{n,d}$ denote the set of general n-input functions where each input is taken from the domain of size d. Currently, the best known PSM protocol for $\mathcal{F}_{n,d}$ has communication complexity $O(d^{n/2}n^3)$ [15] and the best known CDS protocol has communication complexity $2^{\tilde{O}(\sqrt{n \log d})}$ [37]. However, these constructions are inefficient since they require at least sub-exponential communication in n, and are still far from optimal in comparison with the best known lower bounds [3,6,8].

A promising alternative research direction is to design efficient constructions by focusing on functions with specific structure. Among these, *symmetric functions*, whose outputs are invariant under permutations of the n inputs, are one of the most natural function classes with real-world applications such as elections and statistical analysis. We denote the subclass consisting of all symmetric functions by $\mathcal{S}_{n,d}$. For PSM protocols, several efficient constructions exploiting the symmetry of functions have been proposed [12,18,24,25,38,40] and the best known communication complexity for $\mathcal{S}_{n,d}$ is $n^{2d/3+O(1)}$ [25]. This significantly outperforms the general constructions when the number n of parties is much larger than the domain size d (e.g., in an election, there are typically many more voters than candidates).

While symmetry can effectively reduce communication complexity, a natural question is to provide a *quantitative* analysis of the potential efficiency gain from focusing on symmetric functions, which is important for a clear understanding of their benefits. Specifically, we denote the optimal communication complexity of PSM and CDS for a function class $\mathcal{F}$ by $\mathsf{PSM}(\mathcal{F})$ and $\mathsf{CDS}(\mathcal{F})$, respectively. The goal of this work is to clarify the relation between the quantities $\mathfrak{C}(\mathcal{S}_{n,d})$ and $\mathfrak{C}(\mathcal{F}_{n,d})$, for $\mathfrak{C} \in \{\mathsf{PSM}, \mathsf{CDS}\}$. Existing works provide several direct upper bounds on $\mathsf{PSM}(\mathcal{S}_{n,d})$, but the only known relation so far is the trivial inequality $\mathsf{PSM}(\mathcal{S}_{n,d}) \leq \mathsf{PSM}(\mathcal{F}_{n,d})$. Furthermore, to the best of our knowledge, no prior constructions of CDS have achieved any improvement in communication complexity by focusing on $\mathcal{S}_{n,d}$.

1.1   Our Results

In this work, we show upper and lower bounds that relate the optimal communication complexities of PSM and CDS protocols for symmetric functions to those for general functions. Consequently, we obtain close relations between the complexities of $\mathcal{S}_{n,d}$ and $\mathcal{F}_{n,d}$ in two extreme cases. Informally, when the number n of parties is constant, the communication complexity for $\mathcal{S}_{n,d}$ is equal to that for $\mathcal{F}_{n,d}$ up to a constant. This indicates a limitation on the potential efficiency gain achievable by focusing on symmetric functions. In contrast, when the domain size d is constant, the communication complexity for $\mathcal{S}_{n,d}$ is equal to that for $\mathcal{F}_{d-1,n+1}$ up to a factor of $O(n^2)$. This strengthens the previous results on the efficiency improvements of PSM for symmetric functions. In addition, our new constructions for symmetric functions lead to improvements over the state-of-the-art results in related models: (i) ad hoc PSM [11,14], where only a subset of the parties actually send messages and (ii) a new efficient secret sharing scheme for multipartite uniform access structures. See below for more precise statements.

Technically, our bounds are derived by two novel techniques. First, we propose a modular construction of PSM and CDS for symmetric functions. In the PSM case, this improves the communication complexity of the best known construction [25]. In the CDS case, this is the first result to exploit the symmetry of functions to reduce the communication complexity compared to general functions. Second, we introduce a generic technique of expanding the input domains of protocols, which may be of independent interest. This allows us to relate the optimal complexities for functions with different domain sizes. An overview of our techniques will be given in Sect. 2.

Relations to General Functions with Different Domains. Our first theorem relates the optimal communication complexities of PSM and CDS protocols for symmetric functions to those for general functions with different domain sizes.

Theorem 1. *For $\mathfrak{C} \in \{\mathsf{CDS}, \mathsf{PSM}\}$,*

$$\mathfrak{C}(\mathcal{F}_{n,d'}) \leq \mathfrak{C}(\mathcal{S}_{n,d}) \leq \mathfrak{C}(\mathcal{F}_{n,d}), \tag{1}$$

$$\mathfrak{C}(\mathcal{F}_{d-1,n'+1}) \leq \mathfrak{C}(\mathcal{S}_{n,d}) \leq O(n^2) \cdot \mathfrak{C}(\mathcal{F}_{d-1,n+1}), \tag{2}$$

where $d' = \lfloor d/n \rfloor$ and $n' = \lfloor n/(d-1) \rfloor$.

Proof Idea. The upper bound in (1) is trivial as $\mathcal{S}_{n,d} \subseteq \mathcal{F}_{n,d}$. The upper bound in (2) is derived from our novel constructions of PSM and CDS protocols for symmetric functions. By definition, a symmetric function f can be expressed as a function of the *histogram* $\boldsymbol{h}_{\boldsymbol{x}}$ of inputs $\boldsymbol{x}$, that is, $f(\boldsymbol{x}) = f^*(\boldsymbol{h}_{\boldsymbol{x}})$ for some f^*. We devise a modular method to reduce PSM for f to two components: PSM for f^* and basic PSM for message selection. Specifically, the parties first compute all possible messages for the PSM of f^* and then reveal only the messages needed to compute the output for $\boldsymbol{h}_{\boldsymbol{x}}$. The lower bounds follow from the observation that symmetric functions are capable of computing general functions with smaller domains. This allows reducing PSM for general functions to symmetric ones.

By plugging in the best known upper bound for $\mathsf{PSM}(\mathcal{F}_{n,d})$ [15], we obtain a new upper bound of $n^{d/2}$ for $\mathsf{PSM}(\mathcal{S}_{n,d})$, ignoring a polynomial factor of n and d. This improves upon the state-of-the-art bound of $n^{2d/3}$ in [25]. For $\mathsf{CDS}(\mathcal{S}_{n,d})$, we obtain an upper bound of $n^2 2^{\widetilde{O}(\sqrt{d \log n})}$. This improves upon the previously known bound of $2^{\widetilde{O}(\sqrt{n \log d})}$, derived from the best upper bound for $\mathcal{F}_{n,d}$ [37], when $n \gg d$. To the best of our knowledge, this is the first result to exploit the symmetry of functions in reducing the communication complexity of CDS protocols.

On the other hand, our lower bound in (1) indicates a limitation of focusing on symmetric functions: the communication complexity of CDS and PSM for $\mathcal{S}_{n,d}$ cannot be smaller than that for general functions with inputs shorter by $O(\log n)$ bits. An implication of (2) is that any further improvement of our new upper bound for symmetric functions requires improving the best known bounds for general functions [15,37]. For example, an upper bound of n^{cd} on $\mathsf{PSM}(\mathcal{S}_{n,d})$ with $c < 1/2$ would imply an upper bound of $O_d(n^{cd})$ on $\mathsf{PSM}(\mathcal{F}_{d-1,n+1})$. Therefore, improving the exponent in our upper bound requires improving the exponent of the dominant term $d^{n/2}$ in the best known bound for $\mathcal{F}_{n,d}$ [15].

Towards Tight Relations to General Functions. Our next theorem relates the optimal communication complexity of $\mathcal{S}_{n,d}$ to quantities solely based on $\mathcal{F}_{n,d}$ or $\mathcal{F}_{d-1,n+1}$.

First, in the CDS case, we obtain the following theorem.

Theorem 2. *For parameters* $\beta_n = n^{-O(n)}$ *and* $\gamma_d = d^{-O(d)}$,

$$\beta_n \cdot \mathsf{CDS}(\mathcal{F}_{n,d}) \le \mathsf{CDS}(\mathcal{S}_{n,d}) \le \mathsf{CDS}(\mathcal{F}_{n,d}), \tag{3}$$

$$\gamma_d \cdot \mathsf{CDS}(\mathcal{F}_{d-1,n+1}) \le \mathsf{CDS}(\mathcal{S}_{n,d}) \le O(n^2) \cdot \mathsf{CDS}(\mathcal{F}_{d-1,n+1}). \tag{4}$$

As a consequence, we obtain a close relation between the optimal complexities of CDS for symmetric and general functions in the two extreme cases:

- If $n = O(1)$, $\mathsf{CDS}(\mathcal{S}_{n,d})$ is equal to $\mathsf{CDS}(\mathcal{F}_{n,d})$ up to a constant.
- If $d = O(1)$, $\mathsf{CDS}(\mathcal{S}_{n,d})$ is equal to $\mathsf{CDS}(\mathcal{F}_{d-1,n+1})$ up to a factor of $O(n^2)$.

An important implication of (3) is that, for CDS protocols with a constant number of parties, the efficiency gain achievable by focusing on symmetric functions is limited to a constant-factor improvement. This can also be explained intuitively. Suppose, heuristically, that the worst-case complexity of CDS is determined by the maximum representation size of functions, as suggested by existing results. The worst-case representation size for $\mathcal{F}_{n,d}$ is d^n, whereas it is $\binom{n+d-1}{d-1}$ for $\mathcal{S}_{n,d}$. Since $\binom{n+d-1}{d-1} \ge d^n/n^n$ when $n = O(1)$, the complexity of CDS for symmetric functions can be smaller than that for general functions only by a constant factor.

Proof Idea. We show a relation between the complexities of CDS for functions with different domain sizes. Specifically, for $d' < d$, we prove an inequality of the form $\mathsf{CDS}(\mathcal{F}_{n,d}) \leq M \cdot \mathsf{CDS}(\mathcal{F}_{n,d'})$ for some M depending only on n. To this end, we devise a novel method to construct a CDS protocol for $\mathcal{F}_{n,d}$ using only protocols for $\mathcal{F}_{n,d'}$; that is, a technique of expanding the input domains. We can then convert the lower bounds in Theorem 1 to those solely based on $\mathcal{F}_{n,d}$ or $\mathcal{F}_{d-1,n+1}$.

We show an analogous result in the PSM case. A main difference is that, in relating $\mathsf{PSM}(\mathcal{F}_{n,d})$ to $\mathsf{PSM}(\mathcal{F}_{n,d'})$ for some smaller $d' < d$, we reduce PSM for $\mathcal{F}_{n,d}$ to computing compositions of functions in $\mathcal{F}_{n,d'}$ with affine functions, rather than functions in $\mathcal{F}_{n,d'}$. More precisely, we introduce an augmented class $\mathcal{F}_{n,d'}^{\mathrm{affine}}$ consisting of functions of the form $A \circ f$, where $f \in \mathcal{F}_{n,d'}$ and $A(X) = aX + b$ is an affine function. Note that in a PSM protocol for $A \circ f$, the coefficients a, b must be hidden from the referee. Then, we obtain the following theorem.

Theorem 3. *Letting* $\alpha_{n,d} = \mathsf{PSM}(\mathcal{F}_{n,d})/\mathsf{PSM}(\mathcal{F}_{n,d}^{\mathrm{affine}})$,

$$\alpha_{n,d'} \cdot \beta_n \cdot \mathsf{PSM}(\mathcal{F}_{n,d}) \leq \mathsf{PSM}(\mathcal{S}_{n,d}) \leq \mathsf{PSM}(\mathcal{F}_{n,d}), \tag{5}$$

$$\alpha_{d-1,n'+1} \cdot \gamma_d \cdot \mathsf{PSM}(\mathcal{F}_{d-1,n+1}) \leq \mathsf{PSM}(\mathcal{S}_{n,d}) \leq O(n^2) \cdot \mathsf{PSM}(\mathcal{F}_{d-1,n+1}). \tag{6}$$

Since we reduce PSM for $\mathcal{F}_{n,d}$ to PSM for $\mathcal{F}_{n,d'}^{\mathrm{affine}}$ (rather than $\mathcal{F}_{n,d'}$), the lower bounds incur additional overheads of $\alpha_{n,d}$. It remains unclear whether the factor $\alpha_{n,d}$ can be bounded from below by a constant independent of n or d. Nevertheless, we conjecture that $\alpha_{n,d}$ is not very small and, in particular, independent of d. This is heuristically justified, as most existing constructions of PSM are based on certain computational models [4,15,30] and the difference between the computational complexities of f and $A \circ f$ is very small (e.g., only two additional gates when implemented as circuits). Assuming this conjecture, we would obtain a conclusion analogous to the CDS case: $\mathsf{PSM}(\mathcal{S}_{n,d})$ is equal to $\mathsf{PSM}(\mathcal{F}_{n,d})$ up to a constant when $n = O(1)$, and it is determined by $\mathsf{PSM}(\mathcal{F}_{d-1,n+1})$ up to a factor of $O(n^2)$ when $d = O(1)$.

Applications to Related Models. Our new PSM and CDS protocols for symmetric functions have respective applications to ad hoc PSM [11,14] and secret sharing [34,39]. First, ad hoc PSM is an advanced notion of PSM, in which only a subset S of k parties actually send messages, and the referee evaluates a k-input function f on that subset of inputs. It is natural in this model to assume that f is a symmetric function independent of the identities of the parties. There exist generic compilers from PSM to ad hoc PSM [2,19], which incur only a polynomial overhead in k and n to the complexity of the k-party PSM for f. However, the resulting bounds incurred an exponential factor of $d^{k/2}$ in k, since they relied on the trivial bound obtained from $\mathsf{PSM}(\mathcal{F}_{k,d})$. Our improved bound on $\mathsf{PSM}(\mathcal{S}_{k,d})$ immediately implies an ad hoc PSM protocol with communication complexity dominated by $k^{d/2}$, which is polynomial in k when $d = O(1)$. In addition to this immediate application, we also propose a direct construction of ad hoc PSM for symmetric functions, without relying on the generic compiler of [2]. As a result, we further improve the upper bound by a factor of k.

Second, it was shown in [2] that k-party CDS protocols directly imply secret sharing schemes for uniform access structures, in which all sets of size larger than k can recover a secret and all sets of size smaller than k cannot. We show that our CDS protocol for symmetric functions yields an improvement in the share size for a special class of *multipartite* uniform access structures. An access structure is called d-partite [26] if the set of parties is partitioned into d parts and parties within the same part have equivalent roles in the recoverability of secrets[1]. We obtain a secret sharing scheme for d-partite k-uniform access structures whose share size is asymptotically smaller than $k^{\widetilde{O}(\sqrt{d})}$. As a comparison, the general compiler of [2] results in the share size incurring a sub-exponential factor $2^{\widetilde{O}(\sqrt{k \log n})}$ in k; and a folklore construction for arbitrary d-partite access structures based on [34] results in share size $O(k^{d-1})$.

1.2 Related Works

We briefly introduce previous works on the communication complexity of PSM and CDS protocols. Feige, Kilian, and Naor [27] formalized the notion of PSM and presented general feasibility results in the two-party setting, and Ishai and Kushilevitz [30] extended it to the multiparty setting. There exist many constructions of PSM for general functions and for those represented in certain computational models such as branching programs [30] and arithmetic formulas [4] (see [31] for a survey). Beimel et al. [13] successfully devised a more efficient two-party PSM protocol for general functions and this was later generalized and improved by [7,15], leading to the currently best known complexity. To mitigate the exponential communication, PSM protocols tailored to symmetric functions have also been proposed [12,18,24,25,38,40]. On the lower-bound side, Applebaum et al. [3] proved the first non-trivial lower bound on the communication complexity of PSM and Ball and Randolph [8] extended it to the multiparty setting. The notion of CDS was originally introduced by Gertner et al. [29]. Since then, many works have aimed at improving communication complexity, e.g., [16,17,36,37]. Applebaum and Vasudevan [6] showed interesting connections between two-party CDS and other communication games, leading to non-trivial lower bounds. In [17] and [10], nearly tight upper and lower bounds were shown for a restricted class of linear CDS. Despite all these progresses, however, closing the large gaps between the upper and lower bounds in the general setting remains a long-standing open question.

2 Technical Overview

2.1 Proof of Theorem 1

Upper Bounds. The right inequality of (2) is derived by our novel efficient constructions of PSM and CDS protocols for symmetric functions. First, we consider

---

[1] Note that this should not be confused with another definition of "multipartite" access structures in the literature [1,10], where the set is partitioned into k parts and every authorized set of size k contains exactly one party from each parts.

the case of PSM. All the previous constructions [12,24,25] exploited the symmetry of f to obtain its compact representation in certain computation models (e.g., branching programs or truth-tables), and then reduced to the best known PSM protocols in the respective models. However, such "native" approaches can derive only a direct upper bound on $\mathsf{PSM}(\mathcal{S}_{n,d})$ and cannot yield any non-trivial relation between the optimal communication complexities of $\mathcal{S}_{n,d}$ and other classes. In contrast, we show a generic construction of a PSM protocol for $\mathcal{S}_{n,d}$ from that for $\mathcal{F}_{d-1,n+1}$.

If f is symmetric, then $f(\boldsymbol{x})$ is uniquely determined by the *histogram* $\boldsymbol{h_x} = (h^{(0)}, \ldots, h^{(d-1)})$ of $\boldsymbol{x} = (x_0, \ldots, x_{n-1})$, where $h^{(j)}$ counts the frequency of a value j in $\boldsymbol{x}$. Thus, there exists a function $f^* : [n+1]^d \to \{0,1\}$ such that

$$f^*(\boldsymbol{h_x}) = f(\boldsymbol{x}), \ \forall \boldsymbol{x} \in [d]^n. \tag{7}$$

Since $h^{(d-1)} = n - \sum_{j=0}^{d-2} h^{(j)}$, only the $d-1$ variables $(h^{(j)})_{j\in[d-1]}$ are free and we may thus assume that $f^* \in \mathcal{F}_{d-1,n+1}$.

Suppose that a PSM protocol Π_{f^*} for f^* is given, from which we construct a PSM protocol Π_f for f. Let $\mathsf{P}_0, \ldots, \mathsf{P}_{n-1}$ denote the n real parties involved in Π_f and $\mathsf{Q}^{(0)}, \ldots, \mathsf{Q}^{(d-2)}$ denote the $d-1$ virtual parties in Π_{f^*}. Suppose that the real parties receive private randomness r for Π_{f^*} in advance. Each P_i computes the messages $m^{(j)}(h)$ that a virtual party $\mathsf{Q}^{(j)}$ in Π_{f^*} computes on all possible inputs $h \in [n+1]$ and randomness r. Let $(h^{(0)}, \ldots, h^{(d-2)}) = \boldsymbol{h_x}$ denotes the histogram of real parties' inputs $\boldsymbol{x}$. If the parties are able to reveal the message $m^{(j)}(h^{(j)})$ (and nothing else) to the referee, then he can recover $f^*(\boldsymbol{h_x}) = f(\boldsymbol{x})$ using the decoding algorithm of Π_{f^*}, which completes the protocol Π_f. A key observation is that each bin $h^{(j)}$ of the histogram is expressed as $h^{(j)} = \sum_{i\in[n]} \delta_j(x_i)$, where $\delta_j(x) = 1$ if $x = j$ and $\delta_j(x) = 0$ otherwise. Furthermore, $\delta_j(x_i)$ can be locally computed by P_i. Thus, the task of revealing $m^{(j)}(h^{(j)})$ for each j is essentially reduced to the following basic functionality, which we call the *selection function*:

$$\mathsf{Sel}_n(\boldsymbol{m}; a_0, \ldots, a_{n-1}) := \boldsymbol{m}[\sum_{i\in[n]} a_i],$$

where $\boldsymbol{m} = (\boldsymbol{m}[0], \ldots, \boldsymbol{m}[n]) \in \{0,1\}^{n+1}$ is commonly held by all parties and $a_i \in \{0,1\}$ is held by P_i. This functionality was originally introduced by [18] in a different context, and efficient constructions achieving communication complexity $O(n^2)$ are known [18,40]. Since these protocols can also be applied in our purpose of retrieving an entry corresponding to the sum of parties' input bits, we obtain the inequality $\mathsf{PSM}(f) \le O(n^2) \cdot \mathsf{PSM}(f^*)$. We note that the protocol in [40] achieves the currently best communication complexity $O(n^2)$ but is not computationally efficient. Nevertheless, this issue can be mitigated by using the protocol in [18], which achieves polynomial computational complexity at the cost of slightly increasing communication complexity.

Similarly, we can construct a CDS protocol for $f \in \mathcal{S}_{n,d}$ from an arbitrary CDS protocol for the associated function $f^* \in \mathcal{F}_{d-1,n+1}$. A difference is that when evaluating the selection function Sel_n, it is unnecessary to hide the input bits $a_0, \ldots, a_{n-1}$ in CDS protocols, whereas the messages $\boldsymbol{m}$ are still private. We introduce this weaker functionality as the selection function with public inputs, denoted by pSel_n. By leveraging this relaxed setting, we present a PSM protocol for pSel_n whose communication *and computation* complexities are both $O(n^2)$. This should be contrasted with the best known PSM protocol for Sel_n with $O(n^2)$ communication [40], whose computational complexity is $2^{O(n)}$.

Lower Bounds. To derive the left inequality in (1), it suffices to show that for any function $g \in \mathcal{F}_{n,d'}$, there exists a symmetric function $f \in \mathcal{S}_{n,d}$ such that $\mathsf{PSM}(g) \leq \mathsf{PSM}(f)$, that is, any protocol for f can be transformed to a protocol for g with the same communication complexity. Since the following argument can apply to the CDS setting without modification, we only consider the PSM case here. Our approach is to find appropriate embeddings $\psi_i : [d'] \to [d]$ and set f as any function such that $f(\psi_0(x_0), \ldots, \psi_{n-1}(x_{n-1})) = g(x_0, \ldots, x_{n-1})$. Then, any PSM protocol for f can be used to compute g: each party with input $x_i \in [d']$ runs the protocol for f with input $\psi_i(x_i) \in [d]$. Note that the naive embedding $\psi_i(x) = x$ does not satisfy the requirement since g is not necessarily symmetric. Instead, we embed the ith input $x_i \in [d']$ into an element of $[d]$, *storing the index i* in an additional input slot of size $d/d' \geq n$. For the ease of exposition, we assume that n divides d. We can decompose the input domain of each party as $[d] = [n] \times [d'] = \{(i,x) : i \in [n], x \in [d']\}$ and define $\psi_i(x) = (i,x)$ for $i \in [n], x \in [d']$. Then, we set f as a function that first sorts inputs $(i_0, x_0), \ldots, (i_{n-1}, x_{n-1})$ by the indices i_j's and then outputs $g(x_{j_0}, \ldots, x_{j_{n-1}})$, where $((0, x_{j_0}), \ldots, (n-1, x_{j_{n-1}}))$ is the sorted inputs. (We set a value of f to 0 if inputs contain identical indices.) By definition, f satisfies the requirement that $f(\psi_0(x_0), \ldots, \psi_{n-1}(x_{n-1})) = g(x_0, \ldots, x_{n-1})$ and is symmetric as it sorts inputs at the beginning.

Similarly, the proof of the left inequality in (2) is reduced to showing that for any function $g \in \mathcal{F}_{d-1,n'+1}$, there exists $f \in \mathcal{S}_{n,d}$ such that any PSM protocol for f can be transformed to that for g preserving communication complexity. Note that an input to g can be viewed as a histogram $\boldsymbol{h} = (h^0, \ldots, h^{(d-2)})$ with $d-1$ bins. We have chosen $n' = \lfloor n/(d-1) \rfloor$ to ensure that the sum $\sum_{j \in [d-1]} h^{(j)}$ does not exceed n for any input $\boldsymbol{h} \in [n'+1]^{d-1}$. Therefore, we can find a symmetric function $f \in \mathcal{S}_{n,d}$ whose associated function f^* "contains" g, that is, $f^*(\boldsymbol{h}) = g(\boldsymbol{h})$ for every $\boldsymbol{h} \in [n'+1]^{d-1}$. We construct a PSM protocol Π_g for g from any protocol Π_f for f. For ease of exposition, we assume that $d-1$ divides n. The construction proceeds in the *reverse* direction of our previous construction for deriving the upper bound. Let $\{Q^{(j)} : j \in [d-1]\}$ denote the $d-1$ real parties involved in Π_g and $\{P_i^{(j)} : i \in [n'], j \in [d-1]\}$ denote the n virtual parties in Π_f. Each party $Q^{(j)}$ simulates the roles of $\{P_i^{(j)} : i \in [n']\}$. He encodes his input $h^{(j)} \in [n'+1]$ into a vector $(x_0^{(j)}, \ldots, x_{n'-1}^{(j)}) = (\underbrace{j, \ldots, j}_{h^{(j)}}, \underbrace{d-1, \ldots, d-1}_{n'-h^{(j)}})$,

and then computes a message that $P_i^{(j)}$ computes on input $x_i^{(j)}$. The referee receives the messages encoding the inputs $\boldsymbol{x} = (x_i^{(j)})_{i \in [n'], j \in [d-1]}$ where a value $j \in [d-1]$ appears $h^{(j)}$ times and $d-1$ appears $\sum_j (n' - h^{(j)}) = n - \sum_j h^{(j)}$

times. Since the histogram of $\boldsymbol{x}$ is equal to $\boldsymbol{h}$, the decoding of the messages gives $f(\boldsymbol{x}) = f^*(\boldsymbol{h}) = g(\boldsymbol{h})$, which completes the protocol Π_g.

2.2 Proof of Theorem 2

To lower bound $\mathsf{CDS}(\mathcal{F}_{n,d'})$ by $\mathsf{CDS}(\mathcal{F}_{n,d})$ for some $d > d'$, we present a technique for relating the optimal communication complexities of CDS with different domain sizes. Specifically, we prove an inequality of the form $\mathsf{CDS}(\mathcal{F}_{n,d_2}) \leq M \cdot \mathsf{CDS}(\mathcal{F}_{n,d_1})$ for $d_2 > d_1$, where M is a constant depending solely on n. Such bounds have not been considered so far in either the CDS or PSM setting, as the previous works only provided direct upper bounds for $\mathcal{F}_{n,d}$. To this end, we show a construction of a CDS protocol for any function $F \in \mathcal{F}_{n,d_2}$ based on CDS protocols for functions in $\mathcal{F}_{n,d_1}$; that is, a technique of expanding input domains. A key difficulty is that *we cannot assume any structure on given protocols for* $\mathcal{F}_{n,d_1}$. This is because the structure of protocols achieving the optimal communication complexity $\mathsf{CDS}(\mathcal{F}_{n,d_1})$ is currently totally unclear. Therefore, we need to devise a generic construction applicable to arbitrary CDS protocols for $\mathcal{F}_{n,d_1}$.

Here, we show a core construction of expanding each input domain by one bit. Let $F \in \mathcal{F}_{n,2d}$. We decompose the input domain $[2d]$ as $[d] \times \{0,1\}$. Then, F can be expressed as

$$F((x_i, y_i)_{i \in [n]}) = \sum_{\boldsymbol{w} \in \{0,1\}^n} f_{\boldsymbol{w}}(\boldsymbol{x}) \cdot \delta_{w_0}(y_0) \cdots \delta_{w_{n-1}}(y_{n-1}) \tag{8}$$

for any $\boldsymbol{x} \in [d]^n$, $\boldsymbol{y} \in \{0,1\}^n$, where $f_{\boldsymbol{w}}$ is the function $F(\cdot, \boldsymbol{w})$ obtained by fixing each y-component to w_i. Note that $f_{\boldsymbol{w}} \in \mathcal{F}_{n,d}$ and each $\delta_{w_i}(y_i)$ can be locally computed by party i holding y_i. Observe that $F(\boldsymbol{x}, \boldsymbol{y}) = 1$ if and only if there uniquely exists $\boldsymbol{w}$ such that $f_{\boldsymbol{w}}(\boldsymbol{x})\delta_{\boldsymbol{w}}(\boldsymbol{y}) = 1$. A CDS protocol for F is thus obtained by executing 2^n CDS protocols, each for the function $f_{\boldsymbol{w}}(\boldsymbol{x})\delta_{\boldsymbol{w}}(\boldsymbol{y})$. In the sub-protocol corresponding to $\boldsymbol{w} = \boldsymbol{y}$, the referee learns the secret if and only if $F(\boldsymbol{x}, \boldsymbol{y}) = 1$. In all other sub-protocols, the referee learns nothing since $f_{\boldsymbol{w}}(\boldsymbol{x})\delta_{\boldsymbol{w}}(\boldsymbol{y}) = 0$ necessarily holds.

Thus, it suffices to construct a CDS protocol for $G_f(\boldsymbol{x}, \boldsymbol{y}) := f(\boldsymbol{x}) \cdot y_0 \cdots y_{n-1}$ from a CDS protocol Π_f for f. Suppose that each party with input (x_i, y_i) computes a message that encodes an input x_i and a secret s, using Π_f. If $y_i = 1$ for all i and the parties agree on it, then the predicate G_f is equivalent to f and hence the security is guaranteed by Π_f. However, the parties cannot determine in advance whether $y_i = 1$ for all i, and if $y_i = 0$ for some i, then G_f always evaluates to 0 and the secret s must be hidden. Our solution is simply to have party i send nothing if $y_i = 0$. In this case, the referee misses at least one message and cannot proceed to the decoding phase of Π_f. Although a subset of messages may leak information about the secret in plain CDS protocols, it is known that plain CDS can be efficiently upgraded into *strong* CDS [21], in which no information about secrets is leaked as long as at least one of the messages is missing. Therefore, if we use a strong CDS protocol for f as Π_f, then the referee cannot learn the secret whenever $\prod_{i \in [n]} y_i = 0$ (even if $f(\boldsymbol{x}) = 1$). Since the transformation in [21] incurs a communication overhead of n, we obtain $\mathsf{CDS}(F) \le n2^n \cdot \max_{f \in \mathcal{F}_{n,d}} \mathsf{CDS}(f)$.

2.3   Proof of Theorem 3

As in the proof of Theorem 2, we relate the optimal communication complexities of PSM with different domain sizes. We aim at constructing a PSM protocol for any $F \in \mathcal{F}_{n,d_2}$ based on PSM protocols for functions in $\mathcal{F}_{n,d_1}$. We focus on expanding the domain by one bit, that is, $d_2 = 2d$ and $d_1 = d$. Let $F \in \mathcal{F}_{n,2d}$. We attempt to exploit the equality (8) again and reduce PSM for F to $f \in \mathcal{F}_{n,d}$ in a manner similar to the CDS case. However, this does not work for PSM protocols since the referee can immediately learn the inputs $\boldsymbol{y}$ from the index $\boldsymbol{w}$ corresponding to the sub-protocol in which the referee receives all messages. Moreover, the issue cannot be addressed even if the 2^n sub-protocols are randomly permuted. This is because the decoding algorithm of a PSM protocol may depend on the description of the function being computed (i.e., $f_{\boldsymbol{w}}$ in this case), and hence it is impossible to make the referee fully oblivious to the index $\boldsymbol{w}$.

Alternatively, we consider a PSM protocol for computing each summand $f_{\boldsymbol{w}}(\boldsymbol{x})\delta_{w_0}(y_0)\cdots\delta_{w_{n-1}}(y_{n-1}) + b_{\boldsymbol{w}}$. Here, the $b_{\boldsymbol{w}}$'s are random additive shares of zero, which are included in common randomness. The addition by $b_{\boldsymbol{w}}$ ensures that the referee learns the total sum only. Therefore, the computation of F is reduced to 2^n independent invocations of a PSM protocol for a function G'_f defined as $G'_f(b; \boldsymbol{x}, \boldsymbol{y}) := f(\boldsymbol{x}) \cdot y_0 \cdots y_{n-1} + b$, where $f \in \mathcal{F}_{n,d}$ and b is a common bit known by all parties. We obtain $\mathsf{PSM}(\mathcal{F}_{n,2d}) \le 2^n \cdot \max_{f \in \mathcal{F}_{n,d}} \mathsf{PSM}(G'_f)$.

Towards reducing the computation of G'_f to f, our key observation is that G'_f can be expressed as $G'_f(b; \boldsymbol{x}, \boldsymbol{y}) = H'(b, f(\boldsymbol{x}), \boldsymbol{y})$ using a function $H'(b, z, \boldsymbol{y}) := zy_0 \cdots y_{n-1} + b$. Intuitively, this decomposes the computation of G'_f into two parts: the computation of f and that of H', whose complexity depends only on n. It is then sufficient to let the referee learn the value of $H'(b, f(\boldsymbol{x}), \boldsymbol{y})$ and nothing else. For that, we use a *decomposable randomized encoding* (DRE) of H', which is an information-theoretic variant of garbling schemes [31]. Specifically, based on private randomness ρ, it generates a garbled function $\hat{H}'$ encoding H' and garbled inputs $\hat{b}, \hat{z}, \hat{y}$ encoding $b, z, \boldsymbol{y}$ (respectively) such that $\hat{H}'(\hat{b}, \hat{z}, \hat{\boldsymbol{y}}) = H'(b, z, \boldsymbol{y})$ but they leak nothing else. Since the complexity of H' is independent of d, the size of garbled functions and inputs is also independent of d (and is actually polynomial in n) [20,31]. It thus suffices to convey $\hat{H}'$, $\hat{b}$, $\hat{z}$, and $\hat{y}$ to the referee. It is easy to reveal $\hat{H}'$, $\hat{b}$ and each $\hat{y}_i$ since a party who has b, y_i, and ρ can locally compute them on his own. The remaining task is to reveal a garbled input $\hat{z}$ corresponding to $z = f(\boldsymbol{x})$, which depends on $\boldsymbol{x}$ jointly held by all parties. We leverage an additional property that the DRE can be made *affine*, ensuring that $\hat{z}$ takes the form $\alpha f(\boldsymbol{x}) + \beta$, where α and β are functions of ρ only. The task is then completed by invoking a PSM protocol for the function that augments f as

$$f^{\text{affine}}(a, b; x_0, \ldots, x_{n-1}) = af(x_0, \ldots, x_{n-1}) + b,$$

where (a, b) are two auxiliary bits commonly known to all parties but hidden from the referee. In summary, PSM for any $F \in \mathcal{F}_{n,2d}$ can be reduced to PSM for the class $\mathcal{F}_{n,d}^{\text{affine}}$ consisting of all functions f^{affine} with $f \in \mathcal{F}_{n,d}$, and the overhead depends only on n. To iteratively expand the input domain, we rather need an inequality relating $\mathsf{PSM}(\mathcal{F}_{n,2d}^{\text{affine}})$ and $\mathsf{PSM}(\mathcal{F}_{n,d}^{\text{affine}})$. This is easily handled by replacing G'_f and H' in the above argument with $G_f^{\text{affine}}(a, b; \boldsymbol{x}, \boldsymbol{y}) = a f(\boldsymbol{x}) \prod_{i \in [n]} y_i + b$ and $H(a, b, z, \boldsymbol{y}) = a z \prod_{i \in [n]} y_i + b$, respectively.

Remark 1 (The gap between the bounds in Theorem 3). The gap between the upper and lower bounds in (5) is at most

$$\alpha_{n,d'}^{-1} \cdot \beta_n^{-1} = \frac{\mathsf{PSM}(\mathcal{F}_{n,d'}^{\text{affine}})}{\mathsf{PSM}(\mathcal{F}_{n,d'})} \cdot O_n(1).$$

It remains unclear whether the ratio between $\mathsf{PSM}(\mathcal{F}_{n,d}^{\text{affine}})$ and $\mathsf{PSM}(\mathcal{F}_{n,d})$ is generally bounded above by a constant depending only on n. Nevertheless, we conjecture that this ratio is small and particularly independent of d. Under this conjecture, the overall gap would be independent of d and hence the bounds are tight up to a constant when the number n of parties is fixed. As a heuristic argument for this conjecture, consider the case where the computation model is restricted: a formula computing f^{affine} requires only two additional gates compared to f, and the size of a truth table representing f^{affine} is only four times larger than that of f. Since the existing PSM protocols have polynomial communication complexity in the function representation size in the respective models [4,15], the ratio between the communication complexities for f^{affine} and f remains constant.

On the other hand, we also observe a difficulty in proving an upper bound on the above ratio. Consider a simplified case where we attempt to construct a PSM protocol for $f(\boldsymbol{x}) + b$, using only PSM protocols that support an input domain of size d. This functionality corresponds to revealing either $f(\boldsymbol{x})$ or its negation $\overline{f}(\boldsymbol{x})$ to the referee, without telling which one is being revealed. A naive approach would be to run the protocols for f and $\overline{f}$ in parallel but in a random order, which might seem to hide the value of b from the referee. However, since the decoding algorithm of a PSM protocol may depend on the description of the function being computed, the referee may learn b even if the order of protocol executions is randomly permuted.

3   Preliminaries

We define $[n] = \{0, 1, \ldots, n-1\}$ for $n \in \mathbb{N}$ as it will be more convenient to start indexing at 0. For a set X, we write $x \leftarrow_{\$} X$ if x is sampled uniformly at random from X. Let $\mathbb{F}_2 = \{0, 1\}$ denote the finite field of size 2. For $n \in \mathbb{N}$, let $\mathbb{Z}_n$ denote the ring of integers modulo n. For a function $f(n)$, we write $O_t(f(n))$ to denote the set of functions that are asymptotically bounded above by $f(n)$ up to a constant depending on a parameter t but not on n. The notation $\widetilde{O}(f(n))$

hides polylogarithmic factors in $f(n)$. We denote the bit length of a string S by $|S|$. Throughout the paper, we assume by default that n denotes the number of parties and d denotes the cardinality of each party's input domain.

3.1 Symmetric Functions

We define $\mathcal{F}_{n,d}$ as the set of all functions $f : [d]^n \to \{0,1\}$. We call a function $f \in \mathcal{F}_{n,d}$ *symmetric* if $f(x_{\sigma(0)}, \ldots, x_{\sigma(n-1)}) = f(x_0, \ldots, x_{n-1})$ for any input $\boldsymbol{x} = (x_0, \ldots, x_{n-1}) \in [d]^n$ and any permutation σ on $[n]$. Define $\mathcal{S}_{n,d}$ as the subset of $\mathcal{F}_{n,d}$ consisting of all symmetric functions.

For a symmetric function $f \in \mathcal{S}_{n,d}$, the value of $f(\boldsymbol{x})$ is uniquely determined by the *histogram* $\boldsymbol{h} = (h_0, \ldots, h_{d-1})$ of $\boldsymbol{x}$, where $h_j = |\{i \in [n] : x_i = j\}|$. Formally, we encode $x \in [d]$ into a vector $\phi(x) \in \{0,1\}^{d-1}$ defined by $\phi(x) = \boldsymbol{e}_x$ if $x \in \{0, 1, \ldots, d-2\}$ and $\phi(x) = \boldsymbol{0}$ if $x = d-1$, where $\boldsymbol{0}$ is the zero vector and $\boldsymbol{e}_x$ is the unit vector whose entries are 1 at position x and 0 elsewhere Then, according to [25], there exists a function $f^* : [n+1]^{d-1} \to \{0,1\}$ such that for any $(x_0, \ldots, x_{n-1}) \in [d]^n$,

$$f(x_0, \ldots, x_{n-1}) = f^*(\phi(x_0) + \cdots + \phi(x_{n-1})). \tag{9}$$

3.2 Private Simultaneous Messages

A Private Simultaneous Messages (PSM) protocol allows n input parties each holding an input x_i to reveal $f(x_0, \ldots, x_{n-1})$ to an external party called a *referee* without revealing any extra information. For convenience, we define PSM protocols in a more general setting where in addition to their private inputs, the parties share a common input z and reveal $f(z; x_0, \ldots, x_{n-1})$ to the referee.

Definition 1. *Let* $X_0, \ldots, X_{n-1}$, Y, *and* Z *be finite sets. Let* $f : Z \times \prod_{i \in [n]} X_i \to Y$ *be a function. An* n-party *private simultaneous messages (PSM) protocol* Π *for* f *is a tuple of algorithms* (Gen, Enc, Dec), *where:*

- Gen() $\to r$: Gen *is a randomized algorithm that takes no input and outputs common randomness* $r \in \{0,1\}^{\mathsf{rand}}$.
- Enc($i, (z, x_i), r$) $\to m_i$: Enc *is a deterministic algorithm that takes an index* i, $(z, x_i) \in Z \times X_i$, *and* $r \in \{0,1\}^{\mathsf{rand}}$ *as input and outputs a message* $m_i \in \{0,1\}^{\mathsf{comm}_i}$.
- Dec($(m_i)_{i \in [n]}$) $\to y$: Dec *is a deterministic algorithm that takes* $(m_i)_{i \in [n]} \in \prod_{i \in [n]} \{0,1\}^{\mathsf{comm}_i}$ *as input and outputs* $y \in Y$.

satisfying the following properties:

Correctness. *For any* $z \in Z$ *and* $(x_i)_{i \in [n]} \in \prod_{i \in [n]} X_i$, *it holds that*

$$\mathsf{Dec}((\mathsf{Enc}(i, (z, x_i), r))_{i \in [n]}) = f(z; x_0, \ldots, x_{n-1}),$$

with probability 1 over the choice of $r \leftarrow$ Gen().

Privacy. *There exists a randomized algorithm* Sim *such that for any* $z \in Z$ *and* $(x_i)_{i\in[n]} \in \prod_{i\in[n]} X_i$,

$$(\mathsf{Enc}(i,(z,x_i),r))_{i\in[n]} \equiv \mathsf{Sim}(f(z;x_0,\ldots,x_{n-1})),$$

where the probabilities are taken over $r \leftarrow$ Gen() *and the random coins of* Sim.

The communication complexity of Π is defined as $\mathsf{Comm}(\Pi) = \sum_{i\in[n]} \mathsf{comm}_i$. Define $\mathsf{PSM}(f)$ as the minimum of $\mathsf{Comm}(\Pi)$ over all PSM protocols Π for f. For a set $\mathcal{F}$ of functions, define $\mathsf{PSM}(\mathcal{F}) = \max_{f\in\mathcal{F}} \mathsf{PSM}(f)$. The state-of-the-art PSM protocol for general functions is given by [15].

Proposition 1 ([15]). $\mathsf{PSM}(\mathcal{F}_{n,d}) = O(d^{n/2}n^3)$.

We suppose that $\mathsf{PSM}(\mathcal{F}_{n,1}) = 0$ (no communication is required as the value of $f : [1]^n \to \{0,1\}$ is unique), and $\mathsf{PSM}(\mathcal{F}_{1,d}) = 1$ (since the single party can evaluate a function on his own and send the result to the referee).

We also introduce a variant of PSM protocols for functions that are defined only for a subset of inputs. This variant will be used in an application to ad hoc PSM protocols (see Sect. 6.1). Let $X_0,\ldots,X_{n-1}$, Y, and Z be finite sets. Let $\star$ be a special symbol not belonging to Y. We call a function $f : Z \times \prod_{i\in[n]} X_i \to Y \cup \{\star\}$ a *partial function* defined over a subset $S \subseteq Z \times \prod_{i\in[n]} X_i$ if $f(z;\boldsymbol{x}) \in Y$ for all $(z,\boldsymbol{x}) \in S$ and $f(z;\boldsymbol{x}) = \star$ for all $(z,\boldsymbol{x}) \notin S$. Note that $f(z;\boldsymbol{x}) = \star$ indicates that f is not properly defined over $(z,\boldsymbol{x})$. We can naturally extend Definition 1 to partial functions, where correctness and privacy are required only for inputs in S. We defer the formal definition to the full version [22].

3.3 Decomposable Affine Randomized Encoding

We introduce a related notion known as Decomposable Affine Randomized Encoding (DARE). This primitive encodes a function $f(x)$ into a randomized function $\hat{f}(x,r)$ satisfying the following properties:

Correctness. There exists a decoding function Dec such that $\mathsf{Dec}(\hat{f}(x,r)) = f(x)$ for any input x and randomness r.

Privacy. The distribution of $\hat{f}(x,r)$ induced by randomness r depends only on $f(x)$.

Decomposable and Affine. Each component of $\hat{f}(x,r)$ is an affine function of x over some field $\mathbb{F}$ while it may depend arbitrarily on r.

The formal definition can be found, e.g., in [31]. It is known that a DARE of a function f can be obtained from an arithmetic formula computing f.

Proposition 2 ([20,31]). *If* $f : \mathbb{F}^n \to \mathbb{F}$ *is computed by an arithmetic formula of depth* d *over* $\mathbb{F}$, *then there exists a DARE of* f *over* $\mathbb{F}$ *whose output length is* $O_\epsilon(2^{(1+\epsilon)d})$ *for any constant* $\epsilon > 0$.

3.4   Conditional Disclosure of Secrets

A Conditional Disclosure of Secrets (CDS) protocol assumes n input parties each holding an input x_i and sharing a secret s, and a referee who knows all inputs $(x_i)_{i \in [n]}$. The goal is to reveal s to the referee if and only if $f(x_0, \ldots, x_{n-1}) = 1$.

Definition 2. *Let $X_0, \ldots, X_{n-1}$ be finite sets. Let $f : \prod_{i \in [n]} X_i \to \{0,1\}$. An n-party conditional disclosure of secrets (CDS) protocol Π for f is a tuple of algorithms* (Gen, Enc, Dec), *where:*

- Gen() $\to r$: Gen *is a randomized algorithm that takes no input and outputs common randomness* $r \in \{0,1\}^{\text{rand}}$.
- Enc$(i, x_i, s, r) \to m_i$: Enc *is a deterministic algorithm that takes an index* i, $x_i \in X_i$, $s \in \{0,1\}$, *and* $r \in \{0,1\}^{\text{rand}}$ *as input and outputs a message* $m_i \in \{0,1\}^{\text{comm}_i}$.
- Dec$((x_i)_{i \in [n]}, (m_i)_{i \in [n]}) \to s'$: Dec *is a deterministic algorithm that takes* $(x_i)_{i \in [n]} \in \prod_{i \in [n]} X_i$ *and* $(m_i)_{i \in [n]} \in \prod_{i \in [n]} \{0,1\}^{\text{comm}_i}$ *as input and outputs* $s' \in \{0,1\}$.

satisfying the following properties:

Correctness. *For any $s \in \{0,1\}$ and any $(x_i)_{i \in [n]} \in \prod_{i \in [n]} X_i$ such that $f((x_i)_{i \in [n]}) = 1$, it holds that*

$$\mathsf{Dec}((\mathsf{Enc}(i, f, x_i, s, r))_{i \in [n]}) = s,$$

with probability 1 over the choice of $r \leftarrow$ Gen().

Privacy. *For any $(x_i)_{i \in [n]} \in \prod_{i \in [n]} X_i$ such that $f((x_i)_{i \in [n]}) = 0$, it holds that*

$$(\mathsf{Enc}(i, x_i, 0, r))_{i \in [n]} \equiv (\mathsf{Enc}(i, x_i, 1, r'))_{i \in [n]},$$

where the probabilities are taken over independent randomness $r \leftarrow$ Gen() and $r' \leftarrow$ Gen().

We define the communication complexity $\mathsf{Comm}(\Pi)$, $\mathsf{CDS}(f)$, and $\mathsf{CDS}(\mathcal{F})$ as in the case of PSM. The state-of-the-art CDS protocol for general functions is given by [37].

Proposition 3 ([37]). $\mathsf{CDS}(\mathcal{F}_{n,d}) = 2^{O(\sqrt{n \log d} \log(n \log d))} = 2^{\tilde{O}(\sqrt{n \log d})}$.

We suppose that $\mathsf{CDS}(\mathcal{F}_{n,1}) = \mathsf{CDS}(\mathcal{F}_{1,d}) = 1$ since in these cases, a single party can decide to send a secret to the referee.

We also need a stronger notion of CDS protocols, referred to as strong CDS protocols [21], in which no information about the secret is leaked as long as at least one of the messages is missing (see [21] or the full version [22] for the formal definition). The following proposition is obtained by an efficient compiler from CDS to strong CDS [21].

Proposition 4 ([21]). *For any $f \in \mathcal{F}_{n,d}$, the minimum communication complexity of strong CDS protocols for f is upper bounded by $\mathsf{CDS}(f) + n$.*

3.5 Selection Functions

A selection function, denoted by Sel_n, takes as input a bit x_i from each party and a common vector $\boldsymbol{m}$ of length $n + 1$, and outputs the component of $\boldsymbol{m}$ corresponding to the sum of the x_i's. Originally, an efficient PSM protocol for Sel_n was proposed by Benhamouda et al. [18] to upgrade plain PSM protocols into the ones secure against collusion of the referee and parties. Formally, we define a selection function $\mathsf{Sel}_n : \{0,1\}^{n+1} \times \{0,1\}^n \to \{0,1\}$ as

$$\mathsf{Sel}_n(\boldsymbol{m}; (x_i)_{i \in [n]}) = \boldsymbol{m}[s]$$

for any $\boldsymbol{m} \in \{0,1\}^{n+1}$ and any $(x_i)_{i \in [n]} \in \{0,1\}^n$, where $s = \sum_{i \in [n]} x_i$ and $\boldsymbol{m}[s]$ is the sth element of $\boldsymbol{m}$. The best known communication complexity for Sel_n is given by [40].

Proposition 5 ([40]). $\mathsf{PSM}(\mathsf{Sel}_n) = O(n^2)$.

Note that the protocol in [40] requires computational complexity of $2^{O(n)}$. This drawback is mitigated by the protocol in [18,24], which has communication complexity $O(n^2 \log n)$ and computational complexity $\widetilde{O}(n^2)$. We adopt the protocol in [40] as our primary focus is on communication efficiency.

Next, we consider a weaker variant of Sel_n, denoted by pSel_n, which reveals parties' input bits x_i to the referee while keeping the common string $\boldsymbol{m}$ hidden. Then, we can obtain a more efficient PSM protocol that achieves the same communication complexity as the protocol in [40], while simultaneously achieving the same computational complexity as [18]. Our construction is inspired by the PSM protocol for a similar functionality in [9]. Roughly speaking, the difference is that the functionality in [9] reveals the component of a common vector $\boldsymbol{m}$ corresponding to the *product* of the parties' inputs. We define a selection function with public inputs $\mathsf{pSel}_n : \{0,1\}^{n+1} \times \{0,1\}^n \to \{0,1\}^{n+1}$ as

$$\mathsf{pSel}_n(\boldsymbol{m}; (x_i)_{i \in [n]}) = (\boldsymbol{m}[s], x_0, x_1, \ldots, x_{n-1})$$

for any $\boldsymbol{m} \in \{0,1\}^{n+1}$ and any $(x_i)_{i \in [n]} \in \{0,1\}^n$, where $s = \sum_{i \in [n]} x_i$ and $\boldsymbol{m}[s]$ is the sth element of $\boldsymbol{m}$. In a protocol for pSel_n, we assume that the referee knows the values x_i's and executes the decoding algorithm using this information. This assumption is satisfied whenever used for constructing CDS protocols. We prove the following proposition in the full version [22].

Proposition 6. *There exists a PSM protocol for pSel_n whose communication and computational complexities are $O(n^2)$. In particular, $\mathsf{PSM}(\mathsf{pSel}_n) = O(n^2)$.*

We can straightforwardly extend protocols for Sel_n, $\mathsf{Sel}_{k,n}$, and pSel_n to the setting where each component of $\boldsymbol{m}$ is an ℓ-bit strings, rather than a single bit, by executing the protocols in a bit-wise manner. The resulting communication complexity increases by only a multiplicative factor of ℓ.

4   Relations to General Functions with Different Domains

In this section, we give a proof of Theorem 1. The right inequality of (1) is trivial as $\mathcal{S}_{n,d} \subseteq \mathcal{F}_{n,d}$.

4.1   Upper Bounds: New Constructions of PSM and CDS for $\mathcal{S}_{n,d}$

We prove the upper bound in (2) by showing efficient constructions of PSM and CDS protocols for $\mathcal{S}_{n,d}$. First, we consider the case of PSM.

Proposition 7. *Let $f \in \mathcal{S}_{n,d}$ be a symmetric function and $f^* \in \mathcal{F}_{d-1,n+1}$ be a function associated with f satisfying Eq. (9). Then, there exists a PSM protocol Π for f such that* $\mathsf{Comm}(\Pi) = \mathsf{PSM}(f^*) \cdot \mathsf{PSM}(\mathsf{Sel}_n)$. *In particular, it holds that* $\mathsf{PSM}(\mathcal{S}_{n,d}) \le \mathsf{PSM}(\mathcal{F}_{d-1,n+1}) \cdot \mathsf{PSM}(\mathsf{Sel}_n)$.

Notations.
- Let $\Pi_{f^*} = (\mathsf{Gen}_{f^*}, \mathsf{Enc}_{f^*}, \mathsf{Dec}_{f^*})$ be a $(d-1)$-party PSM protocol for f^*.
- Let $\Pi_{\mathsf{sel}} = (\mathsf{Gen}_{\mathsf{sel}}, \mathsf{Enc}_{\mathsf{sel}}, \mathsf{Dec}_{\mathsf{sel}})$ be an n-party PSM protocol for Sel_n.

$\mathsf{Gen}()$.
1. Run $r_{f^*} \leftarrow \mathsf{Gen}_{f^*}()$.
2. For each $k \in [d-1]$, run $r_{\mathsf{sel}}^{(k)} \leftarrow \mathsf{Gen}_{\mathsf{sel}}()$ with independent randomness.
3. For each $k \in [d-1]$ and each $j \in [n+1]$, compute a message $s_j^{(k)} = \mathsf{Enc}_{f^*}(k, j, r_{f^*})$ of the kth party in Π_g encoding an input $j \in [n+1]$.
4. Output $R = ((\boldsymbol{s}^{(k)})_{k \in [d-1]}, (r_{\mathsf{sel}}^{(k)})_{k \in [d-1]})$, where $\boldsymbol{s}^{(k)} = (s_j^{(k)})_{j \in [n+1]}$.

$\mathsf{Enc}(i, x_i, R)$.
1. Let $\phi(x_i) = (v_i^{(0)}, \dots, v_i^{(d-2)}) \in \{0,1\}^{d-1}$.
2. For each $k \in [d-1]$, compute $m_i^{(k)} = \mathsf{Enc}_{\mathsf{sel}}(i, (\boldsymbol{s}^{(k)}, v_i^{(k)}), r_{\mathsf{sel}}^{(k)})$.
3. Output $M_i = (m_i^{(k)})_{k \in [d-1]}$.

$\mathsf{Dec}(M_0, \dots, M_{n-1})$.
1. For each $k \in [d-1]$, compute $t^{(k)} = \mathsf{Dec}_{\mathsf{sel}}(m_0^{(k)}, \dots, m_{n-1}^{(k)})$.
2. Output $y = \mathsf{Dec}_{f^*}(t^{(0)}, \dots, t^{(d-2)})$.

Fig. 1. A PSM protocol for $\mathcal{S}_{n,d}$

Proof. Let Π_{f^*} be a $(d-1)$-party PSM protocol for f^* and Π_{sel} be an n-party PSM protocol for Sel_n. We describe a PSM protocol Π for f in Fig. 1.

Correctness. Let $(x_0, \dots, x_{n-1}) \in [d]^n$ be inputs. Let $(h^{(k)})_{k \in [d-1]} = \sum_{i \in [n]} \phi(x_i) \in [n+1]^{d-1}$. For each $k \in [d-1]$, it follows from the correctness of Π_{sel} that

$$t^{(k)} = \mathsf{Sel}_n((\boldsymbol{s}^{(k)}, v_0^{(k)}), \dots, (\boldsymbol{s}^{(k)}, v_{n-1}^{(k)})) = \mathsf{Enc}_{f^*}(k, h^{(k)}, r_{f^*}).$$

Thus, it holds that $y = f^*(h^{(0)}, \dots, h^{(d-2)}) = f(x_0, \dots, x_{n-1})$.

Privacy. Let $(x_0, \ldots, x_{n-1}) \in [d]^n$ be inputs and $(h^{(k)})_{k \in [d-1]} = \sum_{i \in [n]} \phi(x_i) \in [n+1]^{d-1}$. Let Sim_{f^*} be a simulator for Π_{f^*} and $\mathsf{Sim}_{\mathsf{sel}}$ be a simulator for Π_{sel}. For each $k \in [d-1]$, the messages $m_i^{(k)}$'s can be simulated by $\mathsf{Sim}_{\mathsf{sel}}$ with input $\mathsf{Sel}_n((\boldsymbol{s}^{(k)}, v_0^{(k)}), \ldots, (\boldsymbol{s}^{(k)}, v_{n-1}^{(k)}))$, that is, $(m_i^{(k)})_{i \in [n]} \equiv \mathsf{Sim}_{\mathsf{sel}}(s_{h^{(k)}}^{(k)})$. Since $s_{h^{(k)}}^{(k)} = \mathsf{Enc}_{f^*}(k, h^{(k)}, r_{f^*})$, the $s_{h^{(k)}}^{(k)}$'s can be simulated by Sim_{f^*} with input $g(h^{(0)}, \ldots, h^{(d-2)})$, that is, $(s_{h^{(k)}}^{(k)})_{k \in [d-1]} \equiv \mathsf{Sim}_{f^*}(f^*(h^{(0)}, \ldots, h^{(d-2)}))$. Therefore, since $f^*(h^{(0)}, \ldots, h^{(d-2)}) = f(x_0, \ldots, x_{n-1})$, we obtain a simulator simulating $(M_i)_{i \in [n]} = (m_i^{(k)})_{k \in [d-1], i \in [n]}$ from $f(x_0, \ldots, x_{n-1})$.

Complexity. We have that $|s_j^{(k)}| \leq \mathsf{comm}_k(\Pi_{f^*})$, where $\mathsf{comm}_k(\Pi_{f^*})$ denote the bit length of messages of the kth party in Π_{f^*}. We have that $\sum_{i \in [n]} |m_i^{(k)}| \leq \mathsf{PSM}(\mathsf{Sel}_n) \cdot \mathsf{comm}_k(\Pi_{f^*})$ for each $k \in [d-1]$. Thus, we obtain that $\sum_{i \in [n]} |M_i| \leq \mathsf{PSM}(\mathsf{Sel}_n) \sum_{k \in [d-1]} \mathsf{comm}_k(\Pi_{f^*}) \leq \mathsf{PSM}(f^*) \cdot \mathsf{PSM}(\mathsf{Sel}_n)$. $\square$

By plugging in Propositions 1 and 5, we obtain the following corollary. In particular, this improves the prior upper bound of $n^{2d/3+O(1)}$ in [25].

Corollary 1. $\mathsf{PSM}(\mathcal{S}_{n,d}) \leq \mathsf{PSM}(\mathcal{F}_{d-1,n+1}) \cdot O(n^2) \leq O((n+1)^{d/2} n^{3/2} d^3)$.

Next, in the case of CDS, the following proposition holds. We defer the formal proof to the full version [22] since the construction is analogous to the PSM case except that the selection function Sel_n is replaced with pSel_n.

Proposition 8. *Let $f \in \mathcal{S}_{n,d}$ be a symmetric function and $f^* \in \mathcal{F}_{d-1,n+1}$ be a function associated with f satisfying Eq. (9). Then, there exists a CDS protocol Π for f such that $\mathsf{Comm}(\Pi) = \mathsf{CDS}(f^*) \cdot \mathsf{PSM}(\mathsf{pSel}_n)$. In particular, it holds that $\mathsf{CDS}(\mathcal{S}_{n,d}) \leq \mathsf{CDS}(\mathcal{F}_{d-1,n+1}) \cdot \mathsf{PSM}(\mathsf{pSel}_n)$.*

By plugging in Propositions 3 and 6, we obtain the following corollary.

Corollary 2. $\mathsf{CDS}(\mathcal{S}_{n,d}) \leq \mathsf{CDS}(\mathcal{F}_{d-1,n+1}) \cdot O(n^2) \leq n^2 2^{\widetilde{O}(\sqrt{d \log n})}$.

Prior to this work, the only known bound for $\mathsf{CDS}(\mathcal{S}_{n,d})$ was the trivial one $\mathsf{CDS}(\mathcal{F}_{n,d})$. The currently best known CDS protocol for general functions requires sub-exponential communication in n [37], whereas our protocol achieves polynomial communication when $d = o(\log n)$. This is the first result to demonstrate that the symmetry of functions is effective to reduce the complexity of CDS.

4.2   Lower Bounds

We prove the lower bounds in (1) and (2).

Proposition 9. *For $\mathfrak{C} \in \{\mathsf{PSM}, \mathsf{CDS}\}$, $\mathfrak{C}(\mathcal{S}_{n,d}) \geq \mathfrak{C}(\mathcal{F}_{n,d'})$, where $d' = \lfloor d/n \rfloor$.*

Proof. Let $g : [d']^n \to \{0,1\}$ be a function in $\mathcal{F}_{n,d'}$. Let $S = [n] \times [d']$ and T be a set of size $d - nd'$ that is disjoint from S. Let $X = S \cup T$. We define a symmetric function $f : X^n \to \{0,1\}$ as follows. Let $(a_0,\ldots,a_{n-1}) \in X^n$. If $a_k = (i_k, j_k) \in S$ for all $k \in [n]$ and the i_k's are pairwise distinct, then sort $(a_0,\ldots,a_{n-1})$ in lexicographical order, i.e., according to the values of $(i_0,\ldots,i_{n-1})$. Let $((0,\ell_0),\ldots,(n-1,\ell_{n-1}))$ denote the sorted array. We define $f(a_0,\ldots,a_{n-1}) := g(\ell_0,\ldots,\ell_{n-1})$. Otherwise, we set the value of f to 0. Clearly, $f \in \mathcal{S}_{n,d}$ as it sorts inputs before computing an output.

Given any PSM protocol $\Pi_f = (\mathsf{Gen}_f, \mathsf{Enc}_f, \mathsf{Dec}_f)$ for f, we construct a PSM protocol $\Pi_g = (\mathsf{Gen}_g, \mathsf{Enc}_g, \mathsf{Dec}_g)$ for g with the same communication complexity, which proves $\mathsf{PSM}(\mathcal{S}_{n,d}) \geq \mathsf{PSM}(\mathcal{F}_{n,d'})$. For $i \in [n]$, let P_i and Q_i be the ith party involved in Π_g and Π_f, respectively. Π_g proceeds as follows:

$\mathsf{Gen}_g()$: Run $r_f \leftarrow \mathsf{Gen}_f()$ and output $r_g := r_f$.
$\mathsf{Enc}_g(i, x_i, r_g)$: P_i emulates the roles of Q_i in Π_f with input $a_i = (i, x_i)$. That is, P_i computes $M_i = \mathsf{Enc}_f(i, a_i, r_f)$.
$\mathsf{Dec}_g(M_0,\ldots,M_{n-1})$: Output $y = \mathsf{Dec}_f(M_0,\ldots,M_{n-1})$.

The correctness follows from the fact that $y = f((0,x_0),\ldots,(n-1,x_{n-1})) = g(x_0,\ldots,x_{n-1})$. The privacy directly follows from that of Π_f since what the referee learns is exactly messages resulting from an execution of Π_f.

The statements for CDS follow from the same argument except that the PSM protocols Π_f and Π_g are replaced with CDS protocols for f and g, respectively. $\square$

Proposition 10. *For* $\mathfrak{C} \in \{\mathsf{PSM}, \mathsf{CDS}\}$, $\mathfrak{C}(\mathcal{S}_{n,d}) \geq \mathfrak{C}(\mathcal{F}_{d-1,n'+1})$, *where* $n' = \lfloor n/(d-1) \rfloor$.

Proof. Let $g : [n'+1]^{d-1} \to \{0,1\}$ be a function in $\mathcal{F}_{d-1,n'+1}$. We define a symmetric function $f : [d]^n \to \{0,1\}$ as follows. Due to the symmetry, it suffices to specify all values of f for inputs sorted in ascending order. For any $(x_0,\ldots,x_{d-2}) \in [n'+1]^{d-1}$, define

$$f(\underbrace{0,\ldots,0}_{x_0},\ldots,\underbrace{d-2,\ldots,d-2}_{x_{d-2}},\underbrace{d-1,\ldots,d-1}_{n-\sum_{i\in[d-1]} x_i}) = g(x_0,\ldots,x_{d-2}).$$

Note that $n - \sum_{i\in[d-1]} x_i \geq 0$ since $n \geq n'(d-1)$. For other inputs, set the value of f to an arbitrary value (say, 0). Let $\delta = n - n'(d-1)$.

We show that given any PSM protocol $\Pi_f = (\mathsf{Gen}_f, \mathsf{Enc}_f, \mathsf{Dec}_f)$ for f, it is possible to obtain a PSM protocol $\Pi_g = (\mathsf{Gen}_g, \mathsf{Enc}_g, \mathsf{Dec}_g)$ for g with the same communication complexity, which proves $\mathsf{PSM}(\mathcal{S}_{n,d}) \geq \mathsf{PSM}(\mathcal{F}_{d-1,n'+1})$. For $j \in [d-1]$, let P_j be the jth party involved in Π_g. We partition the set of n parties involved in Π_f, into $d-1$ subsets $S_0,\ldots,S_{d-2}$ such that $|S_j| = n'$ for all $0 \leq j \leq d-3$ and $|S_{d-2}| = n - n'(d-2) = n' + \delta$. We denote $S_j = \{\mathsf{Q}_{j,i} : i \in [n']\}$ for $0 \leq j \leq d-3$ and $S_{d-2} = \{\mathsf{Q}_{d-2,i} : i \in [n'+\delta]\}$. Π_g proceeds as follows:

$\mathsf{Gen}_g()$: Run $r_f \leftarrow \mathsf{Gen}_f()$ and output $r_g := r_f$.

$\mathsf{Enc}_g(j, x_j, r_g)$:

- If $0 \le j \le d-3$, then P_j emulates the roles of parties in S_j by computing $M_j = ((\mu_{j,i}(j))_{i\in[x_j]}, (\mu_{j,x_j+i}(d-1))_{i\in[n'-x_j]})$, where $\mu_{j,i}(x)$ denotes a message of $\mathsf{Q}_{j,i}$ with input x and randomness r_f.
- If $j = d-2$, then P_{d-2} emulates the roles of parties in S_{d-2} by computing $M_{d-2} = ((\mu_{d-2,i}(d-2))_{i\in[x_{d-2}]}, (\mu_{d-2,x_{d-2}+i}(d-1))_{i\in[n'+\delta-x_{d-2}]})$.

$\mathsf{Dec}_g(M_0, \ldots, M_{d-2})$:

1. Parse M_j into $M_j = (M_{j,i})_{i\in[n']}$ for $j \in [d-2]$ and $M_{d-2} = (M_{d-2,i})_{i\in[n'+\delta]}$.
2. Output $y = \mathsf{Dec}_f((M_{j,i})_{j\in[d-2],i\in[n']}, (M_{d-2,i})_{i\in[n'+\delta]})$.

The correctness follows since $\sum_{j\in[d-2]}(n'-x_j)+(n'+\delta-x_{d-2}) = n-\sum_{j\in[d-1]}x_j$ and $y = f(\underbrace{0,\ldots,0}_{x_0},\ldots,\underbrace{d-2,\ldots,d-2}_{x_{d-2}},\underbrace{d-1,\ldots,d-1}_{n-\sum_{j\in[d-1]}x_j}) = g(x_0,\ldots,x_{d-2})$. The second equality follows from the symmetry of f. The privacy directly follows from that of Π_f since what the referee learns is exactly messages resulting from an execution of Π_f.

The statements for CDS follow from the same argument except that the PSM protocols Π_f and Π_g are replaced with CDS protocols for f and g, respectively. $\square$

5   Towards Tight Relations to General Functions

In this section, we give proofs of Theorems 2 and 3. To this end, we relate the optimal communication complexities of general functions with different domain sizes. Specifically, it would be desirable to obtain an inequality of the form $\mathfrak{C}(\mathcal{F}_{n,d_2}) \le M \cdot \mathfrak{C}(\mathcal{F}_{n,d_1})$ for $d_1 < d_2$ and $\mathfrak{C} \in \{\mathsf{PSM}, \mathsf{CDS}\}$. Technically, we present techniques for constructing PSM and CDS protocols for $\mathcal{F}_{n,d_2}$ based on those for $\mathcal{F}_{n,d_1}$.

5.1   The Case of CDS

We begin with the case of CDS, since it is technically easier to handle.

We prepare some notations. Define $\delta_w(y) = 1$ if $y = w$ and 0 if $y \ne w$. For each $\boldsymbol{w} = (w_i)_{i\in[n]} \in \{0,1\}^n$, define $\delta_{\boldsymbol{w}} : \{0,1\}^n \to \{0,1\}$ as $\delta_{\boldsymbol{w}}((y_i)_{i\in[n]}) = \prod_{i\in[n]}\delta_{w_i}(y_i)$. Let $F \in \mathcal{F}_{n,2d}$. We interpret each input $x' \in [2d]$ as a pair (x,y) where $x \in [d]$ and $y \in \{0,1\}$. For each $\boldsymbol{w} \in \{0,1\}^n$, let $f_{\boldsymbol{w}} \in \mathcal{F}_{n,d}$ denote the function obtained by fixing each y-component to w_i, that is, $f_{\boldsymbol{w}}((x_i)_{i\in[n]}) = F((x_i, w_i)_{i\in[n]})$. Furthermore, for a function $f \in \mathcal{F}_{n,d}$, we define a function $G_f \in \mathcal{F}_{n,2d}$ with extended domains as

$$G_f((x_i, y_i)_{i\in[n]}) = f((x_i)_{i\in[n]}) \prod_{i\in[n]} y_i$$

for any $x_i \in [d]$ and $y_i \in \{0,1\}$.

First, we reduce a CDS protocol for $F \in \mathcal{F}_{n,2d}$ to CDS protocols for G_f with $f \in \mathcal{F}_{n,d}$.

Lemma 1. $\mathsf{CDS}(\mathcal{F}_{n,2d}) \le 2^n \cdot \max_{f \in \mathcal{F}_{n,d}} \mathsf{CDS}(G_f)$.

Proof. Let $F \in \mathcal{F}_{n,2d}$. Suppose that for any $f \in \mathcal{F}_{n,d}$, we are given a CDS protocol $\Pi_{G_f} = (\mathsf{Gen}_{G_f}, \mathsf{Enc}_{G_f}, \mathsf{Dec}_{G_f})$ for G_f. We construct a CDS protocol Π_F for F as follows.

$\mathsf{Gen}()$: Output $R = (r_{\boldsymbol{w}})_{\boldsymbol{w} \in \{0,1\}^n}$, where $r_{\boldsymbol{w}} \leftarrow \mathsf{Gen}_{G_{f_{\boldsymbol{w}}}}()$ for each $\boldsymbol{w} \in \{0,1\}^n$.
$\mathsf{Enc}(i, (x_i, y_i), s, R)$: Compute $m_{\boldsymbol{w},i} = \mathsf{Enc}_{G_{f_{\boldsymbol{w}}}}(i, (x_i, \delta_{w_i}(y_i)), s, r_{\boldsymbol{w}})$ for each $\boldsymbol{w} = (w_i)_{i \in [n]} \in \{0,1\}^n$, and output $M_i = (m_{\boldsymbol{w},i})_{\boldsymbol{w} \in \{0,1\}^n}$.
$\mathsf{Dec}((x_i, y_i)_{i \in [n]}; M_0, \dots, M_{n-1})$:
  – If $F((x_i, y_i)_{i \in [n]}) = 0$, then output $z = \perp$.
  – If $F((x_i, y_i)_{i \in [n]}) = 1$, then output $z = \mathsf{Dec}_{G_{f_{\boldsymbol{y}}}}((x_i, 1)_{i \in [n]}; (m_{\boldsymbol{y},i})_{i \in [n]})$.

First, we see the correctness of Π_F. Let $\boldsymbol{x} = (x_i)_{i \in [n]} \in [d]^n$ and $\boldsymbol{y} = (y_i)_{i \in [n]} \in \{0,1\}^n$ be inputs such that $F((x_i, y_i)_{i \in [n]}) = 1$ and $s \in \{0,1\}$ be a secret. Since

$$F((x_i, y_i)_{i \in [n]}) = \sum_{\boldsymbol{w} \in \{0,1\}^n} f_{\boldsymbol{w}}(\boldsymbol{x})\delta_{\boldsymbol{w}}(\boldsymbol{y}),$$

we   have
that $G_{f_{\boldsymbol{y}}}((x_i, \delta_{y_i}(y_i))_{i \in [n]}) = f_{\boldsymbol{y}}(\boldsymbol{x})\delta_{\boldsymbol{y}}(\boldsymbol{y}) = 1$ and $G_{f_{\boldsymbol{w}}}((x_i, \delta_{w_i}(y_i))_{i \in [n]}) = 0$ for $\boldsymbol{w} \ne \boldsymbol{y}$. Thus, it follows from the correctness of $\Pi_{G_{f_{\boldsymbol{y}}}}$ that $z = s$.

Next, we see the privacy of Π_F. Let $\boldsymbol{x} = (x_i)_{i \in [n]} \in [d]^n$ and $\boldsymbol{y} = (y_i)_{i \in [n]} \in \{0,1\}^n$ be inputs such that $F((x_i, y_i)_{i \in [n]}) = 0$. For any $\boldsymbol{w} \in \{0,1\}^n$, we have that

$$G_{f_{\boldsymbol{w}}}((x_i, \delta_{w_i}(y_i))_{i \in [n]}) = \begin{cases} f_{\boldsymbol{y}}(\boldsymbol{x})\delta_{\boldsymbol{y}}(\boldsymbol{y}) = 0, & \text{if } \boldsymbol{w} = \boldsymbol{y}, \\ f_{\boldsymbol{w}}(\boldsymbol{x})\delta_{\boldsymbol{w}}(\boldsymbol{y}) = 0, & \text{if } \boldsymbol{w} \ne \boldsymbol{y}. \end{cases}$$

Thus, the privacy of each $\Pi_{G_{f_{\boldsymbol{w}}}}$ ensures that the distribution of $(m_{\boldsymbol{w},i})_{i \in [n]}$ when $s = 0$ is identical to that when $s = 1$. Since all $\Pi_{G_{f_{\boldsymbol{w}}}}$ are executed on independent randomness, the distribution of messages $(m_{\boldsymbol{w},i})_{i \in [n], \boldsymbol{w} \in \{0,1\}^n}$ when $s = 0$ is identical to that when $s = 1$.

Since $f_{\boldsymbol{w}} \in \mathcal{F}_{n,d}$, the communication complexity of each $\Pi_{G_{f_{\boldsymbol{w}}}}$ is upper bounded by $\max_{f \in \mathcal{F}_{n,d}} \mathsf{CDS}(G_f)$. Since Π_F internally executes 2^n such protocols, the complexity of Π_F is upper bounded by $2^n \cdot \max_{f \in \mathcal{F}_{n,d}} \mathsf{CDS}(G_f)$. $\qquad\square$

Next, we reduce a CDS protocol for G_f with $f \in \mathcal{F}_{n,d}$ to a strong CDS for f. Proposition 4 ensures that the strong CDS is efficiently reduced to a plain CDS for f.

Lemma 2. *For any $f \in \mathcal{F}_{n,d}$, $\mathsf{CDS}(G_f) \le \mathsf{CDS}(f) + n$.*

Proof. Let $f \in \mathcal{F}_{n,d}$ and suppose that a strong CDS protocol Π_f for f is given. We construct a CDS protocol Π_{G_f} for G_f as follows.

$\mathsf{Gen}()$: Output $r \leftarrow \mathsf{Gen}_f()$.
$\mathsf{Enc}(i, (x_i, y_i), s, r)$:

- If $y_i = 0$, output $m_i = \bot$.
- If $y_i = 1$, output $m_i = \mathsf{Enc}_f(i, x_i, s, r)$.

$\mathsf{Dec}((x_i, y_i)_{i \in [n]}; M_0, \ldots, M_{n-1})$:

- If $y_i = 1$ for all i and $f((x_i)_{i \in [n]}) = 1$, output $z = \mathsf{Dec}_f((x_i)_{i \in [n]}; (m_i)_{i \in [n]})$.
- Otherwise, output $z = \bot$.

First, we see the correctness of Π_{G_f}. Let $\boldsymbol{x} = (x_i)_{i \in [n]} \in [d]^n$ and $\boldsymbol{y} = (y_i)_{i \in [n]} \in \{0, 1\}^n$ be inputs such that $G_f((x_i, y_i)_{i \in [n]}) = 1$, and $s \in \{0, 1\}$ be a secret. In particular, $y_i = 1$ for all $i \in [n]$ and $f(\boldsymbol{x}) = 1$. Thus, it follows from the correctness of Π_f that $z = \mathsf{Dec}_f(\boldsymbol{x}; (m_i)_{i \in [n]}) = s$.

Next, we see the privacy of Π_{G_f}. Let $\boldsymbol{x} = (x_i)_{i \in [n]} \in [d]^n$ and $\boldsymbol{y} = (y_i)_{i \in [n]} \in \{0, 1\}^n$ be inputs such that $G_f((x_i, y_i)_{i \in [n]}) = 0$. First, suppose that $y_i = 1$ for all $i \in [n]$. This implies $f(\boldsymbol{x}) = 0$. Thus, the privacy of Π_f ensures that the distribution of messages $(\mathsf{Enc}_f(i, x_i, 0, r))_{i \in [n]}$ is identical to that of $(\mathsf{Enc}_f(i, x_i, 1, r))_{i \in [n]}$. Second, suppose that $y_i = 0$ for some $i \in [n]$. Since Π_f is a strong CDS protocol, the distribution of $(\mathsf{Enc}_f(i', x_{i'}, 0, r))_{i' \in [n] \setminus \{i\}}$ is identical to that of $(\mathsf{Enc}_f(i', x_{i'}, 1, r))_{i' \in [n] \setminus \{i\}}$. Thus, the distribution of messages are independent of a secret.

Clearly, the communication complexity of Π_{G_f} is at most that of Π_f. Thus, it follows from Proposition 4 that $\mathsf{Comm}(\Pi_{G_f}) \leq \mathsf{Comm}(\Pi_f) \leq \mathsf{CDS}(f) + n$. $\square$

Combining Lemmas 1 and 2, we obtain the following inequalities.

Lemma 3. $\mathsf{CDS}(\mathcal{F}_{n,2d}) \leq 2^n(\mathsf{CDS}(\mathcal{F}_{n,d}) + n) \leq n2^n \cdot \mathsf{CDS}(\mathcal{F}_{n,d})$.

By applying Lemma 3 iteratively, we obtain the following proposition.

Proposition 11. *For* $d_1 \leq d_2$, $\mathsf{CDS}(\mathcal{F}_{n,d_2}) \leq (O(d_2/d_1))^{n+\log n} \cdot \mathsf{CDS}(\mathcal{F}_{n,d_1})$.

Proof. Set $\ell = \lceil \log(d_2/d_1) \rceil$. It holds that

$$\mathsf{CDS}(\mathcal{F}_{n,d_2}) \leq 2^n n \cdot \mathsf{CDS}(\mathcal{F}_{n,d_2/2}) \leq \cdots \leq (2^n n)^\ell \cdot \mathsf{CDS}(\mathcal{F}_{n,2^{-\ell}d_2}).$$

Since $2^{-\ell}d_2 \leq d_1$ and $(2^n n)^\ell = (O(d_2/d_1))^{n+\log n}$, the stated inequality is obtained. $\square$

Now, we give a proof of Theorem 2. From Theorem 1, we have an inequality $\mathsf{CDS}(\mathcal{S}_{n,d}) \geq \mathsf{CDS}(\mathcal{F}_{n,d'})$ for $d' = \lfloor d/n \rfloor$. Since $d/d' = O(n)$, it follows from Proposition 11 that $\mathsf{CDS}(\mathcal{F}_{n,d}) \leq n^{O(n)} \cdot \mathsf{CDS}(\mathcal{F}_{n,d'})$, which proves the lower bound in (3). On the other hand, we also have an inequality $\mathsf{CDS}(\mathcal{S}_{n,d}) \geq \mathsf{CDS}(\mathcal{F}_{d-1,n'+1})$ for $n' = \lfloor n/(d-1) \rfloor$. Since $n/n' = O(d)$, it again follows from Proposition 11 that $\mathsf{CDS}(\mathcal{F}_{d-1,n+1}) \leq d^{O(d)} \cdot \mathsf{CDS}(\mathcal{F}_{d-1,n'+1})$, which proves the lower bound in (4).

5.2   The Case of PSM

Next, we give a proof of Theorem 3. We introduce a function class $\mathcal{F}_{n,d}^{\text{affine}}$ that augments $\mathcal{F}_{n,d}$ with affine functions. For $f \in \mathcal{F}_{n,d}$, we define a function f^{affine} : $\{0,1\}^2 \times [d]^n \to \{0,1\}$ as

$$f^{\text{affine}}((a,b); (x_i)_{i \in [n]}) = af((x_i)_{i \in [n]}) + b \bmod 2$$

for any $(a,b) \in \{0,1\}^2$ and $x_i \in [d]$. We set $\mathcal{F}_{n,d}^{\text{affine}} = \{f^{\text{affine}} : f \in \mathcal{F}_{n,d}\}$. We assume that in a PSM protocol for f^{affine}, the coefficients (a,b) are commonly known to all parties but are private and hidden from the referee. Let $\alpha_{n,d}$ denote the ratio $\text{PSM}(\mathcal{F}_{n,d})/\text{PSM}(\mathcal{F}_{n,d}^{\text{affine}})$. Intuitively, it measures the efficiency loss incurred when computing the augmented function f^{affine} as compared to $f \in \mathcal{F}_{n,d}$. Furthermore, for $f \in \mathcal{F}_{n,d}$, we define a function $G_f^{\text{affine}} \in \mathcal{F}_{n,2d}$ as

$$G_f^{\text{affine}}((a,b); (x_i, y_i)_{i \in [n]}) = af((x_i)_{i \in [n]}) \prod_{i \in [n]} y_i + b,$$

where we fix a one-to-one correspondence between $x' \in [2d]$ and $(x,y) \in [d] \times \{0,1\}$. Finally, we define a function $H : \mathbb{F}_2^{n+3} \to \mathbb{F}_2$ as $H(z,a,b,(y_i)_{i \in [n]}) = az \prod_{i \in [n]} y_i + b$ for any $z, a, b, y_i \in \mathbb{F}_2$.

First, we reduce a PSM protocol for $F \in \mathcal{F}_{n,2d}^{\text{affine}}$ to PSM protocols for G_f^{affine} with $f \in \mathcal{F}_{n,d}$.

Lemma 4. $\text{PSM}(\mathcal{F}_{n,2d}^{\text{affine}}) \leq 2^n \cdot \max_{f \in \mathcal{F}_{n,d}} \text{PSM}(G_f^{\text{affine}})$.

Proof. Let $F \in \mathcal{F}_{n,2d}$. Suppose that for any $f \in \mathcal{F}_{n,d}$, we are given a PSM protocol $\Pi_{G_f^{\text{affine}}} = (\text{Gen}_{G_f^{\text{affine}}}, \text{Enc}_{G_f^{\text{affine}}}, \text{Dec}_{G_f^{\text{affine}}})$ for a function G_f^{affine}. We construct a PSM protocol $\Pi_{F^{\text{affine}}}$ for F^{affine} as follows.

Gen():
    1. For each $\boldsymbol{w} \in \{0,1\}^n$, run $r_{\boldsymbol{w}} \leftarrow \text{Gen}_{G_{f_{\boldsymbol{w}}}^{\text{affine}}}()$.
    2. Choose random bits $c_{\boldsymbol{w}} \in \{0,1\}$ for $\boldsymbol{w} \in \{0,1\}^n$ such that $\sum_{\boldsymbol{w}} c_{\boldsymbol{w}} = 0$.
    3. Output $R = ((r_{\boldsymbol{w}})_{\boldsymbol{w} \in \{0,1\}^n}, (c_{\boldsymbol{w}})_{\boldsymbol{w} \in \{0,1\}^n})$.
Enc($i, ((a,b), (x_i, y_i)), R$):
    1. Set $b_{\boldsymbol{w}} \in \{0,1\}$ as $b_{\boldsymbol{w}} = c_{\boldsymbol{w}} + b$ if $\boldsymbol{w} = \boldsymbol{0}$ and $b_{\boldsymbol{w}} = c_{\boldsymbol{w}}$ otherwise.
    2. Compute $m_{\boldsymbol{w},i} = \text{Enc}_{G_{f_{\boldsymbol{w}}}^{\text{affine}}}(i, ((a, b_{\boldsymbol{w}}), (x_i, \delta_{w_i}(y_i))), r_{\boldsymbol{w}})$ for each $\boldsymbol{w} = (w_i)_{i \in [n]} \in \{0,1\}^n$.
    3. Output $M_i = (m_{\boldsymbol{w},i})_{\boldsymbol{w} \in \{0,1\}^n}$.
Dec($M_0, \ldots, M_{n-1}$):
    1. For each $\boldsymbol{w} \in \{0,1\}^n$, compute $z_{\boldsymbol{w}} = \text{Dec}_{G_{f_{\boldsymbol{w}}}^{\text{affine}}}((m_{\boldsymbol{w},i})_{i \in [n]})$.
    2. Output $z = \sum_{\boldsymbol{w} \in \{0,1\}^n} z_{\boldsymbol{w}}$.

First, we see the correctness of $\Pi_{F^{\mathrm{affine}}}$. Let $(a, b) \in \{0, 1\}^2$, $\boldsymbol{x} = (x_i)_{i \in [n]} \in [d]^n$, and $\boldsymbol{y} = (y_i)_{i \in [n]} \in \{0, 1\}^n$. It follows from the correctness of $\Pi_{G^{\mathrm{affine}}_{f_{\boldsymbol{w}}}}$ that

$$z_{\boldsymbol{w}} = G^{\mathrm{affine}}_{f_{\boldsymbol{w}}}((a, b_{\boldsymbol{w}}); (x_i, \delta_{w_i}(y_i))_{i \in [n]}) = a f_{\boldsymbol{w}}(\boldsymbol{x}) \delta_{\boldsymbol{w}}(\boldsymbol{y}) + b_{\boldsymbol{w}}.$$

Since $\sum_{\boldsymbol{w} \in \{0,1\}^n} b_{\boldsymbol{w}} = b + \sum_{\boldsymbol{w} \in \{0,1\}^n} c_{\boldsymbol{w}} = b$, it holds that

$$z = \sum_{\boldsymbol{w} \in \{0,1\}^n} a f_{\boldsymbol{w}}(\boldsymbol{x}) \delta_{\boldsymbol{w}}(\boldsymbol{y}) + b = a f_{\boldsymbol{y}}(\boldsymbol{x}) + b = F^{\mathrm{affine}}((a, b); (x_i, y_i)_{i \in [n]}).$$

Next, we see the privacy of $\Pi_{F^{\mathrm{affine}}}$. We have seen that $z_{\boldsymbol{w}} = a f_{\boldsymbol{w}}(\boldsymbol{x}) \delta_{\boldsymbol{w}}(\boldsymbol{y}) + b_{\boldsymbol{w}}$. Since $(b_{\boldsymbol{w}})_{\boldsymbol{w} \in \{0,1\}^n}$ are random additive shares of b, $(z_{\boldsymbol{w}})_{\boldsymbol{w} \in \{0,1\}^n}$ are random additive shares of $z = \sum_{\boldsymbol{w} \in \{0,1\}^n} z_{\boldsymbol{w}} = F^{\mathrm{affine}}((a, b); (x_i, y_i)_{i \in [n]})$. Thus, we have a randomized algorithm Sim_0 that simulates the distribution of $(z_{\boldsymbol{w}})_{\boldsymbol{w} \in \{0,1\}^n}$ from z. Furthermore, for each $\boldsymbol{w} \in \{0, 1\}^n$, the privacy of $\Pi_{G^{\mathrm{affine}}_{f_{\boldsymbol{w}}}}$ ensures the existence of a simulator $\mathsf{Sim}_{G^{\mathrm{affine}}_{f_{\boldsymbol{w}}}}$ that simulates the distribution of $(m_{\boldsymbol{w}, i})_{i \in [n]}$ from $z_{\boldsymbol{w}}$. Therefore, since all $\Pi_{G^{\mathrm{affine}}_{f_{\boldsymbol{w}}}}$'s are executed on independent randomness, we obtain a simulator that simulates the distribution of messages $(m_{\boldsymbol{w}, i})_{\boldsymbol{w} \in \{0,1\}^n, i \in [n]}$ in $\Pi_{F^{\mathrm{affine}}}$ from z.

Since $f_{\boldsymbol{w}} \in \mathcal{F}_{n,d}$, the communication complexity of each $\Pi_{G^{\mathrm{affine}}_{f_{\boldsymbol{w}}}}$ is upper bounded by $\max_{f \in \mathcal{F}_{n,d}} \mathsf{PSM}(G^{\mathrm{affine}}_f)$. Since $\Pi_{F^{\mathrm{affine}}}$ internally executes 2^n such protocols, the communication complexity of $\Pi_{F^{\mathrm{affine}}}$ is upper bounded by $2^n \cdot \max_{f \in \mathcal{F}_{n,d}} \mathsf{PSM}(G^{\mathrm{affine}}_f)$. $\qquad\square$

Next, we reduce a PSM protocol for G^{affine}_f to that for f^{affine}.

Lemma 5. *For any $f \in \mathcal{F}_{n,d}$, $\mathsf{PSM}(G^{\mathrm{affine}}_f) \leq s \cdot \mathsf{PSM}(f^{\mathrm{affine}})$, where s is the output length of any DARE of H.*

Proof. Let $f \in \mathcal{F}_{n,d}$ and suppose that a PSM protocol for f^{affine} is given. We show a PSM protocol $\Pi_{G^{\mathrm{affine}}_f}$ for G^{affine}_f in Fig. 2.

First, we see the correctness of $\Pi_{G^{\mathrm{affine}}_f}$. Let $(a, b) \in \{0, 1\}^2$, $\boldsymbol{x} = (x_i)_{i \in [n]} \in [d]^n$, and $\boldsymbol{y} = (y_i)_{i \in [n]} \in \{0, 1\}^n$. It follows from the correctness of $\Pi_{f^{\mathrm{affine}}}$ that

$$\hat{z}_j = f^{\mathrm{affine}}(\kappa_j, \lambda_j; (x_i)_{i \in [n]}) = \kappa_j f(\boldsymbol{x}) + \lambda_j$$

for each $j \in [s_0]$, and hence that $\hat{z} = h_0(f(\boldsymbol{x}), \rho)$. Therefore, we have that

$$w = H(f(\boldsymbol{x}), a, b, \boldsymbol{y}) = a f(\boldsymbol{x}) \prod_{i \in [n]} y_i + b = G^{\mathrm{affine}}_f(a, b; (x_i, y_i)_{i \in [n]}).$$

Next, we see the privacy of $\Pi_{G^{\mathrm{affine}}_f}$. The privacy of the DARE $\hat{H}$ ensures the existence of a simulator $\mathsf{Sim}_{\hat{H}}$ that simulates the distribution of $(\hat{z}, \hat{a}, \hat{b}, (\hat{y}_i)_{i \in [n]})$ from $w = H(f(\boldsymbol{x}), a, b, \boldsymbol{y})$. Furthermore, the privacy of $\Pi_{f^{\mathrm{affine}}}$ ensures the existence of a simulator $\mathsf{Sim}_{f^{\mathrm{affine}}}$ that simulates the distribution of $(\mu_i)_{i \in [n]}$ from

Notations.

 – Let $\Pi_{f^{\text{affine}}} = (\text{Gen}_{f^{\text{affine}}}, \text{Enc}_{f^{\text{affine}}}, \text{Dec}_{f^{\text{affine}}})$ be a PSM protocol for f^{affine}.

 – Let $\hat{H} : \mathbb{F}_2^{n+3} \times \mathbb{F}_2^m \to \mathbb{F}_2^s$ be a DARE of H. That is,

$$\hat{H}((z, a, b, (y_i)_{i \in [n]}), \rho) = (h_0(z, \rho), h_1(a, \rho), h_2(b, \rho), (h_i'(y_i, \rho))_{i \in [n]})$$

for any $z, a, b, y_i \in \mathbb{F}_2$ and $\rho \in \mathbb{F}_2^m$. In particular, $h_0(z, \rho)$ can be written as $\kappa(\rho)z + \lambda(\rho)$ for some functions $\kappa, \lambda : \mathbb{F}_2^m \to \mathbb{F}_2^{s_0}$ with $s_0 \leq s$. Let $\text{Dec}_{\hat{H}}$ denote the decoding function of $\hat{H}$.

$\text{Gen}()$.

 1. Choose $\rho \leftarrow_\$ \mathbb{F}_2^m$.

 2. For each $j \in [s_0]$, let κ_j and λ_j be the jth bit of $\kappa(\rho)$ and $\lambda(\rho)$, respectively.

 3. For each $j \in [s_0]$, run $r_j \leftarrow \text{Gen}_{f^{\text{affine}}}()$.

 4. Output $R = (\rho, (\kappa_j, \lambda_j, r_j)_{j \in [s_0]})$.

$\text{Enc}(i, ((a, b), x_i), R)$.

 1. If $i = 0$, compute $\hat{a} = h_1(a, \rho)$ and $\hat{b} = h_2(b, \rho)$.

 2. For each $j \in [s_0]$, compute $m_{i,j} = \text{Enc}_{f^{\text{affine}}}(i, ((\kappa_j, \lambda_j), x_i), r_j)$.

 3. Set $\mu_i = (m_{i,j})_{j \in [s_0]}$.

 4. Compute $\hat{y}_i = h_i'(y_i, \rho)$.

 5. Output $M_i = (\mu_i, \hat{a}, \hat{b}, \hat{y}_i)$.

$\text{Dec}(M_0, \ldots, M_{n-1})$.

 1. Parse μ_i into $(m_{i,j})_{j \in [s_0]}$

 2. For each $j \in [s_0]$, compute $\hat{z}_j = \text{Dec}_{f^{\text{affine}}}((m_{i,j})_{i \in [n]})$.

 3. Set $\hat{z} = (\hat{z}_j)_{j \in [s_0]}$.

 4. Output $w = \text{Dec}_{\hat{H}}(\hat{z}, \hat{a}, \hat{b}, (\hat{y}_i)_{i \in [n]})$.

Fig. 2. A PSM protocol for G_f^{affine}

$\hat{z}$. Therefore, we have a simulator that simulates the distribution of messages $((\mu_i)_{i \in [n]}, \hat{a}, \hat{b}, (\hat{y})_{i \in [n]})$ in $\Pi_{G_f^{\text{affine}}}$ from w.

We have that $\sum_{i \in [n]} |\mu_i| \leq s_0 \cdot \text{PSM}(f^{\text{affine}})$. Furthermore, $|\hat{a}| + |\hat{b}| + \sum_{i \in [n]} |\hat{y}_i| \leq s - s_0 \leq (s - s_0) \cdot \text{PSM}(f^{\text{affine}})$. Thus, the communication complexity of $\Pi_{G_f^{\text{affine}}}$ is at most $s \cdot \text{PSM}(f^{\text{affine}})$. $\qquad\square$

Since H is computed by an arithmetic formula of depth at most $\log(n + 3)$, it follows from Proposition 2 that $s = O(n^{1+\epsilon})$ for any constant $\epsilon > 0$. Thus, Lemmas 4 and 5 yield the following inequality.

Lemma 6. *For a parameter $c_n = O(2^n n^{1+\epsilon})$ where $\epsilon > 0$ is any constant,*

$$\text{PSM}(\mathcal{F}_{n,2d}^{\text{affine}}) \leq c_n \cdot \text{PSM}(\mathcal{F}_{n,d}^{\text{affine}}),$$

By applying Lemma 6 iteratively, we obtain the following proposition.

Proposition 12. *For $d_1 \leq d_2$,*

$$\text{PSM}(\mathcal{F}_{n,d_2}) \leq \text{PSM}(\mathcal{F}_{n,d_2}^{\text{affine}}) \leq (O(d_2/d_1))^{n+O(\log n)} \cdot \text{PSM}(\mathcal{F}_{n,d_1}^{\text{affine}}).$$

Now, we give a proof of Theorem 3. From Theorem 1, we have an inequality $\mathsf{PSM}(\mathcal{S}_{n,d}) \geq \mathsf{PSM}(\mathcal{F}_{n,d'})$ for $d' = \lfloor d/n \rfloor$. Since $d/d' = O(n)$, it follows from Proposition 12 that

$$\mathsf{PSM}(\mathcal{F}_{n,d'}) = \frac{\mathsf{PSM}(\mathcal{F}_{n,d'})}{\mathsf{PSM}(\mathcal{F}_{n,d'}^{\mathrm{affine}})} \cdot \mathsf{PSM}(\mathcal{F}_{n,d'}^{\mathrm{affine}}) \geq \alpha_{n,d'} \cdot n^{-O(n)} \cdot \mathsf{PSM}(\mathcal{F}_{n,d}),$$

which proves the lower bound in (5). On the other hand, we also have an inequality $\mathsf{PSM}(\mathcal{S}_{n,d}) \geq \mathsf{PSM}(\mathcal{F}_{d-1,n'+1})$ for $n' = \lfloor n/(d-1) \rfloor$. Since $n/n' = O(d)$, it similarly follows from Proposition 12 that $\mathsf{PSM}(\mathcal{F}_{d-1,n'+1}) \geq \alpha_{d-1,n'+1} \cdot d^{-O(d)} \cdot \mathsf{PSM}(\mathcal{F}_{d-1,n+1})$, which proves the lower bound in (6).

5.3   Discussion on the Tightness

We discuss the tightness of our bounds on $\mathsf{PSM}(\mathcal{S}_{n,d})$ and $\mathsf{CDS}(\mathcal{S}_{n,d})$. In the CDS case, the bounds (3) in Theorem 2 imply that $\mathsf{CDS}(\mathcal{S}_{n,d})$ is equal to $\mathsf{CDS}(\mathcal{F}_{n,d})$ up to a factor of $n^{O(n)}$. This shows the tightness up to a constant when $n = O(1)$. It is important to note that for CDS protocols with a constant number of parties, the efficiency gain achievable by focusing on the subclass $\mathcal{S}_{n,d}$ is limited to a constant-factor improvement. On the other hand, the bounds (4) imply that $\mathsf{CDS}(\mathcal{S}_{n,d})$ is determined by $\mathsf{CDS}(\mathcal{F}_{d-1,n+1})$ up to a multiplicative factor of $n^2 d^{O(d)}$. For example, if $d = \Theta(\log n/\log \log n)$, this remaining factor is polynomial in n and is asymptotically smaller than the dominant term $2^{O(\sqrt{d \log n} \log(d \log n))} = n^{\omega(1)}$ in the best known bound for $\mathsf{CDS}(\mathcal{F}_{d-1,n+1})$ [37].

In the PSM case, the gap between the upper and lower bounds in (5) is at most

$$\alpha_{n,d'}^{-1} \cdot \beta_n^{-1} = \frac{\mathsf{PSM}(\mathcal{F}_{n,d'}^{\mathrm{affine}})}{\mathsf{PSM}(\mathcal{F}_{n,d'})} \cdot n^{O(n)}.$$

It remains unclear whether the ratio $\mathsf{PSM}(\mathcal{F}_{n,d'}^{\mathrm{affine}})/\mathsf{PSM}(\mathcal{F}_{n,d'})$ is generally bounded above by a constant depending only on n (i.e., belongs to $O_n(1)$). Nevertheless, we conjecture that this ratio is small and independent of d. As a heuristic argument for this conjecture, consider the case where the computation model is restricted. For example, a formula computing f^{affine} requires only two additional gates compared to computing f, and the size of a truth table representing f^{affine} is only four times larger than that of f. Since the state-of-the-art PSM protocols in the respective models have polynomial communication complexity in the function representation size [4,15], the ratio between the communication complexities for f^{affine} and f is constant. Under this conjecture, the gap between $\mathsf{PSM}(\mathcal{S}_{n,d})$ and $\mathsf{PSM}(\mathcal{F}_{n,d})$ is at most a factor $O_n(1)$, implying a limitation on the efficiency of PSM specialized for $\mathcal{S}_{n,d}$ when $n = O(1)$. On the other hand, the gap of (6) is at most

$$\alpha_{d-1,n'+1}^{-1} \cdot \gamma_d^{-1} \cdot O(n^2) = \frac{\mathsf{PSM}(\mathcal{F}_{d-1,n'+1}^{\mathrm{affine}})}{\mathsf{PSM}(\mathcal{F}_{d-1,n'+1})} \cdot n^2 d^{O(d)}.$$

Under the same conjecture as above, $\mathsf{PSM}(\mathcal{S}_{n,d})$ is determined by $\mathsf{PSM}(\mathcal{F}_{d-1,n+1})$ up to a factor of $n^2 d^{O(d)}$. Since the best known bound for $\mathsf{PSM}(\mathcal{F}_{d-1,n+1})$ is dominated by $n^{d/2}$, this remaining factor is asymptotically smaller.

6   Applications to Related Models

Our new constructions of PSM and CDS for symmetric functions lead to improvements over the state-of-the-art results in related models. Our PSM protocol can be extended to ad hoc PSM [11,14] and it improves the best known complexity for symmetric functions [2]. Our CDS protocol implies a new efficient secret sharing scheme for multipartite uniform access structures.

6.1   Ad Hoc PSM for Symmetric Functions

A k-out-of-n ad hoc PSM protocol [14] is an advanced notion of an n-party PSM protocol. In this model, a subset S of k input parties, where S is not known in advance, actually send messages and the referee is able to evaluate a k-input function f on the subset of inputs $(x_i)_{i \in S}$. The formal definition is provided in the full version [22].

It is natural in this ad-hoc setting to assume that f is a symmetric function independent of the identities of the parties. There exist incomparable compilers from a k-party PSM protocol for $f \in \mathcal{S}_{k,d}$ to an ad hoc PSM protocol for f [2,19]. The resulting communication complexity are $O(kn) \cdot \mathsf{PSM}(f)$ [2,19] or $O(k^5 \log n) \cdot \mathsf{PSM}(f)$. However, the symmetry of f was not exploited and the trivial bound $\mathsf{PSM}(f) \leq \mathsf{PSM}(\mathcal{F}_{n,d})$ was applied in [2]. Consequently, the previous upper bounds suffer from an exponential factor of $d^{n/2}$. On the other hand, if our improved upper bound on symmetric functions is applied, then we obtain an ad hoc PSM protocol Π for $f \in \mathcal{S}_{k,d}$ such that

- $\mathsf{Comm}(\Pi) = O(k^3 n) \cdot \mathsf{PSM}(\mathcal{F}_{d-1,k+1}) = O((k+1)^{\frac{d+5}{2}} d^3 n)$; or
- $\mathsf{Comm}(\Pi) = O(k^7 \log n) \cdot \mathsf{PSM}(\mathcal{F}_{d-1,k+1}) = O((k+1)^{\frac{d+13}{2}} d^3 \log n)$.

In addition to this immediate application, we propose a direct construction of ad hoc PSM for symmetric functions without using the generic compiler of [2,19]. This achieves communication complexity $O((k+1)^{\frac{d+3}{2}} d^3 n)$, further improving the first upper bound mentioned above by a factor of k.

Recall that in our PSM protocol for symmetric functions, we build a histogram in which each bin j has the value $\sum_{i \in [n]} \delta_{j,i}$, where $\delta_{j,i} = 1$ if $x_i = j$ and 0 otherwise. Then, the parties run a PSM protocol for the selection function Sel_n to reveal only the message corresponding to $\sum_{i \in [n]} \delta_{j,i}$. In the ad-hoc setting where a set S of k parties participate, we have to reveal the message corresponding to $\sum_{i:P_i \in S} \delta_{j,i}$. This issue can be easily addressed by a method of sharing dummy messages for $P_i \notin S$, inspired by [14,25]: we distribute a message that $P_i \notin S$ would compute on input $\delta_{j,i} = 0$ in the protocol for Sel_n, using a k-out-of-n secret sharing scheme. This ensures that the missing $n - k$ messages are filled with the dummy messages so that the referee can proceed to the decoding phase. However, since the protocol for Sel_n requires $O(n^2)$ communication, this results in $O(kn^2) \cdot \mathsf{PSM}(\mathcal{F}_{d-1,k+1})$, which does not yield improvement. To address this issue, we observe that the value $\sum_{i \in [n]} \delta_{j,i}$

of each bin is always at most k in the ad-hoc setting, since only k parties contribute to the histogram. Consequently, we can reduce an ad hoc PSM protocol to a *restricted version* of the selection function, $\mathsf{Sel}_{k,n}$. Specifically, define a subset $S \subseteq \{0,1\}^{k+1} \times \{0,1\}^n$ as $S = \{(\boldsymbol{m}, (x_i)_{i \in [n]}) : \sum_{i \in [n]} x_i \leq k\}$. Define a partial function $\mathsf{Sel}_{k,n} : \{0,1\}^{k+1} \times \{0,1\}^n \to \{0,1,\star\}$ defined over S as $\mathsf{Sel}_{k,n}(\boldsymbol{m}; (x_i)_{i \in [n]}) = \boldsymbol{m}[s]$ for any $(\boldsymbol{m}, (x_i)_{i \in [n]}) \in S$, where $s = \sum_{i \in [n]} x_i \leq k$ and $\boldsymbol{m}[s]$ is the sth element of $\boldsymbol{m}$. By exploiting the reduced complexity of $\mathsf{Sel}_{k,n}$, we construct a PSM protocol with improved communication complexity $O(kn)$ (see the full version [22] for details). The overall communication complexity of our ad hoc protocol for symmetric functions becomes $O(k^2 n) \cdot \mathsf{PSM}(\mathcal{F}_{d-1,k+1})$. The formal proof is provided in the full version [22].

Theorem 4. *For any $f \in \mathcal{S}_{k,d}$, there exists a k-out-of-n ad hoc PSM protocol Π for f such that* $\mathsf{Comm}(\Pi) = O(k^2 n) \cdot \mathsf{PSM}(\mathcal{F}_{d-1,k+1}) + O(kd \log n)$. *In particular, it holds that* $O((k+1)^{\frac{d+3}{2}} d^3 n)$.

6.2   Secret Sharing for Multipartite Uniform Access Structures

Let $\{\mathsf{P}_0, \ldots, \mathsf{P}_{n-1}\}$ be the set of n parties. We say that a collection Γ of subsets of parties is an access structure if it is monotonically increasing, that is, $A \in \Gamma$ implies $B \in \Gamma$ for any $A \subseteq B$. A secret sharing scheme for an access structure Γ divides a secret s into n shares $(v_i)_{i \in [n]}$ such that a subset of shares $(v_i)_{i \in A}$ can recover s if $A \in \Gamma$ and reveals nothing if $A \notin \Gamma$. We defer the formal definition to the full version [22].

We say that an access structure Γ is k-uniform if $A \in \Gamma$ for any set A with $|A| > k$ and $A \notin \Gamma$ for any set A with $|A| < k$. Thus, Γ uniquely corresponds to a function $g_\Gamma : [n]^k \to \{0,1\}$ defined as $g_\Gamma(i_0, \ldots, i_{k-1}) = 1$ if and only if $A = \{\mathsf{P}_{i_0}, \ldots, \mathsf{P}_{i_{k-1}}\} \in \Gamma$. It was shown in [2] that a k-party CDS protocol Π for g_Γ implies a secret sharing scheme for Γ whose share size is approximately bounded above by $\mathsf{CDS}(g_\Gamma)$. However, while $g_\Gamma \in \mathcal{S}_{k,n}$, exploiting its symmetry cannot yield an improvement since $k < n$. Consequently, the share size for Γ incurs a sub-exponential factor $nk2^{\tilde{O}(\sqrt{k \log n})}$ in k.

We show that our construction of CDS specialized for symmetric functions is effective for a special class of *multipartite* uniform access structures. We say that an access structure Γ is d-partite if there exists a partition $(S_i)_{i \in [d]}$ of the set of n parties such that $A \in \Gamma$ implies $\sigma(A) \in \Gamma$ for any permutation σ that preserves the partition, i.e., $\sigma(S_i) = S_i$ for all i. In particular, as Γ is monotonically increasing, it is uniquely determined by the set of *minimal* vectors in $\mathcal{P}_\Gamma = \{(|A \cap S_i|)_{i \in [d]} : A \in \Gamma\}$. Our key observation is that a d-partite k-uniform access structure Γ uniquely corresponds to a function $h_\Gamma : [d]^k \to \{0,1\}$ defined as

$$A = \{\mathsf{P}_{i_0}, \ldots, \mathsf{P}_{i_{k-1}}\} \in \Gamma \iff h_\Gamma(j_0, \ldots, j_{k-1}) = 1 \tag{10}$$

where each $j_h \in [d]$ denotes the part to which P_{i_h} belongs, i.e., $i_h \in S_{j_h}$. Note that $h_\Gamma \in \mathcal{S}_{k,d}$. We show a transformation from a CDS protocol for h_Γ to a secret sharing scheme for a d-partite k-uniform access structure Γ. Since $h_\Gamma = g_\Gamma$ when $d = n$, this generalizes the previous transformation [2]. The formal proof is given in the full version [22].

Theorem 5. *Let Γ be a d-partite k-uniform access structure over the set of n parties. Then, there exists a secret sharing scheme for Γ whose share size is* $O(nk \cdot \mathsf{CDS}(\mathcal{S}_{k,d}) + kn^2 \log n) = nk^3 2^{\widetilde{O}(\sqrt{d \log k})} + O(kn^2 \log n).$

As a comparison, one can also construct a secret sharing scheme for a d-partite k-uniform access structure Γ, by applying a folklore method inspired by [34] (see, e.g., [23] for a formal description). This construction results in the share size proportional to the total number of minimal vectors in $\mathcal{P}_\Gamma$. Since Γ is d-partite and k-uniform, this number is at most the total number of integer vectors $(x_i)_{i \in [n]}$ such that $x_i \geq 0$ for all i and $\sum_{i \in [d]} x_i \in \{k, k+1\}$. Thus, the share size of this construction is at most $O(k^{d-1})$. Our scheme improves this bound since the share size is asymptotically smaller than $k^{\widetilde{O}(\sqrt{d})}$.

Acknowledgements. This work was supported in part by JST CREST Grant Number JPMJCR22M1, JST K Program Grant Number JPMJKP24U3, and JSPS KAKENHI Grant Number 24K20775.

References

1. Applebaum, B., Arkis, B.: On the power of amortization in secret sharing: d-uniform secret sharing and CDS with constant information rate. ACM Trans. Comput. Theory **12**(4) (2020)
2. Wee, H.: Functional encryption for quadratic functions from k-Lin, revisited. In: Pass, R., Pietrzak, K. (eds.) TCC 2020. LNCS, vol. 12550, pp. 210–228. Springer, Cham (2020). https://doi.org/10.1007/978-3-030-64375-1_8
3. Applebaum, B., Holenstein, T., Mishra, M., Shayevitz, O.: The communication complexity of private simultaneous messages, revisited. J. Cryptol. **33**(3), 917–953 (2020)
4. Applebaum, B., Ishai, Y., Kushilevitz, E.: How to garble arithmetic circuits. In: 2011 IEEE 52nd Annual Symposium on Foundations of Computer Science, pp. 120–129 (2011)
5. Applebaum, B., Nir, O.: Upslices, downslices, and secret-sharing with complexity of 1.5^n. In: Malkin, T., Peikert, C. (eds.) CRYPTO 2021. LNCS, vol. 12827, pp. 627–655. Springer, Cham (2021). https://doi.org/10.1007/978-3-030-84252-9_21
6. Applebaum, B., Vasudevan, P.N.: Placing conditional disclosure of secrets in the communication complexity universe. J. Cryptol. **34**(2), 11 (2021)
7. Assouline, L., Liu, T.: Multi-party PSM, revisited: improved communication and unbalanced communication. In: Theory of Cryptography, pp. 194–223 (2021)
8. Ball, M., Randolph, T.: A note on the complexity of private simultaneous messages with many parties. In: 3rd Conference on Information-Theoretic Cryptography, ITC 2022, pp. 7:1–7:12 (2022)
9. Beimel, A., Farràs, O., Lasri, O.: Improved polynomial secret-sharing schemes. In: Theory of Cryptography, pp. 374–405 (2023)

10. Beimel, A., Farràs, O., Mintz, Y., Peter, N.: Linear secret-sharing schemes for forbidden graph access structures. IEEE Trans. Inf. Theory **68**(3), 2083–2100 (2022)
11. Beimel, A., Gabizon, A., Ishai, Y., Kushilevitz, E.: Distribution design. In: Proceedings of the 2016 ACM Conference on Innovations in Theoretical Computer Science, pp. 81–92. ITCS 2016 (2016)
12. Beimel, A., Gabizon, A., Ishai, Y., Kushilevitz, E., Meldgaard, S., Paskin-Cherniavsky, A.: Non-interactive secure multiparty computation. In: Garay, J.A., Gennaro, R. (eds.) CRYPTO 2014. LNCS, vol. 8617, pp. 387–404. Springer, Heidelberg (2014). https://doi.org/10.1007/978-3-662-44381-1_22
13. Beimel, A., Ishai, Y., Kumaresan, R., Kushilevitz, E.: On the cryptographic complexity of the worst functions. In: Theory of Cryptography, pp. 317–342 (2014)
14. Beimel, A., Ishai, Y., Kushilevitz, E.: Ad hoc PSM protocols: secure computation without coordination. In: Coron, J.-S., Nielsen, J.B. (eds.) EUROCRYPT 2017. LNCS, vol. 10212, pp. 580–608. Springer, Cham (2017). https://doi.org/10.1007/978-3-319-56617-7_20
15. Beimel, A., Kushilevitz, E., Nissim, P.: The complexity of multiparty PSM protocols and related models. In: Nielsen, J.B., Rijmen, V. (eds.) EUROCRYPT 2018. LNCS, vol. 10821, pp. 287–318. Springer, Cham (2018). https://doi.org/10.1007/978-3-319-78375-8_10
16. Beimel, A., Othman, H., Peter, N.: Quadratic secret sharing and conditional disclosure of secrets. IEEE Trans. Inf. Theory **69**(11), 7295–7316 (2023)
17. Beimel, A., Peter, N.: Optimal linear multiparty conditional disclosure of secrets protocols. In: Peyrin, T., Galbraith, S. (eds.) ASIACRYPT 2018. LNCS, vol. 11274, pp. 332–362. Springer, Cham (2018). https://doi.org/10.1007/978-3-030-03332-3_13
18. Benhamouda, F., Krawczyk, H., Rabin, T.: Robust non-interactive multiparty computation against constant-size collusion. In: Katz, J., Shacham, H. (eds.) CRYPTO 2017. LNCS, vol. 10401, pp. 391–419. Springer, Cham (2017). https://doi.org/10.1007/978-3-319-63688-7_13
19. Ciampi, M., Goyal, V., Ostrovsky, R.: Threshold garbled circuits and ad hoc secure computation. In: Canteaut, A., Standaert, F.-X. (eds.) EUROCRYPT 2021. LNCS, vol. 12698, pp. 64–93. Springer, Cham (2021). https://doi.org/10.1007/978-3-030-77883-5_3
20. Cleve, R.: Towards optimal simulations of formulas by bounded-width programs. In: Proceedings of the Twenty-Second Annual ACM Symposium on Theory of Computing, pp. 271–277 (1990)
21. David, T.B., Paskin-Cherniavsky, A.: Tight lower bounds and new upper bounds for evolving CDS. Cryptology ePrint Archive, Paper 2025/292 (2025). https://eprint.iacr.org/2025/292
22. Eriguchi, R.: On the communication complexity of PSM and CDS for symmetric functions. Cryptology ePrint Archive, Paper 2025/1959 (2025). https://eprint.iacr.org/2025/1959
23. Eriguchi, R., Kunihiro, N., Nuida, K.: Multiplicative and verifiably multiplicative secret sharing for multipartite adversary structures. Des. Codes Crypt. **91**(5), 1751–1778 (2023)
24. Eriguchi, R., Ohara, K., Yamada, S., Nuida, K.: Non-interactive secure multiparty computation for symmetric functions, revisited: more efficient constructions and extensions. In: Malkin, T., Peikert, C. (eds.) CRYPTO 2021. LNCS, vol. 12826, pp. 305–334. Springer, Cham (2021). https://doi.org/10.1007/978-3-030-84245-1_11

25. Eriguchi, R., Shinagawa, K.: Efficient multiparty private simultaneous messages for symmetric functions. In: Advances in Cryptology – EUROCRYPT 2025, pp. 240–269 (2025)
26. Farràs, O., Martí-Farré, J., Padró, C.: Ideal multipartite secret sharing schemes. J. Cryptol. 25(3), 434–463 (2012)
27. Feige, U., Kilian, J., Naor, M.: A minimal model for secure computation (extended abstract). In: Proceedings of the Twenty-Sixth Annual ACM Symposium on Theory of Computing, STOC 1994, pp. 554–563 (1994)
28. Gay, R., Kerenidis, I., Wee, H.: Communication complexity of conditional disclosure of secrets and attribute-based encryption. In: Gennaro, R., Robshaw, M. (eds.) CRYPTO 2015. LNCS, vol. 9216, pp. 485–502. Springer, Heidelberg (2015). https://doi.org/10.1007/978-3-662-48000-7_24
29. Gertner, Y., Ishai, Y., Kushilevitz, E., Malkin, T.: Protecting data privacy in private information retrieval schemes. J. Comput. Syst. Sci. 60(3), 592–629 (2000)
30. Ishai, Y., Kushilevitz, E.: Private simultaneous messages protocols with applications. In: Proceedings of the Fifth Israeli Symposium on Theory of Computing and Systems, pp. 174–183 (1997)
31. Ishai, Y.: Randomization techniques for secure computation. Secure Multi-Party Comput. 10, 222–248 (2013)
32. Ishai, Y., Kumaresan, R., Kushilevitz, E., Paskin-Cherniavsky, A.: Secure computation with minimal interaction, revisited. In: Gennaro, R., Robshaw, M. (eds.) CRYPTO 2015. LNCS, vol. 9216, pp. 359–378. Springer, Heidelberg (2015). https://doi.org/10.1007/978-3-662-48000-7_18
33. Ishai, Y., Kushilevitz, E., Paskin, A.: Secure multiparty computation with minimal interaction. In: Rabin, T. (ed.) CRYPTO 2010. LNCS, vol. 6223, pp. 577–594. Springer, Heidelberg (2010). https://doi.org/10.1007/978-3-642-14623-7_31
34. Ito, M., Saito, A., Nishizeki, T.: Secret sharing scheme realizing general access structure. Electron. Commun. Jpn. (Part III: Fundam. Electron. Sci.) 72(9), 56–64 (1989)
35. Liu, T., Vaikuntanathan, V.: Breaking the circuit-size barrier in secret sharing. In: Proceedings of the 50th Annual ACM SIGACT Symposium on Theory of Computing, STOC 2018, pp. 699–708 (2018)
36. Liu, T., Vaikuntanathan, V., Wee, H.: Conditional disclosure of secrets via non-linear reconstruction. In: Katz, J., Shacham, H. (eds.) CRYPTO 2017. LNCS, vol. 10401, pp. 758–790. Springer, Cham (2017). https://doi.org/10.1007/978-3-319-63688-7_25
37. Liu, T., Vaikuntanathan, V., Wee, H.: Towards breaking the exponential barrier for general secret sharing. In: Nielsen, J.B., Rijmen, V. (eds.) EUROCRYPT 2018. LNCS, vol. 10820, pp. 567–596. Springer, Cham (2018). https://doi.org/10.1007/978-3-319-78381-9_21
38. Nuida, K.: Improved private simultaneous messages protocols for symmetric functions with universal reconstruction. Cryptology ePrint Archive, Paper 2025/992 (2025). https://eprint.iacr.org/2025/992
39. Shamir, A.: How to share a secret. Commun. ACM 22(11), 612–613 (1979)
40. Shinagawa, K., Eriguchi, R., Satake, S., Nuida, K.: Private simultaneous messages based on quadratic residues. Des. Codes Crypt. 91(12), 3915–3932 (2023)

Fast and Efficient Perfectly Secure Network-Agnostic Secure Computation

Gilad Asharov[1]([✉])(iD), Fatima Elsheimy[2](iD), and Gilad Stern[3](iD)

[1] Bar-Ilan University, Ramat Gan, Israel
`Gilad.Asharov@biu.ac.il`
[2] Yale University, Connecticut, USA
`Fatima.Elsheimy@yale.edu`
[3] Tel-Aviv University, Tel Aviv, Israel
`giladstern@tauex.tau.ac.il`

Abstract. Secure multiparty computation (MPC) enables mutually distrustful parties to jointly compute over private data without revealing their inputs. While protocols in both synchronous and asynchronous settings have achieved impressive efficiency in either communication or round complexity, combining the two has remained challenging. Only recently, Abraham, Asharov, Patil, and Patra (Eurocrypt'23, Eurocrypt'24) achieved protocols that combine low communication complexity $(O((Cn + Dn^2 + n^4)\log n))$ with fast execution ($O(D)$ rounds) in both synchronous and asynchronous models, for circuits of size C and depth D, in the perfect setting with optimal resilience. However, both protocols crucially assume advanced knowledge of the network type and are fragile under mismatched or varying network conditions.

The fragility of protocols under mismatched network assumptions highlights the need for *network-agnostic* MPC, where security and correctness are preserved in both synchronous and asynchronous settings. Yet, all known perfect network-agnostic protocols incur $\Omega(D+n)$ rounds and communication complexity in the order of n^3 or higher, far worse than their network-specific counterparts.

In this work, we present the first network-agnostic MPC protocol in the perfect security setting, achieving expected round complexity $O(D)$. Our protocol has expected communication complexity $O((Cn^2 + Dn^2 + n^4)\log n)$, improving on the state of the art by a factor of n^3 for small circuits and n^2 for large circuits in communication, in addition to an additive $O(n)$ improvement in round complexity. Our design departs from the

Asharov is supported by the European Union (ERC, FTRC, 101043243). Views and opinions expressed are, however, those of the author(s) only and do not necessarily reflect those of the European Union or the European Research Council. Neither the European Union nor the granting authority can be held responsible for them.
Fatima Elsheimy is supported by the Center for Algorithms, Data, and Market Design at Yale (CADMY).
Gilad Stern is supported in part by ISF 2338/23, AFOSR Award FA9550-23-1-0387, and AFOSR Award FA9550-23-1-0312. Any opinions, findings and conclusions or recommendations expressed in this material are those of the author(s) and do not necessarily reflect the views of the United States Government or AFOSR.

J. Daemen and E. Thomé (Eds.): EUROCRYPT 2026, LNCS 16543, pp. 185–213, 2026.
https://doi.org/10.1007/978-3-032-25324-8_7

structure of prior network-agnostic protocols and introduces several new technical ideas that enable both round and communication efficiency.

1   Introduction

Secure multiparty computation (MPC) is widely regarded as one of the most significant accomplishments of modern cryptography. It enables mutually distrustful parties to jointly compute a function on private inputs without revealing them. In this work, we focus on *perfectly secure computation*. Secure computation protocols fall into two main categories—synchronous and asynchronous—depending on their assumptions about the network.

In the *synchronous* model, all messages between honest parties are delivered within a fixed, known delay bound. This bound must hold for the system's lifetime. Setting it is delicate: if too large, protocols waste time idling; if too small, messages may miss deadlines, risking non-termination or even security failures. In practice, establishing such a bound is difficult, especially under adversarial delays. The *asynchronous* model avoids this assumption: messages are guaranteed to arrive eventually, but with unknown and potentially unbounded delay. This allows protocols to adapt to adversarial conditions and ensures eventual termination even when message delivery is heavily manipulated. Since the introduction of MPC, research both in synchrony and asynchrony has followed two main tracks:

- **Linear-but-slow protocols:** Low communication complexity ($O(n \log n)$ per multiplication gate) but high number of rounds. For example, in the synchronous model, [16] achieves $O(Cn + n^3 \log n)$ communication and $\Omega(D + n^2)$ rounds for a circuit with C multiplication gates and depth D. Similar results hold in the asynchronous setting [15, 17, 42–45].
- **Fast-but-not-linear protocols:** Constant-round per multiplication (total $O(D)$) protocols [5, 12, 19, 28, 32, 37] but with high communication, e.g., $\Omega(Cn^3 + n^3 \log n)$ in the synchronous setting.

Achieving protocols that have both linear communication and are fast – remained elusive. Only recently, two protocols have emerged that achieve both efficiency and speed: $O((Cn + Dn^2 + n^4) \log n)$ communication with $O(D)$ rounds in expectation. This is true for the synchronous setting [2] and the asynchronous setting [3, 4].

A Unified Model. Both synchrony and asynchrony models have drawbacks. The synchronous setting is idealized, demanding round-by-round coordination and an accurate delay bound, which is hard to guarantee even with external clocks. The asynchronous setting, though more realistic, is often viewed as overly pessimistic, and it offers weaker security: perfect synchronous MPC tolerates up to $t < n/3$ corruptions, while perfect asynchronous MPC tolerates only $t < n/4$, for n participants, and those bounds are tight [6, 20].

Even worse, running a synchronous protocol over an asynchronous network provides no guarantees at all: the protocol may fail to terminate, leak secrets, and even correctness can be lost. This is true even if run over a synchronous network, but with an inaccurate bound delay. In contrast, running an asynchronous protocol over a synchronous network does work but does not provide the same level of security as synchronous protocols do. It works only with the weaker $t < n/4$ threshold instead of $t < n/3$, and does not necessarily take the inputs of all honest parties into account.

This leads us to the notion of *network agnostic protocols* – the same code works on both networks without knowing the type of the network [7,9–11,21–23,34]. This eliminates the need to commit to one model in advance. When the delay bound is accurate, such a protocol matches the higher resilience of synchrony. If the delay bound is inaccurate, it degrades gracefully, retaining asynchronous guarantees. In a truly asynchronous network, it naturally provides the robustness of the asynchronous model.

However, designing such a protocol is highly challenging. As opposed to the synchronous or asynchronous setting, all known network agnostic protocols are *not fast* and *not linear*. That is, no protocol is optimal in even one of the dimensions. The protocol of [9] achieves $\Omega(Cn^4 \log n + n^7 \log n)$ communication and $\Omega(D + n)$ rounds. On the other hand, the work of [13] shows a computational MPC and distributed key generation protocols while having $O(n + D)$ rounds and $\tilde{O}(Cn^2)$ communication. This motivates the central questions:

> *Is it possible to construct a fast network-agnostic protocol?*
>
> *Is it possible to construct a fast and linear network-agnostic protocol?*

1.1 Our Results

We answer the first question in the affirmative, achieving the first network-agnostic fast protocol. In addition, we make significant progress towards answering the second:

Theorem 1.1. *Let $n > 3t_s + t_a$ and $t_s \geq t_a$, and assuming $t_s, t_a \in \Theta(n)$. There exists a single network-agnostic multiparty computation protocol for n parties such that for computing a circuit with C multiplication gates and depth-D such that: (1) Communication: The protocol has $O((Cn^2 + Dn^2 + n^4) \log n)$ expected communication complexity; (2) $O(D)$ expected rounds; (3) Resilient to t_s corrupted parties in synchronous networks; (4) and resilient to t_a corrupted parties in asynchronous networks.*

We note that even using many insights from previous synchronous, asynchronous, and network-agnostic protocols, the second question remains open: Is it possible to achieve linear communication per gate? If so, is it possible to do so while keeping the round complexity $O(D)$? Solving this question remains interesting, and would allow us to close the gap between network-agnostic protocols and their synchronous and asynchronous counterparts.

Technically, our protocol contains a different structure compared to previous network-agnostic protocols (e.g., [9,10]), allowing us to use cheaper alternatives for reliably broadcasting messages and agreeing on a core set of inputs asynchronously. This allows us to drastically reduce the use of consensus throughout the whole protocol.

A Limitation. Our protocol does not provide the exact same security guarantee as the asynchronous protocol of [3,4]. Specifically, the latter tolerates $t < n/4$ corruptions and computes on an arbitrary set of $n - t$ (at least $3n/4$) inputs, chosen by the adversary; equivalently, the missing t inputs can be treated as default values. In contrast, in asynchronous executions our protocol may consider only $n - t_s$ (at least $2n/3$) inputs.

Previous works also faced this limitation (e.g., [9,13,41]). We prove that this limitation is *inherent*: every network-agnostic MPC protocol is vulnerable to the following adversarial behavior in asynchronous networks. An adversary can mimic a synchronous execution by delivering all its own messages within the delay bound while delaying those of t_s honest parties. From the protocol's perspective, this is indistinguishable from a synchronous execution where t_s parties are corrupted and remain silent. Consequently, the protocol must proceed with only $n - t_s$ inputs. More formally, we define as $(n - k)$-asynchronous MPC functionality a functionality in which parties send their inputs to the trusted party, and the adversary is allowed to exclude the input of k parties of its choice. In the full version of the paper, we show that:

Theorem 1.2. *Let $t_s \geq t_a$ be two parameters. There does not exist a network-agnostic protocol that is secure against t_s corrupted parties over synchronous network, and t_a corrupted parties theorem asynchronous network, and computes the $(n - t_a)$-asynchronous MPC functionality.*

1.2   Related Work

Synchronous MPC. The first feasibility results in synchronous MPC goes back to the seminal protocol of Ben-Or, Goldwasser and Wigderson [19] and Chaum, Crépeau, and Damgård [28]. Already [19], together with the broadcast protocol of [36] gives $O(D)$-round protocol, but not linear communication. Linear communication was first achieved in 2008 by [16], but with high round complexity of $\Omega(D + n^2)$. Many improvements followed along the years (e.g., [5,12,32,37,38]). The first linear and fast protocol was achieved only recently by [2], with $O((Cn + Dn^2 + n^4) \log n)$ expected communication complexity and $O(D)$ round complexity.

Asynchronous MPC. In asynchronous MPC, the first feasibility result is given by Ben-Or, Canetti and Goldreich [17]. Here, progress has been slower. The work of [17] obtained $\tilde{O}(n^6)$ per gate. [44,45] improved to $\tilde{O}(n^5)$ per gate, followed by [15] with $\tilde{O}(n^3)$ per gate, and [42,43] with $\tilde{O}(n^2)$ per gate. While the known techniques in 2008 by [16] were sufficient to achieve linear communication in synchrony, the same the techniques were not suffice to achieve a similar results in asynchrony. It took 15 more years to reach linear communication compared to the synchronous setting, with the work of [3], achieving the first asynchronous

MPC protocol with $O((Cn+Dn^2+n^5)\log n)$ expected communication complexity and $O(D + \log n)$ expected round complexity. The added $\log n$ term in the round complexity was removed by [4], which also reduced the expected communication to $O((Cn+Dn^2+n^4)\log n)$, matching the efficiency of the synchronous construction.

Network Agnostic. Network-agnostic protocols have been extensively studied since their introduction by Blum, Katz, and Loss [21]. We already mentioned the works of [9], and [41] and [13]. Blum, Katz, and Loss [21] presented a network-agnostic computational consensus protocol, used as an important building block in other protocols. They followed this work by constructing a computational atomic broadcast protocol [22]. Alexandru, Blum, Katz, and Loss [7] solved the highly related task of computational state machine replication, while allowing the network to arbitrarily switch between being synchronous and asynchronous. Network-agnostic MPC with non-perfect security guarantees has also been studied [11,23,34].

On Optimal Resilience. While $n \geq 3t+1$ is the optimal resilience in the synchronous setting and $n \geq 4t+1$ is optimal in the asynchronous setting, the optimal resiliency for network-agnostic constructions remains unclear. When $t_a = 0$, Theorem 1.1 yields a synchronous protocol with $n \geq 3t_s + 1$ participants, which is optimal for the synchronous case. Similarly, when $t_a = t_s$, the network-agnostic protocol of Theorem 1.1 specializes to an asynchronous protocol with $n \geq 4t_a + 1$, achieving optimal resilience in that regime as well. For other parameter choices of (t_s, t_a), however, the optimal bound is unknown. The work of [41] presents a protocol secure when $n > 2t_s + \max\{t_s, 2t_a\}$, which also coincides with $n \geq 3t_s + 1$ when $t_a = 0$ and with $n \geq 4t_a + 1$ when $t_s = t_a$, while offering better resilience for other values of (t_s, t_a). Their protocol, however, requires *exponential* communication, suggesting that characterizing the optimal resiliency for *efficient* network-agnostic protocols is a delicate task.

2   Technical Overview

In this section, we provide a technical overview of our work. We start with clarifying the model, following specifying the structure of our protocol and highlighting our different approach compared to previous works.

The Setting and Modeling. Before proceeding, we recall the setting. Our goal is to design a single MPC protocol in which the parties are unaware of the underlying network. In other words, the same "code" (next-message function) should satisfy the following when computing a function $(y_1, \ldots, y_n) = f(x_1, \ldots, x_n)$:

- *Synchronous:* If the network is synchronous, the protocol securely computes f while tolerating up to t_s corrupted parties. In this setting, the functionality receives inputs from all honest parties, and the adversary controls the inputs of the t_s corrupted parties.

- *Asynchronous:* If the network is asynchronous, the protocol securely computes f while tolerating up to t_a corrupted parties. In this setting, the adversary may exclude up to t_s honest parties from the computation, and the functionality computes f on (at least) $n - t_s$ inputs (see Theorem 1.2), where the adversary can decide which parties to exclude, and with the adversary also supplying the inputs of the t_a corrupted parties.

This already implies that the functionality behaves differently depending on whether the network is synchronous or asynchronous. Hence, the functionality must be aware of the network type, in contrast to the real protocol, where parties remain agnostic. This aligns with other modelings in the UC framework, e.g., where functionalities are aware of the identities of the corrupted parties. In Sect. 3.1, we describe how we model network-agnostic within UC and examine such issues in greater detail.

General Recipe for Network-Agnostic Protocols. We begin with a general recipe for constructing network-agnostic protocols. Suppose we are given a synchronous protocol Π_s for some task, and an asynchronous protocol Π_a for the same task. Clearly, Π_a can also run in a synchronous network, but this often yields weaker security and resilience guarantees. The guiding principle is therefore simple: attempt to run the stronger protocol Π_s; if it fails, fall back to Π_a. Concretely:

- **Synchrony:** Run Π_s, which attempts to compute the task with higher resilience (tolerating up to t_s corruptions). In fact, Π_s *has to be more robust than a regular synchronous protocol*, and provides some security guarantees even when running in an asynchronous network (e.g., it should guarantee privacy of the honest parties' inputs, even if it fails).
- **Agreement:** When Π_s is expected to terminate (this requires local clocks), parties verify whether they obtained outputs as prescribed. They then execute a network agnostic Byzantine agreement protocol to ensure consensus: either all parties confirm the successful completion of Π_s (and output the outputs they obtained), or they all agree to revert to the asynchronous protocol.
- **Asynchrony:** If parties revert to asynchrony, they switch to Π_a. Note that Π_a typically offers weaker guarantees, since $t_a < t_s$.

Indeed, previous works [9–11,41] followed this general recipe, but with significant redundancy. They applied the recipe separately to each component of the protocol—for example, verifiable secret sharing, the broadcast primitive, Beaver triple generation, and so on. While this produces network-agnostic building blocks that can operate independently and are interesting on their own merit, such modularity is unnecessary when the goal is to construct a full MPC protocol for general functionalities. As a result, the approach introduces a large number of redundant Byzantine agreement instances, which are computationally expensive. For example, the protocol of [9] contains $\Omega(n^3)$ such instances, each is expensive (at least $\Omega(n^4 \log n)$).

Our Approach and Concrete Instantiations. We follow two simple design principles:

1. **Whole over parts**: Instead of applying the general recipe separately to each building block, we step back and apply it to the *entire* MPC protocol as a whole.
2. **Async covers sync:** Any asynchronous protocol remains secure when executed in a synchronous network. In general MPC this may yield a suboptimal security threshold ($4t+1$ and not $3t+1$), but for many building blocks where stronger thresholds are attainable in asynchrony, the asynchronous protocol suffices.

Concretely, our baselines for the general recipe are as follows: Π_s, the synchronous protocol of [2]; and Π_a, the asynchronous protocol of [3], augmented with the improved verifiable secret sharing of [4]. As with most secret-sharing based MPC protocols, both follow a similar high-level structure:

1. A *preprocessing* phase, where the parties generate Beaver multiplication triples [14] independently of their inputs;
2. An *input-sharing phase*, where each party secret-shares their inputs to all others;
3. A *circuit-emulation phase*, where the circuit is computed gate-by-gate using the preprocessed triples;
4. An *output-reconstruction phase*.

Our MPC protocol, therefore, has the following high-level structure:

1. **A synchronous attempt:** We modify Steps 1 and 2 of Π_s so that they provide guarantees even in an asynchronous setting. This forms the crux of our technical contribution, detailed in Sect. 2.1.
2. **Agreement:** The parties execute an agreement protocol to determine whether they must fall back to the asynchronous setting. We discuss this step in Sect. 2.2.
3. **Asynchronous fallback:** If a fallback is required, the parties switch to Steps 1 and 2 of Π_a, operating with a lower threshold. Here, we make a direct use of Π_a [3,4].
4. **Circuit evaluation and output reconstruction:** Here we apply the "async covers sync" design principle, and uniformly adopt Steps 3 and 4 of Π_a. Importantly, both Π_s and Π_a enter these phases only after the "committal round" [35], at which point the output is already fixed for all parties, and this asynchronous sub-protocol actually provides the higher security threshold needed for the synchronous protocol. We can therefore we can unify this step and just run its asynchronous variant.

2.1 The Synchronous Attempt

We proceed with a brief overview of the synchronous attempt, i.e., with Steps 1 and 2 in the synchronous protocol Π_s. We emphasize that the security of those steps has to be enhanced in the case where we actually run it in asynchrony, and we elaborate on that in Sects. 2.3 and 2.4.

Step 1–pre-processing. The goal of the pre-processing phase (Step 1) is to generate $|C|$ distinct multiplication triplets, where $|C|$ bounds the number of circuit multiplications. Each triplet consists of three degree-t_s polynomials $A(x), B(x), C(x)$ satisfying $C(0) = A(0) \cdot B(0)$. No party should know these polynomials outright; instead, each P_i should hold only the shares $A(i), B(i), C(i)$. This is achieved as follows:

  1. **Triplet extraction.** To ensure no party knows the final A, B, C, each party P_i first acts as a dealer, generating $A_i(x), B_i(x), C_i(x)$ of degree t_s, with $C_i(0) = A_i(0) \cdot B_i(0)$, and distributing shares to all P_j. A triplet extraction protocol then converts $O(M)$ such dealer-based triplets into $O(M)$ dealer-free triplets.
  2. **Dealer-based triplet generation.** Each party P_i distributes $A_i(x)$, $B_i(x), C_i(x)$ of degree t_s, with $C_i(0) = A_i(0) \cdot B_i(0)$ using the following two sub-components:
     (a) **Verifiable secret sharing (VSS).** The dealer P_i shares $A_i(x), B_i(x), C_i(x)$ of degree t_s. VSS ensures that the distributed values are consistent with degree-t_s polynomials.
     (b) **Multiplication verification with a dealer.** The dealer is supposed to pick those polynomials $A_i(x), B_i(x), C_i(x)$ with the constraint that $C_i(0) = A_i(0) \cdot B_i(0)$. The parties run a distributed zero-knowledge proof to verify that indeed $C_i(0) = A_i(0) \cdot B_i(0)$, where the dealer (who is the only one who actually knows A_i, B_i, C_i) is the prover. If verification fails, the parties substitute a default triplet.

Step 2: Input sharing. In Step 2 of Π_s, each party simply provides its input via VSS, and there is no reason to redesign an additional building block.

First, for triplet extraction, we can once again apply the "async covers synch" principle, as the asynchronous variant of this task suffices also in synchrony. Thus, enhancing Π_s in the asynchronous model reduces to strengthening two components: (1) the underlying VSS; and (2) the multiplication verification with a dealer, and we elaborate on those steps in Sects. 2.3 and 2.4. Note that both of these protocols are still required to maintain privacy in asynchrony, but are not required to terminate, even for an honest dealer. That is because if we are indeed in asynchrony, there will be a fallback to Π_a if the number of successful dealers is not large enough.

2.2   Agreement

We proceed with an overview of Step 2 in our entire MPC protocol. An important goal in our construction is avoiding the many uses of Byzantine Agreement (BA) in all building blocks. The main insight that allows us to avoid multiple instances is the fact that in synchrony, each dealer should be able to eventually complete *all* of its tasks on time, including input sharing, triple sharing, and verification, as we just highlighted above. That is, we not only want to agree on whether to downgrade to asynchrony, but also agree on which dealers finished their task successfully. This step is the turning point of the computation, as it simultaneously determines:

1. Whether or not we stay in synchrony;
2. If we stay in synchrony, which parties successfully provided and completed their input-sharing. This, in turn, fixes the set of parties for whom a default input will be substituted.

Agreeing on such a set is exactly the task of "agreeing on a core set" (ACS) in asynchronous literature [17]. In our case, each party P_i inputs a set S_i, which includes all the dealers that finished their task (by the time they were supposed to, if indeed we are in synchrony). ACS attempts to find a core subset K, of cardinality at least $n - t_s$, that is included in the inputs of at least $n - t_s$ parties. If ACS succeeds in finding a set K of size exactly $n - t_s$, the execution proceeds along the synchronous route: we move on to circuit evaluation and output reconstruction. If, however, no such set is found (i.e., the largest core set has size $< n - t_s$), the protocol falls back to the asynchronous route, which means re-running the input-sharing and preprocessing, over asynchrony, but with a lower threshold. To integrate ACS into our protocol, we require that it satisfy two properties:

- **Synchronous network:** If the network is synchronous, then K must include all honest parties. In particular, by the time ACS is invoked, every honest party must have successfully completed its tasks (sharing and generating multiplication triplets) within the synchronous time bounds.
- **Asynchronous network:** If the network is asynchronous and no core set of size $n - t_s$ is found, then the protocol falls back to asynchrony, and we are fine.

  There is, however, a subtle case: the network may be asynchronous while the adversary delivers all messages promptly, causing the parties to believe the execution is synchronous. In this case, K is allowed not to include all honest parties (as in standard asynchronous MPC). The only requirement is that K contain at least $n - t_s$ parties, and that all parties hold valid shares and multiplication triplets corresponding to those parties in K, ensuring that the remainder of the computation proceeds successfully. This is exactly the case that complements Theorem 1.2.

The ACS Protocol. The ACS protocol that we run in this step is actually n parallel instances of BA. Each party P_i inputs 1 in the jth instance, if P_j as a dealer completed all its tasks. We employ the asynchronous parallel BA protocol of [31], which is also secure under synchrony (the protocol of [31] is statistically-secure, but we discuss how to make it perfect; see more details in the full version of the paper). We use [31] as it achieves an expected constant number of rounds.

Synchronous Network. In synchrony, we make sure that each honest dealer must successfully finish its task on time (i.e., a validity property). If indeed this is guaranteed, then for every honest P_j, all honest parties would input 1 in the jth instance of the parallel BA, and thus all honest parties would include P_j in the core set, as required.

Asynchronous Network. In asynchrony, parties agree on the output of the ACS protocol, but the core set might be either of size $\geq n - t_s$ or not; As mentioned, if indeed $\geq n - t_s$, the parties continue with the computation, resulting in the function being evaluated on a large enough set of inputs, as required. On the other hand, if the set is too small to be considered valid, all parties detect the fact that the network must be asynchronous, and fall back to an asynchronous MPC protocol. (We also remark that inside the asynchronous MPC there will be another invocation of an ACS protocol, as an inside building block of an asynchronous MPC protocol.)

Broadcast. Each one of the VSSes, multiplication triplets with a dealer, ends with a vote whether or not to accept the instance of the dealer or not. Such a vote is a consensus. We observe that we can delay those internal decisions to this global ACS, heavily reducing the number of BAs the protocol performs.

Not only that, we also reduce the costs of broadcasts in those VSSes and multiplication triplets with a dealer. Note that in synchronous there are two options for implementing broadcast:

1. An $O(n)$ round broadcast that we know an exact time when it ends;
2. An expected constant round protocol; here, it is unknown when exactly the broadcast would terminate (this is a random variable), and there is no simultaneous termination.

Both options complicate stuff for us; using the first option implies that we will spend $O(n)$ rounds on the synchronous route, and not achieve a fast protocol; The second option implies that we would not know when exactly to invoke the ACS protocol.

Here we once again apply the "async covers sync" design principle. We replace these broadcasts with reliable broadcast [24]: a weaker asynchronous primitive that, for corrupted senders, only guarantees that if some party receives a message, every party receives the same message. Note that (asynchronous!) reliable broadcast works with the stronger threshold of $n \geq 3t + 1$ (as opposed to $n \geq 4t + 1$ in general MPC), allowing us to use it in synchrony. The important property is that, if the sender is honest, then its message is guaranteed to arrive by a constant number of rounds. This allows us to work within known time bounds without waiting $O(n)$ rounds for synchronous broadcast to terminate.

Using reliable broadcast, all honest parties' messages will arrive on time, allowing honest dealers to make progress on schedule. After the ACS, parties know that they can continue waiting for broadcasts to arrive for all chosen dealers without worrying that they might wait indefinitely, even if they did not hear the messages on time.

We refer the reader to the full version of the paper for further details regarding the ACS.

2.3 Verifiable Secret Sharing

We now move back to Steps 2 of the synchronous protocol, while focusing on the security enhancement it has to guarantee to be run over asynchrony. Our baseline for this overview is the verifiable secret sharing of BGW [19], which proceeds in synchronous steps:

1. The dealer embeds its univariate input polynomial $h(x)$ in a bivariate polynomial $S(x, y)$ such that $S(x, 0) = h(x)$. It sends each party P_i the pair $f_i(x) = S(x, i)$, $g_i(x) = S(i, y)$.
2. The parties exchange sub-shares, i.e., P_i sends to P_j the pair $(f_i(j), g_i(j))$.
3. The parties verify that they received the correct sub-shares; if P_i did not receive the expected sub-shares from P_j, then it publicly complains by broadcasting $(\mathsf{NOK}, i, j, f_i(j), g_i(j))$. Note that it uses the shares it received from the dealer, and not from P_j.
4. If some party P_i falsely complains – the dealer publicly reveals the shares of that P_i.
5. The parties at the end of the protocol have to agree whether to accept the shares of that dealer: Each party should see that the dealer resolved all complaints, and whatever is publicly revealed is consistent with its private share.

What Might Go Wrong? We now analyze what might go wrong when running such a protocol in an asynchronous network.

1. When the dealer is honest, the parties are never supposed to complain about one another. However, in asynchronous networks, a party P_i might not receive the sub-share from an honest P_k, and thus complain about P_k by the time it considers as "the end of the round." In the original protocol, honest parties only complain about corrupted parties, and therefore, making these sub-shares public (as part of the complaint) does not reveal any extra information to the adversary. However, when both parties are honest, making these sub-share *public* leads to a privacy violation since this reveals sub-shares of honest parties.
2. Even when the dealer is honest, we might get non-termination. When the dealer is honest, all parties are supposed to receive messages by known given times, and proceed in the protocol accordingly. Running it in an asynchronous network, parties might receive messages too late, and not be able to proceed on time.
3. When the dealer is corrupted, we might not get the binding property (shares of the honest parties must all lie on the same polynomial). Binding is achieved by having *all* honest parties exchange subshares and having *all* complaints resolved on time. In an asynchronous execution, some honest parties might not talk to each other, and some complaints might not be heard on time.

This demonstrates why we need enhanced guarantees for this building block. Note that we do not need it to fully operate in asynchronous network. We just have to make sure that it does not completely fails.

Low Communication is Challenging. Apart from achieving the two key properties: completeness in the synchronous setting (i.e., an honest dealer can always complete its sharing, and at a fixed time) and binding in the asynchronous setting (i.e., a malicious dealer cannot equivocate, even if the network is synchronous)—our protocol must operate under a tighter resilience threshold while minimizing communication complexity, which is our primary efficiency objective. Our target is to achieve $O(Cn^2)$ communication. For context, in the BGW protocol, the parties exchange $O(n^2 \log n)$ bits over point-to-point channels and an additional $O(n^2 \log n)$ bits over the broadcast channel, resulting in a total communication cost of $O(n^4 \log n)$ when broadcast is realized via standard techniques. Thus, BGW incurs an overhead of $O(n^4 \log n)$ for the sharing of a single value!

To reduce this overhead, our construction relies on packing and batching. Packing means that we increase the degree of the shared polynomial, so that the same messages would encode more secrets, reducing the overall communication per secret; Batching means running multiple instances in parallel, while utilizing the same broadcast messages to resolve all instances simultaneously.

Packing is already nontrivial in asynchronous settings and becomes significantly more challenging under our stricter resilience constraints. To achieve amortization by a factor of n, we embed $t_a \in O(n)$ secrets along the x-dimension of a bivariate polynomial, thereby reducing the per-secret complexity to $O(n^3)$ per secret. We then show how to ensure binding for such packed values, and finally, how batching enables a further reduction to $O(n^2)$.

Ensuring Binding. To solve the issue of parties not talking to each other or complaints not being heard, we adopt techniques from asynchronous MPC [18, 25]. However, the main difficulty is that we are working here with a much tighter threshold.

- When two parties heard from one another, and they do agree with their shares, they broadcast (OK, i, j).
- When two parties heard from one another, but disagree - they send $(\mathsf{NOK}, i, j, f_i(j), g_i(j))$, including the subshares they received from the dealer.
- If a party P_i did not hear from P_j by the end of the round, it broadcasts $(\bot, i, j)$.

The dealer constructs a graph on n indices corresponding to the n parties, where two indices are connected if the associated parties broadcast approval of each other's subshares. Note that if there is a large enough clique of honest parties, then there is binding. However, since finding a clique in a graph is computationally inefficient, the dealer finds instead a "star" which is some approximation of clique [18,25], that suffices to bind a unique bivariate polynomial. Specifically, the dealer searches for a (C,D)-star, which is defined as follows:

(C, D)-Star. $C, D \subseteq [n]$ is a *Star* in G if (1) $C \subseteq D$; (2) $|C| \geq n - 2t$ and $|D| \geq n - t$; (3) for every $c \in C$ and $d \in D$, it holds that $(c, d) \in G$.

In our setting, $n > 3t_s + t_a$. Consequently, $|C| \geq n - 2t_s \geq t_s + t_a + 1$ and $|D| \geq n - t_s \geq 2t_s + t_a + 1$. These conditions are sufficient to bind a bivariate polynomial $S(x, y)$ of degree $t_s + t_a$ in x and t_s in y. Binding is guaranteed in the asynchronous setting (in which at most t_a parties are corrupted), since then $|D|$ provides at least $2t_s + 1 \geq t_s + t_a + 1$ honest parties to fix the x-dimension and $|C|$ ensures at least $t_s + 1$ honest parties to fix the y-dimension. By contrast, if we are in synchronous network (in which case at most t_s parties are corrupted), no binding is guaranteed.

To ensure binding in the synchronous setting, we require the dealer to *filter* the graph. Specifically, if any party sends a NOK message containing wrong information, the dealer removes that party from the graph by deleting all of its edges. Intuitively, this marks the party as faulty and excludes it from further consideration. The filtered graph is then the one in which we actually look for a star. We enforce that the dealer must find such a filtered graph of size at least $n - t_s$, which is guaranteed to exist in the synchronous setting when the dealer is honest. This ensures that if two honest parties receive inconsistent shares, everyone will observe that they complained about each other with differing values. Consequently, parties will reject the dealer's graph if it contains two parties with conflicting shares. Thus, under synchrony, we can be confident that any two honest parties that remain in the graph must have verified their consistency with each other. In this way, the honest parties that survive filtering collectively form a binding clique in the graph. Finally, because $n - 2t_s \geq t_s + t_a + 1$, these honest parties bind one another, ensuring that the bivariate is binding.

Ensuring Completeness. In the asynchronous setting, we abandon the requirement that every honest dealer must complete its sharing attempt. Even honest dealers may fail, in which case their inputs are excluded from the computation. Recall that to decide which inputs are used, the parties execute an agreement on a core-set protocol (see Sect. 2.2). If too few inputs are provided, all parties detect this and fall back to a purely asynchronous execution.

The synchronous setting is stricter: we must ensure that every honest dealer succeeds by a fixed time before running ACS. Note that only parties belonging to the star can be certain they hold correct shares. One might wonder why an honest party in the filtered graph but outside the star should not output its share. The reason is that, in synchrony, correctness hinges on timely NOK messages: honest parties issue NOK complaints on time, ensuring that no two honest parties with conflicting values coexist in the filtered graph. Thus, in synchrony, membership in the filtered graph suffices to ensure correctness. By contrast, in asynchrony, this guarantee no longer holds, and we must rely on the binding properties of the star. Since parties cannot distinguish whether the network is synchronous or asynchronous, they conservatively rely on the star to determine whether their shares are safe to output. This approach works, but there remains a subtle issue: the star has size $n - t_s$, which allows an honest dealer to leave up to t_s honest parties outside the star. To address this, we rely on *extended star*, which is another approximation of a clique (that can be found efficiently) that extends the set C to contain all honest parties [40].

No One is Left Behind. Additionally, we require that if an honest party outputs a share, then every honest party must output a share as well. This requirement is crucial in the circuit evaluation phase: if the dealer is malicious, we cannot allow a situation where some honest parties hold shares while others do not. To prevent this, parties that did not receive shares during the sharing protocol must be able to recover them with the help of others. The standard approach is that parties exchange subshares, followed by error correction to reconstruct the full shares. To correct errors introduced by corrupted parties, each corrupted position requires at least one additional honest party providing subshares. However, the star structure may not contain enough honest parties to guarantee this recovery. Indeed, we can only guarantee stars of size $n - t_s$, which in the worst case $n = 3t_s + t_a + 1$ gives $2t_s + t_a + 1$ parties holding shares. Reconstruction of shares of degree t_s requires $t_s + 1$ correct points, plus one extra honest point for every corrupted point. Thus, if up to t_s parties in the star are corrupted, we require a total of $3t_s + 1$ points to correct t_s errors. This exceeds the $2t_s + t_a + 1$ points guaranteed by the star, and therefore standard error correction alone does not suffice.

To avoid this complication, we force corrupted parties to either provide correct subshares or not provide subshares at all. This is done via an internal *incomplete* sharing protocol. That protocol only guarantees that the dealer provides shares on a low-degree polynomial, but does not guarantee that all parties receive shares. Parties then act as dealers in the *incomplete* sharing in order to provide subshares for the *complete* sharing protocols. Using this technique, we know that if some party is included in the star, the polynomial shared in its *incomplete* sharing must be consistent with all honest parties' shares in the star. This is because to be included in the star, a party must be connected to a large enough number of parties in the star (at least $t_s + t_a + 1$ honest parties in our case). These parties check that the shares received via the *incomplete* sharing are consistent with the ones sent by the dealer in the *complete* sharing. Since the *incomplete* sharing guarantees that all shares are on a low-degree polynomial, any party that receives values from that corrupted party's sharing will also be consistent with the polynomial defined by the honest parties that reported their consistency. Therefore, parties can reconstruct their own shares without the use of error correction. The incomplete sharing has an identical structure to the complete sharing, except that parties outside of the star do attempt to reconstruct their shares using error correction. As stated above, in synchrony, there aren't enough parties to always successfully correct the errors introduced by the corrupted parties, but parties can detect this event and decide not to output shares, making the protocol *incomplete*. In asynchrony, the number of faults is only t_a, meaning errors can always be corrected, and thus the incomplete sharing protocol is actually complete in asynchrony.

Batching. Since both protocols have the same structure, each one requires $O(n^2 \log n)$ bits of direct communication for sharing a bivariate polynomial. However, as we just saw in the complete sharing, each party acts as a dealer for a single instance of incomplete sharing, the total communication of the complete sharing protocol is $O(n^3 \log n)$ for sharing $O(n)$ secrets, resulting in $O(n^2 \log n)$ communication per secret on point-to-point communication channels.

In addition to that, parties broadcast n messages about each other OK/NOK/$\perp$, and the dealer broadcasts a constant number of sets of size $O(n)$ in each sharing. Doing this naïvely, this would require n broadcasts of size $O(n \log n)$, resulting in $O(n^4 \log n)$ total communication when using the protocol of [1] that has communication complexity $O((n^3 + Ln) \log n)$ for broadcasting messages of size L. To reduce the broadcast costs, we batch many instances of the VSS together, and utilize the broadcast messages only once to resolve all the instances simultaneously. We rely here on the techniques of [2]. Using this idea, the total broadcast costs remain $O(n^4 \log n)$ for any number of VSS instances, and thus when sharing X secrets, we get $O((n^4 + n^2 X) \log n)$ complexity, meaning that the complexity becomes $O(n^2 \log n)$ per secret when sharing $O(n^2)$ secrets, or $O(n)$ polynomials.

We refer the reader to Sects. 4, 5 for the full details.

2.4   Multiplication Triplets with a Dealer

The goal of the preprocessing phase of [2] is generating triples of polynomials $A(x), B(x), C(x)$ of degree t such that $A(0) \cdot B(0) = C(0)$, with the adversary only learning its own shares on the polynomials. This is done by first having each party P_i act as a dealer sharing its own triples $A_i(x), B_i(x), C_i(x)$, and proving that for those triples $A_i(0) \cdot B_i(0) = C_i(0)$. Sharing the triples is done using the previously described VSS protocol (for sharing A_i, B_i and C_i), and the proving that indeed $C_i(0) = A_i(0) \cdot B_i(0)$.

We adopt ideas from [2,3], and omit the ith subscript for clarity. For a given triple $(A(x), B(x), C(x))$ of degree-t polynomials, the parties define

$$E(x) := A(x) \cdot B(x) - C(x).$$

If the dealer has shared the polynomials consistently, then the constant term of $E(x)$ must be zero, since correctness requires $A(0) \cdot B(0) = C(0)$. The challenge is thus to verify, in zero knowledge, that this condition holds. The key idea is that the dealer shares the coefficients of E, letting the parties to compute linear combinations on those coefficient, and, in particular, evaluate E on different points. From the sharing of E, we design a protocol in which each P_k can privately recover $E(k)$, and verify that indeed $E(k) = A(k) \cdot B(k) - C(k)$. If this relation holds for $2t + 1$ points, then this binds E. Moreover, the parties publicly reveal $E(0)$ and verify that $E(0) = 0$. This guarantees that $A(0)B(0) = C(0)$. However, sharing E requires shares of $O(n)$ values, and therefore must be performed on a smaller rate than the complete VSS. The key point is that we do not need a full fledged VSS here – in particular, we do not care about reconstruction. We just have to know that there is binding.

Trivariate Sharing. To reduce the rate, we again adopt ideas from asynchronous computation [3]. We embed the coefficients of $E(x)$ into a family of *trivariate* polynomials.

The dealer now packs the coefficients of all such polynomials into a bounded number of trivariate polynomials $S_1, \cdots, S_\ell$, each of degree $t + k$ in the variables x, y, z, where $\ell \in O(1)$. Each trivariate polynomial can hold roughly $(k+1)^3$ coefficients, which suffices to accommodate all the degree-$2t$ constraints for $k \in O(n)$. Concretely, the trivariate would be of degree $t_s + t_a + 1$ in all three dimensions. Verifying the product relation is then reduced to checking that all these trivariate polynomials vanish at the origin, which a party can check locally (see the full version of the paper), and certifies that the dealer's triple satisfies $A(0) \cdot B(0) = C(0)$.

We are left to adapt the trivariate sharing of [3] to our tighter threshold. We proceed as follows.

Synchrony. In the synchronous track, recall that we have t_s corrupted participants, and a total of $n \geq 3t_s + t_a + 1$ participants. This is a higher threshold than the case of $n \geq 4t + 1$ with t corrupted parties as in [3]– we are left with $2t_s + t_a + 1$ honest parties which is less than $3t + 1$.

We therefore combine a restarting technique of [2] which is similar to the player elimination technique (i.e., excluding parties from the computation, once found as corrupted), with excluding $O(n)$ participants at once each time. Whenever a party P_k is excluded, its share becomes some default fixed value (say 0), and the dealer restarts the entire sharing process while choosing new polynomials under the restriction that the shares of P_k are 0s. Restarting allows to reduce the broadcast cost of "revealing" shares of parties, and keep the entire broadcast costs of the protocol low. We prove that after a constant number of restarts, an honest dealer will successfully complete the sharing.

Asynchrony. In the asynchronous track, recall that we have to make sure that the polynomial is binding when t_a parties are corrupted. We use the asynchronous techniques of [3] to bind the polynomial even when it has a high degree in more than one variable. Ideally, if one could find a "larger" star that includes more indices, one could bind the polynomial even though it has a high degree. A major insight of [3] is that if the graph is not "dense" enough (with many parties having very high degrees), a large star can be easily found. On the other hand, if the graph is dense, then using a *trivariate* polynomial can help bind the polynomial.

We refer the reader to the full version of the paper for the full details.

Organization. The rest of the paper is organized as follows. In Sect. 3 we review some preliminaries while some are provided in the full version of the paper. In Sect. 4 we provide the incomplete sharing, followed by the complete sharing in Sect. 5. We review the entire network-agnostic protocol in Sect. 6. Many details are deferred to the full version of the paper. Those include the ACS and multiplication triplets with a dealer.

3   Preliminaries

In this section, we provide an overview of the key setup and assumptions and delegate the rest to the full version of the paper.

3.1   Network and Adversarial Model

We assume a fully connected network of n parties, denoted as $\{P_1, \ldots, P_n\} = \mathcal{P}$, communicating through pairwise, point-to-point channels. Our model is *network agnostic*, meaning that it can be either synchronous or asynchronous, without parties being aware of the specific network type in operation. All parties have access to a global clock and to an upper bound Δ on message delays for synchronous executions. If the network is *synchronous*, the parties' clocks are synchronized and messages that are sent by an honest party at time t are delivered by time $t + \Delta$ to all honest parties. In contrast, if the network is *asynchronous*, the messages are delivered with an arbitrary but finite delay with the only guarantee that the messages are eventually delivered.

We consider a *computationally unbounded* adversary capable of corrupting a subset of the parties and causing them to behave arbitrarily during the execution of the protocol. We assume a *static* adversary, meaning that the adversary selects which parties to corrupt at the beginning of the protocol and cannot change this set during the protocol's execution. In the synchronous setting, the adversary can corrupt up to t_s parties, whereas in the asynchronous setting, up to t_a parties can be corrupted, where $t_a < t_s$.[1] For the corruption threshold, we assume $n > 3t_s + t_a$, which also implies that $t_s < n/3$ and $t_a < n/4$, the respective bounds for secure multi-party computation in synchronous and asynchronous networks. Finally, our protocols are defined over a finite field $\mathbb{F}$, with $|\mathbb{F}| > n$.

3.2   Modeling Network Agnostic Protocols in UC

We consider a protocol that is *network agnostic*, namely, the protocol has the same "next-message functions" when the underlying network is synchronous, or asynchronous. We now show how to model such protocols in the universal-composability (UC) framework due to Canetti [26]. We rely on several papers to simplify the exposition and the analysis.

Our formalization involves the following elements:

The Protocol. We consider a protocol Π between n parties. The parties communicate using a functionality (a trusted party) called Network, which is described below. Moreover, the system contains a global mode functionality that indicates whether the network is synchronous or asynchronous.

Global Mode Functionality. To model the "mode" (either synchronous/ asynchronous), we use the formalization of a global functionality, which we denote as

---

[1] Note that this does not limit the generality of the protocols, as otherwise one could always run an asynchronous protocol with the higher corruption threshold of t_a.

F_{Mode}. The mode functionality is a write-once register, which indicated whether the system is in synchronous or asynchronous. The adversary can write the network state to the register, and all functionalities can read from the register. Once read, no entity can ever write to it again. This is a global functionality that has only one instance. We emphasize that only the other functionalities in the system, and the adversary have access to this functionality. In particular, the honest parties do not have access to it. This is similar to the F_{Lib} functionality as in [27].

The Global Network Functionality. The Network is a functionality that has two modes: Synchronous communication mode, and asynchronous communication mode. Both modes have the same interface, and parties simply communicate by Send command (P_i sends a message to P_j over the communication channel) and Fetch (read the communication channel). In particular, asynchronous communication with eventual delivery is the $F_{\mathsf{ED-SMT}}$ functionality, and synchronous communication is the F_{SYN} functionality, as formalized in [39].

We emphasize that the network decides between the two functionalities (either $F_{\mathsf{ED-SMT}}$ or F_{SYN}) using the global F_{Mode}.

Notice, in particular, that the network functionality has the same interface and implements synchronous or asynchronous communication accordingly.

Clocks and Rounds in Synchronous Functionalities. In the synchronous mode, to implement F_{SYNC} (which is inside F_{Network}), the functionality also uses a clock, i.e., rounds are defined. Therefore, functionalities in the sync might also contain instructions like "in round 3, deliver to the parties the output X", while the communication with F_{Clock}.

Defining Functionalities with a Global Mode. As mentioned, a protocol Π has an access to F_{Network}, and the parties do not know whether they communicate in the synch mode, or asynch mode (while the adversary might know, or even determine, the mode of the computation). The same protocol might have a different input/output behavior depending on the network. In particular, the same protocol might exhibit different behaviors under different network types, but maintain the same interface. For example, synchronous MPC is computed on all honest parties' inputs (in addition to some corrupt parties' inputs), while asynchronous MPC is only expected to use a "large enough" set of inputs. Each party has the same interface to the functionality: sending an input, and (eventually) retrieving an output. The functionality, however, might have different interface with the adversary, depending on the mode.

As previously, this is modeled using the global F_{Mode} functionality. The functionalities check the network state and behave accordingly. Proceeding with the example of MPC, the functionality decides whether to take all inputs into consideration, or whether to take some core of parties into consideration.

Convention. Throughout the paper, we use that convention that each functionality has a variable mode which is either synch or asynch. In general, our statements are in the form of: "Protocol Π implements functionality $\mathcal{F}$ in the global F_{Network}-F_{Mode}-hybrid model".

Non-simultaneous Termination. In some of our synchronous protocols, termination is not guaranteed to occur simultaneously: for instance, certain parties may receive their outputs (and halt) in round r, while others may only do so in round $r+1$. For clarity of exposition, and to cleanly separate the "input–output" behavior of functionalities from other protocol-specific aspects, we model synchronous functionalities as if they terminate simultaneously. This simplification is justified by the work of Cohen et al. [30], which shows that broadcast without simultaneous termination can be treated as an ideal broadcast. Moreover, their compiler converts protocols that rely on simultaneous-termination hybrids into ones using non-simultaneous-termination hybrids, while preserving asymptotic round complexity. We note, however, that the compiler of [30] requires functionalities to follow the structure: (1) inputs from all parties; (2) leakage to the adversary; (3) outputs. Although we do not explicitly present our functionalities in this format, it is straightforward to see that they can be expressed in this way.

Session-Ids. For clarity we omit the specification of sessions ids (sids). We use the convention that: (1) All functionalities are always run in the background; (2) Whenever a party calls a functionality, it provides it with a session id; (3) Each functionality works only once for the same sid, and ignore a command if a previous output to that session-id was already provided; (4) We assume that a unique sid (and the same sid) is given to all parties in the main protocol, and in all invocations of sub-protocols, the calling function's sid is appended using an agreed-upon naming convention.

Notations Regarding Graphs. We use the standard definition of a degree in a graph: if $\mathbb{G} = (V, E)$ is an undirected graph, then $\deg_{\mathbb{G}}(v)$ is defined to be $|\{u \in V | (u, v) \in E\}|$, and $\Gamma(v)$ denote the neighbors of v, i.e., $\{u \mid (u, v) \in E\}$.

In addition, for an undirected graph $\mathbb{G} = (V, E)$ and subset of vertices $W \subseteq V$, we define $\mathbb{G}[W]$ to be the subgraph induced by the vertices in W. We require that our graphs always have the same set of indices for technical reasons, and thus we only remove edges that involve indices not in W. Formally, we define $\mathbb{G}[W] = (V, E')$ where $E' = E \cap (W \times W)$.

3.3   Reliable Broadcast

The following functionality models Bracha's reliable broadcast. This protocol is designed for asynchronous networks, but we will run it also over synchronous networks, which raises some difficulties. If the sender is honest, all parties receive the output at the same round; If the sender is corrupted, then the parties do not necessarily receive output at the same round (yet, if some party receives an output, all parties receive it in at most one round of delay). We model this using the following functionality, while we remark that in the synchronous setting, we model the non-simultaneous termination of [30]:

Functionality 3.1: Reliable Broadcast

In both models, the parties obtain their outputs according to Remark 3.2.

- **Synchronous mode:** The sender sends a message m to the functionality. The functionality delivers to all parties the same message m.
- **Asynchronous mode:** The sender sends a message m to the functionality. Note that in the hybrid-model, the adversary is allowed to set a separate delivery delay for each party.

Remark 3.2 (Non-simultaneous output delivery). *The functionality delivers the output in the following manner:*

- **Synchronous model, honest input provider (sender/dealer):** *when the sender is honest, all parties receive outputs simultaneously in a commonly known round.*
- **Synchronous model, corrupted input provider (sender/dealer):** *the functionality has non-simultaneous termination and therefore we use the wrapper of [30] to allow the adversary to set separate delays for each party, within known upper bounds on the delay. Specifically, in this protocol and other protocols in the paper, if some honest party outputs a value, all honest parties will output a value with a delay of at most one round.*
- **Asynchronous model:** *the adversary is allowed to add a separate unbounded delivery delay for each party.*

Recall that in both models, the parties receive their outputs using a fetch command. By that we mean that when we say that the functionality sends an output to a party, it actually stores its output and sends it after receiving an appropriate fetch *command.*

The reliable broadcast protocols of [1,8,24] are all designed for the asynchornous network, and do not guarantee simultaneous termination when execution over a synchronous network. Nevertheless, by taking the properties of the reliable broadcast as in Abraham, Asharov, and Chandramouli [1], we have:

Theorem 3.3. *Let $n \geq 3t + 1$. There exists a reliable broadcast protocol that securely realizes Functionality 3.1, tolerating at most t corrupted parties over synchronous and asynchronous network. When the sender starts with a message m of size $|m| = L$, then the protocol runs in $O(nL + n^2 \log n)$.*

In the synchronous model, the protocol works in 6 rounds of interaction, but when the sender is corrupted, some honest parties might end in one round later. Therefore, we use $T_{\mathsf{BC}} = 6\Delta$ to denote the optimistic termination of a broadcast, i.e., the time needed for an honest dealer.

4   Incomplete Verifiable Secret Sharing

The following primitive is a variant of verifiable secret sharing. The dealer distributes packed secrets (specifically, $t_a + 1$ secrets). This is a weaker variant of our complete VSS as it is does not ensure completeness in synchrony. Specifically, our protocol achieves the following properties:

1. In asynchronous networks, all honest parties eventually receive verified shares. I.e., this is a complete VSS.
2. In a synchronous network, it is guaranteed that at least $t_s + t_a + 1$ honest parties would have verified shares. The dealer sends to the functionality which parties receive the output. Moreover, it can later decide to deliver to other parties shares on the same polynomial.

4.1   The Functionality

We next define the functionality.

Functionality 4.1: Incomplete VSS

---

1. **Honest dealer:**
   (a) The dealer sends to the functionality the command (input, S), where S is a bivariate polynomial $S(x, y)$ of degree d in x and t_s in y. The functionality sets $K = [n] \setminus I$. The functionality stores (S, K).
   (b) The functionality sends $S(x, i), S(i, y)$ to the adversary for every $i \in I$.
2. **Dishonest dealer:**
   (a) The dealer sends to the functionality the command (input, S, K), where S is a bivariate polynomial $S(x, y)$, and $K \subseteq [n] \setminus I$.
   (b) The functionality verifies that $S(x, y)$ is of degree d in x and t_s in y, and that $|K| \geq t_s + t_a + 1$ and otherwise, replaces it with $S(x, y) = K = \bot$. The functionality stores (S, K).
3. **Output:**
   (a) **Synchronous model:** the functionality sends $S(x, j), S(j, y)$ for every $j \in K$ (non-simultaneously, see Remark 3.2).
   The adversary can additionally send a command $(\mathsf{allowDelivery}, j)$. In this case, if (S, K) are stored, and $j \notin K$, then j is added to K.
   (b) **Asynchronous model:** The functionality ignores K (the VSS is complete in asynchrony), and sends $S(x, j), S(j, y)$ to P_j for every $j \in [n] \setminus I$. Recall that the adversary is allowed to set a separate delivery delay for each party, see Remark 3.2.

The following protocol implements this functionality both in the synchronous and asynchronous models. In the asynchronous model (note that in this case, the number of corruptions is at most t_a), the protocol implements a stronger variant of the functionality, in which the adversary must send $K = [n] \setminus I$, i.e., all parties receive valid shares.

4.2   Protocol Construction

The protocol is implemented in the Reliable-broadcast-hybrid model (as described in Sect. 3.3). The full construction is provided in the full version of the paper. Recall that by our convention, we simply write "the parties broadcast a message m" and do not use directly the functionality. Moreover, we assume that all parties pull broadcast messages at the beginning of each round, and we omit this instruction as well from the protocol. Instead, we can just think as parties receiving broadcast messages in different schedule (with limitations described in the reliable-broadcast functionality).

Security and Deferred Details. In the full version of the paper we provide the security proof of the Incomplete VSS.

The Round Complexity in Synchronous Network $T_{\mathsf{IncompleteVSS}}$. Over synchronous networks, we expect the protocol to terminate after 3 rounds + 2 broadcast rounds if the dealer is honest. As we will use this protocol as a sub-protocol in other protocols (looking ahead, Sect. 5), we denote by $T_{\mathsf{IncompleteVSS}} = 3\Delta + 2T_{\mathsf{BC}}$, where Δ is a bound on a synchronous round, and T_{BC} is a bound on the time needed for broadcast.

4.3   Efficiency and Batching

When considering a single instance of $\Pi_{\mathsf{IncompleteSharing}}$, we can see that the dealer sends $O(n)$ polynomials over the field, each of size field elements of size $O(n \log n)$ in share dissemination round, each party sends $O(n)$ field elements when performing the pair-wise checks, and then both the dealer and participants each broadcast a constant number of vectors of size $O(n \log n)$. Using a broadcast protocol with complexity $O(n^3 \log n + nL)$ for messages of size L, we get a total complexity of $O(n^4 \log n)$ for sharing $O(n)$ secrets.

However, parties can also batch many simultaneous calls to the protocol with the same dealer. When calling ℓ instances to the protocol for sharing ℓn secrets, the dealer will send $O(\ell n)$ field elements of size $O(\log n)$, and each party will send $O(\ell n)$ field elements while performing the consistency checks. Then, instead of sending a message $m_{i,j}$ for each of the sharings separately, parties can send a single message. This is done in an analogous manner to the way OK messages are sent in the full description of the protocol,Z and following the logic of [2].

- If no message is received from P_j in any of the ℓ instances, P_i sets $m_{i,j} = \perp$.
- If values $(a_{j,i}, b_{j,i})$ are received from P_j in all ℓ instances such that $(a_{j,i}, b_{j,i}) = (g_i(j), f_i(j))$, then P_i sets $m_{i,j} = \perp$.
- If values $(a_{j,i}, b_{j,i})$ are received from P_j in all ℓ and for at least one of these pairs $(a_{j,i}, b_{j,i}) \neq (g_i(j), f_i(j))$, P_i sets $m_{i,j} = (\mathsf{NOK}, f_i(j), g_i(j))$ for the instance with the minimal index with inconsistent values.

Note that exactly like in the regular protocol, for any pair of honest parties, parties send OK if all of their received shares are consistent, and send NOK for the same minimal index with inconsistent values. This means that for an honest dealer in synchrony, all honest parties are guaranteed to send OK about each other. On the other hand, if a dishonest dealer chooses to send inconsistent values to honest parties in any of the instances, these parties will send a NOK message about each with inconsistent values in synchrony and either send such a message about each other or $\perp$ if they do not hear from each other in asynchrony. In both cases, the protocol above remains secure, with no edge existing between parties if they claim they are inconsistent even in one instance. Now, instead of constructing a separate graph for each instance and broadcasting it, the dealer constructs a single graph and broadcasts it.

In total, this means that for sharing $O(Xn)$ secrets, the complexity of the batched protocol is $O((n^4 + Xn^2)\log n)$, or $O(n \log n)$ per secret.

5   Complete Verifiable Secret Sharing

The following primitive is a stronger variant of verifiable secret sharing, where now all parties are guaranteed to receive a share. Recall that in the previous primitive (Sect. 4), this was not guaranteed in the synchronous setting, and some parties might not have received a share.

5.1   The Functionality

The functionality is similar to Functionality 4.1, where now there is no set K indicating which parties will receive outputs, as all parties eventually receive output. (Alternatively, this can be viewed as exactly Functionality 4.1, where $K = [n] \setminus I$).

Functionality 5.1: Complete VSS

---

1. **Honest dealer:**
   (a) The dealer sends to the functionality the command (input, S), where S is a bivariate polynomial $S(x, y)$ of degree d in x and t_s in y.
   (b) The functionality sends $S(x, i), S(i, y)$ to the adversary for every $i \in I$.
2. **Dishonest dealer:**
   (a) The dealer sends to the functionality the command (input, S), where S is a bivariate polynomial $S(x, y)$.
   (b) The functionality verifies that $S(x, y)$ is of degree d in x and t_s in y and otherwise, replaces it with $S(x, y) = \perp$. The functionality stores S.
3. **Output:** The functionality sends $S(x, j), S(j, y)$ for every $j \in [n] \setminus I$.
   Recall that in the synchronous model, this is non-simultaneous, while in asynchrony, the adversary is allowed to set a separate delivery delay (see Remark 3.2).

We refer the reader to the full version of the paper for full specification of the protocol that implements Functionality 5.1, the security analysis, and how we batch to improve efficiency.

6   Perfectly Secure Network Agnostic MPC

In this section, we give an overview of the building blocks required for the complete MPC protocol, which follows the common construction in literature as in [2,3,29]. We refer the reader to [29] for detailed explanation. First, we give overview of some building blocks needed for the complete MPC protocol and then, we give explain how to finally get our NA (network agnostic) MPC based on these building blocks.

6.1   Secret Reconstruction

Since the outcome of our VSS is secrets in Shamir-shared format, we discuss how such sharing can be reconstructed efficiently. We use two standard ways of reconstruction: (1) private reconstruction, and (2) batched public reconstruction.

Private Reconstruction. We describe how to privately reconstruct a degree-t_s shared secret at a designated party P. In this procedure, every party sends its share to P, who attempts to recover the underlying secret. The party P collects $2t_s+1$ shares that are consistent with a single degree-t_s polynomial. Note, as $n > 3t_s + t_a$, it is guaranteed that P would receive such shares eventually under any network conditions. To identify this polynomial, P repeatedly applies online error correction (OEC) (see the full version of the paper for more detail). Once such a polynomial is obtained, it is guaranteed to be the correct degree-t_s polynomial, since it coincides with the shares of at least $t_s + 1$ honest parties. However, this is inefficient as it incurs $O(logn)$ communication.

Batched Public Reconstruction. If we reconstruct $t+1$ Shamir-shared secrets would be to perform $(t + 1)n$ private reconstructions, which incurs $O(n^3 \log n)$ communication. To reduce this overhead, a batched reconstruction technique (from [33]) allows the recovery of $t + 1$ shared values with only $O(n^2 \log n)$ bits of communication, yielding an amortized cost of $O(n \log n)$ per secret. The core idea is that instead of reconstructing each secret separately, the parties bundle $t + 1$ sharings together and encode them into n fresh shares using a linear error-correcting code (e.g., Reed–Solomon), which tolerates up to t adversarial errors. Each party then locally reconstructs just one of these new shares via private reconstruction, and by combining their results, all parties can jointly recover the original $t + 1$ values.

6.2   MPC Protocol

The MPC protocol uses the packed VSS (Sect. 5), the verifiable triple sharing (see the full version of the paper for more details) and the rest of the building blocks which are taken from [29]. Our MPC protocol has two phases: (i) Preparing the Beaver triples and input sharing, and (ii) Circuit evaluation using the batched Beaver multiplication.

6.3   Input Sharing and Preparing Beaver Triples

This section is further divided into the following three subsections:

Input and Verifiable Sharing. In this phase, using the verifiable triple sharing protocol (see the full version of the paper for more details), each party acting as a dealer is made to Shamir-share the required number of triples (a, b, c) such that c = ab holds. Each party also uses the packed VSS described in Sect. 5 to share its inputs. The total number of triples each party must share is determined by the size of the computation circuit.

Agreement on Core Set. Given the possibility of the protocol running in the asynchronous communication model, parties cannot wait indefinitely for all others to complete their input and triple sharing. Malicious parties may delay or completely skip their instances, potentially stalling the protocol. To mitigate this, the honest parties agree on a common subset of dealers, referred to as the *Core*, consisting of at least $n - t_s$ parties. This set is guaranteed to have both the input and triple sharing instances eventually terminate for all parties. Once the triple sharing from all dealers in the Core is complete, the parties proceed to execute the triple extraction protocol. Notably, our ACS ensures that all honest parties are in the Core if the network is synchronous.

Triple Extraction. The final component is a triple extraction protocol. The triple extraction protocol, consumes a single verified multiplication triple, $(\langle a_i \rangle,$ $\langle b_i \rangle, \langle c_i \rangle)$, held by each party $P_i \in$ Core from the previous phase. From this, the parties derive $h + 1 - t$ fresh triples unknown to all participants, where $h = \lfloor (|\text{Core}| - 1)/2 \rfloor$. For ease of notation, let $m = |\text{Core}|$ and assume Core $= \{P_1, \ldots, P_m\}$. The communication complexity of the protocol is $\mathcal{O}(n^2)$ point-to-point messages. At a high level, the idea is to transform the m initial shared triples $(\langle a_i \rangle, \langle b_i \rangle, \langle c_i \rangle)$ for $i \in [m]$ into correlated triples $(\langle x_i \rangle, \langle y_i \rangle, \langle z_i \rangle)$ such that the sets $\{x_i, y_i, z_i\}_{i \in [m]}$ interpolate three polynomials $X(\cdot), Y(\cdot), Z(\cdot)$ of degrees h, h, and $2h$, satisfying the relation $X(\cdot) \cdot Y(\cdot) = Z(\cdot)$. Specifically, for each $i \in [m]$, we have $X(i) = x_i, Y(i) = y_i$, and $Z(i) = z_i$, with $1, \ldots, m$ being publicly known, distinct field elements. By construction, the adversary learns (x_i, y_i, z_i) only if P_i is compromised. Therefore, the adversary's knowledge is limited to at most t points on each of the polynomials, preserving a degree of freedom of $h + 1 - t$ in $X(\cdot), Y(\cdot)$ (and hence $Z(\cdot)$). The final output consists of evaluations of these polynomials at $h + 1 - t$ publicly known positions $\beta_1, \ldots, \beta_{h+1-t}$, which serve as the extracted multiplication triples.

The procedure is as follows. For indices $i \in \{1, \ldots, h + 1\}$, the assignments $x_i = a_i, y_i = b_i, z_i = c_i$ are made directly. For indices $i \in \{h + 2, \ldots, m\}$, the values $\langle x_i \rangle$ and $\langle y_i \rangle$ are obtained *non-interactively* as linear combinations of $\{x_j, y_j\}_{j \in [h+1]}$. Subsequently, $\langle z_i \rangle$ for $i \in \{h+2, \ldots, m\}$ is computed via Beaver's method, using $\langle x_i \rangle, \langle y_i \rangle$, and the triple $(\langle a_i \rangle, \langle b_i \rangle, \langle c_i \rangle)$. If P_i is corrupted, then the values (x_i, y_i, z_i) are revealed to the adversary, as expected. Overall, the triple extraction step reduces to a batch of $\mathcal{O}(h)$ Beaver multiplications, requiring $\mathcal{O}((nh + n^2) \log n)$ bits of communication under batched public reconstruction.

6.4 Circuit Evaluation

The second phase of the MPC uses the shares and precomputed degree-t shared multiplication triples to evaluate the circuit. For the linear gates, parties locally apply the linear operation on their respective shares of the inputs. However, the circuit multiplication gates are evaluated via batched Beaver multiplication. This follows the well-known randomization method introduced by Beaver [14], which allows computing the product xy using a random triple $\langle a \rangle$, $\langle b \rangle$, and $\langle c \rangle$, and only requires two public reconstructions. Essentially, each party first locally computes the differences $d = \langle x \rangle - \langle a \rangle$ and $e = \langle y \rangle - \langle b \rangle$, which are then publicly reconstructed. Since the product $z = xy$ can be expanded as $(d+a)(e+b) = de + db + ea + ab$, the parties can locally reconstruct $\langle xy \rangle$ using the formula:

$$\langle xy \rangle = de + d\langle b \rangle + e\langle a \rangle + \langle c \rangle$$

This uses the reconstructed values d and e, along with the pre-shared triple. To improve efficiency, the protocol processes a batch of l multiplications at once, requiring $2l$ public reconstructions. These are grouped into batches of size $t+1$, which ensures that each reconstruction has an amortized communication cost of $\mathcal{O}(n \log n)$ bits. As a result, the total communication complexity of the batched multiplication protocol over l multiplications is $\mathcal{O}((n^2 + nl) \log n)$.

6.5 Efficiency

Parties provide inputs using a single call to the complete VSS protocol, generate triplets with dealers, and call an ACS protocol in the synchronous phase. Following that, parties combine the triplets with dealers to triples without dealers, and continue with computing the circuit. The input sharing and ACS require $O(n^4 \log n)$ communication. In total, C triples need to be generated. Each dealer shares triples at a rate of $O(n^2 \log n)$ per triple (plus $O(n^4 \log n)$ across all sharings), and combining them at rate 1 by taking $O(n)$ triples with dealers and generating $O(n)$ triples without dealers. This means that in total, C triples need to be shared by dealers, for a total cost of $O(Cn^2 \log n)$. Finally, the circuit is evaluated by batch reconstructing triples at each layer. In such a reconstruction, $O(n)$ triples can be reconstructed with $O(n^2 \log n)$ communication, but with at least one reconstruction of cost $O(n^2 \log n)$ at each layer of the circuit. In total, this adds a cost of $O((Dn^2 + Cn) \log n)$. All protocols require $O(1)$ expected rounds, except the evaluation, which must be computed layer-by-layer sequentially, requiring $O(1)$ time per layer. In total, the protocol requires $O(D)$ expected time.

References

1. Abraham, I., Asharov, G., Chandramouli, A.: Simple is COOL: graded dispersal and its applications for byzantine fault tolerance. In: Meka, R. (ed.) ITCS 2025. LIPIcs, vol. 325, pp. 1:1–1:20. Schloss Dagstuhl - Leibniz-Zentrum für Informatik (2025). https://doi.org/10.4230/LIPICS.ITCS.2025.1

2. Abraham, I., Asharov, G., Patil, S., Patra, A.: Detect, pack and batch: Perfectly-secure MPC with linear communication and constant expected time. In: Hazay, C., Stam, M. (eds.) EUROCRYPT 2023, Part II. LNCS, vol. 14005, pp. 251–281. Springer, Cham (2023). https://doi.org/10.1007/978-3-031-30617-4_9

3. Abraham, I., Asharov, G., Patil, S., Patra, A.: Perfect asynchronous MPC with linear communication overhead. In: Joye, M., Leander, G. (eds.) EUROCRYPT 2024, Part V. LNCS, vol. 14655, pp. 280–309. Springer, Cham (2024). https://doi.org/10.1007/978-3-031-58740-5_10

4. Abraham, I., Asharov, G., Patra, A., Stern, G.: Asynchronous agreement on a core set in constant expected time and more efficient asynchronous VSS and MPC. In: Boyle, E., Mahmoody, M. (eds.) TCC 2024, Part IV. LNCS, vol. 15367, pp. 451–482. Springer, Cham (2024). https://doi.org/10.1007/978-3-031-78023-3_15

5. Abraham, I., Asharov, G., Yanai, A.: Efficient perfectly secure computation with optimal resilience. In: Nissim, K., Waters, B. (eds.) TCC 2021. LNCS, vol. 13043, pp. 66–96. Springer, Cham (2021). https://doi.org/10.1007/978-3-030-90453-1_3

6. Abraham, I., Dolev, D., Stern, G.: Revisiting asynchronous fault tolerant computation with optimal resilience. Distrib. Comput. **35**(4), 333–355 (2022)

7. Alexandru, A.B., Blum, E., Katz, J., Loss, J.: State machine replication under changing network conditions. In: Agrawal, S., Lin, D. (eds.) ASIACRYPT 2022, Part I. LNCS, vol. 13791, pp. 681–710. Springer, Cham (2022). https://doi.org/10.1007/978-3-031-22963-3_23

8. Alhaddad, N., Das, S., Duan, S., Ren, L., Varia, M., Xiang, Z., Zhang, H.: Balanced byzantine reliable broadcast with near-optimal communication and improved computation. In: Milani, A., Woelfel, P. (eds.) PODC '22: ACM Symposium on Principles of Distributed Computing, Salerno, Italy, July 25 - 29, 2022, pp. 399–417. ACM (2022). https://doi.org/10.1145/3519270.3538475

9. Appan, A., Chandramouli, A., Choudhury, A.: Perfectly-secure synchronous MPC with asynchronous fallback guarantees. In: Milani, A., Woelfel, P. (eds.) PODC '22: ACM Symposium on Principles of Distributed Computing, Salerno, Italy, July 25 - 29, 2022, pp. 92–102. ACM (2022). https://doi.org/10.1145/3519270.3538417

10. Appan, A., Chandramouli, A., Choudhury, A.: Perfectly-secure synchronous MPC with asynchronous fallback guarantees. IEEE Trans. Inf. Theory **69**(8), 5386–5425 (2023). https://doi.org/10.1109/TIT.2023.3264444

11. Appan, A., Choudhury, A.: Network agnostic MPC with statistical security. In: Rothblum, G.N., Wee, H. (eds.) TCC 2023, Part II. LNCS, vol. 14370, pp. 63–93. Springer, Cham (2023). https://doi.org/10.1007/978-3-031-48618-0_3

12. Asharov, G., Lindell, Y., Rabin, T.: Perfectly-secure multiplication for any $t<n/3$. In: Advances in Cryptology - CRYPTO 2011 (2011)

13. Bacho, R., Collins, D., Liu-Zhang, C., Loss, J.: Network-agnostic security comes (almost) for free in DKG and MPC. In: Handschuh, H., Lysyanskaya, A. (eds.) CRYPTO 2023, Part I. LNCS, vol. 14081, pp. 71–106. Springer, Cham (2023). https://doi.org/10.1007/978-3-031-38557-5_3

14. Beaver, D.: Efficient multiparty protocols using circuit randomization. In: Annual International Cryptology Conference (1991)

15. Beerliová-Trubíniová, Z., Hirt, M.: Simple and efficient perfectly-secure asynchronous mpc. In: Advances in Cryptology – ASIACRYPT 2007, pp. 376–392. Berlin, Heidelberg (2007)

16. Beerliová-Trubíniová, Z., Hirt, M.: Perfectly-secure mpc with linear communication complexity. In: Proceedings of the 5th Conference on Theory of Cryptography, pp. 213–230. TCC'08, Springer, Heidelberg (2008)

17. Ben-Or, M., Canetti, R., Goldreich, O.: Asynchronous secure computation. In: ACM Symposium on Theory of Computing (1993)
18. Ben-Or, M., Canetti, R., Goldreich, O.: Asynchronous secure computation. In: Proceedings of the Twenty-Fifth Annual ACM Symposium on Theory of Computing, STOC '93, pp. 52–61. Association for Computing Machinery, New York, NY, USA (1993). https://doi.org/10.1145/167088.167109
19. Ben-Or, M., Goldwasser, S., Wigderson, A.: Completeness theorems for non-cryptographic fault-tolerant distributed computation (extended abstract). In: Annual ACM Symposium on Theory of Computing (1988)
20. Ben-Or, M., Kelmer, B., Rabin, T.: Asynchronous secure computations with optimal resilience (extended abstract). In: Proceedings of the Thirteenth Annual ACM Symposium on Principles of Distributed Computing, PODC '94, pp. 183–192. Association for Computing Machinery, New York (1994)
21. Blum, E., Katz, J., Loss, J.: Synchronous consensus with optimal asynchronous fallback guarantees. In: Hofheinz, D., Rosen, A. (eds.) TCC 2019, Part I. LNCS, vol. 11891, pp. 131–150. Springer, Cham (2019). https://doi.org/10.1007/978-3-030-36030-6_6
22. Blum, E., Katz, J., Loss, J.: TARDIGRADE: an atomic broadcast protocol for arbitrary network conditions. In: Tibouchi, M., Wang, H. (eds.) ASIACRYPT 2021. LNCS, vol. 13091, pp. 547–572. Springer, Cham (2021). https://doi.org/10.1007/978-3-030-92075-3_19
23. Blum, E., Liu-Zhang, C.-D., Loss, J.: Always have a backup plan: fully secure synchronous MPC with asynchronous fallback. In: Micciancio, D., Ristenpart, T. (eds.) CRYPTO 2020. LNCS, vol. 12171, pp. 707–731. Springer, Cham (2020). https://doi.org/10.1007/978-3-030-56880-1_25
24. Bracha, G.: Asynchronous byzantine agreement protocols. Inf. Comput. **75**(2), 130–143 (1987). https://doi.org/10.1016/0890-5401(87)90054-X
25. Canetti, R.: Asynchronous secure computation. Technion - Computer Science Department - Technical Report CS0755 (1993)
26. Canetti, R.: Universally composable security: A new paradigm for cryptographic protocols. In: FOCS (2001)
27. Canetti, R., Chen, M.: Universally composable succinct vector commitments and applications. IACR Cryptol. ePrint Arch., p. 1103 (2025). https://eprint.iacr.org/2025/1103
28. Chaum, D., Crépeau, C., Damgård, I.: Multiparty unconditionally secure protocols (extended abstract). In: 20th Annual ACM Symposium on Theory of Computing (1988)
29. Choudhury, A., Patra, A.: An efficient framework for unconditionally secure multiparty computation. IEEE Trans. Inf. Theory **63**(1), 428–468 (2017). https://doi.org/10.1109/TIT.2016.2614685
30. Cohen, R., Coretti, S., Garay, J.A., Zikas, V.: Probabilistic termination and composability of cryptographic protocols. J. Cryptol. **32**(3), 690–741 (2019). https://doi.org/10.1007/S00145-018-9279-Y
31. Cohen, R., Forghani, P., Garay, J.A., Patel, R., Zikas, V.: Concurrent asynchronous byzantine agreement in expected-constant rounds, revisited. In: Rothblum, G.N., Wee, H. (eds.) TCC 2023, Part IV. LNCS, vol. 14372, pp. 422–451. Springer, Cham (2023). https://doi.org/10.1007/978-3-031-48624-1_16
32. Cramer, R., Damgård, I., Maurer, U.: General secure multi-party computation from any linear secret-sharing scheme. In: International Conference on the Theory and Applications of Cryptographic Techniques (2000)

33. Damgård, I., Nielsen, J.B.: Scalable and unconditionally secure multiparty computation. In: Annual International Cryptology Conference, pp. 572–590. Springer (2007)

34. Deligios, G., Hirt, M., Liu-Zhang, C.-D.: Round-efficient byzantine agreement and multi-party computation with asynchronous fallback. In: Nissim, K., Waters, B. (eds.) TCC 2021. LNCS, vol. 13042, pp. 623–653. Springer, Cham (2021). https://doi.org/10.1007/978-3-030-90459-3_21

35. Dodis, Y., Micali, S.: Parallel reducibility for information-theoretically secure computation. In: Bellare, M. (ed.) CRYPTO 2000. LNCS, vol. 1880, pp. 74–92. Springer (2000). https://doi.org/10.1007/3-540-44598-6_5

36. Feldman, P., Micali, S.: Optimal algorithms for byzantine agreement. In: 20th Annual ACM Symposium on Theory of Computing (1988)

37. Gennaro, R., Rabin, M.O., Rabin, T.: Simplified vss and fast-track multiparty computations with applications to threshold cryptography. In: ACM Symposium on Principles of Distributed Computing (1998)

38. Goyal, V., Liu, Y., Song, Y.: Communication-efficient unconditional mpc with guaranteed output delivery. In: CRYPTO (2019)

39. Katz, J., Maurer, U., Tackmann, B., Zikas, V.: Universally composable synchronous computation. In: Sahai, A. (ed.) TCC 2013. LNCS, vol. 7785, pp. 477–498. Springer, Heidelberg (2013). https://doi.org/10.1007/978-3-642-36594-2_27

40. Nayak, K., Ren, L., Shi, E., Vaidya, N.H., Xiang, Z.: Improved extension protocols for byzantine broadcast and agreement. arXiv preprint arXiv:2002.11321 (2020)

41. Patil, S., Patra, A.: Perfectly-secure network-agnostic MPC with optimal resiliency. In: Balliu, A., Kuhn, F. (eds.) Proceedings of the ACM Symposium on Principles of Distributed Computing, PODC 2025, Hotel Las Brisas Huatulco, Huatulco, Mexico, June 16-20, 2025, pp. 121–130. ACM (2025). https://doi.org/10.1145/3732772.3733500

42. Patra, A., Choudhury, A., Rangan, C.P.: Communication efficient perfectly secure VSS and MPC in asynchronous networks with optimal resilience. In: Bernstein, D.J., Lange, T. (eds.) AFRICACRYPT 2010. LNCS, vol. 6055, pp. 184–202. Springer, Heidelberg (2010). https://doi.org/10.1007/978-3-642-12678-9_12

43. Patra, A., Choudhury, A., Pandu Rangan, C.: Efficient asynchronous verifiable secret sharing and multiparty computation. J. Cryptol. **28**(1), 49–109 (2015)

44. Prabhu, B., Srinathan, K., Rangan, C.P.: Asynchronous unconditionally secure computation: an efficiency improvement. In: Menezes, A., Sarkar, P. (eds.) INDOCRYPT 2002. LNCS, vol. 2551, pp. 93–107. Springer, Heidelberg (2002). https://doi.org/10.1007/3-540-36231-2_9

45. Srinathan, K., Pandu Rangan, C.: Efficient asynchronous secure multiparty distributed computation. In: INDOCRYPT 2000, pp. 117–129 (2000)

BitGC Made (More) Efficient

Wenhao Zhang[1], Hanlin Liu[1], Kang Yang[2(✉)], Wen-jie Lu[3],
Yu Yu[4,5], Xiao Wang[1], and Chenkai Weng[6]

[1] Northwestern University, Evanston, USA
`{wenhao.zhang,hanlin.liu}@northwestern.edu`
[2] State Key Laboratory of Cryptology, Beijing, China
`yangk@sklc.org`
[3] TikTok, Shanghai, China
[4] Shanghai Jiao Tong University, Shanghai, China
`yuyu@yuyu.hk`
[5] Shanghai Qi Zhi Institute, Shanghai, China
[6] Arizona State University, Tempe, USA
`Chenkai.Weng@asu.edu`

Abstract. Garbled circuits with one-bit-per-gate communication were recently introduced by Liu et al. (BitGC, Eurocrypt 2025), Meyer et al. (Crypto 2025), and Ishai et al. (Crypto 2025). However, these works focus primarily on the theoretical communication complexity, leaving open questions about practical computational efficiency. In this paper, we present a set of optimizations that substantially improve its practical efficiency. First, we eliminate key barriers to enable SIMD support to BitGC, leading to a substantial speedup in its homomorphic operations. Second, we demonstrate that XOR gates can be garbled without any communication, improving both efficiency and simplicity. Finally, we present a computationally efficient garbling scheme that requires zero communication for XOR gates and only 5 bits per AND gate. When applied to an AES-128 circuit, our fastest garbling scheme generates a garbled circuit of just 4 KB in 3 min on a single CPU core.

1 Introduction

Garbled circuit (GC) [55] is a fundamental cryptographic tool that has been widely used to build secure two-party computation (2PC) [42], secure multi-party computation [9], zero-knowledge proofs [38], identity-based encryption [19], etc. It is particularly useful to build protocols with constant-round interaction and active security due to its inherent resilience against a corrupted evaluator.

Optimizing the size of GCs has been studied extensively both in practice and in a theoretical aspect. On the practical side, many optimizations have been proposed to improve the communication [9, 25, 39, 40, 47, 50, 51, 56] and computation [10, 26, 27] of garbling using only symmetric-key primitives. Notably, the scheme by Rosulek and Roy [51] achieves $1.5\lambda + 5$ bits per AND gate and no cost for XOR gates, where λ is the security parameter. It was recently shown to

J. Daemen and E. Thomé (Eds.): EUROCRYPT 2026, LNCS 16543, pp. 214–245, 2026.
https://doi.org/10.1007/978-3-032-25324-8_8

Table 1. Performance of our optimized BitGC variants compared to the original BitGC [44]. An AES-128 circuit includes 6400 AND gates and 28176 XOR gates. The time costs of BitGC-fast and BitGC-small are benchmarked with single-threaded execution and those of BitGC-tiny and BitGC are lower bound estimations assuming the same experimental environment. The communication cost excludes data that is reusable across multiple garblings, and also omits the amortized communication of transmitting encrypted PRG seeds which is arbitrarily small.

	Communication			Computation		
	AND	XOR	AES-128	AND	XOR	AES-128
BitGC-fast (Sec 5.1)	5 bits	0 bit	4.0 KB	22.2 ms	1.66 ms	189 s
BitGC-small (Sec 4)	1 bit	1 bit	4.3 KB	332 ms	119 ms	91 min
BitGC-tiny (Sec 5.2)	1 bit	0 bit	0.8 KB	≥ 1.85 s	≥ 1.31 s	≥ 14 hours
BitGC [44]	1 bit	1 bit	4.3 KB	≥ 10.5 s	≥ 10.5 s	≥ 101 hours

be optimal [37]. In contrast, asymptotically sublinear-size GCs aim for fully succinct constructions [2,13,22,24], typically relying on heavy cryptographic primitives such as fully homomorphic encryption (FHE) or multilinear maps. However, these approaches remain completely impractical so far due to their non-blackbox use of FHE.

More recently, several works by Liu, Wang, Yang and Yu [44], Meyer, Orlandi, Roy and Scholl [46], and Ishai, Li and Lin [36] started to investigate rate-one garbling for Boolean circuits with reasonable efficiency. In particular, these works have shown garbling schemes with one bit per gate communication based on lattice assumptions [36,44] and classical assumptions [36,46]. While these methods represent notable theoretical progress, their concrete efficiency is not clear and likely very far from being practical. Taking BitGC [44] as an example, it requires offline homomorphic evaluation of a pseudorandom generator (PRG) as well as online computation of homomorphic gate assembling and complicated polynomial ring operations. Our conservative estimates show that a direct implementation of their scheme would require at least 4 days to garble an AES-128 circuit.

1.1   Our Contribution

In this paper, we investigate the concrete efficiency of BitGC protocol and propose several important optimizations to maximize its performance. Our most practical scheme is almost 2000× faster than the unoptimized BitGC with a reduced garbling size.

1. BitGC requires using somewhat homomorphic encryption (SWHE) to evaluate a PRG but cannot use the SIMD optimization to accelerate this step. This is because BitGC requires an even ciphertext space while SIMD require primes friendly to number theoretic transformation (NTT). We observed that the

above restriction is due to how BitGC correlates the garbled labels and the permutation bit; by revising the structure of BitGC, we are able to support any ciphertext space and hence bringing back SIMD to accelerate operations on SWHE.

2. Many circuits have been optimized to minimize the number of ANDs with possibly more XOR gates due to the free-XOR optimization [40]. However, all existing one-bit protocols treat all types of gates in the same way. We provide various kinds of free-XOR optimizations to BitGC reducing the communication (sometimes also computation) cost for handling XOR gates.

3. Although the offline homomorphic PRG evaluation can be SIMD-accelerated, the online garbling phase uses ring operations for each gate and cannot use such optimization. We proposed a variant of BitGC with slightly more communication but avoid the need for any homomorphic multiplication in the online phase.

By incorporating all these optimizations, we are able to obtain three schemes (BitGC-small, BitGC-tiny, and BitGC-fast) with different trade-offs as shown in Table 1. While all three schemes can enjoy the SIMD optimizations for improved offline phase, each of them has a different set of feature.

- BitGC-small. This version is direct optimization of the original scheme with SIMD acceleration and slight optimization to make XOR gates cheaper in computation.
- BitGC-tiny. This version further eliminates the communication of XOR gates, but requires larger parameters for SWHE to support free-XOR. As a result, it has the smallest garbling but slow computation (still $10\times$ faster than the unoptimized BitGC).
- BitGC-fast. This is the variant with cheapest computation and the most balanced. XOR gates are additionally $10\times$ cheaper to garble and requires no communication. The downside is that AND gates require 5 bits of communication.

Why not Optimizing HSS-Based Constructions? Ishai et al. [36] and Meyer et al. [46] also proposed protocols for one bit garbling. Both protocols are built from homomorphic secret sharing (HSS) and semi-private HSS (a.k.a. algebraic homomorphic MAC [35]). By working directly over the HSS abstraction, they are able to instantiate one-bit garbling from a variety of assumptions. In this paper, we focus only on the practical efficiency of the garbling schemes and thus focus on lattice-based BitGC. Since these two works share some similar traits as BitGC, we believe some of our optimizations could be applied to their protocols.

2   Technical Overview

Let $\mathcal{R}_p \stackrel{\text{def}}{=} \mathbb{Z}_p[X]/(X^n + 1)$ and $\mathcal{R}_q \stackrel{\text{def}}{=} \mathbb{Z}_q[X]/(X^n + 1)$. For any ring element A, we define $\mathsf{LSB}(A)$ as $A_0 \bmod 2$, where A_0 is the first coefficient of A.

2.1   Recap BitGC Construction

First, we give a brief summary of the BitGC construction [43,44]. In BitGC and many practical garbling schemes, the permutation bit on a wire is defined to be the LSB of the zero label on that wire. For clarity, we store the permutation bit explicitly; thus, each wire has a permutation bit and two garbled labels. The garbler picks a uniform global offset $\Delta \in \mathcal{R}_p$ with $\mathsf{LSB}(\Delta) = 1$. For any wire with (A^0, A^1, π_a), the protocol requires $A^1 = A^0 + (-1)^{\pi_a} \cdot \Delta$. The BitGC sets $\pi_a = \mathsf{LSB}(A^0)$, which implies that $\mathsf{LSB}(A^{\pi_a}) = 0$ where $A^{\pi_a} = A^0 + (-1)^{\pi_a} \cdot \pi_a \cdot \Delta$.

For a message m, we use $[\![m]\!]$ to denote an SWHE ciphertext of m that is encrypted with a private key Δ. Consider a gate g with two inputs and one output. Given the input and output wire masks π_a, π_b, and π_c, the assembled garbled table consists of a set of three ciphertexts:

$$\begin{aligned}
\tau_1 &= [\![(-1)^{\pi_c} \cdot (z_{1,0} - z_{0,0})]\!] \\
\tau_2 &= [\![(-1)^{\pi_c} \cdot (z_{0,1} - z_{0,0})]\!] \\
\tau_3 &= [\![(-1)^{\pi_c} \cdot (z_{0,0} + z_{1,1} - z_{1,0} - z_{0,1})]\!]
\end{aligned} \tag{1}$$

where $z_{i,j} = g(i \oplus \pi_a, j \oplus \pi_b)$. Note that it implicitly defines $\tau_0 = 0$ due to the garbled row reduction [47].

Distributed Evaluation of BitGC. The BitGC scheme crucially requires a special homomorphism enabled by defining two functions Eval and Dec. We defer their instantiations to a later section and focus on their relations here. For any three ciphertexts τ_1, τ_2, τ_3 and uniform $X, Y \in \mathcal{R}_p$, the following equation holds with overwhelming probability:

$$\begin{aligned}
&\mathsf{Eval}_{i,j}(X + i \cdot \Delta, Y + j \cdot \Delta, \tau_1, \tau_2, \tau_3) - \mathsf{Eval}_{0,0}(X, Y, \tau_1, \tau_2, \tau_3) \\
&= i \cdot \mathsf{Dec}(\Delta, \tau_1) + j \cdot \mathsf{Dec}(\Delta, \tau_2) + i \cdot j \cdot \mathsf{Dec}(\Delta, \tau_3) \ .
\end{aligned}$$

When assuming that $\mathsf{Dec}(\Delta, [\![m]\!]) = m \cdot \Delta$ and these τ values are ciphertexts as in Eq. (1), the above equation can be further simplified to

$$\begin{aligned}
&\mathsf{Eval}_{i,j}(X + i \cdot \Delta, Y + j \cdot \Delta, \tau_1, \tau_2, \tau_3) - \mathsf{Eval}_{0,0}(X, Y, \tau_1, \tau_2, \tau_3) \\
&= (-1)^{\pi_c} \cdot (z_{i,j} - z_{0,0}) \cdot \Delta \ .
\end{aligned} \tag{2}$$

For any gate, the garbler always has all the input wire information (A^0, A^1, π_a) and (B^0, B^1, π_b), while the evaluator only holds the labels corresponding to the real values v_a, v_b and masked values, namely $(A^{v_a}, \pi_a \oplus v_a)$ and $(B^{v_b}, \pi_b \oplus v_b)$. One can verify that the labels satisfy the correct correlation: for any bits i and j, we have $A^i = A^{\pi_a} + (\pi_a \oplus i) \cdot \Delta$ and $B^j = B^{\pi_b} + (\pi_b \oplus j) \cdot \Delta$. Using Equation (2), it follows that

$$\begin{aligned}
&\mathsf{Eval}_{\pi_a \oplus i, \pi_b \oplus j}(A^i, B^j, \tau_1, \tau_2, \tau_3) - \mathsf{Eval}_{0,0}(A^{\pi_a}, B^{\pi_b}, \tau_1, \tau_2, \tau_3) \\
&= (-1)^{\pi_c} \cdot (z_{\pi_a \oplus i, \pi_b \oplus j} - z_{0,0}) \cdot \Delta \ .
\end{aligned}$$

However, the computation of π_c encounters a deadlock: by definition, $\pi_c = \mathsf{LSB}(C^0)$ and one can compute labels (C^0, C^1) from ciphertexts (τ_1, τ_2, τ_3), but these ciphertexts rely on π_c. To avoid the "chicken-and-egg" problem, the BitGC computes the permutation bit $\pi_c = \mathsf{LSB}(\mathsf{Eval}_{0,0}(A^{\pi_a}, B^{\pi_b}, \widetilde{\tau}_1, \widetilde{\tau}_2, \widetilde{\tau}_3)) \oplus g(\pi_a, \pi_b)$, where $\widetilde{\tau}_1, \widetilde{\tau}_2, \widetilde{\tau}_3$ are the same as τ_1, τ_2, τ_3 except for replacing $(-1)^{\pi_c}$ with $(-1)^{r_c}$ for a uniform bit r_c. Then, the garbler sets $C^{z_{0,0}} = \mathsf{Eval}_{0,0}(A^{\pi_a}, B^{\pi_b}, \tau_1, \tau_2, \tau_3)$, and is able to compute (C^0, C^1) with $(C^{z_{0,0}}, \Delta, \pi_c, z_{0,0})$. What the evaluator can compute is

$$
\begin{aligned}
\mathsf{Eval}&_{\pi_a \oplus v_a, \pi_b \oplus v_b}(A^{v_a}, B^{v_b}, \tau_1, \tau_2, \tau_3) \\
&= C^{z_{0,0}} + (-1)^{\pi_c} \cdot (z_{\pi_a \oplus v_a, \pi_b \oplus v_b} - z_{0,0}) \cdot \Delta \\
&= C^0 + (-1)^{\pi_c} \cdot z_{0,0} \cdot \Delta + (-1)^{\pi_c} \cdot (z_{\pi_a \oplus v_a, \pi_b \oplus v_b} - z_{0,0}) \cdot \Delta \\
&= C^0 + (-1)^{\pi_c} \cdot g(v_a, v_b) \cdot \Delta = C^{g(v_a, v_b)} = C^{v_c} \ ,
\end{aligned}
$$

where $v_c = g(v_a, v_b)$ is the real bit on the output wire. The BitGC further shows that $\mathsf{LSB}(C^{v_c}) = \pi_c \oplus v_c$, which is the needed masked bit of the output wire. Now, the garbler has the output wire information (C^0, C^1, π_c), and the evaluator holds $(C^{v_c}, \pi_c \oplus v_c)$. Thus, we can continue with the circuit evaluation.

Transmitting BitGC Garbled Table. First of all, transmitting encryptions of random bits is "free" in terms of communication, as the garbler can send an encrypted seed $[\![s]\!]$ to the evaluator, and then both parties can locally and homomorphically expand it using a PRG to generate many pseudorandom bit encryptions. This does not need fully homomorphic encryption as long as a low-depth PRG such as [1,4–6,8,23] is used. Given that, one can transmit the garbled table for a gate with just one bit of communication.

Both garbler and evaluator start with encryptions of input permutation bits and a uniform bit, i.e., $[\![\pi_a]\!]$, $[\![\pi_b]\!]$ and $[\![r_c]\!]$. The garbler has input labels (A^0, A^1), (B^0, B^1). With this setup, the garbler garbles a gate in the following steps:

1. *Compute a candidate garbled table.* The garbler performs homomorphic evaluations on $[\![\pi_a]\!]$, $[\![\pi_b]\!]$ and $[\![r_c]\!]$ to obtain:

$$
\begin{aligned}
\widetilde{\tau}_1 &= [\![(-1)^{r_c} \cdot (z_{1,0} - z_{0,0})]\!] \\
\widetilde{\tau}_2 &= [\![(-1)^{r_c} \cdot (z_{0,1} - z_{0,0})]\!] \\
\widetilde{\tau}_3 &= [\![(-1)^{r_c} \cdot (z_{0,0} + z_{1,1} - z_{1,0} - z_{0,1})]\!]
\end{aligned}
$$

2. *Transmit the garbled-table bit.* The garbler computes

$$
\pi_c = \mathsf{LSB}(\mathsf{Eval}_{0,0}(A^{\pi_a}, B^{\pi_b}, \widetilde{\tau}_1, \widetilde{\tau}_2, \widetilde{\tau}_3)) \oplus g(\pi_a, \pi_b)
$$

   and sends $d_c = r_c \oplus \pi_c$ to the evaluator. Both parties compute $[\![\pi_c]\!] = d_c \oplus [\![r_c]\!]$, and then can locally assemble the garbled table to obtain $\tau_i = (-1)^{d_c} \cdot \widetilde{\tau}_i$ for $i \in \{1, 2, 3\}$. As shown in the BitGC, setting the plaintext modulus p to an even number ensures the correctness of this step.

3. *Obtain Output Labels.* The garbler computes $C^{z_{0,0}}$ as described above, from which the garbler can obtain both output labels, maintaining the invariant.

Constructing Distributed Evaluation. The BitGC presented two constructions of the Eval function under the Ring-LWE assumption [45] and NTRU assumption [32,49]. Both constructions use two basic operations: Dec and $\widehat{\mathsf{Dec}}$. Specifically, for any $X, Y \in \mathcal{R}_p$ and ciphertexts τ_1, τ_2, τ_3, the Eval function is defined as:

$$\mathsf{Eval}_{i,j}(X, Y, \tau_1, \tau_2, \tau_3) \stackrel{\text{def}}{=} \mathsf{Dec}_i(X, \tau_1) + \mathsf{Dec}_j(Y, \tau_2) + \widehat{\mathsf{Dec}}_{i,j}(X, Y, \tau_3) \ .$$

For any ciphertext τ and uniform $X, Y \in \mathcal{R}_p$, the following properties hold with overwhelming probability:

1. Linear distributed decryption: $\mathsf{Dec}_1(X + \Delta, \tau) = \mathsf{Dec}_0(X, \tau) + \mathsf{Dec}(\Delta, \tau)$.
2. Correlated-key distributed decryption:

$$\widehat{\mathsf{Dec}}_{i,j}(X + i \cdot \Delta, Y + j \cdot \Delta, \tau) - \widehat{\mathsf{Dec}}_{0,0}(X, Y, \tau) = i \cdot j \cdot \mathsf{Dec}(\Delta, \tau) \ .$$

The linear distributed decryption function Dec_i above is based on [14]. The BitGC scheme introduces the $\widehat{\mathsf{Dec}}_{i,j}$ function to securely multiply two additive shares. It defines an extended form of the GSW ciphertext and shows how to transform a standard ciphertext into this form. Finally, it applies linear distributed decryption to this extended ciphertext using key-sharings $(X \cdot Y, X, Y, 1)$. Independently, constructions of a similar spirit were also proposed by [36] and [46]. They were proposed under slightly different formulations, but from a broader range of assumptions as well.

Challenges in Making BitGC Practical. Although the BitGC has a lot of potential, its current form is far from practical. Here, we summarize the greatest bottlenecks in concrete efficiency.

- *Incompatible with state-of-the-art SWHE optimizations.* The BitGC requires using a SWHE scheme to homomorphically evaluate a PRG. However, the scheme requires an even plaintext modulus p, which rules out SIMD techniques that rely on an NTT-friendly plaintext modulus. Enabling SIMD could potentially introduce three orders of magnitude improvement on homomorphic PRG evaluation.
- *Incompatible with free-XOR.* The majority of circuits are optimized to minimize the number of AND gates, due to the free-XOR technique [40], which makes XOR gates incur no communication cost and cheap in computational cost. On the other hand, the original BitGC scheme has the same cost across all types of gates; thus, using BitGC on existing free-XOR-optimized circuits would lead to suboptimal performance.
- *High ciphertext space and lattice dimension.* In addition, BitGC has some practical limitations that impact its performance. First, large parameter sizes are necessary due to the high homomorphic depth, specifically to support 1) homomorphic PRG evaluation and 2) homomorphic assembly of the garbled table. A larger modulus increases the cost of modular arithmetic, while a higher

lattice dimension raises the cost of polynomial ring operations. Consequently, homomorphic evaluation remains inefficient, even with optimizations such as the Chinese Remainder Theorem.

Below, we will provide more details of our proposed optimizations and how they can be combined for more practical constructions.

2.2   Enabling SIMD Optimizations for Homomorphic PRG Evaluation

As mentioned above, one major bottleneck is the homomorphic evaluation of PRG over SWHE ciphertexts. Modern lattice-based SWHE schemes are highly efficient due to the use of SIMD optimization. In more detail, plaintext values are packed into polynomial ring elements, where number theoretic transformation (NTT) is used, before being encrypted in SWHE. Due to the high lattice dimension, it is common to pack tens of thousands of plaintext messages into one ring element, thereby significantly amortizing the cost. This optimization requires an NTT-friendly prime as the plaintext modulus, but BitGC, as described above, requires an even plaintext space, thus making it incompatible with the packing technique. We first address this limitation.

Why BitGC Requires Even Plaintext Modulus. The root reason why BitGC requires an even plaintext modulus is the cyclic dependency among values:

1. Garbled-table ciphertexts τ's are dependent on the permutation bit π_c by definition.
2. The output permutation bit π_c is defined from the lowest bit of the output garbled label.
3. The output label is obtained by the garbled-table ciphertext (similar to the garbled row reduction technique [47]).

In the BitGC, this is resolved by an alternative way to compute π_c, where the requirement on the plaintext space is introduced: the garbler instead computes a bit from the "candidate ciphertexts" (namely $\widetilde{\tau}_i$, where π_c is replaced by a uniform bit r_c) as:

$$\mathsf{LSB}(\mathsf{Eval}_{0,0}(A^{\pi_a}, B^{\pi_b}, \widetilde{\tau}_1, \widetilde{\tau}_2, \widetilde{\tau}_3)) \oplus g(\pi_a, \pi_b) \ .$$

The correctness of this procedure can be argued as follows. When $r_c \neq \pi_c$, we have $\widetilde{\tau}_i = -1 \cdot \tau_i$, which means that $\mathsf{Eval}(A^{\pi_a}, B^{\pi_b}, \widetilde{\tau}_1, \widetilde{\tau}_2, \widetilde{\tau}_3) = -\mathsf{Eval}(A^{\pi_a}, B^{\pi_b}, \tau_1, \tau_2, \tau_3)$ when Eval is odd. Now, if the plaintext space is set to even, the resulting permutation bit is still the correct value because for any value a, as the lowest coefficient of the output of Eval, $(a \mod p) \mod 2 = (-a \mod p) \mod 2$ when p is even.

Avoiding Even Plaintext Modulus. BitGC breaks the cyclic dependency by computing the permutation bit without the τ's. Our observation, once writing the permutation bit separate from the garbled labels, is that we can also break the dependency by not enforcing the invariant that $\pi_c = \mathsf{LSB}(C^0)$. In our improved version, we pick all permutation bits uniformly; namely, $[\![\pi_a]\!]$, $[\![\pi_b]\!]$, and $[\![\pi_c]\!]$ are ciphertexts directly from the PRG. Now both parties can assemble the garbled-table ciphertexts τ_1, τ_2, τ_3 directly.

Now, if we look at the values that both parties hold, they remain correlated in the correct manner. The garbler can compute $C^{z_{0,0}} = \mathsf{Eval}_{0,0}(A^{\pi_a}, B^{\pi_b}, \tau_1, \tau_2, \tau_3)$ and hence derive all values (C^0, C^1, π_c) for the output wire. The evaluator can compute $C^{v_c} = \mathsf{Eval}_{\pi_a \oplus v_a, \pi_b \oplus v_b}(A^{v_a}, B^{v_b}, \tau_1, \tau_2, \tau_3)$. However, because this label does not embed the information of the masked bit, the garbler still needs to send one bit to the evaluator to transmit this information. Specifically, the garbler need to send $\pi_c \oplus \mathsf{LSB}(C^0)$ to the evaluator, who computes the masked bit $\pi_c \oplus \mathsf{LSB}(C^0) \oplus \mathsf{LSB}(C^{v_c}) = v_c \oplus \pi_c$, thus maintaining the invariant.

2.3 Supporting Free-XOR

After the above steps of enabling SIMD, the permutation bits of all gates are uniformly random and independent of each other, and we hope further to eliminate the communication for XOR gates. Achieving free-XOR when labels are bit-strings is easy, since the relationship between zero- and one-labels is based on XOR: $A^1 = A^0 \oplus \Delta$. Therefore, in the traditional setting, given that $C^0 = A^0 \oplus B^0$, we have:

$$A^{v_a} \oplus B^{v_b} = (A^0 \oplus v_a \Delta) \oplus (B^0 \oplus v_b \Delta) = A^0 \oplus B^0 \oplus (v_a \oplus v_b)\Delta = C^0 \oplus v_c \Delta.$$

The masked bit is consistent for the same reason. However, in our context, our labels are defined as $A^1 = A^0 + (-1)^{\pi_a} \cdot \Delta$ and thus cannot be directly used in the above approach since it is not XOR homomorphic.

Below, we look at the BitGC scheme after changing it to support an odd modulus. For any gate function g, including the XOR function, two parties can obtain the correct correlation of labels. One bit is communicated so that the evaluator can obtain the masked bit, which is $v_c \oplus \pi_c = (v_a \oplus v_b) \oplus \pi_c$ in our context. We observe that this bit of communication can be eliminated if we can set $\pi_c = \pi_a \oplus \pi_b$, since the permutation bit itself is still "XOR-homomorphic" like a classical bit-string label. Therefore, the task of achieving no communication for XOR gates reduces to ensuring that the evaluator obtains correlated permutation bits: the output permutation bits of AND gates are uniform, while the output permutation bits of XOR gates are the XOR of input permutation bits.

Obtaining correlated permutation bits for free-XOR is not straightforward since the evaluator must obtain the SWHE ciphertexts of all bits. Here we discuss two possible ways, although we acknowledge that none of them are really practical:

- One can use a leveled HE scheme with a large ciphertext space to homomorphically compute the output permutation bits for all XOR gates. In this case, consecutive XOR operations can be evaluated in a binary tree manner. Since the noise does not carry across AND gates, an additional $O(\log N)$ levels of

homomorphic multiplications are needed, where N is the number of XOR gates in the longest sequence of consecutive XOR operations. This method allows zero communication for XOR gates, but in the worst case, the additional number of multiplication levels needed could be $O(\log |C|)$ where $|C|$ is the size of the circuit to be garbled.
– If an SWHE scheme with depth $L+d$ is provided, where d is the depth needed by the original BitGC scheme, then one can achieve $O(1/L)$ bits per XOR gate for a layered circuit. In practice, this approach also leads to significant computational overhead, as increasing L prohibitively increases the computational cost.

In conclusion, it is possible to achieve free communication for XOR gates, but the computational cost becomes even higher than AND gates. Nevertheless, in certain use cases where the garbling size is the most important, it could be of interest. Conceptually, it also enables us to obtain more realistic trade-offs, as described below.

2.4   Better Trade-Off between Computation and Communication

Our third major contribution is to obtain a more realistic trade-off. Note that after applying the SIMD optimization for evaluating the PRG, its cost would be significantly reduced. Now the bottleneck becomes 1) homomorphic assembling of the garbled-table ciphertexts (i.e., $\{\tau_i\}$), which requires two levels of homomorphic evaluation, and 2) distributed evaluation of the table by means of $\mathsf{Eval}_{i,j}$. Note that neither of these two parts can enjoy SIMD acceleration. The first step is dependent on the circuit structure and thus can only be packed if the same circuit needs to be garbled multiple times; the second step involves operations on polynomial rings and is not compatible with packing at all.

To reduce these costs, our goal is to eliminate the need for homomorphic multiplication completely after PRG evaluation. This way, we avoid the heavy operation of table assembling, and only need a smaller ciphertext modulus, which in turn reduces the dimension of the polynomial ring. We plan to accomplish it by slightly increasing the communication.

As an example, the first row of the garbled-table ciphertext τ_1 is an encryption of $t_1 = (-1)^{\pi_c} \cdot (z_{1,0} - z_{0,0})$. One idea would be to first establish encryptions of some random r, where the evaluator only knows the ciphertext, and then the garbler sends $r + t_1$ to the evaluator. The evaluator can recover the encryption of t_1 with homomorphic addition. Note that t_1 can be any of $\{-1, 0, 1\}$, but the above addition works on a very large plaintext domain. Thus r can only be statistical masking with size at least 2^ρ for a statistical security parameter ρ. This would significantly increase the communication.

A better approach is to communicate the high and low bits of $t_1 + 1$, which range between 0 and 2, separately. Let t_H, t_L be the high and low bits of $t_1 + 1$. Suppose the evaluator obtains the SWHE ciphertext of two uniform bits r_H and r_L. The garbler can send $r_H \oplus t_H$ and $r_L \oplus t_L$ to the evaluator, who can compute $[\![t_H]\!] = [\![r_H]\!] \oplus (r_H \oplus t_H)$, and $[\![t_L]\!]$ in a similar way. Then the evaluator can assemble $[\![t_1]\!] = 2 \cdot [\![t_H]\!] + [\![t_L]\!] - 1$. Now, to communicate all three ciphertexts for each gate, the garbler sends 6 bits of communication and needs to use 6 bits from the homomorphically evaluated PRG. One more bit needs to be sent for the evaluator to recover the masked bit as described in Sect. 2.2, meaning that the communication cost is now 7 bits per gate. This is already a fairly competitive baseline, but below we show how to 1) further reduce the cost and 2) support free-XOR cheaply.

A 5-bit Version. There is still hope for improvement because the above scheme is somewhat "wasteful". Each garbled-table ciphertext encrypts a value of three possibilities, while we transmit two bits that can encode four possibilities. Even without considering the correlation between the three values (t_1, t_2, t_3), there are at most 27 possibilities, and thus, less than 6 bits of communication could still be possible. We look back at the plaintext in the garbled rows:

$$
\begin{aligned}
t_1 &= (-1)^{\pi_c} \cdot (z_{1,0} - z_{0,0}) \\
t_2 &= (-1)^{\pi_c} \cdot (z_{0,1} - z_{0,0}) \\
t_3 &= (-1)^{\pi_c} \cdot (z_{0,0} + z_{1,1} - z_{1,0} - z_{0,0})
\end{aligned}
\tag{3}
$$

Our goal is to come up with a minimum number of bits such that their additive linear combination (modulo a large value) produces t_1, t_2, t_3. One may consider decomposing them to small units as $(-1)^{\pi_c} \cdot z_{i,j}$'s but they still range in $\{-1, 0, 1\}$ and thus lead to a total of 8 bits. Instead, we crucially notice that

$$
(-1)^{\pi_c} \cdot (z_{i,j} - z_{0,0}) = z_{i,j} \oplus \pi_c - z_{0,0} \oplus \pi_c .
$$

Note that the right-hand side is a mix of arithmetic operations and Boolean operations. To see why this is true, we note that $(-1)^\pi \cdot (z - \pi) = z \oplus \pi$ for any bits z, π; thus we have:

$$
\begin{aligned}
(-1)^{\pi_c} \cdot (z_{i,j} - z_{0,0}) &= (-1)^{\pi_c} \cdot ((z_{i,j} - \pi_c) - (z_{0,0} - \pi_c)) \\
&= (-1)^{\pi_c} \cdot (z_{i,j} - \pi_c) - (-1)^{\pi_c} \cdot (z_{0,0} - \pi_c) \\
&= z_{i,j} \oplus \pi_c - z_{0,0} \oplus \pi_c .
\end{aligned}
$$

With this observation, one can transmit the garbled-table ciphertext with only 4 bits, sending the masked value of $z_{i,j} \oplus \pi_c$ with the evaluator holding the encrypted mask. The evaluator can homomorphically unmask and compute the difference with only linear operations. One more bit is still needed for the evaluator to obtain the masked bit for the output wire, totaling 5 bits for each gate.

In practice, this leads to significant improvement. Although using more PRG bits, it leads to a 15× improvement in computational cost, due to elimination of homomorphic multiplications and reduction of lattice parameters.

Lightweight Free-XOR. Finally, we would like to further improve this scheme so that the 5-bit communication is only needed for AND gates. We start by plugging the XOR gate function to $z_{i,j}$'s in Equation (3). Note that for a XOR gate, $z_{i,j} = g(i \oplus \pi_a, j \oplus \pi_b) = \pi_a \oplus \pi_b \oplus i \oplus j$. If we set $\pi_c = \pi_a \oplus \pi_b$ similar to Sect. 2.3, then $z_{i,j} \oplus \pi_c = i \oplus j$, and the plaintexts on three garbled rows can be simplified to

$$t_1 = 1$$
$$t_2 = 1$$
$$t_3 = -2,$$

which requires no communication. Essentially, for XOR gates, while Sect. 2.3 eliminates the communication for transmitting the masked value, here we eliminate the need to transmit the garbled tables. Furthermore, we no longer require the encryption of π_c to assemble the garbled table and thus can avoid homomorphic multiplication over a high-depth circuit as needed in Sect. 2.3.

3   Preliminaries

3.1   Notation

We denote the computational and statistical security parameters by λ and ρ, respectively. All logarithms are base 2, i.e., $\log(\cdot)$. For $n \in \mathbb{N}$, let $[n] \overset{\text{def}}{=} \{0, \ldots, n-1\}$. We write $x \overset{\$}{\leftarrow} \mathcal{S}$ for sampling x uniformly at random from a set $\mathcal{S}$, and use $x \leftarrow \mathcal{D}$ to denote that sampling x according to a distribution $\mathcal{D}$. Define the polynomial ring $\mathcal{R} \overset{\text{def}}{=} \mathbb{Z}[X]/(X^n + 1)$ and, for a modulus $q \in \mathbb{N}^+$, the quotient ring $\mathcal{R}_q \overset{\text{def}}{=} \mathcal{R}/q\mathcal{R} = \mathbb{Z}_q[X]/(X^n + 1)$. For a vector or polynomial $\boldsymbol{a}$, we denote its i-th component by a_i, with a_0 being the constant term. For a polynomial $\boldsymbol{a} \in \mathcal{R}$, let $\mathsf{LSB}(\boldsymbol{a}) = a_0 \bmod 2$. We use $\mathsf{negl}(\cdot)$ to represent a negligible function, where $\mathsf{negl}(\lambda) = o(\lambda^{-c})$ for every constant c. Additionally, $\mathsf{poly}(\cdot)$ denotes a polynomial function, with $\mathsf{poly}(\lambda) = O(\lambda^c)$ for some constant c.

For a Boolean circuit f, we use $\mathcal{I}$ to denote the set of circuit-input wires, and denote by $\mathcal{O}$ the set of circuit output wires. We use $\mathcal{W}$, $\mathcal{W}_{\mathsf{AND}}$ and $\mathcal{W}_{\mathsf{XOR}}$ to denote the sets of the output wires of all gates, AND gates and XOR gates, respectively. Each gate in a Boolean circuit is represented by a tuple $(\alpha, \beta, \gamma, T)$, where α and β are the input wires, γ is the output wire, and $T \in \{\mathsf{AND}, \mathsf{XOR}\}$ specifies the type of gate.

3.2   Definition of Garbling Schemes

We recall the definition of a garbling scheme from [51], which modifies the original definition [11] in two ways: (i) correctness allows a negligible probability of failure, and (ii) authenticity is strengthened by giving the adversary an extra decoding information d. As in the previous work [11], we define a side-information function $\Phi(\cdot)$ that deterministically maps a circuit f to a string $\Phi(f)$ specifying which side information is revealed. In this work, we focus on the classical setting $\Phi_{\mathrm{circ}}(f) = f$, where the entire circuit is revealed. The garbler executes the garbling algorithm Gb and encoding algorithm En, while the evaluator runs the evaluation algorithm Ev and decoding algorithm De. These algorithms are defined below.

Definition 1 (Syntax). *A garbling scheme consists of the following four polynomial-time algorithms:*

- $(F, e, d) \leftarrow \mathsf{Gb}(1^\lambda, f)$*: takes as input a security parameter λ and a circuit f, and outputs a garbled circuit F, an encoding information e and a decoding information d.*
- $X \leftarrow \mathsf{En}(e, x)$*: takes as input e and an input x, and outputs a garbled input X.*
- $Y \leftarrow \mathsf{Ev}(F, X)$*: takes as input F and X, and outputs a garbled output Y.*
- $y \leftarrow \mathsf{De}(d, Y)$*: takes as input d and Y, and outputs a circuit output y.*

Correctness. For any circuit f and input x, for $(F, e, d) \leftarrow \mathsf{Gb}(1^\lambda, f)$, then with probability $1 - \mathsf{negl}(\lambda)$,

$$\mathsf{De}\Big(d, \mathsf{Ev}\big(F, \mathsf{En}(e, x)\big)\Big) = f(x).$$

Privacy. The privacy property ensures that the evaluator learns nothing about the input, even when given the transcript (F, X, d). We formalize this as follows.

<table>
<tr><td>

Real World $\mathsf{Exp}^{\mathsf{prv}, \varPhi}_{real}(1^\lambda, f, x)$

1. $(F, e, d) \leftarrow \mathsf{Gb}(1^\lambda, f)$;
2. $X \leftarrow \mathsf{En}(e, x)$;
3. $b \leftarrow \mathcal{D}(F, X, d)$.

</td><td>

Ideal World $\mathsf{Exp}^{\mathsf{prv}, \varPhi}_{ideal, \mathcal{S}}(1^\lambda, f, x)$

1. $(F, X, d) \leftarrow \mathcal{S}(1^\lambda, \varPhi(f), f(x))$
2. $b \leftarrow \mathcal{D}(F, X, d)$.

</td></tr>
</table>

Fig. 1. Experiments for privacy with respect to a side-information function $\varPhi$.

<table>
<tr><td>

Real World $\mathsf{Exp}^{\mathsf{obv}, \varPhi}_{real}(1^\lambda, f, x)$

1. $(F, e, d) \leftarrow \mathsf{Gb}(1^\lambda, f)$;
2. $X \leftarrow \mathsf{En}(e, x)$;
3. $b \leftarrow \mathcal{D}(F, X)$.

</td><td>

Ideal World $\mathsf{Exp}^{\mathsf{obv}, \varPhi}_{ideal, \mathcal{S}}(1^\lambda, f, x)$

1. $(F, X) \leftarrow \mathcal{S}(1^\lambda, \varPhi(f))$
2. $b \leftarrow \mathcal{D}(F, X)$.

</td></tr>
</table>

Fig. 2. Experiments for obliviousness w.r.t. a side-information function $\varPhi$.

Definition 2 (Privacy). *A garbling scheme satisfies privacy if there exists a negligible function $\mathsf{negl}(\cdot)$ and a probabilistic polynomial-time (PPT) simulator*

$\mathcal{S}$ such that, for any probabilistic polynomial time (PPT) distinguisher $\mathcal{D}$, any function f, and any input x,

$$\left| \Pr\left[\mathsf{Exp}^{\mathsf{prv},\Phi}_{real}(1^\lambda, f, x) = 1 \right] - \Pr\left[\mathsf{Exp}^{\mathsf{prv},\Phi}_{ideal,\mathcal{S}}(1^\lambda, f, x) = 1 \right] \right| \leq \mathsf{negl}(\lambda),$$

where $\mathsf{Exp}^{\mathsf{prv},\Phi}_{real}$ and $\mathsf{Exp}^{\mathsf{prv},\Phi}_{ideal,\mathcal{S}}$ are defined in Fig. 1.

Obliviousness. Obliviousness ensures that the evaluator learns nothing about the inputs, even given (F, X). Unlike privacy, the adversary does not receive the decoding information d and thus cannot obtain the output $f(x)$. This property is useful when the evaluator should not learn the output, for example, when the garbling scheme is used as part of a larger system.

Definition 3 (Obliviousness). *A garbling scheme satisfies obliviousness if there exists a negligible function $\mathsf{negl}(\cdot)$ and a PPT simulator $\mathcal{S}$ such that, for any PPT distinguisher $\mathcal{D}$, any function f, and any input x,*

$$\left| \Pr\left[\mathsf{Exp}^{\mathsf{obv},\Phi}_{real}(1^\lambda, f, x) = 1 \right] - \Pr\left[\mathsf{Exp}^{\mathsf{obv},\Phi}_{ideal,\mathcal{S}}(1^\lambda, f, x) = 1 \right] \right| \leq \mathsf{negl}(\lambda),$$

where $\mathsf{Exp}^{\mathsf{obv},\Phi}_{real}$ and $\mathsf{Exp}^{\mathsf{obv},\Phi}_{ideal,\mathcal{S}}$ are defined in Fig. 2.

$$\mathsf{Exp}^{\mathsf{auth}}_{\mathcal{A}}(1^\lambda, f, x)$$

1. $(F, e, d) \leftarrow \mathsf{Gb}(1^\lambda, f)$; $X \leftarrow \mathsf{En}(e, x)$; $\widehat{Y} \leftarrow \mathcal{A}(F, X, d)$;
2. If $\mathsf{De}(d, \widehat{Y}) \neq \bot$ and $\widehat{Y} \neq \mathsf{Ev}(F, X)$, then output 1, else output 0.

Fig. 3. Experiment for authenticity.

Authenticity. Authenticity does not guarantee privacy: the adversary may learn the circuit f and input x. However, it guarantees that the adversary cannot create a forged garbled output $\widehat{Y}$ that decodes successfully while differing from $\mathsf{Ev}(F, X)$, even when given (F, X, d). This property is important for building constant-round zero-knowledge proofs (e.g., [21,31,38,41]).

Definition 4 (Authenticity). *For any PPT adversary $\mathcal{A}$, for any function f and input x, there exists a negligible function $\mathsf{negl}(\cdot)$ such that for any PPT adversary $\mathcal{A}$, the following holds:*

$$\Pr\left[\mathsf{Exp}^{\mathsf{auth}}_{\mathcal{A}}(1^\lambda, f, x) = 1 \right] \leq \mathsf{negl}(\lambda),$$

where $\mathsf{Exp}^{\mathsf{auth}}_{\mathcal{A}}(1^\lambda, f, x)$ is defined in Fig. 3.

3.3   SWHE with Distributed Decryption

We first recall the standard definition of somewhat homomorphic encryption (SWHE) schemes in the private-key setting. Then, we show the definition of a special property called distributed decryption (DD), and refer to SWHE with such a special property as SWHEwDD. Without loss of generality, we adopt two polynomial rings $\mathcal{R}$ and $\mathcal{R}_p$ in the following definition, and note that this definition can be directly extended to other finite fields or rings. We note that Liu et al. [44] presented two instantiations of SWHEwDD under the RLWE and NTRU assumptions respectively, which satisfy our required properties for garbling schemes. To achieve better concrete efficiency, we take an instantiation based on the BGV framework [16,18] under both the RLWE and the Circular Power RLWE (CP-RLWE) [36] assumptions. We give this efficient instantiation in the full version of this paper [57].

Definition 5 (SWHE). *A somewhat homomorphic encryption scheme is a tuple of probabilistic polynomial-time algorithms* (Setup, Gen, Enc, Dec, Eval) *for key space $\mathcal{K} \subseteq \mathcal{R}$, message space $\mathcal{M} \subseteq \mathcal{R}_p$, and ciphertext space $\mathcal{C}$.*

1. params $\leftarrow$ Setup($1^\lambda, 1^L$). *The setup algorithm takes as input a security parameter λ and a maximum multiplication depth L, and outputs a set of parameters* params, *which is an implicit input to the following algorithms and will be omitted for simplicity.*
2. (keypar, Δ) $\leftarrow$ Gen(params). *The key-generation algorithm takes as input a set of parameters* params, *and outputs a set of key-related parameters* keypar *and a secret key $\Delta \in \mathcal{K}$. Similarly,* keypar *is an implicit input to the following algorithms and will be omitted for simplicity.*
3. $[\![m]\!] \leftarrow$ Enc(Δ, m). *The encryption algorithm takes as input a secret key $\Delta \in \mathcal{K}$ and a plaintext $m \in \mathcal{M}$, and outputs a ciphertext $[\![m]\!]$.*
4. $m \leftarrow$ Dec($\Delta, [\![m]\!]$). *The decryption algorithm takes as input a secret key $\Delta \in \mathcal{K}$ and a ciphertext $[\![m]\!] \in \mathcal{C}$, and outputs a plaintext $m \in \mathcal{M}$.*
5. $[\![y]\!] \leftarrow$ HEval($f, [\![m_0]\!], \cdots, [\![m_{\ell-1}]\!]$). *The homomorphic evaluation algorithm takes as input a polynomial-sized arithmetic circuit $f : \mathcal{M}^\ell \to \mathcal{M}$ and ℓ ciphertexts $[\![m_0]\!], \cdots, [\![m_{\ell-1}]\!] \in \mathcal{C}$, and outputs a ciphertext $[\![y]\!] \in \mathcal{C}$.*

For each security parameter λ, depth bound L, circuit $f : \mathcal{M}^\ell \to \mathcal{M}$ with multiplication depth at most L, and $m_0, \ldots, m_{\ell-1} \in \mathcal{M}$, it holds that

$$\Pr\left[\mathsf{Dec}(\Delta, [\![y]\!]) \neq f(m_0, \cdots, m_{\ell-1}) \ \middle| \ \begin{array}{l} \text{params} \leftarrow \mathsf{Setup}(1^\lambda, 1^L), \\ (\text{keypar}, \Delta) \leftarrow \mathsf{Gen}(\text{params}), \\ [\![m_i]\!] \leftarrow \mathsf{Enc}(\Delta, m_i) \ \forall i \in [\ell], \\ [\![y]\!] \leftarrow \mathsf{HEval}(f, [\![m_0]\!], \cdots, [\![m_{\ell-1}]\!]) \end{array}\right] \leq \mathsf{negl}(\lambda) \ .$$

Distributed Decryption Property. The linear distributed decryption (DD) property (i.e., DD of dimension $k = 1$) was introduced by Boyle et al. [14], and was extended to further support the correlated-key DD property (i.e., DD of dimension $k = 2$) by Liu et al. [44]. We recall the DD property in the following definition, and also generalize the definition to support any DD dimension $k \in \mathbb{N}^+$, which may be useful for future garbling constructions. In this work, SWHEwDD refers to SWHE schemes that satisfy the following distributed decryption property on both $k = 1$ and $k = 2$.

Definition 6 (Distributed Decryption). *We say that an SWHE scheme satisfies the distributed decryption property on dimension $k \in \mathbb{N}^+$, if there exist polynomial-time algorithms $\mathsf{DD}_a : \mathcal{R}_p^k \times \mathcal{C} \to \mathcal{R}_p$ for all $a \in \{0,1\}^k$, such that, for all security parameter λ and depth bound L, it holds that*

$$\Pr\left[\begin{array}{l} \mathsf{DD}_x\left(X + x \cdot \Delta, \tau\right) \\ \neq \mathsf{DD}_0(X, \tau) + \left(\prod_{i=0}^{k-1} x_i\right) \cdot \mathsf{Dec}(\Delta, \tau) \end{array} \middle| \begin{array}{l} \mathsf{params} \leftarrow \mathsf{Setup}(1^\lambda, 1^L), \\ (\mathsf{keypar}, \Delta) \leftarrow \mathsf{Gen}(\mathsf{params}), \\ X \xleftarrow{\$} \mathcal{R}_p^k, \\ \forall \tau \in \mathcal{C}, x \in \{0,1\}^k \end{array} \right] \leq \mathsf{negl}(\lambda) \,,$$

where the operation of $X + x \cdot \Delta$ is defined over $\mathcal{R}_p^k$.

That is, if an SWHE scheme satisfies DD on $k = 1$, with overwhelming probability it holds that $\mathsf{DD}_i(X + i \cdot \Delta, \tau) = \mathsf{DD}_0(X, \tau) + i \cdot \mathsf{Dec}(\Delta, \tau)$ for any bit $i \in \{0,1\}$ and uniformly distributed $X \xleftarrow{\$} \mathcal{R}_p$; if one satisfies DD on $k = 2$, with overwhelming probability it holds that $\mathsf{DD}_{i,j}(X + i \cdot \Delta, Y + j \cdot \Delta, \tau) = \mathsf{DD}_{0,0}(X, Y, \tau) + i \cdot j \cdot \mathsf{Dec}(\Delta, \tau)$ for any $i, j \in \{0,1\}$ and uniformly distributed $X, Y \xleftarrow{\$} \mathcal{R}_p$.

To simplify the notation of our garbling scheme, for each $i, j \in \{0,1\}$, we define the function $\mathsf{Eval}_{i,j} : \mathcal{R}_p^2 \times \mathcal{C}^3 \to \mathcal{R}_p$ as

$$\mathsf{Eval}_{i,j}(A, B, \tau_1, \tau_2, \tau_3) := \mathsf{DD}_i(A, \tau_1) + \mathsf{DD}_j(B, \tau_2) + \mathsf{DD}_{i,j}(A, B, \tau_3) \,.$$

CPA and KDM Security Properties. In our garbling schemes, we require that the SWHEwDD scheme satisfies the standard indistinguishability under chosen-plaintext attacks (i.e., IND-CPA in short). Informally, any PPT adversary cannot distinguish $[\![m_0]\!]$ from $[\![m_1]\!]$ for two adversarial-chosen messages m_0, m_1, given that the adversary obtains $(\mathsf{params}, \mathsf{keypar})$ and has access to an encryption oracle $\mathsf{Enc}(\Delta, \cdot)$. Furthermore, we assume that the SWHEwDD scheme also satisfies the key-dependent message (KDM) security [12]. Informally, for any PPT adversary $\mathcal{A}$, it is infeasible that $\mathcal{A}$ can distinguish $[\![f(\Delta)]\!]$ from $[\![0]\!]$ for a function f chosen by itself, given that $\mathcal{A}$ has access to $(\mathsf{params}, \mathsf{keypar})$ as well as $\mathsf{Enc}(\Delta, \cdot)$. For our garbling application, we only need that $[\![\Delta]\!]$ is computationally indistinguishable from $[\![0]\!]$.

4   BitGC-Small: Garbling Scheme with 1 Bit per Gate

4.1   Detailed Construction of BitGC-Small

The details of garbling scheme BitGC-small are shown in Figs. 4 and 5. Compared to the original BitGC scheme [44], BitGC-small achieves the same communication cost but has a much smaller computational cost. The computation is improved by

---

BitGC-small (Part I)

Let $\mathsf{SWHE} = (\mathsf{Setup}, \mathsf{Gen}, \mathsf{Enc}, \mathsf{Dec}, \mathsf{Eval})$ be an SWHEwDD scheme. Let $\mathsf{PRG} : \{0,1\}^{\ell} \to \{0,1\}^{N}$ be a secure t-depth PRG where ℓ is the seed size and $N = |\mathcal{I}| + |\mathcal{W}|$ is the number of wires, $\mathsf{PRF} : \{0,1\}^{\lambda} \times \{0,1\}^{\lambda} \to \mathcal{R}_p$ be a secure PRF, and $\mathsf{H} : \mathcal{R}_p \to \{0,1\}^{\lambda}$ be a random oracle.

$\mathsf{Gb}(1^{\lambda}, f)$:

1. Generate SWHE parameters $\mathsf{params} \leftarrow \mathsf{Setup}(1^{\lambda}, 1^L)$, where $L = t + 2$ is the maximum multiplication depth for SWHE.
2. Produce a set of key-dependent parameters $(\mathsf{keypar}, \Delta) \leftarrow \mathsf{Gen}(\mathsf{params})$ where $\mathsf{LSB}(\Delta) = 1$, and generate $[\![\Delta]\!] := \mathsf{Enc}(\Delta, \Delta)$. Sample a PRF key $K \xleftarrow{\$} \{0,1\}^{\lambda}$.
3. Sample a PRG seed $\boldsymbol{s} \xleftarrow{\$} \{0,1\}^{\ell}$ and compute ciphertext $[\![s_i]\!] := \mathsf{Enc}(\Delta, s_i)$ for each $i \in [\ell]$. Then, compute $(\pi_0, \ldots, \pi_{N-1}) := \mathsf{PRG}(\boldsymbol{s})$, and homomorphically compute ciphertexts $([\![\pi_0]\!], \ldots, [\![\pi_{N-1}]\!]) := \mathsf{PRG}([\![s_0]\!], \ldots, [\![s_{\ell-1}]\!])$.
4. For each input wire $i \in \mathcal{I}$, sample a label $W_i^0 \xleftarrow{\$} \mathcal{R}_p$ and compute $W_i^1 := W_i^0 + (-1)^{\pi_i} \cdot \Delta \in \mathcal{R}_p$.
5. For each gate $(\alpha, \beta, \gamma, T)$ in topological order, do the following:
   - Case 1 ($T = \mathsf{AND}$):
     (a) For each $i, j \in \{0, 1\}$, compute a bit $\hat{z}^{i,j} := (\pi_\alpha \oplus i) \wedge (\pi_\beta \oplus j) \oplus \pi_\gamma$ and homomorphically compute a ciphertext $[\![\hat{z}^{i,j} \cdot \Delta]\!]$ from $[\![\pi_\alpha]\!], [\![\pi_\beta]\!], [\![\pi_\gamma]\!]$ and $[\![\Delta]\!]$ with two levels of homomorphic multiplications.
     (b) Compute $\tau_1 := [\![\hat{z}^{1,0} \cdot \Delta]\!] - [\![\hat{z}^{0,0} \cdot \Delta]\!], \tau_2 := [\![\hat{z}^{0,1} \cdot \Delta]\!] - [\![\hat{z}^{0,0} \cdot \Delta]\!], \tau_3 := [\![\hat{z}^{1,1} \cdot \Delta]\!] - [\![\hat{z}^{0,0} \cdot \Delta]\!] - \tau_1 - \tau_2$.
     (c) Compute a pair of labels $W_\gamma^{\pi_\gamma} := \mathsf{Eval}_{0,0}(W_\alpha^{\pi_\alpha}, W_\beta^{\pi_\beta}, \tau_1, \tau_2, \tau_3) - \hat{z}^{0,0} \cdot \Delta + \mathsf{PRF}_K(\gamma)$ and $W_\gamma^{\pi_\gamma \oplus 1} := W_\gamma^{\pi_\gamma} + \Delta$, along with a bit $d_\gamma := \mathsf{LSB}(W_\gamma^0) \oplus \pi_\gamma$.
   - Case 2 ($T = \mathsf{XOR}$):
     (a) Compute a bit $d_\gamma := \pi_\alpha \oplus \pi_\beta \oplus \pi_\gamma$ as well as three ciphertexts $\tau_1 := (1 - 2 \cdot d_\gamma) \cdot [\![\Delta]\!], \tau_2 := \tau_1$ and $\tau_3 := -\tau_1 - \tau_2$.
     (b) Compute a pair of labels $W_\gamma^{\pi_\gamma} := \mathsf{Eval}_{0,0}(W_\alpha^{\pi_\alpha}, W_\beta^{\pi_\beta}, \tau_1, \tau_2, \tau_3) - d_\gamma \cdot \Delta + \mathsf{PRF}_K(\gamma)$ and $W_\gamma^{\pi_\gamma \oplus 1} := W_\gamma^{\pi_\gamma} + \Delta$.
6. Output a garbled circuit $F := (\mathsf{params}, \mathsf{keypar}, [\![\Delta]\!], K, \{[\![s_i]\!]\}_{i \in [\ell]}, \{d_i\}_{i \in \mathcal{W}})$, an encoding information $e := (\{(\pi_i, W_i^0)\}_{i \in \mathcal{I}}, \Delta)$ and a decoding information $d := \{(\mathsf{H}(W_i^0), \mathsf{H}(W_i^1))\}_{i \in \mathcal{O}}$.

$\mathsf{En}(e, x)$: For each $i \in \mathcal{I}$, compute $\hat{x}_i := x_i \oplus \pi_i$ and $W_i := W_i^0 + (-1)^{\pi_i} \cdot x_i \cdot \Delta \in \mathcal{R}_p$. Output $X := \{(\hat{x}_i, W_i)\}_{i \in \mathcal{I}}$.

Fig. 4. Garbling scheme BitGC-small with 1 bit per gate (Part I).

supporting PRG homomorphic evaluation with SIMD optimization and applying specific optimizations on XOR gates. In particular, for each gate $(\alpha, \beta, \gamma, \mathsf{XOR})$, the masked bit on the output wire γ is equal to

$$\hat{x}_\gamma = (x_\alpha \oplus x_\beta) \oplus \pi_\gamma = (\hat{x}_\alpha \oplus \pi_\alpha) \oplus (\hat{x}_\beta \oplus \pi_\beta) \oplus \pi_\gamma = \hat{x}_\alpha \oplus \hat{x}_\beta \oplus (\pi_\alpha \oplus \pi_\beta \oplus \pi_\gamma) \ .$$

Thus, we let the garbler send $d_\gamma = \pi_\alpha \oplus \pi_\beta \oplus \pi_\gamma$ to the evaluator, who can compute the masked bit $\hat{x}_\gamma = \hat{x}_\alpha \oplus \hat{x}_\beta \oplus d_\gamma$. For each XOR gate with output wire γ, we

---

BitGC-small (Part II)

$\mathsf{Ev}(F, X)$:

1. Homomorphically compute $(\llbracket \pi_0 \rrbracket, \ldots, \llbracket \pi_{N-1} \rrbracket) := \mathsf{PRG}\,(\llbracket s_0 \rrbracket, \ldots, \llbracket s_{\ell-1} \rrbracket)$.
2. For each gate $(\alpha, \beta, \gamma, T)$ in topological order, perform the following steps:
   - Case 1 $(T = \mathsf{AND})$:
     (a) For each $i, j \in \{0, 1\}$, homomorphically compute $\llbracket \hat{z}^{i,j} \cdot \Delta \rrbracket$ from $\llbracket \pi_\alpha \rrbracket$, $\llbracket \pi_\beta \rrbracket$, $\llbracket \pi_\gamma \rrbracket$ and $\llbracket \Delta \rrbracket$.
     (b) Compute $\tau_1 := \llbracket \hat{z}^{1,0} \cdot \Delta \rrbracket - \llbracket \hat{z}^{0,0} \cdot \Delta \rrbracket$, $\tau_2 := \llbracket \hat{z}^{0,1} \cdot \Delta \rrbracket - \llbracket \hat{z}^{0,0} \cdot \Delta \rrbracket$, and $\tau_3 := \llbracket \hat{z}^{1,1} \cdot \Delta \rrbracket - \llbracket \hat{z}^{0,0} \cdot \Delta \rrbracket - \tau_1 - \tau_2$.
     (c) Compute $W_\gamma := \mathsf{Eval}_{\hat{x}_\alpha, \hat{x}_\beta}(W_\alpha, W_\beta, \tau_1, \tau_2, \tau_3) + \mathsf{PRF}_K(\gamma)$.
     (d) Compute a masked bit $\hat{x}_\gamma := \mathsf{LSB}(W_\gamma) \oplus d_\gamma$.
   - Case 2 $(T = \mathsf{XOR})$:
     (a) Compute $\tau_1 := (1 - 2 \cdot d_\gamma) \cdot \llbracket \Delta \rrbracket$, $\tau_2 := \tau_1$ and $\tau_3 := -\tau_1 - \tau_2$.
     (b) Compute $W_\gamma := \mathsf{Eval}_{\hat{x}_\alpha, \hat{x}_\beta}(W_\alpha, W_\beta, \tau_1, \tau_2, \tau_3) + \mathsf{PRF}_K(\gamma)$.
     (c) Compute a masked bit $\hat{x}_\gamma := \hat{x}_\alpha \oplus \hat{x}_\beta \oplus d_\gamma$.
3. Output $Y := \{W_i\}_{i \in \mathcal{O}}$.

$\mathsf{De}(d, Y)$: For each $i \in \mathcal{O}$, if $\mathsf{H}(W_i) = \mathsf{H}(W_i^0)$, set $x_i := 0$; if $\mathsf{H}(W_i) = \mathsf{H}(W_i^1)$, set $x_i := 1$; otherwise, abort and output $\perp$. If not abort, output $y := \{x_i\}_{i \in \mathcal{O}}$.

Fig. 5. Garbling scheme BitGC-small with 1 bit per gate (Part II).

have $d_\gamma = \hat{z}^{0,0}$ according to their definitions. Furthermore, the relationships $\hat{z}^{1,0} = \hat{z}^{0,1} = \hat{z}^{0,0} \oplus 1 = 1 - \hat{z}^{0,0}$ and $\hat{z}^{1,1} = \hat{z}^{0,0}$ hold for each XOR gate. Therefore, the ciphertexts τ_1, τ_2, τ_3 can be computed in a simple manner without any homomorphic multiplications.

The BitGC-small adopts a low-depth PRG, which can be instantiated under different assumptions [1,4–8,23]. Our implementation uses a Goldreich-style random local PRG [1,6], which is able to expand a ℓ-bit seed into ℓ^2 pseudorandom bits using a depth $t = 4$ arithmetic circuit. See Sect. 6 for more details. In this case, BitGC-small requires SWHEwDD to support $t + 2 = 6$ levels of multiplications. We use a pseudorandom function (PRF) to randomize the labels on the output wires of all gates. This makes the DD property be satisfied in the computational sense. Note that PRF is not used to protect the privacy, and instead guarantees the correctness. For a secret key Δ, we assume that $\mathsf{LSB}(\Delta) = 1$. In this case, since $W_i = W_i^0 + (-1)^{\pi_i} \cdot x_i \cdot \Delta = W_i^{\pi_i} + (x_i \oplus \pi_i) \cdot \Delta$ due to the fact that $W_i^{\pi_i} = W_i^0 + (-1)^{\pi_i} \cdot \pi_i \cdot \Delta$ and $(-1)^{\pi_i} \cdot (x_i - \pi_i) = x_i \oplus \pi_i$, we have $\mathsf{LSB}(W_i) = \mathsf{LSB}(W_i^{\pi_i}) \oplus (x_i \oplus \pi_i)$ and $\mathsf{LSB}(W_i^{\pi_i}) = \mathsf{LSB}(W_i^0) \oplus \pi_i$.

The BitGC-small scheme satisfies not only privacy but also obliviousness and authenticity. To achieve authenticity, we use the hash values of a pair of labels for each circuit-output wire as the decoding information, following the standard approach used in prior works [33,44,56]. In proof of security, we model the hash function as a random oracle (RO). In the following subsections, we analyze the correctness of garbling scheme BitGC-small and prove its security. If authenticity is not required, then we can set the permutation bit π_i for each $i \in \mathcal{O}$ as the decoding information; the evaluation algorithm outputs the masked bit $\hat{x}_i$, and the decoding algorithm recovers the output bit $x_i = \hat{x}_i \oplus \pi_i$, for each $i \in \mathcal{O}$. In addition, we note that one can replace the random oracle model with the notion of correlation-robust hash functions (CRHFs) [10,26–28,34] to remove the dependency of RO and achieve better computational efficiency. In particular, while the domain of a CRHF H is often defined over $\{0,1\}^\lambda$, we need to extend the domain of H to $\mathcal{R}_p$ for our garbling schemes. The standard techniques as described above can be applied in not only BitGC-small but also BitGC-fast and BitGC-tiny shown in Sect. 5.

Analysis for Communication Complexity. We focus on the size of a garbled circuit F, as it dominates the communication cost. We can always suppose that the garbler and evaluator have already agreed upon the set of parameters params. The keypar and $[\![\Delta]\!]$ can be reused across multiple garbling executions between the garbler and evaluator, which allows us to amortize the communication cost to negligibly small. Furthermore, the communication cost of transmitting keypar and $[\![\Delta]\!]$ is independent from the circuit size. Excluding the tuple of system parameters (params, keypar, $[\![\Delta]\!]$), the size of garbled circuit F is $|\mathcal{W}| + \ell \cdot |ct| + \lambda$ bits, where $|\mathcal{W}|$ is the number of gates, $\ell = o(|\mathcal{W}|)$ is the seed size of the PRG, and $|ct|$ is the size of an SWHE ciphertext. Therefore, the amortized communication cost for each gate is only 1 bit for sufficiently large circuits.

4.2 Correctness Analysis

In the following, we analyze the correctness of the BitGC-small scheme (Fig. 4 and 5). We replace $\mathsf{PRF}_K(\gamma)$ with a uniform element $R_\gamma \in \mathcal{R}_p$ for each gate-output wire $\gamma \in \mathcal{W}$. This replacement only incurs a negligible difference for the correctness probability, due to the pseudorandomness of PRF outputs, following the correctness analysis in prior works [14,44]. In this case, we have that $W_\gamma^{\pi_\gamma}$ is uniform in $\mathcal{R}_p$ for each $\gamma \in \mathcal{W}$. For each input wire $i \in \mathcal{I}$, we have $W_i^{\pi_i} = W_i^0 + (-1)^{\pi_i} \cdot \pi_i \cdot \Delta$ is uniform in $\mathcal{R}_p$, due to the uniformity of W_i^0.

We prove the correctness by induction following the topological order of the circuit. Throughout this paper, for each wire i, we use x_i and $\hat{x}_i$ to denote the real value and masked value, respectively. For each input wire $i \in \mathcal{I}$, we have that $W_i = W_i^0 + (-1)^{\pi_i} \cdot x_i \cdot \Delta$ and $\hat{x}_i = x_i \oplus \pi_i$. For each gate $(\alpha, \beta, \gamma, T)$, we have the following holds:

$$W_\alpha = W_\alpha^0 + (-1)^{\pi_\alpha} \cdot x_\alpha \cdot \Delta \text{ and } \hat{x}_\alpha = x_\alpha \oplus \pi_\alpha,$$
$$W_\beta = W_\beta^0 + (-1)^{\pi_\beta} \cdot x_\beta \cdot \Delta \text{ and } \hat{x}_\beta = x_\beta \oplus \pi_\beta .$$

According to the definitions of $(W_\alpha^{\pi_\alpha}, W_\beta^{\pi_\beta})$ and $(\hat{x}_\alpha, \hat{x}_\beta)$, it is easy to verify that $W_\alpha = W_\alpha^{\pi_\alpha} + \hat{x}_\alpha \cdot \Delta$ and $W_\beta = W_\beta^{\pi_\beta} + \hat{x}_\beta \cdot \Delta$. For the output wire γ, we show that $W_\gamma = W_\gamma^{\pi_\gamma} + \hat{x}_\gamma \cdot \Delta$ and $\hat{x}_\gamma = \pi_\gamma \oplus x_\gamma$ hold, except with negligible probability. We consider two cases: $T = \mathsf{AND}$ and $T = \mathsf{XOR}$.

Case 1: $T = \mathsf{AND}$. In the Garble algorithm, for the output wire γ, $W_\gamma^{\pi_\gamma}$ is computed as $\mathsf{Eval}_{0,0}(W_\alpha^{\pi_\alpha}, W_\beta^{\pi_\beta}, \tau_1, \tau_2, \tau_3) - \hat{z}^{0,0} \cdot \Delta + R_\gamma$ where $\hat{z}^{0,0} = (\pi_\alpha \wedge \pi_\beta) \oplus \pi_\gamma$. Then, W_γ^0 is computed as $W_\gamma^{\pi_\gamma} - (-1)^{\pi_\gamma} \cdot \pi_\gamma \cdot \Delta$. In the Ev algorithm, we have that $W_\gamma = \mathsf{Eval}_{\hat{x}_\alpha, \hat{x}_\beta}(W_\alpha, W_\beta, \tau_1, \tau_2, \tau_3) + R_\gamma$ and $\hat{x}_\gamma = \mathsf{LSB}(W_\gamma) \oplus d_\gamma$, where $d_\gamma = \mathsf{LSB}(W_\gamma^0) \oplus \pi_\gamma$. Based on the distributed decryption property, with overwhelming probability, we have

$$
\begin{aligned}
W_\gamma &= \mathsf{DD}_{\hat{x}_\alpha}(W_\alpha, \tau_1) + \mathsf{DD}_{\hat{x}_\beta}(W_\beta, \tau_2) + \mathsf{DD}_{\hat{x}_\alpha, \hat{x}_\beta}(W_\alpha, W_\beta, \tau_3) + R_\gamma \\
&= \mathsf{DD}_{\hat{x}_\alpha}(W_\alpha^{\pi_\alpha} + \hat{x}_\alpha \cdot \Delta, \tau_1) + \mathsf{DD}_{\hat{x}_\beta}(W_\beta^{\pi_\beta} + \hat{x}_\beta \cdot \Delta, \tau_2) \\
&\quad + \mathsf{DD}_{\hat{x}_\alpha, \hat{x}_\beta}(W_\alpha^{\pi_\alpha} + \hat{x}_\alpha \cdot \Delta, W_\beta^{\pi_\beta} + \hat{x}_\beta \cdot \Delta, \tau_3) + R_\gamma \\
&= \mathsf{DD}_0(W_\alpha^{\pi_\alpha}, \tau_1) + \mathsf{DD}_0(W_\beta^{\pi_\beta}, \tau_2) + \mathsf{DD}_{0,0}(W_\alpha^{\pi_\alpha}, W_\beta^{\pi_\beta}, \tau_3) + R_\gamma \\
&\quad + \hat{x}_\alpha \cdot \mathsf{Dec}(\Delta, \tau_1) + \hat{x}_\beta \cdot \mathsf{Dec}(\Delta, \tau_2) + \hat{x}_\alpha \cdot \hat{x}_\beta \cdot \mathsf{Dec}(\Delta, \tau_3) \\
&= \mathsf{Eval}_{0,0}(W_\alpha^{\pi_\alpha}, W_\beta^{\pi_\beta}, \tau_1, \tau_2, \tau_3) + R_\gamma + \big(\hat{x}_\alpha \cdot (\hat{z}^{1,0} - \hat{z}^{0,0}) + \\
&\quad \hat{x}_\beta \cdot (\hat{z}^{0,1} - \hat{z}^{0,0}) + \hat{x}_\alpha \cdot \hat{x}_\beta \cdot (\hat{z}^{1,1} + \hat{z}^{0,0} - \hat{z}^{1,0} - \hat{z}^{0,1})\big) \cdot \Delta \\
&= W_\gamma^{\pi_\gamma} + \hat{z}^{0,0} \cdot \Delta + (\hat{z}^{\hat{x}_\alpha, \hat{x}_\beta} - \hat{z}^{0,0}) \cdot \Delta \\
&= W_\gamma^{\pi_\gamma} + \hat{z}^{0,0} \cdot \Delta + (\hat{x}_\gamma - \hat{z}^{0,0}) \cdot \Delta \\
&= W_\gamma^{\pi_\gamma} + \hat{x}_\gamma \cdot \Delta = W_\gamma^{\pi_\gamma} + (x_\gamma \oplus \pi_\gamma) \cdot \Delta \\
&= W_\gamma^{\pi_\gamma} + (-1)^{\pi_\gamma} \cdot (x_\gamma - \pi_\gamma) \cdot \Delta \\
&= W_\gamma^0 + (-1)^{\pi_\gamma} \cdot x_\gamma \cdot \Delta .
\end{aligned}
\tag{4}
$$

In the above analysis, since $\hat{z}^{i,j} = (\pi_\alpha \oplus i) \wedge (\pi_\beta \oplus j) \oplus \pi_\gamma$, $\hat{x}_\alpha = x_\alpha \oplus \pi_\alpha$ and $\hat{x}_\beta = x_\beta \oplus \pi_\beta$, we obtain that $\hat{z}^{\hat{x}_\alpha, \hat{x}_\beta} = (x_\alpha \wedge x_\beta) \oplus \pi_\gamma = x_\gamma \oplus \pi_\gamma = \hat{x}_\gamma$. In addition, we use the fact that $x_\gamma \oplus \pi_\gamma = (-1)^{\pi_\gamma} \cdot (x_\gamma - \pi_\gamma)$ for $x_\gamma, \pi_\gamma \in \{0, 1\}$. Thus, we have

$$
\hat{x}_\gamma = \mathsf{LSB}(W_\gamma) \oplus d_\gamma = \mathsf{LSB}(W_\gamma) \oplus \mathsf{LSB}(W_\gamma^0) \oplus \pi_\gamma = x_\gamma \oplus \pi_\gamma .
$$

Case 2: $T = \mathsf{XOR}$. In the Garble algorithm, for the output wire γ, we still have that $W_\gamma^{\pi_\gamma} = \mathsf{Eval}_{0,0}(W_\alpha^{\pi_\alpha}, W_\beta^{\pi_\beta}, \tau_1, \tau_2, \tau_3) - d_\gamma \cdot \Delta + R_\gamma$ and $W_\gamma^0 = W_\gamma^{\pi_\gamma} - (-1)^{\pi_\gamma} \cdot \pi_\gamma \cdot \Delta$, where $d_\gamma = \pi_\alpha \oplus \pi_\beta \oplus \pi_\gamma$. In the Ev algorithm, we still have $W_\gamma = \mathsf{Eval}_{\hat{x}_\alpha, \hat{x}_\beta}(W_\alpha, W_\beta, \tau_1, \tau_2, \tau_3) + R_\gamma$. Differently, the masked bit $\hat{x}_\gamma = \hat{x}_\alpha \oplus \hat{x}_\beta \oplus d_\gamma$. From the distributed decryption property, except with negligible probability,

$$
\begin{aligned}
W_\gamma &= W_\gamma^{\pi_\gamma} + d_\gamma \cdot \Delta + \hat{x}_\alpha \cdot \mathsf{Dec}(\Delta, \tau_1) + \hat{x}_\beta \cdot \mathsf{Dec}(\Delta, \tau_2) + \hat{x}_\alpha \cdot \hat{x}_\beta \cdot \mathsf{Dec}(\Delta, \tau_3) \\
&= W_\gamma^{\pi_\gamma} + d_\gamma \cdot \Delta + \big(\hat{x}_\alpha + \hat{x}_\beta - 2 \cdot \hat{x}_\alpha \cdot \hat{x}_\beta\big) \cdot (-1)^{d_\gamma} \cdot \Delta \\
&= W_\gamma^{\pi_\gamma} + d_\gamma \cdot \Delta + \big(\hat{x}_\alpha \oplus \hat{x}_\beta\big) \cdot (-1)^{d_\gamma} \cdot \Delta \\
&= W_\gamma^{\pi_\gamma} + d_\gamma \cdot \Delta + \big(\hat{x}_\alpha \oplus \hat{x}_\beta \oplus d_\gamma - d_\gamma\big) \cdot \Delta \\
&= W_\gamma^{\pi_\gamma} + (x_\alpha \oplus x_\beta \oplus \pi_\gamma) \cdot \Delta \\
&= W_\gamma^{\pi_\gamma} + \hat{x}_\gamma \cdot \Delta \\
&= W_\gamma^0 + (-1)^{\pi_\gamma} \cdot x_\gamma \cdot \Delta .
\end{aligned}
\tag{5}
$$

In the above analysis, we omit some intermediate steps, as they can be derived by applying the same approach as in Equation (4). Note that τ_1, τ_2 and τ_3 are now decrypted as

$$\mathsf{Dec}(\Delta, \tau_1) = \mathsf{Dec}(\Delta, \tau_2) = (1 - 2 \cdot d_\gamma) \cdot \Delta = (-1)^{d_\gamma} \cdot \Delta$$
$$\mathsf{Dec}(\Delta, \tau_3) = -2 \cdot (-1)^{d_\gamma} \cdot \Delta,$$

Next, it is easy to verify

$$\hat{x}_\gamma = \hat{x}_\alpha \oplus \hat{x}_\beta \oplus d_\gamma = \hat{x}_\alpha \oplus \hat{x}_\beta \oplus \pi_\alpha \oplus \pi_\beta \oplus \pi_\gamma = x_\alpha \oplus x_\beta \oplus \pi_\gamma = x_\gamma \oplus \pi_\gamma .$$

From the above analysis, for each output wire $i \in \mathcal{O}$, we have $W_i = W_i^0 + (-1)^{\pi_i} \cdot x_i \cdot \Delta$ where $\{x_i\}_{i \in \mathcal{O}} = f(\{x_i\}_{i \in \mathcal{I}})$. Recall that $\mathsf{De}(d, Y)$ outputs 0 if $\mathsf{H}(W_i) = \mathsf{H}(W_i^0)$, and outputs 1 if $\mathsf{H}(W_i) = \mathsf{H}(W_i^1)$. Therefore, $\mathsf{De}(d, Y)$ outputs $y = f(x)$, which completes the correctness proof.

4.3   Security Proof

Before giving the detailed proof, we show an overview of the proof. We complete the proof via a sequence of hybrids, where the real-world execution is **Hybrid 0**. In **Hybrid 1**, the Gb algorithm only computes the labels on the real bits without knowing Δ, following the computation process on the evaluator side. Furthermore, each bit d_γ is computed with the masked bit and $\mathsf{LSB}(W_\gamma)$, given that each masked bit can be computed with the real bit and permutation bit. These changes are computationally indistinguishable from the real-world execution, according to the correctness analysis based on the pseudorandomness of the PRF outputs. In this hybrid, the decoding information is set according to the circuit output $y = f(x)$, and $\mathsf{H}(W_i^{y_i \oplus 1})$ is replaced with a random string V_i. In the random oracle (RO) model, if a PPT adversary can distinguish the decoding information from real values, then we can use it to break the IND-CPA and KDM security of the SWHEwDD scheme. This hybrid allows us to generate a garbled circuit without depending on the secret key Δ, which is crucial for going into the next hybrid. In **Hybrid 2**, we replace $\mathsf{Enc}(\Delta, \Delta)$ and $\mathsf{Enc}(\Delta, s_i)$ for $i \in [\ell]$ with the ciphertexts on zero. It is easy to see that Hybrid 2 is computationally indistinguishable from Hybrid 1, under the assumption that the SWHEwDD scheme is IND-CPA and KDM secure. In **Hybrid 3**, we replace each permutation bit π_i with a random bit, which has a negligible difference based on the pseudorandomness of the PRG output. In **Hybrid 4**, we replace each bit d_γ with a random bit. This hybrid is perfectly distinguishable from Hybrid 3, due to the fact that π_γ is uniform. In Hybrid 4, no real bits are used, and we construct a PPT simulator for BitGC-small. That is, Hybrid 4 is the ideal-world execution. The above overview is used for the proof of privacy. The proof of obliviousness can use the same simulator and hybrids, except that the decoding information would not be sent to the adversary, and thus is unnecessary to be simulated. For authenticity, we can use the simulator of privacy to generate the garbled circuit F and input labels. If a PPT adversary can break authenticity, then it must make a query associated with Δ to the random oracle H. We can extract Δ from the queries of H and use it to break the IND-CPA and KDM security of the SWHEwDD scheme.

Theorem 1. *Garbling scheme* BitGC-small *shown in Figs. 4 and 5 satisfies privacy, obliviousness and authenticity, provided that the SWHEwDD scheme satisfies the IND-CPA and KDM security properties,* PRG *is a secure PRG,* PRF *is a secure PRF, and* H *is a random oracle.*

5 BitGC-Fast and BitGC-Tiny: Garbling Schemes with Free-XOR

5.1 BitGC-Fast with Free-XOR and 5 Bits per AND Gate

The detailed construction of the BitGC-fast garbling scheme is shown in Figs. 6 and 7. The BitGC-fast scheme adopts the En and De algorithms in the BitGC-small scheme (Sect. 4.1). Thus, we omit the description of the two algorithms for BitGC-fast. In Figs. 6 and 7, the steps marked in blue show the differences of the Gb and Ev algorithms between BitGC-fast and BitGC-small. The main differences are listed as follows:

- Homomorphic PRG computation needs to generate the SWHE ciphertexts on $4|\mathcal{W}_{\mathsf{AND}}|$ (instead of $|\mathcal{W}|$) pseudorandom bits
- Each bit $\hat{z}^{i,j}$ is masked with a pseudorandom bit $r_\gamma^{i,j}$ and sent to the evaluator. Then the evaluator can compute the ciphertext $[\![\hat{z}^{i,j} \cdot \Delta]\!]$ with only homomorphic-addition operations.
- For the output wire γ of each AND gate, the permutation bit π_γ is sampled uniformly rather than an output bit of $\mathsf{PRG}(s)$. For each XOR gate, π_γ is defined as $\pi_\alpha \oplus \pi_\beta$. In this case, the bit $d_\gamma = \pi_\alpha \oplus \pi_\beta \oplus \pi_\gamma = 0$, which is unnecessary to be sent and thus communication-free is achieved for XOR gates.

In the amortized setting, BitGC-fast takes 5 bits per AND gate and achieves free-XOR. It requires that the SWHEwDD scheme supports $t+1$ levels of homomorphic multiplications, compared with $t+3$ levels for BitGC-small.

Correctness Analysis. Compared to BitGC-small, the BitGC-fast scheme mainly changes how the bits $\{d_\gamma\}$ are computed. Specifically, for each AND gate, BitGC-fast uses four additional bits of communication to directly transmit $\{\hat{z}^{i,j}\}$ in a secure way. For each XOR gate, BitGC-fast directly sets $d_\gamma = 0$, which realizes free-XOR. Below, we show that these changes do not affect the correctness.

- **Case 1: each AND gate.** The BitGC-fast scheme derives τ_1, τ_2, and τ_3 in the same way as BitGC-small, except that it uses a different method to generate $[\![\hat{z}^{i,j} \cdot \Delta]\!]$. Each term $[\![\hat{z}^{i,j} \cdot \Delta]\!]$ is homomorphically computed as

$$[\![\hat{z}^{i,j} \cdot \Delta]\!] := d_\gamma^{i,j} \cdot [\![\Delta]\!] + (1 - 2 \cdot d_\gamma^{i,j}) \cdot [\![r_\gamma^{i,j} \cdot \Delta]\!].$$

BitGC-fast (Part I)

Let $\mathsf{SWHE} = (\mathsf{Setup}, \mathsf{Gen}, \mathsf{Enc}, \mathsf{Dec}, \mathsf{Eval})$ be an SWHE scheme with distributed decryption. Let $\mathsf{PRG} : \{0,1\}^\ell \to \{0,1\}^{4N}$ be a secure t-depth PRG where ℓ is the seed size and $N = |\mathcal{W}_{\mathsf{AND}}|$ is the number of AND gates, $\mathsf{PRF} : \{0,1\}^\lambda \times \{0,1\}^\lambda \to \mathcal{R}_p$ be a secure PRF, and $\mathsf{H} : \mathcal{R}_p \to \{0,1\}^\lambda$ be a random oracle.

$\mathsf{Gb}(1^\lambda, f)$:

1. Generate a set of setup parameters $\mathsf{params} \leftarrow \mathsf{Setup}(1^\lambda, 1^L)$, where $L = t + 1$ is the maximum multiplication depth for SWHEwDD.

2. Generate a set of key-dependent parameters $(\mathsf{keypar}, \Delta) \leftarrow \mathsf{Gen}(\mathsf{params})$ with $\mathsf{LSB}(\Delta) = 1$, and run $[\![\Delta]\!] := \mathsf{Enc}(\Delta, \Delta)$. Sample a PRF key $K \xleftarrow{\$} \{0,1\}^\lambda$.

3. Sample a PRG seed $s \xleftarrow{\$} \{0,1\}^\ell$ and generate $[\![s_i]\!] := \mathsf{Enc}(\Delta, s_i)$ for each bit s_i with $i \in [\ell]$. Then, compute $\{r_\gamma^{i,j}\}_{\gamma \in \mathcal{W}_{\mathsf{AND}}, i,j \in \{0,1\}} := \mathsf{PRG}(s)$, and homomorphically compute $\mathsf{PRG}([\![s_0]\!], \ldots, [\![s_{\ell-1}]\!])$ to obtain $[\![r_\gamma^{i,j}]\!]$ for each $\gamma \in \mathcal{W}_{\mathsf{AND}}, i,j \in \{0,1\}$.

4. For each $\gamma \in \mathcal{W}_{\mathsf{AND}}, i,j \in \{0,1\}$, homomorphically compute a ciphertext $[\![r_\gamma^{i,j} \cdot \Delta]\!]$ from $[\![r_\gamma^{i,j}]\!]$ and $[\![\Delta]\!]$.

5. For each input wire $i \in \mathcal{I}$, sample $\pi_i \xleftarrow{\$} \{0,1\}$ and $W_i^0 \xleftarrow{\$} \mathcal{R}_p$, and then compute $W_i^1 := W_i^0 + (-1)^{\pi_i} \cdot \Delta \in \mathcal{R}_p$.

6. For each gate $(\alpha, \beta, \gamma, T)$ in topological order, do the following:
   - Case 1 $(T = \mathsf{AND})$:
     (a) Sample $\pi_\gamma \xleftarrow{\$} \{0,1\}$. For each $i,j \in \{0,1\}$, compute $\hat{z}^{i,j} := (\pi_\alpha \oplus i) \wedge (\pi_\beta \oplus j) \oplus \pi_\gamma$, set $d_\gamma^{i,j} := \hat{z}^{i,j} \oplus r_\gamma^{i,j}$, and homomorphically compute $[\![\hat{z}^{i,j} \cdot \Delta]\!] := d_\gamma^{i,j} \cdot [\![\Delta]\!] + (1 - 2 \cdot d_\gamma^{i,j}) \cdot [\![r_\gamma^{i,j} \cdot \Delta]\!]$.
     (b) Compute $\tau_1 := [\![\hat{z}^{1,0} \cdot \Delta]\!] - [\![\hat{z}^{0,0} \cdot \Delta]\!], \tau_2 := [\![\hat{z}^{0,1} \cdot \Delta]\!] - [\![\hat{z}^{0,0} \cdot \Delta]\!], \tau_3 := [\![\hat{z}^{1,1} \cdot \Delta]\!] - [\![\hat{z}^{0,0} \cdot \Delta]\!] - \tau_1 - \tau_2$.
     (c) Compute a pair of labels $W_\gamma^{\pi_\gamma} := \mathsf{Eval}_{0,0}(W_\alpha^{\pi_\alpha}, W_\beta^{\pi_\beta}, \tau_1, \tau_2, \tau_3) - \hat{z}^{0,0} \cdot \Delta + \mathsf{PRF}_K(\gamma)$, $W_\gamma^{\pi_\gamma \oplus 1} := W_\gamma^{\pi_\gamma} + \Delta$, along with a bit $d_\gamma := \mathsf{LSB}(W_\gamma^0) \oplus \pi_\gamma$.
   - Case 2 $(T = \mathsf{XOR})$:
     (a) Compute $\pi_\gamma := \pi_\alpha \oplus \pi_\beta, \tau_1 := [\![\Delta]\!], \tau_2 := \tau_1$, and $\tau_3 := -\tau_1 - \tau_2$.
     (b) Compute a pair of labels $W_\gamma^{\pi_\gamma} := \mathsf{Eval}_{0,0}(W_\alpha^{\pi_\alpha}, W_\beta^{\pi_\beta}, \tau_1, \tau_2, \tau_3) + \mathsf{PRF}_K(\gamma)$ and $W_\gamma^{\pi_\gamma \oplus 1} := W_\gamma^{\pi_\gamma} + \Delta$.

7. Output a garbled circuit $F := (\mathsf{params}, \mathsf{keypar}, [\![\Delta]\!], K, \{[\![s_i]\!]\}_{i \in [\ell]}, \{(d_\gamma, d_\gamma^{0,0}, d_\gamma^{0,1}, d_\gamma^{1,0}, d_\gamma^{1,1})\}_{\gamma \in \mathcal{W}_{\mathsf{AND}}})$, an encoding information $e := (\{(\pi_i, W_i^0)\}_{i \in \mathcal{I}}, \Delta)$ and a decoding information $d := \{\mathsf{H}(W_i^0), \mathsf{H}(W_i^1)\}_{i \in \mathcal{O}}$.

Fig. 6. BitGC-fast with 5 bits per AND gate and free-XOR (Part I), where the differences between BitGC-fast and BitGC-small are marked in blue. (Color figure online)

Therefore, it suffices to show that $\mathsf{Dec}([\![\hat{z}^{i,j} \cdot \Delta]\!]) = \hat{z}^{i,j} \cdot \Delta$. In particular,

$$\mathsf{Dec}([\![\hat{z}^{i,j} \cdot \Delta]\!]) = d_\gamma^{i,j} \cdot \Delta + (1 - 2 \cdot d_\gamma^{i,j}) \cdot r_\gamma^{i,j} \cdot \Delta$$
$$= \left(d_\gamma^{i,j} + r_\gamma^{i,j} - 2 \cdot d_\gamma^{i,j} \cdot r_\gamma^{i,j} \right) \cdot \Delta$$
$$= \left(d_\gamma^{i,j} \oplus r_\gamma^{i,j} \right) \cdot \Delta = \hat{z}^{i,j} \cdot \Delta.$$

BitGC-fast (Part II)

$\mathsf{Ev}(F, X)$:

1. Homomorphically compute $\mathsf{PRG}\,(\llbracket s_0 \rrbracket, \ldots, \llbracket s_{\ell-1} \rrbracket)$ to obtain $\llbracket r_\gamma^{i,j} \rrbracket$ for each $\gamma \in \mathcal{W}_{\mathsf{AND}}, i, j \in \{0,1\}$. Then, for each $\gamma \in \mathcal{W}_{\mathsf{AND}}, i, j \in \{0,1\}$, homomorphically compute $\llbracket r_\gamma^{i,j} \cdot \Delta \rrbracket$ from $\llbracket r_\gamma^{i,j} \rrbracket$ and $\llbracket \Delta \rrbracket$.
2. For each gate $(\alpha, \beta, \gamma, T)$ in topological order, perform the following steps:
   - Case 1 ($T = \mathsf{AND}$):
     (a) For each $i, j \in \{0,1\}$, homomorphically compute $\llbracket \hat{z}^{i,j} \cdot \Delta \rrbracket := d_\gamma^{i,j} \cdot \llbracket \Delta \rrbracket + (1 - 2 \cdot d_\gamma^{i,j}) \cdot \llbracket r_\gamma^{i,j} \cdot \Delta \rrbracket$.
     (b) Compute $\tau_1 := \llbracket \hat{z}^{1,0} \cdot \Delta \rrbracket - \llbracket \hat{z}^{0,0} \cdot \Delta \rrbracket, \tau_2 := \llbracket \hat{z}^{0,1} \cdot \Delta \rrbracket - \llbracket \hat{z}^{0,0} \cdot \Delta \rrbracket, \tau_3 := \llbracket \hat{z}^{1,1} \cdot \Delta \rrbracket - \llbracket \hat{z}^{0,0} \cdot \Delta \rrbracket - \tau_1 - \tau_2$.
     (c) Compute $W_\gamma := \mathsf{Eval}_{\hat{x}_\alpha, \hat{x}_\beta}(W_\alpha, W_\beta, \tau_1, \tau_2, \tau_3) + \mathsf{PRF}_K(\gamma)$.
     (d) Compute a masked bit $\hat{x}_\gamma := \mathsf{LSB}(W_\gamma) \oplus d_\gamma$.
   - Case 2 ($T = \mathsf{XOR}$):
     (a) Set $\tau_1 := \llbracket \Delta \rrbracket$, $\tau_2 := \tau_1$, and $\tau_3 := -\tau_1 - \tau_2$.
     (b) Compute $W_\gamma := \mathsf{Eval}_{\hat{x}_\alpha, \hat{x}_\beta}(W_\alpha, W_\beta, \tau_1, \tau_2, \tau_3) + \mathsf{PRF}_K(\gamma)$.
     (c) Compute a masked bit $\hat{x}_\gamma := \hat{x}_\alpha \oplus \hat{x}_\beta$.
3. Output $Y := \{W_i\}_{i \in \mathcal{O}}$.

Fig. 7. BitGC-fast with 5 bits per AND gate and free-XOR (Part II), where the differences between BitGC-fast and BitGC-small are marked in blue. (Color figure online)

- **Case 2: Each XOR Gate.** The BitGC-fast scheme directly defines $\pi_\gamma = \pi_\alpha \oplus \pi_\beta$, resulting in $d_\gamma = 0$. This modification preserves the correctness of the wire label, since the proof of Equation (5) remains valid. Therefore, it suffices to show that $\hat{x}_\gamma = \pi_\gamma \oplus x_\gamma$. To see this, observe that

$$\hat{x}_\gamma = \hat{x}_\alpha \oplus \hat{x}_\beta = x_\alpha \oplus \pi_\alpha \oplus x_\beta \oplus \pi_\beta = x_\gamma \oplus \pi_\gamma.$$

Therefore, the correctness of BitGC-fast can follow that of the BitGC-small scheme.

Security Proof. The proof of BitGC-fast follows the same hybrid-based strategy as in BitGC-small, except for some modifications tailored to the construction of BitGC-fast. Similarly, we first changes the garbling process without relying on secret key Δ. Then, $\llbracket \Delta \rrbracket$ and $\llbracket s_i \rrbracket$ for $i \in [\ell]$ are replaced with encryptions of zero. The changes are computationally indistinguishable from the real-world execution, under the assumption that the SWHEwDD scheme satisfies the IND-CPA and KDM security and PRF is a secure PRF. Next, each bit $r_\gamma^{i,j}$ is replaced by a uniform bit, justified by the pseudorandomness of the PRG. Finally, the 5-bit communication values for each AND gate are shown to be uniformly random, since they are masked with independent random bits. Note that permutation bits are uniform and independent from the adversary's view in the final hybrid. Through the above proof idea, we are able to obtain a proof for privacy. Using the same approach as in the proof of BitGC-small, we can easily obtain the proofs for both obliviousness and authenticity.

Theorem 2. *Garbling scheme* BitGC-fast *shown in Figs. 6 and 7 satisfies privacy, obliviousness and authenticity, provided that the SWHEwDD scheme satisfies the IND-CPA and KDM security properties,* PRG *is a secure PRG,* PRF *is a secure PRF, and* H *is a random oracle.*

5.2   BitGC-tiny with Free-XOR, 1 Bit per AND Gate and More Computational Cost

We describe a garbling scheme called BitGC-tiny, which supports free-XOR and communication of 1 bit per AND gate. While BitGC-tiny achieves the lowest communication cost among our three garbling schemes, it requires the usage of a leveled HE scheme and brings about much more computational cost. A leveled homomorphic encryption with distributed decryption (LHEwDD) scheme follows the same syntax and security properties as the SWHEwDD scheme (Sect. 3.3), except that the maximum multiplication depth L of the leveled HE scheme can be any positive integer. The LHEwDD scheme can be instantiated in a totally similar method as the SWHEwDD instantiation we discussed in the full version [57], after replacing the BGV-based SWHE scheme with the BGV-based leveled HE scheme.

In the following, we discuss the main differences between BitGC-tiny and BitGC-small.

- In BitGC-tiny, the leveled HE scheme requires $\lceil \log(\ell + 1) \rceil$ more levels of homomorphic multiplications than BitGC-small, where ℓ is the length of the longest consecutive sequence of XOR gates in the circuit.
- Homomorphic PRG computation needs to generate the HE ciphertexts on $|\mathcal{I}| + |\mathcal{W}_{\mathsf{AND}}|$ (instead of $|\mathcal{I}| + |\mathcal{W}|$) pseudorandom bits.
- For each XOR gate $(\alpha, \beta, \gamma, \mathsf{XOR})$, π_γ is directly defined as $\pi_\alpha \oplus \pi_\beta$ rather than an output bit of $\mathsf{PRG}(s)$. Following the approach in BitGC-fast, the bit $d_\gamma = \pi_\alpha \oplus \pi_\beta \oplus \pi_\gamma = 0$ is unnecessary to be sent. Nevertheless, both the Gb and Ev algorithms still need to compute the ciphertext $[\![\pi_\gamma]\!]$, as it remains necessary for garbling subsequent AND gates. To minimize the multiplicative depth, we recursively expand π_γ into its base constituent masks whenever an input itself is an output of an XOR gate. The final $[\![\pi_\gamma]\!]$ then is computed as the homomorphic XOR sum of all flattened masks.

Based on the correctness analysis of BitGC-small and BitGC-fast, the correctness of the BitGC-tiny scheme can be naturally derived. By combining the proof of BitGC-small with that of BitGC-fast, it is easy to obtain the proof of BitGC-tiny, when replacing the IND-CPA and KDM security of SWHEwDD with that of LHEwDD. We state the security of the BitGC-tiny scheme in the following theorem.

Theorem 3. *Garbling scheme* BitGC-tiny *satisfies privacy, obliviousness and authenticity, provided that the LHEwDD scheme satisfies the IND-CPA and KDM security properties,* PRG *is a secure PRG,* PRF *is a secure PRF, and* H *is a random oracle.*

6   Implementation Details

We implement the proposed garbling schemes BitGC-fast and BitGC-small in C++, on top of `Microsoft SEAL 4.1` [52]. In this section, we provide the details of the implementation, including the instantiation of the SWHEwDD scheme and the low-depth PRG, homomorphic evaluation of the PRG with SIMD optimization, and concrete parameters.

SWHEwDD Instantiation. We use the BGV framework [16] under the RLWE assumption as the basic SWHE scheme. We instantiate each $DD_{i,j}$ algorithm for $i, j \in \{0, 1\}$ by replacing the GSW-like ciphertexts in the original scheme [44] with the BGV-like ciphertexts. Furthermore, we adopt the Circular Power RLWE (CP-RLWE) assumption used in the recent work [36] for better efficiency. As a result, we construct an SWHEwDD scheme under the RLWE and CP-RLWE assumptions, which is significantly more efficient than the existing instantiation [44]. We note that the SWHEwDD scheme can also be instantiated under the BFV framework [15,20] in a similar way.

Low-Depth PRG Instantiation. We instantiate our low-depth PRG using Goldreich-style random local PRGs [23]. Let d be the locality of the PRG, ℓ be the seed size, ℓ^s for some $s > 1$ be the polynomial stretch, and $P : \{0,1\}^d \to \{0,1\}$ be the predicate. The i-th bit of the PRG output y_i is associated with a randomly sampled public index set $I_i \in [\ell]^d$, and is evaluated by the predicate P on the input bits indexed by I_i. We choose the predicate P as $\mathsf{XOR}_{k_1}\text{-Majority}_{k_2}$ proposed by Applebaum and Lovett [6], and use the parameters as in [1] with $k_1 = 4$ and $k_2 = 7$ for a high stretch. We set parameters $\ell = 2^{16}, s = 2$, and stretch $\ell^s = 2^{32}$, which can resist the best known attacks [48,53,54]. The predicate P is defined as

$$P(\{x_i\}_{i\in[11]}) = \mathsf{Majority}\left(\{x_i\}_{i\in[7]}\right) \oplus (x_7 \oplus x_8 \oplus x_9 \oplus x_{10})$$

$$= \left(\bigoplus_{0 \le i < j < k < l < 7} (x_i \wedge x_j \wedge x_k \wedge x_l) \right) \oplus (x_7 \oplus x_8 \oplus x_9 \oplus x_{10}).$$

Since the plaintext space in our SWHEwDD instantiation is a polynomial ring $\mathcal{R}_p$, we must arithmetize the Boolean predicate P to enable homomorphic evaluation. We achieve this by mapping logical operations to arithmetic ones: $a \wedge b \mapsto a \cdot b$ and $a \oplus b \mapsto a + b - 2 \cdot a \cdot b$. We further simplify the expression by reducing all higher-degree exponents ($x^k \equiv x$ for $x \in \{0,1\}$). The resulting arithmetic representation of P includes terms of at most $11°$, which can be homomorphically evaluated with a multiplicative depth of 4.

SIMD-Enabled PRG Evaluation. The ring structure of the plaintext space $\mathcal{R}_p$ naturally supports SIMD operations. Let m be the number of slots packed into a polynomial in the plaintext space. An input of $m \cdot \ell$ seed bits, that is divided into m blocks of ℓ bits, is packed into ℓ polynomials then encrypted. For the i-th polynomial, it encodes the i-th bit of all m blocks into its slots. We then homomorphically evaluate the arithmetic expression of the PRG over the ciphertexts, and yield each output ciphertext encrypting a packed polynomial of m bits.

Both the garbler and the evaluator need ciphertexts that only encrypt a single bit instead of a packed polynomial for Garble and Eval algorithms. Therefore, we further need to extract m individual ciphertexts from a ciphertext of a packed polynomial. It can be achieved in two steps. First, we compute the unpacking homomorphically which requires $O(2\sqrt{N})$ homomorphic operations of one multiplicative depth [29,30]. Then, we extract N individual ciphertexts by computing $O(N)$ homomorphic operations of zero multiplicative depth [17]. For a better performance, once the individual ciphertexts are extracted, the ciphertexts can be switched to a smaller modulus with a reduced dimension using the method described in [17].

SWHEwDD Parameters. For our concrete implementation, we take the Residue Number System (RNS) for the ciphertext representation. Let p be the plaintext modulus. Ciphertexts initially use a modulus Q and a lattice dimension N. Following a modulus-switching step after extraction, these are reduced to a smaller modulus q and dimension n. In our BitGC-small implementation, which requires a greater homomorphic depth, we set the modulus bit-length to $\log p = 60$, $\log Q = 1020$ and $\log q = 480$. Consequentially, we set the lattice dimension to $N = 2^{16}$ and $n = 2^{15}$. In BitGC-fast, we set $\log p = 60$, $\log Q = 840$, $\log q = 240$, and lattice dimension $N = 2^{15}$ and $n = 2^{13}$. These parameters are estimated to provide 128-bit security based on [3]. The failing probability per gate of the garbling scheme can be bounded by $O(n/p)$, which is smaller than 2^{-40} with our parameters.

7   Performance Evaluation

In this section, we perform a series of benchmark experiments to study the concrete performance of the BitGC scheme and the proposed variants BitGC-fast, BitGC-small, and BitGC-tiny.

Experimental Setup. Our experimental results are conducted on an AWS EC2 instance of type `m8i.48xlarge`, with up to 768 GiB of memory. All experiments are conducted with *single-threaded* execution. To evaluate the concrete performance of our schemes, we benchmark the end-to-end garbling and evaluation pipeline. We structure the pipeline into two phases:

- **Preprocessing**: this execution only requires an upper bound of the circuit size, and primarily conducted the homomorphic PRG evaluation on the encrypted seed. For our improved SIMD-enabled schemes, two steps are involved: **(1) HE-PRG** which homomorphically evaluates the PRG over encrypted packed polynomials; **(2) Extraction** which extracts individual ciphertexts from the packed ciphertexts. For the original BitGC, only the HE-PRG step is involved.

- **Gate-dependent**: this execution requires the circuit topology. During this phase, the garbler generates the garbled table and computes the output label, while the evaluator takes the garbled table and evaluates the output label of each gate in a topological order. It consists of **(3) Assembly** which assembles three ciphertexts as the input of the Eval function. **(4) Eval** which applies the Eval function on the assembled ciphertexts to obtain the output label.

Experimental Results. We evaluate the performance of our schemes BitGC-fast and BitGC-small by benchmarking an AES-128 circuit with 6400 AND gates and 28176 XOR gates. We utilize a single thread for execution, and note that the preprocessing phase can be further accelerated by parallelizing the execution, as each PRG output bit is associated with an independent index set. Since the computation costs of the garbling and evaluation are nearly identical, we only report the results of the garbling pipeline for simplicity.

In addition, we provide a lower-bound performance estimation for the original BitGC scheme and our BitGC-tiny scheme. For the original BitGC, we estimate the performance by assuming a non-SIMD homomorphic PRG evaluation and assigning the cost of an AND gate to all gates; we apply the same implementation-level optimizations to BitGC as those used in our variants. For the performance estimation of BitGC-tiny, we assume that the additional multiplication depth for homomorphic evaluation is bounded by 5 (supporting circuits with up to 31 consecutive XOR operations). Correspondingly, we set $\log Q = 1500, \log q = 960, N = 2^{18}, n = 2^{17}$ for the parameters underlying the BitGC-tiny scheme. For each XOR gate, we account the cost of homomorphic computing the permutation bit into the "assembly" step.

We note that our instantiated low-depth PRG has an expansion factor of ℓ^{s-1}, and we enable SIMD for homomorphic PRG evaluation. Therefore, the amortized communication cost for transmitting encrypted seeds is $\log Q/\ell^{s-1} \approx 0.02$ bits per homomorphically expanded pseudorandom bit. We need 1 pseudorandom bit per gate for BitGC-small and BitGC, 4 pseudorandom bits per AND gate for BitGC-fast, and 1 pseudorandom bit per AND gate for BitGC-tiny. We therefore omit the amortized communication cost for transmitting encrypted seeds.

The one-time setup communication of SWHEwDD consists of transmitting the public parameters and key-related parameters (including the ciphertext of the secret key Δ, preprocessed ciphertexts for distributed decryption, and all evaluation keys). For BitGC-fast, this cost is about 2.5 GiB, given our SWHEwDD instantiation and parameter selection for 128-bit security. We note that this cost is independent of the circuit size and can be amortized to negligibly small for sufficiently large circuits. Compared to the best-known "Yao-style" garbled circuit [51], BitGC-fast would achieve lower total communication when more than 1.15×10^8 gates (approximately $18,000$ AES-128 circuits) are evaluated.

Table 2. Performance comparison between BitGC and our proposed variants. The communication cost (bits), amortized running time (ms) in total, and amortized running time for each pipeline step (ms) are reported for each AND and XOR gate. Costs for BitGC and BitGC-tiny are lower-bound estimation. Costs are amortized over large circuits and exclude reusable data. The communication cost of transmitting an encrypted seed is negligibly small compared to other components of a garbled circuit and thus is omitted.

	Gate	Comm.	Preprocessing		Gate-dependent		Total time
			HE-PRG	Extraction	Assembly	Eval	
BitGC-fast	AND	5	0.47	19.62	0.44	1.66	22.19
	XOR	0	0	0	0	1.66	1.66
BitGC-small	AND	1	0.16	49.9	232.1	31.6	331.8
	XOR	1			37.7	31.6	119.4
BitGC-tiny	AND	1	≥ 0.16 ·	≥ 798	≥ 928	≥ 126	≥ 1852
	XOR	0			≥ 383	≥ 126	≥ 1307
BitGC [44]	AND	1	10218	0	≥ 232.1	≥ 31.6	≥ 10482
	XOR	1					

The amortized communication and time costs per gate, along with the time costs for each pipeline step, are presented in Table 2.

Analysis. As shown in the table, BitGC scheme incurs a substantial overhead from its non-SIMD homomorphic PRG evaluation. In contrast, with SIMD optimization, our BitGC-small scheme significantly reduces the time cost by $200\times$ during the preprocessing phase. Furthermore, by applying specific optimizations for XOR gates rather than treating them generically, BitGC-small scheme further cuts nearly $4\times$ cost during the gate-dependent phase.

We also note that BitGC-fast scheme provides a powerful trade-off between communication and concrete computational cost. It reduces significantly the per-gate time cost for AND gate and XOR gate by approximately $15\times$ and $70\times$, respectively, compared to BitGC-small scheme, and even further compared to the BitGC-tiny scheme. We acknowledge that it requires more communication per AND gate, but BitGC-fast scheme benefits from the free-XOR property that eliminates communication for XOR gates. This can lead to a comparable total communication cost to BitGC-small scheme, especially in circuits with a high ratio of XOR gates to AND gates like AES-128.

Acknowledgements. The work of Yu Yu is supported by the National Natural Science Foundation of China (Grant Nos. 62125204 and 92270201) and Innovation Program for Quantum Science and Technology (No. 2021ZD0302901/2021ZD0302902).

References

1. Agarwal, A., Baum, C., Braun, L., Scholl, P.: Low-bandwidth mixed arithmetic in VOLE-based ZK from low-degree PRGs. In: EUROCRYPT 2025, Part IV. LNCS (2025). https://doi.org/10.1007/978-3-031-91134-7_14
2. Agrawal, S.: Stronger security for reusable garbled circuits, general definitions and attacks. In: Katz, J., Shacham, H. (eds.) CRYPTO 2017, Part I. LNCS, vol. 10401, pp. 3–35. Springer, Cham (2017). https://doi.org/10.1007/978-3-319-63688-7_1
3. Albrecht, M., et al.: Homomorphic encryption standard. Cryptology ePrint Archive, Report 2019/939 (2019). https://eprint.iacr.org/2019/939
4. Alekhnovich, M.: More on average case vs approximation complexity. In: 44th FOCS (2003). https://doi.org/10.1109/SFCS.2003.1238204
5. Applebaum, B.: Pseudorandom generators with long stretch and low locality from random local one-way functions. In: 44th ACM STOC (2012). https://doi.org/10.1145/2213977.2214050
6. Applebaum, B., Lovett, S.: Algebraic attacks against random local functions and their countermeasures. In: 48th ACM STOC (2016). https://doi.org/10.1145/2897518.2897554
7. Applebaum, B., Raykov, P.: Fast pseudorandom functions based on expander graphs. In: Hirt, M., Smith, A. (eds.) TCC 2016, Part I. LNCS, vol. 9985, pp. 27–56. Springer, Heidelberg (2016). https://doi.org/10.1007/978-3-662-53641-4_2
8. Banerjee, A., Peikert, C., Rosen, A.: Pseudorandom functions and lattices. In: Pointcheval, D., Johansson, T. (eds.) EUROCRYPT 2012. LNCS, vol. 7237, pp. 719–737. Springer, Heidelberg (2012). https://doi.org/10.1007/978-3-642-29011-4_42
9. Beaver, D., Micali, S., Rogaway, P.: The round complexity of secure protocols (extended abstract). In: 22nd ACM STOC (1990). https://doi.org/10.1145/100216.100287
10. Bellare, M., Hoang, V.T., Keelveedhi, S., Rogaway, P.: Efficient garbling from a fixed-key blockcipher. In: 2013 IEEE Symposium on Security and Privacy (2013). https://doi.org/10.1109/SP.2013.39
11. Bellare, M., Hoang, V.T., Rogaway, P.: Foundations of garbled circuits. In: ACM CCS 2012 (2012). https://doi.org/10.1145/2382196.2382279
12. Black, J., Rogaway, P., Shrimpton, T.: Encryption-scheme security in the presence of key-dependent messages. In: Nyberg, K., Heys, H. (eds.) SAC 2002. LNCS, vol. 2595, pp. 62–75. Springer, Heidelberg (2003). https://doi.org/10.1007/3-540-36492-7_6
13. Boneh, D., et al.: Fully key-homomorphic encryption, arithmetic circuit ABE and compact garbled circuits. In: Nguyen, P.Q., Oswald, E. (eds.) EUROCRYPT 2014. LNCS, vol. 8441, pp. 533–556. Springer, Heidelberg (2014). https://doi.org/10.1007/978-3-642-55220-5_30
14. Boyle, E., Kohl, L., Scholl, P.: Homomorphic secret sharing from lattices without FHE. In: Ishai, Y., Rijmen, V. (eds.) EUROCRYPT 2019, Part II. LNCS, vol. 11477, pp. 3–33. Springer, Cham (2019). https://doi.org/10.1007/978-3-030-17656-3_1
15. Brakerski, Z.: Fully homomorphic encryption without modulus switching from classical GapSVP. In: Safavi-Naini, R., Canetti, R. (eds.) CRYPTO 2012. LNCS, vol. 7417, pp. 868–886. Springer, Heidelberg (2012). https://doi.org/10.1007/978-3-642-32009-5_50

16. Brakerski, Z., Gentry, C., Vaikuntanathan, V.: (Leveled) fully homomorphic encryption without bootstrapping. In: ITCS 2012 (2012). https://doi.org/10.1145/2090236.2090262
17. Chen, H., Dai, W., Kim, M., Song, Y.: Efficient homomorphic conversion between (Ring) LWE ciphertexts. In: Sako, K., Tippenhauer, N.O. (eds.) ACNS 2021, Part I. LNCS, vol. 12726, pp. 460–479. Springer, Cham (2021). https://doi.org/10.1007/978-3-030-78372-3_18
18. Chillotti, I., Orsini, E., Scholl, P., Smart, N.P., van Leeuwen, B.: Scooby: Improved multi-party homomorphic secret sharing based on FHE. In: SCN 22. LNCS (2022). https://doi.org/10.1007/978-3-031-14791-3_24
19. Döttling, N., Garg, S.: Identity-based encryption from the Diffie-Hellman assumption. In: Katz, J., Shacham, H. (eds.) CRYPTO 2017, Part I. LNCS, vol. 10401, pp. 537–569. Springer, Cham (2017). https://doi.org/10.1007/978-3-319-63688-7_18
20. Fan, J., Vercauteren, F.: Somewhat practical fully homomorphic encryption. Cryptology ePrint Archive, Report 2012/144 (2012). https://eprint.iacr.org/2012/144
21. Frederiksen, T.K., Nielsen, J.B., Orlandi, C.: Privacy-free garbled circuits with applications to efficient zero-knowledge. In: Oswald, E., Fischlin, M. (eds.) EUROCRYPT 2015, Part II. LNCS, vol. 9057, pp. 191–219. Springer, Heidelberg (2015). https://doi.org/10.1007/978-3-662-46803-6_7
22. Gentry, C., Gorbunov, S., Halevi, S., Vaikuntanathan, V., Vinayagamurthy, D.: How to compress (reusable) garbled circuits. Cryptology ePrint Archive, Report 2013/687 (2013). https://eprint.iacr.org/2013/687
23. Goldreich, O.: Candidate one-way functions based on expander graphs. In: Goldreich, O. (ed.) Studies in Complexity and Cryptography. Miscellanea on the Interplay between Randomness and Computation. LNCS, vol. 6650, pp. 76–87. Springer, Heidelberg (2011). https://doi.org/10.1007/978-3-642-22670-0_10
24. Goldwasser, S., Kalai, Y.T., Popa, R.A., Vaikuntanathan, V., Zeldovich, N.: Reusable garbled circuits and succinct functional encryption. In: 45th ACM STOC (2013). https://doi.org/10.1145/2488608.2488678
25. Gueron, S., Lindell, Y., Nof, A., Pinkas, B.: Fast garbling of circuits under standard assumptions. In: ACM CCS 2015 (2015). https://doi.org/10.1145/2810103.2813619
26. Guo, C., Katz, J., Wang, X., Weng, C., Yu, Yu.: Better concrete security for half-gates garbling (in the multi-instance setting). In: Micciancio, D., Ristenpart, T. (eds.) CRYPTO 2020, Part II. LNCS, vol. 12171, pp. 793–822. Springer, Cham (2020). https://doi.org/10.1007/978-3-030-56880-1_28
27. Guo, C., Katz, J., Wang, X., Yu, Y.: Efficient and secure multiparty computation from fixed-key block ciphers. In: 2020 IEEE Symposium on Security and Privacy (2020). https://doi.org/10.1109/SP40000.2020.00016
28. Guo, C., Wang, X., Yang, K., Yu, Y.: On tweakable correlation robust hashing against key leakages. DCC (8) (2025). https://doi.org/10.1007/s10623-025-01641-9
29. Halevi, S., Shoup, V.: Bootstrapping for **HElib**. In: Oswald, E., Fischlin, M. (eds.) EUROCRYPT 2015, Part I. LNCS, vol. 9056, pp. 641–670. Springer, Heidelberg (2015). https://doi.org/10.1007/978-3-662-46800-5_25
30. Halevi, S., Shoup, V.: Faster homomorphic linear transformations in **HElib**. In: Shacham, H., Boldyreva, A. (eds.) CRYPTO 2018, Part I. LNCS, vol. 10991, pp. 93–120. Springer, Cham (2018). https://doi.org/10.1007/978-3-319-96884-1_4
31. Heath, D., Kolesnikov, V.: Stacked garbling for disjunctive zero-knowledge proofs. In: Canteaut, A., Ishai, Y. (eds.) EUROCRYPT 2020, Part III. LNCS, vol. 12107, pp. 569–598. Springer, Cham (2020). https://doi.org/10.1007/978-3-030-45727-3_19

32. Hoffstein, J., Pipher, J., Silverman, J.H.: NTRU: a ring-based public key cryptosystem. In: Buhler, J.P. (ed.) ANTS 1998. LNCS, vol. 1423, pp. 267–288. Springer, Heidelberg (1998). https://doi.org/10.1007/BFb0054868

33. Huang, Y., Katz, J., Evans, D.: Quid-pro-quo-tocols: strengthening semi-honest protocols with dual execution. In: 2012 IEEE Symposium on Security and Privacy (2012). https://doi.org/10.1109/SP.2012.43

34. Ishai, Y., Kilian, J., Nissim, K., Petrank, E.: Extending oblivious transfers efficiently. In: Boneh, D. (ed.) CRYPTO 2003. LNCS, vol. 2729, pp. 145–161. Springer, Heidelberg (2003). https://doi.org/10.1007/978-3-540-45146-4_9

35. Ishai, Y., Li, H., Lin, H.: Succinct homomorphic MACs from groups and applications. In: 66th FOCS (2025). https://doi.org/10.1109/FOCS63196.2025.00131

36. Ishai, Y., Li, H., Lin, H.: A unified framework for succinct garbling from homomorphic secret sharing. In: CRYPTO 2025, Part IV. LNCS (2025). https://doi.org/10.1007/978-3-032-01884-7_13

37. Januzelli, J., Rosulek, M., Roy, L.: Lower bounds for garbled circuits from shannon-type information inequalities. In: CRYPTO 2025, Part IV. LNCS (2025). https://doi.org/10.1007/978-3-032-01884-7_19

38. Jawurek, M., Kerschbaum, F., Orlandi, C.: Zero-knowledge using garbled circuits: how to prove non-algebraic statements efficiently. In: ACM CCS 2013 (2013). https://doi.org/10.1145/2508859.2516662

39. Kolesnikov, V., Mohassel, P., Rosulek, M.: FleXOR: flexible garbling for XOR gates that beats free-XOR. In: Garay, J.A., Gennaro, R. (eds.) CRYPTO 2014, Part II. LNCS, vol. 8617, pp. 440–457. Springer, Heidelberg (2014). https://doi.org/10.1007/978-3-662-44381-1_25

40. Kolesnikov, V., Schneider, T.: Improved garbled circuit: free XOR gates and applications. In: Aceto, L., Damgård, I., Goldberg, L.A., Halldórsson, M.M., Ingólfsdóttir, A., Walukiewicz, I. (eds.) ICALP 2008, Part II. LNCS, vol. 5126, pp. 486–498. Springer, Heidelberg (2008). https://doi.org/10.1007/978-3-540-70583-3_40

41. Kondi, Y., Patra, A.: Privacy-free garbled circuits for formulas: size zero and information-theoretic. In: Katz, J., Shacham, H. (eds.) CRYPTO 2017, Part I. LNCS, vol. 10401, pp. 188–222. Springer, Cham (2017). https://doi.org/10.1007/978-3-319-63688-7_7

42. Lindell, Y., Pinkas, B.: A proof of security of Yao's protocol for two-party computation. J. Cryptology (2) (2009). https://doi.org/10.1007/s00145-008-9036-8

43. Liu, H., Wang, X., Yang, K., Yu, Y.: Authenticated BitGC for actively secure rate-one 2PC. In: CRYPTO 2025, Part IV. LNCS (2025). https://doi.org/10.1007/978-3-032-01884-7_21

44. Liu, H., Wang, X., Yang, K., Yu, Y.: BitGC: Garbled circuits with 1 bit per gate. In: EUROCRYPT 2025, Part VII. LNCS (2025). https://doi.org/10.1007/978-3-031-91098-2_16

45. Lyubashevsky, V., Peikert, C., Regev, O.: On ideal lattices and learning with errors over rings. In: Gilbert, H. (ed.) EUROCRYPT 2010. LNCS, vol. 6110, pp. 1–23. Springer, Heidelberg (2010). https://doi.org/10.1007/978-3-642-13190-5_1

46. Meyer, P., Orlandi, C., Roy, L., Scholl, P.: Silent circuit relinearisation: sublinear-size (boolean and arithmetic) garbled circuits from DCR. In: CRYPTO 2025, Part IV. LNCS (2025). https://doi.org/10.1007/978-3-032-01884-7_14

47. Naor, M., Pinkas, B., Sumner, R.: Privacy preserving auctions and mechanism design. In: Proceedings of the 1st ACM Conference on Electronic Commerce. pp. 129–139. ACM, New York, NY, USA (1999). https://doi.org/10.1145/336992.337028

48. ODonnell, R., Witmer, D.: Goldreich's PRG: evidence for near-optimal polynomial stretch. In: 2014 IEEE 29th Conference on Computational Complexity (CCC), pp. 1–12 (2014). https://doi.org/10.1109/CCC.2014.9

49. Pellet-Mary, A., Stehlé, D.: On the hardness of the NTRU problem. In: Tibouchi, M., Wang, H. (eds.) ASIACRYPT 2021, Part I. LNCS, vol. 13090, pp. 3–35. Springer, Cham (2021). https://doi.org/10.1007/978-3-030-92062-3_1

50. Pinkas, B., Schneider, T., Smart, N.P., Williams, S.C.: Secure two-party computation is practical. In: Matsui, M. (ed.) ASIACRYPT 2009. LNCS, vol. 5912, pp. 250–267. Springer, Heidelberg (2009). https://doi.org/10.1007/978-3-642-10366-7_15

51. Rosulek, M., Roy, L.: Three halves make a whole? beating the half-gates lower bound for garbled circuits. In: Malkin, T., Peikert, C. (eds.) CRYPTO 2021, Part I. LNCS, vol. 12825, pp. 94–124. Springer, Cham (2021). https://doi.org/10.1007/978-3-030-84242-0_5

52. Microsoft SEAL (release 4.1). https://github.com/Microsoft/SEAL (2023), microsoft Research, Redmond, WA

53. Ünal, A.: Worst-case subexponential attacks on PRGs of constant degree or constant locality. In: EUROCRYPT 2023, Part I. LNCS (2023). https://doi.org/10.1007/978-3-031-30545-0_2

54. Yang, J., Guo, Q., Johansson, T., Lentmaier, M.: Revisiting the concrete security of goldreich's pseudorandom generator. IEEE Trans. Inf. Theory $\mathbf{68}(2)$, 1329–1354 (2022). https://doi.org/10.1109/TIT.2021.3128315

55. Yao, A.C.C.: How to generate and exchange secrets (extended abstract). In: 27th FOCS (1986). https://doi.org/10.1109/SFCS.1986.25

56. Zahur, S., Rosulek, M., Evans, D.: Two halves make a whole. In: Oswald, E., Fischlin, M. (eds.) EUROCRYPT 2015, Part II. LNCS, vol. 9057, pp. 220–250. Springer, Heidelberg (2015). https://doi.org/10.1007/978-3-662-46803-6_8

57. Zhang, W., et al.: BitGC made (more) efficient. Cryptology ePrint Archive, Report 2025/1810 (2025). https://eprint.iacr.org/2025/1810

Succinct Garbled Circuits
with Low-Depth Garbling Algorithms

Hanjun Li[1], Huijia Lin[2], and George Lu[3(✉)]

[1] Carnegie Mellon University, Pittsburgh, PA, USA
[2] University of Washington, Seattle, WA, USA
[3] University of Texas at Austin, Austin, TX, USA
`gclu@cs.utexas.edu`

Abstract. We study the problem of constructing Boolean garbling schemes that are both **succinct**—with garbled circuit size significantly smaller than the original circuit—and have **low-depth** garbling algorithms, where the garbling process runs in parallel time logarithmic in the circuit size. Prior schemes achieve one but not the other, unless relying on indistinguishability obfuscation (iO), which is prohibitively inefficient, relies on a combination of multiple assumptions, and achieves only polynomial garbling depth $\mathsf{poly}(\lambda, \log|C|)$.

We resolve this tension by presenting the first garbling schemes that are both succinct and admit garbling algorithms in NC^1, based only on standard group and lattice assumptions. Our main results include:
- **One-bit-per-gate garbling** with logarithmic garbling depth based on DDH or RLWE and the existence of a local PRG.
- Succinct **Privacy-free garbling** of size linear in the circuit depth D (and sublinear in the circuit size $|C|$), based on DDH or RLWE.
- **Reusable, fully succinct garbling** with logarithmic garbling depth, based on decomposable LWE.

The DDH-based one-bit-per-gate scheme has tunably small inverse polynomial correctness and privacy errors, which can be made negligible at the cost of increasing garbling depth to $\mathsf{poly}(\lambda)$.

As further extension, we also obtain the first attribute-based encryption schemes with *succinct keys* and *low-depth* key generation.

At a conceptual level, our constructions are derived from a **unified framework** that subsumes all prior approaches to succinct garbling. It identifies the common source of high-depth garbling, and provides a general methodology for reducing garbling depth without sacrificing succinctness, applicable across different techniques and assumptions.

1   Introduction

A Boolean garbling scheme transforms a Boolean circuit C and an input x into garbled versions, $(\hat{C}, \mathsf{gk}) \leftarrow \mathsf{GarbC}(1^\lambda, C)$ and $\hat{x} \leftarrow \mathsf{GarbInp}(\mathsf{gk}, x)$, from which the output can be recovered $\mathsf{Eval}(C, \hat{C}, \hat{x}) = y$ without revealing any other information about the input. Garbling schemes are a foundational primitive in cryptography with wide-ranging applications, including multiparty computation [Yao86, BMR90, IPS08, GS17, GS18, BL18], parallel

© International Association for Cryptologic Research 2026
J. Daemen and E. Thomé (Eds.): EUROCRYPT 2026, LNCS 16543, pp. 246–275, 2026.
https://doi.org/10.1007/978-3-032-25324-8_9

cryptography [AIK04, AIK06], and verifiable computation [GGP10, AIK10] etc.; see [App17] for a survey.

Given their central role, a huge amount of work has focused on improving the efficiency of garbled circuits. Two aspects have received particular attention: succinctness, namely minimizing the size of the garbled circuit and garbled inputs; and low-depth garbling, namely reducing the depth, and thus the parallel-time, of the garbling algorithms. Surprisingly, almost all known constructions achieve either succinctness *or* low-depth garbling but not both, except for schemes relying on indistinguishability obfuscation (iO). In this work, we resolve this tension by presenting an array of *succinct* and *low-depth* garbling schemes, based on standard group and lattice assumptions, that are significantly simpler and more efficient than iO-based approaches.

Succinctness. Yao's original construction [Yao82] and subsequent optimizations [BMR90, NPS99, KS08, PSSW09, KMR14, GLNP15, ZRE15, RR21] remain the most computationally efficient general-purpose garbling schemes, owing to their reliance on fast symmetric-key cryptography. They also achieve extremely low garbling depth. The main limitation is their communication complexity: the current state of the art, due to Rosulek and Roy [RR21], devotes $1.5\lambda + 5$ bits to garbling an AND gate, while XOR and NOT gates are free under the random oracle model.

This $\Omega(\lambda)$-bits-per-gate barrier motivated the study of *succinct* garbled circuits, where the bit-length of the garbled circuit $|\hat{C}|$ is asymptotically smaller than the description size of the original circuit C. Since a circuit C with $|C|$ gates requires at least $|C| \log |C|$ bits to describe, succinct garbling demands $|\hat{C}| < |C| \log |C|^1$. Two main approaches have emerged:

- *Fully succinct garbling schemes.* These achieve garbled circuit size independent of $|C|$. Constructions either rely on iO [KLW15, BCG+18], or on combinations of homomorphic encryption (HE) and attribute-based encryption (ABE) [GKP+13, BGG+14, HLL23]. In addition to optimal asymptotic size, these schemes are *reusable* [GKP+13], meaning the same garbled circuit can be used to evaluate arbitrarily many input encodings. However, their concrete efficiency is poor. iO-based constructions are prohibitively expensive, while FHE-plus-ABE approaches are more efficient in a relative sense, they are still far from practical.
- *One-bit-per-gate garbling schemes.* A more recent line of work [LWYY25, ILL25b, MORS25] constructs garbled circuits of size $|\hat{C}| = |C| + o(|C|)$, achieving essentially one bit per gate. These schemes are significantly more efficient than fully succinct ones and have already demonstrated promising concrete performance [ILL25b, LWYY25]. This improvement stems from their reliance on comparatively lightweight techniques, such as homomorphic secret sharing (HSS) [BGI16] and FHE without bootstrapping [GSW13], rather than heavy

---

[1] Note that C and $\hat{C}$ are syntactically different objects. C is a circuit, while $\hat{C}$ is a binary string. Adopting standard notation, $|C|$ denotes the number of *gates* in the original circuit C, while $|\hat{C}|$ denotes the bit-length of the garbled circuit.

tools like iO or the non-black-box combination of FHE and ABE. A further advantage is flexibility in assumptions: one-bit-per-gate constructions can be based on a diverse set of algebraic assumptions, including RLWE, NTRU, DDH over prime-order or Paillier groups, and DCR, in contrast to the narrow reliance of fully succinct approaches on iO or lattice-based primitives.

Low-Depth Garbling. A major drawback of existing succinct garbling schemes in either of these categories is that their garbling algorithms have high depth, growing polynomially with the circuit depth D (namely $\mathsf{poly}(\lambda, D)$). The only exception is constructions based on iO, which achieve garbling depth $\mathsf{poly}(\lambda)$ but at prohibitive concrete cost.

In contrast, a low-depth garbling scheme is one where the garbling depth depends only logarithmically on the circuit size, that is, $\mathsf{poly}(\lambda, \log |C|)$. Such schemes enable highly parallelizable garbling, which are crucial in applications where garbling depth directly translates into round complexity and latency. Yao's garbled circuits exemplify this property: all gates can be garbled in parallel, yielding depth $\mathsf{poly}(\lambda)$ under one-way functions, $O(\log \lambda)$ assuming PRGs in NC^1, and even NC^0 when combined with an NC^0-garbling scheme for NC^1 circuits [IK02, AIK04].

This contrast raises the central questions of our work:

> *Can we construct Boolean garbling schemes that are simultaneously*
> *succinct and low-depth, without relying on iO?*
> *Can succinct garbling be in NC^1, which is unknown even assuming iO?*

Our Results. We give a comprehensive and affirmative answer to the above question by enhancing existing non-iO-based succinct garbling schemes to achieve low – indeed NC^1 – garbling depth while preserving succinctness. Concretely: 1) by enhancing the schemes of [ILL25b], we obtain one-bit-per-gate garbled circuits with NC^1 *garbling*, based on DDH or RLWE, and the existence of local Pseudorandom Generators (PRG) [Gol00]; and 2) by enhancing the "leveled" version of the scheme in [GKP+13, BGG+14], we obtain a *fully succinct, reusable* garbling scheme with NC^1 garbling, based on decomposable LWE [AMR25]. To the best of our knowledge, our succinct garbling schemes are the first to achieve NC^1 garbling depth; this level of parallel efficiency was not attained even by prior iO-based schemes, which have $\mathsf{poly}(\lambda)$ depth.

A key intermediate step towards these constructions is the design of new *privacy-free* garbling schemes that retain various degrees of succinctness while enjoying NC^1 *garbling*, based on the same assumptions. These schemes are of independent interest. Unlike standard garbling, privacy-free garbling [JKO13, FNO15] requires only computational integrity, not privacy: the input x is public, the evaluation algorithm takes it as input explicitly, and the scheme guarantees *authenticity*, namely that it is computationally hard to produce a valid label for an incorrect output (with respect to an authentication key). Privacy-free garbling and the closely related notion of partial garbling [IW14] have found many applications, including efficient zero-knowledge arguments for non-algebraic statements [JKO13,FNO15], CDS and PSM protocols, constrained PRFs [ILL25a], and blockchain applications [Lin25]. Yet in this setting as well, no prior construction achieved both succinctness and low-depth: the only known succinct privacy-free garbling [ILL25a] had depth proportional to the circuit depth. Our work fills this gap.

In essence, our constructions are summarized in the following informal theorems.

Theorem 1.1 (One-Bit-Per-Gate, NC^1-Garbling-Depth, Garbled Circuits, Informal). *Assume DDH over prime-order subgroup of $\mathbb{Z}_p^*$, or DDH over Paillier groups, or RLWE, and the existence of constant-local PRGs. Then there exists garbling schemes for Boolean circuits with the following properties:*

- One-bit-per-gate: *The size of the garbled circuit is $|\hat{C}| = |C| + \mathsf{poly}(\lambda) \cdot (D + o(|C|))^2$, where $|C|$ is the number of gates and D is the depth of the circuit.*
- NC^1 garbling: *The depth of the garbling algorithm is $O(\log \lambda + \log |C|)$.*

The instantiation based on DDH over subgroup of $\mathbb{Z}_p^*$ has a $1/poly(\lambda)$ correctness and privacy errors. The errors can be made negligible, at the price of increasing the garbling depth to $\mathsf{poly}(\lambda)$. Moreover, assuming the same assumptions without local PRGs, there exists garbling schemes for Boolean circuits, with garbled circuit size $\mathsf{poly}(\lambda) \cdot (D + o(|C|))$ and garbling algorithm depth $O(\log \lambda + \log |C|)$.

We note that achieving NC^1 garbling requires the ability to evaluate iterated basic operations of the underlying algebraic structure, such as repeated group operations or ring multiplications, in NC^1. For this reason, we assume DDH over subgroups of $\mathbb{Z}_p^*$. When instantiated under DDH over general groups, our schemes are still low-depth, but with depth complexity $\mathsf{poly}(\lambda)$ rather than NC^1.

Theorem 1.2 (Depth-Succinct, NC^1-Garbling-Depth, Reusable Garbled Circuits, Informal). *Assume decomposable LWE. There exists a reusable garbling scheme for Boolean circuits with the following properties:*

- Depth-succinctness: *The size of the garbled circuit is $\mathsf{poly}(\lambda, D)$, where D is the circuit depth.*
- NC^1garbling: *The depth of the garbling algorithm is $O(\log \lambda + \log |C|)$.*

The decomposable LWE assumption was recently introduced in [AMR25]; it can be viewed as a circular-security assumption for a natural lattice-based public-key encryption scheme and is implied by the hardness of the succinct LWE problem of [Wee24]. See the full version for the formal definition and [AMR25] for further discussion.

---

[2] The exact sublinear factors in $|C|$ varies per construction. Refer to the formal statements in the full version for the exact parameters.

Theorems 1.1 and 1.2 improve upon prior one-bit-per-gate garbling [LWYY25, ILL25b, MORS25] and succinct reusable garbling [GKP+13, BGG+14, QWW18] respectively by reducing the garbling depth from $\mathsf{poly}(\lambda, D)$ to $\mathsf{poly}(\log \lambda, \log |C|)$ while maintaining the same asymptotic garbling size and underlying assumptions (albeit restricted to integer groups for DDH).

Extending Theorem 1.2: ABE with Low-Depth and Succinct Key Generation. We further extend the above theorem to obtain the first attribute-based encryption (ABE) with succinct keys and low-depth key generation.

Reusable garbled circuits and attribute-based encryption (ABE) are closely connected. Existing reusable garbled circuits [GKP+13, BGG+14, QWW18] are typically constructed by combining homomorphic encryption (HE) and ABE, in such a way that the depth of the garbling algorithm mirrors the depth of the ABE key generation, and the garbled circuit size grows with the size of the ABE secret key. Since all prior ABE schemes with succinct secret keys [BGG+14, HLL23] had high-depth key generation, the corresponding reusable garbled circuits also had high-depth garbling. We show that the same techniques we use to reduce garbling depth also apply to ABE, yielding the first ABE scheme with both succinct keys and low-depth key generation.

Theorem 1.3 (ABE with Low-Depth and Succinct Key Generation, Informal). *Assume decomposable LWE. Then there exists an ABE scheme for Boolean circuits with the following properties:*

- Depth-succinct keys: *For a depth-D circuit C, the secret key has size* $\mathsf{poly}(\lambda, D)$.
- NC^1 key generation: *The depth of the key generation algorithm is* $O(\log \lambda + \log |C|)$.

Unified Framework. Our constructions are obtained through a unified framework (described in Sect. 4) that provides a general method for reducing garbling depth without sacrificing succinctness. This framework extends and abstracts the approach of [ILL25b], which combined homomorphic secret sharing (HSS) with algebraic HMAC (aHMAC) [ILL25a] to realize one-bit-per-gate garbled circuits. Unlike that specialized setting, our framework operates at a higher level of abstraction and encompasses both one-bit-per-gate garbling and lattice-based reusable garbling [GKP+13, BGG+14], despite their very different underlying tools (HSS and aHMAC in the former, HE and ABE in the latter).

The framework highlights a common source of high garbling depth in all prior succinct garbling schemes. Conceptually, it views garbling as a two-party protocol between the garbler and the evaluator, who jointly maintain secret shares of every wire value. Evaluation proceeds via local homomorphic computations on each party's shares (corresponding to the garbling and evaluation algorithms), together with one-way communication from the garbler to the evaluator (the garbled circuit itself). In this perspective, the "secret sauce" behind succinctness is the use of homomorphic techniques–HSS, aHMAC, HE, ABE–that reduce communication and thereby garbled circuit size.

The conflict with low-depth garbling arises because these homomorphic techniques typically require *symmetric* (but not identical) local computation by both the garbler and the evaluator, which results in high depth at both ends. Our key idea is to break this symmetry by introducing *periodic share refreshing*. Specifically, the garbler's share of an intermediate value is re-sampled from a fixed distribution, while the evaluator's share is updated accordingly. As a result, the garbler's computation becomes shallow, given all refreshed shares.

A challenge is that naively refreshing all intermediate shares incurs communication linear in $|C|$, destroying succinctness. To overcome this, we compress shares of intermediate values into compact shares of a *hash* and refresh only the latter, which incurs small communication and preserves succinctness. To implement this, we adapt the recent algebraic compression techniques of [AMR25, Wee24], originally developed for succinct garbled RAM and ABE with succinct ciphertexts, to the garbling setting, and provide new group-based instantiation.

Open Questions. The garbling size of our schemes in Theorem 1.1 and Theorem 1.2 all exceed $D \cdot \mathsf{poly}(\lambda)$. Under stronger circular-security variants of the assumptions, prior works can reduce the garbled circuit size further, down to $|\hat{C}| = |C| + \mathsf{poly}(\lambda)$ for one-bit-per-gate garbling [LWYY25, ILL25b, MORS25] and $\mathsf{poly}(\lambda)$ for reusable garbling [HLL23]. Our schemes, however, do not currently admit analogous variants, and we leave closing this gap as an interesting open question.

Another natural question is whether the depth of our schemes can be further reduced to NC^0 using the standard composition technique of [IK02, AIK04]. This technique combines an NC^1 garbling algorithm for general circuits with an NC^0 garbling algorithm for NC^1 circuits. While this approach would indeed reduce the garbling depth to NC^0, it comes at the cost of losing succinctness, since existing NC^0 schemes are not succinct. Whether succinct garbling can be constructed in NC^0 is another extremely interesting question.

2 Technical Overview

The starting point of our ideas will be the high level view of succinct garbling in [MORS24, MORS25, ILL25b], where a garbling scheme is constructed as a 2-party protocol where the garbler and evaluator jointly compute 'shares' of each wire w_i in the circuit $[\![w_i]\!]$. This view captures both privacy-free garbling (where the input is not hidden from the evaluator, who only seeks to produce an authenticated 'label' of the output) as well as the traditional notion of private garbling. In these protocol, only the garbler sends messages, which represents the garbled circuit. This roughly breaks down a garbling protocol into the following steps:

- $\mathsf{Enc}(x) \to [\![x]\!]$: Given an input x, the garbler generates an encoding $[\![x]\!]_G, [\![x]\!]_E$ of the input, and $[\![x]\!]_E$ is sent to the evaluator as the garbled input.

- $\mathsf{HGate}(\llbracket w_1 \rrbracket, \llbracket w_2 \rrbracket, \mathsf{op}) \rightarrow \llbracket \mathsf{op}(w_1, w_2) \rrbracket$: With encodings of input wires, the garbler and evaluator can jointly generate encoding of the output of a gate. Any communication this may require on the garbler's part is part of the garbled circuit.
- $\mathsf{Dec}(\llbracket C(x) \rrbracket) \rightarrow \mathsf{dk}$: Finally, given an encoding of the output wire, the garbler sends some decoding information which allows the evaluator to recover the output of the garbled circuit.

Zooming in a little further, in these prior schemes [ILL25b, MORS25], the garbler's $\llbracket w_i \rrbracket_G = k_i$ and evaluator's $\llbracket w_i \rrbracket_E = \sigma_i = k_i + s \cdot w_i$ shares form an additive secret sharing of $s \cdot w_i$, for some garbling secret s. To advance the computation with some gate $\mathsf{op}(w_1, w_2)$, the garbler publishes some cryptographic material which enables the garbler and evaluator to run HGate to obtain additive shares of $s' \cdot \mathsf{op}(w_1, w_2)$ either completely *noninteractively* (in the case of privacy-free garbling) or with only a single bit of communication (in the setting of private garbling).[3] Importantly, this cryptographic material is reusable, and given shares of every depth j wire, enables the garbler and evaluator to obtain shares of *every* depth $j + 1$ wire, enabling succinctness. Moreover, this HGate protocol works on *any* additive sharing of $s \cdot w$.

Rekeying. This latter observation yields the following simple idea - the garbler 'fixes' their shares k_i of the additive encoding of all the circuit wires before performing any homomorphic evaluation. Since the garbler already has their 'shares' of every wire in the circuit, they can in parallel run HGate for every wire of C, albeit obtaining a 'different' additive share of the output wire k_i'. To ensure the evaluator can proceed with their computation, the garbler simply sends them $\mathsf{rk} = (k_i - k_i')$, which allows the evaluator to realign or 'rekey' their additive share to be consistent with the garbler's independently sampled shares.

   We formalize and abstract this idea through defining a 'rekeying' protocol, which takes the following form:

- $\mathsf{RekeySamp}(1^\lambda) \rightarrow k$: The garbler can sample a fresh share k
- $\mathsf{RekeyGen}(k_i', k_i) \rightarrow \mathsf{rk}$: Given a share k_i' (which will be the output of HGate) and a 'target share' k_i (which will be independently sampled), the garbler computes a rekeying key.
- $\mathsf{RekeyEval}(\sigma_i', \mathsf{rk}) \rightarrow \sigma_i$: When delivered to the evaluator, the rekey rk can be used in conjunction with a share σ_i' to produce a share σ_i.

So long as (k_i', σ_i') and (k_i, σ_i) encode the same value, this will preserve correctness of HGate, and hence the garbling scheme.

Hash Compression. Unfortunately, directly applying this straightforward method of rekeying as described above removes any hope for succinctness, as

---

[3] [ILL25b] also describe an 'unlevelled' variant where $s = s'$ which relies on circular security which achieves depth-independent succinctness. Since our scheme will incur depth-dependent factors for other reasons, we will look at their leveled construction.

the garbler will need to send the evaluator a key for every wire of the circuit. Instead, what we need is a *succinct* rekeying operation where a short rekeying key can re-encode many different wire encodings.

One way to realize this is rather than attempting to rekeying individual wire values, we can instead rekey a short 'hash' of the wire values. For this to be useful with prior gate evaluation procedures, which operates directly on encodings of wire values, there needs to exist non-interactive procedures for both converting an encoding of wires to an encoding of the hash of said wires as well as the reverse. A bit more formally, our hashing scheme should support the following protocols[4]:

- $\mathsf{Compress}(\llbracket x \rrbracket) \rightarrow \llbracket \mathsf{Hash}(x) \rrbracket$: Given an encoding of x, which we recall takes the form $\{k_i\}$ for the garbler and $\{k_i + s \cdot w_i\}$ for the evaluator, they should respectively be able to compute shares k_{Hash} and $(k_{\mathsf{Hash}} + s \cdot \mathsf{Hash}(\{w_i\}))$.
- $\mathsf{Expand}(\llbracket \mathsf{Hash}(x) \rrbracket) \rightarrow \llbracket x \rrbracket$: Conversely, given shares k_{Hash} and $(k_{\mathsf{Hash}} + s \cdot \mathsf{Hash}(\{w_i\}))$, the garbler and evaluator should each compute shares $\{k_i\}$, $\{k_i + s' \cdot w_i\}$ respectively.

This enables the garbler and evaluator to alternate between encodings of the wires (to compute HGate) and encodings of hash of wires (to run Rekey).

It turns out by virtue of the additive structure of the encodings, any linear hash function $\mathsf{Hash}(\mathbf{x}) = \mathbf{x}^\mathsf{T} \cdot \mathbf{u}$ can be 'compressed' while supporting the share format. Thus, the main challenge will be supporting the Expand operation. Much like how succinct gate evaluation HGate is constructed in prior works, this will rely on a publishing some cryptographic 'hints' dependent on garbling secrets s, s' which allow the garbler and evaluator to compute $\llbracket x \rrbracket$ from $\llbracket \mathsf{Hash}(x) \rrbracket$ while simultaneously hiding s, s'. Inspired by the hashing and reconstruction technique recently introduced by $[\mathsf{AMR25}, \mathsf{Wee25}]$ for constructing succinct-time RAM garbling and ABE with succinct ciphertext from lattices, given coefficients $\mathbf{u} = (u_1, \ldots, u_N)^\mathsf{T}$ to a linear hash, we can convert an encoding of $\mathsf{Hash}(\mathbf{x}) = \mathbf{x}^\mathsf{T} \cdot \mathbf{u}$ into an encoding of $\mathbf{x}$ by publishing a random vector $\mathbf{t} = (t_1, \ldots, t_N)^\mathsf{T}$ as well as the matrix $\mathbf{W} = s \cdot \mathbf{t} \cdot \mathbf{u}^\mathsf{T} - s' \cdot \mathbf{I}_N$, embedding s' in the diagonal of $\mathbf{W}$ masked by term $s \cdot t_i \cdot u_i$. Now, given a sharing of the form $(k, k + s \cdot \mathsf{Hash}(\mathbf{x}))$, the garbler and evaluator can recover a share of x_i by first multiplying their respective sharings by t_i

$$t_i \cdot \llbracket \mathsf{Hash}(\mathbf{x}) \rrbracket_G = t_i \cdot k \quad , \quad t_i \cdot \llbracket \mathsf{Hash}(\mathbf{x}) \rrbracket_E = t_i \cdot (k + s \cdot (\mathbf{u}^\mathsf{T} \cdot \mathbf{x})) = t_i \cdot k + s \cdot t_i \cdot \mathbf{u}^\mathsf{T} \cdot \mathbf{x}.$$

This latter term of the evaluator's encoding is in fact exactly the ith row of $\mathbf{W}$ multiplied by $\mathbf{x}$, which allows the evaluator to compute

$$t_i \cdot \llbracket \mathsf{Hash}(\mathbf{x}) \rrbracket_E - \langle \mathbf{w}_i, \mathbf{x} \rangle = t_i \cdot k + s \cdot t_i \cdot \mathbf{u}^\mathsf{T} \cdot \mathbf{x} - (s \cdot (t_i \cdot \mathbf{u}^\mathsf{T}) \cdot \mathbf{x} - s' \cdot \mathbf{e}_i^\mathsf{T} \cdot \mathbf{x}) = t_i \cdot k + s' \cdot x_i.$$

where $\mathbf{e}_i$ is the ith canonical basis vector. The garbler and evaluator can now use

$$t_i \cdot k = \llbracket x_i \rrbracket_G, t_i \cdot k + s' \cdot x_i = \llbracket x_i \rrbracket_E$$

---

[4] In our real scheme, we refer to Expand as HRead which also has the syntax to 'locally' extract/read a single wire value from the hash.

as their new encoding of x_i.

While this gives us the desired functionality, directly giving out $\mathbf{W}$ clearly compromises any sort of secrecy of s, s'. Instead, we will need to give out cryptographic 'encryption' of $\mathbf{W}$ which still enables us to perform the above computation. We discuss how this is instantiated in various contexts below:

Group-Based Construction: In both prime-order and Paillier groups, the high level idea is instead of publishing $\mathbf{t}, \mathbf{W}$, the garbler instead publishes $g^{\mathbf{t}}, g^{\mathbf{W}}$. Intuitively, this allows us to use the secrecy of these terms in the exponent to act as an ElGamal-esque encryption of the secret s'. Since the garbler and evaluator only perform linear operations, this can be directly translated to computing $(g^{\mathbf{t}})^{[\![\mathsf{Hash}(\mathbf{x})]\!]}$, $(g^{\mathbf{W}})^{\mathbf{x}}$, which gives an appropriate additive sharing *in the exponent of* $\mathbb{G}$. Since rekeying is a linear operation, this can be done directly in the exponent of the group! However, while such sharings in the exponent of the group are sufficient for rekeying, such an encoding is insufficient for HGate. Thus, our Expand operation will need to recover a sharing over $\mathbb{Z}$, which we achieve using the techniques of distributed discrete log DDLog protocol [BGI16]. This technique comes with two caveats (in prime-order groups): it incurs some inverse polynomial correctness error, and only works if the additive shares have some bounded polynomial difference. The former will simply reflect as an inverse polynomial correctness error in our 'base' garbling protocol, which can be amplified through generic techniques. With respect to the latter, notice while we can always maintain our initial input $\mathbf{x}$ and the shares of the input encoding $[\![x]\!]$, have bounded distance, the term of $s' \cdot \mathbf{x}$ in $g^{\mathbf{W}}$ could be as large as the group order p itself. However, rather than giving out encryptions of s' directly, we can instead bit-decompose s', using $\mathbf{W}$ to encode the bits of s' which are only 'repacked' after the DDLog returns the encoding to $\mathbb{Z}$.

At a glance, it may not be clear that this hashing has accomplished anything, as although the hash itself is now shorter than the original input, the garbler also has to give out $\mathsf{ct}_{s,s'} = g^{\mathbf{t}}, g^{\mathbf{W}}$, which are at least as long as the input of Hash (and in fact quadratically longer than said input). However, an important distinction between these two quantities is that $\mathsf{ct}_{s,s'}$ are *reusable* (within the same circuit depth of a garbling scheme). Thus, by fixing a compression factor K our garbling scheme pays a one-time cost of $K^2 \cdot D$ to reduce the re-keying communication by a factor of K. We can see this can be asymptotically minimized by setting $K = \left(\frac{|C|}{D}\right)^{\frac{1}{3}}$, incurring $D + |C|^{\frac{2}{3}} D^{\frac{1}{3}}$ total communication (ignoring $\mathsf{poly}(\lambda)$ factors. We also note that by assuming a circular variant of power-DDH, we can reuse the public parameters across layers, incurring a one-time cost of K^2 and rather than $K^2 \cdot D$, meaning our total communication can be brought down to $D + |C|^{\frac{2}{3}}$.

Lattice-Based Construction. In the setting of lattices, this same hashing idea can be executed by simply publishing $\mathbf{t}, \mathbf{u}$ in the clear and an "encryption" as simply a noisy version of $\mathbf{W} + \varepsilon$. In fact, as observed in prior work [AMR25, Wee25], since these hash coefficients can be published in the clear, this enables a recursive

Merkle-style construction where the output of the hash itself is then again taken as input to the compressing hash[5]. This enables the hashing to be instantiated with a *fixed* compression factor[6] independent of the circuit size, meaning unlike in the group-based setting, the size of the rekeying communication can be made independent of $|C|$ (modulo the depth dependence). This recursion introduces one additional constraint - since the output of Hash will need to be taken as input to itself, the hashing must also preserve (up to bounded polynomial factors) the distance of the additive sharing in order for us to apply distributed rounding. In other words, the coefficient $\mathbf{u}$ of Hash must be small. We can accomplish this by once again relying on bit-decomposition, this time using $\mathsf{Bits}(\mathbf{u})$ rather than $\mathbf{u}$ as the coefficients to hash, which allows us to bound the norm of $\|\mathsf{Hash}(\mathbf{x})\|$ relative to $\|\mathbf{x}\|$. Since bit 'recomposition' too is a linear operation (multiplying by $[1, 2, \ldots 2^{\log q}]$), this once again preserves the share format described above. Putting these ideas together, our overall garbling protocol proceeds layer-by-layer over a circuit C as follows:

- On layer j of the circuit, the garbler and evaluator begin with shares $k_{\mathsf{Hash}}^{(j)}, k_{\mathsf{Hash}}^{(j)} + s \cdot \mathsf{Hash}\left(\{w_i^{(j)}\}\right)$, where $k_{\mathsf{Hash}}^{(j)} \leftarrow \mathsf{RekeySamp}(1^\lambda)$ is independently sampled.
- The garbler and evaluator run Expand to obtain shares of the form $\{k^{(j)}\}, \{k^{(j)} + s' \cdot w_i^{(j)}\}$.
- The garbler and evaluator use HGate to compute the outputs of the jth layer of the circuit $\{k^{(j+1)}\}, \{k^{(j+1)} + s'' \cdot w_i^{(j+1)}\}$.
- The wire shares are then hashed down via $\mathsf{Compress}$ to a succinct

$$\left(k_{\mathsf{Hash}}'^{(j+1)}, k_{\mathsf{Hash}}'^{(j+1)} + s'' \cdot \mathsf{Hash}\left(\{w_i^{(j+1)}\}\right)\right).$$

- The garbler sends the evaluator $\left(k_{\mathsf{Hash}}^{(j+1)} - k_{\mathsf{Hash}}'^{(j+1)}\right)$, the difference between the garbler's current share of the hash and a freshly sampled one.

Since both the hash key and rekeying material are sublinear in $|C|$, this yields a succinct and low depth garbling scheme. In the setting of private garbling, this communication is dominated by the 1-bit-per-gate cost of HSS communication.

Reusable Garbling. In the setting of reusable garbling [GKP+13], the garbler can produce a single garbled circuit which can be reused between multiple sets of garbled inputs. Ultimately, we can view the instantiation of reusable garbling through the homomorphic lattice encodings of [BGG+14] as an *approximate*

---

[5] In group instantiations described above, the coefficients $\mathbf{t}, \mathbf{u}$ must be hidden and hence so are the hash values $\mathsf{Hash}(\mathbf{x}) = \mathbf{u}^\mathsf{T} \cdot \mathbf{x}$. However, to apply recursive hashing, the evaluator must know $\mathsf{Hash}(\mathbf{x})$ in the clear.

[6] Prior work generally instantiates this compression factor as a constant such as two. However, for our entire garbling computation to remain in NC^1, our full constructions will require *constant* recursive depth, the compression factor is set proportional to security parameter λ.

additive sharing of $\mathbf{s}^\top \cdot x \otimes \mathbf{G}$ where the garbler holds $\mathbf{s}^\top, \mathbf{B}$ (which can be used to compute $\mathbf{s}^\top \cdot \mathbf{B}$) and the evaluator holds share $\mathbf{s}^\top(\mathbf{B} - x \otimes \mathbf{G}) + \mathbf{e}^\top$ with garbling secret $\mathbf{s}$. The homomorphic evaluation procedures of [BGG+14,BTVW17] directly enable the independent derivation from

$$\mathbf{B} \mapsto \mathbf{B}_C \quad , \quad \mathbf{s}^\top(\mathbf{B} - x \otimes \mathbf{G}) + \mathbf{e}^\top \mapsto \mathbf{s}^\top(\mathbf{B}_C - C(x) \otimes \mathbf{G}) + \mathbf{e}'^\top$$

for a circuit C. In fact, this derivation exactly corresponds to the garbler and evaluator's respective computation of HGate in the context of privacy-free garbling (and the same computation composed under a layer of FHE in the setting of private garbling). However, just like the techniques for gate evaluation in the non-reusable setting, the depth of both sides of this evaluation procedure grow with the circuit it is evaluating.

We can use the same high-level approach of rekeying and hash compression to break this symmetry in computation depth while preserving succinctness. However, the encoding of [BGG+14] puts two additional constraints on our techniques - (1) for the correctness of [BGG+14] homomorphic evaluation, the garbler and evaluator's share now *both* depend on a secret $\mathbf{s}$ and (2) the reusability of this garbling scheme relies on the garbler sampling a *new* $\mathbf{s}$ for each garbled input. Thus, the garbled circuit itself cannot be dependent on $\mathbf{s}$.

While our hashing construction described above suffers from both of these issues (the ciphertexts published for Hash depend on secret $\mathbf{s}$, and the Expand step produces an encoding under a different $\mathbf{s}'$, which would no longer be a [BGG+14] encoding), we can actually directly use the key-homomorphic RAM hash of [AMR25] as the natural [BGG+14]-compatible analogue of our Hash protocol. This comes at the expense of relying on a stronger assumption (decomposed LWE), but otherwise retains the same structure.

We also need to modify our rekeying protocol to respect these constraints. Recall in the non-reusable setting described above, a garbler can 'rekey' an evaluator's share by simply sending them the difference between his current share k' and his freshly sampled share k. This would mean 'rekey' corresponds to $(\mathbf{s}^\top \cdot \mathbf{B}_{\mathsf{Hash}} - \mathbf{s}^\top \cdot \mathbf{B}'_{\mathsf{Hash}})$, which of course is dependent on $\mathbf{s}$. To avoid this, the garbler instead publishes an additional fresh matrix $\mathbf{A}$ in the garbled circuit which it has sampled with a short trapdoor. The rekeying key is now instead computed as a short preimage of the form $\mathbf{A}^{-1}(\mathbf{B}_{\mathsf{Hash}} - \mathbf{B}'_{\mathsf{Hash}})$. When it comes time to garble an input x, the garbler also sends $\mathbf{s}^\top \mathbf{A} + \mathbf{e}^\top$, which, when multiplied by rekeying key, recovers a noisy $(\mathbf{s}^\top \cdot \mathbf{B}_{\mathsf{Hash}} - \mathbf{s}^\top \cdot \mathbf{B}'_{\mathsf{Hash}})$.

With these modifications, however we are able to obtain a succinct NC^1 garbling scheme from decomposed LWE. The same techniques also naturally extend to the setting of attribute-based encryption with succinct and NC^1 key generation.

3   Definitions

Notation. We will refer to (layered) circuit $C : \{0,1\}^\ell \rightarrow \{0,1\}$ computable by a poly-size and depth d circuit as a series of gates, indexed by a tuple $(i,j) \in \mathbb{N}^2$

corresponding to the depth and number of that particular gate. Each gate $g_{(i,j)}$ is of the form (op, lw, rw), where op $\in \{\mathsf{AND}, \mathsf{OR}, \mathsf{NOT}\}$ and lw, rw are the index tuples corresponding to the left and right input wires respectively. We will use C_i to denote the collection of depth i gates and $C_{[i]}(x)$ to denote the circuit which computes all depth $\leq i$ wires of C on x.

Definition 3.1 (Garbled Circuits). *Let λ be a security parameter. A garbling scheme is a tuple of efficient randomized algorithms $\Pi_{\mathsf{garble}} = (\mathsf{Setup}, \mathsf{GarbC}, \mathsf{GarbInp}, \mathsf{Eval})$:*

- $\mathsf{Setup}(1^\lambda, 1^d) \to \mathsf{pp}$: *On input security parameter λ and circuit depth d, the* Setup *algorithm outputs public parameters* pp.
- $\mathsf{GarbC}(\mathsf{pp}, C) \to (\hat{C}, \mathsf{gk})$: *On input public parameters* pp *and circuit C (of depth $\leq d$), the* GarbC *algorithm outputs garbled circuit $\hat{C}$ and garbling key* gk.
- $\mathsf{GarbInp}(\mathsf{gk}, x) \to \hat{x}$: *On input garbling key* gk *and input x, the* $\mathsf{GarbInp}$ *algorithm outputs a garbled input $\hat{x}$.*
- $\mathsf{Eval}(C, \hat{C}, \hat{x}) \to \{0, 1\}$: *On input circuit C, garbled circuit $\hat{C}$ and garbled input $\hat{x}$, the* Eval *algorithm computes the evaluation of the garbling circuit.*

We will consider the following syntactic and semantic properties for a garbling scheme:

- **Correctness:** *For all polynomials $p(\cdot), d(\cdot)$, there exists negligible function* $\mathsf{negl}(\cdot)$ *such that for all $\lambda \in \mathbb{N}$, all circuits $C : \{0, 1\}^\ell \to \{0, 1\}$ of size $|C| \leq p(\lambda)$ and depth $\leq d(\lambda)$, all inputs $x \in \{0, 1\}^\ell$,*

$$\Pr\left[\mathsf{Eval}(C, \hat{C}, \hat{x}) = C(x) \;\middle|\; \begin{array}{l} \mathsf{pp} \leftarrow \mathsf{Setup}(1^\lambda, 1^d) \\ (\mathsf{gk}, \hat{C}) \leftarrow \mathsf{GarbC}(\mathsf{pp}, C) \\ \hat{x} \leftarrow \mathsf{GarbInp}(\mathsf{gk}, x) \end{array}\right] = 1 - \mathsf{negl}(\lambda)$$

- **Decomposability:** *We say a garbling scheme Π_{garble} is decomposable if every bit of the input garbling $\hat{x}$ depends on at most one bit of x.*
- **Succinctness:** *We say a garbling scheme Π_{garble} is succinct if there exists a polynomial p such that for every $\lambda, d \in \mathbb{N}$, circuits C with depth d, input $x \in \{0, 1\}^\ell$, and size $|C| > p(\lambda, d, \ell)$, the garbling size satisfy $|\hat{C}| + |\hat{x}| + |\mathsf{dk}| < |C| \cdot \log |C|$.*
  We say a garbling scheme Π_{garble} is depth-succinct if there exists a polynomial p' such that for every $\lambda, d \in \mathbb{N}$, circuits C with depth d, input $x \in \{0, 1\}^\ell$, the garbling size satisfy $|\hat{C}| + |\hat{x}| + |\mathsf{dk}| < p'(\lambda, d, \ell)$.
  We note that one could consider even stronger definitions of succinctness (and general garbling) which does not a-priori bound or depend on the depth of the circuit. However, our constructions will only consider this depth-dependent case.

We will consider two different distinct 'flavors' of garbled circuits security, each of which will require some additional syntax and algorithms to describe. We will also consider both security definitions in the context of non-reusable and reusable garbled circuits, where changes exclusive to the reusable setting are highlighted in green.

– **Input-Hiding Simulation:** *In the traditional notion of garbled circuits, we require the garbled circuit to 'hide' the input it was evaluated on. To capture this notion, a garbling scheme will also be associated with a tuple of (efficient) simulator algorithms:*
   - $\mathsf{Sim}_0(1^\lambda, 1^d) \to (\mathsf{pp}, \mathsf{st}_0)$*: On input security parameter λ and depth bound d, the zeroth simulator outputs public parameters pp and state st_0.*
   - $\mathsf{Sim}_1(\mathsf{st}_0, C) \to (\hat{C}, \mathsf{gk}, \mathsf{st}_1)$*: On input security prior simulator state st_0 and circuit C, the first simulator outputs garbled circuit $\hat{C}$, the garbling key gk (in the reusable case) and new simulator state st_1.*
   - $\mathsf{Sim}_2(\mathsf{st}_1, b) \to \hat{x}$*: On input simulator state st_1 and circuit output bit b, the second simulator outputs a garbled input $\hat{x}$.*

For an adversary $\mathcal{A}$, define the following as the (selective) input-hiding simulation security experiment $\mathsf{ExptSS}_{\mathcal{A}}^{(b)}(\lambda)$ as follows:

1. *The adversary specifies a depth bound 1^d, a circuit C (of depth $\leq d$), and {one, arbitrarily many} inputs x. The challenger responds as follows:*
   - *If $b = 0$, the challenger computes the real garbling scheme:*
     (a) *The challenger samples public parameters $\mathsf{pp} \leftarrow \mathsf{Setup}(1^\lambda, 1^d)$.*
     (b) *The challenger samples garbled circuit $(\hat{C}, \mathsf{gk}) \leftarrow \mathsf{GarbC}(\mathsf{pp}, C)$.*
     (c) *The challenger samples garbled input(s) $\hat{x} \leftarrow \mathsf{GarbInp}(\mathsf{gk}, x)$ for each x submitted by the adversary.*
   - *If $b = 1$, the challenger computes the simulated garbling scheme:*
     (a) *The challenger samples public parameters $(\mathsf{pp}, \mathsf{st}_0) \leftarrow \mathsf{Sim}_0(1^\lambda, 1^d)$.*
     (b) *the challenger samples garbled circuit $(\hat{C}, \mathsf{gk}, \mathsf{st}_1) \leftarrow \mathsf{Sim}_1(\mathsf{st}_0, C)$.*
     (c) *The challenger samples garbled input(s) $\hat{x} \leftarrow \mathsf{Sim}_2(\mathsf{st}_1, C(x))$ for each x submitted by the adversary.*
2. *The challenger returns $(\mathsf{pp}, \hat{C}, \mathsf{gk}, \{\hat{x}\})$.*
3. *The adversary outputs a bit b', which is the output of the experiment.*

We note that in the reusable setting, the adversary gets two additional 'powers' - it can see the garbling key gk and request as many garbled input labels as desired, while in the non-reusable setting, an adversary makes exactly one such query. We say a scheme Π_{garble} is input-hiding simulation secure if for all PPT adversaries $\mathcal{A}$, there exists a negligible function $\mathsf{negl}(\cdot)$ such that for all $\lambda \in \mathbb{N}$,

$$\left| \Pr[\mathsf{ExptSS}_{\mathcal{A}}^{(0)}(\lambda) = 1] - \Pr[\mathsf{ExptSS}_{\mathcal{A}}^{(1)}(\lambda) = 1] \right| = \mathsf{negl}(\lambda).$$

– **Authenticity:** *An orthogonal property of garbled circuits that could be desirable even in the absence of input hiding is the notion of label authenticity. This is the main security property of interest in the setting of privacy-free garbling [FNO15] where the garbled circuit instead simply represents a way to authenticate computation. To capture this requirement, we additionally assume our garbling algorithms have the following structure:*
   - $\mathsf{GarbInp}(\mathsf{gk}, x) \to \hat{x} = (L_x, \mathsf{dk}), \mathsf{auk}$*: In the input garbling algorithm, let the garbled input $\hat{x}$ be decomposed into two part - a garbled input label L_x and a decoding key dk. In addition, $\mathsf{GarbInp}$ can implicitly compute an authentication key auk.*

- $\mathsf{Eval}(C, \hat{C}, \hat{x}) \to \{0, 1\}$: *The evaluation algorithm can then be decomposed into two steps:*
  * $\mathsf{EvalLabel}(C, \hat{C}, L_x) \to L_{\mathsf{out}}$: *First, the* $\mathsf{EvalLabel}$ *algorithm takes the garbled circuit* $\hat{C}$ *as well as the garbled input labels* L_x *and computes an output label* L_{out}.
  * $\mathsf{DecodeLabel}(\mathsf{dk}, L_{\mathsf{out}}) \to \{0, 1\} \cup \perp$: *Once the output label is computed, a second* $\mathsf{DecodeLabel}$ *algorithm applies the decoding key* dk *to the label, which outputs a bit (which is also the output of* Eval*).*
- $\mathsf{Authenticate}(\mathsf{auk}, L_{\mathsf{out}}) \to \{0, 1\}$: *Privacy-free garbling is also equipped with an 'authentication' algorithm, which takes in authentication key* auk *and a label* L_{out} *and outputs a bit, which is 1 on any label generated by the honest execution of* $\mathsf{GarbInp}, \mathsf{EvalLabel}$.

Now we can define the (selective) authenticity game of a garbling scheme with respect adversary $\mathcal{A}$ *through the following security* $\mathsf{ExptAuth}_{\mathcal{A}}(\lambda)$*:*

1. *The adversary specifies a depth bound* 1^d, *a circuit* C *(of depth* $\leq d$*), and one input* x^*. *The challenger computes the following:*
   - (a) *The challenger samples public parameters* $\mathsf{pp} \leftarrow \mathsf{Setup}(1^\lambda, 1^d)$.
   - (b) *The challenger samples garbled circuit* $(\hat{C}, \mathsf{gk}) \leftarrow \mathsf{GarbC}(\mathsf{pp}, C)$.
   - (c) *The challenger samples garbled input* $\hat{x}^* \leftarrow \mathsf{GarbInp}(\mathsf{gk}, x^*)$, *as well as accompanying authentication key* auk^*.
2. *The challenger returns* $(\mathsf{pp}, \hat{C}, \mathsf{gk}, \hat{x}^* = L_{x^*}, \mathsf{dk}^*)$.
3. *The adversary submits a label* L^*. *The output of the experiment is 1 iff* $1 - C(x^*) = \mathsf{DecodeLabel}(\mathsf{dk}^*, L^*)$ *and* $\mathsf{Authenticate}(\mathsf{auk}^*, L^*) = 1$.

As in the input-hiding simulation security, the setting of reusable authenticity enables the adversary to see the garbling key gk. *As a result, they can generate as many garbled inputs it desires. In either case, we say a scheme* Π_{garble} *satisfies authenticity if for all PPT adversaries* $\mathcal{A}$, *there exists a negligible function* $\mathsf{negl}(\cdot)$ *such that for all* $\lambda \in \mathbb{N}$,

$$\Pr[\mathsf{ExptAuth}_{\mathcal{A}}(\lambda) = 1] = \mathsf{negl}(\lambda).$$

Our constructions will actually realize an intermediate abstraction of garbled circuits with algebraic output labels, whose description (and equivalence to traditional garbled circuits) we defer to the full version of this paper.

4   A General Template for Low-Depth Succinct Garbling

We will take the view of [HK21, HKO22, ILL25b] presenting the (GarbC, $\mathsf{GarbInp}$, Eval) algorithms of a garbling scheme as a two-party protocol between a garbler P_G and evaluator P_E, who jointly hold an encoding of input x and homomorphically compute an encoding of $C(x)$ with one directional communication from the garbler to evaluator (representing the output of $\mathsf{GarbC}, \mathsf{GarbInp}$). This protocol roughly can be decomposed into two algorithms $\mathsf{Setup}, \mathsf{Enc}$ run by P_G, and a subprotocol HGate jointly run by P_G, P_E.

- $\mathsf{Setup}(1^\lambda, 1^d, 1^{|C|}) \to \mathsf{pp}$: The setup algorithm takes in security parameter λ, along with circuit parameters (in our case depth d and (in some instances) circuit size $|C|$), and generates public data pp, which should be sent to P_E and be accessible for all following algorithms and sub-protocols.
- $\mathsf{Enc}(x) \to [\![x]\!], \mathsf{pd}$: The encoding algorithm takes as input the public data pd and a value x and outputs a two-party encoding $[\![x]\!] = ([\![x]\!]_G, [\![x]\!]_E)$ of x, public data pd. The encoding $[\![x]\!]_E$ and public data pd should be sent to P_E. Like pp, we will assume the public data pd is implicitly taken as input and available to all following algorithms and sub-protocols.
- $\mathsf{HGate}(\mathsf{op}, [\![x]\!], [\![y]\!]) \to [\![\mathsf{op}(x, y)]\!]$: The homomorphic gate evaluation protocol takes as input a gate op and input encodings $[\![x]\!], [\![y]\!]$ (jointly held by P_G, P_E) to compute an encoding of the output encoding $[\![\mathsf{op}(x, y)]\!]$ (jointly held by P_G, P_E). In some instances (in particular when relying on homomorphic secret sharing) this could require garbler to evaluator communication.

Once an encoding of $y = C(x)$ has been computed, the shares y_G and y_E can roughly be thought of as the decoding key and output label respectively. To make this general garbling framework low-depth while still retaining succinctness, we can retain the prior encoding Enc and homomorphic evaluation HGate sub-protocols while making use of three additional sub-protocols, a rekeying operation Rekey and a homomorphic $\mathsf{HRead}, \mathsf{HCompress}$, the latter two of which are defined with respect to a homomorphic Hash function. These protocols have the following properties:

- $\mathsf{Rekey}(1^\lambda, [\![x]\!] = ([\![x]\!]_G, [\![x]\!]_E)) \to [\![x]\!]' = ([\![x]\!]'_G, [\![x]\!]'_E)$: The rekeying operation will take a joint encoding of a value x and transform it into a new *fresh* encoding of the same value x. Importantly, the garbler's new share of the encoding $[\![x]\!]'_G$ will be *independent* of the input. To capture this requirement, we will decompose the rekeying protocol into the following steps:
  - $\mathsf{RekeySamp}(1^\lambda) \to [\![x]\!]'_G$: The garbler locally samples a fresh share $[\![x]\!]'_G$.
  - $\mathsf{RekeyGen}([\![x]\!]_G, [\![x]\!]'_G) \to \mathsf{rk}$: Using the freshly generated share $[\![x]\!]'_G$, as well as the original input encoding $[\![x]\!]_G$, the garbler generates a rekeying 'hint' rk, which is sent to the evaluator.
  - $\mathsf{RekeyEval}([\![x]\!]_E, \mathsf{rk}) \to [\![x]\!]'_E$: The evaluator, using their prior encoding share $[\![x]\!]_E$ and the rekey rk, computes their new encoding $[\![x]\!]'_E$.
Such a rekeying immediately enables a low depth garbler by allowing the garbler to generate their shares of each layer of the circuit C independently, then in parallel using HGate to evaluate the wires of each layer, before sending rekeying hints rk to the evaluator to 'bridge' the layers of the circuit.
Unfortunately, in our realisations of such rekeying protocols, the length of rk, and hence the communication between P_G and P_E (which corresponds to the size of the garbled circuit), grows with the length of the value x which needs to be rekeyed. Since we will need to rekey every wire in our circuit, applying this idea naively results in a $\mathsf{poly}(\lambda) \cdot |C|$ overhead, losing any notion of succinctness in the resulting garbled circuit.

- $\mathsf{Hash}(x) \to h_x$: To compress the communication of our garbling protocol, instead of attempting to rekey the wires of circuit directly, we instead rekey a succinct *hash* of our wire labels, while simultaneously ensuring our hash retains enough structure to execute the layer-by-layer homomorphic computation on the underlying encoding.
  - $\mathsf{HRead}(\llbracket h_x \rrbracket, i, P_E : \llbracket x \rrbracket_E) \to \llbracket x_i \rrbracket$: Using an encoding of the hash h_x, along with an index i, the parties can derive an encoding of the ith bit of x. To enable this sub-protocol on the evaluator's side, they will also need their share of the encoding of the original input $\llbracket x \rrbracket_E$. More concretely, the HRead step will require the evaluator to know (in the clear) the input to a linear hash function underlying Hash, which are simply wire values in the case of privacy-free garbling and one time pad encryptions of wire values in the case of private-garbling.
  - $\mathsf{HCompress}(\llbracket x \rrbracket) \to (\llbracket h_x \rrbracket)$: Given encodings of input values $\llbracket x \rrbracket$, the parties can derive an encoding of h_x, the hash of string x, The computational depth of $\mathsf{HCompress}$ will depend *logarithmically* on the length of x.

  Both HRead and $\mathsf{HCompress}$ will be able to be executed *noninteractively*.

Putting these together, we can realise a general framework for low-depth succinct garbling which will proceed as follows:

Inputs: P_G holds input x, circuit C, while P_E just holds circuit C.

Outputs: P_G outputs a decoding key dk, while P_E outputs a label L.

1. **Input Encoding Phase:** Party P_G samples public parameters $\mathsf{pp} \leftarrow \mathsf{Setup}(1^\lambda, 1^d, 1^{|C|})$ and generates encoding and public data $(\llbracket x \rrbracket, \mathsf{pd}, \mathsf{st})$, where $\llbracket x \rrbracket = (\llbracket x \rrbracket_G, \llbracket x \rrbracket_E) \leftarrow \mathsf{Enc}(\mathsf{gk}, x)$, sending $\mathsf{pd}, \llbracket x \rrbracket_E$ to P_E.

2. **Homomorphic Evaluation:** The parties firstly jointly use HGate to evaluate the hash function Hash, obtaining an encoding $\llbracket h_x \rrbracket$. Then, dividing the circuit C into layers $C_1, \ldots, C_d$, P_G and P_E iteratively compute the following for $i \in [d]$:
   - We maintain the invariant that for all $i \in [d]$ computed thus far, $h^{(i)}$ is the hash of all of the output wires $w^{(i)}$ of the ith layer of circuit C, with $h_x = h^{(0)}$.
   - For each gate $j \in |C_i|$, the ith layer of circuit C, take gate $g_{(i,j)} = (\mathsf{op}_j, \mathsf{lw}_j = (\mathsf{ll}_j, \mathsf{li}_j), \mathsf{rw}_j = (\mathsf{rl}_j, \mathsf{ri}_j)) \in C_i$, where ll, rl indicates the "depth" of the left and right input wires, and li, ri indicate their indices. Then compute $\llbracket w^{(i)}_{\mathsf{lw}_j} \rrbracket \leftarrow \mathsf{HRead}(\llbracket h^{(\mathsf{ll}_j)} \rrbracket, \mathsf{li}_j, P_E : \llbracket w^{(\mathsf{ll}_j)} \rrbracket_E)$ and $\llbracket w^{(i)}_{\mathsf{rw}_j} \rrbracket \leftarrow \mathsf{HRead}(\llbracket h^{(\mathsf{rl}_j)} \rrbracket, \mathsf{ri}_j, P_E : \llbracket w^{(\mathsf{rl}_j)} \rrbracket_E)$.
   - For all gates $g_{(i,j)} \in C_i$, compute $\llbracket w^{(i)}_j \rrbracket \leftarrow \mathsf{HGate}(\mathsf{op}_j, \llbracket w^{(i)}_{\mathsf{lw}_j} \rrbracket, \llbracket w^{(i)}_{\mathsf{rw}_j} \rrbracket)$
   - Compute encoding $\llbracket h^{(i)} \rrbracket' \leftarrow \mathsf{HCompress}(\{\llbracket w^{(i)}_j \rrbracket\}_{j \in [|C_i|]})$.
   - Rekey encoding with $\mathsf{Rekey}(\llbracket h^{(i)} \rrbracket') \to \llbracket h^{(i)} \rrbracket$.

3. **Output Phase:** Let j_{out} be the index of the output gate. Derive output encoding $\llbracket y \rrbracket = (\llbracket y \rrbracket_G, \llbracket y \rrbracket_E) \leftarrow \mathsf{HRead}(\llbracket h^{(d)} \rrbracket, \llbracket w^{(d)} \rrbracket, j_{\mathsf{out}})$. The garbler and evaluator derive dk, L from $\llbracket y \rrbracket_G$ and $\llbracket y \rrbracket_E$ respectively.

4.1 Garbling Depth

A garbling procedure following the above-outlined template naturally yields the following parallelization of the garbler's computation.

- **Input Encoding Phase:** Compute as above.
- **Homomorphic Evaluation:** Begin by computing $[\![h_x]\!]_G = [\![h^{(0)}]\!]_G$ as above. *In parallel,* for $i \in [d]$, perform the following:
  - Sample layer key $\mathsf{RekeySamp}(1^\lambda) \to [\![h^{(i)}]\!]_G$.
  - For all gates $g_j = (\mathsf{op}_j, \mathsf{lw}_j, \mathsf{rw}_j) \in C_i$, the garbler computes $[\![w^{(i)}_{\mathsf{lw}_j}]\!]_G \leftarrow$ $\mathsf{HRead}([\![h^{(\mathsf{ll}_j)}]\!], \mathsf{li}_j)$ and $[\![w^{(i)}_{\mathsf{rw}_j}]\!] \leftarrow \mathsf{HRead}([\![h^{(\mathsf{rl}_j)}]\!], \mathsf{ri}_j)^7$.
  - For all gates $g_j \in C_i$, compute $[\![w^{(i)}_j]\!]_G \leftarrow \mathsf{HGate}(\mathsf{op}_j, [\![w^{(i)}_{\mathsf{lw}_j}]\!]_G, [\![w^{(i)}_{\mathsf{rw}_j}]\!]_G)$
  - Compute encoding $[\![h^{(i)}]\!]'_G \leftarrow \mathsf{HCompress}(\{[\![w^{(i)}_j]\!]_G\}_{j \in [|C_i|]})$.
- In parallel for each $i \in [d]$, compute $\mathsf{RekeyGen}([\![h^{(i)}]\!]', [\![h^{(i)}]\!]) \to \mathsf{rk}_i$, which is (in the reusable case), output as part of gk.
- **Output Phase:** Compute as above.

We can see from this rearrangement that any garbling scheme which can be decomposed into our template will naturally have garbling depth independent of the circuit depth C, modulo any depth dependence incurred by the setup or encoding procedures, which we will show is independent or logarithmic for all of our constructions. In fact, in some instantiations, our succinct garbling schemes will be computable in depth $O(\log(\lambda, |C|))$, i.e. NC^1.

5 Non-reusable Succinct Privacy-Free Garbling

In this section, we present our group-based construction of privacy-free succinct garbling, which can be summarized in the following theorem:

Theorem 5.1 (Non-Reusable Succinct Privacy-Free Garbling under DDH). *Assuming any of the following:*

- *DDH in prime-order groups that are subgroups of $\mathbb{Z}_p^*$ for some prime p;*
- *DDH in Paillier groups;*

There exists a succinct privacy-free garbling scheme (i.e., satisfying only authenticity in Definition 3.1) satisfying the following.

- *Garbling sizes of a circuit $C : \{0,1\}^\ell \to \{0,1\}$ with depth D satisfy:*

$$|\hat{C}| < (D + |C|^{2/3} \cdot D^{1/3}) \cdot \mathsf{poly}(\lambda), \quad |\hat{x}| < \ell \cdot \mathsf{poly}(\lambda), \quad |\mathsf{dk}| < \mathsf{poly}(\lambda).$$

- *$\mathsf{GarbC}(\mathsf{pp}, C)$ can be computed in NC^1.*

We show the version in prime-order groups, as the version in Paillier groups is analogous. We defer our other constructions to the full version of this work .

---

^{7} Recall that only the evaluator needs input encodings to execute HRead, while the garbler only needs their share of the hash and the index.

5.1 Preliminaries

We provide a quick review of the standard DDH assumption in prime-order groups, and defer preliminaries on Paillier groups to the full version of this work.

Definition 5.2 (Prime-order Groups). *We consider prime-order groups defined by an instance generation algorithm* Gen *with the following syntax.*

- Gen(1^λ) *outputs* (G, p, g) *where* G *is a group description of prime order* $p > 2^\lambda$, *and* g *is a generator of* G.

Definition 5.3 (DDH Assumption). *We say DDH holds in prime-order groups if the following holds:*

$$\left\{ \mathsf{pp}, g, g^a, g^b, g^{ab} \;\middle|\; \begin{array}{c} \mathsf{pp} = (G, p, g) \leftarrow \mathsf{DDH.Gen}(1^\lambda), \\ a, b \leftarrow \mathbb{Z}_p. \end{array} \right\}_\lambda$$
$$\approx_c \left\{ \mathsf{pp}, g, g^a, g^b, g^c \;\middle|\; \begin{array}{c} \mathsf{pp} = (G, p, g) \leftarrow \mathsf{DDH.Gen}(1^\lambda), \\ a, b, c \leftarrow \mathbb{Z}_p. \end{array} \right\}_\lambda .$$

We will use the distributed discrete log (DDLog) algorithms [BGI16, DKK18, RS21, OSY21] for prime-order and Paillier groups.

Lemma 5.4 Distributed Discrete Log for Prime-Order Groups [BGI16, DKK18]**).** *For a cyclic group* G *with order* p *and a generator* g, *an error bound* $\delta \in (0, 1]$, *a message bound* B, *there exists an algorithm* $\mathsf{DDLog}_{G,g}^{\delta, B}$:

- $\mathsf{DDLog}_{G,g}^{\delta, B}(\varphi : G \to \{0, 1\}^{\lceil \log(2B/\delta) \rceil}, a \in G)$ *takes a function* φ *mapping group elements to bit strings, and an element* a. *It outputs a value* $\alpha \in \mathbb{Z}_p$.

The algorithm requires $O(\sqrt{B/\delta})$ *group operations and evaluations of* φ, *and has the guarantee that for all* $0 < \delta \leq 1$, $B < p$, $a \in G$, *and* $m \leq B$:

$$\Pr\left[\begin{array}{c} \mathsf{DDLog}_{G,g}^{\delta, B}(\varphi, a \cdot g^m) \\ = \mathsf{DDLog}_{G,g}^{\delta, B}(\varphi, a) + m \bmod p \end{array} \;\middle|\; \varphi \leftarrow \$ \right] \geq 1 - \delta,$$

where $\varphi \leftarrow \$$ *means sampling at random from all possible mappings.*

Remark 5.5. We note that the DDLog algorithm can be implemented in depth $O(\log \lambda)$, assuming $B/\delta < \mathsf{poly}(\lambda)$, φ can be evaluated in depth $O(\log \lambda)$. In our constructions using prime-order groups, we instantiate (pseudo)random mappings φ via a PRF $: \{0, 1\}^\lambda \times [2^\lambda] \times G \to \{0, 1\}^\lambda$. In more detail, the parties hold a common random key $\leftarrow \{0, 1\}^\lambda$, and maintain a counter $c \in [2^\lambda]$. Every invocation of DDLog is instantiated with $\varphi(\cdot) := \mathsf{PRF}(\mathsf{key}, c, \cdot)$ (with suitably truncated outputs) for distinct counter values c. Indeed, under the DDH assumption in prime-order subgroups of $\mathbb{Z}_{p'}^*$ for primes p', there exists such PRFs with depth $O(\log \lambda)$ [NR97].

The starting point of our group instantiation is the DDH-based aHMAC scheme of [ILL25a]. In particular, it contains a pair of evaluation algorithms EvalKey, EvalTag that allows two parties P_G, P_E who jointly hold additive shares of the form $\langle \mathbf{s} \cdot x \rangle$, $\langle \mathbf{s} \cdot y \rangle$, to *locally* derive additive shares $\langle \mathbf{s}' \cdot g(x, y) \rangle$, for any Boolean gate g.[8] We will directly use these algorithms to implement our HGate protocol, and our main focus is to design compatible protocols HRead and HCompress for these encodings.

In more detail, in our group instantiation, the encoding of a wire value $[\![x]\!]$ for $x \in \{0, 1\}$ contains a pair of additive shares $\langle \mathbf{s}^{\mathsf{id}} \cdot x \rangle$ over $\mathbb{Z}_p$, and $\mathbf{s}^{\mathsf{id}} \in [p]^2$ are two secret exponents over a modulus p and with an associated id. Additionally, the value x is revealed to the evaluator.

$$[\![x]\!] = ([\![x]\!]_G, [\![x]\!]_E), \quad \text{where } [\![x]\!]_G = (\langle \mathbf{s}^{\mathsf{id}} \cdot x \rangle_G, \mathsf{id}), \quad \text{and } [\![x]\!]_E = (\langle \mathbf{s}^{\mathsf{id}} \cdot x \rangle_E, \mathsf{id}, x).$$

The $\mathsf{id} = (d, \mathsf{type})$ indicates the depth d of the current encoding and its type, i.e., whether it's an InWire (to depth d), or an OutWire. Our encoding of a hash value $[\![\mathbf{h}]\!]$ similarly contains a pair of additive shares $\langle \mathbf{s}^{\mathsf{id}} \otimes \mathbf{h} \rangle$ over $\mathbb{Z}_p$, an id with $\mathsf{type} = \mathsf{hash}$, but without requiring the evaluator to hold $\mathbf{h}$.[9]

Under this encoding, the Rekey steps are as follows, assuming access to public parameters pp that specify the modulus p.

- RekeySamp(id) samples random share $\langle \mathbf{s}^{\mathsf{id}} \cdot x \rangle_G' \leftarrow [p]^2$, and sets $[\![x']\!]_G := (\langle \mathbf{s}^{\mathsf{id}} \cdot x \rangle_G', \mathsf{id})$.
- RekeyGen($[\![x]\!]_G, [\![x']\!]_G$) outputs the difference $\mathsf{rk} \leftarrow \langle \mathbf{s}^{\mathsf{id}} \cdot x \rangle_G' - \langle \mathbf{s}^{\mathsf{id}} \cdot x \rangle_G$.
- RekeyEval($[\![x]\!]_E, \mathsf{rk}$) computes $\langle \mathbf{s}^{\mathsf{id}} \cdot x \rangle_E' \leftarrow \langle \mathbf{s}^{\mathsf{id}} \cdot x \rangle_E + \mathsf{rk}$, and sets $[\![x']\!]_E := (\langle \mathbf{s}^{\mathsf{id}} \cdot x \rangle_E', \mathsf{id}, x)$.

In the following, we make extensive use of the fact that two parties can locally evaluate any linear functions on additive shares (over $\mathbb{Z}_p$). Examples include addition between shares, multiplication by any scalar $c \in \mathbb{Z}_p$, and bit-composition over shares of bits. When two parties want to derive any share $\langle a \rangle$, it suffices for them to derive $\langle \mathsf{Bits}(a) \rangle$. We will omit explicitly writing out bit-compositions in the following to avoid cluttering.

Instantiation of HRead *and* HCompress. We present the two sub-protocols HRead, HCompress in Fig. 1, and 2. We note that the sub-protocols only run the local algorithms $\mathsf{HRead}_G, \mathsf{HRead}_E, \mathsf{HCompress}_G, \mathsf{HCompress}_E$, (Construction 5.8) and don't involve communication between the parties. The sub-protocols assume the parties P_G, P_E hold public data pd produced in the overall protocol by Enc. (See Eq. 5.4.)

Below, we first present our core construction of a pair of fixed-factor hashing algorithms in Construction 5.7, which uses a SecSwitch algorithm

---

[8] The DDH-based algorithms of [ILL25a] incurs a $1/\mathsf{poly}$ correctness error probability. But we note the techniques from a follow-up [ILL25b] for removing this error can be adapted to our constructions.

[9] Note that the hash encoding format is still compatible with the described Rekey steps.

Protocol HRead

The protocol runs between a garbler P_G and an evaluator P_E. It uses the following ingradients:

- The algorithms $\mathsf{HRead}_G, \mathsf{HRead}_E$, from Construction 5.8.

Inputs: P_G, P_E hold public data pd, index i, and jointly encodings $[\![\mathbf{h}]\!]$ (with $\mathsf{id} = (d, \mathsf{hash})$) of a hash and P_E additionally holds encodings $[\![\mathbf{x}]\!]_E$ (without requirements on their ids) of the hashed values.

Outputs: P_G, P_E jointly hold encodings $[\![x_i]\!]$ (with $\mathsf{id}' = (d+1, \mathsf{InWire})$) of the i-th hashed value.

- P_G reads $\mathsf{HR.pd}^{(d)}$ from pd, $\langle \mathbf{s}^{\mathsf{id}} \otimes \mathbf{h} \rangle_G$ from $[\![\mathbf{h}]\!]_G$, and runs

$$\langle \mathbf{s}^{\mathsf{id}'} \cdot x_i \rangle_G \leftarrow \mathsf{HRead}_G^{\mathsf{Hash.pd}^{(d)}}(\langle \mathbf{s}^{\mathsf{id}} \otimes \mathbf{h} \rangle_G, i).$$

  It outputs $[\![x_i]\!]_G := (\langle \mathbf{s}^{\mathsf{id}'} \cdot x_i \rangle_G, \mathsf{id}')$.
- P_E reads $\mathsf{HR.pd}^{(d)}$ from pd, $\langle \mathbf{s}^{\mathsf{id}} \otimes \mathbf{h} \rangle_E$ from $[\![\mathbf{h}]\!]_E$, $\mathbf{x}$ from $[\![\mathbf{x}]\!]_E$, and runs

$$\langle \mathbf{s}^{\mathsf{id}'} \cdot x_i \rangle_E \leftarrow \mathsf{HRead}_E^{\mathsf{Hash.pd}^{(d)}}(\langle \mathbf{s}^{\mathsf{id}} \otimes \mathbf{h} \rangle_E, i, \mathbf{x}).$$

  It outputs $[\![x_i]\!]_E := (\langle \mathbf{s}^{\mathsf{id}'} \cdot x_i \rangle_E, \mathsf{id}', \mathbf{x}[i])$.

Fig. 1. The HRead sub-protocol.

from Construction 5.6 as a building block. Then, we describe wrapper algorithms $\mathsf{HRead}_G, \mathsf{HRead}_E, \mathsf{HCompress}_G, \mathsf{HCompress}_E$ that call fixed-factor hashing in Construction 5.8.

Construction 5.6 (Secret Switching for aHMAC Encodings). The construction is with respect to the following public parameters pp:

- A bound $B < \mathsf{poly}(\lambda)$ on encoded values and $0 < \delta < 1$ on correctness error probability.
- A DDH group instance G with a prime order $p > \lambda^{\omega(1)}$ and a generator $g \in G$.

It uses the DDLog algorithm from Lemma 5.4 instantiated with a suitable $\mathsf{PRF}: \{0,1\}^\lambda \times G \to \{0,1\}^\lambda$ to achieve error probability $< \delta$.

$\mathsf{pd} \leftarrow \mathsf{Setup}^{\mathsf{pp}}(1^\lambda, \mathbf{s} \in [p]^2, \mathbf{s}' \in \{0,1\}^\ell)$: Compute the secret-switching public data as

$$\mathbf{r} \leftarrow [p]^\ell, \quad \mathsf{pd} := (\mathbf{c}_0 = g^{\mathbf{r}}, \mathbf{c}_1 = g^{\mathbf{s}[0] \cdot \mathbf{r} + \mathbf{s}'})$$

Additionally, instantiate $\mathsf{DDLog}_{G,g}$ with a (public) random PRF key $\leftarrow \{0,1\}^\lambda$ which is also included in pd. Since invokations of PRF happens implicitly within invocations of $\mathsf{DDLog}_{G,g}$, we omit it from the following descriptions and similarly from other algorithms in this section.

$\langle s' \cdot x \rangle_{G/E} \leftarrow \mathsf{SecSwitch}^{\mathsf{pd}}(\langle s \cdot x \rangle_{G/E}, \langle x \rangle_{G/E})$: Read $(\mathbf{c}_0, \mathbf{c}_1)$ from pd and compute the following

$$\mathbf{v}_{G/E} \leftarrow (\mathbf{c}_1)^{\langle x \rangle_{G/E}} / (\mathbf{c}_0)^{\langle s[0] \cdot x \rangle_{G/E}},$$
$$\langle s' \cdot x \rangle_{G/E} \leftarrow \mathsf{DDLog}_{G,g}(\mathbf{v}_{G/E}) \bmod p.$$

Construction 5.7 (Fixed Factor Hashing for aHMAC Encodings under DDH). The construction is with respect to the same public parameters $\mathsf{pp} = (B, \delta, G, p, g)$ as specified in Construction 5.6, and additionally

– A hash function $\mathsf{Hash} : \mathbb{Z}^W \to \mathbb{Z}^{\lceil \log p \rceil}$ with compression factor W, *implicitly* defined by W (the exponents of) group elements g^{b_i} for $i \in [W]$;

$$\mathsf{Hash}(\mathbf{x} \in \mathbb{Z}_B^W) := \sum_i \mathsf{Bits}(b_i) \cdot \mathbf{x}[i] \text{ over } \mathbb{Z} \tag{5.1}$$

It uses as ingredients the secret switching algorithms (Construction 5.6, denoted with prefix SS) and the DDLog algorithm from Lemma 5.4 instantiated with a suitable $\mathsf{PRF} : \{0,1\}^\lambda \times G \to \{0,1\}^\lambda$ to achieve error probability $< \delta$.

$\mathsf{pd} \leftarrow \mathsf{Setup}^{\mathsf{pp}}(1^\lambda, s, s' \in [p]^2)$: Read $\{g^{b_i}\}_{i \in [W]}$ from pp, and generate ciphertexts $\{\mathsf{ct}_{i,j,b}\}_{i,j \in [W], b \in \{0,1\}}$ used for extracting hashed values:

$$\mathbf{a}_j \leftarrow [p]^{\lceil \log p \rceil},$$
$$\mathsf{ct}_{i,j,b} \leftarrow (g^{b_i})^{s[b] \cdot \mathbf{a}_j} / g^{\mathbf{u}_j[i] \cdot \mathsf{Bits}(s'[b])} \in G$$

where $\mathbf{u}_j \in \{0,1\}^W$ denote the j-th unit vector. Next, generate public data $\{\mathsf{pd}_{i,b}\}_{i \in [W], b \in \{0,1\}}$ for computing the hash over shares: [10]

$$\mathsf{pd}_{i,b} \leftarrow \mathsf{SS.Setup}(1^\lambda, s, \mathsf{Bits}(s'[b]) \otimes \mathsf{Bits}(b_i)).$$

Finally, output
$$\mathsf{pd} := (\mathsf{pp}, \{\mathsf{ct}_{i,j,b}\}, \{g^{\mathbf{a}_j}\}, \{\mathsf{pd}_i\}).$$

$\langle s' \otimes \mathbf{h} \rangle_{G/E} \leftarrow \mathsf{Compress}^{\mathsf{pd}}(\langle s \otimes \mathbf{x} \rangle_{G/E}, \langle \mathbf{x} \rangle_{G/E})$: Read $\{\mathsf{pd}_{i,b}\}_{i \in [W], b \in \{0,1\}}$ from pd, and compute

$$\langle s' \otimes \mathbf{h} \rangle_{G/E} \leftarrow \sum_i \langle s' \otimes \mathsf{Bits}(b_i) \cdot \mathbf{x}[i] \rangle_{G/E}, \text{ where for } i \in [W], b \in \{0,1\} :$$

$$\langle \mathsf{Bits}(s'[b]) \otimes \mathsf{Bits}(b_i) \cdot \mathbf{x}[i] \rangle_{G/E} \leftarrow \mathsf{SS.SecSwitch}^{\mathsf{pd}_{i,b}}(\langle s \cdot \mathbf{x}[i] \rangle_{G/E},$$
$$\langle \mathbf{x}[i] \rangle_{G/E}).$$

---

[10] We abuse notation here, writing $\mathsf{Bits}(b_i) \otimes \mathsf{Bits}(s[b])$ to mean the flattened vector as the input to $\mathsf{SS.Setup}$.

$\langle \mathbf{s}' \cdot x_j \rangle_{G/E} \leftarrow \mathsf{Extract}^{\mathsf{pd}}(\langle \mathbf{s} \otimes \mathbf{h} \rangle_{G/E}, j, \langle \mathbf{x} \rangle_{G/E})$: First read $\{\mathsf{ct}_{i,j,b}\}_{i,j\in[W], b\in\{0,1\}}$ from pd, and compute

$$\mathsf{diff}_{G/E,j,b} \leftarrow \prod_i (\mathsf{ct}_{i,j,b})^{\langle \mathbf{x}[i] \rangle_{G/E}}.$$

Next read $g^{\mathbf{a}_j}$ and $\alpha, \beta \in [p]^{\lceil \log p \rceil}$ from pd, and compute

$$\langle \mathbf{s} \cdot h \rangle_{G/E} \leftarrow \sum_{k \in [\lceil \log p \rceil]} 2^k \cdot \langle \mathbf{s} \cdot \mathbf{h}[k] \rangle_{G/E},$$

$$\mathbf{v}_{G/E,b} \leftarrow (g^{\mathbf{a}_j})^{\langle \mathbf{s}[b] \cdot h \rangle_{G/E}} / \mathsf{diff}_{G/E,j,b},$$

$$\langle \mathsf{Bits}(\mathbf{s}'[b]) \cdot x_j \rangle_{G/E} \leftarrow \mathsf{DDLog}_{G,g}(\mathbf{v}_{G/E,b}) \bmod p.$$

Construction 5.8 (Hashing for aHMAC Encodings). The construction is with respect to the following public parameters pp:

- A bound γ on the number of parallel instances of fixed factor hashing, and $0 < \delta < 1$ on the correctness error probability.
- A DDH group instance G with a prime order $p > \lambda^{\omega(1)}$ and a generator $g \in G$.
- A hash function $\mathsf{Hash} : \mathbb{Z}^W \to \mathbb{Z}^{\lceil \log p \rceil}$ defined as in Eq. 5.1.

It uses the fixed factor hashing algorithms (Construction 5.7, denoted with prefix FH) as ingradients, with respect to the above G, p, g, Hash and the following additional parameters B, δ'.

- A bound $B = W$ on encoded values;
- An error bound $\delta' < \delta/\gamma$ (s.t. the error probability over all invocations of the ingradient algorithms is $< \delta$).

For a string $\mathbf{x} \in \{0,1\}^\ell$ of length $\ell < W \cdot \gamma$, we define its hash $h_{\mathbf{x}}$ to be the γ hashed values of W chunks of $\mathbf{x}$ by Hash (Eq. 5.1). For an index $i < W \cdot \gamma$, we define $\mathsf{Chunk}_i \in [\gamma]$ to be the (index of the) chunk corresponding to $\mathbf{x}[i]$ during hashing.

$$\mathsf{Chunk}_i = \lfloor i/W \rfloor. \tag{5.2}$$

$\mathsf{pd} \leftarrow \mathsf{Setup}^{\mathsf{pp}}(1^\lambda, \mathbf{s}, \mathbf{s}' \in [p]^2)$: Prepare public data for an instance of fixed factor hashing:

$$\mathsf{FH.pd} \leftarrow \mathsf{FH.Setup}(1^\lambda, \mathbf{s}, \mathbf{s}').$$

Output $\mathsf{pd} := \mathsf{FH.pd}$.

$\langle \mathbf{s}' \cdot x_i \rangle_G \leftarrow \mathsf{HRead}^{\mathsf{pd}}_G(\langle \mathbf{s} \otimes \mathbf{h} \rangle_G, i)$: Assuming $i < W \cdot \gamma$, let $j := \mathsf{Chunk}_i$ as defined in Eq. 5.2 and $i' := i \bmod W$. Read $\mathsf{FH.pd}$ and run the following:

$$\langle \mathbf{s} \otimes \mathbf{h}_j \rangle_G \leftarrow \langle \mathbf{s} \otimes \mathbf{h}[j \cdot \lceil \log p \rceil : (j+1) \cdot \lceil \log p \rceil] \rangle_G,$$

$$\langle \mathbf{s}' \cdot x_i \rangle_G \leftarrow \mathsf{FH.Extract}^{\mathsf{FH.pd}}(\langle \mathbf{s} \otimes \mathbf{h}_j \rangle_G, i', \langle \mathbf{x}_j \rangle_G) \text{ where } \langle \mathbf{x}_j \rangle_G \leftarrow \mathbf{0}.$$

$\langle \mathbf{s}' \cdot x_i \rangle_E \leftarrow \mathsf{HRead}_E^{\mathsf{pd}}(\langle \mathbf{s} \otimes \mathbf{h} \rangle_E, i, \mathbf{x})$: Analogous to HRead_G, except running FH. Extract with $\langle \mathbf{x}_j \rangle_E$ defined as:

$$\mathbf{x}_j := \mathbf{x}[j \cdot W : (j+1) \cdot W], \ \langle \mathbf{x}_j \rangle_E \leftarrow \mathbf{x}_j.$$

$\langle \mathbf{s}' \otimes \mathbf{h} \rangle_G \leftarrow \mathsf{HCompress}_G^{\mathsf{pd}}(\langle \mathbf{s} \otimes \mathbf{x} \rangle_G)$: Read FH.pd from pd, and run FH.Compress on chunks of $\langle \mathbf{s} \otimes \mathbf{x} \rangle_G$ and $\langle \mathbf{x} \rangle_G \leftarrow \mathbf{0}$. For $j \in [\gamma]$:

$$\langle \mathbf{s} \otimes \mathbf{x}_j \rangle_G \leftarrow \langle \mathbf{s} \otimes \mathbf{x}[j \cdot W : (j+1) \cdot W] \rangle_G,$$
$$\langle \mathbf{x}_j \rangle_G \leftarrow \langle \mathbf{x}[j \cdot W : (j+1) \cdot W] \rangle_G,$$
$$\langle \mathbf{s}' \otimes \mathbf{h}_j \rangle_G \leftarrow \mathsf{FH.Compress}^{\mathsf{FH.pd}^{(1)}}(\langle \mathbf{s} \otimes \mathbf{x}_j \rangle_G, \langle \mathbf{x}_j \rangle_G),$$

Finally, concatenate the obtained hashs as $\langle \mathbf{s}' \otimes \mathbf{h} \rangle_G$ and output it.

$\langle \mathbf{s}' \otimes \mathbf{h} \rangle_E \leftarrow \mathsf{HCompress}_E^{\mathsf{pd}}(\langle \mathbf{s} \otimes \mathbf{x} \rangle_E, \mathbf{x})$: Analogous to $\mathsf{HCompress}_G$, except running FH.Compress with chunks of $\langle \mathbf{x} \rangle_E \leftarrow \mathbf{x}$.

Remark 5.9. As presented, a hash computed by HCompress has a fixed size $\gamma \cdot \mathsf{poly}(\lambda)$. In our application to garbling schemes, we optimize to only run $\lceil |\mathbf{x}|/W \rceil$, instead of γ, instances of the fixed factor hash. The resuling hash has size $\lceil |S|/W \rceil \cdot \mathsf{poly}(\lambda)$.

Instantiation of HGate. We set up our encodings for wire values to be directly compatible with the aHMAC evaluation constructions from [ILL25a], which are used for the HGate protocol (Fig. 3). We note that HGate only runs local algorithms EvalKey, EvalTag (Construction 5.11) described below, and doesn't involve communication between the parties. Similarly to HRead and HCompress, the sub-protocol assume the parties P_G, P_E hold public data pd produced in the overall protocol by Enc. (See Eq. 5.4.)

We recall necessary preliminaries from [ILL25a] below (modified slightly for a more modular presentation). When possible, we omit construction details that are not relevant for security proofs and only describe the interfaces.

Construction 5.10 (aHMAC Multiplication under DDH [ILL25a]). The construction is with respect to the same public parameters $\mathsf{pp} = (B, \delta, G, p, g)$ as specified in Construction 5.6.

It uses as ingredients the DDLog algorithm from Lemma 5.4 instantiated with a suitable PRF : $\{0,1\}^\lambda \times G \rightarrow \{0,1\}^\lambda$ to achieve error probability $< \delta$.

$\mathsf{pd} \leftarrow \mathsf{Setup}^{\mathsf{pp}}(1^\lambda, s, s', s'' \in [p])$: takes three secrets $s, s', s'' \in [p]$, and computes pd as follows.

$$\mathbf{r} \leftarrow [p]^{\lceil \log p \rceil}, \ \mathsf{pd} := (\mathsf{pp}, g^{\mathbf{r}}, g^{\mathbf{r}s}, g^{\mathbf{r}s'}, g^{\mathbf{r}ss'+\mathsf{Bits}(s'')}).$$

$\langle s'' \cdot z \rangle_G \leftarrow \mathsf{MultKey}^{\mathsf{pd}}(\langle s \cdot x \rangle_G, \langle s' \cdot y \rangle_G)$: takes as inputs two integers representing the 0-shares of $\langle s \cdot x \rangle_G, \langle s' \cdot y \rangle_E \in \mathbb{Z}$ for some secrets $s, s' \in [p]$. It outputs the 0-share of another share $\langle s'' \cdot z \rangle_G$.

Protocol HCompress

The protocol runs between a garbler P_G and an evaluator P_E. It uses the following ingradients:

- The algorithms $\mathsf{HCompress}_G, \mathsf{HCompress}_E$ from Construction 5.8.

Inputs: P_G, P_E hold public data pd and jointly encodings $[\![\mathbf{x}]\!]$ (with $\mathsf{id} = (d, \mathsf{OutWire})$).

Outputs: P_G, P_E jointly hold the encodings $[\![\mathbf{h}]\!]$ (with $\mathsf{id}' = (d, \mathsf{hash})$) of the hash.

- P_G reads $\mathsf{HW.pd}^{(d)}$ from pd, $\langle \mathbf{s}^{\mathsf{id}} \otimes \mathbf{x} \rangle$ from $[\![x_i']\!]_G$ for $i \in S$, and runs

$$\langle \mathbf{s}^{\mathsf{id}'} \otimes \mathbf{h} \rangle_G \leftarrow \mathsf{HCompress}_G^{\mathsf{HW.pd}^{(d)}}(\langle \mathbf{s}^{\mathsf{id}} \otimes \mathbf{x} \rangle_G).$$

It outputs $[\![\mathbf{h}]\!]_G := (\langle \mathbf{s}^{\mathsf{id}'} \otimes \mathbf{h} \rangle_G, \mathsf{id}')$.

- P_E analogously runs $\mathsf{HCompress}_E$ as follows:

$$\langle \mathbf{s}^{\mathsf{id}'} \otimes \mathbf{h} \rangle_E \leftarrow \mathsf{HCompress}_E^{\mathsf{HW.pd}^{(d)}}(\langle \mathbf{s}^{\mathsf{id}} \cdot \mathbf{x} \rangle_E, \mathbf{x}).$$

where $\mathbf{x}$ is read from $[\![\mathbf{x}]\!]_E$. It outputs $[\![\mathbf{h}]\!]_E := (\langle \mathbf{s}^{\mathsf{id}'} \otimes \mathbf{h} \rangle_E, \mathsf{id}')$.

Fig. 2. The $\mathsf{HCompress}$ sub-protocol.

$\langle s'' \cdot z \rangle_E \leftarrow \mathsf{MultTag}^{\mathsf{pd}}(\langle s \cdot x \rangle_E, \langle s' \cdot y \rangle_E, x, y)$: takes as input the 1-shares of $\langle s \cdot x \rangle_E, \langle s' \cdot y \rangle_E$ for some secret s, s', and the shared values $x, y \in [B]$. It outputs the 1-share of another share $\langle s'' \cdot z \rangle_E$.

We next recall from [ILL25a] the leveled gate evaluation algorithms $\mathsf{EvalKey}$, $\mathsf{EvalTag}$ for aHMAC.

Construction 5.11 (aHMAC (leveled) Gate Evaluation [ILL25a]**).** The construction is with respect to the same public parameters $\mathsf{pp} = (\delta, G, p, g)$ as specified in Construction 5.10.

It uses Construction 5.10 (with prefix Mt) and Construction 5.6 (with prefix SS) as ingredients w.r.t. to G, p, g from above and $B = 2$, $\delta' = \delta/2$.

$\mathsf{pd} \leftarrow \mathsf{Setup}^{\mathsf{pp}}(1^\lambda, \mathbf{s}, \mathbf{s}' \in [p]^2)$: prepare two instances of aHMAC multiplication, and an public data for secret switching from $\mathbf{s}$ to $\mathbf{s}'$.

$$\mathsf{Mt.pd}_0 \leftarrow \mathsf{Mt.Setup}(1^\lambda, \mathbf{s}[0], \mathbf{s}[1], \mathbf{s}'[0]), \quad \mathsf{Mt.pd}_1 \leftarrow \mathsf{Mt.Setup}(1^\lambda, \mathbf{s}[0], \mathbf{s}[1], \mathbf{s}'[1]),$$

$$\mathsf{pd} := (\mathsf{Mt.pd}_0, \mathsf{Mt.pd}_1, \mathsf{SS.pd}), \quad \mathsf{SS.pd} \leftarrow \mathsf{SS.Setup}(1^\lambda, \mathbf{s}, \mathbf{s}').$$

$\langle s' \cdot z \rangle_G \leftarrow \mathsf{EvalKey}^{\mathsf{pd}}(g, \langle \mathbf{s} \cdot x \rangle_G, \langle \mathbf{s} \cdot y \rangle_G)$: We show the case for $g = \mathsf{XOR}$. (The case for $g = \mathsf{AND}$ or any binary gate is analogous.) First read $\mathsf{SS.pd}$ from pd, and compute $\langle \mathbf{s}' \cdot (x + y) \rangle_G$:

$$\langle \mathbf{s}' \cdot (x + y) \rangle_G \leftarrow \mathsf{SecSwitch}^{\mathsf{SS.pd}}(\langle \mathbf{s} \cdot (x + y) \rangle_G, \langle x + y \rangle_G),$$

$$\text{where } \langle \mathbf{s} \cdot (x + y) \rangle_G, \leftarrow \langle \mathbf{s} \cdot x \rangle_G + \langle \mathbf{s} \cdot y \rangle_G, \quad \langle x + y \rangle_G \leftarrow 0.$$

Protocol HGate

The protocol runs between a garbler P_G and an evaluator P_E. It uses the following ingradients:

- The algorithms EvalKey, EvalTag from Construction 5.11.

Inputs: P_G, P_E hold public data pd, an operator op, and jointly encodings of $[\![x]\!]$, $[\![y]\!]$, (with id $= (d, \mathsf{InWire})$).

Outputs: P_G, P_E jointly hold encodings $[\![z]\!]$ (with id$' = (d, \mathsf{OutWire})$), where z should equal $\mathsf{op}(x, y)$.

- P_G reads $\mathsf{GE.pd}^{(d)}$ from pd, $\langle \mathsf{s}^{\mathsf{id}} \cdot x \rangle_G$ $\langle \mathsf{s}^{\mathsf{id}} \cdot y \rangle_G$ from $[\![x]\!]_G$, $[\![x]\!]_G$, and runs

$$\langle \mathsf{s}^{\mathsf{id}'} \cdot z \rangle_G \leftarrow \mathsf{EvalKey}^{\mathsf{GE.pd}^{(d)}}(\mathsf{op}, \langle \mathsf{s}^{\mathsf{id}} \cdot x \rangle_G, \langle \mathsf{s}^{\mathsf{id}} \cdot y \rangle_G).$$

  It outputs $[\![z]\!]_G := (\langle \mathsf{s}^{\mathsf{id}'} \cdot z \rangle_G, \mathsf{id}')$.
- P_E proceeds analogously to P_G by running EvalTag, and outputs $[\![z]\!]_E := (\langle \mathsf{s}^{\mathsf{id}'} \cdot z \rangle_E, \mathsf{id}', \mathsf{op}(x, y))$.

Fig. 3. The HGate sub-protocol.

Then read $\mathsf{Mt.pd}_0, \mathsf{Mt.pd}_1$ from pd, and compute the final output $\langle \mathsf{s}' \cdot z \rangle_G$ as follows:

$$\langle \mathsf{s}'[b] \cdot xy \rangle_G \leftarrow \mathsf{MultKey}^{\mathsf{Mt.pd}_b}(\langle \mathsf{s}[0] \cdot x \rangle_G, \langle \mathsf{s}[1] \cdot y \rangle_G), \text{ for } b \in \{0, 1\},$$
$$\langle \mathsf{s}' \cdot z \rangle_G \leftarrow 2 \cdot \langle \mathsf{s}' \cdot (x + y) \rangle_G - \langle \mathsf{s}' \cdot xy \rangle_G.$$

$\langle \mathsf{s}' \cdot z \rangle_E \leftarrow \mathsf{EvalTag}^{\mathsf{pd}}(g, \langle \mathsf{s} \cdot x \rangle_E, \langle \mathsf{s} \cdot y \rangle_E, x, y)$: Analogous to EvalKey, except when running SecSwitch, set $\langle x + y \rangle_E \leftarrow x + y$, and run MultTag instead of MultKey in the second step.

Instantiation of Setup *and* Enc. We now describe the $\mathsf{Setup}(1^\lambda, 1^D, |C|)$ procedure that selects public parameters $\mathsf{pp} := (1^D, G, p, g, \mathsf{Hash}, \delta, \gamma = \lceil |C|^{2/3} \cdot D^{1/3} \rceil)$ for all sub-protocols HRead, HCompress, HGate.[11]

- Sample a DDH instance $(G, p, g) \leftarrow \mathsf{Gen}(1^\lambda)$, with prime order p.
- Set $W = \lceil (|C|/D)^{1/3} \rceil$, and sample $b_i \leftarrow [p]$ for $i \in [W]$, which define a global hash function $\mathsf{Hash} : \mathbb{Z}^W \to \mathbb{Z}^{\lceil \log p \rceil}$ as specified in Eq. 5.1.
- Set $\delta < 1/(p(\lambda) \cdot (3(D + 1) + |C|))$ s.t. the probability over all invocations of the sub-protocols is $< 1/p(\lambda)$ for any desired polynomial $p(\lambda)$.
- Additionally, pre-compute values $\{g^{2^i}\}_{i \in [\lceil \log p \rceil]}$ for achieving low-depth exponentiations (by the garbler).

We next describe how to sample gk, and the $\mathsf{Enc}(\mathsf{gk}, \mathbf{x})$ procedure that produces encodings $[\![\mathbf{x}]\!]$ and public data pd.

---

[11] In our garbling scheme definition, the Setup algorithm doesn't take $|C|$ or D as input. This syntactical mismatch can be solved by delaying settings of $\mathsf{Hash}, \delta, \gamma$ which depends on $|C|$, D to GarbC, when the circuit is known.

- First choose leveled secrets $\mathbf{s}^{\mathsf{id}} \in [p]^2$ as gk for our encodings:

$$\mathbf{s}^{(0,\mathsf{hash})}, \mathbf{s}^{(0,\mathsf{OutWire})}, \mathbf{s}^{(D+1,\mathsf{InWire})} \leftarrow [p]^2,$$
$$\mathbf{s}^{(d,\mathsf{InWire})}, \mathbf{s}^{(d,\mathsf{OutWire})}, \mathbf{s}^{(d,\mathsf{hash})} \leftarrow [p]^2 \text{ for } d = 1, \ldots, D. \tag{5.3}$$

- Next sets up public data for the sub-protocols:

$$\mathsf{HW.pd}^{(d)} \leftarrow \mathsf{Hash.Setup}(1^\lambda, \mathbf{s}^{\mathsf{id}}, \mathbf{s}^{\mathsf{id}'}), \ \mathsf{HR.pd}^{(d)} \leftarrow \mathsf{Hash.Setup}(1^\lambda, \mathbf{s}^{\mathsf{id}}, \mathbf{s}^{\mathsf{id}''})$$
$$\text{where } \mathsf{id} = (d, \mathsf{OutWire}), \mathsf{id}' = (d, \mathsf{hash}), \mathsf{id}'' = (d+1, \mathsf{InWire})$$
$$\text{for } d = 0, \ldots, D$$
$$\mathsf{GE.pd}^{(d)} \leftarrow \mathsf{GE.Setup}(1^\lambda, \mathbf{s}^{\mathsf{id}}, \mathbf{s}^{\mathsf{id}'})$$
$$\text{where } \mathsf{id} = (d, \mathsf{InWire}), \mathsf{id}' = (d, \mathsf{OutWire}) \text{ for } d = 1, \ldots, D$$
$$\mathsf{pd} := (\{\mathsf{HW.pd}^{(d)}\}, \{\mathsf{HR.pd}^{(d)}\}, \{\mathsf{GE.pd}^{(d)}\}). \tag{5.4}$$

- Finally use $\mathbf{s}^{\mathsf{id}=(0,\mathsf{OutWire})}$ from the above to compute

$$\langle \mathbf{s}^{\mathsf{id}} \cdot \mathbf{x}[i] \rangle_G \leftarrow [p]^2, \quad \langle \mathbf{s}^{\mathsf{id}} \cdot \mathbf{x}[i] \rangle_E \leftarrow \langle \mathbf{s}^{\mathsf{id}} \cdot \mathbf{x}[i] \rangle_G + \mathbf{s}^{\mathsf{id}} \cdot \mathbf{x}[i] \text{ over } \mathbb{Z}_p,$$
$$[\![\mathbf{x}[i]]\!]_G := (\langle \mathbf{s}^{\mathsf{id}} \cdot \mathbf{x}[i] \rangle_G, \mathsf{id}), \quad [\![\mathbf{x}[i]]\!]_E := (\langle \mathbf{s}^{\mathsf{id}} \cdot \mathbf{x}[i] \rangle_E, \mathsf{id}, \mathbf{x}[i]). \tag{5.5}$$

We defer the analysis of correctness and security of this construction to the full version of this paper.

Acknowledgments. Huijia Lin is supported by a Simons collaboration grant for algorithmic fairness and Amazon Research Award. We thank Lawrence Roy for pointing out an error the group-based garbling schemes in an earlier version of this work.

References

[AIK04] Applebaum, B., Ishai, Y., Kushilevitz, E.: Cryptography in NC^0. In: 45th FOCS, Rome, Italy, 17–19 October 2004, pp. 166–175. IEEE Computer Society Press (2004)

[AIK06] Applebaum, B., Ishai, Y., Kushilevitz, E.: Computationally private randomizing polynomials and their applications. Comput. Complex. **15**(2), 115–162 (2006)

[AIK10] Applebaum, B., Ishai, Y., Kushilevitz, E.: From secrecy to soundness: efficient verification via secure computation. In: Abramsky, S., Gavoille, C., Kirchner, C., Meyer auf der Heide, F., Spirakis, P.G. (eds.) ICALP 2010. LNCS, vol. 6198, pp. 152–163. Springer, Heidelberg (2010). https://doi.org/10.1007/978-3-642-14165-2_14

[AMR25] Abram, D., Malavolta, G., Roy, L.: Key-homomorphic computations for ram: fully succinct randomised encodings and more. In: Kalai, Y.T., Kamara, S.F. (eds.) Advances in Cryptology – CRYPTO 2025 (2025)

[App17] Applebaum, B.: Garbled circuits as randomized encodings of functions: a primer. In: Tutorials on the Foundations of Cryptography. ISC, pp. 1–44. Springer, Cham (2017). https://doi.org/10.1007/978-3-319-57048-8_1

[BCG+18]   Bitansky, N., et al.: Indistinguishability obfuscation for ram programs and succinct randomized encodings. SIAM J. Comput. **47**(3), 1123–1210 (2018)

[BGG+14]   Boneh, D., et al.: Fully key-homomorphic encryption, arithmetic circuit ABE and compact garbled circuits. In: Nguyen, P.Q., Oswald, E. (eds.) EUROCRYPT 2014. LNCS, vol. 8441, pp. 533–556. Springer, Heidelberg (2014). https://doi.org/10.1007/978-3-642-55220-5_30

[BGI16]   Boyle, E., Gilboa, N., Ishai, Y.: Breaking the circuit size barrier for secure computation under DDH. In: Robshaw, M., Katz, J. (eds.) CRYPTO 2016. LNCS, vol. 9814, pp. 509–539. Springer, Heidelberg (2016). https://doi.org/10.1007/978-3-662-53018-4_19

[BL18]   Benhamouda, F., Lin, H.: k-round multiparty computation from k-round oblivious transfer via garbled interactive circuits. In: Nielsen, J.B., Rijmen, V. (eds.) EUROCRYPT 2018. LNCS, vol. 10821, pp. 500–532. Springer, Cham (2018). https://doi.org/10.1007/978-3-319-78375-8_17

[BMR90]   Beaver, D., Micali, S., Rogaway, P.: The round complexity of secure protocols (extended abstract). In: 22nd ACM STOC, pp. 503–513, Baltimore, MD, USA, 14–16 May 1990. ACM Press (1990)

[BTVW17]   Brakerski, Z., Tsabary, R., Vaikuntanathan, V., Wee, H.: Private constrained PRFs (and more) from LWE. In: Kalai, Y., Reyzin, L. (eds.) TCC 2017. LNCS, vol. 10677, pp. 264–302. Springer, Cham (2017). https://doi.org/10.1007/978-3-319-70500-2_10

[DKK18]   Dinur, I., Keller, N., Klein, O.: An optimal distributed discrete log protocol with applications to homomorphic secret sharing. In: Shacham, H., Boldyreva, A. (eds.) CRYPTO 2018. LNCS, vol. 10993, pp. 213–242. Springer, Cham (2018). https://doi.org/10.1007/978-3-319-96878-0_8

[FNO15]   Frederiksen, T.K., Nielsen, J.B., Orlandi, C.: Privacy-free garbled circuits with applications to efficient zero-knowledge. In: Oswald, E., Fischlin, M. (eds.) EUROCRYPT 2015. LNCS, vol. 9057, pp. 191–219. Springer, Heidelberg (2015). https://doi.org/10.1007/978-3-662-46803-6_7

[GGP10]   Gennaro, R., Gentry, C., Parno, B.: Non-interactive verifiable computing: outsourcing computation to untrusted workers. In: Rabin, T. (ed.) CRYPTO 2010. LNCS, vol. 6223, pp. 465–482. Springer, Heidelberg (2010). https://doi.org/10.1007/978-3-642-14623-7_25

[GKP+13]   Goldwasser, S., Kalai, Y.T., Popa, R.A., Vaikuntanathan, V., Zeldovich, N.: Reusable garbled circuits and succinct functional encryption. In: Boneh, D., Roughgarden, T., Feigenbaum, J. (eds.) 45th ACM STOC, Palo Alto, CA, USA, 1–4 June 2013, pp. 555–564. ACM Press (2013)

[GLNP15]   Gueron, S., Lindell, Y., Nof, A., Pinkas, B.: Fast garbling of circuits under standard assumptions. In: Ray, I., Li, N., Kruegel, C. (eds.) ACM CCS 2015, Denver, CO, USA, 12–16 October 2015, pp. 567–578. ACM Press (2015)

[Gol00]   Goldreich, O.: Candidate one-way functions based on expander graphs. In: Electronic Colloquium on Computational Complexity (ECCC), vol. 7 (2000)

[GS17]   Garg, S., Srinivasan, A.: Garbled protocols and two-round MPC from bilinear maps. In: Umans, C. (ed.) 58th FOCS, Berkeley, CA, USA, 15–17 October 2017, pp. 588–599. IEEE Computer Society Press (2017)

[GS18]   Garg, S., Srinivasan, A.: Two-round multiparty secure computation from minimal assumptions. In: Nielsen, J.B., Rijmen, V. (eds.) EUROCRYPT 2018. LNCS, vol. 10821, pp. 468–499. Springer, Cham (2018). https://doi.org/10.1007/978-3-319-78375-8_16

[GSW13] Gentry, C., Sahai, A., Waters, B.: Homomorphic encryption from learning with errors: conceptually-simpler, asymptotically-faster, attribute-based. In: Canetti, R., Garay, J.A. (eds.) CRYPTO 2013. LNCS, vol. 8042, pp. 75–92. Springer, Heidelberg (2013). https://doi.org/10.1007/978-3-642-40041-4_5

[HK21] Heath, D., Kolesnikov, V.: One hot garbling. In: Vigna, G., Shi, E. (eds.) ACM CCS 2021, Virtual Event, Republic of Korea, 15–19 November 2021, pp. 574–593. ACM Press (2021)

[HKO22] Heath, D., Kolesnikov, V., Ostrovsky, R.: EpiGRAM: practical garbled RAM. In: Dunkelman, O., Dziembowski, S. (eds.) EUROCRYPT 2022, Part I. LNCS, Trondheim, Norway, 30 May–3 June 2022, vol. 13275, pp. 3–33. Springer, Cham, Switzerland (2022)

[HLL23] Hsieh, Y.-C., Lin, H., Luo, J.: Attribute-based encryption for circuits of unbounded depth from lattices. In: 64th FOCS, Santa Cruz, CA, USA, 6–9 November 2023, pp. 415–434. IEEE Computer Society Press (2023)

[IK02] Ishai, Y., Kushilevitz, E.: Perfect constant-round secure computation via perfect randomizing polynomials. In: Widmayer, P., Eidenbenz, S., Triguero, F., Morales, R., Conejo, R., Hennessy, M. (eds.) ICALP 2002. LNCS, vol. 2380, pp. 244–256. Springer, Heidelberg (2002). https://doi.org/10.1007/3-540-45465-9_22

[ILL25a] Ishai, Y., Li, H., Lin, H.: Succinct homomorphic macs from groups and applications. In: Raz, R., Oshman, R. (eds.) In 66th FOCS (2025)

[ILL25b] Ishai, Y., Li, H., Lin, H.: A unified framework for succinct garbling from homomorphic secret sharing. In: Kalai, Y.T., Kamara, S.F. (eds.) Advances in Cryptology – CRYPTO 2025 (2025)

[IPS08] Ishai, Y., Prabhakaran, M., Sahai, A.: Founding cryptography on oblivious transfer - efficiently. In: Wagner, D. (ed.) CRYPTO 2008. LNCS, Santa Barbara, CA, USA, 17–21 August 2008, vol. 5157, pp. 572–591. Springer, Heidelberg, Germany (2008)

[IW14] Ishai, Y., Wee, H.: Partial garbling schemes and their applications. In: Esparza, J., Fraigniaud, P., Husfeldt, T., Koutsoupias, E. (eds.) ICALP 2014. LNCS, vol. 8572, pp. 650–662. Springer, Heidelberg (2014). https://doi.org/10.1007/978-3-662-43948-7_54

[JKO13] Jawurek, M., Kerschbaum, F., Orlandi, C.: Zero-knowledge using garbled circuits: how to prove non-algebraic statements efficiently. In: Sadeghi, A.-R., Gligor, V.D., Yung, M. (eds.) ACM CCS 2013, Berlin, Germany, 4–8 November 2013, pp. 955–966. ACM Press (2013)

[KLW15] Koppula, V., Lewko, A.B., Waters, B.: Indistinguishability obfuscation for Turing machines with unbounded memory. In: Servedio, R.A., Rubinfeld, R. (eds.) 47th ACM STOC, Portland, OR, USA, 14–17 June 2015, pp. 419–428. ACM Press (2015)

[KMR14] Kolesnikov, V., Mohassel, P., Rosulek, M.: FleXOR: flexible garbling for xor gates that beats free-XOR. In: Garay, J.A., Gennaro, R. (eds.) CRYPTO 2014. LNCS, vol. 8617, pp. 440–457. Springer, Heidelberg (2014). https://doi.org/10.1007/978-3-662-44381-1_25

[KS08] Kolesnikov, V., Schneider, T.: Improved garbled circuit: free XOR gates and applications. In: Aceto, L., Damgård, I., Goldberg, L.A., Halldórsson, M.M., Ingólfsdóttir, A., Walukiewicz, I. (eds.) ICALP 2008. LNCS, vol. 5126, pp. 486–498. Springer, Heidelberg (2008). https://doi.org/10.1007/978-3-540-70583-3_40

[Lin25] Linus, R.: Bitvm 3s – garbled circuits for efficient computation on bitcoin. Technical report, BitVM Alliance (2025)

[LWYY25] Liu, H., Wang, X., Yang, K., Yu, Y.: BitGC: garbled circuits with 1 bit per gate. In: Fehr, S., Fouque, P.-A. (eds.) EUROCRYPT 2025, Part VII, LNCS, Madrid, Spain, 4–8 May 2025, vol. 15607, pp. 437–466. Springer, Cham, Switzerland (2025)

[MORS24] Meyer, P., Orlandi, C., Roy, L., Scholl, P.: Rate-1 arithmetic garbling from homomorphic secret sharing. In: Boyle, E., Mahmoody, M. (eds.) TCC 2024, Part IV, LNCS, Milan, Italy, 2–6 December 2024, vol. 15367, pp. 71–97. Springer, Cham, Switzerland (2024)

[MORS25] Meyer, P., Orlandi, C., Roy, L., Scholl, P.: Silent circuit relinearisation: sublinear-size (Boolean and arithmetic) garbled circuits from DCR. In: Kalai, Y.T., Kamara, S.F. (eds.) Advances in Cryptology – CRYPTO 2025 (2025)

[NPS99] Naor, M., Pinkas, B., Sumner, R.: Privacy preserving auctions and mechanism design. In: Proceedings of the 1st ACM Conference on Electronic Commerce, pp. 129–139 (1999)

[NR97] Naor, M., Reingold, O.: Number-theoretic constructions of efficient pseudorandom functions. In: 38th FOCS, Miami Beach, Florida, 19–22 October 1997, pp. 458–467. IEEE Computer Society Press (1997)

[OSY21] Orlandi, C., Scholl, P., Yakoubov, S.: The rise of Paillier: homomorphic secret sharing and public-key silent OT. In: Canteaut, A., Standaert, F.-X. (eds.) EUROCRYPT 2021. LNCS, vol. 12696, pp. 678–708. Springer, Cham (2021). https://doi.org/10.1007/978-3-030-77870-5_24

[PSSW09] Pinkas, B., Schneider, T., Smart, N.P., Williams, S.C.: Secure two-party computation is practical. In: Matsui, M. (ed.) ASIACRYPT 2009. LNCS, vol. 5912, pp. 250–267. Springer, Heidelberg (2009). https://doi.org/10.1007/978-3-642-10366-7_15

[QWW18] Quach, W., Wee, H., Wichs, D.: Laconic function evaluation and applications. In: Thorup, M. (ed.) 59th FOCS, Paris, France, 7–9 October 2018, pp. 859–870. IEEE Computer Society Press (2018)

[RR21] Rosulek, M., Roy, L.: Three halves make a whole? Beating the half-gates lower bound for garbled circuits. In: Malkin, T., Peikert, C. (eds.) CRYPTO 2021. LNCS, vol. 12825, pp. 94–124. Springer, Cham (2021). https://doi.org/10.1007/978-3-030-84242-0_5

[RS21] Roy, L., Singh, J.: Large message homomorphic secret sharing from DCR and applications. In: Malkin, T., Peikert, C. (eds.) CRYPTO 2021. LNCS, vol. 12827, pp. 687–717. Springer, Cham (2021). https://doi.org/10.1007/978-3-030-84252-9_23

[Wee24] Wee, H.: Circuit ABE with poly(depth, λ)-sized ciphertexts and keys from lattices. In: Reyzin, L., Stebila, D. (eds.) CRYPTO 2024, Part III. LNCS, Santa Barbara, CA, USA, 18–22 August 2024, vol. 14922, pp. 178–209. Springer, Cham, Switzerland (2024)

[Wee25] Wee, H.: Almost optimal KP and CP-ABE for circuits from succinct LWE. In: Fehr, S., Fouque, P.-A. (eds.) EUROCRYPT 2025, Part III. LNCS, Madrid, Spain, 4–8 May 2025, vol. 15603, pp. 34–62. Springer, Cham, Switzerland (2025)

[Yao82] Yao, A.C.-C.: Protocols for secure computations (extended abstract). In: 23rd FOCS, Chicago, Illinois, 3–5 November 1982, pp. 160–164. IEEE Computer Society Press (1982)

[Yao86] Yao, A.C.-C.: How to generate and exchange secrets. In: 27th Annual Symposium on Foundations of Computer Science (SFCs 1986), pp. 162–167. IEEE (1986)

[ZRE15] Zahur, S., Rosulek, M., Evans, D.: Two halves make a whole. In: Oswald, E., Fischlin, M. (eds.) EUROCRYPT 2015. LNCS, vol. 9057, pp. 220–250. Springer, Heidelberg (2015). https://doi.org/10.1007/978-3-662-46803-6_8

Zebra: Arithmetic Garbled RAM for Large Words from DCR

Tianyao Gu[1(✉)], Ashrujit Ghoshal[2], and Elaine Shi[1]

[1] Carnegie Mellon University, Pittsburgh, USA
`tianyaog@andrew.cmu.edu`
[2] Indian Institute of Technology Madras, Chennai, India

Abstract. Garbled RAM is a promising technique for scaling secure two-party computation to large datasets. It features an efficient two-round protocol and supports each memory access with polylogarithmic overhead, thereby avoiding the prohibitive cost of RAM-to-circuit conversion. While earlier works on Garbled RAM primarily focused on establishing theoretical feasibility, recent research has increasingly emphasized concrete efficiency, culminating in constructions that achieve approximately $O(\lambda TW \log N)$ bandwidth cost (up to super-constant factors) for garbling a RAM with running time T, memory size N, and word size W.

We ask whether it is possible to further improve the bandwidth cost of Garbled RAM. In contrast, the Garbled Circuit literature has developed a rich set of techniques that remove the bandwidth's dependence on the security parameter λ, leading to constant-rate or even sub-constant-rate garbling schemes. However, no comparable methods are currently known for Garbled RAM.

We propose a new garbling scheme for arithmetic RAM, called Zebra (short for "Zero Exposure B-bounded Random Accesses"). Specifically, we show that when the word size W is suitably large, we can eliminate the λ-factor dependence and achieve a bandwidth cost of $O(TW \log N)$. In this sense, our scheme can also be viewed as the RAM analogue of "constant-rate garbling for arithmetic circuits". Further, we show how to extend our techniques to support the garbling of boolean RAMs, achieving a bandwidth cost of $O(TW(\log N + \lambda))$ when the word size is suitably large. We implemented Zebra and released our code through open source. Our evaluation shows a $10.1\times$ concrete improvement in bandwidth and a $3.5\times$ improvement in end-to-end time relative to the state-of-the-art Garbled RAM schemes on a 256MB database with 4kB entries.

1   Introduction

The garbled circuit, originally proposed by Yao [59], provides a method for realizing secure two-party computation (2PC), enabling two mutually distrusting parties to jointly perform privacy-preserving data analytics without revealing their private inputs. One compelling feature of the garbled circuit is its round complexity—the protocol requires only two rounds of interaction. However, as a growing body of research [7, 8, 10, 33, 36, 45–47, 52, 60] aimed to make garbled

J. Daemen and E. Thomé (Eds.): EUROCRYPT 2026, LNCS 16543, pp. 276–306, 2026.
https://doi.org/10.1007/978-3-032-25324-8_10

circuits practical for real-world applications, a significant bottleneck manifested in the form of a representation mismatch. Garbled circuit requires that the computation be expressed as a *circuit*, whereas real-world programs are typically expressed in the *Random Access Machine (RAM)* model. Unfortunately, generically converting a RAM program into a circuit incurs a $\Theta(N)$-factor overhead for each memory access, where N denotes the RAM's memory size. This linear per-access penalty becomes prohibitively expensive for computations involving dynamic access patterns over large datasets.

To scale garbled circuits to big data settings, a new line of research—beginning with the seminal work of Lu and Ostrovsky [43]—introduced the notion of Garbled RAM. Specifically, Garbled RAM enables direct garbling of a RAM program without first converting it into a circuit representation, thereby avoiding the linear overhead per memory access inherent in circuit-based approaches. Early works in this area [22–24,43,44] primarily focused on establishing the theoretical feasibility of Garbled RAM under standard cryptographic assumptions. In particular, it was shown that, assuming only one-way functions, a RAM program with time T, space N, and word size W can be compiled into a garbled program of size $T \cdot W \cdot \mathsf{poly}(\lambda, \log N)$ [23]. Throughout this paper, we also refer to the size of the garbled program as the *bandwidth cost*, since the garbler must transmit it to the evaluator during the 2PC protocol. These early constructions, however, remained largely theoretical, with little attention paid to the concrete magnitude of the $\mathsf{poly}(\lambda, \log N)$ factors in their asymptotic cost.

It was not until recently that the community began to witness a paradigm shift in this space. Beginning with the elegant work of Heath et al. [28], a new line of research [26,29,50,58] has advanced Garbled RAM from a purely theoretical construct toward practical realizations. Notably, Park et al. [50] and Heath et al. [29] demonstrated how to achieve a bandwidth cost of $\lambda \cdot TW \cdot \widetilde{O}(\log N)$, where λ denotes the security parameter. Throughout this paper, the notation $\widetilde{O}(f(\mathsf{vars}))$ hides $\mathsf{poly}\log f(\mathsf{vars})$ factors, where vars represents a list of variables. More recently, PicoGRAM further improved the bandwidth cost to $\lambda \cdot T \cdot W \log N \cdot \omega(1)$, where $\omega(1)$ denotes an arbitrarily small super-constant function in λ. For all these concretely efficient instantiations, the computation cost (i.e., the total work of the garbler and evaluator) approximately matches the bandwidth cost up to an $\widetilde{O}(\lambda)$ factor.

We ask whether it is possible to further reduce the bandwidth cost of Garbled RAM while retaining concrete efficiency. If one disregards concrete efficiency, the literature on "succinct Garbled RAM" [5,6,11,15–17,19,37,41] demonstrates how to eliminate the dependence on T in bandwidth by employing heavyweight machinery such as indistinguishability obfuscation (iO) [21,34]. However, since the computation cost of Garbled RAM must inherently scale linearly with T, improving the bandwidth dependence on T alone would not lead to a reduction in the overall cost. In fact, these iO-based constructions [5,6,11,15–17,19,37,41] pay a significant price in overall cost to eliminate the bandwidth's dependence on T—specifically, their computational cost (or overall cost) is a $\mathsf{poly}(\lambda, W, \log(T, N))$ factor worse than known practical constructions [26,28,29,50,58]. Further, the reliance on iO also renders these approaches completely impractical. So far, without relying on iO, we are not aware of any techniques for making the bandwidth's dependence on T even slightly sublinear.

In this paper, we instead focus on understanding whether the dependence on the security parameter λ is necessary. Specifically, we observe that in the garbled circuit literature, a flurry of works [7,32,33,42,45,46] have focused on removing the λ factor dependence in bandwidth costs, resulting in the so-called constant-rate or even sub-constant-rate garbling, for either arithmetic or boolean circuits. However, it is not known whether these techniques can be adapted to the RAM model to achieve similar savings. In fact, even when allowing the use of indistinguishability obfuscation (iO), it remains unknown how to remove the λ-factor dependence in bandwidth. While existing succinct Garbled RAM schemes [5,6,11,15–17,19,37,41] achieve bandwidth that is independent of T, they nevertheless incur a $\mathsf{poly}(\lambda)$ multiplicative overhead in the bandwidth cost. We therefore ask a natural question:

Can we also eliminate or reduce the λ multiplicative factor dependence in the bandwidth cost of Garbled RAM?

1.1 Our Results and Contributions

We answer the above question in the affirmative. Although our approach draws inspiration from the literature on Homomorphic Secret Sharing (HSS) [9,12,45, 46,48,53], we emphasize that existing HSS techniques cannot be directly applied to the RAM setting to achieve our asymptotic improvements. Our results require novel adaptations of known HSS techniques. To the best of our knowledge, this work is the first to establish a concrete connection between the Garbled RAM literature and HSS techniques, yielding non-trivial asymptotic improvements in the RAM setting. Below, we state our main results.

Garbling scheme for arithmetic RAM. We first consider the garbling of a B-bounded *arithmetic* RAM, where B is a λ-bit integer. In a B-bounded arithmetic RAM, every W-bit memory word is expressed as an arithmetic vector in $[-B, B]^{W/\log B}$.[1] In other words, one can imagine that each wire carries a B-bounded value from $[-B, B]$ rather than a boolean value as in a standard boolean RAM. We assume that the CPU supports addition on W-bit words, and coordinate-wise multiplication (of B-bounded integers).

We construct a new arithmetic Garbled RAM scheme called Zebra (short for "Zero Exposure B-bounded Random Accesses"). To the best of our knowledge, Zebra is the first to remove the dependence on the security parameter λ in bandwidth for reasonably large word sizes. More concretely, our result is stated in the following theorem:

Theorem 1 (Garbling arithmetic RAMs). *Assume the Decisional Composite Residuosity (DCR) assumption and the existence of a Random Oracle.*

---

[1] Throughout this paper, we use log to denote the base-2 logarithm.

Table 1. Comparison of Garbled RAM schemes for suitably large memory words, where N is the memory size, W is the bit length of the word, T is the number of CPU steps, λ is the security parameter, and $\omega(1)$ denotes an arbitrarily small super-constant factor in λ. The notation $\widetilde{O}(f(\mathsf{vars}))$ hides $\mathsf{poly}\log f(\mathsf{vars})$ factors. Our arithmetic scheme assumes the word width $W \geq \lambda \cdot \log^2 N$, and our boolean scheme assumes $W \geq \lambda \cdot \log^\epsilon N$ for an arbitrarily small constant $\epsilon > 0$.

Scheme	Bandwidth	Compute	Assumption
Tri-state [29]	$\lambda \cdot TW \cdot \widetilde{O}(\log N)$	$\widetilde{O}(\lambda \log N) \cdot TW$	OWF
PicoGRAM [26]	$\lambda \cdot \omega(1) \cdot TW \log N$	$\widetilde{O}(\lambda^2) \cdot TW \log N$	DDH
Succinct GRAM	$\mathsf{poly}(\lambda, W, \log(T, N))$	$T \cdot \mathsf{poly}(\lambda, W, \log(T, N))$	iO
Our results			
Zebra (arithmetic)	$O(TW \log N)$	$\widetilde{O}(\lambda) \cdot TW \log N$	DCR + RO
Zebra (boolean)	$O(TW(\lambda + \log N))$	$\widetilde{O}(\lambda) \cdot TW(\frac{\lambda^2}{\log T} + \log N)$	DCR + RO

Then, there exists a garbling scheme that achieves $O(TW \log N)$ bandwidth and $\widetilde{O}(\lambda) \cdot TW \log N$ computation cost per CPU step for a B-bounded arithmetic RAM with time T, space N, and word size $W \geq \lambda \cdot \log^2 N$ (in bits)[2].

Relative to prior work [26,29], Theorem 1 improves the bandwidth cost of Garbled RAM by eliminating its dependence on the λ factor. On the other hand, in terms of computation cost, an $\widetilde{O}(\lambda)$-factor dependence still remains. An interesting open question is whether this factor can be further removed. Since the same question remains unresolved even in the context of garbled circuits, achieving such an improvement would likely require fundamentally new techniques.

We also point out that our scheme's dependence on N is optimal—specifically, the well-known ORAM lower bound [13,25,38] implies an $\Omega(W \cdot \log N)$ lower bound on the per-access *computation* cost of any Garbled RAM. Another interpretation of this lower bound is that further improving the $\log N$ factor in bandwidth, even if feasible, would yield only marginal savings in the overall cost of Garbled RAM.

Garbling scheme for boolean RAM. We next extend our results to a standard boolean RAM whose instruction set supports word-level additions and bitwise boolean operations. We prove the following theorem for garbling boolean RAMs (Table 1):

Theorem 2 (Garbling boolean RAMs). *Under the same assumptions as Theorem 1, there exists a garbling scheme that achieves $O(TW(\log N + \lambda))$ bandwidth and $\widetilde{O}(\lambda) \cdot TW(\frac{\lambda^2}{\log T} + \log N)$ computation cost per CPU step for a boolean RAM with time T, space N, and word size $W \geq \lambda \cdot \log^\epsilon N$ (in bits) for an arbitrarily small constant $\epsilon > 0$.*

---

[2] All schemes in this paper still work when the word size W is smaller than the stated threshold, except that the threshold should be used in lieu of the actual W in the asymptotic cost.

For boolean RAM, we improve the bandwidth cost of prior work [26,29] by reducing the $\lambda \log N$ multiplicative factor to an additive $\lambda + \log N$ factor. In comparison with arithmetic RAM (Theorem 1), the $\log N$ factor is now replaced with $\lambda + \log N$ (or $\frac{\lambda^2}{\log T} + \log N$ for computation) in Theorem 2. The additional overhead stems from the need to emulate the CPU's boolean instructions and the associated bit decomposition operations. In practice, due to the heavier dependence on λ in the computation cost, our boolean GRAM may incur a higher end-to-end time than prior works [26,29] in computationally constrained settings, as detailed in Sect. 5. Whether the computation cost of boolean GRAM can be further reduced remains an interesting open question, likely requiring either a more efficient bit-decomposition algorithm or an alternative construction that bypasses arithmetic garbling techniques.

Application: 2-Server Updatable PIR. One important application scenario of Garbled RAM is to realize a two-server Private Information Retrieval (PIR) scheme for a globally shared database. Consider a setting where many clients need to access a shared global database, yet their access patterns may inadvertently reveal highly sensitive information. For instance, in modern cryptocurrencies, queries to blockchain state can leak private details such as a user's identity, trading counterparties, or even intent (e.g., which crypto-asset the user plans to trade). Similarly, accessing a Certificate Transparency (CT) log may expose a user's intent to visit a specific website. Recognizing these privacy risks, several industry leaders—including Signal, Meta, and Ethereum—have acknowledged the importance of enabling oblivious access to globally shared data and have either deployed or announced plans to deploy such oblivious access services [1,3]. Today, most deployed services rely on a combination of Oblivious RAM (ORAM) and trusted hardware. However, industry leaders such as Ethereum have clearly articulated a long-term vision of replacing trusted hardware with cryptography-based solutions [14], motivated both by the desire to eliminate reliance on a small set of hardware vendors, and by the growing body of evidence that off-the-shelf trusted hardware suffers from numerous security vulnerabilities.

Garbled RAM offers an attractive cryptographic alternative for enabling oblivious access to globally shared databases. Informally speaking, trusted hardware is replaced by a cryptographically secure computer jointly realized by the garbler and the evaluator. Further, our large word size assumption is also suitable for many real-life applications such as CT logs, querying the blockchain state at some address along with the corresponding Merkle proofs [35], and fetching one's own cryptographic credentials from a zero-knowledge identity provider [2]. In comparison with the recent line of work on client-preprocessing PIR schemes [20,30,39,51,61], Garbled-RAM-based schemes not only achieve asymptotically better performance, but also readily support frequent updates to the database—a crucial feature in dynamic databases such as blockchains and CT logs. By contrast, in client-preprocessing PIRs [20,30,39,51,61], each database update incurs additional client-side work, rendering such schemes impractical for applications such as light-weight clients for blockchains which often run on weak client devices such as mobile phones.

Specifically, Theorem 1 gives rise to the following corollary.

Corollary 1 (2-server updatable PIR). *Assume the same assumptions as Theorem 1. Given a database with N entries each W-bits long where $W \geq \lambda \log^2 N$, there is a 2-server updatable PIR scheme with the following costs per access or update operation: $O(W \log N)$ bandwidth, $\widetilde{O}(\lambda) \cdot W \log N$ computation, and $O(1)$ rounds of interaction.*

Concrete Performance. We implemented our Zebra scheme and explored its performance for a 2-server PIR scenario as mentioned above. Our code has been published as open source, available at https://github.com/zebragram/zebragram. For a 256 MB database with 4 kB blocks, we improve the bandwidth cost by **10.1×** relative to PicoGRAM [26], from 396 MB to 39.2 MB. Under our test setup, this translates into a 3.53× reduction in end-to-end time, from 11.9 s to 3.36 s per retrieval.

2   Roadmap

2.1   Background: Garbled RAM via Boolean Dynamic Circuits

Our starting point is the garbled RAM scheme of Heath et al. [29]. We begin by giving some background on their blueprint.

RAM expressed as boolean dynamic circuits. A major contribution of Heath et al. [29] is the proposal of a new circuit-based computation model that can efficiently express RAMs, henceforth called *boolean dynamic circuits*[3]. In a standard circuit, gate evaluation is all-or-nothing: only once all input wires are set can the output wires be determined. In contrast, a boolean dynamic circuit supports partial eager evaluation of gates, meaning that as soon as a subset of the input wires is set, certain output wires may already be computed.

This partial eager evaluation capability is crucial for efficiently expressing RAM. Specifically, representing a RAM with time T, space N, and word width W as a standard circuit would result in size $O(T \cdot N \cdot W)$, since each memory access requires a linear-sized selector gadget. By contrast, Heath et al. [29] showed that the same RAM can be represented as a randomized boolean dynamic circuit of size $T \cdot W \cdot \log N \log \log N$, with only negligible (in λ) correctness error. Intuitively, the partial eager evaluation enables the emulation of conditional branching, a key feature that fundamentally distinguishes RAMs from standard circuits.

More specifically, a boolean dynamic circuit comprises not only the standard AND and XOR gates, but also a new switch gate defined as follows[4]. The gate has two data input wires, x_0 and x_1, a control wire c, and a single output wire

---

[3] The original work of Heath et al. [29] refers to a boolean dynamic circuit as a tri-state circuit since every wire can take three values, $\{0, 1, \bot\}$. For convenience of terminology, we adopt the name boolean dynamic circuit instead.

[4] We replace the Buffer and Join gates in the original work [29] with the switch abstraction for ease of understanding.

y. Each wire can take values in $\{0, 1, \bot\}$, where $\bot$ represents the unset state of the wire. The operational semantics of the switch gate are as follows. Initially, all wires are unset. Whenever the control wire c and x_c are both set, the output wire y receives the value x_c (regardless of whether x_{1-c} is set).

Heath et al. [29] showed how to convert a RAM with word width $W \geq \log^2 N$, time T, and space N into a randomized boolean dynamic circuit using:

- $O(T \cdot W \cdot \log N \cdot \log \log N)$ switch gates, and
- $T \cdot W \cdot \log N \cdot \omega(1)$ number of AND and XOR gates, where $\omega(1)$ denotes an arbitrarily small super-constant function in λ.

In the resulting dynamic circuit, the (random) values on all control wires are simulatable without knowing the input to the computation. In other words, the evaluator is allowed to know the values on the control wires.

Garbling Boolean Dynamic Circuits. Assuming the existence of one-way functions, Heath et al. [29] devise a garbling scheme for boolean dynamic circuits where each AND gate and switch gate requires sending $O(\lambda)$ bits of garbling material where λ is the security parameter, whereas XOR gates are free and do not contribute to the bandwidth cost. Therefore, Heath et al.'s garbled RAM incurs a bandwidth cost of $O(\lambda \cdot T \cdot W \cdot \log N \cdot (\log \log N + \omega(1)))$ bits.

2.2 Our Blueprint

Our objective is to eliminate the extraneous multiplicative factors of λ, $\log \log N$, and $\omega(1)$ present in Heath et al.'s scheme, thereby obtaining a Garbled RAM construction with bandwidth cost $O(T \cdot W \cdot \log N)$. In this section, we first address the removal of the λ and $\log \log N$ factors, and defer how to eliminate the super-constant factor to our online version.

Alternative View of the RAM's Dynamic Circuit. Our first key observation is that the boolean dynamic circuit expressing RAM has many synchronized operations on w-bit payloads[5] where $w = O(W + \log N)$. These w-fold synchronized operations are core to the oblivious memory abstraction which can be viewed as a boolean dynamic circuit realization of the Circuit ORAM algorithm [57]. Roughly speaking, they serve the following two purposes: 1) routing memory words (along with some metadata) along paths in the ORAM tree; and 2) reading and writing data to data arrays associated with the nodes in the ORAM tree.

Specifically, consider the following two types of w-synchronized operations:

1. A *w-fold switch gate* has a single-bit control wire $c \in \{0, 1, \bot\}$, two bit-vector inputs denoted $\vec{x}_0 \in \{0, 1, \bot\}^w$ and $\vec{x}_1 \in \{0, 1, \bot\}^w$, and a bit-vector output $\vec{y} \in \{0, 1, \bot\}^w$. If the c and $\vec{x}_c$ are set, then $\vec{y}$ is set to $\vec{x}_c$.

---

[5] Throughout the paper, we use capital letters T, N, and N to denote the parameters of the RAM. We use small letters such as w and n to denote the parameters or the problem sizes seen by an individual circuit gadget or building block.

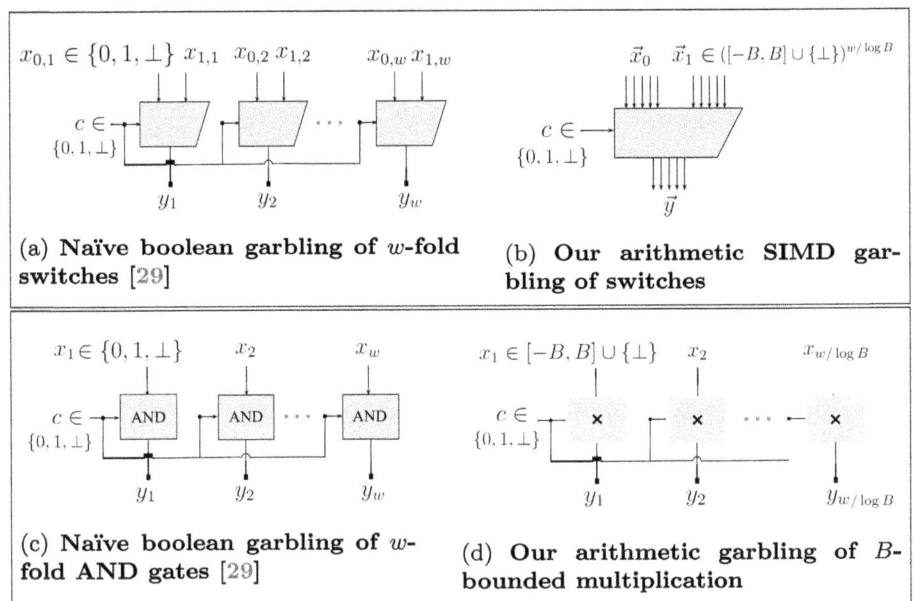

(a) Naïve boolean garbling of w-fold switches [29]

(b) Our arithmetic SIMD garbling of switches

(c) Naïve boolean garbling of w-fold AND gates [29]

(d) Our arithmetic garbling of B-bounded multiplication

Fig. 1. Our blueprint. Each gate in the above picture has $O(\lambda)$ bits of garbling material. B has $O(\lambda)$ bits. Relative to Heath et al. [29], we save a $\lambda \log \log N$ factor for w-fold switches and a λ factor for w-fold AND gates.

2. A *w-fold AND gate* has a single-bit control wire $c \in \{0, 1, \bot\}$, a bit-vector input denoted $\vec{x} \in \{0, 1, \bot\}^w$, and a bit-vector output $\vec{y} \in \{0, 1, \bot\}^w$. Whenever c and $\vec{x}$ are both set, $\vec{y}$ is set to $\vec{y} \leftarrow c \cdot \vec{x}$.

The dynamic circuit expressing RAM [29] can be equivalently viewed as comprising the following operations:

- **w-fold switches:** $O(T \cdot \log N \cdot \log \log N)$ number of $O(W)$-fold switch gates;
- **w-fold ANDs:** $O(T \cdot \log N) \cdot \omega(1)$ number of $O(W)$-fold AND gates;
- **other:** all other gates, including 1) other gates needed for realizing the memory abstraction whose costs are not dominating as long as $W \geq \lambda \log^2 N$; and 2) gates representing the CPU circuit. See Sect. 2.4 for details.

Our Blueprint: Taking Advantage of w-Synchronized Operations. As shown in Fig. 1 (left), the garbling scheme of Heath et al. [29] did not take advantage of the w-synchronized behavior; moreover, it incurs an additional λ-factor blowup because a λ-bit label is used to express each boolean wire. At a very high level, we will shave the λ and $\log \log N$ factors as follows:

1. *B-bounded wires instead of boolean wires: saving the λ factor.* To get rid of the λ factor, we let each wire carry an integer value from the domain $[-B, B]$ (also called a *B-bounded integer*). Each w-bit word can therefore

be expressed as $\lceil w/\log B \rceil = O(w/\lambda)$ number of B-bounded integers. In this way, our garbling scheme aims to spend λ bits of garbling material for each B-bounded arithmetic gate (rather than each boolean gate). By setting $\log B \in \Theta(\lambda)$, this saves us a λ factor. For example, as shown in Fig. 1d, a w-fold AND gate can now be represented as $w/\log B = O(w/\lambda)$ number of multiplication gates, each incurring $O(\lambda)$ bandwidth.

2. **SIMD garbling of switches: saving an extra** $\log\log N$ **factor.** For the switch gates, using B-bounded wires to shave a λ factor alone is not enough for getting our asymptotic results. We need to get rid of an extra $\log\log N$ factor here. To this end, we make the entire w-bit word, expressed as $w/\log B$ number of B-bounded wires, all reuse the same $O(\lambda)$-sized garbling material, as shown in Fig. 1b. For word width $W \geq \lambda \cdot \log\log N$, this lets us save a $w = \Theta(W) = \Theta(1) \cdot \lambda \cdot \frac{W}{\lambda} \geq \Theta(1) \cdot \lambda \cdot \log\log N$ factor for switch gates relative to the naïve approach of Heath et al. [29].

In summary, the first idea enables *intra-wire* savings (where the wires are now B-bounded), and the second idea enables *inter-wire* savings, which we also call SIMD (short for "Single Instruction Multiple Data").

To achieve the $T \cdot W \cdot \log N \cdot \omega(1)$ bandwidth cost, the challenge now boils down to devising a suitable garbling scheme compatible with our blueprint above.

2.3   Realizing the Blueprint with HSS-Like Techniques and Beyond

Primary Encoding Format: Subtractive Sharing. Without risk of ambiguity, we often use the notation x to denote the name of a wire, and use $\mathsf{val}_x \in [-B, B]$ to denote the B-bounded value the wire carries. We introduce the following notations to represent the encoding behind our garbling scheme:

- **Secret key** K **and** Δ: let $K \xleftarrow{\$} [0, \mathcal{N})$ for an RSA modulus $\mathcal{N} = p \cdot q$, and $\Delta = K \cdot B \cdot 2^\lambda + 1$, both sampled by and known only to the garbler.
- **Garbler's share** $\mathcal{R}_x \in \{0,1\}^{\log B + \lambda}$: garbler's share of the wire x—a predetermined mask that does not depend on the wire value val_x at runtime. We often write $\mathcal{R}_x$ in base-$(B \cdot 2^\lambda)$ representation, that is, $\mathcal{R}_x = \mathcal{R}_x^{\Uparrow} \cdot B \cdot 2^\lambda + \mathcal{R}_x^{\Downarrow}$, where $\mathcal{R}_x^{\Uparrow}$ and $\mathcal{R}_x^{\Downarrow}$ denote the higher- and lower-order bits, respectively.
- **Evaluator's share** $\mathcal{L}_x \in \{0,1\}^{\log B + \lambda}$: evaluator's share of wire x which encodes the actual value val_x that wire x takes. Specifically, let val_x be the B-bounded value carried by the wire, then $\mathcal{L}_x = \mathcal{R}_x + \Delta \cdot \mathsf{val}_x$. Similar to the garbler's share, we often write $\mathcal{L}_x$ in base-$(B \cdot 2^\lambda)$ representation, that is, $\mathcal{L}_x = \mathcal{L}_x^{\Uparrow} \cdot B \cdot 2^\lambda + \mathcal{L}_x^{\Downarrow}$, where $\mathcal{L}_x^{\Uparrow} = \mathcal{R}_x^{\Uparrow} + K \cdot \mathsf{val}_x$ and $\mathcal{L}_x^{\Downarrow} = \mathcal{R}_x^{\Uparrow} + \mathsf{val}_x$ denote the higher- and lower-order bits, respectively. For correctness of the base-$(B \cdot 2^\lambda)$ representation, we require that $\mathcal{R}_x^{\Downarrow} \in [B, B \cdot (2^\lambda - 1))$.

Observe that the garbler's and the evaluator's shares jointly form a subtractive secret share of $\Delta \cdot \mathsf{val}_x$, that is, $\mathcal{L}_x - \mathcal{R}_x = \Delta \cdot \mathsf{val}_x$. We can alternatively view their shares as forming subtractive sharings of both x and $K \cdot x$, with the garbler's shares predetermined and independent of the wire's actual value val_x. This

$$\vec{\mathcal{L}}_0 = \vec{\mathcal{R}}_0 + \Delta \cdot \vec{x}_0 \qquad\qquad \vec{\mathcal{L}}_1 = \vec{\mathcal{R}}_1 + \Delta \cdot \vec{x}_1$$

$$\Big\downarrow \vec{\theta}_0 \qquad\qquad\qquad\qquad\qquad \Big\downarrow \vec{\theta}_1$$

$$g^{k_0 \cdot \vec{\gamma}} \exp(\Delta \cdot \vec{x}_0) \qquad\qquad g^{k_1 \cdot \vec{\gamma}} \exp(\Delta \cdot \vec{x}_1)$$

$$\mathrm{Enc}_{\mathcal{L}_{c=0}}(\delta_0) \qquad\qquad \mathrm{Enc}_{\mathcal{L}_{c=1}}(\delta_1)$$

$$g^{k' \cdot \vec{\gamma}} \exp(\Delta \cdot \vec{y}) \xrightarrow{\ \ \mathrm{DDLog}\ \ } \vec{\mathcal{L}}_y = \vec{\mathcal{R}}_y + \Delta \cdot \vec{y}$$

Fig. 2. Garbling a SIMD switch gate: the evaluator's view.

is important since the garbler effectively has to (sample or) evaluate its shares on all wires offline before the actual input to the computation is determined.

Throughout, we assume that a well-formed B-bounded dynamic circuit guarantees the following property: as long as all inputs are B-bounded, every intermediate and output wire also carries a B-bounded value (assuming all additions and multiplications are performed over $\mathbb{Z}$). Consequently, we never need to worry about any wire value underflowing or overflowing the B-bounded range.

The subtractive sharing format is the primary encoding format behind our garbling scheme. With this encoding format, garbling a B-bounded addition gate is easy and free in the sense that it does not contribute to the bandwidth overhead. Suppose we want to garble a gate that computes $z = x + y$: let $(\mathcal{R}_x, \mathcal{L}_x)$ and $(\mathcal{R}_y, \mathcal{L}_y)$ be the garbler and evaluator's shares for the input wires x and y, then $(\mathcal{R}_x + \mathcal{R}_y, \mathcal{L}_x + \mathcal{L}_y)$ would be the shares for the output wire.

Below, we focus on how to garble SIMD switches and multiplication gates—the part that embodies our novel techniques. To this end, we introduce an auxiliary encoding format called divisive sharing.

Auxiliary Encoding Format: Divisive Sharing. Our divisive sharing format follows earlier works on Homomorphic Secret Sharing [48,53]. Let ζ be a positive integer, and g be a generator of unknown order in $\mathbb{Z}_{\mathcal{N}^{\zeta+1}}^{\times}$, where $\mathcal{N}$ is an RSA modulus. Henceforth, we may assume that $\mathcal{N}$ and g are public parameters.

A divisive sharing of a value $\mathsf{val} \in \mathbb{Z}_{\mathcal{N}^{\zeta}}^{+}$ is of the following format:

- **Garbler's share:** $g^k \mod \mathcal{N}^{\zeta+1}$ for some $k \in [0, \mathcal{N})$—again, the garbler's share should not depend on the actual value val which is determined only at runtime;
- **Evaluator's share:** $g^k \cdot \exp(\mathsf{val}) \mod \mathcal{N}^{\zeta+1}$, where $\exp(\cdot) : \mathbb{Z}_{N^{\zeta}} \to 1 + \mathcal{N} \cdot \mathbb{Z}_{\mathcal{N}^{\zeta+1}}^{\times}$ is an efficiently computable function satisfying $\exp(a + b) = \exp(a) \cdot \exp(b)$, with an efficient inverse $\log(\cdot) : 1 + \mathcal{N} \cdot \mathbb{Z}_{\mathcal{N}^{\zeta+1}}^{\times} \to \mathbb{Z}_{N^{\zeta}}$.

Distributed Discrete Log: Divisive Sharing to Subtractive Sharing. Given a divisive sharing of $\Delta \cdot \mathsf{val}$, the garbler and evaluator can convert it back to a subtractive sharing of $\Delta \cdot \mathsf{val}$ by running a distributed discrete log procedure denoted DDLog first proposed by Boyle et al. [12], and later improved by [48,53]. This procedure works by having each party perform a local transformation of their shares, and does not incur any communication (Fig. 2).

SIMD Garbling of Switch Gates. Recall that every w-bit word is expressed as a B-bounded bit vector $[-B, B]^{\lceil w/\log B \rceil}$, since our wires carry B-bounded values. Below, for convenience, we shall call a group of $\lceil w/\log B \rceil$ number of B-bounded wires a *cable*.

1. *Conversion to correlated divisive sharing.* Let $\vec{x}_0 \in ([-B, B] \cup \{\bot\})^{w/\log B}$ and $\vec{x}_1 \in ([-B, B] \cup \{\bot\})^{w/\log B}$ denote the two input cables, and let $c \in \{0, 1, \bot\}$ be a boolean control wire. Without risk of ambiguity, we overload the wires' name $\vec{x}$ or c to also mean the values on the wires. We start with subtractive shares of the input wires, $\langle \vec{\mathcal{R}}_0, \vec{\mathcal{R}}_0 + \Delta \cdot \vec{x}_0 \rangle$ and $\langle \vec{\mathcal{R}}_1, \vec{\mathcal{R}}_1 + \Delta \cdot \vec{x}_1 \rangle$. At this moment, all wires in the two input cables have uncorrelated random masks, i.e., all coordinates of $\vec{\mathcal{R}}_0$ and $\vec{\mathcal{R}}_1$ have uncorrelated randomness (we may view the garbler's share as a random mask).
   The first step is to convert the uncorrelated subtractive shares into correlated divisive shares of the form

   $$\langle g^{k_0 \cdot \vec{\gamma}}, \ g^{k_0 \cdot \vec{\gamma}} \cdot \mathsf{exp}(\Delta \cdot \vec{x}_0) \rangle \quad \text{and} \quad \langle g^{k_1 \cdot \vec{\gamma}}, \ g^{k_1 \cdot \vec{\gamma}} \cdot \mathsf{exp}(\Delta \cdot \vec{x}_1) \rangle$$

   where $k_0, k_1 \in [\mathcal{N}]$ are chosen at random by the garbler. After this conversion, the random masks of the two input cables, $g^{k_0 \cdot \vec{\gamma}}$ and $g^{k_1 \cdot \vec{\gamma}}$ are clearly correlated. Nonetheless, they are indistinguishable from independent random masks under the DCR assumption, as we show in our online version.
   To make this conversion possible, the garbler sends the evaluator two group elements $\vec{\theta}_0$ and $\vec{\theta}_1$ as part of the garbled circuitry[6], where

   $$\vec{\theta}_\beta := g^{k_\beta \cdot \vec{\gamma}} \cdot \mathsf{exp}(-\vec{\mathcal{R}}_\beta) \mod N^{\varsigma+1} \quad \text{for } \beta \in \{0, 1\}.$$

   In the subsequent paragraph "saving the conversion costs", we discuss how to asymptotically reduce the overhead for transmitting these conversion terms.
2. *Encrypt the difference between the source and destination's labels.* As an intermediate goal, we want the garbler and evaluator to have a divisible sharing of $\vec{x}_c$, in the form $\langle g^{k' \cdot \vec{\gamma}}, \ g^{k' \cdot \vec{\gamma}} \cdot \mathsf{exp}(\Delta \cdot \vec{x}_c) \rangle$, where $k' \in \mathbb{Z}_{\mathcal{N}^{\varsigma+1}}^{\times}$ is chosen at random by the garbler. This means that during evaluation, when the evaluator gets the input divisive share $g^{k_c \cdot \vec{\gamma}} \cdot \mathsf{exp}(\Delta \cdot \vec{x}_c)$, it needs to compute the output divisive share $g^{k' \cdot \vec{\gamma}} \cdot \mathsf{exp}(\Delta \cdot \vec{x}_c)$. This is possible if the evaluator simply knows a difference term δ_c such that:

   $$\delta_c \cdot k_c \equiv k' \mod \mathrm{order}(g) \quad \text{and} \quad \delta_c \equiv 1 \mod \mathcal{N}^\varsigma.$$

   Then, the evaluator can compute

   $$\left(g^{k_c \cdot \vec{\gamma}} \cdot \mathsf{exp}(\Delta \cdot \vec{x}_c) \right)^{\delta_c} = g^{\delta_c \cdot k_c \cdot \vec{\gamma}} \cdot \mathsf{exp}(\delta_c \cdot \Delta \cdot \vec{x}_c) = g^{k' \cdot \vec{\gamma}} \cdot \mathsf{exp}(\Delta \cdot \vec{x}_c).$$

---

[6] All terms the garbler sends to the evaluator can be computed offline when the input values are not yet determined.

Therefore, the garbler sends the evaluator the difference term encrypted under the evaluator's share of the control wire value, that is, $\{\mathsf{Enc}_{L_{c=\beta}}(\delta_\beta)\}_{\beta \in \{0,1\}}$ where $L_{c=\beta} := \mathcal{R}_c + \Delta \cdot \beta$ denotes the evaluator's share of the control wire c if it takes on value $\beta \in \{0,1\}$. During evaluation, the evaluator (who is allowed to know the control wire's value c) decrypts one of the two ciphertexts to perform the routing. In Sect. 4.4, we show that $\mathrm{order}(g)$ can be made co-prime to $\mathcal{N}^\varsigma$, and the garbler can solve for δ_c with overwhelming probability. Moreover, we show that if Enc is instantiated from a random oracle, then one can efficiently simulate all the δ_c in the evaluator's view without knowing k_c, k', or $\mathrm{order}(g)$.

Note that exactly because our divisive sharings have correlated masks, we can have all $w/\log B$ B-bounded wires share the same difference term, resulting in a w-factor saving in comparison with the prior work of Heath et al. [29].

3. *Conversion back into subtractive shares.* Finally, the garbler and evaluator convert their divisive sharing of $\vec{x}_c$ back to subtractive sharing using DDLog. This step does not incur any communication.

Saving the Conversion Costs. If we were to perform the conversion between uncorrelated subtractive and correlated divisive shares at every switch gate, the conversion terms (see Step 1 above), whose length matches that of the B-bounded vector itself, would introduce an undesirable $\log \log N$ factor in the bandwidth cost. Fortunately, this conversion is not required at every switch gate. Specifically, switch gates appear only within the routing gadgets of the dynamic circuit representing the RAM. Once the wires are converted into correlated divisive shares, they traverse a sequence of switch gates before needing to be converted back into subtractive shares. On average, we perform only $O(Z)$ conversions for every $O(Z \log Z)$ switch gates, where $Z = \log N \cdot \omega(1)$. This observation allows us to eliminate the extra $\log \log N$ factor, capping the total conversion (bandwidth) cost at $T \cdot W \cdot \log N \cdot \omega(1)$.

Comparison with PicoGRAM's SIMD Switches. Our ideas here are inspired by the recent work PicoGRAM [26]. However, their construction is based on DDH groups and targets boolean wires, leading to two limitations: 1) they suffer from an additional λ-factor overhead, since each boolean wire is assigned an $O(\lambda)$-bit label; and 2) their algebraic techniques are incompatible with supporting arithmetic multiplication over B-bounded values. We devise a novel approach to accomplish SIMD garbling of switch gates—by relying on Decisional Composite Residuosity (DCR) groups, our techniques are compatible with arithmetic garbling over B-bounded values.

Garbling Multiplication Gates. We borrow from Homomorphic Secret Sharing (HSS) [9,12,45,46,48,53] techniques to garble B-bounded multiplication gates. In particular, prior work [9,46] shows that the parties can homomorphically obtain a subtractive share of $a \cdot b \in [-B, B]$ by starting with 1) subtractive shares of both a and $K \cdot a$ and 2) a Damgård-Jurik-ElGamal (DJE) encryption of b under key K. As an intermediate step, they compute divisive shares of $x \cdot y$, then they run the DDLog procedure to convert it back to subtractive shares.

We can rely on this idea to garble a multiplication gate as follows. We want the two parties to end with a subtractive sharing of $x \cdot y \cdot \Delta$. Observe that

$$x \cdot y \cdot \Delta = \underbrace{(x + \mathcal{R}_x^{\Downarrow}) \cdot (y \cdot \Delta + \mathcal{R}_y)}_{=\mathcal{L}_x^{\Downarrow} \cdot \mathcal{L}_y \text{ known by evaluator}} - \underbrace{(\mathcal{R}_x^{\Downarrow} \cdot \Delta) \cdot y - \mathcal{R}_y \cdot x}_{\text{encrypted} \times \text{shared values}} - \underbrace{\mathcal{R}_x^{\Downarrow} \cdot \mathcal{R}_y}_{\text{known by garbler}} \quad (1)$$

Since the first and third terms are known either to the evaluator or garbler, it is trivial to compute a subtractive sharing of these terms (by setting the other party's share to 0). It suffices to compute a subtractive sharing of the middle term. Given our primary encoding format (see Sect. 2.3), both parties start with subtractive sharings of x, y, as well as Kx and Ky. Therefore, it suffices for the garbler to send the evaluator a DJE encryption of $\mathcal{R}_x^{\Downarrow} \cdot \Delta$ and of $\mathcal{R}_y$ under key K. This way, the two parties can rely on the HSS techniques to compute a subtractive share of $x \cdot y \cdot \Delta$. While the messages we encrypt here depend on the secret key K, prior work [9,46] proves that the DJE encryption satisfies KDM-security when the plaintext is an affine function of the secret key K, which holds in our case. Observe also that the DJE encryptions the garbler sends to the evaluator can be precomputed without knowing the actual input to the computation.

Asymptotically Improving the Computation Efficiency. Our techniques so far allow us to shave off a $\lambda \cdot \log \log N$ factor in bandwidth compared to Heath et al. [29]. However, the $\log \log N$ factor improvement does not directly apply to the computational efficiency. In our stack construction, although all $w / \log B$ many B-bounded wires share the same $O(\lambda)$-bit garbling material (namely, the encryption of the difference between the source and destination labels), the evaluator must still apply this difference to each of the $w / \log B$ wires by performing a modular exponentiation during evaluation.

We devise a new technique to let computation benefit from the $\log \log N$ factor saving too. Specifically, we observe that in earlier works [26,29], the switch gates are used to implement a stack gadget—to realize a stack of size $Z = \log N \cdot \omega(1)$, we would need $O(Z \log Z)$ switch gates. Instead of realizing a stack from switch gates, we introduce into our underlying gate set an n-way routing gate that can perform an arbitrary permutation on the inputs. Specifically, an n-way routing gate has inputs $(\vec{x}_1, c_1), \ldots, (\vec{x}_n, c_n)$ and outputs $\vec{y}_1, \ldots, \vec{y}_n$. Each $\vec{x}_i \in ([-B, B] \cup \{\bot\})^{w / \log B}$ is a cable carrying the input value to be routed, and each $c_i \in [n] \cup \{\bot\}$ is a control wire indicating which destination the i-th input cable wants to go to. If $\vec{x}_i$ and c_i are both set, it means that we want to route $\vec{x}_i$ to the c_i-th output cable, and thus we can set $\vec{y}_{c_i} \leftarrow \vec{x}_i$.

Building upon our SIMD garbling techniques in Sect. 2.3, we describe an efficient approach to garble the n-way routing gate, resulting in $O(n \cdot w + n^2 \cdot \lambda)$ bits of bandwidth and $(n \cdot w + n^2) \cdot \widetilde{O}(\lambda)$ computation cost per gate. As long as $w = \Theta(W) \geq \lambda \cdot n$, the bandwidth and computation costs simplify to $O(n \cdot w)$ and $nw \cdot \widetilde{O}(\lambda)$. For the word size $W \geq \lambda \cdot Z$, we can directly implement a Z-sized stack with a single Z-way routing gate, thus avoiding the extra $\log \log N$ cost.

Remark 1 (Comparison with PicoGRAM). PicoGRAM [26] instantiates their stack with a routing network of depth $O(\log Z)$. To save the computation cost, they observe that the evaluator can aggregate all the difference terms δ_c along the routing path with modular multiplication and perform a single exponentiation at the end. However, this trick requires that the evaluator to know the order of the underlying group, which does not apply to our setting.

2.4   Putting Everything Together

In this section, we briefly describe the two remaining components needed to obtain our final result stated in Theorem 1.

Removing the Super-Constant Factor. So far, our costs suffer from an extra super-constant factor denoted $\omega(1)$. If we open up the underlying Circuit ORAM, this $\omega(1)$ factor comes from the super-logarithmically sized buckets in the root and leaf levels of the ORAM tree (whereas all other levels have constant size). The same $\omega(1)$ factor also impacted the performance of earlier works on Garbled RAM [26] or ORAM [55,57]. We make a separate novel contribution by showing how to remove this $\omega(1)$ factor using a Hierarchical ORAM [25] dynamic circuit tailored for polylogarithmic-sized memory. See our online version for details.

Cost of Recursion. Recall that our primary encoding employs a B-bounded arithmetic representation, which is the key reason why we can asymptotically improve the cost for the w-synchronized gates. However, so far, we have neglected the fact that in the dynamic circuit encoding the RAM, there are also many lone boolean gates that are not part of w-synchronized operations. Notably, some of these boolean gates arise due to the recursion structure in the underlying ORAM scheme [57]. At a high level, there are $\log N$ recursion levels providing a memory abstraction for reading and writing $N/2, N/4, \ldots, O(1)$ words of size $O(\log N)$, respectively. The recursion levels store metadata (often called a recursive position map) needed for indexing the ORAM's data structure. Specifically, the i-th recursion level stores which locations to read in the $(i+1)$-th level based on the first i-th bits of the requested address. The key observation here is that these lone boolean operations are performed on *metadata* (such as memory addresses) rather than the memory words themselves.

Earlier, we assumed that we store all data with B-bounded arithmetic representation. However, this would necessitate boolean decomposition and re-composition when we encounter these lone boolean operations. To avoid the extra boolean decomposition costs, we simply store the metadata bit by bit. More concretely, we use $\log N$ number of B-bounded wires to express each memory address that is $\log N$-bits long. For the main data ORAM, as long as $W \geq \lambda \log N$, splitting the metadata into bits does not asymptotically increase the effective word size. Below, we account for the cost of all recursion levels.

We will garble all recursion levels in the same way as we garbled the main ORAM. Because we split $\log N$-sized metadata into bit representations, for the metadata recursion levels, the effective word size is $W' = \lambda \cdot \log N$. We will actually make it slightly worse by blowing up $W' = \lambda \log N \cdot \omega(1)$ to match the word-size assumption for implementing the stack gadget with the Z-way routing gate.

Therefore, the total bandwidth cost across all recursion levels for T steps of RAM computation is

$$\underbrace{\log N}_{\#\text{ rec. levels}} \cdot \underbrace{TW' \log N}_{\text{cost per rec. level}} = T \cdot \lambda \cdot \log^3 N \cdot \omega(1)$$

When $W \geq \lambda \log^2 N \cdot \omega(1)$, this metadata cost is absorbed by the main ORAM's cost $O(T \cdot W \cdot \log N)$. In our online version, we introduce some further optimizations that can relax the word size assumption to $W \geq \lambda \log^2 N$.

Cost of Arithmetic CPU Circuit. Recall that our arithmetic RAM supports word-level additions and coordinate-wise multiplications. Therefore, the CPU circuit can be implemented with $\frac{W}{\lambda} \cdot \operatorname{poly} \log \lambda$ number of B-bounded linear or multiplication gates. Therefore, the total bandwidth cost for garbling all T CPU circuits is at most $T \cdot (W/\lambda) \cdot \operatorname{poly} \log \lambda \cdot \lambda = T \cdot W \cdot \operatorname{poly} \log \lambda$ which is asymptotically absorbed by the costs for implementing the memory abstraction.

Summary and Extension to Boolean RAM. Now, putting everything together, we arrive at our main theorem for garbling an *arithmetic* RAM—see Theorem 1.

If we want to extend our results to a *boolean* RAM whose instruction set supports word-level addition and bitwise operations, we would need to employ extra circuitry for conversion between arithmetic and boolean representations. Specifically, each word of width W will be represented with $O(W/\lambda)$ number of B-bounded arithmetic wires during the memory reads and writes, but will be converted into a boolean representation when performing CPU computation. In Sect. 4.7, we describe techniques for performing such boolean decomposition and composition, inspired by techniques by Ball et al. [7]. We also account for the additional costs associated with boolean decomposition and composition, resulting in Theorem 2.

3 B-Bounded Dynamic Circuit

In this section, we define our computational model, the B-bounded dynamic circuit, which generalizes the tri-state circuits model in prior works [26,27,29].

Definition 1 (Wires and cables). *A wire, denoted as a lowercase letter, such as x, is a variable that can be set to an integer value val_x. A **cable** is a collection of ℓ wires, denoted as $\vec{x}$, where ℓ is called the length of the cable. We use x_i to denote the i-th subwire in a cable $\vec{x}$. Let B be a positive integer, a B-bounded dynamic circuit requires that every wire x's value be B-bounded, that is, $\mathsf{val}_x \in [-B, B]$.*

In the following, we abuse the notation and use x to denote both the wire and its value val_x when the context is clear.

We next define a B-bounded dynamic circuit. In comparison with a standard arithmetic circuit, a *dynamic* circuit allows *eager partial evaluation*. In particular, we introduce the routing and reverse-routing gates, which can be partially evaluated when only a subset of the input wires have been *set*. Previous works [26,27,29] showed that this capability makes it possible to express RAM computations efficiently in dynamic circuits.

Additionally, to support mixed garbling of arithmetic and boolean circuits, we introduce a modulo-2 gate into the gate set for bit-decomposition. Given a B-bounded arithmetic wire $x =: x^{(1)}$, we iteratively compute $y^{(i)} \leftarrow x^{(i)} \bmod 2$ and $x^{(i+1)} \leftarrow \frac{1}{2}\left(x^{(i)} - y^{(i)}\right)$ for $i \in [\log B]$. Meanwhile, bit composition can be achieved easily since it is simply computing a linear combination of the individual bits.

Definition 2 (B-bounded dynamic circuit). *A **dynamic circuit** C consists of wires connected with the following types of gates:*

- **Linear gate**: *The gate is parameterized by a public parameter α. When the two input wires x and y are set, set the output to be $\alpha \cdot x + y$. We do not require α to be an integer, but we require $\alpha \cdot x + y$ to be a B-bounded integer when the arithmetic is performed over the real domain.*
- **Multiplication gate**: *When the two input wires x and y are both set, set the output wire to $x \cdot y$ where the multiplication is over the integer ring $\mathbb{Z}$.*
- **Routing gate**: *Let $n \leq B$ be a positive integer. A routing gate of size $n \times \ell$ takes n input wires $c_1, \ldots, c_n$ called control wires, n input cables $\vec{x}_1, \ldots, \vec{x}_n$ each of length ℓ, and n output cables $\vec{y}_1, \ldots, \vec{y}_n$ each of length ℓ. For any $s \in [n]$, if c_s and $\vec{x}_s$ are set, and $c_s \in [n]$, then the c_s-th output cable $\vec{y}_{c_s}$ is set to $\vec{x}_s$.*
- **Reverse-routing gate**: *Let $n \leq B$ be a positive integer. A reverse-routing gate of size $n \times \ell$ takes n input wires $c_1, \ldots, c_n$ called control wires, n input cables $\vec{x}_1, \ldots, \vec{x}_n$ each of length ℓ, and n output cables $\vec{y}_1, \ldots, \vec{y}_n$ each of length ℓ. For any $s \in [n]$, if c_s and the c_s-th input wire $\vec{x}_{c_s}$ are set, and $c_s \in [n]$, then $\vec{y}_s$ is set to $\vec{x}_{c_s}$.*
- **Modulo-2 gate**: *When the input wire x is set, set the output wire to $y = x \bmod 2$.*

The gates may share the same input wires, but the gates' output wires must be distinct and cannot be the input wires of C. Initially, only the input wires of C is set, and the remaining wires are set based on the gates' definitions above.

Well-Formedness. A B-bounded dynamic circuit C is **well-formed** if the following always hold as long as all input wires are set to B-bounded integers:

1. every wire can be set;
2. every wire's value is an integer within the range $[-B, B]$;
3. for any routing and reverse-routing gate, the control wire values $c_1, \ldots, c_n$ must form a permutation of $[n]$.

Since each wire can only be an input wire of the $\mathcal{C}$ or the output of a unique gate, and moreover, well-formedness requires that the control wires of routing and reverse-routing gates form a permutation, it is easy to see that each wire can only be set to a unique value.

4 Garbling Scheme for B-Bounded Dynamic Circuits

4.1 Definitions: Garbling Scheme

In section, we formally define a garbling scheme and show our construction for garbling B-bounded dynamic circuits in a gate-by-gate manner.

Definition 3 (Garbling scheme). *A garbling scheme, defined for some computation models, consists of a tuple of possibly randomized algorithms:*

- $\widetilde{\mathcal{C}}$, e $\leftarrow$ Garble(1^λ, $\mathcal{C}$)*: upon receiving the security parameter λ and a deterministic program $\mathcal{C}$ under the computation model of concern, output the garbled material denoted $\widetilde{\mathcal{C}}$ and the encoding material* e.
- $\widetilde{\mathsf{inp}}$ $\leftarrow$ Encode(e, inp)*: upon receiving the encoding material* e *and the program's input* inp, *output the encoded input string denoted* $\widetilde{\mathsf{inp}}$.
- out $\leftarrow$ Eval($\widetilde{\mathcal{C}}$, $\widetilde{\mathsf{inp}}$)*: upon receiving the garbled material $\widetilde{\mathcal{C}}$ and encoded input* $\widetilde{\mathsf{inp}}$, *outputs the clear-text output* out.

Definition 4 (Correctness of garbling scheme). *A garbling scheme* (Garble, Encode, Eval) *is **correct** if for polynomial-time program $\mathcal{C}$, there exists a negligible function* negl($\cdot$), *such that for all λ, for any input* inp, *except with* negl($\cdot$) *probability, the following holds: let $\widetilde{\mathcal{C}}$, e $\leftarrow$ Garble(1^λ, $\mathcal{C}$); $\widetilde{\mathsf{inp}}$ $\leftarrow$* Encode(e, inp); out $\leftarrow$ Eval($\widetilde{\mathcal{C}}$, $\widetilde{\mathsf{inp}}$), *then, it must be that* out $=$ $\mathcal{C}$(inp) *where* $\mathcal{C}$(inp) *denotes the outcome of executing the program $\mathcal{C}$ on the input* inp *in clear-text.*

Definition 5 (Security of garbling scheme). *A correct garbling scheme* (Encode, Garble, Eval) *is **secure** with respect to some (deterministic) leakage function* leak, *if and only if there exist probabilistic polynomial-time algorithms* Sim *such that for any program $\mathcal{C}$ and input* inp:

$$\{\widetilde{\mathcal{C}}, \widetilde{\mathsf{inp}}\}_\lambda \stackrel{c}{\approx} \{\mathsf{Sim}(1^\lambda, \mathcal{C}, \mathsf{leak}(\mathcal{C}, \mathsf{inp}), \mathcal{C}(\mathsf{inp}))\}_\lambda$$

where $\widetilde{\mathcal{C}}$, e $\leftarrow$ Garble(1^λ, $\mathcal{C}$) and $\widetilde{\mathsf{inp}}$ $\leftarrow$ Encode(e, inp).

4.2 Setup of Our Garbling Scheme

Next, we present our garbling scheme for B-bounded dynamic circuits. The garbling algorithm Garble can be separated into a circuit-independent part and a circuit-dependent part. We first describe the circuit-independent part also called the setup algorithm, denoted Gen.

$\mathsf{Gen}(1^\lambda)$

1. Samples $\mathcal{N}, \phi(\mathcal{N})$ from $\mathsf{RSA.Gen}(1^\lambda)$, where $\mathcal{N}$ is the product of two λ-bit safe primes p, q, and $\phi(\mathcal{N}) = (p-1)(q-1)$. Let $\zeta = 1 + \lceil 2\log_{\mathcal{N}}(B \cdot 2^\lambda)\rceil$ and $g \leftarrow r^{2\mathcal{N}^\zeta}$ for $r \xleftarrow{\$} \mathbb{Z}^\times_{\mathcal{N}^\zeta+1}$, where B is the bound of the wire values.

2. Samples a global secret key $K \xleftarrow{\$} [\mathcal{N}/4]$, and set $\Delta = K \cdot B \cdot 2^\lambda + 1$.

3. Samples $\gamma_1, \ldots, \gamma_w \xleftarrow{\$} [\mathcal{N}/4]$, where $w = \lceil \frac{W}{B}\rceil$.

4. Let $\left(C^{\mathsf{Mod2}}_{i,1}, C^{\mathsf{Mod2}}_{i,2}\right) \leftarrow \left(g^{r_i}, g^{-r_i \cdot K} \cdot \exp(\Gamma[i])\right)$ where $\Gamma \xleftarrow{\$} \{0,1\}^\lambda$ and $r_i \xleftarrow{\$} [\mathcal{N}/4]$ for each $i \in [\lambda]$, and the exponentiation is done modulo $\mathcal{N}^{\zeta+1}$. Add C^{Mod2} to the public parameter pp

5. Select a hash function H that outputs a $\lceil\log(\mathcal{N}/4)\rceil$-bit string, and a hash function $H_{\mathbb{Z}}$ that outputs an integer in $\mathbb{Z}^\times_{\mathcal{N}^\zeta+1}$. Both hash functions are modeled as random oracles.

6. Let the public parameters $\mathsf{pp} = \left(g, g^K, \mathcal{N}, \zeta, H, H_{\mathbb{Z}}, C^{\mathsf{Mod2}}\right)$ and the secret keys $\mathsf{sk} = (\phi(\mathcal{N}), K, \Delta, \gamma, \Gamma)$.

7. Return $(\mathsf{pp}, \mathsf{sk})$.

Fig. 3. Setup of the garbling scheme. The Gen algorithm is called by the garbler at the beginning of the Garble algorithm, independent of the circuit to be garbled.

Notations. We use $\mathbb{Z}_q$ as a shorthand for $\mathbb{Z}/q\mathbb{Z}$, and $\mathbb{Z}^+_q$ to indicate it is an additive group, and $\mathbb{Z}^\times_q$ to indicate it is a multiplicative group. We use $[n]$ to denote the set of positive integers no greater than n.

Upon receiving the security parameter λ and a dynamic circuit $\mathcal{C}$, the garbler first runs the following Gen algorithm (Fig. 3) to generate the necessary global keys and parameters. In step 1, we set the parameters for the Damgård-Jurik-ElGamal (DJE) cryptosystem [9]. In step 2, we set up the global key for arithmetic garbling. In step 3, we set up the global keys used in the routing gates, where γ_i is used to encode the i-th wire in the cable. In step 4, we set up the parameters used in the modulo-2 gate. Finally, in step 5, we define hash functions that will be used to derive randomness in the garbling of various gates.

Next, we define the garbling of wires used throughout the paper.

Definition 6 (Garbling of wires). *The garbling of a B-bounded wire x consists of a secret share of val_x and a secret share of $K \cdot \mathsf{val}_x$ between the garbler and the evaluator.*

In the first share, the garbler holds a random mask $\mathcal{R}^{\Downarrow}_x$ and the evaluator holds a label $\mathcal{L}^{\Downarrow}_x$, such that $\mathcal{L}^{\Downarrow}_x = \mathcal{R}^{\Downarrow}_x + \mathsf{val}_x$.

In the second share, the garbler holds a random mask $\mathcal{R}^{\Uparrow}_x$ and the evaluator holds a label $\mathcal{L}^{\Uparrow}_x$, such that $\mathcal{L}^{\Uparrow}_x = \mathcal{R}^{\Uparrow}_x + K \cdot \mathsf{val}_x$.

With $\Delta = K \cdot B \cdot 2^\lambda + 1$, the two shares can be combined into a single share of $\Delta \cdot \mathsf{val}_x$, where the garbler holds a combined random mask $\mathcal{R}_x = \mathcal{R}^{\Uparrow}_x \cdot B \cdot 2^\lambda + \mathcal{R}^{\Downarrow}_x$ and the evaluator holds a combined label $\mathcal{L}_x = \mathcal{L}^{\Uparrow}_x \cdot B \cdot 2^\lambda + \mathcal{L}^{\Downarrow}_x$. To correctly decompose the combined share, we require that $B \leq \mathcal{R}^{\Downarrow}_x < B \cdot (2^\lambda - 1)$.

Treating the two shares as one share helps us later simplify the garbling scheme construction and improve the concrete efficiency. Given that $B \leq \mathcal{R}_x^{\Downarrow} < B \cdot (2^\lambda - 1)$, the garbler can decompose the combined random mask $\mathcal{R}_x$ as:

$$\mathcal{R}_x^{\Uparrow} \leftarrow \lfloor \frac{\mathcal{R}_x}{B \cdot 2^\lambda} \rfloor, \quad \mathcal{R}_x^{\Downarrow} \leftarrow \mathcal{R}_x \bmod B \cdot 2^\lambda$$

and the evaluator can decompose the combined label $\mathcal{L}_x$ as:

$$\mathcal{L}_x^{\Uparrow} \leftarrow \lfloor \frac{\mathcal{L}_x}{B \cdot 2^\lambda} \rfloor, \quad \mathcal{L}_x^{\Downarrow} \leftarrow \mathcal{L}_x \bmod B \cdot 2^\lambda$$

In the following, we abuse the notation and simply write x to denote val_x, the value of wire x.

4.3 High-level Garbling Scheme for Dynamic Circuits

In Fig. 4, we present our garbling scheme construction for a dynamic circuit $\mathcal{C}$, with the implementation of each gate type deferred to the later sections. The Garble algorithm first calls Gen to generate the global parameters and keys. Then, it samples random masks for each input wire, adding them to the encoding material, and garbles each gate in a fixed topological order. Finally, it adds the random masks of the output wires to the decoding material. The Encode algorithm takes in the random masks of the input wires and outputs their corresponding labels. The Eval algorithm takes in the input labels, evaluates the garbled gate in an input-dependent topological order, and decodes the output by subtracting the random mask of each output wire from its label. By the well-formedness property, every output wire can be set.

4.4 Routing Gate

In this section, we present the construction of a routing gate that takes n input cables, n control wires, and n output cables, each cable containing $\ell = \frac{W}{B}$ data wires. We omit the construction of the reverse-routing gate, as it is symmetric to the routing gate.

For each $s \in [n]$, the garbler samples a key k_s for the s-th input cable, and k_s' for the s-th output cable. Then, for each input data wire $x_{s,i}$, the garbler sends a group element $\theta_{s,i}$, so that the evaluator can compute $\chi_{s,i} = g^{k_s \cdot \gamma_i} \cdot \exp(\Delta \cdot x_{s,i})$, where γ_i is the key sampled in Gen and tied to the index of the wire in the cable. As we show in our online version, the hard sub-group element $g^{k_s \cdot \gamma_i}$ serves as a pseudorandom one-time pad for the easy sub-group element $\exp(\Delta \cdot x_{s,i})$.

Now suppose that the s-th input data word is routed to the t-th output cable at runtime. We want the evaluator to learn $\chi_{s,i}' = g^{k_t' \cdot \gamma_i} \cdot \exp(\Delta \cdot x_{s,i})$, so that the parties have a divisive share of $\exp(\Delta \cdot x_{s,i})$. To achieve this, the garbler encrypts an exponent $\delta_{s,t}$ such that $(\chi_{s,i})^{\delta_{s,t}} = \chi_{s,i}'$. This exponent $\delta_{s,t}$ can be efficiently computed by the garbler using the following constraints:

$$k_s \cdot \delta_{s,t} \equiv k_t' \mod \phi(\mathcal{N})/4 \,, \quad \delta_{s,t} \equiv 1 \mod \mathcal{N}^\varsigma$$

Garble $(1^\lambda, \mathcal{C})$

1. Run Gen to sample the public parameters pp and the secret keys sk. Parse $\mathcal{N}, \zeta$ from pp. Parse Δ from sk and add it to the encoding material e.
2. For each i-th input wire x_i of $\mathcal{C}$, sample $\mathcal{R}_{x_i} \xleftarrow{\$} [\mathcal{N}^\zeta]$, and add it to the encoding material e.
3. For each gate $\mathcal{G}$ in $\mathcal{C}$, if the random masks of all input wires of $\mathcal{G}$ are already set, run $\mathcal{G}$.Garble and obtain the random masks of all the output wires of $\mathcal{G}$, as well as the garbled gate $\widetilde{\mathcal{G}}$. Store $\widetilde{\mathcal{G}}$ in $\widetilde{\mathcal{C}}$. Repeat until all gates in $\mathcal{C}$ are garbled.
4. For each i-th output wire y_i of $\mathcal{C}$, add $\mathcal{R}_{y_i}^{\Downarrow}$ to the garbled circuit $\widetilde{\mathcal{C}}$.
5. Return $\left(\widetilde{\mathcal{C}}, \mathsf{e}\right)$.

Encode $(\mathsf{e}, \mathsf{inp})$

1. Parse Δ and the random masks $\mathcal{R}_{x_i}$ of the input wires from e.
2. For each i-th input wire x_i of $\mathcal{C}$, compute $\mathcal{L}_{x_i} = \mathcal{R}_{x_i} + \Delta \cdot \mathsf{inp}[i]$.
3. Return $\widetilde{\mathsf{inp}} = \left[\mathcal{L}_{x_1} \cdots \mathcal{L}_{x_{|\mathsf{inp}|}} \right]$.

Eval $\left(\widetilde{\mathcal{C}}, \widetilde{\mathsf{inp}}\right)$

1. Parse the labels of the input wires $\mathcal{L}_{x_1} \cdots \mathcal{L}_{x_{|\mathsf{inp}|}}$ from the encoded input $\widetilde{\mathsf{inp}}$.
2. For each gate $\mathcal{G}$ in $\widetilde{\mathcal{C}}$, if the labels of all input wires of $\mathcal{G}$ are already set, run $\mathcal{G}$.Eval and obtain the labels of all the output wires of $\mathcal{G}$. Repeat until all output wires of $\widetilde{\mathcal{C}}$ are evaluated.
3. For each i-th output wire y_i of $\mathcal{C}$, parse the random mask $\mathcal{R}_{y_i}^{\Downarrow}$ from $\widetilde{\mathcal{C}}$, and compute $\mathsf{out}[i] = \mathcal{L}_{y_i}^{\Downarrow} - \mathcal{R}_{y_i}^{\Downarrow}$. Return out.

Sim$(1^\lambda, \mathcal{C}, \mathsf{leak}(\mathcal{C}, \mathsf{inp}), \mathcal{C}(\mathsf{inp}))$

1. Sample sk and params the same as the Gen function in Figure 3, except that setting $\left(C_{i,1}^{\mathsf{Mod}_2}, C_{i,2}^{\mathsf{Mod}_2} \right) \leftarrow \left(g^r, (g^K)^{-r} \right)$ for each $i \in [\lambda]$.
2. Sample the labels of the input wires $\mathcal{L}_{x_1} \cdots \mathcal{L}_{x_{|\mathsf{inp}|}}$ from $[0, \mathcal{N}^\zeta)$.
3. For each gate $\mathcal{G}$ in $\widetilde{\mathcal{C}}$, if the labels of all input wires of $\mathcal{G}$ are set, run $\mathcal{G}$.Sim and obtain the labels of the output wires. Repeat until all gates of $\widetilde{\mathcal{C}}$ are simulated.
4. Additionally, simulate the random masks of each output wire y_i as $\mathcal{R}_{y_i}^{\Downarrow} \leftarrow \mathcal{L}_{y_i}^{\Downarrow} - \mathcal{C}(\mathsf{inp})[i]$, and add $\mathcal{R}_{y_i}^{\Downarrow}$ to the garbled circuit $\widetilde{\mathcal{C}}$.
5. Return pp, $\widetilde{\mathcal{C}}, \mathcal{L}_{x_1} \cdots \mathcal{L}_{x_{|\mathsf{inp}|}}$.

Fig. 4. Our garbling scheme at a high level, with the implementation of each gate type deferred to the following sections.

where $\phi(\mathcal{N})/4$ is order of the hard sub-group and $\mathcal{N}^\zeta$ is the order of the easy subgroup. Note that the two moduli are co-prime and both are known to the garbler. Since the garbler does not know the routing schedule, she simply encrypts $\delta_{s,t}$ for all pairs $s, t \in [n]$ with the matching labels of the control wires and sends

$\mathsf{Route.Garble}\left(\mathsf{pp}, \mathsf{sk}, [\mathcal{R}_{c_s}]_{s \in [n]} \| [\mathcal{R}_{x_{s,i}}]_{s \in [n], i \in [\ell]}\right)$

1. Parse $g, \zeta, \mathcal{N}, H, H_{\mathbb{Z}}$ from pp and $\phi(\mathcal{N}), K, \gamma$ from sk.
2. For each $s \in [n]$:
   (a) Sample $k_s, k_s' \xleftarrow{\$} [\mathcal{N}/4]$.
   (b) For $i \in [\ell]$, compute $\theta_{s,i} \leftarrow g^{k_s \cdot \gamma_i} \cdot \exp\left(-\mathcal{R}_{x_{s,i}}\right)$ and

   $$\mathcal{R}_{y_{s,i}} \leftarrow \mathsf{DDLog}\left(g^{k_s' \cdot \gamma_i}\right) + H_{\mathbb{Z}}(\mathsf{gid}\|s\|i) \bmod \mathcal{N}^\zeta.$$

   (c) For each $t \in [n]$, let $\delta_{s,t} \leftarrow (k_t'/k_s - 1) \cdot \mathcal{N}^{-\zeta} \bmod \frac{\phi(\mathcal{N})}{4}$ and

   $$\widetilde{\delta}_{s,t} \leftarrow H\left(\mathcal{R}_{c_s}^{\Uparrow} + t \cdot K, \mathsf{gid}\|s\|t\right) \oplus \delta_{s,t}.$$

3. Return the random masks of the output wires $\mathcal{R}_{y_{s,i}}$ for all $s \in [n]$ and $i \in [\ell]$
   and the garbled gate $\widetilde{\mathsf{Route}} = \left(\theta, \widetilde{\delta}, [\mathcal{R}_{c_1}^{\Downarrow} \cdots \mathcal{R}_{c_n}^{\Downarrow}]\right)$.

$\mathsf{Route.Eval}_s\left(\mathsf{pp}, \widetilde{\mathsf{Route}}, \mathcal{L}_{c_s} \| [\mathcal{L}_{x_{s,i}}]_{i \in [\ell]}\right)$

1. Parse $\mathcal{N}, \zeta, H, H_{\mathbb{Z}}$ from pp and $\left(\theta, \widetilde{\delta}, [\mathcal{R}_{c_1}^{\Downarrow} \cdots \mathcal{R}_{c_n}^{\Downarrow}]\right)$ from $\widetilde{\mathsf{Route}}$.
2. Compute $\pi(s) \leftarrow \mathcal{L}_{c_s}^{\Downarrow} - \mathcal{R}_{c_s}^{\Downarrow}$ and decrypt $\delta_{s,\pi(s)} \leftarrow H\left(\mathcal{L}_{c_s}^{\Uparrow}, \mathsf{gid}\|s\|\pi_s\right) \oplus \widetilde{\delta}_{s,\pi(s)}$.
3. For each $i \in [\ell]$, compute $\chi_{s,i} = \theta_{s,i} \cdot \exp(\mathcal{L}_{x_{s,i}})$ and return the output wire
   label

   $$\mathcal{L}_{y_{\pi(s),i}} \leftarrow \mathsf{DDLog}\left((\chi_{s,i})^{\delta_{s,\pi(s)} \cdot \mathcal{N}^\zeta + 1}\right) + H_{\mathbb{Z}}(\mathsf{gid}\|s\|i) \bmod \mathcal{N}^\zeta.$$

$\mathsf{Route.Sim}\left(\mathsf{pp}, \pi, [\mathcal{L}_{c_s}]_{s \in [n]} \| [\mathcal{L}_{x_{s,i}}]_{s \in [n], i \in [\ell]}\right)$

1. Parse $\mathcal{N}, \zeta, H, H_{\mathbb{Z}}$ from pp.
2. For each $i \in [\ell]$, sample $\gamma_i \xleftarrow{\$} [\mathcal{N}/4]$ and reuse it for all the Route gates.
3. For each $s \in [n]$:
   (a) Sample $k_s, \delta_{s,\pi(s)} \xleftarrow{\$} [\mathcal{N}/4]$.
   (b) For $i \in [\ell]$, compute $\theta_{s,i} \leftarrow g^{k_s \cdot \gamma_i}$ and

   $$\mathcal{L}_{y_{\pi(s),i}} \leftarrow \mathsf{DDLog}\left((\theta_{s,i} \cdot \exp(\mathcal{L}_{x_{s,i}}))^{\delta_{s,\pi(s)} \cdot \mathcal{N}^\zeta + 1}\right) + H_{\mathbb{Z}}(\mathsf{gid}\|\pi(s)\|i) \bmod \mathcal{N}^\zeta.$$

   (c) Let $\widetilde{\delta}_{s,\pi(s)} \leftarrow H\left(\mathcal{L}_{c_s}^{\Uparrow}, \mathsf{gid}\|s\|\pi(s)\right) \oplus \delta_{s,\pi(s)}$, and for $t \neq s$, sample $\widetilde{\delta}_{s,\pi(t)} \xleftarrow{\$} \{0,1\}^{\lceil \log(\mathcal{N}/4) \rceil}$.
4. Return the labels of the output wires $\mathcal{R}_{y_{s,i}}$ for all $s \in [n]$ and $i \in [\ell]$ and the
   garbled gate $\widetilde{\mathsf{Route}} = \left(\theta, \widetilde{\delta}, [(\mathcal{L}_{c_1}^{\Downarrow} - \pi(1)) \cdots (\mathcal{L}_{c_n}^{\Downarrow} - \pi(n))]\right)$.

Fig. 5. The routing gate construction. Eval_s denotes the algorithm the evaluator runs to route the s-th input word. The gate incurs $O(\lambda \cdot n \cdot (n + \ell))$ bits of bandwidth and $O(n \cdot w)$ exponentiations, where $\ell = \lceil W/B \rceil$ is the number of cables used to hold each data word.

the ciphertexts to the evaluator. While this incurs quadratic cost in n, where $n \in \omega(\log N)$ in our RAM reduction, the cost does not depend on the word width W and gets amortized when W is large.

Finally, the parties perform a distributed discrete log (DDLog) on their divisive share of $\exp(\Delta \cdot x_{s,i})$, and obtains a subtractive share of $\Delta \cdot x_{s,i}$ on the output wire $y_{t,i}$.

We present the full scheme in Fig. 5 and illustrate an example in our online version.

4.5   Multiplication Gate

As shown in our roadmap (Sect. 2.3), we instantiate the multiplication gate using Homomorphic Secret Sharing (HSS) [53]. Specifically, the garbler encrypts $\mathcal{R}_x^{\Downarrow} \cdot \Delta$ and $\mathcal{R}_y$ under the DJE encryption scheme [9] and includes the ciphertexts in the garbled circuit. Then, based on Equation (1), the parties can locally compute a subtractive share of $\Delta \cdot x \cdot y$ using HSS. In our online version, we show that the ciphertexts can be simulated without knowledge of the wire value assuming the hardness of DCR, since both

$$\mathcal{R}_x^{\Downarrow} \cdot \Delta = (\mathcal{L}_x^{\Downarrow} - x) \cdot (B \cdot 2^{\lambda} \cdot K + 1) \quad \text{and} \quad \mathcal{R}_y = \mathcal{L}_y - y \cdot (B \cdot 2^{\lambda} \cdot K + 1)$$

are affine functions of K (Fig. 6).

Mult.Garble($\mathsf{pp}, \mathsf{sk}, \mathcal{R}_x, \mathcal{R}_y$)
1. Parse $g, \mathcal{N}, \zeta, H_{\mathbb{Z}}$ from pp and K, Δ from sk.
2. Let $(C_{x,1}, C_{x,2}) \leftarrow \left(g^{r_1}, g^{-r_1 \cdot K} \cdot \exp\left(\mathcal{R}_x^{\Downarrow} \cdot \Delta\right)\right)$ where $r_1 \xleftarrow{\$} [\mathcal{N}/4]$.
3. Let $(C_{y,1}, C_{y,2}) \leftarrow \left(g^{r_2}, g^{-r_2 \cdot K} \cdot \exp\left(\mathcal{R}_y\right)\right)$ where $r_2 \xleftarrow{\$} [\mathcal{N}/4]$.
4. Let $R \leftarrow \mathsf{DDLog}\left((C_{x,1})^{\mathcal{R}_y^{\Uparrow}} \cdot (C_{x,2})^{\mathcal{R}_y^{\Downarrow}} \cdot (C_{y,1})^{\mathcal{R}_x^{\Uparrow}} \cdot (C_{y,2})^{\mathcal{R}_x^{\Downarrow}}\right) + H_{\mathbb{Z}}(\mathsf{gid}) \bmod \mathcal{N}^{\zeta}$.
5. Return the random mask of the output wire $\mathcal{R}_z = \left(\mathcal{R}_x^{\Downarrow} \cdot \mathcal{R}_y - R\right) \bmod \mathcal{N}^{\zeta}$, and the garbled gate $\widetilde{\mathsf{Mult}} = (C_x, C_y)$.

Mult.Eval$\left(\mathsf{pp}, \widetilde{\mathsf{Mult}}, \mathcal{L}_x, \mathcal{L}_y\right)$
1. Parse $\mathcal{N}, \zeta, H_{\mathbb{Z}}$ from pp and (C_x, C_y) from $\widetilde{\mathsf{Mult}}$.
2. Let $L \leftarrow \mathsf{DDLog}\left((C_{x,1})^{\mathcal{L}_y^{\Uparrow}} \cdot (C_{x,2})^{\mathcal{L}_y^{\Downarrow}} \cdot (C_{y,1})^{\mathcal{L}_x^{\Uparrow}} \cdot (C_{y,2})^{\mathcal{L}_x^{\Downarrow}}\right) + H_{\mathbb{Z}}(\mathsf{gid}) \bmod \mathcal{N}^{\zeta}$.
3. Return the label of the output wire $\mathcal{L}_z = \left(\mathcal{L}_x^{\Downarrow} \cdot \mathcal{L}_y - L\right) \bmod \mathcal{N}^{\zeta}$.

Mult.Sim($\mathsf{pp}, \mathcal{L}_x, \mathcal{L}_y$)
1. Parse $g^K, \mathcal{N}, \zeta, H_{\mathbb{Z}}$ from pp.
2. Let $(C_{x,1}, C_{x,2}) \leftarrow \left(g^{r_1}, (g^K)^{r_1}\right)$ where $r_1 \xleftarrow{\$} [\mathcal{N}/4]$.
3. Let $(C_{y,1}, C_{y,2}) \leftarrow \left(g^{r_2}, (g^K)^{r_2}\right)$ where $r_2 \xleftarrow{\$} [\mathcal{N}/4]$.
4. Let $L \leftarrow \mathsf{DDLog}\left((C_{x,1})^{\mathcal{L}_y^{\Uparrow}} \cdot (C_{x,2})^{\mathcal{L}_y^{\Downarrow}} \cdot (C_{y,1})^{\mathcal{L}_x^{\Uparrow}} \cdot (C_{y,2})^{\mathcal{L}_x^{\Downarrow}}\right) + H_{\mathbb{Z}}(\mathsf{gid}) \bmod \mathcal{N}^{\zeta}$.
5. Return the label of the output wire $\mathcal{L}_z = \left(\mathcal{L}_x^{\Downarrow} \cdot \mathcal{L}_y - L\right) \bmod \mathcal{N}^{\zeta}$, and the garbled gate $\widetilde{\mathsf{Mult}} = (C_x, C_y)$.

Fig. 6. The multiplication gate construction. Leveraging the HSS technique [53], the gate only requires sending 2 DJE ciphertexts. For computation, Garble incurs 5 exponentiations (with global base g), and Eval incurs 4 exponentiations.

4.6   Linear Gate

We present the construction of the linear gate in Fig. 7. Each party can locally compute the output share by applying the linear combination to its input wire shares. To ensure that all shares remain within $[0, \mathcal{N}^\varsigma)$, both parties add the same random mask to their shares and reduce the result modulo $\mathcal{N}^\varsigma$. This random mask ensures that the probability of shares wrapping around is negligible.

$\mathsf{Linear}_\alpha.\mathsf{Garble}\,(\mathsf{pp},\ \mathcal{R}_x,\ \mathcal{R}_y)$
1. Parse $\mathcal{N}, \varsigma, H_\mathbb{Z}$ from pp.
2. Return the output wire's random mask $\mathcal{R}_z \leftarrow \lfloor \alpha \cdot \mathcal{R}_x \rfloor + \mathcal{R}_y + H_\mathbb{Z}(\mathsf{gid}) \bmod \mathcal{N}^\varsigma$.

$\mathsf{Linear}_\alpha.\mathsf{Eval}\,(\mathsf{pp},\ \mathcal{L}_x,\ \mathcal{L}_y)$
1. Parse $\mathcal{N}, \varsigma, H_\mathbb{Z}$ from pp.
2. Return the output wire's label $\mathcal{L}_z \leftarrow \lfloor \alpha \cdot \mathcal{L}_x \rfloor + \mathcal{L}_y + H_\mathbb{Z}(\mathsf{gid}) \bmod \mathcal{N}^\varsigma$.

$\mathsf{Linear}_\alpha.\mathsf{Sim}\,(\mathsf{pp},\ \mathcal{L}_x,\ \mathcal{L}_y)$
1. Parse $\mathcal{N}, \varsigma, H_\mathbb{Z}$ from pp.
2. Return the output wire's label $\mathcal{L}_z \leftarrow \lfloor \alpha \cdot \mathcal{L}_x \rfloor + \mathcal{L}_y + H_\mathbb{Z}(\mathsf{gid}) \bmod \mathcal{N}^\varsigma$.

Fig. 7. The linear gate construction. The gate does not require any communication or exponentiation.

4.7   Modulo-2 Gate

Finally, we show how to implement a modulo-2 gate that takes an arithmetic garbling of input wire x and outputs an arithmetic garbling of $y = x \bmod 2$.

Leveraging HSS, we simplify the construction of Li and Liu [40], preserving their bandwidth and computation complexity while replacing their programmable random-oracle model with the non-programmable random-oracle model (Fig. 8).

On a high level, we want to first convert our arithmetic garbling of the input wire x into a Boolean garbling of $y = x \bmod 2$. More specifically, we want the parties to obtain an XOR share of $y \cdot \Gamma$, where Γ is a λ-bit global key sampled in Gen. Such type of share has been widely used in practical Boolean garbled circuits due to its Free-XOR property [36].

We observe that for every bit $i \in [\lambda]$, the parties can use HSS to compute a subtractive share of $x \cdot \Gamma[i]$ given the garbling of x and an encryption of $\Gamma[i]$. Since $\Gamma[i] \in \{0, 1\}$, the parties can further get an XOR share of $(x \bmod 2) \cdot \Gamma[i]$ by reducing the subtractive share modulo 2. Repeating this for all bits $i \in [\lambda]$, the parties obtain an XOR share of $\Gamma \cdot (x \bmod 2) = y \cdot \Gamma$.

Finally, the parties convert the Boolean garbling back to the arithmetic garbling of y using a garbled truth table [36,59].

$\mathsf{Mod_2.Garble}\,(\mathsf{pp},\,\mathsf{sk},\,\mathcal{R}_x)$
1. Parse $g,\mathcal{N},\zeta,C^{\mathsf{Mod_2}},H_{\mathbb{Z}}$ from pp and Δ,Γ from sk.
2. Compute the λ-bit string R_{bin} where $R_{\mathrm{bin}}[i] \leftarrow R_i \bmod 2$ and

$$R_i \leftarrow \mathsf{DDLog}\left(\left(C_{i,1}^{\mathsf{Mod_2}}\right)^{\mathcal{R}_x^{\Uparrow}} \cdot \left(C_{i,2}^{\mathsf{Mod_2}}\right)^{\mathcal{R}_x^{\Downarrow}}\right) + H_{\mathbb{Z}}(\mathsf{gid}\|i) \bmod \mathcal{N}^{\zeta}.$$

3. For $b \in \{0,1\}$, compute $h_b \leftarrow H_{\mathbb{Z}}\left(R_{\mathrm{bin}} \oplus b \cdot \Gamma,\, \mathsf{gid}\right) \bmod \mathcal{N}^{\zeta}$.
   - If $\mathcal{R}_x^{\Downarrow}$ is even, set $\mathcal{R}_y \leftarrow h_0$ and $\widetilde{\mathsf{Mod_2}} \leftarrow h_0 - h_1 + \Delta \bmod \mathcal{N}^{\zeta}$.
   - If $\mathcal{R}_x^{\Downarrow}$ is odd, set $\mathcal{R}_y \leftarrow h_1 - \Delta$ and $\widetilde{\mathsf{Mod_2}} \leftarrow -h_0 + h_1 - \Delta \bmod \mathcal{N}^{\zeta}$.
4. Return the random mask of the output wire $\mathcal{R}_y$ and the garbled gate $\widetilde{\mathsf{Mod_2}}$.

$\mathsf{Mod_2.Eval}\,(\mathsf{pp},\,\mathcal{L}_x)$
1. Parse $g,\mathcal{N},\zeta,C^{\mathsf{Mod_2}},H_{\mathbb{Z}}$ from pp.
2. Compute the λ-bit string L_{bin} where $L_{\mathrm{bin}}[i] \leftarrow L_i \bmod 2$ and

$$L_i \leftarrow \mathsf{DDLog}\left(\left(C_{i,1}^{\mathsf{Mod_2}}\right)^{\mathcal{L}_x^{\Uparrow}} \cdot \left(C_{i,2}^{\mathsf{Mod_2}}\right)^{\mathcal{L}_x^{\Downarrow}}\right) + H_{\mathbb{Z}}(\mathsf{gid}\|i) \bmod \mathcal{N}^{\zeta}.$$

3. Compute $h \leftarrow H_{\mathbb{Z}}\left(L_{\mathrm{bin}},\, \mathsf{gid}\right) \bmod \mathcal{N}^{\zeta}$. If $\mathcal{L}_x^{\Downarrow}$ is even, set $\mathcal{L}_y \leftarrow h$, else set $\mathcal{L}_y \leftarrow h + \widetilde{\mathsf{Mod_2}} \bmod \mathcal{N}^{\zeta}$.
4. Return the labels of the output wire $\mathcal{L}_y$.

$\mathsf{Mod_2.Sim}\,(\mathsf{pp},\,\mathcal{L}_x)$
1. Parse $g,\mathcal{N},\zeta,C^{\mathsf{Mod_2}},H_{\mathbb{Z}}$ from pp.
2. Compute the λ-bit string L_{bin} where $L_{\mathrm{bin}}[i] \leftarrow L_i \bmod 2$ and

$$L_i \leftarrow \mathsf{DDLog}\left(\left(C_{i,1}^{\mathsf{Mod_2}}\right)^{\mathcal{L}_x^{\Uparrow}} \cdot \left(C_{i,2}^{\mathsf{Mod_2}}\right)^{\mathcal{L}_x^{\Downarrow}}\right) + H_{\mathbb{Z}}(\mathsf{gid}\|i) \bmod \mathcal{N}^{\zeta}.$$

3. For $b \in \{0,1\}$, compute $h \leftarrow H_{\mathbb{Z}}\left(L_{\mathrm{bin}},\, \mathsf{gid}\right) \bmod \mathcal{N}^{\zeta}$, if $\mathcal{L}_x^{\Downarrow}$ is even, set $\mathcal{L}_y \leftarrow h$ and $\widetilde{\mathsf{Mod_2}} \xleftarrow{\$} [0,\mathcal{N}^{\zeta})$, else set $\mathcal{L}_y \xleftarrow{\$} [0,\mathcal{N}^{\zeta})$ and $\widetilde{\mathsf{Mod_2}} \leftarrow -h + \mathcal{L}_y \bmod \mathcal{N}^{\zeta}$.
4. Return the label of the output wire $\mathcal{L}_y$ and the garbled gate $\widetilde{\mathsf{Mod_2}}$.

Fig. 8. The modulo-2 gate construction. The gate incurs $\zeta \cdot \log \mathcal{N}$ bits of bandwidth, as well as 4λ exponentiations per party.

5 Evaluation

In this section, we demonstrate that our scheme is not only theoretically new but also practical, especially for settings that do not require performing bit decomposition on the memory words, notably, the 2-server updatable PIR application mentioned in Sect. 1.

Implementation and Open Source. We have implemented Zebra in C++ and made our code open-source at https://github.com/zebragram/zebragram. Our implementation builds on top of the open-source PicoGRAM implementation [26]. We use the FLINT (Fast Library for Number Theory) library [56] for large-integer arithmetic and the Intel Paillier Cryptosystem Library [31] to further accelerate modular exponentiation with AVX512 instruction sets. Benchmarks run on an Intel Xeon Platinum 8352S CPU (32 cores at 2.2 GHz), the same model as in [26]. To further improve concrete efficiency:

- We adopt the small-exponent DCR assumption, following [4,7], and reduce the key length to 256 bits for a 128-bit security level against the baby-step giant-step attack [54].
- We additionally assume DDH on the NIST P-256 curve [18] and instantiate position maps as in PicoGRAM.
- We use naive constructions for the root stash and routing gates, which are faster than the theoretical variants at our benchmark scale.

Evaluation Results. We evaluated our implementation and compared the performance with PicoGRAM [26], which is the state-of-the-art Garbled RAM implementation. Our evaluation considers a 2-server PIR-style workload, with a 256 MB database, and 1kB to 4kB word sizes. The word size is chosen to reflect real-world applications such as Certificate Transparency (CT) logs, or the size of a key-value query to the Ethereum blockchain along with its Merkle proofs as specified in EIP-1186 [35].

Table 2 compares our implementation with PicoGRAM [26]. We interpolate PicoGRAM's runtime to our block sizes and core count, since the original implementation would require more than 1 TB of RAM at our test scale.

For 1 kB blocks ($N = 2^{18}$ and $W = 8192$), we obtain a 7.49× reduction in bandwidth and a 1.43× end-to-end speedup over a 300 Mbps link. For 4 kB blocks ($N = 2^{16}$ and $W = 32768$), we obtain a 10.1× reduction in bandwidth and, moreover, a 22% reduction in overall computation despite the use of the Paillier cryptosystem [31,49]. Overall, we achieve a 3.53× end-to-end speedup for 4kB blocks. Larger blocks yield greater speedups because (i) position-map overhead is amortized and (ii) our Eval algorithm exposes more parallelism.

Table 2. Runtime and bandwidth per memory access for our scheme and PicoGRAM [26] on a 256 MB database with 1 kB and 4 kB blocks. The costs do not include bit decomposition. We use 2048-bit RSA keys and 256-bit ElGamal keys under the small-exponent DCR assumption. For both works, the end-to-end time assumes a 300 Mbps network connection, with the garbler's computation pipelined with garbled circuit transmission.

Scheme	Block size	Garble (s)	Eval (s)	Comm. (MB)	End-to-end (s)
PicoGRAM	1 kB	0.695	**0.259**	113.1	3.422
	4 kB	2.667	**0.799**	395.7	11.86
Zebra	1 kB	**0.182**	1.973	**15.11**	**2.396**
	4 kB	**0.455**	2.263	**39.15**	**3.358**
Our Speedup	1 kB	3.82×	0.11×	7.49×	1.43×
	4 kB	5.86×	0.35×	10.1×	3.53×

Table 3. Bit decomposition cost of our scheme at different block sizes. We assume the garbler has precomputed a 10 GB table and the evaluator has precomputed a 100 GB table, which take 14 s and 507 s, respectively.

Block size	Garble (s)	Eval (s)	Comm. (MB)
1 kB	9.020	19.58	2.041
4 kB	33.28	73.93	8.164

Table 3 reports the bit-decomposition cost of our scheme, which is independent of the database size. The evaluation assumes a worst-case workload in which all B-bounded wires in a block are fully decomposed, despite that many applications will not require full decomposition.

Acknowledgements. This work is in part support by NSF under award numbers 2128519, 2212746, and 2044679, a Packard Fellowship, an ONR grant, and a DARPA SIEVE grant under a subcontract from SRI, a JP Morgan Faculty Research Award, and a research grant from 0xPARC. Ashrujit Ghoshal's work is supported by a New Faculty Initiation Grant at IIT Madras, the CyStar Centre of Excellence, and the A. Raghunathan Center for Theoretical CS.

Use of AI. The authors used GPT-5 and Github Copilot to assist with language polishing and proofreading. The authors reviewed and edited the content as needed and take full responsibility for the content of the publication.

References

1. Meta's oram implementation. https://github.com/facebook/oram
2. Private communication with worldcoin
3. Signal's oblivious ram implementation. https://github.com/signalapp/ContactDiscoveryService-Icelake
4. Abram, D., Damgård, I., Orlandi, C., Scholl, P.: An algebraic framework for silent preprocessing with trustless setup and active security. In: Dodis, Y., Shrimpton, T. (eds.) Advances in Cryptology - CRYPTO 2022, pp. 421–452. Springer Nature Switzerland, Cham (2022). https://doi.org/10.1007/978-3-031-15985-5_15
5. Ananth, P., Chen, Y.C., Chung, K.M., Lin, H., Lin, W.K.: Delegating ram computations with adaptive soundness and privacy. In: Hirt, M., Smith, A. (eds.) Theory of Cryptography, pp. 3–30. Springer, Berlin Heidelberg, Berlin, Heidelberg (2016). https://doi.org/10.1007/978-3-662-53644-5_1
6. Ananth, P., Lombardi, A.: Succinct garbling schemes from functional encryption through a local simulation paradigm. In: Beimel, A., Dziembowski, S. (eds.) Theory of Cryptography, pp. 455–472. Springer International Publishing, Cham (2018). https://doi.org/10.1007/978-3-030-03810-6_17
7. Ball, M., Li, H., Lin, H., Liu, T.: New ways to garble arithmetic circuits. In: Hazay, C., Stam, M. (eds.) Advances in Cryptology - EUROCRYPT 2023, pp. 3–34. Springer Nature Switzerland, Cham (2023). https://doi.org/10.1007/978-3-031-30617-4_1

8. Beaver, D., Micali, S., Rogaway, P.: The round complexity of secure protocols. In: Proceedings of the Twenty-Second Annual ACM Symposium on Theory of Computing, pp. 503–513. STOC 1990, Association for Computing Machinery, New York, NY, USA (1990). https://doi.org/10.1145/100216.100287

9. Behera, A.R., Meyer, P., Orlandi, C., Roy, L., Scholl, P.: Privately constrained PRFs from DCR: Puncturing and bounded waring rank. Cryptology ePrint Archive, Paper 2025/230 (2025). https://eprint.iacr.org/2025/230

10. Bellare, M., Hoang, T., Keelveedhi, S., Rogaway, P.: Efficient garbling from a fixed-key blockcipher, pp. 478–492 (2013). https://doi.org/10.1109/SP.2013.39

11. Bitansky, N., Garg, S., Lin, H., Pass, R., Telang, S.: Succinct randomized encodings and their applications. In: Proceedings of the Forty-Seventh Annual ACM Symposium on Theory of Computing, pp. 439–448. STOC 2015, Association for Computing Machinery, New York, NY, USA (2015). https://doi.org/10.1145/2746539.2746574

12. Boyle, E., Gilboa, N., Ishai, Y.: Breaking the circuit size barrier for secure computation under DDH. In: Robshaw, M., Katz, J. (eds.) CRYPTO 2016. LNCS, vol. 9814, pp. 509–539. Springer, Heidelberg (2016). https://doi.org/10.1007/978-3-662-53018-4_19

13. Boyle, E., Naor, M.: Is there an oblivious ram lower bound? In: Proceedings of the 2016 ACM Conference on Innovations in Theoretical Computer Science, pp. 357–368. ITCS 2016, Association for Computing Machinery, New York, NY, USA (2016). https://doi.org/10.1145/2840728.2840761

14. Buterin, V.: A maximally simple l1 privacy roadmap. https://ethereum-magicians.org/t/a-maximally-simple-l1-privacy-roadmap/23459

15. Canetti, R., Chen, Y., Holmgren, J., Raykova, M.: Adaptive succinct garbled ram or: how to delegate your database. In: Proceedings, Part II, of the 14th International Conference on Theory of Cryptography - Volume 9986, pp. 61–90. Springer-Verlag, Berlin, Heidelberg (2016). https://doi.org/10.1007/978-3-662-53644-5_3

16. Canetti, R., Holmgren, J.: Fully succinct garbled ram. In: Proceedings of the 2016 ACM Conference on Innovations in Theoretical Computer Science, pp. 169–178. ITCS 2016, Association for Computing Machinery, New York, NY, USA (2016). https://doi.org/10.1145/2840728.2840765

17. Canetti, R., Holmgren, J., Jain, A., Vaikuntanathan, V.: Succinct garbling and indistinguishability obfuscation for ram programs. In: Proceedings of the Forty-Seventh Annual ACM Symposium on Theory of Computing, pp. 429–437. STOC 2015, Association for Computing Machinery, New York, NY, USA (2015). https://doi.org/10.1145/2746539.2746621

18. Chen, L., Moody, D., Regenscheid, A., Robinson, A., Randall, K.: Recommendations for discrete logarithm-based cryptography: elliptic curve domain parameters. Tech. Rep. NIST Special Publication (SP) 800-186, National Institute of Standards and Technology, Gaithersburg, MD (2023). https://doi.org/10.6028/NIST.SP.800-186

19. Chen, Y.C., Chow, S.S., Chung, K.M., Lai, R.W., Lin, W.K., Zhou, H.S.: Cryptography for parallel ram from indistinguishability obfuscation. In: Proceedings of the 2016 ACM Conference on Innovations in Theoretical Computer Science, Pp. 179–190. ITCS 2016, Association for Computing Machinery, New York, NY, USA (2016). https://doi.org/10.1145/2840728.2840769

20. Corrigan-Gibbs, H., Kogan, D.: Private information retrieval with sublinear online time. In: EUROCRYPT (2020)

21. Garg, S., Gentry, C., Halevi, S., Raykova, M., Sahai, A., Waters, B.: Candidate indistinguishability obfuscation and functional encryption for all circuits. In: 2013 IEEE 54th Annual Symposium on Foundations of Computer Science, pp. 40–49 (2013). https://doi.org/10.1109/FOCS.2013.13
22. Garg, S., Lu, S., Ostrovsky, R.: Black-box garbled ram. In: Proceedings of the 2015 IEEE 56th Annual Symposium on Foundations of Computer Science (FOCS), pp. 210–229. FOCS 2015, IEEE Computer Society, USA (2015). https://doi.org/10.1109/FOCS.2015.22
23. Garg, S., Lu, S., Ostrovsky, R., Scafuro, A.: Garbled ram from one-way functions. In: Proceedings of the Forty-Seventh Annual ACM Symposium on Theory of Computing, Pp. 449–458. STOC 2015, Association for Computing Machinery, New York, NY, USA (2015). https://doi.org/10.1145/2746539.2746593
24. Gentry, C., Halevi, S., Lu, S., Ostrovsky, R., Raykova, M., Wichs, D.: Garbled RAM revisited. In: Nguyen, P.Q., Oswald, E. (eds.) EUROCRYPT 2014. LNCS, vol. 8441, pp. 405–422. Springer, Heidelberg (2014). https://doi.org/10.1007/978-3-642-55220-5_23
25. Goldreich, O., Ostrovsky, R.: Software protection and simulation on oblivious rams. J. ACM **43**(3), 431–473 (1996). https://doi.org/10.1145/233551.233553
26. Gu, T., Tinoco, A., Rajan, S.H.G., Shi, E.: Picogram: practical garbled ram from decisional Diffie-Hellman. In: Tauman Kalai, Y., Kamara, S.F. (eds.) Advances in Cryptology - CRYPTO 2025, pp. 247–281. Springer Nature Switzerland, Cham (2025). https://doi.org/10.1007/978-3-032-01913-4_8
27. Heath, D.: Efficient arithmetic in garbled circuits. In: Advances in Cryptology - EUROCRYPT 2024: 43rd Annual International Conference on the Theory and Applications of Cryptographic Techniques, Zurich, Switzerland, May 26-30, 2024, Proceedings, Part V, pp. 3–31. Springer-Verlag, Berlin, Heidelberg (2024). https://doi.org/10.1007/978-3-031-58740-5_1
28. Heath, D., Kolesnikov, V., Ostrovsky, R.: Epigram: practical garbled ram. In: Advances in Cryptology - EUROCRYPT 2022: 41st Annual International Conference on the Theory and Applications of Cryptographic Techniques, Trondheim, Norway, May 30 - June 3, 2022, Proceedings, Part I, pp. 3–33. Springer-Verlag, Berlin, Heidelberg (2022). https://doi.org/10.1007/978-3-031-06944-4_1
29. Heath, D., Kolesnikov, V., Ostrovsky, R.: Tri-state circuits: a circuit model that captures ram. In: Advances in Cryptology - CRYPTO 2023: 43rd Annual International Cryptology Conference, CRYPTO 2023, Santa Barbara, CA, USA, August 20-24, 2023, Proceedings, Part IV, pp. 128–160. Springer-Verlag, Berlin, Heidelberg (2023). https://doi.org/10.1007/978-3-031-38551-3_5
30. Hoover, A., Patel, S., Persiano, G., Yeo, K.: Plinko: single-server PIR with efficient updates via invertible PRFS. In: Advances in Cryptology - EUROCRYPT 2025 - 44th Annual International Conference on the Theory and Applications of Cryptographic Techniques, Madrid, Spain, May 4-8, 2025, Proceedings, Part VI. LNCS, vol. 15606, pp. 3–33. Springer (2025). https://doi.org/10.1007/978-3-031-91095-1_1
31. Intel: Intel paillier cryptosystem library (pailliercryptolib). https://github.com/intel/pailliercryptolib (2022). version 1.1.4, released December 22, 2022; archived by owner June 30, 2025
32. Ishai, Y., Li, H., Lin, H.: Succinct homomorphic MACs from groups and applications. Cryptology ePrint Archive, Paper 2024/2073 (2024). https://eprint.iacr.org/2024/2073

33. Ishai, Y., Li, H., Lin, H.: A unified framework for succinct garbling from homomorphic secret sharing. In: Tauman Kalai, Y., Kamara, S.F. (eds.) Advances in Cryptology - CRYPTO 2025, pp. 390–425. Springer Nature Switzerland, Cham (2025). https://doi.org/10.1007/978-3-032-01884-7_13

34. Jain, A., Lin, H., Sahai, A.: Indistinguishability obfuscation from well-founded assumptions (2020)

35. Jentzsch, S., Jentzsch, C.: EIP-1186: RPC-method to get merkle proofs — eth_getproof (2018). https://eips.ethereum.org/EIPS/eip-1186

36. Kolesnikov, V., Schneider, T.: Improved garbled circuit: free XOR gates and applications. In: International Colloquium on Automata, Languages and Programming (2008). https://api.semanticscholar.org/CorpusID:7746167

37. Koppula, V., Lewko, A.B., Waters, B.: Indistinguishability obfuscation for turing machines with unbounded memory. In: Proceedings of the Forty-Seventh Annual ACM Symposium on Theory of Computing, pp. 419–428. STOC 2015, Association for Computing Machinery, New York, NY, USA (2015). https://doi.org/10.1145/2746539.2746614

38. Larsen, K.G., Nielsen, J.B.: Yes, there is an oblivious RAM lower bound! In: Shacham, H., Boldyreva, A. (eds.) CRYPTO 2018. LNCS, vol. 10992, pp. 523–542. Springer, Cham (2018). https://doi.org/10.1007/978-3-319-96881-0_18

39. Lazzaretti, A., Papamanthou, C.: Treepir: sublinear-time and polylog-bandwidth private information retrieval from DDH. In: CRYPTO (2023)

40. Li, H., Liu, T.: How to garble mixed circuits that combine Boolean and arithmetic computations. In: Advances in Cryptology – EUROCRYPT 2024: 43rd Annual International Conference on the Theory and Applications of Cryptographic Techniques, Zurich, Switzerland, May 26–30, 2024, Proceedings, Part VI, pp. 331–360. Springer-Verlag, Berlin, Heidelberg (2024). https://doi.org/10.1007/978-3-031-58751-1_12

41. Lin, H., Pass, R.: Succinct garbling schemes and applications. IACR Cryptol. ePrint Arch. **2014**, 766 (2014). https://api.semanticscholar.org/CorpusID:18349655

42. Liu, H., Wang, X., Yang, K., Yu, Y.: BITGC: garbled circuits with 1 bit per gate. In: Advances in Cryptology – EUROCRYPT 2025: 44th Annual International Conference on the Theory and Applications of Cryptographic Techniques, Madrid, Spain, May 4–8, 2025, Proceedings, Part VII, pp. 437–466. Springer-Verlag, Berlin, Heidelberg (2025). https://doi.org/10.1007/978-3-031-91098-2_16

43. Lu, S., Ostrovsky, R.: How to garble ram programs. In: Advances in Cryptology - EUROCRYPT 2013. LNCS, vol. 7881, pp. 719–734. Springer (2013). https://doi.org/10.1007/978-3-642-38348-9_42

44. Lu, S., Ostrovsky, R.: Black-box parallel garbled RAM. In: Katz, J., Shacham, H. (eds.) CRYPTO 2017. LNCS, vol. 10402, pp. 66–92. Springer, Cham (2017). https://doi.org/10.1007/978-3-319-63715-0_3

45. Meyer, P., Orlandi, C., Roy, L., Scholl, P.: Rate-1 arithmetic garbling from homomorphic secret sharing. In: Boyle, E., Mahmoody, M. (eds.) Theory of Cryptography, pp. 71–97. Springer Nature Switzerland, Cham (2025). https://doi.org/10.1007/978-3-031-78023-3_3

46. Meyer, P., Orlandi, C., Roy, L., Scholl, P.: Silent circuit relinearisation: sublinear-size (Boolean and arithmetic) garbled circuits from DCR. In: Tauman Kalai, Y., Kamara, S.F. (eds.) Advances in Cryptology - CRYPTO 2025, pp. 426–458. Springer Nature Switzerland, Cham (2025). https://doi.org/10.1007/978-3-032-01884-7_14

47. Naor, M., Pinkas, B., Sumner, R.: Privacy preserving auctions and mechanism design. In: Proceedings of the 1st ACM Conference on Electronic Commerce, pp. 129–139. EC 1999, Association for Computing Machinery, New York, NY, USA (1999). https://doi.org/10.1145/336992.337028

48. Orlandi, C., Scholl, P., Yakoubov, S.: The rise of paillier: homomorphic secret sharing and public-key silent OT. In: Canteaut, A., Standaert, F.-X. (eds.) EURO-CRYPT 2021. LNCS, vol. 12696, pp. 678–708. Springer, Cham (2021). https://doi.org/10.1007/978-3-030-77870-5_24

49. Paillier, P.: Public-key cryptosystems based on composite degree residuosity classes. In: Stern, J. (ed.) Advances in Cryptology – EUROCRYPT 1999, pp. 223–238. Springer, Berlin Heidelberg (1999). https://doi.org/10.1007/3-540-48910-x_16

50. Park, A., Lin, W.K., Shi, E.: Nanogram: garbled ram with O(LOGN) overhead. In: Advances in Cryptology - EUROCRYPT 2023: 42nd Annual International Conference on the Theory and Applications of Cryptographic Techniques, Lyon, France, April 23-27, 2023, Proceedings, Part I, pp. 456–486. Springer-Verlag, Berlin, Heidelberg (2023). https://doi.org/10.1007/978-3-031-30545-0_16

51. Ren, L., Mughees, M.H., Sun, I.: Simple and practical amortized sublinear private information retrieval using dummy subsets. In: Proceedings of the 2024 on ACM SIGSAC Conference on Computer and Communications Security, pp. 1420–1433. CCS 2024, Association for Computing Machinery, New York, NY, USA (2024)

52. Rosulek, M., Roy, L.: Three halves make a whole? Beating the half-gates lower bound for garbled circuits. In: Advances in Cryptology – CRYPTO 2021: 41st Annual International Cryptology Conference, CRYPTO 2021, Virtual Event, August 16–20, 2021, Proceedings, Part I, pp. 94–124. Springer-Verlag, Berlin, Heidelberg (2021). https://doi.org/10.1007/978-3-030-84242-0_5

53. Roy, L., Singh, J.: Large message homomorphic secret sharing from DCR and applications. In: Advances in Cryptology – CRYPTO 2021: 41st Annual International Cryptology Conference, CRYPTO 2021, Virtual Event, August 16–20, 2021, Proceedings, Part III, pp. 687–717. Springer-Verlag, Berlin, Heidelberg (2021). https://doi.org/10.1007/978-3-030-84252-9_23

54. Shanks, D.: Class number, a theory of factorization and genera. In: Proceedings of the Symposium Pure Mathematics, vol. 20, pp. 415–440. American Mathematical Society, Providence, R.I. (1971)

55. Stefanov, E., et al.: Path Oram: an extremely simple oblivious ram protocol. J. ACM **65**(4) (2018). https://doi.org/10.1145/3177872

56. team, T.F.: FLINT: Fast Library for Number Theory (2025), version 3.3.1. https://flintlib.org

57. Wang, X., Chan, H., Shi, E.: Circuit Oram: on tightness of the goldreich-ostrovsky lower bound. In: Proceedings of the 22nd ACM SIGSAC Conference on Computer and Communications Security, pp. 850–861. CCS 2015, Association for Computing Machinery, New York, NY, USA (2015). https://doi.org/10.1145/2810103.2813634

58. Yang, Y., Peceny, S., Heath, D., Kolesnikov, V.: Towards generic MPC compilers via variable instruction set architectures (visas). In: Proceedings of the 2023 ACM SIGSAC Conference on Computer and Communications Security, pp. 2516–2530. CCS 2023, Association for Computing Machinery, New York, NY, USA (2023). https://doi.org/10.1145/3576915.3616664

59. Yao, A.C.C.: How to generate and exchange secrets. In: 27th Annual Symposium on Foundations of Computer Science (SFCS 1986), pp. 162–167 (1986). https://doi.org/10.1109/SFCS.1986.25

60. Zahur, S., Rosulek, M., Evans, D.: Two halves make a whole - reducing data transfer in garbled circuits using half gates. In: Oswald, E., Fischlin, M. (eds.) Advances in Cryptology - EUROCRYPT 2015 - 34th Annual International Conference on the Theory and Applications of Cryptographic Techniques, Sofia, Bulgaria, April 26-30, 2015, Proceedings, Part II. LNCS, vol. 9057, pp. 220–250. Springer (2015). https://doi.org/10.1007/978-3-662-46803-6_8
61. Zhou, M., Park, A., Shi, E., Zheng, W.: Piano: extremely simple, single-server pir with sublinear server computation. In: IEEE S& P (2024)

Information-Theoretic Network-Agnostic MPC with Polynomial Communication

Xiaoyu Ji[1], Chen-Da Liu-Zhang[2], Daniel Pöllmann[2], and Yifan Song[1,3(✉)]

[1] Tsinghua University, Beijing, China
jixy23@mails.tsinghua.edu.cn, yfsong@mail.tsinghua.edu.cn
[2] Lucerne University of Applied Sciences and Arts, Lucerne, Switzerland
{chen-da.liuzhang,daniel.poellmann}@hslu.ch
[3] Shanghai Qi Zhi Institute, Shanghai, China

Abstract. Network-agnostic MPC protocols tolerate simultaneously a higher number of corruptions $t_s < n/2$ when the network is synchronous, and a lower number $t_a < n/3$ when the network is asynchronous. As such, they provide strong resilience, irrespective of the type of underlying communication network.

We focus on improving the communication complexity of network-agnostic MPC with optimal resilience $2t_s + t_a < n$. In this regime, there are no polynomial-time information-theoretic solutions and current computational protocols (without fully-homomorphic encryption) communicate $O(n^2)$ elements per multiplication gate.

In this work, we significantly advance the landscape by introducing the first information-theoretic protocol with quadratic communication per multiplication gate and the first computational protocol with linear communication per multiplication gate based solely on signatures and symmetric-key encryption.

1 Introduction

The goal of Multi-Party Computation (MPC) is to enable a set of n parties $\mathcal{P} = \{P_1, \ldots, P_n\}$ to jointly compute any arbitrary function on private inputs [Yao82, BGW88, GMW87, CCD88]. The computation is performed in such a way that an adversary does not learn anything beyond the output.

Protocols for MPC can be roughly classified into two models, depending upon the network they operate in. In the synchronous network model, the parties proceed synchronously in rounds. In each round, parties send messages and receive the messages by the end of the round. To implement this round structure, parties are assumed to have synchronized clocks, so they can all start rounds at the same time, and it is also assumed that messages are delivered within a time upper bound Δ, which is an a priori publicly known parameter. In this model, it is possible to achieve MPC for up to $t_s < \frac{n}{2}$ corrupted parties with guaranteed output delivery [RB89, CDD+99, CDN01, DN03, DI05] assuming correlated randomness or broadcast channels. However, the downside is that the protocol may lose all security guarantees if a message is not delivered in time, making

© International Association for Cryptologic Research 2026
J. Daemen and E. Thomé (Eds.): EUROCRYPT 2026, LNCS 16543, pp. 307–336, 2026.
https://doi.org/10.1007/978-3-032-25324-8_11

this model problematic in the real world, where networks may occasionally add significant unpredictable delays.

In the asynchronous model, protocols do not rely on any delay upper-bound, which makes them suitable for even the most unpredictable network conditions. However, this comes at the cost of resilience, and protocols in the asynchronous network model can only support up to $t_a < \frac{n}{3}$ corrupted parties [BKR94, PCR09, CP15, CGHZ16, HNP05, Coh16, CHLZ21, GLZS24, BJK+25b, BJK+25a].

This gave rise to the network-agnostic MPC line of work [BZL20, DHLZ21, BCLZL23, ACC22, AC23, BCV24, PP24] which achieves security guarantees in either network scenario. More precisely, a network-agnostic MPC simultaneously tolerates up to t_s corruptions when the network is synchronous, and t_a corruptions when the network is asynchronous.

Communication Complexity of Network-Agnostic MPC. In the computational setting assuming threshold homomorphic encryption tools and non-interactive zero-knowledge, the first network-agnostic protocols [BZL20, DHLZ21] achieved a communication complexity of $O(n^3)$ field elements per multiplication gate with optimal resilience $t_a + 2t_s < n$. Under the same computational assumptions, the work [BCLZL23] achieved $O(n^2)$ elements per gate. The recent work [BCV24] only makes use of linearly-homomorphic commitments and a PKI for signatures. However, the communication complexity is $O(n^7)$ elements per multiplication gate.

In the information-theoretic setting with optimal resilience $t_a + 2t_s < n$, there are no network-agnostic MPC protocols [AC23] that run in polynomial time against threshold adversaries. The work [ACC22] introduced a polynomial solution communicating $O(n^5/t_a)$ elements in the perfect security setting and $t_a + 3t_s < n$ resilience, and later [PP24] improved the resilience to $2\max(t_s, t_a) + \max(2t_a, t_s) < n$ (albeit with exponential communication).

Compared to the monolithic network setting, recent works in the purely asynchronous setting achieved linear communication per multiplication gate [AAPP24, GLZS24] even with information-theoretic security. This leads to the question of how low one can achieve a similar result with network-agnostic security, or whether there is an inherent communication overhead needed.

Is information-theoretic network-agnostic MPC with linear communication and optimal resilience possible?

1.1   Contributions

We significantly advance the state of the art in the communication complexity of network-agnostic MPC by providing several protocols with optimal resilience. Note that in the setting of information-theoretic protocols with optimal resilience, there are no known solutions even with polynomial time.

Our first result is an information-theoretic MPC with polynomial time and communication as well as optimal resilience. More concretely, our protocol incurs a quadratic communication term next to the circuit size (albeit larger dependencies in the depth). The protocol makes use of a trusted setup for pseudo signatures.

Theorem 1. *Let n, t_s, t_a be positive integers such that $n = 2t_s + t_a + 1$ and κ be the security parameter. Let f be an n-ary function. Assuming a trusted setup for pseudo signatures, there is an unconditionally secure network-agnostic MPC protocol for f among n parties against a malicious adversary who controls up to t_s corrupted parties when the network is synchronous, and t_a corrupted parties when the network is asynchronous.*

For a function f with circuit size $|C|$, input size C_I, output size C_O, and circuit depth D, the MPC protocol requires setup size $O(t_a(n|C|\kappa + n^3 C_I \kappa + n^3 C_O \kappa) + n^6 D\kappa + n^9 \kappa)$ and achieves communication complexity $O(n|C|\kappa + n^3 C_I \kappa + n^3 C_O \kappa + (n^3 + D)n^6 \kappa \log(nD) + n^8 \kappa^2)$ in expectation in the optimistic case and $O(t_a(n|C|\kappa + n^3 C_I \kappa + n^3 C_O \kappa) + n^8 \kappa^2 \cdot D + n^{14} \kappa^2)$ in expectation in the worst case.

We also introduce a computational MPC protocol with linear communication (in the circuit size), but still with larger dependencies in the depth. The protocol also achieves optimal resilience and incurs minimal computational assumptions (only signatures and symmetric-key encryption). The protocol assumes a trusted setup for PKI[1].

Theorem 2. *Let n, t_s, t_a be positive integers such that $n = 2t_s + t_a + 1$ and κ be the security parameter. Let f be an n-ary function. Assuming PKI and symmetric-key encryption schemes, there is a computationally secure network-agnostic MPC protocol for f among n parties against a malicious adversary who controls up to t_s corrupted parties when the network is synchronous, and t_a corrupted parties when the network is asynchronous.*

For a function f with circuit size $|C|$, input size C_I, output size C_O, and circuit depth D, the MPC protocol requires setup size $O(n^2 \kappa)$ and achieves communication complexity $O(n|C|\kappa + n^3 C_I \kappa + n^3 C_O \kappa + (n^3 + D)n^6 \kappa \log(nD) + n^8 \kappa^2)$ in expectation in the optimistic case and $O(n|C|\kappa + n^3 C_I \kappa + n^3 C_O \kappa + n^7 \kappa^2 \cdot D + n^{14} \kappa^2)$ in expectation in the worst case.

1.2 Related Work

The network agnostic model has been studied for multiple primitives including state-machine replication [AMN+20, BKL21, MR21], consensus and broadcast protocols [BKL19, DHLZ21, BKL21, ABKL22, DME24], approximate and convex agreement [GLZW22, GLZW23, CGWW24], secure-message transmission [BCV23, DLZ23], distributed key generation [BCLZL23] and MPC [BZL20, DHLZ21, BCLZL23, ACC22, AC23, BCV24, PP24].

The first network-agnostic (cryptographic) MPC was introduced by Blum, Liu-Zhang and Loss [BZL20], which achieves the optimal resilience of $t_a + 2t_s < n$,

---

[1] Our construction only uses a signature scheme with signature size linearly in the message size.

assuming a trusted setup for threshold additive homomorphic encryption and NIZKs. In the same setting, the work [DHLZ21] proposed a round-efficient solution. Both these works incur $O(n^3)$ per multiplication. The work [BCLZL23] introduced a network-agnostic solution for DKG, which was used to bootstrap the trusted setup of (a more efficient version) of the protocol in [BZL20] from plain bulletin-board PKI, albeit with the same computational assumptions. With the bootstrapping, the incurred cost is still $O(n^3)$ per multiplication; but assuming the trusted setup the authors improved the complexity to $O(n^2)$. The recent work [BCV24] reduced the computational assumptions to linear commitments and signatures, but at the cost of increased communication $O(n^7)$ per multiplication. We further note that assuming fully-homomorphic encryption, it is straightforward to achieve communication independent of the circuit size.

The works [ACC22] introduced provide perfectly secure network-agnostic MPC assuming $t_a + 3t_s < n$ communicating $O(n^5/t_a)$ per multiplication gate. This result was extended to the general adversary setting with perfect security [ACC23] and statistical security [AC23], although the communication complexity grows with the size of the adversary structure, and therefore is exponential for usual choices of threshold adversaries. The work [PP24] defines a perfectly secure MPC protocol under the weaker condition $2\max(t_s, t_a) + \max(2t_a, t_s) < n$, but the efficiency is also exponential.

2   Technical Overview

Recall that we use n for the number of parties, t_s for the synchronous corruption threshold, and t_a for the asynchronous corruption threshold. We further assume that $t_a \leq t_s$ and $n = 2t_s + t_a + 1$. Let Δ be the delivery time-bound for a message sent in the synchronous network.

2.1   Overview of Our Construction

We start with a synchronous MPC protocol $\Pi_{\text{SMPC-GOD}}$ that is secure against t_s corrupted parties with guaranteed output delivery. At a high level, we want to let all parties attempt to execute $\Pi_{\text{SMPC-GOD}}$ in the unknown network setting as follows: (1) In each round, all parties follow $\Pi_{\text{SMPC-GOD}}$ to send messages to each other. (2) Each party, after receiving all messages from other parties, moves on to the next round.

However, this idea may fail entirely when the network is asynchronous due to the following two problems:

- First, a party may not be able to receive all messages from other parties.

When a party A does not receive the desired message from another party B, A cannot distinguish a corrupted B not sending the message from an honest B whose message is delayed due to the large network latency. In the case that B is corrupted, A may wait forever and we lose liveness.

– Second, even if a party has received all messages from other parties in the current round, there is no guarantee that all other parties also have received the desired messages in this round.

Thus, when a party A moves to the next round, another party B may still wait for messages in the current round. However, the security of $\Pi_{\text{SMPC-GOD}}$ may highly rely on the property that when an honest party moves on to the next round, all other honest parties have received their messages in the current round.

Starting Idea. We note that to preserve the security of $\Pi_{\text{SMPC-GOD}}$, it is sufficient to let each party broadcast a confirmation (by using a network-agnostic broadcast protocol Π_{RBC}) claiming that he has received all desired messages in the current round. Then a party only moves to the next round if he has received the confirmations from all parties (including himself). In this way, when an honest party proceeds to the next round, all honest parties have received the desired messages in the current round. Furthermore, by the guarantee of Π_{RBC}, all honest parties will eventually receive all confirmations and move to the next round. This simple modification allows us to prevent an adversary breaking the security of $\Pi_{\text{SMPC-GOD}}$ in the asynchronous setting.

However, it does not resolve the issue of liveness: (1) an honest party A may never receive all desired messages in the current round due to some corrupted party B not sending his message to A, and (2) a corrupted party A may never broadcast the confirmation even if he has received all messages, causing all parties waiting for the confirmations forever. It appears that fully resolving this issue is very difficult or even impossible since in the asynchronous setting, the best resilience one can hope is $t_a < n/3$ whereas in the synchronous setting, the best resilience is $t_s < n/2$.

At the heart of our technique, we propose an ideal functionality $\mathcal{F}_{\text{Channel}}$ that helps all parties pass their messages in each round. Very informally, $\mathcal{F}_{\text{Channel}}$ ensures that for every pair of parties (A, B) where A is the receiver and B is the sender, either (1) A receives his message from B, or (2) all parties identify a party $C \in \{A, B\}$, which is guaranteed to be corrupted if the network is synchronous (but might be an honest party if the network is asynchronous). We refer to this property as *synchronous identifiable abort*.

With $\mathcal{F}_{\text{Channel}}$, in each round, every pair of parties (A, B) use $\mathcal{F}_{\text{Channel}}$ to exchange their messages. Then at the end of this round, all parties would obtain a subset W of identified parties. By the guarantee of $\mathcal{F}_{\text{Channel}}$, for every pair of parties (A, B) that are not in W, they have received desired messages from each other. To deal with parties in W, we note that:

– When the network is synchronous, parties in W are guaranteed to be corrupted. Thus, we may eliminate all parties in W and assume that messages sent by those parties are all-0 strings. This will not break the security of the underlying synchronous protocol $\Pi_{\text{SMPC-GOD}}$.
– When the network is asynchronous, however, W may contain honest parties. Recall that when the network is asynchronous, the number of corrupted parties is bounded by t_a. On the other hand, $\Pi_{\text{SMPC-GOD}}$ can tolerate up to $t_s \geq t_a$

corrupted parties. Thus, as long as $|W| \leq t_s - t_a$, we can still eliminate parties in W and set their messages to be all 0-strings.

Effectively, we just view parties in W as corrupted parties. This is equivalent to an adversary of $\Pi_{\text{SMPC-GOD}}$ who first corrupts t_a parties, and then *adaptively* corrupts parties in W in this round. When $\Pi_{\text{SMPC-GOD}}$ achieves adaptive security, as long as the total number of eliminated parties is bounded by $t_s - t_a$, the security of $\Pi_{\text{SMPC-GOD}}$ remains.

Thus, when $|W| \leq t_s - t_a$, all parties eliminate parties in W and take all 0-strings as messages sent by those parties. When $|W| > t_s - t_a$, further removing parties in W may break the security of $\Pi_{\text{SMPC-GOD}}$ when the network is asynchronous since the total number of effective corrupted parties would be larger than t_s. However, we notice that after eliminating $t_s - t_a$ corrupted parties:

- In the synchronous setting, there are $n - (t_s - t_a) = t_s + 2t_a + 1$ remaining parties and at most $t_s - (t_s - t_a) = t_a$ parties are corrupted (since all eliminated parties are corrupted). In particular, we have $t_s + 2t_a + 1 \geq 3t_a + 1$. Thus for the remaining parties, we are effectively in the $1/3$ corruption case.
- Similarly, in the asynchronous setting, there are $n - (t_s - t_a) = t_s + 2t_a + 1$ remaining parties and at most t_a parties are corrupted (since all eliminated parties can be honest in the worst case). We are still in the $1/3$ corruption case.

Thus, after eliminating $t_s - t_a$ corrupted parties, all parties can fall back to an asynchronous MPC protocol running among the remaining parties with $1/3$ corruption threshold.

2.2 Realization of $\mathcal{F}_{\text{Channel}}$

To realize $\mathcal{F}_{\text{Channel}}$, we first focus on a P2P message from a sender B to a receiver A. As we have discussed above, we want to ensure that either (1) A receives his message from B, or (2) all parties identify a party $C \in \{A, B\}$, which is guaranteed to be corrupted if the network is synchronous (but might be an honest party if the network is asynchronous).

We first assume that when the network is synchronous, for each round, all honest parties enter this round at a similar time. To be more concrete, we assume that the time difference between the starting time of any two honest parties is bounded by Δ. In our compiler, we will ensure this property whenever $\mathcal{F}_{\text{Channel}}$ is invoked when the network is synchronous.

Our construction assumes a signature scheme and makes use of a network-agnostic broadcast protocol Π_{RBC} and a network-agnostic agreement protocol Π_{BA} with the following property:

- When the network is synchronous, if an honest party terminates Π_{RBC} (or Π_{BA}), then all honest parties terminate Π_{RBC} (or Π_{BA}) within Δ time.

We use $\mathtt{Time_{bc}}$ for the running time of Π_{RBC} when the network is synchronous and the dealer is honest. In Sect. 4.3 and Sect. 4.2, we give concrete instantiations of Π_{RBC} and Π_{BA}. At the beginning of the execution, we assume a trusted setup for signatures as described in $\mathcal{F}_{\mathsf{Setup}}$.

Functionality $\mathcal{F}_{\mathsf{Setup}}$

$\mathcal{F}_{\mathsf{Setup}}$ runs with parties $\mathcal{P} = \{P_1, \ldots, P_n\}$ and an adversary $\mathcal{S}$. Let $(\mathtt{Gen}, \mathtt{Sign}, \mathtt{Vrfy})$ be a signature scheme.

1: For each $P_i \in \mathcal{P}$, $\mathcal{F}_{\mathsf{Setup}}$ runs $\mathtt{Gen}(1^\kappa)$ to generate a pair of signing key and verification keys $(\mathsf{sk}^{(i)}, \{\mathsf{vk}_j^{(i)}\}_{j=1}^n)$. Then $\mathcal{F}_{\mathsf{Setup}}$ generates a request-based delayed output to send P_i the signing key $\mathsf{sk}^{(i)}$, and generates a request-based delayed output to send each $P_j \in \mathcal{P}$ the verification key $\mathsf{vk}_j^{(i)}$.

Initial Attempt. At the beginning of each round, A tries to receive the message from B directly. Let $\mathtt{rid}$ denote the index of the current round.

Protocol $\Pi_{\mathrm{P2P\text{-}Send}}(A, B, \mathtt{rid})$

Initial Attempt

1: After B enters the $\mathtt{rid}$-th round, B sends his message m to A.
2: After A enters the $\mathtt{rid}$-th round, A waits for 2Δ time for the message m from B. If A receives the message from B within the time limit, A broadcasts a confirmation $(\mathtt{Confirm}, A, B, \mathtt{rid})$.

Here we set the waiting time to be 2Δ since B may start later than A by Δ, and the message sent by B may require another Δ time to be delivered.

Resend Attempt. Now consider the case where A does not receive the message from B within the time limit. There are two possibilities: either B is corrupted or the network is asynchronous. As observed in [BCV24], for the first case, there is no need to protect the secrecy of B's message. For the second case, we still need to protect the secrecy of B's message but only against t_a corrupted parties.

Thus, to move on, A will ask B to resend his message by distributing a degree-t_a Shamir secret sharing of the message to all parties. Then A will try to collect enough shares from all parties to reconstruct the message. In more details, all parties run the following steps.

Protocol $\Pi_{\mathrm{P2P\text{-}Send}}(A, B, \mathtt{rid})$

Resend Attempt

1: The receiver A broadcasts $(\mathtt{Resend}, A, B, \mathtt{rid})$ to all parties.
2: After entering the $\mathtt{rid}$-th round and receiving $(\mathtt{Resend}, A, B, \mathtt{rid})$ broadcast by A, the sender B samples a random degree-t_a Shamir sharing of his message m, denoted by $[m]_{t_a} := (m_1, \ldots, m_n)$. Then B sends $(\mathtt{Resend}, A, B, \mathtt{rid}, m_i)$ together with his signature to each P_i.

3: For each party P_i, after entering the **rid**-th round and receiving (**Resend**, $A, B,$ **rid**) broadcast by A, if P_i receives (or has received) (**Resend**, $A, B,$ **rid**, m_i) with a valid signature from B within 2Δ time, P_i sends (**Resend**, $A, B,$ **rid**, m_i) and the signature of B to A. Otherwise, P_i sends (**Dispute**, P_i, B) together with his signature to A.

4: Recall that $\mathtt{Time_{bc}}$ is the time required by Π_{RBC} when the dealer is honest and the network is synchronous. The receiver A, after starting Π_{RBC} for (**Resend**, $A, B,$ **rid**), waits for the response from each party P_i for $\mathtt{Time_{bc}} + 4\Delta$ time. A initializes a set **Proof** $= \varnothing$.

- If A receives (**Resend**, $A, B,$ **rid**, m_i) signed by B from P_i, A records m_i.
- If A receives (**Dispute**, P_i, B) with a valid signature from P_i, A adds (**Dispute**, P_i, B) and the signature of P_i to **Proof**.
- Otherwise, A records (**Dispute**, A, P_i).

Finally, A invokes an instance of Π_{RBC} to broadcast a unique message determined as follows:

- If A records m_i from $t_a + 1$ distinct P_i, A reconstructs the secret m and broadcasts a confirmation (**Confirm**, $A, B,$ **rid**).
- If $|\mathbf{Proof}| \geq t_s + 1$, A broadcasts (**Eliminate**, B, **Proof**).
- Otherwise, A broadcasts (**Eliminate**, A).

Note that the last case happens only when A receives at most t_a shares and $|\mathbf{Proof}| \leq t_s$, which implies that A recorded (**Dispute**, A, P_i) for at least $n - t_a - t_s \geq t_s + 1$ distinct P_i.

The key insight of the resending attempt is that a party is eliminated if and only if he has a dispute with at least $t_s + 1$ parties. We ensure that if the network is synchronous, each pair of disputed parties contains at least one corrupted party. Thus, if a party has dispute with $t_s + 1$ parties, this party must be corrupted.

Now we show that if the network is synchronous, no two honest parties will be set dispute in the above process.

- For each pair of honest (P_i, B), when P_i enters the **rid**-th round and receives (**Resend**, $A, B,$ **rid**) broadcast by A, B is guaranteed to enter the **rid**-th round and receive (**Resend**, $A, B,$ **rid**) broadcast by A within Δ time. This also ensures that P_i will receive (**Resend**, $A, B,$ **rid**, m_i) with a valid signature from B within 2Δ time. Thus, P_i will never send (**Dispute**, P_i, B) to A.
- For each pair of honest (A, P_i), A will broadcast (**Resend**, $A, B,$ **rid**) after A enters the **rid**-th round. Then P_i is guaranteed to enter the **rid**-th round and receives (**Resend**, $A, B,$ **rid**) from A within Δ time after A terminates Π_{RBC}. By construction, after another 2Δ time, P_i responses to A either (**Resend**, $A, B,$ **rid**, m_i) signed by B or (**Dispute**, P_i, B). In either case, A will get the response from P_i within 4Δ time and thus A will never record (**Dispute**, A, P_i).

Preserving Liveness. We note that the above process still does not ensure liveness when A is corrupted: A may never broadcast the final message. To preserve liveness, all parties will accuse A if he does not respond in time.

Protocol $\Pi_{\text{P2P-Send}}(A, B, \text{rid})$

Termination

1: Recall that Time_{bc} is the time required by Π_{RBC} when the dealer is honest and the network is synchronous. All parties invoke Π_{BA} and decide their input as follows: After entering the rid-th round, each party P_i waits for $7\Delta + 2\text{Time}_{\text{bc}}$ for the final broadcast message from A.
   - If the received broadcast message is in the form of $(\text{Confirm}, A, B, \text{rid})$, $(\text{Eliminate}, B, \text{Proof})$ (with a valid Proof), or $(\text{Eliminate}, A)$, P_i sets his input of Π_{BA} to be 1.
   - Otherwise P_i sets his input of Π_{BA} to be 0.
2: All parties decide their output based on the result of Π_{BA} and the final broadcast message from A.
   - If Π_{BA} outputs 1 and the final broadcast message from A is $(\text{Confirm}, A, B, \text{rid})$, all parties output $(\text{Confirm}, A, B, \text{rid})$ and A outputs the received message m in addition.
   - If Π_{BA} outputs 1 and the final broadcast message from A is $(\text{Eliminate}, B, \text{Proof})$ (with a valid Proof), all parties output $(\text{Eliminate}, B)$.
   - Otherwise, all parties output $(\text{Eliminate}, A)$.

The analysis of time limit $7\Delta + 2\text{Time}_{\text{bc}}$ is shown in the full version of this paper. When the network is synchronous, an honest P_i will never set his input of Π_{BA} to be 0 for an honest A. When the network is asynchronous, we want agreement on the output of honest parties, that is, all honest parties either agree on that A has received the message m from B or they agree on a party $C \in \{A, B\}$ to be eliminated. The BA protocol, to which honest parties input their bit at time $7\Delta + 2\text{Time}_{\text{bc}}$, guarantees that all honest parties will receive the same output bit and will choose their output accordingly. When the bit is 0, they will all eliminate A, while when the bit is 1, they will accept the output of Π_{RBC} as their output. In this case, Π_{RBC} is guaranteed to terminate as it already terminated for at least one honest party—otherwise BA must have had output 0 due to the validity of BA. Further, we want honest parties to eventually terminate and output the aforementioned decision. It follows directly that all honest parties will terminate $\Pi_{\text{P2P-Send}}$ eventually because all honest parties give input to the BA protocol at time $7\Delta + 2\text{Time}_{\text{bc}}$, which is therefore guaranteed to terminate.

We note that to send a message m of length $|m|$, the resend attempt requires B to send a share of size $|m|$ to each party, which is then passed to A. This results in an $O(n)$ multiplicative factor in the communication complexity. Ideally, A only needs $t_a + 1$ shares to reconstruct the message. In Sect. 5, we show an advanced construction that reduces the overhead to $O(t_a)$ or even $O(1)$ assuming PRG.

Supporting BC Messages. In the synchronous setting, when $t_s \geq n/3$, it is known that guaranteed output delivery is only possible assuming a broadcast channel. Thus, we further extend $\mathcal{F}_{\text{Channel}}$ to support broadcasting messages for each party A. Similar to P2P messages, we want to ensure that either (1) A successfully broadcasts his message m, or (2) all parties identify the party A, which is guaranteed to be corrupted if the network is synchronous (but might be an honest party if the network is asynchronous).

Protocol $\Pi_{\text{BC-Send}}(A, \text{rid})$

1: After A enters the **rid**-th round, A broadcasts his message m to all parties.
2: Recall that Time_{bc} is the time required by Π_{RBC} when the dealer is honest and the network is synchronous. All parties invoke Π_{BA} and decide their input as follows: After entering the **rid**-th round, each party P_i waits for $\Delta + \text{Time}_{\text{bc}}$ for the broadcast message from A.
   - If P_i receives the broadcast message from A within the time limit, P_i sets his input of Π_{BA} to be 1.
   - Otherwise, P_i sets his input of Π_{BA} to be 0.
   If Π_{BA} outputs 1, all parties output the broadcast message m from A. Otherwise, all parties output $(\texttt{Eliminate}, A)$.

We show that when the network is synchronous, an honest party A will not be identified as a corrupted party. It is sufficient to show that in this case, an honest P_i will set his input of Π_{BA} to be 1: After P_i enters the **rid**-th round, A is guaranteed to enter the **rid**-th round within Δ time. Then P_i is guaranteed to receive the broadcast message from A within another Time_{bc}.

When the network is asynchronous, termination for honest parties follows from the termination of Π_{BA} to which all honest parties input their bit at time $\Delta + \text{Time}_{\text{bc}}$. Similar to the argument for $\Pi_{\text{P2P-Send}}$, if Π_{BA} outputs 1, then all honest parties will eventually receive the broadcast message from A.

Summary. To realize $\mathcal{F}_{\text{Channel}}$, we simply invoke $\Pi_{\text{P2P-Send}}$ for every pair of parties and invoke $\Pi_{\text{BC-Send}}$ for every party. To be more concrete,

1. Each party P_i receives $(\text{rid}, m_0^{(i)}, m_1^{(i)}, \ldots, m_n^{(i)})$ as input where **rid** is the round identifier, $m_0^{(i)}$ is the message to be broadcast, and $m_j^{(i)}$ is the message to be sent to P_j.
2. All parties invoke $\Pi_{\text{P2P-Send}}(P_i, P_j, \text{rid})$ to let P_j send his **rid**-th round message $m_i^{(j)}$ to P_i.
3. All parties invoke $\Pi_{\text{BC-Send}}(P_i, \text{rid})$ to let P_i broadcast his **rid**-th round message $m_0^{(i)}$ to all parties.
4. All parties decide the set W as follows.
   - For each call of $\Pi_{\text{P2P-Send}}(P_i, P_j, \text{rid})$, if the output is $(\texttt{Eliminate}, P_i)$, all parties insert P_i in W. If the output is $(\texttt{Eliminate}, P_j)$, all parties insert P_j in W.
   - For each call of $\Pi_{\text{BC-Send}}(P_i, \text{rid})$, if the output is $(\texttt{Eliminate}, P_i)$, all parties insert P_i in W.
5. For each party $P_i \in W$, P_i sets his output to be $(\text{rid}, W, \varnothing)$. For each party $P_i \notin W$, P_i sets his output to be $(\text{rid}, W, \{(m_0^{(j)}, m_i^{(j)})\}_{i \notin W})$.

In Sect. 5, we give the formal descriptions of $\mathcal{F}_{\text{Channel}}$ and our construction, and prove its security.

2.3   Overview of Our Compiler

With $\mathcal{F}_{\mathsf{Channel}}$, we are ready to give a more detailed description of our compiler.

An Initial Attempt. We assume a GOD protocol $\Pi_{\mathsf{SMPC\text{-}GOD}}$ that is secure against t_s corrupted parties in the synchronous setting and a GOD protocol $\Pi_{\mathsf{AMPC\text{-}GOD}}$ that is secure against $1/3$ corruption in the asynchronous setting. All parties initialize a set $W = \varnothing$ at the beginning. Suppose R is the (upper bound of the) number of rounds required by $\Pi_{\mathsf{SMPC\text{-}GOD}}$. From $\mathtt{rid} = 1$ to R, all parties execute the following steps to emulate the $\mathtt{rid}$-th round of $\Pi_{\mathsf{SMPC\text{-}GOD}}$.

1. For each party $P_i \in W$, he sets $m_j^{(i)} = \perp$ for all $j \in \{0, \ldots, n\}$. For each party $P_i \notin W$, he follows $\Pi_{\mathsf{SMPC\text{-}GOD}}$ to compute the broadcast message $m_0^{(i)}$ and each P2P message $m_j^{(i)}$ that is supposed to be sent to P_j for all $j \in \{1, \ldots, n\}$.
2. All parties invoke $\mathcal{F}_{\mathsf{Channel}}$ with inputs $(\mathtt{rid}, m_0^{(i)}, m_1^{(i)}, \ldots, m_n^{(i)})$. Let W' be the set of new identified parties from $\mathcal{F}_{\mathsf{Channel}}$. Then for each party $P_i \in W'$, P_i receives $(\mathtt{rid}, W', \varnothing)$. For each party $P_i \notin W'$, P_i receives $(\mathtt{rid}, W, \{(m_0^{(j)}, m_i^{(j)})\}_{i \notin W})$.
3. All parties set $W = W \cup W'$ and decide their messages received in the $\mathtt{rid}$-th round as follows.
   - For each $P_i \in W$, P_i takes all-0 strings as messages he received in the $\mathtt{rid}$-th round.
   - For each $P_i \notin W$, P_i uses $m_0^{(j)}, m_i^{(j)}$ as the broadcast message and P2P message from P_j for each $P_j \notin W$, and uses all-0 strings as the messages from P_j for each $P_j \in W$.
4. Depending on the size of W and $\mathtt{rid}$, all parties run the following steps.
   - If $|W| \le t_s - t_a$ and $\mathtt{rid} = R$, P_i computes his output following $\Pi_{\mathsf{SMPC\text{-}GOD}}$.
   - If $|W| \le t_s - t_a$ and $\mathtt{rid} < R$, P_i moves to the $(\mathtt{rid} + 1)$-th round of $\Pi_{\mathsf{SMPC\text{-}GOD}}$.
   - Otherwise, all parties take the first $t_s - t_a$ parties in W as the output and terminates.

Recall that in $\mathcal{F}_{\mathsf{Channel}}$, we assume that when the network is synchronous, for each round of $\Pi_{\mathsf{SMPC\text{-}GOD}}$, all honest parties enter the round at a similar time. We show that this is indeed the case in the above sketch. First, this assumption is true for the first round. For each $\mathtt{rid} \ge 2$, an honest party enters the $\mathtt{rid}$-th round after he terminates Π_{RBC} and Π_{BA} in all instances of $\Pi_{\mathsf{P2P\text{-}Send}}$ and $\Pi_{\mathsf{BC\text{-}Send}}$ invoked for the $(\mathtt{rid} - 1)$-th round. By the property of Π_{RBC} and Π_{BA}, every other honest party will terminate these Π_{RBC} and Π_{BA} and thus enter the $\mathtt{rid}$-th round within Δ time.

As we discussed above, after identifying $t_s - t_a$ parties which are guaranteed to be corrupted if the network is synchronous,

- if the network is synchronous, there are at most $t_s - (t_s - t_a) = t_a$ corrupted parties in the remaining $n - (t_s - t_a) = t_s + 2t_a + 1$ parties;

– if the network is asynchronous, there are at most t_a corrupted parties in the remaining $n - (t_s - t_a)$ parties.

In either case, the corruption threshold becomes 1/3 and we can fallback to an asynchronous MPC protocol securely against 1/3 corruption.

Security Issues. Unfortunately, the above construction does not yield a secure network-agnostic MPC protocol. The main issue is that the required security of $\Pi_{\text{SMPC-GOD}}$ does not match the standard adaptive security as we elaborate below.

Recall that when the network is asynchronous, the identified parties can be honest. In our compiler, identified parties are viewed as corrupted parties and all parties just take all-0 strings as messages from identified parties. This means that when the network is asynchronous, an adversary may *adaptively* crash up to $t_s - t_a$ honest parties. Thus, we need $\Pi_{\text{SMPC-GOD}}$ to be secure against the following kind of adversaries:

– The adversary may corrupt a subset of $t \leq t_s$ parties in the beginning of the computation. The adversary will have the full control of the behavior of these parties.
– During the computation, the adversary can adaptively let up to $t_s - t$ honest parties crash. The adversary does *not* have the control of these parties.

Note that by crashing an honest party, the adversary *does not learn* the view, and in particular the input, of this honest party. This is unlike the standard adaptive security where when an honest party is corrupted, the adversary will learn its view and control its behavior.

At a first glance, our required security may sound weaker than the standard adaptive security since the adversary in our case is strictly weaker than that in the standard adaptive security (not being able to access the view and control the behavior of crashed honest parties). Unfortunately, this is not true. The reason is that in our case the ideal adversary (simulator) is also weaker: when crashing an honest party, the ideal adversary does not learn its input. In comparison, in the standard adaptive security, the ideal adversary can learn the input of an honest party when this party becomes corrupted.

We note that this is not an artificial issue. A common strategy of building MPC protocol with GOD is to use party elimination (or dispute control). When a corrupted party is identified, his input can be reconstructed without breaking the security and this trick has been used in [BSFO12] and [GSZ20]. This, however, would break the security in our case since the party being identified can be a crashed honest party.

Another issue is that in our compiler, the emulation of $\Pi_{\text{SMPC-GOD}}$ may fail in the last round. In this case, the adversary may learn the function output but prevent honest parties from learning the function output. Then when falling back to the asynchronous MPC, the adversary can switch to a different set of inputs for corrupted parties, thus breaking the security.

Resolving Security Issues Relying on Robust Secret Sharings. To resolve the above two issues, our idea is to make use of a robust secret sharing (RSS) scheme. Let $[\![s]\!]$ denote a robust secret sharing of the secret s. Very informally, it satisfies that (1) any t_s shares are independent of the secret s, and (2) the secret s can always be reconstructed as long as the number of incorrect shares (from corrupted parties) are bounded by t_s. Such a robust secret sharing scheme can be built with unconditional security for all $t_s < n/2$ [BSFO12].

Recall that the gap between our required security and the standard adaptive security is that when an honest party is crashed in our case, the (ideal) adversary does not learn its input or output. We observe that such a gap can be overcome if either (1) the crashed honest party does not have input/output, or (2) the crashed honest party's input/output are secret shares. In the former case, the view of this crashed honest party can be simulated in the standard adaptive security without requiring any further information. In the latter case, since the total number of crashed honest parties plus the number of corrupted parties is bounded by t_s, by the security of robust secret sharing schemes, this honest party's input/output can be simulated without learning the secrets.

Thus, our construction works in three phases.

Input Phase. We first let each party (acting as the dealer) secret share his input via a robust secret sharing scheme. To be more concrete, we apply our compiler on a synchronous MPC with GOD that securely computes the input sharing functionality with adaptive security.

In this case, only the dealer has input and other parties only have outputs which are secret shares. Thus if the crashed honest party is not the dealer, we may simulate this honest party's share without learning the secret. To deal with the case where the crashed honest party is the dealer, we modify our compiler by letting all parties abort the input sharing protocol when the dealer is crashed and assuming the input sharing protocol fails for this dealer. Intuitively, what an adversary $\mathcal{A}$ can learn in this case is subsumed by the case where $\mathcal{A}$ never crashes the dealer. We show that this can be reduced to an adversary in the standard adaptive security.

Computation Phase. We then apply our compiler on a synchronous MPC with GOD that securely computes from the secret-shared inputs to secret-shared outputs. In this case, all parties' inputs and outputs are secret shares. Following our observation, when an honest party crashed, we may simulate this party's shares without learning the secrets, and reduce the security to the standard adaptive security of the underlying protocol.

Output Phase. Finally, with robust secret sharing of each output value, all parties can reconstruct the outputs. Note that this also addresses the second issue since corrupted parties cannot stop honest parties from reconstructing the outputs at this step.

Fallback Procedure. When a set W of $t_s - t_a$ parties are identified, all parties move to the fallback procedure: Parties that are not in W run an asynchronous MPC with GOD to compute the function output.

Instantiations of Building Blocks. To obtain a network-agnostic MPC only assuming a setup for signatures, we instantiate the building blocks required by our compiler. For robust secret sharing schemes, we follow the technique in [BDOZ11,BFO12] by using pairwise information-theoretic MACs, which is further used in [DEP23]. The sharing size is $O(n^2\kappa)$ bits. Refer to the full version of his paper for more details. For synchronous MPCs, we use the protocols in [BFO12,GSZ20] which can achieve linear communication in the number of parties. For the asynchronous MPC, we use the protocols in [GLZS24,JLS24] that also achieve linear communication. We refer the readers to the full version of this paper for more details.

We note that our compiler can potentially achieve linear communication also in the information-theoretic setting when using a better information-theoretic MPC protocol in the synchronous setting. Recall that in our compiler, it is sufficient to use a synchronous MPC that is secure against t_s corruptions. On the other hand, the instantiations from [BSFO12,GSZ20] are secure in the standard honest majority setting where $t = (n - 1)/2$. In the strong honest majority setting (where there is a gap between the corruption threshold t_s and $n/2$), one can potentially use the packed Shamir secret sharing scheme to further bring down the communication complexity by a factor of $n/2 - t_s = O(t_a)$. This is indeed the case for malicious security with abort [GPS21,GPS22], while the GOD case remains unclear. However, we expect that full security is possible when combining with techniques in [BSFO12,GSZ20].

3   Model

We consider the universal composability (UC) framework [Can01] to prove the security of our protocols. Note that the standard UC framework considers an asynchronous network model where the adversary is allowed to drop messages. We are interested in 1) the synchronous model where parties have access to synchronized clocks and messages are delivered within a publicly known delay, and 2) the asynchronous setting with *eventual delivery*, where messages sent by honest parties are eventually delivered. To capture such models, several variants have been proposed in the literature for synchronous UC [KMTZ13,Can01,LZLM+19,BDD+21] where functionalities keep track of time, and asynchronous UC with eventual delivery [CGHZ16,LZLM+19,CFG+23]. Our protocols can be proven secure in any of those models. When modeling functionalities, we will use the term *request-based delayed output* [Coh16,CP23] to refer to eventual output delivery. Moreover, for functionalities in the synchronous setting, we use the term *time-bound delayed output* to ensure that the output is delivered within a prescribed time-bound, but the adversary may deliver the message earlier. Refer to the full version for more details about the security model.

4   Preliminary

4.1   Signatures

Our construction makes use of a signature scheme. Recall that a signature scheme allows a party P_r to verify the owner and the integrity of a message m received from a sender P_s. We give two instantiations of signature schemes, one with information-theoretic security, and the other one with computational security.

Signature Scheme with Information-Theoretic Security. We first give the syntax of an unconditionally secure signature scheme, which is also referred to as a pseudo-signature, following the definition in [PW96, SHZI02]. Here the key generation algorithm needs to take as input a set $\mathcal{P}$ and two numbers ℓ_s, ℓ_v, where the set $\mathcal{P}$ includes the identities of verifiers who can verify the signatures later ($\mathcal{P}$-verifiable) and the numbers ℓ_s, ℓ_v denote the upper bounds of the signatures that can be generated and verified. To achieve information-theoretic security, each party's verification key cannot be publicly known. That means the signer has a signing key sk and each party $P_i \in \mathcal{P}$ holds a different private verification key vk_i corresponding to sk.

Definition 1. *[PW96, SHZI02] A $\mathcal{P}$-verifiable signature scheme Π consists of three randomized algorithms* (Gen, Sign, Vrfy) *where*

1. ***Key Generation:*** Gen *takes security parameter κ, a set $\mathcal{P}$ and two numbers $\ell_s, \ell_v \in \mathbb{N}$ as inputs and outputs a pair* (sk, **vk**), *where* sk $\in \{0,1\}^\kappa$ *is a signing key,* **vk** $= \{vk_i\}_{i \in \mathcal{P}}$ *and each* $vk_i \in \{0,1\}^\kappa$ *is a verification key corresponding to* sk.
2. ***Signature Generation:*** Sign *takes the message m and the signing key* sk *as inputs and outputs a signature $\sigma \in \{0,1\}^{poly(\kappa)}$.*
3. ***Verification:*** Vrfy *takes the message m, a signature σ and a verification key vk_i as inputs and output a decision-bit $b \in \{0,1\}$.*

We state the security requirement and analyze the cost of an unconditionally secure signature scheme in full version of this paper.

Computationally Secure Signature Scheme. We briefly recall the syntax of a standard signature scheme.

Definition 2. *A computational signature scheme Σ is a triple of efficient algorithms $\Sigma =$* (Gen, Sign, Vrfy), *with the following syntax:*

1. ***Key Generation:*** Gen *takes security parameter κ and outputs a pair* (sk, vk), *where* sk $\in \{0,1\}^\kappa$ *is the signing key, and* vk $\in \{0,1\}^\kappa$ *is the verification key.*
2. ***Signature Generation:*** Sign *takes the message m and the signing key* sk *as inputs and outputs a signature σ.*
3. ***Verification:*** Vrfy *takes the message m, a signature σ and the verification key* vk *as inputs and output a decision-bit $b \in \{0,1\}$.*

We require signatures to satisfy correctness, meaning that Vrfy$(m,$ Sign$(m,$ sk$),$ vk$) = 1$ *for all $m \in \{0,1\}^*$ and for* (sk, vk) $=$ Gen(1^κ). *We also require our signatures to satisfy the standard unforgeability against chosen message attacks [GMR88].*

In our computational protocols we make use of any signature scheme with keys of size $\mathcal{O}(\kappa)$ and signatures of size $\mathcal{O}(\kappa)$ per field element message [ElG85, Sch90, JMV01, BLS01].

4.2   Network Agnostic Byzantine Agreement

In a byzantine agreement (BA) protocol, each party P_i takes a message $m_i \in \mathcal{M}$ as input, where $\mathcal{M}$ is the message space which contains $\perp$. The protocol allows all parties to agree on a common message in $\mathcal{M}$. We recall the property-based definition of a BA protocol as follows.

Definition 3. *Let t be the corruption threshold and Π be a protocol executed by parties $\mathcal{P} = \{P_1, \ldots, P_n\}$, where each party initially holds an input $m_i \in \mathcal{M}$, and all parties terminate upon getting output.*

- *t-**Validity:** If all honest parties have the same input $m \in \mathcal{M}$, then all honest parties take m as output.*
- *t-**Consistency:** Honest parties do not obtain different outputs in $\mathcal{M}$.*
- *t-**Termination:** Suppose all honest parties participate in the protocol with their inputs in $\mathcal{M}$, and they never stop participating until termination. Then all honest parties terminate with a valid output in $\mathcal{M}$.*

For a BA protocol Π, if Π achieves t-validity, t-consistency, and t-termination, we say Π is t-secure. We say Π is a network agnostic BA protocol if Π is t_s-secure in the synchronous setting and t_a-secure in the asynchronous setting. When the network is synchronous, the t_s-termination property guarantees that all honest parties would terminate Π within a deterministic delay, which depends on their starting time. We use $\mathtt{Time}_{\mathsf{ba}}$ to denote the running time when the starting time of all honest parties differ by at most Δ.

In this work, we require all honest parties to terminate the BA protocol at a similar time in the synchronous network. We refer the reader to the full version of this paper to see how this is achieved, and the cost in different settings.

4.3   Network Agnostic Reliably Broadcast

In a reliably broadcast (RBC) protocol, a sender P_s takes a message $m \in \mathcal{M}$ as input, where $\mathcal{M}$ is the message space which contains $\perp$. The protocol allows the sender to consistently distribute the message m among a set of parties. We recall the property-based definition of RBC protocol as follows.

Definition 4. *Let t be the corruption threshold and Π be a protocol executed by parties $\mathcal{P} = \{P_1, \ldots, P_n\}$, where a sender $P_s \in \mathcal{P}$ holds an input $m \in \mathcal{M}$, and all parties terminate upon getting output.*

- *t-**Validity:** If the sender P_s is honest, then every honest parties output m.*
- *t-**Consistency:** If an honest party terminates, then his output is a valid message $m' \in \mathcal{M}$, and all honest parties will eventually terminate with output m'.*

If Π achieves t-validity and t-consistency, we say that Π is t-secure. A network agnostic RBC protocol is t_s-secure in the synchronous setting and t_a-secure in the asynchronous setting. Based on a network agnostic BA protocol Π_{BA}, we can realize RBC protocol by first letting the sender P_s send the message m to all parties, then all parties invoke Π_{BA} with the message received from the sender, and finally terminate with the output of Π_{BA}. We denote this RBC protocol as Π_{RBC} and we can also ensure that all honest parties terminate at a similar time in the synchronous network. The asymptotic cost of Π_{RBC} is identical to that of Π_{BA} in Sect. 4.2. We use $\mathtt{Time}_{\mathsf{bc}}$ to denote the running time of Π_{RBC} when the dealer is honest. Note that if the dealer is honest, then all honest parties will receive the broadcast message within Δ time, which ensures that the starting time of the underlying Π_{BA} of all honest parties differ by at most Δ.

4.4 Robust Secret Sharing

Informally, a (t, n)-robust secret sharing scheme allows a dealer D to share a secret s to all parties such that any t shares are independent of the secret. When needed, all parties can together reconstruct the secret s even with t incorrect shares (provided by corrupted parties). Our construction further requires the robust secret sharing scheme to achieve adaptive secrecy, online reconstruction, and efficient resampling.

Informally, the adaptive secrecy allows the adversary to learn t shares chosen adaptively while still preserving the privacy of the secret. Online reconstruction allows the receiver to reconstruct the secret even if the network is asynchronous (where honest parties' shares come one by one with unknown delay and corrupted parties may not send their shares). Efficient resampling allows us to resample the shares of honest parties given the shares of corrupted parties and the secret. We refer the readers to the full version of this paper for the formal definition and the instantiation.

5 Secure Channel with Synchronous Identifiable Abort

In this section, we give the formal description of the functionality $\mathcal{F}_{\mathsf{Channel}}$. Recall that we use n for the number of parties, t_s for the synchronous corruption threshold, and t_a for the asynchronous corruption threshold. We further assume that $t_a \leq t_s$ and $n = 2t_s + t_a + 1$.

In the beginning, the functionality $\mathcal{F}_{\mathsf{Channel}}$ takes as input two parameters Δ and τ_{synch}, where Δ is the delivery time-bound for a message sent in the synchronous network and τ_{synch} is the time-bound for giving outputs of honest parties in the synchronous mode. The functionality $\mathcal{F}_{\mathsf{Channel}}$ runs in two different modes. In the synchronous mode, we assume that all honest parties enter each round at a similar time (with time difference bounded by Δ). And all parties will move on to the next round only after the current round is finished. In each round, $\mathcal{F}_{\mathsf{Channel}}$ first records the messages $(m_0^{(i)}, m_1^{(i)}, \ldots, m_n^{(i)})$ to be sent by each party P_i. Here $m_0^{(i)}$ represents the broadcast message, and $m_j^{(i)}$ represents the message to be sent to P_j. Before the timeout τ_{synch}, the adversary may choose a subset W of parties in $\mathcal{C}orr$ and $\mathcal{F}_{\mathsf{Channel}}$ will distribute messages to each party that is not in W. The set W represents the identified parties in this round. The functionality $\mathcal{F}_{\mathsf{Channel}}$ guarantees that if an honest party terminates the current round, then all other honest parties terminate the current round within Δ time. In the asynchronous mode, parties may enter each round at a different time. In this case, we allow the adversary $\mathcal{S}$ to choose any subset W of parties in $\mathcal{P}$.

Functionality $\mathcal{F}_{\mathsf{Channel}}$

$\mathcal{F}_{\mathsf{Channel}}$ is parameterized by a set $\mathcal{P} = \{P_1, \ldots, P_n\}$, an adversary $\mathcal{S}$, corruption threshold t_s, t_a, and a variable $\mathsf{mode} \in \{\mathsf{synch}, \mathsf{asynch}\}$. $\mathcal{F}_{\mathsf{Channel}}$ receives the delivery time-bound Δ for a message sent in the synchronous network. In addition, $\mathcal{F}_{\mathsf{Channel}}$ has timeout τ_{synch} for giving outputs of honest parties in the synchronous mode.

$\mathcal{F}_{\mathsf{Channel}}$ receives a set $\mathcal{R}$ of valid round ids.

<u>Initialization</u>

1: $\mathcal{F}_{\mathsf{Channel}}$ receives the set $\mathcal{C}orr$ of corrupted parties from $\mathcal{S}$ and the network configuration $\mathsf{mode} \in \{\mathsf{synch}, \mathsf{asynch}\}$. $\mathcal{F}_{\mathsf{Channel}}$ checks that $|\mathcal{C}orr| \leq t_s$ if $\mathsf{mode} = \mathsf{synch}$ and $|\mathcal{C}orr| \leq t_a$ if $\mathsf{mode} = \mathsf{asynch}$. If not, $\mathcal{F}_{\mathsf{Channel}}$ gives up the security[a].

2: $\mathcal{F}_{\mathsf{Channel}}$ initiates a working round id $\mathtt{wID} = \perp$ and a set of used round ids $\mathcal{U} = \varnothing$.

---

[a] By giving up the security, $\mathcal{F}_{\mathsf{Channel}}$ sends its view to $\mathcal{S}$ and allows $\mathcal{S}$ to arbitrarily decide the output of honest parties and the delivery time.

Functionality $\mathcal{F}_{\mathsf{Channel}}$

Synchronous: $\mathsf{mode} = \mathsf{synch}$

1: Upon receiving a request $(\mathtt{rid}, m_0^{(i)}, m_1^{(i)}, \ldots, m_n^{(i)})$ from P_i such that $\mathtt{rid} \in \mathcal{R}$, $\mathcal{F}_{\mathsf{Channel}}$ records the request and ignores all other requests starting with $\mathtt{rid}$ from P_i. Furthermore, if P_i is honest, $\mathcal{F}_{\mathsf{Channel}}$ does the following: $\mathcal{F}_{\mathsf{Channel}}$ sends $(P_i, \mathtt{rid}, m_0^{(i)}, \{m_j^{(i)}\}_{j \in \mathcal{C}orr})$ and its receiving time τ to $\mathcal{S}$. Then
- If $\mathtt{wID} = \perp$ and $\mathtt{rid} \notin \mathcal{U}$, $\mathcal{F}_{\mathsf{Channel}}$ sets $\mathtt{wID} = \mathtt{rid}$, records its receiving time $\tau_{\mathtt{rid}} := \tau$, and adds $\mathtt{rid}$ to $\mathcal{U}$.
- If $\mathtt{wID} = \mathtt{rid}$ and $\tau \leq \tau_{\mathtt{rid}} + \Delta$, $\mathcal{F}_{\mathsf{Channel}}$ continues.
- In all other cases, $\mathcal{F}_{\mathsf{Channel}}$ gives up the security.

2: Upon reaching time $\tau_{\mathtt{rid}} + \Delta$, $\mathcal{F}_{\mathsf{Channel}}$ checks whether he has recorded $(\mathtt{rid}, m_0^{(i)}, m_1^{(i)}, \ldots, m_n^{(i)})$ for every honest party P_i. If not, $\mathcal{F}_{\mathsf{Channel}}$ gives up the security.

3: Upon receiving $(\mathsf{Proceed}, \mathtt{rid}, W)$ from $\mathcal{S}$ at time τ such that $\mathtt{rid} \in \mathcal{R}$, $\mathcal{F}_{\mathsf{Channel}}$ checks that (1) $\mathtt{wID} = \mathtt{rid}$, (2) $\tau \leq \tau_{\mathtt{rid}} + \tau_{\mathsf{synch}}$, (3) $W \subset \mathcal{C}orr$, and (4) for each $P_i \notin W$, $\mathcal{F}_{\mathsf{Channel}}$ has received the request $(\mathtt{rid}, m_0^{(i)}, m_1^{(i)}, \ldots, m_n^{(i)})$ from P_i. If not, $\mathcal{F}_{\mathsf{Channel}}$ ignores this message. Otherwise, $\mathcal{F}_{\mathsf{Channel}}$ sets $\mathtt{wID} = \perp$ and for each honest P_j, $\mathcal{F}_{\mathsf{Channel}}$ sends a time-bound delayed output $(\mathtt{rid}, W, \{(i, m_0^{(i)}, m_j^{(i)})\}_{i \notin W})$ to P_j with time-bound $\tau + \Delta$.

Here a time-bound delayed output ensures that the functionality $\mathcal{F}_{\mathsf{Channel}}$ will deliver the message within the time-bound, while the adversary $\mathcal{S}$ may ask to deliver the message before the time-bound.

4: Upon reaching time $\tau_{\mathtt{rid}} + \tau_{\mathsf{synch}}$, if $\mathtt{wID} \neq \mathtt{rid}$, $\mathcal{F}_{\mathsf{Channel}}$ continues. Otherwise, $\mathcal{F}_{\mathsf{Channel}}$ checks that for each $P_i \notin \mathcal{C}orr$, $\mathcal{F}_{\mathsf{Channel}}$ has received the request $(\mathtt{rid}, m_0^{(i)}, m_1^{(i)}, \ldots, m_n^{(i)})$ from P_i.
  - If true, $\mathcal{F}_{\mathsf{Channel}}$ sets $\mathtt{wID} = \perp$, and for each honest P_j, $\mathcal{F}_{\mathsf{Channel}}$ sends $(\mathtt{rid}, \mathcal{C}orr, \{(i, m_0^{(i)}, m_j^{(i)})\}_{i \notin \mathcal{C}orr})$ to P_j.
  - Otherwise, $\mathcal{F}_{\mathsf{Channel}}$ gives up the security.

Functionality $\mathcal{F}_{\mathsf{Channel}}$

Asynchronous: mode $=$ asynch

1: Upon receiving a request $(\mathtt{rid}, m_0^{(i)}, m_1^{(i)}, \ldots, m_n^{(i)})$ from P_i such that $\mathtt{rid} \in \mathcal{R}$, $\mathcal{F}_{\mathsf{Channel}}$ records the request and ignores all other requests starting with $\mathtt{rid}$ from P_i. Furthermore, if P_i is an honest party, $\mathcal{F}_{\mathsf{Channel}}$ does the following: $\mathcal{F}_{\mathsf{Channel}}$ sends $(P_i, \mathtt{rid}, m_0^{(i)}, \{m_j^{(i)}\}_{j \in \mathcal{C}orr})$ to $\mathcal{S}$. If this is the first request starting with $\mathtt{rid}$ from an honest party, for each honest party P_j, $\mathcal{F}_{\mathsf{Channel}}$ sends a request-based delayed output $(\mathtt{rid}, \mathcal{P}, \varnothing)$ to P_j.

2: Upon receiving $(\mathsf{Proceed}, \mathtt{rid}, W)$ from $\mathcal{S}$ such that $\mathtt{rid} \in \mathcal{R}$, $\mathcal{F}_{\mathsf{Channel}}$ checks that (1) $\mathtt{rid} \notin \mathcal{U}$, (2) for each $P_i \notin W$, $\mathcal{F}_{\mathsf{Channel}}$ has received the request $(\mathtt{rid}, m_0^{(i)}, m_1^{(i)}, \ldots, m_n^{(i)})$ from P_i, and (3) $(\mathtt{rid}, \mathcal{P}, \varnothing)$ has not been delivered to any honest party. If not, $\mathcal{F}_{\mathsf{Channel}}$ ignores this message. Otherwise, $\mathcal{F}_{\mathsf{Channel}}$ adds $\mathtt{rid}$ in $\mathcal{U}$. Then for each honest $P_j \in W$, $\mathcal{F}_{\mathsf{Channel}}$ replaces the request-based delayed output $(\mathtt{rid}, \mathcal{P}, \varnothing)$ for P_j by $(\mathtt{rid}, W, \varnothing)$. For each honest $P_j \notin W$, $\mathcal{F}_{\mathsf{Channel}}$ replaces the request-based delayed output $(\mathtt{rid}, \mathcal{P}, \varnothing)$ for P_j by $(\mathtt{rid}, W, \{(i, m_0^{(i)}, m_j^{(i)})\}_{i \notin W})$.

5.1 Realizing $\Pi_{\mathsf{P2P\text{-}Send}}$ and $\Pi_{\mathsf{BC\text{-}Send}}$

To realize $\mathcal{F}_{\mathsf{Channel}}$, we first focus on a P2P message from a sender B to a receiver A. Following the discussion in Sect. 2.2, we assume that when the network is synchronous, for each round, all honest parties enter this round at a similar time. To be more concrete, we assume that the time difference between the starting time of any two honest parties is bounded by Δ. Recall that Δ is the delivery time-bound for a message sent in the synchronous network.

Our construction assumes a signature scheme and makes use of a network-agnostic broadcast protocol Π_{RBC} and a network-agnostic agreement protocol Π_{BA} with the following property:

– When the network is synchronous, if an honest party terminates Π_{RBC} (or Π_{BA}), then all honest parties terminate Π_{RBC} (or Π_{BA}) within Δ time.

We use $\mathtt{Time_{bc}}$ for the running time of Π_{RBC} when the network is synchronous and the dealer is honest, and $\mathtt{Time_{ba}}$ for the running time of Π_{BA} when the network is synchronous and the starting time of all honest parties differs by Δ at most. At the beginning of the execution, we assume a trusted setup for signatures as described in $\mathcal{F}_{\mathsf{Setup}}$ (Sect. 2.2).

In the following, we directly present our construction with $O(t_a)$ multiplicative overhead. The initial sending attempt remains unchanged (See Sect. 2.2 for more details).

Advanced Resend Attempt. At a high level, when the initial attempt fails, the receiver A will propose a set of $t_a + 1$ parties which are not disputed with either A or B as the intermediates that pass the shares from B to A. If the resend attempt fails, A will identify new parties that are either disputed with A or B. Then A will repeat the above process. Note that across the whole execution, the resend attempt will fail at most n times. This ensures that the amortized communication overhead of simulating the P2P channel is $O(t_a)$.

Protocol $\Pi_{\mathsf{P2P\text{-}Send}}(A, B, \mathtt{rid})$

Advanced Resend Attempt

The receiver A maintains two sets of parties D_A and D_B, which contain parties that have dispute with A and B respectively. A also maintains the set $\mathtt{Proof}$ which contains $(\mathtt{Dispute}, P_i, B)$ with a valid signature from P_i for each $P_i \in D_B$. A maintains a counter $\mathtt{ReCount}$ representing the number of resend attempts for B's messages, which is set to 0 in the beginning of the whole execution. Let R be the (upper bound of the) number of rounds.

A repeats the following steps until one of the following three conditions is satisfied: (1) A receives $t_a + 1$ message shares; (2) $|D_A| \geq t_s + 1$; (3) $|D_B| \geq t_s + 1$.

1: The receiver A updates $\mathtt{ReCount} := \mathtt{ReCount} + 1$. Then A chooses the set S of the first $t_a + 1$ parties that are not in $D_A \cup D_B$ and broadcasts $(\mathtt{Resend}, A, B, \mathtt{ReCount}, \mathtt{rid}, S)$. Here we use $(\mathtt{Resend}, A, B, \mathtt{ReCount})$ as the unique identifier for the broadcast message $(\mathtt{Resend}, A, B, \mathtt{ReCount}, \mathtt{rid}, S)$. We require that all parties only participate Π_{RBC} with identifier $(\mathtt{Resend}, A, B, \mathtt{ReCount})$ when $1 \leq \mathtt{ReCount} \leq n + R$.

2: The sender B samples a random degree-t_a Shamir sharing of his message m, denoted by $[m]_{t_a} := (m_1, \ldots, m_n)$. This step only runs once.

3: Each party P_i, upon receiving $(\mathtt{Resend}, A, B, \mathtt{ReCount}, \mathtt{rid}, S)$ broadcast by A, if $|S| = t_a + 1$, P_i accepts and records the request. Otherwise, P_i rejects the request.

4: The sender B, after entering the **rid**-th round and accepting $(\texttt{Resend}, A, B, \texttt{ReCount}, \texttt{rid}, S)$, sends $(\texttt{Resend}, A, B, \texttt{rid}, m_i)$ together with his signature to each $P_i \in S$.

5: Each party P_i, after entering the **rid**-th round and accepting $(\texttt{Resend}, A, B, \texttt{ReCount}, \texttt{rid}, S)$, if P_i receives (or has received) $(\texttt{Resend}, A, B, \texttt{rid}, m_i)$ with a valid signature from B within 2Δ time, P_i sends $(\texttt{Resend}, A, B, \texttt{rid}, m_i)$ and the signature of B to A. Otherwise, P_i sends $(\texttt{Dispute}, P_i, B)$ together with his signature to A.

6: Recall that $\texttt{Time}_{\text{bc}}$ is the time required by Π_{RBC} when the dealer is honest and the network is synchronous. The receiver A, after starting Π_{RBC} for $(\texttt{Resend}, A, B, \texttt{ReCount}, \texttt{rid}, S)$, waits for the response from each party $P_i \in S$ for $\texttt{Time}_{\text{bc}} + 4\Delta$ time.

  - If A receives $(\texttt{Resend}, A, B, \texttt{rid}, m_i)$ signed by B from P_i, A records m_i.
  - If A receives $(\texttt{Dispute}, P_i, B)$ with a valid signature from P_i, A adds $(\texttt{Dispute}, P_i, B)$ and the signature of P_i to $\texttt{Proof}$ and adds P_i to D_B.
  - Otherwise, A adds P_i to D_A.

If A records m_i from $t_a + 1$ distinct P_i, A reconstructs the secret m and broadcasts a confirmation $(\texttt{Confirm}, A, B, \texttt{rid})$. If $|D_B| \geq t_s + 1$, A broadcasts $(\texttt{Eliminate}, B, \texttt{Proof})$. Otherwise, A broadcasts $(\texttt{Eliminate}, A)$. Note that the last case happens only when A receives at most t_a shares and $|D_A| \leq t_s$, which implies that A recorded $(\texttt{Dispute}, A, P_i)$ for at least $n - t_a - t_s \geq t_s + 1$ distinct P_i.

In the full version of this paper, we argue that when the network is synchronous, no two honest parties will be set as disputed in the above process. Then to preserve liveness, all parties will accuse A if he does not respond on time.

Protocol $\Pi_{\text{P2P-Send}}(A, B, \texttt{rid})$

Advanced Termination

1: Recall that $\texttt{Time}_{\text{bc}}$ is the time required by Π_{RBC} when the dealer is honest and the network is synchronous. All parties invoke Π_{BA} and decide their input as follows: After entering the **rid**-th round, each party P_i waits for $3\Delta + \texttt{Time}_{\text{bc}} + n(4\Delta + \texttt{Time}_{\text{bc}})$ for the broadcast message from A.

  - If the received broadcast message is in the form of $(\texttt{Confirm}, A, B, \texttt{rid})$, $(\texttt{Eliminate}, B, \texttt{Proof})$ (with a valid $\texttt{Proof}$), or $(\texttt{Eliminate}, A)$, P_i sets his input of Π_{BA} to be 1.
  - Otherwise P_i sets his input of Π_{BA} to be 0.

2: All parties decide their output based on the result of Π_{BA} and the final broadcast message from A.

  - If Π_{BA} outputs 1 and the final broadcast message from A is $(\texttt{Confirm}, A, B, \texttt{rid})$, all parties output $(\texttt{Confirm}, A, B, \texttt{rid})$ and A outputs the received message m in addition.
  - If Π_{BA} outputs 1 and the final broadcast message from A is $(\texttt{Eliminate}, B, \texttt{Proof})$ (with a valid $\texttt{Proof}$), all parties output $(\texttt{Eliminate}, B)$.

> – Otherwise, all parties output (**Eliminate**, A).

The analysis of time limit $3\Delta + \text{Time}_{\text{bc}} + n(4\Delta + \text{Time}_{\text{bc}})$ is shown in the full version of this paper. When the network is synchronous, an honest P_i will never set his input of Π_{BA} to be 0 for an honest A.

Realizing $\Pi_{\text{BC-Send}}$. The realization of $\Pi_{\text{BC-Send}}$ remains the same as described in Sect. 2.2. We omit the repetition and refer the readers to Sect. 2.2 for more details.

5.2   Realization of $\mathcal{F}_{\text{Channel}}$

Now we are ready to present Π_{Channel} that securely realizes $\mathcal{F}_{\text{Channel}}$ in the network-agnostic setting.

Protocol Π_{Channel}

All parties receive as public parameters a set $\mathcal{P} = \{P_1, \ldots, P_n\}$, corruption threshold t_s, t_a, the delivery time-bound Δ for a message sent in the synchronous network, and a set $\mathcal{R}$ of valid round ids.

Initialization

1: All parties invoke $\mathcal{F}_{\text{Setup}}$ to receive the signing keys and verification keys.
2: All parties set $R = |\mathcal{R}|$.

Online Phase

1: Each party P_i, upon receiving the request $(\text{rid}, m_0^{(i)}, m_1^{(i)}, \ldots, m_n^{(i)})$ from the environment $\mathcal{E}$, checks that $\text{rid} \in R$. If true, P_i takes $m_0^{(i)}$ as the broadcast message, and $m_j^{(i)}$ as the P2P message for P_j. Then P_i invokes $\Pi_{\text{P2P-Send}}(A, B, \text{rid})$ for every $A, B \in \mathcal{P}$, and invokes $\Pi_{\text{BC-Send}}(A, \text{rid})$ for every $A \in \mathcal{P}$.
2: All parties decide the set W as follows.
   - For each call of $\Pi_{\text{P2P-Send}}(P_i, P_j, \text{rid})$, if the output is (**Eliminate**, P), all parties insert P in W.
   - For each call of $\Pi_{\text{BC-Send}}(P_i, \text{rid})$, if the output is (**Eliminate**, P_i), all parties insert P_i in W.
3: For each party $P_i \in W$, P_i sets his output to be $(\text{rid}, W, \varnothing)$. For each party $P_i \notin W$, P_i sets his output to be $(\text{rid}, W, \{(m_0^{(j)}, m_i^{(j)})\}_{j \notin W})$.

Lemma 1. *Let n, t_s, t_a be positive integers such that $n = 2t_s + t_a + 1$. Let* (**Gen**, **Sign**, **Vrfy**) *be a signature scheme. Then Π_{Channel} is a network-agnostic MPC protocol in the $\mathcal{F}_{\text{Setup}}$-hybrid model that securely computes $\mathcal{F}_{\text{Channel}}$ against an adversary who may control up to t_s corrupted parties when the network is synchronous, and t_a corrupted parties when the network is asynchronous.*

We refer the readers to the full version of this paper for cost analysis and the proof of Lemma 1.

Realization of $\mathcal{F}_{\mathsf{Channel}}$ with Computational Security and Constant Overhead. Refer to the full version of this paper for the discussion of this part.

6 Agnostic MPC Compiler

In this section, we give the formal description of our compiler.

Required Functionalities in the Synchronous Setting. Let $f : (\{0,1\}^* \cup \{\perp\})^n \to \{0,1\}^*$ be the function that all parties wish to compute. Without loss of generality, we assume all parties receive the same output. Let $(\mathtt{Share}, \mathtt{Recon})$ be a (t_s, n)-robust secret sharing scheme with adaptive secrecy, online reconstruction, and efficient resampling.

We define the following two functionalities $\mathcal{F}_{\mathsf{Input}}, \mathcal{F}_{\mathsf{Comp}}$. Informally, $\mathcal{F}_{\mathsf{Input}}$ allows a single dealer D to distribute a robust secret sharing of his secret s. $\mathcal{F}_{\mathsf{Comp}}$ takes as input a set of robust secret sharings, computes the function f on the secrets of these robust secret sharings, and distributes the robust secret sharing of the function output to all parties.

Functionality $\mathcal{F}_{\mathsf{Input}}(D)$

$\mathcal{F}_{\mathsf{Input}}$ runs with parties $\mathcal{P} = \{P_1, \ldots, P_n\}$, a dealer $D \in \mathcal{P}$, and an adversary $\mathcal{S}$.

1: $\mathcal{F}_{\mathsf{Input}}$ receives the set $Corr$ of up to t_s corrupted parties from $\mathcal{S}$.
2: $\mathcal{F}_{\mathsf{Input}}$ receives the input s from D.
3: $\mathcal{F}_{\mathsf{Input}}$ generates a random robust secret sharing of s, denoted by $[\![s]\!]$. $\mathcal{F}_{\mathsf{Input}}$ distributes the shares of $[\![s]\!]$ to all parties.
4: Whenever $\mathcal{F}_{\mathsf{Input}}$ receives $(\mathtt{corrupt}, P_i)$ from $\mathcal{S}$, if $P_i \notin Corr$ and $|Corr| < t_s$, $\mathcal{F}_{\mathsf{Input}}$ adds P_i in $Corr$ and sends P_i's share of $[\![s]\!]$ to P_i. If $P_i = D$, $\mathcal{F}_{\mathsf{Input}}$ also sends s to $\mathcal{S}$.

Functionality $\mathcal{F}_{\mathsf{Comp}}$

$\mathcal{F}_{\mathsf{Comp}}$ runs with parties $\mathcal{P} = \{P_1, \ldots, P_n\}$ and an adversary $\mathcal{S}$.

1: $\mathcal{F}_{\mathsf{Comp}}$ receives the set $Corr$ of up to t_s corrupted parties from $\mathcal{S}$.
2: $\mathcal{F}_{\mathsf{Comp}}$ receives the set $\mathcal{I} \subset \mathcal{P}$ and for each $P_i \in \mathcal{I}$, $\mathcal{F}_{\mathsf{Comp}}$ receives the shares of $[\![x_i]\!]$ of honest parties.
3: For each $P_i \in \mathcal{I}$, $\mathcal{F}_{\mathsf{Comp}}$ reconstructs x_i from honest parties' shares of $[\![x_i]\!]$. For each $P_i \notin \mathcal{I}$, $\mathcal{F}_{\mathsf{Comp}}$ sets $x_i = \perp$. Then $\mathcal{F}_{\mathsf{Comp}}$ computes $y = f(x_1, \ldots, x_n)$ and generates n random robust secret sharings of y, denoted by $\{[\![y_i]\!]\}_{i=1}^n$. $\mathcal{F}_{\mathsf{Comp}}$ distributes the shares of $\{[\![y_i]\!]\}_{i=1}^n$ to all parties.
4: Whenever $\mathcal{F}_{\mathsf{Comp}}$ receives $(\mathtt{corrupt}, P_i)$ from $\mathcal{S}$, if $P_i \notin Corr$ and $|Corr| < t_s$, $\mathcal{F}_{\mathsf{Comp}}$ adds P_i in $Corr$ and sends P_i's shares of each $[\![s]\!] \in \{[\![x_i]\!]\}_{P_i \in \mathcal{I}} \cup \{[\![y_i]\!]\}_{i=1}^n$ to P_i.

6.1 Our Compiler

Now we are ready to introduce our compiler, which assumes (1) synchronous MPC protocols with GOD, Π_{Input} and Π_{Comp}, that securely compute $\mathcal{F}_{\text{Input}}$ and $\mathcal{F}_{\text{Comp}}$ against t_s corrupted parties (among $2t_s + t_a + 1$ parties) with adaptive security assuming a broadcast channel, and (2) an asynchronous MPC protocol with GOD, $\Pi_{\text{AMPC-GOD}}$, that securely compute $\mathcal{F}_{\text{AMPC}}$ (defined in the full version of this paper) against t_a corrupted parties (among $t_s + 2t_a + 1$ parties). We further assume that the asynchronous MPC will take all honest parties' inputs when running in the synchronous network.

Protocol Π_{Compiler}

Setup

Let Π_{Input} be a synchronous MPC with GOD that securely computes $\mathcal{F}_{\text{Input}}$ against t_s corrupted parties with adaptive security assuming a broadcast channel. Suppose R_I is the (upper bound of the) number of rounds required by Π_{Input}. Let Π_{Comp} be a synchronous MPC with GOD that securely computes $\mathcal{F}_{\text{Comp}}$ against t_s corrupted parties with adaptive security assuming a broadcast channel. Suppose R_C is the (upper bound of the) number of rounds required by Π_{Comp}. Let $\Pi_{\text{AMPC-GOD}}$ be an asynchronous MPC protocol that securely computes $\mathcal{F}_{\text{AMPC}}$ among $t_s + 2t_a + 1$ parties against t_a corruption.

All parties define $\mathcal{R} = \{(\Pi_{\text{Input}}, P_i, j)\}_{i\in[n], j\in[R_I]} \cup \{(\Pi_{\text{Comp}}, j)\}_{j\in[R_C]}$. Then all parties invoke $\mathcal{F}_{\text{Channel}}$.

Input Phase

All parties initialize a set $\mathcal{I} = \varnothing$ at the beginning. For every $D \in \{P_1, \ldots, P_n\}\backslash\mathcal{W}$, from $\mathtt{rid} = 1$ to R_I, all parties execute the following steps sequentially.

1: Each party $P_i \notin \mathcal{W}$ computes his $\mathtt{rid}$-th round message $(m_0^{(i)}, m_1^{(i)}, \ldots, m_n^{(i)})$ following the protocol $\Pi_{\text{Input}}(D)$ where $m_0^{(i)}$ is the broadcast message, and $m_j^{(i)}$ is the P2P message to P_j.

2: Each party $P_i \in \mathcal{W}$ sets $(m_0^{(i)}, m_1^{(i)}, \ldots, m_n^{(i)})$ to be all-0 strings.

3: Each party P_i invokes $\mathcal{F}_{\text{Channel}}$ with input $((\Pi_{\text{Input}}, D, \mathtt{rid}), m_0^{(i)}, m_1^{(i)}, \ldots, m_n^{(i)})$.

4: Upon receiving the output from $\mathcal{F}_{\text{Channel}}$, let W' denote the set received from $\mathcal{F}_{\text{Channel}}$ for the $(\Pi_{\text{Input}}, D, \mathtt{rid})$-th round, each party P_i updates $\mathcal{W} := \mathcal{W}\cup W'$.
  - If $P_i \in \mathcal{W}$, P_i sets all his received messages to be all-0 strings in this round.
  - Otherwise, for each $P_j \notin \mathcal{W}$, P_i takes $(m_0^{(j)}, m_i^{(j)})$ as the messages received from P_j for all $P_j \notin \mathcal{W}$, and takes all-0 strings as the messages received from P_j for all $P_j \in \mathcal{W}$.

5: Depending on the size of $\mathcal{W}$ and $\mathtt{rid}$, all parties run the following steps.
  - If $D \in \mathcal{W}$, all parties stop emulating $\Pi_{\text{Input}}(D)$ and move on to the next dealer.
  - If $|\mathcal{W}| \leq t_s - t_a$,
    - If $\mathtt{rid} = R_I$, P_i computes his output following $\Pi_{\text{Input}}(D)$ and adds D in $\mathcal{I}$.
    - If $\mathtt{rid} < R_I$, P_i moves to the $(\mathtt{rid} + 1)$-th round of $\Pi_{\text{Input}}(D)$.

– Otherwise, all parties move to the fallback procedure.

Computation Phase

From $\mathtt{rid} = 1$ to R_C, all parties execute the following steps.

1: Each party $P_i \notin \mathcal{W}$ computes his $\mathtt{rid}$-th round message $(m_0^{(i)}, m_1^{(i)}, \ldots, m_n^{(i)})$ following the protocol Π_{Comp} where $m_0^{(i)}$ is the broadcast message, and $m_j^{(i)}$ is the P2P message to P_j.

2: Each party $P_i \in \mathcal{W}$ sets $(m_0^{(i)}, m_1^{(i)}, \ldots, m_n^{(i)})$ to be all-0 strings.

3: Each party P_i invokes $\mathcal{F}_{\mathsf{Channel}}$ with input $((\Pi_{\mathsf{Comp}}, \mathtt{rid}), m_0^{(i)}, m_1^{(i)}, \ldots, m_n^{(i)})$.

4: Upon receiving the output from $\mathcal{F}_{\mathsf{Channel}}$, let W' denote the set received from $\mathcal{F}_{\mathsf{Channel}}$ for the $(\Pi_{\mathsf{Comp}}, \mathtt{rid})$-th round, each party P_i updates $\mathcal{W} := \mathcal{W} \cup W'$.

  – If $P_i \in \mathcal{W}$, P_i sets all his received messages to be all-0 strings in this round.

  – Otherwise, for each $P_j \notin \mathcal{W}$, P_i takes $(m_0^{(j)}, m_i^{(j)})$ as the messages received from P_j for all $P_j \notin \mathcal{W}$, and takes all-0 strings as the messages received from P_j for all $P_j \in \mathcal{W}$.

5: Depending on the size of $\mathcal{W}$ and $\mathtt{rid}$, all parties run the following steps.

  – If $|\mathcal{W}| \leq t_s - t_a$,

    • If $\mathtt{rid} = R_C$, P_i computes his output following Π_{Comp} and adds D in $\mathcal{I}$.

    • If $\mathtt{rid} < R_C$, P_i moves to the $(\mathtt{rid}+1)$-th round of Π_{Comp}.

  – Otherwise, all parties move to the fallback procedure.

Reconstruction Phase

For each $[\![y_i]\!]$, all parties send their shares to P_i. Then P_i tries to reconstruct the secret y as follows: Whenever P_i receives a share sh_j from a party P_j, P_i applies Recon on all shares he has received so far. If the output of Recon is not $\perp$, P_i takes the output of Recon as y and halts.

Fallback Procedure

Let $\mathcal{W}'$ be the set of the first $t_s - t_a$ parties in $\mathcal{W}$. Parties in $\mathcal{P} \backslash \mathcal{W}'$ invoke $\Pi_{\mathsf{AMPC\text{-}GOD}}$ to compute the output y. Then parties in $\mathcal{P} \backslash \mathcal{W}'$ send the output to parties in $\mathcal{W}'$ and halt. Each party in $\mathcal{W}'$, after receiving $t_s + t_a + 1$ values from parties in $\mathcal{P} \backslash \mathcal{W}'$, takes the majority as the output and halts.

Lemma 2. *Let n, t_s, t_a be positive integers such that $n = 2t_s + t_a + 1$. Let f be an n-ary function and $(\mathsf{Share}, \mathsf{Recon})$ be a (t_s, n)-robust secret sharing scheme with adaptive secrecy, online reconstruction, and efficient resampling. Suppose that*

– $\Pi_{\mathtt{Input}}$ *is a synchronous MPC with GOD that securely computes $\mathcal{F}_{\mathsf{Input}}$ against t_s corrupted parties with adaptive security assuming a broadcast channel;*

– Π_{Comp} *is a synchronous MPC with GOD that securely computes $\mathcal{F}_{\mathsf{Comp}}$ against t_s corrupted parties with adaptive security assuming a broadcast channel;*

– $\Pi_{\mathtt{AMPC\text{-}GOD}}$ *is an asynchronous MPC with GOD that securely computes $\mathcal{F}_{\mathsf{AMPC}}$ among $t_s + 2t_a + 1$ parties against t_a corrupted parties such that when running in the synchronous network, all honest parties' inputs will be considered.*

Then Π_{Compiler} is a network-agnostic MPC in the $\mathcal{F}_{\text{Channel}}$-hybrid model with GOD that securely computes $\mathcal{F}_{\text{sfe}}$ against an adversary who may control up to t_s corrupted parties when the network is synchronous, and t_a corrupted parties when the network is asynchronous.

We refer the readers to the full version of this paper for cost analysis and the proof of Lemma 2.

Acknowledgments. X. Ji and Y. Song were supported in part by the National Basic Research Program of China Grant 2011CBA00300, 2011CBA00301, the National Natural Science Foundation of China Grant 61033001, 61361136003. Y. Song was also supported in part by the Shanghai Qi Zhi Institute Innovation Program SQZ202313.

References

[AAPP24] Abraham, I., Asharov, G., Patil, S., Patra, A.: Perfect asynchronous MPC with linear communication overhead. In: Joye, M., Leander, G. (eds.) EUROCRYPT 2024, Part V. LNCS, vol. 14655, pp. 280–309. Springer, Cham (2024). https://doi.org/10.1007/978-3-031-58740-5_10

[ABKL22] Alexandru, A.B., Blum, E., Katz, J., Loss, J.: State machine replication under changing network conditions. In: Agrawal, S., Lin, D. (eds.) ASIACRYPT 2022, Part I. LNCS, vol. 13791, pp. 681–710. Springer, Cham (2022). https://doi.org/10.1007/978-3-031-22963-3_23

[AC23] Appan, A., Choudhury, A.: Network agnostic MPC with statistical security. In: Rothblum, G.N., Wee, H. (eds.) TCC 2023, Part II. LNCS, vol. 14370, pp. 63–93. Springer, Cham (2023). https://doi.org/10.1007/978-3-031-48618-0_3

[ACC22] Appan, A., Chandramouli, A., Choudhury, A.: Perfectly-secure synchronous MPC with asynchronous fallback guarantees. In: Milani, A., Woelfel, P. (eds.) 41st ACM PODC, pp. 92–102. ACM (2022)

[ACC23] Appan, A., Chandramouli, A., Choudhury, A.: Network agnostic perfectly secure MPC against general adversaries. In: 37th International Symposium on Distributed Computing (DISC 2023). Schloss Dagstuhl-Leibniz-Zentrum für Informatik (2023)

[AMN+20] Abraham, I., Malkhi, D., Nayak, K., Ren, L., Yin, M.: Sync HotStuff: simple and practical synchronous state machine replication. In: 2020 IEEE Symposium on Security and Privacy, pp. 106–118. IEEE Computer Society Press (2020)

[BCLZL23] Bacho, R., Collins, D., Liu-Zhang, C.-D., Loss, J.: Network-agnostic security comes (almost) for free in DKG and MPC. In: Handschuh, H., Lysyanskaya, A. (eds.) CRYPTO 2023, Part I. LNCS, vol. 14081, pp. 71–106. Springer, Cham (2023). https://doi.org/10.1007/978-3-031-38557-5_3

[BCV23] Bhimrajka, N., Choudhury, A., Varadarajan, S.: Network-agnostic perfectly secure message transmission revisited. In: Chattopadhyay, A., Bhasin, S., Picek, S., Rebeiro, C. (eds.) INDOCRYPT 2023, Part II. LNCS, vol. 14460, pp. 25–44. Springer, Cham (2023). https://doi.org/10.1007/978-3-031-56235-8_2

[BCV24]   Bhimrajka, N., Choudhury, A., Varadarajan, S.: Network-agnostic multi-party computation revisited (extended abstract). In: Tang, Q., Teague, V. (eds.) PKC 2024, Part II. LNCS, vol. 14602, pp. 171–204. Springer, Cham (2024). https://doi.org/10.1007/978-3-031-57722-2_6

[BDD+21]   Baum, C., David, B., Dowsley, R., Nielsen, J.B., Oechsner, S.: TARDIS: a foundation of time-lock puzzles in UC. In: Canteaut, A., Standaert, F.-X. (eds.) EUROCRYPT 2021, Part III. LNCS, vol. 12698, pp. 429–459. Springer, Cham (2021). https://doi.org/10.1007/978-3-030-77883-5_15

[BDOZ11]   Bendlin, R., Damgård, I., Orlandi, C., Zakarias, S.: Semi-homomorphic encryption and multiparty computation. In: Paterson, K.G. (ed.) EUROCRYPT 2011. LNCS, vol. 6632, pp. 169–188. Springer, Heidelberg (2011). https://doi.org/10.1007/978-3-642-20465-4_11

[BFO12]   Ben-Sasson, E., Fehr, S., Ostrovsky, R.: Near-linear unconditionally-secure multiparty computation with a dishonest minority. In: Safavi-Naini, R., Canetti, R. (eds.) CRYPTO 2012. LNCS, vol. 7417, pp. 663–680. Springer, Heidelberg (2012). https://doi.org/10.1007/978-3-642-32009-5_39

[BGW88]   Ben-Or, M., Goldwasser, S., Wigderson, A.: Completeness theorems for non-cryptographic fault-tolerant distributed computation (extended abstract). In: 20th ACM STOC, pp. 1–10. ACM Press (1988)

[BJK+25a]   Bandarupalli, A., et al.: Velox: scalable fair asynchronous MPC from lightweight cryptography. In: Proceedings of the 2025 ACM SIGSAC Conference on Computer and Communications Security, pp. 1799–1813 (2025)

[BJK+25b]   Bandarupalli, A., Ji, X., Kate, A., Liu-Zhang, C.D., Song, Y.: Computationally efficient asynchronous MPC with linear communication and low additive overhead. In: Tauman Kalai, Y., Kamara, S.F. (eds.) CRYPTO 2025, Part IV. LNCS, vol. 16003, pp. 261–294. Springer, Cham (2025). https://doi.org/10.1007/978-3-032-01884-7_9

[BKL19]   Blum, E., Katz, J., Loss, J.: Synchronous consensus with optimal asynchronous fallback guarantees. In: Hofheinz, D., Rosen, A. (eds.) TCC 2019, Part I. LNCS, vol. 11891, pp. 131–150. Springer, Cham (2019). https://doi.org/10.1007/978-3-030-36030-6_6

[BKL21]   Blum, E., Katz, J., Loss, J.: TARDIGRADE: an atomic broadcast protocol for arbitrary network conditions. In: Tibouchi, M., Wang, H. (eds.) ASIACRYPT 2021, Part II. LNCS, vol. 13091, pp. 547–572. Springer, Cham (2021). https://doi.org/10.1007/978-3-030-92075-3_19

[BKR94]   Ben-Or, M., Kelmer, B., Rabin, T.: Asynchronous secure computations with optimal resilience (extended abstract). In: Anderson, J., Toueg, S. (eds.) 13th ACM PODC, pp. 183–192. ACM (1994)

[BLS01]   Boneh, D., Lynn, B., Shacham, H.: Short signatures from the Weil pairing. In: Boyd, C. (ed.) ASIACRYPT 2001. LNCS, vol. 2248, pp. 514–532. Springer, Heidelberg (2001). https://doi.org/10.1007/3-540-45682-1_30

[BSFO12]   Ben-Sasson, E., Fehr, S., Ostrovsky, R.: Near-linear unconditionally-secure multiparty computation with a dishonest minority. In: Safavi-Naini, R., Canetti, R. (eds.) CRYPTO 2012. LNCS, vol. 7417, pp. 663–680. Springer, Heidelberg (2012). https://doi.org/10.1007/978-3-642-32009-5_39

[BZL20]   Blum, E., Liu-Zhang, C.-D., Loss, J.: Always have a backup plan: fully secure synchronous MPC with asynchronous fallback. In: Micciancio, D., Ristenpart, T. (eds.) CRYPTO 2020, Part II. LNCS, vol. 12171, pp. 707–731. Springer, Cham (2020). https://doi.org/10.1007/978-3-030-56880-1_25

[Can01]   Canetti, R.: Universally composable security: a new paradigm for cryptographic protocols. In: 42nd FOCS, pp. 136–145. IEEE Computer Society Press (2001)

[CCD88]   Chaum, D., Crépeau, C., Damgård, I.: Multiparty unconditionally secure protocols (extended abstract). In: 20th ACM STOC, pp. 11–19. ACM Press (1988)

[CDD+99] Cramer, R., Damgård, I., Dziembowski, S., Hirt, M., Rabin, T.: Efficient multiparty computations secure against an adaptive adversary. In: Stern, J. (ed.) EUROCRYPT 1999. LNCS, vol. 1592, pp. 311–326. Springer, Heidelberg (1999). https://doi.org/10.1007/3-540-48910-X_22

[CDN01]   Cramer, R., Damgård, I., Nielsen, J.B.: Multiparty computation from threshold homomorphic encryption. In: Pfitzmann, B. (ed.) EUROCRYPT 2001. LNCS, vol. 2045, pp. 280–300. Springer, Heidelberg (2001). https://doi.org/10.1007/3-540-44987-6_18

[CFG+23] Cohen, R., Forghani, P., Garay, J., Patel, R., Zikas, V.: Concurrent asynchronous byzantine agreement in expected-constant rounds, revisited. In: Rothblum, G., Wee, H. (eds.) TCC 2023, Part IV. LNCS, vol. 14372, pp. 422–451. Springer, Cham (2023). https://doi.org/10.1007/978-3-031-48624-1_16

[CGHZ16] Coretti, S., Garay, J., Hirt, M., Zikas, V.: Constant-round asynchronous multi-party computation based on one-way functions. In: Cheon, J.H., Takagi, T. (eds.) ASIACRYPT 2016, Part II. LNCS, vol. 10032, pp. 998–1021. Springer, Heidelberg (2016). https://doi.org/10.1007/978-3-662-53890-6_33

[CGWW24] Constantinescu, A., Ghinea, D., Wattenhofer, R., Westermann, F.: Convex consensus with asynchronous fallback. In: 38th International Symposium on Distributed Computing (DISC 2024), pp. 15–1. Schloss Dagstuhl–Leibniz-Zentrum für Informatik (2024)

[CHLZ21] Chopard, A., Hirt, M., Liu-Zhang, C.-D.: On communication-efficient asynchronous MPC with adaptive security. In: Nissim, K., Waters, B. (eds.) TCC 2021, Part II. LNCS, vol. 13043, pp. 35–65. Springer, Cham (2021). https://doi.org/10.1007/978-3-030-90453-1_2

[Coh16]   Cohen, R.: Asynchronous secure multiparty computation in constant time. In: Cheng, C.-M., Chung, K.-M., Persiano, G., Yang, B.-Y. (eds.) PKC 2016, Part II. LNCS, vol. 9615, pp. 183–207. Springer, Heidelberg (2016). https://doi.org/10.1007/978-3-662-49387-8_8

[CP15]   Choudhury, A., Patra, A.: Optimally resilient asynchronous MPC with linear communication complexity. In: Proceedings of the 16th International Conference on Distributed Computing and Networking, pp. 1–10 (2015)

[CP23]   Choudhury, A., Patra, A.: On the communication efficiency of statistically secure asynchronous MPC with optimal resilience. J. Cryptol. **36**(2), 13 (2023)

[DEP23]   Damgård, I., Escudero, D., Polychroniadou, A.: Phoenix: secure computation in an unstable network with dropouts and comebacks. In: Chung, K.-M. (ed.) ITC 2023. LIPIcs, vol. 267, pp. 7:1–7:21. Schloss Dagstuhl (2023)

[DHLZ21] Deligios, G., Hirt, M., Liu-Zhang, C.-D.: Round-efficient byzantine agreement and multi-party computation with asynchronous fallback. In: Nissim, K., Waters, B. (eds.) TCC 2021, Part I. LNCS, vol. 13042, pp. 623–

653. Springer, Cham (2021). https://doi.org/10.1007/978-3-030-90459-3_21

[DI05] Damgård, I., Ishai, Y.: Constant-round multiparty computation using a black-box pseudorandom generator. In: Shoup, V. (ed.) CRYPTO 2005. LNCS, vol. 3621, pp. 378–394. Springer, Heidelberg (2005). https://doi.org/10.1007/11535218_23

[DLZ23] Deligios, G., Liu-Zhang, C.-D.: Synchronous perfectly secure message transmission with optimal asynchronous fallback guarantees. In: Baldimtsi, F., Cachin, C. (eds.) FC 2023, Part I. LNCS, vol. 13950, pp. 77–93. Springer, Cham (2023). https://doi.org/10.1007/978-3-031-47754-6_5

[DME24] Deligios, G., Mizrahi Erbes, M.: Closing the efficiency gap between synchronous and network-agnostic consensus. In: Joye, M., Leander, G. (eds.) EUROCRYPT 2024. LNCS, vol. 14655, pp. 432–461. Springer, Cham (2024). https://doi.org/10.1007/978-3-031-58740-5_15

[DN03] Damgård, I., Nielsen, J.B.: Universally composable efficient multiparty computation from threshold homomorphic encryption. In: Boneh, D. (ed.) CRYPTO 2003. LNCS, vol. 2729, pp. 247–264. Springer, Heidelberg (2003). https://doi.org/10.1007/978-3-540-45146-4_15

[ElG85] ElGamal, T.: A public key cryptosystem and a signature scheme based on discrete logarithms. IEEE Trans. Inf. Theory 31(4), 469–472 (1985)

[GLZS24] Goyal, V., Liu-Zhang, C.-D., Song, Y.: Towards achieving asynchronous MPC with linear communication and optimal resilience. In: Reyzin, L., Stebila, D. (eds.) CRYPTO 2024, Part VIII. LNCS, vol. 14927, pp. 170–206. Springer, Cham (2024). https://doi.org/10.1007/978-3-031-68397-8_6

[GLZW22] Ghinea, D., Liu-Zhang, C.-D., Wattenhofer, R.: Optimal synchronous approximate agreement with asynchronous fallback. In: Milani, A., Woelfel, P. (eds.) 41st ACM PODC, pp. 70–80. ACM (2022)

[GLZW23] Ghinea, D., Liu-Zhang, C.-D., Wattenhofer, R.: Multidimensional approximate agreement with asynchronous fallback. In: Proceedings of the 35th ACM Symposium on Parallelism in Algorithms and Architectures, pp. 141–151 (2023)

[GMR88] Goldwasser, S., Micali, S., Rivest, R.L.: A digital signature scheme secure against adaptive chosen-message attacks. SIAM J. Comput. 17(2), 281–308 (1988)

[GMW87] Goldreich, O., Micali, S., Wigderson, A.: How to play any mental game or a completeness theorem for protocols with honest majority. In: Aho, A. (ed.) 19th ACM STOC, pp. 218–229. ACM Press (1987)

[GPS21] Goyal, V., Polychroniadou, A., Song, Y.: Unconditional communication-efficient MPC via hall's marriage theorem. In: Malkin, T., Peikert, C. (eds.) CRYPTO 2021, Part II. LNCS, vol. 12826, pp. 275–304. Springer, Cham (2021). https://doi.org/10.1007/978-3-030-84245-1_10

[GPS22] Goyal, V., Polychroniadou, A., Song, Y.: Sharing transformation and dishonest majority MPC with packed secret sharing. In: Dodis, Y., Shrimpton, T. (eds.) CRYPTO 2022, Part IV. LNCS, vol. 13510, pp. 3–32. Springer, Cham (2022). https://doi.org/10.1007/978-3-031-15985-5_1

[GSZ20] Goyal, V., Song, Y., Zhu, C.: Guaranteed output delivery comes free in honest majority MPC. In: Micciancio, D., Ristenpart, T. (eds.) CRYPTO 2020, Part II. LNCS, vol. 12171, pp. 618–646. Springer, Cham (2020). https://doi.org/10.1007/978-3-030-56880-1_22

[HNP05] Hirt, M., Nielsen, J.B., Przydatek, B.: Cryptographic asynchronous multi-party computation with optimal resilience. In: Cramer, R. (ed.) EURO-CRYPT 2005. LNCS, vol. 3494, pp. 322–340. Springer, Heidelberg (2005). https://doi.org/10.1007/11426639_19

[JLS24] Ji, X., Li, J., Song, Y.: Linear-communication asynchronous complete secret sharing with optimal resilience. In: Reyzin, L., Stebila, D. (eds.) CRYPTO 2024, Part VIII. LNCS, vol. 14927, pp. 418–453. Springer, Cham (2024). https://doi.org/10.1007/978-3-031-68397-8_13

[JMV01] Johnson, D., Menezes, A., Vanstone, S.: The elliptic curve digital signature algorithm (ECDSA). Int. J. Inf. Secur. **1**, 36–63 (2001)

[KMTZ13] Katz, J., Maurer, U., Tackmann, B., Zikas, V.: Universally composable synchronous computation. In: Sahai, A. (ed.) TCC 2013. LNCS, vol. 7785, pp. 477–498. Springer, Heidelberg (2013). https://doi.org/10.1007/978-3-642-36594-2_27

[LZLM+19] Liu-Zhang, C.-D., Loss, J., Maurer, U., Moran, T., Tschudi. D.: Robust MPC: asynchronous responsiveness yet synchronous security. Cryptology ePrint Archive, Report 2019/159 (2019)

[MR21] Momose A., Ren, L.: Multi-threshold byzantine fault tolerance. In: Vigna, G., Shi, E. (eds.) ACM CCS 2021, pp. 1686–1699. ACM Press (2021)

[PCR09] Patra, A., Choudhary, A., Rangan, C.P.: Communication efficient statistical asynchronous multiparty computation with optimal resilience. In: Bao, F., Yung, M., Lin, D., Jing, J. (eds.) Inscrypt 2009. LNCS, vol. 6151, pp. 179–197. Springer, Heidelberg (2010). https://doi.org/10.1007/978-3-642-16342-5_14

[PP24] Patil, S., Patra, A.: Perfectly-secure network-agnostic MPC with optimal resiliency. Cryptology ePrint Archive (2024)

[PW96] Pfitzmann, B., Waidner, M.: Information-theoretic pseudosignatures and byzantine agreement for t $\geq n/3$. Citeseer (1996)

[RB89] Rabin, T., Ben-Or, M.: Verifiable secret sharing and multiparty protocols with honest majority (extended abstract). In: 21st ACM STOC, pp. 73–85. ACM Press (1989)

[Sch90] Schnorr, C.P.: Efficient identification and signatures for smart cards. In: Brassard, G. (ed.) CRYPTO 1989. LNCS, vol. 435, pp. 239–252. Springer, New York (1990). https://doi.org/10.1007/0-387-34805-0_22

[SHZI02] Shikata, J., Hanaoka, G., Zheng, Y., Imai, H.: Security notions for unconditionally secure signature schemes. In: Knudsen, L.R. (ed.) EURO-CRYPT 2002. LNCS, vol. 2332, pp. 434–449. Springer, Heidelberg (2002). https://doi.org/10.1007/3-540-46035-7_29

[Yao82] Yao, A.C.-C.: Protocols for secure computations (extended abstract). In: 23rd FOCS, pp. 160–164. IEEE Computer Society Press (1982)

Perfectly Secure Network-Agnostic MPC Comes for Free

Xiaoyu Ji[1], Chen-Da Liu-Zhang[2], and Yifan Song[1,3(✉)]

[1] Tsinghua University, Beijing, China
`jixy23@mails.tsinghua.edu.cn`, `yfsong@mail.tsinghua.edu.cn`
[2] Lucerne University of Applied Sciences and Arts, Lucerne, Switzerland
`chen-da.liuzhang@hslu.ch`
[3] Shanghai Qi Zhi Institute, Shanghai, China

Abstract. Secure multiparty computation (MPC) allows a set of parties to jointly compute a function while keeping their inputs private. Classical MPC protocols assume either a synchronous or an asynchronous network. Synchronous protocols tolerate more corrupted parties but rely on a timing bound, while asynchronous protocols make no timing assumptions but handle fewer corruptions.

The network-agnostic model aims to combine the advantages of both. It requires security without knowing in advance whether the network is synchronous or asynchronous, guaranteeing resilience against up to t_s corruptions in the synchronous case and t_a corruptions in the asynchronous case. The optimal corruption threshold for perfect security has been established as $n = 2\max(t_s, t_a) + \max(2t_a, t_s) + 1$, but prior work either falls short of this threshold or requires exponential local computation.

In this work, we present the first perfectly secure network-agnostic MPC protocol with polynomial communication and computation complexity under the optimal threshold. Our protocol achieves expected communication complexity $\mathcal{O}((|C|n + (D + C_I)n^2 + n^6)\log n)$ bits for a circuit of size $|C|$ over a finite field $\mathbb{F}$ of size $\mathcal{O}(n)$, depth D, and input size C_I.

Our main technical contribution is a compiler that generates Beaver triples in the network-agnostic setting using synchronous and asynchronous triple-generation protocols in a black-box way. Beyond the cost of the underlying protocols, it only requires $\mathcal{O}(n^2)$ instances of network-agnostic Byzantine agreement.

1 Introduction

Secure multiparty computation (MPC) [Yao82, GMW87, BGW88, CCD88, RB89] enables a set of n parties to jointly compute a function on their private inputs while ensuring that any t corrupted parties learn nothing beyond what can be inferred from their own inputs and outputs.

Traditionally, the design of MPC protocols assumes a fixed communication model: either *synchronous* or *asynchronous*. In the synchronous model, parties proceed in lock-step rounds with synchronized clocks, and every message

© International Association for Cryptologic Research 2026
J. Daemen and E. Thomé (Eds.): EUROCRYPT 2026, LNCS 16543, pp. 337–365, 2026.
https://doi.org/10.1007/978-3-032-25324-8_12

is guaranteed to be delivered within a known time bound Δ. This assumption enables strong security guarantees: statistically secure MPC can be achieved for $t < n/2$ given broadcast [RB89, DN07, BSFO12, GSZ20], and perfectly secure MPC is feasible for up to $t < n/3$ corrupted parties with guaranteed output delivery [BGW88, BH08]. The drawback, however, is brittleness: once messages are delayed beyond Δ, the protocol may completely lose security.

In contrast, the asynchronous model makes no assumptions on delivery time—messages may arrive after any finite delay, but honest parties' messages are guaranteed to eventually be delivered. This makes asynchronous protocols robust to unpredictable networks, but comes with a cost in corruption tolerance: statistically secure asynchronous MPC requires $t < n/3$ [BKR94, CGHZ16, HNP05, Coh16, CHLZ21, GLZS24, BJK+25b, BJK+25a], and perfect security is possible only up to $t < n/4$ corruptions [BCG93, AAPP24]. In other words, synchronous protocols achieve higher resilience but rely on timing assumptions, while asynchronous protocols drop timing assumptions but tolerate fewer corruptions.

This trade-off naturally raises the question: can we design protocols that remain secure without knowing in advance whether the network is synchronous or asynchronous, and thereby inherit the best possible guarantees in either case? This is precisely the goal of the *network-agnostic model*. In this setting, parties are unaware of the underlying network type, yet the protocol guarantees security against up to t_s corruptions if the network is synchronous and up to t_a corruptions if the network is asynchronous. This model has received increased attention in recent years and been considered in the study of multiple primitives including agreement [BKL19, DHLZ21, BKL21, ABKL22, GLZW22, GLZW23], secure-communication [DLZ23], distributed key generation [BCLZL23], and MPC [BZL20, DHLZ21, BCLZL23, ACC22, AC23, BCV24, PP24].

The study of perfectly secure network-agnostic MPC was initiated by [ACC22], who achieved amortized $\mathcal{O}(n^5/t_a \log n)$ bits communication per multiplication gate with an additional $\mathcal{O}(n^7 \log n)$ additive overhead, under the corruption threshold $n = 3t_s + t_a + 1$. Later, [PP24] established the exact optimal threshold for perfectly secure network-agnostic MPC as $n = 2\max(t_s, t_a) + \max(2t_a, t_s) + 1$, and presented a matching feasibility result. Their construction, however, relies on all parties agreeing on a clique of size $n - t_s$, which requires exponential local computation complexity. Consequently, no existing protocol achieves both polynomial communication and computation under the optimal corruption threshold. This motivates our work: constructing the first perfectly secure network-agnostic MPC with polynomial efficiency. At the same time, we are curious whether one can leverage existing synchronous and asynchronous MPC techniques and build a generic compiler for the network-agnostic setting, rather than designing protocols from scratch.

1.1   Our Contributions

In this work, we study the design of perfectly secure network-agnostic MPC with both polynomial communication and computation complexity, under the optimal corruption threshold $n = 2\max(t_s, t_a) + \max(2t_a, t_s) + 1$ [PP24]. Our primary focus is on the amortized communication complexity required to evaluate each gate in the circuit.

For perfect security, existing works have already achieved amortized linear communication per multiplication gate in both the synchronous setting [BH08, GLS19, AAPP23] and the asynchronous setting [AAPP24, AAPS25], while keeping the computation complexity polynomial in the number of parties. This sharp contrast highlights a natural open question:

Can we also obtain a perfectly secure network-agnostic MPC with amortized linear communication and polynomial computation complexity?

We answer this question positively and obtain the following result.

Theorem 1. *Let n, t_s, t_a be positive integers such that $n = 2\max(t_s, t_a) + \max(2t_a, t_s) + 1$. Let f be an n-ary function, there is a perfectly secure network-agnostic MPC protocol for f among n parties against a malicious adversary who controls up to t_s corrupted parties when the network is synchronous, and t_a corrupted parties when the network is asynchronous. For a function f with circuit size $|C|$ and circuit depth D, let C_I denote the input size, the achieved communication complexity is $\mathcal{O}((|C|n + (D + C_I)n^2 + n^6)\log n)$ bits in expectation.*

Note that under the optimal corruption threshold $n = 2\max(t_s, t_a) + \max(2t_a, t_s) + 1$, the case $t_s \leq t_a$ reduces to $n = 4t_a + 1$. In this regime, one can simply run any perfectly secure asynchronous MPC protocol tolerating t_a corruptions. Hence, in the remainder of this work, we focus on the more challenging case $t_a < t_s$ and present our construction for this setting.

Main Technical Result. Following [PP24], we divide the construction of network-agnostic MPC into two phases: the offline phase and the online phase. In the offline phase, the parties prepare random Beaver triples [Bea92], which are then used to evaluate the circuit in the online phase. Unlike prior works [ACC22, PP24], our approach does not construct network-agnostic MPC by first building a network-agnostic secret-sharing scheme. Instead, we build the network-agnostic triple generation protocol by using a synchronous and asynchronous triple generation protocol in a black-box way. This yields the following theorem.

Theorem 2. *Let n, t_s, t_a be positive integers such that $n = 2\max(t_s, t_a) + \max(2t_a, t_s) + 1$. There exists a perfectly secure network-agnostic triple generation protocol that generates N random Beaver triples with communication complexity $\mathcal{O}((Nn + n^6)\log n)$ bits.*

2   Technical Overview

In the following, let n denote the number of parties, t_s denote the synchronous corruption threshold, and t_a denote the asynchronous corruption threshold. We also assume that $t_a < t_s$ and set $n = 2t_s + \max(2t_a, t_s) + 1$.

In this section, we introduce the high-level idea of our network-agnostic triple generation protocol. Concretely, we construct a compiler that combines synchronous and asynchronous triple generation protocols to obtain a network-agnostic one. Recent works [DME24, JLZPS26] also propose compilers for constructing network-agnostic Byzantine agreement and MPC. However, their constructions focus on statistical security and rely on digital signatures, and therefore cannot be applied in the perfectly secure setting.

Throughout this subsection, when we say that a party broadcasts a message, we mean that it invokes an instance of network-agnostic reliable broadcast protocol with that message as input.

2.1 Safely Execute the Synchronous Protocol

We first attempt to let parties invoke the synchronous protocol in the network-agnostic setting. We note that the security of the synchronous protocol relies on two guarantees from the synchronous network: (1) all (honest) parties will receive their messages (from honest parties) within a fixed time bound in each round, and (2) all (honest) parties will proceed to the next round at the same time. However, if the network is asynchronous, we may face the following security and termination issues.

- An honest party A may fail to receive a message from another party B within the expected time bound. However, A cannot distinguish whether this is due to network asynchrony causing message delay, or because a corrupted B drops the message. As a result, A cannot determine whether it has already received the required messages from all honest parties in the current round, and thus may wait indefinitely.
- Even if an honest party receives all messages in a given round, it cannot guarantee that all other honest parties have done so. Since the security of a synchronous protocol may require that honest parties progress round-by-round in a coordinated manner, this prevents the party from safely moving to the next round.

To let parties make progress while maintaining the security, our idea is to design a protocol Π_{Channel} that helps parties to deliver their messages in each round of the synchronous protocol. If all parties acknowledge that all messages are delivered to each other, then they can safely proceed to the next round. Otherwise, if several parties' messages are delayed and cause the protocol stall, Π_{Channel} would help to identify parties that are responsible for this stall, and let all parties abort the protocol. With the help of Π_{Channel}, parties can safely execute a synchronous protocol in the network-agnostic setting, although they cannot guarantee the generation of triples so far. We first introduce the construction of Π_{Channel} as follows, then show how to utilize it in our compiler for triple generation in the next subsection.

Realization of Π_{Channel}. For each ordered pair (A, B), we let the receiver A broadcast a confirmation message $(\mathtt{Confirm}, A, B)$ if it received B's message within the prescribed time bounds, and a conflict message $(\texttt{Conflict}, A, B)$ otherwise. To prevent from waiting indefinitely due to a corrupted receiver A never broadcasting either a confirmation or a conflict message, parties invoke a network-agnostic Byzantine agreement (BA) protocol with input 1 if they have received a broadcast from A regarding whether A has received B's message within the prescribed time bound, and 0 otherwise.

- If BA outputs 1, then at least one honest party has received A's broadcast. Honest parties wait until they receive either $(\texttt{Confirm}, A, B)$ or $(\texttt{Conflict}, A, B)$ from A.
- If BA outputs 0, then not all honest parties received A's broadcast within the time bound. In this case, parties can know that if the network is synchronous, then A is a corrupted party. Then they treat $(\texttt{Conflict}, A, B)$ as the agreed outcome for this pair.

Note that with the help of the time bound, all honest parties eventually will have an input for each BA, thus guaranteeing the termination of these BA protocols. After parties reach an agreement on a confirmation or conflict outcome for every pair, if all outcomes are confirmations, then all required messages for the current round have been received, and parties can safely advance to the next round of the synchronous protocol. Otherwise, if at least one outcome is a conflict, all parties can agree on the identity of parties (A, B) that are responsible for this failure. Refer to Sect. 4.2 for the detailed construction.

A Subtle Issue. In the synchronous case, when we say an honest party A can receive messages from another honest party B within prescribed time bound, we also require that both A and B should enter this round at a similar time. Since the time to enter the next round depends on the termination of BA or broadcast protocol in previous round, we need to ensure that all honest parties should terminate the BA or broadcast protocol at a similar time when the network is synchronous. This issue can be addressed with a modified version of Bracha's reliable broadcast protocol [Bra84], and we show the details in Sect. 4.1.

2.2 High-Level Idea of the Compiler

With the help of $\Pi_{\texttt{Channel}}$, we guarantee that once parties fail to make the progress in the synchronous protocol, they can identify a pair of parties (A, B) that are responsible for this failure. Then our first observation is that in a synchronous case, every honest party will receive all honest parties' messages within the time bound. Consequently, for a pair of parties (A, B) that are responsible for the failure of the synchronous protocol, this ensures the following:

- If the network is synchronous, then at least one of A or B must be corrupted.
- If the network is asynchronous, it is possible that both A and B are honest.

Starting from this observation, we further note that if we directly remove both A and B upon failure, then among the remaining $n - 2$ parties there are at most

$t_s - 1$ corrupted parties in the synchronous case and at most t_a corrupted parties in the asynchronous case. Moreover, the relation $n - 2 = 2(t_s - 1) + \max(2t_a, t_s - 1) + 1$ still holds. Therefore, the optimal corruption threshold is preserved for the remaining parties, and they can rerun the synchronous protocol.

If the protocol fails again, the parties eliminate another pair and repeat the procedure. Note that the number of corrupted parties will decrease by 1 in the synchronous case but 0 in the asynchronous case, so we will only repeats this elimination procedure for $t_s - t_a$ times to reduce the number of corrupt parties to t_a in both network scenarios. We note that in this case, since the number of remaining parties is at least

$$n - 2(t_s - t_a) = 2t_a + \max(2t_a, t_s) + 1 = \max(4t_a, 2t_a + t_s) + 1 \geq 4t_a + 1,$$

the remaining parties can safely switch to a perfectly secure asynchronous triple generation protocol that tolerates up to t_a corrupted parties.

To summarize, now parties can first attempt to safely invoke the synchronous protocol (with the help of Π_{Channel}) to generate triples. If they fail due to the delayed messages of several parties, they would directly eliminate these parties and let the remaining parties rerun the synchronous protocol. Upon eliminating a sufficient number of these parties, the remaining parties can safely switch to execute the asynchronous protocol to generate triples.

Further Optimization. If the remaining parties generate the full set of triples after each elimination, the procedure may repeat $t_s - t_a = \mathcal{O}(n)$ times, leading to at least quadratic amortized communication per triple. To achieve linear amortized cost, we adopt the party elimination framework of [HMP00]. Specifically, we divide triple generation into n segments, where each segment produces $1/n$ fraction of the triples.

However, a subtle issue arises: triples generated in different segments may have different degrees. Let $t_k = t_s - k$ denote the corruption threshold after eliminating $2k$ parties, and let $\mathcal{P}_k$ denote the remaining $n - 2k$ parties. If an arbitrary synchronous protocol is used, the parties in $\mathcal{P}_k$ generate triples of the form $([a]_{t_k}, [b]_{t_k}, [c]_{t_k})$, where each sharing has degree t_k. Thus, triples produced in different segments may have different degrees, which complicates parallel online evaluation and introduces additional overhead.

To resolve this, we use the protocol of [BH08]. Let n' denote the current number of parties, t' the number of corrupted parties, and d the desired degree of the triples. The protocol of [BH08] guarantees that the parties can generate degree-d triples as long as $d + 2t' < n'$.

In our setting, after k elimination steps, we have $n' = n - 2k$ and $t' = t_s - k$. We set the target degree to $d = t_s$. The condition holds as long as $k \leq t_s - t_a$:

$$d + 2t' = t_s + 2(t_s - k)$$
$$< 2t_s + \max(2t_a, t_s) + 1 - 2k = n'.$$

Therefore, throughout the execution, the parties can consistently generate degree-t_s triples when invoking the synchronous triple generation protocols [BH08].

Remark 1. The protocol in [BH08] we used actually only achieves security with identifiable abort. That means when all parties terminate, they either output degree-t_s triples or agree on the identity of a pair of parties who are responsible for the failure of the protocol. Following a similar argument in Sect. 2.2, all parties can directly eliminate this pair of parties and let the remaining parties rerun the current segment.

Putting It All Together. We summarize the compiler as follows. All parties first try to invoke the synchronous protocol to generate degree-t_s triples. During this procedure, triple generation is divided into n segments. In each segment, the parties proceed as follows.

1. All parties execute a synchronous triple generation protocol with identifiable abort [BH08]. Messages in each round are delivered via Π_{Channel}.
2. Upon terminating Π_{Channel}, the parties either agree on a pair of parties to be eliminated or proceed to the next round. At the end of the segment:
   - If valid degree-t_s triples are produced, the parties proceed to the next segment.
   - Otherwise, the identified parties are eliminated and the segment is restarted.

During the execution of these n segments, if a total of $2(t_s - t_a)$ parties have been eliminated, all intermediate results from the synchronous phase are discarded. The remaining $4t_a + 1$ parties then invoke an asynchronous triple generation protocol to produce degree-t_a triples. Refer to Sect. 5.1 for the detailed construction of the compiler.

2.3 Online Error Correction Still Works

During the circuit evaluation, with the help of triples, parties only need to do public reconstruction. We use a modified version of the reconstruction protocol introduced in [DN07], and refer the reader to Sect. 5.2 for more details. It remains to show that the online error-correction procedure works in our setting to guarantee the correctness of the public reconstruction.

Suppose that the parties have terminated the offline phase and agreed on a subset of parties $\mathcal{P}'$ that hold shares of the generated triples. Let $|\mathcal{P}'| = n - 2k$ for some $k \in [0, t_s - t_a]$. If $k = t_s - t_a$, then the parties in $\mathcal{P}'$ hold degree-t_a triples and there are at most t_a corrupted parties. Otherwise, if $k < t_s - t_a$, the parties hold degree-t_s triples and the number of corrupted parties is at most $t_s - k$.

When $|\mathcal{P}'| = 4t_a + 1$ and $t = t_a$, correctness follows directly. We now consider the case $|\mathcal{P}'| = n_k = n - 2k$ for $k \in [0, t_s - t_a)$ and $t = t_s$. In this case, we have

$$\frac{n_k - t - 1}{2} = \frac{n - 2k - t_s - 1}{2} = \frac{t_s + \max(2t_a, t_s) - 2k}{2}$$

$$= \frac{1}{2} \max(2t_a + t_s - 2k, \, 2t_s - 2k) \geq t_s - k.$$

Therefore, the reconstruction procedure can tolerate up to $t_s - k$ incorrect shares. Since there are at most $t_s - k$ corrupted parties in $\mathcal{P}'$, all incorrect values can be corrected, and the online phase succeeds. The same argument guarantees the correctness of output reconstruction.

3   Preliminary

3.1   Model

We consider the universal composability (UC) framework [Can01] to prove the security of our protocols. Note that the standard UC framework considers an asynchronous network model where the adversary is allowed to drop messages. We are interested in 1) the synchronous model where parties have access to synchronized clocks and messages are delivered within a publicly known delay, and 2) the asynchronous setting with *eventual delivery*, where messages sent by honest parties are eventually delivered. To capture such models, several variants have been proposed in the literature for synchronous UC [KMTZ13, Can01, LZLM+19, BDD+21] where functionalities keep track of time, and asynchronous UC with eventual delivery [CGHZ16, LZLM+19, CFG+23]. Our protocols can be proven secure in any of those models. When modeling functionalities, we will use the term *request-based delayed output* [Coh16] to refer to eventual output delivery. Moreover, for functionalities in the synchronous setting, we use the term *time-bound delayed output* to ensure that the output is delivered within a prescribed time-bound, but the adversary may deliver the message earlier.

3.2   Ideal World

We consider the setting of multi-party computation with guaranteed output delivery (GOD). In this setting, we model the ideal MPC functionality $\mathcal{F}_{\mathsf{sfe}}$ defined below with a flag mode, indicating whether the setting is synchronous or asynchronous. When the network is synchronous, the functionality expects the inputs by a certain time and will take into account all inputs from honest parties for the computation, and deliver the outputs by a certain predetermined time. When the network is asynchronous, only $n - t_s - t_a$ honest inputs are guaranteed to be taken into account, which is optimal as proven in [BZL20], and the outputs are eventually delivered.

Functionality $\mathcal{F}_{\mathsf{sfe}}$

$\mathcal{F}_{\mathsf{sfe}}$ is parameterized by a set $\mathcal{P} = \{P_1, \ldots, P_n\}$, an adversary $\mathcal{S}$, an n-party function $f : (\{0,1\}^* \cup \{\perp\})^n \to \{0,1\}^* \cup \{\perp\}$ and a flag mode $\in \{\mathsf{synch}, \mathsf{asynch}\}$. Let t_s (resp. t_a) be the corruption in the synchronous (resp. asynchronous) mode. $\mathcal{F}_{\mathsf{sfe}}$ has timeouts τ_0, τ_f for receiving the inputs and giving outputs of honest parties in the synchronous mode.

For each party P_i, initialize an input value $x^{(i)} = \bot$ and output value $y^{(i)} = \bot$. Set $\mathsf{CoreSet} = \mathcal{H}$.

Initialization

1: $\mathcal{F}_{\mathsf{sfe}}$ receives the set $Corr$ of corrupted parties from $\mathcal{S}$ and the network configuration $\mathsf{mode} \in \{\mathsf{synch}, \mathsf{asynch}\}$. $\mathcal{F}_{\mathsf{sfe}}$ checks that $|Corr| \leq t_s$ if $\mathsf{mode} = \mathsf{synch}$ and $|Corr| \leq t_a$ if $\mathsf{mode} = \mathsf{asynch}$. If not, $\mathcal{F}_{\mathsf{sfe}}$ gives up the security[a].

Synchronous: $\mathsf{mode} = \mathsf{synch}$

1: Upon receiving an input (Input, v) from $P_i \in \mathcal{P}$ by time τ_0, set $x^{(i)} = v$. Send a message (Input, P_i) to $\mathcal{S}$.
2: At time τ_0, if $x^{(i)}$ has been set to a value different from $\bot$ for every honest $P_i \in \mathcal{P}$, then compute $y = f(x^{(1)}, \ldots, x^{(n)})$ and set $y^{(i)} = y$ for every $P_i \in \mathcal{P}$. Otherwise, give up the security.
3: Upon receiving an input $(\mathsf{Deliver}, P_i)$ from $\mathcal{S}$ for an honest party P_i, if the output has been computed but not yet delivered to P_i, output $y^{(i)}$ to P_i.
4: Upon reaching time τ_f, output $y^{(i)}$ to every honest P_i that has not been delivered its output.

Asynchronous: $\mathsf{mode} = \mathsf{asynch}$

1: Upon receiving an input (Input, v) from $P_i \in \mathcal{P}$, set $x^{(i)} = v$. Send a message (Input, P_i) to $\mathcal{S}$.
2: Upon receiving an input $\mathsf{CoreSet}'$ from $\mathcal{S}$ for the first time, verify that $\mathsf{CoreSet}'$ is a subset of $\mathcal{P}$ of size at least $n - t_s$, else ignore the message. Then record $\mathsf{CoreSet} = \mathsf{CoreSet}'$, and for every $P_i \notin \mathsf{CoreSet}$, set $x^{(i)} = \bot$.
3: If $x^{(i)}$ has been set to a value different from $\bot$ for every honest $P_i \in \mathsf{CoreSet}$, then compute $y = f(x^{(1)}, \ldots, x^{(n)})$ and generate a request-based delayed output $y^{(i)} = y$ for every $P_i \in \mathcal{P}$.

---

[a] By giving up the security, $\mathcal{F}_{\mathsf{sfe}}$ sends its view to $\mathcal{S}$ and allows $\mathcal{S}$ to arbitrarily decide the output of honest parties and the delivery time.

3.3 Real World

Network Model. In our protocols, parties have access to a complete network of secure point-to-point channels. Our protocols operate in two possible settings: synchronous or asynchronous.

In the synchronous setting, all parties have access to synchronized clocks and all messages are guaranteed to be delivered within some known upper bound delay Δ. Within Δ, the adversary can schedule the messages arbitrarily. In particular, the adversary is *rushing*, i.e., within the same round, the adversary is allowed to send its messages after seeing the honest parties' messages. Sometimes it is convenient to describe a protocol in rounds, where each round r refers to the interval of time $(r-1)\Delta$ to $r\Delta$. In such case, we say that a party receives a message in round r if it receives the message within that time interval. Moreover, we say a party sends a message in round r when it sends the message at the beginning of the round, i.e., at time $(r-1)\Delta$.

In the asynchronous setting, both assumptions above are removed. That is, parties do not have access to synchronized clocks (but they advance), and the adversary is allowed to arbitrarily schedule the delivery of the messages. However, we assume that all messages are eventually delivered (i.e., the adversary cannot drop messages).

Adversary Model. We consider a static adversary who corrupts parties in an arbitrary manner at the beginning of the protocol, i.e. active corruption. In the synchronous setting, the adversary can corrupt up to t_s parties. In the asynchronous setting, the adversary can corrupt up to t_a parties.

3.4   Network-Agnostic Reliable Broadcast

In a reliable broadcast (RBC) protocol, a sender P_s takes a message $m \in \mathcal{M}$ as input, where $\mathcal{M}$ is the message space which contains $\perp$. The protocol allows the sender to consistently distribute the message m among a set of parties. We recall the property-based definition of RBC protocol as follows.

Definition 1. *Let t be the corruption threshold and Π be a protocol executed by parties $\mathcal{P} = \{P_1, \ldots, P_n\}$, where a sender $P_s \in \mathcal{P}$ holds an input $m \in \mathcal{M}$, and all parties terminate upon getting output.*

- *t-**Validity:** If the sender P_s is honest, then all honest parties output m.*
- *t-**Consistency:** If an honest party terminates, then his output is a valid message $m' \in \mathcal{M}$, and all honest parties will eventually terminate with output m'.*

If Π achieves t-validity and t-consistency, we say that Π is t-secure. A network-agnostic RBC protocol is t_s-secure in the synchronous setting and t_a-secure in the asynchronous setting. The authors in [PP24] give a construction of a network-agnostic RBC protocol with $\mathcal{O}(Ln^2)$ communication bits for broadcasting an L-bit message. We use $\mathtt{Time_{bc}}$ to denote the running time of Π when the dealer is honest and the network is synchronous.

3.5   Network-Agnostic Byzantine Agreement

In a Byzantine agreement (BA) protocol, each party P_i takes a message $m_i \in \mathcal{M}$ as input, where $\mathcal{M}$ is the message space which contains $\perp$. The protocol allows all parties to agree on a common message in $\mathcal{M}$. We recall the property-based definition of a BA protocol as follows.

Definition 2. *Let t be the corruption threshold and Π be a protocol executed by parties $\mathcal{P} = \{P_1, \ldots, P_n\}$, where each party initially holds an input $m_i \in \mathcal{M}$, and all parties terminate upon getting output.*

- *t-**Validity:** If all honest parties have the same input $m \in \mathcal{M}$, then all honest parties take m as output.*
- *t-**Consistency:** Honest parties do not obtain different outputs in $\mathcal{M}$.*

- t-**Termination:** *Suppose all honest parties participate in the protocol with their inputs in $\mathcal{M}$, and they never stop participating until termination. Then all honest parties terminate with a valid output in $\mathcal{M}$.*

For a BA protocol Π, if Π achieves t-validity, t-consistency, and t-termination, we say Π is t-secure. We say Π is a network-agnostic BA protocol if Π is t_s-secure in the synchronous setting and t_a-secure in the asynchronous setting.

To instantiate a perfectly secure network-agnostic BA protocol, the authors in [PP24] give a construction, which invokes n instances of network-agnostic reliable broadcasts and an asynchronous BA protocol in a black-box way. By using the reliable broadcast protocol in [PP24] and asynchronous BA protocol in [AAPP24], it can be achieved with $\mathcal{O}(Ln^3 + n^4 \log n)$ bits of communication for L-bit agreement. When the network is synchronous, the t_s-termination property guarantees that all honest parties will terminate Π within a fixed delay. We use Time_{ba} to denote the running time of Π when the starting time of all honest parties differ by at most Δ and the network is synchronous.

4 Secure Channel with Synchronous Identifiable Abort

4.1 Guarantee a Similar Termination Time for Agreement Protocol in the Synchronous Network

In our later construction, we require that all parties terminate the agreement protocol at a similar time when the network is synchronous. In this subsection, we describe how to ensure that all parties terminate an arbitrary network-agnostic agreement protocol Π at approximately the same time when executed over a synchronous network. We construct a modified protocol Π' as follows. Let Δ denote the maximum message delivery delay in the synchronous network. Then, in the synchronous setting, all parties are guaranteed to terminate Π' within a time difference of at most 2Δ.

Protocol Π'

Let Π denote a network-agnostic agreement protocol, which guarantees all parties terminate with the same output and is secure against $1/3$ fraction of corrupted parties in the synchronous setting and $1/4$ fraction of corrupted parties in the asynchronous setting.

1: All parties participate in Π after they learn their inputs, and we denote the agreement result of Π as m.
2: Upon receiving messages m in the following ways, send (Echo, m) to all parties:
   - Terminate Π with m.
   - The same (Echo, m) from $2t_s + 1$ distinct parties.
   - The same (Ready, m) from $t_s + 1$ distinct parties.
3: Upon receiving messages m in the following ways, send (Ready, m) to all parties:

> - The same $(\mathtt{Echo}, m)$ from $2t_s + 1$ distinct parties.
> - The same $(\mathtt{Ready}, m)$ from $t_s + 1$ distinct parties.
>
> 4: Upon receiving $(\mathtt{Ready}, m)$ from $2t_s + 1$ distinct parties, all parties terminate with output m.

We briefly explain why all parties will terminate within 2Δ time delay in the synchronous setting. Note that all parties may participate in the protocol at different times, and they are message-driven:

1. When the first honest party terminates, he has received $(\mathtt{Ready}, m)$ from $2t_s + 1$ distinct parties, which means that at least $t_s + 1$ honest parties have sent $(\mathtt{Ready}, m)$ to all parties.
2. In the following Δ time delay, the $(\mathtt{Ready}, m)$ sent from these honest parties will be delivered to all honest parties, and they will send $(\mathtt{Ready}, m)$ to all honest parties.
3. In the following Δ time delay, all honest parties are guaranteed to receive $(\mathtt{Ready}, m)$ from $2t_s + 1$ distinct parties, and they will terminate with the same message m.

Building on Π' and the network-agnostic RBC and BA protocols from [PP24], we obtain modified protocols Π'_{rbc} and Π'_{ba} that guarantee all parties terminate at approximately the same time. For an L-bit broadcast or agreement, the resulting communication complexity is $\mathcal{O}(Ln^2)$ bits and $\mathcal{O}(Ln^3 + n^4 \log n)$ bits, respectively.

4.2 Realization of $\Pi_{\mathtt{Channel}}$

As we introduced in Sect. 2.1, we first consider a P2P message from a sender B to a receiver A. Let $\mathtt{rid}$ denote the round id, we assume that all honest parties enter the $\mathtt{rid}$th round within a time difference of at most Δ in the synchronous network. The construction of $\Pi_{\mathtt{P2P\text{-}Send}}(A, B, \mathtt{rid})$ is as follows. It guarantees that when all parties terminate $\Pi_{\mathtt{P2P\text{-}Send}}(A, B, \mathtt{rid})$, all parties will either agree that A receives messages from B or eliminate A and B (or only A).

Protocol $\Pi_{\mathtt{P2P\text{-}Send}}(A, B, \mathtt{rid})$

Sending Message

1: After B enters the $\mathtt{rid}$-th round, B sends his message m to A.
2: After A enters the $\mathtt{rid}$-th round, A waits for 2Δ time for the message m from B. If A receives the message from B within the time limit, A invokes Π'_{rbc} to broadcast a confirmation $(\mathtt{Confirm}, A, B, \mathtt{rid})$. Otherwise, A invokes Π'_{rbc} to broadcast a conflict $(\mathtt{Conflict}, A, B, \mathtt{rid})$.

Termination

1: Recall that $\mathtt{Time}_{\mathrm{bc}}$ is the time required by Π'_{rbc} when the dealer is honest and the network is synchronous. All parties invoke Π'_{ba} and decide their input as

follows: After entering the **rid**-th round, each party P_i waits for $4\Delta + \text{Time}_{\text{bc}}$ for the final broadcast message from A.
- If the received broadcast message is in the form of $(\text{Confirm}, A, B, \text{rid})$ or $(\text{Conflict}, A, B, \text{rid})$, P_i sets his input of Π'_{ba} to be 1.
- Otherwise P_i sets his input of Π'_{ba} to be 0.

2: All parties decide their output based on the result of Π'_{ba} and the final broadcast message from A.
- If Π'_{ba} outputs 1 and the final broadcast message from A is $(\text{Confirm}, A, B, \text{rid})$, all parties output $(\text{Confirm}, A, B, \text{rid})$ and A outputs the received message m in addition.
- If Π'_{ba} outputs 1 and the final broadcast message from A is $(\text{Conflict}, A, B, \text{rid})$, all parties output $(\text{Eliminate}, A, B, \text{rid})$.
- Otherwise, all parties output $(\text{Eliminate}, A, \text{rid})$.

During the execution of synchronous protocol, parties may also need to broadcast the messages in some rounds. Although the broadcast channel can be realized by the P2P channel in the perfectly secure setting, we give a more direct realization of $\Pi_{\text{BC-Send}}$ to handle the broadcast message. The construction of $\Pi_{\text{BC-Send}}$ is similar to $\Pi_{\text{P2P-Send}}$, it takes the identity of party B and the round id **rid** as input, and B will reliable broadcast his messages at the beginning.

Protocol $\Pi_{\text{BC-Send}}(B, \text{rid})$

Sending Message

1: After B enters the **rid**-th round, B invokes Π'_{rbc} to broadcast his message m.
2: For each party A, after he enters the **rid**-th round, A waits for $\Delta + \text{Time}_{\text{bc}}$ time for the message m from B. If A receives the message from B within the time limit, A invokes Π'_{rbc} to broadcast a confirmation $(\text{Confirm}, A, B, \text{rid})$. Otherwise, A invokes Π'_{rbc} to broadcast a conflict $(\text{Conflict}, A, B, \text{rid})$.

Termination

The termination process is the same as $\Pi_{\text{P2P-Send}}$, except that each party P_i waits for $3\Delta + 2\text{Time}_{\text{bc}}$ for the final broadcast message from A.

Putting All It Together. We construct the protocol Π_{Channel} from $\Pi_{\text{P2P-Send}}$ and $\Pi_{\text{BC-Send}}$. Each party takes as input a set $\mathcal{P}'$, which contains the identities of the parties that have been eliminated. For every remaining party $P_i \notin \mathcal{P}'$, it inputs a vector of messages and distributes them using $\Pi_{\text{P2P-Send}}$ and $\Pi_{\text{BC-Send}}$. Once all parties have terminated the executions of $\Pi_{\text{P2P-Send}}(A, B, \text{rid})$ and $\Pi_{\text{BC-Send}}(B, \text{rid})$ for $A, B \in \mathcal{P} \setminus \mathcal{P}'$, they either agree on new parties to be eliminated, or all alive parties in $\mathcal{P} \setminus \mathcal{P}'$ confirm that they have successfully received each other's messages.

Protocol $\Pi_{\texttt{Channel}}$

All parties take a set $\mathcal{P}'$ as input. Each party $P_i \notin \mathcal{P}'$ takes a vector of messages $(\texttt{rid}, m_0^{(i)}, \{m_j^{(i)}\}_{j \notin \mathcal{P}'})$ as input.

1: Each party $P_i \notin \mathcal{P}'$ takes $m_0^{(i)}$ as the broadcast message, and $m_j^{(i)}$ as the P2P message for each $P_j \notin \mathcal{P}'$. Then P_i invokes $\Pi_{\texttt{P2P-Send}}(A, B, \texttt{rid})$ for every $A, B \in \mathcal{P} \setminus \mathcal{P}'$, and invokes $\Pi_{\texttt{BC-Send}}(B, \texttt{rid})$ for every $B \in \mathcal{P} \setminus \mathcal{P}'$.

2: All parties initialize a set $\mathcal{W} = \varnothing$. For the output of each $\Pi_{\texttt{P2P-Send}}(A, B, \texttt{rid})$ and $\Pi_{\texttt{BC-Send}}(B, \texttt{rid})$:
   - If the output is in the form of $(\texttt{Eliminate}, A, B, \texttt{rid})$ or $(\texttt{Eliminate}, A, \texttt{rid})$, all parties add the identities of (A, B) or A to $\mathcal{W}$.

3: All parties terminate with $\mathcal{W}$. If $\mathcal{W} = \varnothing$, then each party $P_i \in \mathcal{P}'$ additionally terminates with $(\texttt{rid}, \mathcal{W}, \{(m_0^{(j)}, m_i^{(j)})\}_{j \notin \mathcal{P}'})$.

Optimization. In the above construction, all parties need to invoke $\Pi'_{\texttt{ba}}$ in each call of $\Pi_{\texttt{P2P-Send}}$ and $\Pi_{\texttt{BC-Send}}$, which adds up to $O(n^2)$ calls of $\Pi'_{\texttt{ba}}$ in each round. We show a simple optimization that reduces the number of calls of $\Pi_{\texttt{ba}}$ and $\Pi'_{\texttt{rbc}}$ to $O(n)$.

In each round, for each party A, we only invoke a single call of $\Pi_{\texttt{ba}}$. Each party P_i sets his input to be 1 if he received the broadcast message from A in $\Pi_{\texttt{P2P-Send}}(A, B, \texttt{rid})$ and $\Pi_{\texttt{BC-Send}}(A, \texttt{rid})$ for all B within the time-bound, and sets his input to be 0 otherwise. Then P_i follows the termination phase of each $\Pi_{\texttt{P2P-Send}}(A, B, \texttt{rid})$ and $\Pi_{\texttt{BC-Send}}(A, \texttt{rid})$ to decide the output. We can similarly show that when the network is synchronous, an honest P_i will never set his input of $\Pi_{\texttt{ba}}$ to be 0 for an honest A.

Based on this optimization, let $L_{\texttt{bc}}, L_{\texttt{P2P}}$ denote be the total broadcast message size and P2P message size, the communication complexity of $\Pi_{\texttt{Channel}}$ is $\mathcal{O}(L_{\texttt{P2P}} n + L_{\texttt{bc}} n^2 + n^5 \log n)$ bits.

5   Construction of Perfectly Secure Agnostic MPC

In this section, we present our construction of network-agnostic MPC. We begin with a perfectly secure agnostic triple-generation protocol, which serves as the foundation for realizing the full agnostic MPC protocol.

5.1   Network-Agnostic Triple Generation Compiler

In this subsection, we give the construction of our triple-generation protocol. Upon terminating the protocol, all parties will output a party set $\mathcal{P}'$, and parties in $\mathcal{P}'$ get their shares of random Beaver triples. If $|\mathcal{P}'| > 4t_a + 1$, then parties in $\mathcal{P}'$ get degree-t_s random Beaver triples. Otherwise, $|\mathcal{P}'| = 4t_a + 1$, and parties in $\mathcal{P}'$ get degree-t_a random Beaver triples.

To build this triple-generation protocol, we rely on two sub-protocols $\Pi_{\texttt{Triple-Id-Sync}}$ and $\Pi_{\texttt{Triple-Async}}$, which realize the functionalities $\mathcal{F}_{\texttt{Triple-Id-Sync}}$ and

$\mathcal{F}_{\text{Triple-Async}}$ defined below, respectively. For the instantiations of these two functionalities:

- For $\mathcal{F}_{\text{Triple-Id-Sync}}$, we use the construction in [BH08] to build $\Pi_{\texttt{Triple-Id-Sync}}$, which securely computes $\mathcal{F}_{\text{Triple-Id-Sync}}$ against $1/3$ corruptions. The communication complexity is $\mathcal{O}((C + n^2)\log n)$ bits, and the round complexity is $\mathcal{O}(n)$.
- For $\mathcal{F}_{\text{Triple-Async}}$, we can use the construction in [AAPS25] to build $\Pi_{\texttt{Triple-Async}}$, which securely computes $\mathcal{F}_{\text{Triple-Async}}$ against $1/4$ corruptions. The communication complexity is $\mathcal{O}((C + n^4)\log n)$ bits, and the expected round complexity is $\mathcal{O}(1)$.

Remark 2. In Appendix A, we give a review of the construction in [BH08]. We note that the $\mathcal{O}(n)$ round complexity of their construction comes from the execution of the BA protocol, the rest of parts only require $\mathcal{O}(1)$ round complexity. Since the round number of the synchronous protocol affects the number of instances $\Pi_{\texttt{Channel}}$ in our construction, a natural optimization here is to use network-agnostic BA to replace the BA protocol used in [BH08]. As a result, parties only need to invoke $\mathcal{O}(1)$ instances of $\Pi_{\texttt{Channel}}$ for the synchronous protocol [BH08] in our compiler.

Functionality $\mathcal{F}_{\text{Triple-Id-Sync}}$

$\mathcal{F}_{\text{Triple-Id-Sync}}$ runs with a party set $\mathcal{P}'$, and an adversary $\mathcal{S}$. Denote N as the number of random degree-t_s Beaver triples to be prepared.

1: Receive the set $Corr$ of corrupted parties. Let $t := |Corr|$ and $n := |\mathcal{P}'|$, if $t_s + 2t < n$, $\mathcal{F}_{\text{Triple-Id-Sync}}$ proceeds. Otherwise, $\mathcal{F}_{\text{Triple-Id-Sync}}$ gives up security and sends all views to $\mathcal{S}$.

2: For all $i \in [N]$, randomly samples a_i, b_i, c_i such that $c_i = a_i \cdot b_i$.

3: For all $i \in [N]$, receive a set of shares $\{u_{i,j}, v_{i,j}, w_{i,j}\}_{j \in Corr}$ of corrupted parties from $\mathcal{S}$. Then sample three random degree-t_s Shamir sharings $([a_i]_{t_s}, [b_i]_{t_s}, [c_i]_{t_s})$ based on the shares of corrupted parties and the secrets a_i, b_i, c_i.

4: Send a request-based delayed output of shares of $\{([a_i]_{t_s}, [b_i]_{t_s}, [c_i]_{t_s})\}_{i=1}^{N}$ to all parties in $\mathcal{P}$.
- Upon receiving a request $(\texttt{Conflict}, P_i, P_j)$ from $\mathcal{S}$, if the output of all parties has not been delivered and $P_i, P_j \in \mathcal{P}$, change it to $(\texttt{Conflict}, P_i, P_j)$. Otherwise, ignore this message.

Functionality $\mathcal{F}_{\text{Triple-Async}}$

$\mathcal{F}_{\text{Triple-Async}}$ runs with a party set $\mathcal{P}'$, and an adversary $\mathcal{S}$. Denote N as the number of random degree-t_a Beaver triples to be prepared.

1: Receive the set $\mathcal{C}orr$ of corrupted parties in $\mathcal{P}$. Let $t := |\mathcal{C}orr|$ and $n := |\mathcal{P}'|$, if $t \leq t_a$ and $4t_a < n$, $\mathcal{F}_{\text{Triple-Async}}$ proceeds. Otherwise, $\mathcal{F}_{\text{Triple-Async}}$ gives up security and sends all views to $\mathcal{S}$.
2: For all $i \in [N]$, randomly samples a_i, b_i, c_i such that $c_i = a_i \cdot b_i$.
3: For all $i \in [N]$, receive a set of shares $\{u_{i,j}, v_{i,j}, w_{i,j}\}_{j \in \mathcal{C}orr}$ of corrupted parties from $\mathcal{S}$. Then sample three random degree-t_a Shamir sharings $([a_i]_{t_a}, [b_i]_{t_a}, [c_i]_{t_a})$ based on the shares of corrupted parties and the secrets a_i, b_i, c_i.
4: Send a request-based delayed output of shares of $\{([a_i]_{t_a}, [b_i]_{t_a}, [c_i]_{t_a})\}_{i=1}^{N}$ to all parties in $\mathcal{P}$.

Then we give our construction of $\Pi_{\text{NA-Triple}}$ for triple generation. Let N be the number of triples to be prepared, the communication complexity is $\mathcal{O}((Nn + n^6)\log n)$ bits, and the round complexity is $\mathcal{O}(n)$.

Protocol $\Pi_{\text{NA-Triple}}$

Let $\Pi_{\text{Triple-Sync}}$ be a synchronous Beaver triple generation protocol that securely computes $\mathcal{F}_{\text{Triple-Id-Sync}}$ with adaptive security. Suppose R is the (upper bound of the) number of rounds required by $\Pi_{\text{Triple-Sync}}$.

All parties define $\mathcal{R} = \{(\Pi_{\text{Triple-Sync}}, j)\}_{j \in [R]}$ and initialize a set $\mathcal{W} = \varnothing$. They also take a public parameter N as input, which denotes the number of random Beaver triples to be prepared.

Regular Procedure

In this procedure, all parties aim to generate N degree-t_s random Beaver triples. They first divide the generation of N degree-t_s Beaver triples into n segments. In each segment, from $\mathbf{rid} = 1$ to R, parties not in $\mathcal{W}$ execute the following steps to generate degree-t_s Beaver triples for all parties in $\mathcal{P} \setminus \mathcal{W}$.

1: Each party $P_i \notin \mathcal{W}$ follows the protocol $\Pi_{\text{Triple-Sync}}$ to compute his $\mathbf{rid}$-th round broadcast message $m_0^{(i)}$ and P2P messages $\{m_j^{(i)}\}_{j \notin \mathcal{W}}$, where each $m_j^{(i)}$ is the P2P message to P_j.
2: All parties invoke an instance of Π_{Channel} with input $\mathcal{W}$, each party $P_i \notin \mathcal{W}$ takes input $(\mathbf{rid}, m_0^{(i)}, \{m_j^{(i)}\}_{j \notin \mathcal{W}})$. Upon receiving the output $\mathcal{W}'$ from Π_{Channel}, all parties compute $\mathcal{W} \leftarrow \mathcal{W} \cup \mathcal{W}'$.
3: All parties first check whether $|\mathcal{W}| \geq 2(t_s - t_a)$. If true, they move to the fallback procedure with the set $\mathcal{W}$. Otherwise, depending on the size of $\mathcal{W}', \mathcal{W}$ and $\mathbf{rid}$, all parties check whether $\mathcal{W}' = \varnothing$,
   - If true, then if $\mathbf{rid} < R$, they move to the ($\mathbf{rid}+1$)-th round of $\Pi_{\text{Triple-Sync}}$. Otherwise, the $\mathbf{rid} = R$, all parties compute their output following $\Pi_{\text{Triple-Sync}}$ and move to the next segment. For the output of $\Pi_{\text{Triple-Sync}}$,
     - If the output is $(\mathbf{Conflict}, P_i, P_j)$, they add the identity of P_i, P_j to set $\mathcal{W}$ and execute the current segment again.

- Otherwise, let $\mathcal{P}' = \mathcal{P} \setminus \mathcal{W}$, all parties in $\mathcal{P}'$ have generated valid degree-t_s Beaver triples. Then all parties terminate with $\mathcal{P}'$, parties in $\mathcal{P}'$ terminate with their degree-t_s Beaver triples.
  - Otherwise, they execute the current segment again.

Fallback Procedure

Let $\mathcal{P}'$ be the set of the first $4t_a + 1$ parties in $\mathcal{P} \setminus \mathcal{W}$, all parties in $\mathcal{P}'$ invoke $\Pi_{\text{Triple-Async}}$ to generate N degree-t_a Beaver triples for parties in $\mathcal{P}'$. Then all parties output the set $\mathcal{P}'$, parties in $\mathcal{P}'$ output their shares of degree-t_a Beaver triples.

Analysis of the Communication Complexity. The total communication costs of $\Pi_{\text{NA-Triple}}$ includes the costs of $\Pi_{\text{Triple-Sync}}$, $\Pi_{\text{Triple-Async}}$ and Π_{Channel}. For at most $\mathcal{O}(n)$ instances of $\Pi_{\text{Triple-Sync}}$ and one instance of $\Pi_{\text{Triple-Async}}$, it costs $\mathcal{O}((Nn + n^4)\log n)$-bit communication. For Π_{Channel}, since there are $\mathcal{O}(n)$ instances of $\Pi_{\text{Triple-Sync}}$, and for each instance of $\Pi_{\text{Triple-Sync}}$ parties need to invoke $R = \mathcal{O}(1)$ instances of Π_{Channel}, there are $\mathcal{O}(Rn) = \mathcal{O}(n)$ instances of Π_{Channel} in total. Each of Π_{Channel} performs an $\mathcal{O}(n^5 \log n)$-bit additive overhead, results in the total communication costs of $\Pi_{\text{NA-Triple}}$ is $\mathcal{O}((Nn + n^6)\log n)$-bit communication.

5.2 Efficient Public Reconstruction

As we introduced in Sect. 2.3, we give the public reconstruction protocol Π_{PubRec} that will be used in the online phase. Let N be the number of sharings to be reconstructed, the communication complexity is $\mathcal{O}((Nn + n^2)\log n)$ bits.

Protocol Π_{PubRec}

All parties in $\mathcal{P}$ take a party set $\mathcal{P}'$ as input. Let N be the number of shares to be reconstructed, $\alpha_1, \ldots, \alpha_n$ be deistinct field elements, t' denote the number of corrupted parties in $\mathcal{P}'$, t denote the degree of Shamir sharings to be reconstructed, and $n' = |\mathcal{P}'|$. The parameter t', t, n' satisfies the relation $(n' - t - 1)/2 \geq t'$. All parties take their shares of $[x_1]_t, \ldots, [x_N]_t$ as inputs.

1: Divide $[x_1]_t, \ldots, [x_N]_t$ into $N/(t+1)$ groups, each of size $t+1$. For each group, each party $P_i \in \mathcal{P}$ does the following.

  (1). Let $[s^{(0)}]_t, \ldots, [s^{(t)}]_t$ denote the degree-t Shamir secret sharings in this group. We define a degree-t polynomial $f(X)$ as follows.

$$f(X) = s^{(0)} + s^{(1)} \cdot X + \cdots + s^{(t)} \cdot X^t$$

      Then if $P_i \in \mathcal{P}'$, he sends his share of $[f(\alpha_j)]_t = [s^{(0)}]_t + [s^{(1)}]_t \cdot \alpha_j + \cdots + [s^{(t)}]_t \cdot \alpha_j^t$ to each $P_j \in \mathcal{P}'$. Otherwise, P_i does nothing in this step.

  (2). Each party $P_i \in \mathcal{P}'$ uses online error correction on shares of $[f(\alpha_i)]_t$ received from parties in $\mathcal{P}'$ to reconstruct $f(\alpha_i)$. Then P_i sends $f(\alpha_i)$ to all parties in $\mathcal{P}$.

> (3). Each party $P_i \in \mathcal{P}$ uses online error correction on $f(\alpha_j)$ received from $P_j \in \mathcal{P}'$ to reconstruct $f(X)$. Then P_i records $s^{(0)}, \ldots, s^{(t)}$.
>
> 2: All parties in $\mathcal{P}$ output $x_1, \ldots, x_N$.

5.3   Construction of Network-Agnostic MPC

We give the construction of $\Pi_{\text{NA-MPC}}$ to realize a perfectly secure agnostic MPC based on $\Pi_{\text{NA-Triple}}$. Let $|C|$ denote the circuit size, D denote the circuit depth, and C_I denote the input size. The achieved communication complexity is $\mathcal{O}((|C|n+n^6)\log n)$ bits in the offline phase and $\mathcal{O}((|C|n+(D+C_I)n^2+n^5)\log n)$ in the online phase. The total expected round complexity is $\mathcal{O}(D+n)$.

A subtle issue in the input phase is that the parties not only agree on a common set of dealers that have distributed their inputs, but also ensure that, in the synchronous case, all honest parties are included in this set. To address this, we introduce a waiting period so that every honest party can complete input distribution in the synchronous case, and only then run agreement to determine the common set. Refer to the following detailed construction.

Protocol $\Pi_{\text{NA-MPC}}$

Let $\mathcal{P} = \{P_1, \ldots, P_n\}$ denote the set of all parties, $|C|$ denote the circuit size, $|C_I|$ denote all parties' input size, and t_s, t_a be the corresponding corruption threshold when the network is synchronous or asynchronous. We use $\Pi_{\text{ba}}, \Pi_{\text{rbc}}$ to denote arbitrary network-agnostic BA and RBC protocols.

Offline Phase

Preparation of Beaver Triples. All parties start by invoking the regular procedure of $\Pi_{\text{NA-Triple}}$ with input parameter $|C| + |C_I|$ to prepare random Beaver triples. All parties will terminate $\Pi_{\text{NA-Triple}}$ with a set $\mathcal{P}'$:
- If all parties terminate the regular phase, parties in $\mathcal{P}'$ get $|C|+|C_I|$ degree-t_s random Beaver triples.
- Otherwise, all parties terminate the fallback procedure, parties in $\mathcal{P}'$ get $|C| + |C_I|$ degree-t_a random Beaver triples.

For the first $|C|$ random Beaver triples, we assign each of them to a multiplication gate. For the last $|C_I|$ Beaver triples, parties in $\mathcal{P}'$ only record the first random sharings in each triple. These random sharings will be used when parties distribute their inputs. In the following, we will use t to denote the degree of random Beaver triples that all parties prepared in the offline phase.

Online Phase

1: **Initialization.** All parties first invoke an instance of Π'_{ba} with input 1. Upon terminating Π'_{ba} with output 1, we know that when the network is synchronous, different honest parties will terminate Π'_{ba} at a similar time (at most 2Δ difference), where Δ is the time bound for each round in the synchronous case.

2: **Distributing Inputs.** For each party P_i's input x_i, all parties assign an unused degree-t sharing $[r]_t$ for it. Then parties in $\mathcal{P}'$ send their shares of $[r]_t$

to P_i, and P_i uses online error correction to reconstruct r. Upon getting r, P_i invokes Π_{rbc} to broadcast $x_i + r$. Upon receiving $x_i + r$ from P_i, parties in $\mathcal{P}'$ locally compute $[x_i]_t = x_i + r - [r]_t$.

3: **Agreement on the Set of Inputs.** All parties initialize n instances of the network-agnostic Π_{ba}, one for each party P_i, denoted by $\Pi_{\text{ba}}^{(i)}$. Then, each party proceeds to the following steps after waiting for an additional $\mathtt{Time}_{\text{bc}} + 2\Delta$ once it terminates Π_{ba}' in Step 1:

(1)   Once a party terminates the P_i's Π_{rbc}, each party sets its input to $\Pi_{\text{ba}}^{(i)}$ as 1.

(2)   After a party has terminated at least $n - t_s$ instances of Π_{ba} with output 1, for all P_i that this party has not terminated P_i's Π_{rbc}, it sets its input to $\Pi_{\text{ba}}^{(i)}$ as 0.

(3)   When all Π_{ba} instances have terminated, all parties define $\mathcal{D}$ as the set of identities corresponding to the all instances of Π_{ba} that output 1.

For every $P_i \in \mathcal{D}$, all parties hold the shares $[x_i]_t$ of its input. For every $P_i \notin \mathcal{D}$, the parties set the shares of P_i's input to 0.

4: **Online Circuit Evaluation.** All parties in $\mathcal{P}'$ evaluate the circuit gate by gate:

- For every addition gate with input sharings $[x]_t, [y]_t$, all parties in $\mathcal{P}'$ locally compute $[z]_t = [x]_t + [y]_t$.
- For a group of at most $t_s + 1$ multiplication gates, suppose the input degree-t Shamir sharings are denoted by $([x_i]_t, [y_i]_t)_{i=1}^{t_s+1}$. Let $([a_i]_t, [b_i]_t, [c_i]_t)_{i=1}^{t_s+1}$ denote the random Beaver triples assigned to these $t_s + 1$ gates.
  1. All parties in $\mathcal{P}'$ locally compute $[x_i + a_i]_t = [x_i]_t + [a_i]_t$ and $[y_i + b_i]_t = [y_i]_t + [b_i]_t$ for all $i \in [t_s + 1]$.
  2. All parties in $\mathcal{P}'$ invoke Π_{PubRec} with their shares and the set $\mathcal{P}'$ to reconstruct $\{x_i + a_i, y_i + b_i\}_{i=1}^{t_s+1}$.
  3. For all $i \in [t_s + 1]$, all parties in $\mathcal{P}'$ locally compute:

$$[z_i]_t = (x_i + a_i)(y_i + b_i) - (x_i + a_i)[b_i]_t - (y_i + b_i)[a_i]_t + [c_i]_t.$$

5: **Output and Termination.** All parties do the following steps.

(1).   For all output sharings $[y]_t$, all parties in $\mathcal{P}$ invoke Π_{PubRec} with input set $\mathcal{P}'$, and parties in $\mathcal{P}'$ additionally take their shares of $[y]_t$ as inputs. All parties in $\mathcal{P}$ will eventually get the output y from Π_{PubRec}.

Analysis of the Communication Complexity. During the offline phase, parties invoke $\Pi_{\text{NA-Triple}}$ to generate triples, which costs $\mathcal{O}(((C+C_I)n+n^6)\log n)$-bit communication. During the input phase, parties need to invoke n instances of Π_{ba}, n instances of Π_{rbc}, and one instance of Π_{ba}', which costs $\mathcal{O}((C_I n^2 + n^5)\log n)$-bit communication. During the evaluation and output phase, parties only need to do public reconstruction and therefore cost $\mathcal{O}((Cn + Dn^2)\log n)$-bit communication. Then the total communication complexity of $\Pi_{\text{NA-MPC}}$ is $\mathcal{O}((Cn + (C_I + D)n^2 + n^6)\log n)$ bits.

Lemma 1. *Protocol $\Pi_{\text{NA-MPC}}$ securely computes $\mathcal{F}_{\text{sfe}}$ against a fully malicious adversary $\mathcal{A}$ who corrupts at most t_s parties in the synchronous setting or t_a parties in the asynchronous setting.*

We prove Lemma 1 as follows. First, we consider the value parameter of τ_0, τ_f (defined in $\mathcal{F}_{\text{sfe}}$). We use $\text{Time}_{\text{bc}}, \text{Time}_{\text{ba}}$ to denote the running time of the network agnostic Π_{ba} and Π_{rbc} in the synchronous case. Let Δ denote the delivery time bound for a message sent in the synchronous network.

In the offline phase, let $R_{\text{sync}}, R_{\text{async}}$ denote the round number of the used synchronous and asynchronous protocol. All parties first invoke Π_{Channel} for each round of the synchronous protocol, and there are at most nR_{sync} instances of Π_{Channel} in our construction. For each Π_{Channel}, the running time is $10\Delta + 2\text{Time}_{\text{bc}} + \text{Time}_{\text{ba}}$ in the synchronous case. Then the total running time of the execution of synchronous protocol is $(10\Delta + 2\text{Time}_{\text{bc}} + \text{Time}_{\text{ba}})nR_{\text{sync}}$ in the synchronous case. For the execution of the asynchronous protocol, each round cost Δ in the synchronous case, results in ΔR_{async} in total. Therefore, the total running time of the offline phase is $(10\Delta + 2\text{Time}_{\text{bc}} + \text{Time}_{\text{ba}})nR_{\text{sync}} + \Delta R_{\text{async}}$ in the worse case.

In the input phase, before all parties eventually agree on the dealer set $\mathcal{D}$, the total running time is $2\Delta + 3\text{Time}_{\text{ba}} + \text{Time}_{\text{bc}}$ in the synchronous case. Therefore, we set

$$\tau_0 = (10\Delta + 2\text{Time}_{\text{bc}} + \text{Time}_{\text{ba}})nR_{\text{sync}} + \Delta R_{\text{async}} + 2\Delta + 3\text{Time}_{\text{ba}} + \text{Time}_{\text{bc}}.$$

During the circuit evaluation the output reconstruction, parties invoke $D+1$ instances of Π_{PubRec} in sequence, which costs $2(D+1)\Delta$ in total when the network is synchronous. Therefore, we set $\tau_f = \tau_0 + 2(D+1)\Delta$.

Then we construct the ideal adversary $\mathcal{S}$ as follows. Let $\mathcal{E}$ be the environment and $\mathcal{A}$ be the real-world adversary. $\mathcal{S}$ receives from $\mathcal{E}$ the party set $\mathcal{P} = \{P_1, \ldots, P_n\}$, the set of corrupted parties $Corr$, and the network configuration $\text{mode} \in \{\text{synch}, \text{asynch}\}$.

Simulator $\mathcal{S}$

Let $Corr$ denote the set of corrupted parties, $|Corr| \leq t_s$ when the network is synchronous, and $|Corr| \leq t_a$ when the network is asynchronous. We denote $\mathcal{S}_{\text{TripleIdSync}}$ and $\mathcal{S}_{\text{TripleAsync}}$ as the simulators used in the security proofs showing that $\Pi_{\text{Triple-Id-Sync}}$ and $\Pi_{\text{Triple-Async}}$ realize $\mathcal{F}_{\text{Triple-Id-Sync}}$ and $\mathcal{F}_{\text{Triple-Async}}$, respectively.

Offline Phase

1: During the **Regular Procedure**, $\mathcal{S}$ does the following steps. Let $\mathcal{A}_{\text{TripleIdSync}}$ be the adversary for the underlying synchronous triple generation protocol $\Pi_{\text{Triple-Id-Sync}}$ who just follows the instructions received from the environment $\mathcal{E}$ and passes the messages received from honest parties in each round. $\mathcal{S}$ acts as $\mathcal{E}_{\text{TripleIdSync}}$ and $\mathcal{F}_{\text{Triple-Id-Sync}}$ and invokes $\mathcal{S}_{\text{TripleIdSync}}$.

2: For the simulation of $\mathcal{F}_{\text{Triple-Id-Sync}}$, $\mathcal{S}$ does the following steps.

    (1). Receive the party set $\mathcal{P}'$ and corrupted party set $Corr'$ from $\mathcal{S}_{\text{TripleIdSync}}$.

(2). Receive a set of shares $\{u_{i,j}, v_{i,j}, w_{i,j}\}_{i\in[N], j\in Corr'}$ of corrupted parties from $\mathcal{S}_{\text{TripleIdSync}}$.

(3). When all honest parties can get their shares of triples, simulate the behavior of sending output messages from $\mathcal{F}_{\text{Triple-Id-Sync}}$ to all honest parties in $\mathcal{P}'$. Upon receiving a request $(\texttt{Conflict}, P_i, P_j)$ from $\mathcal{S}$, if the output of all honest parties has not been delivered and $P_i, P_j \in \mathcal{P}'$, change it to $(\texttt{Conflict}, P_i, P_j)$. Otherwise, ignore this message.

3: In each segment of triple generation, we set $\mathcal{P}' = \mathcal{P} \setminus \mathcal{W}$, and let $Corr'$ denote the corrupted parties in $\mathcal{P}'$. Then from $\texttt{rid} = 1$ to R in the current segment,

(1). $\mathcal{S}$ receives from $\mathcal{A}_{\text{TripleIdSync}}$ the P2P messages and broadcast messages that parties in $\mathcal{P}' \setminus Corr'$ send to parties in $Corr'$.

(2). In $\Pi_{\text{NA-Triple}}$, for each honest party $P_i \in \mathcal{P}'$, after P_i enters the $\texttt{rid}$th round, $\mathcal{S}$ prepares $(m_0^{(i)}, \{m_j^{(i)}\}_{j\notin\mathcal{W}})$ as follows: $\mathcal{S}$ sets $m_0^{(i)}$ as the broadcast messages of P_i received from $\mathcal{A}_{\text{TripleIdSync}}$. For each $P_j \in Corr'$, $\mathcal{S}$ sets $m_j^{(i)}$ as the P2P message sent from P_i to P_j received from $\mathcal{A}_{\text{TripleIdSync}}$. Then $\mathcal{S}$ takes $(m_0^{(i)}, \{m_j^{(i)}\}_{j\notin\mathcal{W}})$ as P_i's input for Π_{Channel} and honestly execute P_i during the Π_{Channel}.

(3). In $\Pi_{\text{NA-Triple}}$, after all parties terminate Π_{Channel} with a set $\mathcal{W}'$, $\mathcal{S}$ follows the protocol to update $\mathcal{W}$. Then, depending on the size of the sets $\mathcal{W}', \mathcal{W}$ and round id $\texttt{rid}$, if $|\mathcal{W}| \geq 2(t_s - t_a)$, $\mathcal{S}$ breaks the loop. Otherwise, $\mathcal{S}$ furthers checks whether $\mathcal{W}' = \varnothing$,

- If true, then if $\texttt{rid} < R$, $\mathcal{S}$ moves to the next round $\texttt{rid}+1$. Otherwise,
  * If $\mathcal{S}$ has received $(\texttt{Conflict}, P_i, P_j)$ during the simulation of $\mathcal{F}_{\text{Triple-Id-Sync}}$, he follows the protocol to update $\mathcal{W}$ and reruns the current segment.
  * Otherwise, $\mathcal{S}$ considers that all parties can terminate the current segment, and $\mathcal{S}$ learns corrupted parties' shares of triples in this segment. Then $\mathcal{S}$ moves to the next segment.
- Otherwise, $\mathcal{S}$ follows the protocol to update $\mathcal{W}$ and reruns the current segment.

If $\mathcal{S}$ terminates the generation of triples for all n segments, $\mathcal{S}$ learns corrupted parties' shares of degree-t_s Beaver triples and moves to the online phase. If $\mathcal{S}$ breaks the loop, $\mathcal{S}$ moves to the fallback procedure.

4: When all parties move to the **Fallback Procedure**, $\mathcal{S}$ does the following steps. $\mathcal{S}$ sets $\mathcal{P}'$ as the first $4t_a + 1$ parties in $\mathcal{P} \setminus \mathcal{W}$. To simulate the fallback procedure, let $\mathcal{A}_{\text{TripleAsync}}$ be the adversary for the underlying asynchronous triple generation protocol $\Pi_{\text{Triple-Async}}$ who follows the instructions received from the environment and passes the messages received from honest parties in each round. $\mathcal{S}$ acts as $\mathcal{E}_{\text{asynch}}$ and $\mathcal{F}_{\text{Triple-Async}}$ and invokes $\mathcal{S}_{\text{TripleAsync}}$.

5: For the simulation of $\mathcal{F}_{\text{Triple-Async}}$,

(1). Define $Corr'$ be the set of corrupted parties in $\mathcal{P}'$.

(2). Receive a set of shares $\{u_{i,j}, v_{i,j}, w_{i,j}\}_{i\in[N], j\in Corr'}$ of corrupted parties from $\mathcal{S}_{\text{TripleAsync}}$.

(3). When all honest parties can get their shares of triples, simulate the behavior of sending output messages from $\mathcal{F}_{\text{Triple-Id-Sync}}$ to all honest parties in $\mathcal{P}'$.

6: For $\mathcal{E}_{\text{asynch}}$, $\mathcal{S}$ instructs $\mathcal{A}_{\text{TripleAsync}}$ to corrupt parties in $Corr'$. Then,

- Whenever $\mathcal{E}$ activates a party $P_i \in \mathcal{P}'$ in $\Pi_{\text{NA-Triple}}$, $\mathcal{S}$ activates P_i in $\Pi_{\text{Triple-Async}}$.
- For each message sent from $P_i \in Corr'$ to $P_j \in \mathcal{P}' \setminus Corr'$ in $\Pi_{\text{NA-Triple}}$, $\mathcal{S}$ receives the message from $\mathcal{A}$ and instructs $\mathcal{A}_{\text{TripleAsync}}$ to let P_i sends the same message to P_j.
- For each message sent from $P_i \in \mathcal{P}' \setminus Corr'$ to $P_j \in Corr'$ in $\Pi_{\text{Triple-Async}}$, $\mathcal{S}$ receives the message from $\mathcal{A}_{\text{TripleAsync}}$ and sends it to P_j on behalf of P_i in $\Pi_{\text{Triple-Async}}$.

Upon terminating $\Pi_{\text{Triple-Async}}$, $\mathcal{S}$ learns corrupted parties' shares of degree-t_a Beaver triples and moves to the online phase.

Online Phase

1: Upon terminating the offline phase, $\mathcal{S}$ learns the set $\mathcal{P}'$. We use $Corr'$ to denote the corrupted parties set in $\mathcal{P}'$ and set $|Corr'| = t' \leq t$, where t is the degree of the random Beaver triples all parties prepared during the offline phase. Let $\mathcal{H}_C$ denote the set of first $t - t'$ honest parties in $\mathcal{P}'$.

2: During the **Initialization**, $\mathcal{S}$ honestly execute honest parties to participate in Π'_{ba}.

3: During the **Distributing Inputs**, for each party $P_i \in \mathcal{P}$:
   - If P_i is corrupted, $\mathcal{S}$ randomly samples the whole sharing $[r]_t$ based on shares of corrupted parties. Then $\mathcal{S}$ honestly executes each honest party to reconstruct r to $\mathcal{S}$. Upon receiving $x_i + r$ from P_i's reliable broadcast, $\mathcal{S}$ extracts P_i's inputs x_i.
   - If P_i is honest, $\mathcal{S}$ simulates the behavior of sending messages between honest parties and P_i. For each share received from an honest party, $\mathcal{S}$ considers this share to be correct. For each share received from a corrupted party, $\mathcal{S}$ checks whether it is the same as the one known to $\mathcal{S}$. If true, $\mathcal{S}$ also considers it correct. When P_i receives $2t + 1$ correct shares, $\mathcal{S}$ considers P_i succeeds in using online error correction to reconstruct the secret r.

   Then, for each honest party $P_i \in \mathcal{P}$, $\mathcal{S}$ randomly samples a value as $x_i + r$ and reliable broadcasts it on behalf of P_i.

4: During the **Agreement on the Set of Inputs**, $\mathcal{S}$ honestly follows the protocol to execute all instances of Π_{ba} with their inputs. Upon terminating, $\mathcal{S}$ learns the set $\mathcal{D}$ of size at least $n - t_s$. Then, $\mathcal{S}$ samples random values for each party in $\mathcal{H}_C$ as their shares of $[x_i]_t$ for each $P_i \in \mathcal{D}$.
   - If $\mathsf{mode} = \mathsf{synch}$, before τ_0, $\mathcal{S}$ sends the set of corrupted parties $Corr$, the set $\mathcal{D}$ which contains the parties who provide inputs, corrupted parties input $\{x_i\}_{Corr' \cap \mathcal{D}}$, and the network mode mode to $\mathcal{F}_{\text{sfe}}$.
   - Otherwise, $\mathcal{S}$ defers this step to the output and termination phase.

5: During the **Online Circuit Evaluation**, for each addition gate, $\mathcal{S}$ follows the protocol to compute the output share for all parties in $Corr' \cup \mathcal{H}_C$. For multiplication gates:
   (1). $\mathcal{S}$ follows the protocol to compute shares of $\{[x_i + a_i]_t, [y_i + x_i]_t\}_{i=1}^{t_s+1}$ for all parties in $Corr' \cup \mathcal{H}_C$.
   (2). $\mathcal{S}$ randomly samples the whole sharings $\{[x_i + a_i]_t, [y_i + b_i]_t\}_{i=1}^{t_s+1}$ based on the shares he computed for parties in $Corr' \cup \mathcal{H}_C$. Then $\mathcal{S}$ gets each shares of $\{[x_i + a_i]_t, [y_i + b_i]_t\}_{i=1}^{t_s+1}$ for honest parties in $\mathcal{P}' \setminus \mathcal{H}_C$, and can honestly execute them during the Π_{PubRec}.

(3). When all parties terminate Π_{PubRec}, $\mathcal{S}$ computes the output shares for all parties in $\mathcal{C}orr' \cup \mathcal{H}_{\mathcal{C}}$.

6: During the **Output and Termination**, upon receiving $\boldsymbol{y}$ from $\mathcal{F}_{\mathsf{sfe}}$, $\mathcal{S}$ computes the whole sharing $[\boldsymbol{y}]_t$ based on the secrets $\boldsymbol{y}$ and shares of $[\boldsymbol{y}]_t$ for parties in $\mathcal{C}orr' \cup \mathcal{H}_{\mathcal{C}}$. With the whole sharing $[\boldsymbol{y}]_t$, $\mathcal{S}$ honestly executes the rest of the steps. When each honest party can get his output, $\mathcal{S}$ delivers the output from $\mathcal{F}_{\mathsf{sfe}}$ to this honest party. In particular, if $\mathsf{mode} = \mathsf{synch}$, an honest party P_i will get his output before τ_f, and $\mathcal{S}$ sends $(\mathtt{Deliver}, P_i)$ to $\mathcal{F}_{\mathsf{sfe}}$ to deliver the output from $\mathcal{F}_{\mathsf{sfe}}$ to this honest party P_i.

Now we show that any computationally unbounded environment $\mathcal{E}$ cannot distinguish the real-world and the ideal-world.

Hyb$_0$: In the initial hybrid, we consider the real-world execution and define the output to be the output of $\mathcal{E}$.

Hyb$_1$: In the following, we focus on the simulation of the offline phase.

Hyb$_{1.1}$: In this hybrid, during the **Regular Procedure**, we change the construction of $\mathcal{S}$ as above. The only difference is that $\mathcal{S}$ learns each honest party P_i's P2P and broadcast messages $(m_0^{(i)}, \{m_j^{(i)}\}_{j \notin \mathcal{W}})$ from $\mathcal{A}_{\mathtt{TripleIdSync}}$. Note that here we also let $\mathcal{S}$ play the role of $\mathcal{A}_{\mathtt{TripleIdSync}}$ during the $\Pi_{\mathtt{Triple\text{-}Id\text{-}Sync}}$, then $\mathcal{A}_{\mathtt{TripleIdSync}}$ will receive honest P_i's P2P and broadcast messages generated by $\mathcal{S}_{\mathtt{TripleIdSync}}$. Since $\Pi_{\mathtt{Triple\text{-}Id\text{-}Sync}}$ realizes $\mathcal{F}_{\mathsf{Triple\text{-}Id\text{-}Sync}}$ with perfect security, then the honest party P_i's P2P and broadcast messages $\mathcal{S}$ received from $\mathcal{A}_{\mathtt{TripleIdSync}}$ have the same distribution as in **Hyb$_1$**. The distributions of **Hyb$_{1.1}$** and **Hyb$_1$** are the same.

Hyb$_{1.2}$: In this hybrid, we let $\mathcal{S}$ play the role of $\mathcal{F}_{\mathsf{Triple\text{-}Id\text{-}Sync}}$ during the **Regular Procedure**, and $\mathcal{S}$ will delay the delivery of honest parties' output shares until the online phase. The distributions of **Hyb$_{1.2}$** and **Hyb$_{1.1}$** are the same.

Hyb$_{1.3}$: In this hybrid, during the **Fallback Procedure**, we change the construction of $\mathcal{S}$ as above, and let $\mathcal{S}$ play the role of $\mathcal{F}_{\mathsf{Triple\text{-}Async}}$. Following the same reason as in **Hyb$_{1.1}$, Hyb$_{1.2}$**, the distributions of **Hyb$_{1.3}$** and **Hyb$_{1.2}$** are the same.

Hyb$_2$: In the following, we focus on the simulation of the online phase.

Hyb$_{2.1}$: In this hybrid, we change the generation of random degree-t sharing $[r]_t$ assigned to an honest party in the input phase. $\mathcal{S}$ first randomly samples a value as $x_i + r$, then computes $r = x_i + r - x_i$ and the whole sharing $[r]_t$ based on the secret r and shares of corrupted parties. Since both r and $x_i + r$ are uniformly random, the distributions of **Hyb$_{2.1}$** and **Hyb$_{2.0}$** are the same.

Hyb$_{2.2}$: In this hybrid, let $\mathcal{H}_{\mathcal{C}}$ be the set of first $t - t'$ honest parties in $\mathcal{P}'$, $\mathcal{S}$ samples random values as their shares of $[x_i]_t$ for each dealer $P_i \in \mathcal{D}$. Since the whole sharing $[x_i]_t$ is still uniformly random given shares of parties in $\mathcal{C}orr \cup \mathcal{H}_{\mathcal{C}}$, the distributions of **Hyb$_{2.2}$** and **Hyb$_{2.1}$** are the same.

Hyb$_{2.3}$: In this hybrid, during the **Online Circuit Evaluation**, when all parties need to reconstruct $\{[x_i + a_i]_t, [y_i + b_i]_t\}_{i=1}^{t_s+1}$, $\mathcal{S}$ first randomly samples the whole sharings $[x_i + a_i]_t, [y_i + b_i]_t$ based on shares of parties in $\mathcal{C}orr \cup \mathcal{H}_{\mathcal{C}}$, then compute $[a_i]_t = [x_i + a_i]_t - [x_i]_t$, $[b_i]_t = [y_i + b_i]_t - [y_i]_t$. The difference is that we change the generation of $[a_i]_t, [b_i]_t$, however, both of the secrets a_i, b_i and $x_i + a_i, y_i + b_i$ are sampled by $\mathcal{S}$, and they are uniformly random given shares of parties in $Corr \cup \mathcal{H}_{\mathcal{C}}$. Therefore, the distributions of $\mathbf{Hyb}_{2.3}$ and $\mathbf{Hyb}_{2.2}$ are the same.

$\mathbf{Hyb}_{2.4}$: In this hybrid, while reconstructing the output sharing $[\boldsymbol{y}]_t$ to a corrupted receiver $\mathcal{S}$ first computes $\boldsymbol{y}$ from all parties' inputs and then computes $[\boldsymbol{y}]_t$ from secret $\boldsymbol{y}$ and the shares for parties in $Corr \cup \mathcal{H}_{\mathcal{C}}$. Finally, $\mathcal{S}$ honestly executes the rest of the steps on behalf of each honest party in $\mathcal{P}'$.

Here, we only change the way of generating the output shares for honest parties not in $\mathcal{H}_{\mathcal{C}}$. We don't change the generation process of shares for parties in $Corr \cup \mathcal{H}_{\mathcal{C}}$ of $[\boldsymbol{y}]_t$ and the secret $\boldsymbol{y}$, and shares of $[\boldsymbol{y}]_t$ for honest parties not in $\mathcal{H}_{\mathcal{C}}$ are fully determined by the shares for parties in $Corr \cup \mathcal{H}_{\mathcal{C}}$ and the secret. Therefore, the honest parties' shares of $[\boldsymbol{y}]_t$ stay unchanged. Thus, $\mathbf{Hyb}_{2.4}$ and $\mathbf{Hyb}_{2.3}$ have the same distribution.

$\mathbf{Hyb}_{2.5}$: In this hybrid, $\mathcal{S}$ doesn't generate shares for honest parties out of $\mathcal{H}_{\mathcal{C}}$ of any Shamir secret sharing. For the computation of output sharings reconstructed to corrupted parties, $\mathcal{S}$ doesn't follow the protocol to compute the secrets. Instead, $\mathcal{S}$ directly uses the corrupted parties' outputs as the secrets. Clearly, by the correctness of the protocol, the outputs computed by following the protocol match the outputs from $\mathcal{F}_{\mathsf{sfe}}$. Besides, the shares for honest parties out of $\mathcal{H}_{\mathcal{C}}$ are not used in the simulation. Thus, $\mathbf{Hyb}_{2.5}$ and $\mathbf{Hyb}_{2.4}$ have the same distribution.

$\mathbf{Hyb}_{2.6}$: In this hybrid, $\mathcal{S}$ no longer requires honest parties' inputs. $\mathcal{S}$ sends the corrupted parties' input, the set of parties who provide input, and the network mode to $\mathcal{F}_{\mathsf{sfe}}$. When each honest party succeeds in using online error correction to reconstruct $\boldsymbol{y}$, $\mathcal{S}$ delivers the output from $\mathcal{F}_{\mathsf{sfe}}$ to this honest party. Thus, $\mathbf{Hyb}_{2.6}$ and $\mathbf{Hyb}_{2.5}$ have the same distribution.

Note that $\mathbf{Hyb}_{2.6}$ is the ideal-world scenario, then we prove that $\Pi_{\mathsf{NA-MPC}}$ realizes $\mathcal{F}_{\mathsf{sfe}}$ with perfect security.

Acknowledgments. X. Ji and Y. Song were supported in part by the National Basic Research Program of China Grant 2011CBA00300, 2011CBA00301, the National Natural Science Foundation of China Grant 61033001, 61361136003. Y. Song was also supported in part by the Shanghai Qi Zhi Institute Innovation Program SQZ202313.

A   Review of the Construction in [BH08]

In this section, we review the triple generation protocol in [BH08] that achieves security with identifiable abort. We use d to denote the degree of triples to be generated, n to denote the number of parties, and t to denote the corruption threshold among these n parties. The parameters d, n, t satisfy that $t \leq d$ and $d + 2t < n$.

At a high level, there are three main stages for their construction.

– **Stage 1: Generating Non-robust Triples.**

- **Stage 2: Agreement on the Success of Triple Generation.**
- **Stage 3: Fault Localization.**

Realization of Stage 1. Parties first prepare random double sharings in the following form.

$$([a]_d, [a]_t), ([b]_d, [b]_t), ([r]_d, [r]_{2t})$$

The authors in [BH08] show how this can be realized with the help of the hyper-invertible matrix, and we refer to the details of this part to their original paper [BH08]. During the generation of these sharings, parties need to verify whether the degree of each sharing is correct and the secrets in each pair of double sharing are the same. If not, at least one honest party would be "unhappy", indicating the generation of triples fails for this party.

Then all parties use these double sharings to generate a triple in the form of $([a]_d, [b]_d, [c]_d)$, where the first two sharings come from their prepared double sharings, and the goal is to compute the third sharing $[c]_d$ such that $c = a \cdot b$. To achieve this goal, all parties do the following steps.

1. Parties locally compute their shares of $[c]_{2t} = [a]_t \cdot [b]_t$. Then they compute $[e]_{2t} = [c]_{2t} - [r]_{2t}$. Note that if a party is "unhappy" with their shares of the double sharings, it will set its share of $[e]_{2t}$ to be $\perp$.
2. Parties exchange their shares of $[e]_{2t}$ to reconstruct the secret e. During this procedure, if a party receives $\perp$ from any party, it will also be "unhappy". If the received n shares do not lie on a unique degree-$2t$ polynomial, parties also become "unhappy".
3. Upon getting e, parties compute their shares of $[c]_d := [r]_d + e$.

As a result, upon terminating the triple generation protocol, we guarantee that parties can either get their shares of $([a]_d, [b]_d, [c]_d)$ or be "unhappy". Then the next step is to let all parties identify whether all of them are "happy". If true, this means all parties have got their shares of triples, and they can terminate. Otherwise, they need to detect a pair of parties that are responsible for the failure of the triple generation process.

In [BH08], the reconstruction of $[e]_{2t}$ is optimized via batch reconstruction that achieves linear communication.

Realization of Stage 2. In this stage, each party P_i that has got its shares of triples will broadcast (P_i, happy), and $(P_i, \mathsf{unhappy})$ otherwise. Then parties wait to receive all these broadcast messages. If all of them are in the form of (P_i, happy), then they can terminate with their shares of triples. Otherwise, this means at least one party P_i considers the triple generation fails, and parties need to do fault localization and detect the reason why P_i is "unhappy".

We note that in the original construction in [BH08], the authors let all parties first exchange their happy bit with each other and then invoke an instance of the BA protocol to reach an agreement. This only costs $\mathcal{O}(n^2 \log n)$-bit communication. However, the BA protocol would require $\mathcal{O}(n)$ rounds to terminate. Here we use n instances of broadcast to replace the BA protocol. Although the communication complexity would blow up to $\mathcal{O}(n^3 \log n)$ bits, the round complexity is reduced to a constant since the broadcast protocol can be realized within constant rounds.

Realization of Stage 3. In this stage, parties proceed with the following steps.

1. Parties first select a party P_r with the smallest index r as the referee, then they send all their views to P_r.
2. With all parties' views, P_r can locally finish all computation for the triple generation procedure. As a result, P_r can detect that there exists a pair of parties (P_i, P_j), and a message with index ℓ where P_i should have sent x to P_j, but P_j claims to have received $x' \neq x$. Then P_r broadcast (ℓ, P_i, P_j, x, x').
3. Upon receiving (ℓ, P_i, P_j, x, x') from P_r, the accused parties P_i and P_j need to broadcast whether they agree with P_r. Let E denote the pair of parties to be eliminated. If P_i disagrees, set $E = \{P_r, P_i\}$. If P_j disagrees, set $E = \{P_r, P_j\}$. Otherwise, set $E = \{P_i, P_j\}$.

For the eliminated parties in E, the authors in [BH08] show that at least one of them is corrupted. Refer to the original paper for more details. During this procedure, each party needs to broadcast $\mathcal{O}(\log n)$ bits, and P_r needs to broadcast $\mathcal{O}(|\ell| + \log n)$ bits.

References

[AAPP23] Abraham, I., Asharov, G., Patil, S., Patra, A.: Detect, pack and batch: perfectly-secure MPC with linear communication and constant expected time. In: Annual International Conference on the Theory and Applications of Cryptographic Techniques, pp. 251–281. Springer (2023)

[AAPP24] Abraham, I., Asharov, G., Patil, S., Patra, A.: Perfect asynchronous MPC with linear communication overhead. In: Annual International Conference on the Theory and Applications of Cryptographic Techniques, pp. 280–309. Springer (2024)

[AAPS25] Abraham, I., Ashsarov, G., Patra, A., Stern, G.: Asynchronous agreement on a core set in constant expected time and more efficient asynchronous VSS and MPC. In: Theory of Cryptography Conference, pp. 451–482. Springer (2025)

[ABKL22] Alexandru, A.B., Blum, E., Katz, J., Loss, J.: State machine replication under changing network conditions. In: Agrawal, S., Lin, D. (eds.) ASIACRYPT 2022, Part I. LNCS, vol. 13791, pp. 681–710. Springer, Cham (2022)

[AC23] Appan, A., Choudhury, A.: Network agnostic MPC with statistical security. In: Rothblum, G.N., Wee, H. (eds.) TCC 2023, Part II. LNCS, vol. 14370, pp. 63–93. Springer, Cham (2023)

[ACC22] Appan, A., Chandramouli, A., Choudhury, A.: Perfectly-secure synchronous MPC with asynchronous fallback guarantees. In: Milani, A., Woelfel, P. (eds.) 41st ACM PODC, pp. 92–102. ACM (2022)

[BCG93] Ben-Or, M., Canetti, R., Goldreich, O.: Asynchronous secure computation. In: 25th ACM STOC, pp. 52–61. ACM Press (1993)

[BCLZL23] Bacho, R., Collins, D., Liu-Zhang, C.-D., Loss, J.: Network-agnostic security comes (almost) for free in DKG and MPC. In: Handschuh, H., Lysyanskaya, A. (eds.) CRYPTO 2023, Part I. LNCS, vol. 14081, pp. 71–106. Springer, Cham (2023)

[BCV24] Bhimrajka, N., Choudhury, A., Varadarajan, S.: Network-agnostic multiparty computation revisited (extended abstract). In: Tang, Q., Teague, V. (eds.) PKC 2024, Part II. LNCS, vol. 14602, pp. 171–204. Springer, Cham (2024)

[BDD+21] Baum, C., David, B., Dowsley, R., Nielsen, J.B., Oechsner, S.: TARDIS: a foundation of time-lock puzzles in UC. In: Canteaut, A., Standaert, F.-X. (eds.) EUROCRYPT 2021. LNCS, vol. 12698, pp. 429–459. Springer, Cham (2021). https://doi.org/10.1007/978-3-030-77883-5_15

[Bea92] Beaver, D.: Efficient multiparty protocols using circuit randomization. In: Feigenbaum, J. (ed.) CRYPTO 1991. LNCS, vol. 576, pp. 420–432. Springer, Heidelberg (1992). https://doi.org/10.1007/3-540-46766-1_34

[BGW88] Ben-Or, M., Goldwasser, S., Wigderson, A.: Completeness theorems for non-cryptographic fault-tolerant distributed computation (extended abstract). In: 20th ACM STOC, pp. 1–10. ACM Press (1988)

[BH08] Beerliová-Trubíniová, Z., Hirt, M.: Perfectly-secure MPC with linear communication complexity. In: Canetti, R. (ed.) TCC 2008. LNCS, vol. 4948, pp. 213–230. Springer, Heidelberg (2008). https://doi.org/10.1007/978-3-540-78524-8_13

[BJK+25a] Bandarupalli, A., Ji, X., Kate, A., Liu-Zhang, C.D., Pöllmann, D., Song, Y.: Velox: scalable fair asynchronous MPC from lightweight cryptography. In: Huang, C.-Y., Chen, J.-C., Shieh, S.-P., Lie, D., Cortier, V. (eds.) ACM CCS 2025, pp. 1799–1813. ACM Press (2025)

[BJK+25b] Bandarupalli, A., Ji, X., Kate, A., Liu-Zhang, C.D., Song, Y.: Computationally efficient asynchronous MPC with linear communication and low additive overhead. In: Kalai, Y.T., Kamara, S.F. (eds.) CRYPTO 2025, Part IV. LNCS, vol. 16003, pp. 261–294. Springer, Cham (2025)

[BKL19] Blum, E., Katz, J., Loss, J.: Synchronous consensus with optimal asynchronous fallback guarantees. In: Hofheinz, D., Rosen, A. (eds.) TCC 2019. LNCS, vol. 11891, pp. 131–150. Springer, Cham (2019). https://doi.org/10.1007/978-3-030-36030-6_6

[BKL21] Blum, E., Katz, J., Loss, J.: TARDIGRADE: an atomic broadcast protocol for arbitrary network conditions. In: Tibouchi, M., Wang, H. (eds.) ASIACRYPT 2021. LNCS, vol. 13091, pp. 547–572. Springer, Cham (2021). https://doi.org/10.1007/978-3-030-92075-3_19

[BKR94] Ben-Or, M., Kelmer, B., Rabin, T.: Asynchronous secure computations with optimal resilience (extended abstract). In: Anderson, J., Toueg, S. (eds.) 13th ACM PODC, pp. 183–192. ACM (1994)

[Bra84] Bracha, G.: An asynchronous [(n - 1)/3]-resilient consensus protocol. In: Proceedings of the Third Annual ACM Symposium on Principles of Distributed Computing, PODC 1984, pp. 154–162. Association for Computing Machinery, New York, NY, USA (1984)

[BSFO12] Ben-Sasson, E., Fehr, S., Ostrovsky, R.: Near-linear unconditionally-secure multiparty computation with a dishonest minority. In: Safavi-Naini, R., Canetti, R. (eds.) CRYPTO 2012. LNCS, vol. 7417, pp. 663–680. Springer, Heidelberg (2012). https://doi.org/10.1007/978-3-642-32009-5_39

[BZL20] Blum, E., Liu-Zhang, C.-D., Loss, J.: Always have a backup plan: fully secure synchronous MPC with asynchronous fallback. In: Micciancio, D., Ristenpart, T. (eds.) CRYPTO 2020. LNCS, vol. 12171, pp. 707–731. Springer, Cham (2020). https://doi.org/10.1007/978-3-030-56880-1_25

[Can01] Canetti, R.: Universally composable security: a new paradigm for cryptographic protocols. In: 42nd FOCS, pp. 136–145. IEEE Computer Society Press (2001)

[CCD88] Chaum, D., Crépeau, C., Damgard, I.: Multiparty unconditionally secure protocols (extended abstract). In: 20th ACM STOC, pp. 11–19. ACM Press (1988)

[CFG+23] Cohen, R., Forghani, P., Garay, J., Patel, R., Zikas, V.: Concurrent asynchronous byzantine agreement in expected-constant rounds, revisited. In: Rothblum, G.N., Wee, H. (eds.) TCC 2023, Part IV. LNCS, vol. 14372, pp. 422–451. Springer, Cham (2023)

[CGHZ16] Coretti, S., Garay, J., Hirt, M., Zikas, V.: Constant-round asynchronous multi-party computation based on one-way functions. In: Cheon, J.H., Takagi, T. (eds.) ASIACRYPT 2016. LNCS, vol. 10032, pp. 998–1021. Springer, Heidelberg (2016). https://doi.org/10.1007/978-3-662-53890-6_33

[CHLZ21] Chopard, A., Hirt, M., Liu-Zhang, C.-D.: On communication-efficient asynchronous MPC with adaptive security. In: Nissim, K., Waters, B. (eds.) TCC 2021. LNCS, vol. 13043, pp. 35–65. Springer, Cham (2021). https://doi.org/10.1007/978-3-030-90453-1_2

[Coh16] Cohen, R.: Asynchronous secure multiparty computation in constant time. In: Cheng, C.-M., Chung, K.-M., Persiano, G., Yang, B.-Y. (eds.) PKC 2016. LNCS, vol. 9615, pp. 183–207. Springer, Heidelberg (2016). https://doi.org/10.1007/978-3-662-49387-8_8

[DHLZ21] Deligios, G., Hirt, M., Liu-Zhang, C.-D.: Round-efficient byzantine agreement and multi-party computation with asynchronous fallback. In: Nissim, K., Waters, B. (eds.) TCC 2021. LNCS, vol. 13042, pp. 623–653. Springer, Cham (2021). https://doi.org/10.1007/978-3-030-90459-3_21

[DLZ23] Deligios, G., Liu-Zhang, C.-D.: Synchronous perfectly secure message transmission with optimal asynchronous fallback guarantees. In: Baldimtsi, F., Cachin, C. (eds.) FC 2023, Part I. LNCS, vol. 13950, pp. 77–93. Springer, Cham (2023). https://doi.org/10.1007/978-3-031-47754-6_5

[DME24] Deligios, G., Mizrahi Erbes, M.: Closing the efficiency gap between synchronous and network-agnostic consensus. In: Annual International Conference on the Theory and Applications of Cryptographic Techniques, pp. 432–461. Springer (2024)

[DN07] Damgård, I., Nielsen, J.B.: Scalable and unconditionally secure multiparty computation. In: Menezes, A. (ed.) CRYPTO 2007. LNCS, vol. 4622, pp. 572–590. Springer, Heidelberg (2007). https://doi.org/10.1007/978-3-540-74143-5_32

[GLS19] Goyal, V., Liu, Y., Song, Y.: Communication-efficient unconditional MPC with guaranteed output delivery. In: Boldyreva, A., Micciancio, D. (eds.) CRYPTO 2019. LNCS, vol. 11693, pp. 85–114. Springer, Cham (2019). https://doi.org/10.1007/978-3-030-26951-7_4

[GLZS24] Goyal, V., Liu-Zhang, C.-D., Song, Y.: Towards achieving asynchronous MPC with linear communication and optimal resilience. In: Reyzin, L., Stebila, D. (eds.) CRYPTO 2024, Part VIII. LNCS, vol. 14927, pp. 170–206. Springer, Cham (2024). https://doi.org/10.1007/978-3-031-68397-8_6

[GLZW22] Ghinea, D., Liu-Zhang, C.D., Wattenhofer, R.: Optimal synchronous approximate agreement with asynchronous fallback. In: Milani, A., Woelfel, P. (eds.) 41st ACM PODC, pp. 70–80. ACM (2022)

[GLZW23] Ghinea, D., Liu-Zhang, C.D., Wattenhofer, R.: Multidimensional approximate agreement with asynchronous fallback. In: Proceedings of the 35th ACM Symposium on Parallelism in Algorithms and Architectures, pp. 141–151 (2023)

[GMW87] Goldreich, O., Micali, S., Wigderson, A.: How to play any mental game or A completeness theorem for protocols with honest majority. In: Aho, A. (ed.) 19th ACM STOC, pp. 218–229. ACM Press (1987)

[GSZ20] Goyal, V., Song, Y., Zhu, C.: Guaranteed output delivery comes free in honest majority MPC. In: Micciancio, D., Ristenpart, T. (eds.) CRYPTO 2020. LNCS, vol. 12171, pp. 618–646. Springer, Cham (2020). https://doi.org/10.1007/978-3-030-56880-1_22

[HMP00] Hirt, M., Maurer, U., Przydatek, B.: Efficient secure multi-party computation. In: Okamoto, T. (ed.) ASIACRYPT 2000. LNCS, vol. 1976, pp. 143–161. Springer, Heidelberg (2000). https://doi.org/10.1007/3-540-44448-3_12

[HNP05] Hirt, M., Nielsen, J.B., Przydatek, B.: Cryptographic asynchronous multi-party computation with optimal resilience. In: Cramer, R. (ed.) EUROCRYPT 2005. LNCS, vol. 3494, pp. 322–340. Springer, Heidelberg (2005). https://doi.org/10.1007/11426639_19

[JLZPS26] Ji, X., Liu-Zhang, C. D., Pöllmann, D., Song, Y.: Information-theoretic network-agnostic MPC with polynomial communication. In: Annual International Conference on the Theory and Applications of Cryptographic Techniques. Springer (2026)

[KMTZ13] Katz, J., Maurer, U., Tackmann, B., Zikas, V.: Universally composable synchronous computation. In: Sahai, A. (ed.) TCC 2013. LNCS, vol. 7785, pp. 477–498. Springer, Heidelberg (2013). https://doi.org/10.1007/978-3-642-36594-2_27

[LZLM+19] Liu-Zhang, C.D., Loss, J., Maurer, U., Moran, T., Tschudi, D.: Robust MPC: asynchronous responsiveness yet synchronous security. Cryptology ePrint Archive, Report 2019/159 (2019)

[PP24] Patil, S., Patra, A.: Perfectly-secure network-agnostic MPC with optimal resiliency. Cryptology ePrint Archive, Paper 2024/990 (2024)

[RB89] Rabin, T., Ben-Or, M.: Verifiable secret sharing and multiparty protocols with honest majority (extended abstract). In: 21st ACM STOC, pp. 73–85. ACM Press (1989)

[Yao82] Yao, A.C.-C.: Theory and applications of trapdoor functions (extended abstract). In: 23rd FOCS, pp. 80–91. IEEE Computer Society Press (1982)

New Upper and Lower Bounds
for Perfectly Secure MPC

Ivan Damgård[1], Shravani Patil[2(✉)], Arpita Patra[2], and Lawrence Roy[1]

[1] Aarhus University, Aarhus, Denmark
[2] IISc Bangalore, Bengaluru, India
patilshravani95@gmail.com

Abstract. We consider perfectly secure MPC for n players and t malicious corruptions. We ask whether requiring only security with abort (rather than guaranteed output delivery, GOD) can help to achieve protocols with better resilience, communication complexity or round complexity. We show that for resilience and communication complexity, abort security does not help, one still needs $3t < n$ for a synchronous network and $4t < n$ in the asynchronous case. And, in both cases, a communication overhead of $O(n)$ bits per gate is necessary.

When $O(n)$ overhead is inevitable, one can explore if this overhead can be pushed to the preprocessing phase and the online phase can be achieved with $O(1)$ overhead. This result was recently achieved in the synchronous setting, in fact, with GOD guarantee. We show this same result in the asynchronous setting. This was previously open since the main standard approach to getting constant overhead in a synchronous on-line phase fails in the asynchronous setting. In particular, this shows that we do not need to settle for abort security to get an asynchronous perfectly secure protocol with overheads $O(n)$ and $O(1)$.

Lastly, in the synchronous setting, we show that perfect secure MPC with abort requires only 2 rounds, in contrast to protocols with GOD that require 4 rounds.

1   Introduction

In secure multiparty computation (MPC), a set of n mutually distrusting parties want to compute an agreed function on inputs held by the parties. The goal is to do this in such a way that the output is correct and is the only new information that is leaked; this must be true even if up to t of the parties are corrupted by an adversary.

In this paper we focus on the model where we want perfect information theoretic security, assuming secure point to point channels between each pair of parties. It is well known that in this model, perfect security is possible if and only if $t < n/3$ for a synchronous network, and $t < n/4$ for the asynchronous case. Moreover, a lower bound is known for the communication complexity [13], indicating that a communication overhead of $\Omega(n)$ bits per gate in the circuit is

J. Daemen and E. Thomé (Eds.): EUROCRYPT 2026, LNCS 16543, pp. 366–396, 2026.
https://doi.org/10.1007/978-3-032-25324-8_13

necessary when t is maximal[1]. Also, a matching upper bound is known [1,5,16]. Finally, regarding round complexity, it is known that 4 rounds are necessary and sufficient for perfectly secure MPC [4]. Based on all this, it may seem that the major questions in this model are answered.

However, a closer look reveals that this is not actually the case: the lower bounds on t are only known to hold for protocols with guaranteed output delivery (GOD), where all honest players always receive output. We could (and should) also consider the weaker property *security with abort*. In the weakest form of abort security, selective abort, the adversary gets the output and can decide whether each honest player gets output or will have to abort. In the following, selective abort is what we mean when talking about abort security. It is natural to ask whether requiring only abort security helps to achieve protocols with better properties, in terms of resilience, communication complexity or round complexity.

Surprisingly, to the best of our knowledge, these questions are open. Considering resilience first, one may note that the standard approach to prove $t < n/3$ is necessary for GOD is to invoke the well-known impossibility of broadcast when $t \geq n/3$. But this fails completely for abort security, as broadcast with abort is known to be possible for $t < n$ [15]. Furthermore, the known lower bound for communication complexity assumes GOD and a synchronous network, and no bounds are known for abort security and an asynchronous network. Finally, the known lower bound on round complexity also assumes GOD.

For completeness, we point out that the corresponding lower bound questions for statistical security are not very interesting, as it is easy to see that settling for abort security does not help in this setting. Namely, a non-trivial abort secure protocol must terminate normally and be secure if all players follow the protocol. So, a synchronous abort secure protocol implies a passively secure protocol for the same n and t, and it is it is well known that this requires $n > 2t$ even for passive corruption. For the asynchronous case, we note that if all players are honest, but we never hear from t of them, an abort secure protocol must terminate and be secure. But this scenario is indistinguishable from one where t players are passively corrupt and we never hear from t honest players, so again the protocol must terminate. This means we can obtain a (synchronous) secure protocol for $n - t$ players and t passive corruptions, which requires $n - t > 2t$, or $n > 3t$.

Finally, on the upper bound front, it is natural to ask if something can be achieved using preprocessing: even if we cannot go below $O(n)$ bits per gate starting from scratch, perhaps we can, assuming preprocessing? Here, the idea is that the protocol executes in two phases: a preprocessing phase where the inputs and function to compute are not known, but where some correlated randomness

---

[1] To be precise, the bound says that there exist functions where perfect security requires communication of $\Omega(nS)$ bits where S is the input size. However, the functions in question have linear size circuits, so this translates to $\Omega(n)$ bits per gate for these circuits – but also for circuits in general, assuming that the protocol applies "the same" approach to any circuit, as is the case for all known general constructions.

is produced, and then this randomness is "consumed" in an on-line phase where the function is computed. The hope is that this phase can be more efficient because the correlated randomness is available. This question on preprocessing was answered very recently for synchronous communication: a GOD protocol exists where the preprocessing has overhead $O(n)$ bits per gate, whereas the on-line phase has overhead $O(1)$ [18]. However, no similar solution is known for the asynchronous case, in particular it is not clear if we would need to settle for abort security to get such a result.

1.1   Our Contribution

In this paper, we settle all of the above questions. Our take-away message is in two parts: first, requiring only abort security does not help to achieve better resilience or communication complexity for general MPC, but it does help significantly in terms of round complexity, and for resilience, if we settle for computing linear functions only. Second, in the off-line/on-line model, it is possible to get overheads $O(n)$ and $O(1)$ even in the asynchronous setting, and with GOD guarantee. In more detail:

- We show that $t < n/3$ is necessary for perfect abort security in general on a synchronous network, and $t < n/4$ is necessary in the asynchronous case.
- On the other hand, we show that Verifiable Secret Sharing (VSS) and secure computation of *linear* functions can be done with perfect abort security assuming only $t < n/2$.
- We show a communication lower bound indicating that an overhead of $\Omega(n)$ bits per gate is necessary to achieve perfect abort security when t is maximal, i.e., $n = 3t + 1$ in the synchronous case and $n = 4t + 1$ in the asynchronous case.
- We present a GOD protocol with preprocessing for an asynchronous network, where the preprocessing phase has communication overhead $O(n)$ bits per gate and the on-line phase has overhead $O(1)^2$.
- We show that two rounds of communication are necessary and sufficient for perfect security with abort.

1.2   Technical Overview

Our lower bounds on resilience and communication share the same proof technique, which is new to the best of our knowledge. We start by assuming an n-party protocol π of the type we want to rule out, π is assumed to do a simple non-linear computation such as an OT from one party to another. We then devise a way to execute π by $n - 1$ parties (that are assumed to follow the protocol),

---

[2] The result for the on-line phase assumes a certain SIMD-like structure of the circuit to compute. Using existing results, we can transform a circuit into an equivalent one with the right structure at the expense of a logarithmic overhead factor. See more details within.

where one party P from π is emulated in a special way by the other players: each time a party expects to get a message m from P, the party chooses a random bit string to play the role of m. This may result in π aborting, but the parties can discard such executions. Note that in case π does not abort, its input/output behaviour is correct, by perfect security against a corrupt P. Also, the probability that π terminates is non-zero. This is because there is a small but non-zero probability that the random messages correspond to P behaving honestly, and π must terminate without aborting if all players are honest. Finally, conditioned on the emulated P being honest, we can invoke perfect security against semi-honest corruption of one of the $n-1$ remaining parties. Based on this, we argue that the $n-1$-party protocol accomplishes something that is not possible.

We show that VSS and linear MPC can be done with abort for honest majority by observing that the standard VSS based on bivariate polynomials becomes abort secure if one requires that no players complain about their shares; and if one requires in reconstruction that all players are on the same polynomial or else we abort. Then a linear function can be evaluated by VSS-ing the inputs and evaluating the function on the shares. Details can be found in the full version [12].

We show that MPC with abort security can be done in two rounds by modifying an existing 2-round protocol with passive security. By adding some checks in the last round and aborting if they fail, we ensure that results are correct if we terminate. Details can be found in the full version [12].

Finally, we consider our asynchronous protocol with $O(1)$ communication overhead per gate in the on-line phase. For this, we apply the well-known strategy of preparing in the preprocessing a number of packed Beaver triples, where a triple consists of 3 random secret-shared vectors $\boldsymbol{a}, \boldsymbol{b}, \boldsymbol{c}$ such that $\boldsymbol{a} * \boldsymbol{b} = \boldsymbol{c}$ where $*$ refers to coordinate-wise multiplication. Here, we are using packed secret-sharing, i.e., Shamir where the degree of the polynomial is increased to preserve privacy even though a vector rather than a single value is shared. However, shares are still single values. We also prepare a number of shared pairs of vectors of form $(\boldsymbol{a}, L(\boldsymbol{a}))$ where L is a linear function. This is useful in the on-line phase for rerouting values between layers of the circuit to compute. Based on existing techniques from [2,14,18], it is relatively straightforward to accomplish this with overhead $O(n)$ per preprocessed gate.

The main technical challenge occurs in the on-line phase. Given the preprocessing material, the communication in the on-line phase essentially reduces to opening a sequence of shared vectors. Doing this in the naive way where all parties send shares to all other parties introduces an overhead we cannot afford. Even though the use of packed secret sharing saves a factor of $\Theta(n)$, sending to all parties still gives a factor n overhead.

The standard solution to this problem is to not send shares to all players, but only to a single player P_{king} who reconstructs locally and sends information back to all players. Intuitively this saves a factor $\Theta(n)$ and so can give us $O(1)$ overhead (here, we are ignoring for the moment how to verifiy what P_{king} does). A second problem is that packed secret sharing only allows coordinate-wise or SIMD-style multiplication and so, for general circuits, one needs to reorder values inside shared blocks. This (and other problems) can be solved if one can apply securely a linear function L to a shared block. Skipping many details, this can be done by having P_{king} apply L to the block she reconstructs.

These observations are the basis for prior work in the synchronous case [18]. Our goal is to get $O(1)$ overhead in the on-line phase for an asynchronous network. For this, several techniques from the synchronous protocol in [18] can be reused. A major challenge, however, is that the technique of using a single P_{king} for reconstruction does not work anymore. We may never hear from P_{king}, even if she is honest. Note that we cannot afford to wait, as we cannot distinguish between a single corrupt player and an honest player whose message is delayed. Assigning $t+1$ or even all parties to all play the role of P_{king} works but reintroduces an overhead of $\Theta(n)$.

We propose instead the following solution: assume we can arrange it such that we can process $m = \Theta(n)$ shared blocks $(\boldsymbol{a}_1, \ldots \boldsymbol{a}_m)$ at the same time and that the same function L is to be applied to all of them. The idea is now to compute a Reed-Solomon style encoding $(\boldsymbol{b}_1, \ldots, \boldsymbol{b}_n)$ of $(\boldsymbol{a}_1, \ldots \boldsymbol{a}_m)$, also in shared form. Since both the encoding and the sharing are linear, this only requires local computation. We then let each party play the role of P_{king} with respect to $\boldsymbol{b}_i$, i.e., players send shares of $\boldsymbol{b}_i$ to P_i who reconstructs, applies L, and sends back to the players shares of $L(\boldsymbol{b}_i)^3$. When these shares are returned, players hold (in shared form) a Reed-Solomon encoding of the desired vector $(L(\boldsymbol{a}_1), \ldots L(\boldsymbol{a}_m))$, possibly with errors corresponding to the corrupt players. Since we can wait for $n-t$ players to return, we are guaranteed $3t+1$ results with t errors which means decoding will work. Note that the vector to decode will be given in shared form, but it turns out that the players can apply decoding to the set of shares they hold. It will be the case that each such set of shares is a Reed Solomon codeword with at most t errors. This is because codewords are characterized by the property that a certain set of linear combinations of the entries (the syndrome) is 0. This property is preserved when applying a linear mapping to codewords, and this is what happens when all parties apply L to what they hold and then secret-share the result.

Now, since we are processing $\Theta(n)$ blocks in one go, this compensates for the cost paid by involving all n players so we still have $O(1)$ overhead. Finally, the decoding automatically corrects the errors introduced by corrupt players, so we need no special procedures for tracking down errors and eliminating players as required in [18].

To apply our solution, we need that the circuit is wide enough and has a sufficiently regular structure so that the same function L can be applied to all blocks coming out of a given layer of the circuit. The circuit may have this SIMD-style structure already, but it can also ensured in general. Either because we evaluate the same circuit in parallel several times, or one can apply the technique from [10] to rewrite the circuit to an equivalent circuit that is a log factor larger, but has the required regular structure.

---

[3] The reconstruction will work, even in the case of packed secret sharing which uses degree larger than t implying that hearing from $n-t$ parties is not necessarily enough to decode to the right polynomial. Using so-called on-line decoding [7] one can detect if enough shares from honest parties are available and wait if not.

1.3   Network Model and Definitions

We consider synchronous and asynchronous network models, where the parties in $\mathcal{P} = \{P_1, \ldots, P_n\}$ are connected via pairwise private and authenticated channels. Additionally, for some of our protocols we assume the availability of a broadcast channel, which allows a party to send an identical message to all the parties. The distrust among the parties is modeled as a centralized, computationally unbounded adversary that can corrupt up to t out of the n parties. When the network is synchronous, every message sent by any party is delivered within a fixed, known time bound Δ. Additionally, all the messages are delivered in the same order they are sent in. Whereas in the asynchronous network, messages are delivered with an arbitrary but finite delay. Moreover, the messages may be delivered in an arbitrary order. The only guarantee is that the messages get delivered eventually. This is modeled by a scheduler which decides on the sequence of message deliveries, and the scheduler itself is assumed to be controlled by the adversary.

2   Lower Bounds

In this section, we show that perfect secure MPC with abort requires $t < n/3$ in the synchronous setting, and $t < n/4$ in the asynchronous setting.

We then prove a communication lower bound. It essentially says that realizing string oblivious transfer for strings of length ℓ with perfect abort security for $n = 3t + k$ parties and t corruptions requires that the total communication complexity is at least $\ell(n - 1)/k$, so when t is maximal, i.e., $k = 1$ we get a factor $\Omega(n)$ overhead. This is the same (type of) bound that was already known for perfectly secure protocols with GOD. Since string OT has a linear size (binary) circuit, we can also conclude that for this family of functions, the communication overhead to get perfect abort security must be a factor $\Omega(n)$ per multiplication gate. Since all known general MPC protocols do "the same" for every circuit, we expect the same overhead factor to be necessary in general.

For the asynchronous case, we get the same bound, but for $n = 4t + k$.

2.1   Some Intuition

We first give an intuitive explanation of the main ideas behind the proofs.

For the communication lower bound, it turns out to be enough to consider a 4 player protocol π for players A, B, C and D, and assume that π implements a string OT from A to B with perfect abort security and is secure against 1 corruption. So, A inputs two string of length ℓ, and B has a selection bit that determines if she receives the first or the second string.

We then construct a 3-party protocol that is executed by A, B and C only where each time they expect a message from D, they will choose a uniformly random string and pretend this was what D sent. We assume all three follow the protocol. This "randomly emulated" D will most of the time not follow the protocol but because π is secure against a corrupt D, its input/output behaviour is correct every time it does not abort. Moreover there is a small but non-zero probability that the random messages correspond to D behaving honestly. In such a case, the protocol will not abort, and we can argue that the transcript of the communication between A and B contains no information on the string B receives because the protocol is secure against passive corruption of A or of B if D is honest.

We then repurpose the protocol to be a key agreement protocol between A and B with C acting as a helper, where the key is the string B receives in the OT. This is (with some non-zero probability) secure even if the adversary sees the communication between A and B. The intuition is now that this can only be the case if C communicates a lot, otherwise there is no way to get the entire string from A to B without the adversary learning anything.

This way we get a lower bound on the communication and this actually also implies the result on resilience: we argue we get a contradiction if C does not communicate (enough), but if we have only 3 players and one corruption this corresponds to C not communicating at all, which of course leads to a contradiction.

The result for the asynchronous case follows quite easily from the synchronous result by observing that if we have an additional player and 1 corruption, the last player could have its message delayed indefinitely, so if the protocol still works (as it should if it is asynchronously secure), we are back in the previous setting.

In the rest of this section we formalize this intuition. This is harder than it might seem at first, the main difficulty is that the 4-party protocol might terminate without aborting even if D was not honest, and in that case we have no privacy guarantees against A or B.

2.2   Leaky Key Agreement Lowerbound

We will reduce everything to a simple information theoretic lowerbound on key agreement extension, i.e., using a pre-existing key of length ℓ' to agree on a random key of length ℓ, where $\ell > \ell'$. This lowerbound will hold even in the presence of leakage and aborts, as long as it is possible for the protocol to complete without leakage. We slightly strengthen the notion of leakage here, by allowing the simulator to program what key is sampled in the case where it is leaked. This simplifies the argument a bit later on, by not requiring the key that is sampled to look random when it gets leaked.

Functionality 2.1: $\mathcal{F}_{\mathsf{AC}}$ - Authenticated Channel Functionality

---

Whenever a message (m, P') is received from a party P:
1. Send (m, P, P') to $\mathcal{A}$.
2. Receive a bit a from $\mathcal{A}$.
3. If $a = 0$, send m to P'.

Functionality 2.2: $\mathcal{F}_{\mathsf{PSK}}^{\ell'}$ - Pre-shared Key

---

The functionality is parameterized by a key length ℓ'.
1. Sample $k' \leftarrow \{0,1\}^{\ell'}$.
2. Send k' to Alice.
3. Receive a bit a from $\mathcal{A}$.
4. If $a = 0$, send k' to Bob.

Functionality 2.3: $\mathcal{F}_{\mathsf{LKA}}^{\ell}$ - Leaky Key Agreement

---

The functionality is parameterized by a message length ℓ.
1. Receive the leakage request $(l, L) \in \{0,1\} \times \{0,1\}^{\ell}$ from $\mathcal{A}$.
2. If $l = 0$ then sample $k \leftarrow \{0,1\}^{\ell}$; else set $k = L$.
3. Send k to Alice.
4. Receive a bit a from $\mathcal{A}$.
5. If $a = 0$, send k to Bob.

Lemma 2.4. *Let π be a synchronous protocol that perfectly realizes $\mathcal{F}_{\mathsf{LKA}}^{\ell}$ between honest parties Alice and Bob, using an authenticated insecure channel and ℓ' bits of correlated randomness. Then $\ell' \geq \ell$, or else it is impossible for SIM_π to send $l = a = 0$ to $\mathcal{F}_{\mathsf{LKA}}^{\ell}$.*

In order to prove this, we need to define a suitable measure of correlation between the states of Alice and Bob. It must ignore the probabilities of leakage or abort. We define a notion that we call common max-information, which measures the max-entropy of everything known to them both.

Definition 2.5. *Let P be a probability distribution, and let $(X, Y) \in \mathcal{X} \times \mathcal{Y}$ be a pair of random variables defined over P. The common max-information $C_P(X; Y)$ of the random variables X and Y is defined as the maximum $\log_2(N)$ such that there exist functions $f \colon \mathcal{X} \to [N] \cup \{\bot\}$ and $g \colon \mathcal{Y} \to [N] \cup \{\bot\}$ where*

$$\Pr_{(X,Y) \leftarrow P}\left[f(X) = g(Y) \vee f(X) = \bot \vee g(Y) = \bot\right] = 1$$

and

$$\forall z \in [N]. \Pr_{(X,Y) \leftarrow P}\left[f(X) = z = g(Y)\right] > 0.$$

We will suppress the distribution P and the write $C(X, Y)$ when P is unimportant or is clear from context. We will need the following basic properties to bound the common max-information of Alice's and Bob's states.

Lemma 2.6 (Symmetry).

$$C(X, Y) = C(Y, X)$$

Lemma 2.7 (Upper bound by max-entropy).

$$C(X,Y) \leq |\log_2(\mathrm{supp}(X))|$$

Proof. To satisfy the second condition, $f(X)$ must have support $[N]$ for $N = 2^{C(X,Y)}$. Since f is deterministic we have $|\mathrm{supp}(f(X))| \leq |\mathrm{supp}(X)|$. □

Lemma 2.8 (Data-processing inequality). *For any randomized function* $u \colon \mathcal{X} \to \mathcal{U}$,

$$C(u(X),Y) \leq C(X,Y)$$

Proof. Let $f(U)$ and $g(Y)$ be some functions that satisfy Definition 2.5 for $U = u(X)$ and Y. For all $x \in \mathcal{X}$, let $f'(x)$ be most probable outcome of $f(u(x))$ other than $\perp$. If $f(u(x))$ is $\perp$ with probability 1, let $f'(x) = \perp$ instead. For any $(x,y) \in \mathrm{supp}(X,Y)$, if there are two possible outcomes $u_1 \neq u_2$ for $u(x)$ then it must be that either $f(u_1) = g(y) = f(u_2)$, $f(u_1) = \perp$, $f(u_2) = \perp$, or $g(y) = \perp$. Otherwise, there would be positive probability of violating the first condition in Definition 2.5. Therefore,

$$\Pr_{(X,Y) \leftarrow P; U \leftarrow u(X)} \left[f'(X) = f(U) \vee f(U) = \perp \vee g(Y) = \perp \right] = 1. \qquad (1)$$

This implies the first condition of Definition 2.5 on (f',g): when $g(Y) \neq \perp$ then either $f'(X) = f(U)$, which implies the condition as it is satisfied by (f,g), or $f(U) = \perp$ and so either $f'(X) = f(U')$ for some other U' (leading to the previous case) or $f'(X) = \perp$ (satisfying the condition directly).

Next, for any $z \in [N]$, there must be some (u_1,y) such that $f(u_1) = z = g(y)$ and there is positive probability that $u_1 = u(X) \wedge y = Y$. Since $z \neq \perp$, by (1) we have $f'(X) = z$ in this event. Therefore the second condition of Definition 2.5 is also satisfied. □

Lemma 2.9 (One-sided conditioning). *For any event $E \subseteq \mathcal{X}$ that has positive probability,*

$$C_{P|E}(X,Y) \leq C_P(X,Y)$$

Proof. Given $f(X)$ and $g(Y)$ satisfying Definition 2.5 for $P \mid E$, define $f'(X)$ to be $f(X)$ if $X \in E$, and otherwise $f'(X) = \perp$. Then $f'(X)$ and $g(Y)$ satisfy Definition 2.5 for P. □

We are now ready to prove our lowerbound on the correlated randomness needed to realize $\mathcal{F}_{\mathsf{LKA}}^{\ell}$.

Proof of Lemma 2.4. Let P be the distribution of the computation trace and communication transcript of Alice and Bob running π, with access to pre-shared key $\mathcal{F}_{\mathsf{PSK}}^{\ell'}$. Let the states of Alice and Bob in round i be S_A^i and S_B^i, respectively, and let r be the number of rounds in π. Without loss of generality, we can assume that $\mathcal{F}_{\mathsf{PSK}}^{\ell'}$ gives Alice and Bob their pre-shared key $k' \in \{0,1\}^{\ell'}$. When Alice and Bob get this pre-shared key, this is the randomness in their states, so we have $C_P(S_A^0, S_B^0) = \ell'$. Let T be the random variable describing Alice and Bob's communication transcript. Let T^* be in the support of T, and let T^i be the event that Alice and Bob's communication matches with T^* for rounds up to (and including) i. The event T^r is equivalent to $T = T^*$.

Next, we show by induction that for all rounds $i \leq r$, $C_P(S_A^i, S_B^i) \leq \ell'$. We already have the base case. For the induction case, we must prove that $C_{P|T^i}(S_A^i, S_B^i) \geq C_{P|T^{i+1}}(S_A^{i+1}, S_B^{i+1})$ for all $i \in [0, r)$. In each round, Alice and Bob can sample randomness and communicate. By Lemma 2.8, sampling local randomness cannot increase the common max-information. There is a unique message m_A^{i+1} that Alice sends to Bob for event T^{i+1} to occur, so Alice sending this message can be interpreted as first conditioning on this message, then modifying Bob's state to include m_A^i. Neither can increase the common max-information: the former by Lemma 2.9, and the latter by Lemma 2.8. A similar argument applies to Bob's messages to Alice.

Consider the keys (k_A, k_B) output by Alice and Bob. (Set a party's output key to $\bot$ if that party aborts.) These are a local function of the party's final states (S_A^r, S_B^r), so by Lemma 2.8 we have $C_{P|T=T^*}(k_A, k_B) \leq \ell'$.

Next, we change to the ideal world to lower bound this common max-information. Let P' be the distribution given by running $\mathcal{F}_{\mathsf{LKA}}^\ell$ and SIM_π, which contains random variables for Alice and Bob's communication transcript T (by SIM_π's simulation of $\mathcal{F}_{\mathsf{AC}}$), the key $k = k_A = k_B$ output by Alice and Bob (again, set a key to $\bot$ if the party aborts), and the bits l and a by which SIM_π requests leakage or abort from $\mathcal{F}_{\mathsf{LKA}}^\ell$. Now consider the distribution $P' \mid T = T^*$, and let $f(k_A) = k_A$ and $g(k_B) = k_B$. These satisfy the first condition of Definition 2.5, as they must agree if no abort occurs. If it is possible that $T = T^*$, $l = 0$, and $a = 0$ all hold simultaneously, then they also satisfy the second condition (with $N = 2^\ell$), as when $l = 0$ the transcript T and abort bit a are both independent of k, so every (k, k) is in the support of the distribution for all $k \in \{0,1\}^\ell$. Therefore, $C_{P'|T=T^*}(k_A, k_B) = \ell$.

Putting this together, if there is some transcript T^* that is possible for SIM_π to produce at the same time as it chooses $l = a = 0$, then $C_{P'|T=T^*}(k_A, k_B) = \ell$. However, we showed in the real world that $C_{P|T=T^*}(k_A, k_B) \leq \ell'$. Since T, k_A, and k_B are all given to the environment, $P \mid T = T^*$ and $P' \mid T = T^*$ must define identical distributions over k_A and k_B. Therefore,

$$\ell' \geq C_{P|T=T^*}(k_A, k_B) = C_{P'|T=T^*}(k_A, k_B) = \ell,$$

unless it is impossible for SIM_π to complete without leaking or aborting. $\square$

2.3   Leakage Auditor Model

We would like to analyze the OT protocol using an OT functionality that allows for leakage, similarly to $\mathcal{F}_{\mathsf{LKA}}^\ell$. Unfortunately, for protocols where a party might be corrupt, modeling this kind of leakage is not so straightforward. Specifically, we must rule out protocols that just randomly choose a party, then just send all the inputs to this party and trust them to do the real computation. Such protocols have a positive probability of not leaking (i.e., of happening to pick an honest party). We rule out this kind of trivial protocol by requiring the leakage to be well-defined in the real world, independent of who is corrupted.

To model this, we add an extra party P_{audit}, who is always honest, but can only receive messages and cannot send any. Because P_{audit} cannot send messages, it cannot help the protocol succeed, so we do not count P_{audit} in the party count n or the threshold t, nor do we count the messages sent to P_{audit} as counting towards the communication complexity. P_{audit}'s only job is to output a bit $l \in \{0,1\}$, indicating whether leakage occurred. This keeps the simulator honest in some sense, because it forces the choice of leakage made by the simulator to correspond to some real world event that is independent of at least semi-honest corruptions.

Here is our leaky OT functionality in this model.

Functionality 2.10: $\mathcal{F}_{\mathsf{LOT}}^{\ell}$ - Leaky Oblivious Transfer Functionality

The functionality is parameterized by a message length ℓ.
1. Receive two strings $m_0, m_1 \in \{0,1\}^{\ell}$ from P_1.
2. Receive the choice bit $b \in \{0,1\}$ from P_2.
3. If P_2 is corrupt, send m_b to $\mathcal{A}$.
4. Receive the leakage bit $l \in \{0,1\}$ from $\mathcal{A}$.
5. Send the leakage bit l to P_{audit}.
6. Compute leakage $L = \begin{cases} (m_0, m_1, b) & \text{if } l = 1 \\ \bot & \text{if } l = 0 \end{cases}$.
7. Send L to $\mathcal{A}$.
8. Receive the abort bit a from $\mathcal{A}$.
9. If $a = 0$ output m_b to P_2. Otherwise, output "abort" to P_2.

Note that any OT protocol without leakage can be converted into a protocol for $\mathcal{F}_{\mathsf{LOT}}^{\ell}$, by adding a dummy P_{audit} who always outputs 0, and having the simulator always send $l = 0$ to $\mathcal{F}_{\mathsf{LOT}}^{\ell}$.

2.4   Execution Transcripts

We use the transcript ts to refer to information that is visible to the environment[4], and so must match between the real and ideal worlds. In addition to the views of the corrupt parties, ts contains at least the following information:

abort(ts): The abort bit a sent received by $\mathcal{F}_{\mathsf{LOT}}^{\ell}$. A value of 1 indicates that the simulator requested an abort, while a value of 0 indicates that the protocol completed successfully.

leak(ts): The leakage bit l sent received by $\mathcal{F}_{\mathsf{LOT}}^{\ell}$. The value 1 means that the simulator requested $\mathcal{F}_{\mathsf{LOT}}^{\ell}$ to leak all inputs.

$\mathsf{SC}_{P,P'}(\mathsf{ts})$: Total size of all messages sent from P to P'. That is, this is the sum of n over all messages (n, P, P') sent by the simulator (pretending to be $\mathcal{F}_{\mathsf{SC}}$) to $\mathcal{A}$.

---

[4] Assuming a dummy adversary that passes on all information.

$\mathsf{TC}_{P,P'}(\mathsf{ts})$: Total size of all messages sent from P to P' or from P' to P. Equals $\mathsf{SC}_{P,P'}(\mathsf{ts}) + \mathsf{SC}_{P',P}(\mathsf{ts})$.

$\mathsf{SC}_P(\mathsf{ts})$: Total sender communication of party P. Equals the sum of $\mathsf{SC}_{P,P'}(\mathsf{ts})$ over all P' (excluding P_{audit}).

$\mathsf{TC}_P(\mathsf{ts})$: Total communication of party P. Equals the sum of $\mathsf{TC}_{P,P'}(\mathsf{ts})$ over all P' (excluding P_{audit}).

$\mathsf{TC}(\mathsf{ts})$: Total communication of the entire protocol. Equals the sum of $\mathsf{SC}_P(\mathsf{ts})$ over all P, or equivalently half the sum of $\mathsf{TC}_P(\mathsf{ts})$ over all P (excluding P_{audit}).

We call ts a "possible transcript" if there exist some inputs to the protocol π such that when all parties behave honestly it is possible for this ts to be produced. This is equivalent whether you take ts to be produced by in the real world or the ideal world, as perfect security implies that ts will have the same distribution for both.

2.5 Communication Lower Bound, Synchronous Protocols

In this section, we lower bound the communication of realizing the string OT functionality $\mathcal{F}_{\mathsf{LOT}}^{\ell}$, in the selective abort setting, from secure channels $\mathcal{F}_{\mathsf{SC}}$.[5] In fact, we prove a statement that is stronger than required for our purpose— even if the protocol is allowed to sometimes leak to the adversary, whenever a leak does not occur the communication complexity is still lower bounded. This strengthening comes for free, as when we replace one of the parties with random behavior there will be a (very high) probability of leaking to the adversary.

Functionality 2.11: $\mathcal{F}_{\mathsf{SC}}$ - Secure Channel Functionality

---

Whenever a message (m, P') is received from a party P:

1. Send $(|m|, P, P')$ to $\mathcal{A}$.
2. Receive a bit a from $\mathcal{A}$.
3. If $a = 0$, send m to P'.

Theorem 2.12. *Let π be a synchronous protocol for $n = 3t + k$ parties and t malicious corruptions that perfectly realizes $\mathcal{F}_{\mathsf{LOT}}^{\ell}$ from $\mathcal{F}_{\mathsf{SC}}$. Then for all possible transcripts ts of π, if $\mathsf{abort}(\mathsf{ts}) = \mathsf{leak}(\mathsf{ts}) = 0$ then every subset X of k parties in π that includes at most one of P_1 and P_2 must always have total communication $\sum_{P \in X} \mathsf{TC}_P(\mathsf{ts}) \geq 2\ell$.[6]*

Averaging over all subsets X of k parties excluding P_2, this gives a lower bound on communication of the entire protocol:

Corollary 2.13. *Let π be a synchronous protocol for $n = 3t + k$ parties and t malicious corruptions that perfectly realizes $\mathcal{F}_{\mathsf{LOT}}^{\ell}$ from $\mathcal{F}_{\mathsf{SC}}$. Then in every possible transcript ts of π such that $\mathsf{abort}(\mathsf{ts}) = \mathsf{leak}(\mathsf{ts}) = 0$, the total communication $\mathsf{TC}(\mathsf{ts})$ is at least $\ell \cdot (n - 1)/k$.*

---

[5] Note that there is only one party with output in $\mathcal{F}_{\mathsf{LOT}}^{\ell}$, so selective and unanimous abort are equivalent.

[6] We defer the proof of this theorem to the end of this subsection.

It also implies that string OT cannot be implemented with perfect abort security if $n \leq 3t$. Namely, if we had a protocol π doing this, say for $n = 3t$, we can construct a protocol π' with $3t + 1$ players by adding a dummy player to π that never communicates. π' clearly contradicts Theorem 2.12, so we have:

Corollary 2.14. *No protocol can perfectly realize $\mathcal{F}_{\mathsf{LOT}}^{\ell}$ in the synchronous setting from secure channels with $n \leq 3t$ parties and t malicious corruptions while supporting a possible transcript ts such that $\mathsf{abort}(\mathsf{ts}) = \mathsf{leak}(\mathsf{ts}) = 0$.*

Our approach to proving Theorem 2.12 will be to reduce from simpler functionalities, eventually reaching one that we can lower bound information theoretically. First, we show that a lowerbound for the case of $n = 4$ and $t = 1$ implies the general case.

Lemma 2.15. *Let π be a synchronous protocol as in Theorem 2.12, and let X be a subset of k parties such that $\{P_1, P_2\} \not\subseteq X$. Then there exists a protocol π' for $n' = 4$ parties and $t' = 1$ malicious corruptions that also perfectly realizes $\mathcal{F}_{\mathsf{LOT}}^{\ell}$. Additionally, there exists a party P_i' of π' such that, for each possible transcript ts of π, there exists a possible transcript ts' of π' such that $\mathsf{abort}(\mathsf{ts}') = \mathsf{abort}(\mathsf{ts})$, $\mathsf{leak}(\mathsf{ts}') = \mathsf{leak}(\mathsf{ts})$, and $\mathsf{TC}_{P_i'}(\mathsf{ts}') \leq \sum_{P \in X} \mathsf{TC}_P(\mathsf{ts})$.*

Proof. Define four the parties $P_1', \ldots, P_4'$ of π', where each part P_j' will emulate a subset S_j of the n parties in π. Let the party corresponding to X be P_i', where $i = 1$ if $X \in P_1$, $i = 2$ if $X \in P_2$, and $i = 3$ otherwise. Define $S_i = X$, and define the three other sets $\{S_j\}_{j \neq i}$ be an arbitrary partition of the remaining $n - k$ parties into three subsets of size t, such that $P_1 \in S_1$ and $P_2 \in S_2$. Then define π' to have each P_j' emulate the parties in S_j in the protocol π, with the inputs of P_1' and P_2' being provided to the emulated P_1 and P_2, respectively, and the output of the emulated P_2 being output by P_2'. P_{audit}' in π' will behave the same as P_{audit} in π, with all messages sent by some $P_j \in S_{j'}$ of π to P_{audit} being sent by $P_{j'}'$ to P_{audit}' in π'.

Every S_j satisfies $|S_j| \leq t$, so a single corruption in π' can be simulated by corrupting up to t parties in π. Therefore, we can simulate π' by running the simulator for π, corrupting S_j if P_j' is corrupted, forgetting all communication between two parties in the same subset, and otherwise passing all messages through. Since all communication between P_i' and P_j' in π' appears as communication between parties in S_i and S_j in π, we have $\mathsf{TC}_{P_i'}(\mathsf{ts}') \leq \sum_{P \in X} \mathsf{TC}_P(\mathsf{ts})$.[7]
□

Next, we show that an $n = 4$ protocol with malicious security implies an $n = 3$ protocol with semi-honest security. Since a simulator for malicious security can lie about the inputs of corrupted parties, malicious security does not always imply semi-honest security. We first show that for $\mathcal{F}_{\mathsf{LOT}}^{\ell}$ malicious security always implies semi-honest security, so we can always assume that the $n = 4$ protocol has semi-honest security when reducing to the $n = 3$ case.

---

[7] Equality fails because communication between two parties in S_i will appear in π, but not in π'.

Lemma 2.16. *Let π be a synchronous protocol that perfectly realizes $\mathcal{F}_{\mathsf{LOT}}^{\ell}$ from secure channels for $n = 4$ and $t = 1$ malicious corruptions. Then π also perfectly realizes $\mathcal{F}_{\mathsf{LOT}}^{\ell}$ for $t = 1$ semi-honest corruptions.*

Proof. The only way in which semi-honest corruptions can make simulation harder is that they do not allow the party's inputs to be controlled by the simulator. To simulate semi-honest corruptions, we ask SIM_π to simulate the case where a party P_s is maliciously corrupted, but make P_s behave identically to an honest P_s. We will show that either leakage occurs, making semi-honest simulation trivial, or the input SIM_π extracts for P_s must be identical to P_s's real input.

This is trivial for $s = 3$, as P_3 has no input. For $s = 1$, if SIM_π extracts some $(m_0', m_1') \neq (m_0, m_1)$, then there will be some b such that $m_b' \neq m_b$. If P_2 inputs b (and SIM_π does not get to see whether it did) then the environment can distinguish, as P_2 will output m_b' in the ideal world and m_b in the real world. Therefore, SIM_π will always extracts $(m_0', m_1') = (m_0, m_1)$. Similarly, if $s = 2$ and SIM_π extracts some $b' \neq b$, then if P_1 inputs uniformly random (m_0, m_1) then the simulators view will only contain $m_{b'}$, and be independent of m_b. Therefore, the simulator has low probability of simulating a protocol execution that causes P_2 (who is behaving honestly, even though it was maliciously corrupted) to output m_b. This would allow the environment to distinguish, because in the real world P_2 would output m_b. $\qquad\square$

Lemma 2.17. *Let π be a synchronous protocol that perfectly realizes $\mathcal{F}_{\mathsf{LOT}}^{\ell}$ from secure channels for $n = 4$ and $t = 1$ corruptions (supporting both malicious and semi-honest corruptions), let P_i be a party (for some $i \in \{1, \ldots, 4\}$), and let ts be a possible transcript of π where $\mathsf{abort(ts)} = \mathsf{leak(ts)} = 0$. Then there exists a protocol π' for $n' = 3$ parties and $t' = 1$ semi-honest corruptions that also perfectly realizes $\mathcal{F}_{\mathsf{LOT}}^{\ell}$, such that there exists a party $P_{i'}'$ of π' (for some $i' \in \{1, 2, 3\}$) and a possible transcript ts' of π', such that $\mathsf{abort(ts')} = \mathsf{leak(ts')} = 0$ and $\mathsf{TC}_{P_{i'}'}(\mathsf{ts}') \leq \mathsf{TC}_{P_i}(\mathsf{ts})$.*

The proof of this lemma is found in the full version of the paper [12]. It is based on the technique mentioned in the introduction, where the three parties in π' run π by emulating directly three parties in π while replacing messages from the fourth party by uniformly random messages. Since there is a small but non-zero probability that this corresponds to the fourth party behaving honestly, we get an implementation of $\mathcal{F}_{\mathsf{LOT}}^{\ell}$, albeit with a small (but non-zero) probability of not leaking.

Next, we reduce to a two party problem: key agreement extension between Alice and Bob (both honest) in the presence of an eavesdropper. It is well know that two-party OT implies key agreement, but this argument relies on having a single communication channel the eavedropper can see. Since we instead have a three-party OT, with communication channels between each pair of parties, we have to do something different. We assume that Alice and Bob have a pre-shared key proportional to the communication complexity along one of the three channels, so that this channel can be masked by a one-time pad. Another channel will be handled by merging two parties, so that communication between these two parties is local to either Alice's or Bob's mind. This leaves just a single channel to eavesdrop on. From here we can use a variation of the usual proof that OT implies key agreement. Later, we will use Lemma 2.4 to show that the pre-shared key must be big enough to one-time pad Alice's entire message, so this in turn lower bounds the communication of along each channel in the OT protocol. The proof of the following lemma is found in the full version [12].

Lemma 2.18. *Let π be a synchronous protocol that perfectly realizes $\mathcal{F}^\ell_{\mathsf{LOT}}$ from secure channels for $n = 3$ and $t = 1$ semi-honest corruptions, and let $i \neq i' \in \{1,\ldots,3\}$ and $\ell' \geq 0$. Then there exists a protocol π' that perfectly realizes $\mathcal{F}^\ell_{\mathsf{LKA}}$ between parties Alice and Bob, using an authenticated insecure channel $\mathcal{F}_{\mathsf{AC}}$ and ℓ' bits of correlated randomness $\mathcal{F}^{\ell'}_{\mathsf{PSK}}$. If it is possible that π neither leaks nor aborts while the channel between P_i and $P_{i'}$ has total communication at most ℓ', then it is also possible that π' neither leaks nor aborts. Additionally, if there is a possible transcript ts of π where $\mathsf{TC}_{P,P'}(\mathsf{ts}) \leq \ell'$ and $\mathsf{abort}(\mathsf{ts}) = \mathsf{leak}(\mathsf{ts}) = 0$, there exists a possible transcript ts' of π' such that $\mathsf{abort}(\mathsf{ts}') = \mathsf{leak}(\mathsf{ts}') = 0$.*

Finally, we put all the above lemmas together into a complete proof.

Proof of Theorem 2.12. From the precondition, let π be a synchronous protocol for $n = 3t + k$ parties and t malicious corruptions, let ts be a possible transcript of π such that $\mathsf{abort}(\mathsf{ts}) = \mathsf{leak}(\mathsf{ts}) = 0$, and let $X \not\supseteq \{P_1, P_2\}$ be an arbitrary subset of k parties whose communication we wish to lowerbound. Assume for contradiction that $\sum_{P \in X} \mathsf{TC}_P(\mathsf{ts}) < 2\ell$. Use Lemma 2.15 to get a four-party malicious protocol π' for $\mathcal{F}^\ell_{\mathsf{LOT}}$ where some party P'_i has total communication at most that of X. That is, there is a possible transcript ts' of π' such that $\mathsf{abort}(\mathsf{ts}') = \mathsf{leak}(\mathsf{ts}') = 0$, and $\mathsf{TC}_{P'_i}(\mathsf{ts}') \leq \sum_{P \in X} \mathsf{TC}_P(\mathsf{ts}) < 2\ell$. Then Lemma 2.17 turns π' into a three-party semi-honest protocol π'' for $\mathcal{F}^\ell_{\mathsf{LOT}}$, in which some party P''_j matches the total communication of P'_i. That is, there exists there exists a party P''_j and a possible transcript ts'' of π', such that $\mathsf{abort}(\mathsf{ts}'') = \mathsf{leak}(\mathsf{ts}'') = 0$ and $\mathsf{TC}_{P''_j}(\mathsf{ts}'') \leq \mathsf{TC}_{P'_i}(\mathsf{ts}') < 2\ell$. For each $k \in \{1, 2, 3\} \setminus \{j\}$, Lemma 2.18 turns π'' into a two-party protocol π''' for $\mathcal{F}^\ell_{\mathsf{LKA}}$ that uses an authenticated channel and ℓ' bits of correlated randomness, where $\ell' = \mathsf{TC}_{P''_j, P''_k}(\mathsf{ts}'')$. Lemma 2.4 then shows that $\ell' \geq \ell$. Finally, there are two possible k for each j, so

$$2\ell > \mathsf{TC}_{P''_j}(\mathsf{ts}'') = \sum_{k \neq j} \mathsf{TC}_{P''_j, P''_k}(\mathsf{ts}'') \geq \sum_{k \neq j} \ell = 2\ell.$$

$\square$

2.6 Communication Lower Bound, Asynchronous Protocols

The standard argument of delaying t parties arbitrarily shows a corresponding lower-bound in the asynchronous setting.

Theorem 2.19. *Let π be an asynchronous protocol for $n = 4t + k$ parties and t malicious corruptions that perfectly realizes $\mathcal{F}_{\mathsf{LOT}}^{\ell}$ from secure channels. If it is possible for π to complete with total communication ℓ' while not leaking or aborting, and while some subset of t parties disjoint from $\{P_1, P_2\}$ is adversarially delayed, then $\ell' \geq \ell \cdot (n - t - 1)/k \geq \ell \cdot \frac{3}{4}(n - 1)/k$.*

Proof. Let D be the set of adversarially delayed parties from the theorem's assumptions. Define a protocol π' that runs π over a synchronous network on $n' = 3t + k$ parties, excluding all parties from D as being adversarially delayed. Then π' perfectly realizes $\mathcal{F}_{\mathsf{LOT}}^{\ell}$ from secure channels, and it is possible for π' to complete with total communication ℓ' without aborting or leaking. By Corollary 2.13, we then have that $\ell' \geq \ell \cdot (n' - 1)/k = \ell \cdot (n - t - 1)/k$. $\square$

Corollary 2.20. *No protocol can perfectly realize $\mathcal{F}_{\mathsf{LOT}}^{\ell}$ in the asynchronous setting from secure channels with $n \leq 4t$ parties and t malicious corruptions, unless π always leaks or aborts when t parties are adversarially delayed.*

3   Asynchronous Perfect MPC with Constant Online Overhead

We design a perfect MPC with malicious security for the optimal resilience of $t < n/4$ in an asynchronous network. The protocol has a communication complexity of $\mathcal{O}(n)$ per multiplication gate in the preprocessing phase while it offers $\mathcal{O}(1)$ online cost per gate[8]. We achieve the aforementioned communication complexity using the techniques of packed secret sharing, which allows us to evaluate a bunch of $\mathcal{O}(n)$ gates of the same kind simultaneously. Below we begin with a brief preliminary, followed by an outline, the online-phase primitives and the MPC protocol. The details of preprocessing phase appear in the full version of the paper [12].

3.1   Preliminaries

Our protocols are defined over a field $\mathbb{F}$ such that $|\mathbb{F}| > 3n/2$ and we denote its elements by $\{-n/2, \ldots, -1, 0, 1, \ldots, n\}$. We use k to denote the number of gates that are "packed" together, or equivalently, evaluated simultaneously. Further, we use degree-d packed Shamir sharing, where $d = t + k - 1$ to ensure privacy of k packed secrets against an adversary that can corrupt up to t parties. In our protocols, the degree of sharing after computation can go up to $d + k - 1 = t + 2k - 2$. To allow honest parties to reconstruct, we have to ensure $n - t > t + 2k - 2$. Hence, when $t < n/4$, we can set $k \leq t/2 + 1$. Unless stated otherwise, we use $k = t/2$ in our protocols. Throughout, we represent by $[v|j]_d$, a degree-d Shamir sharing of a value v via a degree-d polynomial $f(x)$ where $f(-j) = v$ for some

---

[8] The result for the online phase is considering SIMD style of circuit evaluation. Alternatively, using [10], we can transform the circuit into the required structure at the expense of logarithmic (in the circuit size) overhead.

$-j \in \mathbb{F}$. Further, we use $[v]_d$ to denote the packed Shamir sharing of a vector $(v_1, \ldots, v_k)$ via a degree-d polynomial $f(x)$ where $f(-j) = v_j$ for $j \in \{1, \ldots, k\}$. The term e_i denotes the unit vector $(0, \ldots, 0, 1, 0, \ldots, 0)$ which is a k-length vector with 1 in the ith position and 0 in all the remaining positions.

Symmetric Bivariate Polynomials. A degree (ℓ, ℓ) symmetric bivariate polynomial over $\mathbb{F}$ is of the form $S(x, y) = \sum_{i=0}^{\ell} \sum_{j=0}^{\ell} c_{ij} x^i y^j$ where $c_{ij} \in \mathbb{F}$ and $c_{ij} = c_{ji}$ holds for all $i, j \in \{0, ..., \ell\}$. This implies $S(i, j) = S(j, i)$ holds for every i, j. Moreover, $S(x, i) = S(i, y)$ is true for each $i \in \mathbb{F}$. Our protocol uses (t, t)-symmetric bivariate polynomials.

Agreement on a Core Set. In our asynchronous protocols, we also make use of an existing primitive which is called the agreement on a core set or asynchronous common subset, commonly known as ACS. The functionality for the same, $\mathcal{F}_{\mathsf{ACS}}$, appears in the full version [12]. We use the protocol from [3] which has a cost of $\mathcal{O}(n^5)$ field elements of communication with a constant expected run time.

3.2   The Outline

The Preprocessing Phase: In this phase, we generate the input-independent data such as Beaver triples, which is then utilised to evaluate the circuit on the actual inputs of parties in the subsequent online phase. This is particularly useful since we can afford a cost of $\mathcal{O}(n)$ communication per gate in the preprocessing phase to generate correlated data that ensures an efficient online phase. We first abstract out the requirements of the preprocessing phase for a simpler exposition and elaborate on the precise requirements subsequently. Our protocol primarily requires the following types of preprocessing correlations to be generated:

1. **Packed Beaver triples:** We require shared triples of the form $([a]_d, [b]_d, [c]_d)$ where $c_i = a_i b_i$ for all $i \in \{1, \ldots, k\}$. For this, we follow the approach of [14, 18] outlined below:
   (a) First, parties generate standard degree-t shared Beaver triples $([a_i|i]_t, [b_i|i]_t, [c_i|i]_t)$ for each $i \in \{1, \ldots, k\}$ using an existing protocol such as [2, Theorem 6.4 with Sect. 6.1]. The functionality for this appears below.
   (b) Following this, parties convert a group of k such triples $\{(a_i, b_i, c_i)\}_{i \in \{1, \ldots, k\}}$ into a single packed triple $([a]_d, [b]_d, [c]_d)$ locally using techniques from [14]. Specifically, parties can compute $[a]_d = \sum_{i=1}^{k} [e_i]_{k-1} * [a_i|i]_t$, where $[e_i]_{k-1}$ is the default degree-$(k-1)$ Shamir sharing of the unit vector e_i.

Functionality 3.1: $\mathcal{F}_{\mathsf{Triples}}$ - Beaver Triples Functionality

The functionality is parameterized by the set of corrupted parties $\mathcal{C} \subseteq [n]$.

1. The functionality receives the public parameters p and ℓ.
2. For each $k \in \{1, \ldots, p\}$, the functionality does the following:

(a) It samples random elements $x, y \in \mathbb{F}$ and computes $z = xy$. Further, it samples random degree-t polynomials $f(x), g(x), h(x)$ such that $f(-\ell) = x, g(-\ell) = y$ and $h(-\ell) = z$.

(b) The functionality then sends $(f(j), g(j), h(j))$ to each party P_j.

Lemma 3.2 ([6]). *There exists a protocol which realises $\mathcal{F}_{\mathsf{Triples}}$ and has a communication complexity of $\mathcal{O}(np + n^5)$ elements over point-to-point channels to share p random Beaver triples via degree-t Shamir sharing.*

2. **Packed linear transformation pair:** We generate pairs of the form $([\boldsymbol{r}]_d, [L(\boldsymbol{r})]_d)$, where L is a linear transformation to be applied on the vector $\boldsymbol{r}$. At a high level, this will be used to perform a linear transformation of "packed" output wires of every layer in the circuit to match the required sequence for the "packed" input wires of the subsequent layer. We adapt the protocol from [18] in the synchronous network model to suit our setting. Omitting most of the details, the primary challenge we encounter in migrating their protocol to the asynchronous setting is in reconstructing shared vector of k values or alternatively, establishing a default degree-$(k-1)$ sharing of these values without cost inflation. For instance, to reduce $[\boldsymbol{v}]_{d+k-1}$ to $[\boldsymbol{v}]_{k-1}$, their protocol simply reconstructs $\boldsymbol{v}$ to a P_{king}, who further shares $[\boldsymbol{v}]_{k-1}$ with a total cost of $\mathcal{O}(n)$. It is crucial to note that this degree reduction is only used for values that can be revealed publicly without hampering privacy. However, a naive public reconstruction is avoided to prevent $\Omega(n^2)$ communication cost, which is inevitable.

   However, the same technique cannot translate to the asynchronous network setting due to the following reason. It is impossible to distinguish between a corrupt P_{king} which does not distribute $[\boldsymbol{v}]_{k-1}$, and an honest P_{king} which is slow. This may result in an endless wait. On the other hand, using (at least) $t+1$ parties as P_{king} will ensure liveness; however, this will result in cost inflation by a factor of n which we cannot afford. Hence, we require a new mechanism for performing such a degree reduction of values that can be revealed publicly, which comprises our primary contribution in this protocol. The rest of the protocol follows from [18], and we discuss it in the relevant sections.

3. **Packed degree reduction pair:** We require pairs of the form $([\boldsymbol{r}]_d, [\boldsymbol{r}]_{d+k-1})$. During the online phase, $\boldsymbol{r}$ acts as a random pad for a packed Shamir shared vector of k values, say $\boldsymbol{x}$ to facilitate reducing the degree of the sharing polynomial. In particular, given the above pair and $[\boldsymbol{x}]_{d+k-1}$, parties can compute $[\boldsymbol{x} + \boldsymbol{r}]_{d+k-1}$ locally. Given that the elements of $\boldsymbol{r}$ now mask, or pad the elements of $\boldsymbol{x}$, revealing $\boldsymbol{x} + \boldsymbol{r}$ does not raise any privacy concerns. Thus, it can be publicly reconstructed, or even shared with a threshold lower than t. For instance, if we can ensure $[\boldsymbol{x} + \boldsymbol{r}]_{k-1}$ via some procedure such as public reconstruction, then parties can locally compute $[\boldsymbol{x}]_d = [\boldsymbol{x} + \boldsymbol{r}]_{k-1} - [\boldsymbol{r}]_d$. Thus, the task of reducing the degree of a shared

vector $\boldsymbol{x}$ from $(d + k - 1)$ to d while ensuring its privacy now reduces to a simpler task of reducing the degree of the masked vector $\boldsymbol{x} + \boldsymbol{r}$, which can be revealed publicly, from $(d + k - 1)$ to $(k - 1)$. This degree reduction required in the online phase reduces to the same as that required in the earlier case of generating linear transformation pairs.

The protocols for packed linear transformation pair and packed degree reduction pair follow easily from existing work, and we give the complete details of these in the full version of the paper [12]. Moreover, given that the operation to switch from $\{[x_i|i]_t\}_{i \in \{1,\ldots,k\}}$ to $[\boldsymbol{x}]_d$ is local, the protocol in [18] maintains the invariant of degree-t sharing for each wire value instead of the packed sharing described above. The packed sharing of the required values is then computed locally on demand. In our protocol as well, we follow the same approach. For instance, for the packed linear transformation pair, instead of computing $([\boldsymbol{r}]_d, [L(\boldsymbol{r})]_d)$, we maintain $\{([r_i|i]_t, [L_i(\boldsymbol{r})|i]_t)\}_{i \in \{1,\ldots,k\}}$ where $L_i(\boldsymbol{r})$ is the ith element of vector $L(\boldsymbol{r})$. Similarly, for the packed degree reduction pair, we maintain $\{[r_i|i]_t\}_{i \in \{1,\ldots,k\}}$ which in turn allows us to compute $[\boldsymbol{r}]_d$ as described earlier. We can also compute $[\boldsymbol{r}]_{d+k-1} = \sum_{i=1}^{2k-1} [e_i]_{2k-2} * [r_i|i]_t$ using some additional dummy values $\{[r_i|i]_t\}_{i \in \{k+1,\ldots,2k-1\}}$.

The Online Phase: The online phase utilises the preprocessed data to evaluate the circuit on the actual inputs of parties as follows.

1. **Input:** Here, each party holding inputs distributes a degree-t Shamir sharing of each input. For this, we use the VSS protocol from [9] with a $(t+k, t)$-degree bivariate polynomial to share k inputs simultaneously. If the same input is provided to multiple input wires of the circuit, then we require to perform a fan-out operation to copy the same value as many times as required. As observed in prior works such as [14,18], fan-out can be viewed as a linear transformation operation on wire values. Suppose w.l.o.g. that a party has k inputs $\boldsymbol{x} = (x_1, \ldots, x_k)$ such that it has shared $[x_i]_t$ for all $i \in \{1, \ldots, k\}$. As described earlier, parties can locally obtain $[\boldsymbol{x}]_d$. Now let us say that x_1 is used as an input for 4 input wires, then as described in [14,18], we effectively require to create some $\boldsymbol{y} = (x_1, x_1, x_1, x_1, \cdot, \ldots, \cdot)$. It was observed that $\boldsymbol{y}$ can thus be viewed as some linear transformation L applied on the vector $\boldsymbol{x}$, that is, $\boldsymbol{y} = L(\boldsymbol{x})$. We discuss how linear transformation is achieved subsequently.

2. **Linear Transformation:** In addition to fan-out, linear transformations are also required for applying permutation on 'packed' wire values. This is because the values to be packed in a single sharing for evaluation of a layer of gates may not be in the appropriate position in the sharing. For instance, suppose a 'packed' gate in the subsequent layer requires the input $\boldsymbol{x} = (x_1, x_2, \cdot, \ldots, \cdot)$, where x_1 and x_2 are inputs provided by P_1 and P_2 respectively. The procedure for packing k degree-t shared values locally into a degree-$(t + k - 1)$ allows for packing when we have $[x_1|1]_t$ and $[x_2|2]_t$ shared by P_1 and P_2 respectively. That is, when all the values to be packed together are shared

at different positions from $\{-1, \ldots, -k\}$ in their respective sharing. However, it is possible that P_1 and P_2 both shared their inputs at the same position in their respective sharing polynomial. Say $f(x)$ and $g(x)$ are the degree-t polynomials shared by P_1 and P_2 respectively, then we may have $f(-1) = x_1$ and $g(-1) = x_2$. That is, P_1 shared $[x_1|1]_t$, whereas P_2 shared its input as $[x_2|1]_t$, preventing the local packing operation. This issue can be resolved if k inputs shared by P_2 are permuted in order to obtain $[x_2|2]_t$ by replacing the -1th position with some other input. Another caveat in the subsequent layers is that the output of a single gate may be used as an input to multiple gates in the subsequent layer. This requires a fan-out operation to be performed at the output of each layer in the circuit to ensure enough copies of a particular wire value. As observed in the prior works [14,18], this reduces to a linear transformation on the packed wire values. Given that fan-out and permutation are specific types of a linear transformation operations, we discuss the more generic operation of transformation in the subsequent discussion. Again, similar to the earlier phase, we discuss the high level ideas first for a better exposition.

Thus, our goal is as follows: Given packed sharing $[\boldsymbol{x}]_d$ of some $\boldsymbol{x} = (x_1, \ldots, x_k)$, we wish to obtain $[L(\boldsymbol{x})]_d$ where $L(\boldsymbol{x})$ is some linear transformation on the vector $\boldsymbol{x}$. For this, we make use of the linear transformation pair $([\boldsymbol{r}]_d, [L(\boldsymbol{r})]_d)$ generated during the preprocessing. Specifically, parties can locally compute $[\boldsymbol{x} + \boldsymbol{r}]_d$. Note that this value can be publicly revealed since the input $\boldsymbol{x}$ is now masked with the random vector $\boldsymbol{r}$ which is not known to any party, and further it can be permuted to obtain $L(\boldsymbol{x} + \boldsymbol{r})$. Equivalently, parties can also compute $[L(\boldsymbol{x} + \boldsymbol{r})]_{k-1}$ instead of reconstructing. Given this, parties can compute $[L(\boldsymbol{x})]_d = [L(\boldsymbol{x} + \boldsymbol{r})]_{k-1} - [L(\boldsymbol{r})]_d$. Our task is now reduced to computing $[L(\boldsymbol{x} + \boldsymbol{r})]_{k-1}$ from $[\boldsymbol{x} + \boldsymbol{r}]_d$ of the vector $\boldsymbol{x} + \boldsymbol{r}$. That is, we again reduce our task to degree reduction of shared values. Similar to the preprocessing phase, although we have described the ideas with degree-d shared values, the invariant we maintain is degree-t shares of every value. We obtain degree-d packed sharing by packing values on demand via local operations as described earlier.

3. **Computation:** This phase in turn consists of shared evaluation of two types of gates: addition and multiplication.
   (a) Addition gates: These gates can be computed locally as long as the values to be added are shared in the correct position in packed Shamir sharing. The prior step of permutation ensures the required ordering of the values which are inputs to these gates. Hence, for a packed gate with k inputs x_i, y_i and output z_i, parties will hold $[x_i|i]_t$ and $[y_i|i]_t$ for all $i \in \{1, \ldots, k\}$. They can locally compute $[z_i|i]_t = [x_i|i]_t + [y_i|i]_t$. Note that the same gate output z_i may be used as an input to many gates in the subsequent layers, and moreover, z_i may be required to be shared in some other position such as $[z_i|j]_t$ where $i \neq j$. To handle this fan-out and permutation requirement, parties execute the linear transformation protocol as described above after each layer of gate evaluation.

(b) Multiplication gates: Unlike the addition gates, these gates require parties to communicate with each other. Similar to the case of addition, for a packed gate with inputs x_i, y_i and output z_i, parties will hold $[x_i|i]_t$ and $[y_i|i]_t$ for all $i \in \{1, \ldots, k\}$. Thus, parties can compute $[\boldsymbol{x}]_d$ and $[\boldsymbol{y}]_d$ locally and further, utilise one packed Beaver triple from the preprocessing phase to evaluate the gate. The evaluation itself follows Beaver's multiplication protocol, but for packed sharing, as in the prior works [14,18]. Thus given a triple $([\boldsymbol{a}]_d, [\boldsymbol{b}]_d, [\boldsymbol{c}]_d)$, parties first compute $[\boldsymbol{x} + \boldsymbol{a}]_d$ and $[\boldsymbol{y} + \boldsymbol{b}]_d$ which is required to be reconstructed. However, a public reconstruction would result in a communication of $\Omega(n^2)$ which we cannot afford. The work of [18] circumvents this problem by reconstructing to a designated P_{king} as described earlier. To prevent endless wait due to asynchrony in our case while ensuring the desired communication cost, we again follow our approach of degree reduction at this stage to obtain $[\boldsymbol{x} + \boldsymbol{a}]_{k-1}$ and $[\boldsymbol{y} + \boldsymbol{b}]_{k-1}$. While we follow the Beaver's multiplication protocol as in [18] for the rest of the computation, we encounter the same task of public reconstruction again for which we use another instance of our degree reduction protocol. The details are provided in Protocol 3.8. Similar to the case of addition, to handle the fan-out and permutation requirement for the input wires of the next layer gates, parties execute the linear transformation protocol.

4. **Output:** Finally, the output layer ensures that the output of the circuit is reconstructed to the designated party. For instance, suppose a party P_i has to receive the output corresponding to a wire v that is shared as per $[v|i]_t$ among parties. Parties send their respective share of $[v|i]_t$ towards P_i, who can robustly reconstruct the sharing polynomial using online error correction (OEC) [8] and recover v by evaluating the polynomial at $-i^{\text{th}}$ position. In fact, OEC can be used to reconstruct polynomials of higher degrees such as $d + k - 1$ used in our work and we discuss the protocol for reconstruction in the subsequent section.

3.3   Online Phase Primitives

Input Sharing. In the online phase, parties begin by sharing their inputs to the circuit using a degree-t Shamir sharing. For this, parties use the VSS protocol from [9]. The functionality for VSS appears below, followed by our input sharing protocol. Protocol 3.4 has a communication complexity of $\mathcal{O}(n^4)$ elements over point-to-point channels to share $k = \mathcal{O}(n)$ secrets via degree-t Shamir sharing. However, the broadcast cost incurred in their protocol can be batched over many instances for better amortized complexity as mentioned in the below lemma.

Functionality 3.3: $\mathcal{F}_{\text{VSS}}$ - VSS Functionality

---

The functionality is parameterized by the set of corrupted parties $\mathcal{C} \subseteq [n]$.

1. The dealer sends a bivariate polynomial $S(x, y)$ to the functionality.
2. If $S(x, y)$ is of degree at most $2t$ in x and at most t in y, the functionality sends to the ideal adversary the shares $S(x, i), S(i, y)$ for each $i \in \mathcal{C}$ and send

to each party P_j the polynomials $S(x, j), S(j, y)$. Otherwise the functionality does not terminate.

Protocol 3.4: Input Sharing Protocol

- **Input:** A party P_s holding k inputs to the circuit $\boldsymbol{x} = (x_1, x_2, \ldots, x_k)$.
- **The protocol:**
  1. P_s invokes the packed VSS of [9], $\mathcal{F}_{\mathsf{VSS}}$, with a degree $(t + k, t)$-degree bivariate polynomial to share $[x_j | j]_t$ for each $j \in \{1, \ldots, k\}$.

Lemma 3.5. *Protocol 3.4 when run in the batching mode has a communication complexity of $\mathcal{O}(np + n^4)$ elements over point-to-point channels to share p secrets via degree-t Shamir sharing.*

It is possible that the same input is used in many different wires of the circuit. Thus, we require a fan-out operation after the layer of input gates. Since fan-out is a special case of linear transformation, we discuss it in the subsequent section.

Degree Reduction. The degree reduction protocol allows parties holding a packed sharing of k secrets on a degree-$(d + \ell)$ polynomial, to obtain a degree-$(k - 1)$ sharing of the same secrets. In our work, we require degree reduction for two specific cases, when $\ell = 0$ and $\ell = k - 1$. We thus give a protocol for the latter case to reduce the degree from $d + k - 1$ to $k - 1$, and the one for the former case follows naturally by substituting $k = 0$. As already discussed, degree reduction is required in several protocols such as multiplication and linear transformation for obtaining the default degree-$(k - 1)$ sharing of masked vectors of k values. Designing a degree reduction protocol while ensuring $\mathcal{O}(1)$ communication per secret poses significant challenges in the asynchronous network where we cannot rely on a designated P_{king} as in the previous work [18].

At a very high level, our approach for mitigating this issue is to move away from reconstructing towards a single P_{king}, and instead, rely on all the parties to perform the degree reduction in a distributed manner. However, performing a reconstruction towards all the parties would immediately result in an increase in the communication cost. To handle this, instead of performing the degree reduction for a single vector of k values, we batch it over a set of k such vectors. This high level idea omits a lot of technicalities involved in our approach which we elaborate on below while describing the protocol.

At a conceptual level, one can think of our protocol to be an extension of the batched reconstruction from [11] over vectors of values. In our protocol, parties perform the degree reduction of k vectors say $\boldsymbol{u}^1, \ldots, \boldsymbol{u}^k$, each having k components. At the onset of the protocol, parties hold degree-$(d + k - 1)$ sharing of each of these vectors and the goal is to obtain the default degree-$(k - 1)$

sharing of each. For this, parties expand these k sharings of degree-d each to n sharings, each of degree-d using linear error correcting codes that tolerate up to t errors. Further, parties open one sharing per party, which recovers k secrets from it and further distributes a degree-$(k-1)$ sharing of these secrets. Finally, using the shares obtained from each party, parties correct t errors to obtain the shares corresponding to degree-$(k-1)$ sharing of each $\boldsymbol{u}^1, \ldots, \boldsymbol{u}^k$. We now describe why such an error correction is possible. Observe that k vectors $\boldsymbol{u}^1, \ldots, \boldsymbol{u}^k$, each of length k, are encoded to form k codewords of length-n each. In matrix form, this corresponds to mapping a $(k \times k)$ matrix, whose ith column is $\boldsymbol{u}^i$, to a $(k \times n)$ matrix, say $\boldsymbol{P}$, where $\boldsymbol{P} = [\boldsymbol{P}(1), \ldots, \boldsymbol{P}(n)]$ where $\boldsymbol{P}(i)$ is the ith column and where every row is a codeword.

In the protocol, the ith column vector $\boldsymbol{P}(i)$ is reconstructed towards party P_i by sending shares to P_i. Following this, P_i sends to every party P_j a linear combination of the k entries in its column $\boldsymbol{P}(i)$. This is implemented by Step 4 in Protocol 3.6, where it is described as P_i sharing $\boldsymbol{P}(i)$ among the parties with degree $(k-1)$ using VSS from [9] adapted to suit the necessary degree. The details of this VSS apper in the full version [12]. Since we are secret-sharing without privacy here, this is equivalent to sending fixed linear combinations. Crucially, for each party P_j, this linear combination is the same across all the senders P_i. This way, P_j receives a fixed linear combination of the k rows of the matrix P. This is a codeword of length-n, with up to t incorrect values obtained from corrupt parties. This is within the code's decoding capability (since the distance of the code is $n - k$ which is at least $3t + t/2$ since $k \leq t/2 + 1$). Hence, every party gets correct results and we do not rely on decoding being linear.

In case parties wish to obtain the degree reduced form of vectors with some linear transformation L applied on it (as is required in Protocol 3.10), each party locally applies L on the k secrets that it recovers before computing degree-$(k-1)$ sharing. The detailed protocol appears below without including the details for linear transformation since it follows naturally. It has a communication complexity of $\mathcal{O}(n^5)$ elements over point-to-point channels to reduce the degree of sharing of k vectors each with k values (total of $\mathcal{O}(n^2)$ values) from $d + k - 1$ to $k - 1$.

Protocol 3.6: Degree Reduction Protocol

- **Input:** Parties hold $\{[\boldsymbol{u}^i]_{d+k-1}\}_{i=1,\ldots,k}$ and the goal is to obtain $\{[\boldsymbol{u}^i]_{k-1}\}_{i=1,\ldots,k}$.
- **The protocol:**
  1. Parties define a vector of k polynomials $\boldsymbol{P}(x) = \boldsymbol{u}^1 + \boldsymbol{u}^2 \cdot x + \ldots + \boldsymbol{u}^k \cdot x^{k-1}$.
  2. Parties compute $[\boldsymbol{P}(x)]_{d+k-1} = [\boldsymbol{u}^1]_{d+k-1} + [\boldsymbol{u}^2]_{d+k-1} \cdot x + \ldots + [\boldsymbol{u}^k]_{d+k-1} \cdot x^{k-1}$.
  3. Parties compute $[\boldsymbol{P}(i)]_{d+k-1}$ and reconstruct the vector of k values, $\boldsymbol{P}(i)$ to P_i for each $i \in \{1, \ldots, n\}$.
  4. Each P_i shares $[\boldsymbol{P}(i)]_{k-1}$ among all the parties using a VSS protocol with degree-$(k-1)$.

5. Parties run an instance of the ACS protocol to agree on a common set of $n - t$ parties which completed their sharing in the prior step. Let this set be denoted by Com.

6. Parties apply the RS decoding procedure for recovering $[\boldsymbol{P}(x)]_{k-1}$ on $[\boldsymbol{P}(i)]_{k-1}$ for each $P_i \in$ Com instead of applying it directly on $\boldsymbol{P}(i)$ values.

7. Each P_i thus obtains $[\boldsymbol{P}(x)]_{k-1} = [\boldsymbol{u}^1]_{k-1} + [\boldsymbol{u}^2]_{k-1} \cdot x + \ldots + [\boldsymbol{u}^k]_{k-1} \cdot x^{k-1}$ and computes its respective shares $\{[\boldsymbol{u}^i]_{k-1}\}_{i=1,\ldots,k}$.

Lemma 3.7. *Protocol 3.6 when run in the batching mode (with $\Omega(n^3)$ instances in parallel) has a communication complexity of $\mathcal{O}(p+n^5)$ elements over point-to-point channels to reduce the degree of sharing polynomials consisting of p values.*

We note that for the above idea to work, we want a party to verifiably generate degree-$(k - 1)$ sharing of k *non-private* values with constant overhead per value. In the following, we give a protocol for this purpose.

VSS Without Privacy. For degree reduction, we require parties to distribute a default degree-$(k - 1)$ sharing of a vector of k *non-private* values. We observe that the existing VSS protocol of [9] can be tweaked for this task. Specifically, [9] gives a VSS protocol considering a bivariate polynomial with degree $(2t, t)$ that allows parties to create $t+1$ Shamir sharings simultaneously, each with a degree-t. Given that in the standard setting privacy has to be maintained against an adversary that can corrupt up to t parties, we can share 1 secret via each of these $t + 1$ sharings. Thus, we can share $t + 1 = \mathcal{O}(n)$ secrets while ensuring privacy. In contrast, for our case we require to share masked values for which privacy is not a concern, but ensuring the correctness of the degree is. By modifying the VSS of [9] to operate with degree-$(k - 1, k - 1)$ bivariate polynomial, we can precisely achieve this. That is, we can now create k Shamir sharings, each with degree-$(k - 1)$. Each of these k sharings of degree $k - 1$ can be used to share k secrets, thus allowing a total of $k^2 = \mathcal{O}(n^2)$ secrets to be shared simultaneously without privacy. Crucially, the communication cost of VSS in [9] is $\mathcal{O}(n^4)$ field elements for sharing $\mathcal{O}(n)$ secrets simultaneously, while at the same cost we can share $\mathcal{O}(n^2)$ values without privacy. More generally their protocol incurs a cost of $\mathcal{O}(np + n^4)$ for sharing p secrets with privacy whereas a cost of $\mathcal{O}(p + n^4)$ for sharing p secrets without privacy. In the full version [12], we describe the protocol from [9] with degree-$(k - 1, k - 1)$ bivariate polynomial for completeness.

Multiplication. We follow the outline of the multiplication protocol from [18] for evaluating multiplication gates. Due to the invariant maintained in the protocol, parties hold degree-t Shamir sharing of each input wire value x_i, y_i for all $i \in \{1, \ldots, k\}$ from which they can locally obtain $[\boldsymbol{x}]_d, [\boldsymbol{y}]_d$. Additionally, from the preprocessing phase, they also have such sharing of Beaver triples of the form $\{(a_i, b_i, c_i)\}_{i \in \{1,\ldots,k\}}$ using which they can locally compute a degree-d sharing of a packed Beaver triple of the form $(\boldsymbol{a}, \boldsymbol{b}, \boldsymbol{c})$. Following this, as discussed earlier, evaluating a packed multiplication gate essentially reduces to performing degree reduction on shared values, either from degree d or $d + k - 1$, to degree $k - 1$. To achieve this, while ensuring a cost of $\mathcal{O}(1)$ in our network setting, we replace the P_{king} based approach for degree reduction with our new protocol from the earlier section. The rest of the protocol remains the same and it appears below. It has a communication complexity of $\mathcal{O}(n^5)$ elements over point-to-point channels to evaluate $k^2 = \mathcal{O}(n^2)$ multiplication gates simultaneously.

Protocol 3.8: Multiplication Protocol

- **Input:** For k groups of k-packed multiplication gates in the same layer, for all $i \in \{1, \ldots, k\}$ parties hold $\{[x_j^i|j]_t, [y_j^i|j]_t\}_{j=1}^k$. Parties also hold $\{([a_j^i|j]_t, [b_j^i|j]_t, [c_j^i|j]_t)\}_{j=1}^k$ and $\{[r_j^i|j]_t\}_{j=1}^{2k-1}$ from the preprocessing phase for each $i \in \{1, \ldots, k\}$.
- **The protocol:**
  1. Parties locally compute for each $i \in \{1, \ldots, k\}$:
     - $[\boldsymbol{a}^i]_d = \sum_{j=1}^k [e_j]_{k-1} * [a_j^i|j]_t$
     - $[\boldsymbol{b}^i]_d = \sum_{j=1}^k [e_j]_{k-1} * [b_j^i|j]_t$
     - $[\boldsymbol{c}^i]_d = \sum_{j=1}^k [e_j]_{k-1} * [c_j^i|j]_t$
     - $[\boldsymbol{x}^i + \boldsymbol{a}^i]_d = \sum_{j=1}^k [e_j]_{k-1} * [x_j^i|j]_t + [\boldsymbol{a}^i]_d$
     - $[\boldsymbol{y}^i + \boldsymbol{b}^i]_d = \sum_{j=1}^k [e_j]_{k-1} * [y_j^i|j]_t + [\boldsymbol{b}^i]_d$
  2. Invoke the degree reduction protocol (Protocol 3.6 for a batch of k multiplication gates in the same level simultaneously to obtain $[\boldsymbol{x}^i + \boldsymbol{a}^i]_{k-1}$, $[\boldsymbol{y}^i + \boldsymbol{b}^i]_{k-1}$ for all $i \in \{1, \ldots, k\}$.
  3. Parties locally compute
     - $[\boldsymbol{z}^i]_{d+k-1} = [\boldsymbol{x}^i + \boldsymbol{a}^i]_{k-1} * [\boldsymbol{y}^i + \boldsymbol{b}^i]_{k-1} - [\boldsymbol{x}^i + \boldsymbol{a}^i]_{k-1} * [\boldsymbol{b}^i]_d - [\boldsymbol{y}^i + \boldsymbol{b}^i]_{k-1} * [\boldsymbol{a}^i]_d + [\boldsymbol{c}^i]_d$
     - $[\boldsymbol{r}^i]_{d+k-1} = \sum_{j=1}^{2k-1} [e_j]_{2k-2} * [r_j^i|j]_t$
     - $[\boldsymbol{z}^i + \boldsymbol{r}^i]_{d+k-1} = [\boldsymbol{z}^i]_{d+k-1} + [\boldsymbol{r}^i]_{d+k-1}$
  4. Invoke the degree reduction protocol (Protocol 3.6 for a batch of k multiplication gates in the same level simultaneously to obtain $[\boldsymbol{z}^i]_{k-1}$ for all $i \in \{1, \ldots, k\}$.
  5. Parties compute $[z_j^i|j]_t = [\boldsymbol{z}^i + \boldsymbol{r}^i s]_{k-1} - [r_j^i|j]_t$ for all $i \in \{1, \ldots, k\}$.

Lemma 3.9. *Protocol 3.8 when run in the batching mode (with $\Omega(n^3)$ instances in parallel) has a communication complexity of $\mathcal{O}(p + n^5)$ elements over point-to-point channels to evaluate p multiplication gates simultaneously.*

Linear Transformation. As discussed, evaluating a circuit using packed secret sharing involves computing linear transformations on k packed wire values that are shared among parties. Specifically, the linear transformation protocol allows parties to compute degree-d shares of $L(x)$, given the shares of x using some data from the preprocessing stage. We follow the approach of [18], where parties generate the pair $(r, L(r))$ during the preprocessing phase[9]. As noted, the linear transformation operation involves reducing the degree of sharing of a vector of non-private values $x + r$ with the linear transformation L applied it. Specifically, it requires reducing the degree of $x + r$ from d to obtain a degree-$(k - 1)$ sharing of $L(x + r)$.

Once again, we rely on our degree reduction protocol, although with a caveat. Note that, in the case of linear transformations, we don't just reduce the degree of the vector $x + r$, but we also apply a linear transformation on it before reducing the degree. Going back to our degree reduction protocol, it works with a batch of k vectors simultaneously to ensure the desired communication cost. Given that we require to apply the linear transformation on values within each of these vectors during degree reduction, we need all the vectors for which the degree is being reduced to have the same linear transformation being applied. However, this may not be the case in a generic circuit. To circumvent this issue, we can rely on the approach of [10] wherein the circuit C to be computed is first compiled into a new circuit C' such that there is a set of $\log n$ linear transformations which get reused throughout the circuit. This allows us to batch the degree reduction protocol for the same linear transformation with the guarantee that at most $\log n$ different instances of such degree reduction may incur a higher cost in case sufficient values cannot be batched together. Another approach to tackle this is to simply execute our protocol for SIMD circuits, wherein instead of one execution, $m = \mathcal{O}(n^3)$ number of instances of the circuit are executed simultaneously. Here, the batching of degree reduction will happen for the same gates across m circuits. We describe our protocols assuming the latter, and a similar extension can be done for the former case as well. The protocol for linear transformation appears below assuming that the degree reduction occurs on a batch of vectors simultaneously. Specifically, the protocol has a communication complexity of $\mathcal{O}(n^5)$ elements over point-to-point channels to apply the same linear transformation L on k vectors each with k values (total of $\mathcal{O}(n^2)$ values).

Protocol 3.10: Linear Transformation Protocol

- **Input:** Parties hold $\{([r_j|j]_t, [L_j(r)|j]_t)\}_{j=1,\ldots,k}$ from the preprocessing phase where $r = (r_1, \ldots, r_k)$, and $[x_j|j]_t$. The goal is to obtain $[L_j(x)|j]_t$ for all $j \in \{1, \ldots, k\}$ where $x = (x_1, \ldots, x_k)$ and $L_j(x)$ is the jth component of $L(x)$.
- **The protocol:**

---

[9] As in [18], instead of holding degree-d sharing of all the vectors $x, r, L(r)$, parties hold degree-t sharing of each of its components which is then locally converted to a degree-d sharing.

1. Parties compute $[\boldsymbol{x}]_d = \sum_{j=1}^{k} [e_j]_{k-1} * [x_j|j]_t$ and $[\boldsymbol{r}]_d = \sum_{j=1}^{k} [e_j]_{k-1} * [r_j|j]_t$ locally.
2. Parties compute $[\boldsymbol{x} + \boldsymbol{r}]_d = [\boldsymbol{x}]_d + [\boldsymbol{r}]_d$ locally.
3. Invoke the degree reduction protocol (Protocol 3.6) for a batch of k linear transformation gates simultaneously to obtain $[L(\boldsymbol{x} + \boldsymbol{r})]_{k-1}$.
4. Parties compute $[L_j(\boldsymbol{x})|j]_t = [L(\boldsymbol{x} + \boldsymbol{r})]_{k-1} - [L_j(\boldsymbol{r})|j]_t$ locally.

Lemma 3.11. *Protocol 3.10 when run in the batching mode (with $\Omega(n^3)$ instances in parallel) has a communication complexity of $\mathcal{O}(p + n^5)$ elements over point-to-point channels to apply the same linear transformation L on vectors consisting of p values.*

3.4   The Complete MPC Protocol

In this section, we first provide the functionality for MPC, followed by the description of the complete MPC protocol as a composition of all the building blocks defined so far.

Functionality 3.12: AMPC $- \mathcal{F}_{\mathsf{MPC}}$

The functionality is parameterized by a set of corrupted parties $\mathcal{C} \subseteq [n]$. Initialize the sets $S, H, \mathcal{C}' = \phi$. Initialize $x_i = 0$ for every $i \in \mathcal{C}$.
Input: Each P_i holds input $x_i \in \mathbb{F} \cup \{\bot\}$.
Common Input: An n-party function $f(x_1, \ldots, x_n)$.

1. Upon receiving (Input, j, x_j) from an honest party P_j, if $j \notin H$ then add j to S.
2. Receive from the adversary, the sets $H \subset [n] \setminus \mathcal{C}$ and $\mathcal{C}' \subseteq \mathcal{C}$ such that $|H| \leq |\mathcal{C}'| \leq t$. Also receive a set of inputs $\{(\mathsf{Input}, i, x_i)\}_{i \in \mathcal{C}'}$.
3. If $|S| < n - t$, then for each P_j with $j \in H$, the functionality sets $x_j = 0$ and updates $S = S \setminus H$.
4. If $|S \cup \mathcal{C}'| \geq n - t$, then compute $(y_1, \ldots, y_n) = f(x_1, \ldots, x_n)$ and send y_i to P_i for every $i \in [n]$ and terminate.

We divide the MPC protocol in three phases, namely, the circuit transformation, preprocessing and online phase as described below.

(Circuit Transformation Phase)

– Parties first apply the deterministic circuit transformation algorithm from [17] to the circuit C with depth D to obtain a circuit C' which provides packed secret sharing friendliness[10]. The resultant circuit C' is such that $|C'| = \mathcal{O}(|C| + k \cdot (n + D))$ and has the following properties:

---

[10] Alternatively, the circuit could also be transformed using the algorithm from [10] leading to a circuit C' such that $|C'| = \mathcal{O}(|C| \log |C| + nD^2 \log^3 |C|)$ and $D' = \mathcal{O}(D \log^2 |C|)$.

- The number of input gates and the number of output gates belonging to each party are a multiple of k each. Moreover, the number of addition gates and multiplication gates in every intermediate layer are also a multiple of k.
- The number of output wires of the input layer as well as every intermediate layer is a multiple of k. Similarly, the number of input wires of every intermediate layer and the output layer is also a multiple of k. Moreover, every output wire is used exactly once as the input wire in the next layer.
- Gates of the same type in the same layer are divided into groups of k which are evaluated together. Additionally, the number of times the output wires of each group are used as input wires in the subsequent layers is a multiple of k.

(Preprocessing Phase)

- Parties generate the required number of Beaver triples by invoking $\mathcal{F}_{\mathsf{Triples}}$ (Functionality 3.1), degree reduction pairs and linear transformation pairs using existing techniques. The detailed protocols for these appear in the full version [12]. This comprises the preprocessing phase of the MPC protocol.

(Online Phase)

- Parties first divide gates of the same kind in every layer of the circuit into groups of size k.
- Following this, each party uses the VSS protocol from [9] to share their inputs to the circuit via degree-t Shamir sharing.
- Parties then invoke an instance of the ACS protocol to identify a subset of (at least) $n - t$ parties who successfully completed their sharing instances. A default value is considered as input for all the parties outside this set.
- Following this, the inputs to the subsequent layer have to be prepared.
  - For this, parties first apply the fan-out operation on groups of k wires using the linear transformation protocol. This generates the required number of copies of each input value shared by a party.
  - Subsequently, parties apply a permutation on the secrets, again considered in groups of size k. The guarantee offered by [17] is that upon permutation, the resultant shared values hold the following property. For each packed sharing $[z]_d$ that is used as an input to the subsequent layer, the values $z_1, \ldots, z_k$ will be such that they lie at different positions in their respective degree-t sharing obtained as an output of the permutations. This allows parties to locally obtain a packed degree-d sharing of some permutation of z. Finally parties apply permutation again to obtain $[z]_d$.
- The addition and multiplication gates are then evaluated in a topological order. After each layer of evaluation, inputs to the subsequent layer are prepared as discussed above.

- Finally, after evaluating all the computation gates, parties proceed to the output phase. Here, parties reconstruct the packed sharing $[z]_d$ corresponding to a packed output wire belonging to some party P_s towards it by sending their shares. P_s performs online error correction on the received shares to obtain its output.

Protocol 3.13: AMPC – Π_{MPC}

(Circuit Transformation Phase)

- Parties first apply the deterministic circuit transformation algorithm from [17] to the circuit C with depth D to obtain a circuit C' which provides packed secret sharing friendliness [11]. The resultant circuit C' is such that $|C'| = \mathcal{O}(|C| + k \cdot (n + D))$.

(Preprocessing Phase)

- Parties generate $\frac{|C'|}{k}$ groups of Beaver triples of the form $\{[a_i|i]_t, [b_i|i]_t, [c_i|i]_t\}_{i \in \{1,\ldots,k\}}$ by invoking $\mathcal{F}_{\mathsf{Triples}}$ (Functionality 3.1).
- Parties generate $\frac{|C'|}{2k-1}$ groups of random values of the form $\{[r_i|i]_t\}_{i \in \{1,\ldots,2k-1\}}$ required to obtain packed degree reduction pairs for multiplication.
- Parties also generate $\frac{2|C'|}{k}$ linear transformation pairs required in the complete circuit for fan-out and permutation operations.

(Online Phase)

- For every group of k inputs $\boldsymbol{x} = (x_1, \ldots, x_k)$ belonging to a party P_s, it shares its inputs using the VSS protocol from [9] to distribute $[x_i|i]_t$ for all $i \in \{1, \ldots, k\}$.
- Parties then invoke an instance of the ACS protocol (Functionality $\mathcal{F}_{\mathsf{ACS}}$) to identify a subset of (at least) $n - t$ parties who successfully completed their sharing instances. A default value is considered as input for all the parties outside this set.
- Following this, parties evaluate the circuit layer by layer as follows.
  - For every group of k input wires $\boldsymbol{x}$, parties locally obtain $[x_i|p(i)]_t$ for $i \in \{1, \ldots, k\}$ and some permutation p over $\{1, \ldots, k\}$.
  - For every group of k input wires $\boldsymbol{x}$, parties further invoke Protocol 3.10 on $[x_i|p(i)]_t$ for $i \in \{1, \ldots, k\}$ to obtain $[x_i|i]_t$ for all $i \in \{1, \ldots, k\}$.
  - For each group of addition gates with inputs $[x_i|i]_t$ and $[y_i|i]_t$ for $i \in \{1, \ldots, k\}$, parties locally compute $[z_i|i]_t = [x_i|i]_t + [y_i|i]_t$.
  - For each group of multiplication gates with inputs $[x_i|i]_t$ and $[y_i|i]_t$ for $i \in \{1, \ldots, k\}$, parties invoke Protocol 3.8 to compute $[z_i|i]_t = [x_i|i]_t * [y_i|i]_t$.
  - For the group of output wires in a layer $[z_i|i]_t$ and the linear transformation L to be applied on them, parties invoke Protocol 3.10 to obtain $[L_i(\boldsymbol{z})|i]_t$ for all $i \in \{1, \ldots, k\}$.

– For each group of output gates $[z_i|i]_t$ belonging to some party P_s, parties locally compute $[z]_d$ and send their shares to P_s. Party P_s reconstructs its output z using online error correction on the received shares.

Theorem 3.14. *Let $t < n/4$. Protocol Π_{MPC} (Protocol 3.13) securely implements $\mathcal{F}_{\mathsf{MPC}}$ (Functionality 3.12) and has a communication complexity of $\mathcal{O}(|C'|n + n^5)$ bits over point-to-point channels in the preprocessing phase and $\mathcal{O}(|C'| + Dn^5 + n^5)$ bits in the online phase to evaluate a circuit C with depth D.*

The security proof and the complexity analysis appear in the full version [12].

References

1. Abraham, I., Asharov, G., Patil, S., Patra, A.: Detect, pack and batch: perfectly-secure MPC with linear communication and constant expected time. In: Annual International Conference on the Theory and Applications of Cryptographic Techniques, pp. 251–281. Springer (2023)
2. Abraham, I., Asharov, G., Patil, S., Patra, A.: Perfect asynchronous MPC with linear communication overhead. In: Annual International Conference on the Theory and Applications of Cryptographic Techniques, pp. 280–309. Springer (2024)
3. Abraham, I., Asharov, G., Patra, A., Stern, G.: Perfectly secure asynchronous agreement on a core set in constant expected time. IACR Cryptol. ePrint Arch. 1130 (2023). https://eprint.iacr.org/2023/1130
4. Applebaum, B., Kachlon, E., Patra, A.: The round complexity of perfect MPC with active security and optimal resiliency. In: Annual Symposium on Foundations of Computer Science (FOCS) (2020)
5. Beerliová-Trubíniová, Z., Hirt, M.: Perfectly-secure MPC with linear communication complexity. In: Proceedings of the 5th Conference on Theory of Cryptography, TCC 2008, pp. 213–230. Springer, Heidelberg (2008)
6. Beerliová-Trubíniová, Z., Hirt, M.: Perfectly-secure MPC with linear communication complexity. In: Theory of Cryptography Conference (2008)
7. Canetti, R.: Studies in secure multiparty computation and applications (1996). https://www.wisdom.weizmann.ac.il/~oded/PSX/ran-phd.pdf
8. Canetti, R.: Studies in secure multiparty computation and applications. Ph.D. thesis, Citeseer (1996)
9. Choudhury, A., Patra, A.: An efficient framework for unconditionally secure multiparty computation. IEEE Trans. Inf. Theory (2016)
10. Damgård, I., Ishai, Y., Krøigaard, M.: Perfectly secure multiparty computation and the computational overhead of cryptography. In: Gilbert, H. (ed.) EUROCRYPT 2010. LNCS, vol. 6110, pp. 445–465. Springer, Heidelberg (2010). https://doi.org/10.1007/978-3-642-13190-5_23

---

[11] Alternatively, the circuit could also be transformed using the algorithm from [10] leading to a circuit C' such that $|C'| = \mathcal{O}(|C| \log |C| + nD^2 \log^3 |C|)$ and $D' = \mathcal{O}(D \log^2 |C|)$

11. Damgård, I., Nielsen, J.B.: Scalable and unconditionally secure multiparty computation. In: Annual International Cryptology Conference (2007)
12. Damgård, I., Patil, S., Patra, A., Roy, L.: New upper and lower bounds for perfectly secure MPC. Cryptology ePrint Archive (2025)
13. Damgård, I.B., Li, B., Schwartzbach, N.I.: More communication lower bounds for information-theoretic MPC. In: 2nd Conference on Information-Theoretic Cryptography (ITC 2021). Schloss-Dagstuhl-Leibniz Zentrum für Informatik (2021)
14. Escudero, D., Goyal, V., Polychroniadou, A., Song, Y.: Turbopack: honest majority MPC with constant online communication. In: Proceedings of the 2022 ACM SIGSAC Conference on Computer and Communications Security, pp. 951–964 (2022)
15. Fitzi, M., Gottesman, D., Hirt, M., Holenstein, T., Smith, A.: Detectable byzantine agreement secure against faulty majorities. In: Proceedings of the Twenty-First Annual Symposium on Principles of Distributed Computing, pp. 118–126 (2002)
16. Goyal, V., Liu, Y., Song, Y.: Communication-efficient unconditional MPC with guaranteed output delivery. In: Annual International Cryptology Conference, pp. 85–114. Springer (2019)
17. Goyal, V., Polychroniadou, A., Song, Y.: Unconditional communication-efficient MPC via hall's marriage theorem. In: Advances in Cryptology–CRYPTO 2021: 41st Annual International Cryptology Conference, CRYPTO 2021, Virtual Event, 16–20 August 2021, Proceedings, Part II 41, pp. 275–304. Springer (2021)
18. Song, Y., Ye, X.: Perfectly-secure MPC with constant online communication complexity. Cryptology ePrint Archive (2024)

Optimal Good-Case Latency for Sleepy Consensus

Yuval Efron[1](✉) [iD], Joachim Neu[2] [iD], Ling Ren[3] [iD], and Ertem Nusret Tas[2] [iD]

[1] Columbia University, New York, USA
ye2210@columbia.edu
[2] a16z Crypto Research, New York, USA
{jneu,ntas}@a16z.com
[3] University of Illinois at Urbana–Champaign, Champaign, USA
renling@illinois.edu

Abstract. In the context of Byzantine consensus problems such as Byzantine broadcast (BB) and Byzantine agreement (BA), the *good-case* setting aims to study the minimal possible latency of a BB or BA protocol under certain favorable conditions, namely the designated leader being correct (for BB), or all correct parties having the same input value (for BA). We provide a full characterization of the feasibility and impossibility of good-case latency, for both BA and BB, in the synchronous *sleepy* model. Surprisingly to us, we find *irrational* resilience thresholds emerging: 2-round good-case BB is possible if and only if at all times, at least $\frac{1}{\varphi} \approx 0.618$ fraction of the active parties are correct, where $\varphi = \frac{1+\sqrt{5}}{2} \approx 1.618$ is the golden ratio; 1-round good-case BA is possible if and only if at least $\frac{1}{\sqrt{2}} \approx 0.707$ fraction of the active parties are correct.

Keywords: Byzantine agreement · Byzantine broadcast · Good-case latency · Sleepy model · Dynamic participation

1 Introduction

The Byzantine consensus problems [16], such as Byzantine broadcast and Byzantine agreement, are among the most fundamental and well-studied problems in cryptography and distributed computing. The recent surge of cryptocurrencies and blockchain systems has rekindled interest in these problems, and also drawn the community's attention to unconventional system models that were overlooked in the decades of prior research.

One of the most prominent and striking features of the celebrated Nakamoto consensus protocol [11,23] is that it allows correct parties to participate intermittently in the protocol. At any time, only a (possibly tiny) fraction of correct parties are actively following the protocol. The rest of the correct parties are in an *inactive* (or crashed) state. Furthermore, correct parties can transition between active and inactive states at any time without prior notice, and they do not know for sure how many other parties are actively participating in the protocol at any time. A variant of this model (without reliance on proof-of-work) is

J. Daemen and E. Thomé (Eds.): EUROCRYPT 2026, LNCS 16543, pp. 397–426, 2026.
https://doi.org/10.1007/978-3-032-25324-8_14

formalized by Pass and Shi as the *sleepy* model [25], also interchangeably called the *dynamic participation* model.[1] In contrast, we refer to the traditional model where all correct parties are always active as the *static participation* model. Note that a variant of the CAP theorem [12,17,24] shows that a synchronous network is necessary for sleepy consensus, so we assume *synchrony* throughout this paper. The sleepy model is employed by leading blockchains such as Ethereum and Cardano [2,5,15,24].

A line of recent works has designed sleepy Byzantine consensus protocols that match static participation protocols in many aspects. Sleepy Byzantine consensus protocols can tolerate minority Byzantine faults [4,5,7–9,13,15,18,20,22,25], which is the same corruption threshold as in the static model. Protocols in the sleepy model have also achieved expected constant rounds [7–9,18–20,22], again matching the static participation model.

In this paper, we focus on the *good-case* latency T_{gc}, measured in rounds of communication. For the Byzantine broadcast problem, the "good case" refers to the case where the designated sender is correct, while for Byzantine agreement, it refers to the case where all correct parties have the same input value. In addition to a certain latency requirement in the good case, the protocols are required to satisfy the usual consensus desiderata (termination, agreement, validity; see Definitions 1 and 2) even when the good-case conditions are not met. The good-case latency is a metric well-motivated by practical considerations. Most deployed consensus protocols have parties rotate to serve as the *leader*, who proposes a value (a block) for other parties to agree on. Because there are mechanisms to reward or penalize the leader based on its actions, the vast majority of leaders behave correctly. We thus would like the consensus protocol to be as fast as possible under a correct leader.

Note that no Byzantine broadcast protocol can hope to achieve latency $T_{\mathrm{gc}} \leq 1$, even in the good case, for the straightforward reason that it leaves correct parties no time to reconcile (or even detect) equivocating values they may have received from a Byzantine leader in the first communication round. Similarly, no Byzantine agreement protocol can hope to achieve good-case latency $T_{\mathrm{gc}} = 0$, for the analogous reason that it leaves correct parties no time to reconcile different input values they may have. On the other hand, an earlier work [1] has shown that for Byzantine broadcast in the traditional synchronous model with static participation, two rounds are sufficient and necessary in the good case, if the *resilience* ρ (i.e., fraction of Byzantine parties tolerable) is below $1/2$ (see Table 1). For Byzantine agreement in the same model, it is folklore that one-round latency can be achieved in the good case, if and only if at most $1/3$ of parties are Byzantine (see Table 1 and Lemmas 1 and 2).

---

[1] Importantly, the *unexpected temporary crash faults* (what "dynamic participation" refers to) in the sleepy model are not to be confused with *scheduled* reconfiguration of the membership set of parties operating the protocol (also called "stake shift" in the context of proof-of-stake blockchains). No reconfiguration of the set of operating parties takes place throughout this paper.

Table 1. Achievable and impossible resiliences for Byzantine broadcast (BB) and Byzantine agreement (BA) with varying good-case latency T_{gc} in different participation models. Notably, we provide a tight characterization under dynamic participation, where tight irrational resilience thresholds emerge: $1 - 1/\varphi \approx 0.382$ (where $\varphi = \frac{1+\sqrt{5}}{2} \approx 1.618$ is the golden ratio) and $1 - 1/\sqrt{2} \approx 0.293$.

Problem	T_{gc}	Part. Model	Achiev. Resil.	Imposs. Resil.
BB	2	Static P.	1/2 [1]	Open[*]
		Unknown P.	1/2 (Theorem 5)	Open[*]
		Dynamic P.	$1 - 1/\varphi$ (Theorem 3)	$1 - 1/\varphi$ (Theorem 1)
BB	≥ 3	Static P.	1/2 [1][†]	Open[*]
		Unknown P.	1/2 (Theorem 5)[†]	Open[*]
		Dynamic P.	1/2 (Theorem 6)	1/2 [26]
BA	1	Static P.	1/3 (Folk.: Lemma 1)	1/3 (Folk.: Lemma 2)
		Unknown P.	$1 - 1/\sqrt{2}$ (Theorem 4)[‡]	$1 - 1/\sqrt{2}$ (Theorem 2)
		Dynamic P.	$1 - 1/\sqrt{2}$ (Theorem 4)	$1 - 1/\sqrt{2}$ (Theorem 2)[‡]
BA	≥ 2	Static P.	1/2 (Theorem 7)[‡]	1/2 [3]
		Unknown P.	1/2 (Theorem 7)[‡]	1/2[‡]
		Dynamic P.	1/2 (Theorem 7)	1/2[‡]

"Folk." indicates a result is folklore.

[*] The landscape of Byzantine broadcast in the "adversarial majority" regime remains incomplete, even under static participation. The protocol provided in [27] achieves $T_{\mathrm{gc}} = O(\frac{n}{n-f})$. This matches the impossibility results [1] asymptotically, but concrete gaps remain. This lack of clarity seeps into the unknown participation model, since crashed honest parties can be treated as Byzantine for the purpose of protocols tolerating an adversarial majority of parties [26]. For dynamic participation, we fully characterize the good-case latency and resilience achievable for Byzantine broadcast and Byzantine agreement.

[†] Implied by a protocol with better latency.

[‡] Implied by a protocol or impossibility result for a more demanding model.

Results. This paper extends the systematic study of good-case latency of Byzantine consensus to the dynamic participation (sleepy) model. We give a complete characterization of the good-case latency of Byzantine broadcast and Byzantine agreement, and the corresponding resilience (see Table 1). Our results for the dynamic participation model imply a complete characterization of good-case latency and resilience for Byzantine agreement and Byzantine broadcast (in the "honest majority" regime) in the *unknown participation* model [14]. The unknown participation model is weaker than the traditional static participation model, but stronger than the dynamic participation model, in the sense that the number of active correct parties is unknown to the protocol, but does not change once the protocol starts.

Table 2. Earlier protocols and their good-case latency T_{gc} and resilience, for Byzantine broadcast (BB) and Byzantine agreement (BA), in different participation models.

Problem	Part. Model	Protocol	Lat. T_{gc}	Resil.
Broadcast (BB)	Static P.	ANRX'21 [1]	2	1/2
	Unknown P.	KW'21 [14]	3	1/3
	Dynamic P.	MMR'23 [20]	4	1/2
Agreement (BA)	Static P.	Folklore (Lemma 1)	1	1/3
	Static P.	MR'21 [21]	4	1/2
	Unknown P.	KW'21 [14]	3	1/3
	Dynamic P.	LG'23 [9,18]	4	1/2
	Dynamic P.[†]	DSTZ'23 [6][‡]	5	1/2

† Mild stable participation assumption.
‡ Achieves stronger property of conciliation.

Perhaps the most surprising part of our findings is that the critical resilience thresholds that dictate good-case latency under dynamic and unknown participation are *irrational* numbers. For instance, Byzantine broadcast with good-case latency $T_{\text{gc}} = 2$ and resilience ρ can be achieved under dynamic participation if and only if $\rho \leq 1 - 1/\varphi \approx 0.382$, where $\varphi = \frac{1+\sqrt{5}}{2} \approx 1.618$ is the golden ratio. Byzantine agreement with good-case latency $T_{\text{gc}} = 1$ and resilience ρ can be achieved under dynamic participation and under unknown participation if and only if $\rho \leq 1 - 1/\sqrt{2} \approx 0.293$. Interestingly, to the best of our knowledge, the only other appearance, in [10], of an irrational corruption threshold in the context of distributed computing and cryptography also involves the number $1 - 1/\sqrt{2}$.

Our results also establish separations among static, unknown, and dynamic participation. When the corruption threshold is between $1 - 1/\varphi$ and $1/2$, Byzantine broadcast under unknown participation can decide in two rounds in the good case, but requires three rounds under dynamic participation. When the target corruption threshold is between $1 - 1/\sqrt{2}$ and $1/3$, Byzantine agreement under static participation can decide in one round in the good case, but requires two rounds under unknown participation. Conceptually, our results show that these two fundamental consensus primitives exhibit new behavior in the unknown/dynamic participation settings, and this behavior can be captured and characterized with known techniques/frameworks (good-case latency).

Related Work. Table 2 lists earlier consensus protocols with low good-case latency. For Byzantine broadcast, Abraham et al. [1] achieve the optimal $T_{\text{gc}} = 2$ under static participation. For dynamic participation, Malkhi et al. [20] provide $T_{\text{gc}} = 4$ under a majority of correct active parties, which also works under unknown participation, whereas Khanchandani and Wattenhofer [14] achieve improved latency $T_{\text{gc}} = 3$, but only with resilience $1/3$. We provide broadcast protocols for dynamic participation with minimal good-case latency, $T_{\mathrm{gc}} = 2$ and $T_{\mathrm{gc}} = 3$, and optimal resilience, $1 - 1/\varphi$ and $1/2$, respectively (Table 1).

For Byzantine agreement, a folklore result (see Lemmas 1 and 2) achieves the minimal $T_{\mathrm{gc}} = 1$ with $1/3$ resilience despite synchrony and static participation. Under dynamic participation, Losa and Gafni [9,18] achieve $T_{\mathrm{gc}} = 4$ under $1/2$ resilience, while the 3-graded agreement of D'Amato et al. [6] yields a protocol with $T_{\mathrm{gc}} = 5$ at the expense of a mild stable-participation assumption, but that also achieves the stronger property of conciliation. For unknown participation, a result of Khanchandani and Wattenhofer [14] implies an agreement protocol with $T_{\mathrm{gc}} = 3$ but only resilience $1/3$. We provide agreement protocols for dynamic participation (and for unknown participation) with minimal good-case latency, $T_{\mathrm{gc}} = 1$ and $T_{\mathrm{gc}} = 2$, and optimal resilience, $1 - 1/\sqrt{2}$ and $1/2$, respectively (Table 1).

Outline. We briefly review the model and definitions in Sect. 2, before providing a technical overview of our results in Sect. 3. Then, Section 4 proves our impossibility results. Section 5 presents our BB and BA protocols with $T_{\mathrm{gc}} = 2$ and $T_{\mathrm{gc}} = 1$, respectively, and proves their correctness, before Sect. 6 does the same for our BB and BA protocols with $T_{\mathrm{gc}} = 3$ and $T_{\mathrm{gc}} = 2$, respectively.

2   Model and Definitions

2.1   Model

Sleepy Model of Consensus. We work in the *sleepy* model [25] of Pass and Shi, also called the *dynamic participation* model. We consider a setting with N parties in total, identified by a public key infrastructure (PKI). We assume a synchronous pairwise communication network, with a known delay upper-bound of Δ on message delivery. For simplicity, we present both our upper and lower bounds for the case $\Delta = 1$, though both generalize to general Δ in a straightforward manner. We consider some known universe I of possible input values.

The Adversary. We consider a *static corruption* adversary $\mathcal{A}$, i.e., at round $t = 0$, the adversary chooses a set $F \subseteq [N]$ of parties to be *corrupt*. The remaining parties are *correct*. Corrupt parties are entirely controlled by the adversary, and may deviate arbitrarily from the protocol. Furthermore, following [25], at all rounds t, the adversary can adaptively[2] select a subset of the correct parties to be *asleep* (i.e., *inactive*), whereas the remaining correct parties are *awake* (i.e., *active*). Asleep parties are temporarily crashed: they do not execute the protocol or send messages. Messages sent to an asleep party are buffered and delivered to the party (in an adversarially selected order) the next time it wakes up. Upon waking up, parties know the current round number, i.e., we assume synchronized clocks. Note that corrupt parties are awake from round $t = 0$, and

---

[2] The adaptive adversary is not strongly rushing, i.e., it *cannot* observe the contents of a message sent by a party, intercept it, and then put the party to sleep.

never go to sleep throughout the execution. The number of awake parties at round t is denoted by n_t. We drop the subscript when the round is clear from the context. For an adversary $\mathcal{A}$, we denote by $F_{\mathcal{A}}$ the set of parties corrupted by $\mathcal{A}$, and we usually omit the subscript when the adversary is clear from the context. For a value $\rho \in [0, 1]$, we say that an adversary $\mathcal{A}$ is ρ-bounded if for all t, $|F| < \rho n_t$. Finally, whenever relevant, the adversary chooses the input values (from I) of all correct parties.

Unknown Participation Model. Some of our results pertain to the unknown participation model, introduced in [14]. Unknown participation is a special case of the dynamic participation model, which can formally be described by a restricted family of adversaries, as follows. Consider the exact same setup as above, with the following restriction on the adversary model: At time $t = 0$, the adversary picks a set $S \subseteq [N]$ of n awake parties and a set $F \subseteq S$ of corrupt parties. From this point, the adversary cannot wake up or put to sleep any party. In other words, the parties in $S \backslash F$ are correct and awake throughout the entire execution, the parties in F are corrupt and awake throughout the entire execution, and the remaining parties are correct and asleep throughout the entire execution. Similarly to the dynamic participation adversary, we say that an adversary $\mathcal{A}$ is ρ-bounded if $|F| < \rho n$.

Cryptographic Primitives. We use a digital signature scheme on top of our PKI assumption. We assume $\mathcal{A}$ is computationally bounded, i.e., $\mathcal{A}$ cannot forge signatures on any message on behalf of parties outside of $F_{\mathcal{A}}$ (ideal signatures). We denote by $\langle m \rangle_p$ a signed message m by party p.

2.2   Consensus Primitives

We consider two standard consensus problems in this paper, Byzantine broadcast (BB) and Byzantine agreement (BA).

Definition 1 (Byzantine Broadcast (BB)). *In the* BB *problem, there is a designated party ℓ, referred to as the* leader, *with an input $u \in I$. As output, each party p decides a value $o_p \in I$. Let Π be a protocol to be executed by the parties. The following properties constitute the* BB *problem.*

1. **Termination.** *There exists a round T such that every correct party decides and halts in the first round $T' \geq T$ in which it is awake.*
2. **Agreement.** *There exists a value $u' \in I$ such that all correct parties that decide, decide u'.*
3. **Validity.** *If ℓ is correct and awake in round $t = 0$, then all correct parties that decide, decide u, i.e., ℓ's input.*

For a value ρ, we say that a protocol Π for BB *is ρ-secure under dynamic/unknown participation if it satisfies termination, agreement, and validity against any ρ-bounded adversary. The maximum ρ for which Π is ρ-secure is Π's resilience.*

Definition 2 (Byzantine Agreement (BA)). *In the* BA *problem, each party p has an input $u_p \in I$. As output, each party p decides a value $o_p \in I$. Let Π be a protocol to be executed by the parties. The following properties constitute the* BA *problem.*

1. **Termination.** *There exists a round T such that every correct party decides and halts in the first round $T' \geq T$ in which it is awake.*
2. **Agreement.** *There exists a value $u' \in I$ such that all correct parties that decide, decide u'.*
3. **Validity.** *If all correct parties that are awake in round $t = 0$ have u as input, then all correct parties that decide, decide u.*

For a value ρ, we say that a protocol Π for BA *is ρ-secure under dynamic/unknown participation if it satisfies termination, agreement, and validity against any ρ-bounded adversary. The maximum ρ for which Π is ρ-secure is Π's* resilience.

2.3   Good-Case Latency

Decision Latency. For a ρ-bounded adversary $\mathcal{A}$ and a ρ-secure protocol Π for BB or BA, we denote by $\mathsf{DL}_{\mathcal{A}}(\Pi)$ the random variable (over the randomness used by correct parties and the adversary) indicating the smallest round R for which every correct party *decides* (but not necessarily terminates) in the first round $R' \geq R$ in which it is awake, in the presence of $\mathcal{A}$. We say that Π has decision latency R with respect to a ρ-bounded adversary $\mathcal{A}$ if $R = \arg\min_{R' \in \mathbb{N}} \Pr[\mathsf{DL}_{\mathcal{A}}(\Pi) \leq R'] = 1$. For a family $\mathcal{F}$ of ρ-bounded adversaries we define the decision latency of Π with respect to $\mathcal{F}$ to be $\mathsf{DL}_{\mathcal{F}}(\Pi) = \sup_{\mathcal{A} \in \mathcal{F}} \mathsf{DL}_{\mathcal{A}}(\Pi)$.

Good-Case Latency. The efficiency metric we focus on in this work is that of *good-case* decision latency T_{gc}. Intuitively, this measure considers the decision latency of a protocol Π in executions in which certain favorable conditions hold, namely ℓ being correct for BB, or all correct parties having the same input for BA. More formally, we define good-case latency as follows.

1. BB: For a value ρ, and a ρ-secure protocol Π for BB under dynamic/unknown participation, consider the family $\mathcal{F}_{\mathrm{goodcase}}$ of ρ-bounded adversaries $\mathcal{A}$ for which the leader ℓ is correct, i.e., $\ell \notin F$, and the leader is awake at round $t = 0$. We define the good-case latency of Π to be $T_{\mathrm{gc}} \triangleq \mathsf{DL}_{\mathcal{F}_{\mathrm{goodcase}}}(\Pi)$.
2. BA: For a value ρ, and a ρ-secure protocol Π for BA under dynamic/unknown participation, consider the family $\mathcal{F}_{\mathrm{goodcase}}$ of ρ-bounded adversaries $\mathcal{A}$ for which $\mathcal{A}$ gives all correct parties awake at round $t = 0$ the same input value u, for some $u \in I$. We define the good-case latency of Π to be $T_{\mathrm{gc}} \triangleq \mathsf{DL}_{\mathcal{F}_{\mathrm{goodcase}}}(\Pi)$.

Decision vs Termination. As we note above, we distinguish between the event of *decision*, in which a party outputs a value, and the event of *termination*, which is the event where a party stops running the protocol. In all our protocols in Sects. 5 and 6, the event of decision does not imply termination.

3   Technical Overview

The Traditional Case of Synchrony with Static Participation. To develop some intuition about the feasibility of good-case latency, let us begin by considering the traditional synchronous model with static participation, which in our formulation translates to adversaries for which all correct parties are awake in all rounds. Pondering the BB problem for a moment, it definitely seems like in 2 rounds, we cannot do much beyond:

1. Round 0: Have the leader ℓ multicast its value.
2. Round 1: Have all parties report what they heard from the leader.

If the total number of parties is N, keeping this protocol blueprint in mind, for some value $\rho \in [0, \frac{1}{2}]$, we can expect correct parties to collect strictly more than $(1 - \rho)N$ amount of "evidence" for a value u against ρ-bounded adversaries, in executions in which ℓ is correct with input u. An additional observation is that in executions with a correct leader ℓ, correct parties can also expect to collect 0 evidence for any other value. As such, we can have a correct party decide after two rounds if it received sufficient evidence for a value, and *no* evidence for any other value. One can observe that this implies that if a party p decided u, then any other correct party q observed $< \rho N$ evidence for any other value. To allow other parties to break the symmetry, all we need to stipulate is that $(1 - \rho)N \geq \rho N$. Note that this bound holds for all $\rho \leq \frac{1}{2}$, and indeed $\rho = \frac{1}{2}$ turns out to be the correct corruption bound for the feasibility of 2-round good-case BB in the traditional synchronous static participation setting.

Generic Intuition. Given that this approach works for the static participation case, let us test whether the following line of thinking can yield the correct corruption bound for 2-round good-case BB in other settings: *For a bound ρ, derive a lower bound on the amount of evidence c_ρ available for the leader's input in executions with a correct leader. Given this amount, derive an upper bound on the amount of evidence a_ρ a correct party can receive for a different value. Stipulate $c_\rho \geq a_\rho$.*

Dynamic Participation. Let us apply the above intuition to dynamic participation. For a bound ρ, consider a good-case execution (Execution 1), i.e., the leader is correct with some value u and awake at round $t = 0$, for a ρ-bounded adversary $\mathcal{A}$. In a similar fashion to the previous paragraph, consider a correct party p awake in round $t = 2$, and suppose it hears from n_p parties. It can expect to hear evidence for u from at least $c_\rho = (1 - \rho)n_p$ of them, and no evidence for any other value. From the perspective of p, the ρn_p parties reporting no evidence for any value are corrupt and p should ignore them and decide anyway. One might be tempted now to repeat the argument from the previous paragraph, and claim that any other correct party can receive at most ρn_p evidence for any other value, and so we again have $(1 - \rho)n_p \geq \rho n_p$ yielding $\rho = \frac{1}{2}$.

The key observation is that p *does not know that the parties reporting no evidence are actually corrupt*, as it cannot be certain about the total number of participating parties. To make this concrete, consider now an alternative case (Execution 2), in which the leader is corrupt, and although p hears from n_p parties, they are all correct, and there are in fact $\frac{\rho}{1-\rho}n_p$ corrupt parties, and not just ρn_p. The corrupt leader does not send anything to ρn_p of the correct parties, and the rest of the corrupt parties do not send anything to p. From p's perspective at round $t = 2$, execution 2 is identical to execution 1, and so p decides in round $t = 2$ in both of them. In execution 2, however, a different correct party may receive $a_\rho = \frac{\rho}{1-\rho}n_p$ evidence for a value $u' \neq u$. Thus to allow other parties to break the symmetry, we must stipulate $(1-\rho)n_p \geq \frac{\rho}{1-\rho}n_p$, which yields $\rho \leq (1 - \rho)^2$, which in turn gives $\rho \leq 1 - \frac{1}{\varphi}$, where φ is the golden ratio!

This intuition turns out to yield the correct solution, and we provide tight lower and upper bounds in Theorems 1 and 3, respectively. We complement these results by establishing in Theorem 6 that 3-round good-case BB is feasible under dynamic participation for $\rho = \frac{1}{2}$.

Unknown Participation. An astute reader may rush to a premature conclusion upon reading the previous part, as it seems that the same intuition from above should apply to and yield the same bound under unknown participation. At least at first glance, it seems that the only thing we used is p's inability to distinguish between the case of n_p participating parties and $\frac{n_p}{1-\rho}$ participating parties. Perhaps, however, we were too hasty in making that assertion.

This intuition turns out to be deceptive under unknown participation. Specifically, p can more scrupulously rely on the fact that *the same set of correct parties is awake in all rounds*. In protocol terms, parties can multicast a *heartbeat* message both in round $t = 0$ and in round $t = 1$, along with the leader's proposed value; they also relay all received heartbeat messages. Now, a protocol can stipulate that having q's heartbeat relayed by a majority of the parties is a prerequisite for p to count q's contribution to the leader's purported value. It turns out that this technique allows the unknown participation model to boast 2-round good-case BB for $\rho = \frac{1}{2}$, thus establishing a separation between dynamic and unknown participation. The formal details can be found in Theorem 5.

BA. While for BB, the good-case decision latency is either 2 or 3 rounds, the good-case decision latency of BA can be as small as a single round. It turns out that 2-round good-case BA is feasible for $\rho = \frac{1}{2}$ even under dynamic participation! To the best of our knowledge, this result was not known even in the static participation setting, even though it is rather straightforward in that model. For dynamic participation, however, such a result is far from trivial, and involves a novel *report participation* technique. See Theorem 7 for the full details.

This leaves us with the question: what values of ρ make 1-round good-case BA feasible? The same generic intuition we applied for BB under dynamic participation can be repeated, with the caveat that we now have to account for equivocations by corrupt parties when calculating a_ρ. The math yields that we must stipulate $\rho \leq (1 - \rho)^2 - \rho(1 - \rho)$, which is tight for $\rho = 1 - \frac{1}{\sqrt{2}}$. The lower and upper bounds can be found in Theorems 2 and 4, respectively. In fact, our BA lower bound (Theorems 2) applies even for unknown participation (the easier setting), while our BA upper bound (Theorems 4) applies to dynamic participation (the harder setting). Furthermore, this establishes a separation between the static participation model, for which 1-round good-case BA is feasible for $\rho \leq \frac{1}{3}$, and the unknown participation model.

4   Lower Bounds

In this section, we prove the following theorems.

Theorem 1. *Let $\varphi = \frac{1+\sqrt{5}}{2} \approx 1.618$ be the golden ratio. For all $\rho > 1 - \frac{1}{\varphi} \approx 0.382$, there is no ρ-secure protocol solving* BB *under dynamic participation with good-case latency ≤ 2.*

Theorem 2. *For all $\rho > 1 - \frac{1}{\sqrt{2}} \approx 0.293$, there is no ρ-secure protocol solving* BA *under unknown participation with good-case latency ≤ 1.*

4.1   BB Lower Bound

In this section, we prove Theorem 1.

Proof of Theorem 1. Let n be an odd natural number and let $\rho' \in [0, 1]$ such that $\rho' > \rho := 1 - \frac{1}{\varphi}$. In particular, this implies that $\rho' > (1-\rho)^2$, as $1 - \frac{1}{\varphi}$ is a solution of the equation $x = (1 - x)^2$. Assume towards a contradiction that there exists a ρ'-secure BB protocol Π under dynamic participation with good-case latency 2. Let ℓ be the designated leader. We define the following pairwise disjoint sets of parties A, B, C such that $|A| = |C| = \lfloor \rho n \rfloor$, $|B| = \lceil \rho(1 - \rho)n \rceil$. Note that $\rho n + \rho n + \rho(1 - \rho)n = (1 - \rho)^2 n + \rho n + \rho(1 - \rho)n = n$. As such, since none of these added expressions are integers, we have that $|A| + |B| + |C| + |\ell| = n$. We further consider an additional disjoint set S of parties where $|S| = |A| = |C|$.

  We now define and describe four executions of Π, which we denote by G_1, G_2, G_3, G_4. See Fig. 1 for an illustration.

- G_1: In round $t = 0$, the parties in S, B and ℓ are awake. The parties in S are correct. Note that the parties in C are not active at all throughout the protocol. Furthermore, the parties in B are corrupt, and are thus awake at all rounds. The leader ℓ is correct with input 1. In round $t = 1$, the parties in S fall asleep, and the parties in A wake up and remain awake for the remainder of the execution. The parties in A are correct. Note that up to an additive factor of 1 due to the ceiling and floor, one has that $|A| + |B| = \rho n + \rho(1 - \rho)n = \rho(2 - \rho)n = (1 - (1 - \rho)^2)n = (1 - \rho)n$, and thus for a sufficiently large n^3, it holds that $|B| = \lceil (1-\rho)\rho n \rceil < \rho'(|A|+|B|)$, and so the adversary is ρ'-bounded. The parties in B behave correctly in round $t = 0$, and in round $t = 1$ they behave as if they have not received the round $t = 0$ messages of ℓ.

---

[3] Namely, n should be large enough so that the ceiling in $|B|$ does not violate the corruption bound ρ', which is bounded away from ρ by $\rho' - \rho > 0$.

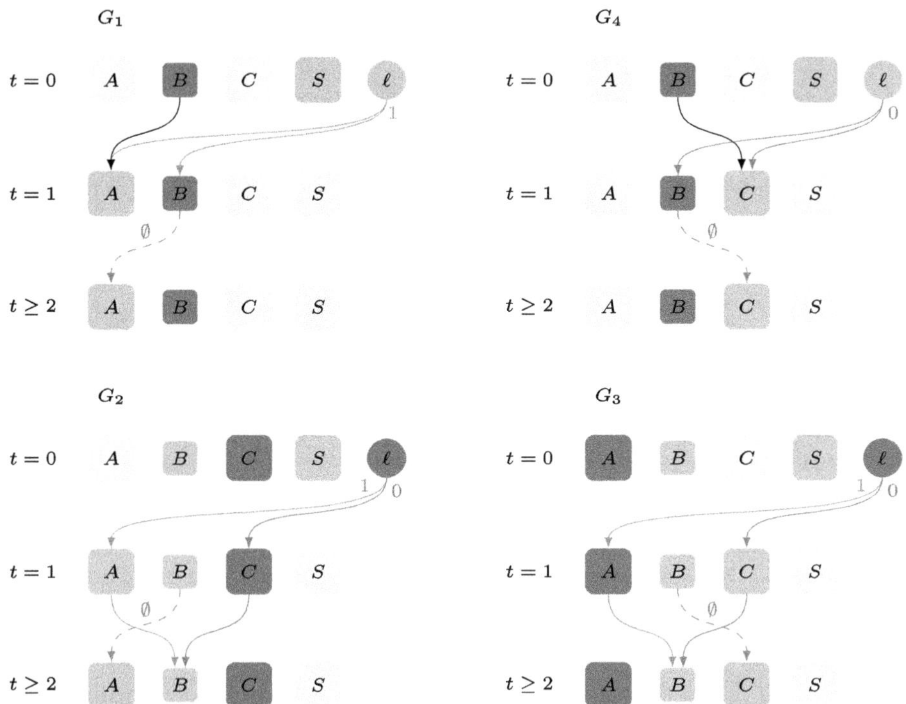

Fig. 1. Illustration of the four executions considered in the proof of Theorem 1. Green labels and arrows indicate correct behavior, or emulation of it, with input 1. Blue labels and arrows indicate correct behavior, or emulation of it, with input 0. Corrupt parties are colored red, correct parties orange. Translucent sets indicate that the set of parties is not awake at that round. The behavior of correct parties is well defined from the protocol description Π, so we omit most of the corresponding arrows to maintain simplicity. Lack of an arrow from a set of corrupt parties to a set of correct parties indicates omission of all corresponding messages. Dashed red arrows labeled "$\emptyset$" indicate messages corresponding to receiving nothing from the leader ℓ in round $t = 0$. Black arrows indicate correct round $t = 0$ behavior. (Color figure online)

- G_2: In round $t = 0$, the parties in S, B, C and ℓ are awake. S, B are correct. The leader ℓ is corrupt and the parties in C are corrupt, and are thus awake throughout the whole execution. In round $t = 1$, S fall asleep, and the parties in A wake up and remain awake for the remainder of the execution. All parties in A, B are correct. Note that for a sufficiently large n, the adversary is ρ'-bounded as $|C| + |\ell| = \lfloor \rho n \rfloor + 1$ by definition and there are n awake parties. The leader ℓ behaves to A as if it were correct with input 1 in rounds $t = 0$ and $t = 1$ and then halts; it does not send any messages to the parties in B. The parties in C do not send any round $t = 0$ messages, and do not send round $t = 1$ messages to A; they behave to B in round $t = 1$ as if they received correct round $t = 0$ messages from ℓ with input 0. Note that this is doable as

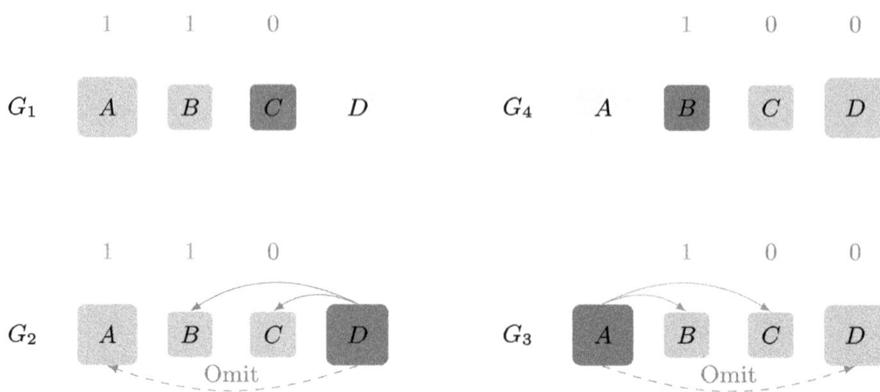

Fig. 2. Illustration of the four executions considered in the proof of Theorem 2. Green labels and arrows indicate correct behavior, or emulation of it, with input 1. Blue labels and arrows indicate correct behavior, or emulation of it, with input 0. Corrupt parties in each execution are colored red, correct parties orange. Translucent sets indicate that the set of parties is not participating in the given execution (inactive). Dashed red arrows labeled "Omit" indicate that no messages are sent from the source set of the arrow to its target set in round $t = 0$. (Color figure online)

ℓ is corrupt. They behave correctly for the remainder of the execution, except for pretending not to have received round $t = 1$ messages from A.

- G_3: This is the dual execution to G_2. In round $t = 0$, the parties in S, B, A and ℓ are awake. S, B are correct. The leader ℓ is corrupt and the parties in A are corrupt, and are thus awake throughout the whole execution. In round $t = 1$, S fall asleep, and the parties in C wake up and remain awake for the remainder of the execution. All parties in C are correct. Note that the adversary is ρ'-bounded by the same argument as in G_2. The leader behaves to C as if it were correct with input 0 in rounds $t = 0$ and $t = 1$ and then halts; it does not send any messages to parties in B. The parties in A do not send any round $t = 0$ messages, and do not send round $t = 1$ messages to C; they behave to B in round $t = 1$ as if they received correct round $t = 0$ messages from ℓ with input 1. Note that this is doable as ℓ is corrupt. They behave correctly for the remainder of the execution, except for pretending not to have received round $t = 1$ messages from C.

- G_4: This is the dual execution to G_1. In round $t = 0$, the parties in S, B and ℓ are awake. The parties in S are correct. Note that the parties in A are not active at all throughout the execution. Furthermore, the parties in B are corrupt, and are thus awake at all times. The leader ℓ is correct with input 0. In round $t = 1$, the parties in S fall asleep, and the parties in C wake up. The parties in C are correct. Note that the adversary is ρ'-bounded by the same argument as in G_1. The parties in B behave correctly in round $t = 0$, and in round $t = 1$ they behave as if they have not received the round $t = 0$ messages of ℓ.

With G_1, G_2, G_3, G_4 defined, we can now proceed with the following observations.

- The parties in A decide 1 in G_1 after 2 rounds. This is a consequence of the assumed good-case latency of 2 property of Π, the leader being correct with input 1 in execution G_1, and the adversary being ρ'-bounded.
- The parties in C decide 0 in G_4 after 2 rounds. This is a consequence of the assumed good-case latency of 2 property of Π, the leader being correct with input 0 in execution G_4, and the adversary being ρ'-bounded.
- In the first two rounds, the parties in A *cannot distinguish* between G_1 and G_2. In both executions, they receive the same set of messages from the exact same parties in the first two rounds. Thus, the parties in A decide 1 in G_2 after 2 rounds.
- In the first two rounds, the parties in C *cannot distinguish* between G_3 and G_4. In both executions, they receive the same set of messages from the exact same parties in the first two rounds. Thus, the parties in C decide 0 in G_3 after 2 rounds.
- The parties in B *cannot distinguish* between G_2, G_3. In G_2, the parties in C are corrupt and falsely claim not to have received round $t = 1$ messages from A, and in G_3, the parties in A are corrupt and falsely claim not to have received round $t = 1$ messages from C. In both G_2, G_3, the parties in A, C behave correctly after round $t = 2$. Thus, throughout both executions, B sees the exact same set of messages, from the exact same sets of parties, with the same delivery timings. Thus, by termination, eventually the parties in B decide the same value in both G_2, G_3.

Putting these observations together, we deduce, by the agreement property of Π, that B outputs 1 in G_2, and 0 in G_3. This contradicts the last observation above, thus concluding the proof. $\qquad\square$

4.2   BA Lower Bound

In this section, we prove Theorem 2.

Proof of Theorem 2 Let n be an even natural number and let $\rho' \in [0, 1]$ such that $\rho' > \rho := 1 - \frac{1}{\sqrt{2}}$. In particular, this implies that $\rho' > (1-\rho)^2 - \rho(1-\rho)$, as $1 - \frac{1}{\sqrt{2}}$ is a solution for $x = (1 - x)^2 - x(1 - x)$. Assume towards a contradiction that there exists a ρ'-secure BA protocol Π with good-case latency 1 under unknown participation. We consider a set of n parties, and a partition of them into disjoint sets A, B, C, D such that $|A| = |D| = \lceil \rho n \rceil$, and $|B| = |C| = \lfloor \rho(1 - \rho)n \rfloor$. Note that by substituting ρ with $(1-\rho)^2 - \rho(1-\rho)$, one gets $\rho n + \rho(1-\rho)n + (1-\rho)^2 n = n$. Since none of these added expressions are integers, and by the fact that A, D are with ceil while B, C are with floor, we get that $|A| + |B| + |C| + |D| = n$. Hence this is a valid partition of the n parties. We now define and describe four executions of Π, which we denote by G_1, G_2, G_3, G_4. See Fig. 2 for an illustration.

- G_1: The participating parties are A, B, C. The parties in A, B are correct and C is corrupt. Note that up to an additive factor of 1, we have that $|A \cup B| = |A| + |B| = (1-\rho)^2 n$, and $|A| + |B| + |C| = \rho(1-\rho)n + (1-\rho)^2 n = (1-\rho)n$, thus for a sufficiently large n, we have that $|C| \leq \rho|A \cup B \cup C| < \rho'|A \cup B \cup C|$, which means the adversary is ρ'-bounded. The parties in A, B have input 1, and the parties in C behave as if they are correct with input 0.
- G_2: The participating parties are A, B, C, D. The parties in A, B, C are correct, and the parties in D are corrupt. Note that $|A \cup B \cup C \cup D| = n$, and that $|D| = \lceil \rho n \rceil$ as $\rho = (1-\rho)^2 - \rho(1-\rho)$. Thus, for a sufficiently large n, one has that $\lceil \rho n \rceil < \rho' n$, and so the adversary is ρ'-bounded. The parties in A, B have input 1, the parties in C have input 0. The parties in D behave as if they are correct with input 0, *except for* not sending any round $t = 0$ messages to A, and pretending not to have received round $t = 0$ messages from A. They behave correctly in all the remaining rounds.
- G_3: This is the dual execution to G_2. The participating parties are A, B, C, D. The parties in C, B, D are correct, and the parties in A are corrupt. Note that the adversary is ρ'-bounded by the same argument as in G_2. The parties in C, D have input 0, the parties in B have input 1. The parties in A behave as if they are correct with input 1, *except for* not sending any round $t = 0$ messages to D, and pretending not to have received round $t = 0$ messages from D. They behave correctly in all the remaining rounds.
- G_4: This is the dual execution to G_1. The participating parties are B, C, D. The parties in C, D are correct, and the parties in B are corrupt. Note that the adversary is ρ'-bounded by the same argument as in G_1. The parties in C, D have input 0, and the parties in B behave as if they are correct with input 1.

With G_1, G_2, G_3, G_4 defined, we can now proceed with the following observations.

- All correct parties in G_1 have the same input 1. Thus, by the validity of BA and the good-case latency of 1 property of Π, the parties in A decide 1 at the end of the first round.
- All correct parties in G_4 have the same input 0. Thus, by the validity of BA and the good-case latency of 1 property of Π, the parties in D decide 0 at the end of the first round.
- At the end of the first round, the parties in A cannot distinguish between G_1, G_2. Thus, also in G_2, the parties in A decide 1 at the end of the first round. By the agreement property of BA, we thus have that both B, C eventually decide 1 in G_2.
- At the end of the first round, the parties in D cannot distinguish between G_3, G_4. Thus, also in G_3, the parties in D decide 0 at the end of the first round. By the agreement property of BA, we thus have that both B, C eventually decide 0 in G_3.
- The parties in B, C cannot distinguish between G_2, G_3, as in both executions they receive the exact same sets of messages, from the same sets of parties,

with the same delivery timings, as both the parties in A and D claim not to have heard from each other in round $t = 1$. Thus, by termination, eventually the parties in B, C decide *the same* value in both G_2, G_3.

From the combination of the last three observations, we arrive at a contradiction, as the parties in B, C output 1 in G_2, 0 in G_3, but also the same value in both G_2, G_3. This concludes the proof. $\square$

5 BB and BA with Optimal Good-Case Latency

In this section, we prove the following theorems.

Theorem 3. *For all $\rho \leq 1 - \frac{1}{\varphi} \approx 0.382$ where $\varphi = \frac{1+\sqrt{5}}{2} \approx 1.618$, there exists a ρ-secure protocol (namely $\Pi_{\mathsf{BB},2}$ below) solving* BB *under dynamic participation with good-case latency $T_{\mathrm{gc}} = 2$.*

Theorem 4. *For all $\rho \leq 1 - \frac{1}{\sqrt{2}} \approx 0.293$, there exists a ρ-secure protocol (namely $\Pi_{\mathsf{BA},1}$ below) solving* BA *under dynamic participation with good-case latency $T_{\mathrm{gc}} = 1$.*

Theorem 5. *For all $\rho \leq 1/2$, there exists a ρ-secure protocol (namely $\Pi_{\mathsf{BB},\mathsf{UP}}$ below) solving* BB *under unknown participation with good-case latency $T_{\mathrm{gc}} = 2$.*

5.1 BB with Good-Case Latency $T_{\mathrm{gc}} = 2$

In this section, we prove Theorem 3. In this protocol, we make black-box use of the BA protocol from [8], which we denote by Π_{BA}, and which is $\frac{1}{2}$-secure under dynamic participation.

Protocol 1: $\Pi_{\mathsf{BB},2}$

1. **Setup.** Leader ℓ with input value b_ℓ. Instructions for party p.
2. **Round $t = 0$:** ℓ multicasts $\langle \mathsf{echo}, b_\ell \rangle_\ell$.
3. **Round $t = 1$:** If received $\langle \mathsf{echo}, u \rangle_\ell$ for some u, then multicast $\langle \mathsf{vote}, u \rangle_p$ along with ℓ's echo message. Else, multicast $\langle \mathsf{vote}, \perp \rangle_p$.
4. **Round $t = 2$:** Let V denote the set of parties from which p received a valid **vote** message. Denote by V_u the set of parties from which p received a valid **vote** for value u. Let u be the value $\arg\max_{u \in I} |V_u|$, breaking ties arbitrarily.

   Multicast $\langle \mathsf{forward}, V_u \rangle_p$, along with the corresponding valid **vote** messages for u from the parties in V_u.

   Early deciding condition: If the following holds:
   (a) Did not detect equivocation from the leader ℓ. I.e., did not receive two **echo** (either forwarded or directly from ℓ) messages signed by the leader ℓ for values $u \neq u'$.
   (b) It holds that $|V_u| > (1 - \rho)|V|$.
   Then decide u and multicast $\langle \mathsf{decided}, u \rangle_p$.
5. **Round $t \geq 3$:**

(a) **Early deciding:** For a value u', denote by $D_{u'}$ the set of parties from which p received a **decided** message for u', and by D^* the set of parties from which p received a **forward** message. If there exists a value u such that $|D_u| > (1 - \rho)|D^*|$, then decide u.

(b) Let u' be the value for which p received the largest V_u set among all received **forward** messages. Run Π_{BA} as instructed that commences in round $t = 3$ with input u', and decide the output of Π_{BA}, if did not decide before, and then terminate.

Proof of Theorem 3. Let ρ be as in the premise of Theorem 3. Our protocol is given in $\Pi_{\mathsf{BB},2}$. We now analyze its security and efficiency. Termination follows from the termination of Π_{BA}, as all parties decide and halt once Π_{BA} terminates. We next handle agreement.

Claim. $\Pi_{\mathsf{BB},2}$ satisfies agreement against any ρ-bounded adversary.

Proof. There are two cases: Either there exists a correct party that decides from the early deciding condition, i.e., prior to participating in Π_{BA}, or not. Agreement is straightforward in the latter case, as no correct party multicasts a **decided** message, and thus no correct party decides due to the early deciding condition in any round $t \geq 2$. Thus, due to Π_{BA} being $\frac{1}{2}$-secure and all correct parties deciding according to its output, agreement holds.

In the former case, let p be a correct party deciding a value u by the early deciding condition. Denote by V^p the set of parties from which p received a valid **vote** message. We first argue that there cannot be two correct parties p, q, both awake at round $t = 2$, that decide different values $u \neq u'$ by the early deciding condition. If this were the case, then p has $|V_u^p| > (1 - \rho)|V^p|$, and $|V_{u'}^q| > (1 - \rho)|V^q|$. As the network is synchronous and $\rho < \frac{1}{2}$, this in particular implies that p has received at least one valid **vote** message for u from a correct party, and q received at least one valid **vote** message for u' from a correct party. This implies, however, that both p, q saw an equivocation from the leader ℓ at round $t = 2$, and thus none of them would have triggered the early deciding condition. This in particular implies that there exists at most one value for which any correct party sends a **decided** message, and thus all correct parties deciding due to the early deciding condition decide the same value.

It remains to show that if some correct party p decides a value u via the early deciding condition at round $t = 2$, then all parties eventually decide u. Denoting the correct parties awake at round $t = 1$ by H, we have that $H \subseteq V^p$. Furthermore, we have that $|V_u^p| > (1 - \rho)|V^p|$, thus $|V_u^p| > (1 - \rho)|H|$. Furthermore, p detected no equivocation from ℓ, hence no party in H multicast a **vote** message for a value $u' \neq u$. Denoting by F the set of corrupt parties, we have that $|F| < \rho(|H| + |F|)$, thus $|F| < \frac{\rho}{1-\rho}|H|$. In particular, we can deduce that any other correct party q receives at most $|F| < \frac{\rho}{1-\rho}|H|$ valid **vote** messages for values different from u. By the behavior of the protocol, p multicasts in round

$t = 2$ the message $\langle \mathsf{forward}, V_u^p \rangle_p$, and so all correct parties awake at rounds ≥ 3 observe at least $(1 - \rho)|H|$ vote messages in the forward message of p. Finally, note that $(1 - \rho)|H| - |F| > (1 - \rho)|H| - \frac{\rho}{1-\rho}|H| = \frac{(1-\rho)^2-\rho}{(1-\rho)}|H| > 0$. The last inequality holds by the assumption that $\rho < (1 - \rho)^2$. Thus, all correct parties awake at round 3 commence Π_{BA} with input u. By the validity guarantee of Π_{BA}, we thus have that all parties decide u, as required. $\square$

Finally, we handle validity and good-case latency.

Claim. $\Pi_{\mathsf{BB},2}$ satisfies validity against any ρ-bounded adversary. Furthermore, $\Pi_{\mathsf{BB},2}$ has good-case latency 2.

Proof. Assume ℓ is correct with input u. Then by the behavior of $\Pi_{\mathsf{BB},2}$, it multicasts $\langle \mathsf{echo}, u \rangle_\ell$ to all correct parties at round $t = 0$. Then, at round $t = 1$, all correct parties multicast $\langle \mathsf{vote}, u \rangle$ along with ℓ's echo message. Note that since ℓ is correct, no valid vote for any value other than u can be sent, by correct or corrupt parties. Thus, at round $t = 2$, no correct party detects equivocation from the leader, and all correct parties awake at $t = 2$ see a valid vote message for u from all correct parties awake at $t = 1$. As the adversary is ρ-bounded, we thus have that $|V_u^p| > (1 - \rho)|V^p|$ for all correct parties p awake at $t = 2$, and they all decide u at $t = 2$ and send corresponding decided messages. The same argument applied to the early deciding condition in rounds $t \geq 3$ then implies that any correct party p decides u in the first round $t \geq 2$ in which it is awake, as required. $\square$

This concludes the proof of Theorem 3. $\square$

5.2   BA with Good-Case Latency $T_{\mathrm{gc}} = 1$

In this section, we prove Theorem 4. In this protocol, we make black-box use of the BA protocol from [8], which we denote by Π_{BA}, and which is $\frac{1}{2}$-secure under dynamic participation.

Protocol 2: $\Pi_{\mathsf{BA},1}$

1. **Setup.** Each party p has input value u_p. Instructions for party p.
2. **Round** $t = 0$: Multicast $\langle \mathsf{echo}, u_p \rangle_p$.
3. **Round** $t = 1$: Denote by E the set of parties from which p received an echo message. Denote by E_u the set of parties from which p received an echo message for value u. Let u be the value $\arg\max_{u \in I} |E_u|$, breaking ties arbitrarily. Multicast $\langle \mathsf{forward}, E_u \rangle_p$, along with the corresponding echo messages for u.

    Early deciding condition: If $|E_u| > (1 - \rho)|E|$, then decide u, and multicast $\langle \mathsf{decided}, u \rangle_p$.
4. **Round** $t \geq 2$:
    (a) **Early Deciding:** For a value u', denote by $D_{u'}$ the set of parties from which p received a decided message for u', and by D^* the set of parties

from which p received a **forward** message. If there exists a value u such that $|D_u| > (1 - \rho)|D^*|$, then decide u.

(b) Let u' be the value for which p received the largest E_u set among all received **forward** messages. Run Π_{BA} as instructed that commences in round $t = 2$ with input u', and decide the output of Π_{BA}, if did not decide before, and then terminate.

Proof of Theorem 4. Let ρ be as in the premise of Theorem 4. Our protocol is given in $\Pi_{\mathsf{BA},1}$. We now analyze its security and efficiency. Termination follows from the termination of Π_{BA}, as all correct parties decide and halt once Π_{BA} decides. Next, we handle agreement.

Claim. $\Pi_{\mathsf{BA},1}$ satisfies agreement against any ρ-bounded adversary.

Proof. There are two cases: either there exists a correct party that decides due to the early deciding condition at round $t = 1$, or not. The proof can be quickly concluded in the latter case, as then no correct party multicasts a **decided** message, and thus no correct party decides according to the early deciding condition in rounds $t \geq 2$. Thus all correct parties decide according to the output of Π_{BA}, which guarantees agreement.

We are now left with the case that there exists a correct party that decides a value u according to the early deciding condition at round $t = 1$. First we prove that this can occur for at most a single value. Assume that there exist two correct parties p, q that decide according to the early deciding condition in round $t = 1$ values u, u', respectively, where $u \neq u'$. Denote by E^p, E^q the sets of echo messages received by p, q, respectively. This implies that $|E_u^p| > (1 - \rho)|E^p|$, and $|E_{u'}^q| > (1 - \rho)|E^q|$. Denoting by H the set of correct parties awake at round $t = 0$, we have that $H \subseteq E^p$ and $H \subseteq E^q$, so $|E_u^p| > (1 - \rho)|H|$, and $|E_{u'}^q| > (1 - \rho)|H|$. Denoting by F^p, F^q the sets of corrupt parties that sent an echo message to p, q, respectively, we have that at least $|E_u^p| - |F^p|$ of the echo messages for u received by p came from correct parties, and similarly at least $|E_{u'}^q| - |F^q|$ of the echo messages for u' received by q came from correct parties. We thus have that:

$$|E_u^p| - |F^p| > (1 - \rho)(|H| + |F^p|) - |F^p| = (1 - \rho)|H| - \rho|F^p|,$$

and similarly:

$$|E_{u'}^q| - |F^q| > (1 - \rho)(|H| + |F^q|) - |F^q| = (1 - \rho)|H| - \rho|F^q|.$$

As $F^q, F^p \subseteq F$, and $|F| < \frac{\rho}{1-\rho}|H|$, we have:

$$|E_u^p| - |F^p| > (1 - \rho)|H| - \frac{\rho^2}{1 - \rho}|H| = \frac{(1 - \rho)^2 - \rho^2}{1 - \rho}|H| = \frac{1 - 2\rho}{1 - \rho}|H|$$
$$= (1 - \frac{\rho}{1 - \rho})|H| > (1 - (1 - 2\rho))|H| = 2\rho|H|.$$

The last inequality holds due to the assumption $\rho < (1-\rho)(1-2\rho)$. This allows us to deduce that fewer than $(1-2\rho)|H|$ correct parties sent an echo message for a value other than u. Thus, $(1-2\rho)|H| \geq |E^q_{u'}| - |F^q| > (1-\rho)|H| - \rho|F^q|$ which implies $|F^q| > |H|$, a contradiction. Thus, there exists at most a single value u for which some correct party decides u via the early deciding condition in round $t = 1$.

This implies that correct parties can only send decided messages for a single value u, and so any correct party deciding according to the early decision condition in round $t \geq 2$ decides u as well, and agreement is maintained.

It remains to show that when a correct party p decides u due to the early deciding condition in round $t = 1$, all correct parties that decide on the Π_{BA} output also decide u. By the early deciding condition in round $t = 1$, $|E^p_u| > (1-\rho)(|H| + |F^p|)$, and at least $|E^p_u| - |F^p| > (1-\rho)|H| - \rho|F^p|$ of those echo messages for u came from correct parties. Thus, fewer than $\rho|H| + \rho|F^p|$ correct parties multicast an echo message for any value $u' \neq u$. This implies that the size of the $E_{u'}$ set in any forward message received by any correct party for a value $u' \neq u$ is bounded by

$$\rho|H| + \rho|F^p| + |F| < \rho(|H| + |F^p|) + \frac{\rho}{1-\rho}|H|$$

$$\stackrel{(1)}{<} \rho|H| + \rho|F^p| + (1-2\rho)|H| < (1-\rho)(|H| + |F^p|) < |E^p_u|.$$

Here, (1) holds due to the assumption $\rho < (1-\rho)(1-2\rho)$. Thus, the forward message sent by p with the set E^p_u is the largest set of echo messages witnessed by any correct party in round $t = 2$, thus by the behavior of $\Pi_{\mathsf{BA},1}$, all correct parties awake at round $t = 2$ commence Π_{BA} with input u. The validity property of Π_{BA} then ensures that all correct parties output u from Π_{BA}, thus all correct parties agree, as required. $\qquad\square$

Next, we handle validity and good-case latency.

Claim. $\Pi_{\mathsf{BA},1}$ satisfies validity against any ρ-bounded adversary. In particular, $\Pi_{\mathsf{BA},1}$ has good-case latency 1.

Proof. Assume that all correct parties awake at round $t = 0$ have the same input value u, then, due to the adversary being ρ-bounded, all correct parties awake at round $t = 1$ observe $|E_u| > (1-\rho)|E|$, as all correct parties send an echo message for u. In particular, *all* correct parties awake in round $t = 1$ decide u by the early deciding condition and multicast a decided message for u. An identical argument then implies that any correct party p, in the first round $t \geq 2$ in which it is awake, observes $|D_u| > (1-\rho)|D^*|$, and thus p decides in the first round $t \geq 1$ in which it is awake. This proves that $\Pi_{\mathsf{BA},1}$ satisfies validity and has $T_{\mathrm{gc}} = 1$. $\qquad\square$

This concludes the proof of Theorem 4. $\qquad\square$

5.3 BB for Unknown Participation with Good-Case Latency $T_{\mathrm{gc}} = 2$

In this section, we prove Theorem 5. In this protocol, we make black-box use of the BA protocol from [8], which we denote by Π_{BA}, and which is $\frac{1}{2}$-secure under dynamic participation.

Protocol 3: $\Pi_{\mathsf{BB,UP}}$

1. **Setup.** Leader ℓ with input value b_ℓ. Instructions for party p.
2. **Round** $t = 0$: If $p = \ell$, multicast $\langle \mathsf{echo}, b_\ell \rangle_\ell$. Else, multicast $\langle \mathsf{echo}, \bot \rangle_p$.
3. **Round** $t = 1$: Denote by E the set of parties from which p received an echo message. Multicast $\langle \mathsf{forward}, E \rangle_p$, along with the corresponding echo messages. If $\ell \in E$ and received $\langle \mathsf{echo}, u \rangle_\ell$, multicast $\langle \mathsf{vote}, u \rangle_p$ along with ℓ's echo. Else, if $\ell \notin E$, multicast $\langle \mathsf{vote}, \bot \rangle_p$.
4. **Round** $t = 2$: Let G denote the set of parties from which p received a forward message, and let V denote the set of parties from which p received a valid vote message. Denote by E the set of parties from which p received an echo message. Denote by $E^* \subseteq E$ the set of parties p for which an echo message from p appeared in more than $\frac{|G|}{2}$ of the received forward messages. Let u be the value $\arg\max_{u \in I} |V_u \cap E^*|$. Multicast $\langle \mathsf{echo2}, V_u \cap E^* \rangle_p$, along with the corresponding valid vote messages.
   Early deciding condition: If the following holds:
   (a) Did not detect equivocation from the leader ℓ, i.e., did not receive two valid vote messages for values $u \neq u'$.
   (b) It holds that $|V_u \cap E^*| > \frac{|E|}{2}$.
   Then decide u and multicast $\langle \mathsf{decided}, u \rangle_p$.
5. **Round** $t \geq 3$:
   (a) Let u' be the value for which p received the largest $V_u \cap E^*$ among all received echo2 messages. Run Π_{BA} as instructed that commences in round $t = 3$ with input u', and decide the output of Π_{BA}, if did not decide before, and then terminate.

Proof of Theorem 5. Our protocol is given in $\Pi_{\mathsf{BB,UP}}$. We now analyze its security and efficiency. Termination follows from the termination of Π_{BA}, as all parties decide and halt once Π_{BA} terminates. We next handle agreement. Denote by n the total number of parties, which is unknown to the correct parties.

Claim. $\Pi_{\mathsf{BB,UP}}$ satisfies agreement against any $\frac{1}{2}$-bounded adversary.

Proof. There are two cases: either there exists a correct party that decides from the early deciding condition, i.e., prior to participating in Π_{BA}, or not. Agreement is straightforward in the latter case, with Π_{BA} being $\frac{1}{2}$-secure and all correct parties deciding its output. We next focus on the former case.

Denote by V^p the set of parties from which p received a valid vote message, and denote by $E^p, E^{*,p}$ the E, E^* sets observed by party p in round $t = 2$, respectively. We first argue that there cannot be two correct parties p, q that decided due to the early deciding condition in round $t = 2$ values $u \neq u'$, respectively. Suppose this was the case, then p has observed $|V_u^p \cap E^{*,p}| > \frac{E^p}{2}$. Denoting by H the set of correct parties, first observe that $H \subseteq E^{*,p}$, as a correct party sends an echo message to all parties, and all correct parties include that echo message in their forward messages. Since H constitutes a majority of the parties, all correct parties observe the echo messages of correct parties as part of their E^* set. This in particular implies that there exists a correct party in $V_u^p \cap E^{*,p}$, and the same argument yields that there exists a correct party in $V_{u'}^q \cap E^{*,q}$. This implies, however, that all correct parties observed in round $t = 2$ a valid vote message for both u, u', and thus no correct party decides by the early deciding condition in round $t = 2$. This implies that there exists at most a single value u, such that a correct party decides u due to the early deciding condition in round $t = 2$. In particular, this also implies that if any correct party decides due to the early deciding condition at a round $t \geq 3$, it can only possibly decide u, as no decided message can be sent by a correct party for any other value.

Now suppose that a correct party p decided u due to the early deciding condition at round $t = 2$. This implies that $|V_u^p \cap E^{*,p}| > \frac{|E^p|}{2}$. This also implies that no correct party multicast a valid vote message for any other value. We next observe that for any correct parties p, q, we have $E^{*,p} \subseteq E^q$, and vice versa. Consider any $z \in E^{*,p}$. The echo message of z appeared in the majority of forward messages received by p, at least one of which was sent by a correct party, and thus all correct parties have seen the echo message of z. For a correct party q, denote by F^q the set of corrupt parties in $E^{*,q}$. We thus have $F^q \subseteq E^{*,q} \subseteq E^p$, and so $|V_{u'}^q \cap E^{*,q}| \leq |F^q| < \frac{|H|+|F^q|}{2} \leq \frac{|E^p|}{2} < |V_u^p \cap E^{*,p}|$. Thus we have that the echo2 message from p constitutes the largest set observed by q, when intersected with $E^{*,q}$. And so, in round $t = 3$, q commences Π_{BA} with input u. This holds for all correct parties, which triggers the validity property of Π_{BA}, and thus all correct parties output u from Π_{BA} and decide u, as required. $\square$

Next, we handle validity and good-case latency.

Claim. $\Pi_{\mathsf{BB,UP}}$ satisfies validity against any $\frac{1}{2}$-bounded adversary. Furthermore, $\Pi_{\mathsf{BB,UP}}$ has good-case latency 2.

Proof. Assume ℓ is correct with input u. Then by the behavior of $\Pi_{\mathsf{BB,UP}}$, it multicasts $\langle\mathsf{echo}, u\rangle_\ell$ to all correct parties at round $t = 0$, and all other correct parties multicast $\langle\mathsf{echo}, \bot\rangle$ at round $t = 0$. Thus, at round $t = 1$, all correct parties multicast $\langle\mathsf{vote}, u\rangle$ and a forward message that includes all echo messages of all correct parties. In round $t = 2$, no party detects equivocation from ℓ due to ℓ being correct, and all parties see a valid vote message for u from all correct parties, and $H \subseteq E^{*,p}$ for all correct parties p. Since the adversary is ρ-bounded, H are a strict majority of the parties, and so any correct party p observes $|V_u^p \cap E^{*,p}| > \frac{|E^p|}{2}$ at round $t = 2$. Thus, all correct parties decide u in round $t = 2$, as required. $\square$

This concludes the proof of Theorem 5. $\square$

6   BB and BA with Optimal Resilience

In this section, we prove the following theorems.

Theorem 6. *For all $\rho \leq 1/2$, there exists a ρ-secure protocol (namely $\Pi_{\mathsf{BB},3}$ below) solving* BB *under dynamic participation with good-case latency $T_{\mathrm{gc}} = 3$.*

Theorem 7. *For all $\rho \leq 1/2$, there exists a ρ-secure protocol (namely $\Pi_{\mathsf{BA},2}$ below) solving* BA *under dynamic participation with good-case latency $T_{\mathrm{gc}} = 2$.*

6.1   BB with Good-Case Latency $T_{\mathrm{gc}} = 3$

In this section, we prove Theorem 6. In this protocol, we make black-box use of the $\frac{1}{2}$-secure dynamic participation BA protocol from [8], which we denote by Π_{BA}.

Protocol 4: $\Pi_{\mathsf{BB},3}$

1. **Setup.** Leader ℓ has input u_ℓ. Instructions for party p.
2. **Round $t = 0$:** ℓ multicasts $\langle \mathsf{echo}, u_\ell \rangle_\ell$.
3. **Round $t = 1$:** If received $\langle \mathsf{echo}, u \rangle_\ell$ for some u, multicast $\langle \mathsf{vote}, u \rangle_p$ along with the corresponding **echo** message from ℓ. Else, multicast $\langle \mathsf{vote}, \bot \rangle_p$.
4. **Round $t = 2$:** Denote by V the set of parties from which p received a **vote** message. Multicast $\langle \mathsf{forward}, V \rangle_p$, along with the corresponding valid **vote** messages.
5. **Round $t = 3$:** Denote by G the set of parties from which p received a **forward** message, and by V the set of parties from which p received a **vote** message, whether directly or via a **forward** message. Denote by V^* the set of parties q for which the following holds.
   (a) p did not detect an equivocation from q, i.e., two valid **vote** messages signed by q for values $u \neq u'$.
   (b) A valid **vote** message from q appears in more than $\frac{|G|}{2}$ of the **forward** messages received by p.
   Let u be the value $\arg\max_{u \in I} |V_u \cap V^*|$. Multicast $\langle \mathsf{echo2}, V_u \cap V^* \rangle_p$, along with the corresponding **vote** messages.
   Early deciding condition: If the following holds:
   (a) p did not detect an equivocation from ℓ, i.e., two valid **vote** messages signed by ℓ for values $u \neq u'$.
   (b) $|V_u \cap V^*| > \frac{|V|}{2}$.
   Then decide u and multicast $\langle \mathsf{decided}, u \rangle_p$.
6. **Round $t \geq 4$:**
   (a) **Early deciding:** Denote by D the set of parties from which p received a **decided** message, and by D^* the set of parties from which p received an **echo2** message. If there exists a value u such that $|D_u| > \frac{|D^*|}{2}$, then decide u.
   (b) Let u' be the value for which p received the largest $V_u \cap V^*$ (intersection with *own* V^*) among all received **echo2** messages. Run Π_{BA} as instructed that commences in round $t = 4$ with input u', and decide the output of Π_{BA}, if did not decide before, and then terminate.

Proof of Theorem 6. Our protocol is given in $\Pi_{\mathsf{BB},3}$. We now analyze its security and efficiency. Termination follows from the termination of Π_{BA}, as all parties decide and halt once Π_{BA} terminates. We next handle agreement.

Claim. $\Pi_{\mathsf{BB},3}$ satisfies agreement against any $\frac{1}{2}$-bounded adversary.

Proof. There are two cases: either there exists a correct party that decides due to the early deciding condition at round $t = 3$, or not. The proof can be quickly concluded in the latter case, as then no correct party multicasts a decided message, and thus no correct party decides according to the early deciding condition in any round $t \geq 3$. Thus, all correct parties decide according to the output of Π_{BA}, which guarantees agreement.

We are now left with the case that there exists a correct party that decides a value u due to the early deciding condition at round $t = 3$. First we prove that this can occur for at most a single value. Assume that there are two correct parties p, q that decide according to the early deciding condition in round $t = 3$ values $u \neq u'$, respectively. We thus have that $|V_u^p \cap V^{*,p}| > \frac{|V^p|}{2}$, and $|V_{u'}^q \cap V^{*,q}| > \frac{|V^q|}{2}$. In particular, both $V_u^p \cap V^{*,p}$ and $V_{u'}^q \cap V^{*,q}$ contain at least one correct party. This implies that both p, q have observed a valid vote message for both u *and* u'. This implies that both p and q have observed an equivocation by ℓ, and thus would not have decided by the early deciding condition in round $t = 3$.

We are thus left with the case that there exists a unique value u such that a correct party p awake in round $t = 3$ decides u via the early deciding condition. First, observe that since no correct party multicasts a decided message for a value $u' \neq u$, we have that any correct party deciding via the early deciding condition in any round $t \geq 4$ decides u as well. If a correct party p awake in round $t = 3$ decides u via the early deciding condition, this implies that p did not detect an equivocation from ℓ, and that $|V_u^p \cap V^{*,p}| > \frac{|V^p|}{2}$. Denoting by H the set of correct parties awake at round $t = 1$, we have that *none* of them multicast a vote message for a value $u' \neq u$, as otherwise, p would have detected an equivocation from ℓ. For some correct party $q \neq p$ awake at round $t = 4$, consider the set $V_{u'}^q \cap V^{*,q}$ for some value $u' \neq u$. Denote by F the set of corrupt parties. As we have just observed, we have that $V_{u'}^q \cap V^{*,q} \subseteq F$. Note, however, that if some $f \in F$ satisfies $f \in V_{u'}^q \cap V^{*,q}$, then a vote message from f for value u' appears in a majority of the forward messages received by q, thus at least one of them was sent by a correct party, and thus all correct parties awake at round $t = 3$, and in particular p, received a valid vote message for u'. This contradicts the assumption that p decided the value u via the early deciding condition at round $t = 3$. We thus have that $V_{u'}^q \cap V^{*,q} = \emptyset$ for all correct parties awake at round $t \geq 4$. This in particular implies that all correct q parties awake at round $t = 4$ observe u to be the value maximizing $V_u^q \cap V^{*,q}$ among all echo2 messages, and commence Π_{BA} with input u. This triggers the validity property of Π_{BA}, which implies that all correct parties output u from Π_{BA}, and thus all correct parties decide u, as required. $\square$

Next, we handle validity and good-case latency.

Claim. $\Pi_{\mathsf{BB},3}$ satisfies validity against any $\frac{1}{2}$-bounded adversary. Furthermore, $\Pi_{\mathsf{BB},3}$ has good-case latency 3.

Proof. Assume ℓ is correct with input u. Then by the behavior of $\Pi_{\mathsf{BB},3}$, it multicasts $\langle \mathsf{echo}, u \rangle_\ell$ to all parties in round $t = 0$. Afterwards, again by protocol behavior, all correct parties awake in round $t = 1$, denoted by H, multicast a valid $\langle \mathsf{vote}, u \rangle_p$ message. In round $t = 2$, all correct parties multicast forward messages containing all vote messages of all correct parties awake in round $t = 1$. In round $t = 3$, note first that no correct party p detects an equivocation from ℓ, due to ℓ being correct. Second, note that $H \subseteq V_u^p \cap V^{*,p}$, and $|V| \leq |H| + |F|$. Thus, we have that $|V_u^p \cap V^{*,p}| > \frac{|V|}{2}$ holds for any correct party p awake in round $t = 3$. Thus, all correct parties awake in round $t = 3$ decide u and multicast a decided message for u. An identical argument then gives that all correct parties decide u in the first round $t \geq 4$ in which they are awake, due to the early deciding condition. $\qquad\square$

This concludes the proof of Theorem 6. $\qquad\square$

6.2   BA with Good-Case Latency $T_{\mathbf{gc}} = 2$

In this section, we prove Theorem 7. In this protocol, we make black-box use of the BA protocol from [8], which we denote by Π_{BA}, and which is $\frac{1}{2}$-secure under dynamic participation. Throughout the protocol, whenever we consider a set of messages S, the notation S^p refers to the local view, or the purported local view, of p of the set S.

Protocol 5: $\Pi_{\mathsf{BA},2}$

1. **Setup.** Each party p has input u_p. Instructions for party p.
2. **Round** $t = 0$: Multicast $\langle \mathsf{echo}, u_p \rangle_p$.
3. **Round** $t = 1$: Denote by E the set of parties from which p received an echo message. Multicast $\langle \mathsf{forward}, E \rangle_p$, along with the corresponding echo messages.
4. **Round** $t = 2$: Denote by G the set of parties from which p received a forward message. Denote by E the set of parties from which p received an echo message, either directly or via a forward message. For a value u, denote by E_u the set of parties from which p received an echo message for u. Denote by E^* the set of parties q for which the following holds.
   (a) p detected no equivocation from q, i.e., two echo messages signed by q for values $u' \neq u$.
   (b) An echo message from q appears in more than $\frac{|G|}{2}$ of the forward messages received by p
   For a value u, denote by E_u^* the set $E_u \cap E^*$.
   Early deciding condition: If there exists a value u such that $|E_u^*| > \frac{|E|}{2}$, then decide u. Multicast $\langle \mathsf{decided}, u, E, E_u^*, \mathsf{forward}_q \mid q \in G \rangle$, where $\mathsf{forward}_q$ indicates the forward message p received from q. Else, multicast $\langle \mathsf{echo2}, E, E^*, \mathsf{forward}_q \mid q \in G \rangle$.

5. **Round $t \geq 3$.**
   - Denote by E the set of parties from which p received an **echo** message, and by E_u the set of parties from which p received an **echo** message for u.
   - Denote by E^* the set defined in an identical manner as in round $t = 2$ above.
   - Denote by G the set of parties from which p received a **forward** message.
   - Denote by T the set of parties from which p received an **echo2** message.
   - Denote by G^* the set of parties q for which a **forward** message from q appeared in more than $\frac{|T|}{2}$ of the echo2 messages.

   (a) **Early deciding:** For a value u, denote by D_u the set of parties from which p received a **decided** message for value u. If there exists a value u such that $|D_u| > \frac{|T|}{2}$, then decide u.

   (b) For a party p, we say a **decided** message from a party q of the form $\langle \mathsf{decided}, u, E^q, E_u^{*,q}, \mathsf{forward}_z \mid z \in G^q \rangle$ is *valid* if the following holds.
   - E^q contains $E^{*,p}$.
   - G^q contains $G^{*,p}$.
   - Each $z \in E_u^{*,q}$ appears in a majority of G^q, and there are no equivocations from z in $\mathsf{forward}_y \mid y \in G^q$.
   - $|E_u^{*,q}| > \frac{|E^q|}{2}$.

   For a valid **decided** message for a value u from a party q, we refer to $|E^q|$ as its *size*. Let u' be the value for which p received the maximum size **decided** message. Run Π_{BA} as instructed that commences in round $t = 3$ with input u', and decide the output of Π_{BA}, if did not decide before, and then terminate.

Proof of Theorem 7. Our protocol is given in $\Pi_{\mathsf{BA},2}$. We now analyze its security and efficiency. Termination follows from the termination of Π_{BA}, as all parties decide and halt once Π_{BA} terminates. We next handle agreement.

Claim. $\Pi_{\mathsf{BA},2}$ satisfies agreement against any $\frac{1}{2}$-bounded adversary.

Proof. There are two cases: either there exists a correct party that decides due to the early deciding condition at round $t = 2$, or not. The proof can be quickly concluded in the latter case, as all correct parties decide according to the output of Π_{BA}, which is $\frac{1}{2}$-secure and guarantees agreement.

We are now left with the case that there exists a correct party that decides a value u due to the early deciding condition at round $t = 2$. First, we prove that this can occur for at most a single value. Assume that two correct parties p, q decide u, u' according to the early deciding condition in round $t = 2$, respectively. In particular, that implies that $|E_u^{*,p}| > \frac{|E^p|}{2}$, and $|E_{u'}^{*,q}| > \frac{|E^q|}{2}$. Note that by the behavior of the protocol we have that $E^{*,p}, E^{*,q} \subseteq E^p$, and similarly $E^{*,p}, E^{*,q} \subseteq E^q$, since every echo in $E^{*,p}, E^{*,q}$ appeared in the **forward** message of at least one correct party. Denote by F_u^p the set of corrupt parties included in $E_u^{*,p}$, and by $F_{u'}^q$ the set of corrupt parties included in $E_{u'}^{*,q}$. Note that $E_u^{*,p} \cap E_{u'}^{*,q} = \emptyset$, as otherwise p, q would have detected an equivocation from the party in the intersection, and would not have included it in their E^* set.

Denote by H^0 the set of correct parties awake at round $t = 0$, and of those, by $H_u^0, H_{u'}^0$ those with input u, u', respectively. One has that

$$|H_u^0| + |F^p| = |E_u^{*,p}| > \frac{|E^p|}{2} \geq \frac{|H^0| + |F^p| + |F^q|}{2}$$

Similarly, one has that

$$|H_{u'}^0| + |F^q| = |E_{u'}^{*,q}| > \frac{|E^q|}{2} \geq \frac{|H^0| + |F^p| + |F^q|}{2}$$

Adding these inequalities, one gets that $|H_u^0| + |H_{u'}^0| > |H^0|$, which is a contradiction.

We are then left with the case that there exists a unique value u such that a correct party p, decides u at round $t = 2$, with reported participation E^p. First note that this implies that any correct party that decides due to the early deciding condition in any round $t \geq 3$ also decides u, as no correct party multicasts a decided message for any value $u' \neq u$. Now, assume that some correct party q, awake in round $t = 3$, received a decided message from a party $z \in F$ for some value u', of the form $\langle \text{decided}, u', E^z, E_{u'}^{*,z}, \text{forward}_s \mid s \in G^z \rangle$, with reported participation E^z, such that $|E^z| \geq |E^p|$. We now prove this cannot happen. Assume otherwise (i.e., $|E^z| \geq |E^p|$), and denote by $E_{u'}^{*,z}$ the claimed such set of z. Denote by F_u^p the set of corrupt parties in $E_u^{*,p}$. We have that $|E_u^{*,p}| = |H_u^0| + |F_u^p|$. We next note that E^p contains the set $E_{u'}^{*,z}$. This holds due to the following: A party $s \in E_{u'}^{*,z}$ must appear in a strict majority of forward messages reported by z, i.e., the set G^z. Since we assume that z sends a *valid* decided message, we have that $G^{*,q} \subseteq G^z$. Denoting by H^1 the set of correct parties awake at round $t = 1$, we have that $H^1 \subseteq G^{*,q} \subseteq G^z$. Thus, if party s appears in a strict majority of the forward messages of the claimed set G^z, then at least one of these forward messages was sent by a correct party at round $t = 1$. Thus, p, which was awake at time $t = 2$, observes an echo message from s for u', and thus $s \in E^p$. This gives $E_{u'}^{*,z} \subseteq E^p$. Denoting by $F_{u'}^z$ the corrupt parties in $E_{u'}^{*,z}$, we in particular have $F_{u'}^z \subseteq E^p$.

In fact, note that this line of arguing actually implies a stronger property, and that is that $E_{u'}^{*,z} \cap E_u^{*,p} = \emptyset$, as p seeing an echo for u' from s implies that $s \notin E_u^{*,p}$.

From $F_{u'}^z \subseteq E^p$, and $E_{u'}^{*,z} \cap E_u^{*,p} = \emptyset$, we can deduce that: $|E_u^{*,p}| = |H_u^0| + |F_u^p| > \frac{|E^p|}{2} \geq \frac{|F_{u'}^z| + |F_u^p| + |H^0|}{2}$. We now have all we need to arrive at a contradiction. Let us summarize our observations.

- $E_{u'}^{*,z} \cap E_u^{*,p} = \emptyset$ which in particular implies that $F_{u'}^z \cap F_u^p = \emptyset$.
- $|E_u^{*,p}| = |H_u^0| + |F_u^p| > \frac{|E^p|}{2} \geq \frac{|F_{u'}^z| + |F_u^p| + |H^0|}{2}$.
- $|E_{u'}^{*,z}| \leq |H_{u'}| + |F_{u'}^z|$. This bound trivially holds.
- $|E^z| \geq |E^p|$, our assumption.
- $|E_{u'}^{*,z}| > \frac{|E^z|}{2}$, from the assumption that z's decided message is valid.

From these observations we deduce that:

$$|H_u^0| + |H_{u'}^0| + |F_u^p| + |F_{u'}^z| \geq |E_{u'}^{*,z}| + |E_u^{*,p}| > |E^p| \geq |H^0| + |F_u^p| + |F_{u'}^z|$$

This finally implies that $|H_u^0| + |H_{u'}^0| > |H^0|$, which is a contradiction. We thus have that all correct parties awake in round $t = 3$ view the decided message from p as the valid decided message with the maximum size ($|E^p|$), and so they all commence Π_{BA} with input u. This triggers the validity property of Π_{BA}, and thus all correct parties output u from Π_{BA} and decide u, and agreement holds. $\square$

Next, we handle validity and good-case latency.

Claim. $\Pi_{\mathsf{BA},2}$ satisfies validity against any $\frac{1}{2}$-bounded adversary. Furthermore, $\Pi_{\mathsf{BA},2}$ has good-case latency 2.

Proof. Assume that all correct parties awake in round $t = 0$ have the same input u. Denoting by H^0 the set of correct parties awake in round $t = 0$ and by F the set of corrupt parties, we thus have that $E_u^{*,p}$ contains H^0 for all correct parties p, as they all send an echo message for u in round $t = 0$, and none of them equivocate. It clearly holds, for every party p, that $|E^p| \leq |H| + |F|$, and since $|H| > |F|$ we thus have that $|E_u^{*,p}| > \frac{|E^p|}{2}$ for all correct parties p in round $t = 2$. Thus, all correct parties awake in round $t = 2$ (denoted by H^2) decide u and multicast a decided message for u. Any correct party q, in the first round $t \geq 3$ in which it is awake, observes decided messages for u from all parties in H^2. This constitutes a majority of the received echo2 messages, and so any correct party q also decides u in the first round $t \geq 3$ in which it is awake. $\square$

This concludes the proof of Theorem 7. $\square$

Acknowledgments. We thank David Tse for fruitful discussions. We thank Yuval Ishai for bringing [10] to our attention. The work of YE was conducted in part while at a16z Crypto Research.

Disclosure of Interests. The authors have no competing interests to declare that are relevant to the content of this article.

A   Folklore BA for Static Participation with $\rho \leq 1/3$ and $T_{\mathsf{gc}} = 1$

In this section we show, for completeness, the following folklore results.

Lemma 1. *For all $\rho \leq 1/3$, there exists a ρ-secure BA protocol (namely $\mathsf{Sync}_{\mathsf{BA},1}$ below) with good-case latency $T_{\mathsf{gc}} = 1$ under static participation in synchrony.*

Lemma 2. *For all $\rho > \frac{1}{3}$, there is no ρ-secure BA protocol with good-case latency ≤ 1 under static participation in synchrony.*

Proof of Theorem. Denote by Π_{BA} an arbitrary choice of BA protocol which is $\frac{1}{3}$-secure under static participation in synchrony. We treat it as a black-box. Our protocol is given below:

Protocol 6: $\mathsf{Sync}_{\mathsf{BA},1}$

1. **Setup.** Each party p has input u_p. Instructions for party p. Denote by n the number of parties and by $f < \frac{n}{3}$ the bound on the number of corrupted parties. Initialize $o_p \leftarrow u_p$.
2. **Round** $t = 0$: Multicast $\langle \mathsf{echo}, u_p \rangle_p$.
3. **Round** $t = 1$: **Early deciding condition.** If there exists a value u such that p received $n - f$ echo messages for u, then decide u. Denote $n - f$ echo messages for a value u by $\mathcal{C}(u)$. Multicast $\langle \mathsf{decided}, \mathcal{C}(u) \rangle$.
4. **Round** $t \geq 2$: If received $\mathcal{C}(u)$ for some value u, set $o_p \leftarrow u$. Run Π_{BA} with input o_p that commences at round $t = 2$, and decide accordingly, if have not decided before, and terminate.

Termination is clear from the termination of Π_{BA}. For agreement, if no correct party decides via the early deciding condition in round $t = 1$, then agreement holds by the agreement property of Π_{BA}. Else, let p be a correct party that decides a value u in round $t = 1$, thus p observed $n - f$ echo messages for u, since $f < \frac{n}{3}$, a quorum intersection argument implies that no $n - f$ echo messages exist for any other value, and so all correct parties set their local o variable to u in round $t = 2$. This triggers the validity property of Π_{BA}, and so all correct parties output u, as required. For validity and good-case latency, consider the case where all correct parties have the same input value u. Then by the behavior of the protocol, all correct parties see in round $t = 1$ $n - f$ echo messages for u, and decide u, as required. This concludes the proof. $\qquad\square$

Next, we prove Lemma 2.

Proof of Theorem. Let $\rho > \frac{1}{3}$, and let n be a natural number, and consider three disjoint sets of parties A, B, C, each of size $\frac{n}{3}$. Assume towards a contradiction that there exists a ρ-secure protocol solving BA under synchrony with static participation and good-case latency 1. We consider three executions G_1, G_2, G_3, as follows.

1. G_1: A, B are correct with input 1. C are corrupt, and behave as if they are correct with input 0. Note that the adversary is ρ-bounded.
2. G_2: A, C are correct, B are corrupt. The adversary is ρ-bounded. A has input 1, C has input 0. B behave in round $t = 0$ to A as if they are correct with input 1, and to C as if they are correct with input 0. B then halt.
3. G_3: Dual to G_1. B, C are correct with input 0. A are corrupt, and behave as if they are correct with input 1. Note that the adversary is ρ-bounded.

Note that in G_1, all correct parties have the same input 1, and so the parties in A decide 1 after one round. Note that up to the end of the first round, G_1, G_2 are indistinguishable from the perspective of A, and so also in G_2, A decides 1 after 1 round. A dual argument gives that C outputs 0 after one round both in G_3 and G_2. Lastly note that in G_2, the adversary is ρ-bounded, and so by the assumption that Π is ρ-secure, agreement must hold and A, C output the same value in G_2, leading to a contradiction. $\qquad\square$

References

1. Abraham, I., Nayak, K., Ren, L., Xiang, Z.: Good-case latency of Byzantine broadcast: a complete categorization. In: PODC, pp. 331–341. ACM (2021)
2. Badertscher, C., Gazi, P., Kiayias, A., Russell, A., Zikas, V.: Ouroboros Genesis: composable proof-of-stake blockchains with dynamic availability. In: CCS, pp. 913–930. ACM (2018)
3. Civit, P., Gilbert, S., Guerraoui, R., Komatovic, J., Paramonov, A., Vidigueira, M.: All Byzantine agreement problems are expensive. In: PODC, pp. 157–169. ACM (2024)
4. D'Amato, F., Losa, G., Zanolini, L.: Asynchrony-resilient sleepy total-order broadcast protocols. In: PODC, pp. 247–256. ACM (2024)
5. D'Amato, F., Neu, J., Tas, E.N., Tse, D.: Goldfish: No more attacks on Ethereum?! In: FC (1). Lecture Notes in Computer Science, vol. 14744, pp. 3–23. Springer (2024)
6. D'Amato, F., Saltini, R., Tran, T., Zanolini, L.: TOB-SVD: total-order broadcast with single-vote decisions in the sleepy model. In: ICDCS, pp. 1033–1043. IEEE (2025)
7. Efron, Y., Neu, J., Pitassi, T.: Fully-fluctuating participation in sleepy consensus. In: AFT. LIPIcs, vol. 354, pp. 17:1–17:22. Schloss Dagstuhl - Leibniz-Zentrum für Informatik (2025)
8. Efron, Y., Tas, E.N.: Dynamically available common subset. Cryptology ePrint Archive, Paper 2025/016 (2025). https://eprint.iacr.org/2025/016
9. Gafni, E., Losa, G.: Brief announcement: Byzantine consensus under dynamic participation with a well-behaved majority. In: DISC. LIPIcs, vol. 281, pp. 41:1–41:7. Schloss Dagstuhl - Leibniz-Zentrum für Informatik (2023)
10. Garay, J., Ishai, Y., Ostrovsky, R., Zikas, V.: The price of low communication in secure multi-party computation. In: Katz, J., Shacham, H. (eds.) CRYPTO 2017. LNCS, vol. 10401, pp. 420–446. Springer, Cham (2017). https://doi.org/10.1007/978-3-319-63688-7_14
11. Garay, J.A., Kiayias, A., Leonardos, N.: The Bitcoin backbone protocol: analysis and applications. J. ACM **71**(4), 25:1–25:49 (2024)
12. Gilbert, S., Lynch, N.A.: Brewer's conjecture and the feasibility of consistent, available, partition-tolerant web services. SIGACT News **33**(2), 51–59 (2002)
13. Goyal, V., Li, H., Raizes, J.: Instant block confirmation in the sleepy model. In: Borisov, N., Diaz, C. (eds.) FC 2021. LNCS, vol. 12675, pp. 65–83. Springer, Heidelberg (2021). https://doi.org/10.1007/978-3-662-64331-0_4
14. Khanchandani, P., Wattenhofer, R.: Byzantine agreement with unknown participants and failures. In: IPDPS, pp. 952–961. IEEE (2021)
15. Kiayias, A., Russell, A., David, B., Oliynykov, R.: Ouroboros: a provably secure proof-of-stake blockchain protocol. In: Katz, J., Shacham, H. (eds.) CRYPTO 2017. LNCS, vol. 10401, pp. 357–388. Springer, Cham (2017). https://doi.org/10.1007/978-3-319-63688-7_12
16. Lamport, L., Shostak, R.E., Pease, M.C.: The Byzantine generals problem. ACM Trans. Program. Lang. Syst. **4**(3), 382–401 (1982)
17. Lewis-Pye, A., Roughgarden, T.: Permissionless consensus. arXiv:2304.14701v5 (2023). http://arxiv.org/abs/2304.14701v5
18. Losa, G., Gafni, E.: Consensus in the unknown-participation message-adversary model. arXiv:2301.04817v2 (2023). http://arxiv.org/abs/2301.04817v2

19. Malkhi, D., Momose, A., Ren, L.: Byzantine consensus under fully fluctuating participation. Cryptology ePrint Archive, Paper 2022/1448, Version 20221024:011919 (2022). https://eprint.iacr.org/archive/2022/1448/20221024:011919
20. Malkhi, D., Momose, A., Ren, L.: Towards practical sleepy BFT. In: CCS, pp. 490–503. ACM (2023)
21. Momose, A., Ren, L.: Optimal communication complexity of authenticated Byzantine agreement. In: DISC. LIPIcs, vol. 209, pp. 32:1–32:16. Schloss Dagstuhl - Leibniz-Zentrum für Informatik (2021)
22. Momose, A., Ren, L.: Constant latency in sleepy consensus. In: CCS, pp. 2295–2308. ACM (2022)
23. Nakamoto, S.: Bitcoin: a peer-to-peer electronic cash system (2008). https://bitcoin.org/bitcoin.pdf
24. Neu, J., Tas, E.N., Tse, D.: Ebb-and-flow protocols: a resolution of the availability-finality dilemma. In: SP, pp. 446–465. IEEE (2021)
25. Pass, R., Shi, E.: The sleepy model of consensus. In: Takagi, T., Peyrin, T. (eds.) ASIACRYPT 2017. LNCS, vol. 10625, pp. 380–409. Springer, Cham (2017). https://doi.org/10.1007/978-3-319-70697-9_14
26. Sridhar, S., Tas, E.N., Neu, J., Zindros, D., Tse, D.: Consensus under adversary majority done right. In: FC (2). Lecture Notes in Computer Science, vol. 15752, pp. 108–126. Springer (2025)
27. Wan, J., Xiao, H., Shi, E., Devadas, S.: Expected constant round Byzantine broadcast under dishonest majority. J. ACM **72**(4), 30:1–30:39 (2025)

Round-Optimal Byzantine Agreement Without Trusted Setup

Diana Ghinea[ID], Ivana Klasovitá[ID], and Chen-Da Liu-Zhang[(✉)][ID]

Lucerne University of Applied Sciences and Arts, Rotkreuz, Switzerland
{diana.ghinea,ivana.klasovita,chen-da.liuzhang}@hslu.ch

Abstract. Byzantine Agreement is a fundamental primitive in cryptography and distributed computing, and minimizing its round complexity is of paramount importance. The seminal works of Karlin and Yao [Manuscript'84] and Chor, Merritt and Shmoys [JACM'89] showed that any randomized r-round protocol must fail with probability at least $(c \cdot r)^{-r}$, for some constant c, when the number of corruptions is linear in the number of parties, $t = \theta(n)$. The work of Ghinea, Goyal and Liu-Zhang [Eurocrypt'22] introduced the first *round-optimal BA* protocol matching this lower bound. However, the protocol requires a trusted setup for unique threshold signatures and random oracles.

In this work, we present the first round-optimal BA protocols without trusted setup: a protocol for $t < n/3$ with statistical security, and a protocol for $t < (1 - \epsilon)n/2$ with any constant $\epsilon > 0$, assuming a bulletin-board PKI for signatures.

1 Introduction

The problem of Byzantine Agreement (BA) [9,18,21,32,33,38] constitutes one of the fundamental building blocks in cryptography and distributed protocols. It allows a set of n parties to reach agreement on a common value even if t of the parties deviate from the protocol.

One of the key measures of efficiency in distributed protocols is their round complexity, which is the number of synchronous communication rounds that a protocol takes until it terminates. On the one hand, it is well known that $t + 1$ rounds are necessary [18,22] and sufficient [18,28,37] when considering deterministic protocols. On the other hand, the foundational works of Ben-Or [4] and Rabin [39] showed that this bound can be circumvented with the use of randomization.

In randomized BA protocols, there is an inherent trade-off between the number of rounds incurred by the protocol versus their probability of failure. More precisely, it is known that any r-round randomized protocol must fail with probability at least $(c \cdot r)^{-r}$, for some constant c, when the number of corruptions is linear in the number of parties $t = \theta(n)$ [10,13,31].

Despite the extensive line of works [1,12,21,23,24,32,36] focusing on improving the round complexity of BA, the optimal trade-off was only achieved recently

J. Daemen and E. Thomé (Eds.): EUROCRYPT 2026, LNCS 16543, pp. 427–456, 2026.
https://doi.org/10.1007/978-3-032-25324-8_15

by the work of Ghinea, Goyal and Liu-Zhang [30], which introduced the first *round-optimal* BA protocol that runs in $O(r)$ rounds and achieves agreement except with probability $(c \cdot r)^{-r}$, for some constant c. The protocol is resilient up to $t = (1 - \epsilon)n/2$ corruptions, for any constant $\epsilon > 0$.

The protocol leverages the Expand-and-Extract paradigm [24] introduced by Fitzi, Liu-Zhang and Loss, which combines a complex deterministic protocol (called Proxcensus), followed by one single multi-valued common coin to achieve BA. This is in contrast to traditional approaches [21] that operate via a sequence of iterations, and execute one coin per iteration. Although the Expand-and-Extract paradigm makes use of a single common coin, it crucially relies on the fact that the common coin protocol is ideal: it distributes the same uniform random value (with no bias nor error) to all parties with overwhelming probability to obtain a round-optimal BA. To achieve this, the authors leverage a trusted setup for unique threshold signatures to implement a 1-round ideal common coin using a random oracle [8,34].

This motivates the question whether it is possible to achieve a round-optimal Byzantine Agreement without trusted setup nor random oracles, or whether these assumptions are inherent.

Is there an r-round BA protocol without trusted setup nor random oracles that achieves agreement except with probability $(c \cdot r)^{-r}$, for some constant c, and secure up to some $t = \theta(n)$ corruptions?

Before stating our results, we note that all current r-round BA protocols without trusted setup or random oracles achieve a success probability of at most $1 - 2^{-r}$. This holds even for any fraction $t = \theta(n)$ of static corruptions.

1.1   Our Contributions

We answer this question in the affirmative by introducing the first round-optimal BA protocols without trusted setup nor random oracles. Our protocols achieve simultaneous termination (all parties simultaneously terminate in the same round) and are secure against a strongly rushing adaptive adversary.

Our first protocol achieves unconditional security and is secure up to $t < n/3$ corruptions.

Theorem 1. *There is an $O(r)$-round BA protocol tolerating an unbounded adversary corrupting up to $t < n/3$ parties, achieving agreement except with probability $(c \cdot r)^{-r}$, for some constant c.*

Our second protocol assumes a bulletin-board PKI[1] and is secure up to $t < (1 - \epsilon)n/2$ corruptions, for any constant $\epsilon > 0$.

Theorem 2. *Assuming a bulletin-board PKI, there is an $O(r)$-round BA protocol tolerating a polynomially-bounded adversary corrupting up to $t < (1 - \epsilon)n/2$ corruptions, for any constant $\epsilon > 0$, achieving agreement except with probability $(c \cdot r)^{-r}$, for some constant c.*

---

[1] In a bulletin-board PKI the keys from corrupted parties can be chosen adversarially. See [7] for a nice discussion.

1.2   Related Work

We give an overview of the progress in the round complexity of BA protocols, focusing on the binary-input case. To achieve multi-valued input BA, one can use standard extension protocols [41], at the cost of an additional 2 rounds in the $t < n/3$ case, and 3 rounds in the $t < n/2$ case.

The foundational work of Feldman and Micali [21] introduced an unconditional protocol for $t < n/3$ with expected constant number of rounds. This was later extended to the $t < n/2$ setting by Fitzi and Garay [23] using number-theoretic assumptions, and Katz and Koo [32] assuming a bulletin-board PKI. Abraham et al. [1] further extended the above results to also achieve expected $O(n^2)$ communication complexity. All these protocols achieve agreement in $O(r)$ rounds except with probability 2^{-r}.

Assuming an ideal 1-round coin-flip protocol with no error nor bias (which can be achieved using unique threshold signatures and random oracle [8,34]), the protocol of Feldman and Micali [21] for $t < n/3$ and Micali and Vaikuntanathan [36] for $t < n/2$ achieve agreement in $2r$ rounds except with probability 2^{-r}.

In the same setting with an ideal coin-flip protocol, Fitzi, Liu-Zhang and Loss [24] introduced the Expand-and-Extract paradigm (which can be seen as a generalized version of the Feldman and Micali iteration paradigm), and introduced a protocol with $r+1$ rounds for $t < n/3$, and $\frac{3}{2}r$ for $t < n/2$, to achieve agreement except with probability 2^{-r}. The result was later improved by Ghinea, Goyal and Liu-Zhang [30] who introduced an $O(r)$-round protocol achieving agreement except with probability $(c \cdot r)^{-r}$ for constant c, and tolerating $t < (1 - \epsilon)n/2$ corruptions, for any constant $\epsilon > 0$.

A line of work focused on achieving round-efficient solutions for *broadcast*, the single-sender version of BA, in the dishonest majority setting [2,11,25,27, 40,42,43].

Karlin and Yao [31], and also Chor, Merritt and Shmoys [13] showed that any r-round randomized protocol must fail with probability at least $(c \cdot r)^{-r}$, for some constant c, when the number of corruptions, $t = \theta(n)$, is linear in the number of parties. This bound was extended to the asynchronous model by Attiya and Censor-Hillel [3].

Protocols with *expected* constant round complexity have probabilistic termination, where parties (possibly) terminate at different rounds, which introduce challenges when composing them. Several works investigated parallel composition [4,23], sequential composition [35], and universal composition [14,15]. Cohen et al. [16] showed lower bounds for Byzantine Agreement with probabilistic termination. The authors give bounds on the probability to terminate after one and two rounds: for a large class of protocols and a combinatorial conjecture, the halting probability after the second round is $o(1)$ (resp. $1/2 + o(1)$) for the case where there are up to $t < n/3$ (resp. $t < n/4$) corruptions.

2   Technical Overview

We summarize the techniques we used in our protocols.

2.1   Modified Expand-and-Extract

Our starting point is the protocol by Ghinea, Goyal and Liu-Zhang [30]. The protocol follows the Expand-and-Extract paradigm introduced by Fitzi, Liu-Zhang and Loss [24], which consists of three steps executed in sequence: expansion, multi-valued coin-flip, and extraction.

In the expansion step, parties jointly execute a deterministic protocol called ℓ-slot Proxcensus, for $\ell \geq 2$. In this protocol, every P_i inputs their input bit $b_i \in \{0, 1\}$, and obtains as output a value $z_i = \mathtt{Prox}_\ell(x_i) \in \{0, \ldots, \ell - 1\}$. Proxcensus guarantees that if every honest party has the input $x_i = 0$ (resp. $x_i = 1$), then every honest party outputs $z_i = 0$ (resp. $z_i = \ell - 1$). Moreover, the honest parties outputs always lie within two consecutive indices, i.e., there is a value $v \in \{0, \ldots, \ell - 2\}$ such that each honest P_i outputs $z_i \in \{v, v + 1\}$.

The multi-valued coin-flip protocol gives a uniform common random value $c \in \{0, \ldots, \ell - 2\}$ to all parties.

In the extraction step, the idea is to perform a cut, where the output bit is $y_i = 0$ if $z_i \leq c$, and $y_i = 1$ otherwise. See Fig. 1.

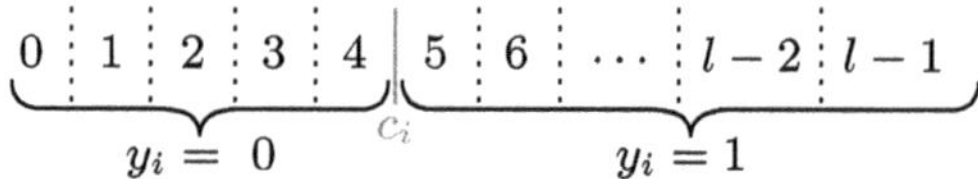

Fig. 1. Party P_i outputs a slot-value in $\{0, \ldots, \ell - 1\}$, and the coin can "cut" the array of slots in any of the $\ell - 2$ intermediate positions (indicated with dotted lines). If the obtained value lies on the left of the cut made by c_i (indicated with a red line), the output is $y_i = 0$. Otherwise, the output is $y_i = 1$.

The rationale is that since honest parties lie within two consecutive slots, there is only one value of c (out of $\ell - 1$ values) that may split the honest parties into outputting different bits. Moreover, if the honest parties start with the same bit, they are guaranteed to output that bit.

This means that the error probability of this protocol is $1/(\ell - 1)$, assuming the coin is perfect. The protocol in [30] introduces a $(3r)$-round Proxcensus with $\ell = (c \cdot r)^r$ for some constant c, which along with a 1-round ideal coin-flip leads to the desired result. The protocol is resilient up to $t = (1 - \epsilon)n/2$, for any $\epsilon > 0$, and uses a bulletin-board PKI (to instantiate the Proxcensus), as well as unique threshold signatures and random oracles (to instantiate the coin).

We note that one can also achieve a Proxcensus protocol secure against $t < n/3$ in the plain model that provides similar guarantees by replacing one of the building blocks in the protocol of [30] (see the full version of the paper).

Our Modification. The first task is to get rid of the 1-round ideal coin-flip based on unique threshold signatures and random oracles. Note that using instead an information-theoretic weak common coin [21,32] that outputs the same random value only with constant probability p would not work, since this would introduce an error of $1 - p$ into the protocol above.

Instead, our first observation is to relax the coin so that with very high probability it provides the honest parties an output from a *uniform interval* of indices. We call this protocol $(\ell - 1, \delta)$-ProxCoin. More precisely, the protocol guarantees that all honest parties output a value $c_i \in [0, \ell - 2]$ (as we need), but the outputs from honest parties may differ in δ units – that is, $|c_i - c_j| \le \delta$. Moreover, at least one honest party outputs a coin that is uniformly distributed over $[0, \ell - 2]$. It is easy to see that the error of the BA protocol becomes $\frac{1+2\delta}{\ell-1}$.

Even though the error is higher, we manage to achieve the result by introducing $O(r)$-round $(\ell - 1, \delta)$-ProxCoin protocols with $\delta = t$ and $\ell = (c \cdot r)^r$ for a constant c. See Sect. 4 for a more complete description of this approach.

2.2   Construction of ProxCoin

The construction of ProxCoin lets each party P_i choose a uniform random value $x_i \in [0, \ell-2]$ and distributes it via a *conditional* verifiable secret sharing protocol cVSS. In the sharing phase of cVSS, each party P_i outputs a flag happy$_i$ and a share s_i. Then, if any honest party P_i sets happy$_i$ = true, the protocol achieves all the guarantees from a standard verifiable secret sharing scheme (for an honest dealer, it is guaranteed that every honest P_j sets happy$_i$ = true). This notion of cVSS is similar to the one considered by Feldman and Micali [21], but with a weaker consistency condition.

The idea is then to reconstruct all the values that were shared via cVSS and take the sum. This approach by itself does not work because a corrupted dealer $\widetilde{D}$ can distribute shares so that each honest party P_i ends up with happy$_i$ = false. In this case, $\widetilde{D}$ can choose their reconstructed value based on the values reconstructed from honest dealers (since cVSS does not guarantee any binding property in this case), arbitrarily biasing the common coin.

Instead, following the idea of Freitas et al. [26], the parties compute a *weighted* sum of the reconstructed values, where the weight of each party is (approximately) agreed upon. That is, the final coin for party P_i is $c_i = \left\lceil \sum_j w_j \cdot x_j \right\rceil$, where w_j is the computed weight for P_j's value and x_j is the reconstructed value from the cVSS where P_j is the dealer. The idea here is that the protocol guarantees that (i) every honest party P_i sets $w_j = 1$ for every honest dealer P_j, (ii) every corrupted P_j must choose their values x_j independently of the honest values and thus cannot influence the common coin, (iii) the weights w_j computed for each corrupted P_j have a bounded small difference, and (iv) if an honest party obtains $w_j > 0$, then the parties successfully reconstruct the same value shared by P_j.

To achieve this, the weights of the parties are computed using a Prox protocol, where each party P_u inputs their flag bit happy$_i$, obtaining an index between $[0, \ell-1]$ (honest indices differ by at most 1). This index is scaled to be a number between $[0, 1]$, simply by dividing by $\ell-1$. This achieves the required guarantees stated above. Note that if the weight is positive for any party P_j, there was one honest party that input flag **true** (meaning the value that was distributed achieves the VSS guarantees, so this value was chosen independently of the other values, and can be reconstructed). Moreover, due to the guarantees from **Prox** and **cVSS**, weights for honestly dealt values are 1 and values dealt by corrupted dealers have a weight that differs by at most $1/(\ell - 1)$. The honest parties' final coins will then differ by at most $\delta \le \lceil t \cdot (\ell - 2)/(\ell - 1) \rceil \le t$, since every value in the weighted sum is between $[0, \ell - 2]$.

2.3   Protocols for Conditional Verifiable Secret Sharing

All that is left is to describe how to achieve *conditional* verifiable secret sharing. We propose two separate protocols – one in the plain model, secure against $t < n/3$ corruptions, and one assuming PKI and digital signatures, secure against $t < n/2$ corruptions. In the following, we discuss these in detail.

Protocol cVSS for t < n/3 with Perfect Security. Our starting point is the protocol by Gennaro, Ishai, Kushilevitz, and Rabin [29] that achieves VSS with perfect security. The sharing phase of the protocol proceeds as follows:

- *Step 1.* First, the dealer D chooses a bivariate polynomial $f(x, y)$ of degree at most t in each variable, such that $f(0, 0) = s$ and sends to each party P_i the i-th projections $a_i(x) = f(x, i)$ and $b_i(y) = f(i, y)$. Moreover, each party P_i sends to each P_j a uniform random pad r_{ij}.
- *Step 2.* Each party P_i broadcasts the blinded values $a_{ij} = a_i(j) + r_{ij}$ and $b_{ij} = b_i(j) + r_{ji}$, where r_{ji} denotes the pad that P_i receives from P_j.
- *Step 3.* For each conflicting pair ($a_{ij} \ne b_{ji}$), the involved parties broadcast their local points: P_i broadcasts $a_i(j)$, P_j broadcasts $b_j(i)$ and D broadcasts $f(j, i)$. A party is then considered *flagged* if their value does not match D's value. If there are more than t flagged parties, D is disqualified.
- *Step 4.* For each flagged party, D broadcasts the polynomial $a_i(x)$, and each party P_j who is unflagged broadcasts $b_j(i)$.
- *Local Computation.* Every party checks whether Step 4 has provided sufficient evidence supporting the flagged parties or D in the conflicts observed in Step 3. If there is sufficient evidence against D, then D is disqualified.

In the reconstruction phase, every party P_i that has completed the sharing phase as unflagged broadcasts $s_i = a_i(0)$. Then, for every party marked as flagged, take $s_i = a_i(0)$ where $a_i(x)$ is the polynomial broadcasted by D in round 4. Let $f'(y)$ be the t-degree polynomial resulting from the Reed-Solomon error-correction interpolation procedure on the shares $s_1, \ldots, s_n$, and output $f'(0)$.

If D is honest, all honest parties remain unflagged, since their broadcasted points always match D's broadcasted points. As a consequence, there are at most t flagged parties and D is not disqualified. The shares of the honest parties then allow for the correct reconstruction of the dealer's secret s. On the other hand, if D is corrupted and was not disqualified during the sharing phase, the shares from unflagged parties completely determine the value that can be reconstructed. This is because there are at least $n - t$ unflagged parties, out of which at least

$n - 2t \geq t+1$ are honest, so their polynomials $b_i(y)$ uniquely determine a degree-t bivariate polynomial $f'(x, y)$. Furthermore, it is not hard to see that the share s_i distributed during the reconstruction for each honest party P_i (including flagged honest parties), will satisfy $s_i = f'(0, i)$.

Our cVSS construction follows the outline of [29], but replaces broadcast with a weaker primitive, called Graded Broadcast GBC. If a sender S distributes a message m via Graded Broadcast, the parties receive a message (if S is honest, this is m) with grade of confidence in $\{0, 1, 2\}$ (if S is honest, this is 2). Moreover, the honest parties' grades differ by at most 1, and agreement on the message received is guaranteed when all honest parties' grades are non-zero.

Graded Broadcast ensures that, when D is honest, the honest parties' view during the sharing phase remains consistent – up to conflicts claimed by corrupted parties, as Graded Broadcast does not always provide agreement under a corrupted sender. Such conflicts will be solved regardless in favor of D, as D is honest, and VSS is achieved. Moreover, note that replacing broadcast by Graded Broadcast does not affect the secrecy guarantees – the adversary has no information about the secret before reconstruction.

The honest parties set their flag happy to false when they observe D deviating from the protocol: this includes receiving messages from D with grades lower than 2, but also reasons for disqualification in the VSS protocol of [29]. We note that we are unable to require the parties to disqualify D upon observing sufficient evidence that D is corrupted. Due to the weaker properties of Graded Broadcast, it is possible that an honest party has not observed this evidence, and believes that D is honest. Hence, upon observing evidence that D is corrupted, an honest party will simply set its flag happy := false. We only need to achieve VSS if at least one honest party has maintained happy = true, i.e., it has not observed evidence of D being corrupted. In such cases, our construction ensures that all honest parties obtain valid shares in the sharing phase, which uniquely determine the secret they obtain in the reconstruction phase – even if some of the honest parties have observed D to be corrupted. Conversely, if an honest party P was not provided with valid shares, then all honest parties will observe this – in such cases, P will be flagged – we make sure that all honest parties indeed flag P, observe that the conflict ends in P's favor, and set happy = false.

Protocol cVSS$_{\text{auth}}$ for t < n/2 Assuming a Bulletin-Board PKI. Our starting point is the VSS protocol of [17]. This protocol follows traditional verifiable secret sharing schemes [6,20] with bivariate polynomials, but uses so-called *information-checking* (IC) signatures, instead of error correction. One can think about such signatures as information-theoretic signatures that can only be forwarded once. We note that our final Byzantine Agreement protocol in the honest-majority setting assumes a bulletin-board PKI for signatures, and therefore our conditional VSS construction in this setting also relies on standard digital signatures as opposed to IC-signatures.

We briefly revisit the protocol of [17]. In order to share a secret s, the dealer D creates a random bivariate polynomial $f(x, y)$ of degree at most t, with $f(0, 0) = s$. The univariate polynomial projections $f(x, i)$ and $f(i, y)$ are sent to party P_i in a signed manner (by sending all the points $(a_{1i}, \ldots, a_{ni}) = (f(1, i), \ldots, f(n, i))$ and $(b_{i1}, \ldots, b_{in}) = (f(i, 1), \ldots, f(i, n))$, where each point is signed using signatures). After this, the parties can bilaterally compare the cross-point values between them, and expose inconsistent behavior by D by broadcasting the signatures. If an inconsistency is detected, D is disqualified. After the cross-checking process, the values held by honest parties are consistent. Since there are at least $n - t \geq t + 1$ honest parties, these values uniquely define a bivariate polynomial $f'(x, y)$ of degree at most t, which in turn defines a fixed secret s' (which is $s' = s$ if D is honest). Therefore, this already ensures that D is committed to a value after the sharing phase. However, the adversary may still corrupt the secret at reconstruction time – the corrupted parties may send arbitrary shares in the reconstruction phase. To prevent this, each share that a party distributes during the reconstruction phase needs to be signed both by D and by other parties in the sharing phase.

Our strategy for achieving Conditional VSS in this setting will be similar to that described for the plain model: we follow the outline of [17], replacing each broadcast invocation with Graded Broadcast. Whenever an honest party observes evidence that D is corrupted, it may set its flag `happy` to `false`, as opposed to disqualifying D – this is important, as the honest parties might not have an identical view over D's behavior. This way, VSS is achieved whenever D is honest. For the case where D is corrupted, we make sure that, unless D provides the honest parties with valid shares that will uniquely determine the secret they obtain in the reconstruction phase, then all honest parties observe this during the sharing phase and set `happy := false`. This way, if D is corrupted and an honest party holds `happy = true` at the end of the sharing phase, then the honest parties are able to reconstruct the same secret in the reconstruction phase, hence VSS is achieved in this case as well.

3   Preliminaries

We are working in a setting with n parties $\mathcal{P} = \{P_1, P_2, \ldots, P_n\}$. We additionally consider a field $\mathcal{K}$ of size at least $n + 1$.

3.1   Communication

We consider a fully-connected network where parties are connected via point-to-point secure channels. The network is synchronous, meaning that the protocol execution proceeds synchronously in rounds, and messages sent at the start of a round are guaranteed to be delivered by the end of the round.

3.2   Adversary

We consider an adversary that can adaptively corrupt up to t parties at any point of the protocol's execution. Corrupted parties can deviate arbitrarily from the protocol. Moreover, the adversary is strongly rushing: they can observe the messages sent by honest parties in a round before choosing their own messages for that round, and, when an honest party sends a message during some round, it can immediately corrupt that party and replace this round's messages with another of its choice (as long as they have not been delivered yet).

3.3   Building Blocks

Signatures. Some of our protocols require the usage of a signature scheme. A signature scheme is a triple of efficient algorithms $(\mathsf{KeyGen}, \mathsf{Sign}, \mathsf{Ver})$, where:

- A key generation algorithm that outputs a pair containing the secret and public key $(\mathsf{sk}, \mathsf{pk}) \leftarrow \mathsf{KeyGen}(1^\kappa)$.
- A signing algorithm Sign that takes as input the secret key sk and a message m, and produces a signature $\sigma \leftarrow \mathsf{Sign}_{\mathsf{sk}}(m)$.
- A verification function, which given the public key pk, a message m and a signature σ, outputs a bit $b \leftarrow \mathsf{Ver}_{\mathsf{pk}}(m, \sigma)$ indicating whether the signature verifies correctly.

The signature scheme is correct, meaning that $\mathsf{Ver}_{\mathsf{pk}}(m, \mathsf{Sign}_{\mathsf{sk}}(m)) = 1$ for every message m and keys generated $(\mathsf{sk}, \mathsf{pk}) \leftarrow \mathsf{KeyGen}(1^\kappa)$.

In this paper, for clarity and ease of exposition, we treat signatures as ideal objects in all of our protocols [19], meaning that a computationally-bounded adversary cannot forge a valid signature without knowing the secret key. When replacing the signatures with real-world instantiations, the results hold against computationally-bounded adversaries except with negligible probability.

In our *authenticated* protocols, parties have access to a bulletin-board public key infrastructure (PKI) for signatures, where all parties hold the same vector of public keys $(\mathsf{pk}_1, \mathsf{pk}_2, \dots, \mathsf{pk}_n)$, and each honest party P_i holds the secret key sk_i associated with pk_i.

Linear Error Correcting Code. We use standard Reed-Solomon (RS) codes with parameters $(n, t + 1)$. There are two algorithms:

- Encoding. Given inputs $m_1, \dots, m_{t+1}$, the encoding function outputs n codewords (a.k.a. shares) $(s_1, \dots, s_n)$ of length n, such that any $t + 1$ codewords uniquely determine the input message and the other codewords.
- Decoding. Given up to c errors and d erasures in codewords $(s_1, \dots, s_n)$, one can reconstruct the original message $(m_1, \dots, m_{t+1})$ if and only if $n - t - 1 \geq 2c + d$.

3.4   Primitives

We define the primitives we consider in the paper.

Byzantine Agreement. We present the definition of Byzantine Agreement with binary inputs below. Note that the *Termination* property is required implicitly.

Definition 1 (Byzantine Agreement). *A protocol Π where initially each party P_i holds an input value $x_i \in \{0,1\}$ and terminates upon generating an output y_i is a Byzantine Agreement protocol, resilient against t corruptions, if the following properties are satisfied whenever up to t parties are corrupted:*

Validity: *If all honest parties have input x, every honest party outputs $y_i = x$.*
Agreement: *Any two honest parties P_i and P_j output the same value $y_i = y_j$.*

Binary Proxcensus. We consider a variant of Byzantine Agreement, called Proxcensus [30], which allows parties to output an index value within an array of ℓ values, so that honest parties' outputs lie within two consecutive indices. Moreover, if parties have the same input bit, they all output an extremal index.

Definition 2 (Binary Proxcensus). *Let $\ell \geq 2$. A protocol Π where initially each party P_i holds an input bit $x_i \in \{0,1\}$ and parties terminate upon generating an output $y_i \in \{0,\ldots,\ell-1\}$ is an ℓ-Proxcensus protocol, resilient against t corruptions, if the following properties hold whenever up to t parties are corrupted:*

Validity: *If all honest parties input $x_i = 0$ (resp. $x_i = 1$), then every honest party outputs $y_i = 0$ (resp. $y_i = \ell - 1$).*
Consistency: *The outputs of any two honest parties P_i and P_j lie within two consecutive slots. That is, there exists a value $v \in 0,\ldots,\ell-2$ such that each honest party P_i outputs $y_i \in \{v, v+1\}$.*

ProxCoin. A protocol ProxCoin allows parties to toss a common *random* index from an array with ℓ indices, such that all honest parties output δ-close indices.

Definition 3 (ProxCoin). *Let $\ell \geq 2$ and $\delta \leq \ell$ be natural numbers. A protocol Π where parties terminate upon generating an output $y_i \in \{0,\ldots,\ell-1\}$ is an (ℓ,δ)-ProxCoin protocol, resilient against t corruptions, if the following properties are satisfied whenever up to t parties are corrupted:*

Consistency: *if one honest party outputs value x and another honest party outputs y, then $|x - y| \leq \delta$.*
One Uniform Randomness: *the value output by at least one honest party must be uniformly distributed over the domain $[0, \ell - 1]$.*

Conditional Verifiable Secret Sharing. We propose a relaxed definition of Verifiable Secret Sharing (VSS), which we denote by *conditional* VSS. In this primitive, each party P_i outputs a share value s_i and a happiness flag happy_i. Intuitively, the guarantees are similar to that of VSS (in terms of correctness and secrecy), except that the binding property only holds when there is an honest party P_i with $\mathsf{happy} = \mathtt{true}$.

Definition 4 (Conditional VSS). *A two-phase protocol Π with a designated party D (called the dealer) is a Conditional VSS protocol resilient against t corruptions, if the following properties hold when up to t parties are corrupted:*

Syntax: *D initially holds an input s. Each honest party P_i holds a boolean happy_i and a share $s_i \in S \cup \{\bot\}$ at the end of the first phase (called the sharing phase), and outputs y_i at the end of the second phase (called the reconstruction phase).*

Sharing-Validity: *If D is honest, then every party P_i holds $s_i \neq \bot$ and $\mathsf{happy}_i = \mathtt{true}$ at the end of the sharing phase.*

Cheating-Prevention: *If any honest party P_i holds share $s_i = \bot$ at the end of the sharing phase, then every honest party P_j holds $\mathsf{happy}_j = \mathtt{false}$.*

Correctness: *If D is honest, every honest party P_i outputs $y_i = s$ after the reconstruction phase.*

Secrecy: *If D is honest, the joint view of the byzantine parties after the sharing phase is independent of s.*

Conditional Binding: *If at least one honest party P_i holds $\mathsf{happy}_i = \mathtt{true}$ at the end of the sharing phase, the joint view of the honest parties at the end of the sharing phase defines a value y' such that all honest parties output y' after the reconstruction phase.*

Graded Broadcast. Our Conditional VSS constructions rely on Graded Broadcast. This is a weakening of broadcast allowing a sender to distribute a value, such that every party P_i obtains a pair of value-grade (y_i, g_i), as described below. For concrete constructions, see [5,21,24,36].

Definition 5 (Graded Broadcast). *A protocol Π where a designated party S (called the sender) holds an input x, and each party P_i terminates upon obtaining an output (y_i, g_i) with $g_i \in \{0, 1, 2\}$, is a Graded Broadcast protocol resilient against t corruptions if the following hold when up to t parties are corrupted:*

Validity *If S is honest, then every honest party P_i outputs $(y_i, g_i) = (x, 2)$.*

Graded Consistency: *If P_i and P_j are honest, they output (y_i, g_i) and (y_j, g_j) such that $|g_i - g_j| \leq 1$. Moreover, if $g_i > 0$ and $g_j > 0$, then $y_i = y_j$.*

4   Expand-and-Extract Paradigm via ProxCoin

We describe the Expand-and-Extract paradigm with the replacement of the ideal coin by a ProxCoin described in Sect. 2. In the protocol below, Prox_ℓ is an ℓ-Proxcensus protocol, and $\mathsf{ProxCoin}_{\ell-1,\delta}$ is an $(\ell - 1, \delta)$-ProxCoin protocol.

Protocol: Π_{EE}^{ℓ}

Let $\ell \geq 2$ be a natural number. The protocol is described from the point of view of party P_i, with input bit $x_i \in \{0, 1\}$.

1: $z_i := \mathtt{Prox}_\ell(x_i);\ c_i := \mathtt{ProxCoin}_{\ell-1,\delta}$.
2: If $z_i \leq c_i$, output 0. Otherwise, output 1.

The honest parties output the same bit whenever either all honest values z_i are on the left side of every coin c_i, i.e., $\max_{P_i} z_i \leq \min_i c_i$, or all honest values z_i are on the right side of every coin c_i, i.e., $\min_{P_i} z_i > \max_i c_i$. This leads us to the following result.

Theorem 3 ([24], Adjusted). *Assume $t < n$. Let $\mathtt{Prox}_\ell$ be an ℓ-slot Prox-census protocol secure up to t corruptions, and $\mathtt{ProxCoin}_{\ell-1,\delta}$ be an $(\ell-1,\delta)$-ProxCoin protocol, secure up to t corruptions. Then, $\Pi_{\mathrm{EE}}^{\ell,\delta}$ achieves binary Byzantine Agreement against an adaptive, strongly rushing adversary with probability $1 - \frac{1+2\cdot\delta}{\ell-1}$.*

Proof. **Validity.** If each P_i inputs 0 to $\mathtt{Prox}_\ell$, they obtain $z_i := 0$. Moreover, since $c_i \geq 0$, all honest parties output 0. Similarly, if each P_i inputs 1 to $\mathtt{Prox}_\ell$, they obtain $z_i := \ell - 1$. As $c_i \leq \ell - 2$, every honest party outputs 1.

Agreement. If all honest parties satisfy the same condition, either $z_i \leq c_i$ or $z_i > c_i$, Agreement is achieved. As $\mathtt{ProxCoin}$ achieves one-process randomness, there is one honest party that outputs a random index $c \in [0, \ell - 2]$. By consistency, all honest parties' coins $c_i \in [c - \delta, c + \delta]$. Then, the protocol achieves Agreement with probability at least $\Pr_c[\max_i z_i \leq c - \delta \text{ or } c + \delta < \min_i z_i]$, hence at least $1 - \Pr_c[c \in [\min_i z_i - \delta, \max_i z_i + \delta)] \geq 1 - \frac{1+2\cdot\delta}{\ell-1}$.

5   Conditional VSS

In this section, we describe our constructions for conditional VSS. As mentioned in Sect. 3.4, this primitive is a weakening of verifiable secret sharing, where the binding property is only achieved when one of the honest parties holds $\mathtt{happy} = 1$.

5.1   Perfect Security with $t < n/3$

We first describe a construction in the plain model without setup. The protocol achieves perfect security against $t < n/3$ corruptions, and is based on the VSS protocol by Gennaro, Ishai, Kushilevitz, and Rabin [29].

Theorem 4. *Protocol $\mathtt{cVSS} = (\mathtt{cVSS.Sh}, \mathtt{cVSS.Rec})$ is a conditional VSS protocol with perfect security up to $t < n/3$ corruptions. The round complexity of $\mathtt{cVSS}$ is $R_{Sh} = 10$ for the sharing phase and $R_{Rec} = 1$ for the reconstruction phase.*

Protocol Description. We describe the complete protocol below, using a Graded Broadcast protocol GBC as a building block. Note that GBC can be achieved for $t < n/3$ without setup [5,21] in 3 rounds and $O(n^2)$ bits of communication.

> **Protocol: cVSS.Sh**
>
> **<u>Distribution:</u>** Let s be the dealer D's input. Every party P_i sets $\mathsf{happy}_i := \mathsf{true}$.
>
> 1: D chooses a random bivariate polynomial $f(x,y)$ over $\mathcal{K}$ of degree at most t in each variable, such that $f(0,0) = s$. For each party P_i, D defines $a_i(x) := f(x,i)$ and $b_i(y) := f(i,y)$ and sends the polynomials a_i, b_i to P_i.
> 2: Party P_i checks whether it has received a_i, b_i from D such that a_i, b_i are polynomials of degree at most t. If not, it sets a_i, b_i to a default polynomial and sets $\mathsf{happy}_i := \mathsf{false}$.
> 3: For every P_j, P_i samples r_{ij} uniformly at random from $\mathcal{K}$ and sends r_{ij} to P_j
> 4: Let r_{ji} be the value P_i receives from P_j (or some default value if no value was received).
>
> **<u>Consistency checks:</u>**
>
> 5: For every P_j, P_i computes $a_{ij} = a_i(j) + r_{ij}$ and $b_{ij} = b_i(j) + r_{ji}$. Then, P_i sends a_{ij}, b_{ij} to all parties via GBC.
> 6: Party P_i checks for each P_j:
>> If it has not received value $b_{ji} = a_{ij}$ with grade 2, it sends $a_i(j)$ via GBC.
>> If it has not received value $a_{ji} = b_{ij}$ with grade 2, it sends $b_i(j)$ via GBC.
> 7: Unless D observes $a_{ij} = b_{ji}$ both with grade 2 in Step 5, it sends $f(j,i)$ to all parties via GBC.
> 8: If P_i has observed $a_{kj} \neq b_{jk}$ with grades at least 1 for some P_j, P_k in Step 6; and P_i has not received a response from D for this pair with grade 2 in Step 7, P_i sets $\mathsf{happy}_i := \mathsf{false}$.
>
> **<u>Flagging parties:</u>**
>
> 9: Party P_i flags party P_j if any of these conditions holds:
>> - In Step 6, P_i has received $a_j(k)$ from P_j with grade 2, and in Step 7 P_i has received $f(k,j) \neq a_j(k)$ from D with grade at least 1.
>> - In Step 6, P_i has received $b_j(k)$ from P_j with grade 2, and in Step 7 P_i has received $f(j,k) \neq b_j(k)$ from D with grade at least 1.
> 10: If P_i has flagged at least $t+1$ parties, it sets $\mathsf{happy}_i := \mathsf{false}$.
> 11: Unless D has observed P_j to be honest (all messages have arrived with grade 2) and consistent (in Step 6, any gradecasted values $a_j(i)$ and $b_j(i)$ satisfy $a_j(i) = f(i,j)$ and $b_j(i) = f(j,i)$), it sends the polynomials $a_j(x) = f(x,j)$ and $b_j(x) = f(j,x)$ to all parties via GBC.
> 12: If P_i has flagged party P_j and P_i has not received from D the polynomials $a_j(x) = f(x,j)$ and $b_j(x) = f(j,x)$ with grade 2, P_i sets $\mathsf{happy}_i := \mathsf{false}$.
> 13: Unless party P_i flagged itself, it checks for each party P_j whether:
>> - In Step 6, P_i has received $a_j(k)$ with grade at least 1 from P_j, and in Step 7, P_i has received $f(k,j) \neq a_j(k)$ from D with grade at least 1.
>> - In Step 6, P_i has received $b_j(k)$ with grade at least 1 from P_j, and in Step 7, P_i has received $f(j,k) \neq b_j(k)$ from D with grade at least 1.

If any of these conditions holds, P_i sends the values $a_i(j), b_i(j)$ via GBC.

Determine share:

14: For each party P_j that P_i flagged, P_i checks that it has received $a_k(j), b_k(j)$ with grade 2 from at least $2t+1$ unflagged parties P_k, such that $a_j(k) = b_k(j)$ and $b_j(k) = a_k(j)$. If this is not the case, it sets $\texttt{happy}_i := \texttt{false}$.

15: Party P_i outputs its share $s_i := a_i(0)$ and the flag $\texttt{happy}_i$.

Protocol: cVSS.Rec

1: Every party P_i sends $s_i = a_i(0)$ to all parties

2: For every party P_j that P_i has flagged in Step 9 of cVSS.Sh, P_i sets $s_j := a_j(0)$, where a_j is the polynomial that P_i has received from D with grade at least 1 via GBC in Step 11 of cVSS.Sh.

3: Let $f_i(x)$ be the polynomial with degree up to t resulting from the Reed-Solomon error-correction interpolation procedure on $s_1, \ldots, s_n$. Party P_i can then compute the secret $y_i = f_i(0)$.

Analysis. We split the proof of Theorem 4 into a sequence of Lemmas. We first note that the Syntax property follows immediately from the protocol description, and the Cheating-Prevention property holds trivially as the parties never output $\bot$. Then, the Sharing-Validity property follows from Lemma 1. Correctness is discussed in Lemma 3, and Secrecy is proven in Lemma 2. Afterwards, we show that Conditional Binding is satisfied in Lemma 5. It remains to discuss the round complexity – cVSS incurs one round of communication plus three sequential steps involving n parallel invocations of GBC for the sharing phase, and n parallel invocations of GBC for the reconstruction phase. As GBC can be achieved within 3 rounds of communication [5,21], this leads to 10 rounds for the sharing phase, and 3 rounds for the reconstruction phase.

Lemma 1. *Assume that the dealer D is honest and holds secret s, and consider the polynomial f that D chooses in Step 1 of cVSS.Sh. Then, every honest party P_i completes cVSS.Sh with $a_i(x) = f(x,i)$, $b_i(y) = f(i,y)$ and $\texttt{happy}_i = \texttt{true}$.*

Proof. Since D is honest, every honest party P_i receives $a_i(x) = f(x,i)$, $b_i(y) = f(i,y)$ in Step 1 – these are t-consistent, thus P_i does not set a_i, b_i to a default polynomial and keeps $\texttt{happy}_i = \texttt{true}$. It remains to analyze the steps of cVSS.Sh where P_i may set $\texttt{happy} := \texttt{false}$ and show that $\texttt{happy}_i = \texttt{true}$ is maintained.

In Step 8, P_i sets $\texttt{happy}_i := \texttt{false}$ only if it observes $a_{kj} \neq b_{jk}$ in Step 5 and has not received a response for this pair from D with grade 2 in Step 7. We note that, if D receives $a_{kj} = b_{jk}$ with grades 2 each in Step 5, P_i receives $a_{kj} = b_{jk}$ with grade at least 1 each. Otherwise, if D does not receive such a pair with grade 2, it responds by sending $f(j,i)$ to all parties via GBC, and P_i receives this response with grade 2. Hence, P_i maintains $\texttt{happy}_i = \texttt{true}$ in this step.

In Step 10, P_i sets $\mathtt{happy}_i := \mathtt{false}$ only if it has flagged at least $t + 1$ parties in Step 9. P_i flags P_j if P_i has received $a_j(k)$ or $b_j(k)$ in Step 6 and a conflicting response from D in Step 7. However, if both D and P_j are honest, the polynomials they distribute match and are received with grade 2, hence P_i does not flag an honest party P_j. Thus, P_i flags at most t parties, and maintains $\mathtt{happy}_i = \mathtt{true}$.

In Step 12, P_i sets $\mathtt{happy}_i := \mathtt{false}$ if it has flagged some party P_j in Step 9 and it has not received the polynomials corresponding to P_j from D with grade 2 in Step 11. We note that, if P_i flags P_j, then D has not observed P_j to be honest in Step 11: P_i has received a polynomial from P_j with grade 2 in Step 6 that did not match D's response in Step 7. GBC guarantees that D has received the same polynomial from P_j in Step 7 with grade at least 1, hence D has not observed P_j to be honest, and therefore D sends the polynomials $a_j(x) = f(x, j)$ and $b_j(x) = f(j, x)$ to all parties via GBC. Then, P_i receives this response with grade 2 in Step 12, and therefore maintains $\mathtt{happy}_i = \mathtt{true}$.

It remains to discuss Step 14. We have already shown that honest parties do not flag honest parties when D is honest in Step 9, hence no honest party flags itself. Then, for every P_j that P_i has flagged in Step 9, P_i checks whether $2t + 1$ unflagged parties P_k have confirmed in Step 13 the values $a_j(k)$ and $b_j(k)$ claimed by D in Step 11. Since no honest party marks itself, every honest party P_k sends $a_k(j) = f(j, k) = b_j(k)$ and $b_k(j) = f(k, j) = a_j(k)$ in Step 13, hence agreeing with D. Then, P_i receives at least $\geq 2t + 1$ values $a_k(j), b_k(j)$ that agree with D, and thus it maintains $\mathtt{happy}_i = \mathtt{true}$. Consequently, P_i completes cVSS.Sh with $\mathtt{happy}_i = \mathtt{true}$, which concludes our proof.

Lemma 2. *cVSS achieves Secrecy.*

Proof. We assume that D is honest with input secret s, and we show that the joint view of the byzantine parties before the start of cVSS.Rec is independent from s. Let f denote the polynomial chosen by D in Step 1.

We first establish that the byzantine parties' views after Step 1 is independent from s. The byzantine parties' view at the end of Step 1 consists of the rows $a_i(x) = f(x, i)$ and columns $b_i(y) = f(i, y)$ where P_i is byzantine. Hence, these are the polynomials corresponding to at most t different rows and at most t different columns. However, this is not sufficient information to determine s: for any secret s', there is a polynomial $f'(x, y)$ of degree at most t in each variable such that $f'(0, 0) = s'$, $f'(x, i) = a_i(x)$ and $f'(i, y) = b_i(y)$ for every byzantine party P_i. Therefore, the byzantine parties' joint view at the end of Step 1 is independent from s. It remains to show that the further steps of cVSS.Sh do not reveal any additional information.

In Step 5, values a_{ij}, b_{ij} are masked by random values r_{ij}, r_{ji} and thus independent of $a_i(k), b_i(k)$: these remain secret to the byzantine parties if P_i and P_j are honest.

In Step 6, an honest party P_i publishes $a_i(j)$ or $b_i(j)$ only if it has not received a matching value with grade 2 from P_j in Step 5. GBC ensures that, if P_j is honest, its value is received with grade 2 by all parties. Moreover, since

D is honest, P_i and P_j hold $a_j(i) = b_i(j) = f(i,j)$ and $a_i(j) = b_j(i) = f(j,i)$. Hence, if P_i publishes the value $a_i(j)$ or $b_i(j)$, P_j must be byzantine, and the published values are already part of the byzantine parties' joint view at the end of Step 1.

In Step 7, D only publishes $f(j,i)$ if it has not observed a pair $a_{ij} = b_{ji}$ with grade 2 in Step 5. As described for Step 6, since D is honest, it has provided the parties with values $a_i(j) = b_j(i) = f(j,i)$. Also, assuming P_i, P_j are honest, they both add the same value r_{ij} to $a_i(j)$ resp. $b_j(i)$ and thus $a_{ij} = b_{ji}$. In addition, since GBC ensures that honest parties' messages are received with grade 2, D receives $a_{ij} = b_{ji}$ both with grade 2 for every pair of honest parties P_i, P_j in Step 5. Hence, if D publishes $f(i,j)$ in Step 7, at least one of the two parties P_i and P_j is corrupted, and therefore the value published was already in the corrupted parties' joint view at the end of Step 1.

We now discuss Step 11: D publishes the polynomials $a_j(x), b_j(x)$ only if it has observed P_j deviating from the protocol: D has either received a message from P_j with a grade ≤ 1 via GBC, or P_j has sent values in Step 6 contradicting the ones it has received from D. Therefore, D only published the polynomials $a_j(x), b_j(x)$ of byzantine parties P_j, hence no new information.

For Step 13, we note that an honest P_i flags a party P_j only if P_j is byzantine (when D is honest): as described in the proof of Lemma 6, P_i flags P_j if P_j has sent a value $a_j(k)$ or $b_j(k)$ in Step 6, and P_i has received a conflicting response from D for P_j in Step 7. However, if both D and P_j are honest, the polynomials they distribute match and are received with grade 2, hence P_i does not flag P_j. Then, in Step 13, an honest party P_i only reveals values $a_i(j), b_i(j)$ where P_j is byzantine, and therefore does not reveal any new information.

Lemma 3. *cVSS achieves Correctness.*

Proof. We assume that D is honest with input s, and we show that every honest party P_i outputs $y_i = s$ at the end of cVSS.Rec.

If f denotes the polynomial chosen by D in Step 1 of cVSS.Sh, Lemma 1 ensures that every honest party P_i completes cVSS.Sh with share $s_i = a_i(0) = f(0,i)$. Then, in cVSS.Rec, every honest party P_i receives $s_j = f(0,j)$ for every honest party P_j. In addition, for every party P_j that P_i has flagged in cVSS.Sh, P_i sets $s_j := a_j(0)$, where $a_j(x)$ is the polynomial published by D in Step 11 of cVSS.Sh: since D is honest, $s_j = a_j(0) = f(0,j)$. P_i sets $f_i(x)$ as the polynomial of degree at most t resulting from the Reed-Solomon error correction interpolation procedure on $s_1, \ldots s_n$. As $n - t \geq 2t + 1$ of these shares agree with $f(0,j)$, there is a unique polynomial of degree at most t that the honest parties can obtain, and this is f. Hence, every honest party P_i outputs $y_i := f(0,0) = s$.

The lemma below notes an additional property of cVSS.Sh that will be helpful when discussing Conditional Binding.

Lemma 4. *Assume that an honest party P_i flags an honest party P_j in Step 9 of cVSS.Sh. Then, if some honest party P_l completes cVSS.Sh with $happy_l = true$, every honest party flags P_j.*

Proof. Since P_i has flagged P_j in Step 9 of cVSS.Sh, P_i has received $a_j(k)$ or $b_j(k)$ from P_j with grade 2 in Step 6. GBC ensures that every honest party P_k has received the same value with grade 2 from P_j in Step 6.

Moreover, since P_l completes cVSS.Sh with $\mathtt{happy}_l = \mathtt{true}$, P_l has observed a response from D to P_j with grade 2 in Step 7. Hence, all honest parties receive this response with grade at least 1. Since P_i flags P_j, this response does not match the value distributed by P_j in Step 6: $a_j(k) \neq f(k,j)$ or $b_j(k) \neq f(j,k)$. Hence, all honest parties observe this and flag P_j.

Lemma 5. *cVSS achieves Conditional Binding.*

Proof. We assume that at least one honest party P_i holds $\mathtt{happy}_i = \mathtt{true}$ at the end of cVSS.Sh, and show that the joint view of the honest parties at the end of cVSS.Sh defines a value y' such that all honest parties output y' in cVSS.Rec.

We first note that, since P_i completes cVSS.Sh with $\mathtt{happy} = \mathtt{true}$, P_i has flagged at most t parties. Moreover, Lemma 4 ensures that the honest parties flag the same honest parties. This implies that there is a set $\mathcal{H}'$ of at least $n - 2t \geq t + 1$ honest parties P_j that have obtained in cVSS.Sh polynomials $a_j(x), b_j(x)$ of degree at most t such that $a_j(k) = b_k(j)$ for every $P_k \in \mathcal{H}'$. In the following, we consider a subset $\mathcal{H} \subseteq \mathcal{H}'$ of size $t + 1$, and define $f'(x, y)$ as the unique polynomial of degree at most t in each variable such that $f'(j, k) = a_k(j) = b_k(k)$ for every pair of parties P_j, P_k in $\mathcal{H}$. Since these are $(t+1) \cdot (t+1)$ constraints, there is a unique such polynomial f'.

Next, we show that the shares $a_j(x), b_j(x)$ of every unflagged honest party $P_j \in \mathcal{H}' \backslash \mathcal{H}$ agree with f'. The polynomial $a_j(x)$ has degree at most t and satisfies $a_j(k) = b_k(j) = f'(k, j)$ for every party $P_k \in \mathcal{H}$. Hence, $a_j(x)$ and $f'(x, j)$ are both polynomials of degree at most t that agree in $|\mathcal{H}| = t + 1$ points, and therefore they are identical. Analogously, $b_j(x)$ is identical with $f'(j, x)$.

Lastly, we consider the polynomial $a_j'(x)$ of a flagged honest party P_j. In Step 14 of cVSS.Sh, P_i has observed at least $2t + 1$ unflagged parties (honest and corrupt), hence at least $t + 1$ unflagged honest parties P_k that confirmed $a_j(k) = b_k(j)$ and $a_k(j) = b_j(k)$. Therefore, $a_j(k) = b_k(j) = f'(k, j)$ for at least $t + 1$ of the honest parties in $\mathcal{H}'$. Since $a_j(x)$ and $f'(x, j)$ are polynomials of degree at most t, it follows that $a_j(x)$ and $f'(x, j)$ are identical. Analogously, $b_j(x)$ is identical with $f'(j, x)$.

Hence, we have obtained that the honest parties' shares uniquely determine a polynomial $f'(x, y)$ of degree at most t in each variable. It remains to discuss cVSS.Rec: in cVSS.Rec, every honest party P_j obtains $s_k = f'(0, k)$ for every honest party P_k. Hence, P_j obtains $n - t \geq 2t + 1$ distinct points that lie on f', plus at most t points that do not. Then, the Reed-Solomon error-correction procedure ensures that the honest parties obtain the same polynomial $f_l(x) = f'(0, x)$ and therefore output $y_l := f_l(0) = f'(0, 0)$.

5.2 Computational Protocol Assuming PKI for $t < n/2$

We now present a construction secure against $t < n/2$ corruptions that assumes a bulletin-board PKI for signatures, and is based on the VSS protocol of Cramer et al. [17]. Our construction is described by the theorem below.

Theorem 5. *Assuming a bulletin-board PKI for signatures, protocol* $cVSS_{auth} = (cVSS_{auth}.Sh,\ cVSS_{auth}.Rec)$ *is a Conditional VSS protocol secure up to* $t < n/2$ *corruptions. The round complexity of* $cVSS_{auth}$ *is* $R_{Sh} = 14$ *for the sharing phase,* $R_{Rec} = 3$ *for the reconstruction phase.*

Protocol Description. We describe the protocol below. Similarly to cVSS, we make use of a Graded Broadcast protocol GBC_{auth} as a building block. GBC_{auth} can be achieved for $t < n/2$ corruptions assuming a bulletin-board PKI in 3 rounds and $O(n^3\kappa)$ bits of communication [24,36].

Protocol: $cVSS_{auth}.Sh$

<u>Distribution</u> Let s be the dealer D's input. Every party P_i sets $\textbf{happy}_i := \textbf{true}$.

1: D chooses a random bivariate polynomial $f(x, y)$ of degree at most t in each variable, such that $f(0, 0) = s$. D sends to party P_i the values $a_{1i} = f(1, i), \ldots, a_{ni} = f(n, i)$ and $b_{i1} = f(i, 1), \ldots, b_{in} = f(i, n)$, along with the corresponding signatures $\sigma_D^{a_{ji}} := \mathsf{Sign}_{sk_D}(a_{ji}, j, i)$ and $\sigma_D^{b_{ij}} := \mathsf{Sign}_{sk_D}(b_{ij}, i, j)$.

<u>Distribution check:</u>

2: Party P_i checks whether it has received t-consistent shares $a_{1i}, \ldots, a_{ni}$ and $b_{i1}, \ldots, b_{in}$ with signatures $\sigma_D^{a_{ji}}, \sigma_D^{b_{ij}}$ from D. If this is the case, P_i sends $\textbf{ok}$ via GBC_{auth}. Otherwise, party P_i sends $\texttt{missing}$ via GBC_{auth} and sets $\textbf{happy}_i := \textbf{false}$.

3: For every party P_i, D checks whether it has received $\textbf{ok}$ with grade 2 via GBC_{auth} from P_i in Step 2. If this is not the case, D sends the shares for P_i, i.e. $a_{1i}, \ldots, a_{ni}$ and $b_{i1}, \ldots, b_{in}$ along with the corresponding signatures $\sigma_D^{a_{ji}}$, $\sigma_D^{b_{ij}}$, to all parties via GBC_{auth}.

4: For every party P_j that P_i has not received $\textbf{ok}$ with grade at least 1 via GBC_{auth} in Step 2, P_i checks whether D has responded in Step 3. Unless P_i has the t-consistent shares with signatures for P_j with grade 2 from D via GBC_{auth} in Step 3, P_i sets $\textbf{happy}_i = \textbf{false}$.

If P_i has not sent an $\textbf{ok}$ message in Step 2, it checks whether it has received its t-consistent shares $a_{1i}, \ldots, a_{ni}$ and $b_{i1}, \ldots, b_{in}$ with signatures $\sigma_D^{a_{ji}}, \sigma_D^{b_{ij}}$ with grade at least 1 from D via GBC_{auth} in Step 3. If this is the case, P_i uses these shares from this point on.

<u>Pair-wise consistency checks:</u>

5: For every party P_j, party P_i sends to P_j its share a_{ji} along with D's signature $\sigma_D^{a_{ji}}$ and its own signature $\sigma_{P_i}^{a_{ji}} := \mathsf{Sign}_{sk_{P_i}}(a_{ji}, j, i)$.

6: Party P_j checks the shares received in Step 5. For every party P_i, unless P_j has received a_{ji} with signatures $\sigma_D^{a_{ji}}, \sigma_{P_i}^{a_{ji}}$ from P_i such that $a_{ji} = b_{ji}$, P_j sends (b_{ji}, j, i) along with D's signature $\sigma_D^{b_{ji}}$ and its own signature $\sigma_{P_j}^{b_{ji}} := \mathsf{Sign}_{sk_{P_j}}(b_{ji}, j, i)$ to all parties via GBC_{auth}.

7: For every party P_j, party P_i checks whether it has received (b_{ji}, j, i) with signatures $\sigma_D^{b_{ji}}, \sigma_{P_j}^{b_{ji}}$ with grade at least 1 via GBC_{auth} in Step 6. If this is the case, P_i sends (a_{ji}, j, i) along with the dealer's signature $\sigma_D^{a_{ji}}$ and its own signature $\sigma_{P_i}^{a_{ji}}$ to all parties via $\mathsf{GBC_{auth}}$.

Determine share:

8: Party P_i checks if it has observed any conflicts in Step 6 and Step 7: if it has received (a_{kj}, k, j) with D's signature $\sigma_D^{a_{kj}}$ with grade at least 1 from P_j via $\mathsf{GBC_{auth}}$ in Step 6, and (b_{kj}, k, j) with D's signature $\sigma_D^{b_{kj}}$ with grade at least 1 from P_k via $\mathsf{GBC_{auth}}$ in Step 7 such that $a_{kj} \neq b_{kj}$. If this is the case, P_i sets $\mathtt{happy}_i := \mathtt{false}$.

9: Party P_i sets $s_i := \perp$ if it has never received t-consistent correctly-signed shares from D. Otherwise, it sets s_i as the list of values b_{ij} with $j \in [n]$ along with D's signatures $\sigma_D^{b_{ij}}$, P_i's signatures $\sigma_{P_i}^{b_{ij}}$, and the signature $\sigma_{P_j}^{a_{ij}} = \sigma_{P_j}^{b_{ij}}$ received from each P_j (if any). Then, P_i outputs s_i and $\mathtt{happy}_i$.

Protocol: $\mathsf{cVSS_{auth}.Rec}$

1: Party P_i sends its shares s_i to all parties via $\mathsf{GBC_{auth}}$ – this is the list of values b_{ij} with $j \in [n]$ along with corresponding signatures from D, P_i, and, for every party P_j, P_j's signature for b_{ij} (if received).

2: If P_i has received the shares of P_j via $\mathsf{GBC_{auth}}$ with grade 2 in the previous step, it checks whether:
   - P_j's claimed shares are t-consistent.
   - For every b_{jk}: P_j has provided its own signature, D's signature and either: the signature from P_k, or in $\mathsf{cVSS_{auth}.Sh}$, P_i has received P_j's signed share with grade 2 in Step 6, and P_i has not observed an appropriate response from P_k with grade 2 in Step 7.

   Unless both of these conditions hold, P_i ignores the shares received from P_j.

3: Party P_i interpolates a polynomial $f_i(x, y)$ of degree at most t in each variable from the undiscarded shares and outputs $y_i := f_i(0, 0)$.

Analysis. We split the proof of Theorem 5 into a sequence of lemmas. We first note that the Syntax property follows directly from the protocol's description. In the following, Lemma 6 implies Sharing-Validity. Afterwards, Lemma 7 proves Cheating-Prevention. We then focus on Secrecy in Lemma 8, and on Correctness in Lemma 9. Finally, we prove Conditional Binding in Lemma 11. Regarding the round complexities, if R_{GBC} denotes the round complexity of the GBC protocol assumed, we note that the Sharing phase takes $R_{\mathsf{Sh}} = 2 + 4 \cdot R$ rounds, while the Reconstruction phase takes $R_{\mathsf{Rec}} = R$ rounds, where R denotes the round complexity of the assumed Graded Broadcast protocol $\mathsf{GBC_{auth}}$. As $R = 3$ by [24, 36], we obtain that $R_{\mathsf{Sh}} = 14$ and $R_{\mathsf{Rec}} = 3$.

Lemma 6. *Assume D is honest and let f denote the polynomial it chose in Step 1 of $\mathsf{cVSS_{auth}.Sh}$. Then, every honest party P_i outputs $s_i \neq \perp$ and $\mathtt{happy}_i := \mathtt{true}$, where s_i contains the list $b_{ij} = f(i, j)$ with $j \in [n]$.*

Proof. As D is honest, every party P_i receives its shares $a_{ji} = f(j,i), b_{ij} = f(i,j)$ with $j \in [n]$. These shares are t-consistent and also pair-wise consistent. Then, in Step 9 of $\mathsf{cVSS_{auth}.Sh}$, every honest party P_i defines s_i as the list $b_{ij} = f(i,j)$ with $j \in [n]$ along with the corresponding signatures, which completes the proof for the first part of the lemma's statement. It remains to show that every honest party P_i completes the protocol with $\mathsf{happy}_i = \mathsf{true}$. To do so, we analyze each of the steps of $\mathsf{cVSS_{auth}.Sh}$ where P_i may update its happy_i flag.

In Step 2, every honest party P_i maintains $\mathsf{happy}_i = \mathsf{true}$ and sends ok via $\mathsf{GBC_{auth}}$. These messages are received with grade 2 by all parties.

Then, in Step 4, P_i checks whether D has responded correctly and with grade 2 to every party P_j that P_i has received a $\mathsf{missing}$ message from with grade at least 1. The Graded Consistency property of $\mathsf{GBC_{auth}}$ guarantees that, if P_i receives $(\mathsf{missing}, g_i)$ from P_j with $g_i \geq 1$, then D either receives $(\mathsf{missing}, g_D)$, or $(\bot, 0)$. That is, D has not received ok with grade 2 from P_j. In Step 3, D sends the t-consistent signed shares corresponding to P_j. Hence, P_i receives the response corresponding to any such P_j with grade 2 and maintains $\mathsf{happy}_i = \mathsf{true}$.

It remains to discuss Step 8: P_i checks whether, in Steps 5-7, it has observed shares (a_{kj}, k, j) and (b_{kj}, k, j) with signatures from D such that $a_{jk} \neq b_{kj}$. Since D is honest, it has provided P_j and P_k with shares a_{kj}, b_{kj} such that $a_{jk} = b_{kj}$. Consequently, at least one of P_j and P_k is byzantine. However, a byzantine party cannot send a different share with a valid signature from D, as it would have to forge D's signature. Consequently, P_i has not observed any conflicting shares in Step 8, and therefore completes $\mathsf{cVSS_{auth}.Sh}$ with $\mathsf{happy}_i = \mathsf{true}$.

Lemma 7. *$\mathsf{cVSS_{auth}}$ satisfies Cheating-Prevention.*

Proof. We assume that an honest party P_i has obtained $s_i = \bot$ in $\mathsf{cVSS_{auth}.Sh}$, while an honest party P_j has completed $\mathsf{cVSS_{auth}.Sh}$ with $\mathsf{happy}_j = \mathsf{true}$.

P_i has not received signed t-consistent shares from D in Step 2, and has announced this by sending $\mathsf{missing}$ to all parties via GBC in Step 2. Every party, including P_j, receives this message with grade 2. Moreover, P_i has not received signed t-consistent shares from D with grade at least 1 in Step 4 either: otherwise, P_i would have obtained $s_i \neq \bot$. However, P_j has not set $\mathsf{happy}_j = \mathsf{false}$ in this step, and therefore it has received signed t-consistent shares for P_i from D with grade 2. We have obtained a contradiction: the Graded Consistency property of GBC ensures that P_i has received, in fact, these shares with grade at least 1, and therefore has completed $\mathsf{cVSS_{auth}.Sh}$ with $s_i \neq \bot$.

Lemma 8. *$\mathsf{cVSS_{auth}}$ achieves Secrecy.*

Proof. We assume that D is honest with input secret s, and we show that the joint view of the byzantine parties before $\mathsf{cVSS_{auth}.Rec}$ starts is independent of s.

As D is honest, if f denotes the polynomial that D has chosen in Step 1 of $\mathsf{cVSS.Sh}$, every party P_i receives its signed shares $a_{ji} = f(j,i)$ and $b_{ij} = f(i,j)$ in Step 1. At this point, the byzantine parties' view contains the evaluations $f(i,j)$

where P_i or P_j is byzantine, hence at most t points on any row $f(i, y)$ and at most t points on any column $f(x, j)$. Since f has degree at most t in each variable, t points along any row or column are insufficient to interpolate the corresponding univariate polynomial. These evaluations impose no restriction on the possible value of $f(0, 0) = s$: for every s' there is a polynomial f' consistent with the byzantine parties' view such that $f'(0, 0) = s'$. Consequently, the byzantine parties' joint view after Step 1 is independent of D's secret s. In the following, we show that the further steps of cVSS.Sh where shares are disclosed do not reveal any additional information.

Since D is honest, every honest party sends ok in Step 2. Then, in Step 3, D publishes the shares of parties it has not received ok with grade 2 from, hence the shares of byzantine parties only, which reveal no new information.

Afterwards, in Step 5, every byzantine party P_j receives a_{ij} from every honest party P_i. Since D is honest, $a_{ji} = f(j, i) = b_{ji}$, which P_j has received from D in Step 1. Hence, no additional information is revealed.

In Step 6, an honest party P_j reveals b_{ji} only if it has not received $a_{ji} = b_{ji}$ in Step 5 from P_j. Since D is honest, P_j has received $b_{ji} = f(j, i) = a_{ji}$ from D in Step 1, and therefore, in this case, P_j is byzantine. Hence, the share b_{ji} was included in the byzantine parties' joint view since Step 1.

Similarly, in Step 7, an honest party P_i reveals a_{ji} only if P_j has revealed b_{ji} in Step 6. Since P_i is honest and D is honest, P_i has sent $a_{ji} = b_{ji} = f(j, i)$ to P_j in Step 5. Therefore P_j is byzantine, and no new information was revealed.

We may therefore conclude that the byzantine parties' joint view before cVSS$_\mathsf{auth}$.Rec is independent of the honest dealer's secret s.

Lemma 9. *cVSS$_{auth}$ achieves Correctness.*

Proof. We assume that D is honest with input s, and we show that each honest party P_i completes cVSS.Rec with output $y_i = s$. Since D is honest, Lemma 6 guarantees that the every honest party P_i completes cVSS$_\mathsf{auth}$.Sh with shares $b_{ij} = f(i, j)$ with $j \in [n]$, where f denotes the polynomial chosen by D in Step 1. In the following, we analyze the shares that each honest party P_i considers in cVSS$_\mathsf{auth}$.Rec.

We note that P_i receives shares from every honest party P_j with grade 2, and we show that P_i does not discard the shares received from P_j. P_i receives from party P_j the shares $b_{jk} = f(j, k)$ for $k \in [n]$, along with a signature from D (since D is honest) and a signature from P_j. If P_j has received P_k's signature $\sigma_{P_k}^{a_{jk}} = \sigma_{P_k}^{b_{jk}}$ for $a_{jk} = b_{jk}$ in Steps 5 or 7 of cVSS.Sh, then this signature is attached as well. Otherwise, P_j has sent (b_{jk}, j, k) along with D's signature and its own signature via GBC$_\mathsf{auth}$ in Step 6 of cVSS.Sh, and P_i has received this message with grade 2. If P_i has received an appropriate response from P_k to P_j with grade 2 via GBC$_\mathsf{auth}$ in Step 7 of cVSS.Sh, then P_i has received this response as well with grade 1, and therefore has attached P_k's signature to the share received by P_i in cVSS$_\mathsf{Rec}$. Hence, if P_j does not attach P_k's signature, P_i observes P_j's signed share b_{jk} in Step 6 of cVSS$_\mathsf{auth}$.Sh and does not observe an appropriate response from P_k in Step 7 of cVSS$_\mathsf{auth}$.Sh. Moreover, P_j's shares are t-consistent, hence P_i does not discard the shares received from P_j.

Next we show that, if P_i does not discard the shares received from a byzantine party P_j, then $b_{jk} = f(j,k)$ for every party P_k: P_i does not discard the shares received from P_j if it has received D's signature for each of these shares. Then, it must be that $b_{jk} = f(j,k)$, as the byzantine parties cannot forge D's signature.

Then, P_i defines $f_i(x,y)$ as a polynomial of degree at most t in each variable such that $f_i(j,k) = b_{jk} = f(j,k)$ for each undiscarded share b_{jk}. These are at least $(t+1) \cdot (t+1)$ (coming from the shares of the $n - t \geq t+1$ honest parties). Then, since $f(x,y)$ is also a polynomial of degree at most t in each variable, $f_i(x,y) = f(x,y)$, and thus P_i outputs $y_i = f_i(x,y) = f(x,y)$.

The next lemma will be useful in proving the Conditional Binding property.

Lemma 10. *If an honest party P_i completes $cVSS_{auth}.Sh$ with $happy_i = true$, then every honest party P_j has obtained t-consistent shares a_{kj}, b_{jk} with $k \in [n]$. Moreover, the honest parties' shares are pair-wise consistent: if P_j and P_k are two honest parties, then $a_{kj} = b_{kj}$.*

Proof. We first note that P_i has not set $\mathtt{happy}_i = \mathtt{false}$ in Step 4. Assuming that an honest party P_j has not received t-consistent shares from D, P_j has sent a $\mathtt{missing}$ message in Step 2, which P_i receives with grade 2. In Step 4, P_i has received D's response to P_j with grade 2, and this response consists of signed t-consistent shares. As P_i has received this response with grade 2, $\mathsf{GBC}_{\mathtt{auth}}$ ensures that P_j has received the same response with grade at least 1, and therefore now holds t-consistent shares.

It remains to show that the honest parties' shares are pair-wise consistent. As P_i has not set $\mathtt{happy}_i = \mathtt{false}$ in Step 8, it has not observed any pair of shares $(a_{kj}, k, j), (b_{kj}, k, j)$ signed by D such that $a_{kj} \neq b_{kj}$. Assuming that two honest parties P_i and P_j hold $a_{kj} \neq b_{kj}$, P_k would have announced this by sending (b_{kj}, k, j) along with D's signature in Step 6. Then, P_j would have responded by sending (a_{kj}, k, j) along with D's signature in Step 7. P_i would have received these messages with grade 2, and would have set $\mathtt{happy}_i = \mathtt{false}$ in Step 8. Therefore, honest parties' shares are pair-wise consistent.

Lemma 11. *$cVSS_{auth}$ achieves Conditional Binding.*

Proof. We assume that at least one honest party P_i holds $\mathtt{happy}_i = \mathtt{true}$, and we show that the joint view of the honest parties at the end of $cVSS_{auth}.Sh$ defines a value y' such that all honest parties output y' in $cVSS_{auth}.Rec$. In the following, we first show that the honest parties' shares at the end of $cVSS_{auth}.Sh$ lie on a unique polynomial $f'(x,y)$ of degree at most t in each variable. Afterwards, we show that, in $cVSS_{auth}.Rec$, every honest party outputs $y_i = f(0,0)$.

By Lemma 10, since P_i has completed $cVSS_{auth}.Sh$ with $\mathtt{happy}_i = \mathtt{true}$, the honest parties have obtained t-consistent shares that are also pair-wise consistent. We may then consider the set $\mathcal{H}$ containing the $t + 1$ honest parties with the lowest indices, and define a polynomial $f'(x,y)$ of degree at most t in each variable based on their consistency cross-checks: $f'(k,j) = a_{kj} = b_{kj}$ for every P_j, P_k in $\mathcal{H}$. These are $(t+1) \cdot (t+1)$ evaluations, and, as a bi-variate polynomial of degree at most t in each variable is uniquely defined by such constraints, they uniquely determine $f'(x, y)$. In the following, we show that all of the honest shares lie on the polynomial f'.

We first consider the shares b_{jk} with $k \in [n]$ of a party $P_j \in \mathcal{H}$. Recall that the shares b_{jk} with $k \in [n]$ of P_j are t-consistent, hence they lie on a unique polynomial $B(x)$ of degree at most t. By construction of f', $f'(j, k) = b_{jk} = B(k)$ for every $P_k \in \mathcal{H}$. The univariate polynomial $f'(j, y)$ also has degree at most t, and $B(x)$ and $f'(j, y)$ agree in $t + 1$ points. Hence they are identical, and $b_{jk} = B(k) = f'(j, k)$ for every $k \in [n]$.

Next, we note that the shares a_{kj} with $k \in [n]$ of any party $P_j \in \mathcal{H}$ also lie on f'. We recall that the shares a_{kj} with $k \in [n]$ are t-consistent, hence they lie on a unique polynomial $A(x)$ of degree at most t: $A(k) = a_{kj}$ for every $k \in [n]$. In addition, $a_{kj} = b_{kj} = f'(k, j)$ for every $P_k \in \mathcal{H}$. The univariate polynomial $f'(x, j)$ also has degree at most t, and $A(x)$ and $f'(x, j)$ agree in $t + 1$ points. Hence, they are identical: $a_{kj} = A(k) = f'(k, k)$ for every $k \in [n]$.

It remains to consider the shares b_{jk} with $k \in [n]$ of honest parties $P_j \notin \mathcal{H}$. These shares are also t-consistent: they lie on a unique polynomial $B(x)$ of degree at most t: $B(k) = b_{jk}$. P_j has obtained $b_{jk} = a_{jk} = f'(j, k)$ for every $P_k \in \mathcal{H}$. Hence $B(x)$ and $f'(j, y)$ agree in at least $t + 1$ points. Since $f'(j, y)$ is also a univariate polynomial of degree at most t, $f'(j, y)$ and $B(x)$ are identical. Hence, $b_{jk} = B(k) = f'(j, k)$ for every $k \in [n]$.

Consequently, the shares of all honest parties lie on a well-defined polynomial $f'(x, y)$ of degree at most t in each variable. We may now analyze $\mathsf{cVSS_{auth}.Rec}$ and show that every honest party P_l obtains $f_l(x, y) = f'(x, y)$ and therefore outputs $y_l = f_l(0, 0) = f'(0, 0)$. Every honest party P_l receives the shares b_{jk} with $k \in [n]$ of each honest party P_j, along with corresponding signatures: D's signature of D, P_j's signature, and possibly P_k's signature. If P_j has received the signature of P_k in Step 5 of $\mathsf{cVSS_{auth}.Sh}$, this signature is attached. Otherwise, P_j has sent (b_{jk}, j, k) along with D's signature via $\mathsf{GBC_{auth}}$ in Step 6 of $\mathsf{cVSS_{auth}.Sh}$, and P_i has received this message with grade 2. If P_l has observed an appropriate response to P_j from P_k with grade 2 in Step 7 of $\mathsf{cVSS_{auth}.Sh}$, then P_j has received this response as well with grade at least 1, thus has attached P_k's signature to its share in $\mathsf{cVSS_{auth}.Rec}$. Moreover, the shares b_{jk} with $k \in [n]$ are t-consistent: otherwise, no honest party P_i would hold $\mathsf{happy}_i = \mathsf{true}$. Hence, P_l does not discard the shares of P_j. Then, it must be that $f_l(j, k) = b_{j,k} = f'(j, k)$ for every honest party P_j, and for every party P_k.

P_l additionally receives shares from up to t byzantine parties. We show that, if P_l does not discard the shares of a byzantine party P_j, then these must also lie on f'. P_l receives the shares b_{jk} with $k \in [n]$ from party P_j, along with corresponding signatures: D's signature, P_j's signature, and possibly P_k's signature. The shares b_{jk} with $k \in [n]$ are t-consistent, hence they lie on a polynomial $B(x)$ degree at most t – otherwise, P_l discards these shares. We then analyze the shares b_{jk} where P_k is honest. If P_j has attached P_k's signature on this share, then $b_{jk} = a_{jk} = f'(j, k)$. Otherwise, since P_l does not discard the share of P_j, P_l has received from P_j the share (b_{jk}, j, k) along with D's signature with grade 2 via $\mathsf{GBC_{auth}}$ in Step 6 of $\mathsf{cVSS_{auth}.Sh}$, and a response with grade 2 from P_k in Step 7.

In Step 8 of $\mathsf{cVSS_{auth}.Sh}$, P_i, holding $\mathsf{happy}_i := \mathsf{true}$, has received these messages from P_j with grade at least 1, and from P_k with grade 2, and has observed that $b_{jk} = a_{jk}$. P_l has also observed the response of P_k with grade 2 in Step 7: hence, in this case P_l discards the shares of P_j. We have therefore obtained that, if P_l does not discard the shares of P_j, then $b_{jk} = B(k) = f'(j,k)$ for the $n - t \geq t + 1$ honest parties P_k. As both $B(x)$ and $f'(j,x)$ are univariate polynomials of degree at most t, $B(x)$ and $f'(j,x)$ must be identical, and $b_{jk} = f'(j,k)$ for every $k \in [n]$.

We have obtained that, if P_l does not discard the shares of P_j, it must be that $b_{jk} = f'(j,k)$ for every $k \in [n]$. As P_l considers the shares of at least $n - t \geq t + 1$ parties, these uniquely determine a polynomial $f_l(x,y)$ of degree at most t in each variable. Then, since both $f_l(x,y)$ and $f'(x,y)$ are polynomials of degree at most t in each variable that agree in at least $(t+1) \cdot (t+1)$ points, it must be that $f_l(x,y) = f'(x,y)$. Consequently, P_l outputs $y_l = f_l(0,0) = f'(0,0)$.

6   ProxCoin

We now introduce the construction of our (ℓ, δ)-ProxCoin protocol $\mathsf{ProxCoin}$. The protocol uses as building blocks: (i) an ℓ_{Prox}-Proxcensus protocol Prox secure up to t corruptions with R_{Prox} rounds, and (ii) a cVSS protocol secure up to t corruptions with R_{Sh} for sharing and R_{Rec} for reconstruction. We first state the theorem achieved from the two building blocks.

Theorem 6. *Let $t < n$, $\ell \geq 2$ and $\ell_{Prox} < \ell$. Further let $\mathbf{Prox}$ and cVSS denote the building blocks as described above. Then, $\mathbf{ProxCoin}$ is a (ℓ, δ)-ProxCoin protocol with $\delta = \lceil t \cdot (\ell - 1)/(\ell_{Prox} - 1) \rceil$ secure up to t corruptions with round complexity $R_{ProxCoin} := R_{Prox} + R_{Sh} + R_{Rec}$.*

By instantiating the underlying building blocks Prox and cVSS, we obtain $\mathsf{ProxCoin}$ protocols secure against $t < n/3$ corruptions in the plain model, and against $t < n/2$ corruptions assuming a bulletin-board PKI. The first corollary is achieved by instantiating Prox with an unauthenticated protocol (which follows from replacing a building block in the protocol of [30] with an unauthenticated version presented in [5]) which we describe in the full version of our paper, and cVSS with that of Theorem 4.

Corollary 1. *Let $L \geq \frac{2t}{n-2t}$ and $\ell = \lfloor \frac{1}{2} \left(\frac{n-2t}{t} \right)^L L^L \rfloor$ be natural numbers. Then, $\mathbf{ProxCoin}$ is a (ℓ, δ)-ProxCoin protocol with $\delta := t$, secure up to $t < n/3$ corruptions with round complexity $R_{ProxCoin} = 3 \cdot L + 11$.*

The second corollary is achieved by instantiating Prox with the protocol introduced in [30] and cVSS with the protocol described by Theorem 5.

Corollary 2. *Consider a constant $\varepsilon > 0$. Let $L \geq \frac{1}{\varepsilon} - 1$, $\ell = \lfloor \frac{1}{2} \left(\frac{2\varepsilon}{1-\varepsilon} \right)^L L^L \rfloor$ be natural numbers. Then, $\mathbf{ProxCoin}$ is (ℓ, δ)-ProxCoin protocol with $\delta := t$, secure up to $t = (1 - \varepsilon)n/2$ corruptions with round complexity $R_{ProxCoin} := 3 \cdot L + 17$.*

Protocol Description. We describe the protocol below. Each party shares a uniform random value using cVSS, and then, following the approach of [26], the final coin will be computed as a *weighted sum* of the reconstructed shares. The weights satisfy a few properties: (i) the weights w^j computed for each corrupted P_j differ by at most $1/(\ell_{\texttt{Prox}} - 1)$; (ii) if the share of a corrupted party P_j cannot be reconstructed, every honest party obtains $w^j = 0$, and (iii) every honest party obtains $w^j = 1$ for every honest party P_j. These properties ensure that the honest parties' coins are well-defined, and differ by at most $\delta := \lceil t \cdot (\ell - 1)/(\ell_{\texttt{Prox}} - 1) \rceil$.

Protocol: ProxCoin

Building Blocks: An $\ell_{\texttt{Prox}}$-Proxcensus Prox, and cVSS.

Parameters: ℓ number of slots and $\delta = \lceil t \cdot (\ell - 1)/(\ell_{\texttt{Prox}} - 1) \rceil$ the difference of number of slots between honest parties.

Player P_i does the following:

1: Choose x_i uniformly at random from $\{0, \ldots, \ell - 1\}$.
2: Distribute the secret x_i to all parties via cVSS.Sh.
3: Denote the outputs of the cVSS.Sh invocation having P_j as dealer by $s_i^j, \texttt{happy}_i^j$.
4: For every party P_j, join Prox with input $\texttt{happy}_i^j$. Upon obtaining output z_i^j, set $w_i^j := z_i^j/(\ell_{\texttt{Prox}} - 1)$.
5: For every party P_j, join the cVSS.Rec invocation having P_j as dealer with input s_i^j and let x_i^j denote the secret obtained. If $x_i^j = \bot$, set $x_i^j := 0$.
6: Output $\left\lceil \sum_{P_j} w_i^j \cdot x_i^j \right\rceil \mod \ell$.

Analysis. We split the proof of Theorem 6 into multiple lemmas: Lemma 15 ensures that One Uniform Randomness holds, and Lemma 16 discusses Consistency, establishing that the ProxCoin requirements are satisfied. The round complexity in Theorem 6 follows from the description. We first discuss some properties.

Lemma 12. *If P_j is honest, every honest party P_i obtains $w_i^j := 1$ and $x_i^j = x_j$.*

Proof. By the Sharing-Validity property of cVSS, every party P_i holds $\texttt{happy}_i^j = \texttt{true}$ for every honest party P_j at the end of the cVSS.Sh invocation with dealer P_j. Then, the Validity property of Prox then ensures that every party obtains $s_i^j = \ell_{\texttt{Prox}} - 1$, and therefore $w_i^j = 1$. In addition, cVSS's Correctness ensures that, at the end of the cVSS.Rec invocation having P_j as dealer, P_i obtains $x_i^j = x_j$.

Lemma 13. *If an honest party P_i obtains $x_i^k := \bot$ for some party P_k, then P_k is corrupted and every honest party P_j obtains $w_j^k := 0$.*

Proof. Due to the Conditional Binding property of cVSS, if P_i obtains $x_i^k := \bot$, every honest party P_j holds $\texttt{happy}_j^k = \texttt{false}$ at the end of the cVSS.Sh invocation having P_k as a dealer. Therefore, all honest parties join Prox with input 0, and the Validity guarantee of Prox ensures that every honest party P_j obtains $s_j^k = 0$, hence sets $w_j^k := 0$. Moreover, the Sharing-Validity property of cVSS ensures that if some honest party P_j obtains $\text{happy}_j^k := \text{false}$, then P_k is corrupted.

Lemma 14. *Assume an honest party P_i obtains $w_i^l > 0$ for some party P_l. Then, there is a value x such that every honest party P_j obtains $x_j^l = x$. Moreover, if both P_j and P_k are honest, $\left| w_j^l - w_k^l \right| \leq 1/(\ell_{Prox-1})$.*

Proof. P_i has obtained $w_i^l > 0$, and therefore $s_i^l > 0$. Prox's Validity property ensures that there is some honest party P_r that has obtained $\text{happy}_r^l = \text{true}$ in the cVSS.Sh invocation with dealer P_l. Then, cVSS's Conditional Binding ensures that there is a value x uniquely defined by the honest parties s^l such that every honest party P_j obtains $x_j^l = x$. Afterwards, Prox's Consistency ensures that, if P_j and P_k are honest, they obtain slots $s_j^l, s_k^l \in [0, \ell_{\text{Prox}} - 1]$, such that $\left| s_j^l - s_k^l \right| \leq 1$ and consequently $\left| w_j^l - w_k^l \right| \leq 1/(\ell_{\text{Prox}-1})$.

Lemma 15. *ProxCoin achieves One Uniform Randomness.*

Proof. As established by Lemma 12, every honest party P_i assigns weight $w_i^j = 1$ and $x_i^j = x_j$ for every honest party P_j. Since honest parties have chosen their secrets x uniformly at random from $\mathbb{Z}_\ell$, the sum $\sum_{\text{honest } P_j} w_i^j \cdot x_i^j \mod \ell$ is also uniformly distributed over $\mathbb{Z}_\ell$.

By Lemma 13, if an honest party P_i obtains $x_i^k = \perp$ at the end of the cVSS.Rec invocation having P_k as a dealer, then P_k is corrupted and every honest party P_j holds $w_j^k = 0$. Note that the summands corresponding to such corrupted parties P_k are not included in the overall weighted sum. Moreover, note that $x_i^k = \perp$ implies that all honest parties obtained $\text{happy}^k = \text{false}$ at the end of cVSS.Sh, so this value is chosen independently of the honest parties' secrets.

Lastly, we consider the corrupted parties P_k such that at least one honest party P_i holds $\text{happy}_k^i = \text{true}$. In this case, cVSS's Conditional Binding ensures that the honest parties obtain the same value x_i^k at the end of the Reconstruction phase, and this value was chosen independently of the honest parties' secrets x_i.

Note that for these parties, the corrupted parties can collude to shift the weights of honest parties. This is however not a problem, as the random values of the honest parties are only revealed once the weights for all parties are set.

As $\sum_{\text{honest } P_j} w_i^j \cdot x_i^j \mod \ell$ is uniformly distributed over $\mathbb{Z}_\ell$, the claim follows.

Lemma 16. *ProxCoin achieves Consistency for $\delta := \lceil t \cdot (\ell - 1)/(\ell_{Prox} - 1) \rceil$.*

Proof. Let c_i and c_j denote the outputs of two honest parties P_i and P_j. We show that $d_\ell(c_i, c_j) \leq \lceil t \cdot (\ell - 1)/(\ell_{\text{Prox}} - 1) \rceil$. We note that $d_\ell(x, y) = \min\{|x -$

$y|, \ell - |x-y|\} \leq |x-y|$, which enables us to upper bound for $d_\ell(c_i, c_j)$ as follows:

$$d_\ell(c_i, c_j) = d_\ell\left(\left\lceil \sum_{P_k} w_i^k \cdot x_i^k \right\rceil \mod \ell, \left\lceil \sum_{P_k} w_j^k \cdot x_j^k \right\rceil \mod \ell\right)$$

$$\leq \left|\left\lceil \sum_{P_k} w_i^k \cdot x_i^k \right\rceil - \left\lceil \sum_{P_k} w_j^k \cdot x_j^k \right\rceil\right|$$

$$\leq \left|\left\lceil \sum_{P_k} w_i^k \cdot x_i^k - \sum_{P_k} w_j^k \cdot x_j^k \right\rceil\right|$$

$$= \left|\left\lceil \sum_{P_k} w_i^k \cdot x_i^k - w_j^k \cdot x_j^k \right\rceil\right|$$

$$\leq \left\lceil \sum_{P_k} \left|w_i^k \cdot x_i^k - w_j^k \cdot x_j^k\right| \right\rceil .$$

We partition the set of parties into three sets: $\mathcal{H}$, denoting the set of honest parties, $\mathcal{B}_0$, denoting the set of corrupted parties P_k such that $w_i^k = w_j^k = 0$, and $\mathcal{B}_w$, denoting the set of corrupted parties P_k such that $w_i^k > 0$ or $w_j^k > 0$ We may then write $\sum_{P_k} \left|w_i^k \cdot x_i^k - w_j^k \cdot x_j^k\right|$ as follows, which enables us to provide an upper bound by analyzing the sums over $\mathcal{H}$, $\mathcal{B}_0$, and $\mathcal{B}_w$ separately:

$$\sum_{P_k} \left|w_i^k \cdot x_i^k - w_j^k \cdot x_j^k\right| = \sum_{P_k \in \mathcal{H}} \left|w_i^k \cdot x_i^k - w_j^k \cdot x_j^k\right| +$$

$$\sum_{P_k \in \mathcal{B}_0} \left|w_i^k \cdot x_i^k - w_j^k \cdot x_j^k\right| +$$

$$\sum_{P_k \in \mathcal{B}_w} \left|w_i^k \cdot x_i^k - w_j^k \cdot x_j^k\right| .$$

We first consider the sum over $\mathcal{H}$: Lemma 12 ensures that, for every honest party P_k, P_i and P_j have obtained weights w_i^k and w_k^j such that $w_i^k = w_j^k = 1$, and secrets x_i^k and x_j^k such that $x_i^k = x_j^k$. This implies that the weighted sums over the honest parties' values are equal, i.e. $\sum_{P_k \in \mathcal{H}} \left|w_i^k \cdot x_i^k - w_j^k \cdot x_j^k\right| = 0$. For the sum over $\mathcal{B}_0$, we obtain $\sum_{P_k \in \mathcal{B}_0} \left|w_i^k \cdot x_i^k - w_j^k \cdot x_j^k\right| = 0$ since $w_i^k = w_j^k = 0$ for every party $P_k \in \mathcal{B}_0$. It remains to discuss the sum over $\mathcal{B}_w$. In this case, Lemma 14 ensures that, for every party $P_k \in \mathcal{B}_w$, P_i and P_j have obtained weights w_i^k and w_j^k satisfying $\left|w_i^k - w_j^k\right| \leq 1/(\ell_{\text{Prox}} - 1)$ and have reconstructed $x_i^k = x_j^k = x$. This implies that, $\left|w_i^k \cdot x_i^k - w_j^k \cdot x_j^k\right| = \left|(w_i^k - w_j^k) \cdot x\right| \leq (\ell - 1)/(\ell_{\text{Prox}} - 1)$. Moreover, we note that $|\mathcal{B}_w| \leq t$, which enables us to conclude that $\sum_{P_k \in \mathcal{B}_w} \left|w_i^k \cdot x_i^k - w_j^k \cdot x_j^k\right| \leq t \cdot (\ell - 1)/(\ell_{\text{Prox}} - 1)$.

Consequently, we have shown that $\sum_{P_k} \left|w_i^k \cdot x_i^k - w_j^k \cdot x_j^k\right| \leq t \cdot (\ell-1)/(\ell_{\text{Prox}} - 1)$, and hence $d_\ell(c_i, c_j) \leq \lceil t \cdot (\ell - 1)/(\ell_{\text{Prox}} - 1)\rceil$. We may therefore conclude that δ-Consistency holds for $\delta = \lceil t \cdot (\ell - 1)/(\ell_{\text{Prox}} - 1)\rceil$.

7 Putting It all Together

We may now combine the results presented in the previous sections and state our final theorems. We defer the complete proofs to the full version of the paper.

In the plain model, we may rely on the Proxcensus protocol described in the full version of the paper and on the ProxCoin protocol of Corollary 1. By using these protocols in $\Pi_{\text{EE}}^{\ell+1}$, Theorem 3 enables us to state the following result.

Theorem 7. *Let $L \geq \frac{2t}{n-2t}$ be a natural number such that $L^L > t^2$ and $\ell = \lfloor \frac{1}{2} \left(\frac{n-2t}{t} \right)^L L^L \rfloor \geq 2$. Then, if $r = L/2$, there is a $(12r + 11)$-round Byzantine Agreement protocol secure against $t < n/3$ corruptions that achieves Agreement except with probability $12 \cdot \left(2 \cdot \left(\frac{n-2t}{t} \right)^2 \right)^{-r} \cdot r^{-r}$.*

In the authenticated setting, Theorem 3 provides the result below, relying on the Proxcensus protocol of [30] and on the ProxCoin protocol of Corollary 2.

Theorem 8. *Consider a constant $\varepsilon > 0$, and let $L \geq \frac{1}{\varepsilon} - 1$ be a natural number such that $L^L > t^2$ and $\ell = \lfloor \frac{1}{2} \left(\frac{2\varepsilon}{1-\varepsilon} \right)^L L^L \rfloor \geq 2$. Then, if $r = L/2$, there is a $(12r + 17)$-round authenticated Byzantine Agreement protocol secure against $t = (1 - \varepsilon)n/2$ corruptions that achieves Agreement except with probability $12 \cdot \left(2 \cdot \left(\frac{2\varepsilon}{1-\varepsilon} \right)^2 \right)^{-r} \cdot r^{-r}$.*

References

1. Abraham, I., Devadas, S., Dolev, D., Nayak, K., Ren, L.: Synchronous Byzantine agreement with expected $O(1)$ rounds, expected $o(n^2)$ communication, and optimal resilience. In: International Conference on Financial Cryptography and Data Security, pp. 320–334. Springer (2019)
2. Alexandru, A.B., Loss, J., Papamanthou, C., Tsimos, G., Wagner, B.: Sublinear-round broadcast without trusted setup. In: Azar, Y., Panigrahi, D. (eds.) 36th SODA, pp. 4132–4171. ACM-SIAM, January 2025
3. Attiya, H., Censor-Hillel, K.: Lower bounds for randomized consensus under a weak adversary. SIAM J. Comput. **39**(8), 3885–3904 (2010)
4. Ben-Or, M.: Another advantage of free choice: Completely asynchronous agreement protocols (extended abstract). In: Proceedings of the 2nd Annual ACM Symposium on Principles of Distributed Computing (PODC), pp. 27–30 (1983)
5. Ben-Or, M., Dolev, D., Hoch, E.N.: Brief announcement: Simple gradecast based algorithms. In: Lynch, N.A., Shvartsman, A.A. (eds.) Distributed Computing, pp. 194–197. Springer, Heidelberg (2010)
6. Ben-Or, M., Goldwasser, S., Wigderson, A.: Completeness theorems for non-cryptographic fault-tolerant distributed computation (extended abstract). In: 20th ACM STOC, pp. 1–10. ACM Press, May 1988
7. Boyle, E., Cohen, R., Goel, A.: Breaking the $O(\sqrt{(n)})$-bit barrier: Byzantine agreement with polylog bits per party. In: Miller, A., Censor-Hillel, K., Korhonen, J.H. (eds.) 40th ACM PODC, pp. 319–330. ACM, July 2021

8. Cachin, C., Kursawe, K., Shoup, V.: Random oracles in Constantinople: Practical asynchronous byzantine agreement using cryptography. J. Cryptol. **18**(3), 219–246 (2005)
9. Castro, M., Liskov, B.: Practical Byzantine fault tolerance. In: OSDI **99**, 173–186 (1999)
10. Hubert Chan, T.-H., Pass, R., Shi, E.: Round complexity of Byzantine agreement, revisited. Cryptology ePrint Archive, Report 2019/886 (2019). https://ia.cr/2019/886
11. Chan, T.-H.H., Pass, R., Shi, E.: Sublinear-Round Byzantine Agreement Under Corrupt Majority. In: Kiayias, A., Kohlweiss, M., Wallden, P., Zikas, V. (eds.) PKC 2020. LNCS, vol. 12111, pp. 246–265. Springer, Cham (2020). https://doi.org/10.1007/978-3-030-45388-6_9
12. Chen, J., Micali, S.: Algorand: A secure and efficient distributed ledger. Theoret. Comput. Sci. **777**, 155–183 (2019)
13. Chor, B., Merritt, M., Shmoys, D.B.: Simple constant-time consensus protocols in realistic failure models. J. ACM (JACM) **36**(3), 591–614 (1989)
14. Cohen, R., Coretti, S., Garay, J.A., Zikas, V.: Probabilistic termination and composability of cryptographic protocols. In: Robshaw, M., Katz, J. (eds.) CRYPTO 2016. Part III, volume 9816 of LNCS, pp. 240–269. Springer, Berlin, Heidelberg (2016)
15. Cohen, R., Coretti, S., Garay, J.A., Zikas, V.: Round-preserving parallel composition of probabilistic-termination cryptographic protocols. In: Chatzigiannakis, I., Indyk, P., Kuhn, F., Muscholl, A. (eds.) ICALP 2017, vol. 80. LIPIcs, pp. 37:1–37:15. Schloss Dagstuhl, July 2017
16. Cohen, R., Haitner, I., Makriyannis, N., Orland, M., Samorodnitsky, A.: On the round complexity of randomized Byzantine agreement. In: Suomela, J. (ed.) 33rd International Symposium on Distributed Computing (DISC 2019), vol. 146. Leibniz International Proceedings in Informatics (LIPIcs), pp. 12:1–12:17, Dagstuhl, Germany (2019). Schloss Dagstuhl–Leibniz-Zentrum fuer Informatik
17. Cramer, R., Damgård, I., Dziembowski, S., Hirt, M., Rabin, T.: Efficient multiparty computations secure against an adaptive adversary. In: Stern, J. (ed.) EUROCRYPT'99. LNCS, vol. 1592, pp. 311–326. Springer, Heidelberg (1999)
18. Dolev, D., Strong, H.: Authenticated algorithms for Byzantine agreement. SIAM J. Comput. **12**, 656–666 (1983)
19. Dolev, D., Yao, A.: On the security of public key protocols. IEEE Trans. Inf. Theory **29**(2), 198–208 (1983)
20. Feldman, P., Micali, S.: Optimal algorithms for byzantine agreement. In: 20th ACM STOC, pp. 148–161. ACM Press, May 1988
21. Feldman, P., Micali, S.: An optimal probabilistic protocol for synchronous Byzantine agreement. SIAM J. Comput. **26**(4), 873–933 (1997)
22. Fischer, M.J., Lynch, N.A.: A lower bound for the time to assure interactive consistency. Inf. Process. Lett. **14**(4), 183–186 (1982)
23. Fitzi, M., Garay, J.A.: Efficient player-optimal protocols for strong and differential consensus. In: Borowsky, E., Rajsbaum, S. (eds.) 22nd ACM PODC, pp. 211–220. ACM, July 2003
24. Fitzi, M., Liu-Zhang, C.-D., Loss, J.: A new way to achieve round-efficient byzantine agreement. In: Miller, A., Censor-Hillel, K., Korhonen, J.H., (eds.) 40th ACM PODC, pages 355–362. ACM, July 2021
25. Fitzi, M., Nielsen, J.B.: On the number of synchronous rounds sufficient for authenticated Byzantine agreement. In: International Symposium on Distributed Computing, pp. 449–463. Springer (2009)

26. Freitas, L., Kuznetsov, P., Tonkikh, A.: Distributed randomness from approximate agreement. In: Scheideler, C., (ed.) 36th International Symposium on Distributed Computing (DISC 2022), vol. 246. Leibniz International Proceedings in Informatics (LIPIcs), pp. 24:1–24:21, Dagstuhl, Germany, Schloss Dagstuhl – Leibniz-Zentrum für Informatik (2022)
27. Garay, J.A., Katz, J., Koo, C.-Y., Ostrovsky, R.: Round complexity of authenticated broadcast with a dishonest majority. In: 48th FOCS, pp. 658–668. IEEE Computer Society Press, October 2007
28. Garay, J.A., Moses, Y.: Fully polynomial byzantine agreement in t+1 rounds. In: Proceedings of the 25th Annual ACM Symposium on Theory of Computing (STOC), pp. 31–41 (1993)
29. Gennaro, R., Ishai, Y., Kushilevitz, E., Rabin, T.: The round complexity of verifiable secret sharing and secure multicast. In: Proceedings of the Thirty-Third Annual ACM Symposium on Theory of Computing, STOC '01, pp. 580–589. Association for Computing Machinery, New York (2001)
30. Ghinea, D., Goyal, V., Liu-Zhang, C.-D.: Round-optimal byzantine agreement. In: Eurocrypt 2022, Trondheim, Norway, May 2022
31. Karlin, A.R., Yao, A.C.: Probabilistic lower bounds for Byzantine agreement and clock synchronization (1984)
32. Katz, J., Koo, C.-Y.: On expected constant-round protocols for byzantine agreement. In: Dwork, C. (ed.) CRYPTO 2006. LNCS, vol. 4117, pp. 445–462. Springer, Heidelberg (2006)
33. Lamport, L., Shostak, R., Pease, M.: The Byzantine generals problem. ACM Trans. Program. Lang. Syst. **4**(3), 382–401 (1982)
34. Libert, B., Joye, M., Yung, M.: Born and raised distributively: fully distributed non-interactive adaptively-secure threshold signatures with short shares. In: Halldórsson, M.M., Dolev, S. (eds.) 33rd ACM PODC, pp. 303–312. ACM, July 2014
35. Lindell, Y., Lysyanskaya, A., Rabin, T.: On the composition of authenticated Byzantine agreement. J.ACM (JACM) **53**(6), 881–917 (2006)
36. Micali, S., Vaikuntanathan, V.: Optimal and player-replaceable consensus with an honest majority (2017)
37. Pease, M., Shostak, R., Lamport, L.: Reaching agreement in the presence of faults. J. ACM **27**(2), 228–234 (1980)
38. Pfitzmann, B., Waidner, M.: Information-theoretic pseudosignatures and Byzantine agreement for $t \geq n/3$. IBM (1996)
39. Rabin, M.O.: Randomized byzantine generals. In: 24th FOCS, pp. 403–409. IEEE Computer Society Press, November 1983
40. Srinivasan, S., Loss, J., Malavolta, G., Nayak, K., Papamanthou, C., Thyagarajan, S.A.K.: Transparent batchable time-lock puzzles and applications to byzantine consensus. In: Proceedings of the 26th International Conference on the Theory and Practice of Public-Key Cryptography (PKC), part I, pp. 554–584 (2023)
41. Turpin, R., Coan, B.A.: Extending binary Byzantine agreement to multivalued Byzantine agreement. Inf. Process. Lett. **18**(2), 73–76 (1984)
42. Wan, J., Xiao, H., Devadas, S., Shi, E.: Round-efficient byzantine broadcast under strongly adaptive and majority corruptions. In: Pass, R., Pietrzak, K. (eds.) TCC 2020. Part I, volume 12550 of LNCS, pp. 412–456. Springer, Cham (2020)
43. Wan, J., Xiao, H., Shi, E., Devadas, S.: Expected constant round byzantine broadcast under dishonest majority. In: Pass, R., Pietrzak, K. (eds.) TCC 2020. Part I, vol. 12550. LNCS, pp. 381–411. Springer, Cham (2020)

When Trying to Catch Cheaters Breaks the MPC: Breaking and Fixing Delayed Consistency Checks in Trident, Fantastic Four, SWIFT, and Quad

Andreas Brüggemann[(✉)] and Thomas Schneider

Technical University of Darmstadt, Darmstadt, Germany
{brueggemann,schneider}@encrypto.cs.tu-darmstadt.de

Abstract. Actively secure multi-party computation in the honest-majority setting often relies on multiple parties computing the same message to be sent. This additional redundancy allows to detect when a party deviates from the protocol. Many works utilize this for efficient protocol design, with some protocols delaying and batching consistency checks to further boost efficiency. In this paper, we show multiple cases where such batched consistency checks render the protocols insecure. Our concrete attacks derive additional knowledge from the batched consistency checks, reconstructing values on intermediate wires. Specifically, we show concrete attacks on Trident (NDSS'20), Fantastic Four (USENIX Security'21) including its implementation in the popular MP-SPDZ framework (CCS'20), and Quad (PoPETS'25). Furthermore, we find how an imprecise specification of SWIFT (USENIX Security'21) can enable a similar attack and reveal a gap in their security proof. Finally, we propose a fix for all protocols with a small performance overhead. Our provably secure fix uses a generic, joint consistency check that replaces the former, insecure consistency checks.

1 Introduction

Secure multi-party computation (MPC) enables multiple parties to compute a function on their joint private inputs without any need to disclose their inputs to each other. Especially MPC with a low number of parties and an honest majority where the adversary can only corrupt less than half of the parties is receiving lots of attention due to the availability of highly efficient protocols, e.g., [1,3,10,21,30]. Motivating applications are secure computations of large functionalities such as privacy-preserving machine learning [10,30] or analysis of large graphs [2,26]. In the active/malicious security model, where the adversary can arbitrarily change the behavior of corrupted parties, an honest majority was shown especially useful, exploiting redundancy of intermediate data to detect deviations from the protocol [6,7,12,14,17,21,28].

In this work, we investigate the family of protocols from [12,14,21,28], designed to be secure against a single malicious party. They detect protocol

© International Association for Cryptologic Research 2026
J. Daemen and E. Thomé (Eds.): EUROCRYPT 2026, LNCS 16543, pp. 457–487, 2026.
https://doi.org/10.1007/978-3-032-25324-8_16

deviations by having for each message sent by some party P_A a second party P_B who can compute and provide the same message, hence introducing redundancy. The party that receives the message from P_A should get the same information from P_B, and in case of any inconsistency between the received messages, securely aborts the protocol execution. To avoid overhead from sending redundant information, the redundant material sent by P_B is delayed during an optimistic protocol execution, where only in the end, before revealing any outputs, redundancy information is transmitted in a batched, compressed way, resulting in zero amortized overhead. Intuitively, this will still detect any inconsistency introduced by a cheating party. In this work, we observe that without an immediate consistency check, a cheater can provide incorrect data to an honest party P_A without immediately being detected, "poisoning" the internal state of P_A. Now, an operation using this poisoned state where P_A sends a message to the cheater eventually requires another honest party P_B to provide the same, redundant information to the cheater to ensure consistency. This may result in an additional inconsistency, given that P_A computes its message on poisoned data so that it can deviate from what P_B sends. The cheater then tries to extract additional information, using the difference between the messages received from P_A, P_B. Such an attack is enabled only by the delayed consistency check. Otherwise, a corrupted party would always receive consistent data from the immediate consistency check, given that the other parties are honest. On the other side, should a party receive inconsistent data during a check, one of the providers would be malicious and, thus, the receiver learns more information, but must be honest, preserving the protocol's security. Yet, the protocols' outstanding performance relies on not having to check for inconsistency immediately after each step.

1.1 Our Contributions

Our contributions are summarized in the following, and an overview of our attacks on the protocols in [12, 14, 21, 28] is given in Table 1.

Vulnerability of Delayed Consistency Checks: We identify and point out the aforementioned generic attack pattern on delayed consistency checks, where a cheater poisons the state of an honest party without immediate detection, using this and later consistency checks to extract private information. Doing that, we observe a dangerous trend where the delayed, batched consistency check is textually described in the respective papers while not being properly included in the formal protocol specification. The original proofs implicitly assume the unoptimized, formal protocol specification, proving secure only an intermediate, simplified, and less efficient version of the protocol. It appears that this discrepancy and the resulting vulnerability have then been carried along in research for more improved protocols without being noticed, given that [14, 21] even cite [28] as the basis for their consistency checks. The reuse of the vulnerable construction appears to be ongoing, given the newness of [21] and the same idea appearing in more works such as [7, 29] while not always opening an attack surface.

Table 1. Number of parties and corrupted parties, exact security model (within active security), amortized cost per multiplication (offline + online), vulnerability to our attack, and global communication cost of our proposed fix w.r.t. the evaluated circuit.

Protocol		#Parties	#Corr.	Security	cost/mult.	Insecure?	Fix overhead
Trident [12]	(§3)	$3+1$	1	Fair	$3+3$	Yes	$\mathcal{O}(1)$
Fantastic Four [14]	(§4)	4	1	Robust	$0+6$	Yes	$\mathcal{O}(1)/\mathcal{O}(d)$ [a]
SWIFT [28]	(§5)	3	1	Robust	$3+3$	Depends [b]	$-$ [c]
Quad [21]	(§6)	$3+1$	1	Fair	$2+3$	Yes	$\mathcal{O}(1)$

[a] d: circuit depth; $\mathcal{O}(1)$ for fair protocol variant; $\mathcal{O}(d)$ for robust variant
[b] Protocol underspecified, possible protocol within the specification is insecure
[c] Protocol appears fixable by appropriate, unambiguous specification

Concrete Attacks: Using our generic attack, we discover explicit attacks on the protocols of Trident [12], Fantastic Four [14], SWIFT [28], and Quad [21]. For Trident, Fantastic Four, and Quad, flaws in the consistency check enable testing for or even extracting values on input wires to multiplication/AND-gates in arithmetic/binary circuits, especially for gates on the last layer of a circuit. In SWIFT, another orthogonal optimization appears to almost inadvertently thwart our attack, still leaving a gap in the security proof, as the optimization is not consciously used for security reasons. Still, we find that SWIFT's under-specified input phase can still enable the extraction of values on some wires.

Efficient Fixes: We provide a generic construction that mitigates our attack by outsourcing the complete consistency check to a small MPC protocol execution. Prior consistency checks consist of multiple partial checks for each pair of sender and receiver, and the partial check where a cheater initially provides incorrect data will always fail. By batching all individual checks in a single protocol that outputs only a single bit, indicating if *any* inconsistency has been detected (but not which one), a cheating attempt will always lead to output 0, leaking nothing. We prove that our fix is secure, i.e., that it maintains soundness of the verification and does not leak any unintended data. It comes at zero amortized and a low concrete overhead with low, constant rounds. We instantiate and use it to fix Trident [12], Fantastic Four [14] with fairness, and Quad [21]. Regarding the robust variant of Fantastic Four, we propose a fix that comes at an overhead linear in the circuit depth, and we fix SWIFT [28] by a less ambiguous specification.

Impact on MPC Implementations: Several MPC implementations were vulnerable to our attacks. Fantastic Four [14] is available in MP-SPDZ [24], the most popular code framework for MPC, and directly inherits the flaw of the insecure protocol specification. Furthermore, the recent framework HPMPC [20] published together with Quad [21] provides not only an implementation of Quad, but also implements Fantastic Four, inheriting the security flaws of two protocols. Finally, the oblivious analytics system ORQ [4] uses a vulnerable implementation of Fantastic Four as one of its protocol back ends.

Responsible Disclosure: We have notified the maintainers of the affected implementations MP-SPDZ [24], HPMPC [20], and ORQ [4]. Together, we have coordinated that the issues were addressed before our attack was publicly disclosed. Simultaneously, we have contacted all authors of the papers proposing vulnerable protocols considered in this work [12,14,21,28]. For more information, see §7.

1.2 Related Work

Our attack essentially introduces an error in one path of the computation and uses another correctly executed path, intended to normally provide redundancy, to generate an inconsistency and extract secrets from that. The concept of introducing errors in some computation paths is related to fault attacks, and a prominent example is [5]. There, random or purposefully induced faults are used to extract secret keys in signature and identification schemes, given that no check for faults is done before faulty data is distributed.

In the space of MPC, our attack is conceptually similar to the "double-dipping attack" of [15,19]. This attack uses redundancy in DN-style [16] protocols for corruption thresholds where the double-degree polynomials are not full-threshold and, hence, not all shares are required for reconstruction. A malicious party exploits that by providing incorrect data to one party during a multiplication. In a subsequent multiplication, this party then provides incorrect data, inconsistent with the shares provided by the other parties. Like our attack, this is enabled as verification is delayed, allowing incorrect data to be used by honest parties before detection, while there also is redundancy. The pattern of attacking two consecutive multiplications is furthermore equal to what we will use for our attack. Our work differs in that the redundancy that is crucial for extracting secrets is introduced by the verification of the protocols we attack, whereas in the double-dipping attack, it is more centrally a part of the main protocol execution without verification. This difference also necessitates a fix to the verification in our case, whereas [15,19] deploy their fix in the protocol's main execution part. For a more detailed comparison to our work, we refer to the full version [8, App. E].

While our attack uses redundancy provided by a verification step of the targeted protocols, we emphasize that it is not a selective failure attack [25], where a malicious party can make the protocol conditionally abort, depending on other parties' private information. In our case, a party cheating is always detected. This detection consists of several partial detection steps, where individual ones may still fail depending on private inputs. Still, we are able to extract significantly more information than this single bit (per detection step).

Our fix (§3.5) generalizes the idea of [22] who compare two hashes with an MPC protocol in the two-party setting to multiple hashes and parties.

Outline. After the preliminaries (§2), we provide a detailed explanation of our attack on Trident [12] in §3, including a generic construction to fix the underlying issues inexpensively. After this introduction of the attack's concept and fix, we translate these to Fantastic Four [14] (§4) while also discussing additional challenges to reach robustness. In §5, we discover that SWIFT's [28] structure almost thwarts our generic attack, but document a gap in its security proof and show possible alternative attacks. Finally, in §6 we briefly remark on how our attack and fix translate to Quad [21] with details in the full version [8, App. D].

2   Preliminaries

Notation. In this work, we mainly consider parties $P_1, \ldots, P_n$. In some cases, we may change the numbering to be consistent with the respective original protocol later. In some protocols, there is one party P_h acting as a helper that is absent from most or all of the protocol's online phase. In this case, we may explicitly define that P_h not to be among $P_1, \ldots, P_n$ for ease of notation. When referring to parties, we may write, e.g., P_{i+1} for $1 \leq i \leq n$ to refer to the next party after P_i in a circular way where P_{n+1} refers to P_1 again. Likewise, we may write P_{i-1} with P_{1-1} referring to P_n. P_h is not considered in this notation.

Computation is over a commutative and finite ring $\mathcal{R}$ which usually is either $\mathbb{Z}_{2^\ell}$ for ℓ-bit integers with $\ell \in \mathbb{N}$, or a finite field $\mathbb{F}_{p^k}$ for prime p and $k \in \mathbb{N}$.[1] Note that this also covers the case of binary computation on $\mathbb{Z}_2 = \mathbb{F}_2$. For sampling a uniformly random value r from $\mathcal{R}$, we write $r \leftarrow_\$ \mathcal{R}$.

We consider protocols based on linear secret sharing. By $[\![x]\!]$, we denote a private value $x \in \mathcal{R}$ which is secret shared between the parties according to the specific secret sharing scheme used in the respective protocol. Linearity of the scheme enables to compute $[\![ax + y + b]\!]$ given arbitrary shares $[\![x]\!], [\![y]\!]$ and public values $a, b \in \mathcal{R}$ without interaction. Some of the considered protocols use different linear secret sharing schemes, in which case we use notation $\langle \cdot \rangle$ with the above properties as an *intermediate sharing semantic*. As for parties, we refer to individual shares in a circular way, e.g., for a sharing $[\![x]\!]$ consisting of $x^1, \ldots x^n$, x^{i+1} corresponds to the next share after x^i and x^1 if $i = n$.

Finally, we denote the statistical security parameter by σ and the computational security parameter by κ. Usual parameter choices are $\sigma = 40$ and $\kappa = 128$ which are consistent with [12, 14, 21, 28] where applicable and stated.

Pseudorandom Functions (PRFs) for Joint, Non-interactive Randomness Generation. The protocols considered in this paper use PRFs to enable one or more parties, holding a random PRF key of length κ, to query a deterministic function (parametrized by the key) with the results being computationally indistinguishable from the results when querying a uniform random function. For details and a formal definition regarding PRFs, see [23]. To enable any subset of parties to sample common random values $r \leftarrow_\$ \mathcal{R}$ non-interactively, we assume that each such subset has established its own independently random and pre-shared PRF key as in [12, 14, 21, 28].

---

[1] Some of the considered protocols are designed for $\mathbb{Z}_{2^\ell}$, but also work for finite fields.

Collision-Resistant Hash Functions. The considered works [12,14,21,28] all utilize collision resistant hash functions. This is a family of functions $\mathsf{H}_k :$ $\{0,1\}^* \rightarrow \{0,1\}^{\ell(\kappa)}$ ($\ell(\kappa)$ is the output size) where for a key k generated by a probabilistic generator in time polynomial in κ, any efficient adversary with access to k is able to find a collision, i.e., $x \neq x'$ s.t. $\mathsf{H}_k(x) = \mathsf{H}_k(x')$ only with probability negligible in κ. For details and a formal definition, we refer to [23]. Throughout this work, we use H as a hash function without a key as used throughout the protocols in [12,14,21,28]. This can be interpreted as the parties jointly and securely computing a key k to use throughout a protocol execution. Furthermore, we denote the output length $\ell(\kappa)$ by $|\mathsf{H}|$.

Security Model. The protocols from [12,14,21,28] considered in this work aim to be secure against an active, nonadaptive adversary $\mathcal{A}$ corrupting one party, corresponding to an honest majority setting as the protocols are for three or four parties. They are in the secure channels setting where each pair of parties has a secure communication channel between them. Furthermore, they consider security in the simulation-based real-world/ideal-world paradigm [9] to formalize that an interactive n-party protocol Π securely implements a functionality $\mathcal{F}$. For completeness, we provide details on this security definition in [8, App. A].

We consider variants of the security model where the adversary can prevent other parties from receiving output (security with abort), where either all or no parties receive outputs (fairness), or where all parties receive outputs irrespective of the adversary's behavior (robustness) [13,18]. For modularization, we also use the *hybrid model* [9]. Details again are provided in [8, App. A].

3 Our Attack and Fix: Trident [12] as an Example

We begin by providing a detailed explanation of our attack against the four-party protocol Trident [12] as its simple and elegant protocol description provides a good starting point to elaborate on our attack which we will later show to generalize to other protocols. We denote the parties by P_1, P_2, P_3, consistent with [12], but rename their party P_0 to P_h here, as it acts as a helper and is of no relevance for our attack. The security model in [12] is either security with abort or even fairness, and our attack works the same for both settings.

Trident uses different secret sharing semantics with the ones provided in Table 2 being the relevant ones for our work. As an *intermediate* sharing semantic, the replicated sharing $\langle \cdot \rangle$ is used. The main sharing semantic in Trident then is $[\![\cdot]\!]$ where a sharing $[\![v]\!]$ can also be viewed as each party holding m_v and a $\langle \cdot \rangle$-sharing of a random mask λ_v s.t. $\mathsf{m}_v = v + \lambda_v$. Note that the sharings are linear, i.e., given $[\![\cdot]\!]$ respectively $\langle \cdot \rangle$-sharings of $x, y \in \mathcal{R}$ and public $a, b \in \mathcal{R}$, $[\![\cdot]\!]$ respectively $\langle \cdot \rangle$-sharings of $ax + y$ can be computed by applying these operations on each separate component of the sharings. Furthermore, a sharing of $x + b$ can be computed by adding b to m_x in $[\![\cdot]\!]$-sharings or adding b to x^1 in $\langle \cdot \rangle$-sharings. Trident uses *function-dependent preprocessing* where all $\langle \cdot \rangle$-sharings of masks λ_v

Table 2. Secret sharing semantics for sharing a value $v \in \mathcal{R}$ in Trident [12]. Party P_h holds $\lambda_v^1, \lambda_v^2, \lambda_v^3$ for a sharing $\llbracket v \rrbracket$ which we abstract away here as it is of no relevance for our attack.

Sharing Type	P_1	P_2	P_3	Correlation
$\langle v \rangle$	(v^2, v^3)	(v^3, v^1)	(v^1, v^2)	$v = v^1 + v^2 + v^3$
$\llbracket v \rrbracket$	$(\mathsf{m}_v, \lambda_v^2, \lambda_v^3)$	$(\mathsf{m}_v, \lambda_v^3, \lambda_v^1)$	$(\mathsf{m}_v, \lambda_v^1, \lambda_v^2)$	$\mathsf{m}_v = v + \lambda_v^1 + \lambda_v^2 + \lambda_v^3$

across the circuit are computed before inputs are provided by the protocol—the online phase only computes the m_v values.

The core of Trident is its multiplication sub-protocol, which also provides the target for our attack. Linear operations are non-interactive, following the linearity of the $\llbracket \cdot \rrbracket$-sharings. Finally, for input and output phases, we simply refer to [12] as they play no role for our attack. To multiply two sharings $\llbracket x \rrbracket, \llbracket y \rrbracket$, observe the following using the linearity of $\langle \cdot \rangle$-sharings:

$$\langle x \cdot y \rangle = \langle (\mathsf{m}_x - \lambda_x) \cdot (\mathsf{m}_y - \lambda_y) \rangle = \mathsf{m}_x \cdot \mathsf{m}_y - \mathsf{m}_x \cdot \langle \lambda_y \rangle - \mathsf{m}_y \cdot \langle \lambda_x \rangle + \langle \lambda_x \cdot \lambda_y \rangle$$

In the preprocessing, we obtain $\langle \gamma_{xy} \rangle$ with $\gamma_{xy} = \lambda_x \lambda_y$. While this is part of the multiplication protocol in [12], we abstract it away into a functionality $\mathcal{F}_{\text{MultPre}}$ (as also used in, e.g., [28]), because its exact instantiation plays no role in our attack. Trident uses helper party P_h for instantiating $\mathcal{F}_{\text{MultPre}}$ which we hence can ignore here. Then, $\langle x \cdot y \rangle = \mathsf{m}_x \cdot \mathsf{m}_y - \mathsf{m}_x \cdot \langle \lambda_y \rangle - \mathsf{m}_y \cdot \langle \lambda_x \rangle + \langle \gamma_{xy} \rangle$ can be computed non-interactively by the linearity of $\langle \cdot \rangle$-sharings. The goal now is to obtain a sharing $\llbracket z \rrbracket$ for $z = x \cdot y$. The parties non-interactively sample random shares for a mask $\langle \lambda_z \rangle$ (using pre-shared keys). They then aim to obtain $\mathsf{m}_z' := \mathsf{m}_z - \mathsf{m}_x \mathsf{m}_y$ from where they can non-interactively add $\mathsf{m}_x \mathsf{m}_y$ to finally obtain m_z and, hence, the output sharing $\llbracket z \rrbracket$.

$$\langle \mathsf{m}_z' \rangle = \langle x \cdot y + \lambda_z - \mathsf{m}_x \mathsf{m}_y \rangle = -\mathsf{m}_x \cdot \langle \lambda_y \rangle - \mathsf{m}_y \cdot \langle \lambda_x \rangle + \langle \gamma_{xy} \rangle + \langle \lambda_z \rangle$$

Now, the resulting sharing $\langle \mathsf{m}_z' \rangle$ is opened interactively to obtain m_z' in the clear, allowing a corrupted party to cheat by sending an incorrect or no message. Trident aims to detect such a cheating attempt by exploiting that each share of $\langle \mathsf{m}_z' \rangle$ is known by two parties. It lets one of these parties send the value and lets the other one send a hash of the value for verification, using a collision-resistant hash function H. The receiver can then hash the plain value and check for equality. In case of a mismatch, it aborts. Hence, one party provides P_i with $\mathsf{m}_z'^i$ while the other provides $\mathsf{H}(\mathsf{m}_z'^i)$. In case of an incorrect $\mathsf{m}_z'^i$ sent, its hash value will differ from the received hash except for negligible probability, leading to any cheating attempt being detected.

The full multiplication sub-protocol is provided in Fig. 1. Note that we decouple the verification here, but for now, assume that it is done in parallel with the remaining online phase for each individual multiplication.

Protocol $\Pi_{\mathsf{mult}}(\llbracket x \rrbracket, \llbracket y \rrbracket) \to \llbracket z \rrbracket$ of Trident [12]

Input: $\llbracket \cdot \rrbracket$-shares of $x, y \in \mathcal{R}$.

Output: $\llbracket \cdot \rrbracket$-shares of $z = x \cdot y$.

Preprocessing:

1. Invoke $\mathcal{F}_{\mathsf{MultPre}}$ on $\langle \lambda_x \rangle$ and $\langle \lambda_y \rangle$ to obtain $\langle \gamma_{xy} \rangle$ with $\gamma_{xy} = \lambda_x \cdot \lambda_y$.
2. Non-interactively generate $\langle \lambda_z \rangle$ by P_{i-1}, P_{i+1} sampling $\lambda_z^i \leftarrow\!\!\$\ \mathcal{R}$ for $i \in \{1, 2, 3\}$.

Online:

1. Each party P_i locally computes:
   - $\mathsf{m}_z'^{i-1} = -\mathsf{m}_x \lambda_y^{i-1} - \mathsf{m}_y \lambda_x^{i-1} + \gamma_{xy}^{i-1} + \lambda_z^{i-1}$.
   - $\mathsf{m}_z'^{i+1} = -\mathsf{m}_x \lambda_y^{i+1} - \mathsf{m}_y \lambda_x^{i+1} + \gamma_{xy}^{i+1} + \lambda_z^{i+1}$.
2. Each party P_i sends $\mathsf{m}_z'^{i-1}$ to P_{i-1}.
3. Each party P_i locally computes $\mathsf{m}_z = \mathsf{m}_x \mathsf{m}_y + \sum_{j=1}^{3} \mathsf{m}_z'^j$.

Verify:

1. Each party P_i sends $h_{i+1} = \mathsf{H}(\mathsf{m}_z'^{i+1})$ to P_{i+1}.
2. Each party P_i proceeds if $h_i = \mathsf{H}(\mathsf{m}_z'^i)$ with $\mathsf{m}_z'^i$ as previously received from P_{i+1} in step 2 of the online phase and aborts otherwise.

Fig. 1. Multiplication protocol of Trident [12] (simplified preprocessing).

3.1 Security of Unoptimized Trident

The security proof of Trident is deferred to the full version [11] of the conference version [12]. Important here is how the simulation of the online and verification phases of multiplications works. According to [11], the simulator emulates the honest parties throughout the protocol by setting their inputs to zero at the start of the protocol and then following the protocol specification. Then, the value $\mathsf{m}_z'^i$ received by a corrupt P_i in the online phase of a multiplication is simulated by handing $\mathsf{m}_z'^i$ (from the emulation of P_{i+1}) to the adversary on behalf of P_{i+1}. Regarding verification, the simulator hands $\mathsf{H}(\mathsf{m}_z'^i)$ to the adversary on behalf of P_{i-1}. For messages sent by the corrupt party P_i, the simulator receives them from the adversary and follows the protocol for the emulated, honest parties.

First, note that the adversary is forced to provide correct messages for each multiplication to avoid the protocol aborting immediately. Should it cheat, the first multiplication where cheating occurs will lead to inconsistent hashes in the multiplication verification except for negligible probability.

Now, note that the message $\mathsf{m}_z'^i$ received by the adversary cannot be distinguished from a real-world execution of the same step. This is because the value is masked by λ_z^i freshly sampled using a PRF key unknown to the adversary—the existence of an efficient distinguisher would contradict the security of the PRF. The second message $\mathsf{H}(\mathsf{m}_z'^i)$ hence too cannot be distinguished from a real-world execution, as in both the real-world and the simulation, it simply is the hash of the other message. Yet, we observe that this only holds because both honest parties have consistent values $\mathsf{m}_z'^i$. This holds true if the verification is done immediately as part of each multiplication, as any inconsistency between the honest parties must be caused by the adversary cheating due to the correctness of the protocol. Yet, in the case of cheating and immediate verification, any inconsistency in resulting shares would lead to an abort before the inconsistent shares can be used as input to other operations. We note that the argument regarding immediate verification is not provided or used in [11,12], an oversight that enables the issues discussed in the following. Yet, the entire proof in [11] appears to implicitly consider an immediate verification, not matching the optimized protocol description in [11,12], which is the topic of the next section.

3.2   Vulnerable Optimization: Delaying and Batching Verifications

To achieve a negligible amortized communication overhead, the verification in Trident batches many individual verification steps from multiple multiplications with the communication of only a single verification. As an example, assume that three independent multiplications yield outputs $[\![u]\!], [\![v]\!], [\![w]\!]$. Then, P_i receives $\mathsf{m}_u'^i, \mathsf{m}_v'^i, \mathsf{m}_w'^i$ from P_{i+1} which can be verified by P_{i-1} sending a single hash (instead of three separate ones) $h_i = \mathsf{H}(\mathsf{m}_u'^i \| \mathsf{m}_v'^i \| \mathsf{m}_w'^i)$ to P_i that then checks for consistency. This still maintains security due to the independence of the multiplications, preventing any inconsistency caused by cheating from influencing the input to other operations (cf. §3.1) besides verification.

Trident goes one step further by *optimistically* executing the protocol without any intermediate verification to then do a single batched verification immediately before any outputs are revealed to parties at the end of the protocol. This makes the verification communication overhead independent of the computed circuit and, hence, yields zero amortized overhead per multiplication. Yet, this optimization is considered only in the protocol specification, not in the security proof, and we will show in §3.3 how this renders the entire protocol insecure. As an example for such delayed verification, we compute $c = a \cdot b$ and use the result to compute $e = c \cdot d$ using the circuit in Fig. 2. Ignoring the input and output phases, the online phase of the protocol hence contains two subsequent online phases of Π_{mult} (Fig. 1) and the batched verification, jointly depicted in Fig. 3.

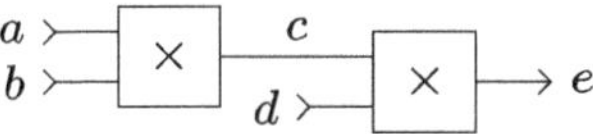

Fig. 2. Simple arithmetic circuit featuring two subsequent multiplications, providing a minimal example to enable our attack in §3.3.

It is easy to see that the batched verification still is sound—any initial incorrect message sent will be mirrored by the different, correct value as part of the input to H, causing at least one of the final comparisons to fail except for negligible probability. The issue arises on the side of privacy: Recall that if verification is not delayed, a party P_i will receive a value which can be simulated as shown

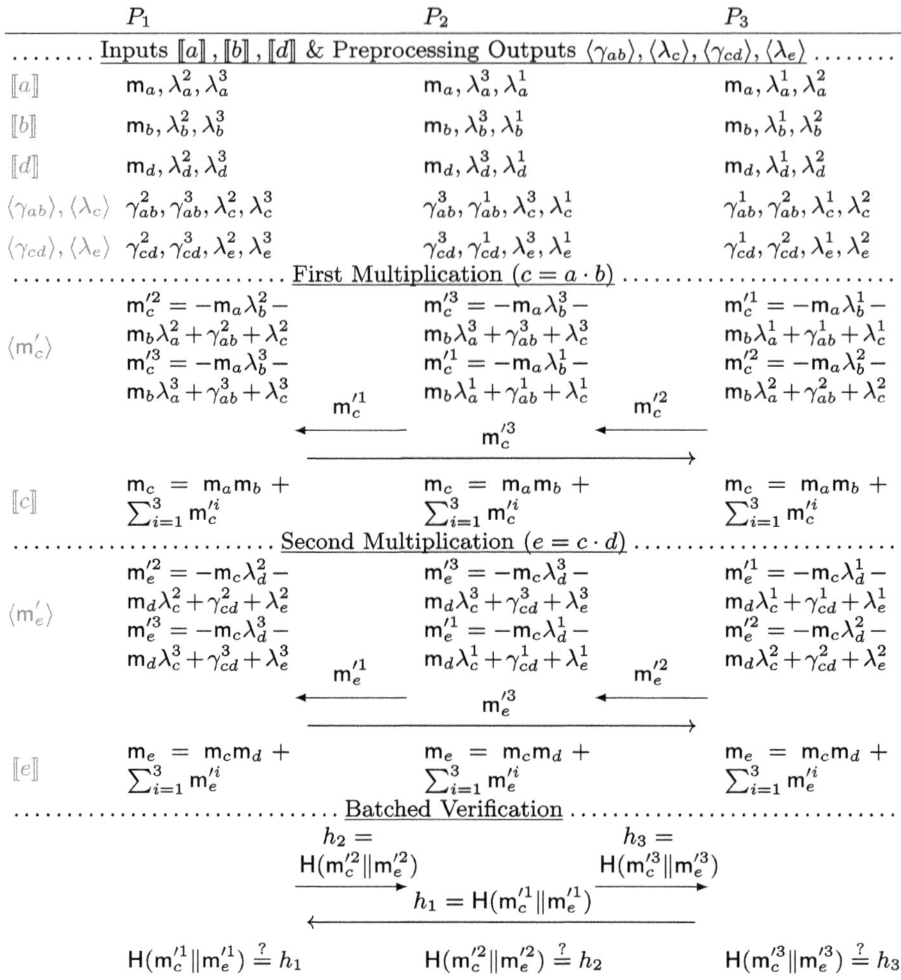

Fig. 3. Online phase of the two multiplications and batched verification required to evaluate the circuit from Fig. 2 in Trident [12], following the notation from Fig. 1.

before. Furthermore, it receives a hash which we simulate by taking the hash of the prior simulated value. If P_i is corrupt, both other parties are honest and hence provide consistent value and hash, yielding indistinguishability of our simulation. If P_i is not corrupt, one of the other parties may be, and inconsistent values may be received, but this does not matter as P_i is honest and hence, no simulation is needed.

Now, by delaying the verification, an incorrect message is not immediately detected. This unfortunately causes the honest parties to reconstruct inconsistent m_z, causing them to have inconsistent states. We proceed to show how a corrupt party can exploit that to cause the honest parties to provide inconsistent values and hashes for a later multiplication in a way that allows the extraction of additional knowledge and, hence, breaking security.

3.3 Our Attack on Trident

Due to the symmetry of Trident, we assume P_1 to be corrupt without loss of generality. We revisit the prior example of computing $c = a \cdot b$ and $e = c \cdot d$ (Fig. 2, Fig. 3). For the first multiplication, P_1 is expected to send $\mathsf{m}_c'^3$ to P_3. Our attack is to instead incorrectly send $\mathsf{m}_c'^3 + 1$. This will cause P_3 to eventually recover $\mathsf{m}_c + 1$ instead of the correct value m_c. This error propagates to further values in the second multiplication. In particular, P_3 has to compute $\mathsf{m}_e'^1 = -\mathsf{m}_c \lambda_d^1 - \mathsf{m}_d \lambda_c^1 + \gamma_{cd}[1] + \lambda_e^1$, but the "$+1$"-offset on m_c causes it to instead compute $\mathsf{m}_e'^1 - \lambda_d^1$. The error has not propagated to P_2 yet which computes the correct $\mathsf{m}_e'^1$ and sends it to P_1. In the verification, P_3 receives $h_3 = \mathsf{H}(\mathsf{m}_c'^3 \| \dots)$ from P_2 which except for negligible probability is unequal to $\mathsf{H}(\mathsf{m}_c'^3 + 1 \| \dots)$. Hence, the cheating attempt is caught as soundness still holds. Yet, the corrupt party P_1 receives from P_3 $h_1 = \mathsf{H}(\mathsf{m}_c'^1 \| \mathsf{m}_e'^1 - \lambda_d^1)$, not necessarily matching $\mathsf{H}(\mathsf{m}_c'^1 \| \mathsf{m}_e'^1)$ given the values received from P_2.

Formal Security Breach. Assuming that the outputs the protocol provides to P_1 and P_1's inputs do not allow to infer knowledge on d, e.g., by P_1 receiving no output and d being another party's input, h_1 cannot be simulated. The simulator from [11] has a value λ_d^1, yet it uses zero-inputs for all honest parties, relying on the adversary not knowing the λ_v^1 values that hence hide all shared values from the adversary (except for those known to the adversary by the design of the evaluated circuit). Assume w.l.o.g. that the simulator hands $h_1 = \mathsf{H}(\mathsf{m}_c'^1 \| \mathsf{m}_e'^1 - \delta)$ to the adversary where δ may depend only on what the simulator knows and, hence, not on value d. In a real execution with $d = 0$, the adversary receives $h_1 = \mathsf{H}(\mathsf{m}_c'^1 \| \mathsf{m}_e'^1 - \lambda_d^1) = \mathsf{H}(\mathsf{m}_c'^1 \| \mathsf{m}_e'^1 - \mathsf{m}_d + \lambda_d^2 + \lambda_d^3)$ and already has $\mathsf{m}_c'^1, \mathsf{m}_e'^1, \lambda_d^2, \lambda_d^3$. For $d = 1$, the adversary receives $\mathsf{H}(\mathsf{m}_c'^1 \| \mathsf{m}_e'^1 - \lambda_d^1) = \mathsf{H}(\mathsf{m}_c'^1 \| \mathsf{m}_e'^1 + 1 - \mathsf{m}_d + \lambda_d^2 + \lambda_d^3)$. Hence, the distributions $\{h_1, \mathsf{m}_c'^1, \mathsf{m}_e'^1, \lambda_d^2, \lambda_d^3\}$ are different for both cases $d = 0$ and $d = 1$ in a real execution except for the negligible probability of a hash collision. Yet, the corresponding distribution induced by the simulation contains $h_1 = \mathsf{H}(\mathsf{m}_c'^1 \| \mathsf{m}_e'^1 - \delta)$ for δ *independent* of d. Hence, it will be distinguishable from at least one of the distributions from the real execution, for $d = 0$ or $d = 1$, and thus, the simulation is distinguishable from a real execution for some input(s).

Concrete Attack. Concretely, a corrupt P_1 can now do an exhaustive search over all $i \in \mathcal{R}$ to find an i s.t. $\mathsf{H}(\mathsf{m}_c'^1 \| \mathsf{m}_e'^1 - i) = h_1$. Except for the unlikely case of a hash collision, it then holds that $i = \lambda_d^1$ and P_1 that already has $\mathsf{m}_d, \lambda_d^2, \lambda_d^3$ can extract the plaintext $d = \mathsf{m}_d - \lambda_d^1 - \lambda_d^2 - \lambda_d^3$ that is another party's input.

This brute-force attack only efficiently works for $|\mathcal{R}| \ll 2^\kappa$, which is given for usual domains, for sure in the binary domain, but even for, e.g., $\mathcal{R} = \mathbb{Z}_{2^{32}}$. Also, $\mathcal{R} = \mathbb{Z}_{2^{64}}$ is too small to properly mitigate such an attack, considering a usual choice of $\kappa = 128$. Furthermore, even for a very large ring $\mathcal{R}$, P_1 is able to check if $d = x$ by testing if $\mathsf{H}(\mathsf{m}_c'^1 \| \mathsf{m}_e'^1 + x - \mathsf{m}_d + \lambda_d^2 + \lambda_d^3) = h_1$, i.e., if $x - \mathsf{m}_d + \lambda_d^2 + \lambda_d^3 = \lambda_d^1 \Leftrightarrow d = x$. Note that depending on the application and circuit, d might be from a much smaller subdomain of $\mathcal{R}$, perhaps even allowing for always efficient extraction of d on a large ring.

Attacks for Larger Circuits. While the circuit from Fig. 2 provides a minimal example for running our attack, attacks on significantly more complex circuits are also feasible. We observe that injecting an offset of 1 for any single targeted multiplication gate may lead to inconsistencies for all further multiplications that (transitively) depend on the output of the targeted gate, i.e., where there exists a path in the circuit from the targeted to the other multiplication gate. In all cases where only one multiplication depends on the targeted one, one of its input wires is the output of the targeted gate, and the other input wire is independent, we can attack the value of the other input wire. To see that, interpret Fig. 2 as part of a larger circuit where a, b, d may be not only inputs, but also outputs from other gates. We only require that intermediate wire c does not (transitively) connect to any other multiplication gate than that which outputs e, also implying that e can only be (transitively) used by linear gates. Then, the injected offset will not cause any inconsistency in the evaluation of multiplication gates beyond what we have used for our attack earlier. Hence, all other multiplications will contribute additional messages to the verification phase, but these will all be consistent. Thus, P_1 receives $h_1 = \mathsf{H}(\ldots \| \mathsf{m}_c'^1 \| \ldots \| \mathsf{m}_e'^1 - \lambda_d^1 \| \ldots)$ to compare to $\mathsf{H}(\ldots \| \mathsf{m}_c'^1 \| \ldots \| \mathsf{m}_e'^1 \| \ldots)$ with the omitted parts being consistent. The attack works as for $h_1 = \mathsf{H}(\mathsf{m}_c'^1 \| \mathsf{m}_e'^1 - \lambda_d^1)$ to compare to $\mathsf{H}(\mathsf{m}_c'^1 \| \mathsf{m}_e'^1)$ before, simply with the consistent values injected in-between.

If the targeted multiplication has paths to multiple other multiplications, the attack becomes more complex, but persists. While the prior example already is sufficient to demonstrate Trident to be insecure, we also provide a further example for a more complex circuit topology in the full version [8, App. B].

3.4 First Attempts on Fixing Trident

One simple fix of Trident is to use the unoptimized multiplication where the verification is used for each individual multiplication. Moreover, as remarked in §3.2, the verification over multiple multiplications can even be batched as long as these multiplications are independent. For that, recall from §3.1 that security is maintained as long as the inputs to a multiplication are consistent between all parties. If we do one batched verification per layer of multiplications in a circuit, this still ensures that no inconsistent data can flow into another multiplication before being detected by a verification step. While fixing the issue that enabled our attack in §3.3, this requires at least d many verifications where each party sends a hash value for a circuit of multiplicative depth d. Hence, this solution results in an overhead that depends on the circuit, hence not amortizing to zero. This is efficient for circuits of very low depth. Yet, with increasing depth it becomes less efficient, adding more verification overhead. We revisit this issue in §3.5, demonstrating a fix that is efficient for circuits of any depth.

We also note that the part of the preprocessing that we abstracted away ($\mathcal{F}_{\text{MultPre}}$ to multiply $\langle \lambda_x \rangle$ and $\langle \lambda_y \rangle$ to obtain $\langle \gamma_{xy} \rangle$ with $\gamma_{xy} = \lambda_x \cdot \lambda_y$) internally also uses the batched verification [12]. As all instances of $\mathcal{F}_{\text{MultPre}}$ are used in parallel by [12], we note that running the batched verification for it at the end of preprocessing is sufficient and has zero amortized overhead, given the aforementioned considerations for the online phase. Hence, we continue to safely ignore the exact instantiation of $\mathcal{F}_{\text{MultPre}}$ in our work.

Searching for a generally less expensive fix, recall that soundness of the batched and delayed verification in Trident still holds—the first incorrect message will always lead to a failed consistency check on the side of the, in this case, honest receiver. Hence, one may aim to do the consistency checks sequentially to cause this cheating attempt being caught and the protocol aborting before the corrupt party receives a hash. Yet, any of the parties may be corrupted, and by the symmetry of the protocol, any fixed, sequential order of consistency checks allows the adversary to corrupt the party receiving a hash first.

Hence, we might aim to completely hide the hash h_i from the party P_i that should receive it in Trident. Each consistency check could then still be implemented using a secure sub-protocol to decide if h_i matches the value expected by P_i, similar to [22]. Yet, this still does not suffice: Considering the prior attack for corrupt P_1 on the simple circuit in Fig. 2, the outcome of the consistency check for h_1 alone already reveals wether $\lambda_d[1] = 0$ which would imply that $d = \mathsf{m}_d + \lambda_d^2 + \lambda_d^3$, which is computable by corrupt P_1.

3.5   Fixing Trident

While Trident could be fixed with an overhead linear in the multiplicative depth of the circuit as discussed in §3.4, we now propose a solution with zero amortized overhead. Our core idea is simple: As proposed in §3.4, we do the consistency checks in any secure MPC protocol as sub-protocol of Trident. While we have seen that the output of an individual check still can leak information, we have also noted that overall soundness holds, i.e., at least one of the checks will always reject if a party cheats. In this case, we now aim to hide the outputs of the other consistency checks to avoid leakage. To this end, instead of running three individual consistency checks, we run a single one inside a secure sub-protocol that executes all three individual checks, but only reveals the AND over all outputs, i.e., if any of the checks failed, but not which specific one. Hence, the output will always be **Reject** if cheating occurred and always be **Accept** otherwise.

We introduce a functionality $\mathcal{F}_{\text{CHECKEQS}}^{A,(s_a)_{a \in A},(t_a)_{a \in A}}$ (formally specified in Fig. 4), which we keep generic to later also allow its utilization in further contexts to fix other protocols in the remainder of the paper. The functionality is parametrized by a set of equality checks A where for each check $a \in A$, parties P_{s_a}, P_{t_a} have a value each with the goal of checking for equality between both. In the current context of Trident (cf. Fig. 1), each party P_i originally computes a hash h_i^1 over its received values while—in the original protocol—receiving hash h_i^2 (originally labeled h_i) to compare to from party P_{i-1}. We let both parties input h_i^1, h_i^2 to the functionality, requiring for Trident to choose $A = \{1,2,3\}$ as labels for its three individual checks and $s_i = i, t_i = i - 1$ for all $i \in \{1,2,3\}$, indicating that h_i^1, h_i^2 are provided by P_i respectively P_{i-1}. For simplicity, we call the functionality with these specific parameters $\mathcal{F}_{\text{CHECKEQS}}^{\text{Trident}}$.

Ideal Functionality $\mathcal{F}_{\text{CHECKEQS}}^{A,(s_a)_{a \in A},(t_a)_{a \in A}}$

Input: $h_a^1, h_a^2 \in \{0,1\}^{|\mathsf{H}|}$ with h_a^1 provided by P_{s_a}, h_a^2 provided by P_{t_a}, for $a \in A$.
Output: `Accept` if $h_a^1 = h_a^2 \; \forall a \in A$, `Reject` otherwise.

Fig. 4. Functionality for joined equality checking.

Using this, we fix Trident's multiplication from Fig. 1 by replacing its original verification with that in Fig. 5, calling the resulting multiplication protocol $\Pi_{\text{mult}}^{\text{FIXED}}$. The "..." here stands for the respective $\mathsf{m}_z'^i, \mathsf{m}_z'^{i+1}$ from all other multiplications as the batched check is done once over all multiplications in the end, before any output is revealed by the protocol.

Protocol Verification step of $\Pi_{\text{mult}}^{\text{FIXED}}(\llbracket x \rrbracket, \llbracket y \rrbracket) \rightarrow \llbracket z \rrbracket$ for Trident [12]

Verify (batched):

1. Each P_i sends $h_i^1 = \mathsf{H}(\dots \|\mathsf{m}_z'^i\| \dots)$ and $h_{i+1}^2 = \mathsf{H}(\dots \|\mathsf{m}_z'^{i+1}\| \dots)$ to $\mathcal{F}_{\text{CHECKEQS}}^{\text{Trident}}$.
2. P_i proceeds if it receives `Accept` from $\mathcal{F}_{\text{CHECKEQS}}^{\text{Trident}}$ and aborts otherwise.

Fig. 5. Fixed, batched verification of the multiplication of Trident [12] in Fig. 1.

We first show that the resulting fixed version of Trident is secure using $\mathcal{F}_{\text{CHECKEQS}}^{\text{Trident}}$ as a hybrid and then provide an instantiation for $\mathcal{F}_{\text{CHECKEQS}}^{\text{Trident}}$.

Theorem 1. *Trident [12] using the fixed multiplication protocol $\Pi_{\text{mult}}^{\text{FIXED}}$ (cf. Fig. 5) is secure in the $\mathcal{F}_{\text{CHECKEQS}}^{\text{Trident}}$-hybrid model.*

Proof. We provide a proof sketch only as the security proof in [11] already covers most of the protocol, including all unchanged components. Proving security requires providing a simulator $\mathcal{S}$, given an adversary $\mathcal{A}$ and a fixed corrupt party P_i. We do this in the following as a single proof over the whole protocol, as the delayed, batched verification allows inconsistent sharings (different m_v-values per party) to propagate through the circuit, being detected only later after execution of the gate that they were introduced by. Throughout the proof, $\mathcal{S}$ locally emulates the honest parties, keeping their internal state (except for their unknown inputs) and following the protocol specification.

First, the preprocessing is simulated following [11]. Also, it is easy to see that the protocol implements the desired functionality. Inputs are provided through the protocols in [12], where $\mathcal{S}$ lets honest parties share 0 instead of their actual inputs and can extract the corrupt party's inputs as described in [11].

The simulator then follows the circuit's topology, using the shares held by the individual parties and noting that different parties might also have different, inconsistent m_v-values introduced by cheating. Additions and multiplications by constants are handled locally on all shares. The remaining multiplications are simulated as follows: $\mathcal{S}$ hands $\mathsf{m}_z'^i$ to $\mathcal{A}$ on behalf of P_{i+1}. Note that this message is masked by $\lambda_z[i]$, sampled using a random PRF key known to both honest parties, but not corrupt P_i and hence, not $\mathcal{A}$. Thus, distinguishing between the simulation and protocol execution from this message would also yield a distinguisher for the used PRF, violating the security assumption regarding the PRF. $\mathcal{S}$ receives from $\mathcal{A}$ a value $\mathsf{m}_z'^{i-1}$ (not necessarily consistent with $\mathsf{m}_z'^{i-1}$ computed internally on behalf of P_{i+1}) or nothing in which case it sends abort to $\mathcal{F}$, simulates the other parties aborting and outputs what $\mathcal{A}$ outputs. $\mathcal{S}$ uses this $\mathsf{m}_z'^{i-1}$ intended for P_{i-1}, emulating P_{i-1}'s behavior using the received value to compute its m_z.

In the batched verification, $\mathcal{S}$ receives from $\mathcal{A}$ values $h_i^1, h_{i+1}^2 \in \{0,1\} \in \{0,1\}^{|H|}$ that P_i is supposed to send to $\mathcal{F}_{\mathrm{CHECKEQS}}^{\mathrm{Trident}}$. If it does not receive these values, it simulates an abort as above. Then, $h_{i-1}^1, h_{i+1}^1, h_{i-1}^2, h_i^2$ are computed by $\mathcal{S}$ on the shares of their respective honest parties. If $h_j^1 \neq h_j^2$ for any $j \in \{1,2,3\}$, then $\mathcal{S}$ hands Reject to $\mathcal{A}$ on behalf of $\mathcal{F}_{\mathrm{CHECKEQS}}^{\mathrm{Trident}}$, sends abort to $\mathcal{F}$, simulates the other parties aborting and outputs what $\mathcal{A}$ outputs. Otherwise, it sends Accept to $\mathcal{A}$ on behalf of $\mathcal{F}_{\mathrm{CHECKEQS}}^{\mathrm{Trident}}$ and proceeds.

To see why this properly simulates the protocol, note that if P_i cheats in any multiplication, it does so the first time for some multiplication with output $[\![z]\!]$ by sending some $\mathsf{m}_z'^{i-1} + \delta, \delta \in \mathcal{R}, \delta \neq 0$ instead of $\mathsf{m}_z'^{i-1}$. As all prior execution was done without cheating by definition, the inputs to the multiplication have consistent shares between all parties. Hence, P_{i+1} computes correct $\mathsf{m}_z'^{i-1}$. Now, P_{i+1} includes $\mathsf{m}_z'^{i-1}$ in h_{i-1}^2 while P_{i-1} includes the received $\mathsf{m}_z'^{i-1} + \delta$ in h_{i-1}^1. Then, except for negligible probability of a hash collision, $h_{i-1}^1 \neq h_{i-1}^2$ so that in the ideal and in the real world, the output of $\mathcal{F}_{\mathrm{CHECKEQS}}^{\mathrm{Trident}}$ will be Reject.

Otherwise, there is no cheating during the multiplications, and all parties have consistent shares. Thus, if $\mathcal{A}$ provides h_i^1, h_{i+1}^2 honestly (it has all required values to compute these values), the output of $\mathcal{F}_{\mathrm{CHECKEQS}}^{\mathrm{Trident}}$ will be Accept as the honest parties compute these hashes on the same input values, given the consistency of all shares. Otherwise, the output of $\mathcal{F}_{\mathrm{CHECKEQS}}^{\mathrm{Trident}}$ will be Reject except for negligible probability, independent of which incorrect h_i^1 or h_{i+1}^2 is chosen exactly.

The output phase is simulated as in [11] and $\mathcal{S}$ outputs what $\mathcal{A}$ outputs. $\square$

Instantiating $\mathcal{F}_{\mathbf{CheckEqs}}^{A,(s_a)_{a \in A},(t_a)_{a \in A}}$. It remains to provide a secure instantiation for generic $\mathcal{F}_{\mathrm{CHECKEQS}}^{A,(s_a)_{a \in A},(t_a)_{a \in A}}$, yielding one for $\mathcal{F}_{\mathrm{CHECKEQS}}^{\mathrm{Trident}}$ too. For that, we require secure evaluation of arithmetic circuits on the domain $\mathcal{R} = \mathbb{F}_{2^{|H|}}$, which can be achieved by any secure MPC protocol in this setting. For now, we abstract this away to functionality $\mathcal{F}_{\mathsf{MPC}}^{\mathsf{sub}}$, evaluating an arithmetic circuit $\mathcal{C}$ on inputs provided by n parties and, in addition, k uniform and secret random values:

$$\mathcal{F}_{\mathsf{MPC}}^{\mathsf{sub}}(\mathcal{C}, x_{1,1}, \dots, x_{1,j_1}, \dots, x_{n,1}, \dots, x_{n,j_n}) =$$
$$\mathcal{C}(x_{1,1}, \dots, x_{1,j_1}, \dots, x_{n,1}, \dots, x_{n,j_n}, r_1 \xleftarrow{\$} \mathbb{F}_{2^{|\mathsf{H}|}}, \dots, r_k \xleftarrow{\$} \mathbb{F}_{2^{|\mathsf{H}|}}),$$

with arithmetic circuit $\mathcal{C}$, inputs $x_{i,1}, \dots, x_{i,j_i} \in \mathbb{F}_{2^{|\mathsf{H}|}}$ being provided by P_i for $1 \leq i \leq n$ (j_i is the number of inputs by P_i), and arbitrary, but fixed $k \in \mathbb{N}_0$. We will later instantiate $\mathcal{F}_{\mathsf{MPC}}^{\mathsf{sub}}$ for the specific case of $\mathcal{F}_{\mathsf{CHECKEQS}}^{\mathsf{Trident}}$, utilizing that Trident is designed for evaluating arithmetic circuits too.

Recall that our goal is to check if $h_a^1 = h_a^2$ for all $a \in A$ at once. We aim to do that efficiently using a small circuit and $\mathcal{F}_{\mathsf{MPC}}^{\mathsf{sub}}$. A simple random linear combination check fits this requirement, having a multiplicative depth of only 1. The resulting instantiation is provided in Fig. 6 and the exact idea of the random linear combination check will become clear in the subsequent proof. Note that it requires computing on a field, which is why we interpret all input hashes as elements of $\mathbb{F}_{2^{|\mathsf{H}|}}$. Note that this field must be and indeed is large, s.t. soundness is violated with probability negligible in the statistical security parameter σ. We then compute a random linear combination using $\mathcal{F}_{\mathsf{MPC}}^{\mathsf{sub}}$ as defined before, output the result x to all parties, and then Accept if $x = 0$.

Protocol $\Pi_{\mathsf{CHECKEQS}}^{A,(s_a)_{a \in A},(t_a)_{a \in A}}$

Input: $h_a^1, h_a^2 \in \{0,1\}^{|\mathsf{H}|}$ (interpreted as elements of $\mathbb{F}_{2^{|\mathsf{H}|}}$) with h_a^1 provided by P_{s_a}, h_a^2 provided by P_{t_a}, for $a \in A$.

Output: Accept if $h_i^1 = h_i^2 \, \forall a \in A$, Reject otherwise.

1. Compute $x = \sum_{a \in A} r_a \cdot (h_a^1 - h_a^2)$ for $r_a \xleftarrow{\$} \mathbb{F}_{2^{|\mathsf{H}|}}, a \in A$, using $\mathcal{F}_{\mathsf{MPC}}^{\mathsf{sub}}$.

2. Accept if $x = 0$, Reject otherwise.

Fig. 6. Protocol instantiating $\mathcal{F}_{\mathsf{CHECKEQS}}^{A,(s_a)_{a \in A},(t_a)_{a \in A}}$.

Theorem 2. *Protocol* $\Pi_{\mathsf{CHECKEQS}}^{A,(s_a)_{a \in A},(t_a)_{a \in A}}$, *given in Fig. 6, securely instantiates* $\mathcal{F}_{\mathsf{CHECKEQS}}^{A,(s_a)_{a \in A},(t_a)_{a \in A}}$ *(Fig. 4) in the* $\mathcal{F}_{\mathsf{MPC}}^{\mathsf{sub}}$-*hybrid model, assuming that* $|\mathsf{H}| > \sigma$.

Proof. For value x computed by $\mathcal{F}_{\mathsf{MPC}}^{\mathsf{sub}}$, it holds that $x = \sum_{a \in A} r_a \cdot (h_a^1 - h_a^2)$. If $h_a^1 = h_a^2$ for all $a \in A$, it trivially follows that $x = 0$ and the protocol outputs Accept. Otherwise, let $\hat{a} \in A$ be such that $h_{\hat{a}}^1 \neq h_{\hat{a}}^2$ which implies that $h_{\hat{a}}^1 - h_{\hat{a}}^2 \neq 0$. If still $x = 0$, then

$$r_{\hat{a}}(h_{\hat{a}}^1 - h_{\hat{a}}^2) = - \sum_{a \in A \setminus \{\hat{a}\}} r_a \cdot (h_a^1 - h_a^2) \implies r_{\hat{a}} = - \frac{\sum_{a \in A \setminus \{\hat{a}\}} r_a \cdot (h_a^1 - h_a^2)}{h_{\hat{a}}^1 - h_{\hat{a}}^2}.$$

Note that $r_{\hat{a}}$ is sampled uniformly at random from $\mathbb{F}_{2^{|\mathsf{H}|}}$, independently of all other r_a and h values. Then, the probability of it satisfying the prior equation and hence accepting is $|\mathbb{F}_{2^{|H|}}|^{-1} = 2^{-|H|} \leq 2^{-\sigma}$ and, hence, negligible. Thus, the protocol correctly instantiates the desired functionality.

Regarding simulation, $\mathcal{S}$ receives from $\mathcal{A}$ all of its inputs to $\mathcal{F}_{\mathsf{MPC}}^{\mathsf{sub}}$ or, if no or insufficient input is provided, sends abort to $\mathcal{F}_{\mathrm{CHECKEQS}}^{A,(s_a)_{a\in A},(t_a)_{a\in A}}$, simulates the other parties aborting, and outputs what $\mathcal{A}$ outputs. It sends $\mathcal{A}$'s inputs to $\mathcal{F}_{\mathrm{CHECKEQS}}^{A,(s_a)_{a\in A},(t_a)_{a\in A}}$, receiving back either Accept or Reject. If $\mathcal{S}$ receives Accept, then it provides 0 to $\mathcal{A}$ on behalf of $\mathcal{F}_{\mathsf{MPC}}^{\mathsf{sub}}$. Otherwise, it samples uniformly random $x' \in \mathbb{F}_{2^{|H|}}$ and provides that to $\mathcal{A}$ on behalf of $\mathcal{F}_{\mathsf{MPC}}^{\mathsf{sub}}$. Finally, it outputs what $\mathcal{A}$ outputs.

Note that the only difference between ideal and real world is that in the case of a Reject, the real x might differ from x' sampled by $\mathcal{S}$. Yet there must exist an $\hat{a}$ such that $h_{\hat{a}}^1 \neq h_{\hat{a}}^2$ as $\mathcal{F}_{\mathrm{CHECKEQS}}^{A,(s_a)_{a\in A},(t_a)_{a\in A}}$ outputs Reject, and

$$x = \sum_{a\in A} r_a \cdot (h_a^1 - h_a^2) = r_{\hat{a}}(h_{\hat{a}}^1 - h_{\hat{a}}^2) + \sum_{a\in A\setminus\{\hat{a}\}} r_a \cdot (h_a^1 - h_a^2).$$

For any fixed r_a for $a \in A \setminus \{\hat{a}\}$, the mapping $r_{\hat{a}} \mapsto r_{\hat{a}}(h_{\hat{a}}^1 - h_{\hat{a}}^2) + \sum_{a\in A\setminus\{\hat{a}\}} r_a \cdot (h_a^1 - h_a^2)$ is bijective as $h_{\hat{a}}^1 - h_{\hat{a}}^2 \neq 0$ is invertible in $\mathbb{F}_{2^{|H|}}$. As $r_{\hat{a}}$ is uniformly random, so is x, proving that x and x' cannot be distinguished. $\square$

Instantiating $\Pi_{\mathsf{mult}}^{\mathbf{FIXED}}$. Now, it easily follows that Trident, using $\Pi_{\mathsf{mult}}^{\mathrm{FIXED}}$ (Fig. 5), is secure in the plain-model if we instantiate $\mathcal{F}_{\mathrm{CHECKEQS}}^{\mathrm{Trident}}$ with $\Pi_{\mathrm{CHECKEQS}}^{\mathrm{Trident}}$ (Fig. 6) and use a secure instantiation of $\mathcal{F}_{\mathsf{MPC}}^{\mathsf{sub}}$ in Trident's setting.

$\mathcal{F}_{\mathsf{MPC}}^{\mathsf{sub}}$ can be instantiated in this setting using any secure MPC protocol for the same setting that supports arithmetic circuits over $\mathbb{F}_{2^{|H|}}$ and generating shares of random values to use inside a circuit. As remarked in §3.4, Trident is still secure if its original verification is not delayed, while this results in higher amortized communication cost. Furthermore, it is easy to generate a random sharing $[\![r]\!]$ for $r \leftarrow_\$ \mathcal{R}$ by for each $i \in \{1, 2, 3\}$, P_{i-1}, P_{i+1} locally sampling $\lambda_r[i] \leftarrow_\$ \mathcal{R}$ using pre-shared keys in the setup and setting $\mathsf{m}_r = 0$. Finally, while Trident is designed for domain $\mathcal{R} = \mathbb{Z}_{2^\ell}$ for performance reasons, it is easy to see that it works on any commutative ring $\mathcal{R}$ and, hence, also $\mathcal{R} = \mathbb{F}_{2^{|H|}}$. Thus, we fix Trident with a new verification that is instantiated with the original, but unoptimized and thus secure Trident (i.e., with immediate verification) on a field.

Given that the verification step is independent of the computed circuit, we achieve the same zero amortized overhead for this step as (optimized) Trident did, but eliminate the security flaw of Trident. The generic $\Pi_{\mathrm{CHECKEQS}}^{A,(s_a)_{a\in A},(t_a)_{a\in A}}$ has a constant multiplicative depth of only one, yielding minimal round overhead. More concretely, the immediate verification within $\Pi_{\mathrm{CHECKEQS}}^{\mathrm{Trident}}$ is only required for three independent multiplications, hence it can be batched (§3.4). The verification only uses three multiplications, three subtractions, two additions, and generates three random shares. Thus, the concrete overhead is negligible and the use of $\mathcal{R} = \mathbb{F}_{2^{|H|}}$ during verification comes at a negligible performance penalty.

4   Attacking and Fixing Fantastic Four [14]

We proceed to extend our attack on Trident [12] from §3 to the robust four-party protocol from Fantastic Four [14].[2] The attack is enabled by the protocol using the same idea for delayed, batched consistency checks as Trident [12]. Fantastic Four utilizes replicated secret sharing among parties P_1, P_2, P_3, P_4 where a secret $v \in \mathcal{R}$ is split into four random values $v^1, v^2, v^3, v^4 \in \mathcal{R}$ subject to $v^1 + v^2 + v^3 + v^4 = v$. Each party P_i knows all shares v^j where $j \neq i$. We denote the sharing of v by $[\![v]\!]$ and note that it is linear.

The intuition to multiply $[\![x]\!], [\![y]\!]$ is that

$$x \cdot y = \left(\sum_{i=1}^{4} x^i \right) \cdot \left(\sum_{i=1}^{4} y^i \right) = \sum_{i=1}^{4} x^i y^i + \sum_{\{i,j\} \subseteq \{1,2,3,4\}, i \neq j} (x^i y^j + x^j y^i).$$

Each $x^i y^i$ can be computed by three parties while for terms $x^i y^j + x^j y^i$, two parties can compute them and then communicate with the remaining parties. This communication can be verified, again using the fact that two parties know the value to be sent and at least one of them must be honest. The multiplication protocol of Fantastic Four is shown in Fig. 7.

Fantastic Four batches the verification at the end of optimistically executed segments which are not explicitly defined in [14]. Yet, in the implementation of the protocol in MP-SPDZ [24] (v0.4.2), the verification is also batched over multiple multiplications where the output of one influences others. Hence, there is an opportunity to deploy a similar attack to that on Trident discussed in §3.

We note that Fig. 7 does not specify for each subset $\{g, h\} \subseteq \{1, 2, 3, 4\}$ who of the two parties is P_g and who is P_h. Similarly, it is not specified who is P_i and who is P_j, i.e., who sends z_{gh}^h to P_g and who later sends the hash in the verification phase. While [14] specifies that $g < h$, it still leaves open the roles of P_i and P_j. Hence, we use the role assignment specified in the implementation in MP-SPDZ [24]. We observe that the implementation does not strictly adhere to the $g < h$ requirement of [14] (which does not affect the correctness and security of the protocol). For consistency, we will follow the role assignment of MP-SPDZ which we provide in Table 3.

We again use our minimal example for computing $c = a \cdot b$ and $e = c \cdot d$ (Fig. 2) to show how our attack from §3 translates to Fantastic Four. We assume here a corrupt P_3. The attack described in the following is also depicted in Fig. 8, highlighting how an injected error propagates through the protocol execution and who sends which messages. In the first multiplication $c = a \cdot b$, we let P_3 send $c_{12}^1 + 1$ instead of $c_{12}^1 = a^2 b^1 + a^1 b^2 - c_{12}^2$, where $c_{12}^2 \leftarrow_\$ \mathcal{R}$. This leads to P_2 having output share $c^1 + 1$ instead of c^1, given that the incorrect received message is one summand of the share. For multiplication $e = c \cdot d$, P_2 is expected to compute $e_{13}^1, e_{14}^4, e_{34}^4$, only the last being independent of incorrect $c^1 + 1$. For

---

[2] For simplicity, we call the protocol "Fantastic Four" here while noting that [14] also contains a three-party protocol that is not relevant to this work.

Protocol $\Pi_{\mathsf{mult}}(\llbracket x \rrbracket, \llbracket y \rrbracket) \to \llbracket z \rrbracket$ of Fantastic Four [14]

Input: $\llbracket \cdot \rrbracket$-shares of $x, y \in \mathcal{R}$.

Output: $\llbracket \cdot \rrbracket$-shares of $z = x \cdot y$.

1. For every $\{g, h\} \subseteq \{1, 2, 3, 4\}, g \neq h$, use parties P_i, P_j with $i, j \notin \{g, h\}$ to generate $\llbracket z_{gh} \rrbracket$ with $z_{gh} = x^g y^h + x^h y^g$.

    – P_i, P_j, P_h non-interactively sample $z_{gh}^g \leftarrow\!\!\$\; \mathcal{R}$.

    – P_i, P_j compute $z_{gh}^h = x^g y^h + x^h y^g - z_{gh}^g$.

    – P_i sends z_{gh}^h to P_g.

    – Set $z_{gh}^i = z_{gh}^j = 0$.

2. Each party P_i sets $z^j = x^j y^j + \sum_{\{g,h\} \subseteq \{1,2,3,4\}, g \neq h} z_{gh}^j$ for $1 \leq j \leq 4, j \neq i$.

Verify:

1. For every $\{g, h\} \subseteq \{1, 2, 3, 4\}, g \neq h$ and parties P_i, P_j with $i, j \notin \{g, h\}$ as above where P_i sends z_{gh}^h to P_g:

    – P_j sends $h_{gh} = \mathsf{H}(z_{gh}^h)$ to P_g.

    – Party P_g proceeds if $h_{gh} = \mathsf{H}(z_{gh}^h)$ (with z_{gh}^h as previously received from P_i).

    – In case of inequality, output error message to other parties and start cheater identification as described in [14].

Fig. 7. Four-party multiplication protocol of Fantastic Four [14] (some operations inlined and separated verification).

Table 3. Assignment of the parties' roles in the MP-SPDZ [24] (`v0.4.2`) implementation of Fantastic Four [14].

$\{g, h\}$	P_g (receives share)	P_h (samples share)	P_i (sends share)	P_j (sends hash)
$\{1, 2\}$	P_2	P_1	P_3	P_4
$\{1, 3\}$	P_3	P_1	P_2	P_4
$\{1, 4\}$	P_1	P_4	P_2	P_3
$\{2, 3\}$	P_3	P_2	P_4	P_1
$\{2, 4\}$	P_4	P_2	P_1	P_3
$\{3, 4\}$	P_4	P_3	P_1	P_2

the other values, the offset on c^1 causes it to compute

$$c^3 d^1 + (c^1 + 1)d^3 - e_{13}^3 = e_{13}^1 + d^3 \text{ instead of } e_{13}^1, \text{ and}$$
$$(c^1 + 1)d^4 + c^4 d^1 - e_{14}^1 = e_{14}^4 + d^4 \text{ instead of } e_{14}^4.$$

These are then sent to P_1 respectively P_3 and cause further errors in the shares for $\llbracket e \rrbracket$ held by P_1, P_2, P_3.

It is easy to see that the consistency check will fail as P_2 receives $h_{12} = \mathsf{H}(c_{12}^1 \| e_{12}^1)$ from P_4, which except for negligible probability does not match $\mathsf{H}(c_{12}^1 + 1 \| e_{12}^1)$ for the values received from P_3. Yet, we observe that the corrupt

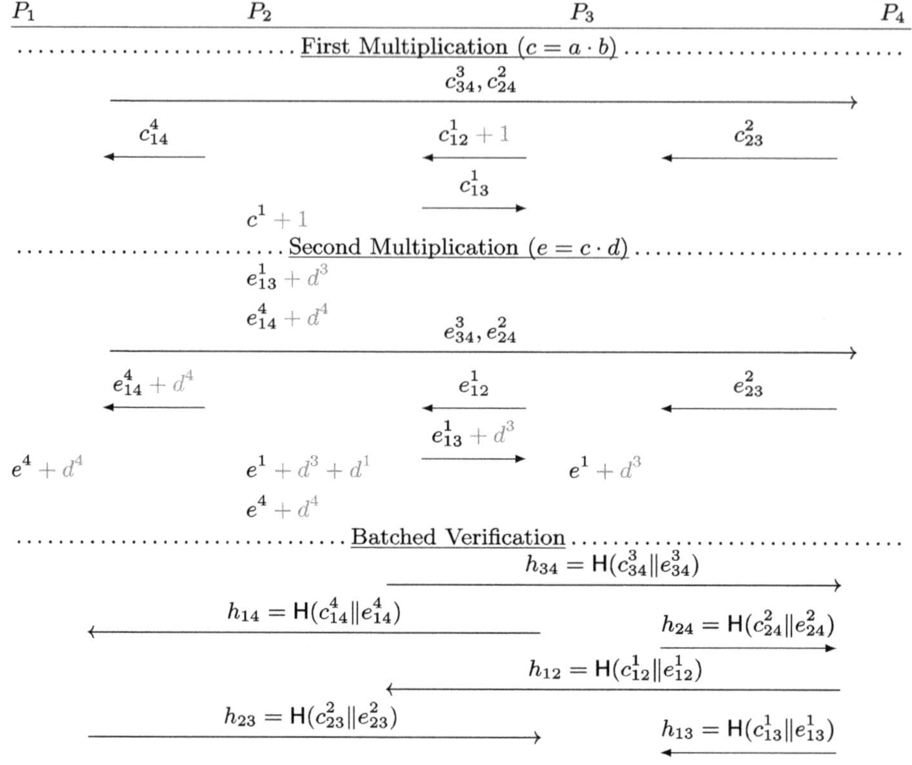

Fig. 8. Two multiplications and batched verification required to evaluate the circuit from Fig. 2 in Fantastic Four [14]. Parts in red are errors introduced by cheating P_3, and we omit all locally held shares that do not contain any error. We also omit the comparison of hash values and cheater identification inside the batched verification, as they play no role in our attack.

party P_3 receives c_{13}^1 and $e_{13}^1 + d^3$ from P_2 while it receives $h_{13} = \mathsf{H}(c_{13}^1 \| e_{13}^1)$ from P_4. Hence, similar to the attack in §3.3, P_3 may for example check for different $x \in \mathcal{R}$ if $\mathsf{H}(c_{13}^1 \| e_{13}^1 + d^3 - x) = h_{13}$. If it succeeds, then except for negligible probability it holds that $x = d^3$ and P_3 can extract $d = d^1 + d^2 + d^3 + d^4$ as it already holds all other shares by the definition of the secret sharing scheme.

We also verified the aforementioned attack to check for a specific $x \in \mathcal{R}$ by implementing a minimal proof-of-concept attack on the protocol implementation in MP-SPDZ [24]. Our code is available at https://encrypto.de/code/F4attack.

4.1   Fixing Fantastic Four

Fantastic Four can be fixed using the exact same approach as our fix for Trident in §3.5. The security flaw again stems from the fact that errors are allowed to propagate through the protocol execution, as outputs of multiplications can be used by further multiplications before being verified. Hence, we are able to instead run an individual verification immediately after each layer of multiplications, decreasing the efficiency of the protocol.

To instead have the verification with zero amortized overhead, we first consider a simplified protocol providing fairness. This is easy to derive from Fantastic Four by simply replacing the cheater identification in the verification step with an immediate abort of the protocol, noting that this abort would always lead to no party receiving any output. Now, we instantiate the verification using $\mathcal{F}_{\text{CHECKEQS}}^{A,(s_a)_{a \in A},(t_a)_{a \in A}}$ (Fig. 4). Recall that for each $\{g,h\} \subseteq \{1,2,3,4\}, g \neq h$, in the original verification (Fig. 7) one hash is sent and then compared. To capture all hash comparisons, we set $A = \{12, 13, 14, 23, 24, 34\}$ and for each $a \in A$, let s_a be the index of the party sending h_a and t_a be the index of the party that receives it in Fig. 7. We call the functionality with these specific parameters $\mathcal{F}_{\text{CHECKEQS}}^{\text{FantasticFour}}$ for simplicity. The fixed verification step is provided in Fig. 9. It again renders the protocol secure, as except for negligible probability, $\mathcal{F}_{\text{CHECKEQS}}^{\text{FantasticFour}}$ exactly outputs Accept if no cheating occurred and Reject otherwise, following the same arguments as in §3.5. The proof is very similar to the one in §3.5, so we omit the details here.

Protocol Verification step of $\Pi_{\text{mult}}^{\text{FIXED}}(\llbracket x \rrbracket, \llbracket y \rrbracket) \to \llbracket z \rrbracket$ for Fantastic Four [14]

Verify (batched):

1. For every $\{g,h\} \subseteq \{1,2,3,4\}, g \neq h$ and parties P_i, P_j with $i,j \notin \{g,h\}$ as above where P_i sends z_{gh}^h to P_g:
   - P_j sends $h_{gh}^1 = \mathsf{H}(\ldots \| z_{gh}^h \| \ldots)$ to $\mathcal{F}_{\text{CHECKEQS}}^{\text{FantasticFour}}$.
   - P_g sends $h_{gh}^2 = \mathsf{H}(\ldots \| z_{gh}^h \| \ldots)$ (z_{gh}^h as received from P_i) to $\mathcal{F}_{\text{CHECKEQS}}^{\text{FantasticFour}}$.

2. P_i proceeds if it receives Accept from $\mathcal{F}_{\text{CHECKEQS}}^{\text{FantasticFour}}$ and aborts otherwise.

Fig. 9. Fixed, batched verification of the multiplication of Fantastic Four [14] in Fig. 7.

To instantiate $\mathcal{F}_{\text{MPC}}^{\text{sub}}$ required for the instantiation of $\mathcal{F}_{\text{CHECKEQS}}^{\text{FantasticFour}}$ (cf. §3.5), we can use Fantastic Four, but with immediate verification after each (layer of) multiplications, resulting in zero amortized overhead as it is used on a small circuit, independent of the circuit to be evaluated by the overall outer protocol.

4.2 Fixing the Robust Version of Fantastic Four

To provide robustness, Fantastic Four [14] is designed to identify honest parties in the case of a verification detecting any inconsistency. For classic robustness, they observe that P_g complaining about receiving a hash from P_j that is inconsistent with the value(s) received from P_i (cf. Fig. 7) indicates that one of these parties is cheating, immediately proving the uninvolved, fourth party to be honest. The protocol then lets all parties hand their shares to the honest party which locally finishes the computation. They also propose a "private robustness" variant which seeks to avoid disclosing clear text values to any party, even if proven honest.

There, a failed verification identifies a set of at most two parties containing the cheater. The protocol then removes parties in this set from the execution until it, in the worst case, ends up with the two parties running a semi-honest protocol, given that the malicious party must be among the previously identified parties.

While both approaches work when verification is not delayed, delaying the verification as in [14] not only breaks security, but also prevents reliable identification of one or multiple honest parties. As we have seen, inconsistencies introduced by a cheater that are not immediately detected cause honest parties to deviate from what an honest protocol execution would appear like. This can lead to honest parties sending incorrect values, which is detected during verification. As an example, note that in Fig. 8, honest P_2 sends incorrect $e_{13}^1 + d^3$ to P_3 while honest P_4 provides an inconsistent hash h_{13} that contains the correct e_{13}^1 without any offset. In the full version of this paper [8, App. C], we provide more detailed examples where, e.g., both senders (of inconsistent value and hash) and the receiver are honest and demonstrate how both notions of robustness in Fantastic Four are broken by delaying verification.

Unfortunately, there appears to be no immediate fix with zero amortized overhead like for fairness (cf. §4.1). More precisely, note that while using $\mathcal{F}_{\text{CHECKEQS}}^{\text{FantasticFour}}$ detects a mismatch resulting from the first incorrect message sent, further mismatches can be produced by continuing to compute on inconsistent shares, and honest parties may send incorrect values. In $\mathcal{F}_{\text{CHECKEQS}}^{\text{FantasticFour}}$, it would then be necessary to additionally identify the original, first inconsistency, which must be caused by the cheater. As $\mathcal{F}_{\text{CHECKEQS}}^{\text{FantasticFour}}$ only receives hashes over data from all multiplications as input, it appears to be unfeasible to identify the exact multiplication causing an inconsistency. Hence, it seems not to be possible to reliably narrow down the cheater's identity using the amortized approach.

A possible solution is to optimistically use the fixed, fair protocol and, should any cheating be detected at the end, run the layer-wise original verification round by round until the first inconsistency is detected. This ensures that the detected inconsistency is directly caused by the cheater, enabling the original robustness mechanisms. Note that this approach yields zero amortized overhead if no cheating occurs and a cheater is not able to abort the protocol execution. Yet, cheating would increase protocol execution cost, given that the round complexity is doubled by sequentially running all verification steps in the end. Given that robustness goes beyond our original attack and fix in §3, we leave it up to future work to formalize how robustness can be achieved securely and investigate if more efficient approaches exist.

5   SWIFT [28]: Almost-Evasion of Our Attack

The three-party protocol of SWIFT [28][3] is another protocol using delayed verification checks and targeting robustness. The core idea (regarding multiplication)

---

[3] For simplicity, we call the protocol "SWIFT" here, noting that [28] also contains a four-party protocol that we do not examine in this paper.

of SWIFT is very close to that of Trident [12] (§3), except for evading the requirement for a fourth party to instantiate preprocessing multiplication $\mathcal{F}_{\mathrm{MultPre}}$, and achieving robustness using a similar approach to cheater identification as that in §4.2 for Fantastic Four [14]. Yet, we note that the close similarity to Trident is present only in more recent rephrased and simplified versions of SWIFT, especially that in [7]. We decide here to target the original protocol in [28], noting that more recent versions are not consistent with each other and do not claim to resolve any security issue. For consistency with [28], note that we label the three parties P_0, P_1, P_2 here, instead of starting with P_1 as before.

The two secret sharing semantics important here are as defined in Table 4. The main sharing semantic is $[\![\cdot]\!]$ and an intermediate additive sharing $\langle\cdot\rangle$ between P_1, P_2 is used. Both sharings are linear. The protocol uses *function-spsdependent preprocessing* where only the β_v-values are computed online.

Table 4. Secret sharing semantics for sharing a value $v \in \mathcal{R}$ in SWIFT [28].

Sharing Type	P_0	P_1	P_2	Correlation
$\langle v \rangle$	—	v^1	v^2	$v = v^1 + v^2$
$[\![v]\!]$	$(\alpha_v^1, \alpha_v^2, \beta_v + \gamma_v)$	$(\alpha_v^1, \beta_v, \gamma_v)$	$(\alpha_v^2, \beta_v, \gamma_v)$	$\beta_v = v + \alpha_v^1 + \alpha_v^2$

The multiplication protocol of SWIFT is depicted in Fig. 10. It already includes optimizations that [28] only describes in text. Importantly, [28] notes that all verification is delayed and batched and that P_1, P_2 can optimistically evaluate the circuit (up to the output phase) alone. Only in the verification, P_0 receives all $\beta_z + \gamma_z$ computed throughout the circuit and immediately verifies their consistency. It then locally computes $\beta_z^{*1}, \beta_z^{*2}$ used by P_1, P_2 before to send hashes, allowing P_1, P_2 to verify consistency of the messages they have previously exchanged in the online phase. Note that P_0 must receive the $\beta_z + \gamma_z$ values first, as it has no knowledge of these if coming out of a multiplication otherwise, while requiring them for computing the hashes for later multiplications, depending on the outcome of the prior one. Finally, the hashes are again computed over the messages over all multiplications to leverage amortization.

We proceed by first discussing in §5.1 how SWIFT almost evades our attack from §3.3, still leaving a gap in its security proof, by making communication more asymmetric, using that P_0 is inactive in the online phase before verification. Then, we show in §5.2 how a modified attack can still be applied, depending on how an underspecified part of the protocol is interpreted.

5.1 Unsuccessful Attack and Gap in the Security Proof

As an example, the flow of messages for computing $c = a \cdot b$ and $e = c \cdot d$ (Fig. 2) is given in Fig. 11. In case of corrupt P_0, our attack from §3.3 cannot be adapted to SWIFT because this party only sends hashes, which will exactly cause a mismatch for one of the other parties if one of these hashes is incorrect by the direct

---

Protocol $\Pi_{\mathsf{mult}}(\llbracket x \rrbracket, \llbracket y \rrbracket) \to \llbracket z \rrbracket$ of SWIFT [28]

Input: $\llbracket \cdot \rrbracket$-shares of $x, y \in \mathcal{R}$.

Output: $\llbracket \cdot \rrbracket$-shares of $z = x \cdot y$.

Preprocessing:

1. Non-interactively generate $\langle a_z \rangle$ by P_0, P_i sampling $a_z^i \leftarrow_\$ \mathcal{R}$ for $i \in \{1, 2\}$.
2. P_1, P_2 non-interactively sample $\gamma_z \leftarrow_\$ \mathcal{R}$.
3. Compute further preprocessing material (check [28] for details):
   - $\langle \chi \rangle$ where in addition, P_0 has both shares χ^1, χ^2.
   - P_1, P_2 have $\psi \in \mathcal{R}$.
   - Prior values are random, subject to $\chi^1 + \chi^2 + \psi = \gamma_x \alpha_y + \alpha_x \gamma_y + \alpha_x \alpha_y$.

Online:

1. Party P_i for $i \in \{1, 2\}$ computes $\beta_z^{*i} = -(\beta_x + \gamma_x)\alpha_y^i - (\beta_y + \gamma_y)\alpha_x^i + \alpha_z^i + \chi^i$.
2. P_1, P_2 exchange $\beta_z^{*1}, \beta_z^{*2}$.
3. P_1, P_2 compute $\beta_z = \beta_z^{*1} + \beta_z^{*2} + \beta_x \beta_y + \psi$.

Verify:

1. P_1 sends $\beta_z + \gamma_z$ and P_2 sends $h_0 = \mathsf{H}(\beta_z + \gamma_z)$ to P_0.
2. If P_0 detects that $h_0 \neq \mathsf{H}(\beta_z + \gamma_z)$ with $\beta_z + \gamma_z$ as received by P_1, it outputs an error message and starts the cheater identification described in [28]. The steps below are not executed in that case.
3. P_0 computes $\beta_z^{*1}, \beta_z^{*2}$ as P_1, P_2 did in step 1 of the online phase.
4. P_0 sends $h_i = \mathsf{H}(\beta_z^{*3-i})$ to P_i for $i \in \{1, 2\}$.
5. If P_i for $i \in \{1, 2\}$ detects that $h_i \neq \mathsf{H}(\beta_z^{*3-i})$ with β_z^{*3-i} as received by P_{3-i}, it outputs an error message and starts the cheater identification described in [28].

Fig. 10. Multiplication protocol of SWIFT [28] (some operations inlined and restructured according to the optimizations that [28] only describes in text).

action of P_0. Yet, it appears that the more sophisticated structure of SWIFT, allowing P_0 to remain absent during most of the protocol execution, also thwarts our attack for another corrupted party, as we will describe in the following.

Assume a corrupt P_1. Furthermore, for a multiplication $x \cdot y = z$, assume that P_1, P_2 hold consistent values $\hat{\beta}_x, \hat{\beta}_y$ on their input wires which do not have to necessarily match the β_x, β_y that they would hold in an honest protocol execution. Now, in a multiplication, P_1 uses $\hat{\beta}_z^{*1} + \delta = -(\hat{\beta}_x + \gamma_x)\alpha_y^1 - (\hat{\beta}_y + \gamma_y)\alpha_x^1 + \alpha_z^1 + \chi^1 + \delta$ for $\delta \in \mathcal{R}$ that P_1 can use to introduce an error to the message. P_2 honestly sends $\hat{\beta}_z^{*2} = -(\hat{\beta}_x + \gamma_x)\alpha_y^2 - (\hat{\beta}_y + \gamma_y)\alpha_x^2 + \alpha_z^2 + \chi^2$. This will cause both parties to eventually compute $\hat{\beta}_z = (\hat{\beta}_z^{*1} + \delta) + \hat{\beta}_z^{*2} + \hat{\beta}_x \hat{\beta}_y + \psi$, offsetting the result by δ. Still, it yields a perhaps incorrect, but consistent $\hat{\beta}_z$ to both parties. For the example circuit from Fig. 2, P_1 could use an error $\delta \neq 0$ in the first multiplication. The parties P_1, P_2 would then obtain $\hat{\beta}_c = \beta_c + \delta$.[4] In

---

[4] Of course, from this, P_1 can also derive β_c given that it selects the error δ.

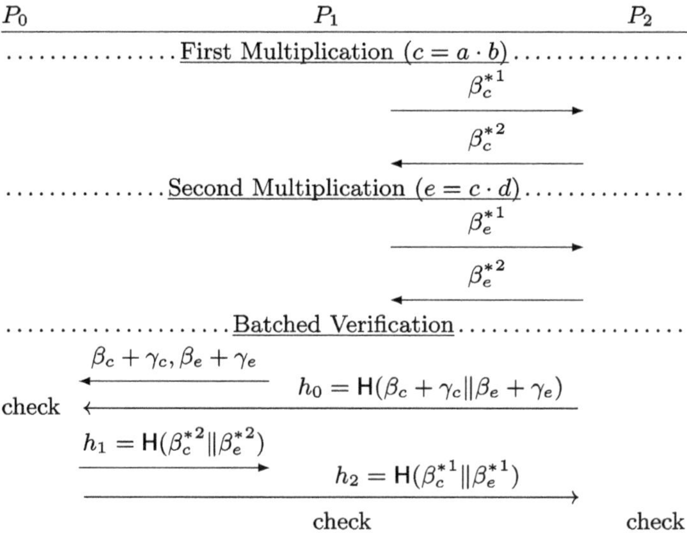

Fig. 11. Online phase of the two multiplications and batched verification required to evaluate the circuit from Fig. 2 in SWIFT [28].

the next multiplication, corrupt P_1 would receive

$$\hat{\beta}_e^{*^2} = -(\hat{\beta}_c + \gamma_c)\alpha_d^2 - (\hat{\beta}_d + \gamma_d)\alpha_c^2 + \alpha_e^2 + \chi^2$$
$$= -(\beta_c + \delta + \gamma_c)\alpha_d^2 - (\beta_d + \gamma_d)\alpha_c^2 + \alpha_e^2 + \chi^2 = \beta_e^{*2} - \delta\alpha_d^2$$

from P_2. Note that this message is still masked by α_e^2.

The difficulty is that the verification towards P_0 is done first. Recall that P_1 can cause P_2 to reconstruct incorrect $\hat{\beta}_z$ along the computation, but it will also learn the same incorrect values. As P_2 sends the hash over all $\hat{\beta}_z + \gamma_z$ to P_0, P_1 can either send consistent, incorrect $\hat{\beta}_z + \gamma_z$, or send other values which except for negligible probability will lead to P_0 detecting an inconsistency and starting cheater identification instead of proceeding with the verification step. This does not allow P_1 to learn anything, as it knows the values that P_2 computes the hash over and, hence, cannot use P_0's reaction as an oracle to derive new information.

In §3.3, our attack relied on P_1 receiving from one party a message, $\hat{\beta}_e^{*^2} = \beta_e^{*2} - \delta\alpha_d^2$ in this case, and from the other party a hash, using an inconsistent message as input, in this case β_e^{*2}. Yet, P_1 is forced for each multiplication $x \cdot y = z$ to send the same incorrect $\hat{\beta}_z + \gamma_z$ that P_2 has to P_0 so that P_0 does not detect an inconsistency. Hence, P_0 uses the same inconsistency used by P_2. Specifically, P_0 will have inputs $\hat{\beta}_x + \gamma_x, \hat{\beta}_y + \gamma_y$, including errors from prior multiplications influencing the input wires but matching the shares of P_2. Then, P_0 will compute

$$\hat{\beta}_z^{*^2} = -(\hat{\beta}_x + \gamma_x)\alpha_y^2 - (\hat{\beta}_y + \gamma_y)\alpha_x^2 + \alpha_z^2 + \chi^2$$

and include this in hash h_1 to send to P_1, but this will be consistent with $\hat{\beta}_z^*$ that P_1 receives from P_2, not disclosing any additional information. For corrupt P_2, the aforementioned arguments are symmetrical.

We note that the prior arguments are neither used in [28] nor in the full version [27] that it refers to for the security proof. Instead, like for Trident [12] as discussed in §3.1, it appears that [27] proves security only for the unoptimized, incomplete protocol without any delayed and batched verification. Hence, the security proof is incomplete. We stress that our prior observations give reason to believe that the multiplication protocol of SWIFT [28] still is secure, but our prior arguments represent only a possible starting point for trying to provide a complete and correct security proof. They do not immediately yield a proof, and while our prior attack did not work, this does not prove SWIFT to be secure. We leave a fix to the security proof to future work. Should it not be possible to fix SWIFT in this way, another option would be the use of $\mathcal{F}_{\text{CHECKEQS}}^{A,(s_a)_{a\in A},(t_a)_{a\in A}}$ as in §3.5, yielding at least a fair protocol, noting prior difficulties in §4.2 to also reach robustness with this approach.

5.2   Potential Attack on SWIFT, Involving the Input Phase

As seen in §5.1, corrupt P_1 and P_2 appear to be unable to exploit causing both honest parties to reach inconsistent states because the honest P_0 will detect any inconsistency before being able to send an inconsistent hash back to the corrupt party. Hence, we now try again to target P_0. For multiplications it only interacts with P_1, P_2 during the verification, sending hashes to both parties and being unable to successfully attack the protocol.

Instead, we investigate the input phase of SWIFT. As described in [28], P_0 can share an input $v \in \mathcal{R}$ as follows:

1. Non-interactively generate $\langle a_v \rangle$ by P_0, P_i sampling $a_v^i \leftarrow_\$ \mathcal{R}$ for $i \in \{1,2\}$ during preprocessing.
2. All parties non-interactively sample $\gamma_v \leftarrow_\$ \mathcal{R}$ during preprocessing.
3. P_0 computes $\beta_v = v + a_v^1 + a_v^2$ (and uses $\beta_v + \gamma_v$ as part of its share).
4. P_0 sends β_v to P_1.
5. P_0, P_1 "jmp-send β_v to P_2" [28, p. 2656].

The "jmp-send" operation denotes that one of the parties P_0, P_1 sends β_v and the other sends $\mathsf{H}(\beta_v)$ to P_2 that then can check for consistency in [28]. While the distribution of roles is ambiguous in the paper, the notation [28, Notation 3.1 and Fig. 1] suggests that the first mentioned party, i.e., P_0 sends the actual value β_v. It is the same primitive that [28] also uses for multiplications—in Fig. 10, we simply inlined it in the overall protocol description. Regarding delaying the consistency check, it is stated that "[t]he communication of hash is done once and for all from P_j to P_k" [28, §3.1] and "while the *verify* for a fixed ordered pair of senders will be executed once and for all in the end" [28, §3.1] in the context of "jmp-send". It is unclear if "in the end" refers to the entire protocol (before the output phase), like for delayed verifications of the multiplications, or only the final "jmp-send"-instance with specific two senders in fixed roles. Unfortunately, [28] provides no public implementation to cross-check. For our attack, we assume that the verification is delayed until immediately before the output phase, just like for multiplications, which appears to be at least within the under-specified protocol description. Furthermore, we assume that the verification towards P_0 remains to be executed first. This would render the input phase part of the optimistic protocol execution.

We now consider a minimal circuit that computes $c = a \cdot b$ where corrupt P_0 provides input a, P_1 provides b, and P_2 receives c. Clearly, P_0 should not gain any information about b. Then, we let P_0 send β_a to P_1 but $\beta_a + 1$ to P_2, yielding the situation depicted in Fig. 12. We label the hash to check the consistency of input a by h_i and note that using that, the inconsistency would be detected. Yet, P_0 receives $\beta_c - \alpha_b^2 + \gamma_c$ and $h_0 = \mathsf{H}(\beta_c + \beta_b - \alpha_b^2 + \gamma_c)$. As in §3.3, this enables P_0 to test for certain or even fully extract β_b while it already has α_b^1, α_b^2 by definition of the secret sharing scheme. Then, it can derive $b = \beta_b - \alpha_b^1 - \alpha_b^2$, the private input of P_1.

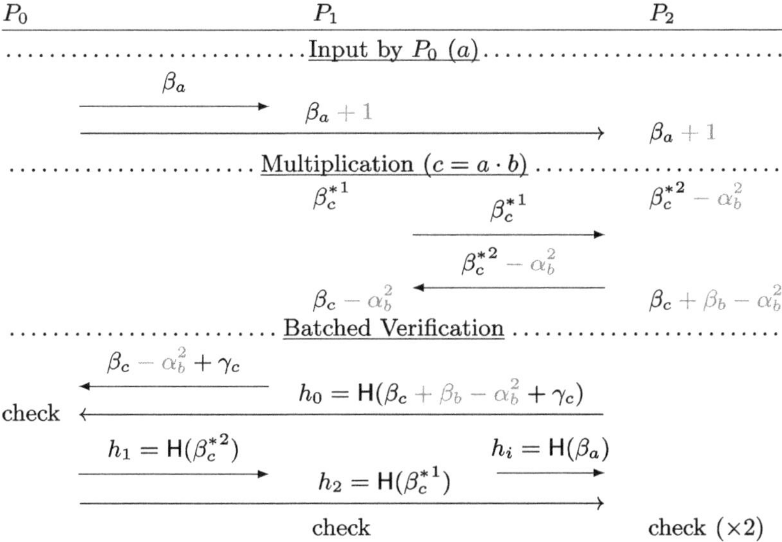

Fig. 12. One input (other correct and omitted), one multiplication and batched verification required to evaluate $c = a \cdot b$ in SWIFT [28]. Parts in red are errors introduced by cheating P_0 and we omit all locally held shares that do not contain any error.

We note that this attack can easily be made impossible by clearly requiring that consistency checks for the input phase run immediately after the input phase, still resulting in zero amortized overhead.

Note on Related Protocols Tetrad [29] and SOCIUM [7]. The four-party protocol Tetrad [29] improves upon Trident [12] with the online phase of multiplications deviating from Tetrad mostly by using the same trick as SWIFT [28] to let two parties run most of the online phase and a third party only joining for the final verification. In contrast to SWIFT, Tetrad has a separate consistency check for the input phase, and this check is not delayed. Hence, we presume that Tetrad evades the original attack from §3.3 similar to SWIFT, still leaving a gap in the security proof (cf. §5.1), and also that it is not vulnerable to the attack from §5.2 involving the input phase. The gap in the proof may result in some details not appearing to be crucial for security. Hence, small optimizations in implementations may appear to still be secure, but create vulnerabilities, see §7.

The three-party protocol SOCIUM from [7] is a modification of SWIFT where only one fixed, known party can be corrupted maliciously, while others cannot deviate from the protocol even when corrupted. It uses only one batched consistency check for messages from the known potentially cheating party. This check fails if any cheating occurred, and as there is no further consistency check, especially none with the potentially cheating party receiving redundant data, it seems that our attack does not apply to SOCIUM.

6   Attacking and Fixing Quad [21]

The last instance of our attack is on the fair four-party protocol Quad [21]. We note that the underlying ideas of Quad are quite similar to those in Trident [12] (discussed in §3), also using a sharing semantic $[\![v]\!]$ consisting of a masked value $\mathsf{m}_v = v + \lambda_v$ and a mask λ_v shared between the parties using a secondary sharing $\langle\lambda_v\rangle$. Multiplication accordingly follows the same intuition as in Trident, and the protocol is optimistically executed while hash-based consistency checks are executed once before revealing any outputs.

This opens exactly the same vulnerability described in §3, also allowing us to deploy a similar fix. For the concrete attack, it again remains to survey how an error introduced by a cheater propagates through the following computation in the exact protocol, enabling the cheater to receive inconsistent data from which it can extract information. This is essentially a technicality that reuses ideas of our attack and fix from §3, used throughout this paper. We provide full details on how the attack and fix exactly translate to Quad in the full version [8, App. D].

7   Responsible Disclosure

We found the vulnerable protocols to be implemented in the MPC frameworks MP-SPDZ[5] [24], HPMPC[6] [20,21], and in the oblivious analytics system ORQ[7] [4]. The frameworks inherited the vulnerabilities from the insecure protocols at the time of disclosure. After acceptance of our paper, we informed the authors of all affected protocols and implementations on January 30, 2026. We

---

[5] https://github.com/data61/MP-SPDZ/, `v0.4.2`: Fantastic Four [14].
[6] https://github.com/chart21/hpmpc/, `a9809dc`: Fantastic Four [14] and Quad [21].
[7] https://github.com/CASP-Systems-BU/orq, `v1.0.0`: Fantastic Four [14].

coordinated with the maintainers of all involved implementations that vulnerabilities were patched or vulnerable protocols were labeled with appropriate warnings before March 15, 2026 when our results were publicly disclosed. Furthermore, this time window provided the authors of vulnerable protocols an opportunity to update the ePrint versions of their papers if desired, given that they are made public not earlier than the patches of all vulnerable implementations.

We consulted with the maintainers of vulnerable implementations about their fixes. MP-SPDZ is now fixed with a round-wise verification, see §3.4. This also includes the input phase so that an attack similar to that from §5.2 is prevented. The fix for HPMPC implements $\mathcal{F}_{\text{CHECKEQS}}^{A,(s_a)_{a\in A},(t_a)_{a\in A}}$ (cf. §3.5) for zero-amortized overhead, but uses an alternative instantiation of that based on binary equality circuits with a higher round complexity. Interestingly, we were notified by the maintainer that HPMPC's implementation of Tetrad [29] is also vulnerable, as minor modifications to the protocol, not contradicting the security proof of Tetrad due to its gap, were made. Finally, ORQ was fixed with our proposed instantiation of $\mathcal{F}_{\text{CHECKEQS}}^{A,(s_a)_{a\in A},(t_a)_{a\in A}}$ from §3.5.

Acknowledgments. We thank Maximilian Stillger (TU Darmstadt) for our insightful discussions about generalizing and improving formalization of existing security proofs. These discussions are what ultimately lead to the discovery of the flaw in SWIFT from where our research presented in this paper started. We also thank the authors and maintainers of affected papers and implementations for their collaboration in the disclosure process and swiftly patching the affected code.

This project received funding from the ERC under the EU's research and innovation programs Horizon Europe (PRIVTOOLS/101124778) and Horizon 2020 (PSOTI/850990). It was co-funded by the DFG within SFB 1119 CROSSING/236615297, and supported by BMFTR and HMWK within ATHENE.

Disclosure of Interests. The authors have no competing interests to declare.

References

1. Araki, T., Furukawa, J., Lindell, Y., Nof, A., Ohara, K.: High-throughput semi-honest secure three-party computation with an honest majority. In: ACM CCS 2016, pp. 805–817 (2016). https://doi.org/10.1145/2976749.2978331
2. Araki, T., Furukawa, J., Ohara, K., Pinkas, B., Rosemarin, H., Tsuchida, H.: Secure graph analysis at scale. In: ACM CCS 2021, pp. 610–629 (2021). https://doi.org/10.1145/3460120.3484560
3. Asharov, G., et al.: Efficient secure three-party sorting with applications to data analysis and heavy hitters. In: ACM CCS 2022, pp. 125–138 (2022). https://doi.org/10.1145/3548606.3560691
4. Baum, E., et al.: ORQ: complex analytics on private data with strong security guarantees. In: ACM SOSP 2025, pp. 802–833 (2025). https://doi.org/10.1145/3731569.3764833
5. Boneh, D., DeMillo, R.A., Lipton, R.J.: On the importance of checking cryptographic protocols for faults. In: Fumy, W. (ed.) EUROCRYPT 1997. LNCS, vol. 1233, pp. 37–51. Springer, Heidelberg (1997). https://doi.org/10.1007/3-540-69053-0_4

6. Boyle, E., Gilboa, N., Ishai, Y., Nof, A.: Practical fully secure three-party computation via sublinear distributed zero-knowledge proofs. In: ACM CCS 2019, pp. 869–886 (2019). https://doi.org/10.1145/3319535.3363227

7. Brüggemann, A., Schick, O., Schneider, T., Suresh, A., Yalame, H.: Don't eject the impostor: fast three-party computation with a known cheater. In: IEEE S&P 2024, pp. 503–522 (2024). https://doi.org/10.1109/SP54263.2024.00164

8. Brüggemann, A., Schneider, T.: When trying to catch cheaters breaks the MPC: Breaking and fixing delayed consistency checks in Trident, Fantastic Four, SWIFT, and Quad. Cryptology ePrint Archive, Report 2026/234 (2026). https://eprint.iacr.org/2026/234

9. Canetti, R.: Security and composition of multiparty cryptographic protocols. J. Cryptol. **13**(1), 143–202 (2000). https://doi.org/10.1007/s001459910006

10. Chaudhari, H., Choudhury, A., Patra, A., Suresh, A.: ASTRA: high throughput 3PC over rings with application to secure prediction. In: ACM Cloud Computing Security Workshop (CCSW) 2019, pp. 81–92 (2019). https://doi.org/10.1145/3338466.3358922

11. Chaudhari, H., Rachuri, R., Suresh, A.: Trident: Efficient 4PC framework for privacy preserving machine learning. Cryptology ePrint Archive, Report 2019/1315 (2019). https://eprint.iacr.org/2019/1315

12. Chaudhari, H., Rachuri, R., Suresh, A.: Trident: efficient 4PC framework for privacy preserving machine learning. In: NDSS 2020 (2020). https://doi.org/10.14722/ndss.2020.23005

13. Cohen, R., Lindell, Y.: Fairness versus guaranteed output delivery in secure multiparty computation. In: Sarkar, P., Iwata, T. (eds.) ASIACRYPT 2014. LNCS, vol. 8874, pp. 466–485. Springer, Heidelberg (2014). https://doi.org/10.1007/978-3-662-45608-8_25

14. Dalskov, A.P.K., Escudero, D., Keller, M.: Fantastic four: honest-majority four-party secure computation with malicious security. In: USENIX Security 2021, pp. 2183–2200 (2021). https://www.usenix.org/conference/usenixsecurity21/presentation/dalskov

15. Dalskov, A.P.K., Escudero, D., Nof, A.: Fully secure MPC and zk-FLIOP over rings: new constructions, improvements and extensions. In: CRYPTO 2024, pp. 136–169. LNCS (2024). https://doi.org/10.1007/978-3-031-68397-8_5

16. Damgård, I., Nielsen, J.B.: Scalable and unconditionally secure multiparty computation. In: Menezes, A. (ed.) CRYPTO 2007. LNCS, vol. 4622, pp. 572–590. Springer, Heidelberg (2007). https://doi.org/10.1007/978-3-540-74143-5_32

17. Furukawa, J., Lindell, Y., Nof, A., Weinstein, O.: High-throughput secure three-party computation for malicious adversaries and an honest majority. In: Coron, J.-S., Nielsen, J.B. (eds.) EUROCRYPT 2017. LNCS, vol. 10211, pp. 225–255. Springer, Cham (2017). https://doi.org/10.1007/978-3-319-56614-6_8

18. Goldreich, O.: Foundations of Cryptography: Basic Applications, vol. 2. Cambridge University Press (2004). https://doi.org/10.1017/CBO9780511721656

19. Goyal, V., Liu, Y., Song, Y.: Communication-efficient unconditional MPC with guaranteed output delivery. In: Boldyreva, A., Micciancio, D. (eds.) CRYPTO 2019. LNCS, vol. 11693, pp. 85–114. Springer, Cham (2019). https://doi.org/10.1007/978-3-030-26951-7_4

20. Harth-Kitzerow, C.: HPMPC: High-performance implementation of secure multiparty computation (MPC) protocols. GitHub (2022). https://github.com/chart21/hpmpc/

21. Harth-Kitzerow, C., Suresh, A., Wang, Y., Yalame, H., Carle, G., Annavaram, M.: High-throughput secure multiparty computation with an honest majority in various network settings. PoPETs **2025**(1), 250–272 (2025). https://doi.org/10.56553/popets-2025-0015

22. Huang, Y., Katz, J., Evans, D.: Quid-Pro-Quo-tocols: strengthening semi-honest protocols with dual execution. In: IEEE S&P 2012, pp. 272–284 (2012). https://doi.org/10.1109/SP.2012.43

23. Katz, J., Lindell, Y.: Introduction to Modern Cryptography, third edn. Chapman and Hall, CRC Press (2014)

24. Keller, M.: MP-SPDZ: a versatile framework for multi-party computation. In: ACM CCS 2020, pp. 1575–1590 (2020). https://doi.org/10.1145/3372297.3417872

25. Kiraz, M.S., Schoenmakers, B.: A protocol issue for the malicious case of yao's garbled circuit construction. In: 27th Symposium on Information Theory in the Benelux, pp. 283–290 (2006), https://berry.win.tue.nl/papers/wic06.pdf

26. Koti, N., Kukkala, V.B., Patra, A., Gopal, B.R.: Graphiti: secure graph computation made more scalable. In: ACM CCS 2024, pp. 4017–4031 (2024). https://doi.org/10.1145/3658644.3670393

27. Koti, N., Pancholi, M., Patra, A., Suresh, A.: SWIFT: Super-fast and robust privacy-preserving machine learning. Cryptology ePrint Archive, Report 2020/592 (2020). https://eprint.iacr.org/2020/592

28. Koti, N., Pancholi, M., Patra, A., Suresh, A.: SWIFT: super-fast and robust privacy-preserving machine learning. In: USENIX Security 2021, pp. 2651–2668 (2021). https://www.usenix.org/conference/usenixsecurity21/presentation/koti

29. Koti, N., Patra, A., Rachuri, R., Suresh, A.: Tetrad: actively secure 4PC for secure training and inference. In: NDSS 2022 (2022)

30. Mohassel, P., Rindal, P.: ABY^3: a mixed protocol framework for machine learning. In: ACM CCS 2018, pp. 35–52 (2018). https://doi.org/10.1145/3243734.3243760

Game Theory Does Not Always Help: The Case of Statistical Multi-party Coin Tossing

Chen-Da Liu-Zhang[1], Elisaweta Masserova[2]([envelope]), João Ribeiro[3,4],
and Sri AravindaKrishnan Thyagarajan[5]

[1] Lucerne University of Applied Sciences and Arts, Lucerne, Switzerland
chen-da.liuzhang@hslu.ch
[2] Carnegie Mellon University, Pittsburgh, PA, USA
elisawem@andrew.cmu.edu
[3] Instituto de Telecomunicações, Lisboa, Portugal
jribeiro@tecnico.ulisboa.pt
[4] Departamento de Matemática, Instituto Superior Técnico, Universidade de Lisboa,
Lisboa, Portugal
[5] University of Sydney, Sydney, Australia

Abstract. The study of coin-tossing protocols lies at the intersection of cryptography and game theory, where parties with potentially conflicting interests aim to jointly generate an unbiased random bit. Classical cryptographic results establish that strong fairness is achievable with an honest majority in the statistical setting, but impossible with a dishonest majority. In parallel, game-theoretic approaches [TCC 2018, Eurocrypt 2022 & CRYPTO 2024] have demonstrated that weaker equilibrium-based fairness guarantees can sometimes circumvent cryptographic lower bounds, raising the question of whether such techniques can overcome impossibility in the statistical regime.

In this work, we answer this question negatively.

- We show that for n parties and $t \geq n/2$ corruptions, there exists no statistically secure, game-theoretic coin-tossing protocol, even assuming broadcast and bounded round complexity—with the sole exception of the case $n = 4$ where all but one party share the same preference. This complements known feasibility results for $t < n/2$, thereby completing the statistical feasibility landscape.
- We further consider the setting without broadcast. Here we prove that no computationally secure game-theoretic coin-tossing protocol exists for $t \geq n/3$ and polynomial-round complexity, except for the corner case $n = 6$ where all but one party share the same preference.

To establish these results, we refine existing frameworks for game-theoretic fairness to capture both broadcast and point-to-point communication models.

Together, our results establish the boundaries of game-theoretic fairness in multi-party coin tossing: while it extends feasibility in the computational setting, it offers no advantage in the statistical setting once an honest majority is lost.

© International Association for Cryptologic Research 2026
J. Daemen and E. Thomé (Eds.): EUROCRYPT 2026, LNCS 16543, pp. 488–514, 2026.
https://doi.org/10.1007/978-3-032-25324-8_17

1   Introduction

Both game theory and cryptography examine the interaction of parties with potentially conflicting interests. Cryptography defines worst-case guarantees, such as privacy, correctness and fairness, that must hold even against fully malicious coalitions. Game theory instead studies rational adversaries, asking whether protocols with incentive structures form equilibria (e.g., Nash or sequential equilibrium) in which deviations are *unprofitable* rather than *impossible*. With the advent of decentralized technologies, an emerging line of work has highlighted how the two fields can mutually inform and strengthen each other.

On the game-theoretic side, cryptographic techniques such as secure multiparty computation (MPC) have been used to replace trusted parties. For example, Dodis and Rabin [22] demonstrated how MPC can help to eliminate the need for a trusted mediator in achieving certain game-theoretic concepts, such as correlated equilibria. Ferreira and Weinberg [24] showed how to use cryptographic commitments to circumvent known impossibility results in auctions by relaxing some of the requirements (instead of ensuring that there exists no profitable deviation, the work ensures that no auctioneer *can find* one without breaking cryptographic assumptions). Timed cryptographic primitives such as time-lock puzzles [31,34] are known to facilitate dishonest majority sealed-bid auctions without a trusted auctioneer.

On the cryptographic side, game-theoretic techniques and notions of security—especially fairness—have been used to circumvent classical impossibility results [16,37,39]. An exciting line of work focuses specifically on the *coin-tossing* functionality. Informally, n parties, each with its own source of randomness, wish to jointly toss a coin in a way that the output is unbiased and unpredictable. Coin-tossing has a long history in cryptography and distributed computing, with applications ranging from leader election to consensus protocols [1–3,6,7,9,10,12,19–21,23,26,27,29,30,32,35,36].

At the heart of this literature are two classical results. Cleve's lower bound [17] showed that a two-party coin toss with one corruption is impossible to achieve—a corrupt party can bias the honest party's outcome by a non-negligible amount. In contrast, Blum's celebrated coin-tossing protocol [11] achieves a weaker but still meaningful guarantee: neither party can bias the outcome towards its *preferred* bit. This distinction is particularly interesting in the game-theoretic setting, where protecting against rational parties seeking to improve utility (rather than arbitrary malicious deviation) may be sufficient [4,5,13–15,38].

More recently, Chung, Guo, Lin, Pass, and Shi [16] explored the feasibility of n-party coin toss under such game-theoretic notions in the presence of a dishonest majority. In more detail, assuming a public preference profile of parties, Chung et al. [16] constructed protocols which satisfy the game-theoretic notion of fairness dubbed *Cooperative-Strategy-Proofness (CSP-fairness)* for an n-party setting with dishonest majority where all parties, except one, prefer the same bit b. On the flip side, Chung et al. proved that when precisely $n - 1$ parties are corrupt, unless all parties except for one have the same preference, CSP-fair coin toss is

Table 1. Feasibility of Coin Tossing

Work	Setting	Security	Threshold	Broadcast	Feasible
Wu et al. [39]	GT	Comp.	$t \leq t^*, n \geq 3$[a]	✓	✓
Wu et al. [39]	GT	Comp.	$t \geq t^* + 1, n \geq 3$	✓	✗
Cleve [17]	Stand.	Comp.	$t \geq \frac{n}{2}, n \geq 2$	✓	✗
Cohen et al. [18]	Stand.	Comp.	$t \geq \frac{n}{3}, n \geq 3$	✗	✗
Rabin and Ben-Or [33]	Stand.	Stat.	$t < \frac{n}{2}, n \geq 2$	✓	✓
Ben-Or et al. [8]	Stand.	Stat.	$t < \frac{n}{3}, n \geq 3$	✗	✓
This work	GT	Stat.	$t \geq \frac{n}{2}, n \geq 2$	✓	✗
This work	GT	Comp.	$t \geq \frac{n}{3}, n \geq 3$	✗	✗

Our impossibility results (last two rows) can be seen as game-theoretic counterparts of the two highlighted results.

[a]The parameter regime has a more fine-grained dependence on the number of parties and their preference profiles. We refer the reader to [39] for more details

impossible to achieve. Wu, Asharov, and Shi [39] then extended this line of work by providing a complete characterization of game-theoretically fair, multi-party coin toss. Specifically, they proposed protocols in the setting where a majority ($\geq \frac{n}{2}$), yet less than $n - 1$, parties are corrupt, and complemented their positive results with matching lower bounds (see Table 1). Most recently, Thyagarajan, Soni, and Wu [37] extended this line of work by considering a multi-sided coin-toss in the same setting, and Zhang and Wu [40] explored the extension of this setting which accommodates arbitrary preference profiles.

We note, however, that the positive results of Wu et al. [39] and Thyagarajan et al. [37] fundamentally rely on computationally secure cryptographic tools in settings with fully malicious adversaries. For instance, Wu et al. employ secure multi-party computation with identifiable abort against a dishonest majority. However, under dishonest majority, MPC with such assumptions is known to be impossible to realize information-theoretically [28]. Consequently, these results do not provide game-theoretic substitutes for *information-theoretic* coin tossing in regimes where strong cryptographic guarantees are known to be impossible (e.g., dishonest-majority fairness).

Motivated by the success of utilizing game-theory to circumvent known cryptographic lower bounds, we thus ask the following natural question:

*Can game theory help us circumvent known lower bounds in the setting of **statistical** n-party coin-toss?*

In this work, we show that, perhaps surprisingly, the answer is **no**. In particular, we show that for $t \geq n/2$ corruptions, fair coin tossing is impossible in the statistical game-theoretic setting (with the exception of a corner case of $n = 4$ where three parties prefer the same bit), thereby complementing the existing positive results for $t < n/2$. Together, these establish a complete characterization of the feasibility landscape (with the exception of our corner case).

1.1   Our Results

Before presenting our formal results, we recall what is already known in the standard (non–game-theoretic) model. It is known [33] that in the standard, non–game-theoretic model, assuming broadcast and an **honest majority**, statistically secure multi-party computation with guaranteed output delivery, and hence, in particular, coin tossing with *strong* fairness, is achievable. Informally, strong fairness means that an adversary controlling up to t parties cannot predict or bias the outcome of the protocol toward *any* coin. Hence, it immediately implies the weaker, game-theoretic notions of fairness (e.g., CSP-fairness), since the adversary in particular cannot bias the outcome towards his preferred coin. In contrast, it is also known that **statistical coin tossing is impossible** when a *dishonest majority* of parties is allowed.

Our first result strengthens this impossibility by showing that, with the exception of one corner case, no statistically secure, **game-theoretic** coin-tossing protocol exists without an honest majority of parties. Formally, we prove the following.

Theorem. *For any fixed maximum number of rounds $\ell(\lambda)$, there exists no statistically secure, game-theoretic coin-toss protocol for n parties when $t \geq \lceil n/2 \rceil$ parties are corrupt, even under a broadcast channel, except for the special case $n = 4$, where all but one party share the same preference.*

Next, we turn our attention to the setting where we have an honest majority but at least a third is corrupt. By the above, we know that even a stronger primitive, like MPC, is possible in this setting *while assuming broadcast*. However, without broadcast (and without setup), the elegant result by Cohen, Haitner, Omri, and Rotem [18] shows that there is no non-trivial (i.e., achieving bias smaller than $\frac{1}{2}$) coin-tossing protocols for $t \geq n/3$, and $n \geq 3$.

As we show in this work, with the exception of one corner case, this lower bound extends to the game-theoretic setting, albeit with a different bias. In more detail, we establish the following.

Theorem. *In the secure point-to-point channel model (no broadcast), given $n \geq 3$ parties and an adversarial threshold $t \geq \frac{n}{3}$, there exists no computationally secure game-theoretic coin-tossing protocol with the round-complexity polynomial in λ, except for the special case $n = 6$, where all but one party share the same preference.*

Note that the above result gives an impossibility not only for the statistical, but also the computational setting. To obtain these results, we need to *extend the coin-tossing framework* of Chung et al. [16] to handle the *absence of broadcast*, which requires a careful treatment. Briefly, prior work on game-theoretic coin tossing typically assumed that the coin output is derived directly from messages sent over a broadcast channel. To capture settings without broadcast, we introduce revised utility and correctness definitions.

We note, however, that our impossibility result for the broadcast setting remains valid in the original model of Chung et al. [16] assuming that parties wish to output an unbiased random bit for any preference profile.[1]

We now describe our results in more detail.

2   Technical Overview

Game-theoretic coin-tossing protocols by Wu et al. [39] and Thyagarajan et al. [37] are built around the following simple yet powerful idea:

In the game-theoretic setting, when parties' preferences are publicly known, any party that misbehaves can be punished by setting the outcome to the opposite of its preferred value.

This idea is particularly compelling in the two-party case. Consider Blum's classical coin-toss protocol [11], and let Alice and Bob have public preferences $p_a, p_b \in \{0, 1\}$. Alice first commits to a random bit r_a by sending $com(r_a)$ to Bob. Bob then samples and publishes his own random bit r_b. Finally, Alice opens her commitment, and the coin is set to $c = r_a \oplus r_b$.

Note that after Bob published his random bit, Alice knows the outcome of the protocol, while Bob does not. In the standard setting, this allows Alice to bias the outcome by aborting after seeing r_b, simply by refusing to open her commitment. In the *game-theoretic* setting, however, such misbehavior can be deterred: if Alice refuses to open, the protocol instead outputs $c = 1 - p_a$, the value *opposite to Alice's preference*.

Such a penalty-based mechanism remains very useful in the *multi-party* setting, although applying it becomes more subtle. At a high level, even if a misbehaving party can be identified, a corrupt coalition may contain multiple parties with *different* preferences. Nevertheless, Wu et al. [39] and Thyagarajan et al. [37] obtain elegant constructions centered around the following ideas. They partition parties into groups according to their public preferences and then running an *MPC with identifiable abort* to toss a coin separately for each group (those preferring 0 and those preferring 1). Malicious parties can be gradually identified and excluded until the protocol reaches a point where either reconstruction succeeds, or – if reconstruction fails – the coalition's adversarial preference is implicitly revealed, allowing the protocol to set the output to the *opposite* of that preference.

While the availability of a *penalty-based approach* that leverages known preferences is powerful for constructing protocols, it makes proving *impossibility results* significantly more challenging. Consider, for example, the cele-

---

brated lower-bound by Cleve [17], which shows that in the standard (non-game-theoretic) setting an unbiased two-party coin-toss is impossible to achieve if an adversary is allowed to corrupt one of the two parties.

At a high level, Cleve's argument defines $4r + 1$ adversarial strategies: the first simply aborts without sending the initial message, while each of the remaining strategies corresponds to a triple (party, bit, message-num). Here, party $\in$ {Alice, Bob} identifies the corrupted party, bit $\in \{0, 1\}$ is its preferred outcome, and message-num is the round after which the party computes the conditional outcome of the protocol. If that outcome disagrees with the preferred bit, the party aborts; otherwise it continues until the next round and may abort there. Cleve then shows that *at least one* of these strategies achieves a bias of $\Omega(\frac{1}{r})$.

This reasoning, however, **breaks down in the game-theoretic setting**: the fact that Alice can bias the output toward 1 does *not* imply that doing so increases her utility. In fact, if Alice prefers zero, she would actively harm herself by performing the attack.

We observe that the key in proving the impossibility of game-theoretic version of fairness is in showing that the adversary can bias the outcome of the protocol *towards his own preference*. Proving this is strictly harder than demonstrating (in line with traditional cryptographic literature) that the adversary can bias the outcome towards *some* value.

2.1 Impossibility of Statistical Game-Theoretic Coin-Toss Without Honest Majority

Establishing an analogue of Cleve's lower bound in the *statistical game-theoretic* setting (note that Wu et al. [39] obtained positive results for certain dishonest-majority regimes in the game-theoretic *computational* setting; see also Table 1) requires new techniques, which we now introduce.

New Tools for Game-Theoretic Reasoning. Inspired by the elegant distributed computing literature which frequently models executions using graphs (e.g., Fischer, Lynch, and Paterson [25]), we introduce the notion of an *execution tree*. Classically, such graphs capture how a protocol evolves: nodes represent the internal states of the parties, and edges correspond to events that advance the system from one state to the next. In our setting, we adapt this idea to two-party protocols by letting each node represent a *partial transcript*, while each directed edge corresponds to one party sending a message and thereby extending the transcript of its parent node. Leaves (representing complete transcripts) are additionally annotated with the protocol's outputs, as well as the probabilities with which each party outputs a given value. This structure will be a key tool in our impossibility arguments.

We further augment the notion of execution trees with the notion we call *black-pink root coloring*. Informally, for the execution tree of a coin-tossing protocol Π, we say the root is *black* if there exists an adversary corrupting Bob who can ensure that the outcome of the protocol matches Bob's preferred bit at least with some probability $\delta(\lambda)$, where λ denotes the security parameter of the protocol. Similarly, the root is *pink* if there exists an adversary corrupting Alice who can ensure that the outcome of the protocol is Alice's preferred bit at least with probability $\delta(\lambda)$. We call $\delta(\lambda) - \frac{1}{2}$ the *bias of the (black-pink) coloring*. If neither of the two applies, the root remains *colorless*. We believe that both the execution-tree formalism and the black–pink root coloring may be useful beyond our specific results, especially for other works at the intersection of game theory and cryptography.

A Note on the Setting. In our presentation below, we consider the model in line with the original one defined by Chung et al. [16], which computes the coin outcome based only on the public broadcast messages. In our later impossibility of coin-tossing without broadcast, however, computing an outcome based on broadcast messages is not possible (given the absence of broadcast), hence in our model (Sect. 3) we require parties to compute the outcome based on their respective views, which in turn means that Alice and Bob may obtain different outputs. Our correctness definitions requires that the output mismatch should not happen except with a negligible probability, but nevertheless, this adjustment introduces a lot of subtleties in our formal proof of security (see Sect. 4).

Thus, for the ease of exposition, for the rest of this subsection we focus on the original model by Chung et al. [16][2]. Briefly, it considers n parties with publicly known preferences encoded in a *preference profile*. A *preference profile* [16] is simply a vector of the parties' preferences, e.g., preference profile $(0, 1)$ means that the first party prefers zero, while the second party prefers one. Parties can communicate with each other through pairwise private channels as well as a public broadcast channel. In this model, a coin-toss protocol is secure if a) all parties are honest, the protocol output is a uniform coin, and b) the protocol is *CSP-fair*, no adversarial coalition of t parties can increase its expected utility, irrespective of the its strategy. The utility of a coalition is a sum of utilities of its members, and a utility of each member is 1 if the protocol output matches the party's preference, and 0 otherwise.

We now outline the intuition behind our proof of impossibility of a statistical game-theoretic coin-toss in the absence of honest majority. Towards this, we first consider the two-party setting, and distinguish between the preference profiles $(0, 0)$ and $(1, 1)$. We start with the $(0, 1)$ case.

Proving Impossibility for the $(0, 1)$-Preference Profile. The core of our argument is to show that for any bound on the number of rounds in the protocol, the root of the execution tree of any given statistical two-party coin-toss for preference profile $(0, 1)$ can be colored either black or pink, where the coloring is for a bias $\frac{1}{2} - \mathsf{negl}(\lambda)$. This, in turn, means that either Alice or Bob can ensure that the outcome of the protocol is their preferred bit with probability $1 - \mathsf{negl}(\lambda)$.

We show this by induction on the number of rounds of the protocol, i.e., depth of the execution tree. Note that in our induction hypothesis we do not assume that the protocol is secure, we simply assume that it is a protocol for two parties which outputs either bit 0 or bit 1. For simplicity, say that in each round

---

[2] With the exception that we require parties to output an unbiased random bit even if all parties have the same preference.

one party speaks. W.l.o.g., assume Alice is the first to send a message in the protocol (in this case, the only one). Intuitively, for single-round protocols, either there exists a message that Alice can send that results in the protocol output being 0 (i.e., her preferred bit according to the preference profile), or all messages of Alice result in the protocol output being 1. In the first case, the root of the execution tree is pink, as Alice can simply choose a message leading to output zero. In the second case, the root is black, as Bob obtains his preferred outcome no matter what an honest Alice does.

To go from protocols with k rounds to those of $k + 1$, we note that removing the root (along with its incident edges) from the execution tree or a $(k+1)$-round protocol Π results in a forest of (sub)trees. Each of this subtrees can be seen as a k-round coin-toss protocol Π' (not necessarily a secure one), where Alice's first message of Π that lead to this subtree is encoded in the description of the new Π', and otherwise the description of the protocol is exactly the same as that of Π (starting with its second round). By induction hypothesis, the roots of each of such subtrees is either black or pink. If there exists at least one pink root, Alice can bias the outcome in Π by choosing the message (corresponding to the execution tree's edge) leading to this subtree. Otherwise, if all roots are black, Bob can bias, as an honest Alice has no choice, but to take some edge leading to a black subtree, from which Bob has a strategy to bias.

We refer the reader to Sect. 4.2 for further details.

Proving Impossibility for the $(1, 1)$-**Preference Profile.** First, note that in contrast to Chung et al. [16], which allow parties to simply output bit b if everyone prefers b, we require (perhaps more in line with traditional cryptographic literature) that parties output an unbiased random coin even in this setting.

To obtain the impossibility in this scenario we follow a similar approach of showing that the root of the execution tree of any given statistical two-party coin-toss for preference profile $(0, 1)$ can be colored either black or pink, however this time with a bias $\delta(\lambda)$ for some non-negligible λ. This, in turn, means that either Alice or Bob can ensure that the outcome of the protocol is their preferred bit with probability $\frac{1}{2} + \delta(\lambda)$.

While the proof structure is similar to the case of the $(0, 1)$ preference profile, there is a subtlety. Intuitively, as Alice and Bob both prefer the same bit, the intuition for the induction begin (i.e., protocols of one round) does not work anymore: If there exists no message of Alice that leads to her preferred outcome, it does *not* mean that all outcomes correspond to the preference of Bob anymore. We need to make use of the fact that the protocol is *correct*, i.e., outputs a fixed bit $b \in \{0,1\}$ with probability at most $\frac{1}{2} + \mathsf{negl}(\lambda)$. Now, we know that (informally) roughly half of Alice's messages lead to bit one, hence the root is pink.

Assuming the correctness of the protocol, however, makes the induction step trickier. Intuitively, the problem now is that in order to make use of the induction hypothesis, we need to show that the obtained subtrees correspond to *correct k-round protocols*. However, this does not immediately follow from the correctness of the $(k + 1)$-round protocol Π: It could be the case that some of the trees are skewed toward, say, zero. Here, skewed towards zero means that an honest execution leads to an outcome zero with probability $\frac{1}{2} + \delta(\lambda)$ for some function δ that is non-negligible in λ. To solve this, we observe that if an honest execution of Π leads to subtrees that are skewed towards zero non-negligibly often, there must be a subtree which is skewed towards one to "even" out the honest execution of Π. Clearly, as long as there exists one subtree which is skewed towards one, a malicious Alice can simply choose the message leading to such subtree, hence the root of Π can be colored pink. Otherwise, except with negligible probability, an honest execution of Π leads to subtrees which correspond to correct protocols. For these, we can apply our induction hypothesis and proceed by a similar argument as in the case the $(0, 1)$-preference profile.

We refer the reader to Sect. 4.3 for further details.

Extending to Multi-party Setting. To prove impossibility in the general multi-party setting, we reduce to our previously shown two-party impossibilities. The key is to partition the parties into two groups of size at most $\frac{n}{2}$ each, such that either

(a) one group prefers 0 and the other prefers 1 (allowing a reduction to the $(0, 1)$-impossibility), or
(b) both groups prefer 1 (allowing a reduction to the $(1, 1)$-impossibility).

Above, a group prefers coin b if the (strict majority) of parties in this group prefer b. We refer the reader to Sect. 4.4 for details.

2.2 Impossibility of Game-Theoretic Coin-Toss for $t \geq \frac{n}{3}$ Without Broadcast

In our second result, we turn to the $t \geq \frac{n}{3}$ setting without broadcast. In the standard (non-game-theoretic) setting, Cohen et al. [18] showed that there exists no secure coin-toss protocol. Naturally, we asked ourselves whether it is possible to achieve statistically secure coin-toss in this setting while a obtaining a game-theoretic fairness guarantee such as CSP-fairness (instead of the strong cryptographic one). However, it turns out that in this regime, it is impossible to achieve even computational protocols. Before we discuss our proof of impossibility, we discuss the implications of this new setting for our model.

Our (Actual) Model. While for the ease of exposition in the prior section we discussed the impossibility result assuming the underlying model of Chung et al. [16], in the setting without broadcast each party must compute its output based on *its own* view. Hence, while prior works assumed that the output is computed deterministically based on the public transcript, and the coin is thus implicitly the same for all parties, we must add an additional correctness requirement stating that the protocol's output of the parties is the same (up to a negligible probability). To account for the fact that parties now have their own outputs, we furthermore have to re-define the utility of the adversarial coalition (otherwise an misbehaving party could "improve" its utility by simply outputting the preferred bit to himself). Instead, we set the utility of a coalition to be the fraction of *honest* parties' outputs that match the adversarial preference, which intuitively corresponds to the idea that the adversary would like to bias the *honest parties*'s outputs towards his preference. As before, in contrast to Chung et al. [16], we aim for an unbiased uniform coin-toss even if all parties have the same preference.

Proving Impossibility for Three Parties, One Corruption In order to show the impossibility of game-theoretic coin-toss in the $t \geq \frac{n}{3}$ setting without broadcast, where $n \geq 3$, we first outline the impossibility of a three-party coin-toss with one corruption. Here, our approach follows the elegant proof by Cohen et al. [18], albeit with adjustments to account for the game-theoretic setting. Intuitively, we consider an execution of a protocol which replicates parties of the original three-party one (which we assume secure) and places them in a ring, so that from the perspective of each party the execution could have been one in which the left party behaves honestly, or one in which the right party behaved honestly. We then show that in this new protocol, as long as the parties are not too many communication links apart, the parties output the same bit – which is furthermore an unbiased random one – except with a negligible probability. Next, we show an adversary who uses the emulation of this protocol to predict the outcome value of the original, real one, at the start of the execution. This will allow us to build an adversary who can bias the protocol's output towards his preferred bit.

Later, we reduce the impossibility of a multi-party coin-toss where at least one third of parties can be corrupt, to that of the three-party case. See Sect. 5 for details.

3   Model and Security Definitions

We use the following model, partially borrowed from Wu et al. [39] and Thyagarajan et al. [37].

Network Model. We consider n parties, denoted by P_1 to P_n, who interact through secure point-to-point channels as well as a public broadcast channel[3]. We assume that all communication channels are authenticated, i.e., messages always carry the true sender's identity. We assume that the network is synchronous and the protocol proceeds in rounds.

Players' Preference Profile. Each party has a publicly stated preference for either the bit 0 or the bit 1. We call the vector of all parties' preferences the *preference profile* $(p_1, \ldots, p_n)$, where p_i denotes the preference of the party P_i.

Adversary. We consider a computationally unbounded fully malicious adversary A that may corrupt up to t parties; the set of corrupted parties is also referred to as the *coalition*. The adversary A is allowed to perform a *rushing attack*: in each round r, the corrupted parties can wait to see all messages sent

---

[3] In Sect. 5 we adjust out model to point-to-point only, no broadcast.

by honest parties (i.e., those not controlled by A) before (jointly) deciding which round-r messages to send.

Strategy. A strategy S_i of a party P_i describes the behavior of a party in each round of the protocol's execution. A strategy S_I for a set I is the union of the strategies of all parties in I.

We let $H = \{H_1, \ldots, H_n\}$ denote the strategy (the code) of the honest execution of protocol Π. That is, H_i is the code that party P_i is supposed to run according to the protocol specification. For a coalition A, we denote by $\bar{A}$ all parties not in A.

Utility. For a number k of honest parties, i.e., total number of parties minus the size of the coalition, let $(\mathsf{out}_1, \ldots, \mathsf{out}_k)$ denote a vector of honest party's outputs. In line with prior works on game-theoretic coin toss [37,39] we consider the adversarial preference to be the preference of the majority of the parties in the coalition. Given A's preference p, we define $\mathsf{util}_A^* = 1 - \frac{\sum_{i \in [k]} |p - \mathsf{out}_i|}{k}$. That is, if no honest party outputs the adversarial preference, util_A^* is zero. If every honest party outputs the adversarial preference, util_A^* of the adversary is one.

Given a strategy profile S_A for A and the honest strategy $H_{\bar{A}}$ for $\bar{A}$, the *expected utility* of A is

$$\mathsf{util}_A(S_A, H_{\bar{A}}) := \mathbb{E}\big[\, \mathsf{util}_A^*(\mathsf{out}_1, \ldots, \mathsf{out}_k)\,\big],$$

where the expectation is over the parties' randomness when parties in A run S_A and parties in $\bar{A}$ run $H_{\bar{A}}$.

Similarly, $\mathsf{util}_A(H_A, H_{\bar{A}})$ denotes the expected utility if everyone follows the honest strategy. In the following, we will refer to expected utility simply by "utility".

Coin Toss Definition. An n-party coin-toss protocol is an interactive protocol, where at the end of the protocol each party P_i computes the coin toss outcome out_i as a deterministic, polynomial-time function over the view of P_i, which includes its randomness r_i, as well as the set of messages sent and received by P_i (including public messages posted to the broadcast channel).

Definition 1. *We say that the coin toss protocol Π, parametrized with a statistical security parameter λ, is **statistically secure** against any t-sized coalition with respect to a preference profile P, if the protocol provides correctness and cooperative-strategy-proofness (CSP-fairness), defined below:*

- ***Correctness.** If everyone behaves honestly, all parties output the same value out with probability at least $1 - \mathsf{negl}(\lambda)$ for some negligible function $\mathsf{negl}(\lambda)$. Further, out is some fixed $b \in \{0,1\}$ with probability at most $1/2 + \mathsf{negl}'(\lambda)$ for some negligible function $\mathsf{negl}'(\cdot)$.*
- ***CSP-fairness.** For all adversaries A corrupting at most t parties, and any strategy S_A adopted by the coalition A, there is a negligible function $\mathsf{negl}(\cdot)$, such that:*

$$\mathsf{util}_A(S_A, H_{\bar{A}}) \leq \mathsf{util}_A(H_A, H_{\bar{A}}) + \mathsf{negl}(\lambda)$$

Informally, the notion of CSP fairness requires that no coalition can increase its expected utility no matter how it deviates from the prescribed strategy. We further define **weak correctness** of a coin-toss protocol Π with a security parameter λ as follows:

- **Weak correctness.** If everyone behaves honestly, all parties output the same value out with probability at least $1 - \mathsf{negl}(\lambda)$ for some negligible function $\mathsf{negl}(\lambda)$.

We refer to the protocols that satisfy the (weak) correctness property as *(weakly) correct*, and to the protocols that satisfy CSP-fairness as *CSP-fair*.

4 Impossibility of Game-Theoretic Statistical Coin-Toss Without Honest Majority

In this section we prove that a game-theoretic coin-toss is impossible to achieve in the information-theoretic setting without assuming honest majority. Towards this, we first introduce two notions that will be helpful in our impossibility results (Sect. 4.1). Next, we discuss two partial results: The impossibility of game-theoretic statistically-secure coin-toss in the two-party setting where one party is corrupt for the $(0, 1)$-preference profile (Sect. 4.2), and for the $(1, 1)$-preference profile (Sect. 4.3). Finally, we use our partial results to prove the impossibility of statistically-secure game-theoretic coin-toss in a setting without honest majority (Sect. 4.4).

4.1 Helper Tools

Before proving our impossibility results, we introduce the following notion of *execution tree* of a two-party protocol Π that we will use throughout this section. **Execution Tree.** At a high level, an execution tree depicts all possible executions of the protocol between two honest parties. In more detail, w.l.o.g., assume exactly one party speaks per round and that the first party (Alice) speaks in odd rounds while the second party (Bob) speaks in even rounds. Let Π be a protocol between Alice and Bob in which each party sends at most K messages. Then:

Definition 2 (Execution tree). *Let $\mathcal{R}_A$ and $\mathcal{R}_B$ denote the randomness spaces of Alice and Bob.*

For a partial transcript $\tau = (m_1, \ldots, m_\ell)$, define the honest support *of the next message for a party $P \in \{A, B\}$ by*

$$\mathrm{Supp}_P(\tau) := \Big\{ m \,\Big|\, \exists (r_a, r_b) \in \mathcal{R}_A \times \mathcal{R}_B : \langle A(r_a), B(r_b) \rangle [1{:}\ell] = \tau \,\wedge\, \mathrm{next}_P^{r_P}(\tau) = m \Big\}.$$

Here $\langle A(r_A), B(r_B) \rangle [1{:}\ell]$ denotes the first ℓ messages of the honest execution of Π when Alice uses randomness r_a and Bob uses randomness r_b, and $\mathrm{next}_P^r(\tau)$ is the next honest message party P produces after seeing τ when running with randomness r.

The execution tree of Π, denoted $\mathcal{T} = (V, E)$, is the rooted directed tree built as follows:

- *The root corresponds to the empty transcript ε and is denoted v_ε.*
- *For each node v_τ already in V:*
  - *if it is Alice's turn next (odd round), then for every $m \in \mathrm{Supp}_A(\tau)$ add a child $v_{\tau\|m}$ and an edge $(v_\tau, v_{\tau\|m})$;*
  - *if it is Bob's turn next (even round), then for every $m \in \mathrm{Supp}_B(\tau)$ add a child $v_{\tau\|m}$ and an edge $(v_\tau, v_{\tau\|m})$.*

Leaves (vertices with no outgoing edges) correspond to full protocol transcripts. For a leaf corresponding to transcript τ, we label it with the outputs and their respective probabilities for each party:

$$\mathrm{SuppOut}(\tau) := \big\{ ((\mathsf{out}_A, p_A), (\mathsf{out}_B, p_B)) \mid \exists (r_A, r_B) \in \mathcal{R}_A \times \mathcal{R}_B : \langle A(r_A), B(r_B) \rangle = \tau$$
$$\wedge\ \mathsf{Output}_A(r_A, \tau) = \mathsf{out}_A$$
$$\wedge\ \mathsf{Output}_B(r_B, \tau) = \mathsf{out}_B$$
$$\wedge\ p_A = \Pr[\mathsf{Output}_A = \mathsf{out}_A \mid \tau]$$
$$\wedge\ p_B = \Pr[\mathsf{Output}_B = \mathsf{out}_B \mid \tau]\big\},$$

where Output_P denotes the output function of party P, and all probabilities are taken over the random tapes of Alice (resp., Bob) conditioned on the honest execution reaching τ.

Intuitively, every node of the tree correspond to a partial transcript between an honest Alice and an honest Bob up to a certain round, and the edge between two vertices corresponds to the message sent by the corresponding party that extends the transcript of the parent by precisely this message.

Black–Pink Root Coloring. Additionally, we introduce the notion of a *black–pink root coloring*, which augments an execution tree by a coloring of its root. Specifically, the root is colored according to whether one of the parties can bias the protocol's outcome toward its preferred value with probability at least p. Formally:

Definition 3 (Black–pink root coloring). *Let $\mathcal{T} = (V, E)$ be the execution tree of a protocol Π as defined above. A* black–pink root coloring *with bias Δ augments $\mathcal{T}$'s root v_ϵ with a color according to a coloring function*

$$\mathsf{c} : \{v_\epsilon\} \longrightarrow \{\mathsf{black}, \mathsf{pink}, \bot\},$$

where the following holds:

- $\mathsf{c}(v_\epsilon) = \mathsf{black}$ *if an adversary that corrupts Bob at the very beginning of the protocol can ensure that Alice's output of Π results in Bob's preferred value with probability at least $\frac{1}{2} + \Delta$;*
- $\mathsf{c}(v_\epsilon) = \mathsf{pink}$ *if an adversary that corrupts Alice at the very beginning of the protocol can ensure that Bob's output of Π results in Alice's preferred value with probability at least $\frac{1}{2} + \Delta$.*
- $\mathsf{c}(v_\tau) = \bot$ *otherwise.*

Note that the distinction between Alice's and Bob's output is minimal: For correct protocols, these are the same except with a negligible probability.

In the following, we will say that a root of an execution tree $\mathcal{T}$ can be *colored black (resp., pink) according to a coloring with bias* Δ, if there exists a black-pink coloring of $\mathcal{T}$ with bias Δ in which the root has the specified color. If there exists no such coloring, we call the root *colorless*.

Finally, before discussing the impossibility results for specific preference profiles, we show that for weakly correct protocols (refer to Sect. 3 for the definition) with one message-sending round holds that honest executions almost always end up in leaves where both parties output the same value except with negligible probability. Formally:

Lemma 1. *Consider a weakly correct two-party coin-tossing protocol Π with security parameter λ consisting of a single message-sending round and an arbitrary preference profile. Then, except with negligible probability, any honest execution of Π finishes in a leaf τ which has a label*

$$((0, 1 - \mathsf{negl}_1(\lambda)), (0, 1 - \mathsf{negl}_2(\lambda)),$$

or a leaf which has a label

$$((1, 1 - \mathsf{negl}_3(\lambda)), (1, 1 - \mathsf{negl}_4(\lambda)),$$

for some functions $\mathsf{negl}_1, \mathsf{negl}_2, \mathsf{negl}_3, \mathsf{negl}_4$ *that are negligible in* λ.

Proof. W.l.o.g., Alice sends the first, and – since Π has a single message-sending round – only message of the protocol. Say there is a non-negligible probability that the honest execution ends up in leaves in which the following holds:

- For a non-negligible $\delta_0(\lambda)$, Bob's output in this leaf is zero, and for (some other) non-negligible $\delta_1(\lambda)$, Bob's output in this leaf is one.

Note that Alice has no knowledge of Bob's randomness. Thus, for each leaf where the above holds Alice will fail to "guess" the output of Bob (in the sense that Alice's output matches Bob's) with a non-negligible probability. Hence, if the executions ends up in non-negligibly many such leaves, it breaks weak correctness.

Thus, except with negligible probability, honest executions end up in nodes in which either a) Bob's output is zero with probability at least $1 - \mathsf{negl}(\lambda)$, or b) Bob's output is one with probability at least $1 - \mathsf{negl}(\lambda)$ for some function negl that is negligible in λ. The lemma statement then follows by weak correctness of Π. $\qquad\square$

In the following, for the ease of notation, for $b \in \{0, 1\}$, we denote labels of the form

$$((b, 1 - \mathsf{negl}_1(\lambda)), (b, 1 - \mathsf{negl}_2(\lambda))$$

simply by $(b, b, 1 - \mathsf{negl}(\lambda))$.

4.2   Impossibility of Game-Theoretic Statistical Coin-Toss for $(0, 1)$-Preference Profile and One Corruption

We now show our first result, namely that there exists no information-theoretic CSP-fair coin tossing protocol in the setting without honest majority. We start with a simpler result for two parties, and one corruption:

Theorem 1. *There exists no statistically secure information-theoretic coin-toss for $n = 2$, a preference profile $P = (0, 1)$, and a fixed maximum number of rounds $\ell(\lambda)$.*

Proof. Towards obtaining the result, we show the following helpful lemmas:

Lemma 2. *The root of the execution tree of any weakly correct information-theoretic two-party coin-toss protocol Π for the preference profile $(0, 1)$, which has a fixed maximum number of rounds ℓ, can be colored either black or pink according to a coloring with bias $\beta = \frac{1}{2} - \mathsf{negl}(\lambda)$ for some function negl that is negligible in λ.*

Proof. We prove the result by induction on the number of rounds k. Our induction hypothesis is that there exists some function negl negligible in λ, so that consistent with the rules of the black-pink coloring with bias $\frac{1}{2} - \mathsf{negl}(\lambda)$, the root of an execution tree of a weakly correct protocol Π, which has a fixed maximum number of rounds k, can be colored black or pink.

Say Alice prefers $b \in \{0, 1\}$ and Bob prefers $1 - b$.

Induction Begin, k = 1. Consider a protocol Π of only round. W.l.o.g., Alice sends the first (and in this case only) message. By Lemma 1, we know that, except with negligible probability, an honest execution of Π ends up in leaves which have either the label $(0, 0, 1 - \mathsf{negl}_0(\lambda))$, or the label $(1, 1, 1 - \mathsf{negl}_1(\lambda))$. There are two cases to consider:

> **Case a.** There exists a leaf with the label $(b, b, 1 - \mathsf{negl}(\lambda))$. Therefore, Alice can bias Bob's output by publishing the message leading to such a leaf, and thus the root can be colored *pink*.
>
> **Case b.** Otherwise, except with negligible probability, an honest execution ends up in leaves which have the label $(1 - b, 1 - b, 1 - \mathsf{negl}(\lambda))$. Thus, except with negligible probability, Bob obtains his preferred outcome (i.e., Alice's output coincides with Bob's preference) regardless of Alice's first message, and the root can be colored *black*.

Induction Step, k $\Rightarrow$ k + 1. Consider a protocol Π of $k + 1$ rounds. If we remove the root and its incident edges from the protocol's execution tree, we get a forest $\mathcal{F}$ of (sub)trees of depth k. Note that each of these subtrees τ can be seen as an execution tree of a (possibly insecure) coin-toss protocol Π_τ with up to k rounds, where the message sent by Alice in the (now removed) edge of Π that lead to this subtree is hardcoded in Π_τ's description, and for all rounds after the first one parties follow the instructions of the original Π. Say that some Π_τ that was defined in this way is not weakly correct, i.e., Alice's and Bob's outputs **do not** coincide with some non-negligible probability $\delta(\lambda)$. As in Π this was the case at most with some negligible probability $\mathsf{negl}'(\lambda)$, it means that an honest Alice chooses an edge leading to any of the subtrees that correspond to such Π_τ at most with some negligible probability $\mathsf{negl}^*(\lambda)$.

For the remaining subtrees, by induction hypothesis, we get that the root of each such subtree can be colored either black or pink. We have two cases:

> **Case 1.** If there is at least one root that is pink, in Π a malicious Alice can choose the message corresponding to the edge that leads to this subtree, and thus bias Bob's output towards her preference with the same probability as in this subtree. Hence, the root of Π's execution tree is pink.
>
> **Case 2.** Otherwise, if all roots of the remaining subtrees are black, in Π, once Alice sent her message, a malicious Bob can bias Alice's output towards his preference with the same probability as in the subtree that an honest Alice "chose" by sending her first message. By above, we get that an honest Alice chooses a subtree with a non-black root at most with probability $\mathsf{negl}^*(\lambda)$, hence Bob can bias Alice's output towards his preference at least with probability $(1-\mathsf{negl}^*(\lambda))*(1-\mathsf{negl}(\lambda)) = 1-\mathsf{negl}'(\lambda)$ for some negligible $\mathsf{negl}'(\lambda)$. Hence, the root of Π's execution tree is black.   □

Theorem 1 follows from Lemma 2 in a straight-forward way. Note that any correct protocol is also weakly correct. Thus, from Lemma 2 we get that the root of an execution tree of any correct protocol can be colored either black or pink according to a coloring with bias $\frac{1}{2} - \mathsf{negl}(\lambda)$. By definition of the black-pink root coloring, we thus get that there exists an adversary who can ensure that the other party's output corresponds to the adversary's preference with probability at least $1 - negl(\lambda)$, thus violating CSP-fairness. Thus, we get that either a) the protocol does not satisfy correctness, or b) the protocol does not satisfy CSP-fairness. In both cases, the protocol is not secure.   □

4.3 Impossibility of Game-Theoretic Statistical Coin-Toss for $(1, 1)$-Preference Profile and One Corruption

Theorem 2. *There exists no statistically secure information-theoretic coin-toss for $n = 2$, a preference profile $P = (1,1)$, and a fixed maximum number of rounds ℓ, where all but one party share the same preference.*

Proof. Similar to the proof of Theorem 1, we first show the following lemma:

Lemma 3. *The root of the execution tree of any **correct** information-theoretic two-party coin-toss protocol Π for a preference profile $(1,1)$, which has a fixed maximum number of rounds $\ell(\lambda)$, can be colored either black or pink according to a coloring with bias $\delta(\lambda)$ for some function δ that is non-negligible in λ.*

Proof. We prove the result by induction on the number of rounds k. Our induction hypothesis is that there exists a function δ that is non-negligible in λ, so that consistent with the rules of the black-pink tree with bias $\delta(\lambda)$, the root of an execution tree of a correct protocol that has at most k rounds, can be colored black or pink.

Induction Begin, k = 1. As every correct protocol is in particular weakly correct, we can apply the same reasoning as in the induction begin of the proof of Lemma 2, and get $\delta(\lambda) = \frac{1}{2} - \mathsf{negl}(\lambda)$.

Induction Step, k $\Rightarrow$ k + 1. Consider a $(k+1)$-round correct protocol Π. If we remove the root and its incident edges from the protocol's execution tree, we get a forest $\mathcal{F}$ of (sub)trees of depth k. Note that each of these trees τ can be seen as an execution tree of a (possibly insecure) coin-toss protocol Π_τ with up to k rounds, where the message sent by Alice in the (now removed) edge of Π that lead to this subtree is hardcoded in Π_τ's description, and for all rounds after the first one parties follow the instructions of the original Π. Say that for some Π' that was defined in this way Alice's and Bob's outputs **do not** coincide with some non-negligible probability. As in Π (by correctness) this was the case at most with some negligible probability $\mathsf{negl}'(\lambda)$, it means that an honest Alice chooses an edge leading to any of the subtrees that correspond to such Π_τ at most with some negligible probability $\mathsf{negl}^*(\lambda)$. We will account for this negligible probability further in the proof when giving a strategy for a malicious Bob (malicious Alice can simply chose the edge where outputs do coincide).

Consider the remaining subtrees, i.e., those in whose corresponding protocols Π_τ the outputs of Alice and Bob coincide except with negligible probability. Denote the forest of such subtrees by $\mathcal{F}'$. There are two cases:

Case 1. All of the subtrees in $\mathcal{F}'$ correspond to the protocols in which the output is a fixed $b^* \in \{0, 1\}$ with probability $\frac{1}{2} \pm \mathsf{negl}(\lambda)$ for some negligible function $\mathsf{negl}(\lambda)$.

In this case, all such protocols are correct, and, as they have at most k rounds, by induction hypothesis we get that the root of every subtree $\in \mathcal{F}'$ is either black or pink. If there is at least one root that is pink, in Π a malicious Alice can choose the message corresponding to the edge that leads to this subtree, and thus bias Bob's output towards her preference with the same probability as in this subtree. Hence, the root of Π's execution tree is pink. Otherwise, if all roots of the remaining subtrees are black, in Π, once Alice sent her message, a malicious Bob can bias Alice's output towards his preference with the same probability as in the subtree that an honest Alice "chose" by sending her first message. By above, we get that an honest Alice chooses a subtree with a non-black root at most with probability $\mathsf{negl}^*(\lambda)$, hence by induction hypothesis Bob can bias Alice's output towards his preference at least with probability $(1 - \mathsf{negl}^*(\lambda))(\frac{1}{2} + \delta(\lambda)) = \frac{1}{2} + \delta'(\lambda)$, for some δ' non-negligible in λ.[4] Hence, the root of Π's execution tree is black.

Case 2. There exists a subtree in $\mathcal{F}'$ in whose corresponding protocol Π' the proportion of 1 and 0 outputs is skewed, i.e., there exists a non-negligible

---

[4] Note that by Bernoulli's inequality $(1 - \mathsf{negl}(\lambda))^{\mathsf{poly}(\lambda)} \geq 1 - \mathsf{poly}(\lambda) * \mathsf{negl}(\lambda)$, hence we can safely repeat this step for polynomial-depth protocols.

$\delta'(\lambda)$ such that in the corresponding subtree the protocol output under honest execution is some fixed b with probability $\frac{1}{2} + \delta'(\lambda)$.

If such subtree exists for $b = 1$, a malicious Alice can always choose this subtree, in which case we can color the root of Π pink.

Otherwise, as the sum of probabilities that Alice chooses a given first edge sums up to 1, if for all "skewed" subtrees $b = 0$, it must be the case that an honest Alice chooses edges leading to the subtrees that correspond to such Π's at most with some negligible probability $\mathsf{negl}^{**}(\lambda)$ (otherwise Π cannot be correct). In this case, as all remaining subtrees correspond to the protocols in which the output is a fixed $b^* \in \{0, 1\}$ with probability $\frac{1}{2} \pm \mathsf{negl}(\lambda)$ for some negligible function $\mathsf{negl}(\lambda)$, by induction hypothesis we get that their roots are either black or pink. Hence, by a similar argument as before, we get that Π's root is also black or pink. $\qquad\square$

Now, from Lemma 3 we get that the root of an execution tree of any correct protocol can be colored either black or pink according to a coloring with bias $\delta(\lambda)$ for some function δ that is non-negligible in λ. By definition of the black-pink root coloring, we obtain that there exists an adversary who can ensure that the other party's output corresponds to the adversary's preference with probability at least $\frac{1}{2} + \delta(\lambda)$, which violates CSP-fairness. Thus, we get that either a) the protocol does not satisfy correctness, or b) the protocol does not satisfy CSP-fairness. In both cases, the protocol is not secure. Hence, Theorem 2 follows. $\square$

4.4 Impossibility of Game-Theoretic Statistical Coin-Toss Without Honest Majority

We now finalize our result and show that without honest majority there exists no game-theoretic statistically secure for an arbitrary number of parties.

Theorem 3. *There exists no statistically secure information-theoretic coin-toss for a fixed maximum number of rounds $\ell(\lambda)$, n parties, and $t \geq \lceil n/2 \rceil$ corruptions, except for the special case $n = 4$, where all but one party share the same preference.*

Proof. Let n_0 denote the number of parties who prefer zero, and let $n_1 = n - n_o$ denote the number of parties who prefer one. W.l.o.g. we assume $n_1 \geq n_0$. There are three cases:

- **Case 1:** $n_0 < \frac{n}{4}$.
- **Case 2:** $n_0 = \frac{n}{4}$.
- **Case 3:** $\frac{n}{4} < n_0 < \frac{n}{2}$.

We now discuss each of these cases in detail.

Case 1. Say there exists a game-theoretic statistically secure coin-toss protocol Π for n parties, where less than $\frac{n}{4}$ parties prefer zero. Split the parties into a group **(a)** of $\lceil \frac{n}{2} \rceil$ parties who prefer one, and **(b)** remaining parties. Given

Π, we can construct a protocol Π' for the two-party, one corruption case with preference profile $(1, 1)$ as follows.

We let Alice execute (next-message functions of) protocol Π for the parties of group $(\mathbf{a})$, while Bob executes protocol Π for the parties of group $(\mathbf{b})$. In the end, Alice takes as output any output produced by a party of group $(\mathbf{a})$, while Bob takes as output any output produced by a party from group $(\mathbf{b})$.

Note that both groups are of size at most $\lceil n/2 \rceil$. Further, note that as $n_0 < \frac{n}{4}$, we get that in group $(\mathbf{b})$ more parties prefer one than zero. As Π is secure against adversaries corrupting up to $\lceil n/2 \rceil$ messages, by CSP-fairness of Π we get that neither group $(\mathbf{a})$, nor group $(\mathbf{b})$ can bias the output of the protocol towards one. Thus, we get that Π' satisfies CSP-fairness for the preference profile $(1, 1)$. By correctness of Π we further get that up to a negligible probability, the output of all parties is the same value, and this value is a bit $b \in \{0, 1\}$ with probability at most $\frac{1}{2} + \mathsf{negl}'(\lambda)$. Thus, we get that Π' satisfies correctness. Together, we obtain that Π' is a statistically secure game-theoretic coin-toss protocol for the preference profile $(1, 1)$ and one corruption - a contradiction to Theorem 2.

Case 2. First, we consider the general case: Say there exists a game-theoretic statistically secure coin-toss protocol Π for $n > 4$ where $n_0 = \frac{n}{4}$. We split the parties into a group $(\mathbf{a})$ of $\frac{n}{2} - 1$ parties who prefer one along with one party who prefers zero, and $(\mathbf{b})$ remaining parties. As $\frac{n}{2} - 1 > 1$, group $(\mathbf{a})$ prefers one. As $n - (\frac{n}{2} - 1) - n_0 = n_0 + 1 > n_0 - 1$, group $(\mathbf{b})$ also prefers one. From here we proceed the same as in **Case 1**, and obtain a contradiction to Theorem 2.

Now, consider the special case with four parties where three parties prefer one. The problem in this scenario is that, no matter how we split parties into groups of size at most two, there exists one group with exactly one party preferring one, and one party preferring zero. Thus, the preference of this group is undefined, and we cannot reduce it to our two-party impossibility. We leave the exploration of this preference profile as an interesting direction for future work.

Case 3. Say there exists a game-theoretic statistically secure coin-toss protocol protocol Π for n parties, where over $\frac{n}{4}$, yet less than $\frac{n}{2}$ parties prefer zero. Split the parties into a group $(\mathbf{a})$ of $\lceil \frac{n}{2} \rceil$ parties who prefer one, and $(\mathbf{b})$ remaining parties. Given Π, we can construct a protocol Π' for the two-party, one corruption case with preference profile $(0, 1)$ as follows.

We let Alice execute (next-message functions of) protocol Π for the parties of group $(\mathbf{a})$, while Bob executes protocol Π for the parties of group $(\mathbf{b})$. In the end, Alice takes as output any output produced by a party of group $(\mathbf{a})$, while Bob takes as output any output produced by a party from group $(\mathbf{b})$.

Note that both groups are of size at most $\lceil n/2 \rceil$. Further, as $n_0 > \frac{n}{4}$, in group $(\mathbf{b})$ more parties prefer zero than one. As Π is secure against adversaries corrupting up to $\lceil n/2 \rceil$ messages, by CSP-fairness of Π we get that group $(\mathbf{a})$ cannot bias the output towards one, while group $(\mathbf{b})$ can bias the output of the protocol towards zero. Thus, we get that Π' satisfies CSP-fairness for the preference profile $(0, 1)$. By correctness of Π we further get that up to a negligible probability, the output of all parties is the same value, and this value is a bit $b \in \{0, 1\}$ with probability at most $\frac{1}{2} + \mathsf{negl}'(\lambda)$. Thus, we get that Π'

satisfies correctness. Together, we obtain that Π' is a statistically secure game-theoretic coin-toss protocol for the preference profile $(0, 1)$ and one corruption - a contradiction to Theorem 1. $\square$

5   Impossibility of Game-Theoretic Coin-Toss for $n \leq 3t$ Without Broadcast

In the standard (non-game-theoretic) setting in the secure point-to-point channel model (without setup and without broadcast) an elegant result by Cohen et al. [18] shows that there exist no non-trivial (i.e., bias smaller than $\frac{1}{2}$) coin-tossing protocols for $n \leq 3t$, $n \geq 3$. We now show that this result extends to the game-theoretic setting, albeit with a different bias. As this result holds even against computational adversaries, we first define the computational version of our coin-tossing notion:

Coin-Tossing, Computational. As before, for a protocol Π, we let H denote the strategy of the honest execution. For a coalition A, we denote by $\bar{A}$ all parties not in A. We denote by $\mathsf{util}_A(S_A, H_{\bar{A}})$ the expected utility of all members in A where the members of A follow some strategy S_A, and the parties who are not in A follow the honest strategy $H_{\bar{A}}$. Similarly, $\mathsf{util}_A(H_A, H_{\bar{A}})$ denotes the expected utility of all members in A where both the members of the coalition A, and the parties who are not in A, follow the honest strategy.

Definition 4. *We say that the coin-toss protocol Π, parametrized with a security parameter λ, is **computationally secure** against any t-sized coalition with respect to a preference profile P, if the protocol provides correctness and cooperative-strategy-proofness (CSP-fairness), defined below:*

- *__Correctness__ If everyone behaves honestly, all parties output the same value* out *with probability at least* $1 - \mathsf{negl}(\lambda)$ *for some negligible function* $\mathsf{negl}(\lambda)$. *Further,* out *is some fixed* $b \in \{0, 1\}$ *with probability at most* $1/2 + \mathsf{negl}(\lambda)$.
- *__CSP-fairness__ For all PPT adversaries A corrupting at most t parties, and any PPT strategy S_A adopted by the coalition A, there is a negligible function* $\mathsf{negl}(\cdot)$, *such that:*

$$\mathsf{util}_A(S_A, H_{\bar{A}}) \leq \mathsf{util}_A(H_A, H_{\bar{A}}) + \mathsf{negl}(\lambda)$$

Theorem 4. *In the secure point-to-point channel model (no broadcast), given $n \geq 3$ parties and an adversarial threshold $t \geq \frac{n}{3}$, there exists no computationally secure coin-toss with round-complexity that is polynomial in λ, except for the special case $n = 6$, where all but one party share the same preference.*

To show this, we adapt the elegant proof by Cohen et al. [18] to the game-theoretic coin-tossing setting.

First, we show the result for three parties:

Theorem 5. *In the secure point-to-point channel model (no broadcast), given $n = 3$ parties and adversarial threshold $t = 1$, for any preference profile, and any maximum number of protocol rounds q which is polynomial in λ, there exists a PPT adversary A that can corrupt any party P_i, and ensure that with probability at least $\frac{3}{4} - \mathsf{negl}(\lambda)$, the output of every honest party is P_i's preference p_i.*

Proof. For the sake of contradiction, assume there exists a computationally secure q-round protocol Π for three parties. Let A, B, and C denote the code executed by each of the three parties in Π. We construct a new protocol Π^* for $12q$ parties as follows. Let the parties be $P_1, \ldots, P_{12q}$. The parties are arranged in a ring: each P_i is connected to P_{i-1} and P_{i+1}, where indices are taken modulo $12q$, and P_1 is connected to P_{12q} and P_2, and P_{12q} is connected to P_{12q-1} and P_1). We define

$$P_i \text{ executes } \begin{cases} \mathsf{A} & \text{if } i \bmod 3 = 1, \\ \mathsf{B} & \text{if } i \bmod 3 = 2, \\ \mathsf{C} & \text{if } i \bmod 3 = 0. \end{cases}$$

In the following, we denote this arrangement as

$$\Pi' = (\mathsf{A}^1, \mathsf{B}^1, \mathsf{C}^1, \ldots, \mathsf{A}^{4q}, \mathsf{B}^{4q}, \mathsf{C}^{4q}).$$

First, we show the following helpful lemma, where distance d between the two parties is the minimal possible number of communication links between them:

Lemma 4. *In an execution of Π^*, where parties have an arbitrary preference profile, and each party's random tape is chosen uniformly at random, any two parties within distance d and every party between them output the same value with probability at least $1 - d \cdot \mathsf{negl}(\lambda)$, and further this output is some fixed $b \in \{0, 1\}$ with probability at most $1/2 + \mathsf{negl}(\lambda)$.*

Proof. First, for any preference profile and any pair of neighboring parties A^j, B^j, we consider an execution of Π, where the adversary A controls party C. In this execution, A internally emulates the execution of Π^*, where the emulated parties A^j, B^j interact exactly as A and B of Π (i.e., upon obtaining a message from A, A emulates A^j sending this message to C^{j-1}, upon obtaining a message from B, A emulates B^j sending this message to C^j, upon C^{j-1} sending a message to A^j, A sends the same message to A, and upon C^j sending a message to B^j, A sends the same message to B). As A corrupts only one party, and Π is a computationally secure coin-tossing protocol, by correctness we get that A and B output the same bit except with a negligible error probability $\mathsf{negl}(\lambda)$. Further, as the joint view of $\mathsf{A}^j, \mathsf{B}^j$ has the same distribution as that of A, B, we get that A^j and B^j output the same value with the same probability as A and B do, i.e., $1 - \mathsf{negl}(\lambda)$, and (by correctness of Π) this output is some fixed $b \in \{0, 1\}$ with probability at most $1/2 + \mathsf{negl}(\lambda)$.

Note that the argument above works analogously for any other pair of neighboring parties, e.g., C^{j-1} together with A^j, and B^j together with C^j. Thus, by union bound we get that any parties within distance d (and everyone in-between), outputs the same value with probability at least $1 - d \cdot \mathsf{negl}(\lambda)$. $\qquad\square$

Now, for any i, and an arbitrary preference profile, we construct an adversary A for Theorem 5 as follows. A corrupts a party $P_i \in \{A, B, C\}$, and emulates an execution of Π^*, sampling the randomness tapes of all parties in Π^* uniformly at random. If the output of party A^{2q} **does not** match the preference of P_i, A simply continues the execution honestly. Otherwise, A proceeds as we outline below. By Lemma 4, we get that the probability of failure is at most $\frac{1}{2} + \mathsf{negl}'(\lambda)$.

Next, in its interaction with the honest parties of Π, the adversary emulates the execution of Π^*, so that the honest parties of Π correspond to B^1 and C^1 (if P_i is A), to A^1 and C^1 (if P_i is B), and to A^1 and B^1 (if P_i is C). That is, whenever an honest party P_j in Π sends a message, A forwards it to the corresponding neighbor of the party acting as P_j in Π^*, and vice versa. In this execution, A sets the randomness tapes of all parties (except those acting as the two honest parties of Π) to match the randomness previously used in the execution in which A^{2q} output P_i's preferred value. We make the following observations:

First, the view of A^{2q} in this attack is the *same* as its view in the execution of Π on the original random tapes that led to the output y. This is because the only random tapes that we changed between the two executions are those of the parties who act as their Π counterparts, these parties are at least q communication links away from A^{2q}, and the execution of Π^* *finishes* after at most q rounds.

Second, note that in the execution of Π^* in which A^{2q}'s output coincided with P_i's preference we set the random tapes of parties uniformly at random, and the distance between A^{2q} and the two parties who act as their Π counterparts is at most $6q$. Thus, by Lemma 4 together with our first observation we get that with probability $1 - 6q \cdot \mathsf{negl}(\lambda)$, the output of the honest parties in Π is the same as that of A^{2q}, i.e., P_i's preference p_i.

Note that if A^{2q}'s output did not coincide with P_i's preference, as the adversary next behaved honestly in Π, by correctness the protocol's output matched the adversarial preference with probability $\frac{1}{2} - \mathsf{negl}(\lambda)$. All in all, we get that our adversary succeeds with probability at least $(\frac{1}{2} - \mathsf{negl}(\lambda)) \cdot (\frac{1}{2} - \mathsf{negl}'(\lambda)) + (\frac{1}{2} - \mathsf{negl}'(\lambda)) \cdot (1 - 6q \cdot \mathsf{negl}(\lambda)) = \frac{3}{4} - \mathsf{negl}^*(\lambda)$ for some negligible function negl^*.
$\square$

Clearly, the existence of adversary A from Lemma 5 implies the impossibility of a three-party, one corruption coin-toss in the setting without broadcast *for any given preference profile*. We now use this result to prove Theorem 4.

Proof. Consider an arbitrary preference profile p, and let n_0 denote the number of parties who prefer zero, and $n_1 = n - n_0$ denote the number of parties who prefer one. W.l.o.g., say $n_1 \geq n_0$, and let $k = n_1 - \lceil \frac{n}{3} \rceil$. We have the following cases:

- **Case 1:** $k \geq n_0$
- **Case 2:** $k < n_0$

Case 1. For the sake of contradiction, say there exists a game-theoretic coin-toss protocol for $n \geq 1$ parties, adversarial threshold $t \geq \frac{n}{3}$ and $k \geq n_0$. Then, if (**case 1a.**) $k - \lceil \frac{n}{3} \rceil \neq n_0$, we can split the parties into the following three groups: **(1)**

$\lceil \frac{n}{3} \rceil$ parties who prefer one, **(2)** $\lceil \frac{n}{3} \rceil$ parties who prefer one, and **(3)** remaining parties. We reduce to the impossibility of the 3-party coin-toss for the preference profile $(1, 1, b)$, where b is the preference of the majority of parties in group **(3)**. Note that b is well-defined, i.e., there is a strict majority as $k - \lceil \frac{n}{3} \rceil \neq n_0$. The reduction is as follows.

Say there exists a protocol Π for n parties which can be split into the three groups as outlined above. We construct a protocol Π' for a three-party coin-toss with the preference profile $(1, 1, b)$ as follows. Call the three parties Alice, Bob, and Charlie. We let Alice execute protocol Π for all parties of group **(1)** and take as output any output value of this group. Bob does the same with group **(2)**, and Charlie with group **(3)**.

Note that all groups are at most size $\frac{n}{3}$. Further, the majority preference of groups **(1)** and **(2)** is one, while the majority preference of group **(3)** is b. By CSP-fairness of Π neither group **(1)** nor group **(2)** can bias the protocol outcome of the honest parties towards one, and group **(3)** cannot bias the honest outcomes toward b. Further, by correctness of Π, all parties output the same bit which is furthermore some fixed $b^* \in \{0, 1\}$ with probability at most $\frac{1}{2} + \mathsf{negl}(\lambda)$. Thus, we get that Π' is secure three-party coin-toss protocol for the preference profile $(1, 1, b)$, hence we reached a contradiction.

Otherwise, if (**case 1b.**) $k - \lceil \frac{n}{3} \rceil = n_0$ and further $n \neq 6$, we split the parties into the following three groups: **(1)** $\lceil \frac{n}{3} \rceil$ parties who prefer one, **(2)** $\lceil \frac{n}{3} \rceil - 1$ parties who prefer one plus one party who prefers zero, and **(3)** remaining parties. We reduce to the impossibility of the 3-party coin-toss for the preference profile $(1, 1, 1)$ by the same argument as above. Otherwise, it remains that $n = 6$ and $k - \lceil \frac{n}{3} \rceil = n_0$, i.e., exactly five parties have preference one. Note that the problem in this scenario is that, no matter how we split parties into groups of size at most two, there exists one group with exactly one party preferring one, and one party preferring zero. Thus, the preference of this group is undefined, and we cannot reduce it to our three-party impossibility. We leave the exploration of this preference profile as an interesting direction for future work.

Case 2. For the sake of contradiction, say there exists a game-theoretic coin-toss protocol for $n \geq 1$ parties, adversarial threshold $t \geq \frac{n}{3}$ and $k < n_0$. Then, if (**case 2a.**) $n_0 - \lceil \frac{n}{3} \rceil \neq k$, we can split the parties into the following three groups: **(1)** $\lceil \frac{n}{3} \rceil$ parties who prefer one, **(2)** $\lceil \frac{n}{3} \rceil$ parties who prefer zero, and **(3)** remaining parties. We reduce to the impossibility of the 3-party coin-toss for the preference profile $(1, 0, b)$, where b is the preference of the majority of parties in group **(3)**. Note that b is well-defined, i.e., there is a strict majority as $n_0 - \lceil \frac{n}{3} \rceil \neq k$.

If (**case 2b.**) $n_0 - \lceil \frac{n}{3} \rceil = k$, and $n \neq 6$, we split the parties into the following three groups: **(1)** $\lceil \frac{n}{3} \rceil$ parties who prefer one, **(2)** $\lceil \frac{n}{3} \rceil - 1$ parties who prefer zero plus one party who prefers one, and **(3)** remaining parties. We reduce to the impossibility of the 3-party coin-toss for the preference profile $(1, 0, 1)$. Otherwise, it remains that $n_0 - \lceil \frac{n}{3} \rceil = k$ and $n = 6$, i.e., exactly five parties have preference zero. As above, we leave a detailed study of this preference profile as an interesting avenue for future work.

6   Conclusion

In this work, we proved two new impossibility results for game-theoretically secure coin tossing. First, we showed that even *assuming broadcast*, a statistically secure, game-theoretic coin-toss protocol is impossible to achieve without an honest majority. Second, we proved that *without broadcast*, once at least one third of the parties may be corrupt, no game-theoretically secure coin toss is possible—even with only computational security. Along the way, we extended the model and security notions of Chung et al. [16] to reason formally about settings *without broadcast*. We further introduced the concepts of *execution trees* and *black–pink root coloring*, which may be of independent interest.

Taken together with known results from the cryptographic literature, our findings yield an (almost) complete picture of the feasibility of *statistical, game-theoretic coin tossing*:

- **With broadcast but without an honest majority:** we show impossibility for all preference profiles, except for the special case $n = 4$ when exactly three parties share the same preference.
- **With broadcast and an honest majority:** strongly fair (and therefore also game-theoretically fair) coin tossing follows from classical results (e.g., Rabin and Ben-Or [33]).
- **Without broadcast and without a strict two-thirds honest majority:** we prove impossibility for all preference profiles, except for the special case $n = 6$ when exactly five parties share the same preference.
- **Without broadcast but with a strict two-thirds honest majority:** strongly fair, statistically secure coin tossing is once again possible (see, e.g., Ben-Or et al. [8]).

We leave the exploration of the two corner cases, i.e., $n = 4$ when exactly three parties share the same preference and $n = 6$ when exactly five parties share the same preference, as an interesting direction for future work.

Acknowledgments. We thank Jason Milionis for helpful discussion in the early stages of this project. J. Ribeiro was supported by national funds through FCT – Fundação para a Ciência e a Tecnologia, I.P., and, when eligible, co-funded by EU funds under project/support UID/50008/2025 – Instituto de Telecomunicações, with DOI 10.54499/UID/50008/2025. E. Masserova was supported by the CBI postdoctoral fellowship.

References

1. Abraham, I., Dolev, D., Gonen, R., Halpern, J.: Distributed computing meets game theory: robust mechanisms for rational secret sharing and multiparty computation. In: PODC (2006)
2. Alon, B., Omri, E.: Almost-optimally fair multiparty coin-tossing with nearly three-quarters malicious. In: TCC (2016)

3. Andrychowicz, M., Dziembowski, S., Malinowski, D., Mazurek, L.: Secure multi-party computations on bitcoin. In: S&P (2014)
4. Aumayr, L., Avarikioti, Z., Maffei, M., Mazumdar, S.: Securing lightning channels against rational miners. In: Luo, B., Liao, X., Xu, J., Kirda, E., Lie, D. (eds.) Proceedings of the 2024 on ACM SIGSAC Conference on Computer and Communications Security, CCS 2024, Salt Lake City, UT, USA, 14–18 October 2024, pp. 393–407. ACM (2024). https://doi.org/10.1145/3658644.3670373
5. Aumayr, L., Avarikioti, Z., Salem, I., Schmid, S., Yeo, M.: X-transfer: enabling and optimizing cross-PCN transactions. In: Garman, C., Moreno-Sanchez, P. (eds.) FC 2025, Part I. LNCS, vol. 15751, pp. 73–90. Springer, Cham (2025). https://doi.org/10.1007/978-3-032-07024-1_5
6. Beimel, A., Haitner, I., Makriyannis, N., Omri, E.: Tighter bounds on multiparty coin flipping via augmented weak martingales and differentially private sampling. SIAM J. Comput. **51**(4), 1126–1171 (2022)
7. Beimel, A., Omri, E., Orlov, I.: Protocols for multiparty coin toss with a dishonest majority. J. Cryptol. **28**(3), 551–600 (2015)
8. Ben-Or, M., Goldwasser, S., Wigderson, A.: Completeness theorems for non-cryptographic fault-tolerant distributed computation. In: Providing sound foundations for cryptography: on the work of Shafi Goldwasser and Silvio Micali, pp. 351–371 (2019)
9. Bentov, I., Kumaresan, R.: How to use bitcoin to design fair protocols. In: Garay, J.A., Gennaro, R. (eds.) CRYPTO 2014. LNCS, vol. 8617, pp. 421–439. Springer, Heidelberg (2014). https://doi.org/10.1007/978-3-662-44381-1_24
10. Berman, I., Haitner, I., Tentes, A.: Coin flipping of any constant bias implies one-way functions. J. ACM (JACM) **65**(3), 1–95 (2018)
11. Blum, M.: Coin flipping by telephone. In: Gersho, A. (ed.) Advances in Cryptology: A Report on CRYPTO 1981, CRYPTO 1981, IEEE Workshop on Communications Security, Santa Barbara, California, USA, 24–26 August 1981, pp. 11–15, U. C. Santa Barbara, Dept. of Elec. and Computer Eng., ECE Report No 82-04 (1981)
12. Buchbinder, N., Haitner, I., Levi, N., Tsfadia, E.: Fair coin flipping: tighter analysis and the many-party case. In: Proceedings of the Twenty-Eighth Annual ACM-SIAM Symposium on Discrete Algorithms, pp. 2580–2600. SIAM (2017)
13. Chung, H., Masserova, E., Shi, E., Thyagarajan, S.A.K.: Ponyta: foundations of side-contract-resilient fair exchange. IACR Cryptol. ePrint Arch., p. 582 (2022). https://eprint.iacr.org/2022/582
14. Chung, H., Masserova, E., Shi, E., Thyagarajan, S.A.K.: Fairness in the wild: Secure atomic swap with external incentives. IACR Cryptol. ePrint Arch., p. 1086 (2025). https://eprint.iacr.org/2025/1086
15. Chung, H., Masserova, E., Shi, E., Thyagarajan, S.A.K.: Rapidash: Atomic swaps secure under user-miner collusion. In: Garman, C., Moreno-Sanchez, P. (eds.) Financial Cryptography and Data Security - 29th International Conference, FC 2025, Miyakojima, Japan, 14–18 April 2025, Revised Selected Papers, Part I. LNCS, vol. 15751, pp. 249–266. Springer, Cham (2025). https://doi.org/10.1007/978-3-032-07024-1_15
16. Chung, K.-M., Guo, Y., Lin, W.-K., Pass, R., Shi, E.: Game theoretic notions of fairness in multi-party coin toss. In: Beimel, A., Dziembowski, S. (eds.) TCC 2018, Part I. LNCS, vol. 11239, pp. 563–596. Springer, Cham (2018). https://doi.org/10.1007/978-3-030-03807-6_21

17. Cleve, R.: Limits on the security of coin flips when half the processors are faulty (extended abstract). In: Hartmanis, J. (ed.) Proceedings of the 18th Annual ACM Symposium on Theory of Computing, Berkeley, California, USA, 28–30 May 1986, pp. 364–369. ACM (1986). https://doi.org/10.1145/12130.12168

18. Cohen, R., Haitner, I., Omri, E., Rotem, L.: Characterization of secure multiparty computation without broadcast. In: Kushilevitz, E., Malkin, T. (eds.) TCC 2016, Part I. LNCS, vol. 9562, pp. 596–616. Springer, Heidelberg (2016). https://doi.org/10.1007/978-3-662-49096-9_25

19. Dachman-Soled, D., Lindell, Y., Mahmoody, M., Malkin, T.: On the black-box complexity of optimally-fair coin tossing. In: Ishai, Y. (ed.) TCC 2011. LNCS, vol. 6597, pp. 450–467. Springer, Heidelberg (2011). https://doi.org/10.1007/978-3-642-19571-6_27

20. Dettling, G., Liu-Zhang, C., Masserova, E., Rambaud, M., Urban, A.: Broadcast for dynamic committees without trusted setup. IACR Cryptol. ePrint Arch., p. 2078 (2025). https://eprint.iacr.org/2025/2078

21. Dodis, Y.: Fault-tolerant leader election and collective coin-flipping in the full information model (2006)

22. Dodis, Y., Rabin, T., et al.: Cryptography and Game Theory. Algorithmic Game Theory, pp. 181–207 (2007)

23. Feige, U.: Noncryptographic selection protocols. In: FOCS (1999)

24. Ferreira, M.V.X., Weinberg, S.M.: Credible, truthful, and two-round (optimal) auctions via cryptographic commitments. In: Biró, P., Hartline, J.D., Ostrovsky, M., Procaccia, A.D. (eds.) EC 2020: The 21st ACM Conference on Economics and Computation, Virtual Event, Hungary, 13–17 July 2020, pp. 683–712. ACM (2020). https://doi.org/10.1145/3391403.3399495

25. Fischer, M.J., Lynch, N.A., Paterson, M.: Impossibility of distributed consensus with one faulty process. J. ACM **32**(2), 374–382 (1985). https://doi.org/10.1145/3149.214121

26. Haitner, I., Omri, E.: Coin flipping with constant bias implies one-way functions. SIAM J. Comput. **43**(2), 389–409 (2014)

27. Haitner, I., Tsfadia, E.: An almost-optimally fair three-party coin-flipping protocol. In: Proceedings of The Forty-Sixth Annual ACM Symposium on Theory of Computing, pp. 408–416 (2014)

28. Kilian, J.: Founding cryptography on oblivious transfer. In: Proceedings of the Twentieth Annual ACM Symposium on Theory of Computing, pp. 20–31 (1988)

29. Liu-Zhang, C., Masserova, E., Ribeiro, J., Soni, P., Thyagarajan, S.A.K.: Improved YOSO randomness generation with worst-case corruptions. In: Clark, J., Shi, E. (eds.) FC 2024, Part II. LNCS, vol. 14745, pp. 73–89. Springer, Cham (2024). https://doi.org/10.1007/978-3-031-78679-2_4

30. Liu-Zhang, C.D., Masserova, E., Ribeiro, J., Soni, P., Thyagarajan, S.A.: Efficient distributed randomness generation from minimal assumptions where parties speak sequentially once. In: Fehr, S., Fouque, P.A. (eds.) Advances in Cryptology - EUROCRYPT 2025, pp. 176–206. Springer, Cham (2025). https://doi.org/10.1007/978-3-031-91092-0_7

31. Malavolta, G., Thyagarajan, S.A.K.: Homomorphic time-lock puzzles and applications. In: Boldyreva, A., Micciancio, D. (eds.) CRYPTO 2019. LNCS, vol. 11692, pp. 620–649. Springer, Cham (2019). https://doi.org/10.1007/978-3-030-26948-7_22

32. Moran, T., Naor, M., Segev, G.: An optimally fair coin toss. J. Cryptol. **29**(3), 491–513 (2016)

33. Rabin, T., Ben-Or, M.: Verifiable secret sharing and multiparty protocols with honest majority. In: Proceedings of the Twenty-First Annual ACM Symposium on Theory of Computing, pp. 73–85 (1989)
34. Rivest, R.L., Shamir, A., Wagner, D.A.: Time-lock puzzles and timed-release crypto (1996)
35. Russell, A., Zuckerman, D.: Perfect information leader election in log* n+ o (1) rounds. J. Comput. Syst. Sci. **63**(4), 612–626 (2001)
36. Thyagarajan, S.A.K., Castagnos, G., Laguillaumie, F., Malavolta, G.: Efficient CCA timed commitments in class groups. In: Proceedings of the 2021 ACM SIGSAC Conference on Computer and Communications Security, pp. 2663–2684 (2021)
37. Thyagarajan, S.A.K., Soni, P., Wu, K.: Game-theoretically fair distributed sampling. In: Reyzin, L., Stebila, D. (eds.) CRYPTO 2024, Part VIII. LNCS, vol. 14927, pp. 207–239. Springer, Cham (2024). https://doi.org/10.1007/978-3-031-68397-8_7
38. Wadhwa, S., Stoeter, J., Zhang, F., Nayak, K.: He-HTLC: revisiting incentives in HTLC. In: 30th Annual Network and Distributed System Security Symposium, NDSS 2023, San Diego, California, USA, February 27 - March 3 2023. The Internet Society (2023). https://www.ndss-symposium.org/ndss-paper/he-htlc-revisiting-incentives-in-htlc/
39. Wu, K., Asharov, G., Shi, E.: A complete characterization of game-theoretically fair, multi-party coin toss. In: Dunkelman, O., Dziembowski, S. (eds.) EUROCRYPT 2022. LNCS, vol. 13275, pp. 120–149. Springer, Cham (2022). https://doi.org/10.1007/978-3-031-06944-4_5
40. Zhang, F., Wu, K.: Game-theoretically fair coin toss with arbitrary preferences. IACR Cryptol. ePrint Arch., p. 1617 (2025). https://eprint.iacr.org/2025/1617

PUFF: Maximally <u>P</u>roactive Sec<u>u</u>rity <u>f</u>or <u>F</u>ree in Perfectly Secure MPC with Guaranteed Output Delivery

Jiarui Li[1,3], Mengzhen Zou[1], Guidong Li[1], Guoyan Zhang[2,3,4,5(✉)], and Chen Qian[1,3,5(✉)]

[1] School of Cyber Science and Technology, Shandong University, Qingdao 266237, Shandong, China
[2] School of Cryptologic Science and Engineering, Shandong University, Jinan 250101, Shandong, China
[3] State Key Laboratory of Cryptography and Digital Economy Security, Shandong University, Jinan 250100, China
[4] Shandong Key Laboratory of Artificial Intelligence Security, Shandong University, Jinan 250100, Shandong, China
[5] Key Laboratory of Cryptologic Technology and Information Security of Ministry of Education, Shandong University, Jinan 250100, Shandong, China
{chen.qian,guoyanzhang}@sdu.edu.cn

Abstract. Achieving proactive security in perfectly-secure Multi-Party Computation (MPC) with guaranteed output delivery is a significant challenge, primarily because traditional protocols require all participants to be continuously online, rendering them impractical for many applications. The recently proposed layered MPC model [DDG+23] addresses this by allowing parties to be offline for extended periods. However, existing protocols for this model incur substantial overhead compared to their counterparts in the standard static setting.

This work introduces a unified framework and essential building blocks for constructing protocols in the layered model, instantiable with both Shamir and CNF secret sharing. Using this framework, we develop highly efficient protocols for Verifiable Secret Sharing (VSS) and secure multiplication for proactive security.

Applying our framework, we construct layered MPC protocols that drastically reduce the communication complexity and the number of layers required to evaluate an arithmetic circuit of depth D. Specifically, our Shamir-based MPC achieves (n^6) per-gate communication with a total layer depth of $D + 13$, representing a significant improvement over the (n^9) complexity and $10D + 8$ depth of [DDG+23].

Keywords: Multi-Party Computation · Verifiable Secret Sharing · Secure Multiplication · Maximally Proactive Security · Dimension Transformation

© International Association for Cryptologic Research 2026
J. Daemen and E. Thomé (Eds.): EUROCRYPT 2026, LNCS 16543, pp. 515–545, 2026.
https://doi.org/10.1007/978-3-032-25324-8_18

1 Introduction

Secure multi-party computation (MPC) [Yao86, GMW87, BGW88, CCD88] allows a set of parties to jointly compute a function on their private inputs without revealing them. Classical MPC protocols, however, typically assume a static set of parties that must remain online for the entire duration of the computation. This assumption is impractical for long-running applications or settings with intermittent participation, such as federated learning and blockchain.

1.1 Synchronous Verifiable Secret Sharing with Perfect Security

Verifiable secret sharing (VSS) is a fundamental building block for secure multiparty computation (MPC). A long line of research has established its theoretical limits, with Dolev et al. [DDWY93] proving that any perfectly secure VSS protocol requires an honest majority of parties, i.e., $n > 3t$. The first protocol to meet this bound was proposed by Ben-Or, Goldwasser, and Wigderson (BGW) [BGW88]. It employed bivariate polynomials to enable cross-checking of shares, but its round complexity was seven.

Subsequent work focused on reducing this round complexity. Gennaro et al. [GIKR01] presented two VSS protocols for the $n > 3t$ setting: a four-round Shamir-based scheme with $O(n^2)$ communication and a three-round scheme based on additive secret sharing with exponential communication. They also proved that three rounds are optimal for this setting. The challenge then shifted to designing a round-optimal Shamir-based VSS. Katz and Koo [KKK08] achieved this by introducing weak VSS (WSS) as a primitive, resulting in a three-round protocol with $O(n^3)$ communication. More recently, Applebaum et al. [AKP20] presented an alternative three-round, (n^3) Shamir-based VSS using a symmetric bivariate polynomial framework.

All the Shamir-based methods above follow the BGW-style complain-and-resolve paradigm: they cross-check shares via a degree-(t, t) bivariate polynomial and, when disputes arise, require the dealer to speak again for resolution. This pattern is ill-suited for dynamic-committee settings as it requires the dealer to remain online.

1.2 Proactive Security and Fluid MPC

The proactive security model, introduced by Ostrovsky and Yung [OY91], considers a mobile adversary that corrupts different parties over time. To counter this, parties periodically execute a refresh protocol to heal from compromises. This paradigm was recently extended to settings with dynamic participation, leading to two main models: YOSO (You-Only-Speak-Once) [GHK+21] and Fluid MPC [CGG+21]. In these models, the computation is carried out by a sequence of committees, where each round may involve a different set of n parties.

In the YOSO model, parties rely on ideal target-anonymous channels to communicate with future, randomly selected committee members, and the adversary is restricted to probabilistic corruptions. In contrast, the Fluid MPC model assumes a stronger, worst-case adversary that can corrupt up to a threshold of parties within any given committee, without requiring specialized communication channels.

Much of the research in the fluid model has focused on constructions security with abort [CGG+21,RS22], where protocols with linear communication complexity have been developed [BEP23,BEP25]. However, security with abort is insufficient for applications like electronic voting and auctions, which require guaranteed output delivery (G.O.D.). Achieving G.O.D. in a fluid setting is particularly challenging because traditional protocols rely on a static set of parties to resolve disputes. To date, the only works to achieve G.O.D. in the fluid model [DDG+23,DKLN24] employ a "Future Messaging" technique, which commits messages required for potential re-broadcasts by the Dealer (or other parties) to future committees. While this effectively adapts the complain-and-resolve to the proactive security model, they do so at the cost of significantly higher complexity compared to their counterparts in the static setting. These protocols operate in the *layered model*, which formalizes the strongest adversarial conditions of fluid MPC and maximal proactivity.

Adopting this layered model, we investigate the feasibility of efficient MPC under the strongest security guarantees: perfect security with guaranteed output delivery. This leads to the central question of our work:

How to build efficient MPC in layered model with perfect security and G.O.D?

1.3 Our Contributions

We answer the above question affirmatively by giving a generic framework to build efficient MPC protocols in the layered model with perfect security and G.O.D. Our framework supports both Shamir and CNF secret sharing schemes. Using our unified framework, our construction of verifiable secret sharing in the layered model is more efficient than the state-of-the-art VSS in the layered model.

We summarize our main contribution as follows:

- A unified view of secret sharing and the introduction of dimension transformation techniques.
- A more efficient VSS in the layered model avoiding the incompatibility between the complaint-and-resolve paradigm and the layered model.
- More efficient offline multiplication and MPC for arithmetic circuits in the layered model.

A Unified View of Secret Sharing and Dimension transformation Techniques. We present a unified framework that generalizes both Shamir and CNF secret sharing schemes as specific instances of a high-dimensional robust secret sharing scheme. This unified perspective enables a modular protocol design, allowing either scheme to be instantiated as needed. The framework achieves maximally proactive security in the layered model using five rounds generically (with Shamir sharing) or four rounds (with CNF sharing).

We also introduce *dimension transformation*, a technique for converting a k-dimensional sharing into a k'-dimensional one. These techniques are essential for achieving maximally proactive secure MPC in the layered model, as they effectively mitigate cross-layer corruption attacks by increasing the dimension of the secret sharing scheme.

A More Efficient VSS in the Layered Model Via avoiding the Complain-and-Resolve Paradigm. By applying this framework, we derive a significantly more efficient verifiable secret sharing protocol in the layered model. Specifically, our Shamir-based VSS achieves five rounds with communication complexity of $O(n^4 \log |\mathbb{F}| + \mathcal{BC}(n^4 \log |\mathbb{F}|))$, improving upon the previous best-known result of six rounds with $O(n^6 \log |\mathbb{F}| + \mathcal{BC}(n^4 \log |\mathbb{F}|))$ in the same maximally-proactive and perfectly secure model. This efficiency gain stems from our VSS construction based on dimension transformation, which avoids the traditional complain-and-resolve paradigm. Consequently, our design eliminates the need for expensive primitives, such as Future Messages, which are typically required to forward secondary broadcast messages from the dealer and participants to subsequent layers in the event of disputes. Here, $\mathcal{BC}$ denotes communication over a broadcast channel. We provide a concrete comparison with other existing VSS protocols in Table 1.

Moreover, when we instantiate our generic VSS protocol with the CNF-based robust secret sharing scheme, we achieve a four-round CNF-based VSS protocol in the layered model, which is one round fewer than the Shamir-based counterpart. This follows from the fact that in the CNF-based VSS protocol, each party

Table 1. Round and communication complexity comparison for perfectly-secure VSS ($n > 3t$), with $\mathcal{BC}$ denoting communication over the broadcast channel.

Shamir-based VSS Scheme	Round	Comm.
[GIKR01]	4	$O(n^2 \log|\mathbb{F}| + \mathcal{BC}(n^2 \log|\mathbb{F}|))$
[AKP20]	3	$O(n^3 \log|\mathbb{F}| + \mathcal{BC}(n^3 \log|\mathbb{F}|))$
[DDG+23] (Layered Setting)	6	$O(n^6 \log|\mathbb{F}| + \mathcal{BC}(n^4 \log|\mathbb{F}|))$
Our work (Layered Setting)	5	$O(n^4 \log|\mathbb{F}| + \mathcal{BC}(n^4 \log|\mathbb{F}|))$
CNF-based VSS[6] Scheme	**Round**	**Comm.**
[GIKR01]	3	$O(n^2 \cdot \binom{n}{t} \log |\mathbb{G}| + \mathcal{BC}(n^2 \cdot \binom{n}{t} \log |\mathbb{G}|))$
[DDG+23] (Layered Setting)	5	$O(n^2 \cdot \binom{n}{t}^3 \log |\mathbb{R}| + \mathcal{BC}(n^2 \cdot \binom{n}{t}^3 \log |\mathbb{R}|))$
Our work (Layered Setting)	4	$O(n^4 \cdot \binom{n}{t}^4 \log |\mathbb{G}| + \mathcal{BC}(n^4 \cdot \binom{n}{t}^4 \log |\mathbb{G}|))$

[6]In CNF-based secret sharing, the secret is first split into $\binom{n}{t}$ additive shares—a share r_T for each set $T \subset [n]$ of size t—and party i receives all shares r_T such that $i \notin T$

can locally identify inconsistent senders in the previous layer using a majority vote. The details of the VSS protocol is presented in Tables 4.

More Efficient Multiplication. Our framework also leads to more efficient protocols for multiplication. Compared to the previous best protocols in the layered model [DDG+23], our Shamir-based multiplication protocol reduces the round complexity from 10 to 8 and the communication complexity from $O(n^9)$ to $O(n^6)$, thereby matching BGW in the standard model. We give a direct comparison in Table 2.

Table 2. Comparison of the round and communication complexity for Shamir Multiplication($n > 3t$). R_{VSS} and $Comm_{VSS}$ denotes round and communication complexity of VSS used in the multiplication

Shamir Multiplication	Round	Comm.
[BGW88] [7]	6 ($R_{VSS} + 3$)	$O(n^2 \cdot Comm_{VSS} + n^5)$
[DDG+23] (Layered Setting)	10 ($R_{VSS} + 4$)	$O(n^9)$
Our work (Layered Setting)	8 ($R_{VSS} + 3$)	$O(n^6)$

[7] The round complexity and communication complexity of the multiplication protocol are not provided in [BGW88]. In [AL17], Sect. 6 presents the details and complexity of the protocol. Additionally, We choose 3-round VSS to obtain optimal round complexity

More Efficient MPC for Arithmetic Circuits in The layered Model. Building on our improved multiplication protocol, we construct Shamir-based and CNF-based MPC protocols in the layered model. Our Shamir-based MPC protocol evaluates an arithmetic circuit of depth D using only $D + 13$ layers, a significant improvement over the prior $10D + 8$ layers [DDG+23]. Similarly, our CNF-based MPC protocol requires only $D + 11$ layers, compared to the previous $7D + 6$ layers. We summarize the round complexity comparison in Table 3. In

Table 3. Round complexity comparison for MPC Protocol(evaluating a depth-D arithmetic circuit). For BGW, we adopt the standard preprocessing with Beaver triples: multiplication triples are generated offline. We treat the rounds of offline as $O(1)$.

MPC protocol	Round(Shamir-based)	Round(CNF-based)
[BGW88]	$D + (1)$	−
[DDG+23] (Layered Setting)	$10D + 8$	$7D + 6$
Our work (Layered Setting)	$D + 13$	$D + 10$

addition, we extend layered MPC, originally defined only for layered arithmetic circuits[1], to support arbitrary arithmetic circuits.

2   Technical Overview

We begin by outlining the main technical challenges in adapting existing secure multi-party computation (MPC) protocols to the layered setting, particularly concerning the preservation of security and efficiency.

2.1   A Unified View of Secret Sharing

Secret sharing is a cornerstone of MPC. The literature is dominated by two primary schemes: the Shamir secret sharing [Sha79], favored for constructing communication-efficient protocols, and the CNF secret sharing [ISN89], often used to achieve minimal round complexity. Although some techniques are transferable, these schemes are typically treated as distinct paradigms.

In this work, we introduce a unified framework that generalizes both. We show that Shamir and CNF sharing are specific instances of a high-dimensional robust secret sharing scheme. This unified perspective enables a modular design for our protocols, allowing either scheme to be plugged in as needed.

Furthermore, we extend this framework to support *dimension transformation*, a mechanism for converting a k-dimensional sharing into a k'-dimensional one. The construction is recursive, with standard 1-dimensional Shamir or CNF sharing as the base case. For instance, a k-dimensional Shamir sharing of a secret s is created by sampling a random polynomial $\mathsf{F}(X_k, \ldots, X_1)$ of degree at most t in each variable, such that $\mathsf{F}(0, \ldots, 0) = s$.

2.2   Dimension Transformation and Proactive Security

A key challenge in achieving maximally proactive security is that the adversary could corrupt different parties in different layers, then create a cross-layer *corruption cohesion* attack. Our first observation is that the corruption cohesion attack can be mitigated by increasing the dimension of the secret sharing scheme.

Example. Consider a protocol spanning two layers using a 2-dimensional (bivariate) Shamir secret sharing scheme in an (n, t)-layered MPC setting. Let a secret s be shared via a random bivariate polynomial $\mathsf{F}(X_1, X_2)$ of degree t in each variable, where $s = \mathsf{F}(0, 0)$. Each party P_i^1 in the first layer, $\mathcal{L}_1$, holds the univariate polynomial $\mathsf{F}(i, X_2)$ as its share. To transfer the sharing to the next

---

[1] *Layered arithmetic circuits* impose a layering on a standard arithmetic circuit: the gates are partitioned into $L_0, \ldots, L_D$ (with inputs in L_0), and every gate $g \in L_i$ takes its inputs only from L_{i-1}. Hence edges go strictly from L_{i-1} to L_i; no skip-layer dependencies are allowed.

layer, P_i^1 sends the point evaluation $\mathsf{F}(i,j)$ to party P_j^2 in $\mathcal{L}_2$. After receiving points from all parties in $\mathcal{L}_1$, each party P_j^2 in $\mathcal{L}_2$ can reconstruct its share, the univariate polynomial $\mathsf{F}(X_1,j)$, by interpolating the points it received.

Now, consider an adversary who corrupts t parties in each layer. In $\mathcal{L}_1$, the adversary learns t polynomials of the form $\mathsf{F}(i,X_2)$. In $\mathcal{L}_2$, the adversary learns another t polynomials of the form $\mathsf{F}(X_1,j)$. This corresponds to learning the values of F on a $\mathsf{t}\times\mathsf{n}$ grid and an $\mathsf{n}\times\mathsf{t}$ grid of points. The union of these points forms a $(\mathsf{t}\times\mathsf{n})\cup(\mathsf{n}\times\mathsf{t})$ grid. Crucially, the largest square subgrid of points known to the adversary is of size $\mathsf{t}\times\mathsf{t}$. Since reconstructing the degree-(t,t) polynomial $\mathsf{F}(X_1,X_2)$ requires knowledge of its values on at least a $(\mathsf{t}+1)\times(\mathsf{t}+1)$ grid of points, the $\mathsf{t}\times\mathsf{t}$ points are insufficient to learn any information about the secret $s=\mathsf{F}(0,0)$.

This example illustrates a general principle. A k-dimensional secret sharing can be visualized as a k-dimensional hypercube of values. Passing shares from one layer to the next corresponds to rotating then projecting this hypercube along one of its dimensions. An adversary corrupting t parties in each of the k layers learns t hyperplanes of values in each of the k dimensions. This information is insufficient to reconstruct the secret, as that would require learning a $(\mathsf{t}+1)\times\cdots\times(\mathsf{t}+1)$ sub-hypercube of values. Thus, by matching the dimension of the secret sharing to the number of layers, we can prevent the adversary from combining information across layers to compromise the secret.

Layered MPC. The above insight leads to a straightforward approach for achieving maximally proactive security in layered MPC: employ a k-dimensional secret sharing scheme for a protocol spanning k layers. Each layer uses one dimension of the sharing, and shares are passed to the next layer by projecting along that dimension. This ensures that even if the adversary corrupts t parties in each layer, they cannot gather enough information to reconstruct the secret. This perspective not only simplifies the design of secure protocols in the layered setting but also provides a clear framework for analyzing their security.

2.3   Dimension Transformation and Complain-Resolve

Another challenge in the layered setting is handling complaints and resolutions when parties are not static but change across layers. In traditional MPC protocols, if a party suspects misbehavior, it can raise a complaint, and the same set of parties can engage in a resolution process. However, in the layered model, the parties involved in the complaint is not present in the future layer, making it unclear who should handle the resolution.

To address this, we leverage our dimension transformation technique. Our second observation is that we do not necessarily need to fold the dimension after handing the hypercube to the next layer. Instead, we can maintain the higher-dimensional structure and allow parties in the future layer to access the relevant information from the previous layer's hypercube. This approach ensures that even if the parties involved in the complaint are not present in the future layer, the necessary information for resolution is still accessible for honest parties.

2.4   Towards the Most Efficient Verifiable Secret Sharing

Combine the above two observations, we can now outline our approach to constructing an efficient verifiable secret sharing (VSS) protocol in the layered setting. We give the intuition behind our 5 layer VSS protocol with the Shamir-based secret sharing and 4 layer VSS one with the CNF-based secret sharing.

To launch the protocol, the dealer first shares its secret using a 4-dimensional secret sharing scheme. Visually, this can be represented as a 4-dimensional cube of values. Then, the dealer distributes the 3-dimensional shares (hyperplanes of the cube) to parties in the first layer, $\mathcal{L}_1$. Each party in $\mathcal{L}_1$ receives a 3-dimensional slice of the hypercube, corresponding to fixing one dimension of the 4-dimensional polynomial.

A key property of VSS is verifiability: the ability for honest parties to detect a faulty dealer. In our protocol, a dealer is deemed faulty if the distributed 3-dimensional cube of shares does not contain any good sub-cube. The error-correction property of the underlying robust secret sharing scheme allows for the recovery of the polynomial from such a sub-cube. To ensure verifiability, our protocol satisfies the following three properties:

- **Correctness:** If the dealer is honest, at least one such good sub-cube exists.
- **Soundness:** If no such good sub-cube exists, all honest parties will detect the dealer's fault.
- **Uniqueness:** If such a good sub-cube exists, all honest parties can reconstruct the same unique secret from it.

The correctness property is straightforward. An honest dealer samples a random 3-dimensional polynomial of degree t in each variable. The resulting cube of shares naturally contains many valid $(t + 1)^3$ sub-cubes. Noticing that the hypercube is only defined by the slices received by honest parties in $\mathcal{L}_1$, the existence of a good sub-cube is guaranteed.

For soundness, the dealer distributes shares such that a good 3-dimensional $(2t + 1)^3$ sub-cube exists. Parties in each layer check for this and publicly broadcast any detected inconsistencies. However, such checks may produce false positives: even if all public checks pass, the dealer may collude with the adversary to introduce inconsistencies into the shares received by parties in the final layer $\mathcal{L}_5$, since among the $2t + 1$ parties claiming inconsistency in each layer, up to t may be malicious. Fortunately, we can rely on the existence of $(t + 1)^2$ "inconsistency-free" sub-cubes, which contain shares only from honest parties and are thus guaranteed to be consistent. Honest parties use these sub-cubes to publicly recover any inconsistent shares held by honest parties outside of the good sub-cube. This public recovery is verifiable by all parties in $\mathcal{L}_5$. If the dealer is faulty and the corrupted parties refuse to publicly recover inconsistent shares, all honest parties in $\mathcal{L}_5$ will detect the fault by verifying consistency. Conversely, if the dealer is honest, all shares from honest parties in $\mathcal{L}_5$ will be consistent, and the dealer is deemed honest.

2.5   Efficient Multiplication and MPC

Building on our efficient VSS protocol and dimension transformation techniques, we construct a multiplication protocol for the layered setting. Our approach adapts the classic BGW multiplication method [BGW88], including its degree-reduction and resharing steps, to the layered model.

Integrating these components, we construct our final MPC protocol. As summarized in Table 3, our protocol achieves significant improvements in both round and communication complexity over prior work [DDG+23]. Notably, our Shamir-based MPC protocol matches the round complexity of the classic BGW protocol in the standard model. This demonstrates that our techniques can bridge the gap between the static and dynamic committee settings without incurring a round-complexity overhead.

3   Organization

This paper is organized as follows. Section 4 introduces the necessary preliminaries, including layered MPC, robust secret sharing, and verifiable secret sharing. Section 5 presents our multi-dimensional robust secret sharing scheme which generalizes both Shamir and CNF secret sharing, a fundamental building block for our constructions. In Sect. 6, we leverage this scheme to build several cross-layer messaging functionalities, which are key to achieving proactive security in our protocols. Section 7 details our main technical contribution: a parallel verifiable secret sharing protocol with low communication and round complexity. Section 8 then presents our offline layered multiplication protocol. Finally, Sect. 9 combines these components to construct a complete MPC protocol for general functionalities that achieves maximal proactive security.

4   Preliminaries

4.1   Notations

We denote by $\mathbb{F}$ a finite field. For a positive integer n, we denote by $[n]$ the set $\{1, 2, \ldots, n\}$. We use bold uppercase letters (e.g., $\boldsymbol{A}$) to denote matrices, bold lowercase letters (e.g., $\boldsymbol{a}$) to denote vectors, and regular lowercase letters (e.g., a) to denote scalars. For a matrix $\boldsymbol{A}$, we use $\boldsymbol{A}[i, j]$ to denote the entry in the i-th row and j-th column of $\boldsymbol{A}$, and $\boldsymbol{A}[i, \cdot]$ to denote the i-th row of $\boldsymbol{A}$. For a vector $\boldsymbol{a}$, we use $\boldsymbol{a}[i]$ to denote the i-th entry of $\boldsymbol{a}$. We use calligraphic uppercase letters (e.g., $\mathcal{A}$) to denote sets. For a set $\mathcal{A}$, we use $|\mathcal{A}|$ to denote its cardinality. We use bold script letters (e.g., ss) to denote vectors of shares.

4.2   Layered MPC

We begin by defining layered MPC [DDG+23] in the UC framework. After this, we recall the definitions of robust secret sharing and verifiable secret sharing, which serve as the core building blocks for constructing MPC protocols.

Maximal Proactive Security. The layered MPC model of [DDG+23] is a specialization of standard MPC with general adversary structures, characterized by: (i) an interaction pattern defined by a layered graph; and (ii) an adversary that may corrupt at most t parties per layer. In [DDG+23], it was shown that, assuming secure erasures, secure layered MPC implies secure maximally proactive MPC. We do not repeat the proof; instead, we recall the formal definition of layered MPC as follows:

Definition 1 (Layered MPC). *Let* n, t, d *be positive integers. An* (n, t, d)-*layered protocol is a synchronous protocol* Π *over secure point-to-point channels and a broadcast channel, with the following special features.*

> **Parties:** *There are* $N = n(d+1)$ *parties, partitioned into* $d+1$ *layers* $\mathcal{L}_i$ *for* $0 \leq i \leq d$, *with* $|\mathcal{L}_i| = n$. *Parties in the last layer* $\mathcal{L}_d$ *are referred to as output clients. Parties in the first layer* $\mathcal{L}_0$ *are referred to as input clients. Parties in intermediate layers* $\mathcal{L}_i$ *for* $1 \leq i < d$ *are referred to as computation parties.*
>
> **Interaction Pattern:** *The execution of the protocol consists of* d *rounds. In round* $i \in \{1, \ldots, d\}$, *parties in* $\mathcal{L}_{i-1}$ *may send messages to parties in* $\mathcal{L}_i$ *over secure point-to-point channels. Each party in* $\mathcal{L}_{i-1}$ *may also broadcast to all parties in* $\mathcal{L}_i$.
>
> **Functionalities:** *We consider functionalities* $\mathcal{F}$ *that take inputs from the input clients and deliver outputs to the output clients.*
>
> **Adversaries:** *We allow an active, rushing, adaptive adversary that may corrupt any number of input and output clients, in addition, up to* t *parties in each intermediate layer* $\mathcal{L}_i$ *for* $0 < i < d$.

We say that a protocol Π *is a layered MPC protocol for* $\mathcal{F}$ *if it realizes* $\mathcal{F}$ *in the standard sense of (stand-alone) secure MPC with general adversary structures [Can00]. We consider the case of perfect security with guaranteed output delivery where* $t < n/3$.

Universal Composability. Following [DDG+23], we develop our protocol for general functionalities in the synchronous, stand-alone model. We prove its perfect security via a straight-line black-box simulator. To extend this result to the Universal Composability (UC) framework, we can adopt one of two standard techniques, as in [DDG+23]:

- Insert dummy layers between every two layers of the original protocol. This ensures synchrony and allows us to apply the result of [KLR06] to establish UC security.
- Broadcast the messages for the initial VSS subprotocols to all parties. Then, the protocol is secure under the Micali-Rogaway definition of security [MR92]. Subsequently, applying the result of Dodis and Micali [DM00] lifts the security guarantee to the UC framework.

4.3 Strongly Robust Secret Sharing

Definition 2 (Robust Secret Sharing). *A* (n, t)-*robust secret sharing scheme over message space* $\mathcal{M}$ *over an Abelian group* $\mathbb{G}$ *consists of a tuple of algorithms* $\mathsf{SS} = (\mathsf{Share}, \mathsf{Reconst})$ *with both message and share space in* $\mathcal{M} = \mathbb{G}$, *and the following syntax:*

$\mathsf{Share}(\mathsf{m}) \rightarrow [\![m]\!]$: *Takes a message* $\mathsf{m} \in \mathcal{M}$ *as input, and outputs a vector of shares* $\mathsf{ss} = ([\![m]\!][1], \ldots, [\![m]\!][n]) \in \mathcal{M}^{\mathsf{n}}$.
$\mathsf{Reconst}([\![m]\!][1], \ldots, [\![m]\!][n]) \rightarrow \mathsf{m}$: *Takes* n *shares as input, and outputs a message* $\mathsf{m} \in \mathcal{M} \cup \{\bot\}$.

We require the following properties to hold:

Correctness: *For any* $\mathsf{m} \in \mathcal{M}$, *we have*

$$\forall I \subseteq [\mathsf{n}] : |I| \geq \mathsf{t} + 1 \implies$$
$$\Pr\left[\mathsf{Reconst}(\{[\![m]\!][i]\}_{i \in I}, \bot, \ldots, \bot) = \mathsf{m} \mid [\![m]\!] \xleftarrow{\$} \mathsf{Share}(\mathsf{m})\right] = 1.$$

Robustness: *For any* $\mathsf{m} \in \mathcal{M}$, *let* $[\![m]\!] \xleftarrow{\$} \mathsf{Share}(\mathsf{m})$, *for all vectors of shares* ss, *we have*

$$\exists I \subseteq [\mathsf{n}], \forall i \in I : \mathsf{ss}[i] = [\![m]\!][i] \wedge |I| \geq \mathsf{n} - \mathsf{t} \implies \mathsf{Reconst}(\mathsf{ss}) = \mathsf{m}.$$

Secrecy: *For all* $\mathsf{m}, \mathsf{m}' \in \mathcal{M}$, *for all* $S \subseteq [\mathsf{n}]$ *with* $|S| < \mathsf{t}$, *the following distributions are identical:*

$$\left\{\{[\![m]\!][i]\}_{i \in S} : [\![m]\!] \xleftarrow{\$} \mathsf{Share}(\mathsf{m})\right\} \equiv \left\{\{[\![m']\!][i]\}_{i \in S} : [\![m']\!] \xleftarrow{\$} \mathsf{Share}(\mathsf{m}')\right\}.$$

Additively Homomorphic: *For all* $\mathsf{m}_1, \mathsf{m}_2 \in \mathcal{M}$, *and all* $\gamma \in \mathbb{F}$, *we have*

$$\Pr\left[\mathsf{Reconst}([\![m_1]\!] + \gamma \cdot [\![m_2]\!]) = \mathsf{m}_1 + \gamma \cdot \mathsf{m}_2 \;\middle|\; \begin{matrix} [\![m_1]\!] \xleftarrow{\$} \mathsf{Share}(\mathsf{m}_1) \\ [\![m_2]\!] \xleftarrow{\$} \mathsf{Share}(\mathsf{m}_2) \end{matrix}\right] = 1.$$

Strong Robustness: *For any* $\mathsf{m} \in \mathcal{M}$, *let* $[\![m]\!] \xleftarrow{\$} \mathsf{Share}(\mathsf{m})$, *for all vectors of shares* ss *such that* $\# \{i \mid \mathsf{ss}[i] \neq [\![m]\!][i]\} \leq \mathsf{t}$, *we have a deterministic polynomial-time algorithm* $\mathsf{ErrorDetect}$ *such that*

$$\mathsf{ErrorDetect}(\mathsf{ss}) = \{i \mid \mathsf{ss}[i] \neq [\![m]\!][i]\}.$$

Moreover, there exists a deterministic polynomial-time algorithm Repair *such that for any* ss *and any* $i \in [\mathsf{n}]$, *we have*

$$\mathsf{Repair}(\mathsf{ss}, i) = [\![m]\!][i].$$

Moreover, we say a vector of shares ss *is* consistent *if* $\mathsf{ErrorDetect}(\mathsf{ss}) = \emptyset$.

4.4   Verifiable Secret Sharing

We adapt the notion of verifiable secret sharing (VSS) to the layered setting. More precisely, since we do not argue the universal composability of the VSS, we define a new ideal functionality in the standalone model for parallel VSS, which consists of l parallel instances of the VSS functionality from $\mathcal{L}_0$ to $\mathcal{L}_d$. The formal definition is provided in the full version of this paper, as well as the ideal functionalities of multiplication and layered-MPC.

4.5   Randomness Generation

We define a randomness generation functionality $\mathcal{F}_{\mathsf{RandGen}}$ that allows parties in layer $\mathcal{L}_i$ to jointly generate a shared random value, which is then secret shared among parties in layer $\mathcal{L}_{i+1}$. The formal definition is provided in the full version of this paper.

In Shamir-based secret sharing, we use a public Vandermonde matrix to linearly mix the shares of n random values, so generating $\mathsf{n} - \mathsf{t}$ globally shared random values requires only one $\mathcal{F}_{\mathsf{Par\text{-}VSS}}$ instance. We provide the detailed construction for Shamir-based secret sharing and CNF-based secret sharing in the full version of this paper.

5   Multi-dimensional Robust Secret Sharing

We generalize the classical robust secret sharing scheme to the higher dimensional one recursively. More precisely, a k-dimensional robust secret sharing scheme is defined recursively using the $(k-1)$-dimensional robust secret sharing scheme, with 1-dimensional robust secret sharing defined as in Definition 2.

Definition 3. (k-Dimensional Secret Sharing scheme). *A k-dimensional* (n,t)*-robust secret sharing scheme consists of a tuple of* PPT *algorithms* $\mathsf{SS}_k =$ (Share, Reconst) *with message space* $\mathcal{M}$*, and the similar syntax as in Definition 2. Formally, we have*

> Share(m) $\rightarrow$ ss : *Takes a message* $\mathsf{m} \in \mathcal{M}$ *as input and outputs a k-dimensional share* ss.
>
> Reconst(ss) $\rightarrow$ m : *Takes a k-dimensional share* ss *as input and outputs a message* $\mathsf{m} \in \mathcal{M} \cup \{\bot\}$.

We require the correctness, robustness, secrecy and additively homomorphic properties as in Definition 2 to hold for the k-dimensional shares.

5.1   Dimension Projection

A secrecy-preserving projection is a procedure that reduces a k-dimensional robust secret sharing to a vector of $(k-1)$-dimensional ones. The "secrecy-preserving" property ensures that an adversary gains no information about the secret, even when corrupting a threshold number of shares from multiple dimension levels simultaneously. This property, formally defined in Definition 4, is crucial for our layered construction, as it prevents information leakage from adversaries corrupting parties across different layers.

Definition 4 (Secrecy-Preserving Projection). *A* (n, t)-*robust secret sharing scheme* SS_k *of dimension* k *supports secrecy-preserving projection if there exists efficient* deterministic *algorithms* $(\mathsf{Proj}, \mathsf{Fold}, \mathsf{ErrorDetect}, \mathsf{Repair}, \mathsf{Rotate})$ *with the following syntax:*

$\mathsf{Proj}(\mathsf{ss}) \to (\mathsf{ss}[1], \ldots, \mathsf{ss}[\mathsf{n}])$: *Takes a* k-*dimensional share* ss *of* m *as input, and outputs a* $(k-1)$-*dimensional vector of shares* $(\mathsf{ss}[1], \ldots, \mathsf{ss}[\mathsf{n}])$.

$\mathsf{Fold}(\{\mathsf{ss}'[i]\}_{i \in [\mathsf{n}]}) \to \mathsf{ss}$: *Takes a vector of* n *shares of a* k-*dimensional share as input, and outputs a* k-*dimensional share.*

$\mathsf{ErrorDetect}(\mathsf{ss}[1], \ldots, \mathsf{ss}[\mathsf{n}]) \to \mathcal{P}([\mathsf{n}]) \cup \bot$: *Takes a vector of* $(k-1)$-*dimensional shares as input and outputs a set of indices of corrupted shares, or* $\bot$ *if the share is inconsistent.*

$\mathsf{Repair}(\mathsf{ss}[1], \ldots, \mathsf{ss}[\mathsf{n}]) \to \mathsf{ss}'$: *Takes a vector of* $(k-1)$-*dimensional shares as input and outputs a repaired* k-*dimensional share* ss'.

We also define the rotation operation that "rotate" a 2-dimensional vector of shares. More precisely, we have

$$\mathsf{Rotate}(\{\mathsf{ss}'[1,j]\}_{j \in [\mathsf{n}]}, \ldots, \{\mathsf{ss}'[\mathsf{n},j]\}_{j \in [\mathsf{n}]}) \to (\{\mathsf{ss}[1,j]\}_{j \in [\mathsf{n}]}, \ldots, \{\mathsf{ss}[\mathsf{n},j]\}_{j \in [\mathsf{n}]})$$

: *Takes a 2-dimensional vector of* k-*dimensional shares and rotates it, outputting a vector of* k-*dimensional shares, such that* $\mathsf{ss}[i,j] = \mathsf{ss}'[j,i]$ *for all* $i, j \in [\mathsf{n}]$.

For simplicity of notation we denote by

$$\mathsf{Proj}(\mathsf{ss}[1], \ldots, \mathsf{ss}[\mathsf{n}]) = (\{\mathsf{ss}[1,j]\}_{j \in [\mathsf{n}]}, \ldots, \{\mathsf{ss}[\mathsf{n},j]\}_{j \in [\mathsf{n}]}),$$

the projection over the vector of shares. Note that ss *is 2-dimensional vector of* $(k-1)$-*dimensional shares of the form* $\mathsf{ss}[i,j]$. *Similarly we have*

$$\mathsf{Fold}(\mathsf{Fold}(\{\mathsf{ss}[1,i]\}_{i \in [\mathsf{n}]}, \ldots, \{\mathsf{ss}[\mathsf{n},i]\}_{i \in [\mathsf{n}]})) = \mathsf{Fold}(\mathsf{ss}'[1], \ldots, \mathsf{ss}'[\mathsf{n}]) = \mathsf{ss}'',$$

for the folding over the 2-dimensional set of shares. The rotation over multi-dimensional shares is defined as the rotation over the last two dimensions.

For simplicity of notation, throughout the paper we use Fold *to denote the robust folding* operator, *which first applies* Repair *to the input vector and then folds the repaired vector. We also extend projection to the abort symbol by defining*

$$\mathsf{Proj}(\bot) := (\bot, \ldots, \bot).$$

The projection, folding, error detection, repair, and rotation operations satisfy the following properties:

Correctness: *For any* $m \in \mathcal{M}$, *we have*

$$\Pr\left[\begin{array}{l}SS_{k-1}.\mathsf{ErrorDetect}(ss) = \emptyset \\ \wedge SS_{k-1}.\mathsf{Reconst}(ss) = m\end{array} \middle| \begin{array}{l}ss' \xleftarrow{\$} SS_k.\mathsf{Share}(m) \\ ss \leftarrow \mathsf{Fold}(\mathsf{Proj}(ss'))\end{array}\right] = 1.$$

Secrecy-Preserving: *For all* $m, m' \in \mathcal{M}$, *for all* $S_k, \ldots, S_1 \subseteq [n]$ *such that* $|S|_i \leq t$ *for all* $i \in [k]$, *the following distributions are identical:*

$$\left\{ \{ss_k[i]\}_{i \in S_k}, \ldots, \{ss_1[i]\}_{i \in S_1} \middle| \begin{array}{l}ss_k \xleftarrow{\$} SS_k.\mathsf{Share}(m) \\ \mathbf{for}\, j \in \{k, \ldots, 2\}: \\ \quad ss_{j-1} \leftarrow \mathsf{Proj}(ss_j)\end{array}\right\}$$

$$\equiv \left\{ \{ss'_k[i]\}_{i \in S_k}, \ldots, \{ss'_1[i]\}_{i \in S_1} \middle| \begin{array}{l}ss'_k \xleftarrow{\$} SS_k.\mathsf{Share}(m') \\ \mathbf{for}\, j \in \{k, \ldots, 2\}: \\ \quad ss'_{j-1} \leftarrow \mathsf{Proj}(ss'_j)\end{array}\right\}.$$

Robust Repair and Error Detection: *For all* k-*dimensional secret shares* ss', *we define the repair functionality as*

$$SS_k.\mathsf{Repair}(ss') = \begin{cases} ss & \textit{if } \exists! m \in \mathcal{M}, \exists! ss, \\ & \quad ss \in \mathsf{Supp}(SS_k.\mathsf{Share}(m)) \\ & \quad \wedge \mathsf{Card}\left(\{i \mid \mathsf{Proj}(ss')[i] \neq \mathsf{Proj}(ss)[i]\}\right) \leq t \\ \bot & \textit{otherwise}\end{cases}.$$

If $\mathsf{Repair}(ss') = \bot$, *we define* $\mathsf{ErrorDetect}(ss') = [n]$. *Otherwise, we define*

$$SS_k.\mathsf{ErrorDetect}(ss') = \{i \in [n] \mid \mathsf{Proj}(ss')[i] \neq \mathsf{Proj}(\mathsf{Repair}(ss'))[i]\}.$$

Additionally, we require that for all distinct $m, m' \in \mathcal{M}$, *for all secret shares* $ss \in \mathsf{Supp}(SS_k.\mathsf{Share}(m))$ *and* $ss' \in \mathsf{Supp}(SS_k.\mathsf{Share}(m'))$, *we have the Hamming distance between their projections is greater than* t, *i.e.,*

$$d_{\mathsf{H}}(\mathsf{Proj}(ss), \mathsf{Proj}(ss')) > t.$$

Commutativity of Projection and Folding: *Let* $k > 1$, *for any vector of* k-*dimensional shares* ss, *we have*

$$\mathsf{Proj}(\mathsf{Fold}(\mathsf{Repair}(ss))) = \mathsf{Fold}(\mathsf{Proj}(\mathsf{Repair}(ss))).$$

Rotation Consistency: *Let* $k > 1$, *for any vector of* k-*dimensional shares* ss, *we have*

$$\mathsf{ErrorDetect}(ss) = \emptyset \implies \mathsf{ErrorDetect}(\mathsf{Rotate}(ss)) = \emptyset.$$

Folding Uniqueness: *For any vector of shares* ss_1, ss_2, *we have*

$$\mathsf{Card}\left(\{i \mid ss_1[i] = ss_2[i]\}\right) \geq n - t$$
$$\implies \mathsf{Fold}(ss_1) = \mathsf{Fold}(ss_2)$$
$$\vee \mathsf{Fold}(ss_1) = \bot \vee \mathsf{Fold}(ss_2) = \bot.$$

The projection operation Proj is a key feature of our multi-dimensional secret sharing scheme. It reduces the dimension of shares while preserving their secrecy. Furthermore, its deterministic nature is essential for the consistency checks in our verifiable secret sharing construction.

Moreover, the projection Proj and the folding Fold generalize the reconstruction procedure. Specifically, reconstructing a secret from a k-dimensional sharing can be viewed as applying a project-rotate-then-fold sequence k times. More specifically, this recursive process can be expressed as:

$$SS_k.\mathsf{Reconst}(\llbracket m \rrbracket) = (\mathsf{Fold} \circ \mathsf{Proj})^k(\llbracket m \rrbracket).$$

This perspective is particularly useful for understanding the structure of our multi-dimensional secret sharing scheme.

5.2 Dimension Lifting

As a complementary operation to dimension projection, dimension lifting allows a party to increase the dimension of a $(k-1)$-dimensional robust vector of secret shares to a k-dimensional one. More precisely, given a $(k-1)$-dimensional (n, t)-robust secret sharing of a message m together with r randomly generated $(k-1)$-dimensional (n, t)-robust secret sharing, a party holding the shares can locally compute a k-dimensional (n, t)-robust secret sharing of the same message m without any interaction with other parties. The formal definition of dimension lifting is provided in Definition 5.

Noticing that the parameter r dependents on the robust secret sharing scheme used. For example, for Shamir's robust secret sharing scheme, we have $r = t$, while for CNF robust secret sharing scheme, we have $r = \binom{n}{t}$.

Definition 5 (Dimension Lifting). *A* (n, t)-*robust secret sharing scheme* SS_k *of dimension k supports dimension lifting if there exists an efficient randomized algorithm* Lift *with the following syntax:*

$\quad$ Lift$(\llbracket m \rrbracket[i], \llbracket r_1 \rrbracket[i], \ldots, \llbracket r_r \rrbracket[i]) \rightarrow$ ss$'[i]$: *Takes a* $(k-1)$-*dimensional share* $\llbracket m \rrbracket[i]$ *of* m *and* r $(k-1)$-*dimensional shares* $\llbracket r_1 \rrbracket[i], \ldots, \llbracket r_r \rrbracket[i]$ *of random messages as input, and outputs a k-dimensional share vector* ss$'[i]$.

For simplicity of notation we denote by Lift$(\llbracket m \rrbracket, \llbracket r_1 \rrbracket, \ldots, \llbracket r_r \rrbracket) =$ ss$'$ *the lifting over the vector of shares. Note that* ss$'$ *is a k-dimensional vector of shares of the form* ss$'[i]$. *Moreover, we require that the lifting operation* Lift *satisfies the following property:*

$\quad$ **Correctness:** *For any* $m \in \mathcal{M}$, *let* $\llbracket m \rrbracket \xleftarrow{\$} SS_{k-1}.\mathsf{Share}(m)$, *and for all* $j \in [t]$, *let* $\llbracket r_j \rrbracket \xleftarrow{\$} SS_{k-1}.\mathsf{Share}(r_j)$ *for random* $r_j \hookleftarrow U(\mathcal{M})$, *we have*

$$\Pr\left[\begin{array}{l} SS_k.\mathsf{Reconst}(\mathsf{ss}') = m \\ \wedge SS_k.\mathsf{ErrorDetect}(\mathsf{ss}') = \emptyset \end{array} \middle| \mathsf{ss}' \leftarrow \mathsf{Lift}(\llbracket m \rrbracket, \llbracket r_1 \rrbracket, \ldots, \llbracket r_t \rrbracket) \right] = 1.$$

Randomness: *For all* $\mathsf{m} \in \mathcal{M}$, *let* $\mathsf{ss} \xleftarrow{\$} \mathsf{SS}_{k-1}.\mathsf{Share}(\mathsf{m})$ *the following distributions are identical:*

$$
\left\{ \mathsf{ss} \,\middle|\, \mathsf{ss} \leftarrow \mathsf{SS}_k.\mathsf{Share}(\mathsf{m}) \right\}
$$

$$
\equiv \left\{ \mathsf{ss} \,\middle|\, \begin{array}{l} \mathsf{ss}' \leftarrow \mathsf{SS}_k.\mathsf{Share}(\mathsf{m}) \\ \mathbf{for}\, i \in [\mathsf{n}] : \\ \quad r_i' \hookleftarrow \mathsf{U}(\mathcal{M}); \quad \mathsf{ss}_i'' \xleftarrow{\$} \mathsf{SS}_k.\mathsf{Share}(r_i') \\ \quad \mathsf{ss} \leftarrow \mathsf{Fold} \circ \mathsf{Proj} \circ \mathsf{Rotate} \circ \mathsf{Lift}(\mathsf{ss}', \mathsf{ss}_1'', \ldots, \mathsf{ss}_\mathsf{t}'') \end{array} \right\}.
$$

In our layered MPC protocol, we employ dimension projection to transmit shares between consecutive layers. While this strategy effectively ensures corruption cohesion, it reduces the dimension of the shares at each layer. Consequently, the sender must start with shares of a sufficiently high dimension to ensure they remain valid (i.e., have a dimension of at least one) upon reaching the final layer. This naïve approach, however, leads to a communication complexity that grows exponentially with the number of layers. To overcome this, we introduce the dimension lifting operation. This operation allows parties to locally increase the dimension of their shares, enabling the maintenance of a constant share dimension across layers without incurring additional communication costs.

5.3 Instantiation with Classic Robust Secret Sharing Schemes

Definition 6. (k-dimensional Shamir's RSS). *A k-dimensional (n, t)-Shamir secret sharing scheme is defined recursively as in Definition 3, where the 1-dimensional (n, t)-Shamir secret sharing scheme is used as the base case. Equivalently, we define the k-dimensional Shamir's RSS as follows:*

$\mathsf{Share}(m)$: *Given a message* $\mathsf{m} \in \mathcal{M}$:
1. *Samples a polynomial* $\mathsf{F} \in \mathcal{M}[X_k, \ldots, X_1]$ *of degree* t *in each variable uniformly at random, such that* $\mathsf{F}(0, \ldots, 0) = \mathsf{m}$.
2. *For each* $i \in [\mathsf{n}]$, *sets the i-th share as* $[\![\mathsf{m}]\!][i] = \mathsf{F}(i, X_{k-1}, \ldots, X_1)$.
3. *Outputs the shares* $([\![\mathsf{m}]\!][1], \ldots, [\![\mathsf{m}]\!][\mathsf{n}])$.
$\mathsf{Reconst}([\![\mathsf{m}]\!][1], \ldots, [\![\mathsf{m}]\!][\mathsf{n}])$:
1. *Using the shares, runs the Berlekamp-Welch algorithm [BW86] to recover a polynomial* $\mathsf{F} \in \mathcal{M}[X_k, \ldots, X_1]$ *of degree* t *in each variable that agrees with at least* $\mathsf{n} - \mathsf{t} \geq 2\mathsf{t} + 1$ *shares.*
2. *If such a polynomial does not exist, outputs* $\perp$. *Otherwise, outputs* $\mathsf{m} \leftarrow \mathsf{F}(0, \ldots, 0)$.

The correctness, robustness, secrecy, and additive homomorphic properties of the k-dimensional Shamir's RSS follow directly from the properties of the 1-dimensional Shamir's RSS. The strong robustness property follows from the Berlekamp-Welch algorithm [BW86], which can efficiently identify and correct up to t erroneous shares.

Definition 7. (Projection for $\mathsf{SS}^{\mathsf{Shamir}}$). *Let* $\mathsf{ss} \xleftarrow{\$} \mathsf{SS}_k^{\mathsf{Shamir}}.\mathsf{Share}(\mathsf{m})$, *we define the projection operation* $\mathsf{Proj}(\mathsf{ss})$ *as follows:*

$\mathsf{Proj}(\mathsf{ss})$: *Parse* ss *as* $\mathsf{F}(X_k, \ldots, X_1)$ *as input, then output*

$$\mathsf{ss}[i] = \mathsf{F}(i, X_{k-1}, \ldots, X_1).$$

$\mathsf{Fold}(\mathsf{ss}[1], \ldots, \mathsf{ss}[n])$: *Takes as input*

$$\mathsf{ss} = (\mathsf{ss}[1], \ldots, \mathsf{ss}[n]) = (\mathsf{F}(1, X_{k-1}, \ldots, X_1), \ldots, \mathsf{F}(n, X_{k-1}, \ldots, X_1)).$$

Compute the corresponding polynomial $\mathsf{F}(X_k, \ldots, X_1)$ *using the Berlekamp-Welch algorithm and outputs* $\mathsf{ss}' = \mathsf{F}(0, X_{k-1}, \ldots, X_1)$.

The correctness of the projection operation follows directly from the definition. The secrecy-preserving property follows from the fact that each share in the projected dimension is a Shamir secret sharing of the corresponding share in the original dimension. We give a proof of the secrecy-preserving property in the full version of this paper.

Definition 8. (Lifting for $\mathsf{SS}^{\mathsf{Shamir}}$). *The lifting operation* Lift *takes a* $(k-1)$-*dimensional share* $[\![\mathsf{m}]\!]$ *of a message* m, *and a vector of* t *many* $(k-1)$-*dimensional shares* $[\![r_1]\!], \ldots, [\![r_{\mathsf{t}}]\!]$ *of random messages as input, and outputs a* k-*dimensional secret share* ss' *as follows:*

$\mathsf{Lift}([\![\mathsf{m}]\!], [\![r_1]\!], \ldots, [\![r_{\mathsf{t}}]\!])$: *Parse* $[\![\mathsf{m}]\!]$ *as* $\mathsf{F}_0(i, X_{k-1}, \ldots, X_1)$, *and for each* $j \in [\mathsf{t}]$, *parse* $[\![r_j]\!]$ *as* $\mathsf{F}_j(i, X_{k-1}, \ldots, X_1)$. *Using the Lagrange interpolation to find the unique degree* t *polynomial* $\mathsf{F}(X_k)$ *such that* $\mathsf{F}(0) = \mathsf{F}_0$ *and* $\mathsf{F}(\mathsf{t}+1) = \mathsf{F}_1, \ldots, \mathsf{F}(2\mathsf{t}) = \mathsf{F}_{\mathsf{t}}$, *output* F *as output.*

More precisely, we define the dimension lifting protocol in ??.

We give the fully instantiation of the k-dimensional CNF RSS in the full version of this paper.

6   Messaging Across Layers - Future Messaging and Resharing

A key functionality in the layered setting is securely sending messages between non-adjacent layers, i.e., from a party in layer $\mathcal{L}_i$ to a party in layer $\mathcal{L}_j$ where $j > i + 1$. While standard MPC models provide this capability directly through secure channels, [DDG+23] transforms the computation model to layered circuits to avoid this problem. To bridge this gap, we introduce three distinct cross-layer messaging functionalities. These will serve as fundamental building blocks for our constructions, each tailored for different scenarios.

The ideal functionality for future messaging provided in the full version of this paper.

We introduce Honest Future Messaging firstly, a variant of this functionality, which guarantees correct message delivery, but relies on the assumption that both the sender and the receiver are honest.

6.1   Honest Future Messaging

This is the simplest cross-layer messaging functionality, which allows a party in layer $\mathcal{L}_i$ to send a message to a party in layer $\mathcal{L}_j$ where $j > i + 1$, with the guarantee that the message will be delivered correctly as long as both the sender and receiver are honest. To send a message m across d layers, the sender embeds m into a d-dimensional robust secret sharing, then successively folds and projects it layer by layer to the next layer. Privacy holds trivially when both the sender and the receiver are honest. Note that this method is suitable only for small d, since the lifting dimension grows with the transmission distance. We provide the details in Table 1 using the multi-dimensional robust secret sharing as described in Definition 2.

Tab. 1: Honest Future Messaging Π_{HFM}

Setup:
  Input Party: $\mathsf{S} \in \mathcal{L}_0$. Without loss of generality, we denote the sender's layer as $\mathcal{L}_0$.
  Output Parties: $\mathsf{R} \in \mathcal{L}_{d+1}$, for some positive integer $d > 0$.
  Protocol parameters
   – d: a positive integer, the number of layers between the sender and the receiver.
   – SS_d: a d-dimensional (n, t)-robust secret sharing scheme with privacy-preserving projection Proj.

- -

Program execution:
Pseudocode of Π_{HFM}:
Layer $\mathcal{L}_0$: S proceeds as follows
  1. **recv** m **from** S **in** $\mathcal{L}_0$
  2. $\mathsf{ss}_d \xleftarrow{\$} \mathsf{SS}_d.\mathsf{Share}(\mathsf{m})$
  3.   **for** $k \in [\mathsf{n}]$: S **send** $\mathsf{ss}_d[k]$ **to** P_k^1 **in** $\mathcal{L}_1$
Layer $\mathcal{L}_1$: P_k^1 proceeds as follows
  1. **recv** $\mathsf{ss}_d[k]$ **from** S **in** $\mathcal{L}_0$
  2. $(\mathsf{ss}_{d-1}[k, 1], \ldots, \mathsf{ss}_{d-1}[k, \mathsf{n}]) \leftarrow \mathsf{Proj}(\mathsf{ss}_d[k])$
  3.   **for** $k' \in [\mathsf{n}]$:
  4.   **send** $\mathsf{ss}_{d-1}[k, k']$ **to** $\mathsf{P}_{k'}^2$ **in** $\mathcal{L}_2$
Layer $\mathcal{L}_\ell$ with $\ell \in [2, d-1]$: P_k^ℓ proceeds as follows
  1. **recv** $\mathsf{ss}'_{d+1-\ell}[k'', k]$ **from** $\mathsf{P}_{k''}^{\ell-1}$ **in** $\mathcal{L}_{\ell-1}$
  2. $\mathsf{ss}_{d+1-\ell}[k] \leftarrow \mathsf{Fold}(\mathsf{Rotate}(\mathsf{ss}'_{d+1-\ell}[1, k], \ldots, \mathsf{ss}'_{d+1-\ell}[\mathsf{n}, k]))$
  3. $(\mathsf{ss}_{d-\ell}[k, 1], \ldots, \mathsf{ss}_{d-\ell}[k, \mathsf{n}]) \leftarrow \mathsf{Proj}(\mathsf{ss}_{d+1-\ell}[k])$
  4.   **for** $k' \in [\mathsf{n}]$:
  5.   **send** $\mathsf{ss}_{d-\ell}[k, k']$ **to** $\mathsf{P}_{k'}^{\ell+1}$ **in** $\mathcal{L}_{\ell+1}$
Layer $\mathcal{L}_d$: P_k^d proceeds as follows
  1. **recv** $\mathsf{ss}'_1[k'', k]$ **from** $\mathsf{P}_{k''}^{d-1}$ **in** $\mathcal{L}_{d-1}$
  2. $\mathsf{ss}_1[k] \leftarrow \mathsf{Fold}(\mathsf{Rotate}(\mathsf{ss}'_1[1, k], \ldots, \mathsf{ss}'_1[\mathsf{n}, k]))$
  3.   **send** $\mathsf{ss}_1[k]$ **to** R **in** $\mathcal{L}_{d+1}$
Layer $\mathcal{L}_{d+1}$: R proceeds as follows
  1. **recv** $\mathsf{ss}_1[1], \ldots, \mathsf{ss}_1[\mathsf{n}]$ **from** $\mathsf{P}_1^d, \ldots, \mathsf{P}_\mathsf{n}^d$ **in** $\mathcal{L}_d$
  2. $\mathsf{m} \leftarrow \mathsf{Fold}(\mathsf{ss}_1[1], \ldots, \mathsf{ss}_1[\mathsf{n}])$

6.2   Honest Future Sharing

A variant of honest future messaging, which we call Honest Future Sharing, is designed to enable a party in an early layer to have a message secret-shared among all parties in a distant future layer. In short, the sender simply lifts the message by one additional dimension compared with Future Messaging, then proceeds exactly as in Future Messaging. Consequently, every party in the receiving layer holds a share of the message. The details of Honest Future Sharing(Π_{HFS}) is provided in the full version of this paper.

6.3   Future Resharing

A core principle of our construction is to maintain secrets in a shared state across all layers. This necessitates a mechanism to transfer a secret sharing from parties in one layer to those in a subsequent layer. We introduce a primitive for this purpose, which we call Future Resharing. Unlike a single party holding the secret(as in future messaging), the secret is already shared among parties in the source layer. The goal is to generate a new, independent sharing of the same secret among parties in a future destination layer. The formal construction is provided in Table 2.

Tab. 2: Future Resharing Π_{FRS}

Setup:
 Input Parties: Parties in $\mathcal{L}_0$ hold 1-dimensional shares of m.
 Output Parties: Parties in $\mathcal{L}_{d+1}$, for some positive integer $d > 0$.
 Protocol parameters
  – d: a positive integer, the target layer of future resharing.
 Preprocess: For each $i \in [0, d]$, each P_k^i receives the shares of C random values(i.e., $[\![r_{i,1}]\!][k], \ldots, [\![r_{i,\mathsf{C}}]\!][k]$). Specifically, $\mathsf{C} = \mathsf{t}$ for Shamir-based secret sharing and $\mathsf{C} = \mathsf{M}$ for CNF-based secret sharing.

- -

Program execution:
 Pseudocode of Π_{FRS}:
 Layer $\mathcal{L}_0$: P_k^0 proceeds as follows
  1. **recv** $[\![\mathsf{m}]\!][k], [\![r_{0,1}]\!][k], \ldots, [\![r_{0,\mathsf{C}}]\!][k]$ **in**$\mathcal{L}_0$
  2. $\mathsf{ss}_2[k] \leftarrow \mathsf{Lift}([\![\mathsf{m}]\!][k], [\![r_{0,1}]\!][k], \ldots, [\![r_{0,\mathsf{C}}]\!][k])$
  3. $(\mathsf{ss}_1[k, 1], \ldots, \mathsf{ss}_1[k, \mathsf{n}]) \leftarrow \mathsf{Proj}(\mathsf{ss}_2[k])$
  4.   **for**$k' \in [\mathsf{n}]$:
  5.   **send** $\mathsf{ss}_1[k, k']$ **to** $\mathsf{P}_{k'}^1$ **in** $\mathcal{L}_1$
 Layer $\mathcal{L}_\ell$ with $\ell \in [1, d]$: P_k^ℓ proceeds as follows
  1. **recv** $\mathsf{ss}_1[k'', k]$ **from** $\mathsf{P}_{k''}^{\ell-1}$ and $[\![r_{\ell,1}]\!][k], \ldots, [\![r_{\ell,\mathsf{C}}]\!][k]$ **in** $\mathcal{L}_{\ell-1}$
  2. $[\![\mathsf{m}]\!][k] \leftarrow \mathsf{Fold}(\mathsf{Rotate}(\mathsf{ss}_1[1, k], \ldots, \mathsf{ss}_1[\mathsf{n}, k]))$
  3. $\mathsf{ss}_2[k] \leftarrow \mathsf{Lift}([\![\mathsf{m}]\!][k], [\![r_{\ell,1}]\!][k], \ldots, [\![r_{\ell,\mathsf{C}}]\!][k])$
  4. $(\mathsf{ss}_1[k, 1], \ldots, \mathsf{ss}_1[k, \mathsf{n}]) \leftarrow \mathsf{Proj}(\mathsf{ss}_2[k])$
  5.   **for**$k' \in [\mathsf{n}]$:
  6.   **send** $\mathsf{ss}_1[k, k']$ **to** $\mathsf{P}_{k'}^{\ell+1}$ **in** $\mathcal{L}_{\ell+1}$
 Layer $\mathcal{L}_{d+1}$: P_k^{d+1} proceeds as follows
  1. **recv** $\mathsf{ss}_1[k'', k]$ **from** $\mathsf{P}_{k''}^d$ **in** $\mathcal{L}_d$
  2. $[\![\mathsf{m}]\!][k] \leftarrow \mathsf{Fold}(\mathsf{Rotate}(\mathsf{ss}_1[1, k], \ldots, \mathsf{ss}_1[\mathsf{n}, k]))$

---

7   Generic Layered VSS Protocol

We give our construction of generic layered VSS protocol Π_{VSS} in Table 3. The protocol is parameterized by three k-dimensional (n, t)-robust secret sharing schemes SS_k for $k = 1, 2, 3, 4$. The protocol proceeds in four layers: the dealer in $\mathcal{L}_0$, internal computation layers $\mathcal{L}_1, \ldots, \mathcal{L}_4$, and the shareholders in $\mathcal{L}_5$.

Overall Structure. The protocol proceeds through the following phases:

$\mathsf{D} \to \mathcal{L}_1$: The dealer shares the secret using SS_4 and sends the resulting shares to $\mathcal{L}_1$.

$\mathcal{L}_1 \to \mathcal{L}_2$: Each party in $\mathcal{L}_1$ projects the received shares and forwards them to $\mathcal{L}_2$.

$\mathcal{L}_2 \to \mathcal{L}_3$: Each party in $\mathcal{L}_2$ performs error detection on the projections received from $\mathcal{L}_1$. Upon detecting an error, the party broadcasts the index of the erroneous share. Subsequently, each party in $\mathcal{L}_2$ projects the shares and sends them to $\mathcal{L}_3$. When P_j^2 detects that P_i^1 is inconsistent, all parties deduce that at least one of P_i^1, P_j^2, or D is corrupted.

$\mathcal{L}_3 \to \mathcal{L}_4$: Leveraging the multi-dimensional structure of the shares, every party in $\mathcal{L}_3$ can locally repair the projections of shares delivered from both the D and $\mathcal{L}_1$ without additional communication, assuming the dealer is honest. Each party in $\mathcal{L}_3$ then broadcasts the repaired shares, enabling all parties to determine whether $\mathcal{L}_1$ or the D is corrupted or whether a $\mathcal{L}_2$ party is maliciously raising false inconsistencies. Finally, each party in $\mathcal{L}_3$ projects the shares and sends them to $\mathcal{L}_4$.

$\mathcal{L}_4 \to \mathcal{L}_5$: Assuming the dealer is honest, every party in $\mathcal{L}_4$ can locally repair the projected shares delivered from the D to $\mathcal{L}_1$ without additional communication. Each party in $\mathcal{L}_4$ broadcasts the repaired shares for parties in $\mathcal{L}_1$ identified as corrupted in the previous phase. Finally, each party in $\mathcal{L}_4$ projects the shares and sends them to $\mathcal{L}_5$. After incorporating the broadcast messages from $\mathcal{L}_4$ regarding $\mathcal{L}_1$, every honest party obtains a consistent view of the shares of $\mathcal{L}_1$.

$\mathcal{L}_5$: Since every honest party in $\mathcal{L}_1$ has a now-consistent share and there are at least $\mathsf{n} - \mathsf{t}$ such parties, every party in $\mathcal{L}_5$ can locally decode to recover the secret share.

Complexity Optimization. A straightforward implementation of the above strategy requires a 5-dimensional robust secret sharing scheme, resulting in communication complexity of (n^5) when instantiated with Shamir secret sharing. This is because each layer contributes a factor of n to the overall complexity by consuming a distinct variable. We optimize this by observing that in $\mathcal{L}_4$, parties in $\mathcal{L}_3$ can directly distribute their shares to all parties in $\mathcal{L}_4$ without projecting them, thereby reducing communication overhead. This optimization trades the structured information of shares in $\mathcal{L}_4$ for improved efficiency. This trade-off is acceptable since $\mathcal{L}_4$ serves only as a relay layer for broadcasting messages and does not require decoding. Consequently, this optimization reduces the protocol's structural communication complexity from n^5 to n^4.

Tab. 3: Generic Verifiable Secret Sharing Protocol Π_{VSS}

Protocol Description:
Participants: Dealer $D \in \mathcal{L}_0$, shareholders in $\mathcal{L}_5$ and internal computation layers $\mathcal{L}_1, \ldots, \mathcal{L}_4$.
Secret Inputs: D inputs $m \in \mathcal{M}$.
Sub-protocols: Protocol SS_4, SS_3, SS_2, SS_1. For clarity, we denote by Proj_i, Fold_i the projection and folding operations for the dimension i.

Protocol Execution:
Dealer D:
1. $ss_4 \overset{\$}{\leftarrow} SS_4.\text{Share}(m)$
2. $(ss_3[1], \ldots, ss_3[n]) \leftarrow \text{Proj}_i(ss_4)$
3. **send** $ss_3[i]$ to P_i^1 in $\mathcal{L}_1$

Layer 1: For each $i \in [n]$, P_i^1 proceeds as follows:
1. **recv** $ss_3[i]$ **from** D **in** $\mathcal{L}_0$
2. **for** $\text{ErrorDetect}(ss_3[i]) \neq \emptyset$ **then** **BCast Complaint**
3. $(ss_2[i, 1], \ldots, ss_2[i, n]) \leftarrow \text{Proj}_j(ss_3[i])$
4. **for** $j \in [n]$: **send** $ss_2[i, j]$ to P_j^2 in $\mathcal{L}_2$

Layer 2: For each $j \in [n]$, P_j^2 proceeds as follows:
1. **for** $i \in [n]$: **recv** $ss_2[i, j]$ **from** P_i^1 **in** $\mathcal{L}_1$
2. $\mathcal{I}_j \leftarrow \text{ErrorDetect}(\{ss_2[i, j]\}_{i \in [n]})$
3. **BCast** $\mathcal{I}_j$
4. **for** $i \in [n]$: $(ss_1[i, j, 1], \ldots, ss_1[i, j, n]) \leftarrow \text{Proj}_k(ss_2[i, j])$
5. **for** $k \in [n]$: **send** $\{ss_1[i, j, k]\}_{i \in [n]}$ to P_k^3 in $\mathcal{L}_3$.

Layer 3: For each $k \in [n]$, P_k^3 proceeds as follows:
1. **for** $j \in [n]$: **recv** $(\{ss_1[i, j, k]\}_{i \in [n]})$ **from** P_j^2 **in** $\mathcal{L}_2$
2. **for** $i, j \in [n]$: $ss_1^1[i, j, k] \leftarrow \begin{cases} ss_1[i, j, k] & \text{if } i \notin \mathcal{I}_j \\ \perp & \text{if } i \in \mathcal{I}_j \end{cases}$
3. $\{ss_1^0[i, j, k]\}_{i, j \in [n]} \leftarrow \text{Repair}_i(\text{Repair}_j(\{ss_1^1[i, j, k]\}_{i, j \in [n]}))$
4. **if** $ss_1^0[i, j, k] \neq ss_1^1[i, j, k]$ **then for** $j \in [n]$: $\mathcal{J}_k[i, j] = 1$ **else for** $j \in [n]$: $\mathcal{J}_k[i, j] = 0$
5. **BCast** $\mathcal{J}_k$
6. **for** $j \in [n]$: **if** $i \in \mathcal{I}_j$ **BCast** $\{ss_1^0[i, j, k], ss_1^1[i, j, k]\}_{i, j \in [n]}$
7. $\{ss_1^0[i, k]\}_{i \in [n]} \leftarrow \text{Repair}_j(\{ss_1^0[i, j, k]\}_{j \in [n]})$
8. $\{ss_1^1[i, k]\}_{i \in [n]} \leftarrow \text{Repair}_j(\{ss_1^1[i, j, k]\}_{j \in [n]})$
9. **for** $i \in [n]$:
10. $\quad (\sigma_{i,k}^0[1], \ldots, \sigma_{i,k}^0[n]) \overset{\$}{\leftarrow} \text{Proj}(SS_2.\text{Share}(ss_1^0[i, k]))$
11. $\quad (\sigma_{i,k}^1[1], \ldots, \sigma_{i,k}^1[n]) \overset{\$}{\leftarrow} \text{Proj}(SS_2.\text{Share}(ss_1^1[i, k]))$
12. **for** $\ell \in [n]$: **send** $\left\{ \sigma_{i,k}^0[\ell], \sigma_{i,k}^1[\ell] \right\}_{i \in [n]}$ to P_ℓ^4 in $\mathcal{L}_4$

Public Computation 1:
1. $M \leftarrow 0^{n \times n \times n}$; $R \leftarrow 0^n$
2. **for** $j \in [n]$: **if** $i \in \mathcal{I}_j$ **then for** $k \in [n]$: $M[i, j, k] \leftarrow 1$
3. **for** $j \in [n] \wedge i \in \mathcal{I}_j$:
4. $\quad ss_p^0[i, j] \leftarrow \text{Fold}_k(\{ss_1^0[i, j, k]\}_{k \in [n]})$; $ss_p^1[i, j] \leftarrow \text{Fold}_k(\{ss_1^1[i, j, k]\}_{k \in [n]})$
5. **if** $ss_p^0[i, j] = \perp$ **then abort**
6. **if** $ss_p^0[i, j] \neq ss_p^1[i, j]$ **then**
7. $\quad$ **for** $j, k \in [n]$: $M[i, j, k] \leftarrow 1$
8. **if** **Complaint** is broadcast from P_i^1 **then**
9. $\quad$ **for** $j, k \in [n]$: $M[i, j, k] \leftarrow 1$
10. **for** $i, j, k \in [n]$: $M[i, j, k] \leftarrow 1$ **if** $\mathcal{J}_k[i, j] = 1$
11. **if** there are not $2t + 1 \times 2t + 1 \times 2t + 1$ zero submatrix in M **then abort**
12. **for** $i \in [n]$: **if** i contains in a $2t + 1 \times 2t + 1 \times 2t + 1$ zero submatrix
13. $\quad$ **then** $R[i] \leftarrow 0$ **else** $R[i] \leftarrow 1$

Layer 4: For each $\ell \in [n]$, P_ℓ^4 proceeds as follows:
1. **for** $k \in [n]$: **recv** $(\left\{ \sigma_{i,k}^0[\ell], \sigma_{i,k}^1[\ell] \right\}_{i \in [n]})$ **from** P_k^3 **in** $\mathcal{L}_3$
2. **for** $R[i] = 1$: **BCast** $\left\{ \sigma_{i,k}^0[\ell] \right\}_{k \in [n]}$
3. **for** $i, k \in [n]$: $(\sigma_{i,k}^1[\ell, 1], \ldots, \sigma_{i,k}^1[\ell, n]) \leftarrow \text{Proj}_m(\sigma_{i,k}^1[\ell])$

4. **for** $m \in [\mathsf{n}]$: **send** $\left\{\sigma^1_{i,k}[\ell, m]\right\}_{i,k \in [\mathsf{n}]}$ **to** P^5_m **in** $\mathcal{L}_5$

Public Computation 2:

1. **for** $R[i] = 1$:
2. $\quad \hat{\sigma}^0_i \leftarrow \mathsf{Fold}_k(\mathsf{Fold}_\ell(\left\{\sigma^0_{i,k}[\ell]\right\}_{k,\ell \in [\mathsf{n}]}))$
3. $\quad$ **if** $\hat{\sigma}^0_i = \perp$ **then abort**
4. $(\hat{\sigma}^0_i[1], \ldots, \hat{\sigma}^0_i[\mathsf{n}]) \leftarrow \mathsf{Proj}_m(\hat{\sigma}^0_i)$

Layer 5: For each $m \in [\mathsf{n}]$, P^5_m proceeds as follows:

1. **for** $\ell \in [\mathsf{n}]$: **recv** $\left\{\sigma^1_{i,k}[\ell, m]\right\}_{i,k \in [\mathsf{n}]}$ from P^4_ℓ in $\mathcal{L}_4$

2. **for** $i \in [\mathsf{n}]$: $\mathsf{F}'[i, m] \leftarrow \begin{cases} \hat{\sigma}^0_i[m] & \text{if } R[i] = 1 \\ \mathsf{Fold}_k(\mathsf{Fold}_\ell(\left\{\sigma^1_{i,k}[\ell, m]\right\}_{k,\ell \in [\mathsf{n}]})) & \text{if } R[i] = 0 \end{cases}$

3. $\hat{\mathsf{F}}[m] \leftarrow \mathsf{Fold}_i(\mathsf{F}'[1, m], \ldots, \mathsf{F}'[\mathsf{n}, m])$
4. Set the share m_m to $\hat{\mathsf{F}}[m]$.

Theorem 1. *Let* SS_k *for* $k \in \{1, 2, 3, 4\}$ *be a* k-*dimensional* (n, t)-*robust secret sharing scheme that supports secrecy-preserving projection. The protocol* $\mathbf{\Pi}_{\mathsf{VSS}}$ *described in Table 3 securely implements the* VSS *functionality against an adaptive adversary corrupting up to* t *parties in each layer.*

The detailed proof of Theorem 1 is provided in the full version of this paper.

7.1   Instantiation with Shamir-Based Robust Secret Sharing

We instantiate the generic VSS protocol in Table 3 using the Shamir-based robust secret sharing scheme from Definition 6. The complete protocol is presented in Table 4.

Tab. 4: Shamir-based Verifiable Secret Sharing Protocol $\mathbf{\Pi}_{\mathsf{VSS}}^{\mathsf{Shamir}}$

Setup:

Participants: Dealer $\mathsf{D} \in \mathcal{L}_0$, shareholders in $\mathcal{L}_5$ and internal computation layers $\mathcal{L}_1, \ldots, \mathcal{L}_4$.

Secret Inputs: D inputs $\mathsf{m} \in \mathcal{M}$.

Sub-protocols:

1. Shamir-based robust secret sharing schemes $\mathsf{SS}^{\mathsf{Shamir}}_4, \mathsf{SS}^{\mathsf{Shamir}}_3, \mathsf{SS}^{\mathsf{Shamir}}_2, \mathsf{SS}^{\mathsf{Shamir}}_1$.
2. Berlekamp-Welch algorithm BW is used to instantiate Fold, ErrorDetect, and Repair for Shamir shares.

- -

Protocol Execution:

Dealer D:

1. Sample a random 4-variate polynomial $\mathsf{F}(W, X, Y, Z)$ of degree at most t in each variable such that $\mathsf{F}(0, 0, 0, 0) = \mathsf{m}$.
2. **for** $i \in [\mathsf{n}]$: **send** $\mathsf{F}(i, X, Y, Z)$ to P^1_i in $\mathcal{L}_1$.

Layer 1: For each $i \in [\mathsf{n}]$, P^1_i proceeds as follows:

1. **recv** $\mathsf{F}(i, X, Y, Z)$ from D in $\mathcal{L}_0$.
2. **for** $\mathsf{ErrorDetect}(\mathsf{F}(i, X, Y, Z)) \neq \emptyset$ **then BCast Complaint.**
3. **for** $j \in [\mathsf{n}]$: **send** $\mathsf{F}(i, j, Y, Z)$ to P^2_j in $\mathcal{L}_2$.

Layer 2: For each $j \in [\mathsf{n}]$, P^2_j proceeds as follows:

1. **for** $i \in [\mathsf{n}]$: **recv** $\mathsf{F}(i, j, Y, Z)$ from P^1_i in $\mathcal{L}_1$.
2. $\mathsf{F}^2(W, j, Y, Z) \leftarrow \mathsf{BW}_W(\{\mathsf{F}(i, j, Y, Z)\}_{i \in [\mathsf{n}]})$.
3. $\mathcal{I}_j \leftarrow \{i \mid \mathsf{F}^2(i, j, Y, Z) \neq \mathsf{F}(i, j, Y, Z) \vee \mathsf{F}^2(i, j, Y, Z) = \perp\}$.
4. **BCast** $\mathcal{I}_j$.

5. **for** $k \in [\mathsf{n}]$: **send** $\{\mathsf{F}(i,j,k,Z)\}_{i \in [\mathsf{n}]}$ **to** P_k^3 **in** $\mathcal{L}_3$.

Layer 3: For each $k \in [\mathsf{n}]$, P_k^3 proceeds as follows:

1. **for** $j \in [\mathsf{n}]$: **recv** $\{\mathsf{F}(i,j,k,Z)\}_{i \in [\mathsf{n}]}$ **from** P_j^2 **in** $\mathcal{L}_2$.

2. **for** $i,j \in [\mathsf{n}]$: $\mathsf{F}^1(i,j,k,Z) \leftarrow \begin{cases} \mathsf{F}(i,j,k,Z) & \text{if } i \notin \mathcal{I}_j \\ \bot & \text{if } i \in \mathcal{I}_j \end{cases}$.

3. $\mathsf{F}^0(W,X,k,Z) \leftarrow \mathsf{BW}_W(\mathsf{BW}_X(\{\mathsf{F}^1(i,j,k,Z)\}_{i,j \in [\mathsf{n}]}))$.

4. **for** $i,j \in [\mathsf{n}]$: **if** $\mathsf{F}^0(i,j,k,Z) \neq \mathsf{F}^1(i,j,k,Z)$ **then**

5.   **for** $j \in [\mathsf{n}]$: $\mathcal{J}_k[i,j] \leftarrow 1$ **else** $\mathcal{J}_k[i,j] \leftarrow 0$.

6. **BCast** $\mathcal{J}_k$.

7. **for** $j \in [\mathsf{n}] \wedge i \in \mathcal{I}_j$: **BCast** $\mathsf{F}^0(i,j,k,Z), \mathsf{F}^1(i,j,k,Z)$.

8. **for** $i \in [\mathsf{n}]$: $\mathsf{F}^0(i,0,k,Z) \leftarrow (\mathsf{BW}_X(\{\mathsf{F}^0(i,j,k,Z)\}_{j \in [\mathsf{n}]}))(0)$.

9. **for** $i \in [\mathsf{n}]$: $\mathsf{F}^1(i,0,k,Z) \leftarrow (\mathsf{BW}_X(\{\mathsf{F}^1(i,j,k,Z)\}_{j \in [\mathsf{n}]}))(0)$.

10. **for** $i \in [\mathsf{n}]$: sample random bivariate polynomials $\mathsf{G}_{i,k}^0(Z,V), \mathsf{G}_{i,k}^1(Z,V)$ of degree at most t such that

11. $\mathsf{G}_{i,k}^0(Z,0) = \mathsf{F}^0(i,0,k,Z)$ and $\mathsf{G}_{i,k}^1(Z,0) = \mathsf{F}^1(i,0,k,Z)$.

12. **for** $\ell \in [\mathsf{n}]$: **send** $\left\{\mathsf{G}_{i,k}^0(Z,\ell), \mathsf{G}_{i,k}^1(Z,\ell)\right\}_{i \in [\mathsf{n}]}$ **to** P_ℓ^4 **in** $\mathcal{L}_4$.

Public Computation 1:

1. $M \leftarrow 0^{\mathsf{n} \times \mathsf{n} \times \mathsf{n}}$; $R \leftarrow 0^{\mathsf{n}}$.

2. **for** $j \in [\mathsf{n}] \wedge i \in \mathcal{I}_j$: **for** $k \in [\mathsf{n}]$: $M[i,j,k] \leftarrow 1$.

3. **for** $j \in [\mathsf{n}] \wedge i \in \mathcal{I}_j$:

4. $\mathsf{H}^0(i,j,Y,Z) \leftarrow (\mathsf{BW}_Y(\{\mathsf{F}^0(i,j,k,Z)\}_{k \in [\mathsf{n}]}))$.

5. $\mathsf{H}^1(i,j,Y,Z) \leftarrow (\mathsf{BW}_Y(\{\mathsf{F}^1(i,j,k,Z)\}_{k \in [\mathsf{n}]}))$.

6.   **if** $\mathsf{H}^0(i,j,Y,Z) = \bot$ **then** abort.

7.   **if** $\mathsf{H}^0(i,j,Y,Z) \neq \mathsf{H}^1(i,j,Y,Z)$ **then for** $j',k \in [\mathsf{n}]$: $M[i,j',k] \leftarrow 1$.

8. **if** **Complaint** is broadcast from P_i^1 **then for** $j,k \in [\mathsf{n}]$: $M[i,j,k] \leftarrow 1$.

9. **for** $i,j,k \in [\mathsf{n}]$: **if** $\mathcal{J}_k[i,j] = 1$ **then** $M[i,j,k] \leftarrow 1$.

10. **if** there are not $2\mathsf{t}+1 \times 2\mathsf{t}+1 \times 2\mathsf{t}+1$ zero submatrix in M **then** abort.

11. **for** $i \in [\mathsf{n}]$: **if** i is in a $2\mathsf{t}+1 \times 2\mathsf{t}+1 \times 2\mathsf{t}+1$ zero submatrix **then** $R[i] \leftarrow 0$ **else** $R[i] \leftarrow 1$.

Layer 4: For each $\ell \in [\mathsf{n}]$, P_ℓ^4 proceeds as follows:

1. **for** $k \in [\mathsf{n}]$: **recv** $\left\{\mathsf{G}_{i,k}^0(Z,\ell), \mathsf{G}_{i,k}^1(Z,\ell)\right\}_{i \in [\mathsf{n}]}$ **from** P_k^3 **in** $\mathcal{L}_3$.

2. **for** $R[i] = 1$: **BCast** $\left\{\mathsf{G}_{i,k}^0(Z,\ell)\right\}_{k \in [\mathsf{n}]}$.

3. **for** $m \in [\mathsf{n}]$: **send** $\left\{\mathsf{G}_{i,k}^1(m,\ell)\right\}_{i,k \in [\mathsf{n}]}$ **to** P_m^5 **in** $\mathcal{L}_5$.

Public Computation 2:

1. **for** $R[i] = 1$:

2. $\hat{\sigma}_i^0(Z) \leftarrow (\mathsf{BW}_Y(\{(\mathsf{BW}_V(\{\mathsf{G}_{i,k}^0(Z,\ell)\}_{\ell \in [\mathsf{n}]}))(0)\}_{k \in [\mathsf{n}]}))(0)$.

3.   **if** $\hat{\sigma}_i^0(Z) = \bot$ **then** abort.

4. $(\hat{\sigma}_i^0[1], \ldots, \hat{\sigma}_i^0[\mathsf{n}]) \leftarrow (\hat{\sigma}_i^0(1), \ldots, \hat{\sigma}_i^0(\mathsf{n}))$.

Layer 5: For each $m \in [\mathsf{n}]$, P_m^5 proceeds as follows:

1. **for** $\ell \in [\mathsf{n}]$: **recv** $\left\{\mathsf{G}_{i,k}^1(m,\ell)\right\}_{i,k \in [\mathsf{n}]}$ **from** P_ℓ^4 **in** $\mathcal{L}_4$.

2. **for** $i \in [\mathsf{n}]$: $\mathsf{F}'[i,m] \leftarrow \begin{cases} \hat{\sigma}_i^0[m] & \text{if } R[i] = 1 \\ (\mathsf{BW}_Y(\{(\mathsf{BW}_V(\{\mathsf{G}_{i,k}^1(m,\ell)\}_{\ell \in [\mathsf{n}]}))(0)\}_{k \in [\mathsf{n}]}))(0) & \text{if } R[i] = 0 \end{cases}$.

3. $\hat{\mathsf{F}}[m] \leftarrow (\mathsf{BW}_W(\{\mathsf{F}'[i,m]\}_{i \in [\mathsf{n}]}))(0)$.

4. Set the share m_m to $\hat{\mathsf{F}}[m]$.

We establish the following theorem regarding the security and efficiency of the Shamir VSS protocol by applying the generic VSS construction from Table 3. Therefore, we omit the proof here. Furthermore, to make the protocol's correctness more intuitive, we provide a toy example for Shamir-based VSS when $\mathsf{t} = 1$ and $\mathsf{n} = 4$ in the full version of this paper.

Theorem 2 (Shamir-based VSS). *The protocol in Table 4 executed in parallel realizes $\mathcal{F}_{\mathsf{Par\text{-}VSS}}$ with perfect t-security for $\mathsf{t} < \mathsf{n}/3$ by consuming 5 layers, and by communicating $O(\mathsf{n}^4 \log |\mathbb{F}|)$ over the point-to-point channel and $O(\mathsf{n}^4 \log |\mathbb{F}|)$ over the broadcast channel for each secret.*

Complexity. In terms of point-to-point communication, the Dealer, Layer 1, and Layer 2 each transmit shares of a 4-variate polynomial to the subsequent layer, incurring a complexity of $O(n^4 \log |\mathbb{F}|)$. Although Layer 3 lifts the polynomial to a 5-variate form, the transmission to the next layer involves evaluating one variable at 0, thus maintaining the cost at $O(n^4 \log |\mathbb{F}|)$. Layer 4 similarly incurs a point-to-point cost of $O(n^4 \log |\mathbb{F}|)$. Additionally, Layer 3 and 4 require a broadcast complexity of $O(n^4 \log |\mathbb{F}|)$.

7.2 Instantiation with CNF-Based Robust Secret Sharing

We instantiate the generic VSS protocol in Table 3 using the CNF-based robust secret sharing scheme from ??. The complete protocol is presented in ?? in the full version of this paper. A key difference is that the CNF-based VSS protocol presents one fewer round than both the Shamir-based variant in Table 4 and the generic VSS protocol in Table 3.

Round Optimization The CNF-based VSS protocol achieves improved round efficiency compared to the Shamir-based variant through a crucial optimization. Specifically, parties P_k^3 in $\mathcal{L}_3$ can set $\mathcal{I}_j$ as the union of all $\mathcal{I}_j^{\mathsf{c}_2}$ for $\mathsf{c}_2 \in \mathcal{S}_j$. This allows P_k^3 to broadcast the corrected values $\mathsf{m}_{i,j,k,\ell}$ when complaints are raised by parties in $\mathcal{L}_2$. In the Shamir-based VSS protocol, this optimization is not possible because an adversary could raise a complaint against an honest party in $\mathcal{L}_2$, forcing P_ℓ^4 to broadcast shares from honest $\mathcal{L}_1$ parties. By contrast, in the CNF-based VSS protocol, although $\mathcal{I}_j$ may contain some honest parties in $\mathcal{L}_1$, there always exists at least one honest set $\mathcal{S}_i$ such that $\mathcal{I}_j \cap \mathcal{S}_i = \emptyset$. This property, together with CNF-based secret sharing, guarantees perfect secrecy. Consequently, the CNF-based VSS protocol eliminates one round of communication compared to the Shamir-based variant, thereby improving efficiency while maintaining security.

8 Layered Multiplication Protocol

In this section, we present our layered multiplication protocols. Our primary focus is on a new Shamir-based multiplication protocol. For completeness, we also adapt the CNF-based protocol from [DDG+23] to our setting by replacing its VSS component. The details of the latter are in the full version of this paper.

Our Shamir-based protocol is constructed by applying our VSS protocol from Sect. 7 and cross-layer messaging technique from Sect. 6 to the BGW multiplication protocol [BGW88], tailored for the layered setting. The resulting protocol uses 8 layers and achieves (n^6) complexity. We begin by recalling the standard BGW multiplication protocol.

- **Step 1 (Masking).** Each party P_i holds shares $[\![a]\!][i]$ and $[\![b]\!][i]$ of secrets a and b. P_i defines $[\![c]\!][i] = [\![a]\!][i] \cdot [\![b]\!][i]$. It then masks these values by polynomials $f_i(x)$ and $g_i(x)$ with random coefficients and constant terms $[\![a]\!][i]$ and $[\![b]\!][i]$ respectively. Let $h_i(x) = f_i(x) \cdot g_i(x)$, which is a degree-$2t$ polynomial.

$$f_i(x) = [\![a]\!][i] + \sum_{l=1}^{t} \alpha_{i,l} x^l \qquad\qquad g_i(x) = [\![b]\!][i] + \sum_{l=1}^{t} \beta_{i,l} x^l$$

$$h_i(x) = f_i(x) \cdot g_i(x) = [\![c]\!][i] + \sum_{l=1}^{2t} \gamma_{i,l} x^l$$

P_i then verifiably secret shares all coefficients of $f_i(x)$, $g_i(x)$, and $h_i(x)$ with all other parties.
- **Step 2 (Share Evaluation).** Upon receiving shares of the coefficients from each P_i, every party P_j can locally compute shares of the polynomial evaluations. Specifically, for each $i, k \in [n]$, P_j computes $[\![f_i(k)]\!][j]$, $[\![g_i(k)]\!][j]$, and $[\![h_i(k)]\!][j]$. For instance:

$$[\![f_i(k)]\!][j] = [\![a]\!][i,j] + \sum_{l=1}^{t} [\![\alpha_{i,l}]\!][j] k^l$$

P_j then sends these evaluation shares to the corresponding party P_k.
- **Step 3 (Verification).** Each party P_k reconstructs the values $f_i(k)$, $g_i(k)$, and $h_i(k)$ from the shares received in the previous step. It then verifies for all $i \in [n]$ that $f_i(k) \cdot g_i(k) = h_i(k)$. If the check fails for some i, P_k broadcasts a complaint (**Complaint**, i, k).
- **Step 4 (Adjudication).** In response to a complaint (**Complaint**, i, k), every party P_j broadcasts its shares of the coefficients of $f_i(x)$, $g_i(x)$, and $h_i(x)$. This allows for a public reconstruction and verification of the check from Step 3. If the check still fails, P_i is identified as dishonest.
- **Step 5 (Output).** Each party P_j computes its final share $[\![c]\!][j]$ of the product $c = ab$ by taking the appropriate linear combination of the shares $\{[\![c]\!][i,j]\}$ received from all parties P_i that were not identified as dishonest.

Apart from replacing directly the VSS protocol used in Step 1 with our VSS layered setting in Sect. 7.1, we identify two main issues when directly adapting the above BGW multiplication protocol to our layered setting to achieve proactive security.

- **Issue 1: Correctness of Shares in Step 2.** In Step 2, each party P_j computes $[\![f_i(k)]\!][j]$, $[\![g_i(k)]\!][j]$, and $[\![h_i(k)]\!][j]$ using the shares it received from each P_i. However, if any P_i is corrupted, it may have shared incorrect values for $[\![a]\!][i]$ or $[\![b]\!][i]$, leading to incorrect computations in Step 2.

- **Issue 2: Cross-Layer Corruption Due to Share Reuse.** The protocol reuses the same shares in multiple steps, specifically between Step 2 and Step 4, and between Step 2 and Step 5. This reuse can lead to vulnerabilities where a corrupted party can exploit the same shares across different layers, potentially compromising the integrity of the protocol.

To address these issues, we employ the honest future resharing technique from Sect. 6.3 to distribute the shares in Step 2 to new layers. This approach effectively mitigates the risks associated with both identified issues. Specifically:

For Issue 1: The resharing technique allows us to securely reshare the values in Step 2 to new layers, ensuring that even if some parties are corrupted, the integrity of the shares is maintained. By doing so, we can effectively mitigate the risks associated with both identified issues.

For Issue 2: By resharing the values to new layers, we ensure that the shares used in Step 4 and Step 5 are independent of those used in Step 2. This independence prevents a corrupted party from exploiting the same shares across different layers, thereby enhancing the protocol's security.

Putting the above countermeasures together, we obtain our Shamir-based multiplication protocol $\Pi_{\mathsf{Mul}}^{\mathsf{Shamir}}$, which is detailed in Table 5.

Tab. 5: Shamir-based Multiplication $\Pi_{\mathsf{Mul}}^{\mathsf{Shamir}}$

Setup:

Public Parameters: Input parties $\mathsf{P}_1^0, \ldots, \mathsf{P}_n^0 \in \mathcal{L}_0$, output parties $\mathsf{P}_1^8, \ldots, \mathsf{P}_n^8 \in \mathcal{L}_8$.

Secret Input: Each P_i^0 inputs $[\![a]\!][i]$ and $[\![b]\!][i]$.

Sub-protocols:
- Protocol $\Pi_{\mathsf{RG}}, \Pi_{\mathsf{FRS}}, \Pi_{\mathsf{HFM}}, \Pi_{\mathsf{HFS}}, \Pi_{\mathsf{VSS}}^{\mathsf{Shamir}}$

Preprocess:
- Each P_i^0 in the layer $\mathcal{L}_0$ obtains two sets of random shares $\{[\![r_1]\!][i], \ldots, [\![r_t]\!][i]\}$ and $\{[\![s_1]\!][i], \ldots, [\![s_t]\!][i]\}$ via Π_{RG}.

Protocol Execution:

Layer 0: For each $i \in [n]$, P_i^0 proceeds as follows:

1. Sample $\{\alpha_{i,l}, \beta_{i,l}\}_{l \in [t]} \xleftarrow{\$} \mathbb{F}$.
2. Define $f_i(x) = [\![a]\!][i] + \sum_{l=1}^{t} \alpha_{i,l} x^l$, $g_i(x) = [\![b]\!][i] + \sum_{l=1}^{t} \beta_{i,l} x^l$.
3. Compute $h_i(x) = f_i(x) \cdot g_i(x) = [\![c]\!][i] + \sum_{l=1}^{2t} \gamma_{i,l} x^l$.
4. Share $\{\alpha_{i,l}\}_{l \in [t]}, \{\beta_{i,l}\}_{l \in [t]}, [\![c]\!][i], \{\gamma_{i,l}\}_{l \in [2t]}$ with $\mathcal{L}_3$ via $\Pi_{\mathsf{VSS}}^{\mathsf{Shamir}}$.
5. $\mathsf{F}_a(i, Y) \leftarrow \mathsf{Lift}([\![a]\!][i], [\![r_1]\!][i], \ldots, [\![r_t]\!][i])$
6. $\mathsf{F}_b(i, Y) \leftarrow \mathsf{Lift}([\![b]\!][i]), [\![s_1]\!][i], \ldots, [\![s_t]\!][i])$
7. **for** $j \in [n]$: **send** $\mathsf{F}_a(i, j), \mathsf{F}_b(i, j)$ **to** P_j^5 **in** $\mathcal{L}_5$ **via** Π_{HFM}

Layer 5: For each $j \in [n]$, P_j^5 proceeds as follows:

1. **recv** $\{[\![\alpha_{i,l}]\!][j]\}_{l \in [t]}, \{[\![\beta_{i,l}]\!][j]\}_{l \in [t]}, [\![c]\!][i, j], \{[\![\gamma_{i,l}]\!][j]\}_{l \in [2t]}$ **from** P_i^0 **via** $\Pi_{\mathsf{VSS}}^{\mathsf{Shamir}}$
2. **recv** $\mathsf{F}_a(i, j), \mathsf{F}_b(i, j)$ **from** P_i^0 **via** Π_{HFM}
3. $\hat{\mathsf{F}}_a(X, j) \leftarrow \mathsf{BW}_X(\{\mathsf{F}_a(i, j)\}_{i \in \mathsf{n}})$
4. $\hat{\mathsf{F}}_b(X, j) \leftarrow \mathsf{BW}_X(\{\mathsf{F}_b(i, j)\}_{i \in \mathsf{n}})$
5. **for** $i, k \in [n]$:
6. $[\![f_i(k)]\!][j] \leftarrow \hat{\mathsf{F}}_a(i, j) + \sum_{l=1}^{t} [\![\alpha_{i,l}]\!][j] \cdot k^l$
7. $[\![g_i(k)]\!][j] \leftarrow \hat{\mathsf{F}}_b(i, j) + \sum_{l=1}^{t} [\![\beta_{i,l}]\!][j] \cdot k^l$
8. $[\![h_i(k)]\!][j] \leftarrow [\![c]\!][i, j] + \sum_{l=1}^{2t} [\![\gamma_{i,l}]\!][j] \cdot k^l$
9.   **send** $([\![f_i(k)]\!][j], [\![g_i(k)]\!][j], [\![h_i(k)]\!][j])$ **to** P_k^6 **in** $\mathcal{L}_6$
10. **for** $i, k \in [n]$: Share $[\![f_i(k)]\!][j], [\![g_i(k)]\!][j], [\![h_i(k)]\!][j]$ with $\mathcal{L}_7$ via Π_{HFS}.
11. **for** $i \in [n]$: Input $[\![c]\!][i, j]$ to Π_{FRS} to reshare $[\![c]\!][i]$ with $\mathcal{L}_8$.

Layer 6: For each $k \in [n]$, P_k^6 proceeds as follows:
1. **recv** $\{[\![f_i(k)]\!][j]\}_{i \in [n]}, \{[\![g_i(k)]\!][j]\}_{i \in [n]}, \{[\![h_i(k)]\!][j]\}_{i \in [n]}$ **from** each P_j^5 in $\mathcal{L}_5$.
2. **for** $i \in [n]$:
3. $\hat{f}_i(k) \leftarrow \mathsf{BW}(\{[\![f_i(k)]\!][j]\}_{j \in [n]})$
4. $\hat{g}_i(k) \leftarrow \mathsf{BW}(\{[\![g_i(k)]\!][j]\}_{j \in [n]})$
5. $\hat{h}_i(k) \leftarrow \mathsf{BW}(\{[\![h_i(k)]\!][j]\}_{j \in [n]})$
6.   **if** $\hat{f}_i(k) \cdot \hat{g}_i(k) \neq \hat{h}_i(k)$: **BCast** (**Complaint**, i, k)

Layer 7: For each $u \in [n]$, P_u^7 proceeds as follows:
1. **recv** $\{[\![f_i(k)]\!][j, u]\}_{i,j,k \in [n]}, \{[\![g_i(k)]\!][j, u]\}_{i,j,k \in [n]}, \{[\![h_i(k)]\!][j, u]\}_{i,j,k \in [n]}$ **from** P_j^5 via Π_{HFS}.
2. **foreach** (**Complaint**, i, k):
3.   **BCast** $\{[\![f_i(k)]\!][j, u]\}_{j \in [n]}, \{[\![g_i(k)]\!][j, u]\}_{j \in [n]}, \{[\![h_i(k)]\!][j, u]\}_{j \in [n]}$

Public computation:
1. **foreach** (**Complaint**, i, k):
2. $\hat{f}_i(k) \leftarrow \mathsf{BW}(\{\mathsf{BW}(\{[\![f_i(k)]\!][j, u]\}_{u \in [n]})\}_{j \in [n]})$
3. $\hat{g}_i(k) \leftarrow \mathsf{BW}(\{\mathsf{BW}(\{[\![g_i(k)]\!][j, u]\}_{u \in [n]})\}_{j \in [n]})$
4. $\hat{h}_i(k) \leftarrow \mathsf{BW}(\{\mathsf{BW}(\{[\![h_i(k)]\!][j, u]\}_{u \in [n]})\}_{j \in [n]})$
5.   **if** $\hat{f}_i(k) \cdot \hat{g}_i(k) \neq \hat{h}_i(k)$: Mark i discarded.

Layer 8: For each $v \in [n]$, P_v^8 proceeds as follows:
1. **recv** $\{[\![c]\!][i, v]\}_{i \in [n]}$ **from** $\mathcal{L}_5$ via $\Pi_{\mathsf{FRS}}^{\mathsf{Shamir}}$.
2. Define a set $G \subseteq [n]$ that for every $i \in G$, i is not discarded.
3. From G, take a subset G' of $2\mathsf{t} + 1$ elements.
4. $[\![c]\!][v] = \sum_{i \in G'} \lambda_i [\![c]\!][i, v]$. $/\!/ \lambda_i$ denotes the Lagrange interpolation coefficients.
5. Set $[\![c]\!][v]$ as its share of c.

Theorem 3 (Shamir-based multiplication). *The protocol in Table 5 realizes the ideal functionality* $\mathcal{F}_{\mathsf{Mult}}$ *in the* $\mathcal{F}_{\mathsf{VSS}}^{(\mathsf{t}, \mathsf{N})}$-*hybrid model as defined in ?? with perfect* t-*security for* $\mathsf{t} < \mathsf{n}/3$ *by consuming 6 layers, and by communicating* $O(\mathsf{n}^6)$ *field elements over the point-to-point channels and* $O(\mathsf{n}^6)$ *field elements over the broadcast channels.*

Proof. The proof and complexity analysis are provided in the full version of this paper. $\qquad\square$

9   Layered MPC for Arithmetic Circuit

In this section, we present a layered MPC construction. The construction follows the BGW paradigm and uses Beaver multiplication triples, and the per-gate layer overhead amortizes to $O(1)$. This paradigm adapts to the layered setting thanks to our future resharing protocol. Our MPC supports both Shamir and CNF secret shares. The protocols of CNF secret shares are provided in the full version of this paper.

9.1   Multiplication Gate

To achieve an amortized cost of one layer per multiplication gate, we adopt an offline-online approach based on Beaver triples. In layered setting, pre-generating all triples in a single setup phase is inefficient, as each triple need to be transported to the layer of its corresponding gate, incurring significant overhead.

Instead, we employ a pipelined approach where the generation of a triple is initiated several layers ahead of its consumption. Specifically, to evaluate a multiplication gate at layer $\mathcal{L}_k$, the process of generating the required triple ($[\![a]\!], [\![b]\!], [\![ab]\!]$) begins at layer $\mathcal{L}_{k-12}$. The shares of a and b are then forwarded to the necessary layers using our future resharing protocol, Π_{FRS}. This pipelined generation, combined with future resharing, ensures that the triples are available at the correct layer when needed, without introducing cross-layer security vulnerabilities. The full protocol is detailed in Table 6.

Complexity. During Triple Generation, Step 1 invokes Π_{RG} twice, incurring a cost of $2 \cdot O(n^5)$. Step 2 invokes $\Pi_{\mathsf{Mul}}^{\mathsf{Shamir}}$ once, which contributes $O(n^6)$ to both point-to-point and broadcast complexities. Step 3 involves eight invocations of Π_{FRS}. Each Π_{FRS} calls Π_{RG} to generate random shares, costing $O(n^5)$, while the execution itself costs only $O(n^2)$. Finally, the execution of the multiplication gate requires a broadcast complexity of only $O(n)$. Consequently, the dominant cost for both point-to-point and broadcast channels is $O(n^6)$, stemming from $\Pi_{\mathsf{Mul}}^{\mathsf{Shamir}}$.

Tab. 6: Shamir-based Multiplication Gate $\Pi_{\mathsf{Mul\text{-}Gate}}^{\mathsf{Shamir}}$

Setup:

Public Parameters: Input parties $\mathsf{P}_1^k, \ldots, \mathsf{P}_n^k$ in layer $\mathcal{L}_k$ with $k \geq 12$, output parties $\mathsf{P}_1^{k+1}, \ldots, \mathsf{P}_n^{k+1} \in \mathcal{L}_{k+1}$.

Secret Inputs: Each P_i^k gets inputs $[\![x]\!][i]$ and $[\![y]\!][i]$.

Sub-protocols:
- Protocol $\Pi_{\mathsf{FRS}}, \Pi_{\mathsf{RG}}, \Pi_{\mathsf{Mul}}^{\mathsf{Shamir}}$.

Triple Generation:
1. $\mathcal{L}_{k-12}$ invokes Π_{RG}, and each $\mathsf{P}_i^{k-7} \in \mathcal{L}_{k-7}$ get random shares $[\![a]\!][i]$ and $[\![b]\!][i]$.
2. $\mathcal{L}_{k-7}$ invokes $\Pi_{\mathsf{Mul}}^{\mathsf{Shamir}}$ with input the shares of a and b, and each $\mathsf{P}_i^{k+1} \in \mathcal{L}_{k+1}$ get $[\![ab]\!][i]$.
3. $\mathcal{L}_{k-7}$ invokes Π_{FRS} to reshare a and b to $\mathcal{L}_{k+1}$, thus $\mathcal{L}_k$ and $\mathcal{L}_{k+1}$ can obtain refresh shares of a and b.

- -

Protocol Execution:

Layer k(Gate Input Layer):
1. Each P_i^k broadcasts $[\![x]\!][i] - [\![a]\!][i]$ and $[\![y]\!][i] - [\![b]\!][i]$.

Layer $k+1$(Gate Output Layer): Each P_j^k proceeds as follows:
1. Obtain $d \leftarrow \mathsf{BW}(\{[\![x]\!][i] - [\![a]\!][i]\}_{i \in [n]})$ and $d \leftarrow \mathsf{BW}(\{[\![y]\!][i] - [\![b]\!][i]\}_{i \in [n]})$.
2. Set $[\![xy]\!][j] = d \cdot [\![b]\!][j] + e \cdot [\![a]\!][j] + [\![ab]\!][j] + de$.

9.2 Layered Secure MPC Protocol

We now present our layered MPC protocol with perfectly secure and guaranteed output delivery. We work with general arithmetic circuit rather than layered arithmetic circuit.

Suppose each input client P_i^0, with $i \in [n]$ in the input layer has $x_i \in \mathbb{F}$ as input, and each party in the output layer wants to compute $f(x_1, \ldots, x_n)$. The secure computation of f proceeds in three phases:

Input Sharing Phase Each client verifiably shares their input using the underlying secret sharing scheme. To facilitate the initial transfer of these shares to the first gate's input layer, clients also generate randomness for the future resharing protocol by sampling and verifiably sharing $n \cdot t$ random values.

Circuit Evaluation Phase The protocol evaluates the circuit gate by gate. In contrast to standard MPC where static parties hold shares, our layered model uses future resharing to pass shares between layers. Specifically, the layer holding a gate's output shares reshares the secret to the layer responsible for the successor gate's input. This approach allows for the direct evaluation of general arithmetic circuits, bypassing the gate alignment issues present in prior work [DDG+23]. The evaluation of the first gate commences only after its inputs have been delivered to the appropriate layer via future resharing.

Output Reconstruction Phase Finally, the parties in the layer holding the output wire of the final gate reveal their shares to the designated output clients, who then reconstruct the final result.

Theorem 4 (Shamir-based MPC). *Let f be an n-party functionality computed by a general arithmetic circuit C over a finite field $\mathbb{F}$, with D levels and M gates. Then, for any $t < n/3$, there is an $(n, t, D + 13)$-layered MPC protocol for f in which the communication is $M \cdot O(n^6)$ field elements over the point-to-point channels and $M \cdot O(n^6)$ field elements over the broadcast channels.*

Tab. 7: Shamir-based Layered MPC Protocol

Setup:
Public Parameters: A arithmetic circuit C over $\mathbb{F}$ with D levels that computes f. Output layer is $d = D + 13$.
Secret Input: Each input client $P_i^0, i \in [n]$ inputs $[\![x]\!]_i$.
Outputs: Each output client receives $f(x_1, \ldots, x_n)$.
Sub-protocols:
- Protocol $\Pi_{\mathsf{RG}}, \Pi_{\mathsf{FRS}}, \Pi_{\mathsf{Mul\text{-}Gate}}^{\mathsf{Shamir}}, \Pi_{\mathsf{VSS}}$.

- -

Protocol Execution:
Input Sharing Phase:
- $\mathcal{L}_0$ invokes nt Π_{RG}[1] in parallel to generate the random numbers required for Π_{FRS}.
- Each P_i^0 invokes Π_{VSS} to share its inputs x_i to $\mathcal{L}_5$. Then, $\mathcal{L}_5$ invokes Π_{FRS} to deliver the share to the **Gate Input Layer** of its input wire.

Circuit Evaluation Phase (Starting at $\mathcal{L}_{12}$):
- **Mutiplication Gate.** Each P_i^k inputs $[\![x]\!][i]$ and $[\![y]\!][i]$ at **Gate Input Layer**$(\mathcal{L}_k)$ and invokes $\Pi_{\mathsf{Mul\text{-}Gate}}^{\mathsf{Shamir}}$, each P_i^{k+1} outputs $[\![xy]\!][i]$ at **Gate Output Layer**$(\mathcal{L}_{k+1})$.
- **Addition Gate.** Each P_i^k inputs $[\![x]\!][i]$ and $[\![y]\!][i]$ at **Gate Input Layer**$(\mathcal{L}_k)$ and each P_i^k outputs $[\![x+y]\!][i] = [\![x]\!][i] + [\![y]\!][i]$ at **Gate Output Layer**$(\mathcal{L}_k)$.
- If the current gate's **Gate Output Layer** does not match its successor's **Gate Input Layer**, invoke Π_{FRS} to reshare input share to its successor's **Gate Input Layer**.

Output Reconstruction Phase:
- Each P_i^{D+12} in $\mathcal{L}_{D+12}$ reveals its share $[\![y]\!][i]$ on the output wire of the output gate to each output clients in $\mathcal{L}_{D+13}$.
- Each output client in $\mathcal{L}_{D+13}$ recovers $y \leftarrow \mathsf{BW}(\{[\![y]\!][i]\}_{i \in [n]})$ as the output of the protocol.

---

[1]Since the adversary may corrupt an arbitrary number of clients, the generation of random shares cannot exploit the Vandermonde matrix trick to reduce communication. We therefore use the same method as in CNF-based secret sharing to generate random shares.

Acknowledgments. This work is supported by the Key R&D Program of Shandong Province, China (Grant 2024ZLGX05), the National Natural Science Foundation of China (Grant 62302272,62472255), the Shandong Provincial Outstanding Young Scientists Fund (Overseas) (Grant 2024HWYQ-013) the National Key R&D Program of China (Grant 2022YFB2702800, Grant 2023YFA1011200)

References

AKP20. Applebaum, B., Kachlon, E., Patra, A.: The round complexity of perfect MPC with active security and optimal resiliency. In: 2020 IEEE 61st Annual Symposium on Foundations of Computer Science (FOCS), pp. 1277–1284. IEEE (2020)

AL17. Asharov, G., Lindell, Y.: A full proof of the BGW protocol for perfectly secure multiparty computation. J. Cryptol. **30**(1), 58–151 (2017)

BEP23. Bienstock, A., Escudero, D., Polychroniadou, A.: On linear communication complexity for (maximally) fluid MPC. In: Annual International Cryptology Conference, pp. 263–294. Springer, Cham (2023). https://doi.org/10.1007/978-3-031-38557-5_9

BEP25. Bienstock, A., Escudero, D., Polychroniadou, A.: Perfectly secure fluid MPC with abort and linear communication complexity. IACR Commun. Cryptol. **1**(4) (2025)

BGW88. Ben-Or, M., Goldwasser, S., Wigderson, A.: Completeness theorems for non-cryptographic fault-tolerant distributed computation (extended abstract). In: 20th ACM STOC, pp. 1–10. ACM Press (1988)

BW86. Berlekamp, E.R., Welzl, M.E.: Error correction of algebraic block codes. US Patent, (4,633,470) (1986)

Can00. Canetti, R.: Security and composition of multiparty cryptographic protocols. J. Cryptol. **13**(1), 143–202 (2000)

CCD88. Chaum, D., Crépeau, C., Damgård, I.: Multiparty unconditionally secure protocols (abstract) (informal contribution). In: Pomerance, C. (ed.) CRYPTO'87, volume 293 of LNCS, page 462. Springer, Berlin, Heidelberg (1988)

CGG+21. Choudhuri, A.R., Goel, A., Green, M., Jain, A., Kaptchuk, G.: Fluid MPC: secure multiparty computation with dynamic participants. In: Malkin, T., Peikert, C. (eds.) CRYPTO 2021. LNCS, vol. 12826, pp. 94–123. Springer, Cham (2021). https://doi.org/10.1007/978-3-030-84245-1_4

DDG+23. David, B., et al.: Perfect MPC over layered graphs. In: Handschuh, H., Lysyanskaya, A. (eds.) CRYPTO 2023. Part I, volume 14081 of LNCS, pp. 360–392. Springer, Cham (2023). https://doi.org/10.1007/978-3-031-38557-5_12

DDWY93. Dolev, D., Dwork, C., Waarts, O., Yung, M.: Perfectly secure message transmission. J. ACM **40**(1), 17–47 (1993)

DKLN24. Deligios, G., Konring, A., Liu-Zhang, C.-D., Narayanan, V.: Statistical layered MPC. In: TCC (4), volume 15367 of Lecture Notes in Computer Science, pp. 362–394. Springer (2024). https://doi.org/10.1007/978-3-031-78023-3_12

DM00. Dodis, Y., Micali, S.: Parallel reducibility for information-theoretically secure computation. In: Bellare, M. (ed.) CRYPTO 2000. LNCS, vol. 1880, pp. 74–92. Springer, Berlin, Heidelberg (2000). https://doi.org/10.1007/3-540-44598-6_5

GHK+21. Gentry, C., Halevi, S., Krawczyk, H., Magri, B., Nielsen, J.B., Rabin, T., Yakoubov, S.: YOSO: you only speak once. In: Malkin, T., Peikert, C. (eds.) CRYPTO 2021. LNCS, vol. 12826, pp. 64–93. Springer, Cham (2021). https://doi.org/10.1007/978-3-030-84245-1_3

GIKR01. Gennaro, R., Ishai, Y., Kushilevitz, E., Rabin, T.: The round complexity of verifiable secret sharing and secure multicast. In: 33rd ACM STOC, pp. 580–589. ACM Press (2001)

GMW87. Goldreich, O., Micali, S., Wigderson, A.: How to play any mental game or a completeness theorem for protocols with honest majority. In: Aho, A., editor, 19th ACM STOC, pp. 218–229. ACM Press (1987)

ISN89. Ito, M., Saito, A., Nishizeki, T.: Secret sharing scheme realizing general access structure. Electr. Commun. Japan (Part III: Fund. Electr. Sci.) **72**(9), 56–64 (1989)

KKK08. Katz, J., Koo, C.-Y., Kumaresan, R.: Improving the round complexity of VSS in point-to-point networks. In: Aceto, L., Damgård, I., Goldberg, L.A., Halldórsson, M.M., Ingólfsdóttir, A., Walukiewicz, I. (eds.) ICALP 2008. LNCS, vol. 5126, pp. 499–510. Springer, Heidelberg (2008). https://doi.org/10.1007/978-3-540-70583-3_41

KLR06. Kushilevitz, E., Lindell, Y., Rabin, T.: Information-theoretically secure protocols and security under composition. In: Proceedings of the Thirty-Eighth Annual ACM Symposium on Theory of Computing, pp. 109–118 (2006)

MR92. Micali, S., Rogaway, P.: Secure computation (abstract). In: Feigenbaum, J. (ed.) CRYPTO'91. LNCS, vol. 576, pp. 392–404. Springer, Berlin, Heidelberg (1992). https://doi.org/10.1007/3-540-46766-1_32

OY91. Ostrovsky, R., Yung, M.: How to withstand mobile virus attacks. In: Proceedings of the Tenth Annual ACM Symposium on Principles of Distributed Computing, pp. 51–59 (1991)

RS22. Rachuri, R., Scholl, P.: Le Mans: dynamic and fluid MPC for dishonest majority. In: Dodis, Y., Shrimpton, T. (eds.) CRYPTO 2022. Part I, volume 13507 of LNCS, pp. 719–749. Springer, Cham (2022). https://doi.org/10.1007/978-3-031-15802-5_25

Sha79. Shamir, A.: How to share a secret. Commun. Assoc. Comput. Mach. **22**(11), 612–613 (1979)

Yao86. Yao, A.C.-C.: How to generate and exchange secrets (extended abstract). In: 27th FOCS, pp. 162–167. IEEE Computer Society Press (1986)

Maintaining Sublinear Locality Over Time: Adaptively Secure MPC on a Reusable Hidden Graph

Elette Boyle[1,2], Ran Cohen[1], and Pierre Meyer[3](✉)

[1] Reichman University, Herzliya, Israel
{elette.boyle,cohenran}@runi.ac.il
[2] NTT Research, Sunnyvale, USA
[3] Aarhus University, Aarhus, Denmark
pierre.meyer@cs.au.dk

Abstract. Communication *locality* of an n-party protocol measures the maximum degree of the communication graph induced by the protocol execution. While secure multi-party computation (MPC) with small, sublinear locality exists in the static-corruption setting, this goal seems nearly paradoxical in the *adaptive*-corruption setting: Even against fail-stop adversaries, small neighbour sets of honest parties lie vulnerable to identification and corruption.

Surprisingly, Chandran et al. [ITCS '15] showed that for a single MPC execution, sublinear locality and adaptive security can be simultaneously achieved, assuming honest-to-honest channels are hidden from the adversary. Their solution works in the "hidden-graph model," where a fresh, initially hidden, low-degree graph is being used in each round. In turn, the combined degree grows with every round—inherently limiting the approach to a single-shot MPC execution, and sublinear total rounds.

This raises the following question, which is the focus of our work:
> *Is it possible to maintain sublinear locality over an* unbounded *number of executions* facing adaptive adversaries?

In this work, we provide an affirmative answer in two settings:

- First, we consider semi-honest adversaries and information-theoretic security, and construct reusable MPC with $\mathsf{polylog}(n)$ locality.
- Second, we consider fail-stop adversaries and computational security, and construct reusable MPC with $\tilde{O}(n^{2/3})$ locality.

Part of this work was conducted while the authors were visiting the Simons Institute for the Theory of Computing.

E. Boyle: Research supported in part by AFOSR Award FA9550-21-1-0046 and ERC Project HSS (852952).

R. Cohen: Research supported in part by NSF grant No. 2055568 and by ISF grant 1834/23.

P. Meyer: Research supported by the European Research Council (ERC) under the European Union's Horizon 2020 research and innovation programme under grants agreement number 852952 (HSS), 803096 (SPEC), and 101124977 (DECRYPSIS), and by a grant from the STIBO foundation.

J. Daemen and E. Thomé (Eds.): EUROCRYPT 2026, LNCS 16543, pp. 546–572, 2026.
https://doi.org/10.1007/978-3-032-25324-8_19

Our results are obtained by devising low-locality protocols while hiding important information about the graph topology, enabling the parties to reuse a *single hidden graph*. As an independent contribution, this serves as new results for adaptively secure topology-hiding computation (Moran et al. [TCC '15]).

1   Introduction

Secure multiparty computation (MPC) [10,26,39,46] enables a set of n parties to compute a joint function of their private inputs while revealing nothing but the output, even when up to t of them might collude and attack the protocol. The design and optimisation of MPC has been the subject of a large body of research in the last 40 years.

A natural metric, which has recently attracted attention, is the number of parties that each party must communicate with during the course of the computation. This is referred to as the *communication locality* of the protocol [16]. Understanding when protocols with sublinear locality (in n) can and cannot be achieved facing linear corruptions (*i.e.* if a constant fraction of parties may be corrupted) has been an important focus of works within both distributed computing and MPC literatures.

Sublinear locality against static *corruptions.* The question was originally explored assuming communication along edges of a *fixed* incomplete graph, where corruptions can take place as a function of the graph structure; however, this setting faces impossibilities for achieving standard security [32,35]. These impossibilities no longer hold when each party may communicate with each other party, but chooses with whom to actually talk during the protocol's execution, *i.e.* when the communication graph evolves dynamically. This "dynamic-graph" setting opens a slew of techniques, such as randomly choosing neighbour sets and transferring information safely via small elected committees. Since corruptions are static, one can argue that high fractions of selected neighbours and elected committees must be honest.

Ultimately, building on distributed protocols such as [11,42–44], protocols secure against linearly many static corruptions have been constructed in this model with sublinear (and as low as $\mathsf{polylog}(n)$) locality, both in the context of broadcast and Byzantine Agreement [12,15,34,37,42–44] and in the context of MPC [13,16,31], even with information-theoretic security [14].

Sublinear locality against adaptive *corruptions?* The picture drastically changes when considering adaptive corruptions, where at a first glance, the goal itself may even sound suspiciously hopeless. Extending the above positive results to the adaptive-corruption regime would seem to reintroduce the very challenges of the fixed-graph setting, where small dynamically elected sets again lie vulnerable to identification and corruption.

Indeed, the same lower bounds on locality do carry over within MPC models presuming that the adversary is privy to the set of active honest-to-honest communication edges. For example, given even fail-stop corruptions, the adversary can simply corrupt and crash all parties who receive a message from a targeted honest party. Even semi-honest adversaries can isolate an honest party and break privacy when considering information-theoretic security in the plain model (with no setup assumptions). Adaptive security faces strong lower bounds in this setting [1,12,14].

Single-Shot Adaptive MPC in the Hidden-Channels Model. However, in many settings (and especially in large-scale MPC), it is overly pessimistic to assume that the adversary sees activity of pairwise communication channels between parties not under its control. Correspondingly, Chandran et al. [21] put forth a (perhaps even more natural) model, in which the adversary does *not* see which honest-to-honest communication channels are exercised, and where the aforementioned adaptive attacks no longer hold. We refer to this as the *hidden-channels model*. Surprisingly, they showed that sublinear locality (and even polylog(n) locality) *can* be achieved with adaptive security within this model, albeit for a single MPC execution.

Chandran et al. [21] cleverly avoided the above-discussed adaptive-corruption attacks by introducing a "hidden-graphs" technique. In this approach, the protocol freshly samples a new low-degree graph G_i for each round i of communication, such that each party only learns its neighbour-set in G_i, but otherwise G_i itself is kept hidden until used. This can be achieved given a secret-key infrastructure (SKI), in which each pair of parties receives a common secret key. Effectively, Chandran et al. first establish an all-to-all reliable message transmission (RMT) mechanism, where the parties flood messages out round by round to their (continually changing) neighbour sets. Neighbours in round i are defined by G_i, ignoring existence of prior G_j for $j < i$. This round-to-round independence loosely allows them to emulate a static-corruption setting, ensuring that future communication-edge selection is independent of any information gleaned by the adversary as a function of the protocol up to this step.

Reusable Adaptive MPC? Unfortunately, a consequence of the many-hidden-graphs approach of [21] is that the overall locality of their protocol grows with the number of *total rounds* of protocol communication. This suffices for the restricted goal of a single MPC execution with computational security, by emulating a single MPC protocol with sublinear round complexity on top of this RMT infrastructure (e.g., a constant-round MPC in the broadcast model, where each broadcast is implemented by a polylog(n)-round protocol). However, it serves as a fundamental limit of their approach toward general protocols, where parties sequentially execute multiple MPC protocols during the course of time. After a linear number of communication rounds, the expected locality of the protocol will already be linear.

This shortcoming holds in all existing adaptively secure MPC with sublinear locality [14,23], each inspired from the many-hidden-graphs approach of [21]. Without the ability to grow the communication graph over time, one is left with a daunting task of somehow protecting a single ultimately fixed low-degree graph. This leads to the following central question:

Is it possible to maintain sublinear locality over an unbounded number of sequential executions facing linear adaptive adversaries?

We emphasise that this remains the case, with no existing approaches to maintain sublinear locality facing adaptive corruptions, even against fail-stop adversaries, and even under cryptographic assumptions. This setting already embodies the core challenges of achieving low locality due to the adversarial ability of honest-party isolation.

In the information-theoretic case (without cryptographic assumptions and without trusted setup), the situation is even worse: sublinear locality is not even known for a *single-shot* MPC with *semi-honest* security. Indeed, for high-depth computations the only known MPC protocols require high round complexity, invalidating the many-hidden-graphs approach altogether.

1.1 Our Results

We present a positive answer to the above question, in two primary settings:

1. Information-theoretic security against *semi-honest* corruptions, and
2. Computational security against *fail-stop* crashes.

Our results are obtained by devising low-locality protocols while hiding important information about the graph topology, enabling the parties to reuse a single hidden graph. Our main technical tools are based on "topology-hiding computation" [45] which is MPC that hides the underlying communication graph. As an independent contribution, we construct new adaptively secure protocol in the *distributional* THC framework of [8].

In the following, by *reusable* general secure function evaluation (SFE) protocol, we mean security that is maintained under *any* (not a priori bounded) polynomially many sequential executions, for an arbitrary sequence of functions, while maintaining the quoted locality. Further, as standard in the literature on large-scale MPC, $\tilde{O}$ notation hides factors of $\log n$ and (when relevant) the computational security parameter λ. We recall that our results are within the hidden-channels model of [21], where the adversary does not see which honest-to-honest communication channels are used.

1.1.1 Information-Theoretic Security Against Semi-honest Adversaries.
We begin with our information-theoretic result, which guarantees $\mathsf{polylog}(n)$ locality against adaptive semi-honest corruption of nearly half of all parties.

Theorem 1 (IT semi-honest). *Let $n \in \mathbb{N}$, let $0 < \varepsilon < 1/2$ be a constant, and let $t = \varepsilon n$. There exist a reusable n-party SFE protocol against adaptive semi-honest t-adversaries with information-theoretic security in the plain model and over hidden channels, maintaining $\mathsf{polylog}(n)$ locality.*

The starting point for our protocol is an observation from [8], showing that if one can establish a protocol for all-to-all secure communication (that is, every party can securely communicate with every other party) that offers information-theoretic security, has sublinear locality, and hides certain aspects of the topology of the underlying communication graph, then it is possible to achieve sequential composition and reuse this protocol within the framework of [21]. However, [8] did not present a candidate protocol for this task (nor does one exist to date). We close this gap by constructing a protocol satisfying these requirements, inspired by Chaum's DC-nets [25].

At a high level, the parties in our protocol operate over a hidden Erdös–Rényi graph where each edge appears with probability $\mathsf{polylog}(n)/n$. Such a graph can be jointly sampled by the parties in the semi-honest setting *without setup* (as observed in [21,22,24], and which we recall in the full version. To enable P_i to privately send a message m to P_j, each party additively secret shares a value with its neighbour-sets: P_i shares m, P_j shares a random mask value r, and all other parties share 0. Next, each party sums up the shares obtained from its neighbours; that is, the parties jointly holds secret shares of the value $m + r$. In the last step, P_j must obtain the sum of all these shares, and recover m.

If we can guarantee the adversary will never corrupt a nontrivial cut in the Erdös–Rényi graph, disconnecting the honest communication subgraph via its corruptions, then the collection of all parties' resulting shares of $m + r$ can be simulated from just the final sum. In this case, it will suffice for parties to simply use a reliable message transmission (RMT) and communicate their shares to P_j in a privacy-free manner.

However, one must take care within this RMT phase. Despite the lack of private inputs, revealing information about the *graph topology* may enable an adversary to adaptively corrupt a cut and disconnect the honest connected component. Unfortunately, there is no known protocol for achieving RMT in Erdös–Rényi graphs with the necessary form of topology hiding.

To fix this issue, we observe that in the context of low-locality MPC, nothing forces us to have the parties communicate their shares within the same graph used to generate them. We implement the semi-honest RMT by augmenting the hidden graph with a fixed, *publicly known* cycle $C = \text{①} - \text{②} - \cdots - \text{ⓝ} - \text{①}$ between the parties (a 1-connected path would also suffice). The parties send and sum their shares along the (fixed) path of length $n - 1$ from P_{j+1} to P_j.

Ultimately, the communication graph of our protocol operates in the union of the two graphs, the Erdös–Rényi graph and the cycle C, and remains this way throughout the course of any (polynomially many) executions of SFE. The role of the Erdös–Rényi graph is to protect the privacy of secret messages; in turn, its topology must remain hidden. We prove that this hiding is preserved as long as the honest parties form a single connected component, in which case the "DC net" messages appear simply as random values independent of the graph structure. And further, as long as the topology is hidden, then with overwhelming probability the adversary will not be able to disconnect the honest component. The role of the cycle graph C, in contrast, is to enable communication of *public* values. As such, there is no issue with the graph being disconnected by (semi-honest) corruptions, and hence its identity need not be hidden. Collectively, the two parts combined translates to the required form of distributionally topology-hiding protocol for the joint graph class of the Erdös–Rényi graph and the cycle C.

1.1.2 Computational Security Against Fail-Stop Adversaries.

Note that the information-theoretic "topology-hiding" protocol above completely breaks if the adversary can crash parties. Although the Erdös–Rényi graph is kept hidden, the cycle C (that is used as a privacy-free RMT channel) is publicly known, so the adversary can disconnect it by crashing any one of the parties. This demonstrates the challenge of combining adaptive security and sublinear locality: where if the adversary obtains enough leakage on the underlying (sub)graph, and identifies a sublinear cut, it can crash all parties on the cut and disconnect the graph. This calls for a drastically different approach from the semi-honest case.

Our second result achieves reusable MPC facing adaptive fail-stop adversaries. We do so by constructing a similar flavour of "topology-hiding" broadcast (THB) in the spirit of [8]), albeit in the computational setting and with partial information *leakage* about the underlying graph. Fortunately, we show that this leakage is sufficiently benign, and still enables sequential executions. This ends up requiring a delicate balance and analysis, ensuring at each step that: (1) If the graph still retains certain structural properties given the current state of corruptions and crashes, then the amount of leakage on the graph structure can be appropriately bounded; (2) Given this nontrivial amount of leakage, then with high probability the adversary will still be unable to violate the corresponding graph property. We defer a deeper discussion to the Technical Overview.

Theorem 2 (Computational fail-stop). *Let $n \in \mathbb{N}$, let $0 < \varepsilon < 1/2$ be a constant, and let $t = \varepsilon n$. Assume the existence of adaptively secure (semi-honest) oblivious transfer. There exist a reusable n-party SFE protocol against PPT adaptive fail-stop t-adversaries with computational security in the plain model and over hidden channels, maintaining $\widetilde{O}(n^{2/3})$ locality.*

It is instructive to compare our results with the lower bounds of Chandran et al. [23]. They showed that secure data erasures are essential for a certain class of low-locality communication protocols; namely, "store-and-forward" protocols, which are a type flooding protocols in which the message identifies the sender (as used by [21]). These protocols are vulnerable to a fail-stop adversary that can passively corrupt a random subset of the parties, and after learning the message trace back and crash parties all the way back to the sender. For this reason, [21] required that when a party P_i starts sending messages to the network, the adversary cannot corrupt P_i until all recipients obtain the messages and until P_i erased the identity of the recipients from its state (*i.e.* atomic-multisend and data erasures in one atomic operation). Chandran et al. [23] used

552   E. Boyle et al.

heavy machinery, combining non-committing encryption (NCE) and fully homomorphic encryption (FHE) in a clever way, to hide the sender's identity from the message and avoid this attack without assuming atomic-multisend and data erasures. Our protocols also do not assume atomic-multisend and data erasures, by using a different approach, based on topology-hiding computation. See Table 1 for a summary of our results and a comparison to prior work.

Table 1. Summary of our results and comparison to prior work.

	adversary	locality	max rounds	assumptions	setup	erasures	atomic multisend
[21]	malicious	$\tilde{O}(n^{1/2})$	$o(n)$	NCE	PKI	✓	✓
[21]	malicious	polylog(n)	$o(n)$	NCE	PKI + SKI	✓	✓
[14]	malicious	polylog(n)	$o(n)$	NCE	PKI + SKI	✓	✓
[23]	malicious	polylog(n)	$o(n)$	NCE	PKI + SKI	✓	✗
[23]	malicious	polylog(n)	$o(n)$	NCE + FHE	PKI + SKI	✗	✗
this work	semi-honest	polylog(n)	**any poly(n)**	-	-	✗	✗
	fail-stop	$\tilde{O}(n^{2/3})$	**any poly(n)**	adaptive OT	-	✗	✗

Organisation of the Paper. In Sect. 2 we present a technical overview of our fail-stop protocol. Preliminaries can be found in Sect. 3. Reusable MPC is defined in Sect. 4 and reduced to the relevant communication functionalities. Distributional THC is discussed in Sect. 5, and our main technical result, of a distributional THB gainst fail-stop adversaries is presented and analyzed in Sect. 6. Due to space limitation, we defer some of the definitions and proofs to the full version of the paper.

2   Technical Overview

We proceed to describe our techniques, focusing on the more challenging fail-stop result.

Reusable MPC. We begin by formally defining the notion of reusable and adaptively secure MPC with sublinear locality, *i.e.* a protocol that can be executed sequentially an unbounded (polynomial) number of times while ensuring security and sublinear locality. Our notion is different than the modular composition of Canetti [17], which guarantees that if a protocol satisfies its security definition, then it can be executed sequentially for an unbounded number of times. As opposed to [17] that ensures "local" properties (security of each protocol on its own when executed sequentially), we require a "global" property, sublinear locality, which must be maintained across all instances. Clearly, requiring each execution on its own to have sublinear locality only suffices to support a sublinear number of executions.

Toward this goal, in Sect. 4 we follow and extend the ideas from [8]. We define an ideal reactive SFE functionality, such that given any q polynomial in

λ and any vector of n-party functions $\mathbf{f} = (f^1, \ldots, f^q)$, the functionality $\mathcal{F}_{\mathsf{sfe}}^{\mathbf{f}}$ operates in q phases, where the jth phase acts like a (standard) SFE of f^j. We allow adaptive corruptions at any point during the ideal computation. In the real world, we consider a generic SFE protocol π that is executed q times sequentially, where the jth execution is for computing f^j; we denote this protocol by $\pi^{\mathbf{f}}$. Finally, we require that for every q that is polynomial in λ and any vector of n-party functions $\mathbf{f} = (f^1, \ldots, f^q)$, the protocol $\pi^{\mathbf{f}}$ securely realises $\mathcal{F}_{\mathsf{sfe}}^{\mathbf{f}}$.

Topology-Hiding Computation (THC). Our main technical tool for realising reusable and adaptively secure MPC with sublinear locality is topology-hiding computation (THC) [45]. These are MPC protocols that operate over an incomplete communication graph, where, in addition to providing input privacy, the topology of the graph is also kept hidden. Specifically, every party knows its own neighbour set, and the view of the adversary can be simulated given the corrupted parties' inputs, outputs, and neighbour sets. A long line of work on THC provided strong feasibility results in the semi-honest setting, *e.g.* [2,3,6–9,40,45].

Ball et al. [8] observed that the standard definition of THC [45] is too strong to be used within adaptively secure MPC in the dynamic-graph setting (as long as the graph is sufficiently sparse, *e.g.* contains a sublinear cut), as this security notion aims to protect against *worst-case* graphs. In this setting, the environment knows the graphs and can signal the adversary which parties to corrupt in order to disconnect the graph. For this reason, [8] put forth the weaker notion of *distributional THC*, where the environment is only aware of the distribution from which the graph is sampled, but not of the actual graph. This is the notion of THC we utilise in this work.

Reusable MPC from Distributional TH Broadcast. The first step toward proving Theorem 2, is reducing the problem of reusable SFE to that of distributional THB. We do so in three steps:

- (*Reusable BC $\Rightarrow$ Reusable SFE*). First, we show that reusable SFE can be realised given reusable broadcast. That is, in a hybrid model where a reactive ideal functionality supports an unbounded number of broadcast operations. This reduction is computationally secure and assumes the existence of adaptively secure key agreement, which is used to generate (over broadcast) a sufficiently long key for one-time pad (OTP) between every pair of parties. Next, given a (standard) honest-majority adaptively secure SFE, *e.g.* [28,29], the parties can send their sensitive messages over broadcast by encrypting them with OTP, which is a symmetric variant of non-committing encryption.
- (*Reusable Distrib-THB $\Rightarrow$ Reusable BC*). Second, we show that reusable broadcast can be realised with locality $\tilde{O}(n^{2/3})$ given distributional, topology-hiding version of reusable broadcast, where the graph distribution samples an Erdös–Rényi graph with parameter $p = n^{-1/3} \cdot \log^2 n$ and where the adversary can ask for leakage about the graph. The specific leakage function Leak is as follows: the simulator may query up to $p^{-2} \log^2 n$ pairs of sets $(S_1, S_2) \in 2^{[n]} \times 2^{[n]}$, and get in return the number of edges in the initial graph (before all crashes) from the set $S_1 \times S_2$. We note that this reduction

translates between two models: the first is the dynamic-graph model where each party can communicate with each other party and the graph evolves over time, and the second is the distributional THC model in which the graph is fixed but hidden.

Initially, the parties execute the hidden-graph sampling from [21,22,24] to agree on their neighbour sets, and later they run the distributional THB protocol while communicating with their neighbour sets and ignoring all other edges.

- (*1-time Distrib-THB $\Rightarrow$ Reusable Distrib-THB*). Third, we show that a distributional, topology-hiding version of reusable broadcast, can be realised with given distributional, topology-hiding version of single-shot broadcast, with the same graph distribution and same leakage. This is based on a hybrid argument in which we additionally show that the specific leakage we consider does not accumulate too much over polynomially many sequential executions.

The remaining task is to construct a distributional THB protocol (for one instance of broadcast) against fail-stop adversaries for the Erdös–Rényi distribution with parameter $p = n^{-1/3} \log^2 n$ and the leakage Leak (described above). This is what we next describe.

2.1   The Distributional THB Protocol

As an initial starting point, consider the trivial protocol of *flooding broadcast*: in the first round, the broadcaster sends the message to its neighbours; then, in successive rounds, each party forwards the message to their neighbours when they receive it for the first time. While this protocol can indeed be run in an "unknown topology" setting (*i.e.* it does not require the parties to know the graph beyond their neighbourhoods), it is however very much *not* topology-hiding. Specifically, each party learns:

- *Distance:* their own distance d to the broadcaster (they receive the message in round d).
- *Direction:* which of their neighbours are at distance $d-1$ from the broadcaster (these are the parties from whom he will receive the message).

Such leakage about the topology can be devastating, as the adversary could *e.g.* corrupt a certain number of parties uniformly at random, learn the identities of neighbours which are one step closer to the broadcaster, corrupt them, and iterate until they reach neighbours of the broadcaster. Indeed, this is precisely the intuition of the lower bound from [23]. Given sufficiently many corruptions, all neighbours of the honest broadcaster will be uncovered this way, and their crashing would disconnect the broadcaster from the network.

"Secure Flooding." A variation on the above flooding protocol can limit this leakage to each party learning just their *own* distance from the broadcaster. Instead of forwarding the message directly, in every round each party performs an MPC with their neighbours which reveals the message to the center party if and only if at least one neighbour knows it. This process can be performed without revealing any information about the central party's degree or neighbour set to the participating parties (see, e.g., [45] and Sect. 6.2). After each iteration of this process, the message reaches parties one hop further from the broadcaster, while hiding the direction from which it was received.

This raises a promising idea: if each party can already infer their exact distance to the broadcaster from their local view of the network alone, then this simple protocol of "flooding enhanced with local MPC" would already be distributionally topology-hiding. For instance, in an $\mathsf{ER}(n, p)$ graph with $p = \omega(\frac{\log n}{\sqrt{n}})$, the diameter is at most 2 with all but negligible probability, so each party initially knows its own distance from every other party.

Unfortunately, leaking each party's distance from the broadcaster is still too much leakage. The source of failure is that adaptive crashes can modify the distance between parties in ways that depend on unknown portions of the graph. Indeed, if the adversary passively corrupts a node $\textcircled{u}$, thereby learning its neighbourhood, then corrupts and crashes all but one of its neighbours $\textcircled{v}$ (which remains honest) (see Fig. 1 for a visual summary of this attack): an honest broadcaster is at distance 2 from $\textcircled{u}$ if and only if it is a neighbour of $\textcircled{v}$. If the adversary were allowed to learn u's distance from each of the honest parties, taking turns acting as broadcasters, the adversary would learn the entire neighbourhood of the honest party v.

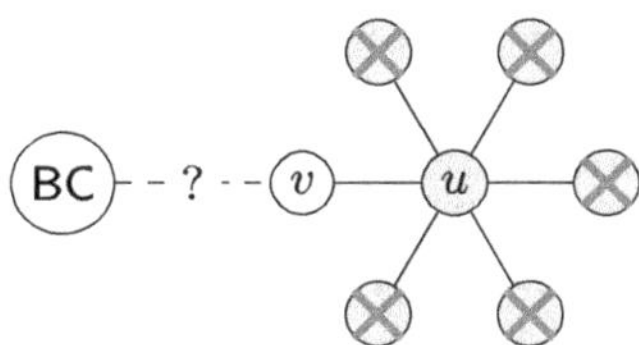

Fig. 1. "Low degree attack": the distance of corrupt u to every possible honest broadcaster BC reveals exactly honest v's neighbourhood.

Excluding Low-degree Parties. Fortunately, there is a way to immunise a protocol against this type of attack. The main idea is that, provided the adversary is not given too much information beyond the corrupted parties' neighbourhoods (specifically, only $o(np)$ bits of leakage on the hidden Erdös–Rényi graph), the adversary cannot identify and thus cannot corrupt more than a constant fraction of an honest party's neighbourhood.

(Informal) Core Lemma 1 (Honest parties have many honest neighbours). *Let $\varepsilon, \delta > 0$. An adversary learning an (n, p)-Erdös–Rényi graph by making up to $t < \varepsilon n$ neighbourhood queries cannot identify $(1 + \delta) \cdot tp$ neighbours of an unqueried node with probability better than $2^{-\mathcal{O}(tp)}$. This probability remains negligible (in n) if the adversary is additionally allowed to make $o(np)$ arbitrary single-bit queries.*

This implies that any party with too many crashed neighbours must (with overwhelming probability) be corrupted, and we are under no obligation to ensure they receive the broadcast message. If we instruct each party to regularly ping their neighbours for a heartbeat, and simply cease any and all communication (which we will refer to as a "self-crash") if too few respond, a party will only learn its distance from the broadcaster if it still has $\Omega(np)$ live neighbours.

The Protocol. The candidate protocol is now to perform "secure flooding" as described above for a given number of iterations (the analysis will show that $t+3$ rounds are sufficient to achieve consistency amongst the honest parties), but with the restriction that at every round each party pings all of its neighbours, then "crashes itself" if it received fewer than δnp such pings itself, where $\delta := \frac{1+\varepsilon}{2}$ (where $\varepsilon > 0$ is the corruption threshold fraction). As it turns out, this relatively simple protocol works, and can be simulated given roughly $1/p^2$ bits of leakage about the graph (ignoring polylogarithmic factors for now). If we choose p such that $1/p^2 = o(np)$ (which translates to locality $\widetilde{\mathcal{O}}(n^{2/3})$), then this leakage will indeed not allow the adversary to corrupt too many neighbours of an honest party.

While the protocol itself is seemingly simple in retrospect, its analysis requires significant care.

2.2   Correctness and Consistency

In order to analyse the protocol's correctness (and determine how many rounds of flooding are required), it is convenient to consider the "flooding trace" of an execution. This is the directed graph, defined after the protocol has terminated, with an edge from u to v if and only if party u ever sent the broadcast message to v (even if u subsequently crashed). Note that the receivers who ever received the message are exactly those who can be reached from the sender—and furthermore, the round in which they received the message is their distance from the sender in the graph (where by "round" here we refer to hops of message communication via the local neighbourhood MPCs). Note in the fail-stop model, parties will never forward an incorrect message: Thus, consistency holds precisely if this set of receiving parties includes either every honest party or none of them.

Assume at least one honest party holds the message by the end of the protocol (either, in the case of the broadcaster, because it held it initially, or, for the other parties, because it was delivered to them in the course of the protocol), and let k be the earliest round in which this happened. There must therefore be an honest party u such that the shortest path from the sender to u exists and is of length k. By minimality of k, all nodes on this path, including the broadcaster but excluding u (unless u is also the broadcaster), must be corrupted. Therefore $k-1 \leq t$. This implies that if the message was ever delivered to an honest party,[1] it was within the first $t+1$ rounds.

---

[1] More precisely: to a party who will not have been corrupted by the end of the protocol.

Once this first honest party got the message, it sent the message to all its honest neighbours,[2] who then sent it to all their honest neighbours. As it turns out, provided the adversary is only ever given $o(np)$ bits of leakage about the graph, it will (with overwhelming probability) not succeed in increasing the distance between any pair of honest parties beyond two. Skipping ahead, however, the security proof will require a slightly stronger version of this statement: any party with $\Omega(np)$ honest neighbours (which with overwhelming probability includes any honest party, by (Informal) Core Lemma 1) must, despite the adversarially caused crashes, be at distance at most two from all honest parties.

(Informal) Core Lemma 2. (Parties with $\Omega(np)$ honest neighbours are within two hops of every honest party). *Let $\varepsilon, \delta > 0$. Consider an adversary learning an (n, p)-Erdős–Rényi graph by making up to $t < \varepsilon n$ neighbourhood queries. Let u be an unqueried node, and let v be a node whose neighbourhood contains at $\Omega(np)$ unqueried nodes (v itself may or may not have been queried). The probability that all the common neighbours between u and v have been queried is at most $2^{-\mathcal{O}(tp)}$. This probability remains negligible (in n) if the adversary is additionally allowed to make $o(np)$ arbitrary single-bit queries.*

2.3 Leakage Analysis

All that remains is showing that our protocol can indeed be simulated with $\widetilde{\mathcal{O}}(1/p^2)$ bits of leakage, even after polynomially many instances of the broadcast protocol, possibly with different broadcasters.

Correctly simulating the protocol boils down to determining each corrupted receiver's output from each of the "neighbourhood MPCs". Note that if a party has fewer than $\delta \cdot np$ live neighbours (we will call such parties "low-degree"), they do not get such an output. However, simulating the views of the other corrupted parties (which we will call "high-degree") requires determining dynamically—as the graph changes with adaptive crashes—which parties are supposed to receive the message in which round.

Our simulation strategy is to juggle between two facts. On the one hand, we show that while the leakage remains bounded by $o(np)$, a certain number of invariants about the graph (*e.g.* that any pair of honest parties will be at distance at most 2) hold with all but negligible probability, and that these invariants are enough to simulate the distance between *almost every pair* of nodes. On the other hand, we show that the pairs of parties whose distance *cannot* be simulated in this way form a specific kind of sparse subgraph. This subgraph is so sparse in fact, that we can show that (n, p) Erdős–Rényi graphs do not admit such structures of size larger than $O(p^{-2} \log^2 n)$. This allows us to argue that (regardless of how the adversary chooses which nodes to corrupt), the simulator will never need more than $\widetilde{O}(p^{-2}) \ll np$ bits of leakage to simulate the protocol, regardless of how many rounds it runs for.

We refer to Sect. 6 for the technical details of our protocol and its analysis.

---

[2] Recall that with overwhelming probability honest parties cannot "self-crash" due to having low degree, so an honest party will indeed send the message to its neighbours.

3   Preliminaries

Notations. For $n \in \mathbb{N}$, let $[n] = \{1, \cdots, n\}$. We denote by λ the security parameter. Let $G = (V, E)$ be an undirected graph of size n, *i.e.* $|V| = n$. The *(open) neighbourhood* of a vertex v in an undirected graph G, denoted $\mathcal{N}_G(v)$, is the set of vertices sharing an edge with v in G. The *closed neighbourhood* of v in G is in turn defined by $\mathcal{N}_G[v] := \mathcal{N}_G(v) \cup \{v\}$.

MPC Model. We consider multiparty protocols in the synchronous model; we require security with guaranteed output delivery and that security remains under sequential composition. We elaborate on the model in Sect. 4.1, and refer the reader to [17,38] for a precise definition of the model. Throughout the paper we assume semi-honest or fail-stop adversaries, that do not deviate from the protocol specification, but might crash. We will consider *adaptive* corruptions, where the adversary can dynamically corrupt parties during the protocol execution, learn their internal state, and potentially crash them (in case of a fail-stop adversary). In addition, we will consider both PPT adversaries (in the fail-stop setting) and computationally unbounded adversaries (in the semi-honest setting).

Recall that in the synchronous model protocols proceed in rounds, where every round consists of a *send phase* followed by a *receive phase*. The adversary is assumed to be *rushing*, meaning that it can obtain the messages sent by the honest parties *before* sending the messages for corrupted parties; this enables the adversary to corrupt additional parties learn their state, and potentially crash them, before sending the corrupted parties' messages. We assume a complete network of point-to-point channels (broadcast is not assumed), where every party has the ability to send a message to every other party. Similarly to [14,21,23], we consider *hidden* channels, where the adversary does not get to see messages exchanged between two honest parties, and not even know whether two honest parties have communicated or not.

We do not consider *secure data erasures* nor the *atomic-multisend model* (also referred to as a weakly adaptive adversary). This means that the adversary can corrupt a party at any point during the protocol (even when it is in the middle of sending messages) and drop messages that were not delivered yet; once corrupted, the adversary learns the entire state of the party, including its input, randomness, incoming messages, and setup information (if relevant). This is the standard model for adaptive corruptions in MPC [18,19,33] (also referred to as a strongly rushing adversary). We refer the reader to a further discussion in [23,27,36,41].

4   Reusable and Adaptively Secure MPC

In this section, we define *reusable* and adaptively secure MPC and present simple reductions to reusable communication tasks.

4.1 Reusable and Adaptively Secure MPC with Low Locality

We start by formulating our notion of an MPC protocol that is secure under (unbounded) sequential composition. Although [17] already considers sequential composition with adaptive corruptions by specifying requirements on each protocol on its own, our notion is different as we require sublinear locality, which is a global property to be maintained jointly across all instances. Clearly, requiring each protocol to maintain sublinear locality independently on its own can only support sequential composition of sublinear many instances.

Toward that end, we adjust the ideal computation from [17] for secure function evaluation of a single function, to an ideal sequential computation of a vector of functions $\mathbf{f} = (f^1, \ldots, f^q)$, for an arbitrary q (which is polynomial in the security parameter), and for arbitrary (efficiently computable) n-party functions $f^1, \ldots, f^q$. We denote this reactive functionality by $\mathcal{F}^{\mathbf{f}}_{\mathsf{sfe}}$. We consider sequential composition by the *same* set of parties. In our definitions below, we will say that an n-party protocol π is a *generic SFE protocol* if for every efficiently computable function $f : (\{0,1\}^*)^n \to (\{0,1\}^*)^n$, the protocol π parameterised with f securely realises the "single-shot" (standard) ideal functionality $\mathcal{F}^{f}_{\mathsf{sfe}}$.

Real-World Computation. In a nutshell, given an n-party generic SFE protocol π and a vector of n-party functions $\mathbf{f} = (f^1, \ldots, f^q)$, we denote by $\pi^{\mathbf{f}}$ the protocol that is obtained by sequentially executing π for q instances, where the jth execution is parameterised with f^j. That is, the protocol $\pi^{\mathbf{f}}$ operates in q phases, where for $j \in [q]$, the jth phase begins where every party P_i obtains its input $x_i^j \in \{0,1\}^*$ from the environment; next, the parties start interacting with one another over the specified communication network (as discussed in Sect. 3); finally, every honest party outputs an output value y_i^j to the environment, and the following phase begins.

The adaptive adversary Adv can corrupt a party at any point during the computation, but is restricted to corrupt at most t parties. Once the adversary corrupts a party, Env learns the identity of the corrupted party and hands some extra auxiliary information to Adv. Once all q phases complete, the environment may send "corrupt P_i" requests to the adversary in the post-execution corruption stage, and the interaction continues until Env halts with an arbitrary output.

Ideal-World Computation. Let $\mathbf{f} = (f^1, \ldots, f^q)$ be a vector of length q of n-party functions to compute, where $f^j : (\{0,1\}^*)^n \to (\{0,1\}^*)^n$. The ideal reactive functionality for computing $\mathbf{f}$ for parties $(P_1, \ldots, P_n)$ is denoted $\mathcal{F}^{\mathbf{f}}_{\mathsf{sfe}}$. The ideal computation sequentially executes q phases, where for every $j \in [q]$, the jth phase proceeds by having every party P_i get its input $x_i^j \in \{0,1\}^*$ from Env and forward it to the ideal functionality. If the adversary is fail-stop, it can crash parties, and the ideal functionality uses default values for the crashed parties who do not provide inputs. The functionality hands the adversary some leakage on the honest parties' inputs, which by default is just the input length $|x_i^j|$ (although for the communication functionalities discussed below the leakage is more substantial). Next, the functionality samples $r_f^j \leftarrow \{0,1\}^*$, computes $(y_1^j, \ldots, y_n^j) = f^j(x_1^j, \ldots, x_n^j; r_f^j)$, and sends y_i^j to party P_i.

The adversary can corrupt a party at any point during the computation, but is restricted to corrupt at most t parties. The environment Env starts with auxiliary information z and once the adversary corrupts a party, Env learns the identity of the corrupted party and hands some extra auxiliary information to Adv. Finally, once all q computations have completed, Adv and Env proceed to the *post-execution corruption (PEC)*, and the interaction continues until Env halts with an arbitrary output.

Security requires that for every real-world adversary there exists and ideal-world adversary (a simulator) such that no environment can distinguish between the two worlds. Formal security definition can be found in the full version.

Communication Locality. The communication locality [14,16] of a protocol corresponds to the maximal degree of any honest party in the communication graph induced by the protocol execution. We consider both incoming communication edges and outgoing communication edges. Note that as we do not consider malicious adversaries, corrupted parties *cannot* "spam" honest parties. In the full version we adjust the definition from [14] to our setting, and refer the reader to [14] for further discussions.

4.2   Semi-honest: Reusable MPC from All-to-All SMT

Having defined reusable MPC, we state (and prove in the full version) a simple reduction of reusable and adaptively secure MPC in the semi-honest setting with information-theoretic security to the task of reusable secure all-to-all communication; namely, realizing an arbitrarily polynomially many instances of *secure message transmission* (SMT) channels between every pair of parties. For q which is polynomial in λ, we denote this functionality by $\mathcal{F}_{\mathsf{psmt}}^q$. This reduction follows immediately by the adaptive security for single-shot computations of the seminal BGW protocol for $t < n/2$ over secure channels [10] (see also [4,5,30]).

Looking ahead, in Sect. 5.2, we will show how to instantiate $\mathcal{F}_{\mathsf{psmt}}^q$ for any q that is polynomial in λ with adaptive security and sublinear locality.

4.3   Fail-Stop: Reusable MPC from Broadcast

For the fail-stop setting, in the full version we present another simple reduction of reusable and adaptively secure MPC to a different communication task: instantiating a reusable broadcast channel, denoted $\mathcal{F}_{\mathsf{bc}}^q$ for any q that is polynomial in λ. This is accomplished by starting with a generic, adaptively secure honest-majority MPC protocol that may communicate over pairwise secure channels and/or via a broadcast channel, *e.g.* [28,29], and encrypting and broadcasting every message that is intendant to be sent over a secure channel. The encryption must also be adaptively secure, so we use an *adaptively secure key agreement* protocol [19], that will be run over the broadcast channel, to establish a sufficiently long random string between every pair of parties and encrypt all communication with a one-time pad. We do not require the broadcast functionality to be corruption-fair [27], meaning that we allow the adversary to first learn an honest sender input (before any honest party) and based on this information corrupt the sender and crash it, preventing the honest parties from ever receiving this message. This is ok in our setting, as every sensitive message that is being broadcasted is first encrypted.

Looking ahead, in Sect. 5.3 and Sect. 6, we will show how to instantiate $\mathcal{F}_{\mathsf{bc}}^q$ for any q that is polynomial in λ with adaptive security and sublinear locality.

5 Distributional Topology-Hiding Computation

In this section, we define our main tool for establishing reusable MPC with sublinear locality: distributional topology-hiding computation.

5.1 Distributional Topology-Hiding Computation

We begin by recalling the definition of distributional THC from [8], who focused on the semi-honest setting with information-theoretic security. We extend the definition to the fail-stop setting with leakage and computational security. Recall that [8] observed that the standard definition of THC [45] is too strong to be used within adaptively secure MPC in the *dynamic graph* setting (as long as the graph is sufficiently sparse, *e.g.* contains a sublinear cut), as this security notion aims to protect against *worst-case* graphs; in this setting, the environment knows the graphs and can signal the adversary which parties to corrupt in order to disconnect the graph. For this reason, [8] put forth the notion of distributional THC, where the environment is only aware of the distribution from which the graph is sampled, but not of the actual graph.

In the setting of "classical" THC [45], the communication graph is fixed but hidden from the protocol. This is captured by an ideal communication functionality, where a special "graph party" forwards the actual graph from the environment to the functionality. The functionality provides each party with its neighbour set, and is in charge of the message delivery (*i.e.* when receiving a message from some P_i to a party P_j, the functionality will forward the message if the parties are neighbours). In contrast, in the setting of distributional THC, the communication functionality samples the graph on its own. To better support compositional capabilities of this notion, [8] allowed the environment to obtain the communication graph before making its decision real/ideal; similarly to classical THC, the communication with the environment is done via the special "graph party" P_{graph}. Once the environment asks for the graph, the communication functionality enters an "out of order" state and stops processing other messages. Ball et al. [8] focused on the semi-honest setting with information-theoretic security (in the plain model), and proved that distributional THC is a non-trivial notion that is indeed weaker than classical THC.

The ideal-model computation of a functionality $\mathcal{F}$ needs to be augmented to provide the simulator with the appropriate information on the graph, *e.g.*

the neighbour-set of each corrupted party. Toward this purpose, [8] defined a *graph-information wrapper* functionality around $\mathcal{F}$, denoted $\mathcal{W}^{\mathcal{D}}_{\text{dist}-\text{graph}-\text{info}}(\mathcal{F})$. Initially, the wrapper samples a graph from the distribution and provides every corrupted party with the neighbour-set; importantly, honest parties do not obtain their neighbour-sets unless adaptively corrupted. The reason is that otherwise, the environment (that immediately learns every value an honest party receives from the ideal functionality) will learn all neighbour-sets, and so will learn the entire graph. All other input messages are forwarded to $\mathcal{F}$ and all messages from $\mathcal{F}$ are delivered to their intendant recipients. We augment the wrapper functionality to be parameterised with a leakage function $\mathsf{Leak}(\cdot)$ and a bound B; the adversary is permitted to ask for leakage queries that are responded by applying the leakage function on the state of the functionality for up to B times. If there is no leakage (*i.e.* if the function $\ell(\cdot)$ always returns $\perp$), we omit its notation from the functionality.

In the full version we extend the definition of the *distributional graph communication* to capture fail-stop adversaries and leakage.

5.2   Semi-honest Distributional TH All-to-All Communication

In the full version, we realise the reusable parallel SMT functionality $\mathcal{F}^q_{\mathsf{psmt}}$ (for an arbitrary q) using a distributional TH-SMT protocol. As discussed in the introduction, we will use an Erdös–Rényi distribution, denoted $\mathcal{D}_{\mathsf{ER}}(n,p)$, where every edge appears in the graph with probability p augmented with a fixed and known cycle $C = ① - ② - \cdots - ⓝ - ①$.

5.3   Fail-Stop Distributional TH Broadcast

The semi-honest protocol completely fails facing fail-stop corruptions, as the adversary can crash the *unhidden* cycle used for broadcast. As discussed in the introduction, our approach in the fail-stop setting is different and more technically involved. In the full version we define the leakage function $\mathsf{Leak}(\cdot)$ and present two reductions: the first is realizing $\mathcal{F}^q_{\mathsf{bc}}$ from $\mathcal{W}^{\mathcal{D}_{\mathsf{ER}}(n,p),\mathsf{Leak},B}_{\text{dist}-\text{graph}-\text{info}}(\mathcal{F}^q_{\mathsf{bc}})$, and the second is realizing $\mathcal{W}^{\mathcal{D}_{\mathsf{ER}}(n,p),\mathsf{Leak},B}_{\text{dist}-\text{graph}-\text{info}}(\mathcal{F}^q_{\mathsf{bc}})$ from $\mathcal{W}^{\mathcal{D}_{\mathsf{ER}}(n,p),\mathsf{Leak},B}_{\text{dist}-\text{graph}-\text{info}}(\mathcal{F}_{\mathsf{bc}})$. In Sect. 6, we will instantiate $\mathcal{W}^{\mathcal{D}_{\mathsf{ER}}(n,p),\mathsf{Leak}}_{\text{dist}-\text{graph}-\text{info}}(\mathcal{F}_{\mathsf{bc}})$; this proves of our second main result, Theorem 2.

6   Adaptively Secure Distributional THB

In Sect. 6.1 we describe our distributional THB protocol in a hybrid model where for every party, the neighbourhood of the party can use an ideal functionality to ideally compute "conditional OR." In Sect. 6.2, we realise this ideal functionality over a star-shape topology.

6.1   Distributional THB in the Neighbourhood MPC Hybrid Model
6.1.1   The Protocol

Protocol Distributional topology-hiding broadcast Π_{BC}

Parties: $P_1, \ldots, P_n$

Parameters: The protocol is parameterised with

1. a number of parties n,
2. a constant $\varepsilon \in (0,1)$ defining the corruption threshold $t \leq \varepsilon n$,
3. a sender index $i^\star \in [n]$,
4. a broadcast message space $\mathcal{M}$ and a special symbol $\perp \notin \mathcal{M}$,
5. the "conditional OR" function $\mathsf{condOR} \colon (\mathcal{M} \cup \{\perp\})^{D+1} \to \mathcal{M} \cup \{\perp\}$ is defined as follows:
    - If condOR is given fewer than $D+1$ inputs, it outputs $\perp$;
    - Otherwise, if all the inputs to condOR are $\perp$, it outputs $\perp$;
    - Otherwise, if all of the inputs in $\mathcal{M}$ are equal, it outputs this common value $m \in \mathcal{M}$;
    - Otherwise (it received at least two different inputs from $\mathcal{M}$), it outputs $\perp$.

Given the above parameters, we further define:

1. $p \leftarrow n^{-1/3} \log^2 n$ // Erdős–Rényi parameter
2. $D \leftarrow \frac{1+\varepsilon}{2} np$ // threshold for a party to be considered "high-degree"

Let $(\mathsf{sid}_{u,r})_{u \in [n], r \in [t+3]}$ be $n(t+3)$ distinct session IDs.
// identifies P_u's "neighbourhood MPC" in the rth round of flooding

Hybrid Model: $(\mathcal{F}_{\mathsf{dist\text{-}graph}}^{\mathsf{ER}(n,p)}, \mathcal{F}_{\mathsf{star\text{-}SFE}})$

Inputs: The sender $P_{i^\star}$ holds as input a message $m \in \mathcal{M}$.

The Protocol: Each party P_i (with $i \in [n]$) does the following:

- **_Initialisation Phase:_**
    1. Send an initialisation message to $\mathcal{F}_{\mathsf{dist\text{-}graph}}^{\mathsf{ER}(n,p)}$, and wait to receive a neighbourhood
    2. Initialise $\mathsf{live\text{-}ctr}_i \leftarrow 0$ // Counter used to track the number of...
       // ...live neighbours in each heartbeat phase
    3. Initialise $\mathsf{high\text{-}degree}_i \leftarrow 1$
    4. Initialise $\mathsf{out}_i \leftarrow \begin{cases} \perp & \text{if } i \neq i^\star \\ m & \text{otherwise} \end{cases}$

Fig. 2. Distributional topology-hiding computation over a class of Erdős–Rényi graphs.

- **Communication Phase:**
  Rounds $1, \ldots, 2n^2(t+3)$:
  // Even rounds are reserved for heartbeats
  // The odd rounds are indexed by $[n] \times [n+1] \times [t+3]$:
  // (1) round $(u,v,r) \in [n] \times [n] \times [t+3]$ is dedicated to P_u's …
  //   …participation in P_v's r^{th} neighbourhood MPC
  // (2) round $(u, n+1, r)$ is a special round dedicated to P_u …
  //   …getting the output of its rth neighbourhood MPC
  - If the round number is even: // Heartbeat
    1. Reset live-ctr$_i \leftarrow 0$
    2. If high-degree$_i$, send $(i,j,0)$ to $\mathcal{F}_{\text{dist-graph}}^{\text{ER}(n,p)}$ for all $j \in \mathcal{N}_G(i)$.
    3. Wait[a] to receive $(i,j,0)$ from $\mathcal{F}_{\text{dist-graph}}^{\text{ER}(n,p)}$ for each $j \in \mathcal{N}_G(i)$; increment live-ctr$_i$ for each such message received.
    4. Update high-degree$_i \leftarrow$ (live-ctr$_i \geq D$)

  - If the round number is of the form $2((u-1)+n(v-1)+n^2(r-1))+1$, with $(u,v,r) \in [n] \times [n] \times [t+3]$:
    // Round dedicated to P_u's (possibly empty)…
    // …contribution to P_v's r^{th} neighbourhood MPC
    If $(i = u) \vee (u \in \mathcal{N}_G(i))$:
        If high-degree$_i$, send $(\text{out}_i, \text{sid}_{u,r})$ to $\mathcal{F}_{\text{star-SFE}}(\text{condOR})$

  - If the round number is of the form $2((u-1)+n^2 r)+1$, with $(u,r) \in [n] \times [t+3]$:
    // Round dedicated to P_u's output from its rth neighbourhood MPC
        Wait to receive a message $(\text{out}, m, \text{sid}_{u,r})$ from $\mathcal{F}_{\text{star-SFE}}(\text{condOR})$ and update out$_i \leftarrow m$

- **Output Phase:** Output out$_i$.

---

[a] Wait until the end of this round's communication phase.

Fig. 2. (*continued*)

Theorem 3. (Distributional THC in the neighbourhood-MPC hybrid model). *Let $\varepsilon \in (0,1)$ be a constant, let $t \leq \varepsilon n$, let $\mathcal{D}$ be the distribution of Erdös–Rényi graphs of parameters (n,p) with $p = n^{1/3} \log^2 n$, let $B = p^{-2} \log^2 n$ (the bound on the number of authorised queries), and let* Leak *be the function which, on input a pair of sets $(S_1, S_2) \in (2^{[n]})^2$, returns the number of edges in $S_1 \times S_2$.*

The protocol of Fig. 2 securely realises $\mathcal{W}_{\text{dist}-\text{graph}-\text{info}}^{\mathcal{D}, \text{Leak}, B}(\mathcal{F}_{\text{BC}})$ (with statistical security) in the $(\mathcal{F}_{\text{graph}}^{\mathcal{D}}, \mathcal{F}_{\text{star}-\text{SFE}}(\text{condOR}))$-hybrid model in the presence of a threshold-t, adaptive, fail-sop adversary.

We refer to the full version of the paper for the proof of Theorem 3. At a high level, this is done by simulating a series of calls to the $\mathcal{F}_{\text{star}-\text{SFE}}(\text{condOR})$ functionality. In order to know what output the corrupted parties should get from an ideal call to this functionality, the simulator estimates the distance of each corrupted party. This is done by running a certain distance estimation algorithm, and making a call to the leakage oracle Leak whenever it fails.

6.1.2   Main Security Arguments

Bounding the Number of Oracle Calls.

Lemma 4. (Bound on the oracle calls made by Sim**).** *Let* Adv *be an adaptive, fail-stop adversary that interacts with parties* $P_1, \ldots, P_n$ *running protocol* Π_{BC} *(Fig. 2) in the* $(\mathcal{F}_{\text{graph}}^{\mathcal{D}}, \mathcal{F}_{\text{star}-\text{SFE}}(\text{condOR}))$*-hybrid model. Let* Sim *be the simulator specified in Theorem 3, which interacts with* $\mathcal{W}_{\text{dist}-\text{graph}-\text{info}}^{\mathcal{D},\text{Leak},+\infty}$ *(the bound* $+\infty$ *means the wrapper does not bound the number of leakage queries it processes).*

The event that Sim *makes at least* $p^{-2} \log^2 n$ *leakage queries to* $\mathcal{W}_{\text{dist}-\text{graph}-\text{info}}^{\mathcal{D},\text{Leak},+\infty}$ *is negligible.*[3]

Proof. Observe that the oracle is never called twice on the same pair (u, i) (where $u, i \in [n]$). Moreover, it only calls the oracle on such a pair if at that point in time (which defines the current flooding prediction graph G_{flooding}):

- i still has $\frac{1+\varepsilon}{2} np$ live neighbours (otherwise **distance** would have terminated on line 1, before making the oracle call of line 11) but fewer than $\frac{1+\varepsilon}{8} np$ honest neighbours in G_{flooding} (otherwise **distance** would have terminated on line 10);
- u is not a neighbour of any of i's corrupted neighbours in G_{flooding} (otherwise **distance** would have terminated on line 9).

We now show there is a negligible probability of the simulator calling the oracle on more than kk' different pairs (u, i), where $k = p^{-1} \log^{1/2} n$ and $k' = p^{-1} \log^{3/2} n$. The only sources of randomness are the coins r_S used by Sim and the coins r_G used to generate the random graph G (note that the oracle itself is deterministic). Fix the randomness (r_S, r_G) and let $\{(u_q, i_q) : q \in \mathcal{Q}\}$ the set of all queries made by the simulator before it terminates.

1. *Claim: there is at most a negligible fraction of the coins for which* $|\{i_q : q \in \mathcal{Q}\}| > k$.
   Let $\mathcal{H}$ be the set of all parties which have not been corrupted by the end of the protocol. The induced subgraph $G[\mathcal{H} \cup \{i_q : q \in \mathcal{Q}\}]$ must have size at least $(1 - \varepsilon)$ (because the adversary Adv can only corrupt up to $t < \varepsilon n$ parties),

---

[3] More precisely, this event is independent of Sim's own randomness tape and occurs with negligible probability over the randomness used to generate the Erdös–Rényi random graph.

and contains at least $|\{i_q : q \in \mathcal{Q}\}|$ nodes with degree at most $\frac{1+\varepsilon}{8}np + k$ (because if party i_q still has more than $\frac{1+\varepsilon}{8}np$ honest neighbours by the end of the protocol, then in particular it would also have had more than $\frac{1+\varepsilon}{8}np$ when it was queried, which is a contradiction). Since asymptotically $\frac{1+\varepsilon}{8}np + k < \frac{1+\varepsilon}{7}np$, we can invoke a lemma proven in the full version, which implies there is only a negligible fraction of the choice of the coins r_G such that $|\{i_q : q \in \mathcal{Q}\}| > k$.

2. *Claim: there is at most a negligible fraction of the coins for which $\exists i \in \{i_q : q \in \mathcal{Q}\}, |\{(u_q, i) : q \in \mathcal{Q}\}| > k'$.*

Let $v = \arg\max_{i \in \{i_q : q \in \mathcal{Q}\}} |\{(u_q, i) : q \in \mathcal{Q}\}|$ (*i.e.* v is one of the nodes for which the simulator has the made the most calls). Denote ℓ the number of queries of the form $(\_, v)$, and let us enumerate these queries $(u_1, v), \ldots, (u_\ell, v)$ in the order they were made. Let $\mathcal{Z}_j$ (resp. $\mathcal{Z}_j$) be the set of live corrupted (resp. honest) neighbours of v at the time query (u_j, v) was made. Observe that:

- $\mathcal{H}_1 \supseteq \cdots \supseteq \mathcal{H}_\ell$ (because a corrupted party cannot later become honest again)
- For every $j \in [\ell - 1]$, $\mathcal{Z}_{j+1} \cap \mathcal{Z}_j \supseteq \mathcal{Z}_{j+1} \cap \overline{\mathcal{H}}_j$. Indeed, any node $x \in \mathcal{Z}_{j+1} \cap \overline{\mathcal{H}}_j$ was still live at the time query (u_{j+1}, v) was made (because $x \in \mathcal{Z}_{j+1}$), so it must have been live when query (u_j, v) was made. The set of live neighbours of v at that time was exactly $\mathcal{Z}_j \cap \overline{\mathcal{H}}_j$. But since $x \in \overline{\mathcal{H}}_j$, this implies that $x \in \mathcal{Z}_j$.

By combining these facts:

$$\bigcap_{j=1}^{\ell} \mathcal{Z}_j = \left(\bigcap_{j=3}^{\ell} \mathcal{Z}_j \right) \cap \underbrace{(\mathcal{Z}_2 \cap \mathcal{Z}_1)}_{\supseteq \mathcal{Z}_2 \cap \overline{\mathcal{H}}_1}$$

$$\supseteq \left(\bigcap_{j=2}^{\ell} \mathcal{Z}_j \right) \cap \overline{\mathcal{H}}_1$$

$$\supseteq \left(\bigcap_{j=4}^{\ell} \mathcal{Z}_j \right) \cap \underbrace{(\mathcal{Z}_3 \cap \mathcal{Z}_2)}_{\supseteq \mathcal{Z}_3 \cap \overline{\mathcal{H}}_2} \cap \overline{\mathcal{H}}_1$$

$$\cdots$$

$$\supseteq \mathcal{Z}_\ell \cap \underbrace{\overline{\mathcal{H}}_{\ell-1} \cap \cdots \cap \overline{\mathcal{H}}_1}_{= \overline{\mathcal{H}}_1}$$

And so $|\bigcap_{j=1}^{\ell} \mathcal{Z}_j| \geq |\mathcal{Z}_\ell \cap \overline{\mathcal{H}}_1| \geq |\mathcal{Z}_\ell| - |\mathcal{H}_1| \geq \frac{1+\varepsilon}{2}np - \frac{1+\varepsilon}{8}np \geq \frac{1+\varepsilon}{4}np$.

Now consider the induced subgraph $G[\left(\bigcap_{j=1}^{\ell} \mathcal{Z}_j\right) \cup \{u_1, \ldots, u_\ell\} \cup \{v\}]$. On the one hand, v has at least $\frac{1+\varepsilon}{4}np$ neighbours in this induced subgraph (by definition of the $\mathcal{Z}_j$, any element of $\bigcap_{j=1}^{\ell} \mathcal{Z}_j$). At the same time, none of the $(u_j)_{j \in [\ell]}$ can be in the 2-neighbourhood of v.[4] By a lemma proven in the full

---

[4] Indeed, suppose there were a party u_j in the 2-neighbourhood of v. Since u_j and v cannot be neighbours (or the query (u_j, v) would never have been made). So

version, such an induced subgraph can only exist for a negligible fraction of the possible coins r_G used to generate the random graph.

By combining the two claims, there is only a negligible probability that the simulator makes more than $kk' = p^{-2} \log^2 n$ calls to the oracle. Therefore, hybrids $\mathcal{H}_1$ and $\mathcal{H}_2$ are indeed statistically indistinguishable.

Correctness of the distance ***Subroutine.*** The main idea behind the subroutine distance is that the simulator, based on the neighbourhoods of the corrupted parties, has perfect knowledge of the "predicted flooding trace graph" G_{flooding} (which is the one the oracle G_{flooding} maintains) up to some distance d away from the sender. This is represented in Fig. 3. The goal of distance is therefore to determine the distance of each corrupted party to the set H_S of the honest parties at distance d from S.

(a) The d-neighbourhood of S in G_k is partitioned as $\mathcal{N}_{G_k}^{(d-1)}(S)$ (the nodes at distance at most $d-1$ from S), H_S (the honest parties at distance exactly d from S), Z_S (the corrupted parties at distance exactly d from S). The (1-)neighbourhood of R is partitioned as H_R (its honest neighbours) and Z_R (its corrupted neighbours).

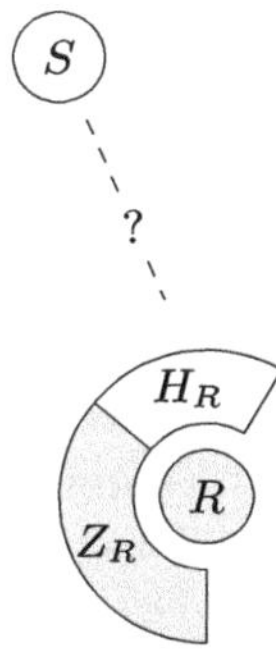

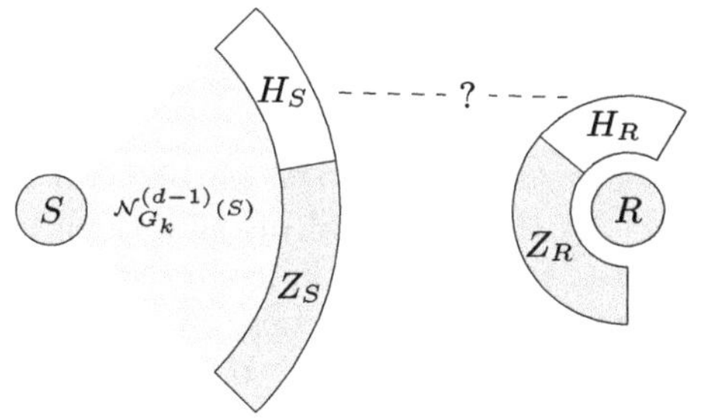

(b) The case where the sender is honest is the special case $d = 0$ (the adversary only has knowledge of the broadcaster, not its neighbourhood) and $H_S = \{S\}$.

Fig. 3. A visual representation of the simulator's partial knowledge of the nodes who have received the message, up to some distance $d \geq 0$ away from the broadcaster S.

Lemma 5. *With the notations of the proof of Theorem 3, the hybrids $\mathcal{H}_{2,t}$ and $\mathcal{H}_{2,t+1}$ are statistically indistinguishable for all $t \in [0, T-1]$.*

We refer to the full version of this paper for the proof of Lemma 5. At a high level, the only difference between these two hybrids is whether the simulator calls the oracle $\mathcal{O}_{\text{predicted-flooding-trace}}$ or runs the subroutine distance for its tth call.

---

they would have to be at distance exactly 2, *i.e.* they have a common neighbour in $S := \left(\bigcap_{j=1}^{\ell} \mathcal{Z}_j\right) \cup \{u_i : i \in [\ell] \setminus \{j\}\}$. Except u_j cannot have a neighbour in $\mathcal{Z}_j \supseteq S$ while v cannot have a neighbour in $\{u_i : i \in [\ell] \setminus \{j\}\} \supseteq S$. This is a contradiction.

One can show, by a case analysis, that there is only a negligible probability that their answers differ. There are ten different cases for what distance can output. In cases $1 - 7$ and 9, the two oracles' outputs are trivially the same, but cases 8 and 10 require non-trivial analysis.

6.2   Instantiating the Hybrid Model

Having the parties perform a "neighbourhood MPC" has been a standard technique of topology-hiding protocols since their inception [45]. If a party u wishes to perform secure computation with its neighbourhood, it issues one-time pseudonyms to its neighbours (so that corrupted parties cannot learn the identities of the honest participants), and simulates "virtual neighbours" in order to pad up its neighbourhood up to some public upper bound (in order to not reveal the degree of u). Note that the simulator knows which corrupted parties participate in which neighbourhood MPCs, as it knows exactly which corrupted parties are neighbours of u.

This solution removes all the topology-hiding aspects of the problem, and we are left to design an adaptively secure fail-stop MPC protocol in a star topology (with a public number of branches). Because we only need to realise functionalities with solitary output to the center u, this is a straightforward task. The parties can use an adaptively secure key-agreement protocol to establish a complete overlay network of secure point-to-point channels (recall that the adversary already knew if two corrupted parties were participating in the same computation, so establishing such channels is not a problem), with the center u acting as a router, passing on unintelligible key-agreement messages.

Once this complete overlay network is established, the parties can use an adaptively secure MPC protocol (*e.g.* [20] that is based on adaptively secure oblivious transfer) to compute the desired function. If the center ever crashes, there is no need to continue because none of the other parties obtains an output anyway (we only deal with solitary output to the center). If one of the other parties crashes, u can simply inform all of its neighbours, and the computation can then be aborted and restarted (note that this can only happens up to $t + 1$ times, so we can set a fixed polynomial upper bound on the number of rounds which should be reserved for each neighbourhood MPC, while still ensuring guaranteed output delivery). Since only corrupted parties can crash (and the simulator therefore knows which neighbourhood MPCs are affected), restarting in this way does not violate the topology-hiding requirement.

Corollary 6. (Distributional Topology-Hiding Computation with Bounded Leakage). *Let $\varepsilon \in (0, 1)$ be a constant, let $t \leq \varepsilon n$, let $p \leftarrow n^{-1/3} \log^2 n$, let $\mathcal{D}$ is the Erdös–Rényi distribution $\mathsf{ER}(n, p)$, let $B \leftarrow p^{-2} \log^2 n$, and let Leak is the function which, on input $(S_1, S_2) \in (2^{[n]})^2$, outputs the number of edges in $S_1 \times S_2$.*

Assuming the existence of adaptive oblivious transfer, there exists a protocol which securely realises $\mathcal{W}_{\mathsf{dist-graph-info}}^{\mathcal{D}, \mathsf{Leak}, B}(\mathcal{F}_{\mathsf{BC}})$ in the $\mathcal{F}_{\mathsf{graph}}^{\mathcal{D}}$-hybrid model.

References

1. Abraham, I., Chan, T.H.H., Dolev, D., Nayak, K., Pass, R., Ren, L., Shi, E.: Communication complexity of byzantine agreement, revisited. In: Robinson, P., Ellen, F. (eds.) 38th ACM PODC, pp. 317–326. ACM (2019). https://doi.org/10.1145/3293611.3331629
2. Akavia, A., LaVigne, R., Moran, T.: Topology-hiding computation on all graphs. In: Katz, J., Shacham, H. (eds.) CRYPTO 2017, Part I. LNCS, vol. 10401, pp. 447–467. Springer, Cham (2017). https://doi.org/10.1007/978-3-319-63688-7_15
3. Akavia, A., Moran, T.: Topology-hiding computation beyond logarithmic diameter. In: Coron, J.S., Nielsen, J.B. (eds.) EUROCRYPT 2017, Part III. LNCS, vol. 10212, pp. 609–637. Springer, Cham (2017). https://doi.org/10.1007/978-3-319-56617-7_21
4. Asharov, G., Cohen, R., Shochat, O.: Static vs. adaptive security in perfect MPC: a separation and the adaptive security of BGW. In: Dachman-Soled, D. (ed.) ITC 2022. LIPIcs, vol. 230, pp. 15:1–15:16. Schloss Dagstuhl (2022). https://doi.org/10.4230/LIPIcs.ITC.2022.15
5. Asharov, G., Lindell, Y.: A full proof of the BGW protocol for perfectly secure multiparty computation. J. Cryptol. **30**(1), 58–151 (2017). https://doi.org/10.1007/s00145-015-9214-4
6. Ball, M., Bienstock, A., Kohl, L., Meyer, P.: Towards topology-hiding computation from oblivious transfer. In: Rothblum, G.N., Wee, H. (eds.) TCC 2023, Part I. LNCS, vol. 14369, pp. 349–379. Springer, Cham (2023). https://doi.org/10.1007/978-3-031-48615-9_13
7. Ball, M., et al.: Topology-hiding communication from minimal assumptions. In: Pass, R., Pietrzak, K. (eds.) TCC 2020, Part II. LNCS, vol. 12551, pp. 473–501. Springer, Cham (2020). https://doi.org/10.1007/978-3-030-64378-2_17
8. Ball, M., Boyle, E., Cohen, R., Malkin, T., Moran, T.: Is information-theoretic topology-hiding computation possible? In: Hofheinz, D., Rosen, A. (eds.) TCC 2019, Part I. LNCS, vol. 11891, pp. 502–530. Springer, Cham (2019). https://doi.org/10.1007/978-3-030-36030-6_20
9. Banoun, D., Boyle, E., Cohen, R.: Information-theoretic topology-hiding broadcast: wheels, stars, friendship, and beyond. In: Aggarwal, D. (ed.) ITC 2024. LIPIcs, vol. 304, pp. 1:1–1:13. Schloss Dagstuhl (2024). https://doi.org/10.4230/LIPIcs.ITC.2024.1
10. Ben-Or, M., Goldwasser, S., Wigderson, A.: Completeness theorems for non-cryptographic fault-tolerant distributed computation (extended abstract). In: 20th ACM STOC, pp. 1–10. ACM Press (1988). https://doi.org/10.1145/62212.62213
11. Bhangale, A., Liu-Zhang, C.D., Loss, J., Nayak, K., Yandamuri, S.: Leader election with poly-logarithmic communication per party. In: Kalai, Y.T., Kamara, S.F. (eds.) CRYPTO 2025, Part II. LNCS, vol. 16001, pp. 37–68. Springer, Cham (2025). https://doi.org/10.1007/978-3-032-01878-6_2
12. Blum, E., Boyle, E., Cohen, R., Liu-Zhang, C.: Communication lower bounds for cryptographic broadcast protocols. In: 37th International Symposium on Distributed Computing, DISC 2023, October 10-12, 2023, L'Aquila, Italy. LIPIcs, vol. 281, pp. 10:1–10:19. Schloss Dagstuhl - Leibniz-Zentrum für Informatik (2023)
13. Boyle, E., Chung, K.M., Pass, R.: Large-scale secure computation: Multi-party computation for (parallel) RAM programs. In: Gennaro, R., Robshaw, M.J.B. (eds.) CRYPTO 2015, Part II. LNCS, vol. 9216, pp. 742–762. Springer, Berlin, Heidelberg (2015). https://doi.org/10.1007/978-3-662-48000-7_36

14. Boyle, E., Cohen, R., Data, D., Hubácek, P.: Must the communication graph of MPC protocols be an expander? In: Shacham, H., Boldyreva, A. (eds.) CRYPTO 2018, Part III. LNCS, vol. 10993, pp. 243–272. Springer, Cham (2018). https://doi.org/10.1007/978-3-319-96878-0_9

15. Boyle, E., Cohen, R., Goel, A.: Breaking the $O(\sqrt{(n)})$-bit barrier: Byzantine agreement with polylog bits per party. In: Miller, A., Censor-Hillel, K., Korhonen, J.H. (eds.) 40th ACM PODC, pp. 319–330. ACM (2021). https://doi.org/10.1145/3465084.3467897

16. Boyle, E., Goldwasser, S., Tessaro, S.: Communication locality in secure multiparty computation - how to run sublinear algorithms in a distributed setting. In: Sahai, A. (ed.) TCC 2013. LNCS, vol. 7785, pp. 356–376. Springer, Berlin, Heidelberg (2013). https://doi.org/10.1007/978-3-642-36594-2_21

17. Canetti, R.: Security and composition of multiparty cryptographic protocols. J. Cryptol. **13**(1), 143–202 (2000). https://doi.org/10.1007/s001459910006

18. Canetti, R.: Universally composable security: a new paradigm for cryptographic protocols. In: 42nd FOCS, pp. 136–145. IEEE Computer Society Press (2001). https://doi.org/10.1109/SFCS.2001.959888

19. Canetti, R., Feige, U., Goldreich, O., Naor, M.: Adaptively secure multi-party computation. In: 28th ACM STOC, pp. 639–648. ACM Press (1996). https://doi.org/10.1145/237814.238015

20. Canetti, R., Lindell, Y., Ostrovsky, R., Sahai, A.: Universally composable twoparty and multi-party secure computation. In: 34th ACM STOC, pp. 494–503. ACM Press (2002). https://doi.org/10.1145/509907.509980

21. Chandran, N., Chongchitmate, W., Garay, J.A., Goldwasser, S., Ostrovsky, R., Zikas, V.: The hidden graph model: communication locality and optimal resiliency with adaptive faults. In: Roughgarden, T. (ed.) ITCS 2015, pp. 153–162. ACM (2015). https://doi.org/10.1145/2688073.2688102

22. Chandran, N., Garay, J., Ostrovsky, R.: Almost-everywhere secure computation with edge corruptions. Cryptology ePrint Archive, Report 2012/221 (2012). https://eprint.iacr.org/2012/221

23. Chandran, N., Garay, J.A., Misra, A.K., Ostrovsky, R., Zikas, V.: Adaptive security, erasures, and network assumptions in communication-local MPC. In: Boyle, E., Mahmoody, M. (eds.) TCC 2024, Part IV. LNCS, vol. 15367, pp. 293–326. Springer, Cham (2024). https://doi.org/10.1007/978-3-031-78023-3_10

24. Chandran, N., Garay, J.A., Ostrovsky, R.: Edge fault tolerance on sparse networks. In: Czumaj, A., Mehlhorn, K., Pitts, A.M., Wattenhofer, R. (eds.) ICALP 2012, Part II. LNCS, vol. 7392, pp. 452–463. Springer, Berlin, Heidelberg (2012). https://doi.org/10.1007/978-3-642-31585-5_41

25. Chaum, D.: The dining cryptographers problem: unconditional sender and recipient untraceability. J. Cryptol. **1**(1), 65–75 (1988). https://doi.org/10.1007/BF00206326

26. Chaum, D., Crépeau, C., Damgård, I.: Multiparty unconditionally secure protocols (extended abstract). In: 20th ACM STOC, pp. 11–19. ACM Press (1988). https://doi.org/10.1145/62212.62214

27. Cohen, R., Garay, J.A., Zikas, V.: Completeness theorems for adaptively secure broadcast. In: Handschuh, H., Lysyanskaya, A. (eds.) CRYPTO 2023, Part I. LNCS, vol. 14081, pp. 3–38. Springer, Cham (2023). https://doi.org/10.1007/978-3-031-38557-5_1

28. Cramer, R., Damgård, I., Dziembowski, S., Hirt, M., Rabin, T.: Efficient multi-party computations secure against an adaptive adversary. In: Stern, J. (ed.) EURO-CRYPT 1999. LNCS, vol. 1592, pp. 311–326. Springer, Berlin, Heidelberg (1999). https://doi.org/10.1007/3-540-48910-X_22

29. Damgård, I., Ishai, Y.: Constant-round multiparty computation using a black-box pseudorandom generator. In: Shoup, V. (ed.) CRYPTO 2005. LNCS, vol. 3621, pp. 378–394. Springer, Berlin, Heidelberg (2005). https://doi.org/10.1007/11535218_23

30. Damgård, I., Nielsen, J.B.: Adaptive versus static security in the UC model. In: Chow, S.S.M., Liu, J.K., Hui, L.C.K., Yiu, S.M. (eds.) ProvSec 2014. LNCS, vol. 8782, pp. 10–28. Springer, Cham (2014). https://doi.org/10.1007/978-3-319-12475-9_2

31. Dani, V., King, V., Movahedi, M., Saia, J., Zamani, M.: Secure multi-party computation in large networks. Distrib. Comput. **30**(3), 193–229 (2017)

32. Dolev, D.: The byzantine generals strike again. J. Algorithms **3**(1), 14–30 (1982)

33. Feldman, P.: Optimal algorithms for byzantine agreement. Ph.D. thesis, Stanford University (1988). https://dspace.mit.edu/handle/1721.1/14368

34. Fernando, R., Gelles, Y., Komargodski, I.: Scalable distributed agreement from LWE: Byzantine agreement, broadcast, and leader election. In: Guruswami, V. (ed.) ITCS 2024, vol. 287, pp. 46:1–46:23. LIPIcs (2024). https://doi.org/10.4230/LIPIcs.ITCS.2024.46

35. Fischer, M.J., Lynch, N.A., Merritt, M.: Easy impossibility proofs for distributed consensus problems. Distrib. Comput. **1**(1), 26–39 (1986)

36. Garay, J.A., Katz, J., Kumaresan, R., Zhou, H.S.: Adaptively secure broadcast, revisited. In: Gavoille, C., Fraigniaud, P. (eds.) 30th ACM PODC, pp. 179–186. ACM (2011). https://doi.org/10.1145/1993806.1993832

37. Gelles, Y., Komargodski, I.: Optimal load-balanced scalable distributed agreement. In: Mohar, B., Shinkar, I., O'Donnell, R. (eds.) 56th ACM STOC, pp. 411–422. ACM Press (2024). https://doi.org/10.1145/3618260.3649736

38. Goldreich, O.: Foundations of Cryptography: Basic Applications, vol. 2. Cambridge University Press, Cambridge, UK (2004). https://doi.org/10.1017/CBO9780511721656

39. Goldreich, O., Micali, S., Wigderson, A.: How to play any mental game or a completeness theorem for protocols with honest majority. In: Aho, A. (ed.) 19th ACM STOC, pp. 218–229. ACM Press (1987). https://doi.org/10.1145/28395.28420

40. Hirt, M., Maurer, U., Tschudi, D., Zikas, V.: Network-hiding communication and applications to multi-party protocols. In: Robshaw, M., Katz, J. (eds.) CRYPTO 2016, Part II. LNCS, vol. 9815, pp. 335–365. Springer, Berlin, Heidelberg (2016). https://doi.org/10.1007/978-3-662-53008-5_12

41. Hirt, M., Zikas, V.: Adaptively secure broadcast. In: Gilbert, H. (ed.) EURO-CRYPT 2010. LNCS, vol. 6110, pp. 466–485. Springer, Berlin, Heidelberg (2010). https://doi.org/10.1007/978-3-642-13190-5_24

42. King, V., Lonargan, S., Saia, J., Trehan, A.: Load balanced scalable byzantine agreement through quorum building, with full information. In: Proceedings of the 12th International Conference on Distributed Computing and Networking (ICDCN), pp. 203–214 (2011)

43. King, V., Saia, J.: Breaking the $O(n^2)$ bit barrier: scalable byzantine agreement with an adaptive adversary. In: Richa, A.W., Guerraoui, R. (eds.) 29th ACM PODC, pp. 420–429. ACM (2010). https://doi.org/10.1145/1835698.1835798

44. King, V., Saia, J., Sanwalani, V., Vee, E.: Scalable leader election. In: 17th SODA, pp. 990–999. ACM-SIAM (2006)

45. Moran, T., Orlov, I., Richelson, S.: Topology-hiding computation. In: Dodis, Y., Nielsen, J.B. (eds.) TCC 2015, Part I. LNCS, vol. 9014, pp. 159–181. Springer, Berlin, Heidelberg (2015). https://doi.org/10.1007/978-3-662-46494-6_8
46. Yao, A.C.C.: Protocols for secure computations (extended abstract). In: 23rd FOCS, pp. 160–164. IEEE Computer Society Press (1982). https://doi.org/10.1109/SFCS.1982.38

On Succinct Non-interactive Secure Computation with Malicious Security

Maya Farber Brodsky[1], Arka Rai Choudhuri[2]([✉]) [iD], Abhishek Jain[3,4], and Omer Paneth[1] [iD]

[1] Tel Aviv University, Tel Aviv, Israel
mayaf2003@gmail.com, omerpa@tauex.tau.ac.il
[2] zkBricks, Sacramento, CA, USA
arka@zkbricks.com
[3] NTT Research, Sunnyvale, USA
abhishek.jain@ntt-research.com
[4] Johns Hopkins University, Baltimore, USA

Abstract. A *non-interactive secure computation (NISC)* protocol allows a client with input x and a server with input y to compute $f(x, y)$ using a single message from the client and a single response from the server. The protocol is called *succinct* if the size of the server's message depends only on the output length and is independent of the size of y and the complexity of f. In the semi-honest setting, succinct NISC is known from fully homomorphic encryption (FHE). In contrast, malicious security is currently known only from non-standard assumptions, such as SNARKs for NP.

In this work, we construct maliciously secure succinct NISC protocols for natural and widely studied functionalities from *standard assumptions*, namely, FHE and batch arguments (BARGs). Our first result is a protocol for *private set membership (PSM)*: the client holds an element x, the server holds a large set S, and the function outputs 1 if and only if $x \in S$. We then give several generalizations:

- *Dictionary lookup:* The server holds a dictionary D of keyvalue pairs, the client's input is a key k, and the output is $D[k]$.
- *Verifiable dictionary lookup:* The server's dictionary must additionally satisfy a predicate P, computable by a read-once machine with small state.
- *UP search:* The client input is an instance x, and the output is $D[w]$, where w is the unique witness for x under some UP relation.

Our protocols achieve *split-simulation* security against a malicious server and standard security against a malicious client. Split-simulation is a relaxation of the standard realideal paradigm, where correctness of the client's output and indistinguishability of the server's view are guaranteed separately.

At the heart of our results lies a *new simulation technique* in which the server's large input is extracted piece by piece and reconstructed into a coherent input. This reconstruction is enabled by a new monotone coupling argument based on Strassen's theorem.

© International Association for Cryptologic Research 2026
J. Daemen and E. Thomé (Eds.): EUROCRYPT 2026, LNCS 16543, pp. 573–603, 2026.
https://doi.org/10.1007/978-3-032-25324-8_20

1   Introduction

Ishai et al. [23] introduced the notion of non-interactive secure computation (NISC): a secure two-party computation protocol that is carried out in one round of interaction. In NISC for a function f, a client, holding an input x sends a single message to a server. The server, holding an input y, responds with a single message from which the client can obtain the output $f(x, y)$. The protocol guarantees that the server does not learn x while the client does not learn anything about y beyond the function output.

The main appeal of NISC is that it does not require any extra rounds beyond the necessary query-response round. In addition to round complexity, previous work has sought to minimize the overhead of the protocol's communication complexity. Ideally, we would like to minimize the overhead compared to the naive insecure protocol where the server evaluates f: The client's message should grow with the size of its input x, and the server's message should grow only with the size of the function output, and not with the size of the input, or with the complexity of computing f.[1] We refer to NISC protocols with such communication as *succinct*.[2]

In the semi-honest setting, succinct NISC for all functions follows from fully homomorphic encryption (FHE) [18]. In contrast, succinct NISC with malicious security in the common reference string (CRS) model[3] is only known from much stronger assumptions: Assuming succinct-non-interactive arguments of knowledge (SNARKs) for NP [5,29], one can compile a semi-honest succinct NISC into a protocol with malicious security. SNARKs are also known to be *necessary* for general purpose succinct NISC with malicious security. The existence of SNARKs, however, is subject to strong barriers [7] and constructions are only known in idealized models or based on non-standard, non-falsifiable assumptions [6,29].

In light of these barriers towards succinct NISC for all functions, we ask:

For which functions can we realize succinct NISC with malicious security?

Focusing on solutions based on *standard* assumptions, we do not know of positive results for any non-trivial function whose output length is shorter than the server's input.

The Extraction Barrier. In order to understand the challenge in achieving malicious security, we focus on the case of malicious server. Recall that simply hiding the client's input x is not sufficient. We must also guarantee that the server

---

[1] We also allow for multiplicative factors that depend polynomially on the security parameter.

[2] Note that this is a stronger requirement than *circuit succinctness*, where the server's message may grow with its input size and the output size, but is otherwise independent of the size of the circuit. See Sect. 1.2 for further discussion.

[3] It is well known that (even non-succinct) NISC with malicious security is impossible in the plain model.

chooses its input *independently* of x (this is referred to as input-independence). This requirement is captured by the standard definition of simulation security: For any malicious server, there should exist an efficient simulator that can produce indistinguishable views for the client and server in the ideal execution of the protocol. In the ideal execution, both the client and the simulator submit inputs to a trusted party that provides the client with the function output. The input submitted by the simulator is typically extracted from the malicious server. However, when the server's message is shorter than its input, we have no techniques for extracting the server's input based on standard assumptions.

Split-Simulation Security. Towards overcoming this barrier, we investigate a weaker notion of security that we refer to as *split-simulation*: The simulator produces views for the client and server that are *individually* indistinguishable from their views in the real execution, however, their joint distribution may not be indistinguishable as required by the standard definition of secure computation. More specifically, split-simulation provides two separate guarantees: (1) Indistinguishability of the server's view in real-world executions with different client inputs, and (2) Indistinguishability of the client's output distribution in the real and ideal world.

As discussed in [19], split-simulation security is weaker than standard simulation. Nevertheless, it provides strong guarantees, including *input independence*. Ben-David et al. [4] demonstrated the feasibility of this notion for a simple function related to private information retrieval (PIR): the client holds an index i, the server holds a database D, and the function output is the i-th entry of D if D satisfies a fixed predicate P, and $\perp$ otherwise. In this work, we show that split-simulation is meaningful and achievable for a much broader class of functions.

1.1 Our Results

In this work, we demonstrate the feasibility of succinct NISC with malicious security for a non-trivial class of functions. All of our constructions satisfy split-simulation security for the clients and standard security for the servers. While our primary focus is on showing feasibility of malicious succinct NISC for a large class of functions and not on applications, our results are for natural and useful functions for which secure computation protocols have been studied and applied extensively. We rely on two cryptographic tools: fully-homomorphic encryption (FHE) and non-interactive batch arguments (BARGs) for NP [10,26]. Both of these tools can be instantiated from the learning with errors (LWE) assumption [11,14].

Private-Set Membership. Our first result is a succinct NISC for the private set-membership (PSM) function. In PSM, the client holds a value x, the server holds a set S, and the function outputs 1 iff $x \in S$. PSM has many real-world applications such as password-breach alert systems [2,20,27] and private contact discovery [28].

Theorem 1 (Informal). *Assuming FHE and BARGs for NP, there exists a succinct NISC for PSM with split-simulation security for clients and standard security for servers.*

Split-simulation for PSM provides important security guarantees that semi-honest security does not. For example, it guarantees that a malicious server cannot make a client output 1 regardless of the client's input. More generally, split-simulation means that the server must "know" some (distribution over) polynomial size sets which is independent of the client's input, and the client's output is consistent with this set.

In the following, we discuss several important extensions of the PSM function. We state our result at the end for the most general setting.

Dictionary Lookup. The dictionary lookup function (aka, key-value search) generalizes PSM from sets to dictionaries. In dictionary lookup, the client holds a key k, and the server holds a dictionary D consisting of key-value pairs where all keys are distinct. The function outputs a value v if D contains an entry of the form (k, v) and $\perp$ otherwise. One can think of dictionary lookup as implementing an arbitrary function whose output is not $\perp$ on at most a polynomial number of inputs.

Verifiability. Next, we extend the above function to *verifiable* dictionary lookup, where we can enforce that the server's dictionary satisfies some public predicate P. That is, the function outputs a value v if $P(D) = 1$ *and* D contains an entry of the form (k, v). Otherwise, the output is $\perp$.

In this work, we consider *bounded-state* predicates P [4]. We say that P is bounded state if it can be computed by reading the entries of D once, maintaining only a logarithmic size state between one entry to the next. For example, a bounded-state predicate can verify that the number of pairs satisfying some efficiently computable property is above/below some threshold. Additionally, we can ensure that D satisfies a bounded-state predicate P when the entries are sorted according to some order.[4]

UP Search. Finally, we further extend the above function to support more general key matching procedures. Instead of directly searching for the key k, the client holds an instance x and we search for a witness for x with respect to some UP relation[5] R_{UP}. That is, the function outputs a value v if $P(D) = 1$ *and*

---

[4] If the size of the entries is super-logarithmic, a bounded-state predicate cannot check if the entries are ordered.

[5] A UP relation is an NP relation with the restriction that each instance x has at most one witness.

D contains an entry of the form (w, v) such that $R_{\mathsf{UP}}(x, w) = 1$. Otherwise, the output is $\bot$.

We now state our final result:

Theorem 2 (Informal). *Assuming FHE and BARGs for NP, there exists a succinct NISC for verifiable dictionary lookup with UP search for the class of (sorted) bounded-state predicates with split-simulation security for clients and standard security for servers.*

We can extend the theorem to predicates with state of super-logarithmic size s at the cost of allowing the server's message to grow with s, assuming FHE and BARGs that are 2^s-secure, and letting the simulator run in time 2^s.

1.2   Related Work

Laconic Cryptography. The notion of laconic function evaluation (LFE) [12,31] can be viewed as the dual of semi-honest succinct NISC. In LFE, a server (holding a *large* input) sends the first message to a client (holding a *small* input). The client responds to the server who then computes the function output. Similar to succinct NISC, LFE requires that the size of the server's message is independent of its input size. For this reason, achieving malicious-secure LFE involves similar barriers as malicious-secure succinct NISC. However, it is possible to achieve distinguisher-dependent simulation security [24] based on standard cryptographic assumptions [16]. In distinguisher-dependent simulation, instead of requiring a universal simulator that works for every distinguisher, we allow the simulator to depend on the distinguisher. Due to the reverse communication pattern in LFE (i.e., server speaks before the client), distinguisher-dependent simulation is enabled by rewinding techniques. However, this is not known to be possible in the setting of succinct NISC.

Recently, Bartusek et al. [3] gave a construction of laconic private-set membership in the generic group model. They consider a notion of authenticated-set security which requires the server's database to contain entries signed by a trusted-third party. It is easy to see that our result in Theorem 2 can also enforce such predicates on the server's database. Unlike their work, we support a broader class of predicates and achieve security from *standard* assumptions. Most significantly, while their protocol requires the server to speak first (and compute the function output), our protocol uses the reverse communication pattern where the client speaks first and learns the output.

Credibility in PSM. In a recent work, Garg et al. [17] investigated malicious-secure succinct NISC for private set membership and present constructions from standard assumptions. Their security definition, however, is significantly weaker than the notion of split-simulation. In particular, their definition only guarantees that for high-entropy client inputs, a malicious server cannot force an accepting output. Split-simulation, in contrast, does not place such restrictions, and is therefore closer to standard simulation security. For this reason, the techniques used in our work are very different from theirs.

Verifiable PIR. Ben-David, Kalai and Paneth [4] consider succinct NISC for the private information retrieval (PIR) functionality with the added guarantee that the database D used by the server must satisfy some bounded-state predicate P. They refer to this notion as verifiable PIR (vPIR) and achieve it with split-simulation security for the client based on BARGs. vPIR can be seen as a special case of verifiable dictionary lookup where the key space is of polynomial size.

Circuit-Succinct Secure Computation. In this work, we consider a strong notion of succinctness where the size of the server's message is independent of both the size of the server's input and the complexity of computing f. Prior works have considered a relaxed notion of *circuit-succinct* secure computation, where the size of the server message may grow with the input length and output length, but is otherwise independent of the circuit complexity of f. Morgan, Pass and Polychroniadou [30] construct circuit-succinct NISC achieving simulation-security, albeit with a simulator whose running time is super-polynomial in the security parameter. Further, they require the underlying primitives used in their construction to also satisfy super-polynomial security.

We also mention recent works [1,15] that study circuit-succinct secure computation in the *interactive* setting. These works construct protocols that achieve standard simulation security (with a polynomial-time simulator) based on standard assumptions.

2   Technical Overview

We first provide an overview of our PSM protocol and then discuss its extensions. Before describing our final protocol, we will present a protocol for general bounded-state functions. While we will not be able to prove that this protocol satisfies split-simulation security, we will show that it satisfies a weaker notion of security that will be useful in our final construction.

Bounded-State Functions. A bounded-state function $f(x, y)$ reads the input $y = (y_1, \ldots, y_k)$, one element at a time, maintaining a logarithmic-size state. More formally, f is bounded state if there exist $s = O(\log \lambda)$, an efficiently computable state update function $U : \{0,1\}^* \times \{0,1\}^s \to \{0,1\}^s$ and an initial state $z_0 \in \{0,1\}^s$ such that:

$$f(x, \epsilon) = z_0 \ ,$$
$$f(x, (y_1, \ldots, y_k)) = U((x, y_k), f(x, (y_1, \ldots, y_{k-1}))) \ .$$

BARGs. The succinct NISC protocol for bounded state f is based on FHE and BARGs, as well as a hash tree. Recall that a BARG is a non-interactive argument system in the CRS model for the conjunction of NP statements where the proof size is polynomial in the size of a single witness and independent of the number of statements. More specifically, we will use BARGs for the index relation [14]: the BARG verifier is given an verification machine M and the number of statements k. The BARG proof asserts that for every $i \in [k]$ there exists a witness w_i such that $M(i, w_i) = 1$.

The security property satisfied by the BARG is called somewhere extraction [14]: For every $i \in [k]$, it is possible to sample a CRS that is "programmed" on i together with a trapdoor τ such that (i) the programmed CRS is indistinguishable from an honestly generated CRS; and (ii) for every poly-size adversary that is given a CRS programmed on i and outputs a verification machine M and a proof π, if π is an accepting proof for (M, k) then using τ we can extract from π a witness w such that $M(i, w) = 1$ with all but negligible probability.

A Protocol for Bounded-State Functions. Next we describe a succinct NISC protocol for any bounded-state function f. In what follows, we focus on split simulation security for the client and ignore server security. To achieve server security, one can simply compose our protocol with a non-succinct NISC protocol with full simulation security for both parties. Such a protocol can be obtained from oblivious transfer and non-interactive zero-knowledge proofs [23]. In this work, we present a simpler transformation tailored to our protocol, using non-interactive zero-knowledge proofs.

The CRS contains two independent BARG CRSs. Given input x, the client sends an FHE encryption $\hat{x}$ of x. Given input $y = (y_1, \ldots, y_k)$ and message $\hat{x}$, the server:

- Homomorphically evaluates $f(\cdot, (y_1, \ldots, y_i))$ on $\hat{x}$ for every $i \in [0, k]$. Let $\hat{z}_0, \ldots, \hat{z}_k$ be the resulting ciphertexts for all intermediate states.
- Computes a hash tree over the strings $y_1, \ldots, y_k$ and $\hat{z}_0, \ldots, \hat{z}_k$. Let h be the root of the hash tree.
- Computes two BARG proofs (one under every CRS) that for every $i \in [k]$ there exist local openings of h to $y_i, \hat{z}_{i-1}$ and $\hat{z}_i$ such that $\hat{z}_i$ is obtained by homomorphically evaluating $U((\cdot, y_i), \cdot)$ on $(\hat{x}, \hat{z}_{i-1})$. Let π_1, π_2 be the BARG proofs.

Finally, the server sends h, π_1, π_2 and local openings of h to $\hat{z}_0$ and $\hat{z}_k$. The verifier checks π_1, π_2, the local openings and that $\hat{z}_0$ is indeed the homomorphic evaluation of $f(\cdot, \epsilon)$ on $\hat{x}$. If all checks pass, it decrypts and outputs z_k.

A Flawed Simulation. Next we describe a flawed split-simulation strategy for the above protocol. The server's view can be simulated by encrypting some dummy input $\perp$ instead of x. This is indistinguishable from the client's message by the security of the FHE. We proceed to describe how to simulate the client's output.[6] For every x and $i \in [k]$, let $(y_i^x, \hat{z}_{i-1}^x, z_i^x)$ be as follows:

---

[6] For readers that are familiar with the simulator of [4], here we use the same strategy, except that it is under homomorphic encryption.

- Sample two CRSs programmed on i and a client message $\hat{x}$ and give these to the adversary.
- Obtain the adversary's answer that contains h, π_1, π_2 and a local openings of h to $\hat{z}_0$ and $\hat{z}_k$. If the answer does not verify, go back to the first step.
- Using the trapdoor for the first CRS, extract from π_1 a witness that contains local openings of h to $y_i, \hat{z}_{i-1}$ and $\hat{z}_i$.
- Decrypt z_{i-1} and z_i and set $(y_i^x, \tilde{z}_{i-1}^x, z_i^x) = (y_i, z_{i-1}, z_i)$.

Set $\tilde{z}_k^x = z_k^x$. Using the CRS indistinguishability and extraction properties of the BARG, we can show by a standard argument that for every x and $i \in [k]$:

- $z_i^x = U((x, y_i^x), \tilde{z}_{i-1}^x)$ except with negligible probability.
- z_i^x and $\tilde{z}_i^x$ are statistically close.

Moreover, $\tilde{z}_0^x = z_0$ except with negligible probability and z_k^x is statistically close to the output of the client in the real experiment on input x.

Since z_i^x and $\tilde{z}_i^x$ are statistically close, we can couple[7] together the k distributions above into a single correlated distribution $(y_i^x, z_i^x)_{i \in [k]}$ such that for every $i \in [k]$, $z_i^x = U((x, y_i^x), z_{i-1}^x)$ except with negligible probability. Denoting $y^x = (y_1^x, \ldots, y_k^x)$ this condition is equivalent to $z_k^x = f(x, y^x)$.

Consider the (flawed) simulator that samples y^x and submits it to the trusted party in the ideal experiment. Indeed, the output of the ideal experiment will be $z_k^x = f(x, y^x)$ which is statistically close to the output of the client in the real experiment on input x. The problem with this simulation strategy is, of course, that it depends on the client's input x. Observe that to sample the variable y_i^x, we only need $\hat{x}$ and not the decryption key or x in the clear. Therefore, for every x, x', we have that y_i^x and $y_i^{x'}$ are computationally indistinguishable. However, this is not the case for the joint distributions y^x and $y^{x'}$ since the coupling depends on the z_i^x variables which we cannot sample without the decryption key. Nonetheless, we observe that the protocol above does satisfy a useful notion of security that we will refer to as *input-dependent simulation*.

Before describing the notion of input-dependent simulation and how to use it, we discuss a couple of subtle technical issues with the proposed simulation strategy (this may be skipped on a first reading). First, the argument above implicitly assumes that the client never outputs $\perp$ in the real experiment. Moreover, if the client outputs $\perp$ with probability $1 - \epsilon$, the expected time to sample from y^x becomes $\mathsf{poly}(1/\epsilon)$ which may not be polynomially bounded. To resolve both issues, we first estimate ϵ by executing the adversary with a random CRS and client message and checking its answer multiple times. Then, with probability $1 - \epsilon$, we simulate the output $\perp$ and with probability ϵ, we sample y^x and proceed as before. In the remainder of this overview, we continue to assume, for simplicity, that the client never outputs $\perp$ (i.e. that $\epsilon = 1$).

The second issue is that, while we can efficiently sample from $(y_i^x, \tilde{z}_{i-1}^x, z_i^x)$ for each i, we may not be able to couple these distributions efficiently. To resolve

---

[7] A coupling of random variables A, B is a joint distribution (A, B) whose marginals match A and B. If A and B are statistically close, there exists a coupling (A, B) such that $A = B$ except with negligible probability.

this, we take $\ell = 2^{O(s)} = \mathsf{poly}(\lambda)$ samples from $(y_i^x, \tilde{z}_{i-1}^x, z_i^x)$ and consider the empirical distribution given by taking one of these ℓ samples at random. Since $|z_i^x| = s$ we get that with high probability over the samples, the value of z_i^x in the empirical distribution and the actual distribution are $1/\mathsf{poly}(\lambda)$-close in statistical distance. Therefore, we can still couple the empirical distributions such that the simulation error is $1/\mathsf{poly}(\lambda)$. Since the empirical distributions have support size $\mathsf{poly}(\lambda)$, we can couple them efficiently by computing a matching on the support of each pair of distributions.

Finally, we note that we can extend the protocol and its simulation to support functions with states of super-logarithmic size s; however, the simulation time will grow with $2^{O(s)}$ since we take $\ell = 2^{O(s)}$ samples, and we need to rely on FHE and BARGs that are 2^s-secure. While super-polynomial time simulation is still meaningful in many settings, it may be problematic when using the NISC protocol for cryptographic functions or when using the protocol in a larger system with other cryptographic primitives.

Input-Dependent Simulation. The strategy above is able to simulate the client's output in the real experiment on input x by using the input x. This task on its own is clearly trivial: we can simply emulate the real experiment on input x and obtain the client's output. What makes the strategy above interesting is that it efficiently extracts a distribution y_x that satisfies the following properties:

> ***Client-Output Indistinguishability***: For every x, the client's output in the real experiment on input x is computationally indistinguishable from $f(x, y^x)$. That is, the server's input distribution y^x "explains" the client's output in the real experiment on input x.
>
> ***Server-Input Indistinguishability***: For every x, x' and $i \in [k]$, y_i^x and $y_i^{x'}$ are computationally indistinguishable. That is, the distribution of each individual entry y_i^x looks independent of x.

Our idea is to use the above protocol that provides input-dependent simulation security for general bounded-state functions, to achieve split-simulation security for specific bounded-state functions such as PSM.

A Flawed PSM Protocol. To implement a PSM protocol we consider the bounded-state function $f^\#(x, y)$ that outputs the number of times x appears in the input $y = (y_1, \ldots, y_k)$. Indeed, $f^\#$ can be implemented with a state of size $\log(k)$. Given a protocol for $f^\#$, we construct a PSM protocol as follows: the client and server execute the protocol for $f^\#(x, y)$ where x is the client's element and y contains the elements of the server's set S in some arbitrary order. The client obtains the outputs $f^\#(x, y)$ and outputs 1 iff $f^\#(x, y) > 0$.

We propose a (flawed) split-simulator for $f^\#$: Simply follow the input-dependent simulation strategy using a dummy input $\perp$. That is, the simulator samples $y^\perp$ and submits it to the trusted party in the ideal experiment. We argue that the output of the simulator is "similar" to the output of the client in the real experiment on input x, in the sense that both variables have almost the same expectation. Indeed, by the server-input indistinguishability property of the input-dependent simulation we have that:

$$\mathbb{E}\left[f^{\#}(x, y^{\perp})\right] = \mathbb{E}\left[\sum_{i \in [k]} \mathbb{1}_{y_i^{\perp} = x}\right] = \sum_{i \in [k]} \mathbb{E}\left[\mathbb{1}_{y_i^{\perp} = x}\right]$$

$$\approx \sum_{i \in [k]} \mathbb{E}\left[\mathbb{1}_{y_i^x = x}\right] = \mathbb{E}\left[\sum_{i \in [k]} \mathbb{1}_{y_i^x = x}\right] = \mathbb{E}\left[f^{\#}(x, y^x)\right] \ .$$

By the client-output indistinguishability property, we know that $f^{\#}(x, y^x)$ is indistinguishable from the client's output in the real experiment on input x. Since the output of f is in a polynomial size set, this means that $\mathbb{E}\left[f^{\#}(x, y^x)\right]$ is negligibly close to the expected client's output in the real experiment. Therefore, the same holds also for $\mathbb{E}\left[f^{\#}(x, y^{\perp})\right]$.

The problem, of course, is that while the client's output distribution has almost the same expectation in the real and in the ideal experiment, the two distributions may be very different. For example, consider an adversary that follows the protocol, but sets its input y as follows: with probability $1/k$ it sets each y_i to x and with probability $1 - 1/k$ its sets each y_i to some $x' \notin \{x, \perp\}$. In both the real and in the ideal experiments, the client output 1 in expectation. However, in the real world on input x the server's input entries are either all x or all x' while in the simulated server input $y^{\perp}$ the distributions of entries are independent. Therefore, in the real experiment the client's output will be > 0 with probability $1/k$ while in the ideal world the client's output is 1 with probability $> 1/2$.

'To fix our PSM protocol, we go back and design a protocol with input-dependent simulation for a richer class of functions.

Sorted Bounded-State Functions. Going beyond bounded-state functions, we give an succinct NISC protocol with input-dependent simulation for the class of *sorted* bounded-state functions. We say that a function f is sorted bounded-state if there exists a bounded-state function g and an efficiently computable total order R (either strict or non-strict) such that:

$$f(x, y = (y_1, \ldots, y_k)) = \begin{cases} g(x, y), & \text{if } \forall i \in [k-1] : \ (y_i, y_{i+1}) \in R \\ \perp, & \text{otherwise} \end{cases} \ .$$

We note that if each entry y_i is of size at most s, then any sorted bounded-state function can be implemented by a function with state of size $O(s)$ which also holds in its state the entry y_i previously read, and compares it to the current entry y_{i+1}. Therefore, if the server's input has bounded-size entries, we can use the protocol for bounded-state functions, however, if the entries are of super-logarithmic size, this will require super-polynomial time simulation. In contrast, our protocol for sorted bounded-state functions has an efficient input-dependent simulator, and it does not require the entries to be bounded in size.

Before describing our protocol with input-dependent simulation for sorted bounded-state functions, we explain how to use it to get a protocol for PSM with split-simulation. The idea is that by forcing the entries $y_1, \ldots, y_k$ to be strictly increasing (and, in particular, distinct), we restrict the output of $f^{\#}(x, y)$ (which counts the number of times x appears in y) to be in $\{0, 1\}$ instead of $[k]$. Since our simulator guarantees that client's output distribution has almost the same expectation in the real and in the ideal experiment, and since these distributions are now supported on $\{0, 1\}$, it follows that the two distributions must also be close in statistical distance.

A Protocol for Sorted Bounded-State Functions. Next we describe our succinct NISC protocol for a sorted bounded-state function f given by a bounded-state function g and a total order R. The protocol is identical to the protocol for bounded-state functions above except that we add another BARG to the server message to prove that y is sorted. That is, the new BARG proves that for every $i \in [k-1]$ there exist local openings of h to y_i and y_{i+1} such that $R(y_i, y_{i+1}) = 1$.

We now describe an input-dependent simulation for this protocol. For simplicity, in this overview we ignore the function g and focus on simulating a sorted server input. Extending this to general sorted bounded-state functions is done by a straightforward combination of the simulation below with the simulation for bounded-state functions above. Similarly to the input-dependent simulator above, for every x and $i \in [k-1]$, we sample $(y_i^x, \tilde{y}_{i+1}^x)$ and set $y_k^x = \tilde{y}_k^x$. From the CRS indistinguishability and extraction properties of the BARG, we can show that for every $i \in [k-1]$:

- $R(y_i^x, \tilde{y}_{i+1}^x)$ except with negligible probability.
- y_{i+1}^x and $\tilde{y}_{i+1}^x$ are computationally indistinguishable.

If y_{i+1}^x and $\tilde{y}_{i-1}^x$ were statistically close, then we could couple together these $k - 1$ distributions into a single correlated distribution $y = (y_1^x, \ldots, y_k^x)$ such that for every $i \in [k - 1]$, $R(y_i^x, y_{i+1}^x)$ (i.e. y is sorted) except with negligible probability. However, in general y_{i-1}^x and $\tilde{y}_{i-1}^x$ may not be statistically close.

Monotone Coupling. To handle the computational case, we prove the following monotone coupling lemma: If a pair of random variables A and B are computationally indistinguishable, there exists a coupling (A, B) such that $R^*(A, B) = 1$ except with negligible probability, where R^* is the non-strict version of R. This lemma follows from a variant of Strassen's theorem that gives necessary and sufficient conditions for the existence of coupling satisfying a relation R. For intuition, we also sketch a direct proof of the lemma: for $r \in [0, 1]$ we denote by $a_r \in A$ and $b_r \in B$ the elements such that:

$$\Pr_{a \leftarrow A}[R^*(a, a_r)] = \Pr_{b \leftarrow B}[R^*(b, b_r)] = r \ .$$

This defines a natural coupling: (a_r, b_r) for a uniform $r \leftarrow [0, 1]$. Note that even if A and B are computationally indistinguishable, it is possible that $R^*(a_r, b_r) = 0$

for most r's. Intuitively, however, a_r and b_r must be "close" to each other with respect to R^*. Therefore, we define a new coupling that is "shifted" by some ϵ: $(a_r, b_{r+\epsilon \bmod 1})$ for a uniform $r \leftarrow [0,1]$. Since A and B are computationally indistinguishable, there exists a negligible ϵ such that $R^*(a_r, b_{r+\epsilon}) = 1$ for every $r \in [0, 1 - \epsilon]$. Otherwise, we can distinguish between A and B since:

$$\Pr_{x \leftarrow B} \left[R^*(x, a_r) = 1 \right] - \Pr_{x \leftarrow A} \left[R^*(x, a_r) = 1 \right] \geq$$
$$\Pr_{x \leftarrow B} \left[R^*(x, b_{r+\epsilon}) = 1 \right] - \Pr_{x \leftarrow A} \left[R^*(x, a_r) = 1 \right] = \epsilon \ .$$

Since r falls outside $[0, 1 - \epsilon]$ with probability ϵ the lemma follows.

Using this lemma we can couple the distributions $(y_{i-1}^x, \tilde{y}_i^x)$ and $(y_i^x, \tilde{y}_{i+1}^x)$ into a joint distribution $(y_{i-1}^x, \tilde{y}_i^x, y_i^x, \tilde{y}_{i+1}^x)$ such that except with negligible probability:

$$R(y_{i-1}^x, \tilde{y}_i^x) \quad \wedge \quad R^*(\tilde{y}_i^x, y_i^x) \quad \wedge \quad R(y_i^x, \tilde{y}_{i+1}^x) \quad \Rightarrow \quad R(y_{i-1}^x, \tilde{y}_{i+1}^x) \ .$$

By repeating this process, we get a single joint distribution $y = (y_1^x, \ldots, y_k^x)$ such that y is sorted except with negligible probability. However, we may not be able to sample y efficiently.

To get efficient sampling, we prove a version of the monotone coupling lemma for empirical distributions: Let A and B be computationally indistinguishable random variables, and let L_A and L_B be the empirical distributions obtained by taking ℓ independent samples from A and from B respectively and considering the uniform distribution over these ℓ samples. Then there exists a coupling (L_A, L_B) such that $R^*(L_A, L_B) = 1$ except with probability $1/\mathsf{poly}(\ell)$. Since the empirical distributions have support size ℓ, we can find this coupling in time $\mathsf{poly}(\ell)$ by computing a matching on the support of the distributions. By taking $\ell = \mathsf{poly}(\lambda)$ to be sufficiently large, we can efficiently sample $y = (y_1^x, \ldots, y_k^x)$ such that y is sorted except with probability $1/\mathsf{poly}(\lambda)$.

Extending to Dictionary Lookup. Next we describe how to extend our PSM protocol to dictionary lookup. Recall that here, a client holds a key k, the server holds a dictionary $D = \{(k_i, v_i)\}_{i \in [m]}$, and the client obtains the value v_i for $i \in [m]$ such that $k_i = k$. If the size of each v_i is logarithmic, then we can use the same protocol for sorted bounded-state functions, replacing $f^\#(k, D)$ with a function that outputs the sum of v_i for each i such that $k_i = k$. We can then use the same argument using expectation to argue that input-dependent simulation of this protocol suffices to achieve split-simulation.

To support values v_i that cannot be stored in bounded state, we extend our protocol from sorted bounded-state functions to sorted *lookup* functions. Given a bounded-state function Search and a total order R, we define the lookup function

$$f(x, y = (y_1, \ldots, y_m)) = \begin{cases} \mathsf{Index}(\mathsf{Search}(x, y), y), & \text{If } \forall i \in [m-1]: (y_i, y_{i+1}) \in R \\ \bot, & \text{otherwise} \end{cases}$$

where the indexing function $\mathsf{Index}(i, y)$ returns y_i if $i \in [m]$, and otherwise $\bot$.

This class of functions captures dictionary lookup: the Search function will return the index of the matching key (which unlike the value, can be stored in bounded state), and the total order is on the keys.

To support this class, we need to modify our protocol. Intuitively, we compose our protocol with a (specific) protocol for private information retrieval. The server, after computing the encrypted output $\hat{z}$ of Search, uses this ciphertext as a PIR query to its input, obtains a PIR answer, and sends it to the client (along with the previous hash, ciphertexts and proofs).

The only remaining issue is to ensure consistency: the server should use the same input for the PIR and for the protocol computing Search. To achieve this, we use a specific PIR scheme, itself given by a BARG. Here, the PIR query is a BARG CRS (which we set to be programmed on $\hat{z}$), and the PIR answer is a BARG proof. The BARG proves that for each i, there exists a local opening of h (the hash value in our original protocol) to y_i. The client then obtains its final output by extracting from this proof, a witness which contains y_z.

The input-dependent simulator for the resulting protocol is almost identical, except that we additionally couple based on the output $\hat{z}$.

Extending to Verifiability and UP Search. Using sorted lookup functions, we can support checking bounded-state predicates P on the server's input, and more general key matching procedures given by a UP relation R_{UP}, by defining appropriate search functions. Namely, we can define $\mathsf{Search}(x, y)$ that returns the index i of the first entry $y_i = (w, v)$ such that $R_{\mathsf{UP}}(x, w) = 1$, or $\perp$ if there is no match or if the predicate $P(y)$ is not satisfied.

The unique witness property is needed to ensure that the sum of matching values (which is what we can argue about in expectation) is a single value. To hide the matching witness w (so that the client only receives the value v), we define a more general Index that additionally applies a projection function $\mathsf{Project}(y_i)$, and the witnesses for the additional BARG only contain the projections.

Roadmap. In the rest of the paper, we start by defining the security notions for non-interactive secure computation considered in this work, including the new notion of *input-dependent simulation* in Sect. 4.

We then state our general theorem achieving input-dependent simulation-security in for a large class of functions in Sect. 5. We present our main protocol for sorted bounded-state functions in Sect. 5.1, and its extension to sorted lookup functions in Sect. 5.2.

We state our main result for verifiable dictionary lookup in Sect. 6. Finally, in Sect. 6.1, we show how to instantiate our general theorems to achieve our main result.

The proofs can be found in the full version of the paper.

3   Preliminaries

Notations. We use PPT to denote probabilistic polynomial-time, and denote the set of all positive integers up to n as $[n] := \{1,\ldots,n\}$. For any finite set S, $x \leftarrow S$ denotes a uniformly random element x from the set S. Similarly, for any distribution $\mathcal{D}$, $x \leftarrow \mathcal{D}$ denotes an element x drawn from the distribution $\mathcal{D}$. By $\{X_\lambda\}_\lambda \approx_c \{Y_\lambda\}_\lambda$ we denote that the two distributions $\{X_\lambda\}_\lambda$ and $\{Y_\lambda\}_\lambda$ are computationally indistinguishable.

We define the primitives used in the work below. Additional preliminaries can be found in the full version of the paper.

3.1   Batch Arguments

We recall the definition of batch arguments [14].

Syntax. A (publicly verifiable and non-interactive) somewhere extractable batch argument for NP (BARG) is given by the following polynomial-time algorithms:

- $\mathsf{Gen}(1^\lambda, i)$: On input the security parameter and index i the generation algorithm returns a CRS crs and a trapdoor τ.
- $\mathsf{Prove}(\mathsf{crs}, \mathsf{M}, 1^t, (w_1, \ldots, w_m))$: On input the CRS crs, a Turing machine M, time bound 1^t, and a sequence of m witnesses $w_1, \ldots, w_m$ the prover algorithm return a proof π.
- $\mathsf{Verify}(\mathsf{crs}, \mathsf{M}, t, m, \pi)$: On input the CRS crs, a Turing machine M, time bound t, a number m and a proof π the verification algorithm returns a bit.
- $\mathsf{Extract}(\tau, \pi)$: On input the trapdoor τ and proof π the extraction algorithm outputs a witness w.

Definition 1 (somewhere extractable BARG). *A somewhere extractable BARG for NP satisfies the following requirements.*

- *(Completeness) For every $\lambda \in \mathbb{N}$, $m, t \leq 2^\lambda$, $i \in [m]$, Turing machine M and witnesses $w_1, \ldots, w_m \in \{0,1\}^n$ such that for every $j \in [m]$, $M(j, w_j)$ accepts in t steps:*

$$\Pr\left[\begin{matrix}\mathsf{Verify}(\mathsf{crs}, \mathsf{M}, t, m, \pi) = 1 \\ \mathsf{Extract}(\tau, \pi) = w_i\end{matrix} : \begin{matrix}(\mathsf{crs}, \tau) \leftarrow \mathsf{Gen}(1^\lambda, i) \\ \pi \leftarrow \mathsf{Prove}(\mathsf{crs}, \mathsf{M}, 1^t, (w_1, \ldots, w_m))\end{matrix}\right] = 1.$$

- *(Efficiency) In the completeness experiment above $|\pi| = \mathsf{poly}(\lambda, n)$. The argument is rate-1 if $|\pi| = n + \mathsf{poly}(\lambda)$.*
- *(Index Hiding) For every polynomial-size adversary $\mathcal{A}$ there exists a negligible function μ such that for every $\lambda \in \mathbb{N}$ and indexes $i_0, i_1 \leq 2^\lambda$:*

$$\Pr\left[\mathcal{A}(\mathsf{crs}) = b : \begin{matrix}b \leftarrow \{0,1\} \\ (\mathsf{crs}, \tau) \leftarrow \mathsf{Gen}(1^\lambda, i_b)\end{matrix}\right] \leq \frac{1}{2} + \mu(\lambda).$$

– *(Somewhere Extraction) For every polynomial-size adversary $\mathcal{A}$ there exists a negligible function μ such that for every $\lambda \in \mathbb{N}$ and $i \leq 2^\lambda$:*

$$\Pr\left[\begin{array}{l} \mathsf{Verify}(\mathsf{crs}, \mathsf{M}, t, m, \pi) = 1 \\ \mathsf{M}(i, w) \text{ does not accept within } t \text{ steps} \end{array} : \begin{array}{l} (\mathsf{crs}, \tau) \leftarrow \mathsf{Gen}(1^\lambda, i) \\ (\mathsf{M}, 1^t, m, \pi) \leftarrow \mathcal{A}(\mathsf{crs}) \\ w \leftarrow \mathsf{Extract}(\tau, \pi) \end{array}\right] \leq \mu(\lambda).$$

BARGs satisfying the above definition can be constructed based on the hardness of LWE, the k-Lin assumption for $k > 1$ or sub-exponential DDH [13,14,22,25,32].

Remark 1. Given a somewhere extractable BARG, one can naturally extend the definition of the key generation algorithm Gen to take as input an index *set* $I \subset [k]$, as opposed to a single index. $\mathsf{Gen}(1^\lambda, I)$ will simply run $\mathsf{Gen}(1^\lambda, i)$ for every $i \in I$. The prover algorithm Prove, given a crs that encodes the $|I|$ indices, will simply generate $|I|$ proofs (one for each crs), and the verifier will check these $|I|$ proofs independently. The size of the proof π now grows linearly in $|I|$. The index hiding property holds for any I and I' as long as $|I| = |I'|$. Lastly, extraction will output the witnesses at all positions indexed by I, i.e. $\mathsf{Extract}$ outputs $\{w_i\}_{i \in I}$.

3.2 Fully Homomorphic Encryption

Syntax. A fully homomorphic encryption scheme FHE consists of a fixed ciphertext size $\ell_{\mathsf{ctxt}} = \ell_{\mathsf{ctxt}}(\lambda)$ and the following polynomial time algorithms.

$\mathsf{Gen}(1^\lambda) \to (\mathsf{pk}, \mathsf{sk})$ This is a probabilistic algorithm that takes as input a security parameter 1^λ. It outputs a public key pk and a secret key sk.

$\mathsf{Enc}(\mathsf{pk}, m) \to c$. This is a probabilistic algorithm that takes as input a public key pk and a message $m \in \{0,1\}^n$. It outputs a ciphertext $c \in \{0,1\}^{n \cdot \ell_{\mathsf{ctxt}}}$.

$\mathsf{Dec}(\mathsf{sk}, c) \to m$. This is a deterministic algorithm that takes as input a secret key pk and a ciphertext $c \in \{0,1\}^{n \cdot \ell_{\mathsf{ctxt}}}$. It outputs a bit $m \in \{0,1\}^n$.

$\mathsf{Eval}(\mathsf{pk}, f, c) \to c^*$. This is a deterministic algorithm that takes as input a public key pk, a circuit representing a function $f : \{0,1\}^n \mapsto \{0,1\}^u$ and ciphertext $c \in \{0,1\}^{n \cdot \ell_{\mathsf{ctxt}}}$. It outputs a ciphertext $c^* \in \{0,1\}^{u \cdot \ell_{\mathsf{ctxt}}}$.

Definition 2 (FHE). *A fully homomorphic encryption scheme* $\mathsf{FHE} = (\mathsf{Gen}, \mathsf{Enc}, \mathsf{Dec}, \mathsf{Eval})$ *is required to satisfy the following properties:*

Encryption Correctness. *For any choice of* $(\mathsf{pk}, \mathsf{sk}) \leftarrow \mathsf{Gen}(1^\lambda)$, *and any* $m \in \{0,1\}^n$ *and any* $c \leftarrow \mathsf{Enc}(\mathsf{pk}, m)$ *we have* $\mathsf{Dec}(\mathsf{sk}, c) = m$.

Evaluation Correctness. *For any choice of* $(\mathsf{pk}, \mathsf{sk}) \leftarrow \mathsf{Gen}(1^\lambda)$, *and any ciphertext* $c \in \{0,1\}^{n \cdot \ell_{\mathsf{ctxt}}}$ *such that* $\mathsf{Dec}(\mathsf{sk}, c) = m \in \{0,1\}^n$ *and any circuit* $f : \{0,1\}^n \mapsto \{0,1\}^u$, *if we set* $c^* = \mathsf{Eval}(f, c)$ *then* $\mathsf{Dec}(\mathsf{sk}, c^*) = f(m)$.

Security. *The encryption scheme must satisfy semantic security, i.e. for every $\lambda \in \mathbb{N}$ and all pairs of messages $m_0, m_1 \in \{0,1\}^n$, it holds that*

$$\mathsf{Enc}(\mathsf{pk}, m_0) \approx_c \mathsf{Enc}(\mathsf{pk}, m_1),$$

where $(\mathsf{pk}, \mathsf{sk}) \leftarrow \mathsf{Gen}(1^\lambda)$.

Compactness. *The ciphertext must be compact, i.e. there exists a polynomial $\mathsf{p}(\cdot)$ such that for every $\lambda \in \mathbb{N}$, $(\mathsf{pk}, \mathsf{sk}) \leftarrow \mathsf{Gen}(1^\lambda)$, message $m \in \{0,1\}^n$, and circuit f with input size n, $|\mathsf{Eval}(f, \mathsf{Enc}(\mathsf{pk}, m))| = |f(m)| \cdot \mathsf{p}(\lambda)$. Note that this also implies that a fresh encryption of m has size $|m| \cdot \mathsf{p}(\lambda)$.*

4   One-Round Two-Party Secure Computation

Syntax. Let $\mathsf{F} = \{\mathsf{F}_\lambda\}_{\lambda \in \mathbb{N}}$ be a two-input polynomial-time computable function. A 1-round 2-party computation protocol for F in the CRS model consist of the following polynomial-time algorithms.

$\mathsf{Gen}(1^\lambda) \to (\mathsf{crs})$ This is a probabilistic algorithm that takes as input a security parameter 1^λ. It outputs a common reference string crs.

$\mathsf{Client}(\mathsf{crs}, x) \to (\mathsf{st}, c)$. This is a probabilistic algorithm that takes as input a common reference string crs and a client input $x \in \{0,1\}^*$. It outputs a state st and a client message c.

$\mathsf{Server}(\mathsf{crs}, y, c) \to s$. This is a probabilistic algorithm that takes as input a common reference string crs, a server input $y \in \{0,1\}^*$ and a client message c. It outputs a server message s.

$\mathsf{Out}(\mathsf{crs}, \mathsf{st}, s) \to z$. This is a deterministic algorithm that takes as input a common reference string crs, a state st and a server message s. It outputs the client output z.

Definition 3 (1-round 2-party Secure Computation). *A 1-round 2-party computation protocol for F in the CRS model $(\mathsf{Gen}, \mathsf{Client}, \mathsf{Server}, \mathsf{Out})$ is required to satisfy the following properties:*

Correctness. *For any $\lambda \in \mathbb{N}$ and inputs $x, y \in \{0,1\}^*$:*

$$\Pr\left[\mathsf{Out}(\mathsf{crs}, \mathsf{st}, s) = \mathsf{F}_\lambda(x, y) \; : \; \begin{array}{l} \mathsf{crs} \leftarrow \mathsf{Gen}(1^\lambda) \\ (\mathsf{st}, c) \leftarrow \mathsf{Client}(\mathsf{crs}, x) \\ s \leftarrow \mathsf{Server}(\mathsf{crs}, y, c) \end{array} \right] = 1.$$

Client Security. *For every polynomial-size adversary $\mathcal{A}$ corrupting the server, and polynomial P there exists a polynomial-size simulator Sim such that for every polynomial-size distinguisher $\mathcal{D}$ there exists a negligible function μ such that for every $\lambda \in \mathbb{N}$ and x such that $|x| \leq P(\lambda)$:*

$$\left| \Pr\left[\mathcal{D}(\mathsf{REAL}_\mathcal{A}(\lambda, x)) = 1 \right] - \Pr\left[\mathcal{D}(\mathsf{IDEAL}_{\mathsf{Sim}}(\lambda, x)) = 1 \right] \right| \leq \mu(\lambda) \; .$$

where the experiments REAL *and* IDEAL *are defined as follows:*

<table>
<tr><td>

$\underline{\mathsf{REAL}_{\mathcal{A}}(\lambda, x)}$

$\mathsf{crs} \leftarrow \mathsf{Gen}(1^\lambda)$

$(\mathsf{st}, c) \leftarrow \mathsf{Client}(\mathsf{crs}, x)$

$(z^*, s) \leftarrow \mathcal{A}(\mathsf{crs}, c)$

$z \leftarrow \mathsf{Out}(\mathsf{crs}, \mathsf{st}, s)$

Output (z^*, z)

</td><td>

$\underline{\mathsf{IDEAL}_{\mathsf{Sim}}(\lambda, x)}$

$(z^*, y) \leftarrow \mathsf{Sim}(1^\lambda)$

If $y = \bot$, *set* $z \leftarrow \bot$

If $y \neq \bot$, *set* $z \leftarrow \mathsf{F}_\lambda(x, y)$

Output (z^*, z)

</td></tr>
</table>

Server security. *For every polynomial-size adversary* $\mathcal{A}$ *corrupting the client, and polynomial* P *there exists a polynomial-size simulator* Sim *such that for every polynomial-size distinguisher* $\mathcal{D}$ *there exists a negligible function* μ *such that for every* $\lambda \in \mathbb{N}$ *and* y *such that* $|y| \leq P(\lambda)$:

$$\left| \Pr\left[\mathcal{D}(\mathsf{REAL}_{\mathcal{A}}(\lambda, y)) = 1 \right] - \Pr\left[\mathcal{D}(\mathsf{IDEAL}_{\mathsf{Sim}}(\lambda, y)) = 1 \right] \right| \leq \mu(\lambda) \ .$$

where the experiments REAL *and* IDEAL *are defined as follows:*

<table>
<tr><td>

$\underline{\mathsf{REAL}_{\mathcal{A}}(\lambda, y)}$

$\mathsf{crs} \leftarrow \mathsf{Gen}(1^\lambda)$

$c \leftarrow \mathcal{A}(\mathsf{crs})$

$s \leftarrow \mathsf{Server}(\mathsf{crs}, y, c)$

Output $\mathcal{A}(\mathsf{crs}, s)$

</td><td>

$\underline{\mathsf{IDEAL}_{\mathsf{Sim}}(\lambda, y)}$

$x \leftarrow \mathsf{Sim}(1^\lambda)$

Output $\mathsf{Sim}(1^\lambda, \mathsf{F}_\lambda(x, y))$

</td></tr>
</table>

4.1 Weak Client Security

A 1-round 2-party computation protocol for F in the CRS model has weak client security if instead of the client security requirement it satisfies the following two requirements: input privacy and weak simulation-security.

Definition 4 (Input Privacy (for the Client)). *A 1-round 2-party computation protocol for* F *in the CRS model* (Gen, Client, Server, Out) *satisfies input privacy if for every polynomial size distinguisher* $\mathcal{D}$ *and polynomial* P *there exists a negligible function* μ *such that for any* $\lambda \in \mathbb{N}$ *and pair of inputs* x_0, x_1 *such that* $|x_0| = |x_1| \leq P(\lambda)$ *it holds that*

$$\Pr\left[\mathcal{D}(\mathsf{crs}, c) = b \ : \ \begin{array}{l} b \leftarrow \{0, 1\} \\ \mathsf{crs} \leftarrow \mathsf{Gen}(1^\lambda) \\ (\mathsf{st}, c) \leftarrow \mathsf{Client}(\mathsf{crs}, x_b) \end{array} \right] \leq \frac{1}{2} + \mu(\lambda).$$

Definition 5 (Weak Simulation-Security (for the Client)). *A 1-round 2-party computation protocol for* F *in the CRS model* (Gen, Client, Server, Out) *satisfies weak simulation-security if for every polynomial-size adversary* $\mathcal{A}$ *corrupting the server, and polynomial* P *there exists a polynomial-size simulator*

Sim *such that for every polynomial-size distinguisher $\mathcal{D}$, large enough $\lambda \in \mathbb{N}$ and x such that $|x| \leq P(\lambda)$:*

$$\left| \Pr\left[\mathcal{D}(\mathsf{REAL}_{\mathcal{A}}(\lambda, x)) = 1 \right] - \Pr\left[\mathcal{D}(\mathsf{IDEAL}_{\mathsf{Sim}}(\lambda, x)) = 1 \right] \right| \leq \frac{1}{P(\lambda)} \ .$$

where the experiments REAL *and* IDEAL *are defined as follows:*

<table>
<tr><td>

$\mathsf{REAL}_{\mathcal{A}}(\lambda, x)$
$\overline{}$
$\mathsf{crs} \leftarrow \mathsf{Gen}(1^{\lambda})$
$(\mathsf{st}, c) \leftarrow \mathsf{Client}(\mathsf{crs}, x)$
$s \leftarrow \mathcal{A}(\mathsf{crs}, c)$
$z \leftarrow \mathsf{Out}(\mathsf{crs}, \mathsf{st}, s)$
Output z

</td><td>

$\mathsf{IDEAL}_{\mathsf{Sim}}(\lambda, x)$
$\overline{}$
$y \leftarrow \mathsf{Sim}(1^{\lambda})$
If $y = \perp$, *set* $z \leftarrow \perp$
If $y \neq \perp$, *set* $z \leftarrow \mathsf{F}_{\lambda}(x, y)$
Output z

</td></tr>
</table>

4.2 Input-Dependent Simulation-Security

Let $n(\lambda), \ell(\lambda), m(\lambda)$ be polynomially bounded functions. Let $\mathsf{F} = \{\mathsf{F}_{\lambda} : \{0,1\}^{n(\lambda)} \times (\{0,1\}^{\ell(\lambda)})^{m(\lambda)} \rightarrow \{0,1\}^{*}\}_{\lambda \in \mathbb{N}}$, be a polynomial-time computable function. A 1-round 2-party computation protocol for F in the CRS model has input-dependent simulation-security if instead of weak simulation-security for the client, it satisfies the following notion of input-dependent simulation-security.

Definition 6 (Input-Dependent Simulation-Security (for the Client)).
A 1-round 2-party computation protocol for F *in the CRS model* (Gen, Client, Server, Out) *satisfies input-dependent simulation-security if for every polynomial-size adversary* $\mathcal{A}$ *corrupting the server, and polynomial* P *there exists a polynomial-size input-dependent simulator* Sim *that satisfies the following requirements:*

Client-Output Indistinguishability. *For every polynomial-size distinguisher* $\mathcal{D}$, *large enough* $\lambda \in \mathbb{N}$ *and* $x \in \{0,1\}^{n(\lambda)}$:

$$\left| \Pr\left[\mathcal{D}(\mathsf{REAL}_{\mathcal{A}}(\lambda, x)) = 1 \right] - \Pr\left[\mathcal{D}(\mathsf{IDEAL}_{\mathsf{Sim}}(\lambda, x)) = 1 \right] \right| \leq \frac{1}{P(\lambda)} \ .$$

where the experiments REAL *and* IDEAL *are defined as follows:*

<table>
<tr><td>

$\mathsf{REAL}_{\mathcal{A}}(\lambda, x)$
$\overline{}$
$\mathsf{crs} \leftarrow \mathsf{Gen}(1^{\lambda})$
$(\mathsf{st}, c) \leftarrow \mathsf{Client}(\mathsf{crs}, x)$
$s \leftarrow \mathcal{A}(\mathsf{crs}, c)$
$z \leftarrow \mathsf{Out}(\mathsf{crs}, \mathsf{st}, s)$
Output z

</td><td>

$\mathsf{IDEAL}_{\mathsf{Sim}}(\lambda, x)$
$\overline{}$
$y \leftarrow \mathsf{Sim}(1^{\lambda}, x)$
If $y = \perp$, *set* $z \leftarrow \perp$
If $y \neq \perp$, *set* $z \leftarrow \mathsf{F}_{\lambda}(x, y)$
Output z

</td></tr>
</table>

Server-Input Indistinguishability. *For every polynomial size distinguisher $\mathcal{D}$ there exists a negligible function μ such that for any $\lambda \in \mathbb{N}$, pair of inputs $x_0, x_1 \in \{0,1\}^{n(\lambda)}$ and $i \in [m(\lambda)]$ it holds that*

$$\Pr\left[\mathcal{D}(y_i) = b \; : \; \begin{array}{l} b \leftarrow \{0,1\} \\ y \leftarrow \mathsf{Sim}(1^\lambda, x_b) \end{array}\right] \leq \frac{1}{2} + \mu(\lambda).$$

where y_i is set to $\perp$ if $y = \perp$.

We also consider a stronger notion of input-dependent simulation-security defined with respect to a function G of the server's input: $\mathsf{G} = \{\mathsf{G}_\lambda : (\{0,1\}^{\ell(\lambda)})^{m(\lambda)} \to \{0,1\}^*\}_{\lambda \in \mathbb{N}}$. We say that a 1-round 2-party computation protocol for F in the CRS model $(\mathsf{Gen}, \mathsf{Client}, \mathsf{Server}, \mathsf{Out})$ satisfies input-dependent simulation-security with respect to G if the server-input indistinguishability requirement is replaced by the following stronger requirement.

Definition 7. (Server-input indistinguishability with respect to G). *For every polynomial size distinguisher $\mathcal{D}$ there exists a negligible function μ such that for any $\lambda \in \mathbb{N}$, pair of inputs $x_0, x_1 \in \{0,1\}^{n(\lambda)}$ and $i \in [m(\lambda)]$ it holds that*

$$\Pr\left[\mathcal{D}(y_i, \mathsf{G}(y)) = b \; : \; \begin{array}{l} b \leftarrow \{0,1\} \\ y \leftarrow \mathsf{Sim}(1^\lambda, x_b) \end{array}\right] \leq \frac{1}{2} + \mu(\lambda).$$

where y_i and $\mathsf{G}(y)$ are set to $\perp$ if $y = \perp$.

5   General Theorem: Input-Dependent Simulation-Security

In this section we present 1-round 2-party protocols satisfying input-dependent simulation-security, for two general function classes: sorted bounded-state functions, and sorted lookup functions.

We first state our theorem for sorted bounded-state functions. This class of functions suffices to obtain protocols for private set membership.

Definition 8 (Function Computable with Bounded State). *Let $s(\lambda)$ be a polynomially bounded function. A function $\mathsf{F} = \{\mathsf{F}_\lambda : \{0,1\}^{n(\lambda)} \times (\{0,1\}^{\ell(\lambda)})^{m(\lambda)} \to \{0,1\}^{s(\lambda)}\}_{\lambda \in \mathbb{N}}$ is computable with state of size s if there exists an efficiently computable function $\mathsf{f} = \{\mathsf{f}_\lambda : \{0,1\}^* \times \{0,1\}^{\ell(\lambda)} \times \{0,1\}^{s(\lambda)} \to \{0,1\}^{s(\lambda)}\}_{\lambda \in \mathbb{N}}$ and $z_0 \in \{0,1\}^{s(\lambda)}$ such that: $\mathsf{F}_\lambda(x, \epsilon) \equiv z_0$, and*

$$\mathsf{F}_\lambda(x, (y_1, \ldots, y_{m(\lambda)})) \equiv \mathsf{f}_\lambda(x, y_{m(\lambda)}, \mathsf{F}(x, (y_1, \ldots, y_{m(\lambda)-1})))$$

Theorem 3. *Let*

$$\mathsf{F} = \{\mathsf{F}_\lambda : \{0,1\}^* \times (\{0,1\}^{\ell(\lambda)})^{m(\lambda)} \to \{0,1\}^{s(\lambda)}\}_{\lambda \in \mathbb{N}}$$

$$\mathsf{G} = \{\mathsf{G}_\lambda : (\{0,1\}^{\ell(\lambda)})^{m(\lambda)} \to \{0,1\}^{s(\lambda)}\}_{\lambda \in \mathbb{N}}$$

be functions computable with state of size $s(\lambda) = O(\log \lambda)$. Let $\mathsf{R} = \{\mathsf{R}_\lambda \subseteq \{0,1\}^{\ell(\lambda)} \times \{0,1\}^{\ell(\lambda)}\}$ be an efficiently computable total order (either strict or non-strict). Let $\mathsf{F}' = \{\mathsf{F}'_\lambda\}_{\lambda \in \mathbb{N}}$ and $\mathsf{G}' = \{\mathsf{G}'_\lambda\}_{\lambda \in \mathbb{N}}$ be the functions:

$$\mathsf{F}'_\lambda(x, y = (y_1, \ldots, y_{m(\lambda)})) = \begin{cases} \mathsf{F}_\lambda(x, y), & \textit{if } \forall i : (y_i, y_{i+1}) \in \mathsf{R}_\lambda \\ \bot, & \textit{otherwise} \end{cases},$$

$$\mathsf{G}'_\lambda(y = (y_1, \ldots, y_{m(\lambda)})) = \begin{cases} \mathsf{G}_\lambda(y), & \textit{if } \forall i : (y_i, y_{i+1}) \in \mathsf{R}_\lambda \\ \bot, & \textit{otherwise} \end{cases}.$$

Assuming NIZK, FHE and BARG, there exists a 1-round 2-party computation protocol for the function F' in the CRS model with input-dependent simulation-security with respect to G' (Definitions 6 and 7) where the client's message is of size $n(\lambda) \cdot \mathsf{poly}(\lambda)$ and the server's message is of size $\ell(\lambda) \cdot \mathsf{poly}(\lambda)$. The protocol additionally satisfies server security (Definition 3) and client input privacy (Definition 4).

To support dictionary lookup (or more generally, VDL with UP search), where dictionary values may be longer than the state, we consider a different class of functions which we call sorted lookup functions.

Theorem 4. *Let*

$$\mathsf{Search} = \{\mathsf{Search}_\lambda : \{0,1\}^* \times (\{0,1\}^{\ell(\lambda)})^{m(\lambda)} \to \{0,1\}^{s(\lambda)}\}_{\lambda \in \mathbb{N}}$$

$$\mathsf{G} = \{\mathsf{G}_\lambda : (\{0,1\}^{\ell(\lambda)})^{m(\lambda)} \to \{0,1\}^{s(\lambda)}\}_{\lambda \in \mathbb{N}}$$

be functions computable with state of size $s(\lambda) = O(\log \lambda)$. Let $\mathsf{R} = \{\mathsf{R}_\lambda \subseteq \{0,1\}^{\ell(\lambda)} \times \{0,1\}^{\ell(\lambda)}\}$ be an efficiently computable total order (either strict or non-strict).

Let $\mathsf{Project} : \{0,1\}^{\ell(\lambda)} \to \{0,1\}^{\ell(\lambda)}$ be a poly-time function. Define the indexing function

$$\mathsf{Index}(x, y) = \begin{cases} \mathsf{Project}(y[x]), & \textit{if } x \in [m(\lambda)] \\ \bot, & \textit{otherwise} \end{cases}.$$

Let $\mathsf{F} = \{\mathsf{F}_\lambda\}_{\lambda \in \mathbb{N}}$ and $\mathsf{G}' = \{\mathsf{G}'_\lambda\}_{\lambda \in \mathbb{N}}$ be the functions:

$$\mathsf{F}_\lambda(x, y = (y_1, \ldots, y_{m(\lambda)})) = \begin{cases} \mathsf{Index}(\mathsf{Search}_\lambda(x, y), y), & \textit{If } \forall i : (y_i, y_{i+1}) \in \mathsf{R}_\lambda \\ \bot, & \textit{otherwise} \end{cases},$$

$$\mathsf{G}'_\lambda(y = (y_1, \ldots, y_{m(\lambda)})) = \begin{cases} \mathsf{G}_\lambda(y), & \textit{if } \forall i : (y_i, y_{i+1}) \in \mathsf{R}_\lambda \\ \bot, & \textit{otherwise} \end{cases}.$$

Assuming NIZK, FHE and BARG, there exists a 1-round 2-party computation protocol for the function F in the CRS model with input-dependent simulation-security with respect to G' (Definitions 6 and 7) where the client's message is of size $n(\lambda) \cdot \mathsf{poly}(\lambda)$ and the server's message is of size $\ell(\lambda) \cdot \mathsf{poly}(\lambda)$. The protocol additionally satisfies server security (Definition 3) and client input privacy (Definition 4).

5.1   Sorted Bounded-State Functions

We present the one-round two-party secure computation protocol for the function $\mathsf{F}' = \{\mathsf{F}'_\lambda\}_{\lambda \in \mathbb{N}}$ defined in Theorem 3. The proof is deferred to the full version of the paper.

Building Blocks. We use the following components for our construction:

- A hash tree scheme $\mathsf{HT} = (\mathsf{HT.Gen}, \mathsf{HT.Hash}, \mathsf{HT.Open}, \mathsf{HT.Verify})$.
- A fully homomorphic encryption (FHE) scheme (Definition 2) $\mathsf{FHE} = (\mathsf{FHE.Gen}, \mathsf{FHE.Enc}, \mathsf{FHE.Dec}, \mathsf{FHE.Eval})$.
- A somewhere extractable batch argument (BARG) scheme (Definition 1) $\mathsf{BARG} = (\mathsf{BARG.Gen}, \mathsf{BARG.Prove}, \mathsf{BARG.Verify}, \mathsf{BARG.Extract})$

Overview. The overall idea of the protocol is for the client to send an FHE $\widehat{c}_0$ of its input x to the server, and have the server compute the encrypted output of F' by performing homomorphic operations on the ciphertext. The client can then simply decrypt the ciphertext to learn its output.

In particular, since the function F can be computed in an iterative manner using f_λ, at step i of this iterative computation the server only needs input y_i defining $\widehat{c}_i$ to be the output of the FHE evaluation f_λ on $\widehat{c}_{i-1}$ using additional input y_i. Further, the output of F' is $\perp$ unless for all i, $(y_{i-1}, y_i) \in \mathsf{R}_\lambda$. To prove that the server updated the ciphertext at each step, while also maintaining the relative ordering, the server computes a BARG that every step i is computed correctly. The iterative (or local) property of both R and F allow the server to compute such a proof. The client then only decrypts if the BARG proof it receives verifies.

For the description of this protocol, we abuse the notation for FHE evaluation and state that $\mathsf{FHE.Eval}(\mathsf{pk}, \mathsf{f}_\lambda, \widehat{c}, y, \widehat{c}_i)$ corresponds to the homomorphic evaluation of the function $\mathsf{f}_\lambda(\cdot, y, \cdot)$ on the plaintext underlying $\widehat{c}$ and $\widehat{c}_i$.

Turing Machine for BARGs. We next describe the family of Turing machine $\mathsf{M} = \{\mathsf{M}_\lambda\}_{\lambda \in \mathbb{N}}$ that the server will need to provide a BARG proof for. The machine M_λ hardcodes the hash key hk, tree root rt, initial and final states $\mathsf{z}_{\mathsf{g},\mathsf{init}}$ and $\mathsf{z}_{\mathsf{g},\mathsf{final}}$ for g, encrypted input $\widehat{c}$, and encrypted initial and final states $\widehat{c}_{\mathsf{init}}$ and $\widehat{c}_{\mathsf{final}}$ for f_λ (Fig. 1).

Note that we can set t, the running time of M, to be the time it takes to perform the above checks, which is polynomial in its inputs.

Protocol. We now describe the protocol below (Fig. 2).

$\mathsf{M}_\lambda[\mathsf{hk}, \mathsf{rt}, \mathsf{z}_{\mathsf{g},\mathsf{init}}, \mathsf{z}_{\mathsf{g},\mathsf{final}}, \widehat{c}, \widehat{c}_{\mathsf{init}}, \widehat{c}_{\mathsf{final}}](i, w_i)$

1. Parse $w_i = (\mathsf{z}_{\mathsf{g},i-1}, \widehat{c}_{i-1}, y_{i-1}, \rho_{i-1}, \mathsf{z}_{\mathsf{g},i}, \widehat{c}_i, y_i, \rho_i)$.

2. if $i = 1$, check $\widehat{c}_0 = \widehat{c}_{\mathsf{init}}$ and $\mathsf{z}_{\mathsf{g},0} = \mathsf{z}_{\mathsf{g},\mathsf{init}}$.
3. if $i = m(\lambda)$, check $\widehat{c}_{m(\lambda)} = \widehat{c}_{\mathsf{final}}$ and $\mathsf{z}_{\mathsf{g},m(\lambda)} = \mathsf{z}_{\mathsf{g},\mathsf{final}}$.
4. Check $\widehat{c}_i = \mathsf{FHE.Eval}(\mathsf{f}_\lambda, \widehat{c}, y_i, \widehat{c}_{i-1})$.
5. Check $\mathsf{z}_{\mathsf{g},i} = \mathsf{g}_\lambda(y_i, \mathsf{z}_{\mathsf{g},i-1})$.
6. Check $\mathsf{HT.Verify}(\mathsf{hk}, \mathsf{rt}, i, (\mathsf{z}_{\mathsf{g},i}, \widehat{c}_i, y_i), \rho_i) = 1$.
7. if $i > 1$, check $\mathsf{HT.Verify}(\mathsf{hk}, \mathsf{rt}, i - 1, (\mathsf{z}_{\mathsf{g},i-1}, \widehat{c}_{i-1}, y_{i-1}), \rho_{i-1}) = 1$ and $(y_{i-1}, y_i) \in \mathsf{R}_\lambda$.
8. Accept if all the checks verify.

Fig. 1: Turing Machine M_λ

Fig. 1. Turing Machine M_λ

5.2   Sorted Lookup Functions

The protocol builds on the one in Sect. 5.1, with an additional building block: a somewhere-extractable hash family

$$\mathsf{SEH} = (\mathsf{SEH.Gen}, \mathsf{SEH.TGen}, \mathsf{SEH.Hash}, \mathsf{SEH.Open}, \mathsf{SEH.Verify}, \mathsf{SEH.Extract}) \ .$$

Specifically, we use the SEH scheme of [21] based on FHE, which has certain additional properties (described in detail in the full version). Namely, we use the fact that the hash key contains an encryption of an index under the FHE scheme, and extraction correctness holds for any ciphertext encrypting i (not only for a fresh ciphertext).

Overview. The protocol is identical to Sect. 5.1, except that we use the SEH scheme to perform the final indexing operation. The server evaluates the FHE ciphertext containing the output of Search, and uses it to construct a hash key for the SEH scheme, programmed on that index. It then computes the SEH of its input y using the evaluated key, and augments the BARG proof to also give openings of its input with respect to this hash. The client then extracts the value from the hash as its final output.

We now describe the protocol, highlighting the changes from Sect. 5.1.

Denote by f_λ, g_λ the state-computing functions for $\mathsf{Search}_\lambda, \mathsf{G}_\lambda$ respectively (as in Definition 8).

Turing Machine for BARGs. We next describe the family of Turing machine $\mathsf{M} = \{\mathsf{M}_\lambda\}_{\lambda \in \mathbb{N}}$ that the server will need to provide a BARG proof for. The machine M_λ hardcodes the hash key hk, tree root rt, SEH key hk^*, SEH root rt^*, and encrypted start state $\widehat{c}_0$ (Fig. 3).

$\mathsf{Gen}(1^\lambda)$

1. $(\mathsf{crs}_{\mathsf{BARG}}, \tau) \leftarrow \mathsf{BARG.Gen}(1^\lambda, \{m(\lambda), m(\lambda)\})$.
2. $\mathsf{hk} \leftarrow \mathsf{HT.Gen}(1^\lambda)$.
3. Output $\mathsf{crs} := (\mathsf{crs}_{\mathsf{BARG}}, \mathsf{hk})$.

$\mathsf{Client}(\mathsf{crs}, x)$

1. $(\mathsf{sk}, \mathsf{pk}) \leftarrow \mathsf{FHE.KeyGen}(1^\lambda)$.
2. $\widehat{c} \leftarrow \mathsf{FHE.Enc}(\mathsf{pk}, x)$.
3. $\widehat{c}_{\mathsf{init}} \leftarrow \mathsf{FHE.Enc}(\mathsf{pk}, \mathsf{z}_{f,0})$.
4. $c := (\mathsf{pk}, \widehat{c}, \widehat{c}_{\mathsf{init}})$.
5. $\mathsf{st} := (c, \mathsf{sk})$.
6. Output (c, st)

$\mathsf{Server}(\mathsf{crs}, y = (y_1, \ldots, y_{m(\lambda)}), c)$

1. Parse c as $(\mathsf{pk}, \widehat{c}, \widehat{c}_{\mathsf{init}})$, and crs as $(\mathsf{crs}_{\mathsf{BARG}}, \mathsf{hk})$.
2. Set $\widehat{c}_0 := \widehat{c}_{\mathsf{init}}$ and $\mathsf{z}_{\mathsf{g},0} := \mathsf{z}_{\mathsf{g},\mathsf{init}}$.
3. For each $i \in [m(\lambda)]$, compute $\widehat{c}_i := \mathsf{FHE.Eval}(f_\lambda, \widehat{c}, y_i, \widehat{c}_{i-1})$.
4. For each $i \in [m(\lambda)]$, compute $\mathsf{z}_{\mathsf{g},i} := \mathsf{g}(y_i, \mathsf{z}_{\mathsf{g},i-1})$.
5. Set $\mathsf{z}_{\mathsf{g},\mathsf{final}} = \mathsf{z}_{\mathsf{g},m(\lambda)}$ and $\widehat{c}_{\mathsf{final}} = \widehat{c}_{m(\lambda)}$.
6. Compute the hash tree root $\mathsf{rt} = \mathsf{HT.Hash}(\mathsf{hk}, ((\mathsf{z}_{\mathsf{g},1}, \widehat{c}_1, y_1) \cdots, (\mathsf{z}_{\mathsf{g},m(\lambda)}, \widehat{c}_{m(\lambda)}, y_{m(\lambda)})))$.
7. Use $\mathsf{hk}, \mathsf{rt}, \mathsf{z}_{\mathsf{g},\mathsf{init}}, \mathsf{z}_{\mathsf{g},\mathsf{final}}, \widehat{c}, \widehat{c}_{\mathsf{init}}$ and $\widehat{c}_{\mathsf{final}}$ to define the Turing machine M_λ as in figure 1.
8. For every $i \in [m(\lambda)]$,
   - $\rho_i = \mathsf{HT.Open}(\mathsf{hk}, ((\mathsf{z}_{\mathsf{g},1}, \widehat{c}_1, y_1) \cdots, (\mathsf{z}_{\mathsf{g},m(\lambda)}, \widehat{c}_{m(\lambda)}, y_{m(\lambda)})), i)$.
   - Construct witness (i, w_i) for with $w_i := (\mathsf{z}_{\mathsf{g},i-1}, \widehat{c}_{i-1}, y_{i-1}, \rho_{i-1}, \mathsf{z}_{\mathsf{g},i}, \widehat{c}_i, y_i, \rho_i)$.

9. Compute the BARG proof $\pi \leftarrow \mathsf{BARG.Prove}(\mathsf{crs}_{\mathsf{BARG}}, \mathsf{M}_\lambda, 1^t, (w_1, \ldots, w_{m(\lambda)}))$.
10. Output $s := (\pi, \mathsf{rt}, \mathsf{z}_{\mathsf{g},m(\lambda)}, \widehat{c}_{m(\lambda)})$.

$\mathsf{Out}(\mathsf{crs}, \mathsf{st}, s)$

1. Parse s as $(\pi, \mathsf{rt}, \mathsf{z}_{\mathsf{g},m(\lambda)}, \widehat{c}_{m(\lambda)})$, crs as $(\mathsf{crs}_{\mathsf{BARG}}, \mathsf{hk})$ and st as (c, sk).
2. Set $\mathsf{z}_{\mathsf{g},\mathsf{final}} = \mathsf{z}_{\mathsf{g},m(\lambda)}$ and $\widehat{c}_{\mathsf{final}} = \widehat{c}_{m(\lambda)}$.
3. Use $\mathsf{hk}, \mathsf{rt}, \mathsf{z}_{\mathsf{g},\mathsf{init}}, \mathsf{z}_{\mathsf{g},\mathsf{final}} \widehat{c}, \widehat{c}_{\mathsf{init}}$ and $\widehat{c}_{\mathsf{final}}$ to define the Turing machine M_λ as in figure 1.
4. If $\mathsf{BARG.Verify}(\mathsf{crs}_{\mathsf{BARG}}, \mathsf{M}_\lambda, 1^t, m(\lambda), \pi) = 1$, set $z = \mathsf{FHE.Dec}(\mathsf{sk}, \widehat{c}_{m(\lambda)})$. Else set $z = \perp$.
5. Output z

Fig. 2: Protocol Π for $\mathsf{F}' = \{\mathsf{F}'_\lambda\}$.

Fig. 2. Protocol Π for $\mathsf{F}' = \{\mathsf{F}'_\lambda\}$.

$\mathsf{M}_\lambda[\mathsf{hk}, \mathsf{rt}, \mathsf{hk}^*, \mathsf{rt}^*, \mathsf{z}_{\mathsf{g},\mathsf{init}}, \mathsf{z}_{\mathsf{g},\mathsf{final}}, \widehat{c}, \widehat{c}_{\mathsf{init}}, \widehat{c}_{\mathsf{final}}](i, w_i)$

1. Parse $w_i = (\mathsf{z}_{\mathsf{g},i-1}, \widehat{c}_{i-1}, y_{i-1}, \rho_{i-1}, \mathsf{z}_{\mathsf{g},i}, \widehat{c}_i, y_i, \rho_i, \rho_i^*)$.
2. if $i = 1$, check $\widehat{c}_0 = \widehat{c}_{\mathsf{init}}$ and $\mathsf{z}_{\mathsf{g},0} = \mathsf{z}_{\mathsf{g},\mathsf{init}}$.
3. if $i = m(\lambda)$, check $\widehat{c}_{m(\lambda)} = \widehat{c}_{\mathsf{final}}$ and $\mathsf{z}_{\mathsf{g},m(\lambda)} = \mathsf{z}_{\mathsf{g},\mathsf{final}}$.
4. Check $\widehat{c}_i = \mathsf{FHE.Eval}(f_\lambda, \widehat{c}, y_i, \widehat{c}_{i-1})$.
5. Check $\mathsf{z}_{\mathsf{g},i} = \mathsf{g}_\lambda(y_i, \mathsf{z}_{\mathsf{g},i-1})$.
6. Check $\mathsf{HT.Verify}(\mathsf{hk}, \mathsf{rt}, i, (\mathsf{z}_{\mathsf{g},i}, \widehat{c}_i, y_i), \rho_i) = 1$.
7. if $i > 1$, check $\mathsf{HT.Verify}(\mathsf{hk}, \mathsf{rt}, i-1, (\mathsf{z}_{\mathsf{g},i-1}, \widehat{c}_{i-1}, y_{i-1}), \rho_{i-1}) = 1$ and $(y_{i-1}, y_i) \in \mathsf{R}_\lambda$.
8. Check $\mathsf{SEH.Verify}(\mathsf{hk}^*, \mathsf{rt}^*, m(\lambda), i, \mathsf{Project}(y_i), \rho_i^*) = 1$.
9. Accept if all the checks verify.

Fig. 3: Turing Machine M_λ

Fig. 3. Turing Machine M_λ

$\mathsf{Gen}(1^\lambda)$

1. $(\mathsf{crs}_{\mathsf{BARG}}, \tau) \leftarrow \mathsf{BARG.Gen}(1^\lambda, \{m(\lambda), m(\lambda)\})$.
2. $\mathsf{hk} \leftarrow \mathsf{HT.Gen}(1^\lambda)$.
3. Output $\mathsf{crs} := (\mathsf{crs}_{\mathsf{BARG}}, \mathsf{hk})$.

$\mathsf{Client}(\mathsf{crs}, x)$

1. $(\mathsf{sk}, \mathsf{pk}) \leftarrow \mathsf{FHE.KeyGen}(1^\lambda)$.
2. $(\mathsf{hk}^*, \mathsf{td}^*) \leftarrow \mathsf{SEH.Gen}(1^\lambda, (\mathsf{sk}, \mathsf{pk}))$.
3. $\widehat{c} \leftarrow \mathsf{FHE.Enc}(\mathsf{pk}, x)$.
4. $\widehat{c}_{\mathsf{init}} \leftarrow \mathsf{FHE.Enc}(\mathsf{pk}, \mathsf{z}_{\mathsf{f},0})$.
5. $\mathsf{st} := (\mathsf{sk}, \mathsf{hk}^*, \mathsf{td}^*)$.
6. $c := (\mathsf{pk}, \widehat{c}, \widehat{c}_{\mathsf{init}}, \mathsf{hk}^*)$.
7. Output (c, st)

$\mathsf{Server}(\mathsf{crs}, y = (y_1, \ldots, y_{m(\lambda)}), c)$

1. Parse c as $(\mathsf{pk}, \widehat{c}, \widehat{c}_{\mathsf{init}}, \mathsf{hk}^*)$, and crs as $(\mathsf{crs}_{\mathsf{BARG}}, \mathsf{hk})$.
2. Set $\widehat{c}_0 := \widehat{c}_{\mathsf{init}}$ and $\mathsf{z}_{\mathsf{g},0} := \mathsf{z}_{\mathsf{g},\mathsf{init}}$
3. For each $i \in [m(\lambda)]$, compute $\widehat{c}_i := \mathsf{FHE.Eval}(f_\lambda, \widehat{c}, y_i, \widehat{c}_{i-1})$.
4. For each $i \in [m(\lambda)]$, compute $\mathsf{z}_{\mathsf{g},i} := \mathsf{g}(y_i, \mathsf{z}_{\mathsf{g},i-1})$.
5. Set $\mathsf{z}_{\mathsf{g},\mathsf{final}} = \mathsf{z}_{\mathsf{g},m(\lambda)}$ and $\widehat{c}_{\mathsf{final}} = \widehat{c}_{m(\lambda)}$.
6. Compute the hash tree root $\mathsf{rt} = \mathsf{HT.Hash}(\mathsf{hk}, ((\mathsf{z}_{\mathsf{g},1}, \widehat{c}_1, y_1) \cdots, (\mathsf{z}_{\mathsf{g},m(\lambda)}, \widehat{c}_{m(\lambda)}, y_{m(\lambda)})))$.
7. Replace the ciphertext in hk^* with $\widehat{c}_{m(\lambda)}$.
8. Let $\mathsf{Project}(y) = (\mathsf{Project}(y_1), \ldots, \mathsf{Project}(y_{m(\lambda)}))$.
9. Compute the SEH root $\mathsf{rt}^* = \mathsf{SEH.Hash}(\mathsf{hk}^*, \mathsf{Project}(y))$.

Fig. 4. Protocol for $\mathsf{F}' = \{\mathsf{F}'_\lambda\}$.

10. Use $\mathsf{hk}, \mathsf{rt}, \mathsf{hk}^*, \mathsf{rt}^*, \mathsf{z}_{\mathsf{g,init}}, \mathsf{z}_{\mathsf{g,final}}, \widehat{c}, \widehat{c}_{\mathsf{init}}$ and $\widehat{c}_{\mathsf{final}}$ to define the Turing machine M_λ as in figure 3.
11. For every $i \in [m(\lambda)]$,
    - $\rho_i = \mathsf{HT.Open}(\mathsf{hk}, ((\mathsf{z}_{\mathsf{g},1}, \widehat{c}_1, y_1) \cdots, (\mathsf{z}_{\mathsf{g},m(\lambda)}, \widehat{c}_{m(\lambda)}, y_{m(\lambda)})), i)$.
    - $\rho_i^* = \mathsf{SEH.Open}(\mathsf{hk}^*, \mathsf{Project}(y), i)$.
    - Construct witness (i, w_i) for with $w_i :=$ $(\mathsf{z}_{\mathsf{g},i-1}, \widehat{c}_{i-1}, y_{i-1}, \rho_{i-1}, \mathsf{z}_{\mathsf{g},i}, \widehat{c}_i, y_i, \rho_i, \rho_i^*)$.
12. Compute the BARG proof $\pi \leftarrow \mathsf{BARG.Prove}(\mathsf{crs}_{\mathsf{BARG}}, \mathsf{M}_\lambda, 1^t, (w_1, \ldots, w_{m(\lambda)}))$.
13. Output $s := (\pi, \mathsf{rt}, \mathsf{rt}^*, \mathsf{z}_{\mathsf{g},m(\lambda)}, \widehat{c}_{m(\lambda)})$.

$\underline{\mathsf{Out}(\mathsf{crs}, \mathsf{st}, s)}$

1. Parse s as $(\pi, \mathsf{rt}, \mathsf{rt}^*, \mathsf{z}_{\mathsf{g},m(\lambda)}, \widehat{c}_{m(\lambda)})$, crs as $(\mathsf{crs}_{\mathsf{BARG}}, \mathsf{hk})$ and st as $(\mathsf{sk}, \mathsf{hk}^*, \mathsf{td}^*)$.
2. Set $\mathsf{z}_{\mathsf{g,final}} = \mathsf{z}_{\mathsf{g},m(\lambda)}$ and $\widehat{c}_{\mathsf{final}} = \widehat{c}_{m(\lambda)}$.
3. Replace the ciphertext in hk^* with $\widehat{c}_{m(\lambda)}$.
4. Use $\mathsf{hk}, \mathsf{rt}, \mathsf{hk}^*, \mathsf{rt}^*, \mathsf{z}_{\mathsf{g,init}}, \mathsf{z}_{\mathsf{g,final}}, \widehat{c}, \widehat{c}_{\mathsf{init}}$ and $\widehat{c}_{\mathsf{final}}$ to define the Turing machine M_λ as in figure 3.
5. If $\mathsf{BARG.Verify}(\mathsf{crs}_{\mathsf{BARG}}, \mathsf{M}_\lambda, 1^t, m(\lambda), \pi) = 1$, set $z = \mathsf{SEH.Extract}(\mathsf{td}^*, \mathsf{rt}^*)$. Else set $z = \perp$.
6. Output z

Fig. 4: Protocol for $\mathsf{F}' = \{\mathsf{F}'_\lambda\}$.

Fig. 4. (*continued*)

Note that we can set t, the running time of M, to be the time it takes to perform the above checks, which is polynomial in its inputs (Fig. 4).

6 Main Result: Private Set Membership and **VDL** with **UP** Search

Our first result is a protocol for the *dictionary lookup* function. Let $n(\lambda), \ell(\lambda), m(\lambda)$ be polynomially bounded functions. The dictionary lookup function:

$$\mathsf{DL} = \{\mathsf{DL}_\lambda : \{0,1\}^{n(\lambda)} \times (\{0,1\}^{n(\lambda)+\ell(\lambda)})^{m(\lambda)} \to \{0,1\}^*\}_{\lambda \in \mathbb{N}} \ ,$$

takes as input a key $k \in \{0,1\}^{n(\lambda)}$ and a dictionary D represented as a sequence of key-value pairs:

$$D = ((k_1, v_1), \ldots, (k_{m(\lambda)}, v_{m(\lambda)})) \in \left(\{0,1\}^{n(\lambda)} \times \{0,1\}^{\ell(\lambda)}\right)^{m(\lambda)} \ .$$

The output is the value v such that $(k, v) \in D$, or $\perp$ if no such value exists, or if the keys $k_1, \ldots, k_{m(\lambda)}$ are not pairwise distinct.

Theorem 5. *Assuming NIZK, FHE and BARG, there exists a 1-round 2-party computation protocol for the function* DL *in the CRS model with weak client security (Sect. 4.1) where the client's message is of size* $n(\lambda) \cdot \mathsf{poly}(\lambda)$ *and the server's message is of size* $(n(\lambda) + \ell(\lambda)) \cdot \mathsf{poly}(\lambda)$.

We also consider an extension that we call *verifiable dictionary lookup* where the server's input D is required to satisfy some predicate. To specify the type of predicates we consider, we first define the notion of a bounded space predicate.

Definition 9 (Bounded State Predicate). *Let* $s(\lambda)$ *be a polynomially bounded function. A predicate* $\mathsf{P} = \{\mathsf{P}_\lambda : (\{0,1\}^{\ell(\lambda)})^{m(\lambda)} \to \{0,1\}\}_{\lambda \in \mathbb{N}}$ *is computable with state of size* s *if there exists an efficiently computable function* $\Gamma = \{\Gamma_\lambda : \{0,1\}^{\ell(\lambda)} \times \{0,1\}^{s(\lambda)} \to \{0,1\}^{s(\lambda)}\}_{\lambda \in \mathbb{N}}$ *and special states* $\mathsf{st}, \mathsf{st}' \in \{0,1\}^{s(\lambda)}$ *such that:*

$$\mathsf{P}_\lambda(y_1, \ldots, y_{m(\lambda)}) = 1 \iff \Gamma_\lambda(y_{m(\lambda)}, \Gamma_\lambda(y_{m(\lambda)-1}, \Gamma_\lambda(\ldots, \Gamma_\lambda(y_1, \mathsf{st})))) = \mathsf{st}' \ .$$

Definition 10 (UP Relation). *A relation* $\mathsf{Rel} = \left\{\mathsf{Rel}_\lambda \subseteq \{0,1\}^{n(\lambda)} \times \{0,1\}^{w(\lambda)}\right\}$ *is a UP relation if it is an NP relation (i.e. there is a polynomial-time algorithm for deciding* $(x,w) \in \mathsf{Rel}_\lambda$*), and for every instance* $x \in \{0,1\}^{n(\lambda)}$*, there exists at most one witness* $w \in \{0,1\}^{w(\lambda)}$ *such that* $(x,w) \in \mathsf{Rel}_\lambda$.

Theorem 6. *Let* $\mathsf{P} = \{\mathsf{P}_\lambda : (\{0,1\}^{n(\lambda)+\ell(\lambda)})^{m(\lambda)} \to \{0,1\}\}_{\lambda \in \mathbb{N}}$ *be a predicate computable with state of size* $s(\lambda) = O(\log \lambda)$. *Let* $\mathsf{R} = \left\{\mathsf{R}_\lambda \subseteq \{0,1\}^{\ell(\lambda)} \times \{0,1\}^{\ell(\lambda)}\right\}$ *be an efficiently computable strict total order, and let* Rel *be a UP relation. Let* $\mathsf{VDL} = \{\mathsf{VDL}_\lambda\}_{\lambda \in \mathbb{N}}$ *be the function:*

$$\mathsf{VDL}_\lambda\left(x, D = ((w_i, v_i))_{i \in [m(\lambda)]}\right) = \begin{cases} \mathsf{DL}_\lambda^{\mathsf{Rel}}(x, D), & \text{if } \mathsf{P}_\lambda(D) = 1 \wedge \forall i : (w_i, w_{i+1}) \in \mathsf{R}_\lambda \\ \bot, & \text{otherwise} \end{cases} ,$$

where $\mathsf{DL}_\lambda^{\mathsf{Rel}}(x, D)$ *outputs* v *such that* $(w, v) \in D$ *and* $(x, w) \in \mathsf{Rel}$, *or* $\bot$ *if no such value exists.*

Assuming NIZK, FHE and BARG, there exists a 1-round 2-party computation protocol for the function VDL *in the CRS model with weak client security (Sect. 4.1) where the client's message is of size* $n(\lambda) \cdot \mathsf{poly}(\lambda)$ *and the server's message is of size* $(n(\lambda) + \ell(\lambda)) \cdot \mathsf{poly}(\lambda)$.

Corollary 1. *Theorem 6 implies Theorem 5.*

Proof sketch. The corollary follows from appropriately setting the predicate P, total order R and UP relation Rel in the function VDL such that a protocol for VDL is also a protocol for DL. Specifically, for all λ, we set P_λ to be the tautology predicate, i.e. $\mathsf{P}_\lambda(\cdot) = 1$, which can be computed with state of size $O(1)$. Next, we set R_λ to be the *strict* total order, i.e. $\forall k, k' \in \{0,1\}^{\ell(\lambda)}, (k, k') \in \mathsf{R}_\lambda \iff k < k'$, where $k < k'$ is interpreted as the standard numerical comparison of the integers represented by the binary strings k and k', and thus checking membership in R_λ efficient. The UP relation Rel is the equality relation, $(x, w) \in \mathsf{Rel}$ if $x = w$.

The server, on input a database $D = ((w_i, v_i))_{i \in [m(\lambda)]}$ first converts D into a database $D' = ((w_i', v_i'))_{i \in [m(\lambda)]}$, which is simply the original database D sorted by the key value. The client and the server then run the protocol for VDL, where the client input remains unchanged, and the server input is D'. $\square$

Given the above corollary, we focus on proving Theorem 6.

Remark 2. We note that while we explicitly assume the existence of NIZKs in addition to BARGs, it was recently shown [8,9] that BARGs, along with one-way functions, imply NIZKs.

6.1 Input-Dependent Simulation to Weak Simulation

In this section, we show how to obtain weak simulation security for verifiable dictionary lookup (VDL).

We show this via a meta-theorem, going from input-dependent to weak simulation-security: for an appropriate choice of G', input-dependent simulation-security for VDL with respect to G' implies weak simulation-security.

Specifically, we define

$$\mathsf{G}_\lambda(D = ((w_i, v_i))_{i \in [m(\lambda)]}) = \begin{cases} 1, & \text{if } \mathsf{P}_\lambda(D) = 1 \\ \bot, & \text{otherwise} \end{cases},$$

and

$$\mathsf{G}'_\lambda(D = ((w_i, v_i))_{i \in [m(\lambda)]}) = \begin{cases} \mathsf{G}(D), & \text{if } \forall i : (w_i, w_{i+1}) \in \mathsf{R}_\lambda \\ \bot, & \text{otherwise} \end{cases}.$$

Observe that if $\mathsf{G}'_\lambda(D) = 1$, then $\mathsf{VDL}_\lambda(x, D) = \mathsf{DL}_\lambda^{\mathsf{Rel}}(x, D)$ and if $\mathsf{G}'_\lambda(D) = \bot$, then $\mathsf{VDL}_\lambda(x, D) = \bot$. G'_λ then effectively acts as an indicator to whether the output of VDL is $\bot$ due to either the total ordering or predicate being violated on D.

Before proving this meta-theorem, we argue that our general theorems (Sect. 5) indeed give us input-dependent simulation-secure protocols for $\mathsf{VDL}, \mathsf{G}'$. In particular, we show that $\mathsf{VDL}, \mathsf{G}'$ can be represented as sorted lookup functions (Theorem 4). For completeness, we first show that for VDL with short values $|v_i| = O(\log \lambda)$, we can represent $\mathsf{VDL}, \mathsf{G}'$ as sorted bounded-state functions (Theorem 3).

Sorted Bounded-State Functions. Define $\mathsf{F} = \{\mathsf{F}_\lambda\}_{\lambda \in \mathbb{N}}$ as

$$\mathsf{F}_\lambda(x, D = ((w_i, v_i))_{i \in [m(\lambda)]}) = \begin{cases} \mathsf{DL}_\lambda^{\mathsf{Rel}}(x, D), & \text{if } \mathsf{P}_\lambda(D) = 1 \\ \bot, & \text{otherwise} \end{cases}$$

Observe that F' instantiated with F described above is indeed VDL. Next we show that F is computable with state of size $s(\lambda) = O(\log \lambda)$. For Theorem 6, we work with predicates $\mathsf{P} = \{\mathsf{P}_\lambda\}_{\lambda \in \mathbb{N}}$ that are computable with state of size $s(\lambda)$. Thus, all that is left to show is that $\mathsf{DL}_\lambda^{\mathsf{Rel}}(x, D)$ can be computed with a state of size $O(\log \lambda)$. This is easy to see when $|v_i| = O(\log \lambda)$ for all i. In particular, we define $\mathsf{f} = \{\mathsf{f}_\lambda\}_{\lambda \in \mathbb{N}}$ as below,

$$\mathsf{f}_\lambda(x, (w_i, v_i), z_{i-1}) = \begin{cases} v_i & \text{if } (x, w_i) \in \mathsf{Rel} \\ z_{i-1} & \text{otherwise} \end{cases}$$

where z_{i-1} is the state so far, and $z_0 = 0$ (or a special string to indicate no match). In words, f simply updates the state to v_i if there is a match, otherwise leaves the state unchanged.

Next, it is easy to observe that G is computable with state of size $O(\log \lambda)$ given that P is computable with state of size $O(\log \lambda)$.

Sorted Lookup Functions. Define $\mathsf{Search} = \{\mathsf{Search}_\lambda\}_{\lambda \in \mathbb{N}}$ as follows: it simply returns the index of the match, if one exists.

$$\mathsf{Search}_\lambda(x, D = ((w_i, v_i))_{i \in [m(\lambda)]}) = \begin{cases} i, & \text{if } (x, w_i) \in \mathsf{Rel} \wedge \mathsf{P}_\lambda(D) = 1 \\ \bot, & \text{otherwise.} \end{cases}$$

For predicates P computable in $O(\log \lambda)$ space, Search can also be computed in $O(\log \lambda)$ space. This follows from the fact that the matched index can be computed using the function f_λ using $O(\log \lambda)$ space as defined below,

$$\mathsf{f}_\lambda(x, (w_i, v_i), (b_{i-1}, z_{i-1})) = \begin{cases} (1, z_{i-1} + 1) & \text{if } \mathsf{Rel}(x, w_i) = 1 \\ (0, z_{i-1} + 1) & \text{otherwise ,} \end{cases}$$

where $(b_0, z_0) = (0, 0)$ is the initial state.

Finally, we define $\mathsf{Project}$ such that $\mathsf{Project}(w, v) = v$.

We now prove the meta-theorem that shows that for our choice of F', G', input-dependent simulation-security can be upgraded to weak-simulation security. This theorem, along with the input privacy of the client directly implies Theorem 6. The proof of the theorem is in the full version of the paper.

Theorem 7. *For the functions* $\mathsf{F}' = \{\mathsf{F}'_\lambda\}_{\lambda \in \mathbb{N}}$ *and* $\mathsf{G}' = \{\mathsf{G}'_\lambda\}_{\lambda \in \mathbb{N}}$ *defined above, any protocol in the CRS model function for* F' *in the CRS model with input-dependent simulation-security with respect to* G' *(Definitions 6 and 7) also satisfies weak simulation-security (Definition 5).*

Acknowledgements. Part of this work was done while Abhishek Jain and Omer Paneth were visiting the Simons Institute for the Theory of Computing.

Abhishek Jain was supported in part by NSF CAREER 1942789, Johns Hopkins University Catalyst award, JP Morgan Faculty Award, and research gifts from Ethereum Foundation, Stellar Development Foundation, and Cisco.

Arka Rai Choudhuri was supported by a grant by Open Philanthropy/Coefficient Giving.

Omer Paneth is a member of the CheckPoint Institute of Information Security and is supported by Len Blavatnik and the Blavatnik Foundation and by AFOSR Award FA9550-23-1-0312. Any opinions, findings and conclusions or recommendations expressed in this material are those of the author(s) and do not necessarily reflect the views of the United States Government or AFOSR.

References

1. Ananth, P., Badrinarayanan, S., Jain, A., Manohar, N., Sahai, A.: From FE combiners to secure MPC and back. In: Hofheinz, D., Rosen, A. (eds.) TCC 2019: 17th Theory of Cryptography Conference, Part I. Lecture Notes in Computer Science, vol. 11891, pp. 199–228. Springer, Cham, Switzerland, Nuremberg, Germany (2019). https://doi.org/10.1007/978-3-030-36030-6_9
2. Apple Inc: Password monitoring - apple support (2021). https://support.apple.com/guide/security/password-monitoring-sec78e79fc3b/web
3. Bartusek, J., Garg, S., Jain, A., Policharla, G.V.: Laconic PSI on authenticated inputs and applications. In: ASIACRYPT. Lecture Notes in Computer Science, Springer (2025)
4. Ben-David, S., Kalai, Y.T., Paneth, O.: Verifiable private information retrieval. In: Kiltz, E., Vaikuntanathan, V. (eds.) TCC 2022: 20th Theory of Cryptography Conference, Part III. Lecture Notes in Computer Science, vol. 13749, pp. 3–32. Springer, Cham, Switzerland, Chicago, IL, USA (2022). https://doi.org/10.1007/978-3-031-22368-6_1
5. Bitansky, N., et al.: The hunting of the SNARK. J. Cryptol. **30**(4), 989–1066 (2017)
6. Bitansky, N., Canetti, R., Chiesa, A., Tromer, E.: Recursive composition and bootstrapping for SNARKS and proof-carrying data. In: Boneh, D., Roughgarden, T., Feigenbaum, J. (eds.) 45th Annual ACM Symposium on Theory of Computing, pp. 111–120. ACM Press, Palo Alto, CA, USA (2013). https://doi.org/10.1145/2488608.2488623
7. Bitansky, N., Canetti, R., Paneth, O., Rosen, A.: On the existence of extractable one-way functions. In: Shmoys, D.B. (ed.) 46th Annual ACM Symposium on Theory of Computing, pp. 505–514. ACM Press, New York, NY, USA (2014). https://doi.org/10.1145/2591796.2591859
8. Bitansky, N., Kamath, C., Paneth, O., Rothblum, R.D., Vasudevan, P.N.: Batch proofs are statistically hiding. In: Mohar, B., Shinkar, I., O'Donnell, R. (eds.) 56th Annual ACM Symposium on Theory of Computing, pp. 435–443. ACM Press, Vancouver, BC, Canada (2024). https://doi.org/10.1145/3618260.3649775
9. Bradley, E., Waters, B., Wu, D.J.: Batch arguments to NIZKs from one-way functions. In: Boyle, E., Mahmoody, M. (eds.) TCC 2024: 22nd Theory of Cryptography Conference, Part II. Lecture Notes in Computer Science, vol. 15365, pp. 431–463. Springer, Cham, Switzerland, Milan, Italy (2024). https://doi.org/10.1007/978-3-031-78017-2_15
10. Brakerski, Z., Holmgren, J., Kalai, Y.T.: Non-interactive delegation and batch NP verification from standard computational assumptions. In: Hatami, H., McKenzie, P., King, V. (eds.) 49th Annual ACM Symposium on Theory of Computing, pp. 474–482. ACM Press, Montreal, QC, Canada (2017). https://doi.org/10.1145/3055399.3055497

11. Brakerski, Z., Vaikuntanathan, V.: Efficient fully homomorphic encryption from (standard) LWE. In: Ostrovsky, R. (ed.) 52nd Annual Symposium on Foundations of Computer Science, pp. 97–106. IEEE Computer Society Press, Palm Springs, CA, USA (2011). https://doi.org/10.1109/FOCS.2011.12

12. Cho, C., Döttling, N., Garg, S., Gupta, D., Miao, P., Polychroniadou, A.: Laconic oblivious transfer and its applications. In: Katz, J., Shacham, H. (eds.) Advances in Cryptology – CRYPTO 2017, Part II. Lecture Notes in Computer Science, vol. 10402, pp. 33–65. Springer, Cham, Switzerland, Santa Barbara, CA, USA (2017). https://doi.org/10.1007/978-3-319-63715-0_2

13. Choudhuri, A.R., Garg, S., Jain, A., Jin, Z., Zhang, J.: Correlation intractability and SNARGs from sub-exponential DDH. In: Handschuh, H., Lysyanskaya, A. (eds.) Advances in Cryptology – CRYPTO 2023, Part IV. Lecture Notes in Computer Science, vol. 14084, pp. 635–668. Springer, Cham, Switzerland, Santa Barbara, CA, USA (2023). https://doi.org/10.1007/978-3-031-38551-3_20

14. Choudhuri, A.R., Jain, A., Jin, Z.: SNARGs for $\mathcal{P}$ from LWE. In: 62nd Annual Symposium on Foundations of Computer Science, pp. 68–79. IEEE Computer Society Press, Denver, CO, USA (2022). https://doi.org/10.1109/FOCS52979.2021.00016

15. Ciampi, M., Misra, A.K., Ostrovsky, R., Shah, A.: Black-box constant-round secure 2PC with succinct communication. In: Fehr, S., Fouque, P.A. (eds.) Advances in Cryptology – EUROCRYPT 2025, Part V. Lecture Notes in Computer Science, vol. 15605, pp. 360–389. Springer, Cham, Switzerland, Madrid, Spain (2025). https://doi.org/10.1007/978-3-031-91092-0_13

16. Döttling, N., Garg, S., Goyal, V., Malavolta, G.: Laconic conditional disclosure of secrets and applications. In: Zuckerman, D. (ed.) 60th Annual Symposium on Foundations of Computer Science, pp. 661–685. IEEE Computer Society Press, Baltimore, MD, USA (2019). https://doi.org/10.1109/FOCS.2019.00046

17. Garg, S., Hajiabadi, M., Jain, A., Jin, Z., Pandey, O., Shiehian, S.: Credibility in private set membership. In: Boldyreva, A., Kolesnikov, V. (eds.) PKC 2023: 26th International Conference on Theory and Practice of Public Key Cryptography, Part II. Lecture Notes in Computer Science, vol. 13941, pp. 159–189. Springer, Cham, Switzerland, Atlanta, GA, USA (2023). https://doi.org/10.1007/978-3-031-31371-4_6

18. Gentry, C.: Fully homomorphic encryption using ideal lattices. In: Mitzenmacher, M. (ed.) 41st Annual ACM Symposium on Theory of Computing, pp. 169–178. ACM Press, Bethesda, MD, USA (2009). https://doi.org/10.1145/1536414.1536440

19. Goldreich, O.: The Foundations of Cryptography - Volume 2: Basic Applications. Cambridge University Press (2004). https://doi.org/10.1017/CBO9780511721656

20. Google Inc: Protect your accounts from data breaches with password checkup (2019). https://security.googleblog.com/2019/02/protect-your-accounts-from-data.html

21. Hubacek, P., Wichs, D.: On the communication complexity of secure function evaluation with long output. In: Roughgarden, T. (ed.) ITCS 2015: 6th Conference on Innovations in Theoretical Computer Science, pp. 163–172. Association for Computing Machinery, Rehovot, Israel (2015). https://doi.org/10.1145/2688073.2688105

22. Hulett, J., Jawale, R., Khurana, D., Srinivasan, A.: SNARGs for P from sub-exponential DDH and QR. In: Dunkelman, O., Dziembowski, S. (eds.) Advances in Cryptology – EUROCRYPT 2022, Part II. Lecture Notes in Computer Science, vol. 13276, pp. 520–549. Springer, Cham, Switzerland, Trondheim, Norway (2022). https://doi.org/10.1007/978-3-031-07085-3_18

23. Ishai, Y., Kushilevitz, E., Ostrovsky, R., Prabhakaran, M., Sahai, A.: Efficient non-interactive secure computation. In: Paterson, K.G. (ed.) Advances in Cryptology – EUROCRYPT 2011. Lecture Notes in Computer Science, vol. 6632, pp. 406–425. Springer Berlin Heidelberg, Germany, Tallinn, Estonia (2011). https://doi.org/10.1007/978-3-642-20465-4_23
24. Jain, A., Kalai, Y.T., Khurana, D., Rothblum, R.: Distinguisher-dependent simulation in two rounds and its applications. In: Katz, J., Shacham, H. (eds.) Advances in Cryptology – CRYPTO 2017, Part II. Lecture Notes in Computer Science, vol. 10402, pp. 158–189. Springer, Cham, Switzerland, Santa Barbara, CA, USA (2017). https://doi.org/10.1007/978-3-319-63715-0_6
25. Kalai, Y., Lombardi, A., Vaikuntanathan, V., Wichs, D.: Boosting batch arguments and RAM delegation. In: Saha, B., Servedio, R.A. (eds.) 55th Annual ACM Symposium on Theory of Computing, pp. 1545–1552. ACM Press, Orlando, FL, USA (2023). https://doi.org/10.1145/3564246.3585200
26. Kalai, Y.T., Paneth, O., Yang, L.: How to delegate computations publicly. In: Charikar, M., Cohen, E. (eds.) 51st Annual ACM Symposium on Theory of Computing, pp. 1115–1124. ACM Press, Phoenix, AZ, USA (2019). https://doi.org/10.1145/3313276.3316411
27. Kannepalli, S., Laine, K., Moreno, R.C.: Password monitor: Safeguarding passwords in Microsoft edge (2021). https://www.microsoft.com/en-us/research/blog/password-monitor-safeguarding-passwords-in-microsoft-edge/
28. Marlinspike, M.: The difficulty of private contact discovery (2014). https://whispersystems.org/blog/contact-discovery/
29. Micali, S.: CS proofs (extended abstracts). In: 35th Annual Symposium on Foundations of Computer Science, pp. 436–453. IEEE Computer Society Press, Santa Fe, NM, USA (1994). https://doi.org/10.1109/SFCS.1994.365746
30. Morgan, A., Pass, R., Polychroniadou, A.: Succinct non-interactive secure computation. In: Canteaut, A., Ishai, Y. (eds.) Advances in Cryptology – EUROCRYPT 2020, Part II. Lecture Notes in Computer Science, vol. 12106, pp. 216–245. Springer, Cham, Switzerland, Zagreb, Croatia (2020). https://doi.org/10.1007/978-3-030-45724-2_8
31. Quach, W., Wee, H., Wichs, D.: Laconic function evaluation and applications. In: Thorup, M. (ed.) 59th Annual Symposium on Foundations of Computer Science, pp. 859–870. IEEE Computer Society Press, Paris, France (2018). https://doi.org/10.1109/FOCS.2018.00086
32. Waters, B., Wu, D.J.: Batch arguments for NP and more from standard bilinear group assumptions. In: Dodis, Y., Shrimpton, T. (eds.) Advances in Cryptology – CRYPTO 2022, Part II. Lecture Notes in Computer Science, vol. 13508, pp. 433–463. Springer, Cham, Switzerland, Santa Barbara, CA, USA (2022). https://doi.org/10.1007/978-3-031-15979-4_15

Author Index

J. Daemen and E. Thomé (Eds.): EUROCRYPT 2026, LNCS 16543, pp. 605–606, 2026.
https://doi.org/10.1007/978-3-032-25324-8